KU-747-200

VOLUME A

THE AMERICAN FILM INSTITUTE CATALOG OF MOTION PICTURES PRODUCED IN THE UNITED STATES

★FILM BEGINNINGS, 1893-1910
A WORK IN PROGRESS

INDEXES

VOLUME

★ A FILM BEGINNINGS, 1893-1910

F1 Feature Films, 1911-1920

F2 Feature Films, 1921-1930

F3 Feature Films, 1931-1940

F4 Feature Films, 1941-1950

F5 Feature Films, 1951-1960

F6 Feature Films, 1961-1970

F7 Feature Films, 1971-1980

F8 Feature Films. 1981-1990

S1 Short Films, 1911-1920

S2 Short Films, 1921-1930

S3 Short Films, 1931-1940

S4 Short Films, 1941-1950

S5 Short Films, 1951-1960

S6 Short Films, 1961-1970

S7 Short Films, 1971-1980

S8 Short Films, 1981-1990

N1 Newsreels, 1908-1920

N2 Newsreels, 1921-1930

N3 Newsreels, 1931-1940

N4 Newsreels, 1941-1950

N5 Newsreels, 1951-1960

N6 Newsreels, 1961-1970

THE AMERICAN FILM INSTITUTE CATALOG

OF MOTION PICTURES PRODUCED IN THE UNITED STATES

★FILM BEGINNINGS, 1893-1910
A WORK IN PROGRESS

INDEXES

Compiled by
Elias Savada

The Scarecrow Press, Inc.
Lanham, Md., & London

British Library Cataloguing-in-Publication Data available

Library of Congress Cataloging-in-Publication Data

(Revised for vol. A, pts. 1–2)

The American Film Institute catalog of motion pictures
produced in the United States.

Publisher and editor vary per vol.
Contents: v. A. Film beginnings, 1893–1910.
pt. [1] Film entries. pt. [2] Indexes. 2 v. —
v. F1. Feature films, 1911–1920. Feature
films, 1911–1920, credit & indexes. 2 v. —
v. F2. Feature films, 1921–1930. Feature
films, 1921–1930, credit & subject indexes.
[etc.] — v. F6. Feature films, 1961–1970.
Feature films, 1961–1970, Feature films,
1961–1970, indexes. 2 v.
1. Motion pictures—United States—Catalogs.
I. Munden, Kenneth W. (Kenneth White), ed.
II. American Film Institute.
PN1998.A57 016.79143´75´0973 79-128587
ISBN 0-8352-0440-5 (v. F1, pt. 1)
ISBN 0-8108-3021-3 (v. A, pts. 1–2)

Manufactured in the United States of America
Printed on acid-free paper

CONTENTS

INTRODUCTION TO THE INDEX VOLUME

★ *Film Beginnings, 1893-1910* has seven separate indexes to assist the researcher. Readers familiar with indexes in other volumes of the *AFI Catalog* will notice some differences here. Previous *AFI Catalog* volumes have indexed film titles chronologically by year, then alphabetically within each year. Because of the importance of the evolution of the medium of motion pictures during the period covered by *Film Beginnings*, it was decided that for this volume films should be listed chronologically, according to the specific *date*, rather than *year* of release. Thus, the reader will find that films released in 1907, for example, can be traced from 5 January through 30 December. Films for which the year of release and the month are known, but with undetermined day of release are listed at the beginning of a specific month. Films for which neither the exact day, month or year of release have been determined, are listed at the end. In cases in which two or more films share the same release date, titles are arranged alphabetically.

While each of the indexes adopts this same basic arrangement, please consult the brief Introduction to each index for specific information on that index. Following the indexes, a Selected Bibliography of books mentioned within the entries is provided. As many of the books listed in the Selected Bibliography are cited by title within the *Film Beginnings* text volume, books are arranged alphabetically by title.

CHRONOLOGICAL INDEX OF FILM TITLES

★ Film titles listed herein are arranged chronologically by year, and within each year, films are arranged chronologically according to specific month and day, then alphabetically under each date.

Films for which the year of release and the month are known, but with undetermined day of release, are listed at the beginning of a specific month. Films for which neither the exact day, month or year of release have been determined, are listed at the end of this index.

CHRONOLOGICAL INDEX OF FILM TITLES

1893 [month undetermined]
Edison Kinetoscopic Records

1894 [month undetermined]
Imperial Japanese Dance
Leonard—Cushing Fight

Jan [day undetermined]
Edison Kinetoscopic Record of a Sneeze, January 7, 1894

Apr [day undetermined]
Edison Kinetoscopic Records

May [day undetermined]
Souvenir Strip of the Edison Kinetoscope [Sandow, the Modern Hercules]

Nov [day undetermined]
Corbett and Courtney Before the Kinetograph

1895 [month undetermined]
Serpentine Dance—Annabelle

1896 [month undetermined]
The Henley Regatta
The Kiss
Lone Fisherman

Aug [day undetermined]
Sparring Contest, Canastota, N.Y.

Sep [day undetermined]
American Falls, Goat Island
American Falls, Luna Island
Annabelle in Flag Dance
Atlantic City Bathers
Atlantic City Boardwalk
Awakening of Rip
Bathers and Lifeboat, Atlantic City
Boys Bathing, Leapfrog—Atlantic City
Busses Leaving R.R. Depot, Atlantic City
Butterfly Dance
Canadian Falls, from American Side
Canadian Falls—Panoramic [View] from Michigan Central R.R.
Canadian Falls—Table Rock
Dancing Darkies
Engine and Pump
Exit of Rip and the Dwarf
Fire Engine at Work
Getting Off Trolley at Atlantic City
A Hard Wash
Li Hung Chang at Grant's Tomb
Li Hung Chang Driving Through 4th St. and Broadway [New York City]
Li Hung Chang, 5th Avenue & 55th Street, N.Y.
Lower Rapids, Niagara Falls
McKinley at Home, Canton, Ohio
The Monkey's Feast
Niagara Gorge from Erie R.R.
On the Boulevard
Panorama of American & Canadian Falls—Taken Opposite American Falls
Panoramic View from Trolley, Atlantic City
Parade, Americus Club, Canton Ohio
Parade at Canton O., Showing Major McKinley in Carriage
Parade, Elkins Cadets, Canton, O.
Parade, Sound Money Club, Canton, O.
Pa. R.R. Cliffs, Jersey City
Pa. R.R., Hattonsfield
Pennsylvania R.R., New Brunswick
Pa. R.R. Train near Phila.
Pointing Down Gorge, Niagara Falls
Rip Leaving Sleepy Hollow
Rip Meeting the Dwarf
Rip Passing over the Mountain
Rip's Toast
Rip's Toast to Hudson
Rip's Twenty Years' Sleep
Sandow
Sawing Wood
Sea Scene
Serpentine Dance by Annabelle
"Shooting the Chutes"
Showing Group of Bathers, Atlantic City Beach
Stable on Fire
Taken from Trolley, Atlantic City
Taken from Trolley in Gorge, Niagara Falls
Tambourine Dance—by Annabelle
Threshing Machine
Train Coming out of Station, Philadelphia, Pa.
Trilby and Little Billee
Union Square and Fourth Avenue
Union Square—New York
Upper Rapids, from Bridge
View on Boulevard, New York City
A Watermelon Feast
West Point Cadet Cavalry
West Point Cadet Drill
Wrestling Pony and Man

Oct [day undetermined]
The Burning Stable
Chicago Fast Mail NYC. R.R.
Clark's Thread Mill
East Side Drive, No. 1
East Side Drive, No. 2
Empire State Express
Empire State Express, N.Y. Central R.R.
Empire State Express No. 2
Feeding the Doves
A Morning Bath
Parade, First Brigade
Park Police Drill Left Wheel and Forward
Park Police Drill Mount and Dismounting
Streets of Cairo
Surf at Long Branch [N.J.]
Train Taking Water, N.Y. Central R.R.
United States Flag
Wine Garden Scene

Nov [day undetermined]
An Arrest at New Haven, Conn.
Charge of West Point Cadets
The Drunken Acrobat
Fighting the Fire
Fire Department, New Haven, Conn.
Fire Department, N.Y. City, 1st and 2nd Alarms
Happy Family
The Human Hen
Imro Fox, Conjuror
Imro Fox Rabbit Trick
A Morning Alarm
Mounted Police Charge
New York Fire Department
The Old Pier and Waves
The Pennsylvania Limited Express
The Runaway in the Park
The Sound Money Parade
Sound Money Parade
Starting for the Fire
The Street Parade
West Point Cadet Cavalry Charge
West Point Cadet Cavalry Drill
Winchester Arms Factory at Noon Time
Yale Football Team at Practice, New Haven, Conn.

Dec [day undetermined]
American Falls from Above, American Side
American Falls from Bottom of Canadian Shore
American Falls—from Incline R.R.
Aquarium
Atlantic City Boardwalk
Black Diamond Express
Broadway & Park Row, Front of U.S. Post Office, N.Y.
Buffalo Horse Market
Chicago and Buffalo Express
Cock Fight
Horseshoe Falls—From Luna Isle
Horseshoe Falls from Table Rock, Canadian Side
Hurdle Race—High Jumpers
The Prodigal's Return; 3 A.M.
Pussy's Bath
Rapids at Cave of the Winds
Sack Race
Snow Men
Special Photographing Train
Tally Ho—Arrival
Tally Ho—Departure
The United States Flag
Whirlpool Rapids—from Bottom of Canadian Shore
Why Papa Cannot Sleep
Wrestling Ponies

1897 [month undetermined]
Babies' Dinner
Babies Quarrel
Barnum's Street Parade, Nos. 1, 2, and 3
Bath Scene
The Bathers
Battery Park
Board Walk, Atlantic City
The Boardwalk
The Book Agent
Breaking Up Housekeeping
Burglar Caught in the Act
Burglars in the Pantry
Butterfly Dance
Corbett and Fitzsimmons Fight
Delaware River, Philadelphia
The Dolorita Passion Dance
Dutch Fishing Boats
East River, New York
Eighth and Vine St. Philadelphia
Elephants at the Zoo
5th Avenue, N.Y.
Fire Rescue Scene
A Good Story
"Has He Hit Me?"
He and She
He Kissed the Wrong Girl
Herald Square
Home Life of a Hungarian Family
The Horse Guards
Indian Club Jugglers
Interesting Parlor Scene
Japanese Rope Walker
Japanese Village
Liberty Statue
Life Rescue
Love in a Broker's Office
Making Love in a Hammock
The Mischievous Monkey
Mr. C. N. Morton
New Pillow Fight
New Watermelon Contest
A Panoramic View in the Grand Canal
Panoramic View of Grand Canal
Panoramic View of Venice
Pelicans at the Zoo
A Race for the Gold Cup
Reading Flyer
The Rocket Coach
Scene in a Popular Oyster Saloon
Scene in Ike Einstein's Pawn Office
Shooting the Chutes
Sir Wilfred Laurier and the New South Wales Lancers
60 Minute Flyer
Ten Nights in a Barroom
"To the Death"
Tourist Train Leaving Livingston, Mont.
Uninvited Guest
Washington Flyer
Watermelon Contest
Yellow Kid
The Zola-Rochefort Duel

Jan [day undetermined]
"Boys Will Be Boys"
Children Playing with Fish
The Farmer's Troubles
The First Sleigh-Ride
Market Square, Harrisburg, Pa.
New England Church Scene
Parisian Dance
Pennsylvania State Militia, Double Time
Pennsylvania State Militia, Single Time
Police Patrol Wagon
Smoking, Eating, and Drinking Scene
Ye Merry Sleigh Bells

Feb [day undetermined]
Broadway, New York, at Madison Square
Champion Rolla O. Heikes, Breaking the Record at Flying Targets with Winchester Shotgun
Ferryboat and Tug Passing Governors Island, New York Harbor
Guard Mount, Ft. Myer [Va.]
Little Egypt
The Milker's Mishap
An Oration
Outbound Vessel Passing Governors Island, N.Y. Harbor
Pennsylvania Avenue, Washington, D.C.
Pile Driving, Washington Navy Yard [Washington, D.C.]
The Pretty Typewriter; or, "Caught in the Act"
Projectile from Ten Inch Disappearing Gun Striking Water, Sandy Hook
The Sausage Machine
Sausage Machine
Ten Inch Disappearing Carriage Gun Loading and Firing, Sandy Hook
13th Infantry, U.S. Army—Bayonet Exercise, Governors Island
13th Infantry, U.S. Army—Blanket Court Martial, Governors Island
13th Infantry, U.S. Army—Full Dress Parade and Manoeuvering, Governors Island
13th Infantry, U.S. Army—Full Dress Parade, Governors Island
13th Infantry, U.S. Army, in Heavy Marching Order, Double-Time, Governors Island
13th Infantry, U.S. Army—Manual of Arms, Governors Island
13th Infantry, U.S. Army—Marching and Counter Marching (Band and Troops), Governors Island
13th Infantry, U.S. Army Marching Through Sallyport, Governors Island
13th Infantry, U.S. Army—Musical Drill, Governors Island
13th Infantry, U.S. Army—Scaling Walls in Retreat, Governors Island
13th Infantry, U.S. Army—Scaling Walls with Wounded and Dying, Governors Island
Waiting for Hubby

Mar [day undetermined]
American and Cuban Flag
Battery A, Light Artillery, U.S. Army
Bicyclers in Inaugural Parade
A Bowery Cafe
The Bungling Waiter
Cavalry Charge
Cavalry Horses at Play
Cavalry Musical Drill
Charge, Through Intervals of Skirmishes
Columbia Bicycle Factory
Columbia School Girls
Deyo
Downey-Monaghan (Round 1)
Downey vs. Monaghan
Drum Corps and Militia
Fencing on Horseback
Fifth Avenue, New York
First Corps Cadets; Mass. National Guard
Gaiety Dance
Geisha Girls
Glimpses of the Grant Parade
A Good Story
Governor Bushnell of Ohio, and Staff
Gov. John A. Tanner, of Virginia, and Staff
His First Smoke
Jumbo
Jumbo, Horseless Fire-Engine
Jumping Hurdles
Keystone Express
Love's Young Dream
McKinley and Cleveland Going to the Capitol
McKinley and Others in Carriage
McKinley Taking the Oath
McKinley Train, Penn. R.R.
Major-General Dodge and Staff
Major-General O. Howard, U.S.A., and Staff
Marines from U.S. Cruiser "New York"
The Miser
Musical Drill; Troop A., Third Cavalry
A Newsboys' Scrap
The Old Guard of New York
Les Parisiennes
A Part of Inaugural Parade, Washington
A Pillow Fight
Playing Doctor
President Cleveland and President McKinley
Return of McKinley from the Capitol
Review of Artillery
S.S. "Middletown"
7th Regiment, N.G.S.N.Y.
71st Regiment, N.G.S.N.Y.
71st Regiment, New York
Sleighing in Central Park
Standing in Stirrups
Steamship "St. Paul" Outward Bound
Theatre Hat
Troop "A" in Inaugural Parade
Troop "A" of Cleveland, O.
Troopers Hurdling
Umbrella Brigade
U.S. Cavalry and Artillery
U.S. Sailors
Vice-President Hobart's Escort
Washington Continental Guards
West Point Cadets
Wrestling, Bareback; 3rd Cavalry
Young Men's Blaine Club of Cincinnati

Apr [day undetermined]
Automatic Piano
Bag Punching by Sadie Leonard
Bareback Hurdle Jumping
Black Diamond Express, No. 1
Black Diamond Express, No. 2
Caught Napping
Cavalry Passing in Review
Chas. Werts, Acrobat
A Coon Cake Walk
A Country Dance
Dance, Franchonetti Sisters
Day After the Circus
Death of Nancy Sykes
Demonstrating the Action of an Automatic Piano
The Elopement
Finish of the Brooklyn Handicap
First Round: Glove Contest Between the Leonards
Foiled Again
French Acrobatic Dance
Girls' Boarding School
Going to the Post
Grace Church, New York
A Hard Scrabble
Hurdle Jumping and Saddle Vaulting
Hurdle Race
Lina & Vani
McKinley Leaving Church
Now I Lay Me Down To Sleep
Panorama of Susquehanna River Taken from the Black Diamond Express
Pennsylvania Avenue, Washington
La Petite Adelaide
Plaguing Grandpa
Receding View, Black Diamond Express
Second Round: Glove Contest Between the Leonards
Seminary Girls
Six Furlong Handicap
Theatre Hats Off
The Washwoman's Troubles
Willie's Hat

May [day undetermined]
An Affair of Honor
Amoskeag Veterans, New Hampshire
Ancient and Honorable Artillery Parade
Battery B, Governor's Troop, Penna.
Bicycle Girl
Buffalo Bill and Escort
Comedy Cake Walk
Corcoran Cadets, Washington
The Daisy Guard
A Dressing Room Scene
Ferryboat "Winthrop"
General Porter's Oration
Girls Wrestling on the Beach
Governor Cook and Staff, Connecticut
Governor of Ohio and Staff
Grant Veterans—G.A.R.
Horse Dancing Couchee Couchee
Husking Bee
Making Soap Bubbles
National Lancers of Boston
O'Brien's Trained Horses
Old Guard, New York City
On the Beach
Pickanninies Dance
Pillow Fight
President McKinley's Address
The Restless Girl
"Ring Around a Rosie"
Saharet
See Saw
7th and 71st Regiment, New York
Shooting the Chutes
Sixth U.S. Cavalry
A "Standard" Picture Animated
Sun Dance—Annabelle
Tandem Hurdle Jumping
Throwing over a Wall
Trick Elephants
U.S.S. "Massachusetts"
Unveiling of the Washington Monument

Jun [day undetermined]
Albany Day Boats
The Biggest Fish He Ever Caught
Boating on the Lake
Chicken Thieves
Children's Toilet
Cornell-Yale-Harvard Boat-Race
Fort Hill Fire Station
Girls Swinging
Harvard Crew
Loading Hay
Mr. Edison at Work in His Chemical Laboratory
Observation Train at the Inter-Collegiate Boat-Races
Peeping Tom
The Picnic
Quick Lunch
A Romp
A Rural Courtship
Still Waters Run Deep
A Surprise Party
Three Jolly Girls and the Fun They Had with the Old Swing
The Tramp and the Bather
Trial Scene
The Troubadour
Trout Poachers
Young America

Jul [day undetermined]
Armour's Electric Trolley
The Bad Boy and Poor Old Grandpa
Beach Scene
Buffalo Fire Department in Action
Buffalo Police on Parade
Buffalo Stockyards
Cattle Driven to Slaughter
A Chicken Farm
Corner Madison and State Streets, Chicago
Expert Driving
Falls of Minnehaha
Free-for-All Race at Charter Oak Park
Giant Coal Dumper
Hauling a Scoop Net
In a Chinese Laundry
In the Surf
A Jolly Crowd of Bathers Frolicking on the Beach at Atlantic City
The Junior Republic on Parade
On the Board Walk
Philadelphia Express, Jersey Central Railway
Promenading on the Beach
Queen's Jubilee
Quick Dressing
Racing at Sheepshead Bay
Sheep Run, Chicago Stockyards
Sprague Electric Train
Suburban Handicap, 1897
Vanishing Lady
Waterfall in the Catskills

Aug [day undetermined]
Admiral Cigarette
Atlantic City Fire Department
A Busy Corner
Catching a Runaway Team
Fire Run
Fire Boat "Edwin S. Stewart"

- A Giant Steam-Shovel
- High Diving
- Making an Arrest
- Mounted Police Drill
- Returning from Drill
- Rough Riding

Sep [day undetermined]

- Aldershot Review
- Bowery Waltz
- Charity Ball
- The Coldstream Guards
- Dancing Girls Limbering Up
- Fisherman's Luck
- Girls' Acrobatic Feats
- Girls Battling for a Hammock
- Gordon Highlanders
- Pretty Girls and the Rail Fence
- Riding on the Merry-Go-Round
- Society Girls Playing "Leap Frog"
- Sutro Baths, No. 2
- Threshing Machine at Work

Oct [day undetermined]

- The Aerial Slide at Coney Island
- Ambulance at the Accident
- Ambulance Call
- Ancient and Honorable Artillery Co.
- Arrest in Chinatown, San Francisco, Cal.
- A Baby Merry-Go-Round
- Beach Apparatus—Practice
- Boat Wagon and Beach Cart
- Boston's Subway
- Boxing for Points
- Capsize of Lifeboat
- The Clarence House Lawn Party
- Crissie Sheridan
- The Crookedest Railroad Yard in the World
- Cupid and Psyche
- Dancing Darkey Boy
- Emperor Francis Joseph of Austria
- Exhibition of Prize Winners
- Facial Expressions by Loney Haskell
- Fall River Boat "Priscilla"
- Fall River Boat Train
- Fastest Wrecking Crew in the World
- Fatima
- First Avenue, Seattle, Washington, No. 8
- Fisherman's Wharf
- A Fishing Schooner
- Fishing Smacks
- Fun on the Steeple-Chase
- Golding Sisters, Champion Swimmers
- Hallow-e'en in Coon-town
- Harvesting Corn
- The Haverstraw Tunnel
- Heads, Hats and Faces
- His Majesty, King Edward VII
- Horses Loading for Klondike
- Hotel Del Monte
- Hotel Vendome, San Jose, Cal.
- The Jealous Monkey
- Jordan, Marsh & Co.'s Store
- Judging Tandems
- Keith's Theatre
- Ladies' Saddle Horses
- Launch of Life Boat
- Launch of Surf Boat
- Leander Sisters
- Lick Observatory, Mt. Hamilton, Cal.
- Loading Baggage for Klondike
- Lurline Baths
- Marshall P. Wilder
- A Maxim Gun in Action
- A Multicycle Race
- New York Elevated Trains
- One-Third Mile Bicycle Race
- Oriten
- A Paced Bicycle Race
- Pie Eating Contest
- Pie-eating Contest
- Rainmakers
- Rescue—Resuscitation
- Return of Lifeboat
- S.S. "Coptic" at Dock
- S.S. "Coptic" in the Harbor
- S.S. "Coptic" Sailing Away
- S.S. "Queen" Leaving Dock
- S.S. "Queen" Loading
- S.S. "Williamette" Leaving for Klondike
- Safety in Four Tracks
- The Sea Lions' Home
- Single Harness Horses
- Soap Bubbles
- Southern Pacific Overland Mail
- Stanford University, California
- Surf at Monterey
- Sutro Baths, No. 1
- Taking on the Pilot
- Teams of Horses
- Wall Scaling
- Washing the Baby

Nov [day undetermined]

- Arrival of His Majesty, King Edward VII (then Prince of Wales) at the Ascot Races, 1897
- Burlesque Cake Walk
- The Dancing Skeleton
- Diving at Bath Beach
- Finish of the English Derby of 1897
- German Warship at Spithead
- H. M. S. Powerful at Spithead
- His Majesty, King Edward VII
- Knock-out Drops
- Maxim Firing Field Gun
- A New Waiter Opening a Fizz
- Philadelphia Police on Parade
- Sad Sea Waves
- Scrub Yacht Race
- Sexless Profiles
- Tramp in a Millionaire's Bed
- A Tramp's Dinner
- Wreck of the Schooner "Richmond"

Nov 27 The Downey and Patterson Fight

Dec [day undetermined]

- The Alarm (Gordon Highlanders)
- The "Amphitrite"
- At the Top of Brooklyn Bridge
- Austrian Mounted Police
- The Battery
- Battleship "Texas"
- Battleships "Maine" and "Iowa"
- Battleships "Marblehead" and "Miantonomah"
- Bayonet Versus Bayonet
- A Camp of Zingari Gypsies
- Charge of Hungarian Hussars
- Charge of the French Cuirassieurs
- A Children's Carnival in Germany
- Christmas Eve
- Christmas Morning
- The Christmas Tree Party
- Cruikshank
- Emperor William of Germany, and Emperor Franz Josef of Austria
- Fast Mail, Northern Pacific Railroad
- Firing by Squad, Gatling Gun
- French Cuirassieurs Charging a Field Battery
- Gatling Gun Crew in Action
- Girard College Cadets
- Girard College Cadets at Double Quick
- Girard College Cadets in Review
- Gordon Highlanders Marching into Camp
- Gymnastic Exercises in the British Army
- Her First Corset
- The Highland Fling, by the Gordon Highlanders
- How a Rat Interrupted an Afternoon Tea
- Hungarian Cavalry Charge
- The Model
- Mount and Dismount, Gatling Gun
- A Mouse in a Girls' Dormitory
- Mulberry Bend
- Night Before Christmas
- Ocean Greyhounds
- Only a Rat
- Place de la Concorde
- Pongo
- A Regimental Calisthenic Drill in the British Army
- Santa Claus Filling Stockings
- Scrambling for Pennies
- Side-Walks of New York
- A Skipping Rope Dance
- "Spike, the Bag-Punching Dog"
- Tipping the Cart in Mulberry Bend
- Trafalgar Square
- Visit of St. Nicholas
- The Workers

1898 [month undetermined]

- After the Battle
- Alciede Capitane
- American Cavalry Charging with Drawn Swords
- American Commissary Wagons Landing on Cuban Soil
- The American Flag
- The Armenian Archbishop, Rome
- Bathing Scene at Rockaway
- Battery Charge
- Battle of Guantanomo [sic]
- Battle of San Juan Hill
- Battleship Indiana
- Battleship Iowa
- The Battleship Maine in the Harbor of Havana
- The Battleship Maine Leaving U.S. Harbor for Havana
- Battleship Massachusetts
- Battleship Oregon
- Battleship Texas
- The Big Monitor Miantonomah Leaving the Navy Yard
- Boxing
- Boxing Cats
- Brave Cubans Firing at Spanish Soldiers
- Broadsword Exercise on the Battleship Texas
- Bucking Broncho
- Caciedo
- Can Can
- Captain Sigsbee on Deck of the U.S. Battleship Texas
- Capture of a Spanish Fort near Santiago
- Capuchin Monks, Rome
- Cavalry Horses Fording a Stream in Santiago de Cuba
- Charge at Las Guasimas
- Cleaning and Firing of the Hotchkiss Revolving Cannon on the Battleship Texas
- Colored Invincibles
- Corbett and Sharkey Fight
- Corpus Christi Procession, Orvieto
- Court Martial
- Crew of the Battleship Texas
- Cruiser Brooklyn
- Cruiser Columbia
- Cruiser Marblehead
- Cruiser New York
- Cubans Drilling, Manual of Arms
- Daily March
- Dispatch Boat Dolphin
- Execution of the Spanish Spy
- Feeding the Pigs
- 15,000 Soldiers Reviewed by the President at Camp Alger May 28
- The Fighting Fifth Cuban Mascot
- Fighting near Santiago
- Flag Film [?]
- Fun in a Spanish Camp
- Fun in the American Camp at Chicamauga
- General Miles and Staff
- Gen'l Sir Herbert Kitchener
- Ghost Dance
- Girls Brigade, of Lansford, Pa.
- Governor Hastings and Mounted Police
- Grand Army Veterans of Chicago
- Grand Army Veterans of New York
- Grand Army Veterans of Philadelphia
- His Holiness, Leo XIII in the Gardens of the Vatican, Being Photographed by the American Biograph Camera
- Hobson and Crew of the Merrimac
- Hoisting of the American Flag at Cavite
- How the Flag Changed in Cuba
- Indian War Council
- Infantry Charge
- Knights of the Golden Eagle
- The Late President Faure of France
- Launch of the Great Battleship Alabama
- Launch of the "Oceanic"
- Massachusetts Regiment Marching
- Mess Call, American Camp at Chicamauga
- Mexican Dance
- The Mysterious Midgets
- Naval Reserves Returning from the War
- New Couchee Dance
- Off for the Front
- Officers of the War Ships
- Outpost Skirmish
- Pennsylvania Academy of Fine Arts
- Philadelphia Letter Carriers
- President Faure Shooting Pheasants
- President McKinley and Cabinet at Camp Alger, May 28, 1898
- Red Cross at the Front
- Return of Our Soldier Boys
- Review of Officers
- Rough Riders
- Rough Riders at Guantanamo
- Sailors Landing Under Fire
- 71st New York
- Soldiers at Play
- Soldiers Firing on Train
- The Spanish Cruiser Vizcaya
- Spanish Infantry Attacking American Soldiers in Camp
- State Fencibles, Pennsylvania

Steam Launch of the Olympia
Surrender of General Toral
Teaching Cavalry to Ride
Third Regiment Pennsylvania
13th Regiment Pennsylvania Volunteers
Torpedo Boat Winslow
U.S. Battleship Texas
The Vatican Guards, Rome
View of Cramp's Shipyard
View of League Island, Philadelphia
Washing the Streets of Porto Rico

Jan [day undetermined]
At the Chorus Girls' Picnic
The Bowery Waiter and the Old Time Ball Player
Charge of the Light Brigade
Clearing a Drift
During the Blizzard
An Early Breakfast
A Fine Day for Sleighing, Boston
Fishing Vessels After the Blizzard
Girls Struggling for a Sofa
Her Morning Exercise
How She Gets Along Without a Maid
An Impromptu Can-can at the Chorus Girls' Picnic
An Interrupted Breakfast
Meeting of Emperor William of Germany and Emperor Franz Josef of Austria
Merry Sleigh Bells
New Year's Carnival
Place de l'Opera
Relieving the Guard at St. James Palace
The See-Saw, at the Chorus Girls' Picnic
Skating
Sleighing Scene
Surf Dashing Against England's Rocky Coast
The Timid Girls and the Terrible Cow
The Tipping Evil
Trinity Church
Unexpected Advent of the School Teacher
What Happened When a Hot Picture Was Taken

Feb [day undetermined]
Battle of San Juan Hill
Branding Cattle
Buck Dance, Ute Indians
Calf Branding
California Limited, A.T. & S.F.R.R.
California Orange Groves, Panoramic View
Cañon of the Rio Grande
Cattle Fording Stream
Cattle Leaving the Corral
Chinese Procession
Circle Dance, Ute Indians
City Hall
Coasting
Cripple Creek Float
Decorated Carriages
Denver Fire Brigade
Dogs Playing in the Surf
Down in Dixie
Eagle Dance, Pueblo Indians
Going Through the Tunnel
Hockey Match on the Ice
Horticultural Floats, No. 9
Indian Day School
Las Viga Canal, Mexico City
Lassoing a Steer
Loading a Mississippi Steamboat
Marching Scene
Mardi Gras Carnival
Market Scene, City of Mexico
Masked Procession
Mexican Fishing Scene
Mexican Rurales Charge
A Mid-Winter Brush
The Monitor "Terror"
Off for the Rabbit Chase
Ostriches Feeding
Ostriches Running, No. 1
Ostriches Running, No. 2
Parade of Coaches
Picking Oranges
Pilot Boat "New York"
Procession of Mounted Indians and Cowboys
Repairing Streets in Mexico
Royal Gorge
Serving Rations to the Indians, No. 1
Serving Rations to the Indians, No. 2
The Skyscrapers of New York
Snowballing the Coasters
South Spring Street, Los Angeles, Cal.
Spanish Ball Game
Spanish Battleship "Viscaya"
Street Scene, San Diego
Sunday Morning in Mexico
Sunset Limited, Southern Pacific Ry.
Surface Transit, Mexico
They're Not So Warm
A Three Masted Schooner
Torpedo Boat, "Dupont"
Train Hour in Durango, Mexico
"Vizcaya" Under Full Headway
Wand Dance, Pueblo Indians
Wash Day in Mexico
'Way Down South

Feb 19 The Passion Play of Oberammergau

Mar [day undetermined]
Acrobatic Monkey
After Launching
American Flag
Boston Navy Yard
Brigadier-General Fitz Hugh Lee
Bull Fight, No. 1
Bull Fight, No. 2
Bull Fight, No. 3
Canadian Artillery Marching on Snow Shoes
Canadian Outdoor Sports
Children Coasting
The Christian Herald's Relief Station, Havana
Coasting in Canada
Coasting Scene in Canada
Cruiser "Montgomery"
Cuban Reconcentrados
Divers at Work on the Maine
Feeding Sea Gulls
Feeding the Ducks at Tampa Bay
Fighting Roosters; in Florida
Freight Train
Harbor Defenses
Hockey Match; Quebec
Launch of Japanese Man-of-War "Chitosa"
Launch, U.S. Battleship "Kentucky"
Launching, No. 2
Lawn Tennis in Florida
Life Saving; Quebec Fire Department
Mexico Street Scene
Mount Tamalpais R.R., No. 1
Mount Tamalpais R.R., No. 2
Mount Taw R.R., No. 3
Native Daughters
Old Glory and Cuban Flag
Parade of Chinese
Procession of Floats
Quebec Fire Department Drill
A Run of the Havana Fire Department
Scene on the Steamship "Olivette"
Sea Waves
The Snow Shoe Club
Spanish Volunteers in Havana
Steamer "Boston"
Steamship "Olivette"
Tampa Bay Hotel, Tampa, Fla.
Union Iron Works
An Unwelcome Visitor
The Wreck of the "Maine"

Apr [day undetermined]
"Away Aloft"
Bareback Riding, 6th Cavalry, U.S.A.
Battleship "Massachusetts"
Captain Sigsbee
Capture of the "Panama"
Conway Castle
Cruiser "Brooklyn"
Cruiser "Minneapolis"
French Can-Can
Her First Lesson in Dancing
Idle Hours of the English Coast Guards
In Camp, Tampa, Fla.
The "Jennie Deans"
Launching of the "Kearsage"
"Me and My Two Friends"
The Monitor "Amphitrite"
Newport News Ship-Building Co.'s Shipyard
The "Panther"
Pile Drivers; Tampa, Fla.
Practice Warfare
Quebec Fire Department
Quebec Fire Department Drill
Ram "Katahdin"
Red Cross Steamer "Texas"
S.S. "Columbia" Sailing
Sailor Nailing Flag to Mast
The Tenth Battalion
A Terrible Spill
Theodore Roosevelt
Three Men in a Boat
Tossing a Nigger in a Blanket
Troop "A"; N.G.S.N.Y.
A Tug in a Heavy Sea
Twelfth Regiment, N.G.S.N.Y.
Water Polo
What Happened to the Dancing Master's Pupil
With the Army at Tampa
Worthing Life-Saving Station

May [day undetermined]
Battery B Pitching Camp
Battleship "Indiana"
Battleship "Iowa"
Between the Acts
Capture of the "Pedro"
A Country Couple's Visit to an Art Gallery
Cuban Patriots
Effect of a Certain Photograph
Folding Beds Are Tricky
A French Quadrille
Fun in the Barn
Harbor of St. Thomas
How Bridget Served the Salad Undressed
In Front of "Journal" Building
An Interrupted Sitting
Karina
The Kiki Dance
Learning To Do Splits
The "Lorenzo"
Moulin Rouge Dancers
The Old Maid's Picture
One Chair Short
The Sleeping Uncle and the Bad Girls
Some Dudes Can Fight
Spinster's Waterloo
A Swift Chappie
Three Views of the 69th Regiment, N.G.S.N.Y.
The Tramp Trapped
The Unexpected Visit
Warships
What Our Boys Did at Manila
When the Clock Strikes Two in the Tenderloin

May 20 The Ball Game
Battery B Arriving at Camp
The Burglar
Burial of the "Maine" Victims
Colored Troops Disembarking
Comedy Set-To
Cruiser "Cincinnati"
Cruiser "Detroit"
Cruiser "Marblehead"
Cuban Refugees Waiting for Rations
Cuban Volunteers Marching for Rations
Flagship "New York"
Heaving the Log
Military Camp at Tampa, Taken from Train
Monitor "Terror"
Morro Castle, Havana Harbor
N.Y. Journal Despatch Yacht "Buccaneer"
9th Infantry Boys' Morning Wash
9th U.S. Cavalry Watering Horses
S.S. "Coptic"
S.S. "Coptic" Lying To
S.S. "Coptic" Running Against the Storm
Secretary Long and Captain Sigsbee
See-Saw Scene
Snow Storm
Steamer "Mascotte" Arriving at Tampa
A Street Arab
The Telephone
10th U.S. Infantry Disembarking from Cars
10th U.S. Infantry, 2nd Battalion Leaving Cars
Transport "Whitney" Leaving Dock
U.S. Battleship "Indiana"
U.S. Battleship "Iowa"
U.S. Cavalry Supplies Unloading at Tampa, Florida
U.S. Cruiser "Nashville"
U.S.S. "Castine"
War Correspondents
Wreck of the Battleship "Maine"

May 28 Cake Walk

Jun [day undetermined]
Afternoon Tea on Board S.S. "Doric"
Anderson Zouaves
Arrival of Tokyo Train
"Balancing in the Basket"
Blanket-Tossing a New Recruit
California Volunteers Marching To Embark

Canton River Scene
Canton Steamboat Landing Chinese Passengers
Chief Devery at Head of N.Y. Police Parade
Church Temperance League
Countryman and Mischievous Boys
Crossing the Line
Cuban Volunteers Embarking
Dalgren Post, G.A.R.
The Deserter
A Duel to the Death
The Foragers
14th U.S. Infantry Drilling at the Presidio
Game of Shovel Board on Board S.S. "Doric"
Giving the General a Taste of It
Going to the Yokohama Races
Government House at Hong Kong
The Greased Pig
He Wanted Too Much for His Pies
Hebrew Orphan Asylum Band
Hong Kong Regiment, No. 1
Hong Kong Regiment, No. 2
Hong Kong, Wharf Scene
Honolulu Street Scene
How the Ballet Girl Was Smuggled into Camp
Irish Volunteers
Japanese Sampans
John A. Dix Post, G.A.R.
Kanakas Diving for Money [Honolulu], No. 1
Kanakas Diving for Money [Honolulu], No. 2
Koltes' Camp, G.A.R.
Landing Wharf at Canton
Loading Horses on Transport
Military Discipline
N. L. Farnum Post, G.A.R.
Naval Post, G.A.R.
Naval Review Spithead
New York Mounted on Parade
New York Police on Parade
New York Police Parade
9th and 13th U.S. Infantry at Battalion Drill
Parade of Buffalo Bill's Wild West Show, No. 1
Parade of Buffalo Bill's Wild West Show, No. 2
Railway Station at Yokohama
The Rainmakers
Returning from the Races
River Scene at Macao, China
Roosevelt's Rough Riders Embarking for Santiago
S.S. "Coptic" Coaling
S.S. "Doric"
S.S. "Doric" in Mid-Ocean
S.S. "Gaelic"
S.S. "Gaelic" at Nagasaki
The Schoolmaster's Surprise
71st N.Y. Volunteers Embarking for Santiago
Shanghai Police
Shanghai Street Scene No. 1
Shanghai Street Scene No. 2
Sikh Artillery, Hong Kong
Soldiers Washing Dishes
Street Boys at the Seashore
Street Scene in Hong Kong
Street Scene in Yokohama, No. 1
Street Scene in Yokohama, No. 2
The Teacher's Unexpected Bath
Theatre Road, Yokohama
Tourists Starting for Canton
Trained Cavalry Horses
The Tramp and the Giant Firecracker
Transport Ships at Port Tampa
Troop Ships for the Philippines
Troops Embarking at San Francisco
Uncle Rube's Visit to the Man-o' War
Veteran Zouaves
The Volunteer Fireman
Wagon Supply Train en Route
Wharf Scene, Honolulu

Jul [day undetermined]

Admiral Cervera and Officers of the Spanish Fleet Leaving the "St. Louis"
Admiral McNair, U.S.N.
An Alarm of Fire in a Soubrettes' Boarding House
The Amateur Trapeze Performers
Army Mules
Bathroom Frivolities
Bayonet Charge; by the 2nd Illinois Volunteers
Blind Man's Bluff
A Breezy Day on a Man-o'-War
The Burglar
A Charge by Cavalry
Children's Tea Party
A Chinese Opium Joint
Cholly's First Moustache
The Chorus Girls' Good Samaraitan
Chorus Girl's Revenge
Col. Torrey's "Rough Riders"
Col. Torrey's Rough Riders and Army Mules
Company "C," 1st Regiment, N.J.V.
The Confetti Dance
Cooling Off
Cooling Off a Hot Baby
Cuban Volunteers
Cubans Sharpening their Machetes
The Daughter of the Regiment
Doing Her Big Brother's Tricks on the Bar
Dressing Paper Dolls
An Execution by Hanging
1st Regiment, N.Y.V.
Follow Your Leader
Fun in a Girl's Dormitory
Fun in a Harlem Flat
Gen. Fitzhugh Lee and Staff
Getting a Shape
Girls Imitating Firemen
Going to Jerusalem
Gymnastic Feats After the Bath
Helping a Good Thing Along
Hot Afternoon in a Bachelor Girl's Flat
A Hot Time in a Hammock
How a Bottle of Cocktails Was Smuggled into Camp
How the Athletic Lover Outwitted the Old Man
How the Dressmaker Got Even with a Dead Beat
Imitation of a College Society Girl
The Inquisitive Girls
An Interrupted Kiss
Joe, the Educated Orangoutang
Joe, the Educated Orangoutang, Undressing
Jumping the Rope After Bed Time
Jumping the Stick
The Katzenjammer Kids in School
A Landing Fight
The Landlady Gives Notice to the Barrasing Sisters
Lasso Throwing
The Lazy Girl
A Letter from Her Soldier Lover
Locked Out, but Not Barred Out
The Locomotive Wheel
"London Bridge Is Falling Down"
The Nearsighted School Teacher
"New York Journal's War Issue"
New York Naval Reserves
The Old Maid and the Burglar
An Overloaded Donkey
Playing Horse
Playing Soldiers
Policemen Play No Favorites
Recruits of the 69th Regiment, N.G.S.N.Y.
A Ride on a Switchback
"Riding the Goat"
The Rivals
Rocky Mountain Riders Rough Riding
"Roly Poly"
A Romp in Camp
Roosevelt's Rough Riders
Rough Riding
"Round and Round the Mulberry Bush"
"Rushing the Growler"
Salt Lake City Company of Rocky Mt. Riders
Second Illinois Volunteers at Double Time
Second Illinois Volunteers in Review
A Second Story Man
A Shoe and Stocking Race
Shooting the Chutes at Home
Siamese Twins
69th Regiment Passing in Review
Smoking Her Out
Some Troubles of House Cleaning
The Soubrettes' Wine Dinner
Spanish Sailors on the "St. Louis"
Spanking the Naughty Girl
The Startled Lover
The Stingy Girl and the Box of Candy
The Stolen Stockings
"Teeter Tauter"
The Telephone
The Third Degree
32nd Regiment, Michigan Volunteers
Three Baths for the Price of One
Three Ways of Climbing over a Chair
Tickling the Soles of Her Feet
A Time and Place for Everything
A Tragedy Averted
Train vs. Donovan
The Tramp and the Muscular Cook
The Tramp Caught a Tartar
Tribulations of a Country Schoolmarm
Tribulations of Sleeping in a Hammock
Troop "H," Denver, Col.
Trying to Jump Her Board Bill
Trying to "Skin the Cat"
Tub Race
U.S. Troop-Ships
An Unsuccessful Raid
The Unwelcome Callers
A Very Laughable Mixup
The Washwoman's Daughter
What's the Matter with the Bed
The Wheelbarrow Race
When the Girls Got Frisky
When the Organ Played in Front of the Hotel
Winding the Maypole
A Windy Corner
Wounded Soldiers Embarking in Row Boats
Wreck of the "Vizcaya"

Aug [day undetermined]

The Baldheaded Dutchman
The Bathing Girls Hurdle Race
A Blast at the Solvay Quarries
Boys Stealing Apples
The Coney Island Bikers
Cuban Ambush
The Dude's Experience with a Girl on a Tandem
Fake Beggar
A Hotel Fire in Paris, and Rescue by Parisian Pompiers
Jumping Net Practice
The Last Round Ended in a Free Fight
"Leapfrog" on the Beach
Little Willie and the Minister
Major General Shafter
Making Love on the Beach
The Minister's Wooing
Mules Swimming Ashore at Daiquiri, Cuba
Naval Constructor Richmond P. Hobson
101st Regiment, French Infantry
Pack Mules with Ammunition on the Santiago Trail, Cuba
Packing Ammunition on Mules, Cuba
Race Between a Multicycle and a Horse
Ready for the Bath
Seventh Ohio Volunteers
Shooting Captured Insurgents
Shooting the Long Sault Rapids
Sixth Pennsylvania Volunteers
65th Regiment at Double Time
65th Regiment, N.Y.V.
A Skirmish Drill
Snap the Whip
Stealing Apples
Steamer "Island Wanderer"
Steamer "New York"
Stolen Sweets
Third Missouri Volunteers
U.S. Troops Landing at Daiquiri, Cuba
Victorious Squadron Firing Salute
Volley Firing

Sep [day undetermined]

Admiral Sampson on Board the Flagship
Agoust Family of Jugglers
The Battleship "Oregon"
Behind the Firing Line
A Bigger Fish Than He Could Manage
Broadsword Drill
Capron's Battery
A Catastrophe in a Sailboat
Charge by Rushes
Close View of the "Brooklyn," Naval Parade
Col. Theodore Roosevelt and Officers of His Staff
Company "H," 3rd N.Y.V.
Crew of the "Yankee"
The Defence of the Flag
18th Pennsylvania Volunteers
Eighth Ohio Volunteers (the President's Own)

Excursion Boats, Naval Parade
Farmer Kissing the Lean Girl
The Farmer's Mishap
The Fat Man and the Treacherous Springboard
Fifteenth Minnesota Volunteers
Fifth Massachusetts Volunteers
First Battalion of the 2nd Massachusetts Volunteers
First Maryland Volunteers
First Rhode Island Volunteers
The Fleet Steaming Up North River
Fourth Infantry, U.S. Regulars
Free Tobacco
A Gallant Charge
The Gallant Young Man
General Wheeler and Secretary of War Alger at Camp Wikoff
The "Glen Island," Accompanying Parade
He Caught More Than He Was Fishing For
How Farmer Jones Made a Hit at Pleasure Bay
How Uncle Reuben Missed the Fishing Party
In the Trenches
The Last Stand
The "Massachusetts," Naval Parade
"Me and Jack"
The Men Behind the Guns
Merry-Go-Round
Ninth Regiment, U.S. Regulars
Observation Train Following Parade
Panoramic View of Camp Wikoff
Peace Jubilee Naval Parade, New York City
Police Boats Escorting Naval Parade
A Poor Landing
A Poor Start
A Precarious Position
President McKinley's Inspection of Camp Wikoff
Queer Fish That Swim in the Sea
Rapid Fire, Charge
Rapid Fire Gun Drill
The Red Cross
Reviewing the "Texas" at Grant's Tomb
Second Battalion; 2nd Massachusetts Volunteers
71st Regiment, N.G.S.N.Y. at Camp Wikoff
A Slippery Landing
Statue of Liberty
Tenth Regiment, Ohio Volunteers
The "Texas," Naval Parade
They Will Never Do It Again
Thirteenth Infantry, U.S. Regulars
33rd Regiment, Michigan Volunteers
The Tramp's Last Bite
The Treacherous Spring Board
Troops Making Military Road in Front of Santiago
Twenty-Fourth Infantry
22nd Regiment, Kansas Volunteers
U.S. Battleship "Oregon"
U.S. Cruiser "Brooklyn," Naval Parade
"Weary Raggles"

Oct [day undetermined]

Advance Guard, Return of N.J. Troops
Allegorical Floats
Balloon Ascension, Marionettes
Beauseant Commandery of Baltimore
Boston Commandery, Boston, Mass.
Cardinal Gibbons
A Chicago Street
Cleveland Commandery, Cleveland, O.
Coronation of Queen Wilhelmina of Holland
County Democracy
Damascus Commandery, Detroit
Dancing Chinaman, Marionettes
Detroit Commandery, No. 1
Ella Lola, a la Trilby [Dance]
Famous Battleship Captains—Philadelphia Peace Jubilee Parade
French Soldiers in a Wall-Climbing Drill
Grand Commandery of the State of New York
Hanselmann Commandery, Cincinnati, O.
How the Gobbler Missed the Axe
Hungarian Women Plucking Geese
In the Adirondacks
An Innocent Victim
Launch of the "Illinois"
Louisville Commandery, Louisville, Ky.
Love in a Cornfield
M. H. Pope Leo in Chair
Major-General Nelson A. Miles, and Staff, in the Peace Jubilee Parade
Naval Constructor Richmond P. Hobson and the Crew of the Merrimac
Officers and Crew of the U.S. Cruiser "Brooklyn"
Parade of Marines, U.S. Cruiser, "Brooklyn"
Pea-Hulling Machine
Peace Parade—Chicago
Philadelphia City Troop and a Company of Roosevelt's Rough Riders
Providence Commandery, Providence, R.I.
Return of 2nd Regiment of New Jersey
Return of Troop C, Brooklyn
St. Bernard Commandery, Chicago
St. Vincent's Cadets
Skeleton Dance, Marionettes
South Gate of the Highlands
Stealing a Ham
Street Fight and Arrest
Tancred Commandery, Pittsburg
The Tenth Cavalry
A Texas Steer
Third Pennsylvania Volunteers
Troop "C"
Turkish Dance, Ella Lola
Twenty-Third Regiment, N.G.S.N.Y.
U.S. Marines
Who's Got the Red Ear?

Nov [day undetermined]

Around the Big Swing
The Dance of the Living Picture
Elopement on Horseback
Gladys Must Be in Bed Before Ten
A Happy Family
Illinois Central Terminal
A Living Picture Model Posing Before a Mirror
Making an Impression
Mr. B. F. Keith
A Narrow Escape
Pope Leo XIII and Count Pecci, No. 1
Pope Leo XIII Approaching Garden
Pope Leo XIII Attended by Guard
Pope Leo [XIII] Blessing in the Garden
Pope Leo XIII Giving Blessing from Chair
Pope Leo XIII in Carriage
Pope Leo XIII in Carriage, No. 1
Pope Leo XIII in Sedan Chair, No. 1
Pope Leo XIII in Vatican Garden, No. 1
Pope Leo XIII, No. 31-56
Pope Leo XIII, No. 57-82
Pope Leo XIII Passing Through Upper Loggia, No. 1
Pope Leo XIII Preparing To Give Blessing from Chair
Pope Leo XIII Seated in Garden
Pope Leo XIII Walking at Twilight, No. 1
Pope Leo [XIII] Walking in the Garden
The Rivals
"Snapping the Whip"
Socks or Stockings
The Tramp in the Kitchen
Underwear Model

Dec [day undetermined]

The Astor Battery
A Boarding School Escape
The Burglar in the Bed Chamber
The Burglar on the Roof
The Cavalier's Dream
The Cop and the Nurse Girl
Country Boarders Locked Out
The Elopement
Ice Yachting
Pope Leo XIII Being Carried in Chair Through Upper Loggia, No. 101
Pope Leo XIII Being Seated Bestowing Blessing Surrounded by Swiss Guards, No. 107
Pope Leo XIII in Canopy Chair, No. 100
Pope Leo XIII in Carriage, No. 102
Pope Leo XIII Leaving Carriage and Being Ushered into Garden, No. 104
Pope Leo XIII, No. 106
Pope Leo XIII Seated in Garden, No. 105
Pope Leo XIII Walking Before Kneeling Guards
S.S. "Coptic" Running Before a Gale
Sleighing Scene
Vanishing Lady
What Demoralized the Barber Shop

1899 [month undetermined]

Admiral Dewey on the Olympia
Admiral Dewey's Flagship Olympia in Action at Manila
Amann
Amann, the Great Impersonator
Armored Train Crossing the Veldt
Battle of El Caney
Battle of Santiago
Battleship Oregon in Action
Beerbohm Tree, the Great English Actor
Bicycling Under Difficulties
The Boxing Horse
British Armored Train
Capt. Coghlan, One of the Manila Heroes, and Crew of the Raleigh, Reviewed by the President
Capture of Porto Rico
Charge at Las Guasimas, Where Capron and Fish Were Killed
Charge of the Rough Riders at El Caney
Chinese Sailors Placing a Wreath on the Monument
Christmas Morning
Church Parade of the Life Guards
The Couchee Couchee Bear
Death of Maceo and His Followers
Departure of the Gordon Highlanders
Destruction of the Spanish Cruiser Maria Theresa
Dewey Arch, New York City
Dewey Land Parade
Dewey Naval Parade
Escort of the President Passing the Monument
Firing the 3 Pounders of the Raleigh
Frere Bridge, as Destroyed by the Boers
Full View of Brooklyn Bridge
General Babbington's Scouts
General Sir Redvers Buller
General Sir Redvers Buller, and Staff, Landing at Cape Town, South Africa
"God Save the Queen"
Her Majesty, Queen Victoria
Her Majesty, Queen Victoria, Reviewing the Honorable Artillery
Her Majesty, Queen Victoria, Reviewing the Household Cavalry at Spital Barracks
Lady Contortionist
Lord Roberts Embarking for South Africa
Lord Wolseley
Morelli and Her Leopards
A Naval Camp
New Lipman Dance
New Umbrella Dance
Plowing Snow in the Park
President McKinley and Wife, Members of His Cabinet and Their Wives and Capt. Coghlan Leaving the Cruiser Raleigh
President McKinley Reviewing the Troops
The Prince of Wales (King Edward VII) at the Aldershot Review
Raid of a New York Bowery Saloon
Repulse of Spanish Troops at Santiago
Rifle Hill Signal Outpost
Rt. Honorable Cecil Rhodes
Ritchie, the Tramp Bicyclist
Santa Claus
Scaling a Fort at Manila
Schoolship Saratoga
Sev. Regiments Passing the Monument
Sleighing in the Park
Sleighing on Diamond Street
Snowballing After School
Tapping a Blast Furnace
The Tramp's Dream
U.S. Cruiser Raleigh
Unveiling of Grant Monument
With the British Ammunition Column

Jan [day undetermined]

Astor Battery on Parade
Coaches Arriving at Mammoth Hot Springs
Coaches Going to Cinnabar from Yellowstone Park
Fifth Avenue Entrance to Central Park
General Lee's Procession, Havana
Lower Falls, Grand Canyon, Yellowstone Park
Spaniards Evacuating
Tourists Going Round Yellowstone Park
Troops at Evacuation of Havana

Feb [day undetermined]

Jones and His Pal in Trouble

Jones' Interrupted Sleighride
Jones' Return from the Club
Larks Behind the Scene
Panoramic View of Brooklyn Bridge
Poker at Dawson City
Rapids below Suspension Bridge
Willie's First Smoke

Feb 11 The Devil's Laboratory
The Infernal Palace

Mar [day undetermined]
Across Brooklyn Bridge
Arabian Gun Twirler
Around the Big Curves
Around the Big Curves on the Manhattan Elevated R.R.
Bicycle Trick Riding, No. 2
Bucking the Blizzard
Can-Can in the Klondike
Dance in a Turkish Harem
The Disappointed Old Maid
Fatima, Star of the Orient
Getting Rid of the Surplus
Grand Military Steeple-Chase
Heavy Sea from Deck of "St. Louis"
Heavy Storm at Sea Taken from S.S. "St. Louis"
A Hot Time in Alaska
How Charlie Got the Dough
In the Grip of the Blizzard
Jones Makes a Discovery
Lockhart's Performing Elephants
Looking Forward S.S. "St. Louis"
Looking Off S.S. "St. Louis" at Sea
Love in the Kitchen
McKinley Leaving State House, Boston
A Mean Trick on a Sleepy Soubrette
A "Moving" Picture
Niagara Falls in Winter
Over the Bannister
Passengers on Port Side S.S. "St. Louis"
Passing Needles—S.S. "St. Louis"
Queen of the Harem
Raising Old Glory over Morro Castle
Rotary Snowplow in Action
Ruins of the Windsor Hotel Fire
A Slide for Life
Storming the Fort
Three Acrobats
Tommy's Ringing Good Joke on His Dad
What Happened to the Burglar

Apr [day undetermined]
Arrival of Boat, Providence, R.I.
The Artist's Dream
As in a Looking Glass
The Astronomer's Dream, or the Trip to the Moon
A Bucking Broncho
Burlesque Queen and Country Photographer
Casey at the Bat
Classic Poses
The Cremation
Cruiser "Raleigh"
A Crusty Old Bachelor
Digging a Trench
The Dusky Serenade
An Easter Parade
Eighth Regiment, Mass. Volunteers
Elevated Railroad and Drawbridge
English Fire Department Run
"Etruria"
Farmer Oatcake Has His Troubles
Ferryboat "St. Louis"
Fire Department Rescue Drill
Frank Gould's Dogs
Going to the Hunt
The Gordon Highlanders
"Graf Waldersee"
Grand National Steeple-Chase
Greater New York
He Thought That He Had 'Em
Her First Pose
High Hurdle Jumping, at Meadowbrook Hunt Club
A High-school Horse
How N.Y. Society Girls Take to the Fad of Tattooing
The Humane Side of Modern Warfare
"It's Unlucky To Pass Under a Ladder"
The Jealous Cook and the Policeman
Johanna's Chase
Liberty Enlightening the World
Little Willie in Mischief Again
Love's Labor Lost
A Marblehead Welcome
Market Square, Providence, R.I.
The Meadowbrook Hunt
Morning Colors on U.S. Cruiser "Raleigh"
"My Ragtime Girl"
Mysterious Disappearance of a Policeman
The Nurse's Joke
Off for China
104th Street Curve, New York, Elevated Railway
Oxford and Cambridge University Boat Crews
Oxford-Cambridge Boat-Race
Panoramic View of Windsor Castle
Parade in Providence, R.I.
Patriot's Day Parade
Pilot Boats in New York Harbor
Pole Vaulting at Columbia University
Prize Winning St. Bernards
The Professor's Fall from Grace
Providence Fire Department
Reginald's First High Hat
Review of First Rhode Island Volunteers
Scots Grey
She Wanted to Be a Boy
South Wales Express
The Startled Lover
Stealing a Bride
Symphony in "A" Flat
Teasing the Cook
Third Avenue Elevated Railroad
Tommy Atkins, Bobby and the Cook
Tremont Street
A Trip over the Manhattan Elevated Railroad
Under Full Sail
U.S. Cruiser "Raleigh"
View of Brooklyn Bridge from a Ferryboat
A Welcome Home
Welcoming the Soldier Boys
Why Clara Was Spanked
Why He Resigned from the Lodge
Wreck of the "Norseman"
A Wringing Good Joke
A Zulu War Dance

Apr 1 Bear Jumping Hurdles
The Trick Bear
The Wrestling Bear

Apr 10 A Trip to the Moon

Apr 29 How Would You Like to Be the Ice Man?

May [day undetermined]
Ambulance Corps Drill
American-Chinese Naval Reserves
The Automatic Prize Fight
A Bare Skin Joke
Board of Trade
The Breeches Buoy
The Burglar and the Bundle
A Burlesque Queen
Burlesque Queen and a Country Photographer
Champion High Jumpers, "Chappie" and "Ben Bolt"
Charlie Wanted the Earth
A Cock Fight
Cramp's Shipyard
Crew of the U.S. Cruiser "Raleigh"
Cripple Creek Bar-Room Scene
Distributing a War Extra
Elephants in a Circus Parade
Farmer Wayback Entertains
First Boston School Regiment
First City Troop of Philadelphia
A Flock of Sheep
Founder's Log Cabin
Frank Melville's Trick Elephant
Gen. Snowden and Staff, and Crew of the U.S.S. "Raleigh"
Getting Up in the World
Girard College Cadets
A Good Shot
Hazing a Freshman
High Jumping
High Steppers in Harness
Hippopotamus "Babe"
Hipwood-Barrett Car Fender
How Little Willie Put a Head on His Pa
Hurdle Jumping
Judging Ladies' Saddle Horses
"Langton Performer 2nd"
A Lark at the French Ball
Launching the Lifeboat
Little Willie and the Burglar
Living Pictures
Lunch Time in the Studio
M. B. Curtis
Mrs. U.S. Grant and President McKinley
Mounted Artillery
New York Mounted Police
Odd Fellows Parade
President McKinley and Mayor Ashbridge of Philadelphia
Running the Hurdles
"Sampson" Champion High Stepper
Schooling Hunters
Second Battalion, 1st Regiment, N. G. of Pennsylvania
Second Boston School Regiment
Second City Troop
The Serenaders
Shooting the Life Line
Spirits in the Kitchen
State Fencibles
Stealing a Dinner
Steamship "Pavonia"
Tent Pegging
Third Boston School Regiment
Troop "F," 3rd Cavalry
A Unique Race
Unveiling the Statue of Gen. U.S. Grant
The Violin Player
What Dumb Animals Can Be Taught
Why Mamie Missed the Masquerade
The Wicked Sister and the Lobster
Yale Athletes
Yale Athletes Broad Jumping
The Yale Crew

May 13 The Enchanted Inn

May 20 The Cavern of the Demons

Jun [day undetermined]
Advance of Kansas Volunteers at Caloocan
Armor vs. Amour
A Bad (K)Night
The Bibulous Clothier
Capture of Trenches at Candaba [Canda Bar]
Chief Devery and Staff
Childhood's Happy Days
Children Feeding Ducklings
The Corset Model
The Demon Barber
The Derby
Down Mount Tom
Eighth Regiment, N.G.S.N.Y.
A Fair Exchange Is No Robbery
Feeding the Pigeons
The Female Drummer
Filipinos Retreat from Trenches
Finish of the Brooklyn Handicap, 1899
First Heavy Artillery
A Football Tackle
For the Most Beautiful
Four A.M. at the French Ball
Going to the Post
Governor Walcott of Massachusetts
"La Grande Duchesse"
Her First Cigarette
How Ducks Are Fattened
Launch of the Porthonstock Life-boat
Lieutenant-General Nelson A. Miles
The Lock-Step
Mesmerist and Country Couple
New York Naval Militia
New York Police
New York Police Parade, June 1st, 1899
Ninth Regiment, N.G.S.N.Y.
The Paddock
Panoramic View, Horseshoe Curve, From Penna. Ltd.
Phillis Was Not Dressed to Receive Callers
President and Mrs. McKinley
President McKinley
The Price of a Kiss
The Pride of the Household
Reproduction of the Fitzsimmons-Jeffries Fight in Eleven Rounds Showing the Knock Out
Rout of the Filipinos
Scrubbem's Washing Machine
Shooting an Artesian Well
Skirmish of Rough Riders
The Soubrette's Birthday
Strange Adventure of New York Drummer
The Suburban
Suckling Pigs
Sunday School Parade
Twenty-Second Regiment, N.G.S.N.Y.
U.S. Infantry Supported by Rough Riders at El Caney
U.S. Troops and Red Cross in the Trenches Before Caloocan [P. I.]

A Whipping Post
Wreck of the "Mohican"
Wreck of the S.S. "Paris"

Jul [day undetermined]

The Approach to Niagara
Aquatic Sports
The Artist's Dream
An Attempt to Escape
Baby Feeding a Kitten
Baby Lund and Her Pets
Baby's Bath
Barrel Fight
A Bluff from a Tenderfoot
Boxing Dogs
Buffalo Fire Department
Canoeing at Riverside
Chorus Girls and the Devil
Chuck Connors vs. Chin Ong
"Columbia" and "Defender" Rounding Stake-Boat
"Columbia" vs. "Defender"
The Dairy Maid's Revenge
Demonstrating the Action of the Cliff-Guibert Hose Reel
Detroit Fire Department
Female Prisoners: Detroit House of Correction
The Finish of Mr. Fresh
Fire Drill at the Factory of Parke, Davis & Co.
A Flock of Export Sheep
G.A.R. Post, Detroit
Glen House Stage
Hazing Affair in a Girls' Boarding School
Her Morning Dip
How Bill the Burglar Got a Bath
How Mamie Had Her Leg Pulled
How Papa Set Off the Fireworks
How the Medium Materialized Elder Simpkin's Wife
How Tottie Coughdrop's Summer Suit Was Spoiled
Hurdle Jumping; by Trained Dogs
An Interrupted Crap Game
A Jest and What Came of It
A Just Cause for Divorce
Kilpatrick's Ride
Love in a Hammock
The Lovers' Quarrel
Lower Rapids of Niagara Falls
Male Prisoners Marching to Dinner
Merlin, the Magician
Michigan Naval Reserves and the Detroit Light Guards
Myopia vs. Dedham
Niagara Falls Station
Panoramic View, Horseshoe Curve, Penna. R.R., No. 2
Panoramic View of Niagara Falls
Parke Davis' Employees
Police Drill
A Ride Through Pack Saddle Mountains, Penna. R.R.
Running through Gallitzen Tunnel, Penna. R.R.
Running Up the Topsail on the "Columbia"
A Scandalous Proceeding
Smallest Train in the World
Steamship "Chippewa"
Steamship "Northland"
The Sweet Girl Graduate
Two Girls in a Hammock
An Up-to-Date Female Drummer
Water for Fair
The Way French Bathing Girls Bathe
What Julia Did to the Ghosts
When Babies' Quarrel
When Their Love Grew Cold
Whirlpool Rapids
The Wizard and the Spirit of the Tree

Aug [day undetermined]

American Soldiers Defeating Filipinos Near Manila
Around Tynsborough Curve
Babies Playing on a Hot Day
Ballet of the Ghosts
"Between the Races"
Bringing a Friend Home for Dinner
Climbing Jacob's Ladder
Crawford Notch
"Ding, Dong, Dell, Johnny's in the Well"
Fancy Diving
A Feast Day in Honolulu
The Fire Boat "New Yorker"
The Flume
43rd Rifles; Royal Canadian Infantry
The Frankenstein Trestle
A Gay Old Boy
The Great Lafayette
The Haunted House
He Didn't Finish the Story
The Henley Regatta
His Masterpiece
Hooksett Falls Bridge
How the Porto Rican Girls Entertain Uncle Sam's Soldiers
How the Tramp Lost His Dinner
The Imperial Limited
"Imperial Limited." Canadian Pacific R.R.
In Fighting Trim
An Intrigue in the Harem
The Jealous Model
Lord and Lady Minto
The Maniac Barber
Miss Jewett and the Baker Family
A Plate of Ice Cream and Two Spoons
The Prentis Trio
Professor Billy Opperman's Swimming School
The Saratoga Limited
Sliding Down Mount Washington
The Spider and the Fly
Stage Coaches Leaving the Hotel Victoria
Summit of Mt. Washington
Topsy-Turvy Quadrille
A Volunteer Fire Company
Water Throwing Contest
What Hypnotism Can Do
Where There's a Will, There's a Way
Why Krausemeyer Couldn't Sleep
Winnisquam Lake
Wonderful Dancing Girls
The X-Ray Mirror

Sep [day undetermined]

Admiral Dewey
Admiral Dewey Landing at Gibraltar
Admiral Dewey Receiving His Mail
Admiral Dewey's Dog, "Bob"
Apple Blossoms
Arabis Patrol
Baxter Street Mystery
The Boston Horseless Fire Department
Chickens Coming Out of the Shell
A Cold Day for Art
Colonel Funston Swimming the Baglag River
Demonstrating the Action of a Patent Street Sprinkler of the American Car Sprinkler Co. of Worcester, Mass
Demonstrating the Action of the Northrop Looms
The Diving Horse
Diving Through Paper Screens
Dreyfus Receiving His Sentence
The Early Morning Attack
Eggs Hatching
Employes of Bausch, Lomb & Co.
The "Erin"
An Exciting Finish
Fancy Diving
Four Corners of Rochester
The Golding Family
The Great Free-for-All Pacing Race
Guardians of the Peace
Heroes of Luzon
The International Alliance
International Collegiate Games
The International Collegiate Games
International Collegiate Games
International Collegiate Games—Half Mile Run
International Collegiate Games—100 Yards Dash
International Collegiate Games—110 Yards Hurdle Race
Jack Tars Ashore
"King" and "Queen," the Great High Diving Horses
Launch of the Battleship "Vengeance"
M'lle. Cathrina Bartho
The Makers of the Kodak
"Man Overboard!"
A Midnight Fantasy
New Brooklyn to New York via Brooklyn Bridge, No. 1
New Brooklyn to New York via Brooklyn Bridge, No. 2
Officers of the "Olympia"
One Mile Dash
Polo—A Dash for Goal
Polo—Hurlingham vs. Ranelagh
The Poster Girls
The Poster Girls and the Hypnotist
Prof. Paul Boynton Feeding His Sea Lions
A Ray of Sunshine After the Rain
Reproduction of the Jeffries and Sharkey Fight
Reproduction of the Pedlar Palmer and Terry McGovern Fight
Reproduction of the Sharkey and Jeffries Fight
Reproduction of the Terry McGovern and Pedlar Palmer Fight
Rochester Fire Department
A Roll Lift Draw Bridge
"Sagasta" Admiral Dewey's Pet Pig
The Sandwich Man
"Shamrock I"
Shamrock Starting on Trial Trip
Shoot the Chutes Series
Sir Thomas Lipton and Party on "Erin's" Launch
Sir Thomas Lipton's Steam Yacht "Erin"
The Skeleton at the Feast
Soldiers of the Future
Some Future Champions
The Summer Girl
A Thrilling Ride
Trial of Captain Dreyfus
Two Hours After Hatching

Sep 30 The Trial of Captain Dreyfus at Rennes, France

Oct [day undetermined]

Admiral Dewey and Mayor Van Wyck Going Down Riverside Drive
Admiral Dewey at State House, Boston
Admiral Dewey Leading Land Parade
Admiral Dewey Leading Land Parade, No. 2
Admiral Dewey Leading Land Parade, (Eighth Ave.)
Admiral Dewey Passing Catholic Club Stand
Admiral Dewey Receiving the Washington and New York Committees
Admiral Dewey Taking Leave of Washington Committee on the U.S. Cruiser 'Olympia'
Admiral Dewey's First Step on American Shore
After the Race—Yachts Returning to Anchorage
Back from Manila
Battery K Siege Guns
Beyond the Great Divide
Chinamen Returning to China
A Close Finish
Col. John Jacob Astor, Staff and Veterans of the Spanish-American War
"Columbia"
"Columbia" Close to the Wind
"Columbia" Winning the Cup
Connecticut Naval Reserves
The "Corsair"
"Corsair" in Wake of Tugboat
Crew of the "Shamrock"
Crew of the "Shamrock," at Work
The Dandy Fifth
The Dewey Arch
Dewey Arch—Troops Passing Under Arch
Dewey Naval Parade
Dewey Parade, 10th Pennsylvania Volunteers
A Dip in the Mediterranean
Down the Western Slope of the Canadian Rockies Through Kicking Horse Pass
The Eastern Slope of the Rockies, Passing Anthracite Station
5th Ohio Volunteers of Cleveland
1st Penn' Volunteers of Philadelphia
Flagship Olympia and Cruiser New York in Naval Parade
Fourth Connecticut Volunteers, Dewey Parade
Full Rigged Ship at Sea
The Gap, Entrance to the Rocky Mountains
Gen. McCrosky Butt and Staff
Governor Roosevelt and Staff
Harbor of Villefranche
The "Havana"
In Busy 'Frisco
In the Canadian Rockies, near Banff
Marines of the Atlantic Fleet
Market Street
Mr. and Mrs. C. Oliver Iselin
Mrs. C. Oliver Iselin and Crew of Columbia

The "Niagara"
Orpheum Theatre, San Francisco
Overland Limited
Panorama at Grant's Tomb, Dewey Naval Procession
Panoramic View of Floral Float "Olympia"
Panoramic View of Olympia in New York Harbor
The "Pennsylvania"
Police Boats and Pleasure Craft on Way to Olympia
Presentation of Loving Cup at City Hall, New York
Presentation of Nation's Sword to Admiral Dewey
The "Richard Peck"
The "Sagamore"
Sailors of the Atlantic Fleet
2nd Battalion, 3rd New York Provisional Regiment, Rochester and Syracuse, Separate Companies
2nd Company Governor's Footguards, Conn.
7th Regiment, New York City
"Shamrock"
"Shamrock" After Carrying Away Topsail
"Shamrock" and "Columbia"
Shamrock and Columbia Jockeying for a Start
"Shamrock" and "Columbia" Rounding the Outer Stake Boat
"Shamrock" and "Columbia" Rounding the Outer Stake Boat, No. 2
"Shamrock" and "Columbia" Yacht Race—First Race
"Shamrock" and "Erin" Sailing
A Spectacular Start
Start of Race Between "Columbia" and "Shamrock"
Start of Second Cup Race
Start of the Second Cup Race
Start of Third Day's Race
Steamer "Grandrepublic"
Steamship "Empress of India"
10th Penn'a Volunteers
Torpedo Boats at the Yacht Race
Training Ship "Lancaster"
Turning Stake Boat; "Columbia" and "Shamrock"
Under the Shadow of Mt. Stephen, Passing Field's Station in the Rocky Mountains
Up the Big Grade in the Valley of the Kicking Horse
West Point Cadets
The West Point Cadets and Band
Yacht Race—Finish

Nov [day undetermined]

After the Ball
Around Gravel Bay
The Astor Tramp
The Bather's Lunch
Battle Flag of the 10th Pennsylvania Volunteers, Carried in the Philippines
The Battle of Jeffries and Sharkey for Championship of the World
The Bride's Trousseau
Bridge No. 804, and Daly's Grade
Bunco on the Seashore
Caribou Bridge
Fougere
Frazer Canyon, East of Yale
Fun in Camp
Grand Trunk R.R. Bridge over Whirlpool
Interior Coney Island Club House, No. 1-4
It's Dangerous to Tickle a Soubrette
Jeffries and a Child at Play
Jeffries and Brother Boxing
Jeffries and Roeber Wrestling
Jeffries Being Rubbed Down
Jeffries Boxing with Tommy Ryan
Jeffries Running with His Trainers
The Jeffries-Sharkey Contest
Jeffries-Sharkey Contest
Jeffries Training on Bicycle
Love and War
The "Make-Up" Thief
Pictures Incidental to Yacht Race
Reproduction of the Corbett and Jeffries Fight
Reproduction of the Jeffries and Corbett Fight
Reproduction of the Jeffries and Ruhlin Fight
Reproduction of the Kid McCoy and Peter Maher Fight
Reproduction of the Peter Maher and Kid McCoy Fight
Reproduction of the Ruhlin and Jeffries Fight
2nd Special Service Battalion, Canadian Infantry, Embarking for So. Africa
2nd Special Service Battalion, Canadian Infantry-Parade
"Shamrock" and "Columbia" Yacht Race—1st Race, No. 2
Tenderloin at Night
Test. Coney Island Athletic Club
Three Hot Babies
Trick Bears
U.S. Cruiser "Olympia" Leading Naval Parade
A Warm Baby with a Cold Deck

Dec [day undetermined]

Blanco Bridge
By Pulpit Rock and Through the Town of Echo
Coolies at Work
Devil's Gate
Devil's Slide
East of Uintah in Weber Canyon
The Escolta
Fighting in the Transvaal
Follow the Girls
The Foster Mother
Going to the Firing Line
Home of Buffalo Bill
One Thousand Mile Tree, Weber Canyon
The "Overland Limited" Passing Witch Rocks
Panoramic View of Manila Harbor
Passing Steamboat and Great Eastern Rocks
Pity the Blind
Port Huron; West End of St. Clair Tunnel
St. Clair Tunnel
33rd Infantry, U.S.A.
Toll Gate and Castle Rock near Green River
Tunnel "No. Three"
West of Peterson; Entrance to Weber Canyon
West Side St. Clair Tunnel

Dec 23 Pianka and her Lions
Dec 25 Cinderella

1900 [month undetermined]

Alladin and the Wonderful Lamp
Birdseye View of Galveston, Showing Wreckage
Boer War Film
Bull Fight
Burning of the Bremen and Main (another view) [Hoboken]
Burning of the Saale [Hoboken]
Darkey Excursionists Bathing, Atlantic City
Earl Roberts
Earl Roberts and General Baden Powell
Earl Roberts and Staff
Fight Between a Lion and a Bull
Fight Between Tarantula and Scorpion
Foreign Palaces
Funeral of Chinese Viceroy, Chung Fing Dang, Marching Through the European Quarter at Peking
Grand Palaces
High Diving
John Philip Sousa
Kansas City Fire Department, Winners of the World's Championship at the Paris Exposition
Mining Operations
Mysterious Acrobat
New Farmer's Mishap
New Sleighing Scene
Niagara Falls in Life Motion Pictures
Old Paris
Oxford-Cambridge Race
Palace of Navigation
Panorama of Both Sides of the River Seine
Panoramic View of Rome
The Parade of Naval Veterans
Parade of the Order of Elks in Atlantic City
Paris Exposition
Queen Victoria's Last Visit to Ireland
Razing a Chimney
The Republican National Convention
Sapho Kiss
South African War Subjects
Speed Trial of the "Albatross"
Sunken Steamer in Galveston Harbor
Taking the Dead from the Ruins [Galveston]
The Trocadero
Vesper Boat Club
View of City of Galveston from the Waterfront

Jan [day undetermined]

Another Picture Showing Demonstration of a Pneumatic Shell Riveter
Battle of Colenso
Blaine Club of Cincinnati
"Caught"
Demonstrating the Action of Pneumatic Shell Riveters on the Underside of the Hull of a Steel Vessel. Taken for the Chicago Pneumatic Tool Co.
Demonstrating the Action of the Chicago Pneumatic Tool Co.'s Deck Machine
Governor Nash of Ohio
"I Had To Leave a Happy Home for You"
Necessary Qualifications of a Typewriter
The Perfect Woman
Pneumatic Tools
Reproduction of the McGovern and Dixon Fight
Unloading Lighters, Manila
Why Jones Discharged His Clerks
Why Mrs. Jones Got a Divorce

Feb [day undetermined]

An Animated Luncheon
Automobile Parade
Battle of the Upper Tugela
Canadian Mounted Rifles on the March
Ching Ling Foo Outdone
Departure of the Second Canadian Contingent
Dick Croker Leaving Tammany Hall
A Dull Razor
Experimental—Handcamera
Faust and Marguerite
Lord Dundonald's Cavalry Seizing a Kopje in Spion Kop
The Magician
Marvin and Casler's Laboratory
Mounted Rifles at Drill
Northwestern Mounted Rifles
On to Ladysmith
The Royal Leinster Regiment
Royal Leinster Regiment on Parade
Royal Leinsters on Review
St. Clair Tunnel
Skating in Central Park
Toronto Mounted Rifles

Mar [day undetermined]

Above the Speedway
An Advance by Rushes
After the Storm
Annie Oakley
Answering the Alarm
An Artist's Dream
The Attack on Magalang
Barroom Scene
The Battle of Mt. Ariat
Betting Field
Boat Rescue
Bowling Green
Bridge of Spain
Brigadier-General Frederick D. Grant and Staff
Bringing General Lawton's Body Back to Manila
British Infantry Marching to Battle
Broadway at Post Office
A Brush on the Speedway
The Call to Arms!
Carnival Dance
Cissy Fitzgerald
Dancing on the Bowery
A Darktown Dance
Dress Parade of the Woodward High School Cadets
Drill of Naval Cadets at Newport
Family Troubles
Fatima's Coochee-Coochee Dance
Foot Ball Game
14th Street and Broadway
Funeral of Major-General Henry W. Lawton
Garden Scene
Getting Ready for the Seashore
The Girl from Paris
Going into Action
Great Foot Ball Game

"How'd You Like To Be the Iceman?"
In the Field
Interrupted Lover
Irish Way of Discussing Politics
Jones Gives a Private Supper
Jones Interviews His Wife
Jones' Return from a Masquerade
The Kiss
Little Mischief
The Little Reb
Lucille Sturgis
Major-General Arthur MacArthur and Staff
Making Manila Rope
Market Place
A Military Inspection
Military Scenes at Newport, R.I.
Miss Lucy Murray
Mr. and Mrs. Califf at Dinner
Morning Fire Alarm
The Mystic Swing
Off for the Boer War
Opening of the Rapid Transit Tunnel
Opera of Martha
Oriental Dance
Paddle Dance
Panoramic View of the Dewey Arch, New York City
Panoramic View of the Ghetto, New York City
Pat vs. Populist
Paterson Falls
Photographing the Ghost
Pickaninnies
Pluto and the Imp
A Quiet Little Smoke
Race Track Scene
Reproduction of the Olsen and Roeber Wrestling Match
Reproduction of the Sharkey and Fitzsimmons Fight
Rosedale
Santa Claus' Visit
Sapho
Scene on the Bois de Boulogne
The 17th Infantry, U.S.A.
Short-Stick Dance
Sidewalks of New York
Silver Dance
Telephone Appointment
The Train for Angeles
The Tramp and the Crap Game
Trial Race Columbia and Defender
Trial Race Columbia and Defender No. 2
Trolley Car Accident
25th Infantry
Umbrella Dance
Uncle Josh in a Spooky Hotel
Uncle Josh's Nightmare
Under Armed Escort
U.S. Marines in Dewey Land Parade
Up-to-Date Cake-Walk
View from the Gorge Railroad
A Visit to the Spiritualist
Walnut Hill Cadets
Water Buffalo, Manila
Watermelon Contest

Mar 10 Feeding Sea Lions

Apr [day undetermined]

After Dark in Central Park
Battle of Mafeking
"Ein Bier"
Birth of Venus
Boer Commissary Train Treking
Boers Bringing in British Prisoners
British Highlanders Exercising
British Troops on Dress Parade
Buffalo Bill's Wild West Show
Capture of Boer Battery
Capture of Boer Battery by British
Charge of Boer Cavalry
The Chimney Sweep and the Miller
The Croton Dam Strike
Demonstrating the Operation of the Harrington Rail Bonding System on the Line of the Coney Island and Brooklyn Railroad Co.
English Lancers Charging
English Transport "Arundel Castle" Leaving for the Transvaal with British Troops
English Troops Boarding Transport
Found a Man Under the Bed
Horsewhipping an Editor
How They Rob Men in Chicago
In Central Park
Not a Man in Sight
Overland Express Arriving at Helena, Mont.
"The Prince of Darkness"
Red Cross Ambulance on Battlefield
The Stocking Scene from "Naughty Anthony"
A Terrible Night
Tommy's Trick on Grandpa
Uncle Si's Experience in a Concert Hall
What Happened to a Fresh Johnnie
White Horse Rapids

Apr 7 Clowns Spinning Hats

Four Heads Better Than One
The Inquisitive Clerks
New Life Rescue
New Morning Bath
Two Old Sparks
Visit to a Spiritualist
The Wonder, Ching Ling Foo

Apr 21 X Rays

May [day undetermined]

After Aguinaldo
Aguinaldo's Navy
The Art of "Making Up"
The Boomerang
Brigadier-General Franklin Bell and Staff
Bringing in the Wounded During the Battle of Grobler's Kloof
Buffalo Bill's Wild West Parade
A Charge of the Insurgents
The Clown and the Mule
Confounding the Art Critic
Discharging a Whitehead Torpedo
The Downward Path: The Fresh Book Agent [Part 1]
The Downward Path: She Ran Away [Part 2]
The Downward Path: The Girl Who Went Astray [Part 3]
The Downward Path: The New Soubrette [Part 4]
The Downward Path: The Suicide [Part 5]
Exploding a Whitehead Torpedo
A Farmer Who Could Not Let Go
The Fighting 36th
A Filipino Town Surprised
A Four-Horse Circus Act
The 4th Cavalry
Gatling Gun Drill
General Bell's Expedition
A Good Time with the Organ Grinder
The Great Ottawa Fire
The Growler Gang Catches a Tartar
A Gun Play in the Klondike
An Historic Feat
How the Farmer Was Buncoed
How the Old Maid Got a Husband
How the Young Man Got Stuck at Ocean Beach
How They Fired the Bum
An Impromptu Hairdresser
Insured Against Loss
Into the Wilderness!
Major-General Lloyd Wheaton
Manila
May Day Parade
Maypole Dance
New Black Diamond Express
On the Advance of Gen. Wheaton
One on the Bum
Panorama of Gorge Railway
Panoramic View of Newport [R.I.]
The Queen's Reception to the Heroes of Ladysmith
A Raid on a Chinese Opium Joint
A Raid on "Dago" Counterfeiters
The Relief of Ladysmith
The Rubberneck Boarders
Sherlock Holmes Baffled
Sidewalks of New York
Slow but Sure
A Somersault on Horseback
A Speedway Parade
The Thief and the Pie Woman
Torpedo Boat "Morris" Running
Tramps in the Old Maid's Orchard
Trial Run of the Battleship "Alabama"
Trial Speed of H. M. Torpedo Boat Destroyer "Viper"
The Troublesome Fly
Uncle Reuben Lands a Kick
Water Babies
Why Mrs. McCarthy Went to the Ball
With the Guns!

Jun [day undetermined]

Alligator Bait
The Approach to Lake Christopher
The Approach to Shelburn
The Arizona Doctor
Brook Trout Fishing
A Cadet Cavalry Charge
A Career of Crime, No. 1: Start in Life
A Career of Crime, No. 2: Going the Pace
A Career of Crime, No. 3: Robbery & Murder
A Career of Crime, No. 4: In the Toils
A Career of Crime, No. 5: The Death Chair
The Census on Cherry Hill
The Champion Beer Drinker
A Close Finish
The Clown and the See-Saw Fairies
A Cold Water Cure
Dewey Land Parade, Detroit
Escape from Sing Sing
The Exposed Seance
Flyers of the Great Lakes
A Gesture Fight in Hester Street
Gilead
Harris Training Tower
High Diving by A. C. Holden
How Bridget Made the Fire
How He Saw the Eclipse
Larchmont Regatta
Love at 55
The Man in the Jimjams
The Masher's Waterloo
Mechanical Hair-Restorer
Monte Myro Troupe of Acrobats
Not the Man She Waited for
Orchard Lake Cadets
Public Square, Cleveland
St. Clair Tunnel
Seeing Things at Night
Shelter Tent Drill
Soldiers of Greater Britain
Steam Yacht "Kismet"
Steeple Chase, Toronto
The Suburban of 1900
Such a Quiet Girl, Too!
The Tell-Tale Kiss
The Tramp and the Burglar
Tramp in the Haunted House
A Tramp in the Well
Valley of the Little Androscoggin
Victoria Jubilee Bridge
Watermelon Contest
Wifie Invades the Studio
A Yard of Frankfurters

Jun 30 A Mysterious Portrait

Neptune and Amphitrite
The Power of the Cross
Spanish Inquisition
Wrestling Extraordinary

Jul [day undetermined]

Allabad, the Arabian Wizard
Amateur Athletic Championships
Arrest of a Shoplifter
Atlantic City Lodge, 276, B.P.O. Elks
Bargain Day
The Black Storm
Blue Ribbon Jumpers
Brooklyn Lodge, No. 22, B.P.O. Elks
The Burglar-Proof Bed
Burning of the Bremen and Main [Hoboken]
Burning of the Standard Oil Co.'s Tanks, Bayonne, N.J.
Burning of the Standard Oil Tanks
A Champion Beer Drinker
Champion Polo Players
Children of the Royal Family of England
A Convict's Punishment
Deep Sea Fishing
Execution of a Spy
The Farmer and the Trolley Car
15th Infantry
Fire Boat "John M. Hutchinson"
From Vaudreuil to St. Anne's
A Hair-Raising Episode
His Dad Caught Him Smoking
His Name Was Mud
Hoboken Fire
The Hoboken Holocaust
How Charlie Lost the Heiress
How They Got Rid of Mamma
A Jersey Skeeter
The Katzenjammer Kids Have a Love Affair
Lawn Tennis
Love in the Dark
The Mail-Man in Coon Town
The Organ Grinder's Fourth of July

Panoramic View of Burning Wharves and Warehouses [Hoboken]
Philadelphia Lodge, No. 2, B.P.O. Elks
Playing Soldier
A Political Discussion
Polo Game: Myopia vs. Dedham
Prize-Winning Coaches
The Promenaders
A Raid on a Woman's Poolroom
Rescue from the Surf
Spirit of the Empire
A Strike in a Dime Museum
Those Wedding Bells Shall Not Ring Out
Too Much of a Good Thing
The Tough Kid's Waterloo
The Tramp Gets Whitewashed
Trouble at the Christening
Trouble in Hogan's Alley
A Wake in "Hell's Kitchen"
Washington Lodge, No. 15, B.P.O. Elks
Who Said Chicken?

Aug [day undetermined]

Annual French Military Carousal
Arrival of Train at Muskoka Wharf
Arrival of Train at Paris Exposition
Beheading Chinese Prisoner
Bombarding and Capturing the Taku Forts by the Allied Fleets
Bombardment of Taku Forts, by the Allied Fleets
Breaking of the Crowd at Military Review at Longchamps
Champs de Mars
Champs Elysees
Chasing the Cherry Pickers
Demonstrating the Action of the Brown Hoisting and Conveying Machine in Unloading a Schooner of Iron Ore, and Loading the Material on the Cars
Departure of Boats from Muskoka Wharf
Eccentricities of an Adirondack Canoe
Eiffel Tower from Trocadero Palace
Esplanade des Invalides
A Farmer's Imitation of Ching Ling Foo
The 'Gator and the Pickaninny
"A Gone Goose"
The Imperial Limited
A Launch Party in the Adirondacks
Life Motion Photographs of the Fitzsimmons and Ruhlin Fight
Living Pictures
M'lle Alma
Massacre of the Christians by the Chinese
The Narrows
Over the Fence and Out
Palace of Electricity
Panorama from the Moving Boardwalk
Panorama of Eiffel Tower
Panorama of Place De L'Opera
Panorama of the Moving Boardwalk
Panorama of the Paris Exposition, from the Seine
Panoramic View of the Champs Elysees
Panoramic View of the Place de la Concorde
Phrosine and Meledore
Pierrot's Problem, or How To Make a Fat Wife Out of Two Lean Ones
Prisoner in the Chinese Pillory in the Streets of Tien Tsin
Reproduction of the Corbett and McCoy Fight
Reproduction of the Fitzsimmons and Sharkey Fight
Rescue from a Harem
Rescue of a White Girl from the Boxers
S.S. Maria Theresa in a Storm
Scene from the Elevator Ascending Eiffel Tower
Scene in the Swiss Village at Paris Exposition
Scene on the Boulevard DeCapucines
The Shah's Return from Paris
The Slave Market
Steamer "Stowell" Running the Narrows
A Storm at Sea
Street Scene at Place de la Concorde, Paris, France
Swiss Village, No. 2
Temptation of St. Anthony
Tug-o-War on Board an Ocean Steamer
The Unfaithful Odalisque

Sep [day undetermined]

"Above the Limit"
Accidents Will Happen
Around the Flip-Flap Railroad
The Barber's Queer Customer
Bird's-Eye View of Dock Front, Galveston
Bryn Mawr Horse Show
Capt. Boynton Feeding His Pets
Children Rolling Down Hill
The Chinese Rubbernecks
A Dog Fight
"Drill, Ye Tarriers, Drill"
Family Troubles
For Ice Cream and Cake
Galveston Disaster
The Galveston Disaster
Ghosts in a Chinese Laundry
H. N. Marvin's Family
A Hand Car and the Imperial Limited
Homer Davenport, the Cartoonist
Hon. B. B. Odell, Jr.
How the Artist Captured the Chinese Boxers
How the Magician Got the Best of the Installment Man
Imperial Limited
Indiana Whitecaps
Launching a Stranded Schooner from the Docks
Lincoln Park
Little Sister
Love in the Suburbs
The Magic Picture
Orpheum Theatre
Panorama of East Galveston
Panorama of Galveston Power House
Panorama of Orphans' Home, Galveston
Panorama of Wreckage of Water Front
Panoramic View of Tremont Hotel, Galveston
Panoramic View, Rescue Work, Galveston
Panoramic View, Wreckage Along Shore, Galveston
Philadelphia's Pride
Republican National Committee of 1900
The "St. Paul" Outward Bound
Scene in Chinatown
A Scene in Fairmount Park, Phila.
Searching Ruins on Broadway, Galveston, for Dead Bodies
"Shoo Fly"
Spooks at School
Tortured by Boxers
The Tribulations of an Amateur Photographer
A Water Duel
What the Bathing Girls Did to the Kodak Fiend
Why Curfew Did Not Ring Last Night
William J. Bryan in the Biograph

Sep 22 The Unexpected Bath

Oct [day undetermined]

Boarding School Girls' Pajama Parade
"Courier"
A Flirtation
Fun in a Photograph Gallery
A Good Time Behind the Scenes
A Hot Time in the Dressing Room
How the Dude Got the Soubrette's Baggage
Jealousy in the Dressing Room
A Joke on the Old Maid
"The Kleptomaniacs"
Knock-out Drops on the Bowery
The Last Alarm
On the Cleveland and Eastern Railway
Pan-American Exposition
President McKinley Laying Corner Stone
Scandal in the Custom House
School Fire Drill
Soubrettes in a Bachelor's Flat
Stallion Championship
They Led Her Husband Astray
A Thief in a Soubrette's Boarding House
"Three Ones"
Through the Key-Hole in the Door
A Visit to Baby Roger
Westminster Street
What the Jay Saw in the Studio
What they Do to Respectable Men in the Tenderloin
Where the Female Smuggler Hid the Lace

Nov [day undetermined]

"Above the Limit"
Another Demonstration of the Cliff-Guibert Fire Hose Reel, Showing a Young Girl Coming from an Office, Detaching the Hose, Running with It 60 Feet, and Playing a Stream, All Inside of 30 Seconds
"Art Studies"
Aunt Jane's Experience with Tabasco Sauce
Bribing the Police
The Clown and the Alchemist
Congress of Nations
Contrary Wind
A Customer Drops In
Employees of Wolfson's Spice Mills, Toledo
The Enchanted Drawing
The Fire at Tarrant & Co.'s Drug Store
Gun Drill by Naval Cadets at Newport [R.I., Naval] Training School
Gymnasium Exercises and Drill at Newport [R.I., Naval] Training School
Hooligan Assists the Magician
In a Chinese Restaurant
Keith's Theater, London
Maude's Naughty Little Brother
Naval Apprentices at Sail Drill on Historic Ship "Constellation"
Naval Sham Battle at Newport
Return of the Canadian Contingent
Scene from "Old Kentucky"
Sham Battle on Land by Cadets at Newport Naval Training School
Showing a Giant Crane Dumping a 40-Ton Car
Two Old Cronies
"Two's Company"
The Ugly Tempered Tramp
"When We Were Twenty-One"

Nov 11 Joan of Arc

Dec [day undetermined]

At Break-Neck Speed
Childhood's Vows
Davy Jones' Locker
The Evidence Was Against Him
From Council Bluffs to Omaha
Grandma and the Bad Boys
Helping Mother
High School Pupils
The Iron Workers
Lawrence Fire Department
Mill Hands
Neptune's Daughters
A Nymph of the Waves
St. Mary's Congregation
"Stop Thief!"
Union Pacific Fast Mail
U.S. Naval Militia
A Wringing Good Joke

1901 [month undetermined]

Amateur Athletic Association Sports
Arrival of Train of Cattle
Beef Extract Room
Beef, Sheep and Hog Killing
"Bend Or"
Branding Hams
Bridge of Sighs
The Builders of Shamrock II
Bull on the Stampede
A Busy Corner at Armour's
Canned Meat Department. No. 1: Filling and Capping
Canned Meat Department. No. 2: Inspecting
Canned Meat Department. No. 5: Vacuum Process
Canned Meat Department. No. 6: Painting and Labeling
Chamberlain and Balfour
Chicago Fat Stock Parade
Chicago Police Parade
Cleaning Pig's Feet
Columbia Post
Coming Out of Scraping Machines and Cutting Off Heads
Cutting Beef
Cutting Meat for Sausage (side view)
Cutting Pork
Dewey Parade
Dressing Beef
Driving Hogs to Slaughter
Drove of Western Cattle
Dumping and Lifting Cattle
Elevated Railroad
Emar De Flon, the Champion Skater
Entrance to Union Stock Yards
Export Packing
Feeding Time
Fire Department of Albany, N.Y.
Hog Slaughtering. No. 6: Opening and Splitting
Hogs on the Rail
Interior of Armour's Power House
Killing Sheep

Koshering Cattle, (Hebrew Method of Killing)
Labeling Cans
Lafayette Post of New York
Lambs Post of Phila.
Lard Refinery
Launch of Shamrock II
Laundry and Sewing Room
Legging Sheep
Li Hung Chang
Loading Cars
Machine and Can Tester
Mince Meat Room
Miscellaneous. No. 6: Panoramic View
Nabbed by the Nipper
Noon Time in Packing Town, (Panoramic)
Noon Time in Packing Town, (Whiskey Point)
Norway Ski Jumping Contests
Oleo Oil Melting
Oleo Oil Pressing
Panoramic View of London Streets, Showing Coronation Decorations
Parade of Horses
Pulling Wool
A Ride on the Elevated R.R. (Panoramic)
Sausage Department. No. 2: Chopping
Scalding and Scraping Hogs
Scenes and Incidents in the G.A.R. Encampment
Sheep Led to Slaughter by Goat
Shipping Department. No. 2: Loading
Signor Marconi—Wireless Telegraphy
Singing Pigs Feet
Skinning Sheep
Slicing Hams and Bacon
Soldering Cans
Soot Versus Suds
Spanish Coronation Royal Bull-Fight
Square Can Machine
Stamping Tin
Sticking Cattle
Sticking Hogs, (Front View)
Street Sweeping Brigade
Stuffing Cans by Machinery
Stuffing Sausage
Stunning Cattle
Sweating Cans
Testing Cans by Machinery
Testing Hams
Testing Horses
Their Majesties the King and Queen
3 Can Testers (side view)
Trimming Room
Weighing Mutton
Winter Life in Sweden

Jan [day undetermined]
After a Rescue at Sea
The Bengal Lancers
Boat Drill in Mid-Ocean
Bolster Sparring
Capt. Reilly's Battery, Bombardment of Pekin
Capt. Reilly's Battery Limbering
Cast Up by the Waves
Charge of Cossack Cavalry
Chinese Junks
A Chinese Market
Cossack Cavalry
Crew of a Pacific Liner
First Bengal Lancers, Distant View
The French Bridge
French Bridge, Tien-Tsin
The Ghost Train
Japanese Artillery
Japanese Infantry on the March
Japanese Soldiers on the Taku Road
Launch of the "Saturn"
Li Hung Chang
Love in a Hammock
An Oriental Highway
Reilly's Light Battery F
Review of Russian Artillery
"Rock of Ages"
Russian Sharp Shooters
Second Squad, Sixth U.S. Cavalry
Sixth U.S. Cavalry Charging
Sixth U.S. Cavalry, Skirmish Line
Street Scene, Tientsin [China]
The Taku Road
Von Waldersee Reviewing Cossacks
The War in China—A British Donkey Train
The War in China—An Army Transport Train
The War in China—Bombay Cavalry
The War in China—British Light Artillery
The War in China—British Rajputs
The War in China—Coolies at Work
The War in China—Japanese Infantry
The War in China—Review of German Troops
The War in China—Ruins of Tien-Tsin
The War in China—Von Waldersee and Staff
The War in China—Von Waldersee's Review

Feb [day undetermined]
Anawanda Club
Charge by 1st Bengal Lancers
Departure of Duke and Duchess of Cornwall for Australia
First Bengal Lancers
The First Procession in State of H. M. King Edward VII
First Procession in State of H. M. King Edward VII
The Forbidden City
The Forbidden City, Pekin
The 14th Sikhs
The Fourth Ghorkhas
God Save the King
In Old China
Locked in the Ice
Main Street, Worcester
Medical Gymnastics
Moline Bag Punching Platform
The 9th Infantry, U.S.A.
On the Pei-Ho
Queen Victoria's Funeral [Number 1]
Queen Victoria's Funeral [Number 2]
Queen Victoria's Funeral [Number 3]
Reading the Proclamation at St. James Palace
Sea Gulls
Second Queen's Rajputs
Shanghai from a Launch
6th Cavalry Assaulting South Gate of Pekin
Squad of Men Clearing the Road
Street in Shanghai
Street Scene in Shanghai
Street Scene, Shanghai
Tien-Tsin
The War in China
The War in China—First Bengal Lancers
The War in China—The Evacuation of Pekin
The War in China—The Fourth Goorkhas
The War in China—The German Contingent

Feb 23 Ice-Boat Racing at Redbank, N.J.
Terrible Teddy, the Grizzly King

Mar [day undetermined]
The Automatic Weather Prophet
Castellane-De Rodays Duel
Codfishing with Trawl
Drawing a Lobster Pot
Fertilizing Codfish Eggs
Fun in a Chinese Laundry
The Old Maid in the Horsecar
President McKinley Leaving the White House for the Capitol
Run of the Worcester Fire Department
The Second Inauguration
Trotters at Worcester
Unloading Cod
Unloading Halibut

Mar 2 The Finish of Bridget McKeen
Follow the Leader
A Joke on Grandma
Mrs. Nation & Her Hatchet Brigade

Mar 9 The Old Maid Having Her Picture Taken
Why Mr. Nation Wants a Divorce

Mar 16 The Kansas Saloon Smashers
President McKinley and Escort Going to the Capitol
President McKinley Taking the Oath

Mar 23 Boxing in Barrels
The Donkey Party
The Fraudulent Beggar
A Hold-Up
Love by the Light of the Moon
Montreal Fire Department on Runners
Photographer's Mishap
Two Rubes at the Theatre

Mar 30 The Cook's Revenge
Photographing the Audience

Apr [day undetermined]
Artillery Drill at Annapolis
Band and Battalion of the U.S. Indian School
Basket Ball
Buffalo Bill's Wild West Parade
Calisthenic Drill
Carrie Nation Smashing a Saloon
Club Swinging, Carlisle Indian School
Deaf Mute Recitation
Demolishing and Building Up the Star Theatre
Dressmaking
Energizing Drill
Forging
General Quarters for Action
Girls Dumbbell Drill
Heavy Gymnastics
The High Jump
The High School Cadets
Japanese Wrestling
Jiu Jitsu, the Japanese Art of Self-Defense
Kindergarten Methods
Laboratory Study
A Language Lesson
Manual Training
A Muffin Lesson
Nature Study, the Rabbit
Physical Training
Pole Vaulting
Springtime in the Park
Star Spangled Banner by a Deaf Mute
U.S. Naval Cadets Marching in Review

Apr 6 The One Man Orchestra
The Queen's Funeral
The Wonderful Trick Donkey

Apr 13 Gans-McGovern Fight
Happy Hooligan April-Fooled
Happy Hooligan Surprised

Apr 20 Barnum and Bailey's Circus

Apr 27 The Gordon Sisters Boxing
Laura Comstock's Bag-Punching Dog
The Life of a Fireman
Pie, Tramp and the Bulldog
The Tramp's Dream

May [day undetermined]
Anna Held
Another Job for the Undertaker
At the Setting of the Sun
Bass Fishing
Boats Under Oars
A Day at the Circus
Fulton Market
Fun in a Butcher Shop
A Good Test of High Explosives
Hauling a Shad Net
The Horticultural Building
How the Dutch Beat the Irish
In a Japanese Tattooing Parlor
In the Gypsy Camp
A Large Haul of Fish
"Laughing Ben"
The Lovers' Yarn
Lubin's Animated Drop Curtain Announcing Slides
Middies Shortening Sails
A Mystic Re-Incarnation
The New Maid
Old Faithful Geyser
On the Old Plantation
Packers on the Trail
Panoramic View of the White Pass Railroad
Riverside Geyser, Yellowstone Park
The Slippery Slide
Steam Tactics
The Tramp's Strategy That Failed
The Tramp's Unexpected Skate
United States Government Gun Test
U.S. Proving Grounds, Sandy Hook
Unloading a Mackerel Schooner
An Unlucky Lover

May 4 Burro Pack Train on the Chilcoot Pass
Miles Canyon Tramway
Rocking Gold in the Klondike
Upper Falls of the Yellowstone
Washing Gold on 20 above Hunker, Klondike

May 18 Affair of Honor

Jun [day undetermined]
An April Fool Joke
Bally-Hoo Cake Walk
Beautiful Orient
"Birth of the Pearl"
The Bridge of Sighs—Pan-American Exposition
A Close Shave
The Court of Fountains—Pan-American Exposition
"The Diskobolus"

Emperor William's Yacht "Meteor"
English Derby, 1901
Esquimaux Dance
An Esquimaux Game
The Esquimaux Village
Experimental
Fair Japan—Pan-American Exposition
"Finishing Touches"
"Forward"
Fountain, Tower, and Basins—Pan-American Exposition
Ham and Eggs
The Heart of New York
Hot Mutton Pies
The Indian Congress
International Yacht Races on the Clyde
A Joke on Whom?
A Legal Hold-Up
A Little Piece of String
Main Entrance to Pan-American Exp.
Meandering Mike
A Non-Union Paper Hanger
On the Benches in the Park
On the Midway—Pan-American Exposition
The Ostrich Farm—On the Midway
Panorama of Midway—Pan-American Exposition
Panoramic View Gov't Building, Pan. Am. Exp.
Panoramic View of the Thames
A Patient Sufferer
"The Pouting Model"
Propylaea and North End of Plaza, Pan. Am. Exp.
Scene in Beautiful Orient—Pan-American Exposition
Sevillenas Dance—Pan-American Exposition
"The Sleeping Child"
Ten Nights in a Bar-Room: Death of Little Mary
Ten Nights in a Bar-Room: Death of Slade
Ten Nights in a Bar-Room: Murder of Willie
Ten Nights in a Bar-Room: The Fatal Blow
Ten Nights in a Bar-Room: Vision of Mary
Triumphal Bridge, Pan-American Exposition
An Unexpected Knockout
U.S. National Cemetery
Venice in America
"Volodyovski"
"Waiting for Santa Claus"
Washington Bridge and Speedway
"You Dirty Boy"

Jun 8 Circular Panorama of the Base of the Electric Tower, Ending Looking Down the Mall
Circular Panorama of the Electric Tower and Pond
Circular Panorama of the Esplanade with the Electric Tower in the Background
Launching of the New Battleship "Ohio" at San Francisco, Cal. When President McKinley Was There
Opening of the Pan-American Exposition showing Vice President Roosevelt Leading the Procession
Panoramic View of the Temple of Music and Esplanade
'Varsity Crew Race on Cayuga Lake, on Decoration Day, Lehigh Valley Observation Train Following the Race, Showing Cornell Crew Finishing First, Columbia Second, University of Pennsylvania Third Ithaca, N.Y., Showing Lehigh Valley Observation Train
View of the Midway

Jun 22 A Trip Around the Pan-American Exposition

Jun 29 Acrobats in Cairo
Buffalo Street Parade
Couchee Dance on the Midway
Fun at a Children's Party
Going to the Fire and the Rescue
A Good Joke
Grand Entry, Indian Congress
Indians No. 1
The Inexhaustible Cab
Midway Dance
Mounted Police Charge
Panorama of the Exposition, No. 1
Panorama of the Exposition, No. 2
Shad Fishing at Gloucester, N.J.
Tramp's Nap Interrupted
Turkish Dance
Twelve in a Barrel
Wedding Procession in Cairo
You Can't Lose Your Mother-in-Law

Jul [day undetermined]
American Falls from Top of Canadian Shore
Ammunition Wagons Arriving on the Battlefield
Arrival of Funeral Cortege at St. George's Chapel
Arrival of Train at Station
The Assembly in the Indian Village
Baby's Meal
The Boston Fire Boat in Action
The Bowery Kiss
Boys Entering Free Bath
Boys Free Public Baths
Breslau Fire Department in Action
Burro Pack Train on Main Street, Dawson City
Circular Panorama of Atlantic City, N.J.
Circular Panorama of Mauch Chunk, Penna.
Circular Panorama of Niagara Falls
Circular Panorama of the American Falls
Circular Panorama of the Esplanade and Forecourt
Circular Panorama of the Midway
The Complete Funeral Cortege Passing Through Windsor
A Composite Picture of the Principal Buildings in Washington, D.C.
The Cragg Family
The Downfall of China
Duel in the Snow
The Educated Chimpanzee
Edward VII, King of England
The Esquimaux Village
The Extensive Wardrobe
F. S. Gibbs and Family
The Falling Walls at the Tarrant Explosion
Feeding the Pigeons
The Finish of Michael Casey; or, Blasting Rocks in Harlem
Fire Dance
The Fire Department of Chelsea, Mass.
Fire Drills at Breslau, Germany
Firemen Fighting the Tarrant Fire
Firemen Rescuing Men and Women
Fish Cut
The Fisherman and the Bathers
Five Minutes to Train Time
Flip-Flap Railway
Flock of Sheep
The Fox Hunt
The Fresh Lover
Fun in a Chinese Laundry
The Funeral Arriving at Hyde Park
The Funeral Cortege Arriving at Trinity Pier
The Georgetown Loop
A German Cuirassier Regiment
Girl's Frolic at the Lake
Great Cavalry Charge
The Great Corpus Christi Procession in Breslau
Great Newark Fire
Great Waterfall of the Rhein at Schaffhausen, Switzerland
Happy Hooligan Has Troubles with the Cook
The Hayseed's Experience at Washington Monument
He Forgot His Umbrella
Herd of Cattle
Hockey Match on the Ice at Montreal, Canada
The Hod Carrier's Revenge
Hooligan and the Summer Girls
Hooligan at the Seashore
Hooligan Causes a Sensation
Hooligan Takes His Annual Bath
Hooligan Visits Central Park
Hooligan's Narrow Escape
How the Professor Fooled the Burglars
Indian Fort, Sherman Hill Tunnel
Japanese Village
Jumping Hurdles
Ladies Day at the Public Baths
Little Algy's Glorious Fourth of July
London Fire Department
Love's Ardor Suddenly Cooled
Market Day in Breslau, Germany
Massacre at Constantinople
The Mechanical Doll
Mine Explosion and What Followed
Miniature Railway
The Mischievous Clerks; or, How the Office was Wrecked
The Mysterious Blackboard
New York Sky-Line from East River and Battery
New York Sky-Line from the North River
Nora's 4th of July
Oh! What a Night; or, The Sultan's Dream
On the Midway—Pan-American Exposition
Opening of Bismarck's Museum
Ostrich Farm
The Overland Limited
Panorama of Brooklyn Bridge, River Front, and Tall Buildings from the East River
Panoramic View of the Bay of Fundy
Panoramic View of the Capitol, Washington, D.C.
Panoramic View of the White House, Washington, D.C.
Parade on the Speedway
The Photographer's Mishap
Piccadilly Circus, London, England
Pine Ridge Bluffs
A Quick Hitch
A Quick Recovery
A Race with the Overland Limited
The Ragtime Waltz
Red Cross of the German Army on the Battlefield
The Reversing Sign Painter
A Rough Day on the Ocean
Royal Artillery and English Sailors Marching Through Hyde Park
Royal Exchange, London, England
Saturday at the Free Baths
Scene in Legation Street, Shanghai
Searching the Ruins of the Tarrant Fire
Shooting the Chutes at Providence, Rhode Island
Snowballing Scene in Halifax
Stage Coach Hold-Up in the Days of '49
The Statue of William Tell
Street Scene in Pekin
Such a Headache
Three of a Kind; or, The Pirate's Dream
Through Gibraltar
The Tough Dance
Train Crossing Dale Creek Fill
Training a Horse to Jump Hurdles
The Tramp's Miraculous Escape
Two Old Cronies
The Wages of Sin—A Mother's Grief
The Wages of Sin—The Assassin's Escape
The Wages of Sin—The Fatal Choice
The Wages of Sin—The Murder of Bess
A Wagon Load of Babies
Washing Down Decks
When Stocks Went Up
Who Said Chicken?
Why Bridget Stopped Drinking
Wild Bear in Yellowstone Park
Women of the Ghetto Bathing

Jul 9 Esquimaux Village
Panorama of a Philippine Village

Aug [day undetermined]
The "Abbot" and "Cresceus" Race
Aunt Sallie's Wonderful Bustle
The Bad Boy's Joke on the Nurse
Bathing at Atlantic City
Bicycle Paced Race
Boys Diving
Broadway and Fourteenth St.
Experimental
The Campus Martius
Canoeing Scene
Centennial Parade
Circular Panorama of Electric Tower
Circular Panorama of Suspension Bridge and American Falls
Circular Panoramic View of Whirlpool Rapids
Cutting Sugar Cane
Detroit Mail Carriers
Esquimaux Game of Snap-the-Whip
Esquimaux Leap-Frog
The Farmer and the Bad Boys
A Flower Parade

Gathering Gladioli
The Henley Regatta, 1901
Industrial Floats
Knight Templars Parade at Louisville, Ky.
Knight Templars Parade Drill
Landing of Cadillac
Loading Sugar Cane
Panorama of Water Front
Panoramic View of Electric Tower from a Balloon
Panoramic View of the Gorge Railroad
Photographing a Country Couple
Professional Handicap Bicycle Race
The Reversible Divers
Sampson-Schley Controversy
Soubrette's Troubles on a Fifth Avenue Stage Coach
Steamboat Leaving for Hilo
Steamship "Bismark"
Steamship "Deutschland"
Steamship "Graf Waldersee"
Swimming Pool at Coney Island
Tally-Ho Departing for the Races
Train of Sugar Cane on Way to Crusher
The Tramp and the Nursing Bottle
Unveiling Chair of Justice
"Weary Willie" and the Gardener
What Happened on Twenty-Third Street, New York City

Sep [day undetermined]
Arrival at Falls View Station
Arrival of Funeral Cortege at the City Hall, Buffalo, N.Y.
Bridge Traffic, Manila
Capt. Schuyler Post of Philadelphia
Chapin Post of Buffalo
A Close Call
Complete Funeral Cortege at Canton, Ohio
Cuyahoga Gorge
The Empire Theatre
Farragut Naval Post, Ohio State
Faust Family of Acrobats
Finish of Futurity
Finish of Futurity, 1901
Finish of Race Sheepshead Bay, Experimental
Funeral of President McKinley
Headquarters, Staff and Band, Ohio State
In Old Hong Kong
Industrial Parade of the Cincinnati Fall Festival
International Field Sports
International Field Sports—Oxford-Cambridge vs. Harvard-Yale
International Track Athletic Meeting—Start and Finish of the One Mile Run
Lambs Club, G.A.R.
Life Rescue at Long Branch
The Living Flag
Lukens, Novel Gymnast
Lyttle Post of Cincinnati
McKinley Funeral—In Solemn State
The Multitude Passing into the City Hall
The Musical Ride
Ox Carts
Panorama of Kobe Harbor, Japan
Panorama, Public Square, Cleveland, O.
Panoramic View of the Crowd Rushing for the City Hall, Buffalo, to View the Body of President McKinley
Panoramic View of the McKinley Homestead
Parade to the Post
President McKinley at the Buffalo Exposition
President McKinley's Funeral
The Queen's Road
Rubes in the Theatre
Sampans Racing Toward Liner
Sampson and Schley Controversy—Tea Party
Sousa and His Band
Street Scene, Tokio, Japan
Street's Zouaves and Wall Scaling
Traveling Men's Association
The Trick Cyclist
What Demoralized the Barber Shop

Sep 21 The Mob Outside the Temple of Music at the Pan-American Exposition [Buffalo]
President McKinley Reviewing the Troops at the Pan-American Exposition
President McKinley's Speech at the Pan-American Exposition

Oct [day undetermined]
Asakusa Temple
Bridal Veil Falls
Captain Nissen Going Through Whirlpool Rapids, Niagara Falls
Coaching for a Record
Duke and Duchess of Cornwall and York Landing at Queenstown, Ontario
The Duke and Duchess of York Arriving at Quebec
Duke and Duchess of York Leaving the Railroad Station at Montreal, Canada
Duke and Duchess of York Marching Through the Streets of Montreal
The Duke and Duchess of York Presenting Medals to Boer War Veterans at the Unveiling of the Queen's Statue
Duke of York at Montreal and Quebec
A Filipino Cock Fight
Finish of Flatbush Stakes, Gravesend Track
Finish of the Third Cup Race
Garden Party in Honor of the Duke and Duchess of York
Hail Columbia!
Horse Parade at the Pan-American Exposition
Horses Jumping Water Jump
International Yacht Races—Columbia vs. Shamrock
Japanese Fencing
A Japanese Railway Train
The Lovers, Coal Box, and Fireplace
Match Race, Endurance by Right vs. Heno
The Matron Stakes
Mr. H. Casler and Baby. Experimental
Natives Leaving Church
A Near View of Shamrock II
Nevada Falls
Panorama, Great Gorge Route over Lewiston Bridge
Panorama of Water Front
A Perilous Proceeding
Rickshaw Parade, Japan
Schooner "Idler" and Revenue Cutter "Gresham"
Shamrock to the Fore
Shamrock's Start
Shimbashi R.R. Station
Spanish Dancers at the Pan-American Exposition
Start of the Third Cup Race
Steam Yacht "American"
Wawona, Big Tree
Working the Breeches Buoy

Oct 5 Arrival of McKinley's Funeral Train at Canton, Ohio
Funeral Leaving the President's House and Church at Canton, Ohio
McKinley's Funeral Entering Westlawn Cemetery, Canton [Ohio]
Panoramic View of the President's House at Canton, Ohio
President McKinley's Funeral Cortege at Buffalo, N.Y.
President McKinley's Funeral Cortege at Washington, D.C.
President Roosevelt at the Canton Station
Taking President McKinley's Body from Train at Canton, Ohio

Oct 19 "Columbia" and "Shamrock II": Finishing Second Race
"Columbia" and "Shamrock II": Jockeying and Starting
"Columbia" and "Shamrock II": Start of Second Race
"Columbia" and "Shamrock II": Starting in the Third Race
"Columbia" and "Shamrock II": Turning the Outer Stake Boat
"Columbia" Winning the Cup
The Martyred Presidents
Pan-American Exposition by Night
Panoramic View of the Fleet After Yacht Race
The Yacht Race Fleet Following the Committee Boat "Navigator" Oct. 4th

Oct 24 Arrival of Tongkin Train
The Bund, Shanghai
The Ch-ien-men Gate, Pekin
Coaling a Steamer, Nagasaki Bay, Japan
Harbor of Shanghai

Oct 25 Convention of Railroad Passengers Agents
Panoramic View, Asheville, N. C.

Oct 26 Little Red Riding Hood

Nov [day undetermined]
Artist's Point
Automobile Parade on the Coney Island Boulevard
Catching an Early Train
A Cavalry Manoeuvre
Coaching Party, Yosemite Valley
In the Yellowstone
Launch
A Mighty Tumble
Panorama, Golden Gate
Panorama of Esplanade by Night
A Phenomenal Contortionist
Picturesque Yosemite
Royal Train with Duke and Duchess of York, Climbing Mt. Hector
Sham Battle at the Pan-American Exposition
Trapeze Disrobing Act
Twentieth Century Flyers
Water Front of San Francisco
A Wonderful Waterfall
Yale Football, Practice Scrimmage
Yale Football Squad of 1901

Nov 16 Execution of Czolgosz, with Panorama of Auburn Prison

Nov 23 A Christmas Dream

Dec [day undetermined]
The Artist's Dilemma
Ascending Mt. Low, California
The Beginning of a Great Enterprise
Building a Harbor at San Pedro
California Oil Wells in Operation
Carrying Out the Snakes
Children Bathing
Children Playing Ball
Cutting Cucumbers and Cauliflower, Heinz
Expert Driving
The Fat and the Lean Wrestling Match
Football Game: West Point vs. Annapolis
Harry Thompson's Imitations of Sousa
Jeffries Exercising in His Gymnasium
Jeffries Side Stepping and Wrestling
Jeffries Skipping the Rope
Jeffries Sparring with His Brother
Jeffries Throwing the Medicine Ball
Leaping Dogs at Gentry's Circus
Line-Up and Teasing the Snakes
The March of Prayer and Entrance of the Dancers
Moki Snake Dance by Walpapi Indians
The Mysterious Cafe
Ostrich Farms at Pasadena
Packing Pickle Jars, Heinz
Panoramic View, Albert Canyon
Panoramic View, Kicking Horse Canyon
Panoramic View, Lower Kicking Horse Canyon
Panoramic View, Lower Kicking Horse Valley
Panoramic View of Boston Subway from an Electric Car
Panoramic View of Moki-Land
Panoramic View of Rubio Canyon, Mt. Low R.R.
Panoramic View, Upper Kicking Horse Canyon
Parade of Snake Dancers before the Dance
Pigeon Farm at Los Angeles, Cal
President Roosevelt at the Army-Navy Game
President Roosevelt Entering Grounds at Army-Navy Football Game
Prize Winners at the Country Fair
Roeber Wrestling Match
Ruhlin at His Training Quarters
Ruhlin Boxing with "Denver" Ed. Martin
Ruhlin Sparring in His Training Quarters
Tally Ho!

Dec 14 Jeffries in His Training Quarters
Ruhlin in His Training Quarters

Dec 21 Jeffries and Ruhlin Sparring Contest at San Francisco, Cal., Nov. 15, 1901—Five Rounds

1902 [month undetermined]
All on Account of Eliza
Arrival of Rex
Ballet Rehearsal
Bathing Made Easy
Black and White Hair Dance
Boating in Lakes of Philippine Village
Bostock's Educated Chimpanzee
The Bryn Mawr Horse Show
Buffalo Bill's Wild West Show

Caught in the Act
The Chicken Thief
Collecting the King's Mail
The Continental Guards
Conture Brothers, Acrobats
Coronation of King Edward VII and Alexandra
Devoy, the Funny Skater
The Dog Caught On
Drawee, the Juggler
The Dull Razor
Eight Japanese Dancing Girls
Electric Tower
The Extensive Wardrobe
Fairmount Park Trolley Panorama
Fire Run, Exposition
The Foot Juggler
Four Hong Kong Sisters
A Frustrated Elopement
Fu Tschi Dancers
Funeral of the German Empress, Frederick
Geisha Girls
Gen. Otis with His Troops in the Philippines
Gipsies Dancing
Grandma and the Bad Boys
Happy Hooligan Turns Burglar
Herald Square, New York
The Hohenzollern
Hu-Ki-Si, Japanese Dancer
Ice Skating
Indians No. 2
Is Ka Trio
Japanese Acrobats
Japanese Bowery
Japanese Dancing Hall
Japanese Yuma Dance
The King and Queen Returning from Westminster
King Edward and Queen Alexandra on Their Way to Westminster
Launch of the Kaiser's Yacht "Meteor"
Life Rescue, Atlantic City
The Lightning Artist
Lohengrin
Loro & Devoy, the Comical Acrobats
Louie Fuliner
Love at 20 and 40 Years After
The Man with the Rubber Head
Mardi Gras Parade
Martha
The Mechanical Doll
Mikado
The Miniature Railway
Mounted Police
Mysterious Transformation Scene
The New Serpentine and Fire Dance
New Year Shooters
An Obstacle Race
Opening Day Parade No. 1
Opening Day Parade No. 2
Opening Day Parade No. 3
Panorama City of Venice
Panorama of Esplanade from Bridge of Triumph
Panorama of Esquimaux Village
Panorama of Midway
Panorama of Ninth Ave. Elevated R.R.
Panorama of Venice
Panoramic View of the French Market
President and Prince at Washington
Prince Henry at Cramp's Shipyard
Pugilist McKeever and Wife Bag Punching
Reuben Buys a Gold Brick
Rube Waddell and the Champion Playing Ball with the Boston Team
Serving Potatoes, Undressed
The Singing Donkey
Skidoo-23
Smoking Smokes
Snicklefritz Has a Hot Time
Soldiers in the Strike District
Sowing Seed on the Farm
Street Scene, Tokio
The Stud Farm, No. 1
The Stud Farm, No. 2
The Stud Farm, No. 3
Stud Pony
Target Practice, and What Happened to Widow Flaherty
Turning Keys over to Rex
The Village Blacksmith
Whose Baby Is You?
Why Jones Left Home
Why the Cook Was Fired
Wonderful Magic
Woodside Park Trolley Panorama
Ye Olde Mill

Jan [day undetermined]

Bird's Eye View of San Francisco, Cal., from a Balloon
A Cable Road in San Francisco, Cal.
Chinese Shaving Scene
Deer in Park
Eeling Through the Ice
Facial Expression
Feeding Geese at Newman's Poultry Farm
Fishing at Faralone Island
Great Sport! Ice Yachting
Ice Yacht Racing
Love in a Hammock
A Mile a Minute on an Ice Yacht
New Year's Mummers Parade
Panoramic View Between Palliser and Field, B. C.
Panoramic View near Mt. Golden on the Canadian Pacific R.R.
Panoramic View of Mt. Tamalpais
Panoramic View of Mt. Tamalpais Between Bow Knot and McKinley Cut
Panoramic View of the Canadian Pacific R.R. near Leauchoil, B. C.
Panoramic View of the Golden Gate
Sea Gulls Following Fishing Boats
A Spill from an Ice Yacht
Starting a Skyscraper
The Twentieth Century Tramp; or, Happy Hooligan and His Airship
Uncle Josh at the Moving Picture Show
The Weary Hunters and the Magician

Feb [day undetermined]

Amateur Ski Jumpers
Arrival of the Governor General, Lord Minto, at Quebec
Battleship "Illinois"
A Big Blaze
"Bouncing"
The Burning of Durland's Riding Academy
Capture of the Biddle Brothers
Christening and Launching Kaiser Wilhelm's Yacht "Meteor"
Circular Panorama of Housing the Ice
Coasting Scene at Montmorency Falls, Canada
Cross-Country Running on Snow Shoes
Cutting and Canaling Ice
Demonstrating the Action of a Mergenthaler-Horton Basket Making Machine
A Devastated City
Docking a Liner
Dog Sleighing
Fire at Durland's Academy, N.Y. City
The Hindoo Fakir
The "Hohenzollern"
A Husky Dog Team
Kent House Slide
"Kronprinz Wilhelm" with Prince Henry [of Prussia] on Board Arriving in New York
Launch of Meteor III
Loading the Ice on Cars, Conveying It across the Mountains and Loading It into Boats
New York City in a Blizzard
Over the Crust
Panorama of the Paterson [N.J.] Fire
Panoramic View of the Hohenzollern
Park Avenue Explosion
The Paterson Fire
Paterson [N.J.] Fire, Showing the Y.M.C.A. and Library
Prince Henry [of Prussia] Arriving in Washington and Visiting the German Embassy
Quebec Fire Department on Sleds
The Royal Salute
Ruins of City Hall, Paterson [N.J.]
Run of a Snow Shoe Club
Skiing in Montreal
Skiing Scene in Quebec
Toboggan Slide
Tobogganing in Canada
Welcome Prince Henry!
"What Ho, She Bumps!"
Working Rotary Snow Ploughs on Lehigh Valley Railroad

Mar [day undetermined]

B. F. Keith's New Million Dollar Theatre
"Deutschland" Leaving New York at Full Speed [with Prince Henry of Prussia]
Experimental. Southwestern Limited Train
Ferryboat Entering Slip
German and American Tableau
Kaiser Wilhelm's Yacht, "Meteor," Entering the Water
Madison Square, New York City
"Meteor III" Afloat
Mice
Prince Henry
Prince Henry and President's Party
Prince Henry at Philadelphia
Prince Henry at West Point
Prince Henry of Germany
Prince Henry [of Prussia] Arriving at West Point
Prince Henry [of Prussia] at Lincoln's Monument, Chicago, Ill.
Prince Henry [of Prussia] at Niagara Falls
Prince Henry [of Prussia] Reviewing the Cadets at West Point
Prince Henry [of Prussia] Visiting Cambridge, Mass. and Harvard University
Sailing of the "Deutschland" with Prince Henry [of Prussia] on Board
"When the Cat's Away, the Mice Will Play"

Mar 15 Arrival of Prince Henry [of Prussia] and President Roosevelt at Shooter's Island

Apr [day undetermined]

Babies Rolling Eggs
The Bessemer Steel Converter in Operation
The Burlesque Suicide
The Burlesque Suicide, No. 2
Century Wheelman, N.Y. City
Charleston Chain Gang
Circular Panoramic View of Jones and Laughlin's Steel Yard
Demonstrating the Action of an Agnew Mailing Machine
Egg Rolling at the White House
Feeding the Bear at the Menagerie
48th Highlanders Regiment
Fun in a Bakery Shop
General Electric Flash Light
The Golden Chariots
Great Bull Fight
Installation Ceremonies, Columbia University
Installation Ceremonies of President Butler
Las Viga Canal, Mexico
Loading a Vessel at Charleston, S. C.
The "Meteor"
Midway of Charleston Exposition [South Carolina]
Miniature Railway
Moonlight on Lake Maggiore, Italy
New Sunset Limited
Panoramic View from Pittsburgh to Allegheny
Panoramic View of Charleston Exposition [South Carolina]
Pontoon Bridge Building
President Roosevelt Reviewing the Troops at Charleston Exposition [South Carolina]
St. Patrick's Cathedral and Fifth Avenue on Easter Sunday Morning [New York City]
Scrambling for Eggs
The Swimming Ducks at Allentown [Pa.] Duck Farm
Tossing Eggs
Trial Trip of "Meteor"

May [day undetermined]

The Absent Minded Clerk, Fly Paper and Silk Hat
The Aerial Railway at the Crystal Palace, London, England
Appointment by Telephone
Arrival of Circus Trains
The Baby and the Pet Bird
The Bibulous Wire Walker
A Bowery Five Cent Shave
The Boys Help Themselves to Foxy Grandpa's Cigars
The Boys, Still Determined, Try It Again on Foxy Grandpa, with the Same Result
The Boys Think They Have One on Foxy Grandpa, but He Fools Them
The Boys Try to Put One Up on Foxy Grandpa

Building Made Easy; or, How Mechanics Work in the Twentieth Century
The Bull and Bear
The Burglars in the Wine Cellar
Burlesque on Romeo and Juliet
The Burlesque Thieves
Burning of St. Pierre [Martinique]
Camels Eating
Camels in a Tent
Carlysle D. Graham Swimming the Whirlpool Rapids
Characteristic Imitations
The Cheese Mites; or, The Lilliputians in a London Restaurant
The Children's Tea Party
The Children's Toys That Came to Life
The Chinese Conjurer and the Devil's Head
A Chinese Mystery
Circus Parade No. 1
Circus Parade No. 2
The Clown and His Burlesque Horse
The Clown and His Mysterious Pictures
The Clown and the Automobile
The Clown with the Portable Body
A Country Groceryman's Revenge
The Creators of Foxy Grandpa
The Darktown Comedians Trip to Paris
Deep Water Diving Illustrated
The Devil in the Schoolhouse
The Devil's Kitchen
Devil's Prison
The Devil's Theatre
Dr. Lehwis Automobile Leaving London for a Trip Around the World
The Double Magician and the Magical Head
Elephants in a Tent
English Army in the Battlefield
English Cavalry on the Battlefield
English Soldiers Exercising
Entire Series of Yacht Race Pictures with Dissolving Effects
Experimental. Moving Picture Machine
Exploding a Land Mine
Exploding a Submarine Mine
Extraordinary Chinese Magic
The Fat and Lean Comedians
Fire Department of Glasgow, Scotland
The Fisherman's Wonderful Catch
Foxy Grandpa and Polly in a Little Hilarity
Foxy Grandpa Shows the Boys a Trick or Two with the Tramp
Foxy Grandpa Tells the Boys a Funny Story
Funeral Procession of Admiral Sampson at Washington
A Gay Old Boy
The Giant and Pygmy
Gibson, the Eccentric American Actor
Going to Bed Under Difficulties
The Great Stag Hunt
The Hair in the Soup
The Haunted Pawnshop
Herrmann, the Great Conjuror
The History of a Crime
The Horrible Nightmare
How the Lover Squared Himself with Papa
How Uncle Josh Defeated the Badgers
The Inexhaustible Wardrobe
Japanese Girl Smoking Cigarettes
Life Rescue Scene at Atlantic City, N.J.
Little Willie's Last Celebration
Magical Changes
The Magical Hen
Magical Sword
The Magician and the Human Pump
The Magician and the Seven Hats
The Mermaid's Ballet
The Mischievous Boys and the Washerwoman
Mt. Pelee in Eruption and Destruction of St. Pierre [Martinique]
Mt. Pelee Smoking Before Eruption [St. Pierre, Martinique]
The Mysterious Doctor
The Mysterious Urn
The Mystic Wreath
The Mystical Burglars
The National Geisha Dance of Japan
Naughty Grandpa and the Field Glass
New Pie Eating Contest
Newsboys and Hokey Pokey Man
The Nurse Maid in the Tunnel
Old Maid Retiring
On the Speedway
Ora Pro Nobis Illustrated
The Other Fellow's Laundry
The Pals and the Clothier's Dummy
Panoramic View of New Haven, Conn.
Panoramic View of Switchback, Mauch Chunk
Peasant Children and Their Rocking Horse
The Pioneer Limited
A Poet's Revenge
A Private Supper at Heller's
The Puppies and Their Mother
A Railroad Wreck (Imitation)
Rube and the Weighing Machine
Rube's Visit to the Studio
The S.S. "Deutschland" in a Storm
The S.S. "Deutschland" in a Storm, No. 2
The S.S. "Deutschland" in Heavy Sea
The S.S. "Deutschland" Leaving Her Dock in Hoboken
Scene on Lower Broadway
A Schoolroom in the Soudan
Shuffleboard on S.S. "Deutschland"
Sir Thomas Lipton on Board the Erin
The Speedway Parade
Street Scene
The Tight Collar
Tommy Atkins Bathing
Transporting a War Balloon
Trouble in a Barnyard
Troubled Dream
Troubles in a Tenement House
Undressing Under Difficulties
Waves at Dover, England
The Weary Traveller and His Wonderful Dream
What Happened to the Inquisitive Janitor
The Wonderful Baby Incubator
Wonderful Feats of Vivisection
The Wonderful Hair Restorer
Worcester High School Eight-Oared Boat Crews in Action

May 3 Blue Beard

Jun [day undetermined]
The Accomodating Cow
Alphonse and Gaston
Aunt Jane and the Tobasco Sauce
Belles of the Beach
Biograph's Improved Incubator
The Bowery Kiss
Daly, of West Point
The Eruption of Mt. Pelee
Eva Tanguay
The Light That Didn't Fail
The Lovers' Knot
Lower New York
Milking Time on the Farm
On a Milk Diet
Over the Rail
Panorama of Lower New York
Panorama of St. Pierre
A Picture from "Puck"
The Polite Frenchman
Rag Time Dance
Rag Time Dance (Hot)
Review of Cadets at West Point
Review of Cadets, West Point
A Seashore Gymkana
A Spill
The Suburban of 1902
The Summer Exodus
"A Sweet Little Home in the Country"
Taking Out the Dead and Wounded
They Found the Leak
A Tough Dance
A Tub Race
Will He Marry the Girl?

Jul [day undetermined]
Baby in a Rage
Baby Playing in Gutter
Black Rock Tunnel on the Rock Island Route
Cavalry Swimming Columbia River
Dancing Skeleton
The DeCarmos
A Delusion
The Draped Model
Explosion of an Automobile
Grandpa's Reading Glass
In a Manicure Parlor
In a Massage Parlor
The Lamp Explodes
Legerdemain Up-to-Date, or the Great Hermann Outdone
A Little Man
Mischievous Willie's Rocking Chair Motor
The New Pillow Fight
No Liberties, Please
Old Mother Hubbard
Panorama, Descending Mt. Blanc
Panoramic View of the Alps, Switzerland
The Photographer's Fourth of July
A Pipe Story of the Fourth
The Prodigal Son
Ringling Bros. Circus Parade
She Meets with Wife's Approval
The Sleeper
Snow White
Thro' Hell Gate
Wrinkles Removed

Jul 15 Jack and the Beanstalk

Aug [day undetermined]
Around the Mulberry Bush
At the Fountain
Baby Parade
The Beach at Atlantic City
Biograph Snapshots at the President
Caught in the Undertow
Demonstrating the Action of an Altman-Taylor Clover Huller
Demonstrating the Action of an Altman-Taylor Threshing Machine
Floral Chair Parade
Gay Girls of Gotham
A Gentleman Burglar
A Heavy Surf at Atlantic City
Jeffries-Fitzsimmons Reproduction Prize Fight Films
The King of Detectives
A Lawn Party
A Little Mix-Up in a Mixed Ale Joint
Old Volunteer Fire Dept.
Rex's Bath
Shut Up!
A Study in Openwork
Sweethearts
Wash Day
Water Nymphs

Aug 30 Crowning of King Edward and Queen Alexandra
The King and Queen Arriving at Westminster Abbey
The King and Queen Leaving Westminster Abbey After the Crowning
King Edward Reviewing Coronation Naval Force at Spithead August 16, 1902
The King's Procession
The New Crowned King and Queen Passing Through Wellington Arch and Down Constitution Hill
Panoramic View of Westminster Abbey and Surroundings

Sep [day undetermined]
Amputating a Leg
A Ball on a Battleship
Bathing at Kiel, Germany
Bologna Eating Contest
Bombardment of Newport
Bowling Alley at a German Picnic
California Naval Reserves
California Naval Reserves Drilling on Board Ship
Ching Ling Foo's Greatest Feats
Circular Panoramic View of St. Pierre from the Lighthouse, Showing Mt. Pelee Smoking in the Distance
Circular Panoramic View of St. Pierre, Showing the Ruins of the Catholic Cathedral and Mt. Pelee Smoking in the Background
Circular Panoramic View of the Market Place at Fort de France, Showing S.S. Korona in the Background
Clearing the Course for the Henley Boat Races, July 10th, 1902
The Columbia-Cornell-Pennsylvania Boat Race at Poughkeepsie
The Cook, Her Lover and the Lady of the House
Coronation Parade
The Crazy Artist and the Pictures That Came to Life
Crying for His Bottle
The Deonzo Brothers in Their Wonderful Barrel Jumping Act
Departure of the Bride and Groom
Down the Mountain Side
A Dutch Soldier's Christmas Box
A Dutchman Shaving
The Dutchman's Interrupted Dinner

The Farmer's Troubles in a Hotel
From the Crow's Nest
The Futurity Crowd
The Futurity of 1902
German Soldiers Starting for War
The Golf Girls and the Tramp
Good Luck Baking Powder Train No. 1
Good Luck Baking Powder Train No. 2
Graduating Day at West Point Military Academy
Grandma Threading Her Needle
The Haunted Dining Room
His First Dose of Medicine
The Hodcarriers' Ping Pong
Horse Racing in Germany
Ice Racing in Stockholm
Kaiser Wilhelm and Emperor Franz Josef, and Prince Henry Riding Horseback
Kaiser Wilhelm and the Empress of Germany Reviewing Their Troops
Kaiser Wilhelm and the German Cuirrassiers Galloping
Kaiser Wilhelm at Stettin
Kaiser Wilhelm at the Launching of a German Battleship
Kaiser Wilhelm in the Tier Garten, Berlin, Germany
Kaiser Wilhelm Inspecting His Soldiers
Kaiser Wilhelm, of Germany, and Emperor Franz Josef, of Austria
Kaiser Wilhelm's Yacht "Meteor" Under Sail
King Edward VII and Queen Alexandra, of Great Britain
Lightning Facial Changes
Loading Cattle in India
The Lovers and the Donkey
The Lovers and the Egg Merchant
The Magical Dish Mender
Michael Casey and the Steam Roller
Mr. Grauman. For Private Use
Mounted Soldiers Fording a River
Moving Picture Operator on a Drunk
Native Bull Cart at Morne Rouge (A Suburb of St. Pierre)
Native Women of Fort de France at Work
Native Women Washing Clothes at Fort de France
Native Women Washing Clothes at the Gueydon Fountain, Fort de France, Martinique
Natives Unloading a Boat of Fire-Wood at Carbet (A Suburb of St. Pierre)
Natives Unloading a Coaling Vessel at Fort de France, Martinique
An Old Fashioned Way of Pulling a Tooth
The Old Maid's Tea Party
Pain's Fireworks
Papa Keeps the Telephone Appointment
A Photographic Contortion
Queen Wilhelmina and Kaiser Wilhelm Riding in the Tier Garten
Queen Wilhelmina Arriving at the Kaiser's Palace
Queen Wilhelmina, of Holland, in Berlin
Reproduction, Coronation Ceremonies—King Edward VII
St. John's Guild. Bathing in Surf and Leaving Water
St. John's Guild. Crippled Children to and from Wagon
St. John's Guild. Dispensary Scene, Floating Hospital
St. John's Guild. Dock to Plank, 35th St.
St. John's Guild. Examination of Patients
St. John's Guild. From Launch to Dock
St. John's Guild. Going in Water.
St. John's Guild. Going to Salt-water Bath Room
St. John's Guild. Julliard and Tug in Narrows
St. John's Guild. Julliard Passing; Fire-Hose Playing
St. John's Guild. Launch Approaching Dock
St. John's Guild. Launch Delivering Patients to F. H.
St. John's Guild. Patients Down Bridge. S.S.H.
St. John's Guild. Plank to Deck, Floating Hospital
Savable Wins
Sea Sick Excursionists
Selling a Pet Dog
Skate Sailing in Sweden
Skating in Stockholm
Skiing in Stockholm, Sweden
Steeplechasing at the Brooklyn Handicap
A Stern Chase
Storm at Sea near St. Pierre, Martinique
Street Scene in Cairo
Street Scene in Fort de France, Martinique
A Telephone Romance
Third Trinity, Cambridge, Winning the Race for the Grand Challenge Cup. Taken at Henley on July 10th, 1902
Torpedo Boats Racing off Newport
Tourists Climbing the Alps
Turning Panorama of Mt. Beacon
Two Germans in a Theatre
The University College of Oxford Winning the Ladies' Challenge Plate
Unveiling the Rochambeau Statue in Washington, D.C.
Unveiling the Rochambeau Statue, Washington, D.C.
Why Papa Reformed, or Setting Back the Clock

Oct [day undetermined]

The Bull and the Picnickers
The Eighth Wonder
General Booth
How They Do Things on the Bowery
The Interrupted Bathers
The Interrupted Picnic
A Lively Scrimmage
Miners at Work Under Guard of Troops
Rock of Ages
"Seeing New York"
Troops Leaving Philadelphia for the Coal Regions

Oct 4 A Trip to the Moon
Who Said Watermelon?

Nov [day undetermined]

The Abbe and the Colonel
Aboard the Aegir
"All Hot"
Allegorical Procession
Arrival of Major Marchand from the Soudan
Arrival on Summit of Pike's Peak
The Attack
An Automobile Parade in the Tuilleries Gardens
The Baby's Meal
Balloon Ascension
Banks of the Elbe
Battleship "Odin"
"Be Good Again"
Beautifyl Beaulieu
Berlin Fire Department
Between the Decks
Bi-Centennial Jubilee Parade
A Blast in a Gravel Bed
The Bogie Man
The Bon Vivant
Boyville Fire Brigade
Bridge of Alexander III
Broncho Busting Scene, Championship of the World
Burlington Flyer
Calling the Pigeons
Captain Dreyfus
The Champs Elysees
The Children and the Frog
The Children of the Czar
Children Playing with Lion Cubs
Clear Creek Canyon
Clever Horsemanship
Climbing Hagerman Pass
The Crown Prince of Germany
A Dance by Kanaka Indians
Dedication of the Alexander Grenadiers' Barracks
Denver Firemen's Race for Life
Dessert at Dan Leno's House
A Dog's Cemetery
The Elephant's Bath
Elevated and Underground
The Emperor and Empress and Crown Prince of Germany
Emperor and Empress of Germany
The Emperor and Empress of Germany
Emperor William II
Emperor William II on Horseback
Emperor William as a Hussar
Emperor William at the Danzig Manoeuvres
Emperor William of Germany on Horseback
Emperor William Returning from Manoeuvres
Empress of Germany at Danzig
Empress of Germany Driving to the Manoeuvres
Field-Marshal Count Von Waldersee
The Flying Train
A Flying Wedge
A French Bicycle Corps
French Boxers
From Monte Carlo to Monaco
Fun in a Clothes Basket
Fun in the Glenwood Springs Pool
Fun on a Sand Hill
Funeral Procession of the Late Empress Frederick
Ganswindt's Flying Machine
George J. Marck and His Lions
German Artillery in Action
German Cavalry Fording a River
German Cavalry Leaping Hurdles
German Garde Kurassiers
German Lancers
German Military Exercises
German Navy Target Practice
German Railway Service
A German Torpedo Boat Flotilla in Action
The Giant Constantin
The Gold Dust Twins
The Gourmand
His Morning Bath
Horse Toboggan Slide
A Hurdle Race
Hydraulic Giants at Work
In a German Bath
In the Friedrichstrasse
In the Heart of the Forest
The India-Rubber Man
Jo Jo, the Dog Faced Boy
King Albert of Saxony
King Edward VII at the Birthday Celebration of the King of Denmark
Launch of the "Koenig Albert"
Launching of the "Kaiser Wilhelm der Grosse"
Lava Slides in Red Rock Canyon
Leaving the Summit of Pike's Peak
Let the Gold Dust Twins Do Your Work
The Longchamps Palace
Marvelous Markmanship
A Mermaid Dance
A Mis-Adventure
Mr. Dan Leno, Assisted by Mr. Herbert Campbell, Editing the "Sun"
Mr. Oldsport's Umbrella
M. Le Comte De Dion
The Murderer's Vision
New York's New Subway
An Obstinate Cork
The Old Port of Marseilles
On Board His Majesty's Battleship "Fuerst Bismark"
On Board His Majesty's Gunboat "Luchs"
On the Elbe
On the Marseilles Tramway
Oom Paul
Panorama of Cog Railway
Panorama of the Famous Georgetown Loop
Panorama of the Royal Gorge
Panorama of Ute Pass
Panorama of Wilhelmshaven
Panoramic View from the Stadtbahn
Panoramic View of Granite Canon
Panoramic View of Hell Gate
Panoramic View of Seven Castles
Panoramic View of the Harbor of Hamburg, Germany
Panoramic View of the Siegesallee
Paris Exposition
A Parisian Ballet
Pike's Peak Toboggan Slide
Prince Tsung of China
Prize-Winning Trip of the Santos-Dumont Airship No. 6
Promenade of the Kings
Rare Fish in an Aquarium
Rare Fish in the Aquarium
A Remarkable Fire
A Rescue at Sea
Return of the German China Fleet
The Rivals
A Romp on the Lawn
Rulers of Half the World
A Run by the Berlin Fire Department, Berlin, Germany

Runaway Stage Coach
Sailing of Battleship "Wurtemberg"
Ten Minutes at Monte Carlo
Torpedo Boat "G-89"
Train in Royal Gorge
The Train to Villefranche
Trains Leaving Manitou
A Tug of War
Umbrella Dance, San Toy
An Unsinkable Skimmer
Unveiling of the Bismarck Monument
An Unwelcome Visitor
Ute Pass Express
The Valiant Pig
Visit of Emperor Francis Josef of Austria to Berlin
A Water Carnival
When Knighthood Was in Flower
When the Bugle Sounds "Charge!"
Where Golden Bars Are Cast
Winter in Germany
With Emperor William's Army
"Zip"

Nov 1 Ali Baba and the Forty Thieves

Dec [day undetermined]

After the First Snow
After the Service
Broadway & Union Square, New York
"Chums"
A Corner in the Play Room
The Horse Market
Officers of National Cash Register Co. Leaving Club House
Sheep and Lambs

1903 [month undetermined]

Actor's Troubles
The Alarm and Hitch
Arrival of Humpty Dumpty
Auntie and the Bee
Automobile Parade
Babies and Kittens
Babies and Puppies
Baby Lund in Lightning Change Act
Barrel Fighters
Bathers with High Diving
Bathing Horses
Beggar's Dream
Beheading Chinese
Birth of a Fairy
Black Magic
Black Serpentine
Bluejackets Scrubbing Their Hammocks
The Bridegroom's Dilemma
Broad Sword Contest
Brothers of the Misericordia, Rome
A Brush in the Snow
Bryan at Home
Buffalo Bill's Parade
Business Rivalry
The Cabinet Trick of the Davenport Brothers
Cake Walk
The California Limited of the Santa Fe Route
Cape Town, South Africa
Chicago Derby Day
Chicago Fire Boats in Action
Chicago Fire Run
Chicago—Michigan Football Game
La Chimera
Christ Walking on the Water
Clown and Automaton
The Coke Ovens of Pennsylvania
Colorado Special, Chicago & Northwestern Ry.
Comic Skater
Comrades
Cook County Democracy Parade
The Cook's Revenge
Corn Harvesting
The Dance of the Little Texas Magnet
Deadwood Coach
The Dells of Wisconsin
Dixon-Palmer Fight
A Donkey Party
Down the Hotel Corridor
Down the Hudson
Down the Slide
The Dull Razor
The Famous Box Trick
Fancy Drill of the Woodmen of America
Feeding Pigeons in the Streets of Venice
Fire Engines at Work
The Fire, the Leap for Life and the Rescue
Flag Dance
Floral Parade
Fool's Parade
Freight Train in the Royal Gorge, Colo.
Fun on the Levee
German Dance
German Torpedo Boat in Action
German Torpedo Boats
The Girl in Blue
Going to Bed Under Difficulties
Going to the Fire
Great Diamond Robbery
The Great Whaleback Steamer, Christopher Columbus
The Hair Dresser
Harper's Ferry
The Harvesters
The Hay Mower
Hermann Looked Like Me
H. H. Pope Leo [XIII] in Chair
The Hold Up
A Hot Time on the Bathing Beach
How Would You Like to Be the Ice Man
Humpty and the Demon
Humpty and the Dude
Humpty and the Piewoman
Humpty Dumpty and the Baby
Humpty's Frolics
Humpty's Troubles with the Policeman
Humpty's Troubles with the Washwoman
The Ice Breaker
Ice Yachting
Illinois Central Flyer
The Infernal Meal
An Innocent Conspirator
Interrupted Crap Game
Jack and Jill
Knights Templar Street Parade, Philadelphia
Krousemeyer Kids
LaSavate
The Last Cartridges
Launching a Steamer
Lightning Artist
The Lightning Change Artist
A Lively Cock Fight
Louis & Nashville Flyer
Louisville Fire Run
Lover's Trouble
Madison Square, New York
The Magician
A Maiden's Paradise
The Man with the Iron Jaw
The Man with the Many Faces
March of the Post Office Employees
Memphis & Ft. Scott Railway Bridge
Memphis Fire Run
Memphis Water Front
Mephisto's Theatre
A Midnight Episode
Military Fire Drill
Mississippi River
Murphy and the Midget
Murphy Has Trouble with His Wife
Murphy Returns from a Masquerade
Murphy's Jealousy
Murphy's Troubles with the Photographer
The Mysterious Trunk
New Serpentine Dance
A Night in Blackville
No Place Like Home
Nymph of the Waves
Old Gentleman Spinkles
Oriental Dance
Outdoing Ching Ling Foo
Overland Flyer
Parade of Roses
Parade through Chicago Streets
Pennsylvania Limited
Pied Piper of Hamelin
Pioneer Limited
Plowing on the Old Farm
Pres. Krueger
Prince Henry Flyer
The Prince Leaving Chicago
Prize Fight in Coon Town
The Puppies and the Little Tease
Reproduction of Fitzsimmons-Gardner Fight
Reproduction of Jeffries-Corbett Fight
The Return to Quarters
Rival Billposters
The Rocky Mountain Limited
Royal Gorge
The Seven Capital Sins
A Shocking Incident
Shooting Craps
Shooting the Chutes
Snow Fight
Soldier's Dream
Something Good-Negro Kiss
Spanish Bull Fight
Start from the House and the Run
State and Madison Sts., Chicago
Street Scene in Port Huron, Mich.
Streets in Cairo, Egypt
The Stump Speaker
Summoning the Spirits
They're Off
Too Cautious
Train on High Bridge
Trick Donkey
Trip Around the Union Loop
Troubles of a Country Visitor
Two of a Kind
Two Old Sports
Umbrella Brigade
Uncle Tom's Cabin Parade
The Undelivered Message
Unveiling of Logan's Monument
The Up-to-Date Spiritualism
The Vanishing Burglars
View of State Street
Wash Day in Camp
Washing Elephants
Who Said Watermelon
Willie's First Smoke
Winter Sports on the Lake
The Wrestlers
Young America Celebrating Dewey's Return

Jan [day undetermined]

After the Ball
After the Hunt
American Falls from Canadian Side
American Falls from Luna Island
Andre at the North Pole
Animal Parade, Hagenbeck's Circus
The Aquarium
Arabian Acrobats
An Arabian Magician
Arrival of the Bull Fighter
Arrival of the Circus Train, No. 1
Arrival of the Circus Train, No. 2
The Artist's Model
At the Grave of Ling Fei Dong
Atlantic City Bathers
Atlantic City Board Walk, Easter Morn
Atlantic City Floral Parade
Aunt Jane's First Lesson in Love
Baby Show Atlantic City
Baby's First Step
Bad Boy and Hod Carrier
Bad Soup
Ballet Scene
Barber Up-to-Date
Bareback Riding
Barnyard Scene
Bathing at Atlantic City
Bathing Horses
Battle of Bladders
Beach at Atlantic City
Beach Scene, Coney Island
Bears Wrestling, Hagenbeck's Circus
The Beauty Show
Behind the Scenes
The Bewildered Astronomer
Bicycle Parade, Philadelphia
Bicyclist and Fisherman
Biddy's Day Off
The Big 4-7 Gun in Action
Birds-eye View of Dawson City on the Yukon River, Alaska
Boat Race
Boer Supply Train Crossing the Veldt
Bostock's Circus Fording a Stream
Bostock's Educated Bears
Boston and New York Express
Boulevard St. Denis, Paris, France
Bowery Street Dancers
Bowling Alley
Boxing Match on Board the U.S. Cruiser Raleigh
Boy Up a Tree; or, Making Love in the Park
Breaker Boys Leaving the Coal Mines
British Troops Leaving for the Transvaal
British, with Music, Leaving for the Transvaal
Buck and Wing Dance
Buck Dance
Bucking Bronchos
Buffalo Bill's Street Parade
Buffaloes Born in the Zoo Gardens
Building the Suez Canal
Bull Fight, No. 1

Bull Fight, No. 2
Bullet vs. Whiskey
Burglar and Fairy
Burglar and Old Maid
Burial of Maine Sailors
Burlesque Cock Fight
Burlesque Lions and Their Tamer, Hagenbeck's Circus
Burning the Rubbish
Butcher Shop No. 1
Butcher Shop No. 2
Cagliostro's Mirror
Cake Walking Horses
Captured
Caravan of Camels
Carlisle's Trained Dogs
Cascade in Switzerland
Cat's Dinner
Chair Dance
Chariot Race
Chicken Thief
Children Saying Their Prayers
A Child's Vision
Chinese Dance
Chinese Laundry
Chinese Silk Mill
Chiquita, the Smallest Woman in the World
Christening Murphy's Baby
Circus Street Parade
City Hall, Philadelphia
Climbing the Greasy Pole
Clog Dance
Clown and Beer-Thief
Clown and Coal Merchant
Clown's Face
Clown's Mixup
Cock Fight
Cock Fight, No. 2
Colored Baby's Morning Bath
Colored Folks Bathing
Colored Sports
Colored Woman Smoking a Pipe
Columbia and Shamrock
Columbia in the Lead
Cossacks
Country Sport and Old Maid
Country Teacher and His Pupils
Courting in Olden Times
Cowboy Fun
Crew of the U.S. Cruiser Raleigh Passing the Grant Monument at Fairmount Park, Philadelphia
Crowd Leaving Athletic Base Ball Grounds
Dance Around the Moon
Dancing for a Chicken
Dancing Skeleton
Darkies' Kiss
Deadly Rivals
Death Curve, New York City
Delaware River Icebound
The Devil's Amusement
The Difficulties of the Manicurist
Digging for Foundation for Large Department Store, Phila.
Disappearing Gun in Action
Doctor's Office
Dolorita
Double-Humped Camels
Driving Cows to Pasture
Drunken Scene
Dutch and Irish Politics
Eating Dinner Under Difficulties
Eating Watermelons for a Prize
Egyptian Sword Dance
Electric Fountain
Electric Treatment
Electrocution of an Elephant
Employees Leaving Fall River Iron Works
The Enchanted Cafe
English Barnyard Scene
Escaped
Essence of Old Virginia
An Evening Chat
Expansion and Contraction
Facial Massage
Fantastic Dining Room
The Farmer and the Old Maid
Farmer Chasing Trespassers
Farmyard Scene
The Fastest Steam Yacht Afloat
Fatima, Couchee Dancer
Feeding Hogs
Feeding the Dogs
Feeding the Elephants
Feeding the Hippopotamus
Feeding the Pigs
Feeding the Swans
Ferris Wheel
Fighting Amazons
Fighting Fifth Northumberland Fusileers
Fire at Triangle Clothing Store, 13th and Ridge Ave., Philadelphia, May 3rd, 1899
Fire Dance
Fisherman's Troubles
The Five Acrobats, St. Leons
The Fooled Policeman
Foreign Train Scenes
Fred Poplar and His Pal
French Couchee Dance
A Fresh Bath
Fun in an Opium Joint
Fun on the Beach
Fun on the Ice
Funeral of Lung Fei Dong, the Chinese Mason
A Funny Story (Facial Expression)
Game of Base Ball
Gardener Sprinkling Bad Boy
Gardener's Joke
Georgia Camp Meeting
German Cruisers Bombarding Venezuelan Forts
Ghost Dancers
Giant Wilkins, the Largest Man in the World
Giant Wilkins Walking No. 2
Giddy Old Maid
Gilbert Saroni Preparing for His Act
Girard College Cadets Reviewed by Governor Hastings, at the Dedication of Stephen Girard's Monument
Girls Rolling Down Hill
Going to the Fire
Goo Goo Eyes
A Good Catch
Grand Entrance into the Hippodrome
Grand Review
Great Gorge R.R., Niagara
Group of Mexicans
Happy Childhood
Hatching Chickens Up-to-Date
Hauling Dirt Up an Incline
He Pulled the Wrong Tooth
Herald Square, New York
Herman the Conjurer
Hey Ding Diddle
Himalayan Bears from India
His Collar Does Not Fit
His First Cigar
His Wife Has Neuralgia
"The Holy City"
Home from the Club
Hon. Wm. Jennings Bryan
Horseshoe Falls from American Side
Horseshoe Falls, from Canadian Side
The House That Jack Built
How a Wife Gets Her Pocket Money
How Murphy Paid His Rent
How Rube Stopped the Trolley Car
The Hungry Countryman
Hunting White Bear
Hurry Up
In the Wrong Room
Indian War Dance
Indians
Inquisitive Models
Introduction of the Rough Riders of the World
The Irate Model
Irish Couple Dancing Breakdown
Irish Reel
James Street, Seattle, Wash.
Japanese Foot Juggler
Japanese Geisha Girls No. 1
Japanese Geisha Girls No. 2
Japanese Sword Fight
Jersey Central Flyer
Jewelry Robbery
Jolly Monks
King Cole
The King's Guardsmen
Kruger and Body Guard Leaving the Volksraad
Kruger Leaving His Residence for the Volksraad
Lafayette Square, Buffalo, N.Y.
L'Argentine Butterfly Dance
L'Argentine Mirror Dance
L'Argentine Silver Dance
Leap Frog
Leaping Tournament over Elephants
Leaving Jerusalem
The Legacy
Lehigh Valley Express "Black Diamond"
Liberty Bell
Lieut. Bagley's Funeral. Escort of Lieut. Bagley's at Raleigh, N. C.
Life of an American Fireman
A Lively Night
The Living Posters
Loading a Train with Stone
Loading and Unloading the Chutes at Willow Grove
Lone Fisherman
Loop the Loop
Loro & Devoy, the Comical Acrobats
Love in a Railroad Train
Love Me Little, Love Me Long
Lovers Interrupted
Lovers Interrupted. New
McKinley's Funeral
The Magical Tramp
Magician
Main Street, Buffalo, N.Y.
Main Street, Fall River
Man Couchee Dance
Manning the Yard Arm on the U.S. Cruiser Raleigh
Mary Had a Little Lamb
Massage Treatment
Max Unger, the Strong Man
May Pole Dance
The Mechanical Head
Merry-Go-Round or Carrousel
Mexican Bull Fight
A Midwinter Blaze
The Miller and Chimney Sweep
Mischievous Boys
Mrs. Schneider's First Pinch of Snuff
Mitchell Day at Wilkes-Barre, Pa.
Morning Exercise on Board the U.S. Cruiser Raleigh
Mules in the Coal Mines
A Narrow Escape
Naval Parade on the Delaware River, Monday, May 1st, in Honor of Admiral Dewey
Never Interfere in Family Troubles
The New Born King
New Chinese Laundry
New Colored Kiss, No. 2
The New Dude and a Market Woman
The New Enchanted Cafe
New Fisherman's Luck
The New Leap Frog
New Passing Train Scene
The New Shooting the Chutes
The New Version of the Two Old Sports
New York's 7th and 71st Regiments
Newell and Chevet, the Famous Acrobats
Nightmare
North American Elk
North American Grey Wolves
Odetta, Chinese Dance
Odetta, Rope Dance No. 1
Odetta, Rope Dance No. 2
Odetta, Spanish Dance
O'Finnegan's Wake
Ohio Colored Troops at Camp Alger
Old Darkey Dancing
Old Maid Courtship
Old Maid's Ballet Dance
Old Maid's First Visit to a Theatre
The Old Maid's Lament
Old Maid's Morning Greeting
On Forbidden Ground
Pacific Avenue, Tacoma, Wash.
Panorama from Elevated Train, New York
Panorama Looking Down Niagara from New Suspension Bridge
Panorama of American Soldiers in Camp
Panorama of Circus Train Unloading Horses
Panorama of City of Venice
Panorama of King's County, N.Y.
Panorama of League Island, Philadelphia
Panorama of New York from Jersey City
Panorama of Schellenen Gorge of Switzerland
Panorama of Thames River
Panorama of the Lehigh Valley Railroad
Panorama of the Menagerie
Panoramic View of Atlantic City Beach
Panoramic View of Haverstraw Tunnel, N.Y.
Parade of the Philadelphia Volunteer Fire Department

Passion Play: Agony in the Garden
Passion Play: Baptism of Jesus
Passion Play: Carrying the Cross
Passion Play: Christ and Disciples Plucking Corn
Passion Play: Christ Before King Herod
Passion Play: Christ Before Pilate and the Condemnation
Passion Play: Christ Before the Two High Priests
Passion Play: Christ Calling Zaccheus from the Tree
Passion Play: Christ Feeding the Multitude
Passion Play: Christ Healing the Sick
Passion Play: Christ in the Carpenter Shop
Passion Play: Christ in the Synagogue
Passion Play: Christ Tempted by the Devil
Passion Play: Flight into Egypt
Passion Play: Herodias Pleads for John the Baptist's Head
Passion Play: Jesus and the Woman of Samaria
Passion Play: Judas' Betrayal and the Messiah's Arrest
Passion Play: Massacre of the Innocents
Passion Play: Placing Jesus in the Tomb
Passion Play: Raising of Lazarus
Passion Play: Shepherds Watching Their Flocks by Night
Passion Play: Suffer Little Children to Come Unto Me
Passion Play: Taking Down the Cross
Passion Play: The Annunciation
Passion Play: The Ascension
Passion Play: The Birth of Christ
Passion Play: The Crucifixion
Passion Play: The Last Supper
Passion Play: The Messiah's Entry into Jerusalem
Passion Play: The Resurrection
Passion Play: The Transfiguration
The Peanut Vendor
Peeping Tom and His Telescope
Performing Elephants
Perkasie Tunnel
Petro in Fairy Land
Philippino War Dance
The Philosopher's Stone
Photographing a Goose
Pie Eating Contest
Pillow Fight, Reversed
Polar Bears
Police Charge on Horseback
Policeman Chasing Bathers
Prairie Emigrant Train Crossing the Plains
President McKinley and His Cabinet on the Reviewing Stand, at Fairmount Park, Phila., May 27, 1899
President Mitchell's Speech
Prince Henry at Washington
Prof. Langtry's Boxing School
Putting Out the Fire
Pygmalion and Galatea
Quadrille in Drawers
Quaker Dance
The Quarrelsome Anglers
Railroad Tunnel Scene
Rapids above American Falls from American Side
Rapids above American Falls from Bridge to Goat Island
Reading a Letter (Facial Expression)
Reading Subway
Rear view of the "Black Diamond Express," Lehigh Valley R.R.
Rear view of the Washington and New York Flyer
Rescue from the Fire
Ricardo Family of Acrobats No. 1
Ricardo Family of Acrobats No. 2
Ricardo Family of Acrobats No. 3
Ricardo Family of Acrobats No. 4
Ricardo Family of Acrobats No. 5
River Drive, Fairmount Park
Riverside Avenue, Spokane, Wash.
Roofs of Paris
Royal Horse Artillery on the March to the Front
The Royal Levee in India [The Delhi 'Durbar']
Rubber Face
Rushing the "Growler"
Sailor's Hornpipe
Scarf Dance
Scene in a Laundry
Scene in Seminary
Scenes of the Wreckage from the Water Front
School Girl's Dance
Scotch Highland Fling
The Sculptor's Studio
Shamrock Placing Her Topsail
Shamrock Rounding Sandy Hook Light Ship
Sharkey-McCoy, 10 Rounds
6th Ave. New York Elevated Railroad
Skating in Fairmount Park
Skating Scene
Skirmish with Boers near Kimberly by a Troop of Cavalry Scouts Attached to Gen. French's Column
Sleigh Riding
Small Boy and Bear, Hagenbeck's Circus
Small Boy and Lion Cub, Hagenbeck's Circus
Snapshot and Its Consequences
Snowballing
Soft Shoe Dance
The Soldier's Return
Spanish Dance
Spokane Falls, Spokane
Squire's Court
Stable on Fire
The Stag Hunt
Station Scene
Stealing Chickens
Steeple Jumping
Submarine Diver
Sunken Vessel in the Harbor
Swimming School
Swiss Training and Breeding Home for St. Bernard Dogs
Taking Out the Dead and Wounded
Teaching Ballet Dancing
Ten Ichi Performing His Wonderful Water Trick
Ten Ichi, the Famous Japanese Magician, with His Troop
10th Pennsylvania Drilling at Manila
There Is No Fool Like an Old Fool
Third Avenue Elevated Train, New York
The Three Bacchantes
Three Bell Sisters in a Fancy Dance
Torpedo Boat in Action
Trained Animals, Hagenbeck's Circus
Trained Bears and Dogs, Hagenbeck's Circus
Trained Goats
The Tramp in the Barber Shop
Tramping on a Rolling Globe
The Tramp's Surprise
Transvaal War Supplies Transported by McKenzie Traction Engines
Trick Dogs, Hagenbeck's Circus
Trick Donkey, Hagenbeck's Circus
Trick Donkey, No. 2
Trick Elephant Bolivar, the Largest Elephant in the World, No. 1
Trick Elephant Bolivar, the Largest Elephant in the World, No. 2
Trick Elephant, Hagenbeck's Circus
Triple Pyramids
Troop Train Conveying the Seaforth Highlanders across the Modder River
Trouble with the Milkmaid
Trouble with the Washerwoman
20th Century Surgeon
24th Chasseurs Steeple Jumping
Two Old Sports
Tyrolienne Dance
Umbrella Dance
U.S. Artillery Drill
U.S. Battleship Indiana
U.S. Monitor Miantonomah Steaming into Key West
U.S. Monitor Terror
Unloading Canal Boat
Unloading the Elephants
An Unpleasant Situation
Upside Down
Vaulting in Saddle and Jumping Hurdle
Venetian Troupe
View of the Residence Section
Volksfest, Philadelphia
Waltz Clog Dance
War Supplies Arriving at Boer Laager by Train of Ox Teams
Washerwoman's Mistake
Washington and New York Flyer
Watering Cavalry Horses
Watermelon Eating Contest
Wedding Procession in a Church at Rome
West Indian Boys Diving for Money
Western Card Game
What Happened to the Milkman
What Was Found in a High Hat
Whirlpool Rapids
Whitewashing a Colored Baby
Wing Dance
The Wire Walker
Woodside Park Trolley Panorama
A Wringing Good Joke
Yacht Columbia
Yacht Race
Yacht Shamrock
Yachting at Atlantic City

Jan 17 The Ascent of Mount Blanc
Picture Hanging Extraordinary

Jan 31 The Magical Egg
S.S. St. Louis
Sensational Hurdle Race
Wonderful Suspension and Evolution

Feb [day undetermined]
Allentown Duck Farm
Annual Circus Parade
Arrival and Departure of President Loubet
Arrival of H.I.M. The German Emperor, at Port Victoria
Arrival of Kaiser Wilhelm in England
Arrival of Lord and Lady Minto at the Barracks, Dawson
Battle Royal
Beauty Show
Before and After
Bootblack and Crossing Sweeper
Broken Trace
Broncho Busting Along the Lines of the Denver & Rio Grande Railway
Bucking Broncho Contest
Bucking Broncho Contest [Sheridan Contest]
C. D. Graham Swimming the Lower Rapids
Cadet's First Smoke
California Limited
Camel Race on the Desert
Canoe Fight
The Canyon of the Grand
Carrying the Crown into Westminster Abbey
Casey's Twins
Cattle Bathing
Cavalry Parade
Chautauqua Aquatic Day. No. 9
Chautauqua Boys' Club. No. 1
Chautauqua Boys' Club. No. 2
Chautauqua Girls' Club. No. 6
Children Coasting
Christian Endeavor Greeting
Dawson City Fire Department Going to a Fire
Dog Teams Hauling Wood to Dawson City, Up the Yukon
The Dude and the Bootblacks
Envelope Folder and Sealer, National Cash Register Co.
Extraordinary Black Art
Fat Man's Race
Feeding Brook Trout at the Pennsylvania State Fishery
Feeding the Pigs
Firing the Royal Salute at Dawson City by the Northwest Mounted Police
French Cavalry Evolutions
Gallery Gods Watching a Funny Act
General Alarm
German Flag Afloat, National Cash Register Co.
Girls Getting on Trolley, National Cash Register Co.
Girls Going to Lunch. National Cash Register Co.
Girls in Physical Culture, National Cash Register Co.
Gravity Fountain
Great French Cavalry Charge
Great German Cavalry Charge
Harvesting Scene
Herring Fishing in the North Sea
Hooligan's Fourth of July
The Human Fly
The Impossible Feat of Balancing
Indian Fire Dance
Indian Hideous Dance
Indian Parade
Indians Charging on the Photographer

Jim Post, the Great Facial Comedian, and His Troubles
Jubilee, National Cash Register Co.
Juvenile Fire Department
King Edward and Queen Alexandra Passing Through London, England
Life Rescue at Atlantic City
Little Wonder Printing Press, National Cash Register Co.
Log-Rolling Contest
Looping the Loop at Coney Island
Lord and Lady Minto with Party, Fording the Rushing Waters of the Klondike on Horseback
The Magic Table
The Magician and the Imp
Market Scene in Cairo, Egypt
Men Getting on Trolley, National Cash Register Co.
Men in Physical Exercise, National Cash Register Co.
Men Leaving Factory, National Cash Register Co.
Mephistopheles' School of Magic
The Minuet. No. 3
Mr. Bickford on Trolley, National Cash Register Co.
Mr. Carney and Friend, National Cash Register Co.
Mr. Carroll and Assistant, National Cash Register Co.
Mr. Chalmers and Mr. Gibbs Arrive at Club, National Cash Register Co.
Mr. Chalmers Going to Officers' Club, National Cash Register Co.
Mr. J. H. Crane, National Cash Register Co.
Mr. Lawer, National Cash Register Co.
Mr. Patterson and Mr. Mark Arriving, National Cash Register Co.
Mrs. Taylor Going over Horseshoe Falls in a Barrel
Mother Goose Nursery Rhymes
Mule Pack Train Taking Gold Dust to Dawson City
North Atlantic Fleet Bombarding Fisher's Island
North Atlantic Fleet Bombarding Fort Adams, Newport Harbor
Officers Leaving Club, National Cash Register Co.
Oh! Shut Up
An Old Squaw on the Trail
1,000 Mile Ride over the Ice on a Bicycle
Panorama and Bathing Scene of Ostend, Belgium
Panorama of Factory from Automobile, National Cash Register Co.
Panoramic View of the Rocky Mountain on the Rock Island System
Panoramic View of the Streets of Paris, France
Panoramic Views and Scenes at the Garden of the Gods
Paternal Affection
Patterson Children in Pony Wagon, National Cash Register Co.
Patterson Children Leaving Home, National Cash Register Co.
Patterson Children on Horseback, National Cash Register Co.
The Peel River Indians with Their Dog Teams and Toboggan Sleighs on the Trail
La Petite Alma, Baby Acrobat
Pike's Peak Cog Wheel Route from Manitou
Policeman and Automobile
Porters in Parade, National Cash Register Co.
Professor Batty's Trained Bears
Race Between Dog Team, Bicycle and Cutter
Reversible Donkey Cart
Sack Race
Santa Fe Colorado Express
Santos Dumont's Airship
Scenes on the Short Line
Seattle Fire Department in Action
Shoshone Indians in Scalp Dance
A Sleigh Load of Squaws
Sluice Mining on Gold Hill in the Klondike, Hutchinson and Johnstone's Claim of No. 6, Eldorado
Smashing a Jersey Mosquito
Smith's Wife Inspects the New Typewriter
Snoqualmie Falls
Sparring Exhibition on Board the U.S.S. "Alabama"
Stage Hold-Up
Start of Endurance Run of the Automobile Club of America
Steam Whistle, National Cash Register Co.
Steer Roping Contest at Cheyenne, Wyo.
Swedish Gymnastics at Chautauqua. No. 8
A Sweep across New York
Team of Horses Hauling Wood to Dawson, Up the Yukon
Testing Jacks, National Cash Register Co.
Trial Run of the Fastest Boat in the World, "The Arrow"
Twentieth Century Conjuring
25 Stories Up!
$25,000 Clean Up on No. 16, Eldorado
United States Mail Leaving Dawson City for White Horse
Up-to-Date Surgery
Ute Indian Snake Dance
Visitors in Wheeling Chairs, National Cash Register Co.
What Casey Won at the Raffle
Window Display Clown, National Cash Register Co.
Window Display Revolving Balls, National Cash Register Co.
Working a Long Tom Rocker on Bonanza Creek
Working the Rocker, Called a Jigger, on Poverty Bar, Fourteen Below Discovery Bonanza Creek

Feb 14 Disagreeable Railroad Passengers
English Barnyard Scene

Mar [day undetermined]
Blasting the Treadwell Mines
Captain Allard Shooting White Horse Rapids
Disposition of Slabs and Waste at Pt. Blakeley
Dog Baiting and Fighting in Valdez
First Snow Storm of the Season, Valdez
Fourth and Market Sts., San Francisco
Horses Swimming Copper River
Hydraulic Mining in Oregon
In the Rapid-Transit Tunnel
Kalama Railroad Ferry Crossing the Columbia River
Leaving Skagway for the Golden North
Oil Fields, Tanks and Lakes of Oil; Kern Co., Cal.
Old Method of Mining, No. 11 Eldorado
Operation on the Famous Chechawko Hill
A Pack Train in the Copper River Country
Pack Train Leaving Valdez for Copper Mines
Panorama of Cal. Oil Fields
Panorama of Kennicott Glacier Port Hole
Panorama of "Miles Canyon"
Panorama of No. 2 Eldorado
Panorama of Taku Glacier
Panorama of White Horse Rapids
Passengers Alighting and Drinking Shasta Water
Past Shasta Spring, California
A Rotary Snow Plow in the Great Northwest
Sacramento Valley, Cal. from Pilot of Engine
Snow-Plow Bucking a 15-foot Snow Slide
Steamer Queen on Ice
Steamer Susie Excursion to Moosehide
Steamer "Yukoner" Leaving Dawson
$35,000 Clean-Up on Eldorado No. 10
Through Cascade Tunnel
Through Miles Canyon on a Cattle Scow
Through Tunnel on the White Pass Route
Through White Horse Rapids
Tunnel Scene of the White Pass Route
Two Miles of the White Pass & Yukon Railroad
Unfair House, Butchers Boycotting, San Francisco
Who Killed Cock Robin?
Willamette Falls
Winter Sport on Snake River, Nome

Mar 7 Robinson Crusoe

Mar 14 Buying a Baby
The Delhi Camp Railway
Logging in Canada
On the Bow River Horse Ranch at Cochrane, North West Territory
Spearing Salmon in the Rivers of the North West Territory

Mar 21 Life of a London Fireman
The Little Match Seller
The Workman's Paradise

Apr [day undetermined]
Acquatic Sports
American Falls, Goat Island
American Falls, Luna Island
Ameta
Artist and the Dummy
Ascending a Rock-Chimney on the Grand Charmoz, 11,293 feet
Ascent and Descent of the Aiguilles Des Grandes Charmoz, 11,293 feet
Bachelor's Paradise
Battle of Confetti at the Nice Carnival
Battle of Flowers at the Nice Carnival
Bewitched Dungeon
The Brahmin and the Butterfly
Breaking a Bronco
The Broncho Horse Race
Coaching in Ireland
Coaching Through the Tunnel on the Kenmere Road
Conjurer and 100 Tricks
Coster Sports
"The Devil of the Deep" and the Sea Urchins
A Devonshire Fair
A Duel with Knives
England's Colonial Troops
An English Prize-Fight
For the Upper Crust
Gigantic Devil
A Gorgeous Pageant of Princes
The Grand Canal, Venice
The Grand Panorama from the Great Schreckhorn, 13,500 feet
The House of Mystery
The House That Jack Built
How He Missed His Train
A Japanese Wrestling Match
A Kennel Club Parade
A Kiss in the Tunnel
Landing Guns
Launch of Shamrock III
Life and Passion of Christ
The Long and Short of It
Looping the Loop
A Majestic Stag
Man's Best Friend
Mary Jane's Mishap; or, Don't Fool with the Parafin
Miracles of Brahmin
The Miser
The Monk in the Monastery Wine Cellar
Mountain Torrents
Native Woman Washing a Negro Baby in Nassau, B. I.
Native Women Coaling a Ship and Scrambling for Money [West Indies]
Native Women Coaling a Ship at St. Thomas, D.W.I.
Native Women Washing Clothes at St. Vincent, B. W. I.
On Horseback, Killarney
On the Grand Canal, Venice
Over London Bridge
Panorama of Alpine Peaks
Panorama of Grindelwald
Panorama of Lucerne Lake
Panorama of Morro Castle, Havana, Cuba
Panorama of Queenstown
Panorama of Willemstadt, Curacao, Taken from the River
Panorama on the St. Gothard Railway
Panoramic View of Monte Carlo
Panoramic View of St. Pierre, Martinique
A Paper Chase
Pa's Comment on the Morning News
Pilot Leaving "Prinzessen Victoria Luise" at Sandy Hook
The Pines of the Rockies
Procession of Floats and Masqueraders at Nice Carnival
Pulling a Seine U.S.F.C.
Push Ball
Railroad Panorama near Spanishtown, Jamaica
Review of Native Chiefs at the Durbar
Review of the Chiefs at the Durbar
Rip Van Winkle
The River Shannon
Ski Jumping Competition
The Sorcerer, Prince and the Good Fairy

Spanish Bull Fight
Spilt Milk
Stag Hunting in England
Stripping Pike Perch U.S.F.C.
A Swiss Carnival
Through the Telescope
Tourists Playing Shuffleboard on "Prinzessen Victoria Luise"
A Triple Balloon Ascent
A Two Handed Sword Contest
Valentine and Orson
A Visit to the London Zoo
A Water Carnival
Weary Willie and the Policeman
West Indian Girls in Native Dance
Wharf Scene and Natives Swimming at St. Thomas, D.W.I.
What Befell the Inventor's Visitor
With the Stag Hounds

Apr 11 Acrobatic Sisters Daines
Reproduction of the Corbett-McGovern Fight (San Francisco, Cal, March 31, 1903)

Apr 13 Gulliver's Travels

May [day undetermined]
The Angler
Animated Dolls
Artillery Exercises
The Artist's Studio
Babes in the Wood
Be Good
Beauty and the Beast
Berlin Fire Department at Drill
Caught Courting
Changing Horses at Glen
Changing Horses at Linden
Child Eating
Chinese National Dance
Coronation Procession Passing Under the Canadian Arch
"Don't Get Gay with Your Manicure!"
Eclipse Car Fender Test
English and French Boxers
English Soldiers at Gun Drill
Experimental
Female Contortionist and Acrobatic Dog
Fighting Rams
Fireboat "New Yorker" Answering an Alarm
Fireboat "New Yorker" in Action
Game of Push Ball
Goody, Goody Two Shoes
The Hairdresser
Hickery, Dickery Dock
Hindoo Street Scene
How the Valet Got into Hot Water
How Tommy Got a Pull on His Grandpa
"I Want My Dinner"
Juvenile Stakes
Landing, Sorting and Gutting Fish
Launching Cup Defender "Reliance"
Lehigh Valley Black Diamond Express
Life of an English Fireman
Little Miss Muffet
Little Snowdrop
London Fire Scene
Market Scene in Hanoi, China
Meadowbrook Steeplechase
Metropolitan Handicap
Miniature Prize Fighters
Modern House Furnishing Methods
New Bull Fight
New York City Dumping Wharf
New York City "Ghetto" Fish Market
New York City Police Parade
N.Y. Fire Department Returning
New York Harbor Police Boat Patrol Capturing Pirates
Old Woman Who Lived in a Shoe
On the Road
Oriental Dancers
Pageant of East Indian Princes
The Pajama Girl
Panorama of Blackwell's Island
Panorama of Riker's Island
Panorama Water Front and Brooklyn Bridge from East River
Panoramic View of Geneva, Switzerland
Panoramic View of Herreshoff Works from Bristol Harbor
Panoramic View of the Alps from an Electric Car
Panoramic View of Torpedo Boat "Winslow" and Yacht "Constitution"
Phantom Ride on the Canadian Pacific
Pres. Roosevelt at the Dedication Ceremonies, St. Louis Exposition
Private Picture for Mr. Hyde
Prize Winners at the Dog Show
Procession of Chinamen in Pekin
Procession of Giant Elephants in India
Pulling Off the Bed Clothes
Resourceful Waiter
Reynard the Fox
Rip Van Winkle
Run of N.Y. Fire Department
A Scarecrow Tramp
A Shocking Incident
Shooting the Chutes
Skyscrapers of New York City, from the North River
Sorting Refuse at Incinerating Plant, New York City
Spilled Milk
Steamscow "Cinderella" and Ferryboat "Cincinnati"
The Still Alarm
Stripping Shad U.S.F.C.
Swiss Family Robinson
Three Bears
Three Little Pigs
Threshing Outfit at Work
Tom, Tom the Piper's Son
Traders of the East Indian Empire
Training the Hounds
Uncle Tom's Cabin
Viceroy of India's Royal Levee
Wheat Harvesting Machines in Operation
White Wings on Review
Window Cleaner's Mishap

May 16 The Gambler's Crime
Smiles and Tears
Spring Cleaning

May 23 Railway Ride in the Alps

Jun [day undetermined]
"Africander" Winning the Suburban Handicap, 1903
Arabian Jewish Dance
Beaver Show Case
Betsy Ross Dance
The Cook Visits the Parlor
Cosy Corner Dance
Crossing the Atlantic
Danger of Dining in Private Dining Rooms
The Doctor's Favorite Patient
Down the Bamboo Slide
Eating Macaroni in the Streets of Naples
Egyptian Boys in Swimming Race
Egyptian Fakir with Dancing Monkey
Egyptian Market Scene
Excavating Scene at the Pyramids of Sakkarah
Feeding Pigeons in Front of St. Mark's Cathedral, Venice, Italy
Fording the River Nile on Donkeys
The Giddy Dancing Master
Gloomy Gus Gets the Best of It
Going to Market, Luxor Egypt
Happy Hooligan Interferes
The Haymarket
Herd of Sheep on the Road to Jerusalem
"Holy Moses" the Camel
How Mike Got the Soap in His Eyes
Jerusalem's Busiest Street, Showing Mt. Zion
A Jewish Dance at Jerusalem
King Edward and President Loubet Reviewing French Troops
King Edward's Visit to Paris
Lake Lucerne, Switzerland
Living Picture Production
Market Street Before Parade
The Necromancer
Over Route of Roosevelt Parade in an Automobile
A Pair of Queens
Panorama of Tivoli, Italy, Showing Seven Falls
Panorama, Union Square, San Francisco
Panoramic View of an Egyptian Cattle Market
Panoramic View of Beyrouth, Syria, Showing Holiday Festivities
Passengers Embarking from S.S. "Augusta Victoria" at Beyrouth
Poor Old Fido!
President Reviewing School Children
The President's Carriage
Primitive Irrigation in Egypt
The Professor of the Drama
Reproduction of Corbett-McGovern Fight
Rock Drill at Work in Subway
Shearing a Donkey in Egypt
69th Regiment, N.G.N.Y.
Snarleyow the Dog Fiend
Street Scene at Jaffa
The Teacher's Unexpected Ducking
Tourists Embarking at Jaffa
Tourists Landing at Island of Capri, Italy
Tourists Returning on Donkeys from Mizpah
Tourists Starting on Donkeys for the Pyramids of Sakkarah
Tourists Taking Water from the River Jordan
An Unprotected Female
Washing Clothes at Sicily

Jun 6 Little Tom Thumb

Jun 13 Beelzebub's Daughters
The Cake Walk Infernal
The Enchanted Basket
The Marvelous Wreath
Misfortune Never Comes Alone
The Mysterious Box
The Queen's Musketeers

Jun 27 The Enchanted Well
The Inn where No Man Rests

Jul [day undetermined]
The American Soldier in Love and War [Number 1]
The American Soldier in Love and War [Number 2]
The American Soldier in Love and War [Number 3]
Battle Flags of the 9th U.S. Infantry
Bayonet Exercises
A Boarding School Prank
The Boy in the Barrel
Catch-as-Catch-Can Wrestling Bout
A Discordant Note
The Divorce: Detected [Part 1]
The Divorce: On the Trail [Part 2]
The Divorce: The Evidence Secured [Part 3]
Expert Bag Punching
The Fate of a Gossip
Happy Hooligan Earns His Dinner
Happy Hooligan in a Trap
How Buttons Got Even with the Butler
Laplanders at Home
Levi & Cohen, The Irish Comedians
Making a Welch Rabbit
Miniature Railway at Wilmington Springs, Delaware
Musical Calisthenics
Musical Drill with Arms
The Physical Culture Girl, No. 1
The Physical Culture Girl, No. 2
The Physical Culture Girl, No. 3
Policemen's Prank on Their Comrade
Pres. Roosevelt's Fourth of July Oration
Razzle Dazzle
A Scrap in Black and White
Shelter Tent Drill
Shooting the Chutes, Luna Park
Strictly Fresh Eggs
A Too Ardent Lover
The Unfaithful Wife: Murder and Suicide [Part 3]
The Unfaithful Wife: The Fight [Part 2]
The Unfaithful Wife: The Lover [Part 1]
A Victim of Circumstantial Evidence
A Welsh Rabbit
Why Foxy Grandpa Escaped a Ducking
Willie's Camera

Jul 11 Sleeping Beauty

Jul 12 Light Heavyweight Championship Contest Between Root and Gardner

Jul 18 The Life of a London Bobby
Pittsburgh Fire Department in Full Run

Jul 25 The Drawing Lesson; or, The Living Statue
The Mystical Flame
The Witch's Revenge

Aug [day undetermined]
Balloon Race
The Burglar
Buying Stamps from Rural Wagon, U.S.P.O.
Cancelling Machine, U.S.P.O.
Carriers at Work, U.S.P.O.
Carriers Leaving Building, U.S.P.O.
Clerks Casing Mail for Bags, U.S.P.O.
Clerks Tying Bags, U.S.P.O.
Clerks Tying Up for Bags, U.S.P.O.
Coach at Rural Post Office, U.S.P.O.
Collecting Mail, U.S.P.O.
Down Where the Wurzburger Flows
The Dude and the Burglars
Exchange of Mail at Rural P.O., U.S.P.O.

Fife Getting Instructions from Committee
Finish of the First Race, Aug. 22
A Funny Story on the Beach
The Gay Shoe Clerk
The Girl at the Window
Gold Dust Twins
A Gypsy Duel
"He Loves Me, He Loves Me Not"
Horses Drawing in Seine
Horses Drawing Salmon Seine
Immigrants Landing at Ellis Island
In My Lady's Boudoir
Jockeying for the Start Aug. 20
Jockeying for the Start Aug. 22
The Kidnapper: At Work [Part 1]
The Kidnapper: In the Den [Part 2]
The Kidnapper: The Rescue [Part 3]
Little Lillian, Toe Danseuse
A Little Tease
Loading Mail Car, U.S.P.O.
"Love Me, Love My Dog"
Lucky Kitten!
Mailing Platform, U.S.P.O.
Men Taking Fish from Salmon Seine
Murder Scene from "King of the Detectives"
Old Mail Coach at Ford, U.S.P.O.
On the Flying Rings
Post Man Delivering Mail, U.S.P.O.
Racing for a Tow
Railroad View—Experimental
Reliance Rounding Turn, August 20th
"Reliance" vs. "Shamrock" III, Aug. 20
The Rose
Routing Mail, U.S.P.O.
Rube and Mandy at Coney Island
Rural Wagon Delivering Mail, U.S.P.O.
Rural Wagon Giving Mail to Branch, U.S.P.O.
A Search for Evidence
Seashore Frolics
Silveon and Emerie "On the Web"
Special Delivery Messenger, U.S.P.O.
Stake Boat with Stake ("John Scully")
Start of the First Race, Aug. 22
Street Car Chivalry
Street Mail Car, U.S.P.O.
Subub Surprises the Burglar
Sweets for the Sweet
Throwing Mail into Bags, U.S.P.O.
A Total Accident
Transporting Internal Rev. Stamps, U.S.P.O.
The Two Sisters!
Tying Up Bags for Train, U.S.P.O.
The Unappreciated Joke
The Waders
The Wages of Sin: A—Murder
The Wages of Sin: B—Retribution
Wagons Loading Mail, U.S.P.O.
"What Are the Wild Waves Saying Sister?"
The Widow
A Yard of Puppies

Aug 1 The Animated Cartoon
DeVoy's Revolving Ladder Act
The Elixir of Life
Fun on Board a Fishing Smack
How to Shut Up a Quarrelsome Wife
Little Tich and His Funny Feet
The Magic Book
Rock of Ages
True Love Never Runs Smooth

Aug 15 The Melomaniac
The Monster
The Oracle of Delphi
A Spiritualistic Photographer

Sep [day undetermined]
(Abandoned)
At Brighton Beach
At Terrific Speed
At the Ford, India. Across the Ravi River
The Baby
Baby Class at Lunch
The Baby Review
Bathing in Samoa
The Busy Bee
Butchering and Cleaning Tables U.S.F.C.
The Camera Fiend
The Chorus Girl and the Salvation Army Lassie
Coasting in the Alps
A Daring Daylight Burglary
The Devonshire Fair
The Devonshire Hunt
The Diamond Robbery
Discovery of Bodies
Experimental
A False Alarm in the Dressing Room
Finish of Yacht Race, Aug. 25th
Firing the Cabin
The Forecastle of the "Kearsage" in a Heavy Sea
From London to Brighton
From Show Girl to Burlesque Queen
The Galloping Tongas
Hammock Scene—(Abandoned)
How to Get a Wife and Baby
In the Dressing Room
Indians Leaving Bald Mountain
The Insurance Collector
Jack Tar Sewing a Patch on the Seat of His Trousers
Jack's Four Footed Friend. Mike the Ship's Mascot
Jockeying and Start of Yacht[s] Aug. 25th
King Edward VII in France
Lady Bountiful Visits the Murphys on Wash Day
Lifting Salmon Trap
The Llamas of Thibet
Love in a Perilous Place
Maypole Dance
The Minister's Hat
Miss Jessie Cameron, Champion Child Sword Dancer
Miss Jessie Dogherty, Champion Female Highland Fling Dancer
New York Caledonian Club's Parade
A Norwegian Waterfall
Old Fashioned Scottish Reel
One of Jack's Games Aboard a Man o' War
Orphans in the Surf
Panorama from Canoe, No. 6
Panorama of Beach and Cliff House
Panorama of Excursion Boats
Parade of Eagles, New York
Piping Down. Wash Clothes. Scrambling for Clothes
Poor Girl, It Was a Hot Night and the Mosquitos Were Thick
Pope [Leo XIII] in His Carriage
Pope [Leo XIII] Passing Through Upper Loggia
President Roosevelt Addressing Crew of "Kearsarge"
Pres. Roosevelt Leaving the Flagship
President Roosevelt's Arrival at "Kearsarge"
President Roosevelt's Departure from "Kearsarge"
Pres. Roosevelt's Sunday Visit to Kearsage
President Roosevelt's Visit to Admiral Barker
Private Picture—Families of H. N. M. & H. C.
Raising Salmon Trap U.S.F.C.
"Reliance" and "Shamrock" III Jockeying and Starting in First Race
Reliance and Shamrock III Turning Outer Stake in Second Race
"Reliance" Crossing the Line and Winning First Race
A Remarkable Group of Trained Animals
Reproduction of Jeffries-Corbett Contest
Rescue of Child from Indians
Rip Van Winkle
Rising Panorama of a Norwegian Waterfall
Rube and the Fender
Salmon Seining on Columbia River U.S.F.C.
The Sand Baby
The Sand Fort
Sea Washing over the Bow of Kearsage
Seeing New York by Yacht
Settler's Home Life
Signal Boys Wig-Wagging
Sir Thomas Lipton's Yacht Fleet Leaving England
Sparring Match on the "Kearsarge"
Start of Race—"Reliance" Ahead
Start of the Gordon-Bennet Cup Race
A Terrific Race
Throwing the Sixteen Pound Hammer
Trained Baby Elephants
Trained Dogs and Elephants
Trappers Crossing Bald Mountain
Tub Race
Turning the Tables
Uncle Tom's Cabin
An Unusual Spectacle
The Wise Elephant

Sep 5 The Fairyland; or, The Kingdom of the Fairies

Sep 18 Trailed by Bloodhounds

Sep 19 Pope Pius X [His Election and the Procession]

Sep 26 The Apothicareric Grotto
The Pigeons, Place St. Marc, Venice

Oct [day undetermined]
Aerial Posing
Alphonse and Gaston 3
Alphonse and Gaston (Journal Thumb Book)
The American Soldier in Love and War
Ancient and Honourable Artillery of London on Parade
The Ancient and Honourables Homeward Bound
The Animated Poster
Arab Act, Luna Park
At the Dressmaker's
The Baby
Ballet of the Nations
Blessed Is the Peacemaker
Burglar's Escape
The Camera Fiend, No. 2
Casey and His Neighbor's Goat
Casey's Nightmare
A Catch of Hard Shell Crabs
Cat's Cradle
Chinaman's Acrobatic Guests
Coal Mine
County Fair
The Cowboy and the Lady
Delivering Mail from Sub-Station [U.S.P.O.]
Dextrous Hand
A Dope in Difficulties
Double Ring Act, Luna Park
An East River Novelty
East Side Urchins Bathing in a Fountain
The Elopement
The Enchanted Cup
The Extra Turn
The Fate of the Artist's Model
Feeding the Sparrows
Flood Scene in Paterson, N.J.
Following the Hounds
Foxy Grandpa [Thumb Book]
From Haverstraw to Newburg
A Frontier Flirtation; or, "How the Tenderfoot Won Out"
Glimpses of Venice
Happy Hooligan's Interrupted Lunch
The Heavenly Twins at Lunch
The Heavenly Twins at Odds
The Honourable Artillery Company of London
Hooligan as a Safe Robber
Hooligan in Jail
Hooligan to the Rescue
Hooligan's Roller Skates
The Impatient Guest
Inside Car, Showing Bag Catcher [U.S.P.O.]
The Irrepressible Burglars
The Julians, Acrobats
King Edward's Visit to Ireland
Kit Carson
Kit Carson #6: Panorama
Leaping Trout
London Zoo
Lovers and the Imp
The Messenger Boy's Mistake
Move On
Neptune's Wife
"Never Touched Him!"
New York City Public Bath
Parade of "Exempt" Firemen
Performing Dogs
Photographer's Victim
The Physical Culture Girl
The Pioneers
Policeman's Interrupted Vision
The Providence Light Artillery
Pulling Against the Stream
Rattan Slide and General View of Luna Park
The Raw Recruit
The Rehearsal
Rent Collector
The Rock of Ages
A Romance of the Rail
Rome and the Vatican
Scenes at the Zoo
Seeing New York by Yacht

Serenader's Difficulties
She Fell Fainting into His Arms
Shooting the Rapids at Luna Park
Slide for Life, Luna Park
The Smoky Stove
Soap vs. Blacking
Springfield Fire Department
Street Scene in Hyderabad
Ten Nights in a Barroom
Toodles and Her Strawberry Tart
Toodles' Strawberry Tart (Journal Thumb Book)
Train Taking Up Mail Bag, U.S.P.O.
Two Chappies in a Box
Uncle Reuben at the Waldorf
U.S. Interior Dept.: Basket Ball, Indian School
U.S. Interior Dept.: Bridal Veil Falls
U.S. Interior Dept.: Changing Coaches, Raymond Coach
U.S. Interior Dept.: Irrigation of Alfalfa Lands
U.S. Interior Dept.: Laguna Indian Chicken-Pulling Race
U.S. Interior Dept.: Laguna Indian Foot Race
U.S. Interior Dept.: Laguna Indian Horse Race
U.S. Interior Dept.: Mail Coach Yosemite Valley
U.S. Interior Dept.: Panorama from Artist's Point
U.S. Interior Dept.: Panorama of Grand Canyon
U.S. Interior Dept.: Santa Fe Coach
U.S. Interior Dept.: Vernal Falls
U.S.P.O. Dept. Santa Fe Mail Train
The Vaidis Sisters, Luna Park
Washerwomen and Chimney-Sweep
Weighing the Baby
"Who Pays for the Drinks?"
The Wrath of a Jealous Wife
"You Will Send Me to Bed, Eh?"

Oct 17 Alice in Wonderland
The Apparition
The Infernal Caldron

Oct 31 Hop Picking
Moses in the Bullrushes
The Poachers

Nov [day undetermined]
Alcrofrisbas, the Master Magician
Alphonse and Gaston and the Burglar (Thumb Book)
Alphonse and Gaston Balcony Scene (Thumb Book)
Alphonse and Gaston Target Practice (Thumb Book)
Arrival of Tourists at the Hotel in Yellowstone Park
Arrival of Train at Gardner
Battleship "Indiana" in Action
Boat Race
Boat Race No. 2
Buster's Joke on Papa
Carpenter Work, Albuquerque School
Crow Indian Festival Dance
Crow Indian War Dance
Crow Indians Harvesting
Down the Bright Angel Trail
Feeding the Russian Bear
Fire Drill: Albuquerque Indian School
Firing the Cook
A Flirtation in Silhouette
Fountain Geyser
Fusion, On to Brooklyn!
Girls' Department, Albuquerque School
Girls Flag Drill, Moqui School
Great Falls of the Yellowstone
The Great Fire Ruins, Coney Island
A Guardian of the Peace
Harvard-Pennsylvania Football Game
Hooligan and Dogs (Journal Thumb Book)
Hooligan's Thanksgiving Dinner (Thumb Book)
An Impartial Lover
Indian Boys, Albuquerque School
Indian Horsemanship
Inspection Aboard Battleship "Indiana"
A Juvenile Elephant Trainer
Katzenjammer Kids (Journal Thumb Book)
Lifting a Wagon from a New York Foundation
The Llamas at Play
Mammouth Paint Pot, Yosemite Valley
Man Overboard! "INDIANA"
Moqui Indian Rain Dance
Navajo Indian Foot Race
Navajo Indian Horse Race
Navajo Indian Tug-of-War
Navajo Indians Wrestling
Navajo Squaw Weaving Blanket
Next!
Off His Beat
"Old Faithful," Yosemite Valley
On Yellowstone Lake
Panorama of Yellowstone Lake
Panoramic View of Hot Springs, Yellowstone Park
Poor Hooligan, So Hungry Too!
Princeton and Yale Football Game
The Professor
Rain Dance at Orabi
Raising Colors, Battleship "Indiana"
Toodles Recites a Recitation
Toodles Recites a Recitation (Thumb Book)
Toodles' Tea Party
Toodles' Tea Party (Thumb Book)
Tying the Red Light on the Tiger's Tail
United States Troops in Yellowstone Park
What Happened in the Tunnel
A Windy Day at the Flatiron Building

Nov 7 Jack Jaggs & Dum Dum
Jupiter's Thunderbolts
Life of Napoleon
10 Ladies in an Umbrella

Nov 14 The Effects of a Trolley Car Collision
A Shocking Accident
Street Car Chivalry
The Tramp's First Bath
A Visit to the Zoo

Nov 21 Animated Picture Studio
Automobile Explosion
Bob Kick, the Mischievous Kid
Cruelty on the High Seas
The Deserter
Down Below
Extraordinary Illusions
Fire and Rescue
The Ghost in the Graveyard
The Goose Takes a Trolley Ride
Hotel and Bath
Letter Came Too Late
Murphy's Wake
The New Cook
Nicholas Nickleby
Over the Garden Wall
A Pugilistic Parson
Quarrelsome Neighbors
Saturday's Shopping
A Trip to Southend

Nov 28 Attack on Chinese Mission
The Bather
Bicycle Dive
Jack's Return
Stop Thief

Dec [day undetermined]
Almost a King
The Ballet Rehearsal
Battleship "Illinois" Passing Under Brooklyn Bridge
Burning of the Academy of Music, Brooklyn
Buster's Joke on Papa
Clarence the Cop
The Dressmaker's Accident
Drill by Providence Police
Dumping Iron Ore
The Gerry Society's Mistake
The Great Train Robbery
Having Her Gown Fitted
Hooligan's Christmas Dream
How Old Is Ann?
How the Old Woman Caught the Omnibus
The Johnnie and the Telephone
Mr. Easy Mark
Noon Hour at Hope Webbing Company
The Office Boy's Revenge
Opening of New East River Bridge, New York
Outcast and Bride
The Over-Anxious Waiter
The Pajama Dance
The Pajama Statue Girls
The Pickpocket
The Porous Plaster
Run of Pawtucket Fire Dept.
Toodles' Christmas (Thumb Book)
Under the Mistletoe
Waiting for Bill

Dec 9 The Ballet Master's Dream

Dec 12 At Work in a Peat Bog
Cliff Scenery at the Fabbins
A Coach Drive from Glengariffe to Kenmore
The Damnation of Faust
A Drove of Wild Welsh Mountain Ponies
Elopement a la Mode
Irish Peasants Bringing Their Milk to a Cooperative Creamery
Jack and Jim
The Mono-Railway Between Listowel and Ballybunion, Ireland
Panorama of the Lakes of Killarney from Hotel
Polo Match for the Championship at Hurlingham
Scenes in an Irish Bacon Factory
Scenes in an Irish Market Place
Scenes of a New Forest Pony Fair
Scenes of Irish Cottage Life
Scenes on a Welsh Pony Farm
Shooting the Rapids of Killarney
A Trip Through the Gap of Dunloe
A Trip to the Giant's Causeway
Trout Fishing, Landing Three Pounder
Wild Mountain Ponies on Dartmoor
Wiring Pike in a Mill Stream

Dec 19 Dear Old Stars and Stripes, Goodbye
Discovered Through an Opera Glass
Every Day Is Sunshine When the Heart Beats True
The Magic Lantern
Only a Soldier Boy

1904 [month undetermined]
Ach du Lieber
After Dark
Algerian Goums in the Desert
Arrival and Release of 40,000 Carrying Pigeons at Ambergate, England
The Baby, the Monkey and the Milk Bottle
Banjo'Lize
Bull-Fight at Juarez, Mexico
Bull Fight with Matadors Senor Don Luis Mazzantini and Bombita
Chicago Portland Special
Clowns
Convention of Red Men, Lancaster, Pa.
The Cook Gets Square
Cook's Joke
Couchee Dance on the Pike
Daisy Donohue
Don't Butt In
Engineers, French Army
Exhibition of the United States Life Saving Crew
Fairbanks
Fish Traps Columbia River
Frivolity
From the South
The Funniest Man in the Exposition
Gavotte
Glimpses of Japan
The Great Toronto Fire, Toronto, Canada, April 19, 1904
Happy Days in Dixie
Hauling in a Big Catch
Hauling in Seines and Pulling Seines into Boat
Herring Fishing on French Coast
Highwaymen
International Winter Sports
The Interrupted Couple
Japanese Coaling a Man-of-War
Japanese Infantry Morning Drill
The Late Senator Mark Hanna
The Liberty Bell on Its Way to the Exposition
Life of an American Fireman
The Little Robin Robbers
Manoeuvres by British Bluejackets, Afloat and Ashore
Mending Seines on the Columbia River
Military Serenade
The Mischievous Kid, the Duck and the Gendarme
The Missing Link
The Monkey and the Ice Cream
Mysterious Clock
Our Own Make Polka
The Oxford and Cambridge Boat Race
Panorama of a Philippine Settlement [Pan-American Exposition]
Panoramic View of Chamonix, Alps
Panoramic View of La Mure, France
Panoramic view of Montreux, Switzerland

Panoramic View of Multnomah Falls
Panoramic View of Spokane Falls
Panoramic View of the Columbia River
The Policeman's Mistake
Preparing the Codfish After the Catch
Roosevelt Dedicating at St. Louis Exposition
Roosevelt Dedication at Lewis and Clark Exposition
A Ruben's Unexpected Bath
The Russian Army in Manchuria
Secret Procession of the Algerian Tribes
Sour Lake Oil Fields
Surf Scene on the Pacific
Toys Competition
Trained Dogs
Trip to the Zoo
The Tunnel Scene
Unloading Fish at Cannery
The Up-to-Date Wizard
View of "La Croisette," Cannes, France
Will He Never Get Undressed
Working in the Charcoal Mines in France
Yum-Yum-Yum

Jan [day undetermined]
And Pat Took Him at His Word
Applicants for Enlistment
The Arbitrator
As Seen on the Curtain
Auction of Deserters' Effects
Awkward Squad
Bag Inspection
The Bench in the Park
The Borrowing Girl
The Boy Under the Table
A Catastrophe in Hester Street
Chameleon Climbing
Chameleons Feeding
The Cheese Mites
Circular Panorama of the Horse Shoe Falls in Winter
Cowboy Justice
Crossing Ice Bridge at Niagara Falls
The Deserter
The Dog and the Baby
Drill
A Drop of Ink
Duel Scene, "By Right of Sword"
The Easy Chair
Elephants at Work
The Escaped Lunatic
Eye Tests, etc., Recruiting
Falling Chimney
First Aid to the Injured
The Furnished Room House—Taking Life Easy
General Quarters
Girl Waving American Flag, National Cash Register Co.
Girls Jumping the Rope
The Heathen Chinese and the Sunday School Teachers
The Homemade Turkish Bath
Ice Skating in Central Park, N.Y.
"In the Springtime, Gentle Annie!"
The Jolly Bill-Posters
Just Before the Raid
A Kiss in the Dark
Lerfoss Waterfall
A Little Bit off the Top
Love and Jealousy Behind the Scenes
The Misdirected Kiss
Nautical Tournament
Obstacle Race
One Way of Taking a Girl's Picture
Physical Examinations
The Picture the Photographer Took
The Power of Authority
Pugilistic Toads
Pull Down the Curtain, Susie
Recruits Embarking
Recruits on "Yorktown"
Sailors Dancing
San Francisco Chinese Funeral
Saved!
The Scene Behind the Scenes
A Scrap in the Dressing Room
Scrubbing Clothes
"Secure"
The Seeress
Serving Outfits to Recruits
Sliding Down Ice Mound at Niagara Falls
The Story the Biograph Told
Stretcher Race over Obstacles
Swearing in Recruits
Three Girls in a Hammock
Tied to Her Apron Strings
The Toad's Luncheon
Torpedo Attack
Treloar and Miss Marshall, Prize Winners at the Physical Culture Show in Madison Square Garden
Trick Bicycle Riding
The Troubles of a Manager of a Burlesque Show
What a Mechanical Toy Did To Some Giddy Girls
What Burglar Bill Found in the Safe
"While Strolling in the Park"

Jan 2 The Somnambulist
William Tell

Jan 9 The Chicago Fire
The Terrible Turkish Executioner

Jan 16 A Burlesque Highway Robbery in "Gay Paree"
Puss in Boots

Jan 23 Amusing Changes
Charming Enchantment
The Kiddies and the Poultry
A Moonlight Serenade; or, The Miser Punished.
Russian Cavalry in Corea [sic]

Jan 30 Alligator Farm
Dogs and Rats
The Monkey Bicyclist
Monkey, Dog and Pony Circus

Feb [day undetermined]
Animated Painting
A Blessing from Above
Blind Man's Buff
The Bold Soger Boy
The Borrowing Girl and the Atomizer
Bubbles!
A Bucket of Cream Ale
A Busy Day for the Corset Model
Casey's Frightful Dream
Clarence, the Cop, on the Feed Store Beat
Cohen's Advertising Scheme
The Committee on Art
Dance of the College Women's Club
Dinah's Defeat
A Fight in the Dormitory
Flour and Feed
Four Beautiful Pairs of Legs
The Four Seasons
Getting Strong; or, The Soubrette's Home Gymnasium
The Girl and the Kitten
A Girl Who Wanted to Rise in the World
The Great Baltimore Fire
Halloween Night at the Seminary
A Hot Time at Home
Ice Boating on the North Shrewsbury, Red Bank, N.J.
An Ice Covered Vessel
A Joke at the French Ball
The Kentucky Squire
Kiss Me!
Let Uncle Ruben Show You How
Little German Band
Mellin's Food Baby
Midnight Intruder
Minuet and Dance—College Women's Club
The Misplaced Signs
An Old Bachelor
Old Maid and Fortune Teller
On the Window Shade
The Opening of the Williamsburg Bridge
Our Deaf Friend, Fogarty
Panorama of Ruins from Baltimore and Charles Street
Panorama of Ruins from Lombard and Charles Street
Panorama of Ruins from Water Front
Photographing a Female Crook
Pity the Blind, No. 2
Quick Work Behind the Scenes
Quick Work for the Soubrettes
S.S. Moro Castle
Sailors Ashore
She Kicked on the Cooking
The Shocking Stockings
The Soubrette's Slide
A Subject for the Rogue's Gallery
Those Troublesome Boys
A Warm Occasion
The Way to Sell Corsets
Wifey's Mistake

Feb 6 The Automobile Race
Devil's Pot
The Falling Palace
A Ferry in the Far East
Fording a Stream
High Diving and Reverse
Hurdle Jumping
An Intelligent Elephant
The Little Greedy Beggar
Marie Antoinette
Metamorphosis of the King of Spades
The Midgets
Tit for Tat; or, A Good Joke on My Head

Feb 13 Every Man His Own Cigar Lighter
The Invisible Sylvia
A Wager Between Two Magicians; or, Jealous of Myself

Feb 20 The Great Baltimore Fire

Feb 23 Diving Lucy
Jack Sheppard—The Robbery of the Mail Coach
The Salmon Fisheries of Vancouver

Mar [day undetermined]
The Attack on Port Arthur
The Battle of Chemulpo
The Battle of the Yalu
Behind the Screen
Buster and Tige Put a Balloon Vendor Out of Business
Buster Brown and the Dude
Buster Makes Room for His Mama at the Bargain Counter
Buster's Dog to the Rescue
The Bustle in the Narrow Door
Butt's Manual, St. John's School
Company Drill, St. John's Military Academy
A Crushed Hat
A Dance on the Pike
Dress Parade, St. John's Academy
The Elopers Who Didn't Elope
A Fair Exchange No Robbery
A Fire in a Burlesque Theatre
The Girls and the Burglar
Grandfather as a Spook
Gun Drill St. John's Academy
The Hoop and the Lovers
How the Cook Made Her Mark
In a Boarding School Gymnasium
The Loaded Cigar
Manual of Arms, St. John's Military Academy
A Misdirected Ducking
Mr. Jack Entertains in His Office
Mr. Jack Is Caught in the Dressing Room
Mr. Jack Visits the Dressing Room
The Model That Didn't Pose
Moneyweight Salesmen
A Novel Way of Catching a Burglar
Panorama of Ruins from Lombard and Hanover Streets, Baltimore, Md.
Pranks of Buster Brown and His Dog Tige
A Railroad Quick Lunch
The Rival Models
School Girl Athletes
School Girl Gymnasts
Section of Buster Brown Series, Showing a Sketch of Buster by Outcault
Shredded Wheat Biscuit No. 1
Shredded Wheat Biscuit No. 2
Sleighing in Central Park, New York
A Snare for Lovers
The Strenuous Life
The Suit of Armor
Torpedo Attack on Port Arthur
A Trick on the Cop
Under the Tree
Waving American Flag—National Cash Register Co.
The Wrong Room

Mar 5 The Bewitched Trunk
The Busy Bee
The Fugitive Apparitions
The Untamable Whiskers

Mar 12 Babe and Dog
Behind a Big Gun
The Clock Maker's Dream
Game of Cards
How the Japs Fought at Port Arthur
Hubby to the Rescue
The Jap Behind the Guns
Japanese Jackies
Lovers' Quarrel
Now, You Stop
Scenes on Every Floor

Mar 26 Benvenuto Cellini; or, A Curious Evasion
The Imperceptible Transmutations
A Miracle Under the Inquisition
The Passion Play

Wonderful Hair Restorer
Apr [day undetermined]
Babe and Puppies
An Escape from the Flames
Fire, Adams Express Co.
Girls Winding Armatures, Westinghouse Works
How to Disperse the Crowd
Japanese Acrobats
Mellin's Food Baby and Bottle
Mellin's Food Cut-Out
Nervy Nat
A Nigger in the Woodpile
Pierrot, Murderer
Review of U.S. Marine Band by Sec'y Moody, U.S. Navy
Shredded Wheat Biscuit
Tracked by Bloodhounds; or, A Lynching at Cripple Creek
The Waif; or, Out in the Street
Welding Big Ring
Westinghouse Sign
A Windy Day on the Roof
Apr 2 Faust and Marguerite
Apr 9 Bombardment of Port Arthur
Living Dummy
The Revolving Table
Russ-Jap Forces Meeting Near Chemulpo
Apr 20 After the Siege Tien-Tsin, Native City, China
Battle of Chemulpo Bay
Camel Caravan, Pekin, China
Coal Carriers Chefoo, China
Fashionable Driving on Palace Quay, St. Petersburg
Flower Parade Race Course, Moscow
Japanese Railroad Scene, Kanagarva, Japan
Japanese Sailors Fencing with Capstan Bars
Japs Loading and Firing a Gun on Battleship "Asama"
Japs Loading and Firing a Six Pounder
A Muddy Street, Tien-Tsin, China
Panorama of Railroad Station at Seoul, Korea, from Departing Train
Panorama Russian Battleship "Gronobia"
Polish Fire Brigade Answering an Alarm, Warsaw
Religious Procession, Moscow
Russian Battleship Repulsing Torpedo Attack
Russian Infantry, Warsaw
Russian Outposts Attacked by Japanese
Skirmish Between Russian and Japanese Advance Guards
Warship in Nagasaki Harbor, Japan
Apr 25 At Sea in a Storm
Automobile Ascending Mt. Snowdon
Belated Husband
Building a Lighthouse
Chambermaid's Revenge
The Dear Boys Home for the Holidays
English Lancers at Drill
An Evil Doer's Sad End
Experienced Waiter
Falls of the Clyde
Fantastic Cake Walk
Herding Polo Ponies and Polo Game
Holbein Swimming the English Channel
Homing Pigeons
Inspector's Birthday
A Juggling Contest
The Lady Juggler
Launching the Steamship "Celtic"
Life Guards Responding to Distress Signals
The Living Picture
Moving Pictures While You Wait
Mysterious Performances
No Bathing Allowed
No Room for Dad
Pleasant Breakfast
The Prodigal Son
Robber of the Dead
The Sailor's Rival
Samson and Delilah
The Smugglers
Surf Scene
That Busy Bee
Washerwoman and Buss
What the Window Cleaner Saw
The Wrong Poison
Apr 30 The Jolly Russian Prophets
Tchin-Chao, the Chinese Conjuror
May [day undetermined]
Annual Parade, New York Fire Department
Assembling a Generator, Westinghouse Works
Assembling and Testing Turbines, Westinghouse Works
Basket ball, Missouri Valley College
Brush Between Cowboys and Indians
Bucking Broncos
Capsized Boat
Casting a Guide Box, Westinghouse Works
Central High School, Calisthenics, Missouri Commission
Coil Winding Machines, Westinghouse Works
Coil Winding Section E, Westinghouse Works
The Cop Fools the Sergeant
Cowboys and Indians Fording River in a Wagon
Dog Factory
Driving Cattle to Pasture
Emerson School, Calisthenics, Missouri Commission
Fencing Class, Missouri Valley College
Free Arm Movement, All Schools, Missouri Commission
Girls Taking Time Checks, Westinghouse Works
Herding Horses across a River
High School Field Exercises, Missouri Commission
Hold Up in a Country Grocery Store
Hyde Park School Graduating Class, Missouri Commission
Hyde Park School Room 2, Missouri Commission
Igorotte Savages, St. Louis Exposition
Kindergarten Ball Game, Missouri Commission
Kindergarten Dance, Missouri Commission
Lathrop School, Calisthenics, Missouri Commission
Linwood School, Calisthenics, Missouri Commission
Opening Ceremonies, St. Louis Exposition
Operation of Westinghouse Block System
Panorama Exterior Westinghouse Works
Panorama from St. Louis Plaza, St. Louis Exposition
Panorama Motor Room, Westinghouse Works
Panorama of Field St., St. Joseph, Mo., Missouri Commission
Panorama of 4th St., St. Joseph, Mo., Missouri Commission
Panorama of Machine Co. Aisle, Westinghouse Co. Works
Panorama of 3rd Street, St. Joseph, Mo., Missouri Commission
Panorama St. Louis Exposition from Launch
Panoramic View Aisle B., Westinghouse Works
Parade of Characters (Asia in America) St. Louis Exposition
Parade of the Pikers, St. Louis Exposition
Railroad Panorama, Pittsburg to Stewart, Westinghouse Works
Rounding Up and Branding Cattle
Sec'y Taft's Address & Panorama
Steam Hammer, Westinghouse Works
Steam Whistle, Westinghouse Works
Taping Coils, Westinghouse Works
Tapping a Furnace, Westinghouse Works
Testing a Rotary, Westinghouse Works
Testing Gas Engine, Westinghouse Works
Testing Large Turbines, Westinghouse Co. Works
Testing Steam Engine, Westinghouse Works
Turning Panorama from Hill, Westinghouse Works
Twenty Mule Team, St. Louis Exposition
War Canoe Race
Western Stage Coach Hold Up
Westinghouse Air Brake Co., Casting Machine
Westinghouse Air Brake Co. Westinghouse Works
Westinghouse Co., No. 3, Moulding Machine
Westinghouse Employees Boarding Train
Westinghouse Employees, Westinghouse Works
Whittier School, Calisthenics, Missouri Commission
May 7 The Wonderful Living Fan
May 14 The Fight on the Bridge Between Russians and Japs
May 21 Barnum's Trunk
May 28 Fishing in Newfoundland—French Shore
Our Jolly French Students
The Restive Chicken
Typical Algerian 'Ouled Nails' Muslin Dance
Jun [day undetermined]
The American Flag, Floating
Art Studies
Atlantic City Floral Parade
Auto Boat Race on the Hudson River
Barnum & Bailey's Circus Street Parade
Beauty Bathing
The Brooklyn Handicap, 1904
Deer Hunting in England
The Devonshire Fair
DeVoy the Wire Walker
Dress Parade of the Filipino Scouts, St. Louis Exposition
Elephants Shooting the Chutes at Luna Park [Coney Island]
The Eviction
Exhibition Fire Drill, Union Square, N.Y.
Filipino Scouts, Musical Drill, St. Louis Exposition
Gymnasium Work, Kirksville, Mo.
Horse-Shoe Curve
Inter-Collegiate Athletic Association Championships, 1904
The International Yacht Race
The Magic Hat
The Magic Hoop
Military Tactics
Pan. of Fifth Ave., Pittsburg, Pa., From a Trolley Car
Panorama of St. Louis Exposition from Wireless Tower
Pan. of St. Railway Building, Pittsburg, Pa.
Parade, Fiftieth Anniversary Atlantic City, N.J.
"Personal"
The Philadelphia Speedway
Physical Culture, Kirksville, Mo.
Pierrot's Mystification
Princess Rajah Dance with Chair, St. Louis Exposition
Princess Rajah, Dance Without Chair
Pushball Game
Rival Conjurers
The Slocum Disaster
Surgical Operation
Surgical Operation by Dr. Hurst
Too Much Mixed Ale
Washing Sheep
"Weary Willie" Kidnaps a Child
West Point Cadets Escorting Liberty Bell, St. Louis Exposition
Willful Murder
Jun 4 The Apple Woman
The Bobby Whitewashed
The Cook in Trouble
The Cook's Lovers
The Coster's Wedding
The Devilish Plank
Jun 18 A Disagreeable Remedy
European Idea of Christopher Columbus Discovering America
The Impossible Dinner
The Lyons Mail
Metamorphosis of a Butterfly
A Scandal on the Staircase
Jun 25 Chased by a Dog
The Child Stealers
Naval Attack on Port Arthur
The Office Boy's Revenge
The Postman Whitewashed
Raid on a Coiner's Den
Jun 26 The Great Train Robbery
Jul [day undetermined]
Acrobat and Pony
All for the Love of a Geisha
Alone
Automobile Race at Ballyshannon, Ireland
Barber's Revenge
Battery "A," Rhode Island Light Artillery
Beyond the Danger Line
Bobby and the Automobile
Boxing Horses, Luna Park, Coney Island
Boys Will Be Boys
Bumping Races
Canoeing on the Charles River, Boston, Mass.

Capture and Execution of Spies by Russians
The Chappie at the Well
Children and White Rats
Chutes of Imaha, Finland
A Circus Romance
Cleaning a Stove Pipe
Clown, Tramp and Cop
Coaching in the White Mountains
Coasting Scene in the Alps
College Sports in England
The Coster's Wedding
A Couple of Lightweights at Coney Island
Courting and Caught
Curate's Love
Dogs Playing Bush Ball
Dorothy's Dream
Driven from Home
Duck Hunt
Dude in an English Railway Coach
Easter Flower Parade in Bois de Boulogne, Paris
Elephants Shooting the Chutes, Luna Park, Coney Island, No. 2
English Locomotive in Shop and on Rail
English Submarine Boat Disaster
Equestrian Bear
Facial Contortions
Fighting the Flames [An Attraction at Coney Island]
The First Baby
Foster Parents
Funny Faces
Game of Old Maid
Giovanni and His Trained Parrots
The Gordon Bennett Automobile Trials, Isle of Man
Hauling in the Fish
Haunted Scene Painter
Holland Submarine Boat Tests
Housemaid's Lovers
Ice Cream Eating Contest Blindfolded
Inter-Collegiate Regatta, Poughkeepsie, N.Y., 1904
Japanese School Children
Japanese State Procession
Japanese Varieties
Kidnapped Child
Landing a "Long Tom" Gun
Launching the Lifeboat
Lion Tamer
London Street Fakirs
Lotto, the Trick Bicyclist
Massachusetts Naval Reserves Leaving the U.S.S. "Alabama"
The Music Hall Manager's Dilemma
Nervous Man Retiring
Night Owl's Return
Obstacle Race, Net and Tank, S.S. "Coptic," Mid-Ocean
Old Maids and the Unfaithful Lovers
Outing, Mystic Shriners, Atlantic City, New Jersey
Panorama of Harvard Class Day
Panorama of Race Track Crowd, St. Louis
Parade, Mystic Shriners, Atlantic City, New Jersey
A Parisienne's Bed Time
The Parson's Cooking Lesson
Peeping Frenchman at the German Bathhouse
Pickpocket
Pillow Fight, S.S. "Coptic," Mid-Ocean
"Pollywogs" 71st Regiment, N.G.S.N.Y., Initiating Raw Recruits
President Roosevelt's Home-coming
Push Ball on Horseback
The Racing Chutes at Dreamland
Rum vs. Cherries
Saturday Afternoon Shopping
Scenes in an Infant Orphan Asylum
Scenes Through a Telescope from Bridge of Russian Battleship
The Seashore Baby
Sick Man's Delirium
Smoked Out
The Snapshot Fiend
Speed Test W. K. Vanderbilt, Jr.'s "Tarantula"
Stolen Puppy
Study, Smoke and Soot
Such Is Life
The Swimming Class
That Impudent Flea
That Terrible Sneeze
Toy Maker and Good Fairy
Tragic Elopement
Troops Landing and Battle Scene
Two Bad Boys in a Church
Two Old Pals at Lunch
Two's Company, Three's None
Voyage of the "Arctic"
What Happened to Jones
Wheelbarrow and Automobile
Zoological Garden

Jul 2 Don Quixote
The Mermaid

Jul 9 A Disaster in a Colliery

Jul 16 Mischances of a Drunkard
The Providence of the Waves; or, The Dream of a Poor Fisherman
White Star S.S. Baltic Leaving Pier on First Eastern Voyage

Jul 23 Annie's Love Story
The Barber of Seville
Dance Plastiques
Japanese Ambush
The Nest Robbers
Tour in Italy

Jul 30 Bold Bank Robbery
Uncle Rube's Birthday

Aug [day undetermined]
Arrival and Departure of the Ice-Crushing Steamer "Baikal" at Baikal, Siberia
The Arrival of the 1st Siberian Sharpshooters at Harbin
Attempted Murder in a Train
Automobiling Among the Clouds
The Baby and the Puppies
Barber's Tricks
The Bewitched Traveler
"The Bushranger." Attack and Robbery of a Mail Convoy
Cairo and the Nile
The Children in the Surf
Children Romping on the Lawn
The Coney Island Beach Patrol
Constantinople and the Bosporus
Curious Sights in Burmah and Cashmere (Section 1)
Curious Sights in Burmah and Cashmere (Section 2)
Democratic National Committee at Esopus
The Execution (Beheading) of One of the Hunchuses (Chinese Bandits) Outside the Walls of Mukden
Extraordinary Feats of Horsemanship
A Fierce Sword Combat at Tokio
Fighting the Flames, Dreamland
Fire and Flames at Luna Park, Coney Island [An Attraction at Coney Island]
The Great International Automobile Race for the Gordon-Bennett Trophy
"He Won't Be Happy till He Gets It"
The International Congress of the Salvation Army
The Japanese Ogre
The Japanese Standard Bearer
Judge Parker & Mayor McClellan at Esopus
Judge Parker Receiving the Notification of His Nomination for the Presidency
Late for Work
The Military Funeral of the "Standard Bearer of the Yalu"
The Moonshiner
"A Newspaper in Making"
Nobles Leaving the Kremlin, Moscow, After a Reception by Czar
Off for the Holidays
Orphan Children on the Beach at Coney Island
Parade of Floats, St. Louis Exposition
Parade of Mystic Shriners, Luna Park, Coney Island
Parade of National Cash Register Co.'s Employees, St. Louis Exposition
Piraeus and Athens (Greece). A Visit to Piraeus
Piraeus and Athens (Greece). Athens and the Acropolis
Piraeus and Athens (Greece). Hoisting Cattle on Steamer
Procession of the "Holy Blood"
A Regiment of the Japanese Imperial Guards and Engineer Corps off to the Front
A Seaside Cakewalk
Speech by President Francis, World's Fair
A Swimming Race at Coney Island
A Trip to Palestine. Jaffa and Its Harbor
A Trip to Palestine. Jerusalem, the Holy City
The Two Bottle Babies
The War Correspondent and the Two Bear Cubs
The Widow and the Only Man

Aug 20 Lookout at Port Arthur

Aug 27 A Boar Hunt
Orla and His Trained Dogs

Sep [day undetermined]
Annual Baby Parade, 1904, Asbury Park, N.J.
Boys' Trick on Grandpa
Brewers' Parade, Philadelphia, Pa.
Burglar, Cop and Barrel
Capture of Yegg Bank Burglars
Children and Rabbits
Defence of Port Arthur
Democratic Presidential Candidate, Judge Parker, and Mayor McClellan, Esopus, N.Y.
Departure 14th Co. Japanese Engineers from Shimbashi Station for Korea
European Rest Cure
Fencing Contest Between Japanese Soldiers, Manchuria
Great Temple Procession, Nikko, Japan
The Hero of Liao Yang
How a French Nobleman Got a Wife Through the New York Herald "Personal" Columns
Imitation Naval Battle—St. Louis Exposition
Japanese Fan Dance
Japanese Flag Dance
Japanese Warriors in Ancient Battle Scene
Military Maneuvers, Manassas, Va.
The Miser's Daughter
Panorama from German Building, World's Fair
Parade of Military, St. Louis Exposition
The Pig That Came to Life
President Theodore Roosevelt
Push Ball on Horseback, No. 2
Pussy's Dinner
The Quarrelsome Washerwoman
War Balloon Ascending and Descending

Sep 3 Falls of the Rhine
Indians and Cowboys
The Strike
The Wrestling Donkey

Sep 7 Linen Shop

Sep 10 Ghezzi and His Circus
Joseph Sold by His Brothers
Life of an American Soldier

Sep 17 Burglar and Girls
The Convict's Escape
A Kiss and a Tumble

Sep 24 The Devil's Seven Castles
Drama in the Air
The Fairy of the Spring
Fox and Rabbits
A Gambler's Quarrel
A Good Story
Ice Cream Eater
Quo Vadis
Ruffian's Dance

Oct [day undetermined]
Advance Guard Fight
Alarm
Alcohol and Its Victims
Amphitrite
Arabian Phantasia
Around Port Arthur (No. 2)
Arrival and Departure of a Train
Arrival of a Train
Attack on a Fortress
Attack on a Train
Automobile Race for the Vanderbilt Cup
A Bad Rich Man
Battleship Leaving Harbor
The Bear and the Sentinel
The Bird Charmer
Bobbie's Downfall
Boy's First Smoke
Bride Retiring
The Brothers Laure
Bullocks Swimming
Cakewalk
Capture of a Gun
Cavalry Crossing a River
Cavalry Fording a Stream
Charging Cuirassiers
Charley's Aunt
Cliffs of Cheddar, England

Cloth Dealer
Convoy of Oxen
Cruelty to Horses
Dance of the Sylphs
Death of Robert McCaire and Bertrand
Decoyed
Diving Scene and Reverse
Dranem Salutes the Audience
Drunkard and Statue
Dwarf's Troubles
Eccentric Tight-rope Walker
Eccentric Waltz
Elephants at Work in India
Embarking Wood in the Far East
The Enchanted Wardrobe
An Englishman's Trip to Paris from London
Extraordinary Fishing
Fairy of the Black Rocks
Fairy of the Lake
The False Cripple
Fire! Fire!
Fisherman, Gendarmes and Bike Thief
Flea
Fly Paper Vendors
Gate Jumping by Unsaddled Horse
Grandma's Glass
Grinning Guillot
A Heavy Sea
Hedge Jumping
Honeymoon Trip
Horse Tied to a Post Jumping
The Illusionist
Impossible to Get a Plunge
In Fair Japan
An Interrupted Flirtation
Iroquois Theatre Fire in Chicago
Japanese Dance
Japanese Girls at Tea
A Jolly Lawn Party
Jumping Horses
Just Like a Girl
Kickapoo
Kissing in a Tunnel
Kissing the Blarney Stone
Ladies of the Court Bathing
Lahury, the Soldier
Launching of the U.S.S. Battleship "Connecticut"
Living Statues; or, Marble Comes to Life
Looping the Loop
The Lost Child
Love or Money
Lover's Crime
Love's Dilemma
Maniac Chase
The Market Woman's Mishap
The Masher's Dilemma
Masks and Faces
Mind! Madame Is Coming
Mixed Bathing
Modern High School Riding
Mysterious Screen
Naval Fight
Night Duty
No Posters Allowed
Old Maid's Flirtation
Otter Hunt
Outpost Skirmishing
Painter's Misfortune
Paris from the Seine
Passing Trains
Pedestrian Jugglers
Pole Jumping
The Porter's Horrible End
Putting Up the Swing
Real Warrior
Revenge!
Rolling Bridge in Tunis
Russian Cavalry
Russian Dance
Russian Infantry
Scenes from My Balcony
Scenes in a Slate Quarry
Sculptor and Model
Sea Gulls at Newlyn, Cornwall, England
The Shadowy Lady
Shooting the Rapids of Killarney
The Shower Bath
Sisters Barrison
Soap Bubbles
A Sorcerer's Night
Spy's Arrest
Spy's Execution
Startling Pursuit
The Statue Dealer
Stop Thief!
Street in Canton, China
Street in Tokio
Swimming Horses
That Poor Insurance Man
Too Hot
Too Late
Tramp on a Farm
The Trials and Troubles of an Automobilist
Two Is Company, Three a Crowd
Up-to-Date Burglars; or, The Mystified Cops
Vision of Art
Water Shoots
A Wedding of Correspondence
Woman's Bath
The Young Farmer Girl

Oct 1 Across the Alps
Dogs and Cats
The Opera Hat
Park in Barcelona by Moonlight
Smoker Too Small

Oct 8 Around Port Arthur
Fantastic Fishing
A Fight on the Yalu

Oct 15 Ascending Mount Pilate
Bathers at Joinville
Greedy Cat
A Railway Tragedy

Oct 17 A Little Boy Called "Taps"

Oct 22 The Animated Costumes
Behind the Lens
The Clever Baker
Disagreeable Five O'Clock
The Girls in the Overalls
In a Hurry to Catch the Train
Mistake in the Door
Simple Simon's Surprise Party

Oct 29 The Fatal Wig
An Impossible Voyage
Three Little Maids
Trained Hogs

Nov [day undetermined]
Avenging a Crime; or, Burned at the Stake
City Hall to Harlem in 15 Seconds, via the Subway Route
Coal Heavers
Don't Butt In
Electric Doorbell
Electric Locomotive Tests and Races, Schenectady, N.Y.
Illustrated Songs
Life of a Race Horse
The Lost Child
Love Will Find a Way
The Lover's Ruse
Miss Lillian Shaffer and Her Dancing Horse
Opening Ceremonies, New York Subway, October 27, 1904
Over the Hedge
Parsifal
Petticoat Lane on Sunday
A Race for a Kiss
Railroad Smashup
Result Too Much Jealousy
A Rube Couple at a County Fair
Shanghaied by Pirates
The Suburbanite
University of Pennsylvania Football Team
"Weary Willie" Kisses the Bride
Wifey's Christmas Gift
Willie's Vacation

Nov 5 Meet Me at the Fountain

Nov 12 August, the Monkey
A Princess in Disguise

Nov 19 A Cheeky Traveler

Dec [day undetermined]
The Amorous Militiaman
At Brighton
Bad Boy's Joke on the Nurse
"Champion Pumpkin Eater"
The Chicken Thief
Disturbed Picnic
Dunloe Women
The Ex-Convict
The Firefall
Great Sea Serpent
The Grotto of Surprises
Guy Fawkes' Day
The Honeymoon
Intresting Story
Lady Plumpton's Motor Car
Lion and Lioness
Mary in the Dock
Mining Operations, Pennsylvania Coal Fields
Mischievous Boys
Oh! What a Surprise
Polar Bears at Play with Cubs
Scarecrow Pump
Stowaway
The "Strenuous" Life; or, Anti-Race Suicide
The Wandering Jew
What Happened to a Camera Fiend

Dec 3 From Christiania to the North Cape
Life of a Race Horse
Saluting the Flag
Sandy McGregor

Dec 10 The Astonishing Frame
The Wonderful Rose Tree

Dec 17 The Baltic Fleet and the North Sea Trawlers
Patrick Street, Cork

Dec 24 Babies Bathing
Burglars at Work
Christmas Angel
His First Hunting Day
Louis XIV
Pilgrimage to Lourdes
Solomon's Judgment
The Swing
Vintage

Dec 31 Russian Antisemitic Atrocities

1905 [month undetermined]
Accelerated (Crazy) Panorama West Shore, Lake of Garda
Accelerated Panorama from Steamer on the Thames, London
"All Day in the Alps" Panorama from Gorner Grat
The Angler's Nightmare
Arrival of the Stage at Wawona Hotel, Enroute to Yosemite
Arrival of Train at Oberammergau
Bacchanale Fete of Vevey
Battalion of Seaforth Highlanders at the Dublin Horse Show
Battery of Artillery Crossing Ball's Bridge, Limerick, Ireland
Bears Feeding at the Lake Hotel, Yellowstone Park
Bird Rock, Nordland, Norway
The "Black Growler" Steam Vent, Yellowstone Park
Blasting in the Glory Hole of the Treadwell Mine, Alaska
Brink of the Upper Falls of the Yellowstone River, Wyoming
Brink of the Vernal Fall, Yosemite Valley
Buffalo Bill Fight
Busses Passing Mansion House, London
Camp Life of the Esquimaux at Cape Nome, Alaska
Capt. John Hance Telling about His 14th Wife, Grand Cañon, Arizona
Capt. John Hance Telling His Famous Fish Story, Grand Cañon, Arizona
Carrying Passengers Ashore Davidson Glacier, Alaska
The Castle Geyser, Yellowstone Park
Cavalcade Descending Eagle Peak Trail, Yosemite Valley
Cavalcade Descending the Nevada Trail, Yosemite Valley
Cavalcade Descending Trail into Grand Cañon of Arizona
Cavalcade on Trail into Grand Cañon of Arizona
Children and Carts of Oberammergau
Children Turning Catherine Wheels on Derby Day, Epsom Downs
Chinese Cook at Hance's Camp, Grand Cañon, Arizona
Chutes of Imatra, Finland
Cloud Play on Dolomite Peaks, Tyrol
Coaching Down the Merced Grade into Yosemite Valley
Coaching Down the Merced Grade, Merced Cañon, California
The Colonel's Friend
Combined Reaper and Thresher at Merced, San Joaquin Valley, California
Congregation Leaving Trondhjlm Cathedral, Norway
Convent Garden Market, London
Corpus Christi Ceremonies, Botzen, Tyrol
Corpus Christi Cortege, Botzen, Tyrol
The "Crazy" Canal Boat, Norway
"Crazy" Congregation Leaving Church, Cortina, Tyrol
The "Crazy" Ferryboat, San Francisco, California

Crazy (or Accelerated) Panoramic Approach to Taku Glacier, Alaska
The "Crazy" Steamer Yellowstone Park
Crazy Steamers on Lake Lucerne
The "Crazy" Tourists on the Nevada Trail, Yosemite Valley
The "Crazy Tourists" on the Pier at Killisnoo, Alaska
The "Crazy" Tourists Starting for the Trail, Yosemite Valley
Crowds Leaving Theatre, Oberammergau
Dad's a Gentleman Too
Dance at Esquimaux Camp, Cape Nome, Alaska
Dance of the Autumn Leaves, Vevey Fete
Deer in Wild Park, Goteborg, Sweden
Dial's Girls' Band, Luna Park
Different Hair Dresses
"Dinner Time" at Camp Curry Yosemite Valley
Dog Teams Dawson City Alaska
Earl of Dudley and Party at the Dublin Horse Show
Embarkation by Crane and Barge at Nome City, Alaska
Empire State Express
Epileptic Seizure
Esquimaux Dance, Cape Nome, Alaska
Falls at Hellesylt, Norway
Falls at Trollhattan, Sweden
Fashionable Folks Leaving the Dublin Horse Show
Feeding Mush Dogs, Mulato, Alaska
Fine Feathers Make Fine Birds
Fire Brigade, Dawson City, Alaska
Fish Carvers, at Fish Market Bergen Norway
Fishmarket, Bergen, Norway
Fjord Panorama from Moving Ship, Norway
Flap-Jack Lady of the Esquimaux, Cape Nome, Alaska
Floral Parade at the Race Track, Moscow, Russia
Floral Parade Festival of Roses, Pasadena, Cal.
Flying Machine, Earl's Court, London
Fourth of July Celebration, Yosemite California
Fourth of July Parade Yosemite California
Gardener's Dance, Vevey Fete
Garland Dance, Vevey Fete
Girls Dancing on Hampstead Heath
The Great Falls of the Yellowstone
Great Fountain Geyser, Yellowstone Park
Henley Regatta, Three Finishes
Herd of Bison, Yellowstone Park
Horse Fair at Randers, Denmark
Hunters Exercising, Dublin Horse Show
Hunters in Exercising Ring, Dublin Horse Show
Hunters Jumping, Dublin Horse Show
Indian Pony Races, Yosemite Valley, California
Irish Constabulary, Keel, Achill Island, Ireland
Irish Hunters Taking the Stone Wall, Dublin Horse Show
An Irish Jig at Dooagh, Achill Island, Ireland
Irish Kiddies Coming out of School, Achill Island
Jaunting Cars Arriving at Dublin Horse Show
Jaunting Cars in Dublin
Jumping by Irish Hunters, Dublin Horse Show
Kicking Football—Harvard
Kiddies Dancing to Hurdy-Gurdy Music, Soho, London
Landing Passengers at Torghattan Island, Norway
Lang (Andreas) and Son, the Two Davids, Oberammergau
Lang (Anton) and Family, Oberammergau
Lapps at Hammerfest, Norway
Latina, Dislocation Act
Latina, Physical Culture Poses [No. 1]
Latina, Physical Culture Poses [No. 2]
[Launching the Ferryboat Richmond—Staten Island]
A Little Jules Verne
London Ladies Looking at Lingerie in Oxford Street Windows, London
Lord Lieutenant of Ireland and Escort, Dublin Horse Show
Love at Each Floor
Market Women Leaving the Railway Station at Galway, Ireland
A Matsuri Procession, Yokohama, Japan
Matsuri Procession, Yokohama, Japan
Meran Fire Brigade Going to a Fire
Minuteman Geyser, Yellowstone Park
Nevada Falls, Yosemite Valley
No Bill Peddlers Allowed
The Old Boys of Dooagh, Achill Island, Iceland
Old Faithful Geyser, Yellowstone Park
Old Spinning Wheel, Dooagh, Achill Island, Ireland
Old Time Miner Rocking for Gold in the Tailings, Klondike
On the Course, Henley Regatta
Out Boating
Panning Gold on a Claim in the Klondike
Panorama from a Moving Train on White Pass & Yukon Railway, Alaska
Panorama from Car on Mendel Pass Cable Railway
Panorama from Car on Oberammergau Electric Railway
Panorama from Dreisprackenspitz Stelvio Pass
Panorama from Electric Car, Lucerne
Panorama from Gortner Grat
Panorama from Moving Steamer on the River Thames, England
Panorama from Moving Train on Albula Railway, Switzerland
Panorama from Moving Train on Murren Electric Railway, Switzerland
Panorama from Train on Visp-Zermatt Railway
Panorama of a Norwegian Fjord from Alvik to Vik from Moving Ship
Panorama of Eismeer, Switzerland
Panorama of Hammerfest Harbor
Panorama of Stockholm from Steam Ferry
Panorama of the Castle of Chillon, Lake Geneva
Panorama of the Course at Henley Showing a Finish
Panorama of the Folgefond Snowfield, Norway
Panorama of the Norwegian Fjord from Moving Ship
Panorama of the Theatre, Vevey Fete
Panorama of Theatre, Vevey Fete
Parade of Passengers Crossing to North Cape, Norway
Passengers Boarding Busses at Hyde Park Corner, London
Passengers Crossing over Open Car, Balley Bunion Railway
Passing Train, Balleybunion Railway, Ireland
Passing Train, Balleybunion Railway, Ireland No. 2
Passing Train (from above) Balleybunion Railway, Ireland
Playful Bear and Dog, Dawson City, Alaska
Procession of Costumed Characters, Vevey Fete
Procession of Performers at Fete of Vevey
Queen Margherita of Italy Arriving in Oberammergau
Railroad Station at Steinach, Tyrol
Railway Panorama from Moving Train Passing Through Conway Castle, Wales
Rapids of the Silver Apron, Yellowstone Park
Religious Cortege on a Rainy Day, Cortina, Tyrol
Retrogressive Jaunting Car, Reverse Panorama from Moving Train, Dublin, Ireland
Reverse Panorama, Maria Theresian Strasse, Innsbruck
Riverside Geyser, Yellowstone Park
Roman Chariot Race, Pasadena, California
Russian Cavalry Review, St. Petersburg
Scene in Oxford Street, London
Scottish Touring Party enroute to the Romsdale, Norway
Scottish Tourist Party in Stockhaeres, Noes, Norway
Servant's Dance, Lake Hotel, Killarney, Ireland
Shepherd's Dance, Vevey Fete
Shooting the Killarney Rapids, Ireland
Slavonian Miners Running to Dinner, Treadwell Mine, Alaska
Sliding River Craft over Boat Railway, River Thames
Sluicing in the Klondike
Spectators Leaving the Theatre Vevey
The "Spokane's" Passengers Descending the Gangplank at Killisnoo Alaska
Squad of Seaforth Highlanders Leaving Bank of Ireland, Dublin
Stage Coaches, Yellowstone Park
Stage Enroute to Hance's Camp, Grand Cañon of Arizona
Stages Leaving Fountain House, Yellowstone Park
Stages Passing Through Wawona Big Tree, Mariposa Grove, California
Storm Effect, Ampezzo Valley
Sunday "Church Parade" Bergen Norway
Sunrise on the Peak, Tyrol
Sunset and Sunrise over the Eiger & Monk Murren
Sunset Clouds over Monte Rosa, Switzerland
Tourist Party in the Gap of Dunloe, Ireland
Tourists Disembarking at Lucerne
Tourists Enroute to the Cliffs of Moher, Ireland
Tourists Leaving Horgheim in the Romsdale Norway
Tourists on the Road to Hotel Stalheim, Norway
Tourists Party near Kate Kearney's Cottage, Gap of Dunloe, Ireland
Tourists Party on the Axenstrasse Switzerland
Train Arriving at Henley Station
Train on the White Pass & Yukon Railway, Alaska
Trains Arriving at Henley Station with Regatta Visitors
Trains on Rigi Railway, Switzerland
A Trip Through Samoa and Fiji Islands
Triumphal Entry of Performers, Vevey Fete
Troop of Horse Guards in St. James Park, London
Turntable of the Ballybunion Railway, Ireland
Tyroler Fest, Steinach, Tyrol
Tyrolese Dance, Innsbruck
Tyrolese Dancers Innsbruck
Unloading Fish, Killisnoo Alaska
Upper Fall of the Yellowstone River
Vernal Falls, Yosemite Valley, California
Voringfos Waterfall Norway
Waterfall from the Road, Stalheim, Norway
Whirlpool Rapids, Niagara, U.S.A.
Wooding Up a River Steamer, Yukon River, Alaska
Working a Scraper on Tailings Klondike

Jan [day undetermined]
Around New York in 15 Minutes
Baby's Day
The Bad Boy and the Grocery Man
Bridget's Troubles
Burlesque Tramp Burglars
Fisherman, Eels or Snakes
The Gentlemen Highwaymen
He Got His Hat
Largest Fat Boy in the World
Masher and Oyster Stand
New Year's Day Parade, Philadelphia
The Paper Hanger in Trouble
Soldier's Romance
Three Jolly Dutchmen
Traction Engine
Tramp and Dump Cart
Tramps in Clover

Jan 14 Big Fountain at Versailles
Christmas, 1904
Wonderful Beehive
Wrestler and Bull

Jan 28 Saved from a Watery Grave

Feb [day undetermined]
Across the New Viaduct of New York
Automobile Races at Ormond, Fla.
Boating Carnival, Palm Beach, Fla.
Duel Between Japanese and Russian Soldiers
In the Swimming Pool, Palm Beach, Fla.
The Kleptomaniac
The Prima Donna's Understudy
The Sleepy Soubrette
Speed Trial of Auto Boat Challenger, Lake Worth, Fla.

Feb 4 Fireworks
Innocent Flirtation
Prompting Phonograph
St. Petersburg Massacre
Feb 11 The Counterfeiters
Feb 25 Bewitched Lover
From Cairo to the Pyramids
Last Attack on the Hill
Love Letter
Riots in St. Petersburg
Surrender at Port Arthur
Mar [day undetermined]
Awful Donkey
Bathing in the Ice at the L Street Bath, Boston
Gov. Wm. L. Douglas, of Mass.
Her First Bicycle Lesson
How She Loves Him
The Inauguration of President Roosevelt
Inauguration of President Roosevelt. Leaving the Capitol
Inauguration of President Roosevelt. President-Elect Roosevelt, Vice-President-Elect Fairbanks and Escort Going to the Capitol
Inauguration of President Roosevelt. Taking the Oath of Office
Inauguration of President Roosevelt. the Grand Inaugural Parade
Life of the New York Policeman
The Nihilists
The Non-Union Bill-Poster
President Roosevelt's Inauguration
Tom, Tom, the Piper's Son
Too Much for Dad
Mar 4 Modern Style House Maids
Mar 11 Gluttonous Negro
President Roosevelt's Inauguration
Mar 18 Samoa and the Fiji Islands
Mar 25 Assassination of the Grand Duke Serge
The Nihilists in Russia
Apr [day undetermined]
Bargain Day on 14th Street, New York
The Bigamist
Children's Hour on the Farm
Employees Leaving Office
Evolution of the Japanese
General Electric Engine Hauling Freight
Gen'l Elec. No. 1 Employees Leaving Work
Gen'l Elec. No. 2 Trolley Changing from Di. to Alter. Cur.
Gen'l Elec. No. 3 Handling Cars at the Barn
N.Y. Life Insurance Co. Pres. McCall & Officers
"Osler"-ising Papa
Panorama from the Roof of the Times Building, New York
Physical Culture Poses
The Pirates
The Seven Ages
Sins and Sorrows of a Great City
Three Cavaliers of the Road
Travels of a Lost Trunk
Wanted: A Dog
Why the Cook Was Not Fired
Women Employee's Dining Room
Apr 1 Winter Sports
Apr 8 Cards and Crime
The Incendiary
The King of Sharpshooters
The Living Playing Cards
The Sign of the Cross
Apr 22 The Black Imp
Apr 29 His Master's Breath
His Master's Voice
The Hold-Up of the Leadville Stage
A Jilted Suitor
May [day undetermined]
The Adjustable Chair
Al Treloar in Muscle Exercises
The Athletic Girl and the Burglar
The Badger Game
The Barber's Dee-Light
The Barber's Pretty Patient
Behind the Scenes
The Bigamist's Trial
The Boarding House Bathroom
The Broker's Athletic Typewriter
The Deadwood Sleeper
The Fake Blind Man
Funeral of Hiram Cronk
"Gee, If Me Mudder Could Only See Me Now"
The Girls, the Burglar, and the Rat
How Jones Lost His Roll
How Mr. Butt-In Benefits by Chauncey's Mishaps
It's a Shame To Take the Money
Kilties' Band
The New Year's Shooters in Philadelphia
N.Y. Police Parade, 1905
Opening of Belmont Park Race Course
Peeping Tom in the Dressing Room
Photographed for the Rogue's Gallery
"Play Ball"—Opening Game, National League, N.Y. City, 1905—New York vs. Boston
Policeman's Pal
Reproduction, Nan Paterson's Trial
Rough House in a New York Honky-Tonk
Spirit of '76
Start of Ocean Race for Kaiser's Cup
A Sweet Kiss
Tramp's Revenge
The Wedding
May 6 A Catching Story
Good Reason for a Divorce
Policeman's Love Affair
Why Papa Could Not Read
May 13 The Crystal Casket
The Lilliputian Minuet
The Moon-Lover
May 27 A Father's Honor
Jun [day undetermined]
A Ballroom Tragedy
Between the Dances
Drills and Exercises, Schoolship "St. Mary's"
How Willie Got the Eggs
Interior N.Y. Subway, 14th St. to 42nd St.
Jack and Jill
Monkey Business
The Pillow Fight, No. 2
A Pipe Dream
Reuben in the Opium Joint
Reuben in the Subway
A Saturday Afternoon at Travers' Island with the New York Athletic Club
The Topers
A Trip to Salt Lake City
2 A.M. in the Subway
Under the Bamboo Tree
The Wine Opener
Jun 3 A Dog Lost, Strayed or Stolen. $25.00 Reward. Apply to Mrs. Brown, 711 Park Ave.
Jun 10 In the Mining District
Jun 17 A Mesmerian Experiment
Jun 24 Christian Martyrs
The Palace of the Arabian Nights
Jul [day undetermined]
The Abductors
Bishop and Burglar
Blowing Bottles
The Bridal Chamber
The Burglar's Slide for Life
Coney Island at Night
Cook and Chimney Sweep
The Darling of the Gallery Gods
Departure of Peary for the North Pole
Duel Scene from "Macbeth"
An Eccentric Burglary
Fatal Necklace
Fixing the Derby Favorite
He Got into the Wrong Bath House
Hippodrome Races, Dreamland, Coney Island
In a Raines Law Hotel
Lifting the Lid
Love's Perfidy
The Lucky Wishbone
Mobilization of the Massachusetts State Troops
A Modern Sappho
Mother's Angel Child
The Mutiny on the Potemkin
New York Athletic Club Crew at Phila., Pa.
[On] a [Good Ole] 5¢ Trolley Ride
On the Beach at Brighton
Only Her Brother
Ore the Banster
Pompey's Honey Girl
A Poor Place for Love Making
The Race for Bed
Raffles, the Dog
Rescued by Rover
Seeing Squashville
Stolen by Gypsies
Torpedo Boats Manoeuvering
The Whole Dam Family and the Dam Dog
Jul 1 Highway Robbery
King of Dollars
A Pleasure Trip
Jul 8 I. B. Dam and the Whole Dam Family
Jul 15 The Gun License
Jul 22 Kidnapped Child
Mr. Dauber and the Whimsical Picture
The Serenade
The Young Tramps
Jul 29 Great Steeplechase
Aug [day undetermined]
An Affair of Honor
Aylesbury Ducks
Blackmail
Blind Man's Bluff
The Broadway Massage Parlor
Dangerous Golfers
The Electric Mule
Elephant's Tub
Empire State Express, the Second, Taking Water on the Fly
Falsely Accused
The Fire-Bug
German Torpedo Boat in Action
His Washing Day
How Jones Saw the Derby
June's Birthday Party
Lady Barber
Leap Frog Railway, Coney Island
Masher and Nursemaid
Mystic Shriners' Day, Dreamland, Coney Island
Peace Envoys at Portsmouth, N.H.
Pennsylvania Tunnel Excavation
Rehearsing a Play at Home
Robbing His Majesty's Mail
Scenes and Incidents, Russo-Japanese Peace Conference, Portsmouth, N.H.
The Society Palmist
The Summer Boarders
Terrible Flirt
Two Strenuous Rubes
Whaling
Wide Awake
Won't You Come Home?
Aug 5 The Chloroform Fiends
Mutiny on Man-of-War in Odessa
The Venetian Looking-Glass
Aug 19 An Adventurous Automobile Trip
Modern Brigandage
Aug 26 On a Vacation Trip
The Vendetta
Sep [day undetermined]
Always a Gentleman
Always Room for One More
Bertha Claiche
The Blacksmith's Daughter
The Boarding School Girls
The Boer War
Burglar and Bull Dog
Burglar and Vapor Bath
Chauncey Explains
Chewing Gum
Cigarette Fiend
The Course of True Love
Cry Baby
Dressing the Baby
Female Crook and Her Easy Victim
Fortune Telling in a Gypsy Camp
Fun on the Joy Line
General Cronje & Mystic Shriners
Girls and "Barrel of Love"
Girls and Moving Stairway
Girls on the "Bumpety Bumps"
Girls Riding Camels
Girls Riding Steeplechase
Girls Riding "Trolley"
Great Buffalo Chase
High Jumping Horses—Sidney Holloway's Farm
His Move
The Horse-Thief
The Little Train Robbery
Lucille Mulhall and Trick Horse
Lucille Mulhall Roping and Tying a Steer
Ludlow's Aerodrome
Nelson-Britt Prize Fight
Nelson-Britt Prize Fight for Lightweight Championship, San Francisco, September 9th, 1905
Odd Fellows Parade, Philadelphia, Pa.
Old Maid and Pet Cat
Old Sweethearts
The River Pirates
Robbed of Her All

Sneezing
Starting on a Coyote Hunt
Steamboat Travel on Long Island Sound
Stop Thief!
Teasing
Unlucky at Cards, Lucky at Love
Western "Bad Man" Shooting Up a Saloon
The White Caps
Sep 16 Impersonation of Britt-Nelson Fight
Life of Moses
Sep 23 A Crazy Composer
Creusot's Metallurgy
The Enchanted Sedan-Chair
Raffles, the Amateur Cracksman
Sep 30 Countryman in Paris
Flower Fairy
Gay Washerwoman
Impatient Customer
Language of Flowers
Loie Fuller
The Servant Girl Problem
Stunning Creations
Wonderful Album
Oct [day undetermined]
Bringing Up a Girl in the Way She Should Go [No. 1]
Bringing Up a Girl in the Way She Should Go [No. 2]
The Cheated Policeman
Chimney Sweep and Pastry Cook
A Country Courtship
The Czar at Czarkoe Selo
Devil's Dice
Dream of the Race Track Fiend
Engagement Ring
Everybody Works But Father (Whiteface)
Fire in New York's Bowery
Firemen's Parade, Scranton, Pa.
A German Warship in a Heavy Sea
The Great Jewel Mystery
Halloween
He Learned Ju Jitsu, So Did the Missus
How Millionaires Sometimes Entertain Aboard Their Yachts
Life Saving Up-to-Date
Meet Me Down at Luna, Lena
Naval Warfare
Pilfered Porker
Scenes in a Police Court
The Scheming Gambler's Paradise
Steel Works
Oct 5 Poor Algy
Oct 14 The Adventures of Sherlock Holmes; or, Held for a Ransom
Behind the Stage
A Henpecked Husband
Ill Rewarded Conjuror
License No. 13; or, The Hoodoo Automobile
The Vicar's Garden Party
Oct 21 The Gay Deceivers
Vanderbilt Auto Race
Oct 24 The Watermelon Patch
Oct 28 Black and White; or, The Mystery of a Brooklyn Baby Carriage
Through the Matrimonial Agency
The Tower of London
Nov [day undetermined]
Airy Fairy Lillian Tries on Her New Corsets
Among the Snakes
Arrival of the Mail Steamer at Larne
The Baby Show
The Barnstormers
Bedelia and the Witch
Brick Making Rotifier
The British Bull Dog
By Rail Through Canadian Rockies
Cake-Walk in Our Alley
Casey's Christening
Cir. of Blood, Frog's Foot
Cir. of Protoplasm in Waterweed
"Clown Sidney on Stilts"
Coaches Starting from Larne and Passing Through Tunnel on the Antrim Coast Road
Convicts' Escape
The Curate's Adventures
Defense of a Pagoda
Defense of Port Arthur
Digesting a Joke (Jas. T. Powers)
Drill Under Oars
Elopement
Empire State Express
An English Gymkana
Everybody Works But Father (Blackface)
The Fat Girl's Love Affair
Father Neptune and Bear
Feeding the Otters
Fiscal Problem
Fresh Water Infusorian
"A Frightful Night"
Getting the Hay
Giant Tortoise Feeding
Head Hunters of Borneo
Hiawatha
Horses Jumping over a Wall
Imp No. 2
Impersonation of the Fitzsimmons-O'Brien Fight
In an English Hayfield
Indian Babies' Bath
The Intruders
Japanese Funeral
A Kentucky Feud
The King and Queen of Italy in Paris
The King Planting a Tree at the Royal Agricultural Society's Show Yard
Latina, Contortionist
The Life Boat
The London Press
Ludlow's Aerodrome, No. 2
Magic Cone
Magic Hair Restorer
Market Day at Kenmore
The Midnight Sun at Scalo
Military Display at Hurlingham
Milking Time: A Kerry Herd
Mr. Martin Duncan
A Moorish Street Minstrel Performing at Morocco City
Motor Boat Race at Monaco
Motor Highwayman
The Naughty Boys and Curate
New York City Fire Department on Parade
The Newt
An Old Maid's Darling
On a Borneo Railway
Over in Jersey
Overturning a Mammoth Chimney
Panorama of the Sultan of Morocco's Troop Forming a Square Awaiting the Arrival of H. M. S.
Panoramic Bird's Eye View of Montreal, Canada
Pillow Fight
Police Raid on a Club
Pond Life
Potters at Work
President Roosevelt at Portland
President Roosevelt at Seattle
President Roosevelt at Tacoma
President Roosevelt at Walla Walla
The Puppies
Railway Panorama Between Green Island and Kilroot
Railway Panorama Between Kilroot and Whitehead
The Rat Trap Pickpocket Detector
Reception of British Fleet
The Red Slug Worm
The Red Snow Germs
Ride on Sprinkler Car
Rock Scene at Ballybunion
Roping and Branding Wild Horses
A Rough Sea on the Derry Coast
Russian Artillery
Russian Field Artillery
Russian Kirgis Troops
Russian Mounted Artillery
Sambo
Scenes at the Zoo
The Servant Girl's Dream
The Servant Question
Shooting the Chutes, Cork Exhibition
A Smart Captive
Snail, Tortoise, Toad
A Snake in the Grass
Sparring at the N.Y.A.C.
The Squire and the Maid
The Stolen Cake
Stork's Tug of War
A Street in Lourdes
A Study in Feet
The Thirteen Club
The Three Honeymoons
Through the Keyhole
Through Tunnel on the Antrim Coast
Tight-Rope Walker Undressing
Torpedo Boat Maneuvering
Tourists Leaving the Lake Hotel, Killarney
Turkish Atrocities in Macedonia
Two Imps
Typhoid Fever Germs
The Waterfalls of Glengariffe
White Rat and Young
The White Rats
Winning a Pair of Gloves
With the German Fleet
Wonderful Hat
Wrestling at the N.Y.A.C.
The Wrestling Elephant
Yantai Episode
Nov 2 Down on the Farm
Nov 4 The Escape from Sing Sing
An Impracticable Journey
The Mysterious Island
The Pastry Cook's Practical Jokes
Unexpected Fireworks
Zoological Garden
Nov 6 The Miller's Daughter
Nov 15 Everybody Works but Father
Nov 18 Burglar Bill
Fun on the Farm
Nov 25 Moving Day; or, No Children Allowed
Rip's Dream
Nov 27 The Train Wreckers
Dec [day undetermined]
A Break for Freedom
Climbing the American Alps
An Execution by Hanging
A Fight for a Bride
Freak Barber
Goaded to Anarchy
Hubby Tries to Keep House
Intercollegiate Cross Country Run
The Night Before Christmas
Reading the Death Sentence
A Reprieve from the Scaffold
Rooms for Gentlemen Only
The Society Raffles
Spectacular Scenes During a New York City Fire
Threshing Scene
Wine, Women & Song [No. 2]
Dec 2 The Green Goods Man; or, Josiah and Samanthy's Experience with the Original "American Confidence Game"
Monsieur Beaucaire, the Adventures of a Gentleman of France
The Newsboy
Oh! You Dirty Boy!
Dec 5 Desperate Encounter Between Burglar and Police
Life of an American Policeman
A River Tragedy
Dec 9 The Hen with the Golden Eggs
Love Is Ingenious
The Postman's Christmas Box
Dec 16 Alcoholism Engenders Tuberculosis
Ceylon
Christmas Miracle
A Tragedy at Sea
Dec 23 The Christmas Goose
Disagreeable Mistake
A Great Discovery
The Photographing Bear
The Three Phases of the Moon
Dec 30 Custom House Search
Man Wanted
Misadventures of a Hat
1906 [month undetermined]
Army Pack Train Bringing Supplies
The Auto-Somnambulist
Before the Ball
Chest and Neck Development
Circular Panorama of Market St. and Stockton
Clown Juggler
Deep Breathing and Chest Expansion
Developing Muscles of Back and Chest
Developing Muscles of Chest and Back
Elk
Epileptic Seizure No. 8
Epileptic Seizure, No. 9
Everybody Works but Mother
Exploded Gas Tanks, U.S. Mint, Emporium and Spreckels' Bld'g.
Game of Chess
Gans-Nelson Contest, Goldfield, Nevada, September 3rd, 1906
General Circular Panorama of the Burned Business District
Good Night
Great Railroad Panorama Through Colorado
Have a Light, Sir
Head-On Collision at Brighton Beach Race Track, July 4th, 1906

Here's to the Prettiest
Irish Reel
It Was Coming to Him
Juvenile Chicken Thieves
Kisses Sweet
Lion Hunt
Military Feeding Starving and Destitute Refugees in Golden Gate Park
Mr. Butt-in-Sky
New Year's Toast
Panorama of Market Street, San Francisco
Panoramic View of Van Ness Ave.
Papa Minds the Baby
Park Lodge, Golden Gate Park
Poker in the West
Punch and Judy
Shad Fishing
She Was Good to Him
Sights in a Great City
A Strenuous Wedding
Substitute for Smoking
Taking His Medicine
Three of a Kind
The Tomboys
Trapped by Pinkertons
Trying It on His Dog
Wash Day at Casey's
Wealthy but Homeless Citizens of San Francisco Cooking Their Meals in the Open Air at Jefferson Sq.
Wrecked Mansions Along Van Ness Avenue
Yale Harvard Boat Race, New London, Conn., 1906
You Won't Cut Any Ice with Me

Jan [day undetermined]
Bicycle Police Chasing Scorching Auto
Deer Stalking with a Camera
Flags and Faces of All Races
The Gossipers
Horse Stealing
A Misguided Bobby at a Fancy Garden Party
Moose Hunt in Canada
Moose Hunt in New Brunswick
Opium Smoker's Dream
The Peashooter
Post No Bills
Quail Shooting at Pinehurst
Salmon Fishing in Quebec
Shaving by Installments
Trout Fishing in Rangeley Lakes
Turkey Hunt at Pinehurst
Two Little Waifs
Whipping Bear
Wine, Women & Song

Jan 6 The Tramp
Jan 13 The Bicycle Robber
Robbers of Children
Jan 20 Fire Cascades
The Wolf's Trap
Jan 27 A Coal Strike
The Deserter
Everybody Works But Mother
A False Alarm
The Henpecked Husband
The Impossible Convicts
The Jolly Monks of Malabar
The Opium Smoker's Dream
The Simple Life
The Streets of New York
Jan 30 The Insurance Solicitor; or, A Story of a Blasted Ambition

Feb [day undetermined]
College Life at Amherst
Dream of a Rarebit Fiend
The Flat Dwellers
The Man with the Ladder and the Hose
The Modern Oliver Twist; or, The Life of a Pickpocket'
Police Raid at a Dog Fight
A Raid on a Cock Fight
Scene in a Rat Pit
Seeing Boston
Terrier vs. Wild Cat
Volunteer Fire Department Parade

Feb 3 Socialism and Nihilism
Feb 10 Beware of My Husband
Tragedy in a Train
Feb 17 Tit-for-Tat
Victims of the Storm
Feb 19 The Critic
A Friend in Need Is a Friend Indeed
Feb 23 Mr. Butt-In
Feb 24 The Heart Governs the Head
The Inventor Crazybrains and His Wonderful Airship
The Last Witch
The Wreckers of the Limited Express

Mar [day undetermined]
Dixon-Chester Leon Contest
Eclipse of Sun
The Lost Collar Button; or, A Strenuous Search
Nelson-McGovern Fight, 1906
Phoebe Snow
Please Help the Blind; or, A Game of Graft
Scenes Washington, D.C.
Stop Thief

Mar 3 Chimney Sweep
Mar 17 Another's Crime
Ascending Mt. Serrat in Spain
Descending Mt. Serrat in Spain
Engadin in Switzerland
I've Lost My Eyeglasses
Passing Trains
The Silver Wedding
Street in Agra, India
Thibidado
A Trip from Naples to Vesuvius, Showing the Volcano in Action
A Trip Through the Island of Ceylon
Mar 29 The Black Hand
Mar 31 A Boarding School Conspiracy

Apr [day undetermined]
The Absent-Minded Shoe Black
Acrobatic Elephant
Aerial Billiard Playing
Apaches in Paris
At Mukden
Baby's Bath
Bad Coffee
Bad Joke
Bad Lodgers
Bath of Sacred Elephants
Bird's Eye View of Paris
Boats on the Nile
Bull Fight
Captain's Inspection
Childish Tricks Baffled
Children's Quarrel
Clown's Revenge
Coal Man's Bath
Compromising Spots
Confession
A Courageous Husband
Dancing Sentry Box
Doorkeeper's Curiosity
Dranem's Dream
Drunkard
The Enchanted Melon
False Alarm
Fantastic Diver
Fencing N.Y.A.C.
First Night Out
Flying Machine
Frog Fishing
Funny Shave
Gaieties of Divorce
Good Pipe
Great Ballet
Hairdresser's Victim
Haunted House
A Heavy Sea
High Sea Fishing
Humorous Phases of Funny Faces
Improvised Suit
In the Polar Regions
The Indiscreet Bathroom Maid
Indiscreet Mystified
Infernal Cave
Ingenious Dauber
Insolvable Guests
Irascible Fisherman
Jack the Bootblack
Japanese Soldier's Return
Joys of Marriage
Keep It Straight
Kids' Practical Jokes
Lady Undressing
Life on Board Ship
Liliputian Dance
Love Letter
Man with 36 Heads
Martyrs of the Inquisition
Matrimonial Agency
Miniature Theatre
Motor-car and Cripple
Nautical Fancy
Nautical Game
Negro and Policeman
Neighbor's Lamp
Nobody Works Like Father
Obstacle Jumping by Attached Horses
Obstinate Drunkard
Old Seducer
Pasha's Nightmare
Penny Milk
Phantom's Guard
Phenomenal Hen
Pierrot's Revenge
Practical Conjuror
Prince of Wales in India
Pussy's Breakfast
Remorse
Retaking a Fort
Revolution in Russia
Robbers Robbed
Room, Please
Runaway in the Park
St. Bartholomew's Day
Sardine Fishing
Scenes of Convict Life
Scholar's Breakfast
Schoolboys' Practical Jokes
Ski Running
Sock
Stupendous Jugglers
Surgical Operation
Temptation of St. Anthony
Ten Wives for One Husband
Terrible Anguish
Topsy-Turvy Dance
Touching Pleading
Trained Bears
Transparent Cards
A Trip Down Mount Tamalpais
Troublesome Fishbone
Tunisian Dance
Two Drunkards
Unforeseen Meeting
Virtue Rewarded
Voice of Conscience
War of Children
When the Masters Are Out
Whence Does He Come?
Where Is My Horse?
The Wig
A Winter Straw Ride
Young Apple Thief

Apr 7 The Maestro Do-Mi-Sol-Do
A Mix-Up in the Gallery
Rescued by Carlo
The Starvelings
Apr 14 Carnival Night
Cruise of the Steamer Ophir, with Prince and Princess of Wales on Board
Fishing Pictures
History of a Pair of Trousers
The Invisible Man
Jewel Robbers Mystified
Living Flowers
Naval Subjects, Merchant Marine, and From All over the World
Old and New Style Conjurors
Railway Panoramas from Every Port of the World
Steamship Panoramas
A Transatlantic Trip of the S.S. Kronprinz Wilhelm, from Bremen to New York
Trip Through Abyssinia
Trip Through America
Trip Through Australia, New Zealand
Trip Through Canada
Trip Through England
Trip Through France
Trip Through Germany
Trip Through India
Trip Through Ireland
Trip Through Italy
Trip Through South Africa
Trip Through Switzerland
Trip Through Transvaal
Turbulent Seas, Waterfalls and Streams
Apr 21 Hello! Hello! Grinder
Life in India
Spontaneous Generation
Apr 28 The Clown's Adventures
Monte Carlo to Monaco
Playing Truant

May [day undetermined]
Arrival of Immigrants, Ellis Island
Dance of Geishas
Dynamiting Ruins and Pulling Down Walls in San Francisco
Her Name Was Maude
Human Apes from the Orient
John Paul Jones Ceremonies
Joke on a Roundsman

Love vs. Title; or, An Up-to-Date Elopement
Oh! That Limburger, the Story of a Piece of Cheese
San Francisco
Scenes in San Francisco
Views in San Francisco
May 1 The Subpoena Server
May 5 A Desperate Crime
Law of Pardon
May 7 Arrival of Refugees at Oakland
City Hall from Market St. and City Hall Ave.
The Doomed City
Effect of Earthquake
Feeding Chinese
The First Trolley Car After the Earthquake
Fun Among the Refugees
Going to the Fire, Showing Chief Sullivan During the Earthquake
The Mission
Panorama from Telegraph Hill
Panorama of Chinatown
Panorama of Market Street before the Fire
Panorama of Nob Hill
Panorama of San Francisco in Smoke and Fire
Panoramas of Market Street, the City Hall, Taken from the Roof of the U.S. Mint
Refugees at the Golden Gate Park
Refugees in Jefferson Square
Refugees on Market St.
St. Francis Hotel
The San Francisco Disaster
Shot for Looting
Thieves in Camp, Golden Gate Park
Waterfront, Refugees Leaving San Francisco
May 12 A Shooting Expedition Accident
The Wig Chase
May 14 Panoramic View from Alamo Square of San Francisco While Burning
Panoramic View of Market Street San Francisco After the Earthquake and Fire
Panoramic View of San Francisco City Hall, Damaged by Earthquake
May 16 San Francisco
May 19 A Childish Match
May 26 Eruption of Mt. Vesuvius
The Lost Leg of Mutton
My Hat
The Olympian Games
Society Ballooning
"23"
Jun [day undetermined]
All Aboard! or, Funny Episodes in a Street Car
Attack on Fort Boonesboro
Bird's Eye View from Hopkins Art Institute
Canoeing in Maine
A College Girl's Affair of Honor
Dynamiting Ruins and Rescuing Soldier Caught in Falling Walls
Earthquake Ruins, New Majestic Theatre and City Hall
Floral Fiesta, Los Angeles, Cal.
Free Show on the Beach
The Jail Bird and How He Flew, a Farce Comedy Escape
Life of a Cowboy
Logging in Maine
Maneuvering a Small Motor Boat
Panorama, City Hall, Van Ness Avenue and College of St. Ignatius
Panorama, Nob Hill and Ruins of Millionaire Residences
Panorama, Notorious "Barbary Coast"
Panorama, Ruins Aristocratic Apartments
Panorama, Russian and Nob Hill from an Automobile
Physical Culture Lesson
Play Ball on the Beach
The Prospectors, a Romance of the Gold Fields
Ruins Bulletin Building, California Theatre and Evening Post
Ruins of Chinatown
Snake Hunting
Spanish Barbecue
The Terrible Kids
They Meet on the Mat
Three American Beauties
A Trip to Berkeley, Cal.
Vertical Panorama City Hall and Surroundings
White Fox Motor Boat
Jun 2 Ephemeral Wealth
Escaped from the Cage
Mrs. Brown's Bad Luck
Jun 14 The Village Cut-Up
Jun 16 A Detective's Trip Around the World
The Holiday
Three Cent Leeks
The Troubles of a Fireman
Jun 23 The Angler's Dream
Blackmailing the Motorists
"A Fresh Bath" or "The Tripper Tripped"
I Fetch the Bread
Marriage of Princess Ena and Alphonse XIII, King of Spain
Me and My Two Pals
The Olympic Games at Athens, Greece
The Rajah's Casket
The Riderless Bicycle
Vengeance Is Mine
Jun 26 Poughkeepsie Regatta
Jun 28 The Paymaster
Jun 30 From North to South
From Tacoma to Seattle
The Gateway to the Catskills
Grand Hotel to Big Indian
Hold-Up of the Rocky Mt. Express
In the Haunts of Rip Van Winkle
In the Heart of the Catskills
Through Austin Glen, Catskill Railway
Trip over Colorado Midland
Trip over Cripple Creek Short Line
Trip Through Colorado
A Trip Through the Chicago Stock-Yards
Trip to Chattanooga and Lookout Mountain
A Trip to Jacksonville, Fla.
A Trip to St. Augustine, Fla.
Trip to Southern Colorado
A Trip to Tampa, Fla.
Ute Pass from a Freight Train
The Valley of Esopus
Who Looks, Pays
Jul [day undetermined]
The Acrobatic Burglars
Fakir and Footpad
House Furnishing Made Easy
The 100 to 1 Shot; or, A Run of Luck
The River Pirates
The Snapshot Fiend; or, Willie's New Camera
Thaw-White Tragedy
The Trading Stamp Craze
Waiting at the Church
Jul 7 The Elections
Follower of Women
A Strange Engagement Bouquet
The Target
Jul 11 Night of the Party
Jul 14 Anything for Peace and Quietness
Butterfly Catching
Corsican Chastisement
Dogs Used as Smugglers
Extraordinary Dislocation
Honor Is Satisfied
A Night Off
The Tramp and the Mattress Maker
The Troublesome Flea
Jul 19 The Masqueraders
Jul 21 The Gambler's Nightmare
The Hilarious Posters
Rival Brothers
Jul 28 Letters Which Speak
Aug [day undetermined]
Arrival Mahukona Express, Kohala, Hawaii
The Convict's Bride
Hauling Sugar Cane, Kohala Plantation, Hawaii
Hawaiians Arriving to Attend a Luau or Native Feast
Hawaiians Departing to Attend a Luau or Native Feast
How the Office Boy Saw the Ball Game
Impersonation of Gans-Nelson Fight
In the Tombs
Kathleen Mavoureen
Pals; or, My Friend, the Dummy
S.S. "Kinau" Landing Passengers, Mahukona, Hawaii
Scenes in Hawaii
Secret Service; or, The Diamond Smugglers
Shearing Sheep, Humunla Ranch, Hawaii
Sheep Coming Through Chute, Humunla Ranch, Hawaii
Washing Sheep, Humunla Beach, Hawaii
Water Tricycle
Weighing the Anchor
Aug 1 No Wedding Bells for Him
The Old Swimming Hole
Aug 4 The Great Mail Robbery
Aug 6 Looking for John Smith
Aug 11 Voyage Around a Star
Aug 18 Fayet-Chamonix: Trip on the New Trolley Line from Le Fayet-St. Gervais to Chamonix
From Menton to Nice
Les Gorges du Fier
Perefitte to Luz
Aug 23 The Cruise of the Gladys
Aug 25 Ascent of Mount Lowe
The Henly Regatta
Ostrich Farm
The Paris-Bordeaux Auto Race
Pigeon Farm
Playmates
Aug 30 The Lone Highwayman
Sep [day undetermined]
The Automobile Thieves
Bryan
E. Forest Fish Gun Assn.
Great Naval Review
Hoe Printing Press in Action
The Indian's Revenge; or, Osceola, the Last of the Seminoles
May's Mechanical Race Track
Trip on Berlin Elevated R.R.
William Jennings Bryan
Sep 1 The Secret of Death Valley
Sep 8 The Paris Students
Reproduction of Nelson-Gans Fight
Sep 20 Brannigan Sets Off the Blast
A Daring Hold-Up in Southern California
The Dog Detective
Rescued in Mid-Air
Sep 22 The Accordion
Sep 29 A Spiritualistic Meeting
The Tenacious Cat
Wanted—A Nurse
Oct [day undetermined]
Getting Evidence, Showing the Trials and Tribulations of a Private Detective
Mother-in-Law, a Domestic Comedy
Motor Race
The 9th Mass. Vol. Militia
A Race for a Wife
Railroad Collision at Los Angeles, Calif.
Scenes and Incidents U.S. Military Academy, West Point
7th Regiment at 69th Army Dedication
Thousand Islands
Vanderbilt Cup 1906
Wanted: A Husband
The Wishbone
Oct 6 A Road Side Inn
Soap Bubbles
Oct 8 The Country Schoolmaster
Oct 13 Custom Officials Bewitched
Fun After the Wedding
Ill Rewarded Honesty
Indian's Revenge
Mephisto's Son
The Merry Frolics of Satan
New Brother
Oct 18 The Fox-Hunt
Oct 27 Dolly's Papa
How to Keep Cool or Our Ice Supply
Whale Hunting
The World Series Baseball Games-White Sox and Cubs
Nov [day undetermined]
And the Villain Still Pursued Her; or, The Author's Dream
Fangere
Fay Templeton
The Honeymoon at Niagara Falls
Humuula Sheep Ranch
Lillian Russell
On Great Western Railway Ldongotten Station
On Great Western Railway Through Dawhistle
Vesta Tilley
Nov 1 Dr. Dippy's Sanitarium
Nov 3 The Bank Defaulter
The Bell Ringer's Daughter
Nov 15 The Tunnel Workers
Nov 24 Algy's New Suit
An Artist's Dream

Caught in a Trap
Colonel's Bicycle
Exmore Stag Hunt
The Female Highwayman
For His Daughter's Honor
Good Night
The Inexperienced Chauffeur
The Lost Hat: He Got It Alright
The Poor Tutor
A Seaside Flirtation
Train Collision
Travels of a Barrel
Two Seedy Rubes: They Have a Hot Time in the Old Town

Dec [day undetermined]
American Falls from Canadian Side, Niagara Falls, N.Y.
American Falls from Goat Island, Niagara Falls, N.Y.
Cave of the Winds
The Drunken Mattress
Horseshoe Falls from American Side, Niagara Falls, N.Y.
Horseshoe Falls from Canadian Side Niagara Falls, N.Y.
A Mid-winter Night's Dream; or, Little Joe's Luck
A Modern Diogenes
O'Brien-Burns Contest, Los Angeles, Cal., Nov. 26th, 1906
Pierce Kids
Singer Building Foundation Co.
A Thrilling Detective Story
A Trip on the "Chippewa," Niagara Falls, N.Y.
A Trip on the "Maid in the Mist," Niagara Falls, N.Y.
Whirlpool Rapids

Dec 1 The Cab
Cross Country
Day in the Country
Honesty's Strange Reward
The Magic Flute
Man Without Scruple
Marble Industry at Carrara
Old Man's Darling
Poor Mother
The Rebellious Walking Stick
Stealing Tomatoes
The Telescope
Tom Moves
The Troubadour
Unquenchable Thirst
Village Witch

Dec 8 At the Seaside
Child's Revenge
Difficult Problem
Japanese Sports
Love's Thermometer
Magic Roses
Skyscrapers

Dec 15 Alladin and His Wonder Lamp
Bobby and His Family
Desperate Girl
The Female Spy
In Search of Adventure
The Murder of His Seventeen Wives
The Mysterious Retort
The Poacher

Dec 20 The Witch

Dec 29 Cabby's Dream
Disappointed
Furnished on Easy Terms
Kiddies Pets
Married for Millions
Tommy's Revenge
Trout Fishing
Weary Willie and His Pal
Won't You Come Home

1907 [month undetermined]
Along the Shore Line of Lake Washington
Bakers in Trouble
Botanist's Misadventures
Cloud Play at Pulfoss, Norway
Dancing Boxing Match, Montgomery and Stone
Delirium in a Studio
The Dutch Kiddies: Montgomery and Stone
Geranger Fjord, Sailing from Merock to Hellisute on a Steamer
Goodbye John
Grant's Tomb
Gratli Vand and Tourists Passing, Panorama
Jim Jeffries on His California Ranch
Laplander Family, Gratli, Norway
[Launching of the Salem at the Fore River Shipyards—Quincy, Mass.—July 27, 1907]
Marceline, the World-Renowned Clown of the N.Y. Hippodrome
Nord Fjord from Loen to Sandene by Steamer [Norway]
Norway: Crazy Canal Boat on the Telemarken Route
Panorama of Market Street, San Francisco
Passion Play: Baptism by Immersion
Pulfoss, Norway, Pulfoss Falls
Sailing thro the Sognia Fjord on a Steamer from Ballholm to Gudvangen [Norway]
Torrents of Zermath
A Trip Up Broadway

Jan [day undetermined]
Base Ball Game
Beaver Hunt
Cheating Justice
Deer Hunt
Following in Father's Footsteps
Foul Play; or, A False Friend
The Gardener's Nap
The Little Globe Trotter
Making Champagne
Man Being Run Over by Automobile
The Moving Picture Man
Philadelphia New Year Shooters
Reformation
Scene at "The Oaks," Portland, Oregon
The Stepmother
Trial Trip of the Airship "La Patrie"
Whale Fishing
Willie Goodchild Visits His Auntie

Jan 5 Life of Christ
The Lighthouse

Jan 12 Between Two Fires
Cousin's Visit
Exciting Honeymoon Trip
Fine Birthday Cake
Forbidden Fruit
Friendship Better Than Riches
Gibelot's Hotel
Hot Chestnuts
Hypnotized Police Inspector
Life in Congo
My Wife's Birthday
Niagara Falls
Paris Slums
Pay Day
Saved by a Melon
Scales of Justice
Six Amorous Dragoons
Skating Lessons
Sportsmen and Lion
Strange Mount
Susan Tastes Our Wine
Tragic Wedding
Unexpected Meal
Venetian Tragedy
Wedding on Bicycles
Who Is Who?

Jan 17 Trial Marriages

Jan 19 Attempted Suicide
Cabby by the Hour
A Colored Man's Revenge
Crime on the Railroad
Little Blind Girl
The Mechanical Statue and the Ingenious Servant

Jan 26 Bad Mother
Fan in Japan
Gans-Herman Fight
The Grafter
The Gypsies
Infants at Breakfast
Joined Lips
Misadventures of a Negro King in Paris
An Officer's Honor
Professor in Difficulties
Servant's Strike
The Stolen Bride
Stormy Winds Do Blow
Wrestler's Wife
Wrestling Matches of 1906

Feb [day undetermined]
Animated Stamp Pad
Baby Cries
The Bad Son
Brown Goes to Mother
Burglar and Policeman
Carmen
Going Away for Holiday
Her First Cake
His First Cigarette
Indian Customs
The Man Monkey
Man Who Hangs Himself
Message from the Sea
The Miner's Daughter
Moonlight on the Ocean
My Master's Coffee Service
My Servant Is a Jewel
My Wife's Birthday
A New Toboggan
Policeman Has an Idea
Poor John
Skiing in Norway
Snowballing
Soldier to Colonel
Stolen Child
Two Rival Peasants
Waiting at the Church
When Friends Meet
Winter in Switzerland
Wrestling Match, Hackenschmidt

Feb 2 The Artful Dodger
The Bad Man: A Tale of the West
Carnival at Venice
College Boy's First Love
Crowds Returning from the Games, Waikiki, H.I.
The Double Life
Faces and Grimaces
The "Float," Waikiki, Honolulu, Hawaiian Islands
Kanaka Fishermen Casting the Throw Net, Hilo, H.I.
The Little Rascal's Tricks
Loading Sugar, Kahului, Maui, H.I.
Native Hawaiian Guards in Bayonet Exercises, H.I.
Pa-u Riders, Hawaiian Island
Panoramic View, Crater of Haleakala, H.I.
Panoramic View, Honolulu Harbor, H.I.
Panoramic View, King St. Honolulu, H.I.
Panoramic View, Oahu Railroad, Haleiwa, H.I.
Panoramic View, Oahu Railroad, Pearl Harbor, Hawaiian Islands
Panoramic View of Waikiki Beach, Honolulu, H.I.
Panoramic View, Waikiki, from an Electric Car, H.I.
Playing a Trick on the Gardener
Playing Truant
S.S. "Kinau" Landing Passengers, Laupahoihoi, H.I.
Scenes on a Sugar Plantation, Hawaiian Islands
Shipping Cattle, Hawaihae, Hawaiian Islands
Snapshots, Hawaiian Islands
Surf Board Riders, Waikiki, Honolulu, H.I.
Surf Scene, Laupahoihoi, Hawaiian Island
Surf Scene, Waikiki, Honolulu, H.I.
A Trip Through the Yellowstone Park, U.S.A.
Two Cabbies for One Passenger
The Underworld of Paris
Wanted, a Governess
Water Buffalo Wallowing, Hawaiian Island
The Zoo at London, Part I
The Zoo at London, Part II

Feb 8 At the Monkey House
Mr. Hurry-Up

Feb 9 Bobby and His Balloon
The Charmer
Constructed Fishing Boat
Determined Creditor
False Coiners
For Mother's Birthday
Forbidden Sport
The Foxy Hoboes
Fun in a Fotograf Gallery
In the Cause of Faith
India Rubberman
Julia at the Barracks
Old Mashers
Policeman's Little Run
Salome "The Dance of the Seven Veils"
Spot at the 'Phone
The Tramp Dog
When We Were Boys

Feb 16 Cavalry School
Difficult Arrest

Phial of Poison
Rat Catching
Robert Macaire and Bertrand; or, The Troubles of a Hobo and His Pal, in Paris
Sea by Moonlight
Two Little Scamps

Feb 23 The Haunted Hotel; or, The Strange Adventures of a Traveler
The Pork Butcher's Nightmare
A Trip Through Yellowstone Park

Mar [day undetermined]
Cassimir's Night Out
Colon to Panama Canal Picture
The Conjuror's Pupil
Conquering the Dolomites
Disturbing His Rest
The Electric Belt
First Snowball
Flashes from Fun City
The Hand of the Artist
His First Camera
His First Dinner at Father-in-Law's
Is Marriage a Failure?
Little Lord Mayor
Looking for Lodgings
Mrs. Smithson's Portrait
Moonlight on Lake
Oh! That Molar
Paying Off Scores
Puck's Pranks on Suburbanite
Quaint Holland
The Runaway Van
Salome
Trap Pigeon Shooting
Traveling Menagerie
Trip to Borneo
Turkey Raffle
Woman Up-to-Date
Wonders of Canada

Mar 2 The Birthday Celebration
The Clever Thief
Fights of Nations
Little Tich
A Set of Dishes
The Teddy Bears
The Unwritten Law: A Thrilling Drama Based on the Thaw White Case

Mar 9 The Girl from Montana
The Murderer
The Spy, a Romantic Story of the Civil War

Mar 16 Ascending Mt. Blanc
Cinderella
A Curious Dream
Hooligans of the Far West
The Life and Passion of Christ
Suicide Impossible
Tommy at Play
The Yawner

Mar 28 Mrs. Smithers' Boarding-School

Mar 30 After the Matinee
The Arlberg Railway
The Atlantic Voyage
The Belle of the Ball
Berlin to Rome
Black Beauty
Captain Kidd and His Pirates
The Carving Doctor
A Championship Won on a Foul
Curfew Shall Not Ring Tonight
Dolomite Towers
Flirting on the Sands
His First Ride
Indian Basket Weavers
The Jota
The Magic Bottle
The Mischievous Sketch
Napoleon and Sentry
An Old Coat Story
Parody on Toreador
Retribution; or, The Brand of Cain
Take Good Care of Baby
Universal Winter Sports
The Yokel's Love Affair

Apr [day undetermined]
Brother Willie's Revenge
Curious Carriage of Klobenstein
Deyo
Dreams of Fair Women
Floral Parade at Pasadena, Calif.
Gay Girl Playing Pool
The Girl on Park Bench
How the World Lives
In a Picture Frame
Me for Water Wagon
Mishaps of a Maid
Miss Kellerman's Diving Feats
Picnic Hampers
Post Office Department Picture
Pranks of Cupid
She Seemed Shy but She Was Fly
Skating on N.Y. Theatre Roof
The Spanish Lovers
This Girl Not Wanted
Tirolean Dance
Undone by a Suit Case
Unloading Mail at Pier 13, N. R., N.Y.
Upset by a Cigarette
Winning a Princess

Apr 6 The Busy Man
Daniel Boone; or, Pioneer Days in America
Drink and Repentance
Father's Picnic
The Fishing Industry
Foiled by a Woman; or, Falsely Accused
The Hero
Quarter Day Conjuring
She Would Sing
Signal Man's Son
Slippery Jim, the Burglar

Apr 11 The Truants

Apr 13 Amateur Night; or, Get the Hook
The Animated Pill Box
Artist's Model
Baby's Peril
The Borrowed Ladder
An Early Round with the Milkman
Street in Frankfort
The Tell-Tale Telephone
Traced by a Laundry Mark
The Vision of a Crime
A Woman's Sacrifice

Apr 20 Anarchist's Mother-in-Law
Auntie's Birthday
The Bad Shilling
Cambridge-Oxford Race
Catch the Kid
Chasing a Sausage
A Cheap Skate
Chef's Revenge
The Coroner's Mistake
Eggs
Father! Mother Wants You
Knight-Errant
Lady Cabby
Land of Bobby Burns
Life and Customs in India
A Mother's Sin
Murphy's Wake
The Naval Nursery
The Poet's Bid for Fame
Polar Bear Hunt
Rogues' Tricks
Sailor's Return
The Terrorist's Remorse
True until Death
The Vacuum Cleaner
Village Fire Brigade
A Winter Day in the Country
Wizard's World

Apr 27 Amateur Photographer
The Baby's First Outing
Boxing Matches in England
Clowns and Statue
The Doll's Revenge
The Fencing Master
The Flat Dwellers; or, The House of Too Much Trouble
From Jealousy to Madness
Golden Beetle
Great Boxing Contest
Herring Fishing
Japanese Women
A Military Prison
On the Stage; or, Melodrama from the Bowery
Picturesque Canada
A Pig in Society
Pompeii
Servant's Revenge
A Smart Capture
The Smugglers
Tragic Rivalry
Wonderful Flames

May [day undetermined]
Examining a Recruit U.S.N.
Governor's Island Taken U.S.N.
A Little Bit of String

May 4 Boss Away, Choppers Play
The Fatal Hand
Johnny's Run
The Park Keeper
The Pirates' Treasure; or, A Sailor's Love Story
The Romany's Revenge
Roof to Cellar
The Skipping Cheeses
Too Much Mother-in-Law
Well-Bred

May 11 Colonial Virginia and Burning of Jamestown
Crayono
Fire Run, Colon Fire Department Under Cocoanut Tree
The Hundred Dollar Bill; or, The Tramp Couldn't Get It Changed
Jamaica Negroes Doing a Two-Step
Jamestown Exposition
Jamestown Exposition International Naval Review, Hampton Roads, Virginia
Jamestown Naval Review
Machete Men Clearing a Jungle [Panama Canal]
Making the Dirt Fly: Scene 1. Steam Shovel in Operation, Culebra Cut
Making the Dirt Fly: Scene 2. Unloading a Dirt Train
Making the Dirt Fly: Scene 3. Dirt Scraper in Operation
Making the Dirt Fly: Scene 4. Railroad Track Lifter in Operation
Making the Dirt Fly: Scene 5. Laborers Lining Up at Mess Tent
Old Market Place, Panama
Panorama from Columbus Point of Atlantic Entrance to the Canal
Panorama La Boca Harbor and Pacific Entrance to Canal
Panorama of Culebra Cut
Panorama Ruins of Old French Machinery
A Tenderloin Tragedy
U.S. Sanitary Squad Fumigating a House

May 18 The Anarchists
Barometer of Love
Clever Detective
Cream Eating Contest
Father's Washing Day
Interesting Reading
Kind-Hearted Girl
Life in India
Lost in the Alps
Papa's Letter
The Pirates
Robbing a Bird's Nest
Spring Cleaning
Stealing Candies
The Stolen Bicycle
The Stolen Pig
Trouble at a Wedding
Wanted, 10,000 Eggs

May 23 If You Had a Wife Like This

May 25 And the Dog Came Back
Beating the Landlord
Buying a Ladder
Catastrophe in the Alps
A Child's Cunning
The Cup and Ball
Dog and the Tramp
A Horse of Another Color
Janitor's Tea Party
Nurse Takes a Walk
Rogie Falls and Salmon Fishing
Salome
Sign of the Times
A Square Deal; or, The End of a Bad Man
Two Cents Worth of Cheese
The Village Celebration

Jun [day undetermined]
Dear Little Sister
Flirty Fan
Jimmie, the Messenger Boy
The Kitchen Terror
Shriners' Conclave at Los Angeles, Cal., May, 1907
Squires, Australian Champion, in His Training Quarters
Wyoming Girl

Jun 1 Anything to Oblige
Artful Husband
Betrothed's Nightmare
Blind Man's Dog
Brigand Story
Cowboys and Red-skins
Distress
Fatal Leap
Forty Winks; or, A Strenuous Dream

Haunted Kitchen
Horrible Adventure
The Human Clock
An Icy Day
Julius, the Sandwich Man
Lawyer Enjoys Himself
Looking for Lodgings
Mines and Forge at Decazeville
Mischievous Sammy
Modern Burglars
The New Policeman
One Man Baseball
One of the Finest
A Perfect Nuisance
To Tame His Wife
The Tramp's Dream
A Trip Through the Holy Land
Winter Amusements
Won by Strategy
The Wrong Chimney; or, Every Man His Own Sweep

Jun 8 Bowser's House Cleaning
The Bunco Steerers; and, How They Were Caught
A Caribou Hunt
The Dog Snatcher
Dolls in Dreamland
The Gentleman Farmer
How to Cure a Cold
The New Hired Man
The Runaway Sleighbelle

Jun 10 The Child Accuser
Dressing in a Hurry
The Faithful Dog; or, True to the End
Saved from the Wreck
The Substitute Drug Clerk

Jun 15 Biker Does the Impossible
Costumes of Different Centuries
A Disturbed Dinner
Dog Police
How Bridget's Lover Escaped
I Never Forget the Wife
The Masher
The Pony Express
Poor Coat
Servant's Vengeance
The Slave, a Story of the South Before the War
Straw Hat Factory in Florence
Washings Badly Marked
Weird Fancies
When Women Vote
The White Slave
Whose Hat Is It?
A Woman's Duel

Jun 17 Rube Brown in Town

Jun 22 The Awkward Man; or, Oh! So Clumsy
The Blackmailer
The Enchanted Mattress
His Cheap Watch
Moving Under Difficulties
The Oyster Industry
Revenge
She Won't Pay Her Rent
That Awful Tooth
Travels of a Lost Trunk
Western Justice
Willie's Dream

Jun 24 Comedy Cartoons
Shoeing the Mail Carrier

Jun 25 The Amateur Rider
Mother-in-Law at the White City

Jun 26 The Legless Runner
The Toilet of an Ocean Greyhound

Jun 27 The Near-Sighted Cyclist

Jun 29 Alps of Chamonix
The Bandit King
The Bandits; or, A Story of Sunny Italy
Because My Father's Dead
Bertie's Love Letter
A Carmen in Danger
Charley Paints
Cohen's Fire Sale
The Comic Duel
Crime in the Mountains
Exciting Night of Their Honeymoon
Frolics of Ding Dong Imps
Fussy Father Fooled
A Hooligan Idea
Humors of Amateur Golf
Mother-in-Law's Race
Mother's Dream
Nervous Kitchenmaid
No More Children
The Orange Peel
Palmistry
Rummy Robbers
A Slave's Love
Struggle for Life
Tragic Moment
Under the Seas

Jul [day undetermined]
Among the Igorrotes
Over the Midland Terminal Railroad: Through Cripple Creek District
Panorama, Crowds at Squires-Burns International Contest, from Center of Ring, Colma, July 4th, 1907
Panorama, Crowds at Squires-Burns International Contest, from Moving Picture Stand, July 4th, 1907
The Sleepy Cop
Through Yellowstone Park

Jul 6 The Book Worm
Diabolo, the Japanese Top Spinner
The Human Incubator
Work for Your Grub
The Wrong Flat; or, A Comedy of Errors

Jul 8 Fatality
Scratch My Back
The Soldier's Helmet
Union Workers Spoil the Food

Jul 13 Drama on the Riviera
A Family Outing
International Contest for the Heavyweight Championship: Squires vs. Burns, Ocean View, Cal., July 4th, 1907
Life's Reality
Lost in an Arizona Desert
A New Death Penalty
Oliver Twist
Quick, I'm on Fire
Seaman's Widow
Troubles of a Gardener
The Window Demonstration
Woodchopper's Daughter

Jul 15 A Hobo Hero

Jul 17 Christy Mathewson, N.Y. National League Baseball Team

Jul 18 Croker's Horse Winning the Derby

Jul 20 Dick Turpin
The Dog Acrobats
Don't Pay Rent—Move
Drama in a Spanish Inn
Father's Quiet Sunday
Getting His Change
Harlequin's Story
The Hypnotist's Revenge
Magic Drawing Room
The Matinee Idol
A Poet and His Babies
Prisoner's Escape
Sambo as Footman
Servant's Generosity
Too Stout
Unlucky Interference
Victim of Science

Jul 27 Caught with the Goods
Chasing a Motorist
Diabolo
Drawing Teacher
Dunhard After All
Elks' Convention Parade
Elks' Convention Parade: "Spirit of '76" and Views of the Grand Stand
Elks' Parade
The Fortune Teller
Genevieve of Brabant
Gypsy's Revenge
Lighthouse Keepers
Lightning Sketches
Looking for the Medal
Nervy Jim and the Cop
The New Apprentice
The Onion Fiend
The Poacher's Daughter
Sham Beggars
Troubles of a Cook
Tunneling the English Channel
Vengeance of the Algerine
Window Cleaner

Jul 31 An Awful Skate; or, the Hobo on Rollers
The Tenderfoot

Aug [day undetermined]
Bigger Than He Looked
Egyptian Princess
An Inquisitive Girl
Pat's Ghost
Post Office Dept. Picture
Smoking Up

Aug 3 Albany, N.Y.
Athletic American Girls
Atlantic City
Baltimore
Boston
The Boy, the Bust and the Bath
Brooklyn
Buffalo
Buying a Donkey
Chester, Pa.
Cincinnati
Cleveland
Colorado Springs
Denver
Detroit
Easton
El Paso
The Express Sculptor
Harrisburg
Jersey City
Kansas City
A Kind Grandfather
New Haven
New Orleans
New York
The Nine Lives of a Cat
Ostrich Farm
Panorama of Court of Honor
Panorama of Market Street Showing the Beautiful Decorations
Paterson, N.J.
Philadelphia
Pittsburg
Poor Little Mites
Reading
The Roller Skate Craze
San Francisco
Scranton
Toledo
Tyron
Wilmington, Del.

Aug 5 Off for the Day; or the Parson's Picnic

Aug 10 Angling in Norway
The Bargain Fiend; or, Shopping a la Mode
The Dancing Swine
Discipline and Humanity
A Double-Barreled Suicide
The Dummy
The Easterner, or, A Tale of the West
First Success
From Barrel to Barrel
From Cairo to Khartoum
A Glorious Start
Grand Canyon of Arizona and the Cliff Dwellers
The Gypsies; or, The Abduction
The Helmet
Life Boat Manoeuvres
Life in a South African Gold Mine
Looking at a Balloon
A Lucky Heiress
The Magnetized Man
A Misunderstanding
Slow but Sure
Spring Gardening
Torpedo Attack on H. M. S. Dreadnought
White Man's First Smoke; or, Puritan Days in America
Young Americans

Aug 13 The Baby Elephant

Aug 14 The Fireman
Fountains of Rome
Kidnapping a Bride
A Modern Youth
The Slavery of Children

Aug 17 The Actor Annoys the Boarders
All's Well That Ends Well
The Book Agent
A Case of Arson
Cock Fight in Seville
The Deaf-Mutes' Ball
The New Stag Hunt
Poor but Proud
The Red Spectre
The Sea Wolf
The Servant Hypnotist
The Smoking Chimney
The Starving Artist, or, Realism in Art
Who's Boss of the House?

Aug 19 The Barber's Daughter
Little Fregoli

Aug 24 Are You an Elk?
A Big Take of Tunny Fish
The Blacksmith's Daughter
The Blacksmith's Strike
Chrysanthemums
The Dervish's Revenge
The Doll Maker's Daughter
Hair Restorer
Her Friend, the Enemy

In an Armchair
Man, Hat and Cocktail, a New Drink, but an Old Joke
Mr. Inquisitive
Nurses' Strike
Robber Robbed
Spanish Views, on Postals
Too Many Children
The Tooth Ache
Two Thousand Miles Without a Dollar
Wandering Willie's Luck

Aug 31 Bathing Under Difficulties
Cab 23
Children's Reformatory
Don Juan
Female Wrestlers
Great Lion Hunt
Half Caste's Revenge
Happy Bob as a Boxer
I'll Dance the Cakewalk
Just Married
Lost Umbrella
Modern Painters
Rival Sisters
Stage Struck
Three Chatterboxes
The Tired Tailor's Dream

Sep [day undetermined]
Attack on Emigrant Train
Bachelor Gets a Baby and Other Things He Don't Want
Bargains
Baxter's Brain Storm
Black-White
Blowing Hard
Buffalo Hunt
Busy Lizzie Loses Her Clothes
The Cannibals
Casey on a Souse—Gives the Bunch a Douse
Chink-Chippie
Chorus Girls
Congested Street Society
Crime Wave
Crooked Dog
The Crush at the Bridge Congested S.S.
Dream Kisses
The Finish of Scrappy Patsey
Fitznoodle's Last Ball
Flip-Rip-Zip
Flirty Fred
Frowsy Lizzie Knocks Them Dizzy
Girl $998
Happy Sport Beards the Manicurer
High Jinks
How Fritz's Pipe Exposed Him to the Maid
How the Lovers Got Rid of Boozy Pa
Hunters Dream
Ironed
Kissers Caught
Light-Fight-White
Mags Jag
A Mash a Smash a Splash
Over the Wall
Peanuts
The Portrait
Pres. Roosevelt Reviewing U.S. Regulars
Pres. Roosevelt Reviewing West Point Cadets
The Punishment of the Horse Thief
[Ranch 101]
Roasted Chestnuts
Row at Rileys
Scenes from Luna Park
Scenes from Miller Bros.
Stripped-Stripped
A Swell Time
A Tenement House Battle
Too Soon
Tramps Angel
Vanishing Friends
Waltzing Walter
Wanted a Man Badly
What His Girl's Voice Did
What the Bum Did to the Dude
What the Fisherman Caught
What the Girls Did to the Bachelor
Wrong Bath

Sep 7 After the Fancy Dress Ball
The Bewildering Cabinet
Cohen's Bad Luck
Disastrous Flirtation
Dot Leedle German Band
A Drink!
Englishman in Harem
The Fountain of Youth
Hanky Panky Cards
Irish Scenes and Types
Knowing Dogs
A Life for a Life
Life in a Burmah Teak Forest
Life of a Bootblack; or, the Street Urchin
The Life of Bee
Liquid Electricity; or, The Inventor's Galvanic Fluid
The Living Silhouette
A Modern Mother
The Motorcyclist
Mount Pilatus Railway
One-Night Stand
Private Atkins Minds the Baby
Rail Lying at Crewe
The Romance of a Singer
The Strength of Cheese
The Warwick Pageant
Who'll Do the Washing?

Sep 12 Lena and the Beaux
The Model's Ma
Neighbors

Sep 14 At the Colonial Exhibition
Cambodian Customs
Cast Up by the Sea
The Cheater's Cheated
A Daring Maid
Electric Pile
For a Woman's Sake
The Ghost Story
The Good Wine
Hunting a Devil
In Sevilla
The Indian's Friendship
John D. and the Reporter
A Modern Samson
Once Upon a Time There Was...
Reggy's Camping Party
Rivals
The Two Fowls
Unlucky Substitution
Who Owns the Pear?

Sep 16 Absent Mindedness
An Acadian Elopement
The Amateur Hunter
Art Student's Frivolities
A Baffled Burglar
The Fly
Roumania, Its Citizens and Soldiers
Woodcutter's Daughter

Sep 21 Arrival of Lusitania
Babes in the Woods
The Blacksmith's Revenge
Charley's Dream
The Dancing Nig
Dieppe Circuit
The Disintegrated Convict
The Eclipse; or, The Courtship of the Sun and the Moon
The Fortune
The Ghost Holiday
Grandpa's Vacation
His Second Childhood
Interrupted Card Party
A Pair of Boots, Please
The Pastry Cook and Musician
Policeman's Boots
Slavery of Children
Wood Industry in Canada
The Wooing of Miles Standish

Sep 23 Amongst the Reptiles
Carl Hagenbeck's Wild Animal Park at Hamburg, Germany
A Chinaman Visits London
Conway to Dublin
Dogs Tracking Burglars
A First Class Restaurant
Glimpses of Erin
Those Boys Again
Uncle's Heritage
Winan's Horses
Wipe Off Your Feet, Please

Sep 25 Terrible Ted

Sep 26 The Persevering Lover

Sep 28 The Adventuress
The Amateur Champion
The Benediction of the Sea
[Building a Railroad in Africa]
The Burglar; or, A Midnight Surprise
Cheekiest Man on Earth
Enchanted Glasses
Getting Even
Gitana; or, The Gypsy
Goldstein's Luck
The Great Brighton Beach Head-On Locomotive Collision
Indian Idyll
Invalid's Adventure
It Served Them Right
Maniac Juggler
The Mill Girl, a Story of Factory Life
Nature Fakirs
Our Band's Going to the Competition
Poor Pig
Purchasing an Automobile
A Race for Millions
The Scheme That Failed
Stilt Race
That Dog Gone Dog
Thursday Is My Jonah Day

Sep 30 Coffee Plantation
The Horse That Ate the Baby
How Isaac Won the Cop
Tamer Hopkins
The Undergraduate

Oct [day undetermined]
The Cleptomaniac
Miraculous Eggs
Mr. Easy Mark
A Night at the Gayety

Oct 1 A Doctor's Conscience
Fisherman's Luck
The Great Victoria Falls

Oct 5 The Amateur Detective
Chinese Slave Smuggling
The Gypsy's Warning
Highwaymen
His First Topper
Interrupted Outing
Late for His Wedding
Lucky Jim
Moses Sells a Collar Button
The New Arrival
The Petticoat Regiment
Returning Good for Evil
Riding School

Oct 7 The Foster Cabby
The Haunted Bedroom
Madame Goes Shopping
Slavery by Circumstance
Tyrolean Alps in the Winter
A Would Be Champion

Oct 12 Asking His Way
Chopin's Funeral March, Burlesqued
A Day of His Own
Drink
Easter Eggs
The First Quarrel
The Girl and the Judge
The Heart's Bidding
Hey There! Look Out!
The Japanese Girl
Little Meg and the Wonderful Lamp
Making Pottery in Japan
Monk's Vengeance
Motoring Under Difficulties
99 in the Shade
The Piker's Dream, a Race Track Fantasy
The Prodigal Son
Serving a Summons
The Sham Sword Swallower
A Soldier's Jealousy
Stolen Chickens
A Too Devoted Wife
The Unveiling Ceremonies of the McKinley Memorial, Canton, Ohio, September 30th, 1907
William, the Poacher

Oct 14 Crazed by a Fad
Farmer Giles' Geese
The Red Man's Way
Rubberneck Reuben
The Spring Gun

Oct 16 Mishaps of a Baby Carriage

Oct 19 All on Account of a Lost Collar Button
The Cigar Box
Clever Tailor
Cricket Terms Illustrated
Don't Go to the Law
A Drama in Seville
Harbor Pirates
Jack the Kisser
Jane Is Furious
Jealousy Punished
Just in Time
Love Microbe
The Masquerade Party
Mischievous Girls
A Modern Don Juan
Naples to Vesuvius
Nathan Hale
Picturesque Wales

A Sailor's Lass
Save the Pieces
A Seaside Girl
Slate Quarries in North Wales
A Story of Eggs
There Is a Rat in the Room
West Africa
Wild Animals
Oct 26 Andalusian Dances
Belle of Bald-Head Row
Brain Storm
Burglary by Motor
A Crime in the Snow
Dog Avenges His Master
A Free Lunch
The Gold Brick
Hamlet, Prince of Denmark
Her First Bike Ride
Ice Cutting in Sweden
The Inquisitive Boy; or, Uncle's Present
International Balloon Races [from the James Gordon Bennett Cup, at St. Louis, Oct. 21, 1907]
It Was Mother-in-law
The Lover's Charm
Magic Lantern
Making Love to the Coalman's Wife
My Mother-in-Law Is an Angel
Pleasant Thoughts
A Quiet Hotel
Red Riding Hood
Satan at Play
Smuggling Chinese into the U.S.A.
The Street Fakir
Tommy in Society
True to Life
The Two Orphans
An Unpleasant Legacy
The Vagabond
The Veiled Beauty; or, Anticipation and Realization
Wonderful Lion Killer
Oct 28 The Absent-Minded Professor
The Adventures of a Bath Chair
Adventures of a Lover
The Athletic Dude
De Beers Diamond Mines, Kimberly, S.A.
An Episode of the Paris Commune
Floor Polisher
A Four Year Old Heroine
The Glue
The Irresistible Piano
Naval Manoeuvres
Onions Make People Weep
Picturesque Brittany
Smoke Without Fire
The Sylvan God
The Thieving Umbrella
Through Hong Kong
Towed by an Automobile
Volunteer's Betrothal
Who Has Stolen My Bicycle
Yale Laundry
Nov [day undetermined]
[Picture taken for Capt. Lovelace]
Nov 2 Across the Ocean on the Lusitania
Bill Butt-in and the Burglars
The Kitchen Maid's Dream
Midnight Ride of Paul Revere
The Rival Motorists
Shakespeare Writing "Julius Caesar"
Smuggled into America
The Soldier's Dream
Nov 4 Accidents Will Happen
An Anonymous Letter
A Good Husband
King Edward on H.M.S. Dreadnought
Launch of the British Battleship Bellerophon
The Lost Bass Drum; or, Where Is That Louie?
Raising the Wind
Under the Old Apple Tree
The White Shoes; or, Looking Out for His Banknote
A Wig Made To Order
Nov 9 Beyond Criticism
The Elixir of Life
The Foundling
Good Glue Sticks
The Handling of the Fleet
His Affinity
A Little Hero
The Mysterious Armor
The Night Watchman
A Pressing Letter
Seek and You Shall Find...Trouble
A Shilling Short in Wages
A Southern Romance
Swedish Sports
Troubles of a Tramp
Tunny Fisheries in Sicily
The Twin Brother's Joke
What a Pipe Did
Nov 11 A Rolling Bed
The Stolen Shoes
Nov 14 The Bomb
Grandfather and the Kitten
Turning the Tables
Nov 16 A Crazy Quilt
A Dramatic Rehearsal
A Drink Cure
Dumb Sagacity
The Eleventh Hour
Even a Worm Will Turn
A Fish Story
How Brown Saw the Baseball Game
The Lost Mine
Neighbors Who Borrow
Sightseeing Through Whiskey
Testing of a Lifeboat
A Tramp's Dream of Wealth
Woman, Cruel Woman
Wooing and Wedding of a Coon
Nov 20 Wife Wanted
Nov 22 In the Dreamland
Where Is My Head
Nov 23 Airship Thieves
Ali Baba and the Forty Thieves
Artistic Woodcarver
The Baboon
A Breeze from the West
Chemist's Mistake
The Collar'd Herring
The Country Girl
Cripple's Duel
The Cupboard
The Despatch Bearer; or, Through the Enemy's Lines
Enchanted Pond
Faith's Reward
Hunting in Canadian Woods
Inexhaustible Barrel
Innkeeper and Wife
The Innkeeper's Wife
Little Conjuror
Mysterious Boudoir
Mystic Shriners at Dreamland
Only Kids
The Parson of Hungry Gulch; or, The Right Man in the Right Place May Work Wonders
The Pirates
The Plank
Presentation of Firemen's Bravery Medals by Mayor McClellan
Satan in Prison
School Days
Three American Beauties [No. 2]
Tippler's Race
The Trainer's Daughter; or, A Race for Love
Venetian Baker; or, Drama of Justice
Watchmaker's Secret
Nov 30 Bad Boy's Joke
Bargain Sales
The Burglar and the Baby
The Clock-Maker's Secret
The Colonial Soldier
Comrade Rations
Daughter's Lover in Difficulties
Economical Trip
A Forester Made King
French Recruit
Master in General
Misadventures of a Street Singer
Modern Hercules at Work
Oh Me! Oh My!
Reedham Boys' Aquatic Sports
Simple-Minded Peasant
Stolen Child's Career
The Tattler
The Tin Wedding
Under False Colors
Unlucky Trousers
Ups and Downs of a Hat
Wood Industry in Norway
Your Wife Is Unfaithful to Us
Dec [day undetermined]
Against the Law
An Angelic Servant
An Animated Dummy
Bulgarian Army
Cabman Mystified
The Cashier
Deaf and Dumb
Diabolo Nightmare
Hatred
Highly Scented Bouquet
Lost, Strayed or Stolen
Love Levels All Ranks
The Shaughraun, an Irish Romance
When the Devil Drives
Willing to Oblige
Youthful Hackenschmidts
Dec 2 Darkest Hour
Harvest Celebration
The Lady Athlete; or, The Jiu Jitsu Downs the Footpads
Tommy's Box of Tools
Wrong Righted
Dec 4 The Elopement
Dec 7 Ben Hur
Bobby's Practical Jokes
College Chums
Doings of a Maniac
An Exciting Ride
Laughing Gas
A Letter in the Sand
The Making of a Modern Newspaper
Mike the Model
The Need of Gold
The Pearl Fisher
The Poor Old Couple
The Rebellious Schoolgirls
A Soldier Must Obey Orders
The Sticky Bicycle
When Cherries are Ripe
Dec 9 Notice to Quit
Saving His Country's Flag
Sunday with the Boss
Dec 14 A Champion After All
The Christmas
Dr. Skinum
Elephants in India
Laughing Gas
A Mother's Secret
Music, Forward!
Nervy Nat
The Pay Train Robbery
Sailor's Practical Joke
A Super's Debut
A Tale of the Sea
Tipsy Tinker
Up to Date Burglars
What Is Home Without a Mother-in-Law
Where Is My Hair?
Dec 20 A Christmas Adoption
Dec 21 Burglar and Old Maids
A Clown's Love Story
The Daily Life of a French Sailor
The Eviction
Father Buys a Hand Roller
The Little Girl Who Did Not Believe in Santa Claus
Madam's Fancies
Manners and Customs of Australia
Mr. Gay and Mrs.
A Night in Dreamland
On the Grass
An Uncle by Marriage
Dec 23 The Gamekeeper's Dog
Nurse's Travels
A Red Hot Day
The Romance of a Fisherman's Daughter
The Two Orphans
The Waters of Life
Dec 27 Burns-Moir
"King Oscar II's Funeral Films"
Dec 28 The Bargeman's Child
The Black Witch
Blue Beard
Doings of a Poodle
Elegant Paris
The First Row
How the Masher Was Punished
Hunting above the Clouds
Japanese Vaudeville "The Flower Kingdom"
The Merry Widow
The Miser's Hoard
The Strong Man
The Talisman or Sheep's Foot
Thieves Caught in Their Own Trap
Thirteen at Table
Unknown Talent
The Witch Kiss
Wonderful Mirrors
Work Made Easy
Dec 30 Cook's Fiancé
False Start

A Tight Fix

1908 [month undetermined]
The Collinwood [Ohio] School Fire
The Collinwood [Ohio] School Fire Funeral

Jan [day undetermined]
The Animated Dummy
The Goebel Tragedy
I Rather Two Step Than Waltz
Impossibilities
A Lucky Horseshoe
Oh Mama
Oh That Curtain
Pipe Dreams

Jan 4 The Bell Boy's Revenge
A Brief Story
The Days of '61
Dog and His Various Merits
The Football Craze
The Four-Footed Hero
An Indian Love Story
The Jealous Wife
A Magistrate's Crime
Professional Jealousy
The Shrimper
The Silver King
Through Darkness to Light
The Tulips

Jan 6 The Affianced
Buying a Cow
The Hypnotist's Pranks
The Marvelous Powder

Jan 11 Afraid of Microbes
"Energizer"
The Farmer
Fatherhood and Drunkenness
Go, Little Cabin Boy
Jack of All Trades
Lovers' Ill Luck
Military Tournament at Saumur
The Rivals: A Love Drama of Pompeii
Such a Good Joke, But— Why Don't He Laugh?

Jan 18 Adventures of a Countryman
Adventures of an Overcoat
Anxious Day for Mother
The Artful Lovers
Bachelor's Wedding Bells
Back to the Farm
Bewitched Son-in-Law
The Diabolical Itching
Dogs of Fashion
Falsely Accused!
First Cigar
Funny Faces Competition
The Gay Vagabonds
Girl's Dream
Going to Switzerland
Have You Seen My Wife?
Heavyweight's Race
A Home at Last
If Wm. Penn Came to Life
In the Bogie Man's Cave
Ingenuity Conquers
Kiri-Kis
The Knight of Black Art
Lady Doctor's Husband
The Last Cartridge, an Incident of the Sepoy Rebellion in India
Man Who Walks on the Water
Medal Winner
The Miser's Fate
Mr. Sleepy Head
Mountaineers
Novice on Stilts
Pied Piper of Hamlin
A Prince's Idea
Quack Doctor
Red Tapism
Rescued from an Eagle's Nest
A Restful Ride
The Ringmaster's Wife
Shipowner's Daughter
The Suburbanite's Ingenious Alarm
Tenor with Leather Lungs
That Squally Beach
The Tramp Hypnotist
Valiant Son
The Viking's Bride
Witch's Secret

Jan 20 The Water Babies; or, The Little Chimney Sweep

Jan 22 Lonesome Junction

Jan 25 Animated Portraits
The Butterflies
Charmed Sword
The Financial Scare
For a Flower
A Gay Old Boy
Good Luck for the Coming Year
The Hostage
The Irish Blacksmith
A Kindhearted Gentleman
The King and the Jester
The Newlyweds First Meal
Pa Takes Up Physical Culture
Picturesque Smyrna
The Pretty Typist
Skillful Policemen
Slave's Hate
Why the Wedding Was Put Off
Will He Overtake Them?

Feb 1 The Blind Boy
Caught, a Detective Story
Classmates
A Cowboy Elopement
Dog's Music Hall
Excursion to Moon
Fireside Reminiscences
A Gypsy's Revenge
His Week's Wages; or, Where's That Quarter?
The Hoosier Fighter
The Intermittent Alarm Clock
London Streets
The Magnetic Eye
A Phlegmatic Gentleman
The Playful Tenant
Sold Again
Soldier's Antics
The Thieving Hand
Under the Star Spangled Banner
A Yankee Man-o-Warsman's Fight for Love

Feb 3 Ancient Headgear
Gainsborough Hat
Music Hath Charms
Oh, That Cat
The Scout

Feb 8 Artistic Rag-Pickers
Babies Will Play
Evangeline
Flower of Youth
Francesca da Rimini; or, The Two Brothers
Gabriel Grub
Galvanic Fluid; or, More Fun with Liquid Electricity
A Gamble for a Woman
The Good Luck of a "Souse"
Home for the Holidays
The Runaway Horse
Sandwich Woman

Feb 10 Bobby's Kodak
The Strenuous War Veteran's Story
Uncle's Clock

Feb 15 Avenged by the Sea
Bobby's Birthday
Cabman's Delusion
A Comedy of Errors
The Count of No Account
A Country Drama
A Day at the Sea Shore
Discharging the Maid
Electrocuted
Farman Aeroplane
Fire Maneuvers in Madrid
Forsaken
Incendiary Foreman
"Louder Please"
Lover and Bicycle
Making Charcoal
Man with Calf's Head
Mr. Shortsighted Goes Shrimping
Monte Cristo
Neapolitan's Revenge
Rival Barbers
A Sculptor's Welsh Rabbit Dream
The Story of an Egg
Touaregs in Their Country
Woman's Army

Feb 17 An Episode of the French Revolution
Satan's Little Jaunt
The Soldier's Wedding

Feb 19 The Snowman

Feb 22 Adventures of a Beggar
Any Barrels to Sell?
I'm Mourning the Loss of Chloe
The Little Cripple
Scullion's Dream
Starting of Around the World Automobile Race

Feb 27 The Princess in the Vase

Feb 28 A Leap Year Proposal

Feb 29 The Banan' Man
Coke Industry
Cold Storage Love
College Days
Cruel Joke
Cupid's Pranks
Custom Officers Mystified
The Deceiver
Esquimaux of Labrador
The Farmer's Daughter; or, The Wages of Sin
Hackenschmidt-Rodgers Wrestling Match
His Sweetheart When a Boy
Hold-Up in Calabria
House to Let; or, The New Tenants
Iceboat Racing on Lake St. Clair
It Is Not the Cowl That Makes the Friar
Jealous Husband
Jerusalem
Mashing the Masher
Michigan vs. Penn Football game
Miracles of a Pain Pad
The One-Legged Man
Othello
Outside Inn
Outwitted
Painless Extraction
Pierrot's Jealousy
Playing at Chess
Poor Little Match Girl
Rag Picker's Christmas
Regattas in London
Reproduction of Burns-Palmer Fight, London [England], February 10th, 1908
The Stowaway
Troubles of a Grass Widower
Unlucky Old Flirt
Up-to-Date Removal

Mar [day undetermined]
The Burglar's Child
Comic Serenade
A Country Girl in Philadelphia
Duel After the Ball
A Faithful Wife
A Fool and His Money
Julius Caesar
Meet Me at the Station
No Children Wanted
A Persistent Actor
Rube Goes to College
Troubles of Too Ardent Admirers
Winning the Gloves

Mar 1 Launching the Roma
Too Much Champagne
What a Razor Can Do

Mar 4 All Is Fair in Love and War

Mar 7 And a Little Child Shall Lead Them
Betrayed by One's Feet
The Boarder Got the Haddock
Captain Kidd
Dr. Jekyll and Mr. Hyde
Duchess' Crime
The Explosive Calf
Henry Hudson
The Mad Musician [An Escape from an Insane Asylum]
The Mattress
Northern Venice
Only Thoughtlessness
Playmates
Sad Awakening
The Squawman's Daughter
A Statue on a Spree
The Tricky Twins
Washington at Valley Forge
'Way Down East
A Workman's Honor
The Yellow Peril

Mar 8 A Bewitching Woman
The Mummy
A New Way of Traveling
The Story of Treasure Island
That Mother-in-Law Is a Bore

Mar 11 The Boy Detective; or, The Abductors Foiled

Mar 14 The Baby Show
Billy Is on Fire
A Briton's Promise
The Curate's Courtship
Custom Officer's Pull
Electric Sword
For the Baby's Sake
The French Spy
The Genii of Fire
In a Difficult Position
The Inquisitive Fly and the Bald Head

Lost, a Pretty Dog
Mr. and Mrs. Jollygood Go Tandeming
My Watch Is Slow
Nellie, the Pretty Typewriter
A New Way to Pay Debts
Our New Errand Boy
A Rape Under Louis XVI
Remorse
See the Point?
Student's Joke on the Porter
Suspicious Husband
Toula's Dream
Mar 15 Angel of the Village
At the Stage Door; or, Bridget's Romance
A Child's Prayer; or, The Good Samaritan
For He's a Jolly Good Fellow
The Frog
Shamus O'Brien
Mar 18 Her First Adventure [Kidnapped with the Aid of a Street Piano]
Mar 21 Animated Snowballs
Beauty Parlors
Caught by Wireless
The Cook Wins
The Devil's Three Sins
The Dream of an Opium Fiend
Easy Money
Engulfed in Quicksands
Gaston Visits Museum
Gendarme Has a Keen Eye
Good-Hearted Sailor
A Good Joke
His Daughter's Voice
The Hot Temper
I Have Won a Pig
Just His Luck
The Magic Bag
The Money Lender
Orderly Jameson
Poor Pa's Folly
The Robbers and the Jew
A Romance of the Fur Country
The Skull and the Sentinel
Stage Memories of an Old Theatrical Trunk
'Twixt Love and Duty; or, A Woman's Heroism
The Vestal
Wedding in Brittany
When Our Sailor Son Comes Home
Whimsical People
Willie's Magic Wand
Mar 28 Avaricious Father
The Caleb Powers Trial
A Country Girl's Seminary Life and Experiences
Different Ways of Smuggling
Do It Now!
A Dream of Youth
Friday, the 13th
The Girl across the Way
The Idler
Jim Gets a New Job
A Narrow Escape
Old Isaacs, the Pawnbroker
Our Own Little Flat
The Pursuit of a Suit
Scarlet Letter
Swashbuckler
Swedish Dances
The Tale of a Shirt
Transformation of a Horse
Mar 29 Cupid's Realm; or, A Game of Hearts
A Modern Samson
The Waif
Apr [day undetermined]
Colored Maid Getting Rid of a Suitor
Crowded Street-Congested Street Society
The Curse of Gold
The Dancing Legs
Dora: A Rustic Idyll
The Drink Cure
The Fake Windstorm
The Fisherman's Model
Gold-Buys
The Hallroom Boys Received Queer Freight
Masked Policeman
The Merry Widow at a Supper Party
Mrs. Trouble
The New Breakfast Food
Scene in a Dressing Room
Selling a Model
That Awful Stork
Then Tramp He Woke Up
What the Dude Lost in the Dressing Room
Apr 4 After the Celebration!
Amateur Acrobat
Big Bow Mystery
Boats
Brigand's Daughter
A False Accusation
Getting Rid of His Dog
Hypnotizing Mother-in-Law
A Mexican Love Story
Moonbeams
The Moonshiner's Daughter
The Mountaineers
The Mystery of a Diamond Necklace
A Night with the Masqueraders in Paris
The Old Maid's Inheritance
The Orphans
Pulcinella
The Robber's Sweetheart
The Soul Kiss
Starvelings
Struck
Terrors of the Deep
What a Good Wine
When the House Rent Was Due
Apr 5 Black Princess
The Fresh-Air Fiend; or, How He Was Cured
Military Airship "Ville de Paris"
The Sacrifice
Sleeping Beauty
The Two Brothers
Apr 6 Romeo and Juliet
Apr 7 A Famous Escape
Apr 11 Angelo, Tyrant of Padua
Antics of Two Spirited Citizens
The Astrologer
The Bad Sister
Basket Mystery or the Traveler's Jest
Boy and the Coalman
The Captain's Wives
Champion Wrestling Bear
A Contagious Nervousness
The Deserter
A Dislocated Veteran
Doctor's Lunch
The Doctor's Monkey
The Dog's Scent
The Door-Keeper's Substitute
The Downfall of the Burglars' Trust
A Dream
Dynamiters
The Edily
The Enchanted Boots
Free Admission
The Gambling Demon
Gotch-Hackenschmidt Wrestling Match
The Half-Moon Tavern
In Morocco
Judith and Holopherne
A Lady Who Likes a Moustache
Lion Hunting
Lion's Tilting Contest
Ma-in-Law Mesmerized
A Magician's Love Test
The Man in the Overalls
The Mayor's Misfortune
The Mishaps of a Bashful Man
Nephew's Luck
The Novice Tight-Rope Walker
£100 Reward
Pierrot and the Devil
Presidential Possibilities
The Professor's Secret
The Scandalous Boys
Shanghai, China
Stone Industry in Sweden
Tale the Autumn Leaves Told
Travels of a Flea
Trip to Norway
Vengeance in Normandy
The Videos
Wanted, a Maid
Willie's Magic Wand
Apr 12 After Midnight; or, A Burglar's Daughter
Champagne Industry
The Cossacks
The Cowboy and the Schoolmarm
James Boys in Missouri
Jealousy
Lottery Ticket
Modern Sculptors
Troubles of a Flirt
Who Needed the Dough?
Why That Actor Was Late
Will Grandfather Forgive?
Apr 13 Neighborly Neighbors
The Parents' Devotion
Apr 15 The King of the Cannibal Islands
Michael Strogoff
Apr 16 The Little Easter Fairy
Something on His Mind
Apr 18 The Accordion
Animated Clock
The Animated Dummy
A Bear in the Flat
Butler's Misdeed
Cider Industry
The Coal Man's Savings
The Consequences of a Night Out
The Crusaders' Return
The Drama on a Roof
The Enchanted Guitar
Engaged Against His Will
False Money
Hunchback Brings Luck
Ice Cream Jack
Improvised Servant
International Illusionist
Just Retribution
Love's Victim
The Miracle
The Misadventures of an Equilibrist
The Nomads
Peggy's Portrait
The Prophetess of Thebes
Railway Tragedy
The Shepherd
The Ski-ing Maniac
The Spirit
Thirsty Moving Men
Tony Has Eaten Garlic
Uncle Bill's Bull
Useful Present for a Child
A Visit to the Public Nursery
Woman's Forbearance
Youthful Treasure Seekers
Apr 19 Christmas Eve
Macbeth, Shakespeare's Sublime Tragedy
A Peaceful Inn
Apr 20 The Fatal Card
Apr 22 The Grandmother's Fables
Hulda's Lovers
Nero and the Burning of Rome
Sappho
Apr 23 Willie's Party
The Wrong Overcoat
Apr 25 The Airship; or, 100 Years Hence
A Disastrous Oversight
The Dog Cop
A French Guard's Bride
Give Me Back My Dummy
Harry, the Country Postman
The Holy City
Ihles & Antonio, Boxers
Juggler Juggles
The Legend of Sleepy Hollow
Long Distance Wireless Photography
A Lord for a Day
A Miser's Punishment
A Mistaken Identity
A Modern Naval-Hero
The Poacher's Wife
A Poor Man's Romance
Rejoicing Dreams
Sausage
Tramp's Revenge
True Hearts Are More Than Coronets
Under the Livery
Unwilling Chiropodist
Well-Thy Water
Workman's Revenge
Apr 27 Acrobatic Pills
The Amateur Hypnotist
Apr 29 The King's Messenger
The Merry Widow Waltz Craze
Apr 30 Beg Pardon!
Oh, My Feet!
May [day undetermined]
A False Alarm
Farmer Greene's Summer Boarders
Fly Paper
Fun in the Hay
The Girl and the Gossip
The Girls Dormitory
Jealousy Behind the Scenes
Man Under the Bed
Nellie's Camera
The Stolen Flask
May 2 The Accusing Vision
Alone at Last
The Baby Strike
Bad Bargain
Bad Boys
The Best Glue

Biarritz
The Blue Bonnet
Briarcliff Auto Race
Cat and Dog Show
The Champagne Bottle
Clogmaking in Brittany
Concealed Love
Cowboy Sports and Pastimes
A Day in the Life of a Suffragette
Diabolical Pickpocket
The Drummer's Day Off
Fiji Islanders
The First Kiss
The First Lottery Prize
For Kate's Health
Forgotten Ones
Fox Hunting
Freddie's Little Love Affair
Frolicsome Powders
Funeral of the Late King of Portugal
Generous Policeman
The Great Trunk Robbery
Greediness Punished
The Greedy Girl
The Hanging Lamp
Harvesting
Humanity Through Ages
In the Land of the Gold Mines
Indian Bitters; or, The Patent Medicine Man
John Is No More a Child
Kidnapped by Gypsies
Lazy Jim's Luck
Life and Customs of Naples
Love's Sacrifice
Mandrel's Feats
Marvelous Pacifier
Men and Women
A Misalliance
The Mission of a Flower
A Mistake in the Dark
Mistaken Identity
Mr. Smith's Difficulties in the Shoe Store
Mrs. Stebbins' Suspicions Unfounded
Modern Hotel
Music Teacher
Mysterious Stranger
The Near-Sighted Hunter
No Divorce Wanted
The Outcast Heroine
Oyster Farming
Panorama of Venice
Parlez Vous Francais? (Do You Speak French?)
The Pastry Cook
Poor Aunt Matilda
Poor Schoolmistress
Portland Stone Industry
The Price of a Favor
A Priest's Conscience
A Ride in a Subway
Rip Van Winkle
The Rival Lovers
Rival Sherlock Holmes
A Sacrifice for Work
Shooting Party
Ski Contest
Soldiers in the Italian Alps
The Statue of Rocco
The Stolen Dagger
A Story of the 17th Century
The Sugar Industry
Sweden
Tell-Tale Cinematograph
Tommy the Fireman
Turning the Tables; or, Waiting on the Waiter
A Useful Beard
What One Small Boy Can Do
A Wife's Devotion
Wrongly Charged
May 4 The Bride's Dream
May 6 Bridal Couple Dodging Cameras
Don't Pull My Leg
Ker-Choo
The Music Master
The Sculptor's Nightmare
May 7 The Mysterious Phonograph
Stop That Alarm!
May 8 Dolly, the Circus Queen
Night Riders
The Under Dog
The White Squaw
With the Fleet in Frisco
May 9 The Bargee's Daughter
The Bargeman's Son
Bloodless Duel
Bogus Magic Powder
The Boxing Englishman
Country about Rome
The Doctor's Dodge
Dog Training
Dreams and Realities
Each in His Turn
Environs of Naples
Excursion to Montreal
The False Coin
Female Police Force
The Flower Girl
The Gambler's Wife
Gathering Indian Figs
Gendarme's Honor
The Guileless Country Lassie
Haunted Castle
In China (Hong Chu Fou)
In the Barber Shop
Indiscreetness of the Kinematograph
The Interrupted Bath
Leap Year; or, She Would Be Wed
A Lover's Hazing
The Lover's Tribulation
The Maid's Last Day
Manoeuvres of Artillery
The Memory of His Mother
A Mother's Crime
My Cabby Wife
Peasant's Difficulties in Society
Professor Bounder's Pills
Sabot Making
She Wanted to Be an Actress
Sicily Illustrated
The Smokeless Stove
Spiritualistic Seance
The Squaw Man
Students' Jokes
Tit for Tat; or, Outwitted by Wit
Tommy Has the Spleen
The Two Guides
The Two Rivals
The Wand Has Lost Its Magic
When Honor Is Lost Everything Is Lost
May 11 The Great Jewel Robbery
May 13 The Gentleman Burglar
May 14 The Automatic Laundry
The "Merry Widow" Hats
May 15 Peck's Bad Boy
May 16 Always Too Late
Artist's Inheritance
Australian Sports and Pastimes
Awkward Orderly
The Basket Maker's Daughter
Bertie's Sweetheart
A Bohemian Romance
The Bond
Canine Sagacity
The Carnival at Nice
Catching a Burglar
Chair, If You Please
The Clown Doctor
Emperor Nero on the Warpath
An Extraordinary Overcoat
A Faithless Friend
Fond of His Paper
The Gambler
A Good Boy
A Good Thief
Japanese Butterflies
Kidnapped for Hate
Little Chimney Sweep
The Little Flower Girl
Locked Up
Lost Pocketbook
Madam Is Capricious
The Magic Powder
Meeting of Kings and Queens
Motoring over the Alps
Mountaineer's Son
Nasty Sticky Stuff
Nellie, the Beautiful Housemaid
Nobleman's Rights
An Odd Pair of Limbs
Oscar's Elopement
The Perverse Statues
Pretty Dairymaid
Pretty Flower Girl
The Ramming of H. M. S. Gladiator by the St. Paul
A Red Man's Justice
The Runaway Lab
Running for Office
St. Patrick's Day in New York
Schoolboy's Joke
Scotland
Sport from All the World
Stolen Boots
Stolen Sausage
The Strong Man's Discretion
These Gentlemen Are with Me
Thirty Years After
The Uncle from America
Waiting upon the Waiter
Why Smith Left Home
The Winning Number
The Young Protector
Youthful Samaritan
May 18 The Cause of All the Trouble
May 20 Curious Mr. Curio
When Knights Were Bold
May 21 The Circus Boy
The Tale of a Pig
May 23 All for a Bird
Bill, the Bill Poster, and Pete, the Paperhanger
Blind Woman's Story
Catholic Centennial Parade
End of a Dream
A Fake Diamond Swindler
Fashionable Hat
The Flight from Seraglio
A Good Medicine
He Got Soap in His Eyes
Imperial Canal
Justinian's Human Torches
Legend of a Ghost
A Lover's Ruse; or, The Miser's Daughter
The Old Story
The Orphan; or, A Mountain Romance
Poverty and Probity
The Stolen Dummy
Summer Boarders Taken In
Troubles of a New Drug Clerk
The Unexperienced Cabman
Unfortunate Pickpocket
Winter Manoeuvres of the Norwegian Army
May 25 The Near-Sighted Professor [His Trials and Tribulations]
Why He Signed the Pledge
May 26 A Night of Terror
May 27 An Animated Doll
The Painter's Revenge
May 28 A Gallant Knight
May 29 His Day of Rest
May 30 Anti-Hair Powder
Around the Coast of Brittany
Artificial Preparation of the Diamond
Athletic Woman
Battle of Flowers in Nice
Burglar's New Trick
Carnival at Nice
The Castle Ghosts
A Complicated Duel
Expensive Marriage
Fire! Fire!
The Fireman's Daughter
A Fool and His Money Are Soon Parted; or, The Prodigal Son Up-to-Date
Hedge Hog Coat
Hide and Seek
A Husband's Revenge; or, The Poisoned Pills
In a Submarine
Inventor's Son's Downfall
Lucky Accident
Magical Suit of Armor
The Marriage of a French Soldier
A Mean Man
The Minstrel's Sacrifice
Mischievous Diabolo
Mr. Drawee
Mr. Farman's Airship
An Occasional Porter
A One Man Band
Oxford and Cambridge Boat Race
The Persistent Beggar
Red Man's Revenge
Remorseful Son
River Avon
River in Norway
Rugby Match
The Salt Did It; or, If You Want To Catch a Bird, Put Salt on It's [sic] Tail
Sammy's Sucker
Steel Industry
Story of a Foundling
Student's Predicament
Unlucky Luck
Warsmen at Play
The Will
May 31 In the Nick of Time

Jun [day undetermined]
The Clown
East Lynne; or, Led Astray
Fluffy's New Corsets
The Girls Boxing Match
Harlem Flats
No Trifling with Love
The Soul Kiss
Special Muto Reel Mellin's Food Co.
Three Weeks
Too Many in Bed
Tracked by a Woman
Two Sides of the Wall

Jun 1 The Greed for Gold
Jun 2 Thompson's Night Out
Jun 3 Skinny's Finish
Jun 4 The Miner's Daughter
Jun 5 The Romance of an Egg
Jun 6 An American Soldier
Arabian Dagger
The Braggart; or, What He Said He Would Do and What He Really Did
The Chimney Sweeper
Coon in Red
Damon and Pythias
Don Juan
East Lynne
Family of Cats
Father's Lesson
Fish Preserving at Astrakhan
Hunting Deer
Justice of the Redskin
Lady Barrister
Mrs. Pimpernell's Gown
Not Yet, But Soon
The Prodigal Son
Romeo and Juliet, a Romantic Story of the Ancient Feud Between the Italian Houses of Montague and Capulet
The Shadow of the Law
Tormented by His Mother-in-Law
The Two Traveling Bags; or, The Adventures of Percy White and Pauline Wells
Weird Symphony
Jun 7 Texas Tex
Jun 8 The Hand of Fate
Magnetic Vapor
Jun 9 'Ostler Joe
Jun 10 The Blue and the Gray; or, The Days of '61
Jun 11 Robbie's Pet Rat
Two Brothers of the G.A.R.
Jun 12 Mixed Babies
Jun 13 Brazil—The Cascades
Cast Off by His Father
The Cat's Revenge
A Chance Shot
Circumstantial Evidence, or, An Innocent Victim
Clarinet Solo
Curiosity Punished
Drama in the Tyrol
Dynamite Duel
The Effective Hair Grower
Faithful Governess Rewarded
The Gentle Sex
Gratitude
Held for Ransom
Hunting Teddy Bears
I Can't Read English
Joyous Surprise
Just Like a Woman
Magic Dice
The Man and His Bottle
Man Hunt
Messenger's Mistake
Misadventures of a Sheriff
The Miser
Mr. Brown Has a Tile Loose
Music and Poetry
A Noble Jester; or, Faint Heart Never Won Fair Lady
The Old Actor
The Paralytic's Vengeance
Penniless Poet's Luck
A Poor Knight and the Duke's Daughter
The Pupa Changes into a Butterfly
The Ragpicker's Daughter
Sailor in Philippines
The Saloon-Keeper's Nightmare
Side Show Wrestlers
Three Sportsmen and a Hat
A Tiresome Play
Tracked by the Police Dog
Two Gentlemen
Up-to-Date Clothes Cleaning
Usefulness at an End
When Casey Joined the Lodge
Winter Time in Northern Europe
Jun 15 An Honest Newsboy's Reward
Two Little Dogs
Jun 16 The Invisible Fluid
Jun 17 Honesty Is the Best Policy
The Little Mad-Cap; or, Oh Splash!
The Tragedian
Jun 18 Adventures of Mr. Troubles
Mephisto's Affinity
Jun 19 The Man in the Box
Jun 20 Astrakhan Fisheries
A Bachelor's Baby; or, A General Misunderstanding
Beatrice Cenci
The Bifton Burglar
The Book Agent
Boston Normal School Pageant
The Chauffeur's Dream
The Courtship of Bessie Barton
The Determined Lovers; or, Where There's a Will, There's a Way
Double Suicide
Driven by Hunger
The Fighting Parson
Grandfather's Pills
The Handy Man at Play
The Little Peace-Maker
Lively Pranks with a Fake Python
Love in 20 Minutes
The Matterhorn
Music Which Hath No Charms
The New Maid
Orphan's Easter Eggs
Peculiar People
Poisoned Pills
The Pony Express
Poor Pussy
The Reprieve, an Episode in the Life of Abraham Lincoln
Ruffians Thrashed
A Russian Bear Hunt
The Selfish Man
Swiss Peasants' Festival
Tribulations of a Mayor
A Trip on the Venetian Canals
Unappreciated Patron
Unlucky Artist
Victim of His Honesty
The Viege Zermatt Railway
Younger Brothers
Jun 22 The Old Maid's Parrot
Romance in a Gypsy Camp
Jun 23 The Outlaw
Jun 24 Love Will Find a Way
Jun 25 Philadelphia, the Cradle of Liberty
The Student's Prank; or, A Joke on His Parents
Jun 26 Over the Hills to the Poor House
Jun 27 Avenged; or, The Two Sisters
Doctor Jink's Liquid Life Restorer
The Fat Baby
For the Sake of a Crown
Held by Bandits
Leap Year Proposals of an Old Maid
The Lost Coin
Magnetic Removal
Mr. Boozer Gets a Fright
Mysterious Flames
Nocturnal Thieves
Our Dog Friends
The Patriot; or, The Horrors of War
The Slaves of the Czar
The Story the Boots Told
Troublesome Theft
Walks in Soudan
Jun 28 Lady Audley's Secret
Jun 29 Held for Ransom
Jun 30 At the French Ball

Jul [day undetermined]
Driven from Home
"June Bug" Aeroplane
Love and Molasses
Jul 1 Pioneers Crossing the Plains in '49
Jul 2 The New Maid
Outwitted by His Wife
Jul 3 At the Crossroads of Life
Jul 4 Ancient Rome
A Bird of Freedom
The Blackmailer
Blessing the Boats in Arcachon
Bull Fight in Arcachon
Busy Fiancé
The Chorus Girl
The Closing Hour
Constantinople
The Country of the "Bogoudens"
The Dressmaker's Surprise
The Dreyfus Affair
A Fine Easter Egg
Fox Hunting
French Dairy Farm
A Gendarme's Tribulations
Heavy Seas
Husband Wanted
Interrupted Romance
A Love Affair of the Olden Days
Love and Fortune
Mr. Smith, the New Recruit
Mother-in-Law and the Artist's Model
Native Life in Sudan
Niagara Falls in Winter
The Nihilist
On Bad Terms with the Janitor
Porcelain Industry
Precipitated Removal
Riviera in Motor Car
A Rustic Heroine; or, In the Days of King George
Scenes in Sicily
Silk Hats Ironed
The Specter
Swiss Alps
They Want a Divorce
A Tragedy of Japan
An Unfortunate Mistake
Unrequited Love
Who Owns the Basket?
The Yale-Harvard Boat Race
Jul 6 Artificial Brooding
A Bad Boy
A Costly Coat
Fountains of Rome
Frightened by Burglars
In the Riviera
Keenest of the Two
The Leaking Glue Pot
Lessons in Jiu Jitsu
Love and Hatred
The Mediterranean Fleet
Nothing to Declare; or, Bested by Custom Officials
The Pastry Cook's Misfortune
A Poacher's Trick
Posthumous Jealousy
St. Marc Place
A Second-Hand Camera
The Troublesome Fly
The Two Pickpockets
Views of New York
Wanted: A Colored Servant
A Western Romance in the Days of '49
Jul 7 The Kentuckian
Jul 9 Two Little Shoes
Jul 10 The Stage Rustler
Jul 11 The Accuser
The Candidate
Cumbersome Baby
Get Me a Stepladder
The Guilty Conscience
The International Horse Show
Jealous Fiancé
John's New Suit; or, Why He Didn't Go to Church
Latest Style Airship
Noisy Neighbors
The Organ-Grinder's Daughter
Over the Sticks
The Perjurer
A Plain Clothes Man
Professor Bric-a-Brac's Inventions
The Shipwreckers
The Spirit of '76
[The Spoilers]
Stockholm
The Stone Breaker
A Trip Through Savoy
'Twixt Love and Duty
Unsuccessful Flirts
The Vanishing Tramp
Votes for Women
Jul 13 The Best Remedy
Consoling the Widow
Disappointing Rehearsal
Father Is Late! Go Fetch Him
Good Night Clown
The Grand Canal in Venice
His Girl's Last Wish
The Lady with the Beard; or, Misfortune to Fortune
The Robbery of the Citizen's Bank
Sammy's Idea
The Simpleton

The Substitute Automatic Servant
Through the Oural Mountains
A Tricky Uncle
The Triumph of Love
Trying to Get Rid of a Bad Dollar
The Two Brothers
Two Little Motorists
A Walking Tree
Wandering Musician
Jul 14 The Adventures of Dollie
Jul 15 The Boston Tea Party
The Little Coxswain of the Varsity Eight
Jul 16 "Captain Molly" or, The Battle of Monmouth
Dr. Curem's Patients
Jul 17 The Fight for Freedom
Jul 18 A Bashful Young Man
Bothersome Husband
The Chieftain's Revenge; or, A Tragedy in the Highlands of Scotland
Contagious Nervous Twitching
Dynamite Man
The Dynamite Man
The Father Is to Blame
Flight of the "June Bug"
In the Government Service
Korea
Motoring Around the World
The Mourners; or, A Clever Undertaking
Mystery of the Mountains
The Poor Officer
Runaway Mother-in-Law
Russian Review of the Fiftieth Regiment
Stricken Blind; or, To Forgive Is Divine
The Wish Bone
Jul 20 Dick's Sister
Jul 21 The Black Viper
Jul 22 The Face on the Barroom Floor
Fly Paper
Jul 23 A Fatal Likeness
Jul 24 The Tavern-Keeper's Daughter
Jul 25 The Affair of the Select Hotel
Bobby White in Wonderland
Crocodile Turns Thief
Cumbersome First Fight
The Directoire Gown
The Girl Nihilist
Hard to Get Arrested
Home Work in China
I Won One Hundred Thousand
It Sticks Everything—Even Iron
King Scatterbrain's Troubles
Lady Jane's Flight, a 17th Century Romance
Levitsky's Insurance Policy; or, When Thief Meets Thief
Living Posters
Matrimonial Stages
Mr. Softhead Has a Good Time
Mrs. Guinness, the Female Bluebeard
A New Fruit
The New Hired Girl
Obeying Her Mother
Off to Morocco
On the War Path
Physical Phenomena
A Pleasant Evening at the Theatre
A Policeman's Dream
The Press Gang; or, A Romance in the Time of King George III
Promoted Corporal
The Renegade
The Saw Mill
Story of a Fishermaiden
The Story of the King of Fregola
Sturdy Sailor's Honor
The Taft Pictures
Three Maiden Ladies and a Bull
Too Polite
The Torrent
Transformation with a Hat Rim
The Tyrant Feudal Lord
Under the Black Flag
Venice and the Lagoon
Weary Waggles' Busy Day
Where Is My Prisoner?
A Wolf in Sheep's Clothing
Jul 27 The White Chief
Jul 28 The Redman and the Child
Jul 29 A Dumb Hero
Jul 30 The Woman Who Gambles
Jul 31 Deceived Slumming Party
Aug [day undetermined]
The Forged Will
French Cops Learning English
H. R. H. The Prince of Wales Decorating the Monument of Champlain and Receiving Addresses of Welcome from the Mayor of Quebec, the Governor General of Canada and Vice-President Fairbanks, Representative of the United States
H. R. H. The Prince of Wales Viewing the Grand Military Review on the Plains of Abraham, Quebec
Hobo's Revenge
Oriental Black Art
The Rainmaker
Tribulations of a Photographer
Aug 1 Baffled Lover
Black Eyed Susan
A Boarding House Acquaintance
Captured by Telephone
The Chronic Life-Saver
A Comical Execution
The Dear Little Heart
An Embarrassing Gift
The Female Politician, Mrs. Bell, Is Nominated for Mayor
Fishing Boats in the Ocean
Follow Your Leader and the Master Follows Last
Head over Heels in Politics
His Mother's Melody
The Indian's Gratitude
An Interesting Conversation
It Smells of Smoke
The Killing Remorse
The Learned Dr. Cornelius
The Little Magician
Love Laughs at Locksmiths, an 18th Century Romance
Making of Tomato Sauce
The Miraculous Flowers
Out of Patience
Overflowing in Italy
Peasant and Prince
Picturesque Naples
The Policeman and the Cook
A Pretty Little Dog
The Road to Ruin
The Roses
Secret of Hypnotism
The Secret of the Iron Mask
Sensational Duel
The Smuggler Automobilist
Too Hungry to Eat
The Tramp's Daughter
The Uncle's Fortune
The Vacuum Cleaner
The Viking's Daughter, the Story of the Ancient Norsemen
Wanderer's Return
Wanted—A Son-in-Law on Trial
War Episode
Water Cure
Aug 3 A Policeman for an Hour
The Sensational Sheath Gown
Aug 4 The Bandit's Waterloo: The Outwitting of an Andalusian Brigand by a Pretty Senora
Aug 5 Tales the Searchlight Told
Aug 6 The Bogus Lord
Aug 7 A Calamitous Elopement: How It Proved a Windfall for Burglar Bill
Aug 8 The Boundary
The Brigand's Daughter
The Child's Forgiveness
A Country Drama
The Cowboy's Baby
The Curse of Drink
Flower Fete on the Bois de Boulogne
The French Airship La Republique
German Dragoons Crossing the Elbe
Grand Prix Motor Race at Dieppe
The Great Northwest
The Gypsy and the Painter
A Gypsy Girl's Love
The Gypsy Model
The Improvised Statue
The Inconvenience of Taking Moving Pictures
An Indian's Honor
Jewel of a Servant
The Knowing Birds
The Little Detective
The Masque Ball
Miss Hold's Puppets
Moscow Under Water
A Prodigal Parson
The Promise! Henri Promises Never to Gamble Again
The Rag Pickers' Wedding
Reedham Boys' Festival Drill
Royal Voyage to Canada
Susceptible Youth
A Tale of a Hat
The Tempter
The Third Degree
Trooping the Colour
Troublesome Husband
Tyrolean Alps Customs
The Walls of Sing Sing
The Water Sprite, a Legend of the Rhine
A Wonderful Fluid
Aug 10 The Light in the Window
Aug 11 The Greaser's Gauntlet
Aug 12 Life's a Game of Cards
Aug 13 The Crushed Tragedian
Wanted: An Artist's Model
Aug 14 The Man and the Woman
Aug 15 Army Dogs
Buried Alive; or, Frolics on the Beach at Coney Island
The Cheese Race
Dieppe Circuit, 1908
The Dog and the Pipe
A Good Repentance
The Gypsy's Revenge
Human Vultures
The Kind-Hearted Bootblack; or Generosity Rewarded
A Kind-Hearted Policeman
Lady-Killer Foiled
Moscow Under Water
Mother's Darling
Music Hall Agent's Dream
New York
The Picture
The Poisoned Bouquet, an Italian Tragedy of the XV Century
The Poor Man, Homeless, Wants to Go to Prison
The Powerful Tenor
Prospective Heirs
The Sailor's Dog
Tercentenary Celebrations to Commemorate the 300th Anniversary of the Founding of Quebec by Champlain
Uncle's Rejected Present
Undesirable Tenants
Aug 17 The King's Diamond
Aug 18 The Fatal Hour
Aug 19 Aeroplane Flights by Henry Farman, Coney Island, N.Y., U.S.A.
When Ruben Comes to Town
Aug 20 Scenes from the Battlefield of Gettysburg, the Waterloo of the Confederacy
Aug 21 For Love of Gold
Aug 22 The Automatic Nurse
The Blue Bird
The Broken Violin
Brothers in Arms
Bryan's Reception in New York
The Checker Fiends
Child Slave Freed
Enchanted Hat
The 50th Regiment Jubilee
The Forester's Remedy
Freedom for All
His First Job
The Indian Sorcerer
Jim Is Fond of Garlic
Just Plain Folks, the Story of a Simple Country Girl
A Kindness Never Goes Unrewarded
The Magic of Catchy Songs
Manual of a Perfect Gentleman
The Merry Widower; or, The Rejuvenation of a Fossil
The Miller, His Son and the Ass
The Mischances of a Photographer
The Mishaps of the New York-Paris Auto Race
The Mystery of the Garrison
Oh, What Lungs!
The Padrone
Picnickers Disturbed
A Trip Through Russia
Two Crazy Bugs
The Village Gossip
The Woes of Roller Skates
A Woman's Jealousy
Wouldn't It Tire You?
Aug 24 Rivals for a Week
The Wrong Valise
Aug 25 Balked at the Altar
Aug 26 Romance of a War Nurse
Aug 27 The Midnight Express
Aug 28 For a Wife's Honor

Aug 29 The Baseball Fan
The Bewitched Tricycle
Biscuits Like Mother Used to Make
The Broken Heart
A Country Lad
A Daughter's Honesty
A Disastrous Flirtation
The Discoverers, a Grand Historical Pageant Picturing the Discovery and Founding of New France, Canada
The Duck's Finish
The Enchanted Mantle
The Eruption of Mt. Vesuvius
The Escape of the Ape
A False Alarm
From Bagdad
The Frontierman's Bride
A Gilded Fool
A Good Dinner Badly Digested
The Grocer's Show
The Hapless Hubby
The Happy Man's Shirt
The Hayseed's Bargain
Head-Dresses Worn in Brittany
How Simpkins Discovered the North Pole
Lonely Gentleman; or, Incompatibility of Temper
Mr. Fuzz
Mrs. Toney's Suitors
Moving by Electricity
Napoleon and the English Sailor
On the Coast of Norway
A Pair of Kids
The Power of Labor
Pretty Flower Girl
Riches, Poverty and Honesty
Robin Hood
Romance of the Old Mill
Salome; or, The Dance of the Seven Veils
Summer in North Europe
A Tale of Two Cities
Troublesome Carbuncle
The Two Models
Under the Sea in a Submarine
Wanted, a Cook
Yusuf the Pirate

Aug 31 Fascinating Fluffy Dimples

Sep [day undetermined]
The Chorus Man's Revenge
A Fatal Temptation
The Hat of Fortune
Heating Powder
It's Never Too Late to Mend
Make Yourself at Home
The Mardi Gras Parade at Coney Island
Reception for the Victorious Olympic Team of American Athletes at City Hall, New York

Sep 1 Betrayed by a Handprint
Samson and Delilah

Sep 2 A Comedy in Black and White
Heard over the Phone

Sep 3 The Pawnbroker

Sep 4 Monday Morning in a Coney Island Police Court

Sep 5 The Clown's Christmas Eve
The Coward
A Dozen of Fresh Eggs
The Dumb Witness
An Enterprising Florist
The Gambler's Fate
The Hidden Hoard
The Hotel Mix-Up
In the Days of the Pilgrims, a Romance of the 15th Century in America
In the Hands of the Enemy
The Laplanders
Lost and Found
The Marathon Race
Oh! What an Appetite
Olympic Games
Professor's Discovery
The School of Life
Stung
The Tramp and the Purse
Two Talented Vagabonds
Western Courtship, a Love Story of Arizona

Sep 8 The Girl and the Outlaw

Sep 9 The Devil
Never Again
Romance of a Taxicab

Sep 11 Behind the Scenes: Where All Is Not Gold That Glitters

Sep 12 Amateur Brigands
Antiquary
The Asphalters' Dilemma
The Beggar
The Blind Woman's Daughter
The Burglar and the Clock
By a Woman's Wit
The Cabby's Wife
The Cattle Rustlers
The Dancing Fiend
The Daughter of the Gypsy
The Diamond Thieves
The Dover Pageant
The Ever-Laughing Gentleman
Fencing Fiend
Fighting the Flames
Goodwood Races
The Great Yellowstone Park Hold-Up
Grotesques
Hamlet
The Hand
The Hand-Cart Race
The Hebrew Fugitive
A Hindoo's Ring
The Isle of Bornholm
King Edward and the German Emperor at Friedrichshof
The Lightning Postcard Artist
The Lion's Bride
Little Walk in Rome
Lottery Ticket
The Marathon Race
The Mesmerist
The Model
Music Hath Its Charms
Olympic Regatta at Henley
Paper Tearing
The Persistent Trombonist
Quebec
Quebec to Niagara
Root in Mexico
Rose, the Flower Girl
The Signalman's Sweetheart
The Son's Crime
The Spiteful Groom
A Stern Father
Strange Inheritance
The Swimming Master
Traveling Through Russia
Tricksy, the Clever Princess
Two Clever Detectives
The Wages of Sin, an Italian Tragedy
The Washerwoman's Revenge
Who Is It?
A Workingman's Dream
The Wrong Lottery Number
Youthful Artist

Sep 13 A Southern Romance of Slavery Days

Sep 15 The Red Girl
Wifey's Strategy

Sep 16 A Wayward Daughter

Sep 18 The Heart of O Yama
Ingomar, the Barbarian

Sep 19 The Amateur Bicyclist
As You Like It
Bathing; or, Charlie and Mary in the Country
Beginning of the Game of Diablo
Brother Lieutenants
Buying a Hat
A Cowboy Escapade
Crazed by Jealousy
His Sweetheart's Birthday
How Glue Is Made
How the Poor Clown's Prayer Was Answered
In the Time of Rebellion
The Lady with the Camellias
The Luckless Spike
The Man with the Big Mouth
A New Electrical Discovery and Its Uses
The New Houseman's Idea
Old Sleuth, the Detective
Paris Fire Brigade at Drill
Policeman's Vision
Salome
The Shepherdess
The Stolen Plans; or, The Boy Detective
A Tale of a Harem: The Caliph and the Pirate
The Umatilla Indians
Unusual Cooking
Willie's Fall from Grace

Sep 20 Custom Officer's Revenge

Sep 21 Gans-Nelson Fight
Hon. William J. Bryan and Hon. John W. Kern
How Rastus Got His Pork Chops
Two Little Breadwinners

Sep 22 Buying a Title
The Leprechaun—An Irish Fairy Story
Not Guilty
A Tricky Painter's Fate
Where the Breakers Roar

Sep 23 Hired-Tired-Fired

Sep 24 In the Nick of Time
The Suicidal Poet

Sep 25 A Smoked Husband

Sep 26 The Artist's Nightmare
The Brahmin's Miracle
The Codfish Industry
Culture of Rice
Duchess of Bracciano
Fatty's Follies
A Great Wrong Righted
The Happiest Day of Her Life
Her Newsboy Friend
How the Coster Sold the Seeds
Magic Dice
The Magic Rubbers
A Magical Tramp
The Magistrate's Conscience
Motor Boat Races, 1908
The Mystery of the Bride, in Black and White
The Thief at the Casino

Sep 28 The Criminal's Daughter
Richard III, a Shakespearian Tragedy
The Ticklish Man

Sep 29 Buncoed Stage Johnnie
Fun with the Bridal Party
Pocahantas — A Child of the Forest
The Stolen Jewels

Sep 30 Beg Pardon
Soul Kiss

Oct [day undetermined]
The Burglar's Ball
The Gondolier's Daughter
Historical Parade
Industrial Parade
The Little Coward
Military Parade, Founders Week Celebration, Philadelphia
Naval Parade
A Rude Awakening
They Forgot the Messenger
What the Copper Saw
The Woman of 1776

Oct 1 A Daughter of Erin
The Masqueraders
Wanted: A Military Man

Oct 2 The Devil
Sandy McPherson's Quiet Fishing Trip
Ten Pickaninnies

Oct 3 The Ayah's Revenge
The Blusterer
Breaking into Society
Bryan in Chicago
Caught Red Handed
Duty Versus Revenge
From the Rococo Times
The Girl I Left Behind Me
Labor Day Parade
The Locket
My Wife's Dog
The Mystery of the Bride in White
Panic in a Village
The Professor's Trip to the Country; or, A Case of Mistaken Identity
Romeo and Juliet
The Sailor's Sweetheart
Sammy's Saw
Spooks Do the Moving
A Sport at the Music Hall

Oct 4 A Basket Party
The Gambler and the Devil
Jap Sports
Jap Women
Palermo and Its Surroundings
The Pardon
Parisian Life in Miniature
A Romance of the Alps
A Strong Gale

Oct 5 Redeemed from Sin
Salome and the Devil to Pay

Oct 6 The Chances of Life
A Grandmother's Story
The Lover's Guide
A Wedding Under Terror
The Zulu's Heart

Oct 7 The Life of Abraham Lincoln
Manon Lescaut

Oct 8 The Ranchman's Love
The Saloon Dance
"When Our Ship Comes In"

Oct 9
- Fantastic Magic
- Father Gets in the Game
- Spending a Holiday
- A Voice from the Dead
- What a Funny Horse

Oct 10
- Andalousie
- Any Rags
- Boxing Mania
- The Countess' Wedding Day
- Deep Down within the Cellar
- A Den of Thieves
- Discharged by the Foreman
- Down in Jungle Town
- The Dynamiter
- Harrigan
- The Helping Hand
- I Want What I Want When I Want It
- I Would Like to Marry You
- I'm Sorry
- I've Taken Quite a Fancy to You
- Just Some One
- L-A-Z-Y
- Leah, the Forsaken
- A Lemon in the Garden of Love
- Lincoln's Speech at Gettysburg
- The Magic Mirror
- Make Believe
- Making Arabian Pottery
- Military Swimming Championship
- A Mother's Fault
- The Old Footlight Favorite
- Paris Fire Brigade
- Rocanbole
- Romance of a School Teacher
- A "Skate" on Skates
- A Stiff Neck
- Stupid Mr. Cupid
- A Talk on Trousers
- Tricked into Giving His Consent
- Troublesome Baby
- Whistle It
- Wouldn't You Like to Have Me for a Sweetheart
- You Got to Love Me a Lot
- Young Heroes of the West

Oct 11
- Doll Making
- The Fake Doctor
- The Innkeeper's Remorse
- The Naughty Little Princess
- Two Broken Hearts, the Story of a Worthless Husband and a Faithful Dog
- Two Great Griefs

Oct 12
- Federal Fete of Wrestling, and Alpino Sports
- The Way They Fooled Dad

Oct 13
- The Barbarian Ingomar
- The Bridge of Sighs
- Jerusalem
- Political Speeches

Oct 14
- His Own Son
- Miscalculated Revenge

Oct 15
- The Bloodstone
- One of the Bravest

Oct 16
- The Court in Session
- Ex-Convict No. 900
- Fire at Sea
- The Puppet's Nightmare
- The Vaquero's Vow
- Victim of Heroism

Oct 17
- An Auto Heroine; or, The Race for the Vitagraph Cup and How It Was Won
- Chauncey Proves a Good Detective
- Crocodile Hunt
- Elixir of Youth
- For the Sake of the Uniform
- Heart of a Gypsy Maid
- His First Frock Coat
- Honeymoon in a Balloon
- Incident from Don Quixote
- A Love Affair
- The Mind Reader
- [Moran-Attel Fight]
- Result of Eating Horseflesh
- A Spanish Romance
- Two's Company, Three's a Crowd
- An Unselfish Guest (?)
- Water Bailiff's Daughter
- What Poverty Leads To
- When Other Lips
- The World's Championship Baseball Series of 1910

Oct 19
- A Desperate Chance
- For His Sister's Sake
- Shadows of Night
- A Treasure of a Pig
- The Witty Ghost

Oct 20
- The Cashier's Romance
- High Jumping at Hurlingham
- Madeira Wicker Chair Industry
- Minstrel Mishaps; or, Late for Rehearsal
- The Planter's Wife
- The Puppet Man's Dream
- Trials of an Educator
- Wheelwright's Daughter

Oct 21
- The Effect of a Shave
- A Father's Will
- The Impersonator's Jokes
- Picturesque Switzerland
- Prince Kin Kin's Malady
- Somnambulic (sic) Bell Ringer
- The Voice of the Heart

Oct 22
- All on Account of a Butterfly
- The Fisherman's Rival
- Hubby's Vacation

Oct 23
- A Fool for Luck; or, Nearly a Policeman
- Over the Hubarthal Railroad
- Romance of a Jewess

Oct 24
- Caught with the Goods
- A Dearly Paid for Kiss
- The Fakir's Dream
- The Free Pass
- How Mabel Found a Husband
- Hunting for Her Better Half
- If I Catch You I Will
- The Little Rope Dancer
- The Merry Widow Hat
- Mysterious Knight
- A Night Out; or, He Couldn't Go Home until Morning
- Pierrette's Talisman
- The Power of Habit
- Preparing for Combat
- The Red Barn Mystery: A Startling Portrayal of the Great Marie Martin Mystery
- The Revengeful Waiter
- A Sicilian Hermit
- Sunny Madeira
- The Witch
- The Young Artist

Oct 25
- Caught in the Web

Oct 26
- Auntie Takes the Children to the Country
- The Convict and the Dove
- Desperately in Love
- How a Pretty Girl Sold Her Hair Restorer
- The Queen's Lover
- When Pa Went Fishing
- The World of Magic

Oct 27
- The Army of Two (An Incident During the American Revolution)
- Bald Headed Actor and Fair Lady
- The Call of the Wild
- The Duke's Good Joke
- He Did Not Know He Was a Monk
- House Cleaning Days; or, No Rest for the Weary
- Jane Shore
- The Mummer's Daughter

Oct 28
- The Arab Band
- A Desperate Character
- First Love Triumphs
- The Fortune Hunters
- Motor Boat Races
- Wrongfully Accused

Oct 29
- Closed on Sundays
- The Flower Thief
- The Lights and Shadows of Chinatown
- The Mountaineer's Revenge
- Pa and the Girls

Oct 30
- Bear Hunt in Canada
- Concealing a Burglar
- A Football Warrior
- The Galley Slave's Return
- The Half Breed
- Mabel's Beau in Trouble
- The Sofa Bed

Oct 31
- Ambulance Dogs
- Cuddle Up a Little Closer
- Cyrano de Bergerac
- Daisy, the Pretty Typewriter
- Don't You Think It's Time to Marry
- Hamlet, Duel Scene with Laertes
- Hep Yo' Self, Peck-a-Boo
- The Honeybees' Honeymoon
- Ideal Policemen
- I'm Afraid to Come Home in the Dark
- I'm Going on the War Path
- In the Barber Shop
- The Moon's Gift
- Precieuses Ridicules
- The Renunciation
- Thunderbolt on the Mill
- Tipperary
- Under Any Old Flag at All
- What It Might Have Been
- Who? Me?
- With Care
- Wouldn't You Like to Flirt with me

Nov [day undetermined]
- The Acrobats
- Automatic Statue
- The Bank Director
- The Child and the Gigantic Animal
- Cupboard Courtship
- The Dance of Death
- The Dancing Girl
- Little Hannie's Last Dream
- The Magic Ring
- The Mill
- On Roller Skates
- The Photographer
- Pierrot's Death
- The Prima Donna of the Ballet Parody
- Rheumatism
- Rose That Makes Everybody Dance
- Scandanavian North
- Supper
- The Tinder Box

Nov 1
- Baseball
- Bear Hunting in Russia
- I've Lost My Ball
- The Stage-Struck Daughter
- Troubles of a Coat
- Unyielding Parent

Nov 2
- The Automatic Hotel
- A Child's Debt
- The Cross Roads
- The Fair Young Lady's Telephone Communication
- A House of Cards
- How the Pair Butted In
- Humpty-Dumpty Circus
- The Legend of Prometheus
- Magic Album
- The Mock Baronets
- My Daughter Will Only Marry a Strong Man
- The Necklace
- The Penalty of His Crime
- Sold by His Parents
- Thou Shalt Not Love
- The Young Tramp

Nov 3
- After Many Years
- Antony and Cleopatra, the Love Story of the Noblest Roman and the Most Beautiful Egyptian
- A Love Tragedy in Spain
- Saved by Love

Nov 4
- Benvenuto Cellini
- Clearing the Mountain Track
- David Garrick
- Don't Fool Your Wife
- Maple Sugar
- The Watchmaker's Wedding

Nov 5
- The Actor's Child
- The Key Under the Mat
- Lunch Time

Nov 6
- Gust of Wind
- The Jester
- The Pirate's Gold
- Pirate's Honor

Nov 7
- All That Trouble for a Drink
- Archie Goes Shopping with the girls
- Ascending Mt. Pilatus in Switzerland
- Barbara Fritchie, the Story of a Patriotic American Woman
- David and Goliath
- A Day in the Life of a Hunt
- The Four-Legged Thief
- His First Experiment in Chemistry
- Jerusalem in the Time of Christ
- A Jilted Woman's Revenge
- The Little Waif
- The Magic Flute
- Mr. Simpson's Artful Ruse
- Nations of the World
- A Night Alarm
- Our Banana Supply
- Our Village Club Holds a Marathon Race
- The Peer's Fancy
- The Pillory
- The Pilot's Daughter
- Push Cart Race
- 'Round Brussels in Ten Minutes
- Time to Get Married
- The Vanderbilt Cup Race
- Yens Yensen, The Swedish Butcher Boy; or, Mistaken for a Burglar
- The Youthful Benefactor

Nov 8 Roman Colonel's Bravado
Nov 9 At Night
Beauty and the Beast
The Cotton Industry of the South
Feeding a Serpent
The First Servant
The Gorges of the Tarn
The Grandfather's Tobacco
Hurry Up, Please
The Lake of Garda, Italy
Looking for the Bald Heads
Monty Buys a Motor
No Race Suicide
Out to Nurse
The Quick Change Mesmerist
The Scare Crow
A Tyrolean Paradise
A Woman's Aid
Nov 10 The Lovers' Telegraphic Code
The Right of the Seigneur
Taming of the Shrew
Two Affinities; or, A Domestic Reunion
The Wonderful Charm
Nov 11 Blood Will Tell
He Who Laughs Last Laughs Best
If It Don't Concern You, Let It Alone
Weather Changes at the Smiths
Nov 12 Jack in Letter Box
The Janitor Falsely Accused
A Mountain Feud
When Women Rule
Nov 13 The Guerrilla
The Railroad Detective
Reception of the American Fleet in Australia
"She"
Nov 14 Blind
Confirmation
The Glacier's Victim
Gypsy's Warning
The Highwayman
The Inn of Death, an Adventure in the Pyrenees Mountains
The Jealous Old Maid; or, No One to Love Her
The Prehistoric Man
Rescue of Children by Dogs
We Close at Noon
Will They Ever Get to Town?
Nov 15 Bear's Fancy
Newfoundland Fisherman
The Village Set
Nov 16 Bicycle Polo
The Doll Maker's Daughter
Madam Flirt and Her Adopted Uncle
Puss in Boots
Through an Orange Grove
Nov 17 Caesar Up-to-Date
Champion Globe Trotter
Colonial Virginia
Disappearing Watch
The Doctor's Wife
The Elf King, a Norwegian Fairy Tale
Having the Time of Their Lives
The Jester's Daughter
The New Stenographer
The Prize Camel
A Serious Joke
The Song of the Shirt
Tarn Mountains
A Visit to Compiegne and Pierrefond
Waterproof Willie
The Young Poacher
Nov 18 Donkey's Skin
The Hoodoo Lounge
Othello
The Tale of a Thanksgiving Turkey
Nov 19 The Engineer
The Hidden Treasure
The Parson's Thanksgiving Dinner
Nov 20 Hannah Dustin: The Border Wars of New England
The Ingrate
Race Prejudice
Wood Floating and Pulp Industry
Nov 21 Cave of the Spooks
Cinderella
The Devil's Bargain
The Fisherman's Life
Grandpa's Pension Day
A Love Affair in Toyland
Old College Chums
The Pirates
The Shoemaker of Coepenick
The Swimming Lesson
A Tale of the Crusades
Wonderful Fertilizer

Nov 23 Circumstantial Evidence; or, Who Ate the Possum Pie
The Dirigible Airship
Marie Stewart
A Pair of Spectacles
Nov 24 The Lady or the Tiger
A Lover's Stratagems
The Peasant Girl's Loyalty
A Woman's Way
Nov 25 Alexandrian Quadrille
An All-Wool Garment
L'Arlesienne
Children of the East
Kind Old Lady
Soldier's Love Token
Nov 26 On Thanksgiving Day
Persistency Wins
The Thanksgiving Turkey
Nov 27 The Clubman and the Tramp
Crack Riders of the Russian Cavalry
The King's Pardon
A Ragged Hero
Sherlock Holmes in the Great Mystery
The Substitute
Nov 28 The Amorous Soldier
An Awful Shock
The Button of Invisibility
Charity Begins at Home, a Story of the South During the Civil War
A Great Shock
Hon. Senator Hayrick
Merry Widow Waltz
The Miner's Daughter
The Standard Bearer
A Strenuous Wedding
Travel
A Trip Through Scotland
The Vagabond
The Vendetta
When the Cat's Away
Nov 30 Her Flowers
The Magic Handkerchief
The Sexton of Longwyn
Weary Willie's Revenge
Dec [day undetermined]
The Bank Robbery
A Female Fire Department
It Happened at Midnight
The Rain-Dear
A Round-Up in Oklahoma
The Snowbird
Ten Minutes with Shakespeare
When Ma Goes Shopping
The Wolf Hunt
Dec 1 A Child's Devotion
Jack of All Trades
Julius Caesar, an Historical Tragedy
Looking for the Sea Serpent
Lord Feathertop
Making Home Attractive
The Valet's Wife
Dec 2 A Dear Old Grandma
Devils in the Farm
Dummies on the Spree
Every Age Has Its Trouble
The Nature Fakir Comes to Grief
An Obstinate Tooth
A Sinner
The Somnambulist
Dec 3 A Dual Life
The Football Fiend
Hobo's Dream
Lady Barbers
Dec 4 For Love of Country: American Patriotism in the Colonial Wars
The Jealous Fisherman
Miss Sherlock Holmes
Money Mad
The Old Maids' Temperance Club
Paris as Seen from a Height of 2600 Feet
Dec 5 The Bewildered Professor
Buying an Automobile
The Country Idyll
The Fast Train
How Jones Saw the Carnival
Modern Magic
She Could Be Happy with Either
A Summer Idyl
Surprise Package
The 10:40 Train
Thompson's Night with the Police
Dec 7 The Clown's Daughter
The Lighthouse-Keeper's Daughter
Rubber Heels
Dec 8 The Feud and the Turkey
Making Moving Pictures
The Tale the Ticker Told

Dec 9 The Acrobatic Maid
A Christmas Carol
The Deadly Plant
Sherlock Holmes
Dec 10 Charlie's Ma-in-Law
Dick's Aunt
The Queen of the Arena
Dec 11 The Angel Child
Maggie, the Dock Rat
The Miniature Circus
Mother-in-Law Breaks All Records
The Reckoning
Dec 12 Animated Matches
A Bike Chase
Christmas in Paradise Alley
Fighting for Gold
Good Resolutions
A Good Watch Dog
It Serves Him Right
The Madman of the Cliff
The Mohammedan at Home
The Quarry Man
Slippery Jim's Repentance
Timid Dwellers
A Trapper on the Frontier
Dec 14 Button, Button, Where Is the Button?
Christmas: From the Birth of Christ to the Twentieth Century
The Face in the Window
A Fatal Present
Father and the Kids
A Free Pardon
Harmless Lunatic's Escape
How the Dodger Secured a Meal
An Interior Cyclone
No Petticoats for Him
Roman Idyl
The Serpent's Tooth
Dec 15 Cocoa Industry, Trinidad, British West Indies
Sheridan's Ride
Slumberland
The Test of Friendship
Dec 16 A Battle Royal
The Changing of Souls
The Installment Collector
The One Best Bet
A Plucky Young Woman
The Spring Lock
Dec 17 A Montana Schoolmarm
On the Stroke of Twelve
Dec 18 An Awful Moment
The Bee and the Rose
The Molly Maguires; or, Labor Wars in the Coal Mines
The Smuggler's Daughter
A Street Waif's Christmas
Dec 19 The Angel of Nativity
Braving Death to Save a Life
The Christmas of a Poacher
The Cobbler Outwitted
The Dancer and the King, a Romantic Story of Spain
Electric Hotel
Faithful to the Test
The Giant Baby
The Good Playthings
Grimsol, the Mischievous Goblin
Hobo on a Bike
In Bitter Rivalry
The Invisible Men
The Legend of Stars
The Little Chimney Sweeps
Love Is Ingenious
Making a Sale
Misdeeds of a Tragical Part
The Police Band
The Poor Singer Girl
Some Dangerous Members of Bostock's Menagerie
Troubles of an Airship
Weary's Christmas Dinner
Willing to Be Courteous
Dec 21 The Baby and the Loafer
Baby's Playmate
The Black Sheep
Cabby's Sweetheart
Christmas Eve at Sunset
Faithful Little Doggie
The Faun
George and Margaret
The Holy Hermit
In Bondage
In the Nick of Time
The Little Marchioness and the Young Shepherdess
My Laundress Inherits

Spoof and His Monkey
Too Much Snuff
Dec 22 The Christmas Burglars
The Merchant of Venice
An Unexpected Santa Claus
Dec 23 Antique Wardrobe
An Awkward Habit
Bill Jones' New Years Resolution
Count Zeppelin's Aerostat
Hercules the Athlete; or, Love Behind the Scenes
"Who Is Smoking That Rope?"
Dec 24 The Duke's Motto
Restored by Repentance
Dec 25 The Gallant Guardsman
Mr. Jones at the Ball
Red Cloud, the Indian Gambler
Silhouettes
Turning over a New Leaf
Dec 26 Bicycle Robbers
Bill Wants to Marry a Toe Dancer
The Flower Girl of Paris
The Hazers
Hermit
Water Sports
Dec 28 Acrobatic Toys
Bobby Has a Pipe Dream
Current News Items
The Devil's Sale
A Heavy Head Piece
Mr. Soaker at the Seaside
A New Year
A New Year's Gift
Not Guilty
St. Moritz
Dec 29 A Dream of Wealth, a Tale of the Gold Seekers of '49
The Helping Hand
The Lost New Year's Dinner
Monkeyland, a Jungle Romance
Dec 30 In Golden Days
The Quack
The Queen's Love (La Tosca)
The Ragtag's Ball
The Sicilian's Revenge
Dec 31 The Forgotten Watch
The House at the Bridge
In the Shenandoah Valley; or, Sheridan's Ride

1909 [month undetermined]
The American Fleet in Hampton Roads, 1909, After Girdling the Globe
Peasant and Princess
Robin Hood and His Merry Men

Jan [day undetermined]
In the Land of Upsidedown
A New Old Master
Satan's Fan
Jan 1 Anonymous Letter
One Touch of Nature
A Persistent Suitor
Strasburg
The Trial of the White Man
Jan 2 Collection of Stamps
The Corsican's Revenge
Cure for Bashfulness
Persistent Suitor
A Sister's Love, a Tale of the Franco-Prussian War
Jan 4 A Bitter Lesson
The Maniac Cook
Mysterious Correspondent
The Old Maid's Dream
Two Very Unlucky Thieves
Jan 5 The Bride of Lammermoor, a Tragedy of Bonnie Scotland
The Painting
Under Northern Skies
Jan 6 The Haunted Lounge
A Lovely Lass
"Mafia," the Secret Society; or, Sicilian Family Honor
The Neighbors' Kids
On Guard at the Powder Magazine
School Children's Strike
Jan 7 Leo's Air Rifle
Mrs. Jones Entertains
Schooldays
The Tenderfoot
Two Orphans of the G.A.R.
The Tyrant's Dream
Jan 8 A Drunkard's Dream
A Florida Feud; or, Love in the Everglades
The Wooden-Headed Veteran
The Worm Will Turn
Jan 9 Burning of Stamboul, Constantinople
For Baby's Sake
He Went to See the Devil Play
Soldier's Heroism
Ted and His Little Sister
A Telepathic Warning, the Story of a Child's Love for Her Father
Tit for Tat
Wright's Aeroplane
Jan 11 The Bewitched Breton
Converted
Duel Under Richeleau
A Gypsy's Jealousy
The Honor of Thieves
Love Finds a Way
Spanish Blood
Visions of a Goldsmith
When Lips Are Sealed
Jan 12 The Castaways
The Heroine of the Forge
Where Is My Wandering Boy To-night?
Jan 13 The Actor's Baby Carriage
A Nervy Thief
The Prehistoric Lid
Professor's Love Tonic
Stilt Walking
Jan 14 How Happy Jack Got a Meal
In Old Arizona
A Rural Elopement
The Sacrifice
The Troubles of a Stranded Actor
Jan 15 Drawing the Color Line
It's Only the Painter
Paper Cock-A-Doodles
The Sponge Fishers of Cuba
Jan 16 The Bride of Tabaiva
The Burglar in a Basket
The Captain's Love
The Coiners, or Catching the Counterfeiters
Gamekeeper's Bride
Holy Fires
The Hunchback
A Little Hero
Mr. Pynhead Out for a Good Time
The Old Schoolmaster
The Poet and the Maid at the Mill
Poetry of the Sea
Porcelain of Good Quality
South African Gold Fields
The Two Sons
An Unprofitable Call
Jan 18 Champion Suffragist
The Criminal Hypnotist
A Hot Remedy
Love's Sweet Melody
Married Twice
The Persevering Insurance Agent
A Pretty Little Milliner
The Sergeant's Stripes
Those Boys!
Troubled Artists
Jan 19 Pagan and Christian
Ruy Blas
Jan 20 Balloon Races
Jim Smith, the Champion Boxer
Life in Russia
The Old Curiosity Shop
The Stepmother
The Stepmother: the Spirit of Unkindness and Jealousy Thwarted
Wonderful Eggs
Jan 21 The Fascinating Mrs. Francis
The Fighting Parson
Love and Law
Mr. Jones Has a Card Party
The Wrong Burglar
Jan 22 Beginning of the Serpentine Dance
Buffin Wins First Prize
A Burglar Cupid
The Girl at the Old Mill
Jan 23 Bobby's Sketches
A Case of Spirits; or, All's Well That Ends Well
A Colonial Romance
A Fish Story
For Mother's Sake
For Their Country's Cause
Going Home to Mother
Lady Cabby's Romance
Messina After the Earthquake
Messina Disaster
The Pleasant Side of a Soldier's Life
Trip on Rhodesian Railway
Jan 25 Sammy Celebrates
The Scar
A Suit Case
Those Awful Hats
The Welcome Burglar
Who Stole Jones' Wood?
Jan 26 The Love of the Pasha's Son, a Turkish Romance
A Romance of Old Madrid
The Treasure; or, The House Next Door
Jan 27 Calling Day
A Cure for Gout
Desert Life
The Gnomes
Nick Carter's Double
Too Much Dog Biscuit
Jan 28 The Cord of Life
Love Germs
The Prairie Town Romance
Jan 29 Messina
A Modest Young Man
The Octoroon: The Story of the Turpentine Forest
A Put Up Job
Jan 30 Cleopatra's Lover; or, A Night of Enchantment
The Frolic of Youth
On the Zambesi
Running Away from Home
Saved by His Dog

Feb [day undetermined]
A B C's of the U.S.A.
At the Dentist
At the Weser (Song)
Bake That Chicken Pie
Believe Me
The Carnival of Venice
Coon Town Parade
Duet from "Martha" (Flotow)
Katrina's Valentine
Mennett [i. e. Menuett]
The Montebank [sic]
Original Cohens
Il Pagliacci (Leoncavallo)
Peaches and Cream
Smile, Smile, Smile
The Taxidermist's Dream
There Never Was a Girl Like You
Torero Song "Carmen"
Il Trovatore
You've Got to Love Me a Lot
Feb 1 Aunt Emmy's Scrap Book
Gendarme's Horses
The Girls and Daddy
The Guard's Alarm
The Living Wreck
Messina Earthquake
A Mother's Heart
The Nurse's Romance
A Sure 'Nuff Tumbler
The Two Bandboxes
A Village Quarrel
Feb 2 The Deacon's Love Letter
The Marathon Race; or, How Tom Paid Off the Mortgage
The Origin of Beethoven's Moonlight Sonata
Feb 3 Incriminating Evidence
Moving Furniture
The Musician's Love Story
Sultan Abdul Hamid, and the Ladies of His Harem
Summer Sport
Feb 4 The Blind Musician
The Brahma Diamond
Stirring Days in Old Virginia
Willie's Water Sprinkler
Feb 5 The Adventures of an Old Flirt
Choosing a Life Partner
The Detectives of the Italian Bureau
He Can Imitate Anything
Feb 6 The Assassination of Abraham Lincoln
Badger Hunt
The Banker
The Delirious Patient
Fatal Wedding
The Great Earthquake in Sicily
The Juggler
A Pirate of Turkey
Riding for Love
The Unwelcome Lover
Virginius
Vulture Hunting in Africa
Why They Fell Out
The Wild Man of Borneo
Feb 8 Buster's Revenge
Edgar Allen Poe
No. 5874
Les Ricochets
Women Chauffeurs

A Wreath in Time
Feb 9 A Bachelor's Supper
A Clever Trick
Jessie, the Stolen Child
The Miner's Will
A Sportive Puppet
Feb 10 Adventures of a Bag of Coal
Baby's Exciting Ride
Charlotte Corday
Dog Outwits Kidnapper
The Double's Fate
Educated Abroad
Following Mother's Footsteps
Grandfather's Birthday
The Guardian of the Bank
Polly's Excursion
A Sign from Heaven
Feb 11 The Bank Messenger
A Secret
Tragic Love
Feb 12 Bess and Her Goose
The High Diver
The Laplanders
The Saleslady's Matinee Idol
Feb 13 The Ambassador's Dispatch Case
The Brazilian's Ring
Circumstantial Evidence
An Evil Day
An Irish Hero
Jones Has Bought a Phonograph
Lost in a Folding Bed
Palmistry
The Showman's Drama
They Lead the Cops on a Chase
Feb 15 The Curtain Pole
The Hand
His Ward's Love
The Silver Dollar
The Unlucky Horseshoe
Feb 16 The American Fleet at Sydney, New South Wales
A Daughter of the Sun
The Hand of a Wizard
The Honor of the Slums
How the Kids Got Even
Outwitted
Feb 17 The Assassination of the Duke of Guise
Bring Me Some Ice
The Caliph's Adventures
Grandfather
A Strong Draught
Tag Day
Feb 18 A Broken Heart
The Hindoo Dagger
The Joneses Have Amateur Theatricals
The King of the Ring
On the Warpath
The Pass Key
Feb 19 The Barber's Christening
Choice of Weapons
His First Flight
How Mother-in-Law Got Even
James and Catherine; or, Love on a Farm
The Making of a Champion
Sporting Days in the Old South
The Uplifting of Mr. Barker
Feb 20 Bernard Palissy
C.Q.D.; or, Saved by Wireless, a True Story of "The Wreck of the Republic"
The Chinamen
Exacting Father-in-Law
The Heroes of St. Bernard
Now I'm Here, I'll Stay
Feb 22 The Galley Slave
A Game of Chess
The Golden Louis
Grand Canal, Venice
Love Me, Love My Dog
The Miser
The Politician's Love Story
Feb 23 The Janitor's Bottle
The Landlady's Portrait
An Obstinate Umbrella
The Perpetual Proposal; or, An Ardent Wooer
The Poor Musician
Some Milk for Baby
Feb 24 Drama Amongst Fishermen
Joel's Wedding
A Little Coquette
Polka on Brain
The Tell-Tale Blotter
What a Uniform Will Do
Feb 25 At the Altar
Holland Cheese
The New Governess
The Skipper's Daughter
Feb 26 The Jolly Trio's Dream
Left Out
Mr. Jonah Gets a Little Dust in His Eyes
The New Minister; or, The Drunkard's Daughter
Sherlock Holmes II: Raffles Escapes from Prison
Topsy-Turvy
Feb 27 A Day's Outing
Edgar and Lucy
Florrie's Birthday
The Foxy Husband
Her Daughter's Dowry
Hypnotic Subject
The Prince and the Dwarf
Saul and David: The Biblical Story of the Shepherd Boy Who Became King of the Israelites
The Shoemaker's Luck
Mar [day undetermined] Buy Matches, Please
It Might Have Been Worse
The Mill Girl
Mar 1 A Dime Novel Detective
His Wife's Mother
The Prussian Spy
The Suffragette's Dream
The Test
Mar 2 And His Coat Came Back
Boyhood Dreams
Mogg Megone, an Indian Romance
100 Per Cent Jealousy
The Piano Teacher
With Taft in Panama
Mar 3 The Blind Foundling; or, Alone in the World
An Embarrassing Present
The False Superintendent
Four Sweethearts
The Guilty Guardian
The Man Monkey
The Sailor's Belt
Shanghaied
Sherlock Holmes III: The Detectives Adventure in the Gas Cellar
Mar 4 A Fool's Revenge
I'll Only Marry a Sport
The Last Call
The Mad Miner
Outing Pastimes in Colorado
Mar 5 A Bad Shot
Behind in His Rent
A Bird in a Gilded Cage
The Old Soldier's Story.
Romance of a Dairy Maid
Mar 6 The Ashes of Hercules
A Day in Washington, the Capital of the United States, Showing Many Points of Interest
Dr. Wright's Invention
Forced to Play Cop
In Sore Straits
Inauguration of President William H. Taft
The Miner's Wife
The Musician
The Story of a Life
Two Violins
Walking on His Toes
Mar 7 Episode in Boer War
A Good Excuse
Mar 8 All's Well That Ends Well
The Capricious Moment
The Chimney Sweep's Birthday
Hurricane of Lovers
The Roue's Heart
Round the Lake of Constanz and the Rhine Falls
The Stowaway
When Love Will
A Widow to Console
The Wooden Leg
Mar 9 Adventures of a Drummer Boy
The Blacksmith's Bride
The Colored Stenographer
Mary Jane's Lovers
Parted, but United Again
The Postal Clerk
A Providential Chance
Story of Every Day
The Student's Predicament
Mar 10 Arrival at the Village
Chances of Life
The Crazy Barber
An Expensive Sky Piece
For the Motherland
Giordono Bruno
He Can't Lose Wifie's Ma
Little Cyril, the Runaway
Mother-in-Law's Day in the Country
Rivalry
Scenes of Morocco
South American Indians
Mar 11 Alcoholic Doctor
The Ironworker
The Little Rag Doll
Love Letter
The New Mirror
Prascovia
Salon in 1820
The Salvation Army Lass
Which Was the Happiest Time in Your Life?
Mar 12 A Canadian Winter Carnival
Convict's Revenge
Educating the Blind
He Is a Cousin Who Eats Truffle
Love and the Motherland
Medieval Episode
The Seminole's Vengeance; or The Slave Catchers of Florida
Mar 13 Buttes Chaumont After a Snow Storm
Father and Son
Grand Maneuvers
The Irresolute Man
Kenilworth
The Presidential Inauguration Film
Sad Awakening
The Smoking Lamp
A Trip to Monte Carlo
Visit from the "Down Home Folks"
Mar 14 The Artist's Model's Sweetheart
For Love of a Fisher Girl
From the North Cape
The Summers-Britt Fight Pictures
Mar 15 A Cowboy Argument
I Did It, Mamma
The Lure of the Gown
Talked to Death
Unusual Elopement
Vampires of the Coast
Mar 16 A Cure for Rheumatism
Devotion and Its Reward
A Home at Last
Innocent, but Found Guilty
Kid's Jest
Love Is Blind
A Midnight Supper
The Musician's Dream
Mar 17 The Celebrated Mountain Climbers
Cremation on the River Ganges
Jealous Hubby
Master Goes Shopping
The Ringleader
The Road Agents
Taming of a Shrew
Mar 18 Boots and Saddles
Reforming a Husband
Uncle Reuben's Courtship
The Voice of the Violin
Mar 19 Child's Vision
The Cracker's Bride
Hungry Hank's Hallucination
The Star of Bethlehem
Summer Home for the School Children of Paris
Tommy's Own Invention
Tramp's Defense
Mar 20 A Brave Irish Lass, the Story of an Eviction in Ireland
The Burden of Debt
A Friend in the Enemy's Camp
The Grand Procession at the King of Siam Jubilee
Mr. Jenkins Washes Up
The Return of Ulysses
The Secretary's Revenge
Sold to Thieves; or, A Deathbed Confession
A Stage Romance; or, An Actor's Love
The Survivor's Story
Western Bill
Mar 22 And a Little Child Shall Lead Them
A Borrowed Suit
Brisquet
The Chambermaid and the Dwarf
Chasi Movement
Chasing the Helmet
Compassion
The Day of the Dog
The Deception
The Dragonad
Dream of Featart
The Duel

Duplicate Vases
The Elixir of Dreams
Fairy Sword
Five Minutes Interview
Foolshead, King of Police
Foolshead Wishes to Commit Suicide
For Honor
Galileo
The Ghost
Goose Chase
Hat Making
High Game
House of Disagreement
In the Land of the Hindoo
Irritable Woman
Italian Cavalry Maneuvers
Jack Has No Clothes
Living Statue
Louis XVII
Magic French Horn
Mail Carrier's Daughter
Main Clues
The Man Who Knows How to Whistle
Marriage in Haste
Master and Servant
Maternal Protection
Matrimonial Agency
The Mesmerist
Mother-in-law Too Kindhearted
Norseman
The Old Grumbler at the Magicians
Our Ice Supply; or, How'd You Like to Be the Iceman
Phantom Games
Lo Piferaro
Pity
Procession in Japan
The Prophecy
Recommended Servant
Removing
Rifle Bill No. 5
Royalist's Wife
Runaway Dog
Service of a Friend
Shooting the Rapids in Japan
Soldier and Witch
Son and Mother-in-law
State Secret
The Statue
The Stolen Inheritance
Taming a Husband
Two Fathers
Tylda and Her Lions
United by Misfortune
Where Stormy Winds Do Blow
A Wild Goose Chase
Zoological Gardens
Mar 23 Cohen at Coney Island
Cohen's Dream of Coney Island
Cross of Honor
Gift
Japanese Magic
Pocket Policeman
Strolling Players
Mar 24 Chivalrous Beggar
An Energetic Street Cleaner
I Have Lost Toby
A Midnight Disturbance
Mr. Pallet Goes Out Landscaping
New Cut Roads Up Mt. Blanc
We Must Have a Butler
Mar 25 A Burglar's Mistake
Four Wise Men
Infant Terrible
A Just Reward
Mad Dog
Mar 26 A Cry from the Wilderness; or, A Tale of the Esquimaux and Midnight Sun
Jolly Sports
The Maid and the Millionaire
The Mysterious Double; or, The Two Girls Who Looked Alike
Mar 27 Across the Border
An Artist's Model's Jealousy
The Beggar's Daughter
Blind Child's Dog
A Convict's Return
A Criminal Invention
Drama in the Forest
Drama in the Village
The Electric Belt
Episode of War
Fishing by Dynamite
Follow Me and I'll Pay for Dinner
Gadbin, the Refractory Suicide
The Good Vicar
The Heart of a Mother
Hero of the Prussian War
Husband's Vengeance
I Want a Moustache
Indians and Cowboys
King Lear
Life on a French Training Ship
Lily Amuses Herself
Love of Travel
Lucia di Lammermoor
Magic Games
The Magician
Misfortunes of a Cobbler
The New Servant
On the Brink
The Paralytic
The Parricide
The Pirate's Daughter
The Poor Schoolma'am
The Reprobate
The Ripe Cheese
The Servant Question Solved
Tracked by a Dog
The Train Robbers
Tubbie's Terrible Troubles
The Unfaithful Cashier
The Warden's Nightmare
Mar 29 The Child of the Regiment
Help! Police!
Jones and His New Neighbors
The Medicine Bottle
The Photograph Habit
What Three Tots Saw in the Land of Nod
Mar 30 Children of the Plains, an Episode of Pioneer Days
Hard to Beat
Oh! Rats!
The Policewoman
The Politician
The Wooden Indian
Mar 31 Arabian Horsemen
Benevolent Employer
The Chauffeur's Adventure
For Love's Sake
His Last Illusion Gone
In Ancient Egypt
The Non-Stop Motor Bicycle
Whale Fishing in Southern Waters
William Tell: The Liberator of Switzerland
Apr [day undetermined]
Henpecked
The House That Jack Built
Inauguration of Taft
A Moroccan Romance
The Over-Eager Heirs
Romance of Engine 999
The Thirteenth at the Table
Through Darkness to Light
The Troubles of the Pretty School Marm
Apr 1 A Drunkard's Reformation
The Guarding Angel
The Sceptical Cowboy
The Settlement Workers
Apr 2 Beware of Evil Companions
The Fish Pirates; or, The Game Warden's Test
Larry, the Limit for Deviltry
Old Aunt Hanna's Cat
On the Western Frontier
Apr 3 The Auto Maniac
Benares
De Comtess de Valeria
Every Lass a Queen
King for an Hour
Life Through a Telescope
Lost in the Snow
The Martins Leave Home for a Week
A Moonlight Trip on the Nile
The Shepherd's Daughter
Stolen for Spite
A Stormy Sea
Uncle's Palm Tree
Apr 5 The Master of Black Rock
Nat Pinkerton: The Anarchists Plot
The Road to the Heart
The Schoolboy's Revenge
Trying to Get Arrested
Vercingetorix—Gaul's Hero
Apr 6 Father's First Half-Holiday
The Life Drama of Napoleon Bonaparte and Empress Josephine of France
The Orange Grower's Daughter
The Prodigal Daughter
The Riviera
Unappreciated Genius
Apr 7 Inviting His Boss for Dinner
The Kiss of Judas
On the Brink of the Precipice
A Tale of the West
Apr 8 Brother Against Brother
The Escaped Melody
Forecastle Tom
A Rude Hostess
Schneider's Anti-Noise Crusade
Apr 9 Any Port in a Storm
Contemptible Theft
A Cup of Tea and She
Moscow Clad in Snow
A Trip to the Wonderland of America
Apr 10 Clarenee and His Cigarette
Disloyal Lover
Eagle's Prey
He Advertised for His Dog
Lost in Chinatown
Mishaps of Lover
Napoleon: the Man of Destiny
Ponto Runs Away with the Milk Cart
Theodore Yearns to be a Tough
The Tramp at the Masquerade
Apr 12 The Curse of Gold
Give Me a Light
Moonstruck
My Friend, Mr. Dummy
Pranks of a Mischievous Kid
A Sound Sleeper
The Winning Coat
Apr 13 Charlie Forced to Find a Job
In the Lime Light
The Interrupted Joy Ride
A Marriage of Convenience
The Other Fellow; or, A Fight for Love
A Tax on Bachelors
Apr 14 Canals of Copenhagen
The Chaperone
Oliver Cromwell
Policeman in Action
The Rubes and the Bunco Men
A Sailor's Life
Under Suspicion
Apr 15 After the Bachelors' Ball
Confidence
Love Under Spanish Skies
Slip-Powder
Apr 16 Bangkok
The General's Fiancée
In the Days of Witchcraft
The Teamster's Daughter
We're Backing Up
Apr 17 Automatic Nursing Bottle
A Bachelor's Persistence
The Deacon's Holiday
Forgiven; or, Father and Son
Jack's Successful Bluff
The Magic Purse
Nellie's Love Story
A Plot Foiled
A Plucky Little Girl
Puritan Maid
The State Secret
Story of a Calf's Head
Student Days
A Traitor to the King
Unforgiving Father
Violets
A War Time Tale
Apr 19 Lady Helen's Escapade
The Legend of the Forget-Me-Not
Paul Has Decided to Marry
The Queen of the Ranch
A Troublesome Satchel
World's Heavyweight Championship Pictures Between Tommy Burns and Jack Johnson
The Yiddisher Boy
Apr 20 The Dynamite Waistcoat
Outcast, or Heroine
The Poet's Vision
Too Much Advice
The Wood-Chopper's Child
Apr 21 The Artist's Dream
Magic Eggs
Miller's Dream
One Touch of Nature
A Pair of Garters
A Pair of White Gloves
Sentenced to Death
The Short Circuit House
A Walk Through the Zoo
Apr 22 The Dairy Maid's Lovers
The Drive for a Life
A Fatal Flirtation
A Fighting Chance

A School for Lovemaking
Apr 23 The Northern Schoolmaster
There's No Fool Like an Old Fool
Who's Who
Apr 24 Artful Art
Bailiff Makes a Seizure
Burglary in the Year 2000
The Cabin Boy's Dog
The Deserter
The Dog Came Back
A Faithful Fool
Foolshead Looks for a Duel
Found on the Rocks
The Game of Pallone
A Heartless Mother
High Game
Hungary
It Was a Beautiful Dream
Last Year's Time Table
The Lost Sheep
A Lover's Quarrel
The Magic of Music
The Magnetizer
Married Under Difficulties
Martyrdom of Louis XVII
A Marvelous Ointment
Modern Egypt
Nancy; or, The Burglar's Daughter
Professor's Anti-Gravitation
The Regimental Barber
The Rival Cyclists
Runaway Kids
The Squire and the Noble Lord
The Stolen Bride
A Thoughtless Beauty
The Unlucky Thief
The Viking's Love; or, True to His Chief
The Villain's Wooing
Apr 26 The Clever Reporter
The Gold Prospectors
Inventions of an Idiot
Lucky Jim
Twin Brothers
Why the Mail Was Late
Apr 27 The Automatic Monkey
The Bandits
Before and After
A Belated Meal
Earthenware Industry
His First Girl
How They Propose
The Little Shepherd of "Tumbling Run"
Apr 28 The Fairy's Presents
How Chauncey Became a Champion
The Love-sick Barber
Nat Pinkerton [Series II]
Old Heidelberg
The Suspicious Fencing Master
An Unwritten Letter
Apr 29 Boys Will Be Boys
The House of Terror
Mephisto and the Maiden
'Tis an Ill Wind That Blows No Good
Apr 30 The Artist and the Girl
Playing Patience
Uncle Tom Wins
An Unsuccessul Substitution
Wilbur Wright's Aeroplane
May [day undetermined]
The Conjuror's Outing
An Old Man's Bride
Persistent Jane
Pressing Business
May 1 The Anarchist's Sweetheart
The Bohemian Girl
Countess Valleria of Issogne
The Donkey That Was Not an Ass
The Dragoons Under Louis XIV
Dream Spectres
Easter Bells
Farmer Jones Goes to the Market
The Fickle Husband
Hunting the Hippopotamus
The Marathon Craze
Misplaced Confidence
Removal Under Difficulties
The Sculptor's Love
Siamese Actors and Actresses Play a Siamese Drama
Two Ladies and a Beggar
An Unfortunate Bath
Winter Sports and Games at Stockholm, Sweden, 1909
May 3 Between Love and Honor
The Eavesdropper
The Falling Arrow
Puzzle Mad
The Suicide Club
Your Turn, Marquis
May 4 Grin and Win; or, Converted by a Billiken
Plain Mame; or, All That Glitters Is Not Gold
A Road to Love
May 5 Boxing Match [by Hallberg of Denmark and Young Joe Gaines "Baltimore Black"]
Forgotten
Hard Working Elephants
A Mexican's Gratitude
Paza Did It
The Peddler's Reward
Thanksgiving Turkey
Zou-Zou, the Lucky Dog
May 6 Adventures of a Keg
Chinatown Slavery
The Note in the Shoe
The Old Hall Clock
One Busy Hour
May 7 A Chinese Wedding
The Doctored Dinner Pail
Fuss and Feathers
Haunted by the Cops
Instantaneous Nerve Powder
Love's Triumphs
May 8 Arrest of the Orderly
Artillery Manoeuvers in the Mountains
An Awful Toothache
Baby's Chum
Cat in the Pot
The Cavalier's Wife
Chauffeur Out for a Good Time
A Cowboy's Sweetheart
Danish Capitol Under Snow
Dressed for the Occasion
Earthly Paradise
Eddie Is a Real Live One
Ellen
Filial Devotion
First Comes the Fatherland
Four Footed Hawkshaw
Frolics of Gamins
Funeral of Joe Petrosino: The American Detective in Merino, Italy
The Gambler's Vow
Glimmeramm
The Haunted Bridge
High Art
House Full of Agreeables
Husband Goes to Market
I Will Have a Husband
The Immortal Goose
Indiscretion of Moving Picture
The Inheritance of Baptiste Durand
Jammer-bach
Johnny Is No Longer a Child
The Land of the Pharoah
Love with Love Is Paid
The Magic Wand
The Milkman's Wooing
Modern Tramp
Neptune's Daughter; or, The Shoemaker's Dream
New Pain Killer
Novel Invitation
An Old Man's Honor
Peasant and Photographers
Romance of the Crafty Usurper and the Young King
Shark Fishing
Snowball
Sportsmen in Switzerland
Taking Home the Eggs
Tragedy at the Circus
The Tramp's Luck
Tribulations of a Lover
Trick Well Played
Tricks of the Photographer
Unlucky Smuggler
Unpleasant Substitution
The Way to Happiness
What William Did
Where There's a Will There's a Way
Why the Wedding Didn't Come Off
May 10 The French Duel
A Golden Lie
Jones and the Lady Book Agent
Mirielle's Sincere Love
A Striking Resemblance
May 11 The Cyclone Sneezer
For Her Country's Sake
The Infernal Machine
Lunatics in Power
An Uneven Keel
May 12 The Bachelor's Wife
Bamboo Pole Equilibrist
The Beggarmaid
The Hunter's Grief
Mr. Flip
Moscow
Roosevelt in Africa
A Timely Apparition
Wilbur Wright and His Majesty King Edward VII
May 13 A Baby's Shoe
The Bad Lands
The Right to Labor
May 14 A Faithful Old Horse
Good for Evil
Manufacturing Steel Rails
The Pony Express
See a Pin and Pick It Up, All That Day You'll Have Good Luck
May 15 The Actor's Mother
Carnival at Nice
The Detective's Ruse
Dime Novel Dan
Disappointed Heirs
A Distracted Man
An Exciting Hunt
A False Accusation, a Story of Paternal Devotion
Fishing Industry
Foolshead on the Alps
For a Woman's Sake
For Honor's Sake
Free Champagne
Galileo, Inventor of the Pendulum
Humble Heroes
In the Service of the King
Magic Sack
A New Policeman
On the French Littoral
The Ponce de Leon Fete
Rosin Industry
The Spoilt Child
The Temptation of John Gray
Tower of London
The Two Donkeys
Unlucky Bridegroom
Who Has Seen My Head?
A Woman's Heart
May 17 The Beggar's Coin
Faded Flowers
Fountain of Youth
The Intruder
The Jilt
The Press Gang
Summering in the Austrian Alps
Winter Landscapes Round Stockholm
May 18 Bridget on Strike
The Defaulting Solicitor
He Couldn't Lose Her
The Policeman Sleeps
A Somnambulistic Hero
Teddy in Jungleland
The World Upset
May 19 Blessings Sometimes Come in Disguise
Caught on the Cliffs
The Farmer's Grandson
The Indian Trailer
Objections Overcome
Père Milon
May 20 Resurrection
The Smuggler's Daughter
With Grant
May 21 Daunted by His First Love
Disinherited Son's Loyalty
The Girl Spy: An Incident of the Civil War
Hunting Big Game in Africa
Land of the Midnight Sun
Little Miss Moffit and Simian Stone
The Sandman
May 22 The Attack
Black Coated Brigands
Black's Funeral
Boys' Holiday
Cartouche
A Clever Detective
Copenhagen Zoo
Favorite Doll
A Guest's Predicament
In Quest of Health
In Sardinia
Jepthah's Daughter, a Biblical Tragedy
Johnny and the Indians
The Judgment of Solomon
Justice or Mercy
Longing for Gold
The Master Detective; or, The Attack on the Strong Room

94 89 93

276

Neurasthenique
Perilous Expedition
Present for Her Husband
River Panorama
Sapho
Scenes in Ceylon
Stratagem Rewarded
Tom's Misfit
Two Pickpockets
Unprofitable Experiment
Why Father Learned to Ride
You Shall Pay for It

May 24 Arabian Cavalry
The Artist's Dummy
Berthold in Paris
Blind Farmer
Blind Man's Daughter
The Bondsman's Fate
Boy's Adventure
Champagne Party
Cured by Gymnastics
Deserved Punishment
Dr. Clown
Dog and Baby
Dreamer
Eloping with Aunty
Flat Hunting
The Flirt, a Tale of the Plains
Good People
Grand Stag Hunting
Great Flood in India, September, 1908
Grip in the Family
Happy Artist
Heart of Genevieve
Henry Farman, King of the Air
His First Pants
Home of the Arabians
Hurt
Hypnotism
Innocence
King Edward's Visit to Berlin
Lead and Zinc Mines
Life of a Wood Ant
Little Mother
Masquerade Costume
Military Review
A Miracle
Miracle of Love
Mishaps of a Governess
Mr. Inquisitive
New Style Airship
The Newlyweds
Officer McCue
Only a Dog
Poor Life
Repairing Railroad Tracks
Servant
Sleep Walker
Soldier Manoeuvres in Morocco
Son's Sacrifice
Stronger Than Death
Sweetheart's Bouquet
Sweetheart's Christmas
Telltale Graphophone
Tommy's Tricks
Tragedy in the Family
Tragedy of a Ghost
Troubles of a Fisherman
Two Memories
Useful Young Man

May 25 A Blind Man of Jerusalem
Brothers in Arms
Cigarette Making: From Plantation to Consumer
The Glories of Sunset
Old Sweethearts of Mine, a Phantasy in Smoke

May 26 Annie Laurie
How Jones Paid His Debts
The Human Ape; or, Darwin's Triumph
An Obliging Friend
Panther Hunting on the Isle of Java
A Profitable Marriage
Scenes from the World's Largest Pigeon Farm
The Seventh Clerk

May 27 A Bride Won by Bravery
The Cricket on the Hearth
A Wartime Sweetheart

May 28 Alphonse Gets in Wrong
A Child's Prayer
Miss Faust
A Pig in a Poke
A Poor Wife's Devotion
Professor Fix Fixed
Romance of a Fishermaid

May 29 The Accusing Double
Apostle of Gaul
The Bear in the Staircase
Bottled Up
Count of Monte Cristo
The Emperor
The Empty Sleeve; or, Memories of By-Gone Days
Forester's Son
Frost Bound Nature
The Hasty Tempered Father; or, The Blacksmith's Love
He Couldn't Dance, but He Learned
He Was 25 Cents Short of His Salary
His Only Quid
King's Jester
Lesson in Electricity
Mimosa and the Good Prince
Morganatic Marriage
Motherly Love of Animals
Nantilda
A Piano Lesson
Reveler's Dream
Scrappy Bill
The Suffragist Wants a Husband
Vaccination Against Injuries
A Visit to the London Zoological Gardens

May 31 Advantages of Aviation
Father's Glue
The Lost Heiress
An Uninvited Guest
What Drink Did

Jun [day undetermined]
The Awakening of Mr. Coon
The Fighting Cigar
The Innocent Bystander
Under the Steam Hammer

Jun 1 The Cripple's Marriage
The Curfew Bell
The Good Omen
Oliver Twist
Wep-Ton-No-Mah, the Indian Mail Carrier

Jun 2 Cab Number 519
The Dog and the Sausage
Magic Carpet
Making Tambourines
Saved by a Waif
The Sleeping Tonic
Tender Cords

Jun 3 Are You the Man?
Eradicating Aunty
Fighting Bob
His Duty
My Friend, the Indian

Jun 4 A Bruised Heart
Carnival at Nice, 1909
A Child of the Sea
"Davy" Crockett in Hearts United
$5,000 Reward
The Hold-Up Held Up
The Omnibus Taxicab
A Wife's Ordeal

Jun 5 Airship Zeppelin
Cat Came Back
Debut of an Alpinist
Dentist's Daughter
Face to Face
False Piano Professor
Gambler's Honor
Game of Hearts
Gypsy's Child
Happy Man
Italian Artillery
Legend of the Erring Jew
A Nevada Girl
On the Zuider Zee
The Oriental Mystic
Protector of Animals
Resuscitated
Saved from Conviction
A Soldier's Heart
Trollhattan in Winter
A True Friend
The Truer Lover

Jun 7 The Blue Legend
A Cork Leg Legacy
The Pulverizer
Saucy Sue
Two Frolicking Youths
The Violin Maker of Cremona

Jun 8 A Conspiracy
A Friend in Need Is a Friend Indeed
The Legend of Sterling Keep
Mr. Physical Culture's Surprise Party
A Mother's Choice
Victim of a Crisis

Jun 9 The Brothers Laurento
The Convict
The General and the Sentry
The Race Course
Street Life in North Siam
Ten Nights in a Bar-room
La Tosca
A True Girl from the West
Two Heroes

Jun 10 The Lonely Villa
The Moonstone
A New Trick
Prof. Wise's Brain Serum Injector
Through Jealousy

Jun 11 The Boots He Couldn't Lose
Buying Manhattan
The Little Angel of Roaring Springs
The Mystic Swing
Snake Skin Industry
The Squaw's Revenge
A Woman's Intrigue

Jun 12 Achill's Rocky Shores
The Birth of a Big Gun
The Brave Page Boy
Caught at Last
Cingalese Village Life
The Consequences of a Bad Action
Cyrano de Bergerac's Adventure
Drama at Messina
Early Days in the West
Episode of Cuban War
A False Friend
His Lucky Day
Historical Fan
Hobo's Dream
How Jones Got a New Suit
Killarney's Lakes
The Man Housemaid
Man with the Cut Throat
A Message from the Sea
Only a Dart
Private Brown
Rapids and Falls of Tannfossen and Rista
A Romance of Old Mexico
Ski Runners of the Italian Army
Skylight Theater Seat
Special License
A Strong Diet
Too Clean a Servant
Weary Willie Wheeling

Jun 14 Cupid's Four Darts
The Dog Detective
Ingratitude
The Son's Return
Through Shadow to Sunshine

Jun 15 The Foundling—A Dressing Room Waif
Hunted to the End
A Paying Business
A Rural Tragedy

Jun 16 The Brave Girl on the Fifteenth Floor
Don Juan; or, A War Drama of the Eighteenth Century
A Hustling Advertiser
Life's Disappointment
The Little Peacemaker
Modern Algeria
The New Footman
The Reckoning
Strenuous Sneezer
The Wages of Sin

Jun 17 The Conjuror
Curing a Jealous Husband
Cyrano de Bergerac
The Faded Lillies
Flossie's New Peach-Basket Hat
The Girl Heroine
Her First Biscuits
In the Sultan's Power
It Takes Gasoline to Win a Girl
Officer's Revenge
Recompense

Jun 18 Closed on Sunday
How the Tramp Got the Lunch
Looking for His Umbrella
Mardi Gras in Havana
Mixed in His Dinner Dates
A Priest of the Wilderness: Father Jogue's Mission to the Iroquois
A Terrible Attempt
Why Mr. Jones Was Arrested

Jun 19 The Art of Fencing
The Bachelor's Dream
The Cry from the Well
The English Derby
A Good Birthday Present
Lesson in Cycling
Love Wins

The Loyal Indian
A Maker of Diamonds
Making Lace
The Plot That Failed
Poor Little Kiddies
A Russian Romance
The Stolen Princess

Jun 21 For His Daughter's Sake
The Red Man
The Story of Two Lives
Was Justice Served?

Jun 22 The Duke's Jester; or, A Fool's Revenge
A Good Hearted Policeman
The Lost Invitation
The Troublesome Lamppost

Jun 23 The Curse of Cocaine
The Grandfather
Mrs. Simpson's Attractiveness
Winning a Princess
A Woman of the People

Jun 24 A Country Girl's Peril
The Hypnotic Cure
The Mexican Sweethearts
The Peachbasket Hat
Saved by His Sweetheart

Jun 25 An Affair of Art
An Affair of Honor
An Assortment of Aeroplanes
Cowboy's Narrow Escape
Famine in the Forest; or, The Trapper's Gratitude
Never Again
The Whole World Kin

Jun 26 Aboard the German Navy
The Buffoon
Bully and Recruit
Chimney Sweep's Debut
A Cowboy's Romance
Dollar in Each Egg
Egyptian Princess
Foolshead Wrestling
Fratricide
Good for Nothing Nephew
Heroine of the Balkans
His Wedding Morn
Joan of Arc
Louis the XI
Lover's Mistake
Maddened Players
Misadventures of a Bench
Moonlight on the Thames
The Mother-in-Law Phantasm
Officer's Lodgment
The Old Organ
A Painful Joke
Percy Wanted a Moustache
Police Dogs
Quiet Day at the Cafe
The Shepherd's Dog
Stung by a Bee
Sunshine After Storm
To the Custody of the Father
The Troubles of an Amateur Detective
Winter Horseplay
The Wrong Coat
The Wrong Medicine

Jun 28 Broke Again
The Great Rose Festival of Portland
Mary Jane Visits Her Country Cousin
The Oysterman's Gold
The Way of Man
A Western Hero

Jun 29 A Man Without a Country
No Appetite for Dinner
Saved from the Flames
Washington under the British Flag

Jun 30 The Phantom Sirens
The Policeman's Romance
Psyche
Rulers of the World
The Slavey

Jul 1 Ben's Kid
The Necklace
The Old Army Chest
The Spanish Girl

Jul 2 The Bogey Woman
Fun with a Manikin
He Wouldn't Go Under a Ladder
The Japanese Invasion
Parted on their Honeymoon
A True Indian's Heart

Jul 3 American Squadron in France
Bee's Eviction
Bink's Toreador
Book Taught Hypnotism
The Crystal Ball
Determined Wooer
Dissolution of Parliament
The Dog and the Bone
The Egg Race
Fancy Dress Ball
The Great Automobile Race
The Hand Bell
Infernal Salamandre
An Inspiring Sunset
A Joke on Teddy
Lighthouse
Lord of Montmorency
Modern Cinderella
A Mother's Grief
The Mouse
A Pair of Truants
Pity and Love
Policeman's Rest
The Prince and the Actor
The Sentimental Burglar
Ski Jumping
The Snow Man
The Sunny South of France
Washington Under the American Flag

Jul 5 A Child's Love
A Great Wrong Righted
The Love Plotters
The Message
Spanish Army

Jul 6 The Coin Collector
The Dramatist's Dream
Led Astray
Raised in the Country
Up the Ladder with Tom Bowline

Jul 7 The Black Sheep
Exciting Steeple-Chase
The Pretty Fisher-Maiden
A Tragic Ending of Shrove Tuesday
Tunisian Industries

Jul 8 The Country Doctor
The Lion Tamer
Roommates
The Sideboard Folding Bed

Jul 9 An Absent-Minded Cupid
The Blacksmith's Wife
The Fan
A Little Detective
A Soldier of the U.S. Army
A Squeedunk Sherlock Holmes

Jul 10 A Bad Case
Comrade's Rations
Flirtation Collar
Gaffles, Vice King of Police
The Gambler's Son
Herring Fishing
Horse to the Rescue
The Interrupted Jollification
The Life of a Pierrot
Mine at Last
The Origin of Man
The Persistent Lover
Phonographic Message of Love
Pierrot as a Grocer
Prince of Chalant
The Reason of the Strongest
The Salome Craze
The Sheriff's Pet
Trained Falcon
A Tramp Show Heart
Visions of Mother
Wearybones Seeks Rest, and Gets It
The Witch's Donkey

Jul 12 The Aborigine's Devotion
The Cardinal's Conspiracy
Different Rulers of the World
Driven from Home
Wood Floating in Morvan

Jul 13 The Cobbler and the Caliph
Only a Dream
The Secret of the Locket
Ski-ing at Ispheming, Mich.
A Sure Cure

Jul 14 Conchita, the Spanish Belle
The Evil Spirit in a Girl's Boarding School
The New Cop
True to Her First Love
Which Is Which?
The Wizard's Walking Stick

Jul 15 The Friend of the Family
The Peasant Prince
Tender Hearts
Two Cousins

Jul 16 Caught by the Coupon Craze
The Egyptian Mystery
The Escape from Andersonville
The Hand of Justice
I Love My Wife, but Oh, You Kid

Jul 17 Automatic Umbrella Seller
Ballad of the Pumpkin
Billy's Bugle
The Birth and Adventures of a Fountain Pen
Born for Trouble
Brave Little Organ Boy
Carnival Merriment in the North
Count Ugolini
The Curate of the Races
Expiation
Fate and Poverty
His First Drink
In the Hands of the Enemy
Inexperienced Angler
The Invisible Thief
A Jealous Woman
A Kind Hearted Tough
The Lost Tie
A Luckless Nap
The Magic Fountain Pen
Miraculous Fluid
Mr. Stubborn
Motor Skates
Mysterious Lodger
Never Gamble for Your Trousers
An Old Soldier
Pietro, the Bandit
The Poisoned Flower
A Princess' Love Affair
The Punch Register
The Sacrifice
A Shadow of the Past
The Step-Mother
Too Much Lobster for Supper
Tragic Night

Jul 19 Behind the Mask
Catching Turtles
The Fiddlers
A Nugget of Gold
The Renunciation

Jul 20 The Adventures of Fifine
Instruction by Correspondence
McGinty's Sudden Rise
The Man in the Moon
The Missionary and the Maid
True to His Master

Jul 21 Bewitched Manor House
The King's Conspiracy
Little Busybody
Pennsylvania Monument at Fort Mahone near Petersburg, Va.
Reception of President Taft in Petersburg, Virginia, May 19th, 1909
The Romance of a Stranded Actress
A Tale of Texas

Jul 22 Her Favorite Tune
Hiring a Girl
Jealousy and the Man
Mexican Bill
Sweet and Twenty
Won in the Desert

Jul 23 The Bridegroom's Dilemma
A Case of Lumbago
Casey's Jumping Toothache
The Gypsy Artist
Holding Up the Wedding
Sweet Toothed Dogs
Tickle Mary
The Tom-Boy

Jul 24 Admirer of a Mustache
Bachelor's Misfortune
Brown's Moving Day
A Clever Nurse
Columbine's Return
The Good Shepherd
The Harp Player
John Maxwell's Medal
Little Imp
The Monk's Mother
Off the Coast of Norway
Poor Kid
Professor of Dancing
The Sword and the King
Territory on Brain
Treacherous Policeman
Two Turtle Doves
The Would-Be Acrobats

Jul 26 Champion Heavyweight Lifter
A Convict's Sacrifice
A Hot Time at Atlantic City
Living Dolls
Sweet Dreams Intermingled with Nightmares

Jul 27 The Last Confession
The Little Orphan; or, All Roads Lead to Rome

Midwinter Sports
Mother Goose
Papa's Hat
Taking His Photograph
Jul 28 Amazons of Different Periods
The Barber's Revenge
A Case of Seltzer
His Rival's Hand
Maryland 1777
Parks in Berlin
The Tramp Story
Jul 29 The Heart of a Race Tout
Mr. Buttinsky
The Slave
Sporting Blood
Jul 30 Charity Begins at Home
The Factory Girl
Love's Sacrifice
A Mother's Sorrow
Mulligan's Waterloo
My Wife's Gone to the Country
Jul 31 The Artist's Revenge
An Easy Job
A Game for a Life
Game of Nine Pins
The Gamekeeper's Son
A Georgia Wedding
In Hot Water
Little Gypsy
Missionary
Picturesque Tunis
Three-Wheeled Car
Wine a Gent
Wonderful Rose Designs
Aug 2 The Butler's Tricks
Fantastic Heads
A Strange Meeting
When the Flag Falls
Aug 3 The Bugle Call
The Morning After
The Prince and the Pauper
The Sentinel on Duty
The Truant; or, How Willie Fixed His Father
Aug 4 Much Ado about Nothing
The Mustard Plaster
Stripping a Forest in Winter
Thelly's Heart
The Turning Point
Aug 5 Before the Mast
His Little Girl
The Mended Lute
She Would Be an Actress
Aug 6 Lochinvar
Sailor's Child
The Tobacco Edict, Old New York, 1648
Traced by a Kodak
The Tragedy of Meudon
Aug 7 Arabian Pilgrimage
Baby Is King
Butcher Boy
Clever Horse Hans
The Course of True Love
Double Awakening
The Hidden Treasure
Japanese Prince
King of Spain
The Orphan of Messina
Sympathetic Tippler
Troubles of a Coachman
The Two Pigeons
A Woman's Way
Wonderful Compound
Aug 9 Charity Rewarded
Drunkard's Child
Jones' Burglar
The Newest Woman
The Sacrifice
Satan's Smithy
They Would Elope
Aug 10 Apprentice Boys at Newport [R.I.] Naval Training Station
A Coward
Cyclist's Horn
Dust in His Eye
For Her Sweetheart's Sake
Princess Nicotine; or, The Smoke Fairy
Retaliation
Aug 11 Laurels
A Long Reach
A Maid of the Mountains
Pompey's Dream
The Power of Love
Aug 12 The Better Way
The Leopard Queen
An Unexpected Guest
Aug 13 Cigar-Butt Pickers in Paris
Furnished Rooms to Let
Out of Work
The Price of a Soul
Sheltered Under Stars and Stripes
A Trip to Jupiter
The Yiddisher Cowboy
Aug 14 An Amazing Story
Black Hand
Bouquet Gallantly Offered
The Burning Home
Foolshead Sportsman of Love
The Foxy Farmer
The Gift of Youth, a Fairy Story
Her Beautiful Hair
A Hero of the Italian Independence
The Iron Mask
Mr. Isaacs and the Mice
The Mysterious Crime
A Near Tragedy
Nightmare of a Single Man
The Obdurate Father
Peddling Shoes
Race for a Farmer's Cup
Satan's Retreat
A Smart Trick
A Soldier's Wife
The Spy
A Trying Position
Water Sports
Why She Didn't Marry
The Wild Ass's Skin
Aug 16 A Cold Plunge in Moscow
A Heroic Father
How Brown Got Married
How the Loser Won
The Hungry Actor
With Her Card
The Young Bachelor's Dream
Aug 17 The Cobbler and the Millionaire
Far from the Madding Crowd
The Judge's Whiskers and the Magic Hair Restorer
Liberty for an Hour; or, An Act of Unselfishness
The Little Drummer of 1792
A Simple Home Dinner
Aug 18 Building Barrels
Elastic Transformation
The Lost Letter
The Strikers
Two Lovers and a Coquette
Wonders of Nature
Aug 19 His Wife's Visitor
Measure for Measure
Mrs. Jones' Lover; or, "I Want My Hat"
The Yellow Jacket Mine
Aug 20 The Dog Circus Rehearsal
Doomed
Half Breed's Treachery
Queen of the Quarry
The Web of Fate: An Incident of the French Revolution
The Wright Brothers Aeroplane
Aug 21 The Betrothed's Nightmare
False Alarm
False Lunatic
Getting Even with Everybody
He Preferred to Smoke His Pipe
Honesty Rewarded
Hooligan Against His Will
The King's Protege
Madam Lydia's Little Trick
Mishaps of a Policeman
The New General
Niccolo' De' Lapi
Rival Sisters
Rover Turns Santa Claus
The Spy
Story of a Picture
Surroundings of Copenhagen
Up the Mountain from Hong Kong
The Vengeance of the Lion Tamer
The Way of the Cross, the Story of Ancient Rome
When Jack Gets His Pay
Aug 23 Before the Dawn
Dances of Various Countries
The Hat Juggler
The Indian Runner's Romance
Wifey Away, Hubby at Play
Aug 24 Borrowed Clothes; or, Fine Feathers Make Fine Birds
A Child of the Forest
The Frock Coat
Judge Not That Ye Be Not Judged
The Patience of Miss Job
Too Gentlemanly
Aug 25 The Blacksmith's Daughter
Broken Ties
The Eternal Romance
On Another Man's Pass
Sevres Porcelain
Tennessee Guards
Aug 26 The Midnight Sons
Nearsighted Mary
"Oh, Uncle"
A Royal Outcast
The Seventh Day
A Strange Reunion
Aug 27 A Billposter's Trials
The Conspirators: An Incident of a South American Revolution
A Dash to Death
The Dyspeptic and His Double
Manufacturing Bamboo Hats
Secret Service Woman
Aug 28 Ancestral Treasures
A Cheap Removal
Cowboys in Argentina
The Evil That Men Do
The Farmer's Joke
Foolshead Matrimony
[G.A.R. Procession]
A Generous Emperor
Grandmother's Birthday
Great Event at Podunk
Henpeck's Revolt
The Horse and the Haystack
The Hypnotic Wife
Little Seller of Cyclamens
The Professor's Dilemma
Rival Mesmerists
The Shell; or, "A Madman's Revenge"
The Spy's Revenge
Squaring the Account
The Two Friends
Aug 30 The Doctor's Bride
The Haunted Hat
The Heart of an Outlaw
The Mills of the Gods
Mrs. Jones' Birthday
The New Mail Carrier
Pranks
Ralph Benefits by People's Curiosity
Winning a Widow
Aug 31 The French Battleship "Justice"
The Hunchback
Niagara in Winter Dress
Professor Puddenhead's Patents
Suffer Little Children...For of Such Is the Kingdom of Labor
Sep 1 An Awakened Conscience
The Little Street Singer
Magic Cartoons
My Wife's Gone to the Country (Hooray! Hooray!)
Peaceful Jones
Sam Not Wanted in the Family
Sep 2 The Blight of Sin
The Little Darling
The Sealed Room
The Woman Hater
Sep 3 Backward, Turn Backward, O Time, in Your Flight
Ethel's Luncheon
His Two Children
The Pay Car
Show Your License
A Visit to Biskra
Sep 4 An Apostle of Temperance
Baby's Revenge
Bad Brother
Bad Day for Lavinsky
Biskra, Garden of Allah
The Boy and His Kite
The Boy Scouts
By Path of Love
The Crusader's Return
Cycle Rider and the Witch
Day After a Spree
Fancy Soldier
Florian De Lys
Foolshead, King of Robbers
Frontier Days
Gaffy's King of Detectives
The Galley Slave
A Grave Disappointment
The Henpecked Husband
How the Bulldog Paid the Rent
How the Page Boy Cured a Flirt
In Hot Pursuit
A Jealous Husband
Launching the "Voltaire"

Leap of Alola
The Life of a Red Man
Little Jim
Louisa of Lucerne
Love and Revenge
Love of a Hunchback
Madwoman's Child
Mexican Drama
Mr. A. Nutt
Mosimilla
Norrkobing
Only a Tramp
Romantic Italy
A Strong Woman's Lover
Training Bulls for the Fight
A Troublesome Malady
The Village Idiot
Who Laughs Last
Sep 6 The Call of the Heart
Our Country in Arms
"1776" or, The Hessian Renegades
Spring Has Come
The Stampede
They Robbed the Chief of Police
Versailles
Sep 7 A Dangerous Pair
First Airships Crossing the English Channel
The Fisherman; or, Men Must Work and Women Must Weep
He Tried on Hand Cuffs
The Mason's Paradise
The Temptation
Sep 8 The Diamond Necklace
Glimpses of Paris
Justified
The Little Soldier
Sleepy Jim
The Stolen Gems
Sweden—Gotha Canal
The Wishing Charm
Sep 9 Comata, the Sioux
The Engagement Ring
Glimpses of Yellowstone Park
A True Patriot
Sep 10 The Amateur William Tell
Hiram's Bride
The Making of Honey
The Paymaster
Tom Thumb
Sep 11 An Alpine Echo; or, The Symphony of a Swiss Music Box
Chasing a Sea Lion in the Arctics
The Gray Dame
Great Airship Flights at Rheims
How to Tame a Mother-in-Law
Mozart's Last Requiem
Sports in Java
Sep 13 The Amateur Detective
The Boy and the Convict
The Children's Friend
The Child's Prayer
Daughter of an Anarchist
Don Carlos
The Freebooters
From Millionaire to Porter
Getting Even
Her Face Was Her Fortune
Importune Neighbor
The Justifier
Love of Adventures
The Rivals
The Story of a Bad Cigar
Uncle Rube's Visit
Votes for Women
Sep 14 The Fiddle and the Fan
Her Busy Day
The Little Father; or, The Dressmaker's Loyal Son
Little Sister
The Tricky Dummies
The Wealthy Rival; or A Summer Story That Needs No Explanation
Sep 15 The Bull Fight
A Case of Tomatoes
City of Naples
The Fatal Love
Pontine Marshes, Italy
The Pretty Girl of Nice
Three Reasons for Haste
A White Lie
Sep 16 The Actor Burglar
All on Account of a Letter
The Broken Locket
Crooked Path
The Fortune Hunters
Sep 17 How the Landlord Collected His Rents
A Kentucky Planter
The Mountebank's Son
The Story of a Rose
'Tis Now the Very Witching Hour of Night
Winning a Dinner
Sep 18 Aeroplane Contests at Rheims
Arab Life in South Algeria
The Arithmetic Lesson
A Broken Heart
Calino Objects to Work
Construction of Balloons
A Dream of Paradise
The End of the Terror
The Farmer's Treasure
For My Children
The Fresh Kid
German Spring Parade
A Girl of the Woods
How Dr. Nicola Procured the Chinese Cane
How Money Circulates
If at First You Don't Succeed
Luck of the Cards
Making of a Sailor
Man with the Sack in Society
The Marble Heart; or, The Sculptor's Dream
Oh, What a Beard!
Pietro, the Candy Kid
Pietro, the Mule Driver
The Railroad Wreck
Runaway Model
A Tricky Convict
A Villain's Downfall
Sep 20 Aviation Contests at Rheims
The Bachelor's Visit
Blind Against His Will
The Bull Fight of Oran
Caught in His Own Trap
False Alarm
His Wife's Troublesome Twitching
In Old Kentucky
Taft in Chicago, and at the Ball Game
Tragical Love
When Woman Hates
Sep 21 Carlo and the Baby
Eleanora
Meskal, the Smuggler
Old Servants
The Ordeal
Saved from the Quicksands
The Siren's Necklace
Strike Time in Paris
Taking in a Reef
The Unspoken Goodbye
Sep 22 Dan Blake's Rival
Dr. Cook at Copenhagen
Dropped from the Clouds
The Five Divorcees
Gratitude
The Legend of the Lighthouse
The Tower of Nesle
Sep 23 An Aerial Elopement
The Conquering Hero
A Fair Exchange
Jackson's Last Steeple Chase
A Lucky Man
Nobody Loves a Fat Man
Stricken Blind
Sep 24 Careless Tramp
Caucasian Customs
A Knight for a Night
Love and War: An Episode of Waterloo
Marriage of Yvonne
Mrs. Minta's Husband
A Squaw's Sacrifice
True Love Never Runs Smoothly
The Winning Boat
Sep 25 The Adopted Child
All for a Nickel
The Eccentric Barber
Fantine; or, A Mother's Love
Father's Beautiful Beard
From Portofino to Nervi
The Good Samaritan
The Great Prize
Life on Board a Training Ship
The Little Milliner and the Thief
A Mother's Love
Necessity Is the Mother of Invention
Not Wanted on Voyage
On the Crest of the Waves
Phaedra
Servant's Good Joke
Theodora
Towards Immortalidated [sic]
Trained Birds
Sep 27 Across the Divide
A Fish Story
Grand Naval Parade
He Learns the Trick of Mesmerism
Leather Stocking
Mother-in-Law's Parrot
Naval Parade of the Hudson-Fulton
[Nelson-Hyland Fight Pictures]
Old Love Letters
The Priest's Niece
Suitor's Competition
Sep 28 Breach of Promise
Onawanda; or, An Indian's Devotion
The Romance of an Umbrella
Why Girls Leave Home
Wife or Child
Sep 29 The Blind Detective
The Brothers
Chasing the Ball
A Close Call
An Embarrassing Portfolio
Jane Is Unwilling to Work
Love, the Conqueror
Pierrot, the Fuddler
Sep 30 The Awakening
The Drunkard's Fate
Historic Parade
The Judge's Ward
The Man and the Law
Rats
Wanted, a Child
Oct 1 An Eventful Trip
Faithful Wife
A Game of Chess
The Mystery of the "Sleeper" Trunk
Two of a Kind
The Wallace Jewels
Oct 2 Arab Life
The Cremation
The Garbage of Paris
Good Cigars
Heroism Reconciles
Mady Millicent's Visitor
The Masterpiece
Mr. Muddlehead's Mistake
The Poacher
Romance of a Pierrot
The Scales of Justice
Vendetta
Oct 4 Billiken
Careless Life
Commander R. E. Peary
Entertaining Grandfather
Eve of the Wedding
How Binks Butted In
Love and Sacrifice
Military Parade
Pippa Passes; or, The Song of Conscience
The Story of a Banknote
A Trip to Yosemite
Who Discovered the North Pole?
Oct 5 Betty's Choice
Breaking the Bank
Forgiven at Last
Hot Time in Cold Quarters
Laddie
Never Eat Green Apples
The Pill Box
Oct 6 A Birthday Affair
Deputy
The Devil and the Painter
Female Sleuth
Gambling Passion
The Magic Melody
The Music Lesson
The Mysterious Motor
The Sheriff's Girl
Yachting off Cowes
Oct 7 A Blank Check
A Child's Plea
The Curse of Money
Fools of Fate
The North Pole Craze
Was It a Snake Bite?
Wheels of Justice
Oct 8 Dove Eye's Gratitude
Expert Glass Blowing
The Hand-Organ Man
How Jack Helped His Little Sister
The Minister's Daughter
Sister Angelica
United States Military Tournament
Oct 9 Adventures of an Emigrant
Anti-Fat Sanitarium
The Dog Pickpocket

For Her Sake; or, Two Sailors and a Girl
Napoleon
Sleuth and the Wig
Vagabond Life
Wedding Party in Luna Park
Oct 11 The Convict's Wife
Invisibility
The Little Teacher
Love Stronger Than Revenge
Maneuvers of Ambulance Corps.
Mistaken Identity
Out for the Day
Papa's Honeymoon
Pet of the Big Horn Ranch
The Trappers
Who Owned the Coat?
Oct 12 Convicting Evidence
How He Earned His Medal
A New Life
The New Servant
Noble and Commoner
Red Wing's Gratitude
Too Many on the Job
Winter Sports
Oct 13 The Cook's Mistake
His Mexican Bride
Liquid Air
The Love Trip
A Lucky Husband
Princess of the Sea
The Stolen Wireless
The Twelfth Juror
The Two Sergeants
A Wonderful Remedy
Oct 14 Bear and Forbear
A Change of Heart
Lost in Siberia
Sandy, the Poacher
The Telephone Call
Oct 15 Blessington's Bonny Babies
The Gold Seeker's Daughter
Hansel and Gretel
The Man and the Girl
The Romance of a Poor Girl
Whitler's Witless Wanderings
Oct 16 Alphonse, the Dead Shot
The Broken Violin
Chums
The Diver's Remorse
Life Behind the Bars at Joliet
One-Legged Pete and Pat
Physical Culture Fiend
The Red Domino
Oct 18 The Belated Wedding
Berlin Jack the Ripper
Bob's Electric Theater
A Drunkard's Son
Escaped Lunatic
Foolshead's Trousers
Haps and Mishaps
His Lost Love
Lobster Fishing
The Major and the Judge
A No Man's Land
Reformation of a Wine-Loving Artist
Roosevelt's Route Through Africa
Oct 19 A Dull Knife
His Helpmate
Husband's Strategy
Man in Pieces
The Mexican's Revenge
The Phantom Ship
Sardinian Brigand
Their Social Education
Winter Sports in Hungary
Oct 20 Almost a Suicide
Casting Bread upon the Water
Crown Prince of Germany Drilling Battery
For the Cause of Suffrage
A Good Trick
A Home Without Children
Hunting Jack Rabbits in Hungary
The Ogress
The Purse
The Widow
A Woman's Wit
Oct 21 Artful Dodger
Aunt Lena's Visit
A Broken Melody
The Cowboy Millionaire
The Expiation
Mignon
Oct 22 A Brother's Wrong
Drink
A Great Game
Iona, the White Squaw
The Lost Handbag
Oct 23 The Bracelet
Cosette
Country Life in a Flat
Gotacanal—over Norway's Rockies
A Lunatic's Day Off
Pittsburgh-Detroit Ball Game
Special Peary Film
Tickled to Death
Oct 24 [Johnson-Ketchel Fight Films]
Oct 25 The Boating Party
The Bogus Heir
The Brigand's Repentance
Briton and Boer
A Buried Secret
The False Oath
The Great Lottery
Hiawatha
In the Watches of the Night
The Indian Phantasy
Love and Vendetta
A Prince's Love
Romance in the Andes
The Strength of Love
A Visit to Uncle
The Would-Be Champion
Oct 26 Ambulance Ventilators
He Fell in Love with His Wife
The Lie
The Old Lord of Ventnor
The Two Mr. Whites
Oct 27 Awakened Memories
Brother and Sister
Cinderella Up-to-Date
The Gambler
Grotesque Make-Up
Maud Muller
The Plundered Museum
Sunday at Douarenez
Volcanoes of Java
Oct 28 Dope Head Clancy
Lines of White on a Sullen Sea
The Love Hunter
More Precious Than Gold
The Senorita
Oct 29 All's Fair in Love
Buffalo Racing in Madoera
The Girl Scout; or the Canadian Contingent in the Boer War
Life Behind the Scenes
Mexican's Crime
The Three Kisses
Oct 30 A Barrow Race
Burglar in the Trunk
Entombed Alive
[Judge Gaynor and Hon. John H. McCooey]
Mountebank's Watchcase
[Otto T. Bannard, Republican Candidate for Mayor of New York]
The Song of the Cradle
Nov [day undetermined]
The Fox Hunt
Nov 1 Across the Island of Ceylon
Brave Women of '76
The Gibson Goddess
A Lesson in Palmistry
The Lonely Bachelor
Love's Stratagem
Nero; or, The Burning of Rome
What's Your Hurry?
The Witches' Cavern
Nov 2 Adele's Wash Day
Change of Complexion
Comedy and Tragedy
Don Quixote
Honest John, the Coachman
Miss Annette Kellerman
Mystic Melodies
A Race for the Monkey
Nov 3 A Bachelor's Love Affair
Dynamite
Eat Your Soup
For Sale: A Baby
The General's Birthday Present
Hanson & Co.
The Hypnotist's Revenge
Life in Dalerne (Sweden)
The Lost Years
Tale of the Fiddle
"Ursula," World's Fastest Motor Boat
Nov 4 Actress and Child
Let Bygones Be Bygones
Napoleon and Princess Hatzfeld
Nursing a Viper
Sealed Instructions
The Trouble Kiss
Villainness Still Pursued Him
Nov 5 Bill, the Bill Poster
The Cattle Thieves
A Duel in Mid-Air
The Prodigal Son
A Very Attractive Gentleman
The Witch
Young Deer's Bravery
Nov 6 Belgrade, Capital of Servia
Cops on a Strike
The Destiny of Paul Wang
Elephant Hunting in Cambodge
From Cabin Boy to King
Malicious Rival
Princess and Slave
The Sack Race
The Silk Worm Series
Spartacus
Two Brothers
The Warrior's Sacrifice
Nov 8 Bandits of the Atlas Gorges
The Bearskin
Boatman of the Riviera
Culture of Tea in Java
Destiny
Enthusiastic Hand Ball Player
Father's Holiday
For Love's Sweet Sake
Force of Love
Henry the Third
Lines of the Hand
Miracle of a Necklace
Misadventures of a Pair of Trousers
Musical Waiter
Orange Growing in Palestine
Pirates of the Sea
The Restoration
The Stage Driver
Woes of a Cinematographer
Nov 9 All for the Love of a Girl
A Bride and Groom's Visit to the New York Zoological Gardens
Good for Evil
Into the Shadow
A Peace Agitator
The Pigmy World
A Sticky Proposition
Telltale Reflections
Nov 10 The Flight of Monsieur Valette
The Game
The Haunted Castle
A Heavy Gale at Biarritz
The Necklace of the Holy Virgin
The Robber Duke
A Serious Error
The Short-Sighted Governess
The Suicide Woods
A Tumultuous Elopement
Yachting on the Baltic
Nov 11 Across the Isthmus
Bertha's Birthday
The Blue Garter
Found in a Taxi
"Hello, Bill"
The Kissing Germ
The Light That Came
Nov 12 Dora
The Farmer's Son
His Masterpiece
Logging in the Italian Alps
Man with the Dolls
A Man with Three Wives
The Ranchman's Wife
Running in Hard Luck
Nov 13 Balloon Trip over Turin
A Broken Life
The Cabman's Good Fairy
Good Lesson in Charity
Harlequin's Nightmare
How Foolshead Paid His Debts
The Invaders
Launcelot and Elaine
Life for a Life
A Message to Napoleon; or, An Episode in the Life of the Great Prisoner at Elba
Mischief of a Big Drum
Nana's Mother
Now Keep Smiling
The Rhymester's Ruse
Romance of Life
Sam's Artistic Beard
The Street Arab
Substitute Pig
Two Little Runaways
Nov 14 Rigoletto

Nov 15 The Brave (?) Policeman
Children of the Sea
The Cursed Cage
Electrified Hunchback
The Fisherman's Bride
The Forest Ranger's Daughter
High Treason
In India, Marriage of the Nephew of the Maharajah of Tagore
Two Chums Looking for Wives
Two Women and a Man
Nov 16 Benedict Arnold
A Convict's Heroism
The Gypsy's Secret
The Imp of the Bottle
Indian Basket Making
Mysterious Luggage
A Set of Teeth
A Winter's Tale
Nov 17 The Count's Wooing
Fighting Suffragettes
Goddess of the Sea
Her Dramatic Career
A Mislaid Baby
Mr. and Mrs. Duff
The Personal Conduct of Henry
Workhouse to Mansion
Nov 18 The Cost of Forgetfulness
Foiled
An Hour of Terror
Julius Caesar
A Midnight Adventure
A Millionaire Bootblack
Servant's Revenge
Sweet Revenge
Up San Juan Hill
Nov 19 How French Perfumes Are Made
An Indian's Bride
The Love of Little Flora
The Nobleman's Dog
The Pale Face's Wooing
Three Thanksgivings
Nov 20 Adonis Is Robbed of His Clothes
The Best Man Wins
A Girl's Cross Roads
Moon for Your Love
A Mother's Heart
The Patient from Punkville
The Sins of the Fathers
Visions of a Nag
Nov 22 Ali Bey's Dancing Drops
Honest Little Rag Picker
Honor Among Thieves
The Hostage
In Wrong Simms
John Farley's Redemption
Late for the Recital
Legend of the Good Knight
Levitsky Sees the Parade
Napoleon's Game of Chess
On the Border
The Open Gate
The Rubber Man
When Women Win
Nov 23 Belle of the Harvest
Marriage of Love
A Red Man's Love
A Rose of the Tenderloin
Why They Married
Nov 24 A Convenient Lamp-Post
A Heart's Devotion
A Lady's Purse
On the Wrong Scent
The Red Star Inn
The Sleeper
Tulips
Nov 25 The Delayed Telegram
Finnigan's Initiation
Martyr or Crank?
The Mountaineer's Honor
On the Little Big Horn; or, Custer's Last Stand
President Taft in the Far West
Nov 26 Annual Celebration of School Children at Newark, NJ
The Bigamist
Bluebeard
Dooley's Thanksgiving Turkey
The Governor's Daughter
The Parson's Prayer
Thanksgiving, Then and Now
Nov 27 Chinese Amusements
Dream of a Fisherman
Jean Valjean
Judgment
Mix-Up at Court
The Mixed Letters
The Village Scare
Nov 29 Brought to Terms
A Bunch of Lilacs
The Double Six
Her Generous Way
In the Window Recess
Leopard Hunting in Abyssinia
A Life for a Life
Making It Pleasant for Him
Marvelous Shaving Soap
The Motor Cyclist
The Painter's Idol
Professor Short Sight's Surprise
The Servant of the Actress
Spanish Marriage
The Trick That Failed
Nov 30 Atlanta Automobile Speedway Races
The Bridegroom's Joke
The Broken Vase
Dirigible Balloons at St. Louis
The Heart of a Clown
In the Consomme
Pressing Business
The Wonderful Electro-Magnet
Dec [day undetermined]
Marie Dressler
Dec 1 Baby Swallows a Nickel
A Boy Hero; or, The Fisherman's Son
Consul Crosses the Atlantic
Fortune Favors the Brave
Legend of Orpheus
Seeing Things
Trollhattan
Two Sides to a Story
The Wolf Hunt
Dec 2 The Answered Prayer
The Cub Reporter
The Death Disc: A Story of the Cromwellian Period
An Indian Wife's Devotion
The Lemon Sisters at Muldoon's Picnic
A Million Dollar Mix-Up
Dec 3 Forced into Marriage
The Geisha Who Saved Japan
The Keeper of the Light
The Message of an Arrow
The Three Neighbors
Dec 4 A Cask of Good Old Wine
The Crocodile Hunt
From the Egg to the Spit
His Reformation
How to Get a City Job
Indiscreet Father and Son
The Life of Moses
Little Willie's Trip to the North Pole
Punishment of an Athlete
An Unlucky Acquisition
Wrestling
X-Ray Glasses
Dec 6 An Athlete of a New Kind
Captain Fracassee
The Disguised Bridegroom
The Electric Safe
The Engineer's Daughter
He Wanted a Baby
The Heir of Clavencourt Castle
His Last Game
The Lady's Companion
The Little Vendean
Mr. Sadman's Cure
She Took Mother's Advice
The Song That Reached Her Heart
Through the Breakers
Dec 7 A Day with Our Soldier Boys
In a Pickle
A Lesson in Domestic Economy
Listen
My Lord in Livery
A Run for the Money
Top-Heavy Mary
What the Cards Foretold
Dec 8 The Bachelor and the Maid
Capturing the North Pole; or, How He Cook'ed Peary's Record
The End of the Tragedy
The Evil Philter
The Fatal Ball; or, The Miner's Daughter
Gerhardi Mohr
Impossible to Get Sleep
A Pair of Slippers
The Secret Chamber
Temptations of the Gold Fields; or, The Two Gold Diggers
Dec 9 A Bad Case of Grip
The Heroine of Mafeking
If Love Be True
July 4th, 1910
The Redman's View
Dec 10 Bear Hunt in Russia
The House of Cards
Masquerader's Charity
The Rally Round the Flag
Re-united at the Gallows
Dec 11 Daughters of Poverty
Exploits of a Cowboy
Gambling with Death
Macbeth
The Ranchman's Rival
Santa Claus and the Miner's Child
Willyboy Gets His
Dec 12 La Grande Breteche
Dec 13 Beethoven
The Beggarman's Gratitude
A Corner in Wheat
Dr. Lyvenemup's Elixir
Dottynob's Dancing
Jinks the Grouch
Pine Ridge Feud
Repairing the House
The Smuggler's Sweetheart
The Tramp's Romance
A Trip to the Arctic
The Two Sons
When Courage Fled
Dec 14 Comrades Under General Grant
Fenton of the 42nd
The Life Buoy
Manhood's Reward
A Merry Christmas and a Happy New Year
The New Policeman
Nothing Is Ever Lost
The Professor and the Thomas Cats
Dec 15 An Amateur Hold-Up
A Female Reporter
The Living Doll
Punch and Judy
The Red Signal
Switzerland, Conquering the Alps
The Ugly Girl
Dec 16 Her Mother's Mistake
In a Hempen Bag
The Indian
Romance of the Rocky Coast
The Test
Dec 17 A Gift from Santa Claus
The Law of the Mountains
The Love of a Savage
The Lucky Number
The Strong Tonic
Dec 18 Beyond the Rockies
The Butcher's Bill
Cambyses, King of Persia
The Forced Loan
Hector, the Angel Child
The Honey Industry
In Southern Sweden
Mr. Nosey Parker
Mother-in-Law Crazy with Music
Off to the Wedding
Reformed Thief
The Shepherd's Flute
The Spanish Girl
Two Christmas Tides
Dec 20 The Chemist's Bell
The Death of the Duke D'Enghien
Don Quixote
The Drunkard's Christmas
Explorer's Dream
Granny's Darling
Lest We Forget
A Little Disagreement
Lorenzi De Medica
Mac Nabb Wants to Get Arrested
A Modern Dr. Jekyll
Mother-in-Law Must Fly
A Persistent Lover
A Policeman's Xmas Eve
The Prisoner's Strategy
Three Christmas Dinners
Through the Hood River Valley and Along the Columbia in Oregon
A Trap for Santa Claus
Vindicated
Dec 21 The Cook Makes Madeira Sauce
The Forgotten Watch
A Happy Accident
The Mischievous Elf
Re-united by Santa Claus
The Stranger
Dec 22 Contest for a Handkerchief
Fiorella, the Bandit's Daughter
From the Fighting Top of a Battleship in Action

A Kiss in the Dark
The Love Token
Object: Matrimony
Dec 23 Blissville the Beautiful
The Christian Martyrs
In Little Italy
Dec 24 Agriculture in Hungary
The Birth of Jesus
The Cardboard Baby
Faust
An Italian Love Story
Dec 25 Absorbing Tale
Alberno & Rosamunda
Bath Chair
The Deceiver
The Deserter
Drama in the Far West
Drama of Villasgne
Electra
Father's Busy Papering
The Good Doctor
The Greek Slave's Passion
Gypsy Child
The Happy Widower
The Heart of a Cowboy
Interrupted Rendezvous
The Kidnapped King
Magda
A Midsummer Night's Dream
Mule Driver's Bride
Original Sausage Tale
An Outcast's Christmas
Pork Butcher
Pretty Fisher-Woman
Real Brittany
Reincarnated Mummy
Repentance
The Sailor's Son
Silly Billy
Spring Heeled Jack
Suicide Club
A Surprising Powder
The Thames in Winter
Theodora
Turning Out of Time
Who Seeks Finds
The Wonderful Pearl
Dec 27 Admiral Nelson's Son
The Awakening of Bess
A Bad Bargain
Buried Alive
Marvellous Garlands
The New Chief
The Persistent Poet
To Save Her Soul
Dec 28 The Cap of Fortune
A Clever Sleuth
Excelsior
The Fallen Idol
Foolshead Pays a Visit
Hush Money
Mug Chump's Early Morning Excursion
The Power of the Press
Tobacco Mania
Dec 29 Battle in the Clouds
The Gold Digger's Son
Jack's Birthday
Oh, You Doggie!
The Park of Caserta
The Policeman's Revolver
The Story of My Life
A Well Earned Medal
Dec 30 Choosing a Husband
A Daughter of the Sioux
The Day After
The Justice of Solomon
The Motherless Waif
The Rheumatic Bridegroom
A Romance of the South
Three Fingered Jack
Dec 31 A Christmas Legend
Corsican Hospitality
The Emperor's Staff Officer
Fishing Industry at Gloucester, Mass.
A Live Corpse
The Red Cross Heroine
A Slave to Drink

1910 [month undetermined]
The Comet
Kinematographic X-Ray Picture of a Human Stomach During Digestion, Taken During One Inspiration
Love-Making Under Difficulties
[Roosevelt at the Arkansas State Fair]
With Roosevelt in Africa

Jan [day undetermined]
A Lucky Knock
The Story of a Shoe
Victims of Jealousy
Jan 1 Cupid and the Motor Boat
The Legion of Honor
Refreshing Bath
Tabby's Finish
Trials of a Schoolmaster
Vengeance; or, The Forester's Sacrifice
A Western Maid
Why He Did Not Win Out
Jan 3 Foolshead's Holiday
A Happy New Year
Madam's Favorite
The Marriage of the Cook
Patrician and Slave
The Poem of Life
The Rocky Road
The Salted Mine
Seal and Walrus Hunting
The Smuggler's Game
The Strolling Players
Their Chaperoned Honeymoon
A Victim of Circumstances
A Wall Street Chance
The Winning Punch
Jan 4 The Avenging Dentist
Forty Years in the Land of Midian [The Life of Moses Part II]
A Frozen Ape
Pardners
The Wreck at Sea
Jan 5 The Adventuress
Drama at Sea
Football Craze
How Hubby Made Good
The King's Command
The Overzealous Domestic
Shanghai of To-day
Tragedy at the Mill
The Wife's Sacrifice
Jan 6 Alderman Krautz's Picnic
The Dancing Girl of Butte
The Highlander's Defiance
The Nemesis
The Tattooed Arm
Jan 7 Ashes
The Deacon's Daughter
The Engineer's Romance
An English Boxing Bout
Modern Highwayman
Red Girl's Romance
Jan 8 Child as Benefactor
His Only Child
His Opponent's Card
How the Dog Saved the Flag
The Last Look
On the Bank of the River
Richelieu; or, The Conspiracy
The Rivals
A Seat in the Balcony
Jan 10 Brave Little Heart
By Right of Love
The Garibaldi Boy
Glimpses of an Indian Village
Her Terrible Ordeal
Hotstuff Takes on the Champions
The Law of Destiny
Miss Moneybags Wishes to Wed
Monarchs of All Nations
Over the Wire
The Rebel's Fate
Rudolph of Hapsburg
A Tale of the Backwoods
The Terrors of the Family
Toes and Teeth
Women in India
Jan 11 Bear Hunt in the Rockies
The Call Boy's Vengeance
The Old Maid's Valentine
A Redman's Devotion
Shooting in the Haunted Woods
Towser's New Job
Jan 12 Broken Happiness
Camille
Electric Insoles
An Episode of Napoleon's War with Spain
Home of the Gypsies
My Aunt's Birthday
The Old Maid and the Burglar
Robert Macaire; or, The Two Vagabonds
True to His Oath
Jan 13 All on Account of the Milk
The Celebrated Case (Part I): Convicted by His Own Child
Forgiven
He Joined the Frat
Mishaps of Bonehead
Under the Stars and Stripes
Wild Duck Hunting on Reel Foot Lake
Jan 14 The Beggar's Repentance
A Forester's Sweetheart
The Parson's Umbrella
The Romance of a Trained Nurse
Story of a Leg
Troop "B", 15th U.S. Cavalry Bareback Squad in the Monkey Drill at Fort Myer, Virginia
A Warrior Bold
Jan 15 An Absorbing Tale
Amorous Minstrel
At the Carnival
Bogus General
Boy Scouts
Church Robber
Consequence of a Lie
Death of the Brigand Chief
Decorated by the Emperor
The Double
Drama Under Richelieu
Episode of French Revolution
A Father's Love
Follow Me
Forced Treatment
Foster Brothers
Getting Rid of Uncle
Good Tramp
Human Squib
Marvelous Indeed
Mind, I Catch You Smoking
Naughty Boys
On a Racket
Patent Glue
Railway on the Ice Sea
Review of U.S. Troops—Fort Leavenworth
Rivals
Roast Chicken
Simple Simon
A Sister's Sacrifice
The Son of the Wilderness
A Stag Hunt in Java
The Twine
Tyrolean Tragedy
Jan 17 Arthur's Little Love Affair
The Freebooter's Captive
He Got Rid of the Moths
His Vacation
Jealousy, a Bad Counsellor
Mammy's Boy Joins the Army
The Miners
Muggins
A New Divorce Cure
On the Reef
Romeo and Juliet at the Seaside
A Slippery Day
Testing Their Love
The Tide of Fortune
A Visit to Bombay
A Young Girl's Sacrifice
Jan 18 A Cowboy's Reward
Fatal Fascination
Getting Square with the Inventor
In the Nick of Time
The Little Heroine
Out with It
The Toymaker's Secret
Jan 19 Adventures of a Sandwich Man
An Aerial Acrobat
The Bareback Rider
The Brothers
The Coast Guard
Flower Parade at Pasadena, California
Italian Artillery
Pauli
The Refugee
Riva, Austria, and the Lake of Garda
Won by a Hold-Up
Jan 20 The Call
The Celebrated Case (Part II): Saved by His Own Child
The Courtship of Miles Standish
Martyrs of Pompeii
The Usurper
The Wages of Sin
Jan 21 The Coquette
Fickle Fortune
The Luck of Roaring Camp
The Magic Flower
The Painter's Sweetheart
Romany Rob's Revenge
Jan 22 Anarchists on Board; or, The Thrilling Episode on the S.S. "Slavonia"
The Confession

Count Tolstoi
The Devil Is Loose
Five Minutes to Twelve
Football Player
A Pair of Schemers; or, My Wife and My Uncle
A Russian Heroine
Swallowed by the Deep
The Tempting Collar
There Are Some Ghosts
Jan 24 Acrobatic Exercises by the Colibris Dwarfs
Adoring an Ad.
An Afternoon Off
Cupid, D. D. S.
The Honor of His Family
Never Again
The Ranch King's Daughter
A Rose of the Philippines
The Unlucky Fisherman
Jan 25 The Plagues of Egypt and the Deliverance of the Hebrew [The Life of Moses Part III]
The Price of Patriotism
A Romance of the Prairie
Seaside Adventures at Home
A Woman's Strategy
Jan 26 Angler and the Cyclist
An Artist's Inspiration
A Choice Policeman
He Would Be an Acrobat
The Lass Who Loves a Sailor
The Last Keepsake
The Modern Messenger Boy
Motherless
Tommy in Dreamland
Uncle Learns to Hypnotize
Walkaway's New Boots
Jan 27 Bear Hunting
Bonehead's Second Adventure
The Devil, the Servant, and the Man
The Flirto-Maniac
The Last Deal
Marble Quarrying in Tennessee
The Ordeal
Jan 28 A Georgia Possum Hunt
His Imaginary Crime
The Leather Industry
The Man Who Lost
The Scarecrow
The Skipper's Yarn
Jan 29 The Burglar Trap
Cousin Lou for Mine
The Girl and the Judge; or A Terrible Temptation
A Good Winning
The Great Divide
Her City Beaux
The Montana Ranchman
The Mystery of the Lama Convent; or, Dr. Nicola in Thibet
On the Firing Line
An Outlaw's Sacrifice
The Strong Man
Tale of Colonial Days: An Episode in the Life of Alexander Hamilton and Aaron Burr
The Timid One
Wild Waves at St. Jean-de-Lux
Jan 31 Bill's Boots
The Cloister's Touch
Coffee Culture
Coquette's Suitors
Dick's a Winner
Our German Cousin
Shooting an Oil Well
Sports in the Snow
Too Much Protection
Feb [day undetermined]
New York of Today
Feb 1 Ascending the Jura Mountains
Caught in His Own Trap
The Female Bandit
The Golden Lily
A Japanese Peach Boy
The Skeleton
Feb 2 The Clown's Big Moment
Hamlet, Prince of Denmark
Hero and Leander
The Might of the Waters
The Postmistress
Sheltered in the Woods
The Step-Mother
A Voice from the Fireplace
The Wrong Man
Feb 3 Foxy Hobo Married for Love
A Heroine of Chance
It Might Have Been
Justice
Politics
Sentimental Sam
Tom's Last Steeple Chase
The Woman from Mellon's
Feb 4 The Bad Man from Riley's Gulch
By His Own Hands
His Just Deserts
The Little Old Men of the Woods
The Model Drama
Roller Skating in Australia
Strike Instigator
The Surprise Party
Winter Days in Sweden
Feb 5 Adam II — Miscellaneous
Civil War
A Critical Situation
The Foxy Soldiers; or, How Schmidt Got to the Masquerade
His Daughter's Legacy
Love and Treason
Sensational Logging
Submarines in Paris
Twelfth Night
A Woman's Destiny
Feb 7 The Bandit
The Child and the Dancing-Jack
The Course of True Love
In the Serpent's Power
Justice in the Far North
Mr. Giddy's Revenge
The Samaritan's Courtship
The Two Raffles
Feb 8 Doctor's Peculiar Treatment
In Winter's Grip
The Livingston Case
The Passing Shadow
Servant from the Country
Settled Out of Court
The Ten of Spades; or, A Western Raffle
Feb 9 Coals of Fire
The Confederate Spy
The Consequence of a Nod
Cora, the Contraband's Daughter
In Ancient Greece
The Longing for Gaol
The Mountaineer
Pirate's Fiancée
The Price of Fame
Spike's Battle
The Strongest
Venetian Isles
Feb 10 Celestial Vengeance
A Child of the Prairie
The Duke's Plan
In the Shadow of Mt. Shasta
[Salt Lake City]
Feb 11 Before and After
An Equine Hero
The Feud
Hard Heart
A Queen of the Burlesque
Souvenirs of Paris
The Troubadour
Young Deer's Gratitude
Feb 12 A Bag Race
Bitter-Sweet
False Oath
Foolshead Preaches Temperance
Foolshead Receives
The Foot Juggler
The Gambler's Doom
The Jockey
Nema Lescout
Never Despair; or, From Misery to Happiness
The Paris Disaster
The Untimely Visit
The Victory of Israel [The Life of Moses Part IV]
Vulture of Seine
Western Chivalry
Worried to Death
Feb 14 The Blind Man's Tact
A Bootblack's Daily Labor in Algiers
Brown's Gouty Foot
Druid Remains in Brittany
The Enterprising Clerk
The Hand of the Heiress
Loving Hearts
One Night, and Then —
Paris Flood
[Paris Flood Pictures]
The Roman
The Serum; or, The Antidote
Feb 15 Daring Lion's Bride
The Ghost
Government Rations
Pastoral Scenes
The President's Special
Tragedy at Sea
The Wayside Shrine
Feb 16 The Acrobatic Fly
Aviation at Los Angeles, Calif.
Baby's First Tooth
The Blue Swan Inn
Carmen
A Daughter's Devotion
The Fisherman's Granddaughter
Her Dolly's Revenge
I Have Lost My Latch Key
The Man Who Could Not Sit Down
The Old Maid and Bonehead
The Silent Messenger
The Silent Piano
Feb 17 Camargo
Easy Job
The Englishman and the Girl
The Girls of the Range
A Honeymoon Through Snow to Sunshine
Feb 18 Dooley's Holiday
Hobo's Dream of Wealth
The Impostor
The Little Beggar
The Miniature
Muriel's Stratagem
A Panicky Picnic
"That's What They All Say"
The Trapper and the Redskins
Trip Through North of England
A Trip to Mars
Feb 19 Better Than Gold
The Comedy-Graph
The Cowboy and the Squaw
Fate Against Her
Louise Strozzi
The Promised Land [The Life of Moses Part V]
Ruined by His Son
Three Queens and a Jack
Feb 21 A Corsican's Revenge
Duty and Conscience
Face to Face
The Gunby's Sojourn in the Country
His Last Burglary
Jane and the Stranger
The New Marshall at Gila Creek
Saved from the Tide
Feb 22 Duped
For Her Father's Honor
His Fears Confirmed
Paid in Full
A Victim of Bridge
Feb 23 The Buried Secret
The Dog of the Cheese Monger
A Family Outing
The Fisherman's Honour
Foolshead at the Ball
In Arizona
The Lamp-Post Inspector
The Miser's Child
Oh, So Sick!
The Runaway Stove
The Third Degree
The Winning of Father
Feb 24 Back Among the Old Folks
The Death of Minnehaha
The District Attorney
Taming a Husband
Feb 25 Dooley Referees the Big Fight
The Harry Brothers
The Indian Scout's Vengeance
Iron Arm's Remorse
A Lesson by the Sea
Lost and Regained
Ouchard, the Merchant
That Girl of Dixon's
Feb 26 Blue Fishing Nets
Doctor's Sacrifice
Granny's Birthday
In the Gulf of Salerno
The Legend of King Midas
The Mexican's Faith
The Soul of Venice
Why Fricot Was Sent to College
The Witch's Ballad
Feb 28 The Castles on the Rhine from Bingen to Coblenz
The Final Settlement
The Governor's Pardon
Industries in Southern California
Joseph Sold by His Brethren

A Mica Mine, the Ullugura Mountains
Nick Carter as Acrobat
The Ranger and the Girl
Mar 1 The Cowboy and the School Marm
An Eye for an Eye
The Plucky Suitor
Ranson's Folly
Scenes of the Australian Gold Fields
The Vale of Aude
Mar 2 Baby Bet
The Court Jester
The Egg Trust
Electrical Safe
From Beyond the Seas
The Golf Mania
Jack's Return
Lines of the Hand
The Mysterious Track
Rags, Old Iron!
The Sailor's Dog
The Shirtwaist Strike
The Treachery of the Pequots
The Two Mothers
The Violin Maker of Cremona
The Wrestling Match
Mar 3 The Millionaire's Adventure
The New Minister
The Newlyweds
Samuel of Posen
Mar 4 At the Eleventh Hour
Brittany Lassies
The Door
The Electric Bathtub
The Girl Thief
The Man Under the Bed
The New Partners
On the Border Line
Retaliation
Mar 5 The Beautiful Snow
A Happy Turn
The History of a Sardine Sandwich
The Mad Drainpipe
The Ostrich and the Lady
Pierrot
A Pleasant Walk
The Poet of the Revolution
The Ranch Girl's Legacy
Supreme Recognition
The Vindictive Foreman
Mar 7 The Cage (An Episode in the Adventures of Morgan the Pirate)
Marriage in Haste
Mother Love
Strenuous Massage
Taming Wild Horses at Buenos Aires
The Thread of Destiny
Told in the Golden West
Tragic Idyl
Mar 8 A Brother's Devotion
Drama on the Britain Coast
The Great Scoop
Her Cowboy Lover
The Indian and the Cowgirl
The Legend of Daphne
My Milliner's Bill
The Right Decision
Mar 9 The Arrest of Duchess de Berry
At the Bar of Justice
A Father's Patriotism
Foolshead Chief of the Reporters
He Knew Best
Her Soldier Sweetheart
An Interrupted Honeymoon
On the Little Big Horn
Salome
The Town Traveler's Revenge
A Tragic Adventure
The Water-Flyer
A Wolf in Sheep's Clothing
Mar 10 Across the Plains
The Devotion of Women
Hearts Are Trump
In Old California
Sacred Fire
We Will Die Together, Love
Mar 11 "Conscience;" or, The Baker Boy
A Cure for Timidity
His First Valentine
Love Drops
Mr. Short Sighted
The Mysterious Armour
The Robber Baron
The Rose of the Ranch
A Seaside Flirtation
Mar 12 Count of Monte Christo
Fatal Imprudence
The Fence on Bar Z Ranch
The Pirate Airship
Rabelais' Joke
Sporty Dad
A Tale of a Tenement
Taming a Grandfather
They Have Vanished My Wife
A Wedding During the French Revolution
Mar 14 Aspirants to the Hand of Helen
The Blunderer
The Broken Oath
The Converts
A Crowded Hotel
The Dawn of Freedom
Her First Love
Mamma's Angel Child
Nelson-Wolgast Fight
The Revenge of Dupont L'Anguille
Tobacco Culture
Uncle's Money
Mar 15 The Actor's Children
For His Sister's Honor
Fruit Growing, Grand Valley, Colorado (The Results of Irrigation)
In the Shadow of the Cliffs
A Mountain Blizzard
The Saraband Dance
Victims of Fate
War Time Pals
Mar 16 A Bullfight in Mexico
Burglar's Daughter
The Captive
The Country Schoolmaster
Insidious Weapons
The Inventor's Model
Life in the Next Century
Loisette
Method in His Madness
Peter's Patent Paint
The Seminole's Trust
The Shepherdess
The Silver Lining
A Trip Along the Rhine
The Two Brothers
Mar 17 After Four Generations
In the Frozen North
The Irish Boy
The Love of Lady Irma
The Man
The Time-Lock Safe
Mar 18 The Enchanted Castle
The Exile
Frankenstein
Mexican's Ward
The Mystery of Temple Court
Mar 19 The Betraying Mirror
The Courting of the Merry Widow
The Girl and the Fugitive
In the Foothills of Savoy
Little Jack's Letter
The Parson's Poster
A Quiet Honeymoon
The Theft of the Diamonds
Wild Birds in Their Haunts
A Willful Dame
Mar 21 Faithful
His Sick Friend
Honesty, Its Own Reward
The Lover's Embarrassment
A Mother's Heart
Stung!
The Village Inventor
A Woman's Repentance
Mar 22 Capital vs. Labor
John Hardy's Invention
The Man from Texas
The Man with the Weak Heart
The Queen and the Mirror
St. Elmo
A Western Romance
The Wild Coast of Belle Island
A Winter Romance at Niagara Falls
Mar 23 For the King
The Girl and the Bandit
The Hand of Uncle Sam
The Horseshoe
A Maid of the Mountains
Military Dirigible
Over the Appennines of Italy
The Sea's Vengeance
The Tenderfoot
Mar 24 Adventures of Princess Lovelock
A Family Feud
How a Bad Tempered Man Was Cured
The Stage Note
Stunts on Skates
Troublesome Lad
The Twisted Trail
Two Gentlemen of the Road
The Wonderful Wizard of Oz
Mar 25 The Banks of the Ganges
Company "D" to the Rescue
Double Six
Dwarf Detective
The Hand of Fate
No Trifling with Love
The Railway Mail Clerk
The Suit Case Mystery
Mar 26 The Airship Gaze
The Broken Spell
A Conquest
The Fall of Babylon
Foolshead Wishes to Marry the Governor's Daughter
Foxy Ernest
Innkeeper's Daughter
A Ranchman's Wooing
The Rivalry of the Two Guides
Sleeping Pills
Tsing Fu, the Yellow Devil
Mar 28 Gold Is Not All
His Spanish Wife
The Little Vixen
The Polar Bear Hunt in the Arctic Seas
Transfusion
The Treasure Hunters
The Treasure of Louis
A Trip to Berne
Mar 29 Bradford's Claim
The Capture of the Burglar
The Diary of a Nurse
The End of the Trail
The Indiscretion of Betty
The Man Who Waited
Nannina
She's Done It Again
Uncle's Will
Mar 30 The Cowboy Preacher
Cured by a Tip
Drama on the Reef
Driven to Steal
His Hunting Trip
Inventive Trouser
Lo, the Poor Indian
Making Sherry Wine at Xeres
The Midnight Escape
Out of Sight, Out of Mind
Red Hawk's Last Raid
Robber's Ruse
A Sudden Telephone Call
An Unworthy Fiancé
Mar 31 The Daughter's Choice
Hard Cash
His Last Dollar
The Smoker
The Wife of Marcius
Apr 1 Andrea Chenier
The Further Adventures of the Girl Spy
Michael Strogoff
Pa, Ma and Baby
A Race for Inheritance
The Rhine Falls at Schaffhausen
A Shot in Time
The Tongue of Scandal
A Woman's Caprice
Apr 2 Amateur Billiards
Athletic Sports in India
The Dreamer
The Flower of the Ranch
The Fruits of Vengeance
Lorenzo, the Wolf
Madame Sans Gene; or, The Duchess of Danzig
O'er Crag and Torrent
The Servant and the Tutor
Apr 4 After the Fall of the "Eagle"
Agra
As It Is in Life
Back to Boarding
The Common Enemy
The Good Boss
The Miser's Daughter
The Right House, But —
The Theater of Phenomenons
Apr 5 The Actress
Boxing Fever
Daddy's Double
A Drama of the Mountain Pass
From Shadow to Sunshine
The Heart of a Rose
It Pays to Advertise
Love and Art
Poetry of the Waters
Romance of a Snake Charmer

Apr 6 The Duchess of Langeais
The Fly Pest
Frontier Day in the West
Henry's New Hat
Her Father's Choice
Honest Little Urchin
Imagination
My Life Remembrances of a Dog
Partners
Rico, the Jester
The Snake Man
An Unpleasant Dream
The Uprising of the Utes
The Vintage
Wandering Wilfred's April Fool's Day
Apr 7 Cyclone Pete's Matrimony
First Love Is Best
His Second Wife
Hugo, the Hunchback
Mother Land
A Rich Revenge
Roosevelt at Messina
Roosevelt's Reception
Apr 8 Come to Supper with Me
Elektra
The Gipsy Girl's Love
The Hunchbacked Fiddler
Motherless Waif
New Little Mother
Paula Peters and Her Trained Animals
Red Wing's Loyalty
Sandy the Substitute
Apr 9 At the Farm
The Conqueror
A Family Quarrel
A Hasty Operation
Honest Peggy
Hustling Mr. Brown
The Kiss Was Mightier Than the Sword
A New Burglar Alarm
O'er Hill and Vale
The Ranger's Bride
The Valuable Hat
Apr 11 The Clay Baker
The Fisherman's Luck
Hemlock Hoax, the Detective
Her Sister's Sin
Jones' Watch
Musical Masterpiece
One-Legged Acrobats
A Romance of the Western Hills
The Rosary
Spanish Fandalgo
The Strength of Duty
Apr 12 For Her Sister's Sake
The Girl in the Barracks
His Mother's Letter
King Cotton
Rivalry in the Oil Fields
The Stubborn Lover
Vintage in Lanquedoc
The Volcano of Chinyero
Apr 13 An Artist's Temptation
At Double Cross Ranch
The Attack upon the Train
Fricot in College
Ice Scooters on Lake Ronkonkoma
The Legend of the Cross
The Lookout; or, Saved from the Sea
The Miniature
The Old Fiddler
A Ramble Through the Isle of Sumatra
Their Sea Voyage
Uncle Eph's Dream
Washed Ashore
Apr 14 The Ace of Hearts
Branding a Thief
Dorothy and the Scarecrow in Oz
The Kid
Western Justice
Apr 15 The Call of the Heart
The Forager
Her First Appearance
Johnny's Pictures of the Polar Regions
The Mask Maker
The Old Shoe Came Back
Red Wing's Constancy
Sam Langford and John Flynn Fight
A 29-Cent Robbery
Apr 16 The Bad Man and the Preacher
The Bully
Egyptian Village Market
The Hidden Treasure
In Africa
Mephisto at a Masquerade
The Merry Widow Takes Another Partner
A Mistake
The Mistaken Bandit
The Pillagers
[Talking Moving Picture]
The Three Brothers
Touring the Canary Islands
Apr 18 Ascending the Sea of Ice
The Greenhorns
In War Time
Love the Conqueror
Mr. A. Jonah
The Queen's Attendant
The Rival Cooks
Roosevelt in Africa
Simone
Thou Shalt Not
When the Cat's Away
Apr 19 A Case of Identity
A Husband's Mistake
Love's Awakening
A Penitent of Florence
Re-Making of a Man
Apr 20 The Cowboy and the Lieutenant
Down in Mexico
Fighting the Iroquois in Canada
Grandpa's Darling
The Heart of a Vagabond
The Lover's Oracle
Othello
Petit Jean Louis d'Or & Co.
She Wanted a Bow-Wow
Through the Tunnel
Trawler Fishing in a Hurricane
A Wise Guy
A Young Aviator's Dream
Apr 21 The Angel of Dawson's Claim
Davy Crockett
The First-Born
The Maelstrom
The Tenderfoot's Triumph
Apr 22 Adventures of a Cowpuncher
The Bravest Girl in the South
Delhi
Her Battle for Existence
Her Sweet Revenge
The Miner and Camille
Ready in a Minute
Sand Man's Cure
The Wreath
Apr 23 The Chivalrous Stranger
The Conjuror
The Cowboy's Sweetheart
A Day Off
The Four Seasons
Isabella of Arragon
Judith and Holofernes
St. Elmo
The Storm
Apr 25 A Child of the Sea
Mr. Mix at the Mardi Gras
On Time for Business
The Parisian
The Power of a Smile
The Six-Legged Sheep
Venice
The Way of the World
Apr 26 Among the Snowy Mountains
Gallegher
Grandfather's Story
Hazel, the Heart Breaker
A Newspaper Error
Paying Attention
The Penalty of Beauty
The Potter's Wheel
Rattlesnakes
Solving the Puzzle
Through the Darkness
Apr 27 Baby Has the Colic
The Bagpipe Player
Bethlehem
Days of '49
A Doctor's Revenge
Flat to Rent
Fricot Is Learning a Handicraft
Jim Wants to Get Punched
The Latest in Garters
The Rival Miners
The Sacred Turquoise of the Zuni
Saved by an Indian
Volcanic Eruptions of Mt. Aetna
Apr 28 The Angelus
Artist's Child
Indian Blood
The New Shawl
The Reservists
The Seal of the Church
Tommy and the Powder
Twenty Francs
Up a Tree
Apr 29 The Cigars His Wife Bought
Drowsy Dick, Officer No. 73
The Love Romance of the Girl Spy
The Merry Medrano Circus Clowns
The Portrait
The Rescue of the Pioneer's Daughter
She Wanted to Marry a Hero
The Subterfuge
A Yorkshire School
Apr 30 Bud's Escapade
The Captain of the Guard
The Cheese Box
Deep Sea Fishing
The False Friar
The Fashionable Sport
Hope of the Village
The Minotaur
Saved from the Sultan's Sentence
The Sculptor's Dream
A Vein of Gold
May [day undetermined]
Panoramic Railway View from Front of Train
May 2 The Broken Friendship
The Cow-Boy Girls
The Gold-Seekers
The Master Mechanic
Mrs. Nosey
My Maid Is Too Slow
Only a Faded Flower
The Picturesque Pyrenees
Safety Suit for Skaters
Scratch
Two Men
May 3 The Banks of the Danube
The Cigarette Maker of Seville
The Flood
Legally Dead
The Lost Trail
The Money Bag
A Sister's Devotion
May 4 Blue Jackets' Manoeuvres on a Sailing Vessel
Called to the Sea
Chief Blackfoot's Vindication
A Daughter of the Mine
Diamond Cut Diamond
Hunting Adventure
Immigrants' Progress in Canada
A Soldier's Sweetheart
The Stolen Fortune
Who Killed Her?
The Witch of the Ruins
May 5 Aunt Maria's Substitute
The Debt Repaid
Fury of the Waves
The Little Beggar Maid
The Miner's Sweetheart
Negro's Sacrifice
Papinta
They Would Roller Skate
The Unchanging Sea
Village Beauty
May 6 Customs of the Buddhists in India
The Egret Hunter
Jane Eyre
Love and Marriage in Poster Land
Love and Money
One of the Finest
A Romantic Girl
The Senator and the Suffragettes
May 7 Artist's Good Joke
The Call of the Forest
The Cherries
Father's Crime
Gigantic Waves
How the Great Field Marshall Villars Had an Adopted Daughter
The Mad Miner Recovers
Mario's Swan Song
Medium Wanted as Son-in-Law
The Sentinel's Romance
The Sheriff's Sacrifice
The Shriners' Pilgrimage to New Orleans
The Somnambulist
May 9 Beatrice Cenci
Kidd's Treasure
Love Among the Roses
Mother's Victory
The Mulligans Hire Out
Pete Wants a Job
The Prisoner of the Golden Isle
Rastus in Zululand
A Rural Romeo
Saved by Faith

7 Days
Villainy Defeated
May 10 Cupid's Comedy
History Repeats Itself
A Little Vagrant
Mystery of the Cossacks
"Salvation" Smith
A Sea of Clouds
The Stuff That Americans Are Made Of
The Three Wishes
May 11 Cleopatra
Fricot Gets in a Libertine Mood
He Stubs His Toe
Hearts and Home
In the Dark Valley
The Indian Princess
Purged by Fire
A Quiet Boarding House
Roosevelt in Cairo
The Secret of the Lake
May 12 Chicken
The Cowboy's Devotion
Her Two Suitors
The Invisible Dog
A Mother's Grief
Speed Versus Death
There, Little Girl, Don't Cry
Three Fingered Kate
The Turn of the Dice
Two Betrothed
The Two Brothers
Wearing of the Green
May 13 Accidents Will Happen
Berlin
The Best Man Wins
Between Love and Duty
Carminella
The Closed Door
Lost for Many Years
The Surgeon's Visit
May 14 Bobby, the Boy Scout
The Card Party
Christopher Columbus
The Club of the Corpulent
The Convict's Dream
The Cowpuncher's Ward
Foolshead Learns to Somersault
Honor of the Alpine Guide
The Little Truant
The Marvelous Cure; or, The Wonderful Hair-Growing Fluid
The Minister's New Suit
The Special Agent
That Gentleman Has Won a Million
The Tramp Organist
The Wrong Road
May 16 Barberine
A Doctor's Perfidy
The Girl from Arizona
The Heart of a Heathen Chinee
The Heart of Tessa
Johnson Training for His Fight with Jeffries
Lucretia
Over Silent Paths
The Regeneration of Father
May 17 Child's Doctor
The Feud
A Funny Story
His Yankee Girl
Marvellous Waters
Music Hath Charms
The Princess and the Peasant
Racing for a Bride
May 18 The Aztec Sacrifice
The Danger Line
The Devil on Two Sticks
The Electric Servant
The Fighting Parson
For the Flag
The Girl Conscript
The Gold Spider
Love and a Palette
Love and a Pallette
Modern Railway Construction
Who Will Win My Heart?
Wonderful Machine Oil
May 19 An Affair of Hearts
Fruit and Flowers
He Did Not Die
In the Name of Allah
The Indian Girl's Romance
The Lace Maker's Dream
The Land of Oz
A Race for a Bride
A Rough Night on the Bridge
Werther
May 20 A Brave Little Girl
Cuban War
Cupid at the Circus
Gee I Am Late
The Mexican's Jealousy
Out of the Past
Parting His Hair
The Seminole Halfbreeds
Sisters
May 21 The Centenarian
Conquered Again
A Father's Grief
The Little Doctor of the Foothills
The Masher's Delirium
The Milk Industry in the Alps
Mont Blanc
On Parole
The Temperance Leader
A Tempestuous Adventure
The Wings of Love
May 22 Proposing Under Difficulties
May 23 Brotherly Love
A Desperate Duel
Devoted Playmates
The Eternal Triangle
Good Business
Juan, the Pelota Player
Little Mary and Her Dolly
Madness for Love
The Messenger Boy Magician
Ramona
Romeo Turns Bandit
The Unmailed Letter
Winter Bathing in the West Indies
May 24 All on Account of a Laundry Mark
Convict No. 796
The Curse of Gambling
Deserter
The Doctor's Love Story
Drive Through Central Park
Floral Studies
Fortune's Fool
Kind-Hearted Tramp
Over the Cliffs
Sunday Afternoon on Fifth Avenue
May 25 Capturing Cub Bears
The Cliff Dwellers
Estrellita; or, The Invasion of the French Troops in Portugal
His Wife's Testimony
Love's Great Tragedy
Max Leads Them a Novel Chase
Motherless Child
Reconciled
The Red Man's Honor
A Sagacious Animal
Tin Wedding Presents
Where Is Mulcahy?
May 26 The Brave Deserve the Fair
Don Carlos
In the Great Northwest
A Knot in the Plot
Midsummer Night's Dream
A New Excuse
The Paleface Princess
Roosevelt in Paris
The Sisal Industry in the Bahamas
May 27 Auntie at the Boat Race
Faust and Marguerite
Friends
'Mid the Cannon's Roar
A Mirror of the Future
Perils of the Plains
A Prince of Worth
The Winter's Tale
May 28 The Amateur Hypnotist
The Brother, Sister and Cowpuncher
The Eagle's Egg; or The Rival Lovers
Foolshead Marries Against His Will
His Revenge
King Edward's Funeral
The Knot in the Handkerchief
Love Amidst Historic Ruins
The Love of Chrysanthemum
The Messenger's Dog
Pete Has Nine Lives
Roosevelt in Denmark
A Sailor's Friendship
May 29 Love Your Neighbor as Yourself, but Leave His Wife Alone!
May 30 After Many Years
Down with the Women
The Impalement
King Edward's Funeral
Life of the Alpine Shooters in the Frontier Outposts
A Reno Romance
Russia, the Caucasian Mountains
The Squatter's Daughter
The Trimming of Paradise Gulch
A Veteran of the G.A.R.
The Watchmaker's Hat
May 31 The Crack Shot
Jarnac's Treacherous Blow
The Little German Band
The Mule Driver and the Garrulous Mute
The Peacemaker
The Tie That Binds
Won and Lost
Jun [day undetermined]
The Funeral of King Edward
Jun 1 Custer's Last Stand
Henry's Package
Her Life for Her Love
Ines de Castro
A Just Revenge
Levi's Dilemma
The Lily of the Ranch
Making Salt
The Navajo's Bride
One Can't Believe One's Eyes
Prascovia
Jun 2 A Bachelor's Love
Gardner at the Convent
In the Season of Buds
The Padre's Secret
Percy, the Cowboy
A Stray Dog
Thief
Valgeres Blood
Vitellius and Heliogabalus
Jun 3 The Castaways
Davy Jones' Parrot
The Girl of the Northern Woods
Lillian and Anetta
Married on Horseback
The Piece of Lace
The Slave's Love
The Two Portraits
What Happened to a Cinematograph Party
Jun 4 Adopting a Child
Am I Mad?
Animated Cotton
Away Out West
Battles of Soul
Beneath the Walls of Notre Dame
Boy and Purse
Burglar's Dog
The Carman's Dream
A Drink of Goat's Milk
A Father's Mistake
A Fool's Paradise
Foolshead as a Porter
Gipsy's Baby
Her Portrait
Jane of Montressor
The Jump to Death
[King Edward's Funeral]
The Last of the Dandies
Macbeth
The Majesty of the Law
Negro's Gratitude
O! That Indian
The Office Seeker
A Pennyworth of Potatoes
Picturesque Sentari
Quarrelsome Man
A Race for a Bride
Scratch as Scratch Can
Servant and Guardian
The Slave's Sacrifice
Teaching a Husband a Lesson
A Trip on the Seine
Two Friends
Jun 6 The Barge Man of Old Holland
The Bucking Broncho
A Child of the Ghetto
The Flag of Company "H"
Grandfather's Gift
A Martyr of Love
The Nichols on a Vacation
Officer Muldoon's Double
A Sculptor Who Has Easy Work
Jun 7 Girls
His Duty
Mr. Bumptious on Birds
A Modern Cinderella
The Monastery in the Forest
A Night on the Coast
The Shyness of Shorty
The Two Roses
Jun 8 Burly Bill
The Empty Cradle

A Jealous Wife
Lucy Consults the Oracle
The Mountain Lake
The Nightmare
The Outlaw's Redemption
The Price of Jealousy
The Shipwrecked Man
The Vivandiera

Jun 9 Blind Love
The Children of Edward IV
A Discontented Woman
Love's "C.Q.D."
Mr. Swell in the Country
The New Boss of Bar X Ranch
The Range Riders
A Victim of Jealousy

Jun 10 The Bellringer's Daughter
Dmitri Donskoj
The Exiled Chief
Over the Garden Wall
Russia—The Land of Oppression
Saved from the Redmen
24-Hour Automobile Race
The Writing on the Wall

Jun 11 The Altar of Love
The Duel
Floating to Wealth
Her Romance
Lerin's Abbey on St. Honorat's Island
Limburger and Love
Linda of Chamouny
The Marriage of Esther
The Ranchman's Feud
An Unexpected Friend

Jun 13 Artist's Dream
The Biter Bit
Childish Escapade
In Love with the Charcoal Woman
In the Border States
Micro-Cinematography: Sleeping Sickness
On Panther Creek
Romeo and Juliet in Our Town
The Sheriff's Daughter
Views of England
The Way to Win
The Wild Man of Borneo

Jun 14 At the Dawning; or, The Fear of the Comet
A Bitter Enemy
An Engineer's Sweetheart
The House on the Hill
The Russian Lion
United States Life Saving Drills
Wenonah
The Woman Hater

Jun 15 The Barry Sisters
The Battle of Legnano; or, Barbarossa
The Bone-Setter's Daughter
Caught Red-Handed
A Child of the Regiment
The Emperor's Message
The Gum-Shoe Kid
A Honeymoon for Three
How Championships Are Won—and Lost
Jeffries on His Ranch
A Message from the East
Mistaken Identity
Rape of the Sabines
Settling a Boundary Dispute
A Trip to Brazil

Jun 16 Caught in the Rain
The Face at the Window
Her Lesson
The Legend of the Holy Chapel
The Old Maid's Picnic
A Policeman's Son
Red Eagle's Love Affair
Seeing the Real Thing
Spirit of the Sword
A Texas Joke

Jun 17 A Central American Romance
A Cowboy's Race for a Wife
Davy Jones' Landladies
The Little Hero of Holland
MacNab Visits the Comet
Married in Haste
Max Makes a Touch
Poor, but Proud
The White Captive of the Sioux

Jun 18 The Bandit's Wife
Col. Theodore Roosevelt's Reception
Distractions of Foolshead
Esther and Mordecai
Her Dad's Pistol
How Brother Cook Was Taught a Lesson
Ito, the Beggar Boy
Lake of Lucerne
The New Sign of the Globe Hotel
The Phrenologist
Roosevelt's Reception in New York
Roosevelt's Return
The Spanish Frontier
A Tragic Evening
The Turn of the Tide
[Welch-Daniels Fight]
White Fawn's Devotion

Jun 20 Boss of Circle E Ranch
Eugenie Grandet
Hebrew's Gratitude
In the Mesh of the Net
May and December
Never Again
Opening an Oyster
Poetical Jane
Reconciliation of Foes
The Road to Happiness
A Wasted Effort

Jun 21 Bootles' Baby
The Devil's Wand
Drowsy Dick's Dream
Hercules and the Big Stick
The Little Mother at the Baby Show
Love Is Stronger Than Life
Nevada
Princess and Pigeon
The Sea Wolves
Tempered with Mercy
Thelma

Jun 22 A Child of the Squadron
An Excursion into Wales
Grandpa's Will
An Interrupted Courtship
Perseverance Rewarded
Riding School in Belgium
Sheriff's Daughter
The Story of Lulu Told by Her Feet
Taft for a Day
The Tricky Umbrella of Fricot
A Victim of Hate
The Wanderers

Jun 23 Claim Jumpers
From Love to Martyrdom
Getting Rid of Uncle
The Marked Time-Table
The Motion Picture Man
No Smoking
Oliver Twist
One Good Turn
Our New Minister
Sea Cave and Cliffs
A Self-Made Hero
The Stranded Actor
White-Doe's Lover

Jun 24 Catching Fish with Dynamite
The Cheyenne Raiders; or, Kit Carson on the Santa Fe Trail
A Curious Invention
An Exciting Yarn
A Family Feud
The Governor's Daughter
Isis
The Judgment of the Mighty Deep
Lieutenant Rose, R. N.
A Mexican Lothario
Too Many Girls
We Want Your Vote

Jun 25 By the Faith of a Child
The Captain's Wife
Cash on Delivery
The Clown and His Dogs
Does Nephew Get the Cash?
The Forest Ranger
Forget Me Not
The Great Train Hold Up
Lakes at Eventide
The Man Suffragette for the Abolition of Work for Women
A Plucky Girl
A White Lie
Who Owned the Coat
Why Jones Reformed

Jun 27 Apache Gold
The Brothers' Feud
Caesar in Egypt
A Child's Impulse
The Crooked Trail
The Heroine of Pawnee Junction
Juliet Wants to Marry an Artist
The Long Trail
Save Us from Our Friends
The Sorceress of the Strand

Jun 28 The Elder Sister
Her Terrible Peril
The Little Fiddler
Mother and Daughter
Tempest and Sunshine
Under the Reign of Terror
The Unlimited Train
When Old New York Was Young
The Witch's Spectacles

Jun 29 All's Well That Ends Well
C-H-I-C-K-E-N Spells Chicken
Fishery in the North
A Millionaire Tramp
The Miner's Sacrifice
Napoleon
Pat and the 400
St. Paul and the Centurion
The Taking of Saragossa
The Tenderfoot Parson

Jun 30 Faith Lost and Won
False Accusation
Faust
The Fire Chief's Daughter
For Her Son's Sake
Fort Du Bitche
A Game for Two
Muggsy's First Sweetheart
The Ruling Passion
She Would Be a Business Man

Jul [day undetermined]
Great Ball Game Between the East and West
St. George and the Dragon
Sea Waves
[Train Wreck in Middletown, Ohio]

Jul 1 Charles the Fifth
The Colonel's Errand
The Flag of His Country
The Fresh Air Fiend
Inside the Earth
The Plumber
A Quiet Pipe
A Ranchman's Simple Son
Rebellious Betty
Saved by the Flag
Saved from Himself
The Stars and Stripes
Wilson's Wife's Countenance

Jul 2 The Bad Man's Last Deed
Catherine, Duchess of Guisa
Gotch-Zbyszko World's Championship Wrestling Match
The Lady Doctor
The Man Behind the Curtain
Max Foils the Police
Motoring Among the Cliffs and Gorges of France
Old Glory
On the Threshold
Riding Feats by Cossacks
The Sons of the Minister
Trapped by His Own Mark

Jul 4 The Derby
The Fallen Idol
The Ghetto Seamstress
Go West, Young Woman, Go West
His Child's Captive
The King of the Beggars
The Purgation
The Rhine from Cologne to Bingen
The Runaway Dog
A Soldier's Sacrifice

Jul 5 A Boarding School Romance
Booming Business
The Boy and His Teddy Bear
The Clink of Gold
Equal to the Emergency
Gone to Coney Island
Life in Senegal, Africa
On the Border
A Sinner's Sacrifice
A Tale of Two Coats

Jul 6 A Darling Confusion
The Hero Engineer
Jeffries-Johnson World's Championship Boxing Contest, Held at Reno, Nevada, July 4, 1910
Jinks Has the Shooting Mania
Love Ye One Another
Manoeuvers of the New York Police Force
No Questions Asked
The Other Johnson
A Russian Spy
The Tamer; Alfred Schneider and His Lions
That Little German Band
Tropical Java of the South Sea Islands

Jul 7 The Call of the Circus
Ferdie's Vacation

Giorgione
Jemmy
The Little Preacher
A Midnight Cupid
One Man's Confession
The Way of the Red Man

Jul 8 Attacked by Arapahoes; or, The Gold Seekers and the Indians
Between Love and Honor
Big-Hearted Mary
Colonel Roosevelt Reviewing French Troops
From Gypsy Hands
The Girl Strike Leader
The Girl Who Dared
The Money Lender's Son
Must Be Without Encumbrance
A New Hat for Nothing
Reproduction of Jeffries-Johnson Championship Contest
The Sheriff of Black Gulch
A Wireless Romance

Jul 9 The Abyss
Becket
The Burglar and the Baby
The Champion of the Race
The Invincible Sword
The Laughing Machine
Ruins of Mediaeval Fortifications in France
Sally's Beaux
The Unknown Claim
Vengeance of Millesaunte
The Wonderful Cigar

Jul 11 The Almighty Dollar
Aviation at Montreal: June 25th to July 5th, 1910
The Call of the West
The Faithless Lover
The Hall-Room Boys
The Highbinders
John, the Usher
Just for Good Luck
Old Heads and Young Hearts
The Pirate's Dower
What the Daisy Said

Jul 12 A Deal in Broken China
A Hidden Serpent
In the Realm of the Czar
The Lucky Shot
A Mexican Love Affair
A Mightier Hand
Nellie's Farm
Out of the Night
Prince of Kyber

Jul 13 Abernathy Kids to the Rescue
An Advertisement Answered
Among the Breakers
The Clergyman and His Ward
Grandmother
The Moonlight Flitting
The Overland Coach Robbery
The Struggle of Two Souls
Tweedle Dum's Aeronautical Adventure
Verona
The Wicked Baron and the Page

Jul 14 The Adopted Daughter
The Badgers
A Child's Faith
The End of a Dynasty
The Golden Secret
Granddad's Extravagance
A Hunting Story
The Saloon Next Door
The Sheriff

Jul 15 Bill's Serenade
A Bridegroom's Mishap
The Converted Deacon
Corporal Truman's War Story
The Greatest of These Is Charity
Her Uncle's Will
The Hindoo's Treachery
How Bumptious Papered the Parlor
[Kinemacolor Films]
Please Take One
A Political Discussion
Red Fern and the Kid
Retribution
A Vacation in Havana

Jul 16 Algerian Stud
A Broken Symphony
A Good Loser
A Jealous Wife
The Jolly Whirl
Jupiter Smitten
Mother-in-law, Son-in-law and Tanglefoot
The Prodigal Son

The Tattler
Trailed to the Hills
The Voice of the Blood

Jul 18 An Awful Symphony
A Flash of Light
Mistaken Identity
The Nurse's Trunk
The Phoenix
The Right to Labor
Rosemary for Remembrance
Summertime
To-morrow Is Pay-day

Jul 19 The Failure of Success
A Game of Hearts
The Girls of the Ghetto
A Message of the Sea
The Old Loves and the New
Twa Hieland Lads

Jul 20 Back in the Mountains
Catching Lobsters
Haunted by Conscience
Levi and Family at Coney Island
Manon
Only a Hobo
Pekin, the Walled City
The Power from Above
The Romance of a Jockey
A Romance of an Anvil
Some Riding Exercises of the Italian Cavalry
The Thief
Through the Enemy's Line

Jul 21 Andromache
As the Bells Rang Out!
John Graham's Gold
Mateo Falcone
Mazeppa; or, The Wild Horse of Tartary
The Mistake
A Postal Substitute
Serious Sixteen

Jul 22 Black Pete's Reformation
Brave Hearts; or, Saved from the Indians by a Woman's Wit
The Cowboy's Sweetheart and the Bandit
Davy Jones and Captain Bragg
A Devoted Little Brother
A Frontier Hero
Lazy Farmer Brown
Ma's New Dog
The Playwright's Love
Repaid with Interest

Jul 23 A Cannon Duel
Cohen and Murphy
The Desperado
The Elopement
Fabian Cleaning Chimney
The Foxy Lawyer
Hako's Sacrifice
Let Us Die Together
More of Betty's Pranks
Our Housemaid
Pete Has a Good Time
The Princess and the Fishbone

Jul 25 Breaking Up Ice in Finland
The Call to Arms
Getting Even with the Lawyer
The Mad Dog Scare
The Silversmith to King Louis XI
A Sleep Walking Cure
The Step-Daughter
Two Maids
The Ungrateful Daughter-In-Law
Wifie's Mamma

Jul 26 An Angler's Dream
The Beautiful Margaret
Love in Mexico
Making Wooden Shoes
The Missing Bridegroom
Peg Woffington
Uncle Tom's Cabin
Uncle Tom's Cabin, Part 1

Jul 27 The Art Lover's Strategy
The Cow-Boy and the Squaw
A Daughter in Dixie
The Detective's Dream
A Fair Exchange
The Kissing Bug
Mexican Domain
On the Ethiopian Frontier
A Personal Matter
The Prospector's Treasure
The Room of the Secret
A True Pal

Jul 28 Bear Ye One Another's Burdens
The Cowboy's Stratagem
The Hiding Place
Three Hearts

Unexpected Help
The Woman in the Case

Jul 29 The Bailiff
Bumptious as an Aviator
In the Wild West
The Mermaid
Pure Gold
Tommy Gets His Sister Married
Uncle Tom's Cabin, Part 2
The Unexpected Reward

Jul 30 Broncho Billy's Redemption
Cagliostro
Fabian Arranging Curtain Rods
For the Sake of a Child
The Forbidden Novel; or, Don't Do as I Do, Do as I Say
A Little Confederate
The Sculptor's Ideal
The Two Bears
Uncle Tom's Cabin, Part 3
The Vixen
Where Can We Hang this Picture?

Jul 31 Ranch Life in the Great South-West

Aug [day undetermined]
Carrie de Mar
Pickaninny and the Pup

Aug 1 An Arcadian Maid
B.P.O.E.
Betty as an Errand Girl
Her First Long Dress
Hunting Bats in Sumatra
Irony of Fate
She Surveys Her Son-in-Law
Shrimps
The Soldier's Honor
The United States Revenue Detective

Aug 2 The Ace of Hearts
An Ancient Mariner
Her Private Secretary
Jenk's Day Off
A Miner's Sweetheart
An Unfair Game
With Bridges Burned

Aug 3 The Barrel Jumper
Camel and Horse Racing in Egypt
A College Chicken
A Colonial Belle
Fricot Drinks a Bottle of Horse Embrocation
The Glove
Mulcahy's Raid
The Rest Cure
Sons of the West
The Spitfire
Under Both Flags
The Witch of Carabosse

Aug 4 Ah Sing and the Greasers
The Eagle and the Eaglet
Her Father's Pride
The Law of the West
Mrs. Bargainday's Baby
Yankeeanna

Aug 5 A Cowboy's Generosity
The Legend of Scar-Face
The Moths and the Flame
No Man's Land
No Rest for the Weary
The Restoration
U.S. Submarine "Salmon"
The Wooing O't

Aug 6 Almost a Hero
Fiftieth Anniversary of Yokohama
Her Mother's Wedding Gown
His Baby's Shirt
The Latest Fashion in Skirts
The Lord's Prayer
Louisa Miller
Magdalene; or, The Workman's Daughter
Teneriffe, the Gem of the Canaries
Under Western Skies

Aug 8 The Broker's Daughter
The Buried Man of Tebessa
Competition of the Police and Guard Dogs
Forgiven
The Heart of a Sioux
The House with Closed Shutters
Jewish Types in Russia
Once upon a Time
The Troubles of a Flirt

Aug 9 The Death of Michael Grady
The Lady and the Burglar
The Mad Hermit
A Man's Way
Picturesque Waters of Italy
A True Country Heart
The Water Cure

Aug 10 The Animated Scare-Crow
The Borrowed Baby
A Favour Admission to a Play
Feeding Seals at Catalina Isle
Hearts of Gold
Her Photograph
The Hermit of the Rockies
The "Ibis"
On the Banks of the Zuyder Zee, Holland
The Silent Witness
Truth Beyond Reach of Justice
Up-to-Date Servants
The Wrong Bag

Aug 11 Beyond Endurance
A Change of Heart
Charles Le Tremeraire
Hoodoo Alarm Clock
Indian Squaw's Sacrifice
Lost in the Soudan
The Oedipus King
The Return of Ta-Wa-Wa
A Salutary Lesson

Aug 12 The Attack on the Mill
The Call of the Blood
Lena Rivers
Mrs. Barrington's House Party
The Prairie Post Mistress
The Red Girl and the Child

Aug 13 A Cloud
Drifts of Snow in Chamonix Valley
Entombed Alive
The Girl on Triple X
The Life Boat
Madame Clairo
Oliver Twist
Papa's Cane
The Stolen Policeman
The Turn of the Balance
Winning a Husband

Aug 15 Among the Roses
Back to Life After 2,000 Years
The Colonel's Boot
The District Attorney's Triumph
The Duck Farm
The Heroic Coward
Max Has to Change
The Monkey Showmen of Djibah
The Usurer
Willie

Aug 16 Across Russian Poland
Daisies
The Estrangement
The Girl Reporter
His New Family
The Sewing Girl
A Woman's Better Nature

Aug 17 A Cheyenne Brave
Count of Noaccount
The Count That Counted
A Cowboy's Pledge
The Hump's Secret
Paris Viewed from the Eiffel Tower
The Perversity of Fate
The Rival Serenaders
Tweedle Dum Has Missed the Train
Why Dad Was Held Up

Aug 18 Carmen
Her Winning Way
Human Hearts
Knights Templars Conclave
An Old Story with a New Ending
Senator's Double
Shanghaied
Shorty at the Shore
When We Were in Our Teens

Aug 19 Back to Nature
Bumptious Takes Up Automobiling
The Eriks
How the Squire Was Captured
The Redmen's Persecution
Running Fire
She Stoops to Conquer
A Short-Lived Triumph
True to His Trust

Aug 20 Agnes Visconti
Buying a Mother-in-Law
The Dumb Half Breed's Defence
[Jack Johnson's Own Story of the Big Fight]
Refusing a Mansion
A School in New Guinea
The Shepherd's Dog
Under the Old Apple Tree
A Woman's Power

Aug 22 Butter Making in Normandy
Cowboy Chivalry
Dora Thorne
The Firemen of Cairo
The Gang Leader's Reform
A Miscalculation
Musette's Caprice
The Sorrows of the Unfaithful
The Taming of Jane

Aug 23 A Dainty Politician
The Deceivers
Four Little Tailors
The Gunsmith
Love and the Law
The Mascot of Company "D"
Neighbors; or, Yvonne's Daughter
The Three Cherry Pits; or, The Veteran's Honor

Aug 24 A Bully's Waterloo
Escape of the Royalists
A Fatal Vengeance
Fricot's Itching Powder
In the Black Hills
The Romany Wife
Scenes in Norway
The Sheriff and His Son
Shipbuilders of Toulon
Take Me Out to the Ball Game
The Tale of a Hot Dog
The Troubles of a Policeman

Aug 25 The Acrobat's Son
The Anarchistic Grip
The Chemist's Mistake
The Dream Pill
For the Sunday Edition
Hazing a New Scholar
In the Time of the First Christians
The Indian Raiders
The Romance of Circle Ranch
Wilful Peggy

Aug 26 The Canadian Moonshiners
Kit Carson
The Latchkey
The Lovers' Well
The Men Hater's Club
The Valet's Vindication

Aug 27 The Cantiniere
The Castaway's Return
The Deputy's Love
An Enemy of the Dust
Fabian's Hollow Tooth
Foolshead in the Lion's Cage
How Jack Won His Bride
In the Pyrenees
The Mail Carrier
Rose Leaves
A Society Sinner
The Vow, or, Jephthah's Daughter

Aug 29 The Emigrant
Fantastic Furniture
Kids Will Be Kids
Memento of the Past
The Modern Prodigal
The Stronger Sex
An Unexpected Servant
Who Killed John Dare?
The Widow

Aug 30 Ancient Castles of Austria
An Assisted Elopement
The Burlesque Queen
Dan, the Arizona Scout
From Tyranny to Liberty
The Horse Shoer's Girl
Jean and the Calico Doll
The Shepherd and the Maid
The Templars Conclave

Aug 31 Advertising for a Wife
The Blazed Trail
Buying a Bear
The Cowboy and the Easterner
A Cruise in the Mediterranean
The Fisherman's Crime
A Game with Fame
Turning the Tables
Tweedle Dum's Forged Bank Note
The Unsophisticated Book Agent
Who's Who
You Stole My Purse

Sep [day undetermined]
Only a Jew

Sep 1 The Affair of an Egg
Great Marshall Jewel Case
King of a Day
The Man Who Died
Muggsy Becomes a Hero
The Right Girl
The Road to Richmond
That Letter from Teddy
Won in the Fifth

Sep 2 Deer Hunting in Celebes Islands
A Fresh Start
A Life for a Life
The Man Who Learned
The Night Rustlers
Saved from Ruin
White Man's Money, the Indian Curse

Sep 3 Calino Takes New Lodgings
Fabian Hunting Rats
The Little Drummer Boy
Maggie Hollihan Gets a Job
The Matinee Idol
The Millionaire and the Ranch Girl
Unrequited Love
The Vestal
The Wrong Box

Sep 5 The Healing Faith
Judge Ye Not in Haste
Led by Little Hands
The Little Blind Girl
The Lost Chance
The New Moving Picture Operator
A Summer Idyll
Who Is Boss?
You Saved My Life
Zoological Gardens in Antwerp

Sep 6 The Big Scoop
Chew-Chew Land; or, The Adventures of Dolly and Jim
The Girl Next Door
The Inconstant
Mother
A Rough Weather Courtship
The Way of the Transgressor Is Hard
Western Justice

Sep 7 The Caprice of a Dame
A Dog on Business
Fricot Has Lost His Collar Button
The Gambler's Wife
His Indian Bride
Ingratitude; or, The Justice of Providence
[Jones, the Burglar Catcher]
Mama's Birthday Present
Military Kite Flying at Rheims
The Moonshiner's Daughter
The Snorer

Sep 8 Baseball, That's All
Conscience of a Child
Cowboy's Courtship
Jim, the Ranchman
Little Angels of Luck
Matilda's Winning Ways
The Minister's Speech
A Sister's Sacrifice
Wanted: An Athletic Instructor

Sep 9 Alice's Adventures in Wonderland
The Belgian Army
The Cow Puncher's Sweetheart
The Doctor's Carriage
How She Won Him
Lucy at Boarding School
A True Indian Brave

Sep 10 The Appeal of the Prairie
Elgin National Trophy Races
For the Girl's Sake
An Indian Girl's Love
The Messenger Boy's Sweetheart
Mr. Coward
Robert the Devil
Robinson Crusoe
A Thief Well Received
The Three of Them

Sep 11 Lame Woman

Sep 12 Between Duty and Honor
Captured by Wireless
A Good Glue
The Greenhorn and the Girl
Hunting the Panther
Little Boy
A Mohawk's Way
The Two Daughters

Sep 13 A Cowboy's Matrimonial Tangle
A Day of Pleasure
An Easy Winner
The Great Secret
A Powerful Voice
The Sepoy's Wife
Tangled Lives
The Tell Tale Perfume

Sep 14 Animated Powders
The Artisan
He Met the Champion
The Iron Foundry
The Law and the Man
The Little Mother
Monkeyshines
The Tramps

The Two Sisters
Whist
A Wild Goose Chase
Sep 15 An Attempted Elopement
Aunt Tabitha's Monkey
Buffalo Bill's Wild West and Pawnee Bill's Far East
Dixie
A Game for Life
In Life's Cycle
In the Mission Shadows
Mrs. Rivington's Pride
Resourceful Robert
The Schoolmaster of Mariposa
The Selfish Man's Lesson
The Temptation of Sam Bottler
Sep 16 Bumptious as a Fireman
For a Western Girl
From the Arctics to the Tropics
A Leap for Life
The Sacking of Rome
The Stolen Invention
Two Waifs and a Stray
Unconscious Heroism
Sep 17 Cowboy and Indian Frontier Celebration
Danish Dragoons
A Dummy in Disguise
Fabian Out for a Picnic
The Falconer
Hank and Lank Joyriding
A Lunatic at Large
Poems in Pictures
The Pony Express Rider
The Pugilist's Child
Round Trip $5.98
The Vagaries of Love
World's Championship Motor Races
Sep 19 Bertie's Elopement
Big Medicine
The Blind Man's Dog
Debt
The Falls of the Rhine
The False Friend
A Summer Tragedy
Trip to the Isle of Jersey
The White Squaw
Zeb, Zeke and the Widow
Sep 20 Aunt Hannah
For the Love of Red Wing
A Husband's Sacrifice
Jean the Matchmaker
Not Guilty
Sunset
Tactics of Cupid
An Unselfish Love
Sep 21 An Arizona Romance
A Close Shave
A Corsican Vendetta
A Flirty Affliction
The Japanese Spy
The Last Friend
Molly at the Regiment—Her Adventures
Scenes in the Celestial Empire
Strayed from the Range
Trailing the Black Hand
The White Princess of the Tribe
Sep 22 The Bobby's Dream
The Cattle Thief's Revenge
Love's Old Sweet Song
Ma-in-Law as a Statue
The New Butler
The Oath and the Man
Only a Bunch of Flowers
The Salt on the Bird's Tail
The Sergeant
That Typist Again
Sep 23 Almost a Hero
A Cattle Rustler's Daughter
The Conspiracy of Pontiac; or, At Fort Detroit in 1763
The Convict
A Husband's Jealous Wife
A Jar of Cranberry Sauce; or, The Crime in Room 13
Julie Colonna
Max in a Dilemma
The Mexican Tumblers
A Modern Knight Errant
Tontolini as a Ballet Dancer
Sep 24 The Bad Luck of an Old Rake
Bill Mason's Ride
Dr. Jekyll and Mr. Hyde; or, A Strange Case
Foolshead as a Policeman
His Lordship
In Need of a Painter
Renunciation
The Reserved Shot
A Simple Mistake
The Times Are Out of Joint
The Tout's Remembrance
Sep 25 The Ole Swimmin Hole
Sep 26 Colombo and Its Environs
Max Is Absent-Minded
Pressed Roses
Rose O' Salem-Town
The Sheriff's Capture
The Street Arab of Paris
The Yankee Girl's Reward
Sep 27 A Cowboy for Love
The Footlights or the Farm
Her Adopted Parents
Home Made Mince Pie
"Oh! You Wives"
Over Mountain Passes
The Sunken Submarine
The Taming of Buck
Too Much Water
Sep 28 Curing a Masher
Hank and Lank: They Dude Up Some
The Heart of Edna Leslie
The Hoodoo
The Laugh's on Father
Levi, the Cop
The Quarrel
Reedham's Orphanage Festival, 1910
The Virgin of Babylon
A Western Girl's Sacrifice
Where the Sun Sets
Sep 29 Annie
Examination Day at School
How Jones Won the Championship
The Kentucky Pioneer
Kindness Abused and Its Results
The Path of Duty
A Plucky American Girl
The School-Marm's Ride for Life
The Stenographer's Friend
Sep 30 Dots and Dashes
Giovanni of Medici
A Home Melody
Ononko's Vow
The Ranch Raiders
The Sick Baby
Spotted Snake's Schooling
Oct 1 The Adoption of Helen
The Bachelor and the Baby
Bird's Eye View from World's Highest Buildings
The Diver's Honor
The Flight across the Atlantic
Foolshead Employed in a Bank
Foolshead Has Been Presented with a Foot Ball
A High-Speed Biker
The Music Teacher
Patricia of the Plains
Rip Van Winkle
Southern Tunis
Who Owns the Rug?
Oct 3 All the World's a Stage
The Baggage Smasher
Behind the Scenes of the Cinema Stage
Betty Is Still at Her Old Tricks
A Cold Storage Romance
The Iconoclast
Molucca Islands
My Friend, the Doctor
Through the Ruins of Carthage
Women of the West
Oct 4 The Beechwood Ghost
Her Fiancé and the Dog
Leon of the Table d'Hote
The Little Acrobat
More Than His Duty
Ransomed; or, A Prisoner of War
War
Young Deer's Return
Oct 5 All on Account of a Lie
City of the Hundred Mosques, Broussa, Asia Minor
The Cowboys to the Rescue
Different Trades in Bombay
The Dishonest Steward
The Engineer's Sweetheart
The Golden Hoard
Mirth and Sorrow
The Pit That Speaks
Tweedledum's Duel
When Cupid Sleeps
Oct 6 Auntie in the Fashion
Billy's Sister
The Deciding Vote
For Her Country's Sake
A Gold Necklace
The Golf Fiend
How Hubby Got a Raise
Mother's Portrait
Wild Bill's Defeat
Woman's Vanity
Oct 7 Avenged
Big Elk's Turndown
Bumptious Plays Baseball
The Farmer's Daughter
The Girl Scout
The Last of the Saxons
A Life for Love
Slippery Jim
Oct 8 All's Fair in Love and War
The Bearded Bandit
The Dunce Cap
Foolshead Fisherman
An Indian's Gratitude
Jealousy
Mrs. Cannon Is Warm
The Sage, the Cherub and the Widow
A Skier Training
The Storms of Life
Within an Inch of His Life
Oct 10 Betty Is Punished
The Carmelite
The Clown and the Minister
A Game of Hearts
Jes' Plain Dog
The Monogrammed Cigarette
The Order Is to March
The Sanitarium
The Stigma
That Chink at Golden Gulch
Oct 11 Actors' Fund Field Day
Brother Man
A Cowboy's Daring Rescue
The Lovers' Mill
A Man and a Girl
Pocahontas
Simpson's Skate
The Song That Reached His Heart
The Three Friends
Oct 12 The Betrothed's Secret
Curing a Grouch
Foiled by a Cigarette; or, The Stolen Plans of the Fortress
45 Minutes from Broadway
Hank and Lank: They Get Wise to a New Scheme
How the Tenderfoot Made Good
Papa's First Outing
The S.S. Mauretania
Silver Plume Mine
A Summer Flirtation
Tweedledum on His First Bicycle
Oct 13 Bill and the Missing Key
The Garden of Fate
In the Golden Harvest Time
Liz's Career
A Lucky Toothache
The Masher
Mysteries of Bridge of Sighs at Venice
Out for Mischief
Runaway Star
The Tale a Camera Told
Oct 14 The Chuncho Indians of the Amazon River, Peru
Delightful Dolly
The Mad Lady of Chester
On Her Doorsteps
The Prayer of a Miner's Child
The Stolen Father
Werther
Winona
Oct 15 Aeroplanes in Flight and Construction
The Aviation Craze
The Cowboy's Mother-in-Law
The Legacy
Paid Boots and Stolen Boots
A Pearl of Boy
The Romance of a Necklace
Saved by Bosco
A Shot in the Night
Tracked across the Sea
Willie Visits a Moving Picture Show
A Woman's Wit
Oct 17 The Broken Doll
The Copper and the Crook
Dr. Geoffrey's Conscience
The Foreman
Hearts and Politics
An Indian Chief's Generosity
Jinks Wants to Be an Acrobat
Mother and Child
One on Max

Oct 18 Auld Robin Grey
The Devil
Grandmother's Plot
The House of the Seven Gables
The Lure of Gold
Oh, What a Knight!
Phantom Ride from Aix-les-Bains
Sleepy Jones
Oct 19 Around Pekin
The Boys of Topsy-Turvy Ranch
The Cat Came Back
Excursion on the Chain of Mont Blanc
Hank and Lank: Uninvited Guests
Hiring a Gem
Imperfect Perfectos
In the Shadow of the Night
Outwitted
Stolen by Indians
Tunny Fishing off Palermo, Italy
Tweedledum's Sleeping Sickness
The Tyranny of the Dark
Oct 20 Archie's Archery
The Banker's Daughters
The Calumny
The Fur Coat
Gilson and Those Boys
Hawkins' Hat
The Heart of a Cowboy
Two Boys in Blue
The Tyrant
Uncle Jim
Oct 21 A Child's Sacrifice
Davy Jones' Domestic Troubles
The Education of Elizabeth
His Life for His Queen
The Last of the Savelli
Their Child
A Wedding Trip from Montreal Through Canada to Hong Kong
The Wrong Trail
Oct 22 The Artist's Luck
Breaking Home Ties
The Cheat
Clothes Make the Man
The False Coin
Foolshead Between Two Fires
Hearts of Gold
In the Gray of the Dawn
The Locket
The Mystery of Lonely Gulch
Pals of the Range
Oct 24 The Absent-Minded Doctor
Another's Ghost
The Count of Montebello
The Ghost in the Oven
Hagenbeck's Menagerie
The Message of the Violin
Oh You Skeleton
Romance in the Rockies
Saved by Her Dog
Solving the Bond Theft
Oct 25 The Amazon
The Breach of Discipline
The First Gray Hair
The Girl Cowboy
Jean Goes Foraging
The Lord and the Lady
The Plot That Failed
Young Lord Stanley
Oct 26 The Bouquet
Bruges, Belgium
Doings at the Ranch
Hank and Lank: They Take a Rest
In the Spreewald
Launching the First Italian Dreadnought
The Motor Fiend
Rev. John Wright of Missouri
The Signet Ring
The Strongest Tie
A Touching Mystery
Tweedledum Wants to be a Jockey
Oct 27 Bewitched
Blasted Hopes
A Clause in the Will
Edith's Avoirdupois
False Love and True
The Hobble Skirt
Mendelssohn's Spring Song
The Passing of a Grouch
The Proposal
Ruin
She Required Strength and Got It
Under the Stars and Bars
Where You Go I Go
Oct 28 Buffalo Fight
Captain Barnacle's Chaperone
The Fairies' Hallowe'en
Indian Pete's Gratitude
Max in the Alps
The Pretty Dairy Maid
A Red Girl's Friendship
The Sergeant's Daughter
The Swiss Guide
Tontolini Is in Love
World's Championship Series
Oct 29 Adventure of a Millionaire
The Armorer's Daughter
A Day on the French Battleship "Justice"
An Excursion on the Lake of Garda
Foolshead Volunteer on the Red Cross
In the Web
The Indian and the Maid
The Life of Molière
The Silent Message
The Telephone
Who Is She?
Why They Signed the Pledge
Oct 31 Brothers
Darjiling
The Idol's Eye
The Italian Sherlock Holmes
The Little Mother
The Manufacture of Cheese at Roquefort
Max Has Trouble with His Eyes
New Style Inkwell
Settled Out of Court
Two Little Waifs
Nov 1 Both Were Stung
A Double Elopement
The Fatal Gold Nugget
A Fortunate Misfortune
The Key of Life
Mental Science
Mistress and Maid
Picturesque Majorca
The Sheriff and Miss Jones
Nov 2 Boy Scouts of America in Camp at Silver Bay, Lake George, N.Y.
Caught by Cowboys
Cowboy Justice
Crossing the Andes
The Facori Family
The Girl from the East
Riders of the Plains
The Rough Rider's Romance
The Slave of Carthage
That Doggone Dog
Tragical Concealment
Turning of the Worm
Nov 3 Birthday Cigars
Cohen's Generosity
The Early Settlers
Fatty Taking a Bath
The Fault of Grandmother
Generous Customers
Her Diary
Mike the Housemaid
Willie
Nov 4 The Children's Revolt
A Fateful Gift
The Little Station Agent
Red Wing and the White Girl
Silver Cloud's Sacrifice
Ten Nights in a Bar Room
The Woman of Samaria
A Wooden Sword
Nov 5 Abraham Lincoln's Clemency
A Fatal Picnic
The Fishing Smack
In the Mountains of Kentucky
The Jewel Case
A Russian Romance
A Sufferer of Insomnia
A Westerner's Way
Where Have I Put My Fountain Pen?
Where Sea and Shore Doth Meet
Nov 7 The Bachelor
The Fugitive
Keeping His Word
The Lady Barbers
Micro-Cinematography: Recurrent Fever
Religious Fetes at Thibet
The Resurrection of Lazarus
Spirit of the West
The Taming of Wild Bill
Waiter No. 5
Nov 8 The Branded Man
Hank and Lank: Life Savers
The Lassie's Birthday
The Little Fire Chief
The Masquerade Cop
Moonshine and Love
Pharoah; or, Israel in Egypt
A Tale of a Hat
A Trip over the Rocky and Selkirk Mountains in Canada
When Love Is Young
Nov 9 A Floating Message
For a Woman's Honor
The King of Beggars
A Mexican Legend
The Ranchman and the Miser
Secret of the Cellar
The Ship's Husband
A Trip Through Scotland
The Woodsman
Nov 10 The Black Gondola
The Gambler's Charm
The Last Straw
The Model's Redemption
A Mountain Wife
The Mystery of the Torn Note
Simple Charity
A Stormy Seas
The Vampire
Nov 11 The Adoption
The American and the Queen
The Attack on Fort Ridgely
Bill as a Boxer
A Black Heart
Bud's Triumph
Dutch Types
The Nine of Diamonds
The Truth Revealed
A Widow and Her Child
Nov 12 The Coalman's Soap
Faithful until Death
Foolshead Knows All and Does All
A Gambler's End
The Heroine of 101 Ranch
Jean Goes Fishing
The Marked Trail
Mexican Centennial
Mother-in-Law Arrives
The Ordeal
A Trip to the Blue Grotto, Capri, Italy
Under a Changing Sky
World's Wrestling Champions
Nov 14 The Case of the Missing Heir
The Devil's Billiard Table
The Double
Ginhara or Faithful Unto Death
Mr. Four Flush
Romantic Redskins
A Shadow of the Past
The Street Preacher
Sunshine Sue
Nov 15 Drumsticks
The Flight of Red Wing
How Women Love
Into the Jaws of Death
Love at First Sight
Nebuchadnezzar's Pride
Paul and Virginia
That Woman Lawyer
Nov 16 An Alpine Retreat
A Drama of the Present
The Hand of Providence
Love Laughs at Locksmiths
The Mermaid
The Ranchman's Bride
The Rival Barons
Russian Wolf Hunt
The Stolen Claim
Tweedledum Gets Employed in the Corporation Body
The Way of the West
Nov 17 The Education of Mary Jane
Fortune's Wheel
Gratitude
His Sergeant's Stripes
Judge and Father
Love in Quarantine
The Lure of the City
Right in Front of Father
The Troublesome Baby
Nov 18 Bill as a Lover
Blopps in Search of the Black Hand
The Bum and the Bomb
The City of Her Dreams
Her Father's Sin
An Indian Maiden's Choice
Jim Bridger's Indian Bride
Military Cyclists of Belgium
A Modern Courtship
Phaedra
The Toymaker, the Doll and the Devil
Nov 19 The Diamond Swindler
Foolshead Victim of His Honesty
Francesca Da Rimini
Lisbon, Before and During the Revolution

The Little Prospector
Moulders of Souls
The New Magdalene
Oklahoma Bill
An Original Palette
The Other Way
Spanish Loyalty
The Way of Life

Nov 21 Caught by the Camera
The Dull Razor
The Exiled Mother
Lone Wolf's Trust
New South Wales Gold Mine
The Old Longshoreman
The Song of the Wildwood Flute
Starlight's Devotion
Their Day of Thanks
There's No Place Like Home

Nov 22 Absent Minded Arthur
Cast into the Flames
Hank and Lank: as Sandwich Men
His Mother's Thanksgiving
Suspicion
A Thanksgiving Surprise
That Popular Tune
Thou Shalt Not Kill
True Western Honor
A Woman's Wit

Nov 23 Behind a Mask
Cast Thy Bread upon the Waters
A Deal in Indians
Gounod's 'Ave Maria'
How Rastus Gets His Turkey
The Lad from Old Ireland
Let Us Give Thanks
Nantes and Its Surroundings
The Story of a Pair of Boots
Through the Clouds
Wonderful Plates

Nov 24 A Big Joke
The Country Boarder
The Cowboys and the Bachelor Girls
Forgiven
His New Lid
The Merry Wives of Windsor
Not So Bad as It Seemed
Nothing but Money
Romance of the Lazy K Ranch
Sacrificed

Nov 25 A Cheyenne's Love for a Sioux
A Daughter of the Mines
A Dog's Instinct
A Four-Footed Pest
In Friendship's Name
Isis
One Touch of Nature
The Roses of the Virgin
The Statue Dog
The Wild Flower and the Rose

Nov 26 Calino Travels as a Prince
A Chosen Marksman
An Eleventh Hour Redemption
Kean; or, The Prince and the Actor
Love, Luck and Gasoline
Samson's Betrayal
So Runs the Way
Stage Coach Tom
A Western Woman's Way
A Windy Day
The Woman Hater

Nov 28 A Border Tale
A Difficult Capture
A Freak
The Heart of an Actress
A Plain Song
The Queen of Hearts
The Regeneration
The Revolving Doors
Shadows and Sunshine
The Wreck

Nov 29 The Flat Next Door
The Greater Love
The Ranchman's Personal
Tarascon on the Rhone
The Tie That Binds
Value—Beyond Price
Wanted—A Baby
Who Wins the Widow?
A Woman's Love

Nov 30 Arms and the Woman
Finland—Falls of Imatra
The Indian Land Grab
The Judas Money; or, An Episode of the War in Vendee
Ramble Through Ceylon
The Return at Midnight
Saved by a Vision
The Touch of a Child's Hand
Up the Thames to Westminster
Valley Folks
Who Is Nellie?

Dec [day undetermined]
[Artillery Drill at West Point]
Aviation Meet of the Aero Club, St. Louis, Mo.
Biskra and the Sahara Desert
Farm Yard Friends
Floral Fiends
From Bud to Blossom
[Lake Garda, Northern Italy]
[Liquors and Cigars]
[The London Fire Brigade]
[London Zoological Gardens]
Motor and Yacht Boating in England
[Picking Strawberries]
[Potomac Falls, Virginia]
[The Richmond Horse Show]
Scenes in Algeria
A Visit to the Seaside at Brighton Beach, England
[Washington's Home and Ground at Mount Vernon]

Dec 1 A Child's Judgment
Effecting a Cure
A Painful Debt
Pals
Spoony Sam
The Stepmother
A Touching Affair

Dec 2 Bill as an Operator
A Child of the Wild
The Cowpuncher's Glove
Elder Alden's Indian Ward
Jack Fat and Jim Slim at Coney Island
John Halifax, Gentleman
Necessity Is the Mother of Invention
Queen of the Nihilists
The Tale the Mirror Told
What a Dinner!
What Is to Be, Will Be

Dec 3 The Big Drum
The Birthday Present
Circle "C" Ranch Wedding Present
The Dog Keeper
Lured by a Phantom; or, The King of Thule
The Maid of Niagara
Nancy's Wedding Trip
The Ohami Troupe of Acrobats
The Preacher's Wife
When the World Sleeps
When Woman Wills

Dec 5 The Aspirations of Gerald and Percy
A Child's Stratagem
The Clever Domestic
In the Czar's Name
The Laundry Girl's Good Night
On the Mexican Border
The Price of a Sacrifice
Vera, the Gypsy Girl
The Widow of Mill Creek Flat

Dec 6 Love's Awakening
A Man of Honor
The Medicine Man
Professor's Hat
The Rehearsal
Rip Van Winkle
A Sioux's Reward
A Tin-Type Romance
The Winning of Miss Langdon

Dec 7 Amateur Night
An Animated Armchair
Cocoanut Plantation
The Conquering Hero
The Death of Admiral Coligny
Hearts of the West
The Life of a Salmon
Nature's Nobleman
Rachel
The Tell-Tale Portrait
Tweedledum Learns a Tragical Part

Dec 8 Happy Jack, a Hero
In the Wilderness
Reggie's Engagement
The Soldier of the Cross
Turning the Tables
'Twixt Loyalty and Love
Two Lucky Jims
What Great Bear Learned

Dec 9 And She Came Back
A Brave Western Girl
The Captain's Bride
The Girls He Left Behind Him
He Who Laughs Last
The Iron Clad Lover
Lady Betty's Strategy
The Rescue of Molly Finney
Saved in the Nick of Time
Soap in His Eyes
Western Justice
What Will It Be

Dec 10 The Color Sergeant's Horse
A Cowboy's Vindication
The Dispensation
Foolshead Knows How to Take His Precautions
The Good Samaritan
Her First Husband's Return
The Poacher
The Revolt
A Ride to Death

Dec 12 The Bowling Craze
A Clever Ruse
An Exile's Love
Faithful Max
A Fight for Millions
The Golden Supper
In Her Father's Absence
The Julians
Our Dear Uncle from America
The Rummage Sale
A Tale of the Sea

Dec 13 Closed Gate
An Indian's Test
The Law and the Man
Love and Law
A Mountain Maid
An Old Silver Mine in Peru
The Phantom Rider
A Plucky Western Kid
A Tangled Masquerade
The Tramp Bicyclist

Dec 14 Brothers
Charlie and Kitty in Brussels
Dido Forsaken by Aeneas
Hoboes' Xmas
The Little Matchseller's Christmas
Pigs Is Pigs
The Pilgrim
Scenes in British India
Seth's Temptation
The Sheriff and the Detective

Dec 15 The Binding Shot
County Fair
The False Accusation
His Sister-in-Law
The Musical Ranch
Old Norris' Gal
The Poor Student
The Renowned International Aviation Meet

Dec 16 A Girl of the Plains
Her Favorite Tune
Her Indian Mother
How We Won Her
The International Motor Boat Races
Little Snowdrop
The Millionaire Milkman
The Old Miner's Doll
Playing at Divorce
The Red Cross Seal
Two Suits

Dec 17 A Christmas Letter
Dickey's Courtship
A Dixie Mother
Herod and the New Born King
His Gypsy Sweetheart
The Mother's Shadow
Saved by Divine Providence
The Tenderfoot Messenger
Thieves as Quick Change Artists
The Thin Dark Line

Dec 19 The Child of Two Mothers
The Crippled Teddy Bear
The Dead Letter
Get Rich Quick
Her Fatal Mistake
Hunting Sea Lions in Tasmania
John Dough and the Cherub
The Lesson
The Museum of Sovereigns
A Ward of Uncle Sam

Dec 20 The Bachelor's Finish
The Cattle Baron's Daughter
The Greater Call
Hank and Lank
His Cinderella Girl
Jack Logan's Dog
The Kingdom of Flowers
The Light in the Window
Looking Forward

The Police Force of New York City
Dec 21 The Arm of the Law
A Chamois Hunt
A Desperate Remedy
His Mother
The Joke They Played on Bumptious
Little Peter's Xmas Day
The Little Spreewald Maiden
Love's Sorrow
Max Goes Skiing
The Romance of Count de Beaufort
The Runaway Motor Car
Tweedledum and Frothy Want to Get Married
The Tyrant of Florence
Dec 22 An American Count
Her Husband's Deception
Little Nell's Tobacco
Neapolitan Volcanic Islands
Overland to Freemont
The Recreation of an Heiress
A Troublesome Parcel
A Western Welcome
White Roses
Who Was the Culprit?
Dec 23 Betty's Fireworks
Bill Plays Bowls
The Childhood of Jack Harkaway
A Christmas Carol
Clancy
The Lucky Charm
The Pale Faced Princess
The Pawnshop
Rosalie's Dowry
The Terror of the Plains
When Lovers Part
Dec 24 The Bad Man's Christmas Gift
Cain and Abel
The Cattlemen's Feud
A Father's Love
Grand Central Power House Explosion
Greediness Spoiled Foolshead's Christmas
In Norway
Jean and the Waif
The Necklace of the Dead
The Old Home
Owen Moran vs. Battling Nelson
The Refuge
Sunshine in Poverty Row
Dec 26 The Atonement
The Bowling Fiend
The Fear of Fire
Girlies
An Insane Heiress
The Lock-Keeper
Making a Man of Him
The Rustlers
The Unexpected Honeymoon
Winning Back His Love
Dec 27 The Adventuress
Eldora, the Fruit Girl
Freddie's Courtship
Girls Will Be Boys
In Neighboring Kingdoms
An Indian's Elopement
The Station Agent's Daughter
The Vicar of Wakefield
Dec 28 The American Fleet in French Waters
Coaching in Devonshire, England
Drama of the Engine Driver
Elda of the Mountains
A Family of Vegetarians
The Girl Spy Before Vicksburg
The Golden Gates
Grandfather's Pipe
In Full Cry
A Mexican Romance
The Outcast's Salvation
Running Away from a Fortune
Thoughtfulness Remembered by the Ute
Dec 29 After the Ball
Blue Horse Mine
His Wife's Sweethearts
In the Tall Grass Country
Justinian and Theodora
The Rustic
The Squaw and the Man
Unreasonable Jealousy
Dec 30 Aunt Julia's Portrait
Carnival of Japanese Firemen in Tokio
Catalan, the Minstrel
Crazy Apples
Hypnotized
The Missing Bridegroom
Mrs. Richard Dare
The Romance of Hefty Burke
The Stranger
Taming the Terror
Tim Writes a Poem
Dec 31 Bearhunting
The Boy City
A Daughter of Virginia
The Doctor's Secretary
A Gambler of the West
The Jealous Wife's New Year Day
Norwegian Water Falls
A Sacrifice — And Then
The Scarecrow
Trapped
Where the Winds Blow
The Yaqui Girl

1911
Jan [day undetermined]
Alice in Funnyland
Alice's New Year's Party
The Birth of the Gnomes
Feb 12 Lassoing Wild Animals in Africa

PERSONAL NAME INDEX

★ Entries in the Personal Name Index are arranged alphabetically according to name. Film title entries are then arranged chronologically, following the pattern of other indexes in *Film Beginnings, 1893-1910*, by year, month and day. The reader will notice that some film titles are followed by an **asterisk** (*), indicating that the participation of that person in the film noted is uncertain.

Unlike the *AFI Catalog of Feature Films, 1911-20* and *AFI Catalog of Feature Films, 1931-40*, *Film Beginnings, 1893-1910*, which is a work in progress, does not provide extensive cross-references. Establishment of authoritative name entries will be an ongoing project until complete cataloging of all films of the period can be completed.

The reader should also consult the Keyword Index for personal names which may also provide insights into the appearance of actual historical persons in specific films.

PERSONAL NAME INDEX

Li Hung Chang
An Oriental Highway
Reilly's Light Battery F
Review of Russian Artillery
Russian Sharp Shooters
Second Squad, Sixth U. S. Cavalry
Sixth U. S. Cavalry Charging
Sixth U. S. Cavalry, Skirmish Line
Street Scene, Tientsin [China]
The Taku Road
Von Waldersee Reviewing Cossacks
The War in China—A British Donkey Train
The War in China—An Army Transport Train
The War in China—Bombay Cavalry
The War in China—British Light Artillery
The War in China—British Rajputs
The War in China—Coolies at Work
The War in China—Japanese Infantry
The War in China—Review of German Troops
The War in China—Ruins of Tien-Tsin
The War in China—Von Waldersee and Staff
The War in China—Von Waldersee's Review

Feb [day undetermined]
Charge by 1st Bengal Lancers
First Bengal Lancers
The Forbidden City
The Forbidden City, Pekin
The 14th Sikhs
The Fourth Ghorkhas
In Old China
The 9th Infantry, U. S. A.
On the Pei-Ho
Second Queen's Rajputs
Shanghai from a Launch
6th Cavalry Assaulting South Gate of Pekin
Squad of Men Clearing the Road
Street in Shanghai
Street Scene in Shanghai
Street Scene, Shanghai
Tien-Tsin
The War in China
The War in China—First Bengal Lancers
The War in China
The War in China—The Evacuation of Pekin
The War in China—The Fourth Goorkhas
The War in China—The German Contingent

Acton, Miss
1907
Dec 7 College Chums

Adams, Stella
1909
Jun 17 In the Sultan's Power

Adolfi, John G.
1907
Mar 9 The Spy, a Romantic Story of the Civil War
1908
Jun 6 Romeo and Juliet, a Romantic Story of the Ancient Feud Between the Italian Houses of Montague and Capulet
Dec 1 Julius Caesar, an Historical Tragedy
1909
Jan 19 Ruy Blas
Apr 10 Napoleon: the Man of Destiny

Ainsworth, William Harrison
1909
May 15 Tower of London

Alaska, Harry
1903
Oct [day undetermined]
Chinaman's Acrobatic Guests

Albens
1903
Feb [day undetermined]
Cadet's First Smoke

Alexandra, Queen
1910
Jun 4 [King Edward's Funeral]

Alexandre, M.
1909
Sep 22 The Tower of Nesle
1910
Jul 28 The Hiding Place

Alfonso of Spain, King
1910
Jun 4 [King Edward's Funeral]

Alger, Russell A.
1898
Sep [day undetermined]
General Wheeler and Secretary of War Alger at Camp Wikoff
President McKinley's Inspection of Camp Wikoff

Allen, D. R.
1906
Aug [day undetermined]
Kathleen Mavoureen

Allen, E. H.
1910
Jul 1 A Ranchman's Simple Son

Allen, Maude
1910
Feb 9 In Ancient Greece

Alstrup, Oda
1908
Sep 19 The Lady with the Camellias

Alter, Lottie
1910
Aug 31 Advertising for a Wife
Sep 21 An Arizona Romance

Amann
1899 [month undetermined]
Amann
Amann, the Great Impersonator

Ambrosio, Arturo
1910
Nov 2 The Slave of Carthage

Americus Quartet
1897
Nov [day undetermined]
Burlesque Cake Walk

Andersen, Hans Christian
1903
Mar 21 The Little Match Seller

Anderson, Broncho Billy *see* **Anderson, G. M.**

Anderson, C.
1910
Apr 7 Cyclone Pete's Matrimony

Anderson, G. M. *same as* **Anderson, Broncho Billy**
1903
Oct [day undetermined]
The Messenger Boy's Mistake
Dec [day undetermined]
The Great Train Robbery
1905
Sep 23 Raffles, the Amateur Cracksman
1906 [month undetermined]
Sights in a Great City
The Tomboys
Oct 27 Dolly's Papa
Nov 24 The Female Highwayman
1907
Jan 12 Who Is Who?
Mar 9 The Girl from Montana
Mar 30 His First Ride
Jul 31 An Awful Skate; or, the Hobo on Rollers
1908
Apr 12 James Boys in Missouri
1909
Feb 17 Tag Day
Apr 7 A Tale of the West
May 5 A Mexican's Gratitude
May 19 The Indian Trailer
Nov 20 The Best Man Wins*
Dec 4 His Reformation*
Dec 11 The Ranchman's Rival*
The Ranchman's Rival
Dec 25 The Heart of a Cowboy
1910
Feb 19 The Cowboy and the Squaw
Feb 26 The Mexican's Faith
Mar 5 The Ostrich and the Lady
The Ranch Girl's Legacy
Mar 19 The Girl and the Fugitive
Apr 9 The Ranger's Bride
May 14 The Cowpuncher's Ward
May 21 The Little Doctor of the Foothills
Jun 4 Away Out West
Jun 11 The Ranchman's Feud
Jun 18 The Bandit's Wife
Jun 25 The Forest Ranger
Jul 2 The Bad Man's Last Deed
Jul 9 The Unknown Claim
Jul 16 Trailed to the Hills
Jul 30 Broncho Billy's Redemption
Aug 6 Under Western Skies
Aug 13 The Girl on Triple X
Aug 20 The Dumb Half Breed's Defence
Aug 24 Take Me Out to the Ball Game
Aug 27 The Deputy's Love
Sep 3 The Millionaire and the Ranch Girl
Sep 10 An Indian Girl's Love
Sep 24 The Tout's Remembrance
Oct 8 The Bearded Bandit
Oct 22 Pals of the Range
Nov 19 The Little Prospector
Dec 24 The Bad Man's Christmas Gift
Dec 31 A Gambler of the West

Anderson, Helen
1910
Dec 16 The Old Miner's Doll

André, Victor
1902
Oct 4 A Trip to the Moon

Angelo, Jean
1909
Dec 15 The Ugly Girl

Annabelle
1896
Sep [day undetermined]
Tambourine Dance—by Annabelle
1897
May [day undetermined]
Sun Dance—Annabelle
1902
Nov [day undetermined]
A Mermaid Dance

Antoinette, Miss
1907
Dec 7 College Chums

Arbuckle, Fatty
1910
Oct 10 The Sanitarium

L'Argentine
1902 [month undetermined]
The New Serpentine and Fire Dance
1903
Jan [day undetermined]
L'Argentine Butterfly Dance
L'Argentine Mirror Dance
L'Argentine Silver Dance

Arguilliere, Alexandre
1909
Oct 22 Drink

Armitage, F. S.
1897
Jun [day undetermined]
Trout Poachers
1898
Feb [day undetermined]
Torpedo Boat, "Dupont"
Jul [day undetermined]
New York Naval Reserves
Sep [day undetermined]
Peace Jubilee Naval Parade, New York City*
71st Regiment, N. G. S. N. Y. at Camp Wikoff
1899
May [day undetermined]
The Automatic Prize Fight
The Burglar and the Bundle
Champion High Jumpers, "Chappie" and "Ben Bolt"
Charlie Wanted the Earth
Farmer Wayback Entertains
A Good Shot
High Steppers in Harness
How Little Willie Put a Head on His Pa
Judging Ladies' Saddle Horses
"Langton Performer 2nd"
Little Willie and the Burglar
Living Pictures
M. B. Curtis
New York Mounted Police
"Sampson" Champion High Stepper
The Serenaders
Spirits in the Kitchen
The Violin Player
Jun [day undetermined]
Armor vs. Amour
A Bad (K)Night
Chief Devery and Staff
Childhood's Happy Days
The Corset Model
The Demon Barber
Eighth Regiment, N. G. S. N. Y.
The Female Drummer
Finish of the Brooklyn Handicap, 1899
For the Most Beautiful

Four A. M. at the French Ball
Her First Cigarette
Lieutenant-General Nelson A. Miles
New York Naval Militia
New York Police
Ninth Regiment, N. G. S. N. Y.
Phillis Was Not Dressed to Receive Callers
The Price of a Kiss
The Pride of the Household
Scrubbem's Washing Machine
The Soubrette's Birthday
Sunday School Parade
Twenty-Second Regiment, N. G. S. N. Y.

Jul [day undetermined]
The Approach to Niagara
The Artist's Dream
Baby Feeding a Kitten
Baby Lund and Her Pets
Baby's Bath
Barrel Fight
A Bluff from a Tenderfoot
Buffalo Fire Department
Chorus Girls and the Devil
Chuck Connors vs. Chin Ong
"Columbia" and "Defender" Rounding Stake-Boat
"Columbia" vs. "Defender"
The Dairy Maid's Revenge
Demonstrating the Action of the Cliff-Guibert Hose Reel
Detroit Fire Department
Female Prisoners: Detroit House of Correction
The Finish of Mr. Fresh
Fire Drill at the Factory of Parke, Davis & Co.
A Flock of Export Sheep
G. A. R. Post, Detroit
How Bill the Burglar Got a Bath
How Mamie Had Her Leg Pulled
How the Medium Materialized Elder Simpkin's Wife
An Interrupted Crap Game
Love in a Hammock
The Lovers' Quarrel
Lower Rapids of Niagara Falls
Male Prisoners Marching to Dinner
Merlin, the Magician
Michigan Naval Reserves and the Detroit Light Guards
Niagara Falls Station
Panoramic View of Niagara Falls
Parke Davis' Employees
Police Drill
Running Up the Topsail on the "Columbia"
Steamship "Chippewa"
Steamship "Northland"
Two Girls in a Hammock
An Up-to-Date Female Drummer
Water for Fair
The Way French Bathing Girls Bathe
When Babies' Quarrel
When Their Love Grew Cold
Whirlpool Rapids
The Wizard and the Spirit of the Tree

Aug [day undetermined]
Babies Playing on a Hot Day
Ballet of the Ghosts
Bringing a Friend Home for Dinner
"Ding, Dong, Dell, Johnny's in the Well"
A Feast Day in Honolulu
A Gay Old Boy
His Masterpiece
How the Porto Rican Girls Entertain Uncle Sam's Soldiers
The Jealous Model
The Maniac Barber
A Plate of Ice Cream and Two Spoons
The Saratoga Limited
The Spider and the Fly
A Volunteer Fire Company
Water Throwing Contest
What Hypnotism Can Do

Sep [day undetermined]
Apple Blossoms
Arabis Patrol
Baxter Street Mystery
A Cold Day for Art
Diving Through Paper Screens
Dreyfus Receiving His Sentence
Employes of Bausch, Lomb & Co.
The "Erin"
An Exciting Finish
Fancy Diving
Four Corners of Rochester
The Golding Family
The Great Free-for-All Pacing Race
Guardians of the Peace
The International Alliance
"King" and "Queen," the Great High Diving Horses
The Makers of the Kodak
A Midnight Fantasy
One Mile Dash
The Poster Girls
The Poster Girls and the Hypnotist
Prof. Paul Boynton Feeding His Sea Lions
A Ray of Sunshine After the Rain
Rochester Fire Department
The Sandwich Man
"Shamrock I"
Shamrock Starting on Trial Trip
Sir Thomas Lipton and Party on "Erin's" Launch
Sir Thomas Lipton's Steam Yacht "Erin"
The Skeleton at the Feast
Soldiers of the Future
The Summer Girl
A Thrilling Ride
Trial of Captain Dreyfus

Oct [day undetermined]
A Close Finish
Col. John Jacob Astor, Staff and Veterans of the Spanish-American War
"Columbia"
"Columbia" Close to the Wind
Connecticut Naval Reserves
The "Corsair"
"Corsair" in Wake of Tugboat
Crew of the "Shamrock"
Crew of the "Shamrock," at Work
The Dandy Fifth
The Dewey Arch
Dewey Naval Parade
5th Ohio Volunteers of Cleveland
1st Penn' Volunteers of Philadelphia
Fourth Connecticut Volunteers, Dewey Parade
Full Rigged Ship at Sea
Gen. McCrosky Butt and Staff
Governor Roosevelt and Staff
The "Havana"
Marines of the Atlantic Fleet
Mr. and Mrs. C. Oliver Iselin
Mrs. C. Oliver Iselin and Crew of Columbia
The "Niagara"
The "Pennsylvania"
The "Richard Peck"
The "Sagamore"
Sailors of the Atlantic Fleet
2nd Battalion, 3rd New York Provisional Regiment, Rochester and Syracuse, Separate Companies
2nd Company Governor's Footguards, Conn.
7th Regiment, New York City
"Shamrock"
"Shamrock" After Carrying Away Topsail
"Shamrock" and "Columbia"
A Spectacular Start
Start of Race Between "Columbia" and "Shamrock"
Start of Second Cup Race
Start of the Second Cup Race
Start of Third Day's Race
Steamer "Grandrepublic"
10th Penn'a Volunteers
Torpedo Boats at the Yacht Race
Training Ship "Lancaster"
Turning Stake Boat; "Columbia" and "Shamrock"
The West Point Cadets and Band

Nov [day undetermined]
After the Ball
The Bather's Lunch
The Bride's Trousseau
Bunco on the Seashore
Fougere*
It's Dangerous to Tickle a Soubrette
The "Make-Up" Thief
Three Hot Babies
A Warm Baby with a Cold Deck

Dec [day undetermined]
Follow the Girls
The Foster Mother
Pity the Blind

1900

Jan [day undetermined]
Another Picture Showing Demonstration of a Pneumatic Shell Riveter
Blaine Club of Cincinnati
Demonstrating the Action of Pneumatic Shell Riveters on the Underside of the Hull of a Steel Vessel. Taken for the Chicago Pneumatic Tool Co.
Demonstrating the Action of the Chicago Pneumatic Tool Co.'s Deck Machine
Governor Nash of Ohio
Pneumatic Tools

Feb [day undetermined]
St. Clair Tunnel
Skating in Central Park

Mar [day undetermined]
Above the Speedway
A Brush on the Speedway
Getting Ready for the Seashore
"How'd You Like To Be the Iceman?"
Off for the Boer War
Opening of the Rapid Transit Tunnel

Apr [day undetermined]
"Ein Bier"
Buffalo Bill's Wild West Show
Demonstrating the Operation of the Harrington Rail Bonding System on the Line of the Coney Island and Brooklyn Railroad Co.
Horsewhipping an Editor
In Central Park
Not a Man in Sight
"The Prince of Darkness"
The Stocking Scene from "Naughty Anthony"
A Terrible Night
Uncle Si's Experience in a Concert Hall
What Happened to a Fresh Johnnie

May [day undetermined]
The Boomerang
Confounding the Art Critic
A Farmer Who Could Not Let Go
The Great Ottawa Fire
A Gun Play in the Klondike
How the Young Man Got Stuck at Ocean Beach
A Raid on a Chinese Opium Joint
A Raid on "Dago" Counterfeiters
Tramps in the Old Maid's Orchard

Jun [day undetermined]
The Approach to Lake Christopher
The Approach to Shelburn
Brook Trout Fishing
A Cadet Cavalry Charge
Dewey Land Parade, Detroit
Flyers of the Great Lakes
Gilead
Harris Training Tower
Orchard Lake Cadets
St. Clair Tunnel
Shelter Tent Drill
Valley of the Little Androscoggin
Victoria Jubilee Bridge

Jul [day undetermined]
Atlantic City Lodge, 276, B. P. O. Elks
Blue Ribbon Jumpers
Brooklyn Lodge, No. 22, B. P. O. Elks
Burning of the Standard Oil Tanks
Champion Polo Players
15th Infantry
Fire Boat "John M. Hutchinson"
Philadelphia Lodge, No. 2, B.P.O. Elks
Prize-Winning Coaches
The Promenaders
Rescue from the Surf
Washington Lodge, No. 15, B. P. O. Elks

Aug [day undetermined]
Demonstrating the Action of the Brown Hoisting and Conveying Machine in Unloading a Schooner of Iron Ore, and Loading the Material on the Cars

Sep [day undetermined]
"Above the Limit"
Around the Flip-Flap Railroad
Bryn Mawr Horse Show
Capt. Boynton Feeding His Pets
Children Rolling Down Hill
For Ice Cream and Cake
H. N. Marvin's Family
Philadelphia's Pride
Republican National Committee of 1900

The "St. Paul" Outward Bound
A Scene in Fairmount Park, Phila.
Oct [day undetermined]
"Courier"
School Fire Drill
Stallion Championship
"Three Ones"
Nov [day undetermined]
"Above the Limit"
Another Demonstration of the Cliff-Guibert Fire Hose Reel, Showing a Young Girl Coming from an Office, Detaching the Hose, Running with It 60 Feet, and Playing a Stream, All Inside of 30 Seconds
"Art Studies"
Aunt Jane's Experience with Tabasco Sauce
Bribing the Police
Contrary Wind
A Customer Drops In
The Fire at Tarrant & Co.'s Drug Store
In a Chinese Restaurant
Scene from "Old Kentucky"
Two Old Cronies
"Two's Company"
The Ugly Tempered Tramp
"When We Were Twenty-One"
Dec [day undetermined]
The Evidence Was Against Him
Helping Mother
"Stop Thief!"
1901
Jan [day undetermined]
The Ghost Train
Feb [day undetermined]
Anawanda Club
Locked in the Ice
Moline Bag Punching Platform
Sea Gulls
Mar [day undetermined]
Castellane-De Rodays Duel
The Second Inauguration
Apr [day undetermined]
Buffalo Bill's Wild West Parade
Carrie Nation Smashing a Saloon
Demolishing and Building Up the Star Theatre
Japanese Wrestling
Jiu Jitsu, the Japanese Art of Self-Defense
Springtime in the Park
May [day undetermined]
Anna Held
In a Japanese Tattooing Parlor
The Lovers' Yarn
The New Maid
An Unlucky Lover
Jun [day undetermined]
An April Fool Joke
"Birth of the Pearl"
A Close Shave
"The Diskobolus"
Experimental
"Finishing Touches"
"Forward"
Ham and Eggs
The Heart of New York
Hot Mutton Pies
A Joke on Whom?
A Legal Hold-Up
A Little Piece of String
Meandering Mike
A Non-Union Paper Hanger
On the Benches in the Park
A Patient Sufferer
"The Pouting Model"
"The Sleeping Child"
Ten Nights in a Bar-Room: Death of Little Mary
Ten Nights in a Bar-Room: Death of Slade
Ten Nights in a Bar-Room: Murder of Willie
Ten Nights in a Bar-Room: The Fatal Blow
Ten Nights in a Bar-Room: Vision of Mary
An Unexpected Knockout
"Waiting for Santa Claus"
Washington Bridge and Speedway
"You Dirty Boy"
Jul [day undetermined]
The Downfall of China
F. S. Gibbs and Family
Five Minutes to Train Time
The Fresh Lover
He Forgot His Umbrella
The Hod Carrier's Revenge
Little Algy's Glorious Fourth of July
Nora's 4th of July
A Quick Recovery
The Wages of Sin—A Mother's Grief
The Wages of Sin—The Assassin's Escape
The Wages of Sin—The Fatal Choice
The Wages of Sin—The Murder of Bess
When Stocks Went Up
Sep [day undetermined]
A Close Call
Finish of Futurity, 1901
Finish of Race Sheepshead Bay, Experimental
Parade to the Post
Sousa and His Band
Oct [day undetermined]
Finish of the Third Cup Race
Hail Columbia!
International Yacht Races—Columbia vs. Shamrock
A Near View of Shamrock II
Schooner "Idler" and Revenue Cutter "Gresham"
Shamrock to the Fore
Shamrock's Start
Start of the Third Cup Race
Steam Yacht "American"
Dec [day undetermined]
Expert Driving
Tally Ho!
1903
Apr [day undetermined]
Ameta
May [day undetermined]
Caught Courting
Eclipse Car Fender Test
How Tommy Got a Pull on His Grandpa
Jun [day undetermined]
Reproduction of Corbett-McGovern Fight
Oct [day undetermined]
From Haverstraw to Newburg
Parade of "Exempt" Firemen
Seeing New York by Yacht
U. S. Interior Dept.: Basket Ball, Indian School
U. S. Interior Dept.: Bridal Veil Falls
U. S. Interior Dept.: Changing Coaches, Raymond Coach
U. S. Interior Dept.: Irrigation of Alfalfa Lands
U. S. Interior Dept.: Laguna Indian Chicken-Pulling Race
U. S. Interior Dept.: Laguna Indian Foot Race
U. S. Interior Dept.: Laguna Indian Horse Race
U. S. Interior Dept.: Mail Coach Yosemite Valley
U. S. Interior Dept.: Panorama from Artist's Point
U. S. Interior Dept.: Panorama of Grand Canyon
U. S. Interior Dept.: Santa Fe Coach
U. S. Interior Dept.: Vernal Falls
U. S. P. O. Dept. Santa Fe Mail Train
Nov [day undetermined]
Arrival of Tourists at the Hotel in Yellowstone Park
Arrival of Train at Gardner
Carpenter Work, Albuquerque School
Crow Indian Festival Dance
Crow Indian War Dance
Crow Indians Harvesting
Down the Bright Angel Trail
Fire Drill: Albuquerque Indian School
Fountain Geyser
Girls' Department, Albuquerque School
Girls Flag Drill, Moqui School
Great Falls of the Yellowstone
Indian Boys, Albuquerque School
Indian Horsemanship
Mammouth Paint Pot, Yosemite Valley
Moqui Indian Rain Dance
Navajo Indian Foot Race
Navajo Indian Horse Race
Navajo Indian Tug-of-War
Navajo Indians Wrestling
Navajo Squaw Weaving Blanket
"Old Faithful," Yosemite Valley
On Yellowstone Lake
Panorama of Yellowstone Lake
Panoramic View of Hot Springs, Yellowstone Park
Rain Dance at Orabi
United States Troops in Yellowstone Park
Dec [day undetermined]
Drill by Providence Police
Noon Hour at Hope Webbing Company
Run of Pawtucket Fire Dept.
1904
Apr [day undetermined]
Review of U. S. Marine Band by Sec'y Moody, U. S. Navy
Jul [day undetermined]
Battery "A," Rhode Island Light Artillery
Aug [day undetermined]
Parade of Mystic Shriners, Luna Park, Coney Island
1905
Feb [day undetermined]
Across the New Viaduct of New York
Mar [day undetermined]
The Nihilists
Apr [day undetermined]
Bargain Day on 14th Street, New York
Children's Hour on the Farm
Physical Culture Poses
Three Cavaliers of the Road
Wanted: A Dog
1908
Jul 15 The Boston Tea Party
1909
Dec 24 Faust
1910
Apr 5 The Heart of a Rose

Armstrong, Charles
1909
Aug 14 Mr. Isaacs and the Mice
Sep 13 Votes for Women

Armstrong, E. A.
1905
Nov [day undetermined]
Hiawatha

Arnaud, Etienne
1909
Jul 20 The Man in the Moon

Arthur, Julie
1909
Apr 10 Napoleon: the Man of Destiny
1910
Jan 4 Forty Years in the Land of Midian [The Life of Moses Part II]
Jan 25 The Plagues of Egypt and the Deliverance of the Hebrew [The Life of Moses Part III]
Feb 12 The Victory of Israel [The Life of Moses Part IV]
Feb 19 The Promised Land [The Life of Moses Part V]

Arthur, Timothy Shay
1909
May 31 What Drink Did
1910
Nov 4 Ten Nights in a Bar Room

Artressi, Joseph
1903
Jan [day undetermined]
Leaping Tournament over Elephants

Arvidson, Linda
1907
Dec 21 Mr. Gay and Mrs.*
1908
Feb 1 Classmates
Feb 27 The Princess in the Vase*
Apr 15 The King of the Cannibal Islands
Apr 29 The King's Messenger
Jul 10 The Stage Rustler
Jul 14 The Adventures of Dollie
Jul 28 The Redman and the Child
Aug 4 The Bandit's Waterloo: The Outwitting of an Andalusian Brigand by a Pretty Senora
Aug 7 A Calamitous Elopement: How It Proved a Windfall for Burglar Bill
Aug 11 The Greaser's Gauntlet
Aug 14 The Man and the Woman
Aug 18 The Fatal Hour
Aug 25 Balked at the Altar
Aug 28 For a Wife's Honor
Sep 1 Betrayed by a Handprint
Sep 15 The Red Girl
Sep 22 Where the Breakers Roar
Sep 25 A Smoked Husband
Sep 29 The Stolen Jewels

Nov 6 The Pirate's Gold
Nov 10 Taming of the Shrew
Nov 17 The Song of the Shirt
Nov 24 A Woman's Way
Nov 27 The Clubman and the Tramp
Dec 8 The Feud and the Turkey
Dec 15 The Test of Friendship
Dec 18 An Awful Moment
Dec 29 The Helping Hand
1909
Jan 1 One Touch of Nature
Jan 14 A Rural Elopement
The Sacrifice
Jan 18 Those Boys!
Jan 21 Mr. Jones Has a Card Party
Jan 25 Those Awful Hats
Feb 8 Edgar Allen Poe
Feb 11 Tragic Love
Feb 15 The Curtain Pole
His Ward's Love
Mar 15 I Did It, Mamma
Mar 29 The Medicine Bottle
Apr 1 A Drunkard's Reformation
May 3 The Eavesdropper
May 13 A Baby's Shoe
Aug 30 The Heart of an Outlaw
The Mills of the Gods
Pranks
Sep 9 Comata, the Sioux
Sep 13 The Children's Friend
Sep 27 Leather Stocking
Oct 28 Lines of White on a Sullen Sea
Dec 13 A Corner in Wheat
1910
Jan 24 The Honor of His Family
Mar 7 The Thread of Destiny
Mar 14 The Converts
Mar 28 Gold Is Not All
May 5 The Unchanging Sea
Dec 5 A Child's Stratagem

Ashbridge, Mayor
1899
May [day undetermined]
President McKinley and Mayor Ashbridge of Philadelphia

Astor, John Jacob, Col.
1898
Sep [day undetermined]
President McKinley's Inspection of Camp Wikoff
1899
Oct [day undetermined]
Col. John Jacob Astor, Staff and Veterans of the Spanish-American War

Auer, Florence
1905
Oct 24 The Watermelon Patch*
1908
May 6 The Sculptor's Nightmare*
Jun 26 Over the Hills to the Poor House
Jul 3 At the Crossroads of Life
Jul 7 The Kentuckian
Jul 17 The Fight for Freedom
Jul 24 The Tavern-Keeper's Daughter
Aug 18 The Fatal Hour*

August, Edwin
1910
Jun 28 The Little Fiddler
Jul 1 The Stars and Stripes
Aug 2 With Bridges Burned
Aug 23 Love and the Law
Sep 6 The Big Scoop
Oct 11 The Song That Reached His Heart*
Nov 7 The Fugitive
Nov 10 Simple Charity
Nov 15 Into the Jaws of Death
Dec 5 A Child's Stratagem
Dec 12 The Golden Supper
Dec 26 Winning Back His Love

Avcock, Governor
1902
Apr [day undetermined]
President Roosevelt Reviewing the Troops at Charleston Exposition [South Carolina]

Avery, Charles
1908
Oct 9 Father Gets in the Game
Dec 1 The Valet's Wife
Dec 29 The Helping Hand
1909
Apr 29 'Tis an Ill Wind That Blows No Good
May 6 One Busy Hour
May 10 The French Duel
May 20 Resurrection
Jun 3 Eradicating Aunty
Aug 16 With Her Card
Nov 26 Dooley's Thanksgiving Turkey
1910
Jan 25 A Romance of the Prairie
Feb 18 Dooley's Holiday
Feb 25 Dooley Referees the Big Fight
Mar 22 The Man from Texas
May 27 Perils of the Plains
Jul 1 A Ranchman's Simple Son

Aylott, Dave
1909
Jun 12 Only a Dart
Jul 17 Billy's Bugle
Sep 4 The Boy Scouts
Sep 13 The Boy and the Convict
Sep 18 A Tricky Convict*
Oct 7 Was It a Snake Bite?*
1910
Jan 17 Muggins
Jun 4 The Last of the Dandies
A Race for a Bride
Scratch as Scratch Can
Jul 8 From Gypsy Hands
Jul 15 The Hindoo's Treachery

Babcock, Louis L.
1901
Jun 8 Opening of the Pan-American Exposition showing Vice President Roosevelt Leading the Procession

Bacon, Robert
1910
May 26 Roosevelt in Paris

Baden-Powell, General
1900 [month undetermined]
Earl Roberts and General Baden Powell

Badet, Mlle.
1910
Aug 18 Carmen

Baggot, King
1910
Apr 4 The Miser's Daughter
Sep 26 Pressed Roses
Oct 24 The Count of Montebello
Nov 14 The Double
Dec 5 The Aspirations of Gerald and Percy
Dec 29 Unreasonable Jealousy

Baker, Johnny
1910
Sep 15 Buffalo Bill's Wild West and Pawnee Bill's Far East

Balfour, A. J.
1901 [month undetermined]
Chamberlain and Balfour

Balshofer, Fred J.
1909
May 21 Disinherited Son's Loyalty
May 28 Romance of a Fishermaid
Jun 4 "Davy" Crockett in Hearts United
Jun 11 The Squaw's Revenge
Jun 18 A Terrible Attempt
Why Mr. Jones Was Arrested
Jun 25 Cowboy's Narrow Escape
Jul 2 A True Indian's Heart
1910
Jun 17 A Cowboy's Race for a Wife
Jun 21 The Sea Wolves
Jun 24 A Mexican Lothario
Jun 28 Her Terrible Peril

Balzac, Honoré de
1909
Sep 2 The Sealed Room
Oct 30 Entombed Alive
Dec 12 La Grande Breteche
1910
Apr 6 The Duchess of Langeais
Jun 20 Eugenie Grandet
Jul 25 The Silversmith to King Louis XI

Barat, Mlle.
1909
Aug 6 The Tragedy of Meudon

Barker, Captain
1898
Sep [day undetermined]
U. S. Battleship "Oregon"

Barker, Florence
1909
Dec 30 Choosing a Husband
1910
Jan 6 The Dancing Girl of Butte
Jan 10 Her Terrible Ordeal
Jan 20 The Call
Feb 7 The Course of True Love
Mar 3 The Newlyweds
Mar 17 The Love of Lady Irma
The Man
Mar 21 Faithful
Apr 14 The Kid
Apr 21 The Tenderfoot's Triumph
Apr 25 The Way of the World
Apr 28 Up a Tree
May 2 The Gold-Seekers
May 19 An Affair of Hearts
May 26 A Knot in the Plot
May 30 The Impalement
Jun 9 A Victim of Jealousy
Jul 7 A Midnight Cupid
Jul 14 A Child's Faith
Jul 21 Serious Sixteen
Jul 28 Unexpected Help
Sep 19 A Summer Tragedy
Sep 22 The Oath and the Man
Dec 8 Happy Jack, a Hero

Barker, Kenneth
1904
Jun 25 The Child Stealers

Barker, Reginald
1910
Aug 6 Under Western Skies
Aug 27 The Deputy's Love

Barker, Will
1904
Apr 25 The Smugglers
Jun 25 The Child Stealers

Barleon, Amelia
1910
May 6 Jane Eyre
May 27 The Winter's Tale

Barnard, Anne, Lady
1910
Oct 18 Auld Robin Grey

Barnes, George
1903
Dec [day undetermined]
The Great Train Robbery
1910
Oct 11 Pocahontas
Dec 30 Hypnotized

Barnes, William, State Committeeman
1900
Sep [day undetermined]
Hon. B. B. Odell, Jr.

Barrington, Rutland
1902
Nov [day undetermined]
Umbrella Dance, San Toy

Barry, Mr.
1908
Feb 29 Cupid's Pranks

Bartet, Mme.
1909
Mar 20 The Return of Ulysses

Bartho, Cathrina
1899
Sep [day undetermined]
M'lle. Cathrina Bartho
1900
Dec [day undetermined]
A Nymph of the Waves

Bartlett, Mr.
1908
Oct 9 A Voice from the Dead

Bartlett, Franklin, Col.
1899
Jun [day undetermined]
Twenty-Second Regiment, N. G. S. N. Y.

Barton, Winnie
1908
Apr 4 Brigand's Daughter

Bascom, H. L.
1906
Aug [day undetermined]
Kathleen Mavoureen

Bass, Lyman M.
1901
Jun 8 Opening of the Pan-American Exposition showing Vice President Roosevelt Leading the Procession

Bates, Charles F.
1897
Oct [day undetermined]
Exhibition of Prize Winners

Baum, L. Frank
1910
Mar 24 The Wonderful Wizard of Oz
Dec 19 John Dough and the Cherub
Baumann, C.
1909
Jun 4 "Davy" Crockett in Hearts United
Baur, Harry
1909
Nov 22 Legend of the Good Knight
Bayer, T. P.
1910
Dec 8 Turning the Tables
Bayley, Eve
1902
Sep [day undetermined]
Grandma Threading Her Needle
Beach, Rex
1910
Jan 4 Pardners
May 31 The Mule Driver and the Garrulous Mute
Jun 7 The Shyness of Shorty
Jul 12 Out of the Night
Aug 2 With Bridges Burned
Beachey
1910
Feb 16 Aviation at Los Angeles, Calif.
Beal
1907
Dec 7 Ben Hur
Beal, Frank
1910
Jan 27 The Devil, the Servant, and the Man
Apr 28 The Angelus
Nov 28 The Regeneration
Beaudine, William
1910
Sep 19 A Summer Tragedy
Beck, Lieutenant
1910
Feb 16 Aviation at Los Angeles, Calif.
Bell, J. Franklin, Brigadier-General
1900
May [day undetermined]
Brigadier-General Franklin Bell and Staff
Bell Sisters
1903
Jan [day undetermined]
Three Bell Sisters in a Fancy Dance
Bergen, Nella
1899
Sep [day undetermined]
The Summer Girl
Berlioz, Hector
1903
Dec 12 The Damnation of Faust
Bernard, Dorothy
1910
Feb 21 His Last Burglary
Feb 24 Taming a Husband
Feb 28 The Final Settlement
Bernhardt, Sarah
1908
Oct 31 Hamlet, Duel Scene with Laertes
Bernon, Bleuette
1902
Oct 4 A Trip to the Moon
1903
Sep 5 The Fairyland; or, The Kingdom of the Fairies
Bernstein, Henri
1910
Aug 27 A Society Sinner
Bert, Hal
1909
Feb 10 The Guardian of the Bank
May 8 Baby's Chum
Besserer, Eugenie
1910
Mar 24 The Wonderful Wizard of Oz
Besserer, L.
1909
Dec 25 The Heart of a Cowboy
Biehl, Conrad, Mayor
1901
Jun 8 Opening of the Pan-American Exposition showing Vice President Roosevelt Leading the Procession

Bishop Brothers, The
1903
Jan [day undetermined]
Leaping Tournament over Elephants
Bitzer, G. W.
1898
Jul [day undetermined]
The Katzenjammer Kids in School
The Nearsighted School Teacher
Tribulations of a Country Schoolmarm
1899
Apr [day undetermined]
Farmer Oatcake Has His Troubles
Going to the Hunt
High Hurdle Jumping, at Meadowbrook Hunt Club
The Meadowbrook Hunt
Pole Vaulting at Columbia University
May [day undetermined]
Ambulance Corps Drill
Board of Trade
The Breeches Buoy
Distributing a War Extra
First Boston School Regiment
A Flock of Sheep
Founder's Log Cabin
Hipwood-Barrett Car Fender
Launching the Lifeboat
Mounted Artillery
Schooling Hunters
Second Boston School Regiment
Shooting the Life Line
Stealing a Dinner
Third Boston School Regiment
Troop "F," 3rd Cavalry
A Unique Race
Jun [day undetermined]
Children Feeding Ducklings
Down Mount Tom
Feeding the Pigeons
First Heavy Artillery
Governor Walcott of Massachusetts
"La Grande Duchesse"
How Ducks Are Fattened
President and Mrs. McKinley
President McKinley
Jul [day undetermined]
Aquatic Sports
Canoeing at Riverside
Glen House Stage
Kilpatrick's Ride
Myopia vs. Dedham
Smallest Train in the World
Aug [day undetermined]
Around Tynsborough Curve
Climbing Jacob's Ladder
Crawford Notch
The Flume
The Frankenstein Trestle
The Great Lafayette
He Didn't Finish the Story
Hooksett Falls Bridge
Miss Jewett and the Baker Family
Sliding Down Mount Washington
Summit of Mt. Washington
Winnisquam Lake
Sep [day undetermined]
Demonstrating the Action of a Patent Street Sprinkler of the American Car Sprinkler Co. of Worcester, Mass
Demonstrating the Action of the Northrop Looms
A Roll Lift Draw Bridge
Some Future Champions
Oct [day undetermined]
Beyond the Great Divide
Chinamen Returning to China
Down the Western Slope of the Canadian Rockies Through Kicking Horse Pass
The Eastern Slope of the Rockies, Passing Anthracite Station
The Gap, Entrance to the Rocky Mountains
In the Canadian Rockies, near Banff
Steamship "Empress of India"
Under the Shadow of Mt. Stephen, Passing Field's Station in the Rocky Mountains
Up the Big Grade in the Valley of the Kicking Horse
Nov [day undetermined]
Around Gravel Bay
Bridge No. 804, and Daly's Grade
Caribou Bridge
Frazer Canyon, East of Yale
Grand Trunk R. R. Bridge over Whirlpool*
Dec [day undetermined]
By Pulpit Rock and Through the Town of Echo
Devil's Gate
Devil's Slide
East of Uintah in Weber Canyon
Home of Buffalo Bill
One Thousand Mile Tree, Weber Canyon
The "Overland Limited" Passing Witch Rocks
Passing Steamboat and Great Eastern Rocks
Toll Gate and Castle Rock near Green River
Tunnel "No. Three"
West of Peterson; Entrance to Weber Canyon
1900
Mar [day undetermined]
Dress Parade of the Woodward High School Cadets
Walnut Hill Cadets
May [day undetermined]
The Clown and the Mule
A Four-Horse Circus Act
Gatling Gun Drill
A Somersault on Horseback
A Speedway Parade
Water Babies
Jun [day undetermined]
A Close Finish
Larchmont Regatta
Public Square, Cleveland
Soldiers of Greater Britain
Steam Yacht "Kismet"
Steeple Chase, Toronto
The Suburban of 1900
Jul [day undetermined]
Champion Polo Players
Deep Sea Fishing
From Vaudreuil to St. Anne's
Polo Game: Myopia vs. Dedham
The Tough Kid's Waterloo
Aug [day undetermined]
Arrival of Train at Muskoka Wharf
Chasing the Cherry Pickers
Departure of Boats from Muskoka Wharf
A Farmer's Imitation of Ching Ling Foo
The Imperial Limited
Over the Fence and Out
Sep [day undetermined]
Galveston Disaster
The Galveston Disaster
A Hand Car and the Imperial Limited
Imperial Limited
Little Sister
Love in the Suburbs
Panoramic View, Rescue Work, Galveston
Panoramic View, Wreckage Along Shore, Galveston
A Water Duel
Oct [day undetermined]
The Last Alarm
On the Cleveland and Eastern Railway
Pan-American Exposition
Nov [day undetermined]
Employees of Wolfson's Spice Mills, Toledo
Showing a Giant Crane Dumping a 40-Ton Car
Dec [day undetermined]
At Break-Neck Speed
Childhood's Vows
From Council Bluffs to Omaha
High School Pupils
The Iron Workers
Lawrence Fire Department
Mill Hands
St. Mary's Congregation
U. S. Naval Militia
Union Pacific Fast Mail
1901
Jan [day undetermined]
Launch of the "Saturn"
Feb [day undetermined]
Main Street, Worcester
Mar [day undetermined]
Run of the Worcester Fire Department
Trotters at Worcester
Apr [day undetermined]
General Quarters for Action
May [day undetermined]
At the Setting of the Sun

Boats Under Oars
A Good Test of High Explosives
The Horticultural Building
Middies Shortening Sails
Steam Tactics
U. S. Proving Grounds, Sandy Hook
United States Government Gun Test
Jun [day undetermined]
U. S. National Cemetery
Jul [day undetermined]
Arrival of Train at Station
Fish Cut
Flock of Sheep
The Georgetown Loop
Herd of Cattle
Indian Fort, Sherman Hill Tunnel
The Overland Limited
Pine Ridge Bluffs
A Race with the Overland Limited
Through Gibraltar
Train Crossing Dale Creek Fill
Sep [day undetermined]
Industrial Parade of the Cincinnati Fall Festival
Traveling Men's Association
Oct [day undetermined]
Bridal Veil Falls
Nevada Falls
Wawona, Big Tree
Dec [day undetermined]
The Beginning of a Great Enterprise
1902
Jun [day undetermined]
The Suburban of 1902
Jul [day undetermined]
Baby in a Rage
Baby Playing in Gutter
A Little Man
A Pipe Story of the Fourth
Aug [day undetermined]
Baby Parade
The Beach at Atlantic City
Biograph Snapshots at the President
Caught in the Undertow
Floral Chair Parade
A Heavy Surf at Atlantic City
Sep [day undetermined]
A Ball on a Battleship
Bombardment of Newport
Nov [day undetermined]
A Remarkable Fire
Dec [day undetermined]
The Horse Market
Sheep and Lambs*
1903
Jan [day undetermined]
A Midwinter Blaze
Feb [day undetermined]
Children Coasting
A Sweep across New York
25 Stories Up!
Mar [day undetermined]
In the Rapid-Transit Tunnel
Apr [day undetermined]
For the Upper Crust
Pulling a Seine U. S. F. C.
Spilt Milk
Stripping Pike Perch U. S. F. C.
May [day undetermined]
The Artist's Studio
Changing Horses at Glen
Changing Horses at Linden
"Don't Get Gay with Your Manicure!"
The Hairdresser
"I Want My Dinner"
Juvenile Stakes
Meadowbrook Steeplechase
Metropolitan Handicap
N. Y. Fire Department Returning
On the Road
The Pajama Girl
Private Picture for Mr. Hyde
Pulling Off the Bed Clothes
Run of N. Y. Fire Department
A Shocking Incident
Shooting the Chutes
Stripping Shad U. S. F. C.
Jun [day undetermined]
Beaver Show Case
Betsy Ross Dance
The Cook Visits the Parlor
Cosy Corner Dance
Danger of Dining in Private Dining Rooms
The Doctor's Favorite Patient
Down the Bamboo Slide
The Giddy Dancing Master
Gloomy Gus Gets the Best of It
Happy Hooligan Interferes
The Haymarket
"Holy Moses" the Camel
How Mike Got the Soap in His Eyes
The Necromancer
A Pair of Queens
Poor Old Fido!
The Professor of the Drama
Rock Drill at Work in Subway
Snarleyow the Dog Fiend
The Teacher's Unexpected Ducking
An Unprotected Female
Jul [day undetermined]
The American Soldier in Love and War [Number 1]
The American Soldier in Love and War [Number 2]
The American Soldier in Love and War [Number 3]
The Boy in the Barrel
Catch-as-Catch-Can Wrestling Bout
A Discordant Note
The Divorce: Detected [Part 1]
The Divorce: On the Trail [Part 2]
The Divorce: The Evidence Secured [Part 3]
Expert Bag Punching
The Fate of a Gossip
Happy Hooligan Earns His Dinner
Happy Hooligan in a Trap
How Buttons Got Even with the Butler
Levi & Cohen, The Irish Comedians
Making a Welch Rabbit
The Physical Culture Girl, No. 1
The Physical Culture Girl, No. 2
The Physical Culture Girl, No. 3
Pres. Roosevelt's Fourth of July Oration
Shooting the Chutes, Luna Park
Strictly Fresh Eggs
A Too Ardent Lover
The Unfaithful Wife: Murder and Suicide [Part 3]
The Unfaithful Wife: The Fight [Part 2]
The Unfaithful Wife: The Lover [Part 1]
A Victim of Circumstantial Evidence
A Welsh Rabbit
Why Foxy Grandpa Escaped a Ducking
Willie's Camera
Aug [day undetermined]
The Dude and the Burglars
Gold Dust Twins
A Gypsy Duel
The Kidnapper: At Work [Part 1]
The Kidnapper: In the Den [Part 2]
The Kidnapper: The Rescue [Part 3]
Lucky Kitten!
Murder Scene from "King of the Detectives"
On the Flying Rings
The Rose
A Search for Evidence
Silveon and Emerie "On the Web"
Sweets for the Sweet
The Wages of Sin: A—Murder
The Wages of Sin: B—Retribution
The Widow
Sep [day undetermined]
The Forecastle of the "Kearsage" in a Heavy Sea
The Insurance Collector
Jack Tar Sewing a Patch on the Seat of His Trousers
Jack's Four Footed Friend. Mike the Ship's Mascot
One of Jack's Games Aboard a Man o' War
Piping Down. Wash Clothes. Scrambling for Clothes
President Roosevelt Addressing Crew of "Kearsarge"
Pres. Roosevelt Leaving the Flagship
President Roosevelt's Arrival at "Kearsarge"
President Roosevelt's Departure from "Kearsarge"
Pres. Roosevelt's Sunday Visit to Kearsage
President Roosevelt's Visit to Admiral Barker
Reproduction of Jeffries-Corbett Contest
Sea Washing over the Bow of Kearsage
Signal Boys Wig-Wagging
Sparring Match on the "Kearsarge"
Oct [day undetermined]
Arab Act, Luna Park
At the Dressmaker's
The Baby
Blessed Is the Peacemaker
The Camera Fiend, No. 2
A Catch of Hard Shell Crabs
Cat's Cradle
The Cowboy and the Lady
Double Ring Act, Luna Park
The Elopement
The Fate of the Artist's Model
A Frontier Flirtation; or, "How the Tenderfoot Won Out"
The Honourable Artillery Company of London
Hooligan as a Safe Robber
Hooligan in Jail
Hooligan to the Rescue
The Providence Light Artillery
The Rehearsal
The Rock of Ages
She Fell Fainting into His Arms
Slide for Life, Luna Park
The Vaidis Sisters, Luna Park
Weighing the Baby
"You Will Send Me to Bed, Eh?"
Nov [day undetermined]
Battleship "Indiana" in Action
Boat Race
Boat Race No. 2
Feeding the Russian Bear
A Flirtation in Silhouette
Harvard-Pennsylvania Football Game
Hooligan and Dogs (Journal Thumb Book)
An Impartial Lover
Inspection Aboard Battleship "Indiana"
Katzenjammer Kids (Journal Thumb Book)
The Llamas at Play
Man Overboard! "INDIANA"
Poor Hooligan, So Hungry Too!
Raising Colors, Battleship "Indiana"
Dec [day undetermined]
Battleship "Illinois" Passing Under Brooklyn Bridge
Hooligan's Christmas Dream
Toodles' Christmas (Thumb Book)
1904
Jan [day undetermined]
Applicants for Enlistment
Auction of Deserters' Effects
Awkward Squad
Bag Inspection
Cowboy Justice
Drill
Eye Tests, etc., Recruiting
First Aid to the Injured
General Quarters
Obstacle Race
Physical Examinations
Recruits Embarking
Recruits on "Yorktown"
Sailors Dancing
Scrubbing Clothes
"Secure"
Serving Outfits to Recruits
Stretcher Race over Obstacles
Swearing in Recruits
Torpedo Attack
Feb [day undetermined]
The Four Seasons
Mellin's Food Baby
The Misplaced Signs
The Opening of the Williamsburg Bridge
Mar [day undetermined]
The Battle of the Yalu
Butt's Manual, St. John's School
Company Drill, St. John's Military Academy
Dress Parade, St. John's Academy
Gun Drill St. John's Academy
Manual of Arms, St. John's Military Academy
Apr [day undetermined]
Girls Winding Armatures, Westinghouse Works
Welding Big Ring
Westinghouse Sign
May [day undetermined]
Assembling a Generator, Westinghouse Works
Assembling and Testing Turbines, Westinghouse Works
Casting a Guide Box, Westinghouse Works

Coil Winding Machines, Westinghouse Works
Coil Winding Section E, Westinghouse Works
Girls Taking Time Checks, Westinghouse Works
Operation of Westinghouse Block System
Panorama Exterior Westinghouse Works
Panorama Motor Room, Westinghouse Works
Panorama of Machine Co. Aisle, Westinghouse Co. Works
Panoramic View Aisle B., Westinghouse Works
Railroad Panorama, Pittsburg to Stewart, Westinghouse Works
Steam Hammer, Westinghouse Works
Steam Whistle, Westinghouse Works
Taping Coils, Westinghouse Works
Tapping a Furnace, Westinghouse Works
Testing a Rotary, Westinghouse Works
Testing Gas Engine, Westinghouse Works
Testing Large Turbines, Westinghouse Co. Works
Testing Steam Engine, Westinghouse Works
Turning Panorama from Hill, Westinghouse Works
Westinghouse Air Brake Co., Casting Machine
Westinghouse Air Brake Co. Westinghouse Works
Westinghouse Co., No. 3, Moulding Machine
Westinghouse Employees Boarding Train
Westinghouse Employees, Westinghouse Works

Jun [day undetermined]
Auto Boat Race on the Hudson River
The Brooklyn Handicap, 1904
"Personal"
The Slocum Disaster

Jul [day undetermined]
Alone
Beyond the Danger Line
Coaching in the White Mountains
A Couple of Lightweights at Coney Island
Fighting the Flames [An Attraction at Coney Island]
The First Baby
Holland Submarine Boat Tests
Panorama of Harvard Class Day
President Roosevelt's Home-coming
The Racing Chutes at Dreamland
The Seashore Baby
Speed Test W. K. Vanderbilt, Jr.'s "Tarantula"
The Swimming Class

Aug [day undetermined]
Automobiling Among the Clouds
The Baby and the Puppies
The Children in the Surf
The Coney Island Beach Patrol
Democratic National Committee at Esopus
Fighting the Flames, Dreamland
Judge Parker & Mayor McClellan at Esopus
The Moonshiner
Orphan Children on the Beach at Coney Island
A Seaside Cakewalk
A Swimming Race at Coney Island
The Two Bottle Babies
The Widow and the Only Man

Sep [day undetermined]
The Hero of Liao Yang

Oct [day undetermined]
Automobile Race for the Vanderbilt Cup
Launching of the U. S. S. Battleship "Connecticut"
The Lost Child

Nov [day undetermined]
Electric Locomotive Tests and Races, Schenectady, N. Y.

Dec [day undetermined]
The Chicken Thief

1905 [month undetermined]
Latina, Dislocation Act

Jan [day undetermined]
Baby's Day
The Bad Boy and the Grocery Man
The Gentlemen Highwaymen
New Year's Day Parade, Philadelphia

Feb [day undetermined]
Automobile Races at Ormond, Fla.
Boating Carnival, Palm Beach, Fla.
In the Swimming Pool, Palm Beach, Fla.
The Prima Donna's Understudy
The Sleepy Soubrette
Speed Trial of Auto Boat Challenger, Lake Worth, Fla.

Mar [day undetermined]
Bathing in the Ice at the L Street Bath, Boston
Gov. Wm. L. Douglas, of Mass.
The Inauguration of President Roosevelt
Tom, Tom, the Piper's Son

Apr [day undetermined]
Children's Hour on the Farm
Employees Leaving Office
Gen'l Elec. No. 1 Employees Leaving Work
Gen'l Elec. No. 2 Trolley Changing from Di. to Alter. Cur.
Gen'l Elec. No. 3 Handling Cars at the Barn
General Electric Engine Hauling Freight
N. Y. Life Insurance Co. Pres. McCall & Officers
"Osler"-ising Papa
Women Employee's Dining Room

May [day undetermined]
The Adjustable Chair
Al Treloar in Muscle Exercises
The Athletic Girl and the Burglar
The Badger Game
The Barber's Dee-Light
The Barber's Pretty Patient
The Bigamist's Trial
The Boarding House Bathroom
The Broker's Athletic Typewriter
The Deadwood Sleeper
Funeral of Hiram Cronk
"Gee, If Me Mudder Could Only See Me Now"
The Girls, the Burglar, and the Rat
It's a Shame To Take the Money
N. Y. Police Parade, 1905
Peeping Tom in the Dressing Room
Reproduction, Nan Paterson's Trial
Rough House in a New York Honky-Tonk
Spirit of '76
The Wedding

Jun [day undetermined]
A Ballroom Tragedy
Between the Dances
How Willie Got the Eggs
Interior N. Y. Subway, 14th St. to 42nd St.
Monkey Business
The Pillow Fight, No. 2
A Pipe Dream
Reuben in the Opium Joint
Reuben in the Subway
A Saturday Afternoon at Travers' Island with the New York Athletic Club
The Topers
A Trip to Salt Lake City
2 A. M. in the Subway
Under the Bamboo Tree
The Wine Opener

Jul [day undetermined]
The Abductors
The Bridal Chamber
The Darling of the Gallery Gods
Departure of Peary for the North Pole
Duel Scene from "Macbeth"
He Got into the Wrong Bath House
In a Raines Law Hotel
Lifting the Lid
Love's Perfidy
Mobilization of the Massachusetts State Troops
A Modern Sappho
On the Beach at Brighton
Ore the Banster
Pompey's Honey Girl
A Poor Place for Love Making
Seeing Squashville

Aug [day undetermined]
Blackmail
The Broadway Massage Parlor
The Fire-Bug
Leap Frog Railway, Coney Island
Peace Envoys at Portsmouth, N.H.
Pennsylvania Tunnel Excavation
The Society Palmist
The Summer Boarders

Sep [day undetermined]
Always Room for One More
Bertha Claiche
The Boer War
Chauncey Explains
Female Crook and Her Easy Victim
Fun on the Joy Line
General Cronje & Mystic Shriners
High Jumping Horses—Sidney Holloway's Farm
His Move
The Horse-Thief
Ludlow's Aerodrome
The River Pirates
Robbed of Her All
Teasing
Unlucky at Cards, Lucky at Love

Oct [day undetermined]
Bringing Up a Girl in the Way She Should Go [No. 1]
Bringing Up a Girl in the Way She Should Go [No. 2]
A Country Courtship
Dream of the Race Track Fiend
Everybody Works But Father (Whiteface)
The Great Jewel Mystery
Halloween
How Millionaires Sometimes Entertain Aboard Their Yachts

Nov [day undetermined]
Airy Fairy Lillian Tries on Her New Corsets
The Barnstormers
Everybody Works But Father (Blackface)
The Fat Girl's Love Affair
A Kentucky Feud
Latina, Contortionist
Ludlow's Aerodrome, No. 2
The Rat Trap Pickpocket Detector
Reception of British Fleet
Sparring at the N. Y. A. C.
The Thirteen Club
Wrestling at the N.Y.A.C.

Dec [day undetermined]
A Break for Freedom
Climbing the American Alps
Reading the Death Sentence

1906

Jan [day undetermined]
Deer Stalking with a Camera
The Gossipers
Moose Hunt in New Brunswick
Quail Shooting at Pinehurst
Salmon Fishing in Quebec
Trout Fishing in Rangeley Lakes
Turkey Hunt at Pinehurst
Wine, Women & Song

Jan 27 The Henpecked Husband
The Impossible Convicts
The Simple Life

Jan 30 The Insurance Solicitor; or, A Story of a Blasted Ambition

Feb [day undetermined]
College Life at Amherst
Police Raid at a Dog Fight
A Raid on a Cock Fight
Scene in a Rat Pit
Seeing Boston
Terrier vs. Wild Cat
Volunteer Fire Department Parade

Feb 19 The Critic
A Friend in Need Is a Friend Indeed

Feb 23 Mr. Butt-In

Mar [day undetermined]
Dixon-Chester Leon Contest
Eclipse of Sun
Scenes Washington, D. C.

Mar 29 The Black Hand

May [day undetermined]
Arrival of Immigrants, Ellis Island
Her Name Was Maude
Human Apes from the Orient
John Paul Jones Ceremonies

May 1 The Subpoena Server

May 16 San Francisco
May 26 Eruption of Mt. Vesuvius
Society Ballooning
"23"
Jun [day undetermined]
Attack on Fort Boonesboro
Canoeing in Maine
A College Girl's Affair of Honor
Free Show on the Beach
Logging in Maine
Maneuvering a Small Motor Boat
Physical Culture Lesson
Play Ball on the Beach
They Meet on the Mat
White Fox Motor Boat
Jun 14 The Village Cut-Up
Jun 26 Poughkeepsie Regatta
Jun 28 The Paymaster
Jun 30 The Gateway to the Catskills
Grand Hotel to Big Indian
Hold-Up of the Rocky Mt. Express
In the Haunts of Rip Van Winkle
In the Heart of the Catskills
Through Austin Glen, Catskill Railway
The Valley of Esopus
Jul [day undetermined]
Thaw-White Tragedy
Jul 11 Night of the Party
Jul 19 The Masqueraders
Sep [day undetermined]
Bryan
E. Forest Fish Gun Assn.
Hoe Printing Press in Action
May's Mechanical Race Track
Oct [day undetermined]
Motor Race
The 9th Mass. Vol. Militia
7th Regiment at 69th Army Dedication
Thousand Islands
Oct 8 The Country Schoolmaster
Oct 18 The Fox-Hunt
Nov 1 Dr. Dippy's Sanitarium
Dec [day undetermined]
Singer Building Foundation Co.
Dec 29 Married for Millions

1907

Jan [day undetermined]
Man Being Run Over by Automobile
Jan 5 The Lighthouse
Jan 17 Trial Marriages
Feb [day undetermined]
Carmen
Feb 8 At the Monkey House
Mr. Hurry-Up
Mar [day undetermined]
Salome
Trap Pigeon Shooting
Mar 2 Fights of Nations
Mar 28 Mrs. Smithers' Boarding-School
Apr [day undetermined]
Brother Willie's Revenge
Deyo
Dreams of Fair Women
The Girl on Park Bench
Mishaps of a Maid
Post Office Department Picture
Skating on N. Y. Theatre Roof
The Spanish Lovers
This Girl Not Wanted
Undone by a Suit Case
Unloading Mail at Pier 13, N. R., N. Y.
Upset by a Cigarette
Apr 11 The Truants
Apr 27 The Fencing Master
May [day undetermined]
Examining a Recruit U.S.N.
Governor's Island Taken U.S.N.
May 11 Crayono
Jamestown Exposition
A Tenderloin Tragedy
May 23 If You Had a Wife Like This
Jun [day undetermined]
Dear Little Sister
Flirty Fan
The Kitchen Terror
Wyoming Girl
Jun 17 Rube Brown in Town
Jun 29 Exciting Night of Their Honeymoon
Fussy Father Fooled
Jul 20 The Hypnotist's Revenge
Aug [day undetermined]
Bigger Than He Looked
Egyptian Princess
Pat's Ghost
Post Office Dept. Picture
Smoking Up
Aug 17 The Deaf-Mutes' Ball
Aug 31 The Tired Tailor's Dream
Sep [day undetermined]
Bachelor Gets a Baby and Other Things He Don't Want
Bargains
Black-White
Blowing Hard
Busy Lizzie Loses Her Clothes
Chink-Chippie
Chorus Girls
Congested Street Society
Crime Wave
Crooked Dog
The Crush at the Bridge Congested S. S.
Dream Kisses
The Finish of Scrappy Patsey
Flip-Rip-Zip
Flirty Fred
Frowsy Lizzie Knocks Them Dizzy
High Jinks
Hunters Dream
Ironed
Kissers Caught
Light-Fight-White
Mags Jag
Pres. Roosevelt Reviewing U. S. Regulars
Pres. Roosevelt Reviewing West Point Cadets
Row at Rileys
Stripped-Stripped
A Swell Time
A Tenement House Battle
Too Soon
Tramps Angel
Vanishing Friends
Wanted a Man Badly
What His Girl's Voice Did
Sep 12 The Model's Ma
Neighbors
Sep 25 Terrible Ted
Oct [day undetermined]
Mr. Easy Mark
Oct 19 Love Microbe
Oct 28 Yale Laundry
Nov [day undetermined]
[Picture taken for Capt. Lovelace]
Nov 4 Under the Old Apple Tree
Nov 20 Wife Wanted
Dec 4 The Elopement
Dec 14 Dr. Skinum
Dec 21 Mr. Gay and Mrs.

1908

Jan [day undetermined]
Oh Mama
Oh That Curtain
Jan 4 Professional Jealousy
Jan 18 Falsely Accused!
Jan 22 Lonesome Junction
Feb 1 Classmates
Feb 10 Bobby's Kodak
Feb 19 The Snowman
Feb 27 The Princess in the Vase
Mar 7 The Yellow Peril
Mar 11 The Boy Detective; or, The Abductors Foiled
Mar 18 Her First Adventure [Kidnapped with the Aid of a Street Piano]
Mar 21 Caught by Wireless
Mar 28 Old Isaacs, the Pawnbroker
Apr [day undetermined]
Gold-Buys
Masked Policeman
Mrs. Trouble
Selling a Model
Apr 7 A Famous Escape
Apr 15 The King of the Cannibal Islands
Apr 22 Hulda's Lovers
Apr 29 The King's Messenger
May [day undetermined]
Fly Paper
The Girl and the Gossip
The Girls Dormitory
Jealousy Behind the Scenes
May 6 The Music Master
The Sculptor's Nightmare
May 20 When Knights Were Bold
May 26 A Night of Terror
May 29 His Day of Rest
Jun [day undetermined]
Special Muto Reel Mellin's Food Co.
Three Weeks
Jun 2 Thompson's Night Out
Jun 5 The Romance of an Egg
Jun 9 'Ostler Joe
Jun 12 Mixed Babies
Jun 16 The Invisible Fluid
Jun 19 The Man in the Box
Jun 23 The Outlaw
Jun 26 Over the Hills to the Poor House
Jun 30 At the French Ball
Jul 3 At the Crossroads of Life
Jul 7 The Kentuckian
Jul 10 The Stage Rustler
Jul 17 The Fight for Freedom
Jul 21 The Black Viper
Jul 31 Deceived Slumming Party
Aug 7 A Calamitous Elopement: How It Proved a Windfall for Burglar Bill
Aug 14 The Man and the Woman
Sep [day undetermined]
The Chorus Man's Revenge
Sep 1 Betrayed by a Handprint
Sep 4 Monday Morning in a Coney Island Police Court
Sep 22 Where the Breakers Roar
Sep 25 A Smoked Husband
Sep 29 The Stolen Jewels
Oct [day undetermined]
They Forgot the Messenger
What the Copper Saw
Oct 2 The Devil
Oct 6 The Zulu's Heart
Oct 9 Father Gets in the Game
Oct 13 The Barbarian Ingomar
Oct 16 The Vaquero's Vow
Oct 20 The Planter's Wife
Oct 23 Romance of a Jewess
Oct 27 The Call of the Wild
Oct 30 Concealing a Burglar
Nov 3 After Many Years
Nov 6 The Pirate's Gold
Nov 10 Taming of the Shrew
Nov 13 The Guerrilla
Nov 17 The Song of the Shirt
Nov 20 The Ingrate
Nov 27 The Clubman and the Tramp
Dec 1 The Valet's Wife
Dec 4 Money Mad
Dec 8 The Feud and the Turkey
Dec 11 The Reckoning
Dec 15 The Test of Friendship
Dec 22 The Christmas Burglars
Dec 25 Mr. Jones at the Ball

1909

Jan 1 One Touch of Nature
Jan 4 The Maniac Cook
Jan 7 Mrs. Jones Entertains
Jan 11 The Honor of Thieves
Love Finds a Way
Jan 14 A Rural Elopement
The Sacrifice
Jan 18 The Criminal Hypnotist
Those Boys!
Jan 21 The Fascinating Mrs. Francis
Mr. Jones Has a Card Party
Jan 25 Those Awful Hats
The Welcome Burglar
Jan 28 The Cord of Life
Feb 1 The Girls and Daddy
Feb 4 The Brahma Diamond
Feb 8 Edgar Allen Poe
A Wreath in Time
Feb 11 Tragic Love
Feb 15 The Curtain Pole
His Ward's Love
Feb 18 The Hindoo Dagger
The Joneses Have Amateur Theatricals
Feb 22 The Golden Louis*
The Politician's Love Story
Feb 25 At the Altar
Mar 1 His Wife's Mother
The Prussian Spy
Mar 4 A Fool's Revenge
Mar 8 The Roue's Heart
The Wooden Leg
Mar 11 The Salvation Army Lass
Mar 15 I Did It, Mamma
The Lure of the Gown
Mar 18 The Voice of the Violin
Mar 22 And a Little Child Shall Lead Them
The Deception
Mar 25 A Burglar's Mistake
Mar 29 Jones and His New Neighbors
The Medicine Bottle
Apr 1 A Drunkard's Reformation
Apr 5 Trying to Get Arrested
Apr 8 A Rude Hostess
Schneider's Anti-Noise Crusade
Apr 12 A Sound Sleeper
The Winning Coat

Apr 15 Confidence
Apr 19 Lady Helen's Escapade
A Troublesome Satchel
Apr 22 The Drive for a Life
Apr 26 Lucky Jim
Apr 29 'Tis an Ill Wind That Blows No Good
May 3 The Eavesdropper
The Suicide Club
May 6 The Note in the Shoe
One Busy Hour
May 10 The French Duel
Jones and the Lady Book Agent
May 13 A Baby's Shoe
May 17 The Jilt
May 20 Resurrection
May 24 Eloping with Aunty
Two Memories
May 27 The Cricket on the Hearth
May 31 What Drink Did
Jun 3 Eradicating Aunty
His Duty
Jun 7 The Violin Maker of Cremona
Jun 10 The Lonely Villa
A New Trick
Jun 14 The Son's Return
Jun 17 The Faded Lillies
Her First Biscuits
Jun 21 Was Justice Served?
Jun 24 The Mexican Sweethearts
The Peachbasket Hat
Jun 28 The Way of Man
Jul 1 The Necklace
Jul 5 The Message
Jul 8 The Country Doctor
Jul 12 The Cardinal's Conspiracy
Jul 15 The Friend of the Family
Tender Hearts
Jul 19 The Renunciation
Jul 22 Jealousy and the Man
Sweet and Twenty
Jul 26 A Convict's Sacrifice
Jul 29 The Slave
Aug 2 A Strange Meeting
Aug 5 The Mended Lute
Aug 9 Jones' Burglar
They Would Elope
Aug 12 The Better Way
Aug 16 With Her Card
Aug 19 His Wife's Visitor
Mrs. Jones' Lover; or, "I Want My Hat"
Aug 23 The Indian Runner's Romance
Aug 26 "Oh, Uncle"
The Seventh Day
Aug 30 The Heart of an Outlaw
The Mills of the Gods
Sep 2 The Little Darling
The Sealed Room
Sep 6 "1776" or, The Hessian Renegades
Sep 9 Comata, the Sioux
Sep 13 The Children's Friend
Getting Even
Sep 16 The Broken Locket
Sep 20 In Old Kentucky
Sep 23 A Fair Exchange
Sep 27 Leather Stocking
Sep 30 The Awakening
Wanted, a Child
Oct 4 Pippa Passes; or, The Song of Conscience
Oct 7 Fools of Fate
Oct 11 The Little Teacher
Oct 14 A Change of Heart
Oct 18 His Lost Love
Oct 21 The Expiation
Oct 25 In the Watches of the Night
Oct 28 Lines of White on a Sullen Sea
Nov 1 The Gibson Goddess
What's Your Hurry?
Nov 4 Nursing a Viper
Nov 8 The Restoration
Nov 11 The Light That Came
Nov 15 Two Women and a Man
Nov 18 A Midnight Adventure
Sweet Revenge
Nov 22 The Open Gate
Nov 25 The Mountaineer's Honor
Nov 29 In the Window Recess
The Trick That Failed
Dec 2 The Death Disc: A Story of the Cromwellian Period
Dec 6 Through the Breakers
Dec 9 The Redman's View
Dec 13 A Corner in Wheat
Dec 16 In a Hempen Bag
The Test
Dec 20 A Trap for Santa Claus
Dec 23 In Little Italy
Dec 27 To Save Her Soul
Dec 30 Choosing a Husband
The Day After

1910
Jan 3 The Rocky Road
Jan 6 The Dancing Girl of Butte
Jan 10 Her Terrible Ordeal
Jan 17 On the Reef
Jan 20 The Call
Jan 24 The Honor of His Family
Jan 27 The Last Deal
Jan 31 The Cloister's Touch
Feb 3 The Woman from Mellon's
Feb 10 The Duke's Plan
Feb 14 One Night, and Then —
Feb 17 The Englishman and the Girl
Feb 21 His Last Burglary
Feb 24 Taming a Husband
Feb 28 The Final Settlement
Mar 3 The Newlyweds
Mar 7 The Thread of Destiny
Mar 10 In Old California
Mar 14 The Converts
Mar 17 The Man
Mar 21 Faithful
Mar 24 The Twisted Trail
Mar 28 Gold Is Not All
Apr 4 As It Is in Life
Apr 7 A Rich Revenge
Apr 11 A Romance of the Western Hills
Apr 18 Thou Shalt Not
Apr 25 The Way of the World
May 2 The Gold-Seekers
May 5 The Unchanging Sea
May 9 Love Among the Roses
May 12 The Two Brothers
May 16 Over Silent Paths
May 23 Ramona
May 30 The Impalement
Jun 2 In the Season of Buds
Jun 6 A Child of the Ghetto
Jun 9 A Victim of Jealousy
Jun 13 In the Border States
Jun 16 The Face at the Window
Jun 23 The Marked Time-Table
Jun 27 A Child's Impulse
Jun 30 Muggsy's First Sweetheart
Jul 4 The Purgation
Jul 7 A Midnight Cupid
Jul 11 What the Daisy Said
Jul 14 A Child's Faith
Jul 18 A Flash of Light
Jul 21 As the Bells Rang Out!
Serious Sixteen
Jul 25 The Call to Arms
Jul 28 Unexpected Help
Aug 1 An Arcadian Maid
Aug 4 Her Father's Pride
Aug 8 The House with Closed Shutters
Aug 11 A Salutary Lesson
Aug 15 The Usurer
Aug 22 The Sorrows of the Unfaithful
Aug 25 Wilful Peggy
Aug 29 The Modern Prodigal
Sep 5 A Summer Idyll
Sep 8 Little Angels of Luck
Sep 12 A Mohawk's Way
Sep 15 In Life's Cycle
Sep 22 The Oath and the Man
Sep 26 Rose O' Salem-Town
Sep 29 Examination Day at School
Oct 3 The Iconoclast
Oct 10 That Chink at Golden Gulch
Oct 17 The Broken Doll
Oct 20 The Banker's Daughters
Oct 24 The Message of the Violin
Oct 31 Two Little Waifs
Nov 7 The Fugitive
Waiter No. 5
Nov 10 Simple Charity
Nov 14 Sunshine Sue
Nov 21 The Song of the Wildwood Flute
Nov 28 A Plain Song
Dec 5 A Child's Stratagem
Dec 12 The Golden Supper
Dec 15 His Sister-in-Law
Dec 19 The Lesson
Dec 26 Winning Back His Love

Bizet, Georges
1910
Feb 16 Carmen

Blaché, Alice *same as* **Blaché, Alice Guy**
1904
Jun 18 The Lyons Mail
1906
Apr [day undetermined]
Bad Lodgers
1907
Jan 5 Life of Christ*
1910
Oct 21 A Child's Sacrifice*

Blaché, Alice Guy *see* **Blaché, Alice**

Blackman, A. Noel
1901
Mar 16 President McKinley and Escort Going to the Capitol

Blackton, B.
1908
May 9 Tit for Tat; or, Outwitted by Wit

Blackton, J. Stuart
1905
Dec 2 Monsieur Beaucaire, the Adventures of a Gentleman of France
1906
Jun [day undetermined]
The Jail Bird and How He Flew, a Farce Comedy Escape
Nov [day undetermined]
And the Villain Still Pursued Her; or, The Author's Dream
1907
Feb 23 The Haunted Hotel; or, The Strange Adventures of a Traveler*
Jul 13 Oliver Twist
Jul 27 Lightning Sketches*
Aug 10 The Easterner, or, A Tale of the West*
Dec [day undetermined]
The Shaughraun, an Irish Romance
1908
Feb 8 Francesca da Rimini; or, The Two Brothers*
Aug 29 Salome; or, The Dance of the Seven Veils
1909
Feb 27 Saul and David: The Biblical Story of the Shepherd Boy Who Became King of the Israelites*
Mar 6 Inauguration of President William H. Taft
Apr 10 Napoleon: the Man of Destiny
Jun 1 Oliver Twist
Jul 17 The Magic Fountain Pen
Aug 21 The Way of the Cross, the Story of Ancient Rome*
Sep 27 Grand Naval Parade
Sep 30 Historic Parade
Oct 4 Military Parade
Dec 25 A Midsummer Night's Dream
1910
Jan 4 Forty Years in the Land of Midian [The Life of Moses Part II]
Jan 25 The Plagues of Egypt and the Deliverance of the Hebrew [The Life of Moses Part III]
Feb 5 Twelfth Night
Feb 12 The Victory of Israel [The Life of Moses Part IV]
Feb 19 The Promised Land [The Life of Moses Part V]
Jul 6 Jeffries-Johnson World's Championship Boxing Contest, Held at Reno, Nevada, July 4, 1910
Oct 7 The Last of the Saxons*
Nov 19 Francesca Da Rimini

Blackton, W.
1909
Nov 13 Launcelot and Elaine

Blackwell, Carlyle
1910
Jul 26 Uncle Tom's Cabin, Part 1
Jul 29 Uncle Tom's Cabin, Part 2
Jul 30 Uncle Tom's Cabin, Part 3
Oct 11 Brother Man
Oct 14 On Her Doorsteps
Dec 17 A Dixie Mother

Blair, a dog
1909
Feb 10 Dog Outwits Kidnapper

Blaisdell, E.
1910
Oct 28 Captain Barnacle's Chaperone

Blanchard, Bertha
1910
Dec 27 The Vicar of Wakefield

Bleckyrden, W.
1898
May 20 Heaving the Log
S. S. "Coptic"
S. S. "Coptic" Lying To
S. S. "Coptic" Running Against the Storm
Jun [day undetermined]
Honolulu Street Scene
Kanakas Diving for Money [Honolulu], No. 1
Kanakas Diving for Money [Honolulu], No. 2
S. S. "Coptic" Coaling
S. S. "Doric"
S. S. "Doric" in Mid-Ocean
S. S. "Gaelic" at Nagasaki
Shanghai Police
Shanghai Street Scene No. 1
Shanghai Street Scene No. 2
Sikh Artillery, Hong Kong
Street Scene in Hong Kong
Street Scene in Yokohama, No. 1
Street Scene in Yokohama, No. 2
Theatre Road, Yokohama
Tourists Starting for Canton
Wharf Scene, Honolulu
Dec [day undetermined]
S. S. "Coptic" Running Before a Gale

Bliss, Cornelius
1900
Sep [day undetermined]
Republican National Committee of 1900

Blom, August
1909
Nov 13 A Message to Napoleon; or, An Episode in the Life of the Great Prisoner at Elba

Blount, F. A.
1899
Sep [day undetermined]
International Collegiate Games—100 Yards Dash

Bob, a dog
1910
Dec 21 The Romance of Count de Beaufort

Bodoni
1904
Oct [day undetermined]
Eccentric Waltz

Boggs, Frank
1907
Dec 23 The Two Orphans
1908
Jan 4 The Four-Footed Hero
Mar 7 The Squawman's Daughter
Aug 8 The Cowboy's Baby
1909
Mar 4 Outing Pastimes in Colorado
Apr 29 Mephisto and the Maiden
May 13 The Bad Lands
Jun 17 In the Sultan's Power
Nov 25 On the Little Big Horn; or, Custer's Last Stand
1910
Feb 14 The Roman
Mar 10 Across the Plains
May 30 The Trimming of Paradise Gulch
Jun 27 The Long Trail
Jul 31 Ranch Life in the Great South-West

Bonifanti, Decoroso
1909
Nov 1 Nero; or, The Burning of Rome

Bonine, Robert K.
1897
Oct [day undetermined]
Horses Loading for Klondike
Loading Baggage for Klondike*
S. S. "Williamette" Leaving for Klondike
1898
May [day undetermined]
The Kiki Dance
1901
May [day undetermined]
Packers on the Trail
The Slippery Slide
May 4 Burro Pack Train on the Chilcoot Pass
Rocking Gold in the Klondike
Washing Gold on 20 above Hunker, Klondike
Aug [day undetermined]
Boys Diving
Cutting Sugar Cane
Loading Sugar Cane
Panorama of Water Front
Steamboat Leaving for Hilo
Train of Sugar Cane on Way to Crusher
Sep [day undetermined]
Bridge Traffic, Manila
In Old Hong Kong
Ox Carts
Panorama of Kobe Harbor, Japan
The Queen's Road
Sampans Racing Toward Liner
Street Scene, Tokio, Japan
Oct [day undetermined]
Asakusa Temple
A Filipino Cock Fight
Japanese Fencing
A Japanese Railway Train
Natives Leaving Church
Panorama of Water Front
Rickshaw Parade, Japan
Shimbashi R. R. Station
Oct 24 Arrival of Tongkin Train
The Bund, Shanghai
The Ch-ien-men Gate, Pekin
Coaling a Steamer, Nagasaki Bay, Japan
Harbor of Shanghai
Nov [day undetermined]
Artist's Point
A Cavalry Manoeuvre
Coaching Party, Yosemite Valley
In the Yellowstone
Panorama, Golden Gate
Picturesque Yosemite
Water Front of San Francisco
A Wonderful Waterfall
1902
Jan [day undetermined]
Eeling Through the Ice
Great Sport! Ice Yachting
Ice Yacht Racing
A Mile a Minute on an Ice Yacht
A Spill from an Ice Yacht
Starting a Skyscraper
Feb [day undetermined]
Amateur Ski Jumpers
A Big Blaze
"Bouncing"
Dog Sleighing
Fire at Durland's Academy, N. Y. City
A Husky Dog Team
Kent House Slide
Launch of Meteor III
Over the Crust
Quebec Fire Department on Sleds
Run of a Snow Shoe Club
Toboggan Slide
Welcome Prince Henry!
"What Ho, She Bumps!"
Mar [day undetermined]
B. F. Keith's New Million Dollar Theatre
Ferryboat Entering Slip
Madison Square, New York City
"Meteor III" Afloat
Mice
Prince Henry
Prince Henry at Philadelphia
Prince Henry at West Point
Prince Henry of Germany
"When the Cat's Away, the Mice Will Play"
Apr [day undetermined]
Demonstrating the Action of an Agnew Mailing Machine
General Electric Flash Light
The "Meteor"
Trial Trip of "Meteor"
May [day undetermined]
The Boys Help Themselves to Foxy Grandpa's Cigars
The Boys, Still Determined, Try It Again on Foxy Grandpa, with the Same Result
The Boys Think They Have One on Foxy Grandpa, but He Fools Them
The Boys Try to Put One Up on Foxy Grandpa
The Creators of Foxy Grandpa
Experimental. Moving Picture Machine
Foxy Grandpa and Polly in a Little Hilarity
Foxy Grandpa Shows the Boys a Trick or Two with the Tramp
Foxy Grandpa Tells the Boys a Funny Story
On the Speedway
A Poet's Revenge
A Private Supper at Heller's
Scene on Lower Broadway
The Speedway Parade
Street Scene
Jun [day undetermined]
The Accomodating Cow
Alphonse and Gaston
Belles of the Beach
Biograph's Improved Incubator
The Bowery Kiss
Daly, of West Point
Eva Tanguay
The Light That Didn't Fail
The Lovers' Knot
Milking Time on the Farm
On a Milk Diet
Panorama of Lower New York
A Picture from "Puck"
The Polite Frenchman
Rag Time Dance
Rag Time Dance (Hot)
Review of Cadets at West Point
Review of Cadets, West Point
A Seashore Gymkana
A Spill
The Summer Exodus
"A Sweet Little Home in the Country"
They Found the Leak
A Tough Dance
A Tub Race
Will He Marry the Girl?
Jul [day undetermined]
A Delusion
The Draped Model
Grandpa's Reading Glass
In a Manicure Parlor
In a Massage Parlor
The Lamp Explodes
Mischievous Willie's Rocking Chair Motor
No Liberties, Please
The Photographer's Fourth of July
She Meets with Wife's Approval
The Sleeper
Thro' Hell Gate
Wrinkles Removed
Aug [day undetermined]
Around the Mulberry Bush
At the Fountain
Demonstrating the Action of an Altman-Taylor Clover Huller
Demonstrating the Action of an Altman-Taylor Threshing Machine
Gay Girls of Gotham
A Gentleman Burglar
The King of Detectives
A Lawn Party
A Little Mix-Up in a Mixed Ale Joint
Old Volunteer Fire Dept.
Rex's Bath
Shut Up!
A Study in Openwork
Sweethearts
Wash Day
Water Nymphs
Sep [day undetermined]
Down the Mountain Side
The Futurity Crowd
The Futurity of 1902
Good Luck Baking Powder Train No. 1
Good Luck Baking Powder Train No. 2
Mr. Grauman. For Private Use
Pain's Fireworks
St. John's Guild. Bathing in Surf and Leaving Water
St. John's Guild. Crippled Children to and from Wagon
St. John's Guild. Dispensary Scene, Floating Hospital
St. John's Guild. Dock to Plank, 35th St.
St. John's Guild. Examination of Patients
St. John's Guild. From Launch to Dock
St. John's Guild. Going in Water.
St. John's Guild. Going to Salt-water Bath Room
St. John's Guild. Julliard and Tug in Narrows
St. John's Guild. Julliard Passing; Fire-Hose Playing
St. John's Guild. Launch Approaching Dock
St. John's Guild. Launch Delivering Patients to F. H.
St. John's Guild. Patients Down Bridge. S.S.H.

St. John's Guild. Plank to Deck, Floating Hospital
Savable Wins
A Stern Chase
Turning Panorama of Mt. Beacon
Oct [day undetermined]
The Eighth Wonder
General Booth
"Seeing New York"
Nov [day undetermined]
"All Hot"
Boyville Fire Brigade
The Gold Dust Twins
Let the Gold Dust Twins Do Your Work
New York's New Subway
A Romp on the Lawn
An Unsinkable Skimmer
Dec [day undetermined]
After the First Snow
After the Service
Broadway & Union Square, New York
"Chums"
A Corner in the Play Room
1903
Feb [day undetermined]
Envelope Folder and Sealer, National Cash Register Co.
German Flag Afloat, National Cash Register Co.
Girls Getting on Trolley, National Cash Register Co.
Girls Going to Lunch. National Cash Register Co.
Girls in Physical Culture, National Cash Register Co.
Jubilee, National Cash Register Co.
Little Wonder Printing Press, National Cash Register Co.
Men Getting on Trolley, National Cash Register Co.
Men in Physical Exercise, National Cash Register Co.
Men Leaving Factory, National Cash Register Co.
Mr. Bickford on Trolley, National Cash Register Co.
Mr. Carney and Friend, National Cash Register Co.
Mr. Carroll and Assistant, National Cash Register Co.
Mr. Chalmers and Mr. Gibbs Arrive at Club, National Cash Register Co.
Mr. Chalmers Going to Officers' Club, National Cash Register Co.
Mr. J. H. Crane, National Cash Register Co.
Mr. Lawer, National Cash Register Co.
Mr. Patterson and Mr. Mark Arriving, National Cash Register Co.
Officers Leaving Club, National Cash Register Co.
Panorama of Factory from Automobile, National Cash Register Co.
Patterson Children in Pony Wagon, National Cash Register Co.
Patterson Children Leaving Home, National Cash Register Co.
Patterson Children on Horseback, National Cash Register Co.
Porters in Parade, National Cash Register Co.
Steam Whistle, National Cash Register Co.
Testing Jacks, National Cash Register Co.
Visitors in Wheeling Chairs, National Cash Register Co.
Window Display Clown, National Cash Register Co.
Window Display Revolving Balls, National Cash Register Co.
1905
Mar [day undetermined]
Inauguration of President Roosevelt. President-Elect Roosevelt, Vice-President-Elect Fairbanks and Escort Going to the Capitol
Inauguration of President Roosevelt. Taking the Oath of Office
Inauguration of President Roosevelt. the Grand Inaugural Parade
President Roosevelt's Inauguration
1906
Aug [day undetermined]
Arrival Mahukona Express, Kohala, Hawaii
Hauling Sugar Cane, Kohala Plantation, Hawaii
Hawaiians Arriving to Attend a Luau or Native Feast
Hawaiians Departing to Attend a Luau or Native Feast
S. S. "Kinau" Landing Passengers, Mahukona, Hawaii
Shearing Sheep, Humunla Ranch, Hawaii
Sheep Coming Through Chute, Humunla Ranch, Hawaii
Washing Sheep, Humunla Beach, Hawaii
1907
Feb 2 Crowds Returning from the Games, Waikiki, H.I.
The "Float," Waikiki, Honolulu, Hawaiian Islands
Kanaka Fishermen Casting the Throw Net, Hilo, H.I.
Loading Sugar, Kahului, Maui, H.I.
Native Hawaiian Guards in Bayonet Exercises, H.I.
Pa-u Riders, Hawaiian Island
Panoramic View, Crater of Haleakala, H.I.
Panoramic View, Honolulu Harbor, H.I.
Panoramic View, King St. Honolulu, H.I.
Panoramic View, Oahu Railroad, Haleiwa, H.I.
Panoramic View, Oahu Railroad, Pearl Harbor, Hawaiian Islands
Panoramic View of Waikiki Beach, Honolulu, H.I.
Panoramic View, Waikiki, from an Electric Car, H.I.
S. S. "Kinau" Landing Passengers, Laupahoihoi, H.I.
Scenes on a Sugar Plantation, Hawaiian Islands
Shipping Cattle, Hawaihae, Hawaiian Islands
Snapshots, Hawaiian Islands
Surf Board Riders, Waikiki, Honolulu, H.I.
Surf Scene, Laupahoihoi, Hawaiian Island
Surf Scene, Waikiki, Honolulu, H.I.
A Trip Through the Yellowstone Park, U.S.A.
Water Buffalo Wallowing, Hawaiian Island
May 11 Fire Run, Colon Fire Department Under Cocoanut Tree
Jamaica Negroes Doing a Two-Step
Machete Men Clearing a Jungle [Panama Canal]
Old Market Place, Panama
Panorama from Columbus Point of Atlantic Entrance to the Canal
Panorama Ruins of Old French Machinery
U. S. Sanitary Squad Fumigating a House

Booth, Edwin
1910
Jan 8 Richelieu; or, The Conspiracy

Booth, Elmer
1910
Sep 22 The Oath and the Man

Booth, Walter R.
1902
May [day undetermined]
The Cheese Mites; or, The Lilliputians in a London Restaurant
The Haunted Pawnshop*
Magical Sword
Ora Pro Nobis Illustrated*
A Railroad Wreck (Imitation)
Undressing Under Difficulties*
The Wonderful Baby Incubator
1903
May [day undetermined]
Miniature Prize Fighters
Oct [day undetermined]
Soap vs. Blacking*
1904
Jul [day undetermined]
Haunted Scene Painter*
The Music Hall Manager's Dilemma*
Voyage of the "Arctic"
1907
Jan [day undetermined]
Following in Father's Footsteps*
Willie Goodchild Visits His Auntie*
Mar [day undetermined]
The Conjuror's Pupil*
The Hand of the Artist
Puck's Pranks on Suburbanite*
Mar 30 The Magic Bottle*
Apr 20 The Vacuum Cleaner*
Jun 24 Comedy Cartoons
Sep 7 Hanky Panky Cards
Sep 16 A Baffled Burglar*
Oct 7 The Haunted Bedroom
Nov 4 Accidents Will Happen*
Dec [day undetermined]
Diabolo Nightmare
When the Devil Drives
1908
Mar 21 His Daughter's Voice
Willie's Magic Wand
May 30 Sammy's Sucker
Jun 20 The Chauffeur's Dream
Jul 13 Two Little Motorists*
Sep 12 The Lightning Postcard Artist
Paper Tearing
Nov 9 The Quick Change Mesmerist
Nov 14 The Prehistoric Man
Nov 17 Champion Globe Trotter
Disappearing Watch
Waterproof Willie
1909
Feb 1 The Guard's Alarm
Feb 10 Following Mother's Footsteps
Feb 16 The Hand of a Wizard
Feb 24 Polka on Brain
Jun 2 Magic Carpet
Jul 14 The Wizard's Walking Stick
Aug 31 Professor Puddenhead's Patents
Nov 17 Workhouse to Mansion*
Dec 8 Capturing the North Pole; or, How He Cook'ed Peary's Record
Dec 29 Battle in the Clouds
1910
Jan 15 An Absorbing Tale
May 12 The Invisible Dog
May 18 The Electric Servant
Jun 4 Animated Cotton

Boothby, Guy
1910
Jan 29 The Mystery of the Lama Convent; or, Dr. Nicola in Thibet

Bosetti, Roméo
1906
May 12 The Wig Chase
1907
Aug 10 The Magnetized Man

Boss, Yale
1910
Mar 15 The Actor's Children

Bostwick, H.
1910
Feb 8 The Livingston Case
Apr 19 A Case of Identity

Bosworth, Hobart
1909
Jun 3 Fighting Bob
Jun 17 In the Sultan's Power
1910
Jan 20 The Courtship of Miles Standish
Feb 14 The Roman
Mar 10 Across the Plains
Mar 24 The Wonderful Wizard of Oz
May 26 In the Great Northwest
Jun 6 The Barge Man of Old Holland
Jun 27 The Long Trail
Jul 14 The Sheriff
Dec 12 A Tale of the Sea*

Bosworth, Robert
1910
Aug 15 Willie

Bouchier, Bob
1904
Dec [day undetermined]
Lady Plumpton's Motor Car

Boucicault, Dion
1903
Nov 21 Murphy's Wake
1906
Aug [day undetermined]
Kathleen Mavoureen
1907
Apr 20 Murphy's Wake

Boulden, Edward
1907
Nov 23 The Trainer's Daughter; or, A Race for Love
Dec 7 College Chums
Dec 14 Laughing Gas
Bourgeois, Gerard
1910
Feb 2 Hamlet, Prince of Denmark*
Boutet de Monvel, Louis
1900
Aug [day undetermined]
Living Pictures
Bouwmeester, Theo
1909
May 1 The Anarchist's Sweetheart*
Jun 12 Special License*
Jun 26 To the Custody of the Father*
The Wrong Coat*
Jul 24 Treacherous Policeman*
Sep 4 Only a Tramp*
Sep 18 Luck of the Cards*
Oct 7 The Curse of Money*
Oct 11 Mistaken Identity*
Oct 12 The New Servant*
1910
Jun 4 A Father's Mistake*
Teaching a Husband a Lesson*
Bovy, Berthe
1909
Feb 17 The Assassination of the Duke of Guise
Boyce, W. D.
1910
Apr 16 In Africa
Boyd, Aline
1905
Feb [day undetermined]
The Kleptomaniac
Brabin, Charles J.
1909
Oct 22 The Lost Handbag
1910
Aug 23 Love and the Law
Bracey, Clara T.
1910
Jun 23 The Marked Time-Table
Aug 18 An Old Story with a New Ending
Aug 25 Wilful Peggy
Aug 29 The Modern Prodigal
Sep 8 Little Angels of Luck
Sep 26 Rose O' Salem-Town
Oct 24 The Message of the Violin
Nov 7 The Fugitive
Nov 14 Sunshine Sue
Bradlet, J. M.
1908
Jan 4 The Four-Footed Hero
Bradshaw, C. H.
1900
Nov [day undetermined]
Scene from "Old Kentucky"
Brecy, Rene
1910
Dec 26 The Lock-Keeper
Brennan, Harry
1902
Nov [day undetermined]
Broncho Busting Scene, Championship of the World
1903
Feb [day undetermined]
Bucking Broncho Contest [Sheridan Contest]
Brenon, Herbert
1907
Aug 17 The Sea Wolf
Brent, Mrs.
1910
Dec 24 Jean and the Waif
Brevil, Beta
1910
May 7 Mario's Swan Song
Aug 27 Rose Leaves
Briscoe, L.
1909
Aug 5 She Would Be an Actress
Brontë, Charlotte
1910
May 6 Jane Eyre

Brooke, Van Dyke
1909
Feb 20 C. Q. D.; or, Saved by Wireless, a True Story of "The Wreck of the Republic"
1910
May 24 Convict No. 796
May 28 The Love of Chrysanthemum
May 31 The Peacemaker
Aug 6 Her Mother's Wedding Gown
Oct 28 Captain Barnacle's Chaperone
Brown, John P.
1906
Feb [day undetermined]
Dream of a Rarebit Fiend
Browning, E.
1909
Sep 3 Ethel's Luncheon
Sep 14 Little Sister
Browning, Robert
1908
Jan 18 Pied Piper of Hamlin
1909
Oct 4 Pippa Passes; or, The Song of Conscience
Bruce, Kate
1909
Jun 3 His Duty
Jul 8 The Country Doctor
Aug 9 They Would Elope
Aug 12 The Better Way
Sep 6 "1776" or, The Hessian Renegades
Sep 16 The Broken Locket
Sep 20 In Old Kentucky
Sep 23 A Fair Exchange
Sep 30 The Awakening
Wanted, a Child
Oct 11 The Little Teacher
Oct 14 A Change of Heart
Oct 18 His Lost Love
Oct 25 In the Watches of the Night
Oct 28 Lines of White on a Sullen Sea
Nov 1 What's Your Hurry?
Nov 11 The Light That Came
Nov 15 Two Women and a Man
Nov 18 A Midnight Adventure
Nov 22 The Open Gate
Nov 25 The Mountaineer's Honor
Dec 6 Through the Breakers
Dec 9 The Redman's View
Dec 16 In a Hempen Bag
Dec 27 To Save Her Soul
1910
Jan 13 All on Account of the Milk
Jan 20 The Call
Jan 24 The Honor of His Family
Feb 14 One Night, and Then —
Feb 17 The Englishman and the Girl
Feb 21 His Last Burglary
Mar 3 The Newlyweds
Mar 21 Faithful
Mar 24 The Twisted Trail
Mar 28 Gold Is Not All
Apr 11 A Romance of the Western Hills
May 2 The Gold-Seekers
May 9 Love Among the Roses
May 12 The Two Brothers
May 23 Ramona
May 26 A Knot in the Plot
Jun 2 In the Season of Buds
Jun 6 A Child of the Ghetto
Jun 20 May and December
Aug 1 An Arcadian Maid
Aug 4 Her Father's Pride
Aug 15 The Usurer
Aug 29 The Modern Prodigal
Sep 1 The Affair of an Egg
Sep 29 Examination Day at School
Oct 6 A Gold Necklace
How Hubby Got a Raise
Oct 13 A Lucky Toothache
The Masher
Oct 17 The Broken Doll
Oct 31 Two Little Waifs
Nov 7 The Fugitive
Waiter No. 5
Nov 10 Simple Charity
Nov 28 A Plain Song
Dec 1 Effecting a Cure
Dec 29 His Wife's Sweethearts
Brule, André
1910
May 19 Werther

Bryan, William Jennings
1900
Sep [day undetermined]
William J. Bryan in the Biograph
1903 [month undetermined]
Bryan at Home
Jan [day undetermined]
Hon. Wm. Jennings Bryan
Buckwalter, Harry
1902
Nov [day undetermined]
Arrival on Summit of Pike's Peak
Balloon Ascension*
Burlington Flyer
Clear Creek Canyon
Climbing Hagerman Pass
Denver Firemen's Race for Life
Fun in the Glenwood Springs Pool
Horse Toboggan Slide
Hydraulic Giants at Work*
Lava Slides in Red Rock Canyon
Leaving the Summit of Pike's Peak*
Panorama of Cog Railway*
Panorama of the Famous Georgetown Loop
Panorama of the Royal Gorge
Panorama of Ute Pass
Panoramic View of Granite Canon
Panoramic View of Hell Gate
Panoramic View of Seven Castles
Pike's Peak Toboggan Slide*
Runaway Stage Coach
Train in Royal Gorge
Trains Leaving Manitou
Ute Pass Express
Where Golden Bars Are Cast
1903 [month undetermined]
Freight Train in the Royal Gorge, Colo.*
1904 [month undetermined]
Chicago Portland Special*
Fish Traps Columbia River*
Hauling in a Big Catch*
Hauling in Seines and Pulling Seines into Boat*
Mending Seines on the Columbia River*
Panoramic View of Multnomah Falls*
Panoramic View of Spokane Falls*
Panoramic View of the Columbia River*
Sour Lake Oil Fields*
Surf Scene on the Pacific*
Unloading Fish at Cannery*
Apr [day undetermined]
Tracked by Bloodhounds; or, A Lynching at Cripple Creek
Oct 22 The Girls in the Overalls
1905
Apr 29 The Hold-Up of the Leadville Stage
1906
Jun 30 Trip over Cripple Creek Short Line
Buffons, The
1899
Mar [day undetermined]
Three Acrobats
Bull, H. A., Captain
1901
Jun 8 Opening of the Pan-American Exposition showing Vice President Roosevelt Leading the Procession
Buller, Redvers, General Sir
1899 [month undetermined]
General Sir Redvers Buller
General Sir Redvers Buller, and Staff, Landing at Cape Town, South Africa
Bulwer-Lytton, Sir Edward
1910
Jan 8 Richelieu; or, The Conspiracy
Bunny, John
1910
Dec 2 Jack Fat and Jim Slim at Coney Island
Dec 27 In Neighboring Kingdoms
Bunting, S. W.
1910
Nov 24 His New Lid
Burby, Gordon
1906
Jun 28 The Paymaster
Aug 30 The Lone Highwayman
Burgess, Neil
1910
Dec 15 County Fair

Burne-Jones, Edwin, Sir
1910
Nov 10 The Vampire
Burns, Frankie
1910
Oct 22 In the Gray of the Dawn
Burns, Robert P.
1908
Jun 20 The Fighting Parson
Burroughs, W. F.
1906
Aug [day undetermined]
Kathleen Mavoureen
Burt, Laura
1900
Nov [day undetermined]
Scene from "Old Kentucky"
1905
Sep [day undetermined]
The Horse-Thief
Bushnell, Governor
1897
Mar [day undetermined]
Governor Bushnell of Ohio, and Staff
Buss, Harry
1909
Jul 17 The Curate of the Races
Butler, Ellis Parker
1910
Dec 14 Pigs Is Pigs
Butler, William J.
1909
Aug 12 The Better Way
Aug 30 The Mills of the Gods
1910
Jun 13 In the Border States
Jun 27 A Child's Impulse
Jul 21 Serious Sixteen
Aug 11 A Salutary Lesson
Aug 22 The Sorrows of the Unfaithful
Aug 25 Wilful Peggy
Sep 12 A Mohawk's Way
Sep 22 The Oath and the Man
Oct 3 The Iconoclast
Oct 27 The Proposal
Oct 31 Two Little Waifs
Nov 17 The Troublesome Baby
Nov 24 Not So Bad as It Seemed
Nov 28 A Plain Song
Dec 1 Effecting a Cure
Dec 8 Turning the Tables
Dec 22 White Roses
Dec 29 After the Ball
Cahill, L.
1910
Oct 27 The Passing of a Grouch
Dec 5 A Child's Stratagem
Caines, Eleanor
1910
Jun 9 The New Boss of Bar X Ranch
Aug 29 The Stronger Sex
Sep 26 The Sheriff's Capture
Oct 13 Liz's Career
Caldwell
1910
Aug 30 The Horse Shoer's Girl
Nov 26 The Woman Hater
Calmettes, André
1909
Feb 17 The Assassination of the Duke of Guise
Jun 9 La Tosca
Dec 12 La Grande Breteche
1910
Apr 6 The Duchess of Langeais
The Duchess of Langeais*
Jul 21 Mateo Falcone
Calvert, Charles
1910
May 12 Three Fingered Kate
Cameron, Jessie
1903
Sep [day undetermined]
Miss Jessie Cameron, Champion Child Sword Dancer
Cameron Highlanders' Band
1910
Dec [day undetermined]
A Visit to the Seaside at Brighton Beach, England
Cannon, Joseph G., Representative
1901
Mar 16 President McKinley and Escort Going to the Capitol
President McKinley Taking the Oath

Capellani, Albert
1906
May 5 Law of Pardon
Dec 1 Poor Mother
Dec 15 Alladin and His Wonder Lamp
1907
Jul 20 Harlequin's Story
1909
Jun 26 Joan of Arc
Oct 22 Drink
1910
Jun 4 Macbeth
Sep 14 The Two Sisters
Capozzi, Alberto A.
1909
Jun 26 Louis the XI
Nov 1 Nero; or, The Burning of Rome
Nov 22 The Hostage
1910
Jan 15 The Son of the Wilderness
Jan 19 Pauli
Nov 2 The Slave of Carthage
Cappelli, Dante
1909
Dec 11 Macbeth*
1910
Jan 12 Camille
Feb 16 Carmen
Cappilani, M.
1909
Nov 14 Rigoletto
Carl, Renée
1909
May 25 A Blind Man of Jerusalem
Carleton, Lloyd B.
1910
Mar 22 St. Elmo
Mar 29 She's Done It Again
Carleton, Will
1908
Jun 26 Over the Hills to the Poor House
Carlile, C. A.
1909
Dec 25 The Kidnapped King
Carlile, C. Douglas
1909
Dec 25 The Kidnapped King
Carmen
1903
Jan [day undetermined]
The Wire Walker
Carney, Augustus
1909
Feb 17 Tag Day
1910
Sep 17 Hank and Lank Joyriding
Sep 28 Hank and Lank: They Dude Up Some
Oct 12 Hank and Lank: They Get Wise to a New Scheme
Oct 15 The Cowboy's Mother-in-Law
Oct 19 Hank and Lank: Uninvited Guests
Oct 26 Hank and Lank: They Take a Rest
Nov 8 Hank and Lank: Life Savers
Nov 22 Hank and Lank: as Sandwich Men
Dec 17 The Tenderfoot Messenger
Dec 20 Hank and Lank
Carny, A.
1909
Nov 17 Her Dramatic Career
Carol, J.
1909
Nov 3 For Sale: A Baby
Carré, Michel
1909
Jun 16 The Reckoning
Nov 1 The Lonely Bachelor
1910
Nov 15 Paul and Virginia
Carrington, William
1903
Sep [day undetermined]
Rip Van Winkle
Nov 21 Nicholas Nickleby
A Pugilistic Parson
1904
Jun 4 The Apple Woman
Carroll, J.
1910
Jul 14 A Child's Faith
Carroll, Lewis
1903
Oct 17 Alice in Wonderland

Carthy, Arthur
1904
Jun [day undetermined]
The Eviction
Carus, Emma
1910
Oct 11 Actors' Fund Field Day
Carver, W.
1907
Apr 6 Daniel Boone; or, Pioneer Days in America
Caserini, Mario
1908
Apr 6 Romeo and Juliet
1909
Dec 11 Macbeth
1910
May 9 Beatrice Cenci
Jun 15 The Battle of Legnano; or, Barbarossa
Casey, Kenneth
1910
Sep 6 Chew-Chew Land; or, The Adventures of Dolly and Jim
Sep 16 Two Waifs and a Stray
Oct 4 Ransomed; or, A Prisoner of War
Nov 4 The Children's Revolt
Nov 12 Jean Goes Fishing
Nov 15 Drumsticks
Cash, Morney
1904
Jun [day undetermined]
The Eviction
Casler, Herman
1901
Oct [day undetermined]
Mr. H. Casler and Baby. Experimental
1902
Jan [day undetermined]
Love in a Hammock
Cervera y Topete, Pascual, Admiral
1898
Jul [day undetermined]
Admiral Cervera and Officers of the Spanish Fleet Leaving the "St. Louis"
Chadwick, French E., Captain
1898 [month undetermined]
Cruiser New York
Chaffee, Adna R., Major-General
1901
Feb [day undetermined]
The War in China
Chamberlain, Joseph
1901 [month undetermined]
Chamberlain and Balfour
Chance, Anna
1900
Nov [day undetermined]
"Above the Limit"
Charrington, Arthur
1910
Jan 17 Muggins
Jun 4 A Race for a Bride
Chart, Jack
1909
Jun 26 Bully and Recruit
Chase, Walter D., M. D.
1905
Dec [day undetermined]
Threshing Scene
Chelles, M.
1909
May 12 The Hunter's Grief
Cheriff, Hadji
1899
Mar [day undetermined]
Arabian Gun Twirler
Chester, Virginia
1910
Dec 31 The Yaqui Girl
Chevet
1903
Jan [day undetermined]
Newell and Chevet, the Famous Acrobats
Chiquita
1903
Jan [day undetermined]
Chiquita, the Smallest Woman in the World

Chomón, Segundo de
1905
Sep 30 Stunning Creations
Dec 9 The Hen with the Golden Eggs
1906
Apr [day undetermined]
Haunted House
1907
Jan 26 Servant's Strike
Oct 19 The Cigar Box
1908
Jan 18 Kiri-Kis
Apr 12 Modern Sculptors
Nov 9 Beauty and the Beast

Church, Frederick
1908
Aug 8 The Cowboy's Baby
1909
Feb 17 Tag Day
Mar 4 The Mad Miner

Claire, Gertrude
1910
Apr 25 The Way of the World
May 23 Ramona

Clarges, Verner
1909
Aug 12 The Better Way
Sep 9 Comata, the Sioux
Sep 13 The Children's Friend
Sep 20 In Old Kentucky
Sep 23 A Fair Exchange
1910
Jan 17 On the Reef
Jan 24 The Honor of His Family
Apr 29 A Yorkshire School
May 3 The Cigarette Maker of Seville
Jun 9 A Victim of Jealousy
Jun 16 The Face at the Window
Jul 7 A Midnight Cupid
Jul 11 What the Daisy Said
Jul 18 A Flash of Light
Sep 8 Little Angels of Luck
Oct 6 How Hubby Got a Raise
Oct 20 The Banker's Daughters
Oct 24 The Message of the Violin
Oct 27 The Passing of a Grouch
Oct 31 Two Little Waifs
Nov 17 Love in Quarantine
Nov 24 Not So Bad as It Seemed
Dec 19 The Lesson
Dec 22 The Recreation of an Heiress

Clark, C. E., Captain
1898 [month undetermined]
Battleship Oregon

Clark, Mabel
1905
Jul [day undetermined]
Rescued by Rover

Clark, Marion, Baby
1899
Jun [day undetermined]
Childhood's Happy Days
The Pride of the Household

Clark, May
1902 [month undetermined]
A Frustrated Elopement
1903
Oct 17 Alice in Wonderland
Nov [day undetermined]
The Professor
1904
Jul [day undetermined]
The Parson's Cooking Lesson
1905
Nov [day undetermined]
The Servant Girl's Dream
The Servant Question
The Three Honeymoons
1907
Oct 19 A Seaside Girl
1908
Jan 18 The Artful Lovers
1909
Apr 24 The Villain's Wooing

Clarke, N. B.
1906
Aug [day undetermined]
Kathleen Mavoureen

Clary, Charles
1910
Nov 10 The Vampire

Claudel
1902
Oct 4 A Trip to the Moon

Clay, Bertha M.
1910
Aug 22 Dora Thorne

Clayton, Ethel
1909
Sep 8 Justified
Sep 22 Gratitude
Sep 29 The Brothers
Oct 13 The Twelfth Juror
1910
Sep 24 The Tout's Remembrance

Clayton, Marguerite
1910
Aug 27 The Deputy's Love

Cleary, Master
1910
Nov 30 The Touch of a Child's Hand

Clemens, Katherine Boland
1910
Nov 14 The Double

Clemens, Samuel *see* **Twain, Mark**

Cleveland, Grover, President
1897
Mar [day undetermined]
President Cleveland and President McKinley

Clifford, J.
1906
Aug [day undetermined]
Kathleen Mavoureen

Clifford, William
1910
Aug 31 The Blazed Trail
Dec 1 Pals

Cockshott, F. G.
1901
Sep [day undetermined]
International Track Athletic Meeting—Start and Finish of the One Mile Run

Cody, William F. *same as* **Cody, Buffalo Bill**
1898 [month undetermined]
Indian War Council
1910
Sep 15 Buffalo Bill's Wild West and Pawnee Bill's Far East

Coffin, Hayden
1902
Nov [day undetermined]
Umbrella Dance, San Toy

Cogan, James P.
1908
Mar 21 Caught by Wireless
Apr 7 A Famous Escape
Jul 15 The Boston Tea Party
Sep 22 The Leprechaun—An Irish Fairy Story

Coghlan, Captain
1899 [month undetermined]
President McKinley and Wife, Members of His Cabinet and Their Wives and Capt. Coghlan Leaving the Cruiser Raleigh

Cogley, Nick
1909
Sep 20 The Bachelor's Visit

Cohan, George M.
1910
Oct 11 Actors' Fund Field Day

Cohen, Sally
1900
Oct [day undetermined]
"The Kleptomaniacs"

Cohl, Emile
1908
Oct 16 The Puppet's Nightmare
Nov 2 A House of Cards*
Nov 21 A Love Affair in Toyland
Dec 12 Animated Matches
Dec 28 Acrobatic Toys
1909
Feb 9 A Sportive Puppet
Feb 13 The Ambassador's Dispatch Case
Mar 13 The Smoking Lamp
Mar 23 Japanese Magic
Pocket Policeman
Apr 21 Magic Eggs
Apr 27 The Automatic Monkey
May 18 The World Upset*
Jun 12 Historical Fan
Jul 10 A Bad Case
Jul 20 The Man in the Moon
Aug 11 Laurels
Aug 25 Sevres Porcelain
Sep 1 Magic Cartoons
Nov 2 Don Quixote
Nov 9 Telltale Reflections*
Nov 20 Moon for Your Love
Dec 4 X-Ray Glasses
1910
Feb 19 The Comedy-Graph
Apr 26 Solving the Puzzle
May 21 The Masher's Delirium
May 24 Floral Studies
May 31 Jarnac's Treacherous Blow
Jun 21 Hercules and the Big Stick
Jul 16 The Jolly Whirl
Jul 26 The Beautiful Margaret
Aug 23 Four Little Tailors

Cohn, Jack
1909
Oct 25 Hiawatha

Coleby, A. E.
1907
Oct 12 Serving a Summons
Oct 19 Don't Go to the Law*
Nov 16 A Drink Cure*
Even a Worm Will Turn*
1908
Mar 14 For the Baby's Sake
Mar 21 'Twixt Love and Duty; or, A Woman's Heroism
May 2 Freddie's Little Love Affair
The Mission of a Flower
May 9 The Interrupted Bath
Leap Year; or, She Would Be Wed
Professor Bounder's Pills
Nov 21 The Devil's Bargain
Dec 14 How the Dodger Secured a Meal
1909
Feb 10 Grandfather's Birthday
The Guardian of the Bank
Polly's Excursion
Apr 17 A Traitor to the King
Apr 24 High Game
Jun 12 How Jones Got a New Suit
The Man Housemaid
Jun 26 His Wedding Morn
Aug 7 Butcher Boy
Aug 21 When Jack Gets His Pay
Sep 4 Little Jim
Oct 19 The Phantom Ship
Dec 30 The Motherless Waif
1910
Mar 30 Robber's Ruse
Apr 5 Boxing Fever
Apr 30 The Sculptor's Dream*
May 14 The Convict's Dream
Jun 4 Adopting a Child

Coleman, H.
1910
Jun 2 Percy, the Cowboy
Nov 3 Mike the Housemaid

Colibris Dwarfs
1910
Jan 24 Acrobatic Exercises by the Colibris Dwarfs

Colla, Albert
1902
Nov 1 Ali Baba and the Forty Thieves
1903
Jul 11 Sleeping Beauty

Collart, Stella W.
1910
Nov 24 Not So Bad as It Seemed

Collinge, P.
1910
Oct 14 Winona

Collins, Alf
1903
Sep [day undetermined]
Rip Van Winkle
Oct [day undetermined]
Dextrous Hand*
Photographer's Victim*
Nov 21 The Ghost in the Graveyard
Murphy's Wake
The New Cook
Nicholas Nickleby
A Pugilistic Parson
Dec [day undetermined]
The Pickpocket
Dec 12 Elopement a la Mode
1904
Jan 2 The Somnambulist*
Apr 25 Inspector's Birthday*
No Room for Dad*

Pleasant Breakfast*
The Sailor's Rival
Jun [day undetermined]
The Eviction
Military Tactics*
Jun 4 The Apple Woman
The Cook's Lovers*
The Coster's Wedding
Jun 25 Chased by a Dog
The Office Boy's Revenge*
Raid on a Coiner's Den
Jul [day undetermined]
Old Maids and the Unfaithful Lovers*
Such Is Life*
Oct [day undetermined]
The Masher's Dilemma
Mixed Bathing
Night Duty
Revenge!
Oct 29 The Fatal Wig*
Nov [day undetermined]
Electric Doorbell
Dec [day undetermined]
The Amorous Militiaman*
At Brighton
1905
May [day undetermined]
Behind the Scenes
Nov [day undetermined]
A Smart Captive*
1906
Jan [day undetermined]
The Peashooter*
Jan 27 A False Alarm*
May 26 The Lost Leg of Mutton*
1907
Jan [day undetermined]
The Gardener's Nap*
Mar 30 Curfew Shall Not Ring Tonight
Apr 20 Catch the Kid
Sep 7 The Motorcyclist*
Sep 30 The Undergraduate*
Nov 9 A Shilling Short in Wages*
Dec 2 The Lady Athlete; or, The Jiu Jitsu Downs the Footpads
Dec 21 Father Buys a Hand Roller*
1908
Feb 3 Oh, That Cat*
Apr 18 Ice Cream Jack
Aug 29 Napoleon and the English Sailor
Oct 26 The Convict and the Dove*
Collins, Wilkie
1909
Jun 10 The Moonstone
Colosse
1910
Nov 12 World's Wrestling Champions
Colton, George
1910
May 16 Johnson Training for His Fight with Jeffries
Columbia, Joe
1903
Jan [day undetermined]
The New Shooting the Chutes
Compton, Charles
1910
May 6 Jane Eyre
Congdon
1901
Aug [day undetermined]
Gathering Gladioli
Steamship "Bismark"
Steamship "Graf Waldersee"
Sep [day undetermined]
Arrival at Falls View Station
Funeral of President McKinley
International Field Sports
International Field Sports—Oxford-Cambridge vs. Harvard-Yale
International Track Athletic Meeting—Start and Finish of the One Mile Run
Panoramic View of the McKinley Homestead
President McKinley's Funeral
Oct [day undetermined]
Finish of Flatbush Stakes, Gravesend Track
Horses Jumping Water Jump
Match Race, Endurance by Right vs. Heno
A Perilous Proceeding
Nov [day undetermined]
A Mighty Tumble
Twentieth Century Flyers
Yale Football, Practice Scrimmage
Yale Football Squad of 1901
Dec [day undetermined]
Children Playing Ball
Cutting Cucumbers and Cauliflower, Heinz
Football Game: West Point vs. Annapolis
Packing Pickle Jars, Heinz
President Roosevelt at the Army-Navy Game
President Roosevelt Entering Grounds at Army-Navy Football Game
1902
Jan [day undetermined]
Deer in Park
Feb [day undetermined]
Battleship "Illinois"
Demonstrating the Action of a Mergenthaler-Horton Basket Making Machine
A Devastated City
Docking a Liner
The "Hohenzollern"
Park Avenue Explosion
The Paterson Fire
The Royal Salute
Mar [day undetermined]
Prince Henry
Prince Henry and President's Party
Conger, Minister
1901
Feb [day undetermined]
The War in China
Connes, Robert
1910
Apr 15 Her First Appearance
Jun 3 The Piece of Lace
Jun 21 Bootles' Baby
Consoli, Mlle.
1906
Apr [day undetermined]
Great Ballet
Constantin
1902
Nov [day undetermined]
The Giant Constantin
Converse, J. H.
1901
Sep [day undetermined]
International Field Sports—Oxford-Cambridge vs. Harvard-Yale
Cook, F. A., Captain
1898 [month undetermined]
Cruiser Brooklyn
Cooper, Professor
1910
Jun 15 How Championships Are Won—and Lost
Cooper, Arthur
1904
Jul [day undetermined]
Toy Maker and Good Fairy
1905
Aug [day undetermined]
His Washing Day
Robbing His Majesty's Mail
Nov [day undetermined]
Motor Highwayman
1907
Feb [day undetermined]
Her First Cake
Mar [day undetermined]
Oh! That Molar
Apr 13 The Animated Pill Box
Apr 20 The Poet's Bid for Fame
Oct 26 The Lover's Charm*
1908
Feb 29 His Sweetheart When a Boy*
Mar 7 The Boarder Got the Haddock
The Tricky Twins*
May 2 A Sacrifice for Work*
Nov 21 Grandpa's Pension Day
1909
May 22 Boys' Holiday
In Quest of Health
Jun 5 Happy Man
Cooper, Claude Hamilton
1910
Oct 21 A Child's Sacrifice*
Oct 28 The Sergeant's Daughter*
Nov 4 A Fateful Gift*
Nov 11 A Widow and Her Child*
Nov 18 Her Father's Sin*
Nov 25 One Touch of Nature*
Dec 2 What Is to Be, Will Be*
Dec 9 Lady Betty's Strategy*
Dec 16 Two Suits*
Dec 23 The Pawnshop*
Dec 30 Mrs. Richard Dare*
Cooper, James Fenimore
1909
Sep 27 Leather Stocking
Coppée, François
1909
Jun 7 The Violin Maker of Cremona
1910
Mar 2 The Violin Maker of Cremona
Coquelin
1908
Oct 31 Cyrano de Bergerac
Precieuses Ridicules
Corbett, James J.
1894
Nov [day undetermined]
Corbett and Courtney Before the Kinetograph
1910
Jun 15 How Championships Are Won—and Lost
Oct 11 Actors' Fund Field Day
Corelli, Marie
1910
Jun 21 Thelma
Cormon, Eugène
1903
Apr [day undetermined]
A Duel with Knives
Cortelyou, George B., Private Secretary
1896
Sep [day undetermined]
McKinley at Home, Canton, Ohio
1901
Mar 16 President McKinley and Escort Going to the Capitol
Costello, Dolores
1910
Oct 29 The Telephone
Costello, Maurice
1908
Aug 29 Salome; or, The Dance of the Seven Veils
1909
Feb 27 Saul and David: The Biblical Story of the Shepherd Boy Who Became King of the Israelites
Sep 28 The Romance of an Umbrella
Nov 27 Jean Valjean
Dec 25 A Midsummer Night's Dream
1910
Jan 22 A Pair of Schemers; or, My Wife and My Uncle
Apr 8 Elektra
Apr 23 St. Elmo
Apr 26 Through the Darkness
May 24 Convict No. 796
May 28 The Love of Chrysanthemum
Jun 10 Over the Garden Wall
Aug 13 The Turn of the Balance
Aug 27 Rose Leaves
Sep 9 How She Won Him
Sep 13 The Sepoy's Wife
Nov 29 A Woman's Love
Dec 6 A Tin-Type Romance
Dec 13 The Law and the Man
Cottens, Victor de
1904
Oct 29 An Impossible Voyage
Cotton, Lucy
1910
Nov 7 The Fugitive
Courtney, Helen
1905
Feb [day undetermined]
The Kleptomaniac
Courtney, Peter
1894
Nov [day undetermined]
Corbett and Courtney Before the Kinetograph
Cowles, W. S., Captain
1898
Oct [day undetermined]
Famous Battleship Captains—Philadelphia Peace Jubilee Parade

1910
Apr 1 Michael Strogoff
May 17 The Princess and the Peasant
Jun 17 A Central American Romance
Jul 1 The Stars and Stripes
Sep 20 An Unselfish Love
Oct 4 More Than His Duty
Oct 11 The Song That Reached His Heart*
Dec 23 A Christmas Carol*

Day, U. S. W., Brigadier-General
1901
Mar 16 President McKinley and Escort Going to the Capitol

Dean, P.
1905
Dec 2 Monsieur Beaucaire, the Adventures of a Gentleman of France

Dean, Ralph
1910
Jun 7 The Shyness of Shorty

Dearly, M.
1910
Aug 18 Carmen

de Beaufort, Count
1910
Dec 21 The Romance of Count de Beaufort

Deed, André
1902
May [day undetermined]
The Clown with the Portable Body
1906
May 12 The Wig Chase
1908
Apr 12 Modern Sculptors
May 2 Diabolical Pickpocket*
Sep 5 A Dozen of Fresh Eggs
1909
Apr 24 Foolshead Looks for a Duel
May 15 Foolshead on the Alps
Nov 13 How Foolshead Paid His Debts
1910
Mar 9 Foolshead Chief of the Reporters
Mar 26 Foolshead Wishes to Marry the Governor's Daughter
May 14 Foolshead Learns to Somersault
May 28 Foolshead Marries Against His Will
Foolshead Marries Against His Will*
Aug 27 Foolshead in the Lion's Cage
Oct 1 Foolshead Employed in a Bank
Foolshead Has Been Presented with a Foot Ball
Oct 22 Foolshead Between Two Fires
Dec 24 Greediness Spoiled Foolshead's Christmas

De Flon, Emar
1901 [month undetermined]
Emar De Flon, the Champion Skater

Defoe, Daniel
1910
Sep 10 Robinson Crusoe

De Garde, Adele
1908
Dec 22 The Christmas Burglars
1909
Feb 22 The Golden Louis
Mar 15 I Did It, Mamma
Mar 22 And a Little Child Shall Lead Them
The Deception
Mar 25 A Burglar's Mistake
Mar 29 The Medicine Bottle
Apr 1 A Drunkard's Reformation
Apr 26 Twin Brothers
May 31 What Drink Did
Jul 8 The Country Doctor
Nov 29 In the Window Recess
Dec 2 The Death Disc: A Story of the Cromwellian Period
Dec 6 Through the Breakers
Dec 16 In a Hempen Bag
1910
Sep 2 A Life for a Life
Sep 6 Chew-Chew Land; or, The Adventures of Dolly and Jim
Nov 4 The Children's Revolt
Nov 12 Jean Goes Fishing
Dec 24 Jean and the Waif

Dehelly, M.
1910
Jul 20 Manon

Delaney, Billy
1901
Dec [day undetermined]
Jeffries Exercising in His Gymnasium

Delaney, Leo
1909
Nov 13 Launcelot and Elaine
1910
Aug 27 Rose Leaves
Oct 4 Ransomed; or, A Prisoner of War
Oct 29 The Telephone
Nov 12 Jean Goes Fishing
Dec 6 A Tin-Type Romance

Delannoy, Henri
1902
Oct 4 A Trip to the Moon

Delaplanche, Eugène
1900
Aug [day undetermined]
Living Pictures

De La Roy, Mlle.
1899 [month undetermined]
Lady Contortionist

De La Ruese, Mlle.
1903 [month undetermined]
Broad Sword Contest

Delauny, M.
1909
Mar 20 The Return of Ulysses

Delibes, Clément Philbert Léo
1910
Jan 18 The Toymaker's Secret

De Liguoro, A.
1910
Jan 20 Martyrs of Pompeii

Delvair, Jeanne
1910
Jun 4 Macbeth
Jul 21 Andromache

De Mar, Carrie
1902
May [day undetermined]
The Creators of Foxy Grandpa
Foxy Grandpa and Polly in a Little Hilarity

Demidoff, Olga
1910
Jun 9 The Children of Edward IV

Denham, J. B.
1900
Jul [day undetermined]
Amateur Athletic Championships

D'Ennery, Adolphe-Philippe
1903
Apr [day undetermined]
A Duel with Knives
1904
Oct 29 An Impossible Voyage

Denny, Archibald
1901 [month undetermined]
The Builders of Shamrock II

Dermoz, Mlle.
1910
Apr 6 The Duchess of Langeais

Desfontaines, Henri
1904
Oct [day undetermined]
Bride Retiring

Dettloff
1910
Nov 12 World's Wrestling Champions

De Varney, Miss
1907
Nov 23 The Trainer's Daughter; or, A Race for Love

Devery, Chief
1899
Jun [day undetermined]
New York Police Parade, June 1st, 1899

Dewey, George, Admiral
1899
Sep [day undetermined]
Admiral Dewey
Admiral Dewey Landing at Gibraltar
Admiral Dewey Receiving His Mail
Admiral Dewey's Dog, "Bob"
"Sagasta" Admiral Dewey's Pet Pig
Oct [day undetermined]
Admiral Dewey and Mayor Van Wyck Going Down Riverside Drive
Admiral Dewey at State House, Boston
Admiral Dewey Leading Land Parade
Admiral Dewey Leading Land Parade, No. 2
Admiral Dewey Leading Land Parade, (Eighth Ave.)
Admiral Dewey Passing Catholic Club Stand
Admiral Dewey Receiving the Washington and New York Committees
Admiral Dewey Taking Leave of Washington Committee on the U. S. Cruiser 'Olympia'
Admiral Dewey's First Step on American Shore
Presentation of Loving Cup at City Hall, New York
Presentation of Nation's Sword to Admiral Dewey
1901 [month undetermined]
Dewey Parade
Mar 16 President McKinley and Escort Going to the Capitol
President McKinley Taking the Oath

Deyo
1897
Mar [day undetermined]
Deyo
Gaiety Dance
1907
Apr [day undetermined]
Deyo

de Yonson, Carlotta
1909
Dec 25 The Kidnapped King

Dezac, Sacha
1910
Feb 9 In Ancient Greece

Dickens, Charles
1897
Apr [day undetermined]
Death of Nancy Sykes
1903
Nov 21 Nicholas Nickleby
1906
Feb [day undetermined]
The Modern Oliver Twist; or, The Life of a Pickpocket'
1907
Jul 13 Oliver Twist
1908
Feb 8 Gabriel Grub
Dec 9 A Christmas Carol
1909
Jan 20 The Old Curiosity Shop
May 27 The Cricket on the Hearth
Jun 1 Oliver Twist
Sep 24 A Knight for a Night
1910
Apr 29 A Yorkshire School
Jun 23 Oliver Twist
Aug 13 Oliver Twist
Aug 23 Love and the Law

Dickson, W. K. L.
1894
Jan [day undetermined]
Edison Kinetoscopic Record of a Sneeze, January 7, 1894
1896
Sep [day undetermined]
American Falls, Goat Island
American Falls, Luna Island
Canadian Falls, from American Side
Canadian Falls—Panoramic [View] from Michigan Central R. R.
Canadian Falls—Table Rock
Li Hung Chang at Grant's Tomb
Li Hung Chang Driving Through 4th St. and Broadway [New York City]
Li Hung Chang, 5th Avenue & 55th Street, N. Y.
Lower Rapids, Niagara Falls
McKinley at Home, Canton, Ohio
Niagara Gorge from Erie R. R.
Panorama of American & Canadian Falls—Taken Opposite American Falls
Parade, Americus Club, Canton Ohio
Parade at Canton O., Showing Major McKinley in Carriage
Parade, Elkins Cadets, Canton, O.
Parade, Sound Money Club, Canton, O.
Pointing Down Gorge, Niagara Falls
Taken from Trolley in Gorge, Niagara Falls
Upper Rapids, from Bridge
West Point Cadet Cavalry
West Point Cadet Drill
1897 [month undetermined]
Butterfly Dance
1898 [month undetermined]
The Vatican Guards, Rome*

Dec [day undetermined]
Pope Leo XIII Being Carried in Chair Through Upper Loggia, No. 101
Pope Leo XIII Being Seated Bestowing Blessing Surrounded by Swiss Guards, No. 107
Pope Leo XIII in Canopy Chair, No. 100
Pope Leo XIII in Carriage, No. 102
Pope Leo XIII Leaving Carriage and Being Ushered into Garden, No. 104
Pope Leo XIII Seated in Garden, No. 105
Pope Leo XIII Walking Before Kneeling Guards
1899
Jun [day undetermined]
Wreck of the "Mohican"*
Wreck of the S. S. "Paris"
Sep [day undetermined]
Admiral Dewey*
Jack Tars Ashore*
Officers of the "Olympia"*
"Sagasta" Admiral Dewey's Pet Pig*
Oct [day undetermined]
A Dip in the Mediterranean*
Harbor of Villefranche*
1903
Sep [day undetermined]
Pope [Leo XIII] in His Carriage
Pope [Leo XIII] Passing Through Upper Loggia

Dieudonné, Albert
1909
Feb 17 The Assassination of the Duke of Guise

Dieudonné, Alphonse
1906
Apr [day undetermined]
Surgical Operation

Dillon, Eddie
1905
Mar [day undetermined]
The Nihilists*
1906
Jun 14 The Village Cut-Up
1908
Jan 18 Falsely Accused!
Jan 22 Lonesome Junction
Feb 1 Classmates
Feb 10 Bobby's Kodak
Feb 27 The Princess in the Vase
Mar 11 The Boy Detective; or, The Abductors Foiled
Mar 21 Caught by Wireless
Mar 28 Old Isaacs, the Pawnbroker
May 6 The Sculptor's Nightmare
May 29 His Day of Rest
Jun 2 Thompson's Night Out
Jun 5 The Romance of an Egg
Jun 9 'Ostler Joe
Jun 12 Mixed Babies
Jun 16 The Invisible Fluid
Jun 19 The Man in the Box
Jun 23 The Outlaw
Jun 26 Over the Hills to the Poor House
Jun 30 At the French Ball
Jul 3 At the Crossroads of Life
Jul 7 The Kentuckian
Jul 10 The Stage Rustler
Jul 17 The Fight for Freedom
Jul 21 The Black Viper
Jul 31 Deceived Slumming Party
Sep 22 Where the Breakers Roar
1909
Oct 11 The Little Teacher
Oct 14 A Change of Heart
1910
Jun 30 Muggsy's First Sweetheart
Jul 4 The Purgation
Aug 1 An Arcadian Maid
Aug 15 The Usurer
Aug 22 The Sorrows of the Unfaithful
Sep 1 The Affair of an Egg
Muggsy Becomes a Hero
Sep 19 A Summer Tragedy
Sep 29 Examination Day at School
Oct 20 The Banker's Daughters
Nov 7 The Fugitive
Nov 14 Sunshine Sue
Nov 28 A Plain Song
Dec 1 Effecting a Cure
Dec 8 Turning the Tables
Dec 15 His Sister-in-Law
Dec 22 White Roses
Dec 29 After the Ball

Dillon, J. T.
1908
Jan 22 Lonesome Junction
1910
Jul 21 As the Bells Rang Out!
Aug 1 An Arcadian Maid
Sep 1 The Affair of an Egg
Sep 12 A Mohawk's Way
Dec 29 After the Ball

Dion, Hector
1907
Sep 28 The Mill Girl, a Story of Factory Life
Oct 5 The Gypsy's Warning

Dixey, Henry E.
1908
Nov 4 David Garrick

Dobson, F. A.
1899
Apr [day undetermined]
"My Ragtime Girl"
1904
Jun [day undetermined]
The Slocum Disaster
1905
Jul [day undetermined]
Mother's Angel Child
The Mutiny on the Potemkin
Sep [day undetermined]
The Boer War
The Course of True Love
Oct [day undetermined]
The Great Jewel Mystery
Nov [day undetermined]
Casey's Christening
The Thirteen Club
Dec [day undetermined]
Climbing the American Alps
An Execution by Hanging
A Fight for a Bride
A Reprieve from the Scaffold
Rooms for Gentlemen Only
The Society Raffles
Wine, Women & Song [No. 2]
1906
Jan 27 A Coal Strike
Everybody Works But Mother
The Henpecked Husband
The Jolly Monks of Malabar
The Streets of New York
Feb 19 The Critic
Mar 17 The Silver Wedding
Apr [day undetermined]
Fencing N. Y. A. C.
Jun 14 The Village Cut-Up
Jul 19 The Masqueraders
Aug [day undetermined]
The Convict's Bride
In the Tombs
Water Tricycle
Weighing the Anchor
Aug 1 No Wedding Bells for Him
The Old Swimming Hole
Aug 6 Looking for John Smith
Aug 23 The Cruise of the Gladys
Aug 30 The Lone Highwayman
Sep 20 Brannigan Sets Off the Blast
Sep 29 Wanted—A Nurse
Oct 18 The Fox-Hunt
Nov [day undetermined]
Fangere
Fay Templeton
Lillian Russell
Vesta Tilley
Nov 15 The Tunnel Workers
Dec 8 Skyscrapers
1907
Jan [day undetermined]
The Moving Picture Man
Apr [day undetermined]
Gay Girl Playing Pool
Me for Water Wagon
Pranks of Cupid
She Seemed Shy but She Was Fly
Jun 8 A Caribou Hunt
Dolls in Dreamland
Aug 31 The Tired Tailor's Dream
Sep [day undetermined]
Attack on Emigrant Train
Buffalo Hunt
The Cannibals
Casey on a Souse—Gives the Bunch a Douse
Fitznoodle's Last Ball
Girl $998
Happy Sport Beards the Manicurer
How the Lovers Got Rid of Boozy Pa
A Mash a Smash a Splash
Over the Wall
Peanuts
The Portrait
The Punishment of the Horse Thief [Ranch 101]
Scenes from Luna Park
Scenes from Miller Bros.
Waltzing Walter
What the Bum Did to the Dude
What the Fisherman Caught
What the Girls Did to the Bachelor
Wrong Bath
Sep 12 Lena and the Beaux
Sep 25 Terrible Ted
Oct [day undetermined]
Mr. Easy Mark
Oct 19 Love Microbe
1908
Jan 11 "Energizer"
Nov 2 Humpty-Dumpty Circus

Dockstader, Lew
1905
Oct [day undetermined]
Everybody Works But Father (Whiteface)
Nov [day undetermined]
Everybody Works But Father (Blackface)
1908
Oct 20 Minstrel Mishaps; or, Late for Rehearsal

Dodge, Major-General
1897
Mar [day undetermined]
Major-General Dodge and Staff

Dodson, F. A.
1907
Sep [day undetermined]
How Fritz's Pipe Exposed Him to the Maid

Dogherty, Jessie
1903
Sep [day undetermined]
Miss Jessie Dogherty, Champion Female Highland Fling Dancer

Dolorita
1897 [month undetermined]
The Dolorita Passion Dance
1903
Jan [day undetermined]
Dolorita

Don Fulano, a horse
1910
Feb 11 An Equine Hero
Mar 29 Bradford's Claim

Dondini, Cesare
1910
Apr 20 Othello

Donnelly, A.
1910
Dec 26 Winning Back His Love
Dec 29 After the Ball

Donovan, Miss
1910
Dec 20 The Greater Call

Donovan, Mike, Professor
1898
Jul [day undetermined]
Train vs. Donovan

Dorny, André
1910
Nov 21 The Exiled Mother

Dougherty, Lee
1899
Apr [day undetermined]
"My Ragtime Girl"

Dougherty, Lee, Mrs.
1899
Apr [day undetermined]
"My Ragtime Girl"

Doyle, Arthur Conan, Sir
1909
Jun 2 Cab Number 519

Drachmann, Holger
1907
Sep 14 Once Upon a Time There Was...

Dranem
1904
Jun 18 A Disagreeable Remedy
Sep 24 Ice Cream Eater
Oct [day undetermined]
Lahury, the Soldier

Oct 22 The Clever Baker
1906
Apr [day undetermined]
Dranem's Dream
Dressler, Marie
1910
Oct 11 Actors' Fund Field Day
Duffy, A. F.
1900
Jul [day undetermined]
Amateur Athletic Championships
Dulac, Mlle.
1910
May 19 Werther
Dumas, Alexandre, *fils*
1908
Sep 19 The Lady with the Camellias
1909
Sep 22 The Tower of Nesle
1910
Jan 12 Camille
Dumas, Alexandre, *père*
1908
Feb 15 Monte Cristo
1910
Nov 26 Kean; or, The Prince and the Actor
Du Maurier, George
1896
Sep [day undetermined]
Trilby and Little Billee
du Montel, Hélène
1910
Jul 30 Cagliostro
Duncan, F. Martin
1904
Jan [day undetermined]
The Cheese Mites
Duncan, Grace
1910
Oct 6 A Gold Necklace
Duncan, J.
1909
Dec 25 The Kidnapped King
Duncan, William
1909
Jan 21 Love and Law
Eagan, Deputy Chief
1899
Apr [day undetermined]
Parade in Providence, R. I.
Earl, Miss
1908
Jan 18 Rescued from an Eagle's Nest
Eberman, C. E., Field Secretary Dr.
1903
Feb [day undetermined]
Christian Endeavor Greeting
Edwards, Billy
1898 [month undetermined]
Boxing
Edwin, Walter
1908
Nov 3 Saved by Love
Egan, Gladys
1908
Sep 11 Behind the Scenes: Where All Is Not Gold That Glitters
Oct 6 The Zulu's Heart
Oct 23 Romance of a Jewess
Nov 3 After Many Years
1909
May 31 What Drink Did
Jun 10 The Lonely Villa
Jun 21 Was Justice Served?
Jun 28 The Way of Man
Jul 5 The Message
Jul 8 The Country Doctor
Jul 22 Jealousy and the Man
Jul 26 A Convict's Sacrifice
Aug 26 The Seventh Day
Aug 30 The Heart of an Outlaw
Sep 13 The Children's Friend
Sep 30 Wanted, a Child
Oct 25 In the Watches of the Night
Nov 1 What's Your Hurry?
Dec 13 A Corner in Wheat
Dec 16 In a Hempen Bag
Dec 20 A Trap for Santa Claus
Dec 23 In Little Italy
1910
Jan 17 On the Reef
Jan 20 The Call
Feb 14 One Night, and Then —
Feb 17 The Englishman and the Girl
Mar 28 Gold Is Not All
Apr 4 As It Is in Life
Apr 18 Thou Shalt Not
May 5 The Unchanging Sea
Jun 13 In the Border States
Jul 14 A Child's Faith
Jul 28 Unexpected Help
Aug 8 The House with Closed Shutters
Aug 11 A Salutary Lesson
Aug 22 The Sorrows of the Unfaithful
Sep 8 Little Angels of Luck
Sep 29 Examination Day at School
Oct 3 The Iconoclast
Oct 17 The Broken Doll
Nov 17 The Troublesome Baby
Dec 5 A Child's Stratagem
Dec 15 His Sister-in-Law
Egleston, Ann
1905
Feb [day undetermined]
The Kleptomaniac
Elder, E.
1910
Nov 14 The Street Preacher
Eldridge, Charles
1910
Oct 15 The Legacy
Eline, Grace
1910
Apr 15 A 29-Cent Robbery
Eline, Marie "The Thanhouser Kid"
1910
Apr 15 A 29-Cent Robbery
May 6 Jane Eyre
Jun 7 The Two Roses
Jun 17 The Little Hero of Holland
Jun 24 The Governor's Daughter
Jul 1 The Flag of His Country
Jul 19 The Girls of the Ghetto
Jul 22 The Playwright's Love
Jul 26 Uncle Tom's Cabin
Sep 9 The Doctor's Carriage
Sep 20 Not Guilty
Oct 14 Delightful Dolly
Oct 21 Their Child
Oct 28 The Fairies' Hallowe'en
Nov 4 Ten Nights in a Bar Room
Nov 8 The Little Fire Chief
Nov 22 A Thanksgiving Surprise
Dec 27 The Vicar of Wakefield
Eliot, George
1909
Sep 23 A Fair Exchange
Elisier, Mme.
1909
Aug 25 The Eternal Romance
Ely, Mr.
1910
Oct 15 Aeroplanes in Flight and Construction
Emerie
1903
Aug [day undetermined]
On the Flying Rings
Silveon and Emerie "On the Web"
Erb, Ludwig G. B.
1910
Apr 16 [Talking Moving Picture]
Erskine, W., Mrs.
1910
Aug 19 How the Squire Was Captured
Ethier, Alphonse
1910
May 6 Jane Eyre
Jun 21 Thelma
Evans, August J.
1910
Mar 22 St. Elmo
Apr 23 St. Elmo
Evans, Frank
1909
Sep 23 A Fair Exchange
1910
Jan 6 The Dancing Girl of Butte
Jan 17 On the Reef
Jun 13 In the Border States
Jun 27 A Child's Impulse
Jul 7 A Midnight Cupid
Sep 12 A Mohawk's Way
Evans, Fred
1910
Jun 4 The Last of the Dandies
Evans, Robley D., Admiral
1898 [month undetermined]
Battleship Iowa
Oct [day undetermined]
Famous Battleship Captains—Philadelphia Peace Jubilee Parade
1902 [month undetermined]
President and Prince at Washington
Fabian, Victor
1910
Jul 23 Fabian Cleaning Chimney
Jul 30 Fabian Arranging Curtain Rods
Aug 27 Fabian's Hollow Tooth
Sep 3 Fabian Hunting Rats
Sep 17 Fabian Out for a Picnic
Nov 12 Mother-in-Law Arrives
Fabre, Marcel
1910
Jul 13 Tweedle Dum's Aeronautical Adventure
Aug 31 Tweedle Dum's Forged Bank Note
Oct 26 Tweedledum Wants to be a Jockey
Faithfull, Geoffrey
1903
Oct 17 Alice in Wonderland
Faithfull, Stanley
1903
Oct 17 Alice in Wonderland
Falena, Ugo
1910
Jan 12 Camille
Falero, Louis
1900
Aug [day undetermined]
Living Pictures
Fangere
1906
Nov [day undetermined]
Fangere
Farley, Dot
1910
Nov 14 Romantic Redskins
Nov 21 Starlight's Devotion
Farnham, Henry A.
1909
May 21 The Girl Spy: An Incident of the Civil War
1910
Apr 1 The Further Adventures of the Girl Spy
Apr 29 The Love Romance of the Girl Spy
Nov 23 The Lad from Old Ireland
Dec 28 The Girl Spy Before Vicksburg
Farren, Fred
1904
Jul [day undetermined]
Voyage of the "Arctic"
Fatima
1900
Mar [day undetermined]
Fatima's Coochee-Coochee Dance
1903
Jan [day undetermined]
Fatima, Couchee Dancer
Faust, August
1901
Dec [day undetermined]
Roeber Wrestling Match
Faust, Martin J.
1910
May 6 Jane Eyre
May 13 The Best Man Wins
May 27 The Winter's Tale
Dec 2 John Halifax, Gentleman
Dec 27 The Vicar of Wakefield
Fechter, Charles
1908
Feb 15 Monte Cristo
Fenton, Mabel
1897
Apr [day undetermined]
Death of Nancy Sykes
Ferdinand of Bulgaria, King
1910
Jun 4 [King Edward's Funeral]
Fernandez, Escamillo
1910
Jun 3 The Piece of Lace
Feuillade, Louis
1907
Mar [day undetermined]
The Electric Belt
May 25 Janitor's Tea Party
Jul 8 Union Workers Spoil the Food

Aug 10 The Magnetized Man
1909
May 25 A Blind Man of Jerusalem
Aug 17 The Cobbler and the Millionaire
Sep 11 Mozart's Last Requiem
Sep 22 The Legend of the Lighthouse
1910
Apr 23 Judith and Holofernes
Jun 11 The Marriage of Esther
Jun 18 Esther and Mordecai
Fields, Lew
1910
Oct 11 Actors' Fund Field Day
Finch, Flora
1908
Dec 29 The Helping Hand
1909
Jan 7 Mrs. Jones Entertains
Jan 25 Those Awful Hats
May 10 Jones and the Lady Book Agent
Jun 28 The Way of Man
1910
Jul 30 Uncle Tom's Cabin, Part 3
Fisher, Lenore
1907
Jun 22 Willie's Dream
Fitz-Allen, A.
1904
Nov [day undetermined]
Parsifal
Fitzgerald, Cissy
1900
Mar [day undetermined]
Cissy Fitzgerald
Fitzhamon, Lewin
1904
Jul [day undetermined]
The Coster's Wedding
The Parson's Cooking Lesson
Stolen Puppy
Aug [day undetermined]
The Bewitched Traveler
Sep [day undetermined]
Boys' Trick on Grandpa
Oct [day undetermined]
Decoyed
An Englishman's Trip to Paris from London
Lover's Crime
Nov [day undetermined]
Coal Heavers
The Lover's Ruse
Over the Hedge
A Race for a Kiss
Dec [day undetermined]
The Honeymoon
Lady Plumpton's Motor Car
1905
Jul [day undetermined]
Only Her Brother
Rescued by Rover
Aug [day undetermined]
Falsely Accused
Rehearsing a Play at Home
Terrible Flirt
Nov [day undetermined]
The Servant Girl's Dream
The Servant Question
The Three Honeymoons
Two Imps
1907
Mar 30 After the Matinee
Black Beauty
Apr 6 The Busy Man
Apr 27 The Doll's Revenge
A Smart Capture
Jun 1 Fatal Leap
The New Policeman
The Tramp's Dream
Jul 20 A Poet and His Babies
Aug 24 The Doll Maker's Daughter
Hair Restorer
Her Friend, the Enemy*
Sep 21 The Ghost Holiday
Oct 12 Drink
Little Meg and the Wonderful Lamp
A Soldier's Jealousy
A Too Devoted Wife
Oct 19 Mischievous Girls
A Modern Don Juan
A Sailor's Lass
A Seaside Girl
Nov 16 Dumb Sagacity
A Tramp's Dream of Wealth
Dec 7 A Letter in the Sand
The Rebellious Schoolgirls
The Sticky Bicycle
1908
Jan 18 The Artful Lovers
The Viking's Bride*
Feb 29 Painless Extraction
Mar 14 The Curate's Courtship
May 2 The Greedy Girl
Tell-Tale Cinematograph
May 9 The Doctor's Dodge
May 16 Catching a Burglar
A Faithless Friend
Jun 6 Father's Lesson
Jun 13 The Man and His Bottle
Sep 5 The Hidden Hoard
The Tramp and the Purse
Sep 12 The Burglar and the Clock
Sep 26 The Thief at the Casino
Oct 10 A Den of Thieves
Nov 12 Jack in Letter Box
When Women Rule
Nov 25 Soldier's Love Token
Dec 14 A Free Pardon
Harmless Lunatic's Escape*
The Serpent's Tooth*
Dec 21 Baby's Playmate
Cabby's Sweetheart
1909
Feb 10 Dog Outwits Kidnapper
Mar 22 Fairy Sword
Apr 17 A Plucky Little Girl
Apr 24 The Deserter*
The Dog Came Back
A Heartless Mother*
Last Year's Time Table
A Lover's Quarrel
Married Under Difficulties*
Professor's Anti-Gravitation
Runaway Kids
A Thoughtless Beauty
The Unlucky Thief*
The Villain's Wooing
May 1 The Fickle Husband
An Unfortunate Bath
May 8 The Milkman's Wooing
May 15 The Detective's Ruse
In the Service of the King
The Spoilt Child*
Unlucky Bridegroom
May 22 Present for Her Husband*
Why Father Learned to Ride
Jun 5 Cat Came Back
Dentist's Daughter
Gypsy's Child
Jun 26 The Shepherd's Dog
Jul 3 The Dog and the Bone
Fancy Dress Ball
A Pair of Truants
Jul 17 The Curate of the Races
Too Much Lobster for Supper*
Aug 14 Race for a Farmer's Cup
Aug 21 The Spy*
Story of a Picture*
Aug 28 A Cheap Removal*
Rival Mesmerists*
Sep 4 The Boy and His Kite
Sep 13 The Rivals*
Sep 18 A Villain's Downfall*
Sep 25 The Little Milliner and the Thief
Necessity Is the Mother of Invention
Oct 11 Invisibility
Oct 18 A Drunkard's Son
Oct 21 Artful Dodger
Nov 13 The Cabman's Good Fairy
The Street Arab
1910
Apr 26 The Penalty of Beauty
May 2 Safety Suit for Skaters*
Jun 4 Boy and Purse
Gipsy's Baby
Jun 21 Tempered with Mercy*
Jul 8 A New Hat for Nothing
Floyd, W. R.
1906
Aug [day undetermined]
Kathleen Mavoureen
Foley, Kid
1901
Jul [day undetermined]
The Bowery Kiss
The Ragtime Waltz
The Tough Dance
1902
Jun [day undetermined]
A Tough Dance
Folger, William M., Captain
1898
Oct [day undetermined]
Famous Battleship Captains—Philadelphia Peace Jubilee Parade
Foli, Ling
1903
May [day undetermined]
Chinese National Dance
Fonleney, C.
1909
Oct 22 Drink
Ford, Mistress
1910
Nov 24 The Merry Wives of Windsor
Ford, Francis
1910
Sep 8 Baseball, That's All
Oct 13 Out for Mischief
Oct 27 Under the Stars and Bars
Dec 1 Pals
Dec 22 A Western Welcome
Dec 29 In the Tall Grass Country
Forde, Victoria
1910
Nov 17 Love in Quarantine
Fortune, T.
1909
Jan 12 Where Is My Wandering Boy To-night?
Foster, Dorothy
1910
Jul 5 The Boy and His Teddy Bear
Foster, William C.
1910
Nov 10 The Vampire
Fougere, Eugenie
1899
Nov [day undetermined]
Fougere
Fox, F. B.
1899
Sep [day undetermined]
International Collegiate Games—110 Yards Hurdle Race
Fox, Imro
1896
Nov [day undetermined]
The Human Hen
Imro Fox, Conjuror
Imro Fox Rabbit Trick
Fox, J.
1909
Sep 14 Little Sister
Foy, Eddie
1910
Oct 11 Actors' Fund Field Day
Foy, Magda
1910
Oct 21 A Child's Sacrifice
Fragson
1905
Aug 19 An Adventurous Automobile Trip
Fraidora, Mlle.
1898 [month undetermined]
Can Can
Franchonetti Sisters
1897
Apr [day undetermined]
Dance, Franchonetti Sisters
Francis, Miss
1910
Dec 19 The Dead Letter
François, a dog
1909
Dec 29 Oh, You Doggie!
Franklin, Irene
1910
Oct 11 Actors' Fund Field Day
Fratellini Brothers
1906
Apr [day undetermined]
Acrobatic Elephant
Frawley, Jack
1904
Jun 26 The Great Train Robbery*
Jul 30 Bold Bank Robbery
Frean, W.
1904
Jun [day undetermined]
The Eviction

French, Miss
1910
Jul 26 Uncle Tom's Cabin, Part 1
Jul 29 Uncle Tom's Cabin, Part 2
Jul 30 Uncle Tom's Cabin, Part 3
French, Charles K.
1909
May 28 Romance of a Fishermaid
Jun 4 "Davy" Crockett in Hearts United
Aug 27 Secret Service Woman
Sep 3 His Two Children
Oct 29 Mexican's Crime
Dec 10 Re-united at the Gallows
1910
Apr 15 Red Wing's Constancy
Apr 22 Adventures of a Cowpuncher
Frusta, Arrigo
1908
May 2 Rival Sherlock Holmes
1909
Sep 23 Jackson's Last Steeple Chase
Nov 1 Nero; or, The Burning of Rome
Nov 22 The Hostage
1910
Jan 19 Pauli
Feb 9 The Longing for Gaol
Apr 13 Fricot in College
Apr 20 The Heart of a Vagabond
May 25 Estrellita; or, The Invasion of the French Troops in Portugal
Jun 8 The Shipwrecked Man
Jun 22 The Story of Lulu Told by Her Feet
Jul 20 The Romance of a Jockey
Jul 27 The Room of the Secret
Aug 17 The Hump's Secret
Sep 28 The Virgin of Babylon
Oct 19 Excursion on the Chain of Mont Blanc
Nov 2 The Slave of Carthage
Nov 23 The Story of a Pair of Boots
Fuentes, Antonio
1902
Apr [day undetermined]
Great Bull Fight
Fuller, Lawson N.
1897
Jul [day undetermined]
Expert Driving
Fuller, Loie
1901
Jul [day undetermined]
Fire Dance
Fuller, Mary
1910
Jan 21 The Luck of Roaring Camp
Apr 8 Elektra
May 31 The Peacemaker
Jun 7 A Modern Cinderella
Jul 30 Uncle Tom's Cabin, Part 3
Sep 30 Ononko's Vow*
Fuller, Melville W., Chief Justice
1901
Mar 16 President McKinley Taking the Oath
Gage, Lyman J., Secretary
1901
Mar 16 President McKinley and Escort Going to the Capitol
Galipaux
1904
Oct [day undetermined]
Boy's First Smoke
1905
Aug 19 An Adventurous Automobile Trip
Gallinger, Senator
1901
Jun 8 Opening of the Pan-American Exposition showing Vice President Roosevelt Leading the Procession
Gallop, Gloria
1910
Apr 29 The Cigars His Wife Bought
May 6 Jane Eyre
Gans, Joe
1901
Apr 13 Gans-McGovern Fight
Garavaglia, Ferruccio
1910
Apr 20 Othello
Gardner, Helen
1910
Sep 9 How She Won Him
Garnier, Phillipe
1909
Dec 12 La Grande Breteche
1910
May 19 Werther
Jun 9 The Children of Edward IV
Aug 11 Charles Le Tremeraire
Garros, Paul de
1909
Dec 25 Drama of Villasgne
Garwood, William
1910
May 6 Jane Eyre
Dec 27 The Vicar of Wakefield
Gasnier, Louis
1908
Jan 18 First Cigar
Sep 5 A Dozen of Fresh Eggs
1910
Mar 11 A Cure for Timidity
May 6 A Romantic Girl
May 16 The Girl from Arizona
Gasperini, Maria Caserini
1909
Dec 11 Macbeth*
1910
May 9 Beatrice Cenci
Gates, General
1898
Sep [day undetermined]
President McKinley's Inspection of Camp Wikoff
Gauntier, Gene
1906
Jun 28 The Paymaster
Jul [day undetermined]
Thaw-White Tragedy
Dec 8 Skyscrapers
1907
Dec 7 Ben Hur
1908
Apr 22 Hulda's Lovers
Jun 2 Thompson's Night Out*
Jun 5 The Romance of an Egg
Sep 1 Betrayed by a Handprint
Sep 8 The Girl and the Outlaw*
1909
May 21 The Girl Spy: An Incident of the Civil War
1910
Apr 1 The Further Adventures of the Girl Spy
Apr 22 The Bravest Girl in the South
May 6 The Egret Hunter
Aug 3 A Colonial Belle
Aug 17 The Perversity of Fate
Sep 9 The Cow Puncher's Sweetheart
Sep 28 The Heart of Edna Leslie
Nov 23 The Lad from Old Ireland
Dec 21 The Little Spreewald Maiden
Dec 28 The Girl Spy Before Vicksburg
Dec 30 The Stranger
Gautier, Théophile
1909
Dec 6 Captain Fracassee
Dec 25 Alberno & Rosamunda
Gebhardt, George
1908
Jun 19 The Man in the Box
Jul 7 The Kentuckian
Jul 10 The Stage Rustler
Jul 17 The Fight for Freedom
Jul 21 The Black Viper
Jul 24 The Tavern-Keeper's Daughter
Jul 28 The Redman and the Child
Jul 31 Deceived Slumming Party
Aug 7 A Calamitous Elopement: How It Proved a Windfall for Burglar Bill
Aug 11 The Greaser's Gauntlet
Aug 14 The Man and the Woman
Aug 18 The Fatal Hour
Aug 21 For Love of Gold
Aug 25 Balked at the Altar
Aug 28 For a Wife's Honor
Sep 1 Betrayed by a Handprint
Sep 4 Monday Morning in a Coney Island Police Court
Sep 8 The Girl and the Outlaw
Sep 11 Behind the Scenes: Where All Is Not Gold That Glitters
Sep 15 The Red Girl
Sep 18 The Heart of O Yama
Sep 22 Where the Breakers Roar
Sep 25 A Smoked Husband
Sep 29 The Stolen Jewels
Oct 2 The Devil
Oct 6 The Zulu's Heart
Oct 9 Father Gets in the Game
Oct 13 The Barbarian Ingomar
Oct 16 The Vaquero's Vow
Oct 20 The Planter's Wife
Oct 23 Romance of a Jewess
Oct 27 The Call of the Wild
Nov 6 The Pirate's Gold
Nov 10 Taming of the Shrew
Nov 13 The Guerrilla
Nov 17 The Song of the Shirt
Nov 20 The Ingrate
Nov 24 A Woman's Way
Nov 27 The Clubman and the Tramp
Dec 1 The Valet's Wife
Dec 4 Money Mad
Dec 8 The Feud and the Turkey
Dec 11 The Reckoning
Dec 15 The Test of Friendship
Dec 18 An Awful Moment
Dec 22 The Christmas Burglars
Dec 25 Mr. Jones at the Ball
Dec 29 The Helping Hand
1909
Jan 4 The Maniac Cook
Jan 14 A Rural Elopement
Jan 18 The Criminal Hypnotist
Jan 25 The Welcome Burglar
Jan 28 The Cord of Life
Feb 4 The Brahma Diamond
Feb 8 A Wreath in Time
Feb 18 The Joneses Have Amateur Theatricals
Feb 22 The Politician's Love Story
May 10 Jones and the Lady Book Agent
Genetoo, Mlle.
1903
Jan [day undetermined]
Chair Dance
Geniat, Marcele
1909
Nov 14 Rigoletto
George of England, King
1910
Jun 4 [King Edward's Funeral]
George of Greece, King
1910
Jun 4 [King Edward's Funeral]
Gérôme, Jean Léon
1900
Aug [day undetermined]
The Slave Market
Geronimo
1905
Sep [day undetermined]
Great Buffalo Chase
Gherardini
1909
May 22 Sapho
Ghezzi
1904
Sep 3 The Wrestling Donkey
Gibbs, Frederick D.
1900
Sep [day undetermined]
Republican National Committee of 1900
Gibson, Frances
1910
Nov 22 A Thanksgiving Surprise
Gilbert, Lee
1909
Dec 25 The Kidnapped King
Gillette, George W.
1901
Jun 8 Opening of the Pan-American Exposition showing Vice President Roosevelt Leading the Procession
Gilmore, Paul
1897
Jul [day undetermined]
Vanishing Lady
Gilmour, J. H.
1909
Sep 8 Justified
1910
Jan 5 The Adventuress
May 18 The Danger Line
Gilroy, W.
1904
Nov [day undetermined]
Opening Ceremonies, New York Subway, October 27, 1904

Ginnett, Mrs.
1907
Jul 20 Dick Turpin
Ginnett, Fred
1907
Jul 20 Dick Turpin
Girard, Adelaide
1910
Apr 23 The Four Seasons
Gobbett, T. J.
1909
Sep 4 Bad Day for Lavinsky*
Gobbett, William David
1911
Feb 12 Lassoing Wild Animals in Africa
Godfrey, Cossie
1907
Oct 19 Mischievous Girls
Godfrey, Gladys
1907
Oct 19 Mischievous Girls
Goethe, Johann Wolfgang von
1909
Apr 29 Mephisto and the Maiden
1910
May 19 Werther
Jun 30 Faust
Jul 30 Cagliostro
Oct 14 Werther
Golden, Joseph A.
1907
Jul 20 The Hypnotist's Revenge
Aug 17 The Deaf-Mutes' Ball
Aug 31 The Tired Tailor's Dream
Sep 25 Terrible Ted
1909
Aug 25 The Blacksmith's Daughter
1910
Apr 12 His Mother's Letter
Apr 16 [Talking Moving Picture]
Aug 30 The Horse Shoer's Girl
Nov 19 The New Magdalene
Nov 26 The Woman Hater
Golding, Elaine
1899
Sep [day undetermined]
The Golding Family
Golding, Ethel
1899
Sep [day undetermined]
The Golding Family
Goldsmith, Oliver
1910
Aug 19 She Stoops to Conquer
Dec 27 The Vicar of Wakefield
Goodman, H. B.
1910
Dec 22 The Recreation of an Heiress
Goodman, R.
1910
Apr 28 The Seal of the Church
May 26 The Paleface Princess
Jun 30 The Ruling Passion
Jul 21 A Postal Substitute
Sep 1 Won in the Fifth
Gordon, Belle
1898
May 20 Comedy Set-To
Gordon, Julia Swayne
1908
Sep 28 Richard III, a Shakespearian Tragedy
Dec 22 The Merchant of Venice
1910
Feb 5 Twelfth Night
Apr 2 The Fruits of Vengeance
Nov 12 Jean Goes Fishing
Gorman, William
1903
Jan [day undetermined]
Cake Walking Horses
Gotch, Frank
1910
Jul 2 Gotch-Zbyszko World's Championship Wrestling Match
Gould, George
1900
Jul [day undetermined]
Champion Polo Players
Gounod, Charles
1904
Apr 2 Faust and Marguerite
1909
Dec 24 Faust
Gove, O. M.
1906
May [day undetermined]
Scenes in San Francisco
Views in San Francisco
Jun [day undetermined]
Spanish Barbecue
A Trip to Berkeley, Cal.
Aug 25 Ascent of Mount Lowe
Ostrich Farm
Pigeon Farm
Sep 20 A Daring Hold-Up in Southern California
1907
Sep 16 An Acadian Elopement
Graham, Carlysle D.
1902
May [day undetermined]
Carlysle D. Graham Swimming the Whirlpool Rapids
1903
Feb [day undetermined]
C. D. Graham Swimming the Lower Rapids
Graham, Evelyn
1909
May 28 Romance of a Fishermaid
Jun 4 "Davy" Crockett in Hearts United
Jul 2 A True Indian's Heart
1910
Jun 21 The Sea Wolves
Graham, H. E.
1899
Sep [day undetermined]
International Collegiate Games
Grammar, Henry
1910
Jul 31 Ranch Life in the Great South-West
Grandon, Francis J.
1910
Jan 6 The Dancing Girl of Butte
Feb 3 The Woman from Mellon's
Feb 7 The Course of True Love
Feb 10 The Duke's Plan
Feb 21 His Last Burglary
Feb 24 Taming a Husband
Mar 7 The Thread of Destiny
Mar 10 In Old California
Mar 17 The Man
Mar 31 His Last Dollar
Apr 7 A Rich Revenge
Apr 25 The Way of the World
Apr 28 Up a Tree
May 2 The Gold-Seekers
May 9 Love Among the Roses
May 19 An Affair of Hearts
May 23 Ramona
May 26 A Knot in the Plot
Jun 16 The Face at the Window
Jul 11 What the Daisy Said
Jul 28 Unexpected Help
Aug 4 Her Father's Pride
Aug 15 The Usurer
Sep 22 The Oath and the Man
Oct 10 That Chink at Golden Gulch
Oct 17 The Broken Doll
Nov 10 Simple Charity
Nov 21 The Song of the Wildwood Flute
Grant, Frederick D., Brigadier-General
1900
Mar [day undetermined]
Brigadier-General Frederick D. Grant and Staff
Grant, Ulysses S., Mrs.
1899
May [day undetermined]
Mrs. U. S. Grant and President McKinley
Grapewin, Charles E.
1900
Sep [day undetermined]
"Above the Limit"
Nov [day undetermined]
"Above the Limit"
Gravier, Mlle.
1910
Jun 11 The Marriage of Esther
Jun 18 Esther and Mordecai
Gray
1910
Jul 27 The Room of the Secret
Gray, M.
1910
Aug 19 How the Squire Was Captured
Aug 26 The Valet's Vindication
Graybill, Joe
1910
Jun 16 The Face at the Window
Jun 23 The Marked Time-Table
Jun 27 A Child's Impulse
Jun 30 Muggsy's First Sweetheart
Jul 4 The Purgation
Jul 11 What the Daisy Said
Jul 18 A Flash of Light
Jul 25 The Call to Arms
Aug 8 The House with Closed Shutters
Aug 18 An Old Story with a New Ending
When We Were in Our Teens
Dec 8 Turning the Tables
Dec 19 The Lesson
Green, Francis V., Major-General
1901
Mar 16 President McKinley and Escort Going to the Capitol
1903
Jan [day undetermined]
New York's 7th and 71st Regiments
Green, Jennie
1906
Jan [day undetermined]
Horse Stealing
Green, Tom
1903 [month undetermined]
Two Old Sports
Feb [day undetermined]
Mother Goose Nursery Rhymes
Jul 18 The Life of a London Bobby
1905
Jul [day undetermined]
Fixing the Derby Favorite*
1906
Jan [day undetermined]
Horse Stealing
1907
Mar [day undetermined]
Turkey Raffle*
Apr 6 Drink and Repentance*
Foiled by a Woman; or, Falsely Accused*
Quarter Day Conjuring*
Slippery Jim, the Burglar*
Apr 13 The Tell-Tale Telephone*
A Woman's Sacrifice*
Jun 1 The Wrong Chimney; or, Every Man His Own Sweep*
Jun 29 Bertie's Love Letter*
The Comic Duel*
Greene, Francis V., Colonel *see* **Green, Francis V.**
Greene, K.
1909
Aug 5 She Would Be an Actress
Greenway, Lieutenant
1898
Sep [day undetermined]
Col. Theodore Roosevelt and Officers of His Staff
Greenwood, Winnifred
1910
Mar 24 The Wonderful Wizard of Oz
Gregory, Carl Lewis
1910
Mar 22 St. Elmo
Gretillat, M.
1909
Oct 22 Drink
Griffith, D. W.
1908
Jan 4 Professional Jealousy
Jan 18 Falsely Accused!
Rescued from an Eagle's Nest
Feb 1 Classmates
Feb 27 The Princess in the Vase
Feb 29 Cupid's Pranks
Mar 7 The Yellow Peril
Mar 18 Her First Adventure [Kidnapped with the Aid of a Street Piano]*
Mar 21 Caught by Wireless
Mar 28 Old Isaacs, the Pawnbroker
Apr 7 A Famous Escape
Apr 15 The King of the Cannibal Islands
Apr 22 Hulda's Lovers*
Apr 29 The King's Messenger
May 6 The Music Master
The Sculptor's Nightmare
May 20 When Knights Were Bold

Jun 9 'Ostler Joe
Jun 12 Mixed Babies
Jun 16 The Invisible Fluid
Jun 19 The Man in the Box
Jun 23 The Outlaw
Jun 26 Over the Hills to the Poor House*
Jun 30 At the French Ball
Jul 3 At the Crossroads of Life
Jul 7 The Kentuckian
Jul 10 The Stage Rustler*
The Stage Rustler
Jul 14 The Adventures of Dollie
Jul 17 The Fight for Freedom*
Jul 21 The Black Viper
Jul 24 The Tavern-Keeper's Daughter
Jul 28 The Redman and the Child
Jul 31 Deceived Slumming Party
Aug 4 The Bandit's Waterloo: The Outwitting of an Andalusian Brigand by a Pretty Senora
Aug 7 A Calamitous Elopement: How It Proved a Windfall for Burglar Bill
Aug 11 The Greaser's Gauntlet
Aug 14 The Man and the Woman
Aug 18 The Fatal Hour
Aug 21 For Love of Gold
Aug 25 Balked at the Altar
Aug 28 For a Wife's Honor
Sep 1 Betrayed by a Handprint
Sep 4 Monday Morning in a Coney Island Police Court
Sep 8 The Girl and the Outlaw
Sep 11 Behind the Scenes: Where All Is Not Gold That Glitters
Sep 15 The Red Girl
Sep 18 The Heart of O Yama
The Heart of O Yama*
Sep 22 Where the Breakers Roar
Sep 25 A Smoked Husband
Sep 29 The Stolen Jewels
Oct 2 The Devil
Oct 6 The Zulu's Heart
Oct 9 Father Gets in the Game
Oct 13 The Barbarian Ingomar
Oct 16 The Vaquero's Vow
Oct 20 The Planter's Wife
Oct 23 Romance of a Jewess
Oct 27 The Call of the Wild
Oct 30 Concealing a Burglar
Nov 3 After Many Years
Nov 6 The Pirate's Gold
Nov 10 Taming of the Shrew
Nov 13 The Guerrilla
Nov 17 The Song of the Shirt
Nov 20 The Ingrate
Nov 24 A Woman's Way
Nov 27 The Clubman and the Tramp
Dec 1 The Valet's Wife
Dec 4 Money Mad
Dec 8 The Feud and the Turkey
Dec 11 The Reckoning
Dec 15 The Test of Friendship
Dec 18 An Awful Moment
Dec 22 The Christmas Burglars
Dec 25 Mr. Jones at the Ball
Dec 29 The Helping Hand

1909

Jan 1 One Touch of Nature
Jan 4 The Maniac Cook
Jan 7 Mrs. Jones Entertains
Jan 11 The Honor of Thieves
Love Finds a Way
Jan 14 A Rural Elopement
The Sacrifice
Jan 18 The Criminal Hypnotist
Those Boys!
Jan 21 The Fascinating Mrs. Francis
Mr. Jones Has a Card Party
Jan 25 Those Awful Hats
The Welcome Burglar
Jan 28 The Cord of Life
Feb 1 The Girls and Daddy
Feb 4 The Brahma Diamond
Feb 8 Edgar Allen Poe
A Wreath in Time
Feb 11 Tragic Love
Feb 15 The Curtain Pole
His Ward's Love
Feb 18 The Hindoo Dagger
The Joneses Have Amateur Theatricals
Feb 22 The Golden Louis
The Politician's Love Story
Feb 25 At the Altar
Mar 1 His Wife's Mother
The Prussian Spy
Mar 4 A Fool's Revenge
Mar 8 The Roue's Heart
The Wooden Leg
Mar 11 The Salvation Army Lass
Mar 15 I Did It, Mamma
The Lure of the Gown
Mar 18 The Voice of the Violin
Mar 22 And a Little Child Shall Lead Them
The Deception
Mar 25 A Burglar's Mistake
Mar 29 Jones and His New Neighbors
The Medicine Bottle
Apr 1 A Drunkard's Reformation
Apr 5 The Road to the Heart
Trying to Get Arrested
Apr 8 A Rude Hostess
Schneider's Anti-Noise Crusade
Apr 12 A Sound Sleeper
The Winning Coat
Apr 15 Confidence
Apr 19 Lady Helen's Escapade
A Troublesome Satchel
Apr 22 The Drive for a Life
Apr 26 Lucky Jim
Twin Brothers
Apr 29 'Tis an Ill Wind That Blows No Good
May 3 The Eavesdropper
The Suicide Club
May 6 The Note in the Shoe
One Busy Hour
May 10 The French Duel
Jones and the Lady Book Agent
May 13 A Baby's Shoe
May 17 The Jilt
May 20 Resurrection
May 24 Eloping with Aunty
Two Memories
May 27 The Cricket on the Hearth
May 31 What Drink Did
Jun 3 Eradicating Aunty
His Duty
Jun 7 The Violin Maker of Cremona
Jun 10 The Lonely Villa
A New Trick
Jun 14 The Son's Return
Jun 17 The Faded Lillies
Her First Biscuits
Jun 21 Was Justice Served?
Jun 24 The Mexican Sweethearts
The Peachbasket Hat
Jun 28 The Way of Man
Jul 1 The Necklace
Jul 5 The Message
Jul 8 The Country Doctor
Jul 12 The Cardinal's Conspiracy
Jul 15 The Friend of the Family
Tender Hearts
Jul 19 The Renunciation
Jul 22 Jealousy and the Man
Sweet and Twenty
Jul 26 A Convict's Sacrifice
Jul 29 The Slave
Aug 2 A Strange Meeting
Aug 5 The Mended Lute
Aug 9 Jones' Burglar
They Would Elope
Aug 12 The Better Way
Aug 16 With Her Card
Aug 19 His Wife's Visitor
Mrs. Jones' Lover; or, "I Want My Hat"
Aug 23 The Indian Runner's Romance
Aug 26 "Oh, Uncle"
The Seventh Day
Aug 30 The Heart of an Outlaw
The Mills of the Gods
Pranks
Sep 2 The Little Darling
The Sealed Room
Sep 6 "1776" or, The Hessian Renegades
Sep 9 Comata, the Sioux
Sep 13 The Children's Friend
Getting Even
Sep 16 The Broken Locket
Sep 20 In Old Kentucky
Sep 23 A Fair Exchange
Sep 27 Leather Stocking
Sep 30 The Awakening
Wanted, a Child
Oct 4 Pippa Passes; or, The Song of Conscience
Oct 7 Fools of Fate
Oct 11 The Little Teacher
Oct 14 A Change of Heart
Oct 18 His Lost Love
Oct 21 The Expiation
Oct 25 In the Watches of the Night
Oct 28 Lines of White on a Sullen Sea
Nov 1 The Gibson Goddess
What's Your Hurry?
Nov 4 Nursing a Viper
Nov 8 The Restoration
Nov 11 The Light That Came
Nov 15 Two Women and a Man
Nov 18 A Midnight Adventure
Sweet Revenge
Nov 22 The Open Gate
Nov 25 The Mountaineer's Honor
Nov 29 In the Window Recess
The Trick That Failed
Dec 2 The Death Disc: A Story of the Cromwellian Period
Dec 6 Through the Breakers
Dec 9 The Redman's View
Dec 13 A Corner in Wheat
Dec 16 In a Hempen Bag
The Test
Dec 20 A Trap for Santa Claus
Dec 23 In Little Italy
Dec 27 To Save Her Soul
Dec 30 Choosing a Husband
The Day After

1910

Jan 3 The Rocky Road
Jan 6 The Dancing Girl of Butte
Jan 10 Her Terrible Ordeal
Jan 17 On the Reef
Jan 20 The Call
Jan 24 The Honor of His Family
Jan 27 The Last Deal
Jan 31 The Cloister's Touch
Feb 3 The Woman from Mellon's
Feb 10 The Duke's Plan
Feb 14 One Night, and Then —
Feb 17 The Englishman and the Girl
Feb 21 His Last Burglary
Feb 24 Taming a Husband
Feb 28 The Final Settlement
Mar 3 The Newlyweds
Mar 7 The Thread of Destiny
Mar 10 In Old California
Mar 14 The Converts
Mar 17 The Man
Mar 21 Faithful
Mar 24 The Twisted Trail
Mar 28 Gold Is Not All
Apr 4 As It Is in Life
Apr 7 A Rich Revenge
Apr 11 A Romance of the Western Hills
Apr 18 Thou Shalt Not
Apr 25 The Way of the World
May 2 The Gold-Seekers
May 5 The Unchanging Sea
May 9 Love Among the Roses
May 12 The Two Brothers
May 16 Over Silent Paths
May 19 An Affair of Hearts
May 23 Ramona
May 30 The Impalement
Jun 2 In the Season of Buds
Jun 6 A Child of the Ghetto
Jun 9 A Victim of Jealousy
Jun 13 In the Border States
Jun 16 The Face at the Window
Jun 23 The Marked Time-Table
Jun 27 A Child's Impulse
Jun 30 Muggsy's First Sweetheart
Jul 4 The Purgation
Jul 7 A Midnight Cupid
Jul 11 What the Daisy Said
Jul 14 A Child's Faith
Jul 18 A Flash of Light
Jul 21 As the Bells Rang Out!
Serious Sixteen
Jul 25 The Call to Arms
Jul 28 Unexpected Help
Aug 1 An Arcadian Maid
Aug 4 Her Father's Pride
Aug 8 The House with Closed Shutters
Aug 11 A Salutary Lesson
Aug 15 The Usurer
Aug 22 The Sorrows of the Unfaithful
Aug 25 Wilful Peggy
Aug 29 The Modern Prodigal
Sep 5 A Summer Idyll
Sep 8 Little Angels of Luck
Sep 12 A Mohawk's Way
Sep 15 In Life's Cycle
Sep 22 The Oath and the Man
Sep 26 Rose O' Salem-Town
Sep 29 Examination Day at School
Oct 3 The Iconoclast
Oct 10 That Chink at Golden Gulch

Oct 17 The Broken Doll
Oct 20 The Banker's Daughters
Oct 24 The Message of the Violin
Oct 31 Two Little Waifs
Nov 7 The Fugitive
Waiter No. 5
Nov 10 Simple Charity
Nov 14 Sunshine Sue
Nov 21 The Song of the Wildwood Flute
Nov 28 A Plain Song
Dec 5 A Child's Stratagem
Dec 12 The Golden Supper
Dec 15 His Sister-in-Law
Dec 19 The Lesson
Dec 26 Winning Back His Love

Griffith, K., Mrs.
1907
Dec 7 College Chums

Griggs, John W., Attorney General
1901
Mar 16 President McKinley and Escort Going to the Capitol

Grimm, Jakob Ludwig Karl
1909
Oct 15 Hansel and Gretel
1910
Feb 4 The Little Old Men of the Woods

Grimm, Wilhelm
1909
Oct 15 Hansel and Gretel
1910
Feb 4 The Little Old Men of the Woods

Griswold, W.
1906
Aug [day undetermined]
Kathleen Mavoureen

Guazzoni, Enrico
1910
Jun 30 Faust
Sep 16 The Sacking of Rome

Guéroult, Edmund
1909
Jun 23 The Grandfather

Gugusse
1906
Apr [day undetermined]
Clown's Revenge

Haakon of Norway, King
1910
Jun 4 [King Edward's Funeral]

Hacker, Captain
1900
May [day undetermined]
Brigadier-General Franklin Bell and Staff

Haddock, W. F.
1909
Jul 23 Casey's Jumping Toothache

Haggar, Henry
1907
Feb [day undetermined]
Message from the Sea

Haggar, Violet
1908
Oct 24 The Red Barn Mystery: A Startling Portrayal of the Great Marie Martin Mystery

Haggar, Walter
1908
Oct 24 The Red Barn Mystery: A Startling Portrayal of the Great Marie Martin Mystery

Haggar, William
1903
Apr [day undetermined]
A Duel with Knives
Oct 31 The Poachers
1904
Jun 4 The Bobby Whitewashed
Dec [day undetermined]
Mary in the Dock
1905
Nov [day undetermined]
Convicts' Escape
1907
Feb [day undetermined]
Message from the Sea

Haggard, Henry Rider
1908
Nov 13 "She"

Haldeman, E.
1909
Sep 30 Wanted, a Child
Nov 22 The Open Gate
Dec 2 The Death Disc: A Story of the Cromwellian Period
1910
Jan 3 The Rocky Road
Jan 27 The Last Deal
Jan 31 The Cloister's Touch
Feb 28 The Final Settlement
Sep 8 Little Angels of Luck
Sep 12 A Mohawk's Way
Sep 29 Examination Day at School
Oct 3 The Iconoclast
Oct 31 Two Little Waifs

Hale, Edward Everett
1909
Jun 29 A Man Without a Country

Halévy, Ludovic
1910
Feb 16 Carmen

Haley, Bill
1910
Jul 12 A Deal in Broken China

Hall, Emmett Campbell
1910
Apr 28 Indian Blood
Jun 16 Red Eagle's Love Affair
Jun 27 Apache Gold
Aug 8 The House with Closed Shutters
Sep 1 The Road to Richmond
Sep 5 The Healing Faith
Sep 23 Almost a Hero
Sep 26 Rose O' Salem-Town
Oct 10 That Chink at Golden Gulch
Dec 13 A Mountain Maid

Hall, Robert, General
1900
Mar [day undetermined]
Funeral of Major-General Henry W. Lawton

Hall, Sherman R.
1901
Jun 8 Opening of the Pan-American Exposition showing Vice President Roosevelt Leading the Procession

Halm, Friedrich
1908
Oct 13 The Barbarian Ingomar

Hamilton
1910
Feb 16 Aviation at Los Angeles, Calif.

Hamilton, F.
1908
Jul 11 A Plain Clothes Man

Hamilton, Gilbert P.
1908
Jun 20 Younger Brothers
1910
Feb 26 The Mexican's Faith*

Hamilton, S.
1909
Oct 29 Mexican's Crime

Hanaway, Frank
1903
Dec [day undetermined]
The Great Train Robbery

Handworth, Octavia
1910
May 16 The Girl from Arizona

Hanibal
1910
Nov 12 World's Wrestling Champions

Hanlon, Alfred
1910
May 27 The Winter's Tale

Hanna, Mark, Senator
1900
Sep [day undetermined]
Republican National Committee of 1900
1901
Mar 16 President McKinley and Escort Going to the Capitol
President McKinley Taking the Oath
Jun 8 Opening of the Pan-American Exposition showing Vice President Roosevelt Leading the Procession

Hargrave, N. H.
1901
Sep [day undetermined]
International Field Sports—Oxford-Cambridge vs. Harvard-Yale

Harrington
1906
Jun 28 The Paymaster

Harris, C.
1909
Jul 1 The Necklace*

Harris, Thurston
1907
Sep 21 The Ghost Holiday
Oct 19 A Seaside Girl
Nov 16 A Tramp's Dream of Wealth
Dec 7 A Letter in the Sand
1908
Jan 18 The Artful Lovers
Jun 13 The Man and His Bottle
Sep 12 The Burglar and the Clock

Harron, Robert
1907
Dec 14 Dr. Skinum
Dec 21 Mr. Gay and Mrs.
1908
Jan 4 Professional Jealousy
Feb 10 Bobby's Kodak
Feb 19 The Snowman
Mar 11 The Boy Detective; or, The Abductors Foiled
Mar 18 Her First Adventure [Kidnapped with the Aid of a Street Piano]
Jun 2 Thompson's Night Out
Jun 12 Mixed Babies
Jun 30 At the French Ball
Jul 3 At the Crossroads of Life
Aug 7 A Calamitous Elopement: How It Proved a Windfall for Burglar Bill
Aug 25 Balked at the Altar
Sep 4 Monday Morning in a Coney Island Police Court
Sep 11 Behind the Scenes: Where All Is Not Gold That Glitters
Sep 22 Where the Breakers Roar
Sep 25 A Smoked Husband
Oct 30 Concealing a Burglar
Nov 17 The Song of the Shirt
Nov 27 The Clubman and the Tramp
Dec 1 The Valet's Wife
Dec 8 The Feud and the Turkey
Dec 11 The Reckoning
Dec 15 The Test of Friendship
1909
Feb 1 The Girls and Daddy
Feb 4 The Brahma Diamond
Feb 18 The Hindoo Dagger
Feb 25 At the Altar
Mar 25 A Burglar's Mistake
Apr 1 A Drunkard's Reformation
Apr 12 A Sound Sleeper
Apr 19 A Troublesome Satchel
Jul 5 The Message
Aug 9 They Would Elope
Aug 30 Pranks
Nov 18 Sweet Revenge
1910
Jan 10 Her Terrible Ordeal
Apr 25 The Way of the World
Jun 27 A Child's Impulse
Sep 5 A Summer Idyll

Hart, Joseph
1902
May [day undetermined]
The Boys Help Themselves to Foxy Grandpa's Cigars
The Boys, Still Determined, Try It Again on Foxy Grandpa, with the Same Result
The Boys Think They Have One on Foxy Grandpa, but He Fools Them
The Boys Try to Put One Up on Foxy Grandpa
The Creators of Foxy Grandpa
Foxy Grandpa and Polly in a Little Hilarity
Foxy Grandpa Shows the Boys a Trick or Two with the Tramp
Foxy Grandpa Tells the Boys a Funny Story
1903
Jul [day undetermined]
Why Foxy Grandpa Escaped a Ducking
Oct [day undetermined]
Foxy Grandpa [Thumb Book]
1904
Sep [day undetermined]
European Rest Cure

Hart, R.
1909
Nov 4 Nursing a Viper
Nov 11 The Light That Came
Nov 15 Two Women and a Man
Nov 18 A Midnight Adventure
Nov 22 The Open Gate
Dec 9 The Redman's View
Dec 16 In a Hempen Bag
1910
Jan 24 The Honor of His Family
Jan 27 The Last Deal
Feb 17 The Englishman and the Girl
Feb 24 Taming a Husband
Mar 17 The Love of Lady Irma

Harte, Betty
1909
Jun 17 In the Sultan's Power
1910
Mar 10 Across the Plains

Harte, Bret
1910
Jan 21 The Luck of Roaring Camp

Hartigan, C. P.
1909
Dec 4 The Life of Moses

Haskell, Loney
1897
Oct [day undetermined]
Facial Expressions by Loney Haskell

Hastings, Govenor
1903
Jan [day undetermined]
Girard College Cadets Reviewed by Governor Hastings, at the Dedication of Stephen Girard's Monument

Hastings, Carey L.
1910
Mar 22 St. Elmo

Hatot, Georges
1904
Oct [day undetermined]
Bride Retiring
1905
Oct 14 Behind the Stage
1906
Apr [day undetermined]
A Courageous Husband
Doorkeeper's Curiosity*
The Indiscreet Bathroom Maid
Lady Undressing*
1907
Jan 5 Life of Christ*

Havel
1896
Nov [day undetermined]
The Drunken Acrobat

Havey, M. B.
1910
Dec 15 His Sister-in-Law

Hawkins, Cleve
1910
Jul 8 Reproduction of Jeffries-Johnson Championship Contest

Hawthorne, Nathaniel
1908
Mar 28 Scarlet Letter
1910
Oct 18 The House of the Seven Gables

Hay, John M., Secretary
1901
Mar 16 President McKinley and Escort Going to the Capitol

Hedlund, Guy
1906
Nov 15 The Tunnel Workers
1910
Feb 24 Taming a Husband
Aug 29 The Modern Prodigal
Sep 26 Rose O' Salem-Town
Oct 17 The Broken Doll

Hegard, A.
1909
Sep 22 The Tower of Nesle

Heikes, Rollo
1897
Feb [day undetermined]
Champion Rolla O. Heikes, Breaking the Record at Flying Targets with Winchester Shotgun

Heilbronn, Lorant
1904
Sep 24 The Fairy of the Spring
1907
Mar 16 Cinderella*
1908
Nov 9 Beauty and the Beast

Held, Anna
1910 [month undetermined]
The Comet

Heming, Violet
1910
Jun 14 The Woman Hater
Jun 28 Tempest and Sunshine
Jul 29 The Mermaid
Aug 12 Lena Rivers
Nov 15 Paul and Virginia

Henderson, Dell
1910
Jan 31 The Cloister's Touch
Feb 7 The Course of True Love
Feb 10 The Duke's Plan*
Feb 24 Taming a Husband
Mar 3 The Newlyweds
Mar 14 The Converts
Mar 17 The Love of Lady Irma
Mar 21 Faithful
Mar 24 The Twisted Trail
Mar 28 Gold Is Not All
Apr 11 A Romance of the Western Hills
Apr 21 The Tenderfoot's Triumph
May 2 The Gold-Seekers
May 5 The Unchanging Sea
May 12 The Two Brothers
May 16 Over Silent Paths
May 30 The Impalement
Jun 6 A Child of the Ghetto
Jun 16 The Face at the Window
Jul 4 The Purgation
Jul 28 Unexpected Help
Aug 25 Wilful Peggy
Aug 29 The Modern Prodigal
Oct 17 The Broken Doll
Oct 24 The Message of the Violin
Nov 21 The Song of the Wildwood Flute
Nov 28 A Plain Song
Dec 8 Happy Jack, a Hero
Dec 19 The Lesson

Henderson, Grace
1909
Dec 13 A Corner in Wheat
Dec 16 In a Hempen Bag
1910
Jun 23 The Marked Time-Table
Jun 30 Muggsy's First Sweetheart
Jul 21 As the Bells Rang Out!
Jul 25 The Call to Arms
Aug 4 Her Father's Pride
Aug 8 The House with Closed Shutters
Aug 15 The Usurer
Sep 1 Muggsy Becomes a Hero
Sep 8 Little Angels of Luck
Oct 3 The Iconoclast
Oct 6 How Hubby Got a Raise
Oct 13 The Masher
Oct 24 The Message of the Violin
Oct 31 Two Little Waifs
Nov 7 Waiter No. 5
Nov 10 Simple Charity
Nov 17 Love in Quarantine
Nov 24 Not So Bad as It Seemed
Dec 8 Happy Jack, a Hero
Dec 22 The Recreation of an Heiress
Dec 29 His Wife's Sweethearts

Hendrie, Anita
1908
Dec 29 The Helping Hand
1909
Jan 4 The Maniac Cook
Jan 11 Love Finds a Way
Jan 18 Those Boys!
Jan 21 The Fascinating Mrs. Francis
Jan 28 The Cord of Life
Feb 1 The Girls and Daddy
Feb 18 The Joneses Have Amateur Theatricals
Feb 22 The Golden Louis
Feb 25 At the Altar
Mar 4 A Fool's Revenge
Mar 11 The Salvation Army Lass
Mar 15 I Did It, Mamma
The Lure of the Gown
Mar 22 And a Little Child Shall Lead Them
The Deception
Mar 29 Jones and His New Neighbors
Apr 5 The Road to the Heart
Trying to Get Arrested
Apr 8 A Rude Hostess
Schneider's Anti-Noise Crusade
Apr 12 The Winning Coat
Apr 19 Lady Helen's Escapade
A Troublesome Satchel
Apr 26 Lucky Jim
Twin Brothers
May 6 The Note in the Shoe
May 10 The French Duel
May 13 A Baby's Shoe
May 24 Eloping with Aunty
Two Memories
Jun 14 The Son's Return
Jun 17 Her First Biscuits
Jun 24 The Peachbasket Hat

Henry, O.
1909
Jan 14 The Sacrifice
Mar 22 The Deception
Apr 5 Trying to Get Arrested
1910
Sep 19 A Summer Tragedy

Hepworth, Barbara
1905
Jul [day undetermined]
Rescued by Rover
1909
Feb 10 Dog Outwits Kidnapper

Hepworth, Cecil
1902 [month undetermined]
Bathing Made Easy
Explosion of an Automobile
1903
Feb [day undetermined]
Policeman and Automobile
Oct 17 Alice in Wonderland
Nov [day undetermined]
The Professor
Nov 21 Fire and Rescue
Hotel and Bath
Letter Came Too Late
Saturday's Shopping
1904
Aug [day undetermined]
The Bewitched Traveler
1905
Jul [day undetermined]
Rescued by Rover
Nov [day undetermined]
The Three Honeymoons
1909
Oct 11 Invisibility

Hepworth, Cecil, Mrs.
1903
Oct 17 Alice in Wonderland
Nov 21 Letter Came Too Late
1905
Jul [day undetermined]
Rescued by Rover
Nov [day undetermined]
The Three Honeymoons

Hepworth, T. C.
1903
Feb [day undetermined]
Policeman and Automobile

Heuzé, André
1906
Apr [day undetermined]
Ten Wives for One Husband
May 5 Law of Pardon
May 12 The Wig Chase
Jul 14 Dogs Used as Smugglers
1907
Feb 9 Policeman's Little Run
Jun 15 Dog Police*
Jun 29 Mother-in-Law's Race

Heyes, Percy
1904
Jun [day undetermined]
The Eviction

Hicks, Elinor
1910
May 12 The Two Brothers

Higginson, N. J., Captain
1898 [month undetermined]
Battleship Massachusetts

Higginson, Percy
1909
Aug 9 They Would Elope
Oct 4 Pippa Passes; or, The Song of Conscience

Jan 25 The Welcome Burglar
Jan 28 The Cord of Life
Feb 4 The Brahma Diamond
Feb 25 At the Altar
Mar 1 His Wife's Mother
Mar 4 A Fool's Revenge
Mar 11 The Salvation Army Lass
Mar 15 The Lure of the Gown
Mar 25 A Burglar's Mistake
Apr 15 Confidence
May 3 The Eavesdropper
May 6 The Note in the Shoe
Jul 2 A True Indian's Heart
Oct 1 Faithful Wife*

Irving, Washington
1903
Sep [day undetermined]
Rip Van Winkle
1908
Apr 25 The Legend of Sleepy Hollow
May 2 Rip Van Winkle
1910
Dec 6 Rip Van Winkle

Irwin, Charlie
1903
Feb [day undetermined]
Steer Roping Contest at Cheyenne, Wyo.

Irwin, May
1896 [month undetermined]
The Kiss

Iselin, C. Oliver, Mrs.
1899
Oct [day undetermined]
A Close Finish

Jackson, Mr.
1901 [month undetermined]
The Builders of Shamrock II

Jackson, Helen Hunt
1910
May 23 Ramona

James, Mr.
1903
Nov 28 Attack on Chinese Mission

Jamison, W. L.
1903
Jun [day undetermined]
Panoramic View of an Egyptian Cattle Market
1904
Dec [day undetermined]
Mining Operations, Pennsylvania Coal Fields

Jarvis, F. W.
1900
Jul [day undetermined]
Amateur Athletic Championships

Jarvis, J. M., Col.
1899
Jun [day undetermined]
Eighth Regiment, N. G. S. N. Y.

Jasset, Victorin
1905
Apr 8 The Incendiary
1907
Jan 5 Life of Christ*
Mar 16 Cinderella*

Jean, a dog
1910
Aug 30 Jean and the Calico Doll
Sep 20 Jean the Matchmaker
Oct 25 Jean Goes Foraging
Nov 12 Jean Goes Fishing
Dec 6 A Tin-Type Romance
Dec 24 Jean and the Waif
Dec 31 Where the Winds Blow

Jeannie
1908
Jan 18 Rescued from an Eagle's Nest

Jefferson, Joseph
1896
Sep [day undetermined]
Awakening of Rip
Exit of Rip and the Dwarf
Rip Leaving Sleepy Hollow
Rip Meeting the Dwarf
Rip Passing over the Mountain
Rip's Toast
Rip's Toast to Hudson
Rip's Twenty Years' Sleep
1903
May [day undetermined]
Rip Van Winkle

Jeffries, Jack
1901
Dec [day undetermined]
Jeffries Side Stepping and Wrestling
Jeffries Sparring with His Brother

Jeffries, James J.
1899
Nov [day undetermined]
Jeffries-Sharkey Contest
1901
Dec [day undetermined]
Jeffries Exercising in His Gymnasium
Jeffries Side Stepping and Wrestling
Jeffries Skipping the Rope
Jeffries Sparring with His Brother
Jeffries Throwing the Medicine Ball
Dec 21 Jeffries and Ruhlin Sparring Contest at San Francisco, Cal., Nov. 15, 1901—Five Rounds

Jennings, Al
1908
Dec [day undetermined]
The Bank Robbery

Jennings, William
1899
Apr [day undetermined]
A Bucking Broncho

Jerrold, Douglas
1908
Aug 1 Black Eyed Susan

Jewell, Theodore, Captain
1898
Oct [day undetermined]
Famous Battleship Captains—Philadelphia Peace Jubilee Parade

Johnson, Arthur
1905
Sep [day undetermined]
The White Caps
1908
Jul 14 The Adventures of Dollie
Aug 11 The Greaser's Gauntlet
Aug 25 Balked at the Altar
Aug 28 For a Wife's Honor
Sep 8 The Girl and the Outlaw
Sep 22 Where the Breakers Roar
Sep 25 A Smoked Husband
Oct 2 The Devil
Oct 6 The Zulu's Heart
Oct 16 The Vaquero's Vow
Oct 20 The Planter's Wife
Oct 23 Romance of a Jewess
Oct 27 The Call of the Wild
Oct 30 Concealing a Burglar
Nov 13 The Guerrilla
Nov 17 The Song of the Shirt
Nov 20 The Ingrate
Nov 24 A Woman's Way
Dec 1 The Valet's Wife
Dec 4 Money Mad
Dec 8 The Feud and the Turkey
Dec 11 The Reckoning
Dec 15 The Test of Friendship
Dec 25 Mr. Jones at the Ball
1909
Jan 1 One Touch of Nature
Jan 11 The Honor of Thieves
Jan 14 The Sacrifice
Jan 18 The Criminal Hypnotist
Jan 25 Those Awful Hats
Feb 1 The Girls and Daddy
Feb 4 The Brahma Diamond
Feb 8 Edgar Allen Poe
A Wreath in Time
Feb 11 Tragic Love
Feb 15 The Curtain Pole
His Ward's Love
Feb 18 The Hindoo Dagger
Feb 22 The Politician's Love Story
Feb 25 At the Altar
Mar 1 The Prussian Spy
Mar 18 The Voice of the Violin
Mar 22 And a Little Child Shall Lead Them
Apr 1 A Drunkard's Reformation
Apr 5 The Road to the Heart
Apr 8 A Rude Hostess
Schneider's Anti-Noise Crusade
Apr 15 Confidence
Apr 22 The Drive for a Life
Apr 26 Twin Brothers
May 10 The French Duel
May 17 The Jilt
May 20 Resurrection
May 24 Eloping with Aunty
Jun 3 Eradicating Aunty
His Duty
Jun 10 A New Trick
Jun 17 Her First Biscuits
Jun 28 The Way of Man
Jul 15 Tender Hearts
Jul 29 The Slave
Aug 2 A Strange Meeting
Aug 5 The Mended Lute
Aug 12 The Better Way
Aug 16 With Her Card
Aug 23 The Indian Runner's Romance
Aug 30 The Heart of an Outlaw
The Mills of the Gods
Pranks
Sep 2 The Little Darling
The Sealed Room
Sep 9 Comata, the Sioux
Sep 16 The Broken Locket
Sep 30 The Awakening
Oct 11 The Little Teacher
Oct 14 A Change of Heart
Oct 21 The Expiation
Nov 1 The Gibson Goddess
Nov 4 Nursing a Viper
Nov 11 The Light That Came
Nov 18 Sweet Revenge
Nov 25 The Mountaineer's Honor
Nov 29 The Trick That Failed
Dec 6 Through the Breakers
Dec 16 The Test
Dec 27 To Save Her Soul
Dec 30 The Day After
1910
Jan 13 All on Account of the Milk
Jan 31 The Cloister's Touch
Feb 24 Taming a Husband
Feb 28 The Final Settlement
Mar 3 The Newlyweds
Mar 10 In Old California
Mar 14 The Converts
Mar 21 Faithful
Mar 24 The Twisted Trail
Apr 11 A Romance of the Western Hills
Apr 21 The Tenderfoot's Triumph
May 5 The Unchanging Sea
May 9 Love Among the Roses
May 12 The Two Brothers
May 16 Over Silent Paths
Jul 28 Unexpected Help
Oct 22 In the Gray of the Dawn
Oct 29 The Armorer's Daughter
Nov 5 Where Sea and Shore Doth Meet
Dec 24 The Refuge

Johnson, Jack
1910
May 16 Johnson Training for His Fight with Jeffries
Aug 20 [Jack Johnson's Own Story of the Big Fight]

Johnson, John S., Lieut. Col.
1901
Mar 16 President McKinley and Escort Going to the Capitol

Johnson, Tefft
1909
Sep 3 Ethel's Luncheon
Sep 14 Little Sister
1910
Feb 5 Twelfth Night

Johnston
1899
Sep [day undetermined]
M'lle. Cathrina Bartho*

Jones, James K., Senator
1901
Mar 16 President McKinley Taking the Oath

Jones, S. S.
1901 [month undetermined]
Amateur Athletic Association Sports

Jordan, Nicholas
1910
Mar 15 The Actor's Children
Jul 5 Booming Business

Joyce, Alice
1910
Sep 28 The Heart of Edna Leslie
Oct 5 The Engineer's Sweetheart
Oct 21 The Education of Elizabeth
Nov 25 The Roses of the Virgin
Dec 7 Rachel
Dec 9 The Rescue of Molly Finney

Jusserand, Jules
1910
May 26 Roosevelt in Paris
Katzer, M.
1907
Dec 28 The Merry Widow
Kauser, F. J.
1901 [month undetermined]
Amateur Athletic Association Sports
Kearton, Cherry
1910
Apr 18 Roosevelt in Africa
1911
Feb 12 Lassoing Wild Animals in Africa*
Keith, B. F.
1898
Nov [day undetermined]
Mr. B. F. Keith
Keller, Gus
1903
Jul [day undetermined]
Expert Bag Punching
Kelly, James T.
1897
Sep [day undetermined]
Bowery Waltz
Kennedy, Mr.
1907
Dec 7 College Chums
Kennedy, Tom
1910
Jun 15 How Championships Are Won—and Lost
Kent, Charles
1909
Nov 13 Launcelot and Elaine
Dec 4 The Life of Moses
1910
Jan 4 Forty Years in the Land of Midian [The Life of Moses Part II]
Jan 8 Richelieu; or, The Conspiracy
Jan 25 The Plagues of Egypt and the Deliverance of the Hebrew [The Life of Moses Part III]
Feb 5 Twelfth Night
Feb 12 The Victory of Israel [The Life of Moses Part IV]
Feb 19 The Promised Land [The Life of Moses Part V]
Jul 9 Becket
Aug 27 Rose Leaves
Sep 20 Jean the Matchmaker
Kent, Dorothy
1897
Sep [day undetermined]
Bowery Waltz
Kent, J. B.
1908
Dec [day undetermined]
The Bank Robbery
A Round-Up in Oklahoma
Kerrigan, J. Warren
1910
Feb 2 A Voice from the Fireplace
Feb 12 Bitter-Sweet
Mar 23 The Hand of Uncle Sam
Apr 27 The Latest in Garters
May 4 The Stolen Fortune
May 25 Where Is Mulcahy?
Jun 15 A Honeymoon for Three
Jun 22 A Victim of Hate
Jul 6 A Darling Confusion
The Other Johnson
Jul 13 An Advertisement Answered
Aug 17 The Count That Counted
Oct 26 The Bouquet
Nov 21 Starlight's Devotion
Kershaw, Eleanor
1910
Feb 7 The Course of True Love
Feb 24 Taming a Husband
Keys, Nelson
1910
Jun 21 Drowsy Dick's Dream
Kilgore, Joseph
1909
Jun 29 Washington under the British Flag
Jul 3 Washington Under the American Flag
Kilpatrick
1899
Jul [day undetermined]
Kilpatrick's Ride
King, Bob
1904
Jun [day undetermined]
The Eviction
King, R.
1909
Jul 1 The Necklace
Jul 8 The Country Doctor
Aug 26 The Seventh Day
Kingsley, Charles
1908
Jan 20 The Water Babies; or, The Little Chimney Sweep
1910
May 5 The Unchanging Sea
Kipling, Rudyard
1910
Nov 10 The Vampire
Kirkwood, James
1909
Jun 17 The Faded Lillies
Jun 21 Was Justice Served?
Jun 24 The Mexican Sweethearts
Jun 28 The Way of Man
Jul 5 The Message
Jul 12 The Cardinal's Conspiracy
Jul 15 Tender Hearts
Jul 19 The Renunciation
Jul 22 Jealousy and the Man
Sweet and Twenty
Jul 26 A Convict's Sacrifice
Jul 29 The Slave
Aug 5 The Mended Lute
Aug 9 They Would Elope
Aug 12 The Better Way
Aug 19 His Wife's Visitor
Aug 23 The Indian Runner's Romance
Aug 26 "Oh, Uncle"
The Seventh Day
Aug 30 The Heart of an Outlaw
Sep 6 "1776" or, The Hessian Renegades
Sep 9 Comata, the Sioux
Sep 13 Getting Even
Sep 23 A Fair Exchange
Oct 4 Pippa Passes; or, The Song of Conscience
Oct 7 Fools of Fate
Oct 14 A Change of Heart
Oct 18 His Lost Love
Oct 28 Lines of White on a Sullen Sea
Nov 1 The Gibson Goddess
Nov 8 The Restoration
Nov 25 The Mountaineer's Honor
Nov 29 In the Window Recess
Dec 2 The Death Disc: A Story of the Cromwellian Period
Dec 6 Through the Breakers
Dec 9 The Redman's View
Dec 13 A Corner in Wheat
Dec 30 The Day After
1910
Jan 20 The Call
Jan 27 The Last Deal
Feb 10 The Duke's Plan
Feb 14 One Night, and Then —
Feb 21 His Last Burglary
Feb 28 The Final Settlement
Jun 9 A Victim of Jealousy
Oct 22 In the Gray of the Dawn
Oct 29 The Armorer's Daughter
Nov 5 Where Sea and Shore Doth Meet
Dec 17 The Thin Dark Line
Kitamura
1903
Jan [day undetermined]
Japanese Foot Juggler
Kitchell, W. H.
1910
Jul 15 How Bumptious Papered the Parlor
Sep 1 The Man Who Died
Nov 3 Mike the Housemaid
Nov 7 The Taming of Wild Bill
Dec 21 The Runaway Motor Car
Kline, Mamie
1903
Jan [day undetermined]
Cake Walking Horses
Knabenshue
1910
Feb 16 Aviation at Los Angeles, Calif.
Knowles, James Sheridan
1909
Feb 6 Virginius
Komura, Jutaro, Baron
1905
Aug [day undetermined]
Scenes and Incidents, Russo-Japanese Peace Conference, Portsmouth, N.H.
Krauss, Henri
1909
Jun 16 The Reckoning
Jun 23 The Grandfather
Sep 22 The Tower of Nesle
1910
Jun 9 The Children of Edward IV
Aug 11 Charles Le Tremeraire
Kreighoff, B.
1910
Dec 23 Clancy
Krone, John
1909
Mar 14 The Summers-Britt Fight Pictures
Apr 19 World's Heavyweight Championship Pictures Between Tommy Burns and Jack Johnson
Kurtis, Mr.
1907
Dec 7 College Chums
La Blanche, Prof.
1903
Jan [day undetermined]
Man Couchee Dance
Lafayette, the Great
1899
Aug [day undetermined]
The Great Lafayette
Sep [day undetermined]
Dreyfus Receiving His Sentence
Trial of Captain Dreyfus
Lagrange, Louise
1907
Mar 16 Cinderella
Lambert, Albert
1909
Feb 17 The Assassination of the Duke of Guise
Mar 20 The Return of Ulysses
Apr 7 The Kiss of Judas
1910
Sep 1 King of a Day
Lamberton, Captain
1899
Sep [day undetermined]
Officers of the "Olympia"
Lamy, Edmund
1910
Mar 24 Stunts on Skates
Land, M.
1910
Jun 20 The Road to Happiness
Landelle, Charles
1900
Aug [day undetermined]
Living Pictures
Landers, M.
1909
Aug 25 The Eternal Romance
Lanning, Frank
1910
May 4 Chief Blackfoot's Vindication
Aug 5 The Legend of Scar-Face
Aug 12 The Call of the Blood
Oct 7 Big Elk's Turndown
Oct 14 Winona
Oct 28 Indian Pete's Gratitude
Lapham, F. DeWitt
1899
Apr [day undetermined]
Patriot's Day Parade
Larkin, George
1908
Mar 21 Animated Snowballs
Oct 13 The Bridge of Sighs
Dec 11 The Angel Child
1910
Aug 3 Under Both Flags
Aug 17 A Cheyenne Brave
Oct 8 An Indian's Gratitude
Nov 2 Cowboy Justice
Larsen, Viggo
1907
Apr 20 Anarchist's Mother-in-Law
1908
Apr 4 The Robber's Sweetheart
Apr 11 Lion Hunting
Sep 19 The Lady with the Camellias

1909
Mar 31 The Non-Stop Motor Bicycle
Sep 4 Cycle Rider and the Witch
Nov 13 A Message to Napoleon; or, An Episode in the Life of the Great Prisoner at Elba
1910
Jan 8 Child as Benefactor

Lassie
1910
Dec 12 Faithful Max

Laurier, Wilfred, Sir
1897 [month undetermined]
Sir Wilfred Laurier and the New South Wales Lancers

Lavėdan, Henri
1909
Feb 17 The Assassination of the Duke of Guise
Nov 5 The Prodigal Son

Lawley, Henry
1902
Jul [day undetermined]
Explosion of an Automobile

Lawrence, Florence
1907
Apr 6 Daniel Boone; or, Pioneer Days in America
Aug 3 Athletic American Girls
The Boy, the Bust and the Bath
Nov 23 The Despatch Bearer; or, Through the Enemy's Lines
Dec [day undetermined]
The Shaughraun, an Irish Romance
1908
Jun 6 Romeo and Juliet, a Romantic Story of the Ancient Feud Between the Italian Houses of Montague and Capulet
Aug 29 Salome; or, The Dance of the Seven Veils
Sep 1 Betrayed by a Handprint
Sep 8 The Girl and the Outlaw
Sep 11 Behind the Scenes: Where All Is Not Gold That Glitters
Sep 15 The Red Girl
Sep 18 The Heart of O Yama
Sep 22 Where the Breakers Roar
Sep 25 A Smoked Husband
Sep 29 The Stolen Jewels
Oct 2 The Devil
Oct 6 The Zulu's Heart
Oct 9 Father Gets in the Game
Oct 13 The Barbarian Ingomar
Oct 16 The Vaquero's Vow
Oct 20 The Planter's Wife
Oct 23 Romance of a Jewess
Oct 27 The Call of the Wild
Oct 30 Concealing a Burglar
Nov 3 After Many Years
Nov 10 Taming of the Shrew
Nov 17 The Song of the Shirt
Nov 20 The Ingrate
Nov 27 The Clubman and the Tramp
Dec 1 The Valet's Wife
Dec 4 Money Mad
Dec 11 The Reckoning
Dec 15 The Test of Friendship
Dec 18 An Awful Moment
Dec 22 The Christmas Burglars
Dec 25 Mr. Jones at the Ball
Dec 29 The Helping Hand
1909
Jan 1 One Touch of Nature
Jan 7 Mrs. Jones Entertains
Jan 11 The Honor of Thieves
Jan 14 The Sacrifice
Jan 18 Those Boys!
Jan 21 Mr. Jones Has a Card Party
Jan 25 Those Awful Hats
Jan 28 The Cord of Life
Feb 1 The Girls and Daddy
Feb 4 The Brahma Diamond
Feb 8 A Wreath in Time
Feb 11 Tragic Love
Feb 15 The Curtain Pole
His Ward's Love
Feb 18 The Joneses Have Amateur Theatricals
Mar 1 His Wife's Mother
Mar 8 The Wooden Leg
Mar 11 The Salvation Army Lass
Mar 15 The Lure of the Gown
Mar 22 The Deception
Mar 29 Jones and His New Neighbors
The Medicine Bottle
Apr 1 A Drunkard's Reformation
Apr 5 The Road to the Heart
Trying to Get Arrested
Apr 8 Schneider's Anti-Noise Crusade
Apr 12 A Sound Sleeper
The Winning Coat
Apr 15 Confidence
Apr 19 Lady Helen's Escapade
A Troublesome Satchel
Apr 22 The Drive for a Life
Apr 29 'Tis an Ill Wind That Blows No Good
May 6 The Note in the Shoe
May 10 The French Duel
Jones and the Lady Book Agent
May 13 A Baby's Shoe
May 17 The Jilt
May 20 Resurrection
May 24 Eloping with Aunty
May 31 What Drink Did
Jun 3 Eradicating Aunty
Jun 17 Her First Biscuits
Jun 24 The Peachbasket Hat
Jun 28 The Way of Man
Jul 8 The Country Doctor
Jul 12 The Cardinal's Conspiracy
Jul 15 Tender Hearts
Jul 22 Jealousy and the Man
Sweet and Twenty
Jul 29 The Slave
Aug 5 The Mended Lute
Aug 9 Jones' Burglar
Aug 19 Mrs. Jones' Lover; or, "I Want My Hat"
Nov 1 Love's Stratagem
Nov 15 The Forest Ranger's Daughter
1910
Jan 31 Coquette's Suitors
Mar 7 Mother Love
Apr 4 The Miser's Daughter
Apr 21 The Maelstrom
Sep 26 Pressed Roses

Leander Sisters, The
1897
Oct [day undetermined]
Cupid and Psyche
Leander Sisters

Le Bargy, Charles
1909
Feb 17 The Assassination of the Duke of Guise
Jun 9 La Tosca
1910
Jun 16 The Legend of the Holy Chapel

Lee, E. Lawrence
1908
Jun 20 Younger Brothers

Lee, Fitzhugh, General
1898
Mar [day undetermined]
Brigadier-General Fitz Hugh Lee
Jul [day undetermined]
Gen. Fitzhugh Lee and Staff
1899
Jan [day undetermined]
General Lee's Procession, Havana

Lee, H.
1908
Jul 11 A Plain Clothes Man

Legrand, M.
1910
Jun 11 The Marriage of Esther
Jun 18 Esther and Mordecai

Lehrmann, Henry
1910
Feb 7 The Course of True Love
Mar 17 The Love of Lady Irma
Aug 1 An Arcadian Maid

Leigh, Grace
1902
Nov [day undetermined]
Umbrella Dance, San Toy

Leigh Sisters
1900
Mar [day undetermined]
Umbrella Dance
1903
Jan [day undetermined]
Umbrella Dance

Leighton, Lillian
1910
Mar 24 The Wonderful Wizard of Oz

Leist, Bernadine Prissi
1909
Nov 23 A Rose of the Tenderloin
1910
Apr 15 Her First Appearance
Jun 3 The Piece of Lace
Oct 3 The Iconoclast
Nov 7 Waiter No. 5

Le Las, M.
1909
Feb 8 Les Ricochets

Lemaître, Jules
1909
Mar 20 The Return of Ulysses

Leno, Dan
1902
Nov [day undetermined]
Dessert at Dan Leno's House
Mr. Dan Leno, Assisted by Mr. Herbert Campbell, Editing the "Sun"
An Obstinate Cork

Leonard, Al, Professor
1896
Aug [day undetermined]
Sparring Contest, Canastota, N.Y.

Leonard, Marion
1908
Jul 3 At the Crossroads of Life
Jul 24 The Tavern-Keeper's Daughter
Aug 4 The Bandit's Waterloo: The Outwitting of an Andalusian Brigand by a Pretty Senora
Aug 11 The Greaser's Gauntlet
Dec 8 The Feud and the Turkey
Dec 22 The Christmas Burglars
1909
Jan 1 One Touch of Nature
Jan 4 The Maniac Cook
Jan 11 Love Finds a Way
Jan 14 A Rural Elopement
The Sacrifice
Jan 18 The Criminal Hypnotist
Jan 21 The Fascinating Mrs. Francis
Jan 25 The Welcome Burglar
Jan 28 The Cord of Life
Feb 18 The Hindoo Dagger
Feb 22 The Politician's Love Story
Feb 25 At the Altar
Mar 1 The Prussian Spy
Mar 4 A Fool's Revenge
Mar 15 The Lure of the Gown
Mar 18 The Voice of the Violin
Mar 22 And a Little Child Shall Lead Them
Mar 25 A Burglar's Mistake
Mar 29 The Medicine Bottle
Apr 1 A Drunkard's Reformation
Apr 8 A Rude Hostess
Apr 12 The Winning Coat
Apr 22 The Drive for a Life
Apr 26 Lucky Jim
May 3 The Eavesdropper
May 6 The Note in the Shoe
May 17 The Jilt
May 20 Resurrection
May 24 Two Memories
Jun 3 His Duty
Jun 10 The Lonely Villa
A New Trick
Aug 16 With Her Card
Aug 30 The Heart of an Outlaw
The Mills of the Gods
Pranks
Sep 2 The Sealed Room
Sep 9 Comata, the Sioux
Sep 13 The Children's Friend
Sep 27 Leather Stocking
Oct 7 Fools of Fate
Oct 18 His Lost Love
Oct 21 The Expiation
Oct 25 In the Watches of the Night
Oct 28 Lines of White on a Sullen Sea
Nov 1 The Gibson Goddess
Nov 4 Nursing a Viper
Nov 8 The Restoration
Nov 11 The Light That Came
Nov 18 Sweet Revenge
Nov 29 In the Window Recess
Dec 2 The Death Disc: A Story of the Cromwellian Period
Dec 6 Through the Breakers
Dec 16 The Test
Dec 20 A Trap for Santa Claus
Dec 23 In Little Italy
Dec 30 The Day After
1910
Jan 17 On the Reef
Jan 31 The Cloister's Touch
Feb 10 The Duke's Plan
Mar 10 In Old California
Mar 28 Gold Is Not All
Mar 31 His Last Dollar
Apr 4 As It Is in Life

MacArthur, Arthur, Major-General
1900
Mar [day undetermined]
Major-General Arthur MacArthur and Staff
McCabe, Harry
1908
Apr 12 James Boys in Missouri
McCay, Winsor
1906
Feb [day undetermined]
Dream of a Rarebit Fiend
McClellan, George B., Mayor
1904
Aug [day undetermined]
Judge Parker & Mayor McClellan at Esopus
Nov [day undetermined]
Opening Ceremonies, New York Subway, October 27, 1904
McCutcheon, John T.
1910
Apr 16 In Africa
McCutcheon, M.
1907
Nov 20 Wife Wanted
McCutcheon, Wallace
1897
Oct [day undetermined]
Fastest Wrecking Crew in the World*
1899
Aug [day undetermined]
The Fire Boat "New Yorker"
A Gay Old Boy
How the Tramp Lost His Dinner
An Intrigue in the Harem
Topsy-Turvy Quadrille
Where There's a Will, There's a Way
Wonderful Dancing Girls
The X-Ray Mirror
1900
Jan [day undetermined]
"Caught"
"I Had To Leave a Happy Home for You"
Necessary Qualifications of a Typewriter
The Perfect Woman
1901
Sep [day undetermined]
Finish of Futurity
McKinley Funeral—In Solemn State
President McKinley's Funeral
Oct [day undetermined]
The Matron Stakes
1903
Aug [day undetermined]
Balloon Race
The Girl at the Window
"He Loves Me, He Loves Me Not"
In My Lady's Boudoir
"Love Me, Love My Dog"
A Total Accident
A Yard of Puppies
Sep [day undetermined]
(Abandoned)
The Camera Fiend
Discovery of Bodies
Experimental
Firing the Cabin
Hammock Scene—(Abandoned)
Indians Leaving Bald Mountain
Love in a Perilous Place
Private Picture—Families of H. N. M. & H. C.
Rescue of Child from Indians
Settler's Home Life
Trappers Crossing Bald Mountain
Oct [day undetermined]
Kit Carson
Kit Carson #6: Panorama
Nov [day undetermined]
Battleship "Indiana" in Action
Boat Race
Boat Race No. 2
Harvard-Pennsylvania Football Game
Inspection Aboard Battleship "Indiana"
A Juvenile Elephant Trainer
Man Overboard! "INDIANA"
Raising Colors, Battleship "Indiana"
1904
Jun [day undetermined]
"Personal"
Aug [day undetermined]
The Moonshiner
The Widow and the Only Man
Oct [day undetermined]
Launching of the U. S. S. Battleship "Connecticut"
The Lost Child
Dec [day undetermined]
The Chicken Thief
1905
Mar [day undetermined]
The Inauguration of President Roosevelt
The Nihilists
Apr [day undetermined]
Panorama from the Roof of the Times Building, New York
Wanted: A Dog
Jul [day undetermined]
Stolen by Gypsies
Sep [day undetermined]
The White Caps
1906
Mar 29 The Black Hand
Apr [day undetermined]
A Winter Straw Ride
Jun 30 Hold-Up of the Rocky Mt. Express*
Aug 6 Looking for John Smith
1907
Apr 6 Daniel Boone; or, Pioneer Days in America
Oct 19 Love Microbe
Nov 20 Wife Wanted
1908
Feb 1 Classmates
Feb 10 Bobby's Kodak
Feb 19 The Snowman
Feb 27 The Princess in the Vase
Mar 7 The Yellow Peril
Mar 11 The Boy Detective; or, The Abductors Foiled
Mar 18 Her First Adventure [Kidnapped with the Aid of a Street Piano]
Mar 21 Caught by Wireless
Mar 28 Old Isaacs, the Pawnbroker
Apr 7 A Famous Escape
Apr 15 The King of the Cannibal Islands
Apr 22 Hulda's Lovers
Apr 29 The King's Messenger
May 6 The Music Master
The Sculptor's Nightmare
May 20 When Knights Were Bold
May 29 His Day of Rest
Jun 2 Thompson's Night Out
Jun 5 The Romance of an Egg
Jun 9 'Ostler Joe
Jun 12 Mixed Babies
Jun 16 The Invisible Fluid
Jun 19 The Man in the Box
Jun 23 The Outlaw
Jun 30 At the French Ball
Jul 7 The Kentuckian
Jul 10 The Stage Rustler
Jul 21 The Black Viper
Jul 31 Deceived Slumming Party
McCutcheon, Wallace, Jr.
1908
Jul 3 At the Crossroads of Life
McDermott, Marc
1909
Nov 2 Comedy and Tragedy
1910
Aug 19 How the Squire Was Captured
Dec 23 A Christmas Carol
McDonagh, John
1910
Nov 7 The Fugitive
McDovall, J.
1906
Aug [day undetermined]
Kathleen Mavoureen
McDowell, Claire
1908
Oct 2 The Devil
Oct 20 The Planter's Wife
Oct 27 The Call of the Wild
1910
Aug 25 Wilful Peggy
Sep 12 A Mohawk's Way
Oct 3 The Iconoclast
Oct 6 How Hubby Got a Raise
Nov 7 Waiter No. 5
Nov 24 His New Lid
Dec 5 A Child's Stratagem
Dec 12 The Golden Supper
Dec 15 His Sister-in-Law
McDowell, J. B.
1909
Sep 4 Baby's Revenge*
McDuffee, Eddie
1897
Oct [day undetermined]
A Paced Bicycle Race
McGee, James L.
1909
Apr 29 Mephisto and the Maiden
McGinnis, D. J.
1906
Aug [day undetermined]
Kathleen Mavoureen
McGlynn, Frank
1910
Jan 4 Pardners
Apr 8 Sandy the Substitute
May 27 'Mid the Cannon's Roar
Sep 6 The Big Scoop
Sep 30 Ononko's Vow
McGovern, A.
1910
Aug 15 The District Attorney's Triumph
Oct 10 The Clown and the Minister
Oct 31 Brothers
Nov 14 The Street Preacher
McGovern, Terry
1901
Apr 13 Gans-McGovern Fight
1910
Oct 11 Actors' Fund Field Day
McGowan, John P.
1910
Dec 14 Seth's Temptation
McGowan, R. F.
1910
Sep 1 The Affair of an Egg
McGrath, Jim
1904
Jun [day undetermined]
The Eviction
Mack, Hayward
1910
Dec 22 Little Nell's Tobacco
McKenzie, M. S., Captain
1898
Oct [day undetermined]
Famous Battleship Captains—Philadelphia Peace Jubilee Parade
Mackin, Laurie, Mrs.
1910
Jan 13 All on Account of the Milk
McKinley, William
1896
Sep [day undetermined]
McKinley at Home, Canton, Ohio
1897
Mar [day undetermined]
President Cleveland and President McKinley
1898
Sep [day undetermined]
President McKinley's Inspection of Camp Wikoff
1899 [month undetermined]
President McKinley and Wife, Members of His Cabinet and Their Wives and Capt. Coghlan Leaving the Cruiser Raleigh
May [day undetermined]
Mrs. U. S. Grant and President McKinley
President McKinley and Mayor Ashbridge of Philadelphia
Jun [day undetermined]
President McKinley
Oct [day undetermined]
Presentation of Nation's Sword to Admiral Dewey
1901
Mar [day undetermined]
President McKinley Leaving the White House for the Capitol
The Second Inauguration
Mar 16 President McKinley and Escort Going to the Capitol
President McKinley Taking the Oath
McKinnel, Norman
1899 [month undetermined]
Beerbohm Tree, the Great English Actor

Macklin, A.
1909
Feb 17 Tag Day
Maclarty, Basil
1905
Nov [day undetermined]
Motor Highwayman
McNair, Admiral
1898
Jul [day undetermined]
Admiral McNair, U.S.N.
Macpherson, Jeanie
1908
Oct 30 Concealing a Burglar
Nov 27 The Clubman and the Tramp
Dec 4 Money Mad
Dec 22 The Christmas Burglars
1909
Jan 7 Mrs. Jones Entertains
Feb 15 The Curtain Pole
Nov 18 Sweet Revenge
1910
Aug 11 A Salutary Lesson
Aug 18 An Old Story with a New Ending
Dec 5 A Child's Stratagem
Dec 15 His Sister-in-Law
Dec 19 The Lesson
Dec 26 Winning Back His Love
McRae, Representative
1901
Mar 16 President McKinley and Escort Going to the Capitol
President McKinley Taking the Oath
McSweeney, Governor
1902
Apr [day undetermined]
President Roosevelt Reviewing the Troops at Charleston Exposition [South Carolina]
Maggi, Luigi
1909
Jun 26 Louis the XI
Nov 1 Nero; or, The Burning of Rome
Nov 20 A Mother's Heart
1910
Jan 15 The Son of the Wilderness
Nov 2 The Slave of Carthage
Mailes, Charles Hill
1909
Jun 17 The Faded Lillies
Manley, Charles
1900
Mar [day undetermined]
Uncle Josh's Nightmare
1902
Jan [day undetermined]
Uncle Josh at the Moving Picture Show
Mann, Louis
1910
Oct 11 Actors' Fund Field Day
Mannie, a dog
1905
Jul [day undetermined]
The Burglar's Slide for Life
1906
Jun [day undetermined]
The Terrible Kids
Mansfield, R.
1908
Mar 28 Scarlet Letter
Manthey, C.
1907
Dec 28 The Merry Widow
Manuel of Portugal, King
1910
Jun 4 [King Edward's Funeral]
Mapes, A.
1910
Nov 23 The Lad from Old Ireland
Maquier, Pierre
1908
Oct 31 Hamlet, Duel Scene with Laertes
March, Anita
1909
Sep 4 The Boy Scouts
1910
Jan 17 Muggins
Marck, George J.
1902
Nov [day undetermined]
George J. Marck and His Lions
Marconi, Gugliemo
1901 [month undetermined]
Signor Marconi—Wireless Telegraphy
Marelli, Pietro
1909
Dec 25 Alberno & Rosamunda
Marion, Frank J.
1910
Apr 27 The Sacred Turquoise of the Zuni
Mars, "Bud"
1910
Oct 15 Aeroplanes in Flight and Construction
Marsh
1899
Sep [day undetermined]
A Thrilling Ride
Marshall, Mr.
1910
Jul 20 The Thief
Martin, Ed
1901
Dec [day undetermined]
Ruhlin Boxing with "Denver" Ed. Martin
Martin, J. H.
1905
Jul [day undetermined]
Cook and Chimney Sweep*
Fatal Necklace*
The Race for Bed*
Oct [day undetermined]
Devil's Dice*
He Learned Ju Jitsu, So Did the Missus*
Dec [day undetermined]
Freak Barber*
Hubby Tries to Keep House*
1906
Jan [day undetermined]
A Misguided Bobby at a Fancy Garden Party*
Opium Smoker's Dream*
Shaving by Installments*
Jul [day undetermined]
Fakir and Footpad*
House Furnishing Made Easy
1907
Apr 6 Signal Man's Son*
Apr 20 Chef's Revenge*
Knight-Errant
A Mother's Sin*
May 4 The Fatal Hand*
Sep 14 The Cheater's Cheated*
Oct 5 His First Topper*
1909
Oct 19 The Phantom Ship
Martin, Lee
1898 [month undetermined]
Bucking Broncho
Martin, Lucy
1900
Mar [day undetermined]
Miss Lucy Murray
Martinek, H. O.
1910
May 12 Three Fingered Kate
Jun 21 Drowsy Dick's Dream
Jul 5 The Boy and His Teddy Bear
Jul 12 A Deal in Broken China
Martinek, Ivy
1910
May 12 Three Fingered Kate
Jun 21 Drowsy Dick's Dream
Marvin, Arthur
1897
Mar [day undetermined]
A Bowery Cafe
1899
Apr [day undetermined]
Farmer Oatcake Has His Troubles
Symphony in "A" Flat
May [day undetermined]
Distributing a War Extra
A Unique Race
Aug [day undetermined]
43rd Rifles; Royal Canadian Infantry
The Imperial Limited
"Imperial Limited." Canadian Pacific R. R.
In Fighting Trim
Lord and Lady Minto
Sep [day undetermined]
Heroes of Luzon
Nov [day undetermined]
Jeffries and a Child at Play
Jeffries and Brother Boxing
Jeffries and Roeber Wrestling
Jeffries Being Rubbed Down
Jeffries Boxing with Tommy Ryan
Jeffries Running with His Trainers
Jeffries-Sharkey Contest
Jeffries Training on Bicycle
Dec [day undetermined]
Port Huron; West End of St. Clair Tunnel
St. Clair Tunnel
West Side St. Clair Tunnel
1900
Feb [day undetermined]
Canadian Mounted Rifles on the March
Departure of the Second Canadian Contingent
Mounted Rifles at Drill
Northwestern Mounted Rifles
The Royal Leinster Regiment
Royal Leinster Regiment on Parade
Royal Leinsters on Review
Toronto Mounted Rifles
Apr [day undetermined]
After Dark in Central Park
The Chimney Sweep and the Miller
The Croton Dam Strike
How They Rob Men in Chicago
Tommy's Trick on Grandpa
May [day undetermined]
The Art of "Making Up"
Buffalo Bill's Wild West Parade
The Downward Path: She Ran Away [Part 2]
The Downward Path: The Fresh Book Agent [Part 1]
The Downward Path: The Girl Who Went Astray [Part 3]
The Downward Path: The New Soubrette [Part 4]
The Downward Path: The Suicide [Part 5]
A Good Time with the Organ Grinder
The Growler Gang Catches a Tartar
How the Farmer Was Buncoed
How the Old Maid Got a Husband
How They Fired the Bum
An Impromptu Hairdresser
Insured Against Loss
May Day Parade
Maypole Dance
One on the Bum
The Rubberneck Boarders
Sherlock Holmes Baffled
Sidewalks of New York
The Thief and the Pie Woman
The Troublesome Fly
Uncle Reuben Lands a Kick
Why Mrs. McCarthy Went to the Ball
Jun [day undetermined]
Alligator Bait
The Arizona Doctor
A Career of Crime, No. 1: Start in Life
A Career of Crime, No. 2: Going the Pace
A Career of Crime, No. 3: Robbery & Murder
A Career of Crime, No. 4: In the Toils
A Career of Crime, No. 5: The Death Chair
The Census on Cherry Hill
The Champion Beer Drinker
The Clown and the See-Saw Fairies
A Cold Water Cure
Escape from Sing Sing
The Exposed Seance
A Gesture Fight in Hester Street
How Bridget Made the Fire
How He Saw the Eclipse
Love at 55
The Man in the Jimjams
The Masher's Waterloo
Mechanical Hair-Restorer
Not the Man She Waited for
Seeing Things at Night
Such a Quiet Girl, Too!
The Tell-Tale Kiss
The Tramp and the Burglar
Tramp in the Haunted House
A Tramp in the Well
Wifie Invades the Studio
A Yard of Frankfurters
Jul [day undetermined]
Allabad, the Arabian Wizard
Arrest of a Shoplifter
Bargain Day
The Black Storm

The Burglar-Proof Bed
A Champion Beer Drinker
A Convict's Punishment
Execution of a Spy
A Hair-Raising Episode
His Dad Caught Him Smoking
His Name Was Mud
Hoboken Fire
The Hoboken Holocaust
How Charlie Lost the Heiress
How They Got Rid of Mamma
A Jersey Skeeter
The Katzenjammer Kids Have a Love Affair
Love in the Dark
The Mail-Man in Coon Town
The Organ Grinder's Fourth of July
A Political Discussion
A Raid on a Woman's Poolroom
A Strike in a Dime Museum
Those Wedding Bells Shall Not Ring Out
Too Much of a Good Thing
The Tramp Gets Whitewashed
Trouble at the Christening
Trouble in Hogan's Alley
A Wake in "Hell's Kitchen"
Who Said Chicken?

Aug [day undetermined]
Eccentricities of an Adirondack Canoe
The 'Gator and the Pickaninny
"A Gone Goose"
A Launch Party in the Adirondacks
Living Pictures
M'lle Alma
The Narrows
Phrosine and Meledore
Pierrot's Problem, or How To Make a Fat Wife Out of Two Lean Ones
Rescue from a Harem
Rescue of a White Girl from the Boxers
The Shah's Return from Paris
The Slave Market
Steamer "Stowell" Running the Narrows
Temptation of St. Anthony
The Unfaithful Odalisque

Sep [day undetermined]
Accidents Will Happen
The Barber's Queer Customer
The Chinese Rubbernecks
A Dog Fight
"Drill, Ye Tarriers, Drill"
Family Troubles
Ghosts in a Chinese Laundry
Homer Davenport, the Cartoonist
Hon. B. B. Odell, Jr.
How the Artist Captured the Chinese Boxers
How the Magician Got the Best of the Installment Man
Indiana Whitecaps
The Magic Picture
"Shoo Fly"
Spooks at School
Tortured by Boxers
The Tribulations of an Amateur Photographer
What the Bathing Girls Did to the Kodak Fiend
Why Curfew Did Not Ring Last Night

Oct [day undetermined]
Boarding School Girls' Pajama Parade
A Flirtation
Fun in a Photograph Gallery
A Good Time Behind the Scenes
A Hot Time in the Dressing Room
How the Dude Got the Soubrette's Baggage
Jealousy in the Dressing Room
A Joke on the Old Maid
"The Kleptomaniacs"
Knock-out Drops on the Bowery
Scandal in the Custom House
Soubrettes in a Bachelor's Flat
They Led Her Husband Astray
A Thief in a Soubrette's Boarding House
Through the Key-Hole in the Door
A Visit to Baby Roger
Westminster Street
What the Jay Saw in the Studio
What they Do to Respectable Men in the Tenderloin
Where the Female Smuggler Hid the Lace

Nov [day undetermined]
Return of the Canadian Contingent

1901

Feb [day undetermined]
Medical Gymnastics

Mar [day undetermined]
Codfishing with Trawl
Drawing a Lobster Pot
Fertilizing Codfish Eggs
Unloading Cod
Unloading Halibut

Apr [day undetermined]
Artillery Drill at Annapolis
Band and Battalion of the U. S. Indian School
Basket Ball
Calisthenic Drill
Club Swinging, Carlisle Indian School
Deaf Mute Recitation
Dressmaking
Energizing Drill
Forging
Girls Dumbbell Drill
Heavy Gymnastics
The High Jump
The High School Cadets
Kindergarten Methods
Laboratory Study
A Language Lesson
Manual Training
A Muffin Lesson
Nature Study, the Rabbit
Physical Training
Pole Vaulting
Star Spangled Banner by a Deaf Mute
U. S. Naval Cadets Marching in Review

May [day undetermined]
Bass Fishing
Fulton Market
Hauling a Shad Net
In the Gypsy Camp
A Large Haul of Fish
"Laughing Ben"
A Mystic Re-Incarnation
On the Old Plantation
Unloading a Mackerel Schooner

Jun [day undetermined]
Bally-Hoo Cake Walk
Beautiful Orient
The Bridge of Sighs—Pan-American Exposition
The Court of Fountains—Pan-American Exposition
Esquimaux Dance
An Esquimaux Game
The Esquimaux Village
Fair Japan—Pan-American Exposition
Fountain, Tower, and Basins—Pan-American Exposition
The Indian Congress
Main Entrance to Pan-American Exp.
On the Midway—Pan-American Exposition
The Ostrich Farm—On the Midway
Panorama of Midway—Pan-American Exposition
Panoramic View Gov't Building, Pan. Am. Exp.
Propylaea and North End of Plaza, Pan. Am. Exp.
Scene in Beautiful Orient—Pan-American Exposition
Sevillenas Dance—Pan-American Exposition
Triumphal Bridge, Pan-American Exposition
Venice in America

Jul [day undetermined]
Boys Entering Free Bath
Boys Free Public Baths
Ladies Day at the Public Baths
On the Midway—Pan-American Exposition
Saturday at the Free Baths
Women of the Ghetto Bathing

Aug [day undetermined]
Broadway and Fourteenth St. Experimental
The Campus Martius
Centennial Parade
Detroit Mail Carriers
A Flower Parade
Industrial Floats
Landing of Cadillac
Steamship "Deutschland"
Unveiling Chair of Justice

Sep [day undetermined]
Arrival at Falls View Station
Capt. Schuyler Post of Philadelphia
Chapin Post of Buffalo
Cuyahoga Gorge
The Empire Theatre
Farragut Naval Post, Ohio State
Funeral of President McKinley
Headquarters, Staff and Band, Ohio State
Lambs Club, G. A. R.
The Living Flag
Lyttle Post of Cincinnati
Panorama, Public Square, Cleveland, O.

Oct [day undetermined]
Coaching for a Record

Oct 25 Convention of Railroad Passengers Agents
Panoramic View, Asheville, N. C.

1902

Mar [day undetermined]
Experimental. Southwestern Limited Train

Apr [day undetermined]
Century Wheelman, N. Y. City
48th Highlanders Regiment
Installation Ceremonies, Columbia University
Installation Ceremonies of President Butler
Pontoon Bridge Building

May [day undetermined]
A Private Supper at Heller's
Street Scene

Jun [day undetermined]
Lower New York
Over the Rail
They Found the Leak

Sep [day undetermined]
From the Crow's Nest

1903

Aug [day undetermined]
Railroad View—Experimental

1904

Jun [day undetermined]
Exhibition Fire Drill, Union Square, N. Y.

1907

Dec 21 Mr. Gay and Mrs.

1908

Jan 4 Professional Jealousy

Apr [day undetermined]
Colored Maid Getting Rid of a Suitor
Crowded Street-Congested Street Society
The Fisherman's Model
The Hallroom Boys Received Queer Freight
The Merry Widow at a Supper Party
Scene in a Dressing Room
That Awful Stork
Then Tramp He Woke Up
What the Dude Lost in the Dressing Room

May [day undetermined]
A False Alarm
Farmer Greene's Summer Boarders
Fun in the Hay
Man Under the Bed
Nellie's Camera

Jun [day undetermined]
Fluffy's New Corsets
The Girls Boxing Match
The Soul Kiss
Three Weeks
Too Many in Bed

Jun 19 The Man in the Box
Jun 26 Over the Hills to the Poor House
Jul 3 At the Crossroads of Life
Jul 7 The Kentuckian
Jul 10 The Stage Rustler
Jul 14 The Adventures of Dollie
Jul 17 The Fight for Freedom
Jul 21 The Black Viper
Jul 24 The Tavern-Keeper's Daughter
Jul 28 The Redman and the Child
Jul 31 Deceived Slumming Party
Aug 4 The Bandit's Waterloo: The Outwitting of an Andalusian Brigand by a Pretty Senora
Aug 7 A Calamitous Elopement: How It Proved a Windfall for Burglar Bill
Aug 11 The Greaser's Gauntlet
Aug 14 The Man and the Woman
Aug 18 The Fatal Hour
Aug 21 For Love of Gold

Aug 25 Balked at the Altar
Aug 28 For a Wife's Honor
Sep 1 Betrayed by a Handprint
Sep 8 The Girl and the Outlaw
Sep 11 Behind the Scenes: Where All Is Not Gold That Glitters
Sep 15 The Red Girl
Sep 18 The Heart of O Yama
Sep 22 Where the Breakers Roar
Oct 27 The Call of the Wild
Nov 3 After Many Years
Nov 6 The Pirate's Gold
Nov 10 Taming of the Shrew
Nov 13 The Guerrilla
Nov 20 The Ingrate
Nov 24 A Woman's Way
Dec 1 The Valet's Wife
Dec 8 The Feud and the Turkey
Dec 18 An Awful Moment
Dec 29 The Helping Hand

1909

Jan 1 One Touch of Nature
Jan 11 Love Finds a Way
Jan 18 Those Boys!
Jan 28 The Cord of Life
Feb 1 The Girls and Daddy
Feb 11 Tragic Love
Feb 22 The Golden Louis*
The Politician's Love Story
Feb 25 At the Altar
Mar 1 His Wife's Mother
Mar 4 A Fool's Revenge
Mar 8 The Wooden Leg
Mar 11 The Salvation Army Lass
Mar 15 The Lure of the Gown
Mar 18 The Voice of the Violin
Mar 25 A Burglar's Mistake
Apr 5 The Road to the Heart
Trying to Get Arrested
Apr 8 Schneider's Anti-Noise Crusade
Apr 12 A Sound Sleeper
Apr 15 Confidence
Apr 19 A Troublesome Satchel
Apr 22 The Drive for a Life
Apr 26 Lucky Jim
Twin Brothers
Apr 29 'Tis an Ill Wind That Blows No Good
May 3 The Eavesdropper
The Suicide Club
May 6 One Busy Hour
May 10 The French Duel
May 13 A Baby's Shoe
May 17 The Jilt
May 20 Resurrection
May 24 Eloping with Aunty
May 27 The Cricket on the Hearth
Jun 3 Eradicating Aunty
His Duty
Jun 10 The Lonely Villa
Jun 14 The Son's Return
Jun 17 The Faded Lillies
Jun 21 Was Justice Served?
Jun 24 The Peachbasket Hat
Jun 28 The Way of Man
Jul 1 The Necklace
Jul 5 The Message
Jul 15 The Friend of the Family
Jul 19 The Renunciation
Aug 9 Jones' Burglar
Aug 30 Pranks
Sep 6 "1776" or, The Hessian Renegades
Sep 27 Leather Stocking
Oct 4 Pippa Passes; or, The Song of Conscience
Oct 11 The Little Teacher
Nov 18 A Midnight Adventure
Dec 16 The Test
Dec 27 To Save Her Soul

1910

Jan 3 The Rocky Road
Jan 13 All on Account of the Milk
Jan 24 The Honor of His Family
Jan 31 The Cloister's Touch
Feb 7 The Course of True Love
Feb 28 The Final Settlement
Mar 3 The Newlyweds
Mar 17 The Love of Lady Irma
Mar 21 Faithful
Mar 31 His Last Dollar
The Smoker
Apr 14 The Kid
Apr 21 The Tenderfoot's Triumph
Apr 28 Up a Tree
May 2 The Gold-Seekers
May 9 Love Among the Roses
May 12 The Two Brothers
May 19 An Affair of Hearts
May 26 A Knot in the Plot
May 30 The Impalement
Jun 2 In the Season of Buds
Jun 6 A Child of the Ghetto
Jun 20 May and December
Never Again
Jun 27 A Child's Impulse
Jul 21 Serious Sixteen
Aug 18 An Old Story with a New Ending
When We Were in Our Teens
Sep 1 The Affair of an Egg
Muggsy Becomes a Hero
Sep 19 A Summer Tragedy
Oct 6 A Gold Necklace
How Hubby Got a Raise
Oct 13 A Lucky Toothache
The Masher
Oct 27 The Passing of a Grouch
The Proposal
Nov 10 Simple Charity
Nov 17 Love in Quarantine
The Troublesome Baby
Nov 24 His New Lid
Not So Bad as It Seemed
Dec 1 Effecting a Cure
Dec 8 Happy Jack, a Hero
Turning the Tables
Dec 22 The Recreation of an Heiress
White Roses
Dec 29 After the Ball
His Wife's Sweethearts

Marvin, Yvonne
1910
Jun 21 Thelma

Mary, Jules
1909
Aug 6 The Tragedy of Meudon

Masnier, M.
1909
May 12 The Hunter's Grief

Mathieu, Julienne
1908
Apr 12 Modern Sculptors
Nov 9 Beauty and the Beast

Matler
1907
Dec 7 Ben Hur

Matrowsky
1900
Aug [day undetermined]
Living Pictures

Matthews, Mr.
1910
Oct 10 The Monogrammed Cigarette
Oct 17 The Copper and the Crook

Maupassant, Guy de
1909
May 19 Père Milon
Jul 1 The Necklace
Aug 10 A Coward
1910
Feb 2 A Voice from the Fireplace

Maurice, Mary Birch
1910
Oct 15 The Legacy

Maxim, Hiram
1897
Oct [day undetermined]
A Maxim Gun in Action
Nov [day undetermined]
Maxim Firing Field Gun

Mazzantini, Luis
1902
Apr [day undetermined]
Great Bull Fight

Mead, William M., Admiral
1898
Oct [day undetermined]
Famous Battleship Captains—Philadelphia Peace Jubilee Parade
1905
Aug [day undetermined]
Scenes and Incidents, Russo-Japanese Peace Conference, Portsmouth, N.H.

Meade, Harry, Dr.
1901
Jun 8 Opening of the Pan-American Exposition showing Vice President Roosevelt Leading the Procession

Meilhac, Henri
1910
Feb 16 Carmen

Melford, George
1910
Aug 3 A Colonial Belle
Oct 26 The Strongest Tie
Nov 30 The Touch of a Child's Hand
Dec 7 Rachel

Melford, J.
1910
Nov 30 The Touch of a Child's Hand

Méliès, Gaston
1908
May 23 Catholic Centennial Parade
Jun 20 Boston Normal School Pageant
1909
Oct 13 The Stolen Wireless
Nov 24 The Red Star Inn
Dec 8 The Fatal Ball; or, The Miner's Daughter

Méliès, Georges
1899
Apr 10 A Trip to the Moon
May 13 The Enchanted Inn
Dec 25 Cinderella
1900
Apr 7 Four Heads Better Than One
Jun 30 A Mysterious Portrait
1901
Apr 6 The One Man Orchestra
Nov 23 A Christmas Dream
Dec [day undetermined]
The Fat and the Lean Wrestling Match
1902 [month undetermined]
The Man with the Rubber Head
May [day undetermined]
The Clown with the Portable Body
May 3 Blue Beard
Sep [day undetermined]
Reproduction, Coronation Ceremonies—King Edward VII
Oct 4 A Trip to the Moon
1903 [month undetermined]
The Cook's Revenge
The Famous Box Trick
Going to Bed Under Difficulties
A Midnight Episode
The Seven Capital Sins
Feb [day undetermined]
The Human Fly
The Impossible Feat of Balancing
Mephistopheles' School of Magic
Apr [day undetermined]
The Brahmin and the Butterfly
Gigantic Devil
Jun 13 The Cake Walk Infernal
The Enchanted Basket
The Marvelous Wreath
The Mysterious Box
Jun 27 The Enchanted Well
The Inn where No Man Rests
Jul 25 The Drawing Lesson; or, The Living Statue
The Mystical Flame
The Witch's Revenge
Aug 15 The Melomaniac
The Monster
The Oracle of Delphi
A Spiritualistic Photographer
Sep 5 The Fairyland; or, The Kingdom of the Fairies
Oct 17 The Apparition
The Infernal Caldron
Nov [day undetermined]
Alcrofrisbas, the Master Magician
Nov 7 Jack Jaggs & Dum Dum
Jupiter's Thunderbolts
10 Ladies in an Umbrella
Nov 21 Bob Kick, the Mischievous Kid
Extraordinary Illusions
Dec 9 The Ballet Master's Dream
Dec 12 The Damnation of Faust
Jack and Jim
Dec 19 The Magic Lantern
1904
Jan 9 The Terrible Turkish Executioner
Jan 23 A Moonlight Serenade; or, The Miser Punished.
Feb 6 Tit for Tat; or, A Good Joke on My Head
Feb 13 The Invisible Sylvia
Mar 5 The Bewitched Trunk
The Fugitive Apparitions
The Untamable Whiskers

Mar 12 The Clock Maker's Dream
Mar 26 A Miracle Under the Inquisition
Apr 2 Faust and Marguerite
Apr 30 Tchin-Chao, the Chinese Conjuror
May 7 The Wonderful Living Fan
Jun 4 The Cook in Trouble
The Devilish Plank
Jul 2 The Mermaid
Oct 29 An Impossible Voyage
Dec [day undetermined]
The Firefall
The Wandering Jew
1905
Apr 8 The King of Sharpshooters
The Living Playing Cards
May 13 The Lilliputian Minuet
Jun 17 A Mesmerian Experiment
Jun 24 The Palace of the Arabian Nights
Aug 19 An Adventurous Automobile Trip
Sep [day undetermined]
Stop Thief!
Sep 23 A Crazy Composer
Oct [day undetermined]
The Scheming Gambler's Paradise
Nov 4 Unexpected Fireworks
1906
Apr 7 A Mix-Up in the Gallery
May 5 A Desperate Crime
Jul 14 The Tramp and the Mattress Maker
Jul 21 The Hilarious Posters
Oct 6 Soap Bubbles
Oct 13 The Merry Frolics of Satan
Dec 15 The Mysterious Retort
Dec 20 The Witch
1907 [month undetermined]
Delirium in a Studio
Feb 16 Robert Macaire and Bertrand; or, The Troubles of a Hobo and His Pal, in Paris
Apr 20 Rogues' Tricks
Jun 29 Under the Seas
Jul 27 Tunneling the English Channel
Sep 21 The Eclipse; or, The Courtship of the Sun and the Moon
Nov 16 Sightseeing Through Whiskey
1908
Jan 18 The Knight of Black Art
Feb 8 The Good Luck of a "Souse"
Apr 12 Why That Actor Was Late
Apr 18 The Prophetess of Thebes
Apr 25 Long Distance Wireless Photography
May 9 In the Barber Shop
Jun 13 Side Show Wrestlers
Up-to-Date Clothes Cleaning
Aug 22 His First Job
The Indian Sorcerer
The Mischances of a Photographer
Sep 22 Not Guilty
A Tricky Painter's Fate
Sep 29 Buncoed Stage Johnnie
Fun with the Bridal Party
1909
Oct 27 Cinderella Up-to-Date

Melrose, Mat
1902
May [day undetermined]
The Absent Minded Clerk, Fly Paper and Silk Hat

Melville, Frank
1903
Jan [day undetermined]
Cake Walking Horses

Mérimée, Prosper
1910
Feb 16 Carmen
May 3 The Cigarette Maker of Seville

Mersereau, Violet
1909
May 3 The Suicide Club
May 27 The Cricket on the Hearth

Merwin, Bannister
1909
Jan 12 Where Is My Wandering Boy To-night?

Mesnier, M.
1910
Jul 28 The Hiding Place

Metenier, Oscar
1910
Mar 14 The Revenge of Dupont L'Anguille

Michealis, Sophus
1910
Mar 12 A Wedding During the French Revolution

Migé, Clement
1909
Sep 18 Calino Objects to Work
1910
Sep 3 Calino Takes New Lodgings
Nov 26 Calino Travels as a Prince

Miles, David
1908
Dec 29 The Helping Hand
1909
Jan 11 The Honor of Thieves
Jan 14 A Rural Elopement
Jan 18 The Criminal Hypnotist
Jan 28 The Cord of Life
Feb 1 The Girls and Daddy
Feb 4 The Brahma Diamond
Feb 11 Tragic Love
Feb 25 At the Altar
Mar 1 The Prussian Spy
Mar 8 The Roue's Heart*
The Wooden Leg
Mar 18 The Voice of the Violin
Mar 22 And a Little Child Shall Lead Them
Apr 1 A Drunkard's Reformation
Apr 5 The Road to the Heart
Apr 15 Confidence
Apr 19 Lady Helen's Escapade
Apr 26 Lucky Jim
Twin Brothers
Apr 29 'Tis an Ill Wind That Blows No Good
May 3 The Eavesdropper
May 20 Resurrection
May 24 Eloping with Aunty
Two Memories
May 27 The Cricket on the Hearth
May 31 What Drink Did
Jun 3 Eradicating Aunty
His Duty
Jun 7 The Violin Maker of Cremona
Jun 10 The Lonely Villa
Jun 17 The Faded Lillies
Jun 21 Was Justice Served?

Miles, E. C.
1909
Oct 24 [Johnson-Ketchel Fight Films]

Miles, Herbert J.
1903
Jun [day undetermined]
Market Street Before Parade
Over Route of Roosevelt Parade in an Automobile
Panorama, Union Square, San Francisco
President Reviewing School Children
The President's Carriage
Aug [day undetermined]
Horses Drawing in Seine
Horses Drawing Salmon Seine
Men Taking Fish from Salmon Seine
Sep [day undetermined]
Butchering and Cleaning Tables U. S. F. C.
Lifting Salmon Trap
Panorama of Beach and Cliff House
Raising Salmon Trap U. S. F. C.
Salmon Seining on Columbia River U. S. F. C.
1906 [month undetermined]
Head-On Collision at Brighton Beach Race Track, July 4th, 1906*
Apr [day undetermined]
A Trip Down Mount Tamalpais*
Dec [day undetermined]
O'Brien-Burns Contest, Los Angeles, Cal., Nov. 26th, 1906*
1907
Jun [day undetermined]
Shriners' Conclave at Los Angeles, Cal., May, 1907*
Squires, Australian Champion, in His Training Quarters*
Jul 13 International Contest for the Heavyweight Championship: Squires vs. Burns, Ocean View, Cal., July 4th, 1907*

Miles, Nelson A., General
1898 [month undetermined]
General Miles and Staff
Oct [day undetermined]
Major-General Nelson A. Miles, and Staff, in the Peace Jubilee Parade
1899
Jun [day undetermined]
Lieutenant-General Nelson A. Miles
Oct [day undetermined]
Admiral Dewey Leading Land Parade
1901
Mar 16 President McKinley and Escort Going to the Capitol
President McKinley Taking the Oath

Miller, Ashley
1910
Feb 1 A Japanese Peach Boy
Feb 11 A Queen of the Burlesque
Feb 18 A Trip to Mars
Feb 22 A Victim of Bridge
Feb 25 That Girl of Dixon's
Apr 15 Her First Appearance
Apr 26 Gallegher
Jun 3 The Piece of Lace
Jun 7 Mr. Bumptious on Birds
Jun 21 Bootles' Baby
Jul 15 How Bumptious Papered the Parlor
Sep 2 The Man Who Learned

Miller, Joseph, Captain
1899
Jun [day undetermined]
New York Naval Militia

Miller, W. C.
1909
Dec 9 The Redman's View
Dec 13 A Corner in Wheat
Dec 23 In Little Italy
Dec 27 To Save Her Soul
1910
Jan 6 The Dancing Girl of Butte
Jan 10 Her Terrible Ordeal
Jan 17 On the Reef
Jan 20 The Call
Feb 10 The Duke's Plan
Mar 7 The Thread of Destiny
Mar 21 Faithful
Mar 24 The Twisted Trail
Apr 18 Thou Shalt Not
May 16 Over Silent Paths
May 23 Ramona
Jun 2 In the Season of Buds
Jun 6 A Child of the Ghetto
Jun 13 In the Border States
Jun 23 The Marked Time-Table
Jul 14 A Child's Faith
Aug 4 Her Father's Pride
Aug 18 An Old Story with a New Ending
Aug 22 The Sorrows of the Unfaithful
Sep 5 A Summer Idyll
Sep 22 The Oath and the Man
Sep 26 Rose O' Salem-Town
Sep 29 Examination Day at School
Oct 10 That Chink at Golden Gulch
Oct 13 A Lucky Toothache
Nov 7 The Fugitive
Nov 10 Simple Charity
Nov 14 Sunshine Sue
Nov 28 A Plain Song
Dec 19 The Lesson
Dec 22 White Roses
Dec 29 His Wife's Sweethearts

Millet, Jean François
1910
Apr 28 The Angelus

Mills, Edward M.
1901
Jun 8 Opening of the Pan-American Exposition showing Vice President Roosevelt Leading the Procession

Minor, Thomas F.
1902
Nov [day undetermined]
Broncho Busting Scene, Championship of the World

Mistinguett, Mlle.
1909
Nov 17 Her Dramatic Career

Mitchell, Mr.
1910
Aug 3 A Colonial Belle

Mitchell, H. M.
1910
Mar 17 The Irish Boy
Jun 20 The Road to Happiness
Jul 7 Ferdie's Vacation
Dec 26 Making a Man of Him

Mitchell, James McC.
1901
Jun 8 Opening of the Pan-American Exposition showing Vice President Roosevelt Leading the Procession

Nau, E.
1909
Oct 22 Drink
Neason, Hazel
1909
Nov 27 Jean Valjean
1910
Oct 13 The Garden of Fate
Neidert
1899
Mar [day undetermined]
Bicycle Trick Riding, No. 2
Neil, Roy
1910
Jul 8 A Wireless Romance
Jul 29 The Unexpected Reward
Oct 4 More Than His Duty
Nov 15 Into the Jaws of Death
Dec 2 The Cowpuncher's Glove
Dec 30 The Romance of Hefty Burke
Neilson, Julia
1899 [month undetermined]
Beerbohm Tree, the Great English Actor
Nelson, J.
1910
Dec 1 Spoony Sam
Nepoti, Alberto
1910
Jan 12 Camille
Feb 16 Carmen
Apr 20 Othello
Nesbitt, Miriam
1908
Nov 3 Saved by Love
Newell
1903
Jan [day undetermined]
Newell and Chevet, the Famous Acrobats
Nicholls, George O.
1908
Sep 11 Behind the Scenes: Where All Is Not Gold That Glitters
Sep 18 The Heart of O Yama*
1909
May 13 A Baby's Shoe
May 17 The Jilt
Sep 27 Leather Stocking
Sep 30 Wanted, a Child
Oct 4 Pippa Passes; or, The Song of Conscience
Oct 11 The Little Teacher
Oct 14 A Change of Heart
Oct 18 His Lost Love
Oct 25 In the Watches of the Night
Oct 28 Lines of White on a Sullen Sea
Nov 1 What's Your Hurry?
Nov 8 The Restoration
Nov 11 The Light That Came
Nov 18 A Midnight Adventure
Nov 22 The Open Gate
Nov 25 The Mountaineer's Honor
Nov 29 In the Window Recess
The Trick That Failed
Dec 2 The Death Disc: A Story of the Cromwellian Period
Dec 6 Through the Breakers
Dec 23 In Little Italy
Dec 27 To Save Her Soul
Dec 30 The Day After
1910
Jan 3 The Rocky Road
Jan 10 Her Terrible Ordeal
Jan 24 The Honor of His Family
Jan 27 The Last Deal
Feb 3 The Woman from Mellon's
Feb 14 One Night, and Then —
Feb 17 The Englishman and the Girl
Feb 21 His Last Burglary
Mar 14 The Converts
Mar 24 The Twisted Trail
Apr 4 As It Is in Life
Apr 18 Thou Shalt Not
Apr 25 The Way of the World
Jun 6 A Child of the Ghetto
Jun 16 The Face at the Window
Jun 23 The Marked Time-Table
Jun 30 Muggsy's First Sweetheart
Jul 7 A Midnight Cupid
Jul 14 A Child's Faith
Jul 21 As the Bells Rang Out!
Jul 28 Unexpected Help
Aug 1 An Arcadian Maid
Aug 15 The Usurer
Aug 29 The Modern Prodigal
Sep 8 Little Angels of Luck
Sep 12 A Mohawk's Way
Sep 15 In Life's Cycle
Sep 26 Rose O' Salem-Town
Oct 3 The Iconoclast
Oct 24 The Message of the Violin
Nov 7 Waiter No. 5
Nov 14 Sunshine Sue
Nielsen, Martinius
1910
Nov 26 Kean; or, The Prince and the Actor
Nobles, Dolly
1910
Jul 18 The Phoenix
Nobles, Milton
1910
Jul 18 The Phoenix
Nomand, M.
1909
Aug 25 The Eternal Romance
Nonguet, Lucien
1903
Nov 7 Life of Napoleon
1904
Jan 16 Puss in Boots
Mar 26 The Passion Play
Oct 8 Around Port Arthur
1905
Jun 10 In the Mining District
Jun 24 Christian Martyrs
Aug 5 Mutiny on Man-of-War in Odessa
1906
Jan 27 The Deserter
Apr [day undetermined]
Revolution in Russia
Ten Wives for One Husband*
Jul 14 Dogs Used as Smugglers
Dec 15 The Female Spy
1907
Jun 29 Struggle for Life
1908
Nov 9 Beauty and the Beast
1910
Dec 21 Max Goes Skiing
Normand, Mabel
1910
Jun 10 Over the Garden Wall
Norris, Frank
1909
Dec 13 A Corner in Wheat
Norton, Roy
1910
Mar 11 His First Valentine
Apr 8 Sandy the Substitute
Aug 16 His New Family
Sep 13 The Great Secret
Novelli, Amleto
1910
Jun 30 Faust
Nuitter, Charles Louis Etienne
1910
Jan 18 The Toymaker's Secret
Nunes, M.
1909
Nov 17 Her Dramatic Career
Oakley, Annie
1900
Mar [day undetermined]
Annie Oakley
1910
Oct 11 Actors' Fund Field Day
O'Brien
1896
Nov [day undetermined]
The Drunken Acrobat
O'Brien, Mr.
1897
May [day undetermined]
Horse Dancing Couchee Couchee
O'Brien, Daniel
1903
Jan [day undetermined]
Leaping Tournament over Elephants
O'Brien, J.
1910
Oct 22 Pals of the Range
O'Brien, J. J.
1901
Apr [day undetermined]
Japanese Wrestling
Jiu Jitsu, the Japanese Art of Self-Defense
Odell, B. B., Jr., Governor
1900
Sep [day undetermined]
Hon. B. B. Odell, Jr.
1901
Jun 8 Opening of the Pan-American Exposition showing Vice President Roosevelt Leading the Procession
Odetta
1903
Jan [day undetermined]
Odetta, Chinese Dance
Odetta, Rope Dance No. 1
Odetta, Rope Dance No. 2
Odetta, Spanish Dance
Ogle, Charles
1910
Jan 4 Pardners
Mar 18 Frankenstein
Apr 1 Michael Strogoff
Apr 15 Her First Appearance
Nov 23 Through the Clouds
Olcott, Sidney
1906
Jun 14 The Village Cut-Up
1907
Dec 7 Ben Hur
1908
Mar 7 Henry Hudson
Nov 20 Hannah Dustin: The Border Wars of New England
1909
Jan 8 A Florida Feud; or, Love in the Everglades
Jan 29 The Octoroon: The Story of the Turpentine Forest
May 21 The Girl Spy: An Incident of the Civil War
Jun 18 A Priest of the Wilderness: Father Jogue's Mission to the Iroquois
Oct 15 The Man and the Girl
Dec 17 The Law of the Mountains
1910
Jan 28 The Man Who Lost
Apr 1 The Further Adventures of the Girl Spy
Apr 27 The Sacred Turquoise of the Zuni
May 18 The Aztec Sacrifice
May 25 The Cliff Dwellers
Jun 22 The Wanderers
Sep 23 The Conspiracy of Pontiac; or, At Fort Detroit in 1763
Nov 23 The Lad from Old Ireland
Dec 14 Seth's Temptation
Dec 28 The Girl Spy Before Vicksburg
Dec 30 The Stranger
Oldfield, Barney
1910
Sep 17 World's Championship Motor Races
Omegna, Roberto
1909
Nov 29 Leopard Hunting in Abysinnia
Omers, Les
1903
Jul 11 Sleeping Beauty
O'Neil, Barry
1910
Mar 15 The Actor's Children
Mar 22 St. Elmo
Apr 15 A 29-Cent Robbery
Jun 3 The Girl of the Northern Woods
Jun 10 The Writing on the Wall
Jul 26 Uncle Tom's Cabin
O'Neil, K.
1906
Aug [day undetermined]
Kathleen Mavoureen
Opperman, Frank
1910
Mar 31 The Smoker
Apr 4 As It Is in Life
Apr 7 A Rich Revenge
Apr 21 The Tenderfoot's Triumph
Apr 28 Up a Tree
May 23 Ramona
May 26 A Knot in the Plot
Orman, James B., Governor
1903
Feb [day undetermined]
Christian Endeavor Greeting
Ormiston-Smith, F.
1903
Jan 17 The Ascent of Mount Blanc
1907
Mar 30 The Arlberg Railway

Osterman, Kathryn
1900
May [day undetermined]
The Art of "Making Up"
1903
Jul [day undetermined]
Making a Welch Rabbit
Strictly Fresh Eggs
The Unfaithful Wife: Murder and Suicide [Part 3]
The Unfaithful Wife: The Fight [Part 2]
The Unfaithful Wife: The Lover [Part 1]
A Welsh Rabbit
Aug [day undetermined]
The Girl at the Window
"He Loves Me, He Loves Me Not"
In My Lady's Boudoir
Lucky Kitten!
The Rose
A Search for Evidence
Sweets for the Sweet
The Widow
1904
Oct [day undetermined]
The Lost Child
Dec [day undetermined]
The "Strenuous" Life; or, Anti-Race Suicide
O'Sullivan, Anthony
1906
Mar 29 The Black Hand
1907
Oct 28 Yale Laundry
Dec 14 Dr. Skinum
Dec 21 Mr. Gay and Mrs.
1908
Jan 22 Lonesome Junction
Mar 7 The Yellow Peril
Apr 7 A Famous Escape
Apr 15 The King of the Cannibal Islands
Apr 22 Hulda's Lovers
May 6 The Sculptor's Nightmare
Jun 2 Thompson's Night Out
Jun 9 'Ostler Joe
Jun 16 The Invisible Fluid
Jun 19 The Man in the Box
Jul 3 At the Crossroads of Life
Jul 7 The Kentuckian
Jul 10 The Stage Rustler
Jul 17 The Fight for Freedom
Jul 21 The Black Viper
Jul 31 Deceived Slumming Party
Aug 11 The Greaser's Gauntlet
Sep 4 Monday Morning in a Coney Island Police Court
1909
Apr 29 'Tis an Ill Wind That Blows No Good
May 3 The Suicide Club
May 6 The Note in the Shoe
May 24 Eloping with Aunty
Two Memories
May 31 What Drink Did
Jun 14 The Son's Return
Jun 17 The Faded Lillies
Jul 1 The Necklace
Jul 19 The Renunciation
Jul 22 Jealousy and the Man
Jul 26 A Convict's Sacrifice
Aug 19 Mrs. Jones' Lover; or, "I Want My Hat"
Aug 23 The Indian Runner's Romance
Aug 30 The Heart of an Outlaw
Sep 13 Getting Even
Sep 23 A Fair Exchange
Sep 30 The Awakening
Wanted, a Child
Oct 18 His Lost Love
Oct 25 In the Watches of the Night
Nov 1 The Gibson Goddess
Nov 11 The Light That Came
Nov 15 Two Women and a Man
Nov 29 The Trick That Failed
Dec 20 A Trap for Santa Claus
Dec 30 Choosing a Husband
1910
Jan 10 Her Terrible Ordeal
Feb 3 The Woman from Mellon's
Feb 24 Taming a Husband
Feb 28 The Final Settlement
Mar 7 The Thread of Destiny
Mar 21 Faithful
Mar 31 His Last Dollar
Apr 4 As It Is in Life
Apr 7 A Rich Revenge
Apr 28 Up a Tree
May 2 The Gold-Seekers
May 19 An Affair of Hearts
May 26 A Knot in the Plot
Jun 9 A Victim of Jealousy
Jun 20 Never Again
Jul 18 A Flash of Light
Aug 15 The Usurer
Sep 12 A Mohawk's Way
Oct 6 How Hubby Got a Raise
Oct 10 That Chink at Golden Gulch
Oct 13 The Masher
Oct 20 The Banker's Daughters
Oct 27 The Proposal
Otis, Elita P.
1909
Jun 1 Oliver Twist
Otis, Harrison Gray, General
1900
Mar [day undetermined]
Funeral of Major-General Henry W. Lawton
1902 [month undetermined]
Gen. Otis with His Troops in the Philippines
Ott, Fred
1894
Jan [day undetermined]
Edison Kinetoscopic Record of a Sneeze, January 7, 1894
Otter, Lieut.-Col.
1899
Aug [day undetermined]
In Fighting Trim
Outcault, R. T.
1904
Mar [day undetermined]
Section of Buster Brown Series, Showing a Sketch of Buster by Outcault
Overton, Winfield S., Lieutenant
1901
Mar 16 President McKinley and Escort Going to the Capitol
Page, Mistress
1910
Nov 24 The Merry Wives of Windsor
Page, Arthur
1908
Aug 29 Napoleon and the English Sailor
Paget, Alfred
1909
Jul 29 The Slave
Aug 5 The Mended Lute
1910
Feb 10 The Duke's Plan
Apr 11 A Romance of the Western Hills
May 9 Love Among the Roses
May 16 Over Silent Paths
Jun 23 The Marked Time-Table
Jul 7 A Midnight Cupid
Jul 14 A Child's Faith
Jul 21 As the Bells Rang Out!
Jul 25 The Call to Arms
Jul 28 Unexpected Help
Aug 15 The Usurer
Aug 25 Wilful Peggy
Sep 26 Rose O' Salem-Town
Oct 17 The Broken Doll
Dec 26 Winning Back His Love
Paley, William
1898 [month undetermined]
Battle of San Juan Hill
Red Cross at the Front
Sailors Landing Under Fire
Surrender of General Toral
Aug [day undetermined]
Cuban Ambush
Major General Shafter
Mules Swimming Ashore at Daiquiri, Cuba
Pack Mules with Ammunition on the Santiago Trail, Cuba
Packing Ammunition on Mules, Cuba*
Shooting Captured Insurgents
U. S. Troops Landing at Daiquiri, Cuba
Sep [day undetermined]
Troops Making Military Road in Front of Santiago
1899
Jun [day undetermined]
Skirmish of Rough Riders
U. S. Infantry Supported by Rough Riders at El Caney
Panzer, Paul
1905
Jul [day undetermined]
Stolen by Gypsies
Nov 4 The Escape from Sing Sing
Dec 2 Monsieur Beaucaire, the Adventures of a Gentleman of France
1906
Nov [day undetermined]
And the Villain Still Pursued Her; or, The Author's Dream
1908
Feb 1 The Thieving Hand
Feb 8 Francesca da Rimini; or, The Two Brothers
Jun 6 Romeo and Juliet, a Romantic Story of the Ancient Feud Between the Italian Houses of Montague and Capulet
1909
Aug 10 Princess Nicotine; or, The Smoke Fairy
Sep 11 An Alpine Echo; or, The Symphony of a Swiss Music Box
Nov 13 Launcelot and Elaine
1910
Nov 12 A Gambler's End
Dec 24 Sunshine in Poverty Row
Papillon, Zizi
1903
Dec 9 The Ballet Master's Dream
Parker, Alton B., Judge
1904
Aug [day undetermined]
Judge Parker & Mayor McClellan at Esopus
Parkman, Francis
1910
Sep 23 The Conspiracy of Pontiac; or, At Fort Detroit in 1763
Pasquali, Ernesto M.
1909
Dec 25 Alberno & Rosamunda
Paul, Robert W.
1902
May [day undetermined]
The Children's Tea Party
Paulham
1910
Feb 16 Aviation at Los Angeles, Calif.
Pearson, Virginia
1910
Oct 14 On Her Doorsteps
Pereiet, Monsieur
1903 [month undetermined]
Broad Sword Contest
Perier, J.
1910
Jul 20 Manon
Periolat, George
1909
Apr 17 Forgiven; or, Father and Son*
Perley, Charles G.
1909
Feb 8 Edgar Allen Poe
Jun 24 The Mexican Sweethearts*
Perrault, Charles
1901
Oct 26 Little Red Riding Hood
1902
May 3 Blue Beard
1904
Jan 16 Puss in Boots
1907
Mar 16 Cinderella
1909
Aug 14 The Wild Ass's Skin
Sep 10 Tom Thumb
Perret, Leonce
1909
Apr 21 A Pair of White Gloves
1910
Jun 11 The Marriage of Esther
Jun 18 Esther and Mordecai
Aug 27 The Vow, or, Jephthah's Daughter*
Oct 29 The Life of Molière
Perrot, Phillipe
1900
Aug [day undetermined]
Living Pictures
Perry, Pansy
1907
Mar 9 The Girl from Montana

Persons, Thomas
1908
Jan 4 The Four-Footed Hero
Peters, Madison C., Reverend
1909
Dec 4 The Life of Moses
1910
Jan 4 Forty Years in the Land of Midian [The Life of Moses Part II]
Jan 25 The Plagues of Egypt and the Deliverance of the Hebrew [The Life of Moses Part III]
Feb 12 The Victory of Israel [The Life of Moses Part IV]
Feb 19 The Promised Land [The Life of Moses Part V]
La Petite Adelaide
1897
Apr [day undetermined]
La Petite Adelaide
Pezzaglia, A.
1910
Apr 20 Othello
Phelan, B.
1909
May 21 The Girl Spy: An Incident of the Civil War
Philip, John W., Admiral
1898 [month undetermined]
Battleship Texas
Oct [day undetermined]
Famous Battleship Captains—Philadelphia Peace Jubilee Parade
Philippe, D.
1908
Mar 14 Remorse
Phillips, Edwin R.
1909
Apr 10 Napoleon: the Man of Destiny
May 29 He Couldn't Dance, but He Learned
1910
Jan 22 A Pair of Schemers; or, My Wife and My Uncle
Mar 12 Taming a Grandfather
Apr 15 The Call of the Heart
May 24 Convict No. 796
Jun 11 The Altar of Love
Sep 2 A Life for a Life
Oct 8 The Sage, the Cherub and the Widow
Nov 19 Francesca Da Rimini
Dec 9 He Who Laughs Last
Pickett, Bill
1910
Mar 16 A Bullfight in Mexico
Pickford, Jack
1909
Aug 30 Pranks
Sep 30 Wanted, a Child
Dec 16 In a Hempen Bag
Dec 27 To Save Her Soul
1910
Jan 13 All on Account of the Milk
Mar 31 The Smoker
Apr 14 The Kid
Apr 21 The Tenderfoot's Triumph
May 19 An Affair of Hearts
Aug 29 The Modern Prodigal
Sep 29 Examination Day at School
Oct 17 The Broken Doll
Nov 7 Waiter No. 5
Nov 28 A Plain Song
Dec 22 White Roses
Pickford, Lottie
1909
Jul 12 The Cardinal's Conspiracy
Jul 15 Tender Hearts
Aug 23 The Indian Runner's Romance*
1910
Feb 3 The Woman from Mellon's
Oct 6 A Gold Necklace
Dec 15 His Sister-in-Law
Pickford, Mary
1909
May 24 Two Memories
Jun 3 His Duty
Jun 7 The Violin Maker of Cremona
Jun 10 The Lonely Villa
Jun 14 The Son's Return
Jun 28 The Way of Man
Jul 1 The Necklace
Jul 8 The Country Doctor
Jul 15 Tender Hearts
Jul 19 The Renunciation
Jul 22 Sweet and Twenty
Aug 9 They Would Elope
Aug 19 His Wife's Visitor
Aug 23 The Indian Runner's Romance
Aug 26 "Oh, Uncle"
The Seventh Day
Aug 30 The Heart of an Outlaw
Sep 2 The Little Darling
Sep 6 "1776" or, The Hessian Renegades
Sep 13 Getting Even
Sep 16 The Broken Locket
Sep 30 The Awakening
Oct 11 The Little Teacher
Oct 18 His Lost Love
Oct 25 In the Watches of the Night
Nov 1 What's Your Hurry?
Nov 8 The Restoration
Nov 11 The Light That Came
Nov 18 A Midnight Adventure
Nov 25 The Mountaineer's Honor
Nov 29 The Trick That Failed
Dec 16 The Test
Dec 27 To Save Her Soul
Dec 30 The Day After*
1910
Jan 13 All on Account of the Milk
Feb 3 The Woman from Mellon's
Feb 17 The Englishman and the Girl
Mar 3 The Newlyweds
Mar 7 The Thread of Destiny
Mar 24 The Twisted Trail
Mar 31 The Smoker
Apr 4 As It Is in Life
Apr 7 A Rich Revenge
Apr 11 A Romance of the Western Hills
May 5 The Unchanging Sea
May 9 Love Among the Roses
May 23 Ramona
Jun 2 In the Season of Buds
Jun 9 A Victim of Jealousy
Jun 20 May and December
Never Again
Jun 27 A Child's Impulse
Jun 30 Muggsy's First Sweetheart
Jul 11 What the Daisy Said
Jul 25 The Call to Arms
Aug 1 An Arcadian Maid
Aug 18 When We Were in Our Teens
Aug 22 The Sorrows of the Unfaithful
Aug 25 Wilful Peggy
Sep 1 Muggsy Becomes a Hero
Oct 6 A Gold Necklace
Oct 13 A Lucky Toothache
Nov 7 Waiter No. 5
Nov 10 Simple Charity
Nov 21 The Song of the Wildwood Flute
Nov 28 A Plain Song
Dec 22 White Roses
Pilar-Morin, Mme.
1909
Nov 2 Comedy and Tragedy
1910
Feb 1 A Japanese Peach Boy
May 3 The Cigarette Maker of Seville
May 13 Carminella
Jun 3 The Piece of Lace
Aug 30 From Tyranny to Liberty
Nov 29 The Greater Love
Pineschi, Lamberto
1909
May 22 Sapho
Plessis
1906
Apr [day undetermined]
Troublesome Fishbone
Plumb, E. Hay
1907
Jun 1 The New Policeman*
Pomeroy, Robert W.
1901
Jun 8 Opening of the Pan-American Exposition showing Vice President Roosevelt Leading the Procession
Poore, O. L.
1907
Sep 16 An Acadian Elopement
Poplar, Fred
1903
Jan [day undetermined]
Fred Poplar and His Pal
Porter, Edwin S.
1899
Jun [day undetermined]
Strange Adventure of New York Drummer
Oct [day undetermined]
After the Race—Yachts Returning to Anchorage
"Columbia" Winning the Cup
"Shamrock" and "Columbia" Rounding the Outer Stake Boat
"Shamrock" and "Columbia" Rounding the Outer Stake Boat, No. 2
"Shamrock" and "Columbia" Yacht Race—First Race
"Shamrock" and "Erin" Sailing
Nov [day undetermined]
Pictures Incidental to Yacht Race
"Shamrock" and "Columbia" Yacht Race—1st Race, No. 2
1900
Mar [day undetermined]
An Artist's Dream
The Mystic Swing*
Uncle Josh in a Spooky Hotel
Uncle Josh's Nightmare
Nov [day undetermined]
Congress of Nations
Dec [day undetermined]
A Wringing Good Joke
1901
Feb 23 Terrible Teddy, the Grizzly King
Mar 2 The Finish of Bridget McKeen
Follow the Leader
A Joke on Grandma
Apr 27 Pie, Tramp and the Bulldog
The Tramp's Dream
May [day undetermined]
Another Job for the Undertaker
Fun in a Butcher Shop
Jul [day undetermined]
The Esquimaux Village
The Photographer's Mishap
The Tramp's Miraculous Escape
Aug [day undetermined]
Aunt Sallie's Wonderful Bustle
Circular Panorama of Electric Tower
Esquimaux Game of Snap-the-Whip
Esquimaux Leap-Frog
Panoramic View of Electric Tower from a Balloon
Photographing a Country Couple
The Tramp and the Nursing Bottle
"Weary Willie" and the Gardener*
What Happened on Twenty-Third Street, New York City
Oct 19 The Martyred Presidents
Pan-American Exposition by Night
Nov [day undetermined]
Catching an Early Train
Panorama of Esplanade by Night
A Phenomenal Contortionist
Nov 16 Execution of Czolgosz, with Panorama of Auburn Prison
Dec [day undetermined]
The Artist's Dilemma
The Mysterious Cafe
1902 [month undetermined]
Happy Hooligan Turns Burglar
Jan [day undetermined]
The Twentieth Century Tramp; or, Happy Hooligan and His Airship
Uncle Josh at the Moving Picture Show
Feb [day undetermined]
Capture of the Biddle Brothers
Apr [day undetermined]
The Burlesque Suicide
Fun in a Bakery Shop
May [day undetermined]
Appointment by Telephone
Burning of St. Pierre [Martinique]
Mt. Pelee in Eruption and Destruction of St. Pierre [Martinique]*
Mt. Pelee Smoking Before Eruption [St. Pierre, Martinique]*
Jul 15 Jack and the Beanstalk
Oct [day undetermined]
The Bull and the Picnickers
1903
Jan [day undetermined]
Life of an American Fireman
May [day undetermined]
Fireboat "New Yorker" in Action
Lehigh Valley Black Diamond Express
New York City Police Parade
New York Harbor Police Boat Patrol Capturing Pirates
Panorama of Blackwell's Island
Panorama of Riker's Island
Panorama Water Front and Brooklyn Bridge from East River
Sorting Refuse at Incinerating Plant, New York City

Steamscow "Cinderella" and Ferryboat "Cincinnati"
The Still Alarm
Jun [day undetermined]
"Africander" Winning the Suburban Handicap, 1903
69th Regiment, N. G. N. Y.
Aug [day undetermined]
Down Where the Wurzburger Flows
The Gay Shoe Clerk
Rube and Mandy at Coney Island
Seashore Frolics
Street Car Chivalry
Subub Surprises the Burglar
The Unappreciated Joke
Sep [day undetermined]
Baby Class at Lunch
Miss Jessie Cameron, Champion Child Sword Dancer
Miss Jessie Dogherty, Champion Female Highland Fling Dancer
New York Caledonian Club's Parade
Old Fashioned Scottish Reel
Orphans in the Surf
Throwing the Sixteen Pound Hammer
Uncle Tom's Cabin
Oct [day undetermined]
The Animated Poster
Casey and His Neighbor's Goat
An East River Novelty
East Side Urchins Bathing in a Fountain
The Extra Turn
The Heavenly Twins at Lunch
The Heavenly Twins at Odds
The Messenger Boy's Mistake
New York City Public Bath
The Physical Culture Girl
A Romance of the Rail
Two Chappies in a Box
Nov [day undetermined]
Buster's Joke on Papa
What Happened in the Tunnel
Dec [day undetermined]
Buster's Joke on Papa
The Great Train Robbery
How Old Is Ann?
The Office Boy's Revenge
Under the Mistletoe

1904
Jan [day undetermined]
Circular Panorama of the Horse Shoe Falls in Winter
Crossing Ice Bridge at Niagara Falls
Ice Skating in Central Park, N. Y.
Sliding Down Ice Mound at Niagara Falls
Treloar and Miss Marshall, Prize Winners at the Physical Culture Show in Madison Square Garden
Feb [day undetermined]
Animated Painting
Casey's Frightful Dream
Cohen's Advertising Scheme
Halloween Night at the Seminary
Ice Boating on the North Shrewsbury, Red Bank, N. J.
Little German Band
Midnight Intruder
Old Maid and Fortune Teller
Wifey's Mistake
Mar [day undetermined]
Buster and Tige Put a Balloon Vendor Out of Business
Buster Brown and the Dude
Buster Makes Room for His Mama at the Bargain Counter
Buster's Dog to the Rescue
Pranks of Buster Brown and His Dog Tige
Section of Buster Brown Series, Showing a Sketch of Buster by Outcault
Sleighing in Central Park, New York
Apr [day undetermined]
Babe and Puppies
Japanese Acrobats
Apr 20 Battle of Chemulpo Bay
Skirmish Between Russian and Japanese Advance Guards
May [day undetermined]
Annual Parade, New York Fire Department
The Cop Fools the Sergeant
Dog Factory
Hold Up in a Country Grocery Store
Jun [day undetermined]
Elephants Shooting the Chutes at Luna Park [Coney Island]
Inter-Collegiate Athletic Association Championships, 1904
"Weary Willie" Kidnaps a Child
Jul [day undetermined]
Canoeing on the Charles River, Boston, Mass.
Inter-Collegiate Regatta, Poughkeepsie, N. Y., 1904
Scenes in an Infant Orphan Asylum
Jul 16 White Star S. S. Baltic Leaving Pier on First Eastern Voyage
Aug [day undetermined]
Fire and Flames at Luna Park, Coney Island [An Attraction at Coney Island]
Sep [day undetermined]
Capture of Yegg Bank Burglars
European Rest Cure
How a French Nobleman Got a Wife Through the New York Herald "Personal" Columns
Oct [day undetermined]
Maniac Chase
Nov [day undetermined]
City Hall to Harlem in 15 Seconds, via the Subway Route
Miss Lillian Shaffer and Her Dancing Horse
Opening Ceremonies, New York Subway, October 27, 1904
Parsifal
Railroad Smashup
A Rube Couple at a County Fair
"Weary Willie" Kisses the Bride
Dec [day undetermined]
Bad Boy's Joke on the Nurse
The Ex-Convict
Scarecrow Pump
The "Strenuous" Life; or, Anti-Race Suicide*
The "Strenuous" Life; or, Anti-Race Suicide

1905
Feb [day undetermined]
The Kleptomaniac
Mar [day undetermined]
Inauguration of President Roosevelt. President-Elect Roosevelt, Vice-President-Elect Fairbanks and Escort Going to the Capitol
Inauguration of President Roosevelt. Taking the Oath of Office
Inauguration of President Roosevelt. the Grand Inaugural Parade
President Roosevelt's Inauguration
Apr [day undetermined]
The Seven Ages
May [day undetermined]
How Jones Lost His Roll
Opening of Belmont Park Race Course
Start of Ocean Race for Kaiser's Cup
Jul [day undetermined]
The Burglar's Slide for Life
Coney Island at Night
Hippodrome Races, Dreamland, Coney Island
[On] a [Good Ole] 5¢ Trolley Ride
Raffles, the Dog
Stolen by Gypsies
The Whole Dam Family and the Dam Dog
Aug [day undetermined]
The Electric Mule
Empire State Express, the Second, Taking Water on the Fly
June's Birthday Party
Mystic Shriners' Day, Dreamland, Coney Island
Scenes and Incidents, Russo-Japanese Peace Conference, Portsmouth, N.H.
Sep [day undetermined]
The Boarding School Girls
The Little Train Robbery
The White Caps
Oct 5 Poor Algy
Oct 24 The Watermelon Patch
Nov 2 Down on the Farm
Nov 6 The Miller's Daughter
Nov 15 Everybody Works but Father
Nov 27 The Train Wreckers
Dec [day undetermined]
The Night Before Christmas
Dec 5 Desperate Encounter Between Burglar and Police
Life of an American Policeman
A River Tragedy

1906
Feb [day undetermined]
Dream of a Rarebit Fiend
Mar [day undetermined]
Phoebe Snow
Apr [day undetermined]
A Winter Straw Ride
Jun [day undetermined]
Life of a Cowboy
The Terrible Kids
Three American Beauties
Jul [day undetermined]
Waiting at the Church
Aug [day undetermined]
How the Office Boy Saw the Ball Game
Kathleen Mavoureen
Oct [day undetermined]
Getting Evidence, Showing the Trials and Tribulations of a Private Detective
Nov [day undetermined]
The Honeymoon at Niagara Falls

1907
Feb [day undetermined]
Poor John
Waiting at the Church
Mar 2 The Teddy Bears
Apr 6 Daniel Boone; or, Pioneer Days in America
May 18 Lost in the Alps
Jun 29 Cohen's Fire Sale
Aug 3 The Nine Lives of a Cat
Aug 31 Stage Struck
Sep 14 Rivals
Sep 28 A Race for Millions
Oct 19 Jack the Kisser
Nov 2 Midnight Ride of Paul Revere
Nov 23 Three American Beauties [No. 2]
The Trainer's Daughter; or, A Race for Love
Dec 7 College Chums
Dec 14 Laughing Gas
Dec 21 The Little Girl Who Did Not Believe in Santa Claus

1908
Jan 18 Rescued from an Eagle's Nest
The Suburbanite's Ingenious Alarm
Feb 1 Fireside Reminiscences
A Yankee Man-o-Warsman's Fight for Love
Feb 15 A Sculptor's Welsh Rabbit Dream
Feb 29 Cupid's Pranks
Mar 7 Playmates
Mar 14 Nellie, the Pretty Typewriter
Mar 21 Animated Snowballs
Stage Memories of an Old Theatrical Trunk
Mar 28 A Country Girl's Seminary Life and Experiences
Apr 11 Tale the Autumn Leaves Told
Apr 12 The Cowboy and the Schoolmarm
Apr 22 Nero and the Burning of Rome
Apr 29 The Merry Widow Waltz Craze
May 6 Bridal Couple Dodging Cameras
May 13 The Gentleman Burglar
May 20 Curious Mr. Curio
May 27 The Painter's Revenge
Jun 3 Skinny's Finish
Jun 10 The Blue and the Gray; or, The Days of '61
Jun 17 Honesty Is the Best Policy
Jun 24 Love Will Find a Way
Jul 1 Pioneers Crossing the Plains in '49
Jul 15 The Boston Tea Party
The Little Coxswain of the Varsity Eight
Jul 22 The Face on the Barroom Floor
Fly Paper
Aug 5 Tales the Searchlight Told
Aug 19 When Ruben Comes to Town
Sep 2 A Comedy in Black and White
Heard over the Phone
Sep 9 The Devil
Sep 15 Wifey's Strategy
Sep 22 Buying a Title
Sep 29 Pocahantas — A Child of the Forest
Oct 2 Sandy McPherson's Quiet Fishing Trip
Ten Pickaninnies
Oct 9 A Voice from the Dead
Oct 16 Ex-Convict No. 900
Oct 20 Minstrel Mishaps; or, Late for Rehearsal
Oct 27 The Army of Two (An Incident During the American Revolution)

Nov 3 Saved by Love
Nov 10 The Lovers' Telegraphic Code
Nov 17 Colonial Virginia
The New Stenographer
Nov 27 The King's Pardon
Dec 4 Miss Sherlock Holmes
The Old Maids' Temperance Club
Dec 11 The Angel Child
Dec 15 Cocoa Industry, Trinidad, British West Indies
Dec 22 An Unexpected Santa Claus
1909
Jan 1 A Persistent Suitor
Jan 12 Where Is My Wandering Boy To-night?
Jan 22 A Burglar Cupid
Jan 29 A Modest Young Man
May 4 A Road to Love
May 7 The Doctored Dinner Pail
May 14 The Pony Express
1910
Jan 11 Bear Hunt in the Rockies
Jan 21 The Luck of Roaring Camp
Mar 15 Fruit Growing, Grand Valley, Colorado (The Results of Irrigation)
Apr 5 The Heart of a Rose
Apr 6 Partners

Potel, Victor
1910
Sep 7 A Dog on Business
Sep 17 Hank and Lank Joyriding
Sep 28 Hank and Lank: They Dude Up Some
Oct 12 Hank and Lank: They Get Wise to a New Scheme
Oct 19 Hank and Lank: Uninvited Guests
Oct 26 Hank and Lank: They Take a Rest
Nov 8 Hank and Lank: Life Savers
Nov 22 Hank and Lank: as Sandwich Men
Dec 20 Hank and Lank

Potter, Bertie
1907
Apr 27 The Doll's Revenge
1909
Apr 24 Professor's Anti-Gravitation

Potter, Gertie
1907
Apr 27 The Doll's Revenge
Jun 1 The New Policeman
Sep 21 The Ghost Holiday
Oct 12 A Soldier's Jealousy
Oct 19 A Modern Don Juan
Nov 16 Dumb Sagacity
A Tramp's Dream of Wealth
1908
Nov 12 When Women Rule
1909
Apr 24 A Thoughtless Beauty
May 1 An Unfortunate Bath

Potter, Henry
1907
Jun 1 The New Policeman

Potter, Hetty
1907
Jun 1 The Tramp's Dream

Powell, Frank
1909
Jun 3 His Duty
Jun 17 The Faded Lillies
Jun 21 Was Justice Served?
Jul 5 The Message
Jul 8 The Country Doctor
Jul 12 The Cardinal's Conspiracy
Jul 15 The Friend of the Family
Tender Hearts
Jul 29 The Slave
Aug 2 A Strange Meeting
Aug 5 The Mended Lute
Aug 16 With Her Card
Aug 19 His Wife's Visitor
Aug 23 The Indian Runner's Romance
Aug 26 The Seventh Day
Aug 30 The Heart of an Outlaw
The Mills of the Gods
Sep 6 "1776" or, The Hessian Renegades
Sep 13 The Children's Friend
Sep 16 The Broken Locket
Oct 7 Fools of Fate
Oct 25 In the Watches of the Night
Nov 4 Nursing a Viper
Nov 15 Two Women and a Man
Nov 18 Sweet Revenge
Dec 2 The Death Disc: A Story of the Cromwellian Period
Dec 13 A Corner in Wheat
1910
Jan 3 The Rocky Road
Jan 13 All on Account of the Milk
Feb 7 The Course of True Love
Mar 3 The Newlyweds
Mar 10 In Old California
Mar 17 The Love of Lady Irma
The Man
Mar 31 The Smoker
Apr 14 The Kid
Apr 21 The Tenderfoot's Triumph
Apr 28 Up a Tree
May 26 A Knot in the Plot
May 30 The Impalement
Jun 20 May and December
Never Again
Aug 18 An Old Story with a New Ending
When We Were in Our Teens
Sep 1 The Affair of an Egg
Muggsy Becomes a Hero
Sep 19 A Summer Tragedy
Oct 6 A Gold Necklace
How Hubby Got a Raise
Oct 13 A Lucky Toothache
The Masher
Oct 27 The Passing of a Grouch
The Proposal
Nov 17 Love in Quarantine
The Troublesome Baby
Nov 24 His New Lid
Not So Bad as It Seemed
Dec 1 Effecting a Cure
Dec 8 Happy Jack, a Hero
Turning the Tables
Dec 22 The Recreation of an Heiress
White Roses
Dec 29 After the Ball
His Wife's Sweethearts

Powers, James T.
1905
Nov [day undetermined]
Digesting a Joke (Jas. T. Powers)

Powers, Pat
1910
Jul 8 Reproduction of Jeffries-Johnson Championship Contest

Pratt, William W.
1901
Jun [day undetermined]
Ten Nights in a Bar-Room: Death of Little Mary
Ten Nights in a Bar-Room: Death of Slade
Ten Nights in a Bar-Room: Murder of Willie
Ten Nights in a Bar-Room: The Fatal Blow
Ten Nights in a Bar-Room: Vision of Mary
1909
Jun 9 Ten Nights in a Bar-room

Pre, Renee
1910
Jun 3 The Two Portraits

Prescott, Vivian
1910
Jun 16 The Face at the Window
Jun 27 A Child's Impulse
Jul 18 A Flash of Light
Jul 25 The Call to Arms
Aug 11 A Salutary Lesson
Dec 26 Winning Back His Love

Prescott, William H.
1910
May 18 The Aztec Sacrifice

Price, Kate
1910
Dec 2 Jack Fat and Jim Slim at Coney Island

Prince, M.
1909
Nov 17 Her Dramatic Career

Principi, Mirra
1910
May 25 Estrellita; or, The Invasion of the French Troops in Portugal

Prion, L.
1900
Aug [day undetermined]
Living Pictures

Prior, Herbert
1907
Aug 31 Stage Struck
1909
Feb 22 The Politician's Love Story
Mar 4 A Fool's Revenge*
Mar 11 The Salvation Army Lass
Apr 8 Schneider's Anti-Noise Crusade
Apr 19 Lady Helen's Escapade
Apr 26 Twin Brothers
Apr 29 'Tis an Ill Wind That Blows No Good
May 3 The Suicide Club
May 6 One Busy Hour
May 24 Two Memories
May 27 The Cricket on the Hearth
Jun 3 Eradicating Aunty
Jun 7 The Violin Maker of Cremona
Jun 10 A New Trick
Jun 14 The Son's Return
Jun 21 Was Justice Served?
Jul 1 The Necklace
1910
Mar 11 His First Valentine
Aug 12 The Attack on the Mill
Nov 4 The Little Station Agent
Nov 23 Through the Clouds

Pugacheff
1910
Nov 12 World's Wrestling Champions

Quinlan, J. F.
1899
Sep [day undetermined]
International Collegiate Games—100 Yards Dash

Quirk, William A.
1909
Jun 24 The Mexican Sweethearts
Jul 12 The Cardinal's Conspiracy
Jul 19 The Renunciation
Jul 22 Sweet and Twenty
Aug 2 A Strange Meeting
Aug 9 They Would Elope
Aug 19 His Wife's Visitor
Aug 26 "Oh, Uncle"
Aug 30 The Heart of an Outlaw
Sep 2 The Little Darling
Sep 13 Getting Even
Sep 27 Leather Stocking
Oct 11 The Little Teacher
Oct 14 A Change of Heart
Oct 28 Lines of White on a Sullen Sea
Nov 1 The Gibson Goddess
What's Your Hurry?
Nov 4 Nursing a Viper
Nov 18 A Midnight Adventure
Dec 6 Through the Breakers
Dec 16 The Test
Dec 30 Choosing a Husband
1910
Jan 6 The Dancing Girl of Butte
Jan 20 The Call
Jan 27 The Last Deal
Feb 3 The Woman from Mellon's
Feb 14 One Night, and Then —
Mar 31 His Last Dollar
The Smoker
Apr 7 A Rich Revenge
Apr 28 Up a Tree
May 19 An Affair of Hearts
May 26 A Knot in the Plot
Jun 20 May and December
Never Again
Jun 30 Muggsy's First Sweetheart
Jul 21 Serious Sixteen
Aug 18 When We Were in Our Teens
Sep 1 Muggsy Becomes a Hero
Sep 24 A Simple Mistake
Nov 19 The Other Way
Nov 23 How Rastus Gets His Turkey
Dec 28 Running Away from a Fortune

Raleigh, Walter, Sir
1909
Aug 6 Lochinvar

Randall, Bernard
1910
Apr 29 She Wanted to Marry a Hero

Randall, D. L.
1910
Aug 2 An Unfair Game

Ranous, William V.
1907
Mar 9 The Spy, a Romantic Story of the Civil War
Aug 10 The Easterner, or, A Tale of the West
Aug 24 Man, Hat and Cocktail, a New Drink, but an Old Joke
1908
Apr 12 Jealousy
Apr 19 Macbeth, Shakespeare's Sublime Tragedy

Jun 6 Romeo and Juliet, a Romantic Story of the Ancient Feud Between the Italian Houses of Montague and Capulet
Sep 28 Richard III, a Shakespearian Tragedy
1909
Feb 27 Saul and David: The Biblical Story of the Shepherd Boy Who Became King of the Israelites
Mar 27 King Lear
Sep 4 The Galley Slave
Oct 25 Hiawatha
Nov 1 Love's Stratagem
Nov 27 Jean Valjean
1910
Feb 5 Twelfth Night

Ransdall, Sergeant-at-Arms
1901
Mar 16 President McKinley Taking the Oath

Rasmussen, Holger
1910
Nov 26 Kean; or, The Prince and the Actor

Raymond, Charles
1905
Jul [day undetermined]
Bishop and Burglar*
Aug [day undetermined]
How Jones Saw the Derby*
1907
Jul 20 Dick Turpin*
1908
May 2 Lazy Jim's Luck*
May 30 The Fireman's Daughter*
Aug 15 Uncle's Rejected Present*
Sep 12 The Diamond Thieves*
Oct 17 When Other Lips*
Nov 7 A Jilted Woman's Revenge*
A Night Alarm*
Our Village Club Holds a Marathon Race*
1909
Mar 22 Royalist's Wife*
May 8 Baby's Chum
Jul 24 The Would-Be Acrobats*

Rea, Isabel
1910
Aug 25 For the Sunday Edition
Dec 29 Unreasonable Jealousy

Reade, Charles
1910
Jul 26 Peg Woffington

Red Wing
1908
May 8 The White Squaw
1909
Jun 25 Cowboy's Narrow Escape
Jul 2 A True Indian's Heart
Oct 9 For Her Sake; or, Two Sailors and a Girl
Oct 12 Red Wing's Gratitude
1910
Mar 1 The Cowboy and the School Marm
Mar 8 The Indian and the Cowgirl
Apr 8 Red Wing's Loyalty
Apr 15 Red Wing's Constancy
Apr 22 Adventures of a Cowpuncher
May 6 Love and Money
May 20 The Mexican's Jealousy
Sep 20 For the Love of Red Wing
Nov 4 Red Wing and the White Girl
Nov 15 The Flight of Red Wing

Redfern, Jasper
1904 [month undetermined]
The Monkey and the Ice Cream

Reed, Langford
1908
Jan 18 Anxious Day for Mother
Pied Piper of Hamlin
Jan 20 The Water Babies; or, The Little Chimney Sweep
Feb 17 The Soldier's Wedding
Apr 11 The Captain's Wives
The Downfall of the Burglars' Trust
The Scandalous Boys
May 2 Poor Aunt Matilda
May 9 The Memory of His Mother
Jun 13 Mr. Brown Has a Tile Loose
Three Sportsmen and a Hat
Jul 25 Three Maiden Ladies and a Bull
Aug 1 Follow Your Leader and the Master Follows Last
1909 [month undetermined]
Robin Hood and His Merry Men
Mar 22 A Wild Goose Chase
Apr 17 Puritan Maid
Apr 24 Nancy; or, The Burglar's Daughter

May 8 The Cavalier's Wife
Romance of the Crafty Usurper and the Young King
May 22 Favorite Doll
Jul 3 Modern Cinderella

Regent Street Rajah
1909
Feb 10 The Guardian of the Bank

Regnier, Mlle.
1910
Jul 20 Manon

Regustus, B.
1907
Dec 14 Laughing Gas

Reichgott, D.
1910
Sep 8 Baseball, That's All

Reid, Hal
1910
Aug 18 Human Hearts
Dec 12 A Tale of the Sea

Reid, Wallace
1910
Jul 18 The Phoenix

Renee, Carl
1910
Aug 27 The Vow, or, Jephthah's Daughter

Renot, Delphine
1910
Jun 27 Caesar in Egypt

Reviere
1897
Oct [day undetermined]
A Paced Bicycle Race

Reynolds, Lynn
1910
Jun 9 The Range Riders

Rhodes, Cecil
1899 [month undetermined]
Rt. Honorable Cecil Rhodes

Rianz, Mlle.
1910
Jun 27 Caesar in Egypt

Rice
1899
Sep [day undetermined]
International Collegiate Games

Rice, John C.
1896 [month undetermined]
The Kiss
1900
Oct [day undetermined]
"The Kleptomaniacs"

Ricketts, Thomas
1908
Dec 9 A Christmas Carol
1909
Sep 8 Justified
Sep 22 Gratitude
Oct 20 A Woman's Wit
Oct 27 Maud Muller
Nov 10 The Game
1910
Jan 5 The Adventuress
Jan 8 His Only Child
Mar 23 The Hand of Uncle Sam
May 4 The Stolen Fortune
Jul 13 An Advertisement Answered
Jul 20 The Thief
Jul 27 A Fair Exchange
Nov 17 The Lure of the City
Dec 5 Vera, the Gypsy Girl

Riley, James Whitcomb
1910
May 12 There, Little Girl, Don't Cry
Sep 25 The Ole Swimmin Hole

Ringheim, Viking
1909
Sep 4 Cycle Rider and the Witch

Rising, W. H.
1905
Feb [day undetermined]
The Kleptomaniac

Rixey, Dr.
1899
Jun [day undetermined]
President McKinley

Robbas, Henry
1901
Jun 8 Opening of the Pan-American Exposition showing Vice President Roosevelt Leading the Procession

Robbins, A. D.
1904
Jan [day undetermined]
Trick Bicycle Riding

Robbins, J.
1909
Aug 18 Wonders of Nature
Dec 25 The Heart of a Cowboy

Roberti, Lydia De
1909
Nov 1 Nero; or, The Burning of Rome
1910
Feb 16 The Silent Piano
May 25 Estrellita; or, The Invasion of the French Troops in Portugal

Roberts, Frederick, Earl
1899 [month undetermined]
Lord Roberts Embarking for South Africa
1900 [month undetermined]
Earl Roberts
Earl Roberts and General Baden Powell
Earl Roberts and Staff

Robertson
1910
Sep 17 World's Championship Motor Races

Robinne, Gabrielle
1909
Feb 17 The Assassination of the Duke of Guise

Robinson, Gertrude
1908
Dec 8 The Feud and the Turkey
Dec 15 The Test of Friendship
Dec 18 An Awful Moment
1909
Jan 1 One Touch of Nature
Jan 21 The Fascinating Mrs. Francis
Feb 1 The Girls and Daddy
Mar 25 A Burglar's Mistake
Apr 22 The Drive for a Life
Aug 30 The Heart of an Outlaw
Sep 6 "1776" or, The Hessian Renegades
Sep 16 The Broken Locket
Oct 4 Pippa Passes; or, The Song of Conscience
Oct 18 His Lost Love
Nov 4 Nursing a Viper
Nov 22 The Open Gate
Dec 2 The Death Disc: A Story of the Cromwellian Period
1910
Feb 3 The Woman from Mellon's
Feb 14 One Night, and Then —
Mar 17 The Love of Lady Irma
Jul 4 The Purgation
Jul 11 What the Daisy Said
Jul 14 A Child's Faith
Aug 18 An Old Story with a New Ending
Sep 1 The Affair of an Egg
Sep 5 A Summer Idyll
Sep 19 A Summer Tragedy
Oct 10 That Chink at Golden Gulch
Oct 13 The Masher
Oct 22 In the Gray of the Dawn

Robinson, Walter C. "Spike"
1910
Feb 9 Spike's Battle

Robinson, William C.
1910
Jul 18 A Flash of Light
Jul 21 As the Bells Rang Out!
Oct 27 The Proposal
Nov 24 His New Lid
Dec 1 Effecting a Cure
Dec 22 White Roses
Dec 29 His Wife's Sweethearts

Robson, May
1908
Oct 24 A Night Out; or, He Couldn't Go Home until Morning

Roche, Madaline
1910
May 11 Cleopatra

Rodriguez, Mlle.
1898 [month undetermined]
Mexican Dance

Roe, Nat
1910
Apr 13 Ice Scooters on Lake Ronkonkoma

Roeber, Ernest
1901
Dec [day undetermined]
Roeber Wrestling Match

Rogers, George
1904 [month undetermined]
The Russian Army in Manchuria
Rollini, Z.
1904
Sep 24 Drama in the Air
Roma, Roma T.
1897 [month undetermined]
He and She
Roosevelt, Alice
1902 [month undetermined]
Launch of the Kaiser's Yacht "Meteor"
Feb [day undetermined]
Christening and Launching Kaiser Wilhelm's Yacht "Meteor"
Roosevelt, Kermit
1910
May 26 Roosevelt in Paris
Roosevelt, Theodore
1898
Apr [day undetermined]
Theodore Roosevelt
Sep [day undetermined]
Col. Theodore Roosevelt and Officers of His Staff
1902 [month undetermined]
Launch of the Kaiser's Yacht "Meteor"
President and Prince at Washington
Feb [day undetermined]
Christening and Launching Kaiser Wilhelm's Yacht "Meteor"
Apr [day undetermined]
President Roosevelt Reviewing the Troops at Charleston Exposition [South Carolina]
1910
Apr 18 Roosevelt in Africa
May 26 Roosevelt in Paris
Jun 4 [King Edward's Funeral]
Jun 18 Roosevelt's Reception in New York
Sep 17 Cowboy and Indian Frontier Celebration
Roosevelt, Theodore, Mrs.
1902
Apr [day undetermined]
President Roosevelt Reviewing the Troops at Charleston Exposition [South Carolina]
Root, Elihu, Secretary
1901
Mar 16 President McKinley and Escort Going to the Capitol
Rosaman
1905
Dec [day undetermined]
Intercollegiate Cross Country Run
Rose, Frank O.
1907
Dec 7 Ben Hur
Rosemond, Anna
1910
Mar 22 St. Elmo
Mar 29 She's Done It Again
Apr 29 She Wanted to Marry a Hero
May 13 The Best Man Wins
May 20 Cupid at the Circus
May 27 The Winter's Tale
Jun 3 The Girl of the Northern Woods
Jun 7 The Two Roses
Jun 21 Thelma
Jun 28 Tempest and Sunshine
Jul 26 Uncle Tom's Cabin
Aug 12 Lena Rivers
Aug 19 She Stoops to Conquer
Oct 11 Pocahontas
Rosen, Roman Romanovich, Count
1905
Aug [day undetermined]
Scenes and Incidents, Russo-Japanese Peace Conference, Portsmouth, N.H.
Rosenthal, Joe
1905
Nov [day undetermined]
Hiawatha
1909
May 8 What William Did
Rosetti, Romeo
1907
Mar [day undetermined]
The Electric Belt
Ross, Charles
1897
Apr [day undetermined]
Death of Nancy Sykes
Rostand, Edmond
1909
Jun 17 Cyrano de Bergerac
Rottjer, H.
1907
Dec 7 Ben Hur
Roubert, M.
1910
Jul 26 Uncle Tom's Cabin, Part 1
Jul 29 Uncle Tom's Cabin, Part 2
Jul 30 Uncle Tom's Cabin, Part 3
Rouet
1909
Jun 23 The Grandfather
Rowe, Nicholas
1908
Oct 27 Jane Shore
Rubenstein, L. M.
1910
Nov 21 Caught by the Camera
Ruhlin, Gus
1901
Dec [day undetermined]
Ruhlin at His Training Quarters
Ruhlin Boxing with "Denver" Ed. Martin
Ruhlin Sparring in His Training Quarters
Dec 14 Ruhlin in His Training Quarters
Dec 21 Jeffries and Ruhlin Sparring Contest at San Francisco, Cal., Nov. 15, 1901—Five Rounds
Russell, Lillian
1906
Nov [day undetermined]
Lillian Russell
Russell, W.
1909
Feb 17 Tag Day
Russell, William
1910
Dec 2 John Halifax, Gentleman
Dec 20 Looking Forward
Dec 27 The Vicar of Wakefield
Dec 30 Hypnotized
Rust, E. C.
1901
Sep [day undetermined]
International Field Sports
Ryan, J. H., Mrs.
1910
Oct 31 Two Little Waifs
Nov 21 The Song of the Wildwood Flute
Sackville, Gordon
1910
Sep 30 Ononko's Vow
St. Clair, Miss *could be same as* **Sinclair,**
1908
Dec 11 The Angel Child
St. Elmo
1901
Nov [day undetermined]
A Phenomenal Contortionist
St. Leons, The
1903
Jan [day undetermined]
The Five Acrobats, St. Leons
St. Pierre, Bernardine
1910
Nov 15 Paul and Virginia
Sais, Marin
1910
Feb 5 Twelfth Night
Sampson, William T., Rear Admiral
1898 [month undetermined]
Cruiser New York
1899
Oct [day undetermined]
Admiral Dewey Leading Land Parade
Sandeau, Jules
1909
May 12 The Hunter's Grief
Sandow, Eugene
1894
May [day undetermined]
Souvenir Strip of the Edison Kinetoscope [Sandow, the Modern Hercules]
1896
Sep [day undetermined]
Sandow
Sanger, Eugene
1910
Oct 22 In the Gray of the Dawn
Santley, Fred
1910
Apr 5 Daddy's Double
Santschi, Tom
1909
Apr 29 Mephisto and the Maiden
Jun 17 In the Sultan's Power
1910
Mar 10 Across the Plains
Sarashe Sisters
1894 [month undetermined]
Imperial Japanese Dance
Sardou, Victorien
1908
Sep 18 The Heart of O Yama
1909
Jun 9 La Tosca
Saroni, Gilbert
1901
Mar [day undetermined]
The Old Maid in the Horsecar
Mar 9 The Old Maid Having Her Picture Taken
1903
Jan [day undetermined]
Gilbert Saroni Preparing for His Act
Goo Goo Eyes
Old Maid's First Visit to a Theatre
The Old Maid's Lament
Sarony
1900
Aug [day undetermined]
Living Pictures
Saulle, Mr.
1907
Nov 23 The Trainer's Daughter; or, A Race for Love
Savage, Cowden
1900
Jul [day undetermined]
Champion Polo Players
Sawyer, Laura
1909
Jan 12 Where Is My Wandering Boy To-night?
Dec 24 Faust
1910
Sep 20 An Unselfish Love
Nov 23 Through the Clouds
Scalanghe, Angelo
1910
Nov 2 The Slave of Carthage
Schiller, Johann
1909
Nov 22 The Hostage
1910
Aug 3 The Glove
Schley, Winfield S., Rear Admiral
1898 [month undetermined]
Cruiser Brooklyn
1899
Oct [day undetermined]
Admiral Dewey Leading Land Parade
Schneider, Max
1910
Oct 22 In the Gray of the Dawn
Schultze, Carl E.
1902
May [day undetermined]
The Boys Help Themselves to Foxy Grandpa's Cigars
The Boys, Still Determined, Try It Again on Foxy Grandpa, with the Same Result
The Boys Think They Have One on Foxy Grandpa, but He Fools Them
The Boys Try to Put One Up on Foxy Grandpa
The Creators of Foxy Grandpa
Foxy Grandpa and Polly in a Little Hilarity
Foxy Grandpa Shows the Boys a Trick or Two with the Tramp
Scott, Senator
1900
Sep [day undetermined]
Republican National Committee of 1900

Scott, Walter, Sir
1909
Mar 13 Kenilworth
Seabert, C. F.
1906
Aug [day undetermined]
Kathleen Mavoureen
Seay, Charles M.
1910
Dec 14 Pigs Is Pigs
Seigmann, George
1909
May 6 The Note in the Shoe
Sennett, Mack
1908
Mar 28 Old Isaacs, the Pawnbroker*
Apr 29 The King's Messenger
May 6 The Sculptor's Nightmare
Jun 2 Thompson's Night Out
Jun 16 The Invisible Fluid
Jun 26 Over the Hills to the Poor House
Jul 7 The Kentuckian
Jul 10 The Stage Rustler
Jul 21 The Black Viper
Jul 31 Deceived Slumming Party
Aug 18 The Fatal Hour
Sep 1 Betrayed by a Handprint
Sep 4 Monday Morning in a Coney Island Police Court
Sep 8 The Girl and the Outlaw*
Sep 11 Behind the Scenes: Where All Is Not Gold That Glitters
Sep 15 The Red Girl
Sep 18 The Heart of O Yama
Sep 22 Where the Breakers Roar
Sep 25 A Smoked Husband
Oct 2 The Devil
Oct 9 Father Gets in the Game
Oct 16 The Vaquero's Vow
Oct 23 Romance of a Jewess
Oct 27 The Call of the Wild
Oct 30 Concealing a Burglar
Nov 6 The Pirate's Gold
Nov 13 The Guerrilla
Nov 17 The Song of the Shirt
Nov 27 The Clubman and the Tramp
Dec 1 The Valet's Wife
Dec 4 Money Mad
Dec 8 The Feud and the Turkey
Dec 11 The Reckoning
Dec 15 The Test of Friendship
Dec 18 An Awful Moment
Dec 25 Mr. Jones at the Ball
Dec 29 The Helping Hand
1909
Jan 4 The Maniac Cook
Jan 11 The Honor of Thieves
Love Finds a Way
Jan 14 A Rural Elopement
The Sacrifice
Jan 25 Those Awful Hats
Feb 1 The Girls and Daddy
Feb 4 The Brahma Diamond
Feb 8 A Wreath in Time
Feb 11 Tragic Love
Feb 15 The Curtain Pole
Feb 22 The Politician's Love Story
Feb 25 At the Altar
Mar 1 His Wife's Mother
The Prussian Spy
Mar 4 A Fool's Revenge
Mar 8 The Wooden Leg
Mar 18 The Voice of the Violin
Mar 22 And a Little Child Shall Lead Them
Mar 25 A Burglar's Mistake
Mar 29 Jones and His New Neighbors
Apr 1 A Drunkard's Reformation
Apr 5 The Road to the Heart
Apr 8 A Rude Hostess
Apr 12 A Sound Sleeper
Apr 19 A Troublesome Satchel
Apr 26 Lucky Jim
Apr 29 'Tis an Ill Wind That Blows No Good
May 3 The Suicide Club
May 6 One Busy Hour
May 10 Jones and the Lady Book Agent
May 17 The Jilt
May 20 Resurrection
May 31 What Drink Did
Jun 10 The Lonely Villa
A New Trick
Jun 14 The Son's Return
Jun 17 Her First Biscuits
Jun 21 Was Justice Served?
Jun 24 The Mexican Sweethearts
Jun 28 The Way of Man
Jul 5 The Message
Jul 22 Jealousy and the Man
Jul 26 A Convict's Sacrifice
Jul 29 The Slave
Aug 2 A Strange Meeting
Aug 5 The Mended Lute
Aug 9 Jones' Burglar
Aug 12 The Better Way
Aug 16 With Her Card
Aug 23 The Indian Runner's Romance
Aug 26 The Seventh Day
Aug 30 The Heart of an Outlaw
Sep 2 The Little Darling
Sep 13 Getting Even
Sep 16 The Broken Locket
Sep 20 In Old Kentucky
Sep 23 A Fair Exchange
Sep 27 Leather Stocking
Sep 30 The Awakening
Oct 21 The Expiation
Oct 25 In the Watches of the Night
Nov 18 A Midnight Adventure
Dec 20 A Trap for Santa Claus
Dec 23 In Little Italy
Dec 30 Choosing a Husband
The Day After
1910
Jan 6 The Dancing Girl of Butte
Jan 13 All on Account of the Milk
Jan 20 The Call
Feb 24 Taming a Husband
Mar 7 The Thread of Destiny
Mar 10 In Old California
Mar 14 The Converts
Mar 17 The Love of Lady Irma
Mar 21 Faithful
Mar 24 The Twisted Trail
Mar 28 Gold Is Not All
Apr 4 As It Is in Life
Apr 7 A Rich Revenge
Apr 28 Up a Tree
May 2 The Gold-Seekers
May 12 The Two Brothers
May 19 An Affair of Hearts
May 26 A Knot in the Plot
Jun 2 In the Season of Buds
Jun 9 A Victim of Jealousy
Jun 20 Never Again
Jun 27 A Child's Impulse
Jul 4 The Purgation
Jul 7 A Midnight Cupid
Jul 14 A Child's Faith
Aug 1 An Arcadian Maid
Aug 18 When We Were in Our Teens
Sep 1 The Affair of an Egg
Sep 19 A Summer Tragedy
Sep 29 Examination Day at School
Oct 6 A Gold Necklace
Oct 13 A Lucky Toothache
Oct 17 The Broken Doll
Oct 27 The Passing of a Grouch
Nov 17 Love in Quarantine
Nov 24 Not So Bad as It Seemed
Dec 1 Effecting a Cure
Dec 29 His Wife's Sweethearts
Serena, Gustavo
1910
Jun 30 Faust
Sergine, Mlle.
1909
Dec 12 La Grande Breteche
Severin, M.
1909
Feb 3 Incriminating Evidence
Seylor, Suzanne
1908
Oct 31 Hamlet, Duel Scene with Laertes
Shaffer, Mr.
1907
Aug 31 Stage Struck
Shaffer, Lillian
1903
Jan [day undetermined]
Cake Walking Horses
1904
Nov [day undetermined]
Miss Lillian Shaffer and Her Dancing Horse
Shafter, Major General
1898 [month undetermined]
Surrender of General Toral
Aug [day undetermined]
Major General Shafter
Shakespeare, William
1899 [month undetermined]
Beerbohm Tree, the Great English Actor
1908
Feb 29 Othello
Sep 19 As You Like It
Nov 10 Taming of the Shrew
Dec 1 Julius Caesar, an Historical Tragedy
1909
Dec 11 Macbeth
Dec 25 A Midsummer Night's Dream
1910
Feb 2 Hamlet, Prince of Denmark
Feb 5 Twelfth Night
Apr 20 Othello
May 27 The Winter's Tale
Jun 4 Macbeth
Nov 24 The Merry Wives of Windsor
Sharkey, Tom
1899
Nov [day undetermined]
Jeffries-Sharkey Contest
Shaw, Brinsley
1910
Jul 20 The Thief
Shea, William
1905
Sep 30 The Servant Girl Problem
1907
Dec [day undetermined]
The Shaughraun, an Irish Romance
1908
Jun 6 Romeo and Juliet, a Romantic Story of the Ancient Feud Between the Italian Houses of Montague and Capulet
1909
Jul 3 Washington Under the American Flag
1910
Jun 3 Davy Jones' Parrot
Jun 17 Davy Jones' Landladies
Jul 9 Becket
Jul 22 Davy Jones and Captain Bragg
Oct 18 Auld Robin Grey
Oct 21 Davy Jones' Domestic Troubles
Sheffield Fire Brigade
1903
Sep [day undetermined]
A Daring Daylight Burglary
Sheldon, Edward
1909
Mar 11 The Salvation Army Lass
Shelley, Mr.
1907
Sep 14 Rivals
Shelley, Mary Wollstonecraft
1910
Mar 18 Frankenstein
Shepard, Iva
1910
Mar 31 The Wife of Marcius
Apr 7 Hugo, the Hunchback
Sheridan
1907
Dec 7 Ben Hur
Sherry, J. Barney
1905
Sep 23 Raffles, the Amateur Cracksman
1909
Sep 10 The Paymaster
Oct 29 Mexican's Crime
1910
Jan 21 The Luck of Roaring Camp
Jan 25 A Romance of the Prairie
Feb 8 The Ten of Spades; or, A Western Raffle
Mar 18 Mexican's Ward
Mar 22 The Man from Texas
May 13 Lost for Many Years
May 27 Perils of the Plains
Jun 10 Saved from the Redmen
Jun 21 The Sea Wolves
Jun 28 Her Terrible Peril
Shubert, Marie
1903 [month undetermined]
German Dance
Shumway, Leonard C.
1909
Aug 5 She Would Be an Actress
Sicotte, E.
1909
Nov 24 The Red Star Inn

Sigsbee, Charles D., Captain
1898 [month undetermined]
Captain Sigsbee on Deck of the U. S. Battleship Texas
Apr [day undetermined]
Captain Sigsbee
Silvain, M.
1909
Nov 14 Rigoletto
Silveon
1903
Aug [day undetermined]
On the Flying Rings
Silveon and Emerie "On the Web"
Simone, Charles
1910
Sep 15 In Life's Cycle
Sims, George R.
1908
Jun 9 'Ostler Joe
Sinclair, Miss *could be same as* **St. Clair,**
1909
Jan 12 Where Is My Wandering Boy To-night?
Slevin, Jim
1906
Jun 28 The Paymaster
Nov 15 The Tunnel Workers
Dec 8 Skyscrapers
Smalley, Phillips
1910
Oct 22 In the Gray of the Dawn
Oct 29 The Armorer's Daughter
Smith *could be same as* **Smith, Blair**
1905
Dec 2 Monsieur Beaucaire, the Adventures of a Gentleman of France
Smith, Postmaster General
1901
Mar 16 President McKinley and Escort Going to the Capitol
Smith, Albert
1900
Nov [day undetermined]
Congress of Nations
Smith, Albert E.
1907
Jul 13 Oliver Twist
1910
Feb 5 Twelfth Night
Smith, B. *could be same as* **Smith, Blair**
1901
Sep 21 President McKinley's Speech at the Pan-American Exposition
1902
May [day undetermined]
Mt. Pelee in Eruption and Destruction of St. Pierre [Martinique]
Mt. Pelee Smoking Before Eruption [St. Pierre, Martinique]
Smith, Blair *could be same as* **Smith, B.**
1903
Dec [day undetermined]
The Great Train Robbery
1910
Mar 22 St. Elmo
Mar 29 She's Done It Again
Apr 5 Daddy's Double
Apr 15 The Old Shoe Came Back
A 29-Cent Robbery
Smith, E.
1908
May 9 Tit for Tat; or, Outwitted by Wit
Smith, F. Percy
1909
Jul 3 Dissolution of Parliament
Smith, George A.
1900
Mar [day undetermined]
Photographing the Ghost
1901
Jun 29 The Inexhaustible Cab
1902
May [day undetermined]
The Absent Minded Clerk, Fly Paper and Silk Hat
Sep [day undetermined]
Grandma Threading Her Needle
1903 [month undetermined]
Two Old Sports
Feb [day undetermined]
Mother Goose Nursery Rhymes
Apr [day undetermined]
The House That Jack Built
A Kiss in the Tunnel
Mary Jane's Mishap; or, Don't Fool with the Parafin
The Monk in the Monastery Wine Cellar
Pa's Comment on the Morning News
Through the Telescope
Jul 18 The Life of a London Bobby
1904 [month undetermined]
The Baby, the Monkey and the Milk Bottle
Jul [day undetermined]
Dorothy's Dream
1910
Dec [day undetermined]
A Visit to the Seaside at Brighton Beach, England
Smith, George A., Mrs.
1903
Apr [day undetermined]
A Kiss in the Tunnel
Smith, J. B.
1903
May [day undetermined]
Fireboat "New Yorker" Answering an Alarm
Fireboat "New Yorker" in Action
New York City Dumping Wharf
New York City "Ghetto" Fish Market
New York City Police Parade
New York Harbor Police Boat Patrol Capturing Pirates
Skyscrapers of New York City, from the North River
The Still Alarm
White Wings on Review
Sep [day undetermined]
Reliance and Shamrock III Turning Outer Stake in Second Race*
"Reliance" and "Shamrock" III Jockeying and Starting in First Race
"Reliance" Crossing the Line and Winning First Race
Dec [day undetermined]
Opening of New East River Bridge, New York
Smith, Jack
1908
Mar 21 The Robbers and the Jew*
1909
Aug 14 The Burning Home*
Smith, John A., Dr.
1901
Jun 8 Opening of the Pan-American Exposition showing Vice President Roosevelt Leading the Procession
Smith, Orrilla
1910
Mar 15 The Actor's Children
Smith, Sebastian
1905
Jul [day undetermined]
Rescued by Rover
1907
Jun 1 The Tramp's Dream
Smith, Sebastian, Mrs.
1905
Jul [day undetermined]
Rescued by Rover
Smyth, Mayor
1902
Apr [day undetermined]
President Roosevelt Reviewing the Troops at Charleston Exposition [South Carolina]
Solinski
1904
Oct [day undetermined]
Eccentric Waltz
Solter, Harry
1908
Apr 7 A Famous Escape
Apr 15 The King of the Cannibal Islands
Apr 22 Hulda's Lovers
May 6 The Sculptor's Nightmare
May 20 When Knights Were Bold
Jun 2 Thompson's Night Out
Jun 9 'Ostler Joe
Jul 7 The Kentuckian
Jul 10 The Stage Rustler
Jul 24 The Tavern-Keeper's Daughter
Jul 28 The Redman and the Child
Jul 31 Deceived Slumming Party
Aug 4 The Bandit's Waterloo: The Outwitting of an Andalusian Brigand by a Pretty Senora
Aug 7 A Calamitous Elopement: How It Proved a Windfall for Burglar Bill
Aug 11 The Greaser's Gauntlet
Aug 14 The Man and the Woman
Aug 18 The Fatal Hour
Aug 21 For Love of Gold
Aug 28 For a Wife's Honor
Sep 1 Betrayed by a Handprint
Sep 4 Monday Morning in a Coney Island Police Court
Sep 8 The Girl and the Outlaw
Sep 18 The Heart of O Yama*
Sep 22 Where the Breakers Roar
Sep 25 A Smoked Husband
Sep 29 The Stolen Jewels
Oct 2 The Devil
Oct 6 The Zulu's Heart
Oct 9 Father Gets in the Game
Oct 13 The Barbarian Ingomar
Oct 16 The Vaquero's Vow
Oct 20 The Planter's Wife
Oct 23 Romance of a Jewess
Oct 27 The Call of the Wild
Oct 30 Concealing a Burglar
Nov 3 After Many Years
Nov 10 Taming of the Shrew
Nov 13 The Guerrilla
Nov 17 The Song of the Shirt
Nov 24 A Woman's Way
Nov 27 The Clubman and the Tramp
Dec 1 The Valet's Wife
Dec 4 Money Mad
Dec 8 The Feud and the Turkey
Dec 11 The Reckoning
Dec 15 The Test of Friendship
Dec 18 An Awful Moment
1909
Jan 1 One Touch of Nature
Jan 4 The Maniac Cook
Jan 7 Mrs. Jones Entertains
Jan 11 The Honor of Thieves
Love Finds a Way
Jan 14 A Rural Elopement
The Sacrifice
Jan 21 The Fascinating Mrs. Francis
Jan 25 The Welcome Burglar
Feb 4 The Brahma Diamond
Feb 8 A Wreath in Time
Feb 15 The Curtain Pole
Feb 18 The Hindoo Dagger
Mar 1 The Prussian Spy
Mar 8 The Roue's Heart
Mar 11 The Salvation Army Lass
Mar 15 The Lure of the Gown
Mar 25 A Burglar's Mistake
Apr 12 The Winning Coat
Apr 26 Lucky Jim
May 6 One Busy Hour
May 13 A Baby's Shoe
Jun 14 The Son's Return
Jun 21 Was Justice Served?
Jul 19 The Renunciation
Jul 26 A Convict's Sacrifice
Jul 29 The Slave
Sonne, Petrine
1909
Mar 31 The Non-Stop Motor Bicycle
Sep 4 Cycle Rider and the Witch
Nov 10 The Short-Sighted Governess
Sorel, Cécile
1909
Jun 9 La Tosca
Sorelle, William J.
1910
Feb 18 The Miniature
Mar 1 Ranson's Folly
Sørensen, Axel
1909
Nov 10 The Short-Sighted Governess
Sousa, John Philip
1900 [month undetermined]
John Philip Sousa
1901
Sep [day undetermined]
Sousa and His Band
Sowder, Martin Thad
1902
Nov [day undetermined]
Broncho Busting Scene, Championship of the World
1903
Feb [day undetermined]
Bucking Broncho Contest

Spencer, Allan, Chief
1901
Jul [day undetermined]
The Fire Department of Chelsea, Mass.
Spencer, G.
1910
Dec 6 The Winning of Miss Langdon
Spier, Martha
1910
Jun 1 Levi's Dilemma
Jun 22 A Victim of Hate
Dec 24 Sunshine in Poverty Row
Spooner, Senator
1901
Mar 16 President McKinley Taking the Oath
Spooner, Cecil
1909
Aug 3 The Prince and the Pauper
Springfield, E. M.
1908
May 2 The Blue Bonnet
Stanley, Henry
1910
Aug 25 The Romance of Circle Ranch
Stanton, Walter
1903
Jan [day undetermined]
Burlesque Cock Fight
The Mechanical Head
Stark, M.
1907
Aug 31 Stage Struck
Stedman, Marshall
1909
Jan 21 Love and Law
1910
Dec 29 Justinian and Theodora
Stevenson, Robert Louis
1909
Nov 16 The Imp of the Bottle
1910
Sep 24 Dr. Jekyll and Mr. Hyde; or, A Strange Case
Stewart, Jane
1905
Feb [day undetermined]
The Kleptomaniac
Stewart, L. L.
1910
Nov 17 Love in Quarantine*
Stone, F. A.
1907 [month undetermined]
Dancing Boxing Match, Montgomery and Stone
Goodbye John
Storey, Edith
1908
Feb 8 Francesca da Rimini; or, The Two Brothers
1910
Jan 4 Forty Years in the Land of Midian [The Life of Moses Part II]
Jan 25 The Plagues of Egypt and the Deliverance of the Hebrew [The Life of Moses Part III]
Feb 5 Twelfth Night
Feb 12 The Victory of Israel [The Life of Moses Part IV]
Feb 19 The Promised Land [The Life of Moses Part V]
Dec 22 A Western Welcome
Storm-Petersen, Robert
1908
Apr 4 The Robber's Sweetheart
Sep 19 The Lady with the Camellias
Stoughton, M.
1908
Aug 25 Balked at the Altar
Oct 23 Romance of a Jewess*
Stow, Percy
1902 [month undetermined]
A Frustrated Elopement
1903
Feb [day undetermined]
Policeman and Automobile
Reversible Donkey Cart
Sep [day undetermined]
The Diamond Robbery*
Oct 17 Alice in Wonderland
Nov [day undetermined]
The Professor
Nov 21 Animated Picture Studio
Letter Came Too Late
Dec [day undetermined]
How the Old Woman Caught the Omnibus
1904
Aug [day undetermined]
Attempted Murder in a Train
Off for the Holidays
Sep [day undetermined]
The Pig That Came to Life
The Quarrelsome Washerwoman
Sep 7 Linen Shop
Sep 17 Burglar and Girls
The Convict's Escape
A Kiss and a Tumble
Dec [day undetermined]
Guy Fawkes' Day
Dec 3 Sandy McGregor
1905 [month undetermined]
Fine Feathers Make Fine Birds
Feb 25 Love Letter
Aug [day undetermined]
Blind Man's Bluff
Dangerous Golfers
Nov [day undetermined]
Ride on Sprinkler Car
1906
Sep 20 Rescued in Mid-Air
1907
Jan 26 The Stolen Bride
Feb 2 The Artful Dodger
The Double Life
Mar [day undetermined]
Disturbing His Rest
Paying Off Scores
The Runaway Van
Sep 23 Those Boys Again
Sep 30 The Horse That Ate the Baby
Oct 28 The Absent-Minded Professor
The Adventures of a Bath Chair
1908
Jan 18 Anxious Day for Mother
Pied Piper of Hamlin
Jan 20 The Water Babies; or, The Little Chimney Sweep
Feb 17 The Soldier's Wedding
Apr 11 The Captain's Wives
The Downfall of the Burglars' Trust
The Scandalous Boys
May 2 Poor Aunt Matilda
May 9 The Memory of His Mother
Jun 13 Mr. Brown Has a Tile Loose
Three Sportsmen and a Hat
Jul 25 Three Maiden Ladies and a Bull
Aug 1 Follow Your Leader and the Master Follows Last
1909 [month undetermined]
Robin Hood and His Merry Men
Mar 22 A Wild Goose Chase
Apr 17 Puritan Maid
Apr 24 Nancy; or, The Burglar's Daughter
May 8 The Cavalier's Wife
Romance of the Crafty Usurper and the Young King
May 22 Favorite Doll
May 29 Lesson in Electricity
Morganatic Marriage
Jul 3 Modern Cinderella
Jul 17 Motor Skates
Sep 23 An Aerial Elopement
Nov 13 The Invaders
1910
Mar 16 Peter's Patent Paint
May 14 Bobby, the Boy Scout
Jun 4 A Drink of Goat's Milk
Jun 24 Lieutenant Rose, R. N.
Jul 1 The Plumber
Stowe, Harriet Beecher
1903
May [day undetermined]
Uncle Tom's Cabin
Sep [day undetermined]
Uncle Tom's Cabin
1910
Jul 26 Uncle Tom's Cabin
Uncle Tom's Cabin, Part 1
Jul 29 Uncle Tom's Cabin, Part 2
Jul 30 Uncle Tom's Cabin, Part 3
Straub, Major
1900
May [day undetermined]
Brigadier-General Franklin Bell and Staff
Streator's Zouaves
1901
Sep [day undetermined]
Street's Zouaves and Wall Scaling
Strickland, Mabel
1907
Jun 22 Willie's Dream
Stuart, Ralph
1904
Jan [day undetermined]
Duel Scene, "By Right of Sword"
Sturgeon, Rollin S.
1909
Dec 4 The Life of Moses
1910
Jan 4 Forty Years in the Land of Midian [The Life of Moses Part II]
Jan 25 The Plagues of Egypt and the Deliverance of the Hebrew [The Life of Moses Part III]
Feb 12 The Victory of Israel [The Life of Moses Part IV]
Feb 19 The Promised Land [The Life of Moses Part V]
Jul 26 Uncle Tom's Cabin, Part 1
Jul 29 Uncle Tom's Cabin, Part 2
Jul 30 Uncle Tom's Cabin, Part 3
Sturgis, Lucille
1900
Mar [day undetermined]
Lucille Sturgis
Sullivan, Mr.
1907
Dec 14 Laughing Gas
Sullivan, Tim
1910
Oct 11 Actors' Fund Field Day
Sunshine, Marion
1910
Nov 14 Sunshine Sue
Sutherland, Mrs.
1909
Sep 4 The Boy Scouts
Sutherland, Frank
1909
Sep 4 The Boy Scouts
Sweet, Blanche
1909
Nov 12 A Man with Three Wives
Dec 13 A Corner in Wheat
Dec 30 Choosing a Husband
The Day After
1910
Jan 3 The Rocky Road
Jan 13 All on Account of the Milk
Apr 11 A Romance of the Western Hills
Taft, Secretary
1908
Apr 11 Presidential Possibilities
Taillade, Mlle.
1909
May 12 The Hunter's Grief
Tainguy, Lucien
1899
Apr 10 A Trip to the Moon*
1902
Oct 4 A Trip to the Moon
Takahira, Kogoro, Baron
1905
Aug [day undetermined]
Scenes and Incidents, Russo-Japanese Peace Conference, Portsmouth, N.H.
Talbot, Henry
1901
May [day undetermined]
Bass Fishing
Talmadge, Norma
1910
May 28 The Love of Chrysanthemum
Dec 17 A Dixie Mother
Dec 27 In Neighboring Kingdoms
Tanguay, Eva
1902
Jun [day undetermined]
Eva Tanguay
Tannehill, M.
1909
Sep 3 Ethel's Luncheon
Tanner, Miss
1910
Jul 25 The Step-Daughter

Tanner, John A., Governor
1897
Mar [day undetermined]
Gov. John A. Tanner, of Virginia, and Staff
Tansey, John
1908
Jul 28 The Redman and the Child
1909
Aug 26 The Seventh Day
Tapley, Rose
1910
Oct 29 The Telephone
Tarlarini, Mary Cleo
1909
Nov 20 A Mother's Heart
1910
Jan 19 Pauli
Sep 28 The Virgin of Babylon
Nov 2 The Slave of Carthage
Taylor, Alma
1907
Jun 1 The New Policeman
1909
Aug 21 Story of a Picture
Sep 25 The Little Milliner and the Thief
1910
Jul 8 A New Hat for Nothing
Taylor, Belle
1910
Dec 5 A Child's Stratagem
Taylor, H. C., Captain
1898 [month undetermined]
Battleship Indiana
Taylor, Irma
1910
May 6 Jane Eyre
Taylor, Julia M.
1910
Dec 13 Love and Law
Taylor, K.
1909
Sep 3 Ethel's Luncheon
Taylor, S. E. V.
1908
Jun 26 Over the Hills to the Poor House
Nov 20 The Ingrate
1909
Oct 28 Lines of White on a Sullen Sea
1910
Feb 21 His Last Burglary
Mar 17 The Man
Apr 7 A Rich Revenge
Apr 21 The Tenderfoot's Triumph
May 30 The Impalement
Jun 2 In the Season of Buds
Jun 6 A Child of the Ghetto
Jun 9 A Victim of Jealousy
Jun 13 In the Border States
Jun 16 The Face at the Window
Jun 27 A Child's Impulse
Jul 4 The Purgation
Jul 7 A Midnight Cupid
Jul 11 What the Daisy Said
Jul 18 A Flash of Light
Jul 21 As the Bells Rang Out!
Serious Sixteen
Aug 1 An Arcadian Maid
Aug 4 Her Father's Pride
Aug 18 When We Were in Our Teens
Aug 22 The Sorrows of the Unfaithful
Sep 12 A Mohawk's Way
Sep 22 The Oath and the Man
Oct 22 In the Gray of the Dawn
Nov 28 A Plain Song
Taylor, Tom
1910
Jul 26 Peg Woffington
Tempest, Marie
1902
Nov [day undetermined]
Umbrella Dance, San Toy
Templeton, Fay
1906
Nov [day undetermined]
Fay Templeton
Tennyson, Alfred Tennyson, Baron
1908
Nov 3 After Many Years
1909
Nov 12 Dora
Nov 13 Launcelot and Elaine
1910
Dec 12 The Golden Supper
Terwilliger, George W.
1910
Oct 13 A Lucky Toothache
Tessandier, A.
1909
Aug 6 The Tragedy of Meudon
Tewkesbury, T. W. B.
1900
Jul [day undetermined]
Amateur Athletic Championships
Thanhouser, Gertrude
1910
Mar 15 The Actor's Children
Mar 22 St. Elmo
Thaw, Evelyn Nesbitt
1907
Mar 2 The Unwritten Law: A Thrilling Drama Based on the Thaw White Case
Theodore Lorch Company *see* **Lorch Company, Theodore**
Thomas, C. H.
1899
Sep [day undetermined]
International Collegiate Games—100 Yards Dash
Thomas, G.
1907
Nov 20 Wife Wanted
Thompson, Harry
1901
Dec [day undetermined]
Harry Thompson's Imitations of Sousa
Thompson, N. E., Major-General
1901
Mar 16 President McKinley and Escort Going to the Capitol
Thompson, R., Mr.
1907
Sep 14 Rivals
Thomson, Frederick
1910
Jul 30 Uncle Tom's Cabin, Part 3
Thorpe, Rose H.
1907
Mar 30 Curfew Shall Not Ring Tonight
Thurman
1900
Aug [day undetermined]
Living Pictures
Tilghman, William Matthew
1908
Dec [day undetermined]
The Bank Robbery
Tilley, Vesta
1906
Nov [day undetermined]
Vesta Tilley
Timmory, G.
1909
Nov 20 The Patient from Punkville
Tissot, Alice
1909
May 25 A Blind Man of Jerusalem
Tobin, Miss
1910
Jul 30 Uncle Tom's Cabin, Part 3
Todd, Harry
1909
Feb 17 Tag Day
Apr 29 Mephisto and the Maiden
Tolstoy, Leo
1909
May 20 Resurrection
Toncray, Kate
1905
Sep [day undetermined]
The White Caps
1906
Nov 15 The Tunnel Workers
1910
Sep 8 Little Angels of Luck
Toohey, John P.
1910
Sep 19 A Summer Tragedy
Oct 27 The Passing of a Grouch
Topley
1910
Sep 30 A Home Melody
Toral, General
1898 [month undetermined]
Surrender of General Toral
Toto
1906
Apr [day undetermined]
Clown's Revenge
Townsend, Edward W.
1909
Sep 14 Little Sister
Oct 19 Their Social Education
Nov 23 A Rose of the Tenderloin
1910
Feb 22 A Victim of Bridge
Mar 25 The Suit Case Mystery
May 6 The Senator and the Suffragettes
May 13 Carminella
Jun 3 The Piece of Lace
Aug 26 The Valet's Vindication
Townsend, Frederick DeP.
1901
Jun 8 Opening of the Pan-American Exposition showing Vice President Roosevelt Leading the Procession
Townsend, V. R.
1909
Nov 26 Thanksgiving, Then and Now
Train, George Francis
1898
Jul [day undetermined]
Train vs. Donovan
Travis, Charles W.
1909
Jun 4 "Davy" Crockett in Hearts United
Tray, J.
1904
Jun [day undetermined]
The Eviction
Tree, Beerbohm
1899 [month undetermined]
Beerbohm Tree, the Great English Actor
Trimble, Lawrence
1910
Oct 18 Auld Robin Grey
Trouhanova, Mlle.
1909
Nov 14 Rigoletto
Dec 15 The Ugly Girl
Trunnelle, Mabel
1908
Nov 24 A Woman's Way*
1910
May 17 The Princess and the Peasant
Jul 8 A Wireless Romance
Aug 2 With Bridges Burned
Nov 4 The Little Station Agent
Dec 27 Eldora, the Fruit Girl
Turner, Florence
1907
Jun 8 How to Cure a Cold
Sep 14 Cast Up by the Sea
Sep 28 The Mill Girl, a Story of Factory Life
Oct 5 The Gypsy's Warning
1908
Feb 8 Francesca da Rimini; or, The Two Brothers
Apr 11 Tale the Autumn Leaves Told
1909
Mar 13 Kenilworth
Nov 13 Launcelot and Elaine
1910
Jan 22 A Pair of Schemers; or, My Wife and My Uncle
Feb 5 Twelfth Night
Apr 23 St. Elmo
Jun 10 Over the Garden Wall
Jun 15 How Championships Are Won—and Lost
Jul 1 Wilson's Wife's Countenance
Jul 30 Uncle Tom's Cabin, Part 3
Aug 6 Her Mother's Wedding Gown
Aug 27 Rose Leaves
Sep 20 Jean the Matchmaker
Sep 24 Renunciation
Oct 11 Brother Man
Oct 18 Auld Robin Grey
Nov 5 In the Mountains of Kentucky
Nov 19 Francesca Da Rimini
Dec 17 A Dixie Mother

Turner, Otis
1908
Jun 20 The Fighting Parson
Jul 11 The Spirit of '76
1909
Feb 4 Stirring Days in Old Virginia
May 21 Hunting Big Game in Africa
Oct 21 The Cowboy Millionaire
1910
Mar 24 The Wonderful Wizard of Oz
Jul 7 The Way of the Red Man
Jul 31 Ranch Life in the Great South-West
Aug 11 Lost in the Soudan
Oct 20 Two Boys in Blue
Turpin, Ben
1908
Aug 22 Oh, What Lungs!
Oct 3 Breaking into Society
1909
Mar 24 A Midnight Disturbance
Apr 14 The Rubes and the Bunco Men
Jul 28 A Case of Seltzer
Twain, Mark *same as* **Clemens, Samuel**
1907
Mar 16 A Curious Dream
1909
Aug 3 The Prince and the Pauper
Dec 2 The Death Disc: A Story of the Cromwellian Period
Tysoe, A. E.
1900
Jul [day undetermined]
Amateur Athletic Championships
Unger, Max
1903
Jan [day undetermined]
Max Unger, the Strong Man
U.S. 9th Infantry
1903
Jul [day undetermined]
Musical Calisthenics
Musical Drill with Arms
Urban, Charles
1902
Sep [day undetermined]
Reproduction, Coronation Ceremonies—King Edward VII
Van Arden, Mr.
1910
Apr 13 Ice Scooters on Lake Ronkonkoma
Van Buren, Mabel
1910
Aug 18 An Old Story with a New Ending
Vanderbilt, Alfred G.
1901
Oct [day undetermined]
Coaching for a Record
Van Guysling, A. H.
1906
Oct [day undetermined]
Railroad Collision at Los Angeles, Calif.
1907
Apr [day undetermined]
Floral Parade at Pasadena, Calif.
Vani
1897
Apr [day undetermined]
Lina & Vani
Van Wyck, Mayor
1899
Jun [day undetermined]
Lieutenant-General Nelson A. Miles
Oct [day undetermined]
Admiral Dewey Leading Land Parade
Varennes, M.
1909
Jun 23 The Grandfather
Aug 6 The Tragedy of Meudon
Oct 22 Drink
Vaser, Ernesto
1910
Apr 13 Fricot in College
Vassail
1899
Sep [day undetermined]
The International Collegiate Games
Vaughan, Vivian
1903
Jan [day undetermined]
Life of an American Fireman
Velle, Gaston
1904
Feb 6 Metamorphosis of the King of Spades
May 21 Barnum's Trunk
Jun 18 Metamorphosis of a Butterfly*
Jul [day undetermined]
Japanese Varieties
Sep 24 Drama in the Air
Oct [day undetermined]
Mysterious Screen
Dec 24 Burglars at Work
1905
Jan 14 Wonderful Beehive
May 13 The Moon-Lover
Sep 30 Flower Fairy
Dec 9 The Hen with the Golden Eggs
Dec 16 A Tragedy at Sea
1906
Feb 17 Tit-for-Tat
Victims of the Storm
Apr [day undetermined]
Infernal Cave
Phantom's Guard
Transparent Cards*
Apr 14 The Invisible Man
Jun 16 A Detective's Trip Around the World
Jun 23 The Rajah's Casket
Aug 11 Voyage Around a Star
1907
Nov 30 The Clock-Maker's Secret
Verdi, Giuseppe
1909
Nov 14 Rigoletto
Verne, Jules
1902
Oct 4 A Trip to the Moon
1904
Oct 29 An Impossible Voyage
1908
Apr 15 Michael Strogoff
1910
Apr 1 Michael Strogoff
Vernoud, M.
1909
Nov 17 Her Dramatic Career
Victoria, Vesta
1907
Feb [day undetermined]
Poor John
Waiting at the Church
Vignola, Robert
1906
Mar 29 The Black Hand
1910
Aug 3 A Colonial Belle
Dec 30 The Stranger
Vincent, James
1910
May 6 The Egret Hunter
Aug 3 A Colonial Belle
Aug 17 The Perversity of Fate
Nov 30 The Touch of a Child's Hand
Vitaliani, I.
1910
Nov 18 Phaedra
Vitrotti, Giovanni
1908
May 2 Frolicsome Powders
Modern Hotel
Panorama of Venice
May 9 Sicily Illustrated
Oct 20 The Cashier's Romance
1909
Apr 24 A Marvelous Ointment
May 1 Countess Valleria of Issogne
May 8 Artillery Manoeuvers in the Mountains
May 15 Galileo, Inventor of the Pendulum
May 29 Count of Monte Cristo
Jun 5 A True Friend
Jun 26 Louis the XI
Jul 10 Phonographic Message of Love
Jul 24 Little Imp
Nov 1 Nero; or, The Burning of Rome
Nov 8 Musical Waiter
Pirates of the Sea
Nov 22 The Hostage
Dec 6 The Little Vendean
Dec 29 The Story of My Life
1910
Jan 15 The Son of the Wilderness
Jan 19 Pauli
Jan 26 The Last Keepsake
Feb 2 Hero and Leander
Feb 9 The Longing for Gaol
Feb 16 I Have Lost My Latch Key
The Silent Piano
Feb 26 Why Fricot Was Sent to College
The Witch's Ballad
Mar 2 The Mysterious Track
The Two Mothers
Mar 12 Fatal Imprudence
They Have Vanished My Wife
Mar 16 Insidious Weapons
Mar 23 The Sea's Vengeance
Mar 30 An Unworthy Fiancé
Apr 13 The Legend of the Cross
Apr 20 The Heart of a Vagabond
Petit Jean Louis d'Or & Co.
Apr 27 A Doctor's Revenge
Fricot Is Learning a Handicraft
May 4 Who Killed Her?
May 11 Fricot Gets in a Libertine Mood
The Secret of the Lake
May 18 The Devil on Two Sticks
May 25 Estrellita; or, The Invasion of the French Troops in Portugal
Jun 8 A Jealous Wife
The Shipwrecked Man
Jun 22 The Story of Lulu Told by Her Feet
The Tricky Umbrella of Fricot
Jul 6 The Tamer; Alfred Schneider and His Lions
Jul 13 The Struggle of Two Souls
Jul 27 The Room of the Secret
Aug 3 The Glove
Aug 17 The Hump's Secret
Tweedle Dum Has Missed the Train
Aug 24 A Fatal Vengeance
Aug 31 The Fisherman's Crime
Tweedle Dum's Forged Bank Note
Sep 7 The Caprice of a Dame
Fricot Has Lost His Collar Button
Sep 21 The Last Friend
Molly at the Regiment—Her Adventures
Sep 28 The Virgin of Babylon
Oct 12 The Betrothed's Secret
Tweedledum on His First Bicycle
Oct 19 Excursion on the Chain of Mont Blanc
Oct 26 Tweedledum Wants to be a Jockey
Nov 9 A Floating Message
Nov 23 Gounod's 'Ave Maria'
The Story of a Pair of Boots
Dec 21 Tweedledum and Frothy Want to Get Married
Dec 28 Drama of the Engine Driver
Grandfather's Pipe
Vivian, E.
1909
Jun 17 In the Sultan's Power
Voijere, George
1905
Feb [day undetermined]
The Kleptomaniac
Volbert, M.
1910
Feb 21 Face to Face
Vosberg, Mr.
1910
Aug 3 A Colonial Belle
Vosburgh, Harold
1904
Aug [day undetermined]
The Moonshiner
Waddell, Rube
1903
Jan [day undetermined]
Game of Base Ball
Wagener, F. W., Captain
1902
Apr [day undetermined]
President Roosevelt Reviewing the Troops at Charleston Exposition [South Carolina]
Wagner, Richard
1904
Nov [day undetermined]
Parsifal
Wainwright, Richard, Captain
1898
Oct [day undetermined]
Famous Battleship Captains—Philadelphia Peace Jubilee Parade
Walcott, Governor
1899
Jun [day undetermined]
Governor Walcott of Massachusetts
Oct [day undetermined]
Admiral Dewey at State House, Boston

Walker, Lewis
1899 [month undetermined]
Beerbohm Tree, the Great English Actor
Walker, Lillian
1909
Feb 20 C. Q. D.; or, Saved by Wireless, a True Story of "The Wreck of the Republic"
1910
Apr 19 Love's Awakening
Wall, Dave
1908
Jun 10 The Blue and the Gray; or, The Days of '61
Jul 22 The Face on the Barroom Floor
1909
Sep 28 Why Girls Leave Home
1910
Jan 29 The Girl and the Judge; or A Terrible Temptation
Wallace, Lew
1907
Dec 7 Ben Hur
Walters, George W., Mrs.
1910
Jul 8 The Girl Strike Leader
Walthall, H. B.
1909
Jul 26 A Convict's Sacrifice
Aug 2 A Strange Meeting
Aug 5 The Mended Lute
Aug 12 The Better Way
Aug 16 With Her Card
Aug 30 The Heart of an Outlaw
Pranks
Sep 2 The Little Darling
The Sealed Room
Sep 13 Getting Even
Sep 20 In Old Kentucky
Dec 13 A Corner in Wheat
Dec 20 A Trap for Santa Claus
Dec 23 In Little Italy
Dec 30 The Day After
1910
Jan 17 On the Reef
Jan 20 The Call
Jan 24 The Honor of His Family
Jan 31 The Cloister's Touch
Feb 14 One Night, and Then —
Feb 21 His Last Burglary
Mar 3 The Newlyweds
Mar 7 The Thread of Destiny
Mar 10 In Old California
Mar 14 The Converts
Apr 14 The Kid
Apr 18 Thou Shalt Not
Apr 21 The Tenderfoot's Triumph
Apr 25 The Way of the World
May 2 The Gold-Seekers
May 9 Love Among the Roses
May 12 The Two Brothers
May 23 Ramona
May 30 The Impalement
Jun 6 A Child of the Ghetto
Jun 13 In the Border States
Jun 16 The Face at the Window
Jul 25 The Call to Arms
Aug 8 The House with Closed Shutters
Aug 15 The Usurer
Aug 22 The Sorrows of the Unfaithful
Aug 25 Wilful Peggy
Sep 5 A Summer Idyll
Sep 15 In Life's Cycle
Sep 22 The Oath and the Man
Sep 26 Rose O' Salem-Town
Oct 3 The Iconoclast
Oct 20 The Banker's Daughters
Oct 22 In the Gray of the Dawn
Oct 29 The Armorer's Daughter
Waltham, J.
1909
Nov 1 The Gibson Goddess
Walton, Fred
1910
Jul 11 The Hall-Room Boys
Ward, Jean
1909
Apr 29 Mephisto and the Maiden
Ward, John
1901 [month undetermined]
The Builders of Shamrock II
Warver, Mrs.
1907
Apr 6 Daniel Boone; or, Pioneer Days in America
Warwick
1898 [month undetermined]
Boxing
Waterbury Brothers
1900
Jul [day undetermined]
Champion Polo Players
Watson, G. L.
1901 [month undetermined]
The Builders of Shamrock II
Weber, Miss
1907
Aug 31 Stage Struck
Webster
1900
Mar [day undetermined]
The Kiss*
Weed, A. E.
1903
Jul [day undetermined]
Battle Flags of the 9th U. S. Infantry
Bayonet Exercises
A Boarding School Prank
Musical Calisthenics
Musical Drill with Arms
Shelter Tent Drill
Aug [day undetermined]
The Burglar
Buying Stamps from Rural Wagon, U. S. P. O.
Cancelling Machine, U. S. P. O.
Carriers at Work, U. S. P. O.
Carriers Leaving Building, U. S. P. O.
Clerks Casing Mail for Bags, U. S. P. O.
Clerks Tying Bags, U. S. P. O.
Clerks Tying Up for Bags, U. S. P. O.
Coach at Rural Post Office, U. S. P. O.
Collecting Mail, U. S. P. O.
Exchange of Mail at Rural P. O., U. S. P. O.
Fife Getting Instructions from Committee
Finish of the First Race, Aug. 22
A Funny Story on the Beach
Jockeying for the Start Aug. 20
Jockeying for the Start Aug. 22
A Little Tease
Loading Mail Car, U. S. P. O.
Mailing Platform, U. S. P. O.
Old Mail Coach at Ford, U. S. P. O.
Post Man Delivering Mail, U. S. P. O.
Reliance Rounding Turn, August 20th
"Reliance" vs. "Shamrock" III, Aug. 20
Routing Mail, U. S. P. O.
Rural Wagon Delivering Mail, U. S. P. O.
Rural Wagon Giving Mail to Branch, U. S. P. O.
Special Delivery Messenger, U. S. P. O.
Stake Boat with Stake ("John Scully")
Start of the First Race, Aug. 22
Street Mail Car, U. S. P. O.
Throwing Mail into Bags, U. S. P. O.
Transporting Internal Rev. Stamps, U. S. P. O.
The Two Sisters!
Tying Up Bags for Train, U. S. P. O.
The Waders
Wagons Loading Mail, U. S. P. O.
"What Are the Wild Waves Saying Sister?"
Sep [day undetermined]
The Baby
Bathing in Samoa
The Chorus Girl and the Salvation Army Lassie
A False Alarm in the Dressing Room
Finish of Yacht Race, Aug. 25th
From Show Girl to Burlesque Queen
In the Dressing Room
Jockeying and Start of Yacht[s] Aug. 25th
Lady Bountiful Visits the Murphys on Wash Day
The Minister's Hat
Panorama of Excursion Boats
Parade of Eagles, New York
Poor Girl, It Was a Hot Night and the Mosquitos Were Thick
The Sand Baby
The Sand Fort
Seeing New York by Yacht
Start of Race—"Reliance" Ahead
Oct [day undetermined]
Alphonse and Gaston 3
Alphonse and Gaston (Journal Thumb Book)
Delivering Mail from Sub-Station [U. S. P. O.]
Foxy Grandpa [Thumb Book]
From Haverstraw to Newburg
Happy Hooligan's Interrupted Lunch
Hooligan's Roller Skates
Inside Car, Showing Bag Catcher [U. S. P. O.]
"Never Touched Him!"
Seeing New York by Yacht
The Smoky Stove
Toodles and Her Strawberry Tart
Toodles' Strawberry Tart (Journal Thumb Book)
Train Taking Up Mail Bag, U. S. P. O.
Uncle Reuben at the Waldorf
"Who Pays for the Drinks?"
The Wrath of a Jealous Wife
Nov [day undetermined]
Alphonse and Gaston and the Burglar (Thumb Book)
Alphonse and Gaston Balcony Scene (Thumb Book)
Alphonse and Gaston Target Practice (Thumb Book)
Firing the Cook
Fusion, On to Brooklyn!
A Guardian of the Peace
Harvard-Pennsylvania Football Game
Hooligan's Thanksgiving Dinner (Thumb Book)
Lifting a Wagon from a New York Foundation
Next!
Off His Beat
Toodles Recites a Recitation
Toodles Recites a Recitation (Thumb Book)
Toodles' Tea Party
Toodles' Tea Party (Thumb Book)
Tying the Red Light on the Tiger's Tail
A Windy Day at the Flatiron Building
Dec [day undetermined]
Almost a King
The Ballet Rehearsal
Burning of the Academy of Music, Brooklyn
Clarence the Cop
The Dressmaker's Accident
Dumping Iron Ore
The Gerry Society's Mistake
Having Her Gown Fitted
The Johnnie and the Telephone
Mr. Easy Mark
The Over-Anxious Waiter
The Pajama Dance
The Pajama Statue Girls
The Porous Plaster
Waiting for Bill
1904
Jan [day undetermined]
And Pat Took Him at His Word
The Arbitrator
As Seen on the Curtain
The Bench in the Park
The Borrowing Girl
The Boy Under the Table
A Catastrophe in Hester Street
The Dog and the Baby
A Drop of Ink
Duel Scene, "By Right of Sword"
The Easy Chair
The Escaped Lunatic
The Furnished Room House—Taking Life Easy
Girl Waving American Flag, National Cash Register Co.
Girls Jumping the Rope
The Heathen Chinese and the Sunday School Teachers
The Homemade Turkish Bath
"In the Springtime, Gentle Annie!"
The Jolly Bill-Posters
Just Before the Raid
A Kiss in the Dark
A Little Bit off the Top
Love and Jealousy Behind the Scenes
The Misdirected Kiss
One Way of Taking a Girl's Picture
The Picture the Photographer Took
The Power of Authority

1909
Jun 9 La Tosca
Jul 17 The Invisible Thief
1910
May 11 Cleopatra
Oct 7 Slippery Jim

Zola, Émile
1909
Oct 22 Drink
1910
Aug 12 The Attack on the Mill

CORPORATE NAME INDEX

★ Film titles listed herein are listed under specific corporate name headings and, like other indexes in *Film Beginnings, 1893- 1910*, are arranged chronologically by year, month and day, then alphabetically by date of release. Please note that, in many cases, films are listed under both the Production and the Distribution company. Thus, each film may be listed more than once if two or more companies were involved in its production and distribution. This is often the case of foreign-made films that were released in the United States by a different company or under an anglicized name of the foreign company.

Cross-references are provided to assist the user in identifying companies which evolved, merged or changed names over the course of their existence.

CORPORATE NAME INDEX

A. G. Whyte
1909
Dec 11 Santa Claus and the Miner's Child
Dec 18 Beyond the Rockies
Dec 20 Vindicated
Dec 25 The Deceiver
Dec 30 The Justice of Solomon
1910
Jan 6 The Nemesis
Jan 13 Forgiven
Mishaps of Bonehead
Jan 27 Bonehead's Second Adventure
The Ordeal
Feb 3 Justice
Feb 5 Submarines in Paris
Feb 9 The Mountaineer
Feb 14 Paris Flood
Feb 16 A Daughter's Devotion
The Old Maid and Bonehead
Feb 23 In Arizona
Mar 5 The Vindictive Foreman
Mar 9 On the Little Big Horn
Mar 23 The Tenderfoot
Mar 30 The Cowboy Preacher
Apr 6 Frontier Day in the West
Apr 13 At Double Cross Ranch
Apr 27 Days of '49
May 4 A Daughter of the Mine
May 11 The Indian Princess
May 18 The Fighting Parson
May 25 The Red Man's Honor
Jun 1 The Lily of the Ranch
Jun 6 The Bucking Broncho
Jun 13 The Sheriff's Daughter
Jun 15 A Message from the East
Jun 16 Her Lesson
The Old Maid's Picnic
Jun 18 The Turn of the Tide
Jun 20 Boss of Circle E Ranch
Jun 22 An Interrupted Courtship
Jun 23 Getting Rid of Uncle
One Good Turn
Jun 25 Cash on Delivery
Jun 27 The Crooked Trail
Jun 29 All's Well That Ends Well
Jun 30 For Her Son's Sake
She Would Be a Business Man
Jul 4 A Soldier's Sacrifice
Jul 6 No Questions Asked
Jul 7 One Man's Confession
Jul 11 Aviation at Montreal: June 25th to July 5th, 1910
Jul 13 Among the Breakers
Jul 14 The Badgers
Granddad's Extravagance
Jul 20 The Power from Above

A. J. Clapham
1910
Dec 21 Love's Sorrow
Dec 28 Thoughtfulness Remembered by the Ute

Actograph Co.
1907
Nov 23 Hunting in Canadian Woods
Mystic Shriners at Dreamland
Presentation of Firemen's Bravery Medals by Mayor McClellan

Actophone Co.
1910 [month undetermined]
Love-Making Under Difficulties
Jan 5 The Wife's Sacrifice
Jan 12 Robert Macaire; or, The Two Vagabonds
Jan 19 The Brothers
Jan 26 An Artist's Inspiration
Feb 2 The Clown's Big Moment
Feb 9 Spike's Battle
Feb 16 The Silent Messenger
Feb 23 The Third Degree
Mar 2 Jack's Return
The Shirtwaist Strike
Mar 9 A Wolf in Sheep's Clothing
Mar 12 Count of Monte Christo
Mar 19 The Parson's Poster
Mar 22 A Winter Romance at Niagara Falls
Mar 29 The End of the Trail
Apr 6 Partners
Apr 13 An Artist's Temptation
Uncle Eph's Dream
Apr 20 Down in Mexico
Apr 27 Baby Has the Colic
Saved by an Indian
May 4 A Soldier's Sweetheart
May 11 Hearts and Home
May 18 Love and a Palette
Love and a Pallette
May 25 Love's Great Tragedy

Alfred Duskes
1909
Oct 25 The Great Lottery
Nov 13 Romance of Life
Nov 22 Ali Bey's Dancing Drops
Dec 13 Dottynob's Dancing

Alfred L. Harstyn & Co.
1909
Apr 24 Bailiff Makes a Seizure
May 1 Countess Valleria of Issogne
The Donkey That Was Not an Ass
Easter Bells
Farmer Jones Goes to the Market
The Fickle Husband
Removal Under Difficulties
Aug 21 Mishaps of a Policeman
The Vengeance of the Lion Tamer

The All Star Hadley Exhibition Moving Picture Co.
1907
Sep 28 The Great Brighton Beach Head-On Locomotive Collision

Alpha Trading Co.
1904
Jul [day undetermined]
Toy Maker and Good Fairy
1905
Aug [day undetermined]
His Washing Day
Robbing His Majesty's Mail
Nov [day undetermined]
Motor Highwayman
1908
Nov 21 Grandpa's Pension Day
1909
Jun 5 Happy Man

The American Cinephone Co.
1910
Aug 20 [Jack Johnson's Own Story of the Big Fight]

American Film Mfg. Co.
1910
Nov 14 Romantic Redskins
Nov 17 The Lure of the City
Nov 21 Starlight's Devotion
Nov 24 A Big Joke
Nothing but Money
Nov 28 The Regeneration
Dec 1 A Touching Affair
Dec 5 Vera, the Gypsy Girl
Dec 8 Two Lucky Jims
Dec 12 The Rummage Sale
Dec 15 The Binding Shot
Dec 19 Her Fatal Mistake
Dec 22 Her Husband's Deception
A Troublesome Parcel
Dec 26 Girlies
Dec 29 The Squaw and the Man

American Fotophone Co.
1910
Apr 16 [Talking Moving Picture]

American Kinograph Co.
1910
Apr 5 Boxing Fever
May 30 King Edward's Funeral
Jun 21 Drowsy Dick's Dream
Tempered with Mercy
Jun 24 Lieutenant Rose, R. N.
Jun 28 Under the Reign of Terror
Jul 1 The Fresh Air Fiend
The Plumber
Jul 5 The Boy and His Teddy Bear
Jul 8 From Gypsy Hands
A New Hat for Nothing
Jul 12 A Deal in Broken China
Prince of Kyber
Jul 15 The Hindoo's Treachery

American Motor Racing Picture Co.
1910
Sep 10 Elgin National Trophy Races

American Moving Picture Co.
1910
Jan [day undetermined]
The Story of a Shoe

American Mutoscope and Biograph Co. *see also* **American Mutoscope Co.; The Biograph & Mutoscope Co. for France, Ltd.; Biograph Co.; British Mutoscope and Biograph Co.; Deutsche Mutoskop und Biograph G.m.b.H.**
1896
Sep [day undetermined]
Awakening of Rip
Exit of Rip and the Dwarf
A Hard Wash
The Monkey's Feast
Rip Leaving Sleepy Hollow
Rip Meeting the Dwarf
Rip Passing over the Mountain
Rip's Toast
Rip's Toast to Hudson
Rip's Twenty Years' Sleep
Sandow
Oct [day undetermined]
Empire State Express
United States Flag
Dec [day undetermined]
Sack Race
Why Papa Cannot Sleep
1897 [month undetermined]
The Mischievous Monkey
Feb [day undetermined]
The Pretty Typewriter; or, "Caught in the Act"
Projectile from Ten Inch Disappearing Gun Striking Water, Sandy Hook
The Sausage Machine
Ten Inch Disappearing Carriage Gun Loading and Firing, Sandy Hook
Mar [day undetermined]
A Bowery Cafe
Cavalry Charge
Downey vs. Monaghan
Geisha Girls
Jumbo, Horseless Fire-Engine
Love's Young Dream
A Pillow Fight
Theatre Hat
Apr [day undetermined]
A Coon Cake Walk

Dance, Franchonetti Sisters
French Acrobatic Dance
Theatre Hats Off
Willie's Hat

May [day undetermined]
An Affair of Honor
Comedy Cake Walk
Shooting the Chutes

Jun [day undetermined]
The Biggest Fish He Ever Caught
Girls Swinging
A Rural Courtship
Still Waters Run Deep
The Tramp and the Bather
Trout Poachers
Young America

Aug [day undetermined]
Atlantic City Fire Department

Sep [day undetermined]
Girls' Acrobatic Feats
Riding on the Merry-Go-Round

Oct [day undetermined]
A Baby Merry-Go-Round
Fastest Wrecking Crew in the World
Fun on the Steeple-Chase
The Haverstraw Tunnel
A Multicycle Race
A Paced Bicycle Race
Washing the Baby

Nov [day undetermined]
Scrub Yacht Race

Dec [day undetermined]
At the Top of Brooklyn Bridge
The Battery
Battleships "Maine" and "Iowa"
Christmas Morning
The Christmas Tree Party
Night Before Christmas
Ocean Greyhounds
Santa Claus Filling Stockings
"Spike, the Bag-Punching Dog"

1898 [month undetermined]
The Armenian Archbishop, Rome
Capuchin Monks, Rome
Corpus Christi Procession, Orvieto
The Mysterious Midgets
The Vatican Guards, Rome

Jan [day undetermined]
Charge of the Light Brigade
Her Morning Exercise
An Impromptu Can-can at the Chorus Girls' Picnic
Merry Sleigh Bells
The See-Saw, at the Chorus Girls' Picnic
Sleighing Scene

Feb [day undetermined]
Torpedo Boat, "Dupont"
"Vizcaya" Under Full Headway

Mar [day undetermined]
Launch, U. S. Battleship "Kentucky"

Apr [day undetermined]
Practice Warfare
S. S. "Columbia" Sailing
Theodore Roosevelt

May [day undetermined]
How Bridget Served the Salad Undressed
Karina
The Kiki Dance
Moulin Rouge Dancers
The Old Maid's Picture
Some Dudes Can Fight

Jun [day undetermined]
The Schoolmaster's Surprise

Jul [day undetermined]
How the Athletic Lover Outwitted the Old Man
An Interrupted Kiss
Joe, the Educated Orangoutang
The Katzenjammer Kids in School
A Landing Fight
The Old Maid and the Burglar
A Ride on a Switchback
Roosevelt's Rough Riders
The Tramp and the Muscular Cook
The Washwoman's Daughter
Wounded Soldiers Embarking in Row Boats
Wreck of the "Vizcaya"

Aug [day undetermined]
The Bathing Girls Hurdle Race
The Coney Island Bikers
The Dude's Experience with a Girl on a Tandem
The Last Round Ended in a Free Fight
The Minister's Wooing
Shooting the Long Sault Rapids
Steamer "Island Wanderer"
Steamer "New York"
Stolen Sweets

Sep [day undetermined]
Col. Theodore Roosevelt and Officers of His Staff
18th Pennsylvania Volunteers
The Fat Man and the Treacherous Springboard
General Wheeler and Secretary of War Alger at Camp Wikoff
"Me and Jack"
Peace Jubilee Naval Parade, New York City
President McKinley's Inspection of Camp Wikoff
71st Regiment, N. G. S. N. Y. at Camp Wikoff
U. S. Battleship "Oregon"

Oct [day undetermined]
Cardinal Gibbons
An Innocent Victim
Launch of the "Illinois"
Love in a Cornfield
Street Fight and Arrest
Who's Got the Red Ear?

Nov [day undetermined]
A Living Picture Model Posing Before a Mirror
Making an Impression
Gladys Must Be in Bed Before Ten
The Rivals

Dec [day undetermined]
The Elopement
Ice Yachting

1899 [month undetermined]
Amann
Amann, the Great Impersonator
Ritchie, the Tramp Bicyclist

Mar [day undetermined]
Around the Big Curves
Bucking the Blizzard
The Disappointed Old Maid
Grand Military Steeple-Chase
In the Grip of the Blizzard
Lockhart's Performing Elephants
A "Moving" Picture
Niagara Falls in Winter
Tommy's Ringing Good Joke on His Dad
What Happened to the Burglar

Apr [day undetermined]
The Artist's Dream
As in a Looking Glass
A Bucking Broncho
Farmer Oatcake Has His Troubles
Going to the Hunt
High Hurdle Jumping, at Meadowbrook Hunt Club
"It's Unlucky To Pass Under a Ladder"
The Meadowbrook Hunt
Pole Vaulting at Columbia University
Prize Winning St. Bernards
The Startled Lover
Symphony in "A" Flat

May [day undetermined]
Ambulance Corps Drill
American-Chinese Naval Reserves
The Automatic Prize Fight
A Bare Skin Joke
Board of Trade
The Breeches Buoy
The Burglar and the Bundle
A Burlesque Queen
Burlesque Queen and a Country Photographer
Champion High Jumpers, "Chappie" and "Ben Bolt"
Charlie Wanted the Earth
A Cock Fight
Cramp's Shipyard
Crew of the U. S. Cruiser "Raleigh"
Distributing a War Extra
Elephants in a Circus Parade
Farmer Wayback Entertains
First Boston School Regiment
First City Troop of Philadelphia
A Flock of Sheep
Founder's Log Cabin
Frank Melville's Trick Elephant
Gen. Snowden and Staff, and Crew of the U. S. S. "Raleigh"
Getting Up in the World
Girard College Cadets
A Good Shot
Hazing a Freshman
High Jumping
High Steppers in Harness
Hippopotamus "Babe"
Hipwood-Barrett Car Fender
How Little Willie Put a Head on His Pa
Hurdle Jumping
Judging Ladies' Saddle Horses
"Langton Performer 2nd"
A Lark at the French Ball
Launching the Lifeboat
Little Willie and the Burglar
Living Pictures
Lunch Time in the Studio
M. B. Curtis
Mrs. U. S. Grant and President McKinley
Mounted Artillery
New York Mounted Police
Odd Fellows Parade
President McKinley and Mayor Ashbridge of Philadelphia
Running the Hurdles
"Sampson" Champion High Stepper
Schooling Hunters
Second Battalion, 1st Regiment, N. G. of Pennsylvania
Second Boston School Regiment
Second City Troop
The Serenaders
Shooting the Life Line
Spirits in the Kitchen
State Fencibles
Stealing a Dinner
Steamship "Pavonia"
Tent Pegging
Third Boston School Regiment
Troop "F," 3rd Cavalry
A Unique Race
Unveiling the Statue of Gen. U. S. Grant
The Violin Player
What Dumb Animals Can Be Taught
Why Mamie Missed the Masquerade
The Wicked Sister and the Lobster
Yale Athletes
Yale Athletes Broad Jumping
The Yale Crew

Jun [day undetermined]
Armor vs. Amour
A Bad (K)Night
Chief Devery and Staff
Childhood's Happy Days
Children Feeding Ducklings
The Corset Model
The Demon Barber
The Derby
Down Mount Tom
Eighth Regiment, N. G. S. N. Y.
Feeding the Pigeons
The Female Drummer
First Heavy Artillery
For the Most Beautiful
Four A. M. at the French Ball
"La Grande Duchesse"
Her First Cigarette
How Ducks Are Fattened
Launch of the Porthonstock Life-boat
Lieutenant-General Nelson A. Miles
The Lock-Step
New York Naval Militia
New York Police
Ninth Regiment, N. G. S. N. Y.
The Paddock
Phillis Was Not Dressed to Receive Callers
President and Mrs. McKinley
President McKinley

The Price of a Kiss
The Pride of the Household
Scrubbem's Washing Machine
Shooting an Artesian Well
The Soubrette's Birthday
Suckling Pigs
Sunday School Parade
Twenty-Second Regiment, N. G. S. N. Y.
A Whipping Post
Wreck of the "Mohican"
Wreck of the S. S. "Paris"

Jul [day undetermined]

The Approach to Niagara
The Artist's Dream
An Attempt to Escape
Baby Feeding a Kitten
Baby Lund and Her Pets
Baby's Bath
Barrel Fight
A Bluff from a Tenderfoot
Boxing Dogs
Buffalo Fire Department
Canoeing at Riverside
Chorus Girls and the Devil
Chuck Connors vs. Chin Ong
"Columbia" and "Defender" Rounding Stake-Boat
"Columbia" vs. "Defender"
The Dairy Maid's Revenge
Detroit Fire Department
Female Prisoners: Detroit House of Correction
The Finish of Mr. Fresh
Fire Drill at the Factory of Parke, Davis & Co.
A Flock of Export Sheep
G. A. R. Post, Detroit
Glen House Stage
Hazing Affair in a Girls' Boarding School
Her Morning Dip
How Bill the Burglar Got a Bath
How Mamie Had Her Leg Pulled
How Papa Set Off the Fireworks
How the Medium Materialized Elder Simpkin's Wife
How Tottie Coughdrop's Summer Suit Was Spoiled
Hurdle Jumping; by Trained Dogs
An Interrupted Crap Game
A Jest and What Came of It
A Just Cause for Divorce
Kilpatrick's Ride
Love in a Hammock
The Lovers' Quarrel
Male Prisoners Marching to Dinner
Merlin, the Magician
Michigan Naval Reserves and the Detroit Light Guards
Niagara Falls Station
Panoramic View of Niagara Falls
Parke Davis' Employees
Police Drill
Running Up the Topsail on the "Columbia"
A Scandalous Proceeding
Smallest Train in the World
Steamship "Chippewa"
Steamship "Northland"
The Sweet Girl Graduate
Two Girls in a Hammock
An Up-to-Date Female Drummer
Water for Fair
The Way French Bathing Girls Bathe
What Julia Did to the Ghosts
When Babies' Quarrel
When Their Love Grew Cold
The Wizard and the Spirit of the Tree

Aug [day undetermined]

Around Tynsborough Curve
Babies Playing on a Hot Day
Ballet of the Ghosts
"Between the Races"
Bringing a Friend Home for Dinner
Climbing Jacob's Ladder
Crawford Notch
"Ding, Dong, Dell, Johnny's in the Well"
Fancy Diving
A Feast Day in Honolulu
The Fire Boat "New Yorker"
The Flume
43rd Rifles; Royal Canadian Infantry
The Frankenstein Trestle
A Gay Old Boy
The Great Lafayette
He Didn't Finish the Story
The Henley Regatta
His Masterpiece
Hooksett Falls Bridge
How the Porto Rican Girls Entertain Uncle Sam's Soldiers
How the Tramp Lost His Dinner
The Imperial Limited
"Imperial Limited." Canadian Pacific R. R.
In Fighting Trim
An Intrigue in the Harem
The Jealous Model
Lord and Lady Minto
The Maniac Barber
Miss Jewett and the Baker Family
A Plate of Ice Cream and Two Spoons
Professor Billy Opperman's Swimming School
The Saratoga Limited
Sliding Down Mount Washington
The Spider and the Fly
Stage Coaches Leaving the Hotel Victoria
Summit of Mt. Washington
Topsy-Turvy Quadrille
A Volunteer Fire Company
Water Throwing Contest
What Hypnotism Can Do
Where There's a Will, There's a Way
Winnisquam Lake
Wonderful Dancing Girls

Sep [day undetermined]

Admiral Dewey
Admiral Dewey Receiving His Mail
Admiral Dewey's Dog, "Bob"
Apple Blossoms
Arabis Patrol
Baxter Street Mystery
Chickens Coming Out of the Shell
A Cold Day for Art
Demonstrating the Action of a Patent Street Sprinkler of the American Car Sprinkler Co. of Worcester, Mass
Demonstrating the Action of the Northrop Looms
Diving Through Paper Screens
Dreyfus Receiving His Sentence
Eggs Hatching
Employes of Bausch, Lomb & Co.
The "Erin"
An Exciting Finish
Fancy Diving
Four Corners of Rochester
The Golding Family
The Great Free-for-All Pacing Race
Guardians of the Peace
Heroes of Luzon
The International Alliance
International Collegiate Games
The International Collegiate Games
International Collegiate Games
International Collegiate Games—Half Mile Run
International Collegiate Games—110 Yards Hurdle Race
International Collegiate Games—100 Yards Dash
Jack Tars Ashore
"King" and "Queen," the Great High Diving Horses
Launch of the Battleship "Vengeance"
M'lle. Cathrina Bartho
The Makers of the Kodak
"Man Overboard!"
A Midnight Fantasy
Officers of the "Olympia"
One Mile Dash
Polo—A Dash for Goal
Polo—Hurlingham vs. Ranelagh
The Poster Girls
The Poster Girls and the Hypnotist
Prof. Paul Boynton Feeding His Sea Lions
A Ray of Sunshine After the Rain
Rochester Fire Department
A Roll Lift Draw Bridge
"Sagasta" Admiral Dewey's Pet Pig
The Sandwich Man
"Shamrock I"
Shamrock Starting on Trial Trip
Sir Thomas Lipton and Party on "Erin's" Launch
Sir Thomas Lipton's Steam Yacht "Erin"
The Skeleton at the Feast
Soldiers of the Future
Some Future Champions
The Summer Girl
A Thrilling Ride
Trial of Captain Dreyfus
Two Hours After Hatching

Oct [day undetermined]

Back from Manila
Beyond the Great Divide
Chinamen Returning to China
A Close Finish
Col. John Jacob Astor, Staff and Veterans of the Spanish-American War
"Columbia"
"Columbia" Close to the Wind
Connecticut Naval Reserves
The "Corsair"
"Corsair" in Wake of Tugboat
Crew of the "Shamrock"
Crew of the "Shamrock," at Work
The Dandy Fifth
The Dewey Arch
Dewey Naval Parade
A Dip in the Mediterranean
Down the Western Slope of the Canadian Rockies Through Kicking Horse Pass
The Eastern Slope of the Rockies, Passing Anthracite Station
5th Ohio Volunteers of Cleveland
1st Penn' Volunteers of Philadelphia
Fourth Connecticut Volunteers, Dewey Parade
Full Rigged Ship at Sea
The Gap, Entrance to the Rocky Mountains
Gen. McCrosky Butt and Staff
Governor Roosevelt and Staff
Harbor of Villefranche
The "Havana"
In Busy 'Frisco
In the Canadian Rockies, near Banff
Marines of the Atlantic Fleet
Market Street
Mr. and Mrs. C. Oliver Iselin
Mrs. C. Oliver Iselin and Crew of Columbia
The "Niagara"
Orpheum Theatre, San Francisco
Overland Limited
The "Pennsylvania"
The "Richard Peck"
The "Sagamore"
Sailors of the Atlantic Fleet
2nd Battalion, 3rd New York Provisional Regiment, Rochester and Syracuse, Separate Companies
2nd Company Governor's Footguards, Conn.
7th Regiment, New York City
"Shamrock"
"Shamrock" After Carrying Away Topsail
"Shamrock" and "Columbia"
A Spectacular Start
Start of Race Between "Columbia" and "Shamrock"
Start of Second Cup Race
Start of the Second Cup Race
Start of Third Day's Race
Steamer "Grandrepublic"
Steamship "Empress of India"
10th Penn'a Volunteers
Torpedo Boats at the Yacht Race
Training Ship "Lancaster"
Turning Stake Boat; "Columbia" and "Shamrock"

Under the Shadow of Mt. Stephen, Passing Field's Station in the Rocky Mountains
Up the Big Grade in the Valley of the Kicking Horse
The West Point Cadets and Band
Yacht Race—Finish

Nov [day undetermined]
After the Ball
Around Gravel Bay
The Bather's Lunch
The Bride's Trousseau
Bridge No. 804, and Daly's Grade
Bunco on the Seashore
Caribou Bridge
Fougere
Frazer Canyon, East of Yale
Grand Trunk R. R. Bridge over Whirlpool
Interior Coney Island Club House, No. 1-4
It's Dangerous to Tickle a Soubrette
Jeffries and a Child at Play
Jeffries and Brother Boxing
Jeffries and Roeber Wrestling
Jeffries Being Rubbed Down
Jeffries Boxing with Tommy Ryan
Jeffries Running with His Trainers
Jeffries-Sharkey Contest
Jeffries Training on Bicycle
The "Make-Up" Thief
Test. Coney Island Athletic Club
Three Hot Babies
A Warm Baby with a Cold Deck

Dec [day undetermined]
Blanco Bridge
By Pulpit Rock and Through the Town of Echo
Coolies at Work
Devil's Gate
Devil's Slide
East of Uintah in Weber Canyon
The Escolta
Follow the Girls
The Foster Mother
Going to the Firing Line
Home of Buffalo Bill
One Thousand Mile Tree, Weber Canyon
The "Overland Limited" Passing Witch Rocks
Panoramic View of Manila Harbor
Passing Steamboat and Great Eastern Rocks
Pity the Blind
Port Huron; West End of St. Clair Tunnel
St. Clair Tunnel
33rd Infantry, U. S. A.
Toll Gate and Castle Rock near Green River
Tunnel "No. Three"
West of Peterson; Entrance to Weber Canyon
West Side St. Clair Tunnel

Dec 25 Cinderella

1900 [month undetermined]
Fight Between Tarantula and Scorpion
Kansas City Fire Department, Winners of the World's Championship at the Paris Exposition
Oxford-Cambridge Race
Panoramic View of Rome
Paris Exposition
Speed Trial of the "Albatross"

Jan [day undetermined]
Another Picture Showing Demonstration of a Pneumatic Shell Riveter
Blaine Club of Cincinnati
"Caught"
Demonstrating the Action of Pneumatic Shell Riveters on the Underside of the Hull of a Steel Vessel. Taken for the Chicago Pneumatic Tool Co.
Demonstrating the Action of the Chicago Pneumatic Tool Co.'s Deck Machine
Governor Nash of Ohio
"I Had To Leave a Happy Home for You"
Necessary Qualifications of a Typewriter
The Perfect Woman
Pneumatic Tools
Unloading Lighters, Manila

Feb [day undetermined]
Canadian Mounted Rifles on the March
Departure of the Second Canadian Contingent
Experimental—Handcamera
Marvin and Casler's Laboratory
Mounted Rifles at Drill
Northwestern Mounted Rifles
The Royal Leinster Regiment
Royal Leinster Regiment on Parade
Royal Leinsters on Review
St. Clair Tunnel
Skating in Central Park
Toronto Mounted Rifles

Mar [day undetermined]
Above the Speedway
An Advance by Rushes
The Attack on Magalang
The Battle of Mt. Ariat
Bridge of Spain
Brigadier-General Frederick D. Grant and Staff
Bringing General Lawton's Body Back to Manila
A Brush on the Speedway
The Call to Arms!
Dress Parade of the Woodward High School Cadets
Funeral of Major-General Henry W. Lawton
Getting Ready for the Seashore
Going into Action
"How'd You Like To Be the Iceman?"
In the Field
Major-General Arthur MacArthur and Staff
Making Manila Rope
Market Place
A Military Inspection
Off for the Boer War
Opening of the Rapid Transit Tunnel
The 17th Infantry, U. S. A.
The Train for Angeles
25th Infantry
Under Armed Escort
Walnut Hill Cadets
Water Buffalo, Manila

Apr [day undetermined]
After Dark in Central Park
"Ein Bier"
Buffalo Bill's Wild West Show
The Chimney Sweep and the Miller
The Croton Dam Strike
Demonstrating the Operation of the Harrington Rail Bonding System on the Line of the Coney Island and Brooklyn Railroad Co.
Found a Man Under the Bed
Horsewhipping an Editor
How They Rob Men in Chicago
In Central Park
Not a Man in Sight
"The Prince of Darkness"
The Stocking Scene from "Naughty Anthony"
A Terrible Night
Tommy's Trick on Grandpa
Uncle Si's Experience in a Concert Hall
What Happened to a Fresh Johnnie

May [day undetermined]
After Aguinaldo
Aguinaldo's Navy
The Art of "Making Up"
A Charge of the Insurgents
The Boomerang
Brigadier-General Franklin Bell and Staff
Buffalo Bill's Wild West Parade
The Clown and the Mule
Confounding the Art Critic
The Downward Path: She Ran Away [Part 2]
The Downward Path: The Fresh Book Agent [Part 1]
The Downward Path: The Girl Who Went Astray [Part 3]
The Downward Path: The New Soubrette [Part 4]
The Downward Path: The Suicide [Part 5]
A Farmer Who Could Not Let Go
The Fighting 36th
A Filipino Town Surprised
A Four-Horse Circus Act
The 4th Cavalry
Gatling Gun Drill
General Bell's Expedition
A Good Time with the Organ Grinder
The Great Ottawa Fire
The Growler Gang Catches a Tartar
A Gun Play in the Klondike
An Historic Feat
How the Farmer Was Buncoed
How the Old Maid Got a Husband
How the Young Man Got Stuck at Ocean Beach
How They Fired the Bum
An Impromptu Hairdresser
Insured Against Loss
Into the Wilderness!
Major-General Lloyd Wheaton
Manila
May Day Parade
Maypole Dance
On the Advance of Gen. Wheaton
One on the Bum
A Raid on a Chinese Opium Joint
A Raid on "Dago" Counterfeiters
The Rubberneck Boarders
Sherlock Holmes Baffled
Sidewalks of New York
Slow but Sure
A Somersault on Horseback
A Speedway Parade
The Thief and the Pie Woman
Tramps in the Old Maid's Orchard
Trial Speed of H. M. Torpedo Boat Destroyer "Viper"
The Troublesome Fly
Uncle Reuben Lands a Kick
Water Babies
Why Mrs. McCarthy Went to the Ball
With the Guns!

Jun [day undetermined]
Alligator Bait
The Approach to Lake Christopher
The Approach to Shelburn
The Arizona Doctor
Brook Trout Fishing
A Cadet Cavalry Charge
A Career of Crime, No. 1: Start in Life
A Career of Crime, No. 2: Going the Pace
A Career of Crime, No. 3: Robbery & Murder
A Career of Crime, No. 4: In the Toils
A Career of Crime, No. 5: The Death Chair
The Census on Cherry Hill
The Champion Beer Drinker
A Close Finish
The Clown and the See-Saw Fairies
A Cold Water Cure
Dewey Land Parade, Detroit
Escape from Sing Sing
The Exposed Seance
Flyers of the Great Lakes
A Gesture Fight in Hester Street
Gilead
Harris Training Tower
How Bridget Made the Fire
How He Saw the Eclipse
Larchmont Regatta
Love at 55
The Man in the Jimjams
The Masher's Waterloo
Mechanical Hair-Restorer
Not the Man She Waited for
Orchard Lake Cadets
Public Square, Cleveland
St. Clair Tunnel
Seeing Things at Night
Shelter Tent Drill
Soldiers of Greater Britain
Steam Yacht "Kismet"
Steeple Chase, Toronto

The Suburban of 1900
Such a Quiet Girl, Too!
The Tell-Tale Kiss
The Tramp and the Burglar
Tramp in the Haunted House
A Tramp in the Well
Valley of the Little Androscoggin
Victoria Jubilee Bridge
Wifie Invades the Studio
A Yard of Frankfurters
Jun 30 The Power of the Cross
Jul [day undetermined]
Allabad, the Arabian Wizard
Amateur Athletic Championships
Arrest of a Shoplifter
Atlantic City Lodge, 276, B.P.O. Elks
Bargain Day
The Black Storm
Blue Ribbon Jumpers
Brooklyn Lodge, No. 22, B.P.O. Elks
The Burglar-Proof Bed
Burning of the Standard Oil Tanks
A Champion Beer Drinker
Champion Polo Players
A Convict's Punishment
Deep Sea Fishing
Execution of a Spy
The Farmer and the Trolley Car
15th Infantry
Fire Boat "John M. Hutchinson"
From Vaudreuil to St. Anne's
A Hair-Raising Episode
His Dad Caught Him Smoking
His Name Was Mud
Hoboken Fire
The Hoboken Holocaust
How Charlie Lost the Heiress
How They Got Rid of Mamma
A Jersey Skeeter
The Katzenjammer Kids Have a Love Affair
Lawn Tennis
Love in the Dark
The Mail-Man in Coon Town
The Organ Grinder's Fourth of July
Philadelphia Lodge, No. 2, B.P.O. Elks
A Political Discussion
Polo Game: Myopia vs. Dedham
Prize-Winning Coaches
The Promenaders
A Raid on a Woman's Poolroom
Rescue from the Surf
A Strike in a Dime Museum
Those Wedding Bells Shall Not Ring Out
Too Much of a Good Thing
The Tough Kid's Waterloo
The Tramp Gets Whitewashed
Trouble at the Christening
Trouble in Hogan's Alley
A Wake in "Hell's Kitchen"
Washington Lodge, No. 15, B.P.O. Elks
Who Said Chicken?
Aug [day undetermined]
Arrival of Train at Muskoka Wharf
Chasing the Cherry Pickers
Demonstrating the Action of the Brown Hoisting and Conveying Machine in Unloading a Schooner of Iron Ore, and Loading the Material on the Cars
Departure of Boats from Muskoka Wharf
Eccentricities of an Adirondack Canoe
A Farmer's Imitation of Ching Ling Foo
The 'Gator and the Pickaninny
"A Gone Goose"
The Imperial Limited
A Launch Party in the Adirondacks
Living Pictures
M'lle Alma
The Narrows
Over the Fence and Out
Phrosine and Meledore
Pierrot's Problem, or How To Make a Fat Wife Out of Two Lean Ones
Rescue from a Harem
Rescue of a White Girl from the Boxers
The Shah's Return from Paris
The Slave Market
Steamer "Stowell" Running the Narrows
Temptation of St. Anthony
The Unfaithful Odalisque
Sep [day undetermined]
"Above the Limit"
Accidents Will Happen
Around the Flip-Flap Railroad
The Barber's Queer Customer
Bryn Mawr Horse Show
Capt. Boynton Feeding His Pets
Children Rolling Down Hill
The Chinese Rubbernecks
A Dog Fight
"Drill, Ye Tarriers, Drill"
Family Troubles
For Ice Cream and Cake
Galveston Disaster
The Galveston Disaster
Ghosts in a Chinese Laundry
H. N. Marvin's Family
A Hand Car and the Imperial Limited
Homer Davenport, the Cartoonist
Hon. B. B. Odell, Jr.
How the Artist Captured the Chinese Boxers
How the Magician Got the Best of the Installment Man
Imperial Limited
Indiana Whitecaps
Lincoln Park
Little Sister
Love in the Suburbs
The Magic Picture
Orpheum Theatre
Panoramic View, Rescue Work, Galveston
Panoramic View, Wreckage Along Shore, Galveston
Philadelphia's Pride
Republican National Committee of 1900
The "St. Paul" Outward Bound
Scene in Chinatown
A Scene in Fairmount Park, Phila.
"Shoo Fly"
Spooks at School
Tortured by Boxers
The Tribulations of an Amateur Photographer
A Water Duel
What the Bathing Girls Did to the Kodak Fiend
Why Curfew Did Not Ring Last Night
William J. Bryan in the Biograph
Oct [day undetermined]
Boarding School Girls' Pajama Parade
"Courier"
A Flirtation
Fun in a Photograph Gallery
A Good Time Behind the Scenes
A Hot Time in the Dressing Room
How the Dude Got the Soubrette's Baggage
Jealousy in the Dressing Room
A Joke on the Old Maid
"The Kleptomaniacs"
Knock-out Drops on the Bowery
The Last Alarm
On the Cleveland and Eastern Railway
Pan-American Exposition
Scandal in the Custom House
School Fire Drill
Soubrettes in a Bachelor's Flat
Stallion Championship
They Led Her Husband Astray
A Thief in a Soubrette's Boarding House
"Three Ones"
Through the Key-Hole in the Door
A Visit to Baby Roger
Westminster Street
What the Jay Saw in the Studio
What they Do to Respectable Men in the Tenderloin
Where the Female Smuggler Hid the Lace
Nov [day undetermined]
"Above the Limit"
Another Demonstration of the Cliff-Guibert Fire Hose Reel, Showing a Young Girl Coming from an Office, Detaching the Hose, Running with It 60 Feet, and Playing a Stream, All Inside of 30 Seconds
"Art Studies"
Aunt Jane's Experience with Tabasco Sauce
Bribing the Police
Contrary Wind
A Customer Drops In
Employees of Wolfson's Spice Mills, Toledo
The Fire at Tarrant & Co.'s Drug Store
In a Chinese Restaurant
Keith's Theater, London
Return of the Canadian Contingent
Scene from "Old Kentucky"
Showing a Giant Crane Dumping a 40-Ton Car
Two Old Cronies
"Two's Company"
The Ugly Tempered Tramp
"When We Were Twenty-One"
Nov 11 Joan of Arc
Dec [day undetermined]
At Break-Neck Speed
Childhood's Vows
Davy Jones' Locker
The Evidence Was Against Him
From Council Bluffs to Omaha
Helping Mother
High School Pupils
The Iron Workers
Lawrence Fire Department
Mill Hands
Neptune's Daughters
A Nymph of the Waves
St. Mary's Congregation
"Stop Thief!"
U. S. Naval Militia
Union Pacific Fast Mail
1901 [month undetermined]
Amateur Athletic Association Sports
"Bend Or"
The Builders of Shamrock II
Chamberlain and Balfour
Emar De Flon, the Champion Skater
Launch of Shamrock II
Li Hung Chang
Nabbed by the Nipper
Norway Ski Jumping Contests
Panoramic View of London Streets, Showing Coronation Decorations
Signor Marconi—Wireless Telegraphy
Soot Versus Suds
Spanish Coronation Royal Bull-Fight
Their Majesties the King and Queen
Winter Life in Sweden
Jan [day undetermined]
After a Rescue at Sea
The Bengal Lancers
Boat Drill in Mid-Ocean
Bolster Sparring
Capt. Reilly's Battery, Bombardment of Pekin
Capt. Reilly's Battery Limbering
Cast Up by the Waves
Charge of Cossack Cavalry
Chinese Junks
A Chinese Market
Cossack Cavalry
Crew of a Pacific Liner
First Bengal Lancers, Distant View
The French Bridge
French Bridge, Tien-Tsin
The Ghost Train
Japanese Artillery
Japanese Infantry on the March
Japanese Soldiers on the Taku Road
Launch of the "Saturn"
Li Hung Chang
An Oriental Highway
Reilly's Light Battery F
Review of Russian Artillery
"Rock of Ages"
Russian Sharp Shooters
Second Squad, Sixth U. S. Cavalry
Sixth U. S. Cavalry Charging
Sixth U. S. Cavalry, Skirmish Line
Street Scene, Tientsin [China]

The Taku Road
Von Waldersee Reviewing Cossacks
The War in China—A British Donkey Train
The War in China—An Army Transport Train
The War in China—Bombay Cavalry
The War in China—British Light Artillery
The War in China—British Rajputs
The War in China—Coolies at Work
The War in China—Japanese Infantry
The War in China—Review of German Troops
The War in China—Ruins of Tien-Tsin
The War in China—Von Waldersee and Staff
The War in China—Von Waldersee's Review

Feb [day undetermined]
Anawanda Club
Charge by 1st Bengal Lancers
Departure of Duke and Duchess of Cornwall for Australia
First Bengal Lancers
The First Procession in State of H. M. King Edward VII
First Procession in State of H. M. King Edward VII
The Forbidden City
The Forbidden City, Pekin
The 14th Sikhs
The Fourth Ghorkhas
God Save the King
In Old China
Locked in the Ice
Main Street, Worcester
Medical Gymnastics
Moline Bag Punching Platform
The 9th Infantry, U. S. A.
On the Pei-Ho
Queen Victoria's Funeral [Number 1]
Queen Victoria's Funeral [Number 2]
Queen Victoria's Funeral [Number 3]
Reading the Proclamation at St. James Palace
Sea Gulls
Second Queen's Rajputs
Shanghai from a Launch
6th Cavalry Assaulting South Gate of Pekin
Squad of Men Clearing the Road
Street in Shanghai
Street Scene in Shanghai
Street Scene, Shanghai
Tien-Tsin
The War in China
The War in China—First Bengal Lancers
The War in China
The War in China—The Evacuation of Pekin
The War in China—The Fourth Goorkhas
The War in China—The German Contingent

Mar [day undetermined]
Castellane-De Rodays Duel
Codfishing with Trawl
Drawing a Lobster Pot
Fertilizing Codfish Eggs
Run of the Worcester Fire Department
The Second Inauguration
Trotters at Worcester
Unloading Cod
Unloading Halibut

Apr [day undetermined]
Artillery Drill at Annapolis
Band and Battalion of the U. S. Indian School
Basket Ball
Buffalo Bill's Wild West Parade
Calisthenic Drill
Carrie Nation Smashing a Saloon
Club Swinging, Carlisle Indian School
Deaf Mute Recitation
Demolishing and Building Up the Star Theatre
Dressmaking
Energizing Drill
Forging
General Quarters for Action
Girls Dumbbell Drill
Heavy Gymnastics
The High Jump
The High School Cadets
Japanese Wrestling
Jiu Jitsu, the Japanese Art of Self-Defense
Kindergarten Methods
Laboratory Study
A Language Lesson
Manual Training
A Muffin Lesson
Nature Study, the Rabbit
Physical Training
Pole Vaulting
Springtime in the Park
Star Spangled Banner by a Deaf Mute
U. S. Naval Cadets Marching in Review

May [day undetermined]
Anna Held
At the Setting of the Sun
Bass Fishing
Boats Under Oars
Fulton Market
A Good Test of High Explosives
Hauling a Shad Net
The Horticultural Building
In a Japanese Tattooing Parlor
In the Gypsy Camp
A Large Haul of Fish
"Laughing Ben"
The Lovers' Yarn
Middies Shortening Sails
A Mystic Re-Incarnation
The New Maid
On the Old Plantation
The Slippery Slide
Steam Tactics
U. S. Proving Grounds, Sandy Hook
United States Government Gun Test
Unloading a Mackerel Schooner
An Unlucky Lover

Jun [day undetermined]
An April Fool Joke
Bally-Hoo Cake Walk
Beautiful Orient
"Birth of the Pearl"
The Bridge of Sighs—Pan-American Exposition
A Close Shave
The Court of Fountains—Pan-American Exposition
"The Diskobolus"
Emperor William's Yacht "Meteor"
English Derby, 1901
Esquimaux Dance
An Esquimaux Game
The Esquimaux Village
Experimental
Fair Japan—Pan-American Exposition
"Finishing Touches"
"Forward"
Fountain, Tower, and Basins—Pan-American Exposition
Ham and Eggs
The Heart of New York
Hot Mutton Pies
The Indian Congress
International Yacht Races on the Clyde
A Joke on Whom?
A Legal Hold-Up
A Little Piece of String
Main Entrance to Pan-American Exp.
Meandering Mike
A Non-Union Paper Hanger
On the Benches in the Park
On the Midway—Pan-American Exposition
The Ostrich Farm—On the Midway
Panorama of Midway—Pan-American Exposition
Panoramic View Gov't Building, Pan. Am. Exp.
Panoramic View of the Thames
A Patient Sufferer
"The Pouting Model"
Propylaea and North End of Plaza, Pan. Am. Exp.
Scene in Beautiful Orient—Pan-American Exposition
Sevillenas Dance—Pan-American Exposition
"The Sleeping Child"
Ten Nights in a Bar-Room: Death of Little Mary
Ten Nights in a Bar-Room: Death of Slade
Ten Nights in a Bar-Room: Murder of Willie
Ten Nights in a Bar-Room: The Fatal Blow
Ten Nights in a Bar-Room: Vision of Mary
Triumphal Bridge, Pan-American Exposition
U. S. National Cemetery
An Unexpected Knockout
Venice in America
"Volodyovski"
"Waiting for Santa Claus"
Washington Bridge and Speedway
"You Dirty Boy"

Jul [day undetermined]
Arrival of Train at Station
Boys Entering Free Bath
Boys Free Public Baths
The Downfall of China
F. S. Gibbs and Family
Fish Cut
Five Minutes to Train Time
Flock of Sheep
The Fresh Lover
The Georgetown Loop
He Forgot His Umbrella
Herd of Cattle
The Hod Carrier's Revenge
Indian Fort, Sherman Hill Tunnel
Ladies Day at the Public Baths
Little Algy's Glorious Fourth of July
Nora's 4th of July
Oh! What a Night; or, The Sultan's Dream
On the Midway—Pan-American Exposition
The Overland Limited
Pine Ridge Bluffs
A Quick Recovery
A Race with the Overland Limited
Saturday at the Free Baths
Through Gibraltar
Train Crossing Dale Creek Fill
The Wages of Sin—A Mother's Grief
The Wages of Sin—The Assassin's Escape
The Wages of Sin—The Fatal Choice
The Wages of Sin—The Murder of Bess
When Stocks Went Up
Women of the Ghetto Bathing

Aug [day undetermined]
Boys Diving
Broadway and Fourteenth St. Experimental
The Campus Martius
Centennial Parade
Cutting Sugar Cane
Detroit Mail Carriers
A Flower Parade
Gathering Gladioli
The Henley Regatta, 1901
Industrial Floats
Landing of Cadillac
Loading Sugar Cane
Panorama of Water Front
Steamboat Leaving for Hilo
Steamship "Bismark"
Steamship "Deutschland"
Steamship "Graf Waldersee"
Train of Sugar Cane on Way to Crusher
Unveiling Chair of Justice

Sep [day undetermined]
Arrival at Falls View Station
Bridge Traffic, Manila
Capt. Schuyler Post of Philadelphia
Chapin Post of Buffalo
A Close Call
Cuyahoga Gorge

The Empire Theatre
Farragut Naval Post, Ohio State
Finish of Futurity
Finish of Futurity, 1901
Finish of Race Sheepshead Bay, Experimental
Funeral of President McKinley
Headquarters, Staff and Band, Ohio State
In Old Hong Kong
Industrial Parade of the Cincinnati Fall Festival
International Field Sports
International Field Sports—Oxford-Cambridge vs. Harvard-Yale
International Track Athletic Meeting—Start and Finish of the One Mile Run
Lambs Club, G. A. R.
The Living Flag
Lyttle Post of Cincinnati
McKinley Funeral—In Solemn State
Ox Carts
Panorama of Kobe Harbor, Japan
Panorama, Public Square, Cleveland, O.
Panoramic View of the McKinley Homestead
Parade to the Post
President McKinley's Funeral
The Queen's Road
Sampans Racing Toward Liner
Sampans Racing toward Liner
Sousa and His Band
Street Scene, Tokio, Japan
Traveling Men's Association

Oct [day undetermined]
Asakusa Temple
Bridal Veil Falls
Coaching for a Record
A Filipino Cock Fight
Finish of Flatbush Stakes, Gravesend Track
Finish of the Third Cup Race
Hail Columbia!
Horses Jumping Water Jump
International Yacht Races—Columbia vs. Shamrock
Japanese Fencing
A Japanese Railway Train
Match Race, Endurance by Right vs. Heno
The Matron Stakes
Mr. H. Casler and Baby. Experimental
Natives Leaving Church
A Near View of Shamrock II
Nevada Falls
Panorama of Water Front
A Perilous Proceeding
Rickshaw Parade, Japan
Schooner "Idler" and Revenue Cutter "Gresham"
Shamrock to the Fore
Shamrock's Start
Shimbashi R. R. Station
Start of the Third Cup Race
Steam Yacht "American"
Wawona, Big Tree

Oct 24 Arrival of Tongkin Train
The Bund, Shanghai
The Ch-ien-men Gate, Pekin
Coaling a Steamer, Nagasaki Bay, Japan
Harbor of Shanghai

Oct 25 Convention of Railroad Passengers Agents
Panoramic View, Asheville, N. C.

Oct 26 Little Red Riding Hood

Nov [day undetermined]
Artist's Point
A Cavalry Manoeuvre
Coaching Party, Yosemite Valley
In the Yellowstone
Launch
A Mighty Tumble
Panorama, Golden Gate
Picturesque Yosemite
Twentieth Century Flyers
Water Front of San Francisco
A Wonderful Waterfall
Yale Football, Practice Scrimmage
Yale Football Squad of 1901

Nov 23 A Christmas Dream

Dec [day undetermined]
The Beginning of a Great Enterprise
Children Playing Ball
Cutting Cucumbers and Cauliflower, Heinz
Expert Driving
Football Game: West Point vs. Annapolis
Packing Pickle Jars, Heinz
President Roosevelt at the Army-Navy Game
President Roosevelt Entering Grounds at Army-Navy Football Game
Tally Ho!

1902 [month undetermined]
A Frustrated Elopement
The Man with the Rubber Head

Jan [day undetermined]
Deer in Park
Eeling Through the Ice
Great Sport! Ice Yachting
Ice Yacht Racing
Love in a Hammock
A Mile a Minute on an Ice Yacht
A Spill from an Ice Yacht
Starting a Skyscraper

Feb [day undetermined]
Amateur Ski Jumpers
Battleship "Illinois"
A Big Blaze
"Bouncing"
Demonstrating the Action of a Mergenthaler-Horton Basket Making Machine
A Devastated City
Docking a Liner
Dog Sleighing
Fire at Durland's Academy, N. Y. City
The "Hohenzollern"
A Husky Dog Team
Kent House Slide
Launch of Meteor III
Over the Crust
Park Avenue Explosion
The Paterson Fire
Quebec Fire Department on Sleds
The Royal Salute
Run of a Snow Shoe Club
Toboggan Slide
Welcome Prince Henry!
"What Ho, She Bumps!"

Mar [day undetermined]
B. F. Keith's New Million Dollar Theatre
Experimental. Southwestern Limited Train
Ferryboat Entering Slip
Madison Square, New York City
"Meteor III" Afloat
Mice
Prince Henry
Prince Henry and President's Party
Prince Henry at Philadelphia
Prince Henry at West Point
Prince Henry of Germany
"When the Cat's Away, the Mice Will Play"

Apr [day undetermined]
Century Wheelman, N. Y. City
Demonstrating the Action of an Agnew Mailing Machine
48th Highlanders Regiment
General Electric Flash Light
Installation Ceremonies, Columbia University
Installation Ceremonies of President Butler
The "Meteor"
Pontoon Bridge Building
Trial Trip of "Meteor"

May [day undetermined]
The Boys Help Themselves to Foxy Grandpa's Cigars
The Boys, Still Determined, Try It Again on Foxy Grandpa, with the Same Result
The Boys Think They Have One on Foxy Grandpa, but He Fools Them
The Boys Try to Put One Up on Foxy Grandpa
The Clown with the Portable Body
The Creators of Foxy Grandpa
Experimental. Moving Picture Machine
Foxy Grandpa and Polly in a Little Hilarity
Foxy Grandpa Shows the Boys a Trick or Two with the Tramp
Foxy Grandpa Tells the Boys a Funny Story
Herrmann, the Great Conjuror
The Magician and the Human Pump
On the Speedway
A Poet's Revenge
A Private Supper at Heller's
Scene on Lower Broadway
The Speedway Parade
Street Scene

May 3 Blue Beard

Jun [day undetermined]
The Accomodating Cow
Alphonse and Gaston
Aunt Jane and the Tobasco Sauce
Belles of the Beach
Biograph's Improved Incubator
The Bowery Kiss
Daly, of West Point
Eva Tanguay
The Light That Didn't Fail
The Lovers' Knot
Lower New York
Milking Time on the Farm
On a Milk Diet
Over the Rail
Panorama of Lower New York
A Picture from "Puck"
The Polite Frenchman
Rag Time Dance
Rag Time Dance (Hot)
Review of Cadets at West Point
Review of Cadets, West Point
A Seashore Gymkana
A Spill
The Suburban of 1902
The Summer Exodus
"A Sweet Little Home in the Country"
They Found the Leak
A Tough Dance
A Tub Race
Will He Marry the Girl?

Jul [day undetermined]
Baby in a Rage
Baby Playing in Gutter
A Delusion
The Draped Model
Explosion of an Automobile
Grandpa's Reading Glass
In a Manicure Parlor
In a Massage Parlor
The Lamp Explodes
A Little Man
Mischievous Willie's Rocking Chair Motor
No Liberties, Please
The Photographer's Fourth of July
A Pipe Story of the Fourth
She Meets with Wife's Approval
The Sleeper
Thro' Hell Gate
Wrinkles Removed

Aug [day undetermined]
Around the Mulberry Bush
At the Fountain
Baby Parade
The Beach at Atlantic City
Biograph Snapshots at the President
Caught in the Undertow
Demonstrating the Action of an Altman-Taylor Clover Huller
Demonstrating the Action of an Altman-Taylor Threshing Machine
Floral Chair Parade
Gay Girls of Gotham
A Gentleman Burglar
A Heavy Surf at Atlantic City
The King of Detectives
A Lawn Party
A Little Mix-Up in a Mixed Ale Joint
Old Volunteer Fire Dept.

Rex's Bath
Shut Up!
A Study in Openwork
Sweethearts
Wash Day
Water Nymphs
Sep [day undetermined]
A Ball on a Battleship
Bombardment of Newport
Coronation Parade
Down the Mountain Side
From the Crow's Nest
The Futurity Crowd
The Futurity of 1902
Good Luck Baking Powder Train No. 1
Good Luck Baking Powder Train No. 2
Mr. Grauman. For Private Use
Pain's Fireworks
A Photographic Contortion
Reproduction, Coronation Ceremonies—King Edward VII
St. John's Guild. Bathing in Surf and Leaving Water
St. John's Guild. Crippled Children to and from Wagon
St. John's Guild. Dispensary Scene, Floating Hospital
St. John's Guild. Dock to Plank, 35th St.
St. John's Guild. Examination of Patients
St. John's Guild. From Launch to Dock
St. John's Guild. Going in Water.
St. John's Guild. Going to Salt-water Bath Room
St. John's Guild. Julliard and Tug in Narrows
St. John's Guild. Julliard Passing; Fire-Hose Playing
St. John's Guild. Launch Approaching Dock
St. John's Guild. Launch Delivering Patients to F. H.
St. John's Guild. Patients Down Bridge. S.S.H.
St. John's Guild. Plank to Deck, Floating Hospital
Savable Wins
A Stern Chase
A Telephone Romance
Turning Panorama of Mt. Beacon
Oct [day undetermined]
The Eighth Wonder
General Booth
"Seeing New York"
Oct 4 A Trip to the Moon
Nov [day undetermined]
The Abbe and the Colonel
Aboard the Aegir
"All Hot"
Allegorical Procession
Arrival of Major Marchand from the Soudan
The Attack
An Automobile Parade in the Tuilleries Gardens
The Baby's Meal
Banks of the Elbe
Battleship "Odin"
"Be Good Again"
Beautifyl Beaulieu
Berlin Fire Department
Between the Decks
Bi-Centennial Jubilee Parade
A Blast in a Gravel Bed
The Bogie Man
The Bon Vivant
Boyville Fire Brigade
Bridge of Alexander III
Calling the Pigeons
Captain Dreyfus
The Champs Elysees
The Children and the Frog
The Children of the Czar
Children Playing with Lion Cubs
Clever Horsemanship
The Crown Prince of Germany
A Dance by Kanaka Indians
Dedication of the Alexander Grenadiers' Barracks
Dessert at Dan Leno's House
A Dog's Cemetery
The Elephant's Bath
Elevated and Underground
The Emperor and Empress and Crown Prince of Germany
Emperor and Empress of Germany
The Emperor and Empress of Germany
Emperor William II
Emperor William II on Horseback
Emperor William as a Hussar
Emperor William at the Danzig Manoeuvres
Emperor William of Germany on Horseback
Emperor William Returning from Manoeuvres
Empress of Germany at Danzig
Empress of Germany Driving to the Manoeuvres
Field-Marshal Count Von Waldersee
The Flying Train
A Flying Wedge
A French Bicycle Corps
French Boxers
From Monte Carlo to Monaco
Fun in a Clothes Basket
Fun on a Sand Hill
Funeral Procession of the Late Empress Frederick
Ganswindt's Flying Machine
George J. Marck and His Lions
German Artillery in Action
German Cavalry Fording a River
German Cavalry Leaping Hurdles
German Garde Kurassiers
German Lancers
German Military Exercises
German Navy Target Practice
German Railway Service
A German Torpedo Boat Flotilla in Action
The Giant Constantin
The Gold Dust Twins
The Gourmand
His Morning Bath
A Hurdle Race
In a German Bath
In the Friedrichstrasse
In the Heart of the Forest
The India-Rubber Man
Jo Jo, the Dog Faced Boy
King Albert of Saxony
King Edward VII at the Birthday Celebration of the King of Denmark
Launch of the "Koenig Albert"
Launching of the "Kaiser Wilhelm der Grosse"
Let the Gold Dust Twins Do Your Work
The Longchamps Palace
Marvelous Markmanship
A Mermaid Dance
A Mis-Adventure
Mr. Dan Leno, Assisted by Mr. Herbert Campbell, Editing the "Sun"
Mr. Oldsport's Umbrella
M. Le Comte De Dion
The Murderer's Vision
New York's New Subway
An Obstinate Cork
The Old Port of Marseilles
On Board His Majesty's Battleship "Fuerst Bismark"
On Board His Majesty's Gunboat "Luchs"
On the Elbe
On the Marseilles Tramway
Oom Paul
Panorama of Wilhelmshaven
Panoramic View from the Stadtbahn
Panoramic View of the Harbor of Hamburg, Germany
Panoramic View of the Siegesallee
Paris Exposition
A Parisian Ballet
Prince Tsung of China
Prize-Winning Trip of the Santos-Dumont Airship No. 6
Promenade of the Kings
Rare Fish in an Aquarium
Rare Fish in the Aquarium
A Remarkable Fire
A Rescue at Sea
Return of the German China Fleet
The Rivals
A Romp on the Lawn
Rulers of Half the World
A Run by the Berlin Fire Department, Berlin, Germany
Sailing of Battleship "Wurtemberg"
Ten Minutes at Monte Carlo
Torpedo Boat "G-89"
The Train to Villefranche
A Tug of War
Umbrella Dance, San Toy
An Unsinkable Skimmer
Unveiling of the Bismarck Monument
An Unwelcome Visitor
The Valiant Pig
Visit of Emperor Francis Josef of Austria to Berlin
A Water Carnival
When Knighthood Was in Flower
When the Bugle Sounds "Charge!"
Winter in Germany
With Emperor William's Army
"Zip"
Dec [day undetermined]
After the First Snow
After the Service
Broadway & Union Square, New York
"Chums"
A Corner in the Play Room
The Horse Market
Officers of National Cash Register Co. Leaving Club House
Sheep and Lambs
1903 [month undetermined]
Brothers of the Misericordia, Rome
A Donkey Party
Down the Hotel Corridor
Down the Hudson
Flag Dance
German Torpedo Boat in Action
H. H. Pope Leo [XIII] in Chair
Ice Yachting
An Innocent Conspirator
Madison Square, New York
Old Gentleman Spinkles
Jan [day undetermined]
A Midwinter Blaze
The Soldier's Return
What Was Found in a High Hat
Jan 31 Wonderful Suspension and Evolution
Feb [day undetermined]
Children Coasting
Envelope Folder and Sealer, National Cash Register Co.
German Flag Afloat, National Cash Register Co.
Girls Getting on Trolley, National Cash Register Co.
Girls Going to Lunch. National Cash Register Co.
Girls in Physical Culture, National Cash Register Co.
The Human Fly
The Impossible Feat of Balancing
Jubilee, National Cash Register Co.
Little Wonder Printing Press, National Cash Register Co.
The Magician and the Imp
Men Getting on Trolley, National Cash Register Co.
Men in Physical Exercise, National Cash Register Co.
Men Leaving Factory, National Cash Register Co.
Mephistopheles' School of Magic
Mr. Bickford on Trolley, National Cash Register Co.
Mr. Carney and Friend, National Cash Register Co.
Mr. Carroll and Assistant, National Cash Register Co.
Mr. Chalmers and Mr. Gibbs Arrive at Club, National Cash Register Co.
Mr. Chalmers Going to Officers' Club, National Cash Register Co.

Mr. J. H. Crane, National Cash Register Co.
Mr. Lawer, National Cash Register Co.
Mr. Patterson and Mr. Mark Arriving, National Cash Register Co.
Officers Leaving Club, National Cash Register Co.
Panorama of Factory from Automobile, National Cash Register Co.
Patterson Children in Pony Wagon, National Cash Register Co.
Patterson Children Leaving Home, National Cash Register Co.
Patterson Children on Horseback, National Cash Register Co.
Policeman and Automobile
Porters in Parade, National Cash Register Co.
Steam Whistle, National Cash Register Co.
A Sweep across New York
Testing Jacks, National Cash Register Co.
Twentieth Century Conjuring
25 Stories Up!
Up-to-Date Surgery
Visitors in Wheeling Chairs, National Cash Register Co.
Window Display Clown, National Cash Register Co.
Window Display Revolving Balls, National Cash Register Co.

Mar [day undetermined]
Blasting the Treadwell Mines
Captain Allard Shooting White Horse Rapids
Disposition of Slabs and Waste at Pt. Blakeley
Dog Baiting and Fighting in Valdez
First Snow Storm of the Season, Valdez
Fourth and Market Sts., San Francisco
Horses Swimming Copper River
Hydraulic Mining in Oregon
In the Rapid-Transit Tunnel
Kalama Railroad Ferry Crossing the Columbia River
Leaving Skagway for the Golden North
Oil Fields, Tanks and Lakes of Oil; Kern Co., Cal.
Old Method of Mining, No. 11 Eldorado
Operation on the Famous Chechawko Hill
A Pack Train in the Copper River Country
Pack Train Leaving Valdez for Copper Mines
Panorama of Cal. Oil Fields
Panorama of Kennicott Glacier Port Hole
Panorama of "Miles Canyon"
Panorama of No. 2 Eldorado
Panorama of Taku Glacier
Panorama of White Horse Rapids
Passengers Alighting and Drinking Shasta Water
Past Shasta Spring, California
A Rotary Snow Plow in the Great Northwest
Sacramento Valley, Cal. from Pilot of Engine
Snow-Plow Bucking a 15-foot Snow Slide
Steamer Queen on Ice
Steamer Susie Excursion to Moosehide
Steamer "Yukoner" Leaving Dawson
$35,000 Clean-Up on Eldorado No. 10
Through Cascade Tunnel
Through Miles Canyon on a Cattle Scow
Through Tunnel on the White Pass Route
Through White Horse Rapids
Tunnel Scene of the White Pass Route
Two Miles of the White Pass & Yukon Railroad
Unfair House, Butchers Boycotting, San Francisco
Willamette Falls
Winter Sport on Snake River, Nome

Mar 7 Robinson Crusoe

Mar 14 The Delhi Camp Railway
Logging in Canada
On the Bow River Horse Ranch at Cochrane, North West Territory
Spearing Salmon in the Rivers of the North West Territory

Apr [day undetermined]
Acquatic Sports
American Falls, Goat Island
American Falls, Luna Island
Ameta
Artist and the Dummy
Ascending a Rock-Chimney on the Grand Charmoz, 11,293 feet
Ascent and Descent of the Aiguilles Des Grandes Charmoz, 11,293 feet
Bachelor's Paradise
Bewitched Dungeon
The Brahmin and the Butterfly
Breaking a Bronco
The Broncho Horse Race
Coaching in Ireland
Coaching Through the Tunnel on the Kenmere Road
Conjurer and 100 Tricks
Coster Sports
"The Devil of the Deep" and the Sea Urchins
A Devonshire Fair
A Duel with Knives
England's Colonial Troops
An English Prize-Fight
For the Upper Crust
Gigantic Devil
A Gorgeous Pageant of Princes
The Grand Canal, Venice
The Grand Panorama from the Great Schreckhorn, 13,500 feet
The House of Mystery
The House That Jack Built
How He Missed His Train
A Japanese Wrestling Match
A Kennel Club Parade
A Kiss in the Tunnel
Landing Guns
Launch of Shamrock III
Life and Passion of Christ
The Long and Short of It
Looping the Loop
A Majestic Stag
Man's Best Friend
Mary Jane's Mishap; or, Don't Fool with the Parafin
Miracles of Brahmin
The Miser
The Monk in the Monastery Wine Cellar
Mountain Torrents
On Horseback, Killarney
On the Grand Canal, Venice
Over London Bridge
Panorama of Alpine Peaks
Panorama of Grindelwald
Panorama of Lucerne Lake
Panorama of Queenstown
Panorama on the St. Gothard Railway
A Paper Chase
Pa's Comment on the Morning News
The Pines of the Rockies
Pulling a Seine U. S. F. C.
Push Ball
Review of Native Chiefs at the Durbar
Review of the Chiefs at the Durbar
The River Shannon
Ski Jumping Competition
The Sorcerer, Prince and the Good Fairy
Spanish Bull Fight
Spilt Milk
Stag Hunting in England
Stripping Pike Perch U. S. F. C.
A Swiss Carnival
Through the Telescope
A Triple Balloon Ascent
A Two Handed Sword Contest
A Visit to the London Zoo
A Water Carnival
Weary Willie and the Policeman
What Befell the Inventor's Visitor
With the Stag Hounds

Apr 13 Gulliver's Travels

May [day undetermined]
The Angler
The Artist's Studio
Be Good
Caught Courting
Changing Horses at Glen
Changing Horses at Linden
Child Eating
"Don't Get Gay with Your Manicure!"
Eclipse Car Fender Test
Experimental
The Hairdresser
How Tommy Got a Pull on His Grandpa
"I Want My Dinner"
Juvenile Stakes
Life of an English Fireman
Meadowbrook Steeplechase
Metropolitan Handicap
N. Y. Fire Department Returning
On the Road
The Pajama Girl
Private Picture for Mr. Hyde
Pulling Off the Bed Clothes
Rip Van Winkle
Run of N. Y. Fire Department
A Shocking Incident
Shooting the Chutes
Stripping Shad U. S. F. C.

May 16 Spring Cleaning

Jun [day undetermined]
Beaver Show Case
Betsy Ross Dance
The Cook Visits the Parlor
Cosy Corner Dance
Danger of Dining in Private Dining Rooms
The Doctor's Favorite Patient
Down the Bamboo Slide
The Giddy Dancing Master
Gloomy Gus Gets the Best of It
Happy Hooligan Interferes
The Haymarket
"Holy Moses" the Camel
How Mike Got the Soap in His Eyes
Living Picture Production
Market Street Before Parade
The Necromancer
Over Route of Roosevelt Parade in an Automobile
A Pair of Queens
Panorama, Union Square, San Francisco
Poor Old Fido!
President Reviewing School Children
The President's Carriage
The Professor of the Drama
Reproduction of Corbett-McGovern Fight
Rock Drill at Work in Subway
Snarleyow the Dog Fiend
The Teacher's Unexpected Ducking
An Unprotected Female

Jul [day undetermined]
The American Soldier in Love and War [Number 1]
The American Soldier in Love and War [Number 2]
The American Soldier in Love and War [Number 3]
Battle Flags of the 9th U. S. Infantry
Bayonet Exercises
A Boarding School Prank
The Boy in the Barrel
Catch-as-Catch-Can Wrestling Bout
A Discordant Note
The Divorce: Detected [Part 1]
The Divorce: On the Trail [Part 2]
The Divorce: The Evidence Secured [Part 3]
Expert Bag Punching
The Fate of a Gossip
Happy Hooligan Earns His Dinner
Happy Hooligan in a Trap
How Buttons Got Even with the Butler
Laplanders at Home
Levi & Cohen, The Irish Comedians
Making a Welch Rabbit
Musical Calisthenics
Musical Drill with Arms

The Physical Culture Girl, No. 1
The Physical Culture Girl, No. 2
The Physical Culture Girl, No. 3
Pres. Roosevelt's Fourth of July Oration
Shelter Tent Drill
Shooting the Chutes, Luna Park
Strictly Fresh Eggs
A Too Ardent Lover
The Unfaithful Wife: Murder and Suicide [Part 3]
The Unfaithful Wife: The Fight [Part 2]
The Unfaithful Wife: The Lover [Part 1]
A Victim of Circumstantial Evidence
A Welsh Rabbit
Why Foxy Grandpa Escaped a Ducking
Willie's Camera

Aug [day undetermined]
Balloon Race
The Burglar
Buying Stamps from Rural Wagon, U. S. P. O.
Cancelling Machine, U. S. P. O.
Carriers at Work, U. S. P. O.
Carriers Leaving Building, U. S. P. O.
Clerks Casing Mail for Bags, U. S. P. O.
Clerks Tying Bags, U. S. P. O.
Clerks Tying Up for Bags, U. S. P. O.
Coach at Rural Post Office, U. S. P. O.
Collecting Mail, U. S. P. O.
The Dude and the Burglars
Exchange of Mail at Rural P. O., U. S. P. O.
Fife Getting Instructions from Committee
Finish of the First Race, Aug. 22
A Funny Story on the Beach
The Girl at the Window
Gold Dust Twins
A Gypsy Duel
"He Loves Me, He Loves Me Not"
Horses Drawing in Seine
Horses Drawing Salmon Seine
In My Lady's Boudoir
Jockeying for the Start Aug. 20
Jockeying for the Start Aug. 22
The Kidnapper: At Work [Part 1]
The Kidnapper: In the Den [Part 2]
The Kidnapper: The Rescue [Part 3]
A Little Tease
Loading Mail Car, U. S. P. O.
"Love Me, Love My Dog"
Lucky Kitten!
Mailing Platform, U. S. P. O.
Men Taking Fish from Salmon Seine
Murder Scene from "King of the Detectives"
Old Mail Coach at Ford, U. S. P. O.
On the Flying Rings
Post Man Delivering Mail, U. S. P. O.
Racing for a Tow
Railroad View—Experimental
Reliance Rounding Turn, August 20th
"Reliance" vs. "Shamrock" III, Aug. 20
The Rose
Routing Mail, U. S. P. O.
Rural Wagon Delivering Mail, U. S. P. O.
Rural Wagon Giving Mail to Branch, U. S. P. O.
A Search for Evidence
Silveon and Emerie "On the Web"
Special Delivery Messenger, U. S. P. O.
Stake Boat with Stake ("John Scully")
Start of the First Race, Aug. 22
Street Mail Car, U. S. P. O.
Sweets for the Sweet
Throwing Mail into Bags, U. S. P. O.
A Total Accident
Transporting Internal Rev. Stamps, U. S. P. O.
The Two Sisters!
Tying Up Bags for Train, U. S. P. O.
The Waders
The Wages of Sin: A—Murder
The Wages of Sin: B—Retribution
Wagons Loading Mail, U. S. P. O.
"What Are the Wild Waves Saying Sister?"
The Widow
A Yard of Puppies

Sep [day undetermined]
(Abandoned)
At Brighton Beach
At Terrific Speed
At the Ford, India. Across the Ravi River
The Baby
Bathing in Samoa
The Busy Bee
Butchering and Cleaning Tables U. S. F. C.
The Camera Fiend
The Chorus Girl and the Salvation Army Lassie
Coasting in the Alps
A Daring Daylight Burglary
The Devonshire Fair
The Devonshire Hunt
The Diamond Robbery
Discovery of Bodies
Experimental
A False Alarm in the Dressing Room
Finish of Yacht Race, Aug. 25th
Firing the Cabin
The Forecastle of the "Kearsage" in a Heavy Sea
From London to Brighton
From Show Girl to Burlesque Queen
The Galloping Tongas
Hammock Scene—(Abandoned)
How to Get a Wife and Baby
In the Dressing Room
Indians Leaving Bald Mountain
The Insurance Collector
Jack Tar Sewing a Patch on the Seat of His Trousers
Jack's Four Footed Friend. Mike the Ship's Mascot
Jockeying and Start of Yacht[s] Aug. 25th
King Edward VII in France
Lady Bountiful Visits the Murphys on Wash Day
Lifting Salmon Trap
The Llamas of Thibet
Love in a Perilous Place
The Minister's Hat
A Norwegian Waterfall
One of Jack's Games Aboard a Man o' War
Panorama from Canoe, No. 6
Panorama of Beach and Cliff House
Panorama of Excursion Boats
Parade of Eagles, New York
Piping Down. Wash Clothes. Scrambling for Clothes
Poor Girl, It Was a Hot Night and the Mosquitos Were Thick
Pope [Leo XIII] in His Carriage
Pope [Leo XIII] Passing Through Upper Loggia
President Roosevelt Addressing Crew of "Kearsarge"
Pres. Roosevelt Leaving the Flagship
President Roosevelt's Arrival at "Kearsarge"
President Roosevelt's Departure from "Kearsarge"
Pres. Roosevelt's Sunday Visit to Kearsage
President Roosevelt's Visit to Admiral Barker
Private Picture—Families of H. N. M. & H. C.
Raising Salmon Trap U. S. F. C.
A Remarkable Group of Trained Animals
Reproduction of Jeffries-Corbett Contest
Rescue of Child from Indians
Rip Van Winkle
Rising Panorama of a Norwegian Waterfall
Salmon Seining on Columbia River U. S. F. C.
The Sand Baby
The Sand Fort
Sea Washing over the Bow of Kearsage
Seeing New York by Yacht
Settler's Home Life
Signal Boys Wig-Wagging
Sparring Match on the "Kearsarge"
Start of Race—"Reliance" Ahead
Start of the Gordon-Bennet Cup Race
A Terrific Race
Trained Baby Elephants
Trained Dogs and Elephants
Trappers Crossing Bald Mountain
An Unusual Spectacle
The Wise Elephant

Sep 18 Trailed by Bloodhounds

Oct [day undetermined]
Alphonse and Gaston 3
Alphonse and Gaston (Journal Thumb Book)
The American Soldier in Love and War
Arab Act, Luna Park
At the Dressmaker's
The Baby
Blessed Is the Peacemaker
The Camera Fiend, No. 2
A Catch of Hard Shell Crabs
Cat's Cradle
The Cowboy and the Lady
Delivering Mail from Sub-Station [U. S. P. O.]
Double Ring Act, Luna Park
The Elopement
The Fate of the Artist's Model
Foxy Grandpa [Thumb Book]
From Haverstraw to Newburg
A Frontier Flirtation; or, "How the Tenderfoot Won Out"
Happy Hooligan's Interrupted Lunch
The Honourable Artillery Company of London
Hooligan as a Safe Robber
Hooligan in Jail
Hooligan to the Rescue
Hooligan's Roller Skates
Inside Car, Showing Bag Catcher [U. S. P. O.]
Kit Carson
Kit Carson #6: Panorama
"Never Touched Him!"
Parade of "Exempt" Firemen
The Pioneers
The Providence Light Artillery
The Rehearsal
The Rock of Ages
Seeing New York by Yacht
She Fell Fainting into His Arms
Slide for Life, Luna Park
The Smoky Stove
Toodles and Her Strawberry Tart
Toodles' Strawberry Tart (Journal Thumb Book)
Train Taking Up Mail Bag, U. S. P. O.
U. S. Interior Dept.: Basket Ball, Indian School
U. S. Interior Dept.: Bridal Veil Falls
U. S. Interior Dept.: Changing Coaches, Raymond Coach
U. S. Interior Dept.: Irrigation of Alfalfa Lands
U. S. Interior Dept.: Laguna Indian Chicken-Pulling Race
U. S. Interior Dept.: Laguna Indian Foot Race
U. S. Interior Dept.: Laguna Indian Horse Race
U. S. Interior Dept.: Mail Coach Yosemite Valley
U. S. Interior Dept.: Panorama from Artist's Point
U. S. Interior Dept.: Panorama of Grand Canyon
U. S. Interior Dept.: Santa Fe Coach
U. S. Interior Dept.: Vernal Falls
U. S. P. O. Dept. Santa Fe Mail Train
Uncle Reuben at the Waldorf
The Vaidis Sisters, Luna Park
Weighing the Baby
"Who Pays for the Drinks?"
The Wrath of a Jealous Wife
"You Will Send Me to Bed, Eh?"

Oct 17 Alice in Wonderland
Oct 31 Hop Picking

Moses in the Bullrushes
The Poachers
Nov [day undetermined]
Alphonse and Gaston and the Burglar (Thumb Book)
Alphonse and Gaston Balcony Scene (Thumb Book)
Alphonse and Gaston Target Practice (Thumb Book)
Arrival of Tourists at the Hotel in Yellowstone Park
Arrival of Train at Gardner
Battleship "Indiana" in Action
Boat Race
Boat Race No. 2
Carpenter Work, Albuquerque School
Crow Indian Festival Dance
Crow Indian War Dance
Crow Indians Harvesting
Down the Bright Angel Trail
Feeding the Russian Bear
Fire Drill: Albuquerque Indian School
Firing the Cook
A Flirtation in Silhouette
Fountain Geyser
Fusion, On to Brooklyn!
Girls' Department, Albuquerque School
Girls Flag Drill, Moqui School
Great Falls of the Yellowstone
A Guardian of the Peace
Harvard-Pennsylvania Football Game
Hooligan and Dogs (Journal Thumb Book)
Hooligan's Thanksgiving Dinner (Thumb Book)
An Impartial Lover
Indian Boys, Albuquerque School
Indian Horsemanship
Inspection Aboard Battleship "Indiana"
A Juvenile Elephant Trainer
Katzenjammer Kids (Journal Thumb Book)
Lifting a Wagon from a New York Foundation
The Llamas at Play
Mammouth Paint Pot, Yosemite Valley
Man Overboard! "INDIANA"
Moqui Indian Rain Dance
Navajo Indian Foot Race
Navajo Indian Horse Race
Navajo Indian Tug-of-War
Navajo Indians Wrestling
Navajo Squaw Weaving Blanket
Next!
Off His Beat
"Old Faithful," Yosemite Valley
On Yellowstone Lake
Panorama of Yellowstone Lake
Panoramic View of Hot Springs, Yellowstone Park
Poor Hooligan, So Hungry Too!
The Professor
Rain Dance at Orabi
Raising Colors, Battleship "Indiana"
Toodles Recites a Recitation
Toodles Recites a Recitation (Thumb Book)
Toodles' Tea Party
Toodles' Tea Party (Thumb Book)
Tying the Red Light on the Tiger's Tail
United States Troops in Yellowstone Park
A Windy Day at the Flatiron Building
Nov 21 Animated Picture Studio
Automobile Explosion
Cruelty on the High Seas
The Deserter
Down Below
Fire and Rescue
The Ghost in the Graveyard
Hotel and Bath
Letter Came Too Late
Murphy's Wake
The New Cook
Nicholas Nickleby
Over the Garden Wall
A Pugilistic Parson
Quarrelsome Neighbors
Saturday's Shopping
A Trip to Southend
Nov 28 Attack on Chinese Mission
The Bather
Bicycle Dive
Jack's Return
Stop Thief
Dec [day undetermined]
Almost a King
The Ballet Rehearsal
Battleship "Illinois" Passing Under Brooklyn Bridge
Burning of the Academy of Music, Brooklyn
Clarence the Cop
The Dressmaker's Accident
Drill by Providence Police
Dumping Iron Ore
The Gerry Society's Mistake
Having Her Gown Fitted
Hooligan's Christmas Dream
How the Old Woman Caught the Omnibus
The Johnnie and the Telephone
Mr. Easy Mark
Noon Hour at Hope Webbing Company
The Over-Anxious Waiter
The Pajama Dance
The Pajama Statue Girls
The Pickpocket
The Porous Plaster
Run of Pawtucket Fire Dept.
Toodles' Christmas (Thumb Book)
Waiting for Bill
Dec 12 At Work in a Peat Bog
Cliff Scenery at the Fabbins
A Coach Drive from Glengariffe to Kenmore
Elopement a la Mode
Irish Peasants Bringing Their Milk to a Cooperative Creamery
The Mono-Railway Between Listowel and Ballybunion, Ireland
Panorama of the Lakes of Killarney from Hotel
Polo Match for the Championship at Hurlingham
Scenes in an Irish Bacon Factory
Scenes in an Irish Market Place
Scenes of a New Forest Pony Fair
Scenes of Irish Cottage Life
Scenes on a Welsh Pony Farm
Shooting the Rapids of Killarney
A Trip Through the Gap of Dunloe
A Trip to the Giant's Causeway
Trout Fishing, Landing Three Pounder
Wild Mountain Ponies on Dartmoor
Wiring Pike in a Mill Stream
1904 [month undetermined]
The Late Senator Mark Hanna
Jan [day undetermined]
And Pat Took Him at His Word
Applicants for Enlistment
The Arbitrator
As Seen on the Curtain
Auction of Deserters' Effects
Awkward Squad
Bag Inspection
The Bench in the Park
The Borrowing Girl
The Boy Under the Table
A Catastrophe in Hester Street
Cowboy Justice
The Dog and the Baby
Drill
A Drop of Ink
Duel Scene, "By Right of Sword"
The Easy Chair
The Escaped Lunatic
Eye Tests, etc., Recruiting
First Aid to the Injured
The Furnished Room House—Taking Life Easy
General Quarters
Girl Waving American Flag, National Cash Register Co.
Girls Jumping the Rope
The Heathen Chinese and the Sunday School Teachers
The Homemade Turkish Bath
"In the Springtime, Gentle Annie!"
The Jolly Bill-Posters
Just Before the Raid
A Kiss in the Dark
A Little Bit off the Top
Love and Jealousy Behind the Scenes
The Misdirected Kiss
Obstacle Race
One Way of Taking a Girl's Picture
Physical Examinations
The Picture the Photographer Took
The Power of Authority
Pull Down the Curtain, Susie
Recruits Embarking
Recruits on "Yorktown"
Sailors Dancing
Saved!
The Scene Behind the Scenes
A Scrap in the Dressing Room
Scrubbing Clothes
"Secure"
The Seeress
Serving Outfits to Recruits
The Story the Biograph Told
Stretcher Race over Obstacles
Swearing in Recruits
Three Girls in a Hammock
Tied to Her Apron Strings
Torpedo Attack
The Troubles of a Manager of a Burlesque Show
What a Mechanical Toy Did To Some Giddy Girls
What Burglar Bill Found in the Safe
"While Strolling in the Park"
Jan 2 The Somnambulist
Feb [day undetermined]
A Blessing from Above
Blind Man's Buff
The Bold Soger Boy
The Borrowing Girl and the Atomizer
Bubbles!
A Bucket of Cream Ale
A Busy Day for the Corset Model
Clarence, the Cop, on the Feed Store Beat
The Committee on Art
Dance of the College Women's Club
Dinah's Defeat
A Fight in the Dormitory
Flour and Feed
Four Beautiful Pairs of Legs
The Four Seasons
Getting Strong; or, The Soubrette's Home Gymnasium
The Girl and the Kitten
A Girl Who Wanted to Rise in the World
The Great Baltimore Fire
A Hot Time at Home
An Ice Covered Vessel
A Joke at the French Ball
The Kentucky Squire
Kiss Me!
Let Uncle Ruben Show You How
Mellin's Food Baby
Minuet and Dance—College Women's Club
The Misplaced Signs
An Old Bachelor
On the Window Shade
The Opening of the Williamsburg Bridge
Our Deaf Friend, Fogarty
Photographing a Female Crook
Pity the Blind, No. 2
Quick Work Behind the Scenes
Quick Work for the Soubrettes
S. S. Moro Castle
Sailors Ashore
She Kicked on the Cooking
The Shocking Stockings
The Soubrette's Slide
A Subject for the Rogue's Gallery
Those Troublesome Boys
A Warm Occasion
The Way to Sell Corsets
Feb 23 Diving Lucy
Jack Sheppard—The Robbery of the Mail Coach
The Salmon Fisheries of Vancouver
Mar [day undetermined]
The Battle of the Yalu

Behind the Screen
The Bustle in the Narrow Door
Butt's Manual, St. John's School
Company Drill, St. John's Military Academy
A Crushed Hat
A Dance on the Pike
Dress Parade, St. John's Academy
The Elopers Who Didn't Elope
A Fair Exchange No Robbery
A Fire in a Burlesque Theatre
The Girls and the Burglar
Grandfather as a Spook
Gun Drill St. John's Academy
The Hoop and the Lovers
How the Cook Made Her Mark
In a Boarding School Gymnasium
The Loaded Cigar
Manual of Arms, St. John's Military Academy
A Misdirected Ducking
Mr. Jack Entertains in His Office
Mr. Jack Is Caught in the Dressing Room
Mr. Jack Visits the Dressing Room
The Model That Didn't Pose
Moneyweight Salesmen
A Novel Way of Catching a Burglar
A Railroad Quick Lunch
The Rival Models
School Girl Athletes
School Girl Gymnasts
Shredded Wheat Biscuit No. 1
Shredded Wheat Biscuit No. 2
A Snare for Lovers
The Strenuous Life
The Suit of Armor
A Trick on the Cop
Under the Tree
Waving American Flag—National Cash Register Co.
The Wrong Room

Mar 12 Behind a Big Gun
How the Japs Fought at Port Arthur
The Jap Behind the Guns
Japanese Jackies

Apr [day undetermined]
An Escape from the Flames
Fire, Adams Express Co.
Girls Winding Armatures, Westinghouse Works
Mellin's Food Baby and Bottle
Mellin's Food Cut-Out
Nervy Nat
A Nigger in the Woodpile
Review of U. S. Marine Band by Sec'y Moody, U. S. Navy
Shredded Wheat Biscuit
The Waif; or, Out in the Street
Welding Big Ring
Westinghouse Sign
A Windy Day on the Roof

May [day undetermined]
Assembling a Generator, Westinghouse Works
Assembling and Testing Turbines, Westinghouse Works
Basket ball, Missouri Valley College
Casting a Guide Box, Westinghouse Works
Central High School, Calisthenics, Missouri Commission
Coil Winding Machines, Westinghouse Works
Coil Winding Section E, Westinghouse Works
Emerson School, Calisthenics, Missouri Commission
Fencing Class, Missouri Valley College
Free Arm Movement, All Schools, Missouri Commission
Girls Taking Time Checks, Westinghouse Works
High School Field Exercises, Missouri Commission
Hyde Park School Graduating Class, Missouri Commission
Hyde Park School Room 2, Missouri Commission
Igorotte Savages, St. Louis Exposition
Kindergarten Ball Game, Missouri Commission
Kindergarten Dance, Missouri Commission
Lathrop School, Calisthenics, Missouri Commission
Linwood School, Calisthenics, Missouri Commission
Opening Ceremonies, St. Louis Exposition
Operation of Westinghouse Block System
Panorama Exterior Westinghouse Works
Panorama from St. Louis Plaza, St. Louis Exposition
Panorama Motor Room, Westinghouse Works
Panorama of Field St., St. Joseph, Mo., Missouri Commission
Panorama of 4th St., St. Joseph, Mo., Missouri Commission
Panorama of Machine Co. Aisle, Westinghouse Co. Works
Panorama of 3rd Street, St. Joseph, Mo., Missouri Commission
Panorama St. Louis Exposition from Launch
Panoramic View Aisle B., Westinghouse Works
Parade of Characters (Asia in America) St. Louis Exposition
Parade of the Pikers, St. Louis Exposition
Railroad Panorama, Pittsburg to Stewart, Westinghouse Works
Sec'y Taft's Address & Panorama
Steam Hammer, Westinghouse Works
Steam Whistle, Westinghouse Works
Taping Coils, Westinghouse Works
Tapping a Furnace, Westinghouse Works
Testing a Rotary, Westinghouse Works
Testing Gas Engine, Westinghouse Works
Testing Large Turbines, Westinghouse Co. Works
Testing Steam Engine, Westinghouse Works
Turning Panorama from Hill, Westinghouse Works
Twenty Mule Team, St. Louis Exposition
Westinghouse Air Brake Co., Casting Machine
Westinghouse Air Brake Co. Westinghouse Works
Westinghouse Co., No. 3, Moulding Machine
Westinghouse Employees Boarding Train
Westinghouse Employees, Westinghouse Works
Whittier School, Calisthenics, Missouri Commission

Jun [day undetermined]
Auto Boat Race on the Hudson River
The Brooklyn Handicap, 1904
Dress Parade of the Filipino Scouts, St. Louis Exposition
The Eviction
Exhibition Fire Drill, Union Square, N. Y.
Filipino Scouts, Musical Drill, St. Louis Exposition
Gymnasium Work, Kirksville, Mo.
Military Tactics
Panorama of St. Louis Exposition from Wireless Tower
"Personal"
Physical Culture, Kirksville, Mo.
Princess Rajah Dance with Chair, St. Louis Exposition
Princess Rajah, Dance Without Chair
The Slocum Disaster
West Point Cadets Escorting Liberty Bell, St. Louis Exposition
Willful Murder

Jun 4 The Apple Woman
The Bobby Whitewashed
The Cook's Lovers
The Coster's Wedding

Jun 25 Chased by a Dog
The Child Stealers
Naval Attack on Port Arthur
The Office Boy's Revenge
The Postman Whitewashed
Raid on a Coiner's Den

Jul [day undetermined]
Alone
Battery "A," Rhode Island Light Artillery
Beyond the Danger Line
Coaching in the White Mountains
A Couple of Lightweights at Coney Island
Fighting the Flames [An Attraction at Coney Island]
The First Baby
Holland Submarine Boat Tests
Panorama of Harvard Class Day
Panorama of Race Track Crowd, St. Louis
President Roosevelt's Home-coming
The Racing Chutes at Dreamland
The Seashore Baby
Speed Test W. K. Vanderbilt, Jr.'s "Tarantula"
The Swimming Class

Jul 9 A Disaster in a Colliery

Aug [day undetermined]
Automobiling Among the Clouds
The Baby and the Puppies
The Bewitched Traveler
The Children in the Surf
The Coney Island Beach Patrol
Democratic National Committee at Esopus
Fighting the Flames, Dreamland
Judge Parker & Mayor McClellan at Esopus
The Moonshiner
Orphan Children on the Beach at Coney Island
Parade of Floats, St. Louis Exposition
Parade of Mystic Shriners, Luna Park, Coney Island
Parade of National Cash Register Co.'s Employees, St. Louis Exposition
A Seaside Cakewalk
Speech by President Francis, World's Fair
A Swimming Race at Coney Island
The Two Bottle Babies
The Widow and the Only Man

Sep [day undetermined]
Brewers' Parade, Philadelphia, Pa.
The Hero of Liao Yang
Imitation Naval Battle—St. Louis Exposition
Panorama from German Building, World's Fair
Parade of Military, St. Louis Exposition
The Pig That Came to Life
The Quarrelsome Washerwoman

Sep 7 Linen Shop

Sep 17 Burglar and Girls
The Convict's Escape
A Kiss and a Tumble

Oct [day undetermined]
Automobile Race for the Vanderbilt Cup
Cruelty to Horses
Decoyed
An Englishman's Trip to Paris from London
In Fair Japan
Kissing in a Tunnel
Kissing the Blarney Stone
Ladies of the Court Bathing
Launching of the U. S. S. Battleship "Connecticut"
The Lost Child
The Masher's Dilemma
Mixed Bathing
Night Duty
Paris from the Seine
Putting Up the Swing
Revenge!
Shooting the Rapids of Killarney

Soap Bubbles
Oct 15 A Railway Tragedy
Oct 17 A Little Boy Called "Taps"
Oct 29 Three Little Maids
Nov [day undetermined]
Coal Heavers
Electric Locomotive Tests and Races, Schenectady, N. Y.
The Lover's Ruse
Over the Hedge
Petticoat Lane on Sunday
A Race for a Kiss
The Suburbanite
University of Pennsylvania Football Team
Dec [day undetermined]
The Amorous Militiaman
At Brighton
The Chicken Thief
Dunloe Women
The Honeymoon
Lady Plumpton's Motor Car
Mary in the Dock
Dec 3 Life of a Race Horse
Sandy McGregor
Dec 17 The Baltic Fleet and the North Sea Trawlers
Dec 24 The Swing
1905 [month undetermined]
Dial's Girls' Band, Luna Park
Epileptic Seizure
Fine Feathers Make Fine Birds
Kicking Football—Harvard
Latina, Dislocation Act
Latina, Physical Culture Poses [No. 1]
Latina, Physical Culture Poses [No. 2]
Jan [day undetermined]
Baby's Day
The Bad Boy and the Grocery Man
The Gentlemen Highwaymen
New Year's Day Parade, Philadelphia
Feb [day undetermined]
Across the New Viaduct of New York
Automobile Races at Ormond, Fla.
Boating Carnival, Palm Beach, Fla.
In the Swimming Pool, Palm Beach, Fla.
The Prima Donna's Understudy
The Sleepy Soubrette
Speed Trial of Auto Boat Challenger, Lake Worth, Fla.
Mar [day undetermined]
Bathing in the Ice at the L Street Bath, Boston
Gov. Wm. L. Douglas, of Mass.
The Inauguration of President Roosevelt
The Nihilists
Tom, Tom, the Piper's Son
Apr [day undetermined]
Bargain Day on 14th Street, New York
Children's Hour on the Farm
Employees Leaving Office
Gen'l Elec. No. 1 Employees Leaving Work
Gen'l Elec. No. 2 Trolley Changing from Di. to Alter. Cur.
Gen'l Elec. No. 3 Handling Cars at the Barn
General Electric Engine Hauling Freight
N. Y. Life Insurance Co. Pres. McCall & Officers
"Osler"-ising Papa
Panorama from the Roof of the Times Building, New York
Physical Culture Poses
Three Cavaliers of the Road
Wanted: A Dog
Women Employee's Dining Room
May [day undetermined]
The Adjustable Chair
Al Treloar in Muscle Exercises
The Athletic Girl and the Burglar
The Badger Game
The Barber's Dee-Light
The Barber's Pretty Patient
The Bigamist's Trial
The Boarding House Bathroom
The Broker's Athletic Typewriter
The Deadwood Sleeper
Funeral of Hiram Cronk
"Gee, If Me Mudder Could Only See Me Now"
The Girls, the Burglar, and the Rat
It's a Shame To Take the Money
N. Y. Police Parade, 1905
Peeping Tom in the Dressing Room
Reproduction, Nan Paterson's Trial
Rough House in a New York Honky-Tonk
Spirit of '76
The Wedding
Jun [day undetermined]
A Ballroom Tragedy
Between the Dances
How Willie Got the Eggs
Interior N. Y. Subway, 14th St. to 42nd St.
Monkey Business
The Pillow Fight, No. 2
A Pipe Dream
Reuben in the Opium Joint
Reuben in the Subway
A Saturday Afternoon at Travers' Island with the New York Athletic Club
The Topers
A Trip to Salt Lake City
2 A. M. in the Subway
Under the Bamboo Tree
The Wine Opener
Jul [day undetermined]
The Abductors
The Bridal Chamber
The Darling of the Gallery Gods
Departure of Peary for the North Pole
Duel Scene from "Macbeth"
He Got into the Wrong Bath House
In a Raines Law Hotel
Lifting the Lid
Love's Perfidy
Mobilization of the Massachusetts State Troops
A Modern Sappho
Mother's Angel Child
The Mutiny on the Potemkin
New York Athletic Club Crew at Phila., Pa.
On the Beach at Brighton
Ore the Banster
Pompey's Honey Girl
A Poor Place for Love Making
Rescued by Rover
Seeing Squashville
Aug [day undetermined]
Blackmail
The Broadway Massage Parlor
The Fire-Bug
German Torpedo Boat in Action
Leap Frog Railway, Coney Island
Peace Envoys at Portsmouth, N.H.
Pennsylvania Tunnel Excavation
The Society Palmist
The Summer Boarders
Sep [day undetermined]
Always Room for One More
Bertha Claiche
The Boer War
Chauncey Explains
The Course of True Love
Female Crook and Her Easy Victim
Fun on the Joy Line
General Cronje & Mystic Shriners
High Jumping Horses—Sidney Holloway's Farm
His Move
The Horse-Thief
Ludlow's Aerodrome
The River Pirates
Robbed of Her All
Teasing
Unlucky at Cards, Lucky at Love
Sep 30 Gay Washerwoman
Oct [day undetermined]
Bringing Up a Girl in the Way She Should Go [No. 1]
Bringing Up a Girl in the Way She Should Go [No. 2]
A Country Courtship
Dream of the Race Track Fiend
Everybody Works But Father (Whiteface)
A German Warship in a Heavy Sea
The Great Jewel Mystery
Halloween
How Millionaires Sometimes Entertain Aboard Their Yachts
Nov [day undetermined]
Airy Fairy Lillian Tries on Her New Corsets
The Barnstormers
By Rail Through Canadian Rockies
Casey's Christening
Everybody Works But Father (Blackface)
The Fat Girl's Love Affair
A Kentucky Feud
Latina, Contortionist
Ludlow's Aerodrome, No. 2
The Rat Trap Pickpocket Detector
Reception of British Fleet
Sparring at the N. Y. A. C.
The Thirteen Club
Wrestling at the N.Y.A.C.
Dec [day undetermined]
A Break for Freedom
Climbing the American Alps
An Execution by Hanging
A Fight for a Bride
Intercollegiate Cross Country Run
Reading the Death Sentence
A Reprieve from the Scaffold
Rooms for Gentlemen Only
The Society Raffles
Threshing Scene
Wine, Women & Song [No. 2]
Dec 23 Disagreeable Mistake
Dec 30 Custom House Search
1906 [month undetermined]
Epileptic Seizure No. 8
Epileptic Seizure, No. 9
Jan [day undetermined]
Deer Stalking with a Camera
The Gossipers
Moose Hunt in New Brunswick
Quail Shooting at Pinehurst
Salmon Fishing in Quebec
Trout Fishing in Rangeley Lakes
Turkey Hunt at Pinehurst
Wine, Women & Song
Jan 27 A Coal Strike
Everybody Works But Mother
A False Alarm
The Henpecked Husband
The Impossible Convicts
The Jolly Monks of Malabar
The Opium Smoker's Dream
The Simple Life
The Streets of New York
Jan 30 The Insurance Solicitor; or, A Story of a Blasted Ambition
Feb [day undetermined]
College Life at Amherst
Police Raid at a Dog Fight
A Raid on a Cock Fight
Scene in a Rat Pit
Seeing Boston
Terrier vs. Wild Cat
Volunteer Fire Department Parade
Feb 19 The Critic
A Friend in Need Is a Friend Indeed
Feb 23 Mr. Butt-In
Mar [day undetermined]
Dixon-Chester Leon Contest
Eclipse of Sun
Scenes Washington, D. C.
Mar 17 The Silver Wedding
Mar 29 The Black Hand
Apr [day undetermined]
The Absent-Minded Shoe Black
Baby's Bath
Bad Coffee
Compromising Spots
Confession
Dancing Sentry Box
Fencing N. Y. A. C.
Lady Undressing
Touching Pleading
Troublesome Fishbone
May [day undetermined]
Arrival of Immigrants, Ellis Island

Dance of Geishas
Her Name Was Maude
Human Apes from the Orient
John Paul Jones Ceremonies
San Francisco
Scenes in San Francisco
Views in San Francisco
May 1 The Subpoena Server
May 16 San Francisco
May 26 Eruption of Mt. Vesuvius
The Lost Leg of Mutton
The Olympian Games
Society Ballooning
"23"
Jun [day undetermined]
Attack on Fort Boonesboro
Canoeing in Maine
A College Girl's Affair of Honor
Free Show on the Beach
Logging in Maine
Maneuvering a Small Motor Boat
Physical Culture Lesson
Play Ball on the Beach
Spanish Barbecue
They Meet on the Mat
A Trip to Berkeley, Cal.
White Fox Motor Boat
Jun 14 The Village Cut-Up
Jun 26 Poughkeepsie Regatta
Jun 28 The Paymaster
Jun 30 The Gateway to the Catskills
Grand Hotel to Big Indian
Hold-Up of the Rocky Mt. Express
In the Haunts of Rip Van Winkle
In the Heart of the Catskills
Through Austin Glen, Catskill Railway
The Valley of Esopus
Jul [day undetermined]
Thaw-White Tragedy
Jul 11 Night of the Party
Jul 19 The Masqueraders
Aug [day undetermined]
The Convict's Bride
In the Tombs
Water Tricycle
Weighing the Anchor
Aug 1 No Wedding Bells for Him
The Old Swimming Hole
Aug 6 Looking for John Smith
Aug 18 Fayet-Chamonix: Trip on the New Trolley Line from Le Fayet-St. Gervais to Chamonix
From Menton to Nice
Les Gorges du Fier
Perefitte to Luz
Aug 23 The Cruise of the Gladys
Aug 25 Ascent of Mount Lowe
The Henly Regatta
Ostrich Farm
The Paris-Bordeaux Auto Race
Pigeon Farm
Playmates
Aug 30 The Lone Highwayman
Sep [day undetermined]
Bryan
E. Forest Fish Gun Assn.
Hoe Printing Press in Action
May's Mechanical Race Track
Trip on Berlin Elevated R. R.
Sep 20 Brannigan Sets Off the Blast
A Daring Hold-Up in Southern California
The Dog Detective
Rescued in Mid-Air
Sep 29 Wanted—A Nurse
Oct [day undetermined]
Motor Race
The 9th Mass. Vol. Militia
Railroad Collision at Los Angeles, Calif.
7th Regiment at 69th Army Dedication
Thousand Islands
Oct 8 The Country Schoolmaster
Oct 18 The Fox-Hunt
Nov [day undetermined]
Fangere
Fay Templeton
Lillian Russell
On Great Western Railway Ldongotten Station
On Great Western Railway Through Dawhistle
Vesta Tilley
Nov 1 Dr. Dippy's Sanitarium
Nov 15 The Tunnel Workers
Dec [day undetermined]
The Drunken Mattress
A Modern Diogenes
Pierce Kids
Singer Building Foundation Co.
Dec 8 Skyscrapers
Dec 29 Married for Millions

1907

Jan [day undetermined]
Man Being Run Over by Automobile
The Moving Picture Man
Jan 5 Life of Christ
The Lighthouse
Jan 17 Trial Marriages
Feb [day undetermined]
Carmen
Feb 8 At the Monkey House
Mr. Hurry-Up
Mar [day undetermined]
Colon to Panama Canal Picture
Salome
Trap Pigeon Shooting
Mar 2 Fights of Nations
Mar 28 Mrs. Smithers' Boarding-School
Apr [day undetermined]
Brother Willie's Revenge
Deyo
Dreams of Fair Women
Floral Parade at Pasadena, Calif.
Gay Girl Playing Pool
The Girl on Park Bench
Me for Water Wagon
Mishaps of a Maid
Post Office Department Picture
Pranks of Cupid
She Seemed Shy but She Was Fly
Skating on N. Y. Theatre Roof
The Spanish Lovers
This Girl Not Wanted
Undone by a Suit Case
Unloading Mail at Pier 13, N. R., N. Y.
Upset by a Cigarette
Apr 11 The Truants
Apr 27 The Fencing Master
May [day undetermined]
Examining a Recruit U.S.N.
Governor's Island Taken U.S.N.
May 11 Crayono
Jamestown Exposition
A Tenderloin Tragedy
May 23 If You Had a Wife Like This
Jun [day undetermined]
Dear Little Sister
Flirty Fan
The Kitchen Terror
Wyoming Girl
Jun 8 A Caribou Hunt
Dolls in Dreamland
Jun 17 Rube Brown in Town
Jun 29 Exciting Night of Their Honeymoon
Fussy Father Fooled
Jul 20 The Hypnotist's Revenge
Aug [day undetermined]
Bigger Than He Looked
Egyptian Princess
Pat's Ghost
Post Office Dept. Picture
Smoking Up
Aug 17 The Deaf-Mutes' Ball
Aug 31 The Tired Tailor's Dream
Sep [day undetermined]
Attack on Emigrant Train
Bachelor Gets a Baby and Other Things He Don't Want
Bargains
Black-White
Blowing Hard
Buffalo Hunt
Busy Lizzie Loses Her Clothes
The Cannibals
Casey on a Souse—Gives the Bunch a Douse
Chink-Chippie
Chorus Girls
Congested Street Society
Crime Wave
Crooked Dog
The Crush at the Bridge Congested S. S.
Dream Kisses
The Finish of Scrappy Patsey
Fitznoodle's Last Ball
Flip-Rip-Zip
Flirty Fred
Frowsy Lizzie Knocks Them Dizzy
Girl $998
Happy Sport Beards the Manicurer
High Jinks
How Fritz's Pipe Exposed Him to the Maid
How the Lovers Got Rid of Boozy Pa
Hunters Dream
Ironed
Kissers Caught
Light-Fight-White
Mags Jag
A Mash a Smash a Splash
Over the Wall
Peanuts
The Portrait
Pres. Roosevelt Reviewing U. S. Regulars
Pres. Roosevelt Reviewing West Point Cadets
The Punishment of the Horse Thief [Ranch 101]
Row at Rileys
Scenes from Luna Park
Scenes from Miller Bros.
Stripped-Stripped
A Swell Time
A Tenement House Battle
Too Soon
Tramps Angel
Vanishing Friends
Waltzing Walter
Wanted a Man Badly
What His Girl's Voice Did
What the Bum Did to the Dude
What the Fisherman Caught
What the Girls Did to the Bachelor
Wrong Bath
Sep 12 Lena and the Beaux
The Model's Ma
Neighbors
Sep 16 An Acadian Elopement
Sep 25 Terrible Ted
Oct [day undetermined]
Mr. Easy Mark
Oct 19 Love Microbe
Oct 28 Yale Laundry
Nov [day undetermined]
[Picture taken for Capt. Lovelace]
Nov 4 Under the Old Apple Tree
Nov 20 Wife Wanted
Dec 4 The Elopement
Dec 14 Dr. Skinum
Dec 21 Mr. Gay and Mrs.

1908

Jan [day undetermined]
Oh Mama
Oh That Curtain
Jan 4 Professional Jealousy
Jan 11 "Energizer"
Jan 18 Falsely Accused!
Jan 22 Lonesome Junction
Feb 1 Classmates
Feb 10 Bobby's Kodak
Feb 19 The Snowman
Feb 27 The Princess in the Vase
Mar 7 The Yellow Peril
Mar 11 The Boy Detective; or, The Abductors Foiled
Mar 18 Her First Adventure [Kidnapped with the Aid of a Street Piano]
Mar 21 Caught by Wireless
Mar 28 Old Isaacs, the Pawnbroker
Apr [day undetermined]
Colored Maid Getting Rid of a Suitor
Crowded Street-Congested Street Society
The Fisherman's Model
Gold-Buys
The Hallroom Boys Received Queer Freight
Masked Policeman
The Merry Widow at a Supper Party

Mrs. Trouble
Scene in a Dressing Room
Selling a Model
That Awful Stork
Then Tramp He Woke Up
What the Dude Lost in the Dressing Room
Apr 7 A Famous Escape
Apr 15 The King of the Cannibal Islands
Apr 22 Hulda's Lovers
Apr 29 The King's Messenger
May [day undetermined]
A False Alarm
Farmer Greene's Summer Boarders
Fly Paper
Fun in the Hay
The Girl and the Gossip
The Girls Dormitory
Jealousy Behind the Scenes
Man Under the Bed
Nellie's Camera
May 6 The Music Master
The Sculptor's Nightmare
May 20 When Knights Were Bold
May 26 A Night of Terror
May 29 His Day of Rest
Jun [day undetermined]
Fluffy's New Corsets
The Girls Boxing Match
The Soul Kiss
Special Muto Reel Mellin's Food Co.
Three Weeks
Too Many in Bed
Jun 2 Thompson's Night Out
Jun 5 The Romance of an Egg
Jun 9 'Ostler Joe
Jun 12 Mixed Babies
Jun 16 The Invisible Fluid
Jun 19 The Man in the Box
Jun 23 The Outlaw
Jun 26 Over the Hills to the Poor House
Jun 30 At the French Ball
Jul 3 At the Crossroads of Life
Jul 7 The Kentuckian
Jul 10 The Stage Rustler
Jul 14 The Adventures of Dollie
Jul 17 The Fight for Freedom
Jul 21 The Black Viper
Jul 24 The Tavern-Keeper's Daughter
Jul 28 The Redman and the Child
Jul 31 Deceived Slumming Party
Aug 4 The Bandit's Waterloo: The Outwitting of an Andalusian Brigand by a Pretty Senora
Aug 7 A Calamitous Elopement: How It Proved a Windfall for Burglar Bill
Aug 11 The Greaser's Gauntlet
Aug 14 The Man and the Woman
Aug 18 The Fatal Hour
Aug 21 For Love of Gold
Aug 25 Balked at the Altar
Aug 28 For a Wife's Honor
Sep [day undetermined]
The Chorus Man's Revenge
Sep 1 Betrayed by a Handprint
Sep 4 Monday Morning in a Coney Island Police Court
Sep 8 The Girl and the Outlaw
Sep 11 Behind the Scenes: Where All Is Not Gold That Glitters
Sep 15 The Red Girl
Sep 18 The Heart of O Yama
Sep 22 Where the Breakers Roar
Sep 25 A Smoked Husband
Sep 29 The Stolen Jewels
Oct [day undetermined]
They Forgot the Messenger
What the Copper Saw
Oct 2 The Devil
Oct 6 The Zulu's Heart
Oct 9 Father Gets in the Game
Oct 13 The Barbarian Ingomar
Oct 16 The Vaquero's Vow
Oct 20 The Planter's Wife
Oct 23 Romance of a Jewess
Oct 27 The Call of the Wild
Oct 30 Concealing a Burglar
Nov 3 After Many Years
Nov 6 The Pirate's Gold
Nov 10 Taming of the Shrew
Nov 13 The Guerrilla
Nov 17 The Song of the Shirt
Nov 20 The Ingrate
Nov 24 A Woman's Way
Nov 27 The Clubman and the Tramp
Dec 1 The Valet's Wife
Dec 4 Money Mad
Dec 8 The Feud and the Turkey
Dec 11 The Reckoning
Dec 15 The Test of Friendship
Dec 18 An Awful Moment
Dec 22 The Christmas Burglars
Dec 25 Mr. Jones at the Ball
Dec 29 The Helping Hand
1909
Jan 1 One Touch of Nature
Jan 4 The Maniac Cook
Jan 7 Mrs. Jones Entertains
Jan 11 The Honor of Thieves
Love Finds a Way
Jan 14 A Rural Elopement
The Sacrifice
Jan 18 The Criminal Hypnotist
Those Boys!
Jan 21 The Fascinating Mrs. Francis
Mr. Jones Has a Card Party
Jan 25 Those Awful Hats
The Welcome Burglar
Jan 28 The Cord of Life
Feb 1 The Girls and Daddy
Feb 4 The Brahma Diamond
Feb 8 Edgar Allen Poe
A Wreath in Time
Feb 11 Tragic Love
Feb 15 The Curtain Pole
His Ward's Love
Feb 18 The Hindoo Dagger
The Joneses Have Amateur Theatricals
Feb 22 The Golden Louis
The Politician's Love Story
Feb 25 At the Altar
Mar 1 His Wife's Mother
The Prussian Spy
Mar 4 A Fool's Revenge
Mar 8 The Roue's Heart
The Wooden Leg
Mar 11 The Salvation Army Lass
Mar 15 I Did It, Mamma
The Lure of the Gown
Mar 18 The Voice of the Violin
Mar 22 And a Little Child Shall Lead Them
The Deception
Mar 25 A Burglar's Mistake
Mar 29 Jones and His New Neighbors
The Medicine Bottle
Apr 1 A Drunkard's Reformation
Apr 5 The Road to the Heart
Trying to Get Arrested
Apr 8 A Rude Hostess
Schneider's Anti-Noise Crusade
Apr 12 A Sound Sleeper
The Winning Coat
Apr 15 Confidence
Apr 19 Lady Helen's Escapade
A Troublesome Satchel
Apr 22 The Drive for a Life
Apr 26 Lucky Jim
Twin Brothers
Apr 29 'Tis an Ill Wind That Blows No Good
May 3 The Eavesdropper
The Suicide Club
May 6 The Note in the Shoe
One Busy Hour
May 10 The French Duel
Jones and the Lady Book Agent
May 13 A Baby's Shoe
May 17 The Jilt

American Mutoscope Co. *see also* **American Mutoscope and Biograph Co.; The Biograph & Mutoscope Co. for France, Ltd.; Biograph Co.; British Mutoscope and Biograph Co.; Deutsche Mutoskop und Biograph G.m.b.H.**
1896 [month undetermined]
The Henley Regatta
Aug [day undetermined]
Sparring Contest, Canastota, N.Y.
Sep [day undetermined]
American Falls, Goat Island
American Falls, Luna Island
Annabelle in Flag Dance
Atlantic City Bathers
Atlantic City Boardwalk
Awakening of Rip
Bathers and Lifeboat, Atlantic City
Boys Bathing, Leapfrog—Atlantic City
Busses Leaving R. R. Depot, Atlantic City
Butterfly Dance
Canadian Falls, from American Side
Canadian Falls—Panoramic [View] from Michigan Central R. R.
Canadian Falls—Table Rock
Dancing Darkies
Engine and Pump
Exit of Rip and the Dwarf
Fire Engine at Work
Getting Off Trolley at Atlantic City
A Hard Wash
Li Hung Chang at Grant's Tomb
Li Hung Chang Driving Through 4th St. and Broadway [New York City]
Li Hung Chang, 5th Avenue & 55th Street, N. Y.
Lower Rapids, Niagara Falls
McKinley at Home, Canton, Ohio
The Monkey's Feast
Niagara Gorge from Erie R. R.
On the Boulevard
Panorama of American & Canadian Falls—Taken Opposite American Falls
Panoramic View from Trolley, Atlantic City
Parade, Americus Club, Canton Ohio
Parade at Canton O., Showing Major McKinley in Carriage
Parade, Elkins Cadets, Canton, O.
Parade, Sound Money Club, Canton, O.
Pa. R. R. Cliffs, Jersey City
Pa. R. R., Hattonsfield
Pennsylvania R. R., New Brunswick
Pa. R. R. Train near Phila.
Pointing Down Gorge, Niagara Falls
Rip Leaving Sleepy Hollow
Rip Meeting the Dwarf
Rip Passing over the Mountain
Rip's Toast
Rip's Toast to Hudson
Rip's Twenty Years' Sleep
Sandow
Sawing Wood
Sea Scene
Serpentine Dance by Annabelle
"Shooting the Chutes"
Showing Group of Bathers, Atlantic City Beach
Stable on Fire
Taken from Trolley, Atlantic City
Taken from Trolley in Gorge, Niagara Falls
Tambourine Dance—by Annabelle
Threshing Machine
Train Coming out of Station, Philadelphia, Pa.
Trilby and Little Billee
Union Square and Fourth Avenue
Union Square—New York
Upper Rapids, from Bridge
View on Boulevard, New York City
A Watermelon Feast
West Point Cadet Cavalry
West Point Cadet Drill
Wrestling Pony and Man
Oct [day undetermined]
Chicago Fast Mail NYC. R. R.
Empire State Express
Empire State Express No. 2
Empire State Express, N. Y. Central R. R.
Parade, First Brigade
Train Taking Water, N. Y. Central R. R.
United States Flag
Nov [day undetermined]
An Arrest at New Haven, Conn.
The Drunken Acrobat
Fire Department, New Haven, Conn.
Fire Department, N. Y. City, 1st and 2nd Alarms
Happy Family
The Human Hen
Imro Fox, Conjuror

Imro Fox Rabbit Trick
New York Fire Department
The Pennsylvania Limited Express
The Sound Money Parade
Sound Money Parade
Winchester Arms Factory at Noon Time
Yale Football Team at Practice, New Haven, Conn.

Dec [day undetermined]
Aquarium
Atlantic City Boardwalk
Broadway & Park Row, Front of U. S. Post Office, N. Y.
The Prodigal's Return; 3 A. M.
Pussy's Bath
Sack Race
Snow Men
The United States Flag
Why Papa Cannot Sleep
Wrestling Ponies

1897 [month undetermined]
Bath Scene
Burglars in the Pantry
Dutch Fishing Boats
Elephants at the Zoo
A Good Story
"Has He Hit Me?"
He and She
He Kissed the Wrong Girl
Home Life of a Hungarian Family
The Horse Guards
The Mischievous Monkey
Mr. C. N. Morton
A Panoramic View in the Grand Canal
Panoramic View of Grand Canal
Panoramic View of Venice
Pelicans at the Zoo
A Race for the Gold Cup
The Rocket Coach
Sir Wilfred Laurier and the New South Wales Lancers
"To the Death"
The Zola-Rochefort Duel

Jan [day undetermined]
"Boys Will Be Boys"
Children Playing with Fish
New England Church Scene
Smoking, Eating, and Drinking Scene
Ye Merry Sleigh Bells

Feb [day undetermined]
Broadway, New York, at Madison Square
Champion Rolla O. Heikes, Breaking the Record at Flying Targets with Winchester Shotgun
Ferryboat and Tug Passing Governors Island, New York Harbor
Little Egypt
An Oration
Outbound Vessel Passing Governors Island, N.Y. Harbor
The Pretty Typewriter; or, "Caught in the Act"
Projectile from Ten Inch Disappearing Gun Striking Water, Sandy Hook
The Sausage Machine
Sausage Machine
Ten Inch Disappearing Carriage Gun Loading and Firing, Sandy Hook
13th Infantry, U. S. Army—Bayonet Exercise, Governors Island
13th Infantry, U. S. Army—Blanket Court Martial, Governors Island
13th Infantry, U. S. Army—Full Dress Parade and Manoeuvering, Governors Island
13th Infantry, U. S. Army—Full Dress Parade, Governors Island
13th Infantry, U. S. Army, in Heavy Marching Order, Double-Time, Governors Island
13th Infantry, U.S. Army—Manual of Arms, Governors Island
13th Infantry, U. S. Army—Marching and Counter Marching (Band and Troops), Governors Island
13th Infantry, U. S. Army Marching Through Sallyport, Governors Island
13th Infantry, U. S. Army—Musical Drill, Governors Island
13th Infantry, U. S. Army—Scaling Walls in Retreat, Governors Island
13th Infantry, U. S. Army—Scaling Walls with Wounded and Dying, Governors Island
Waiting for Hubby

Mar [day undetermined]
Bicyclers in Inaugural Parade
A Bowery Cafe
The Bungling Waiter
Cavalry Charge
Cavalry Horses at Play
Cavalry Musical Drill
Charge, Through Intervals of Skirmishes
Columbia Bicycle Factory
Columbia School Girls
Deyo
Downey-Monaghan (Round 1)
Downey vs. Monaghan
Fencing on Horseback
First Corps Cadets; Mass. National Guard
Gaiety Dance
Geisha Girls
Glimpses of the Grant Parade
A Good Story
Governor Bushnell of Ohio, and Staff
Gov. John A. Tanner, of Virginia, and Staff
His First Smoke
Jumbo
Jumbo, Horseless Fire-Engine
Jumping Hurdles
Keystone Express
Love's Young Dream
McKinley and Others in Carriage
McKinley Train, Penn. R. R.
Major-General Dodge and Staff
Major-General O. Howard, U. S. A., and Staff
The Miser
Musical Drill; Troop A., Third Cavalry
A Newsboys' Scrap
The Old Guard of New York
Les Parisiennes
A Part of Inaugural Parade, Washington
A Pillow Fight
Playing Doctor
President Cleveland and President McKinley
Review of Artillery
S. S. "Middletown"
7th Regiment, N. G. S. N. Y.
71st Regiment, N. G. S. N. Y.
Standing in Stirrups
Steamship "St. Paul" Outward Bound
Theatre Hat
Troop "A" in Inaugural Parade
Troop "A" of Cleveland, O.
Troopers Hurdling
U. S. Cavalry and Artillery
U. S. Sailors
West Point Cadets
Wrestling, Bareback; 3rd Cavalry

Apr [day undetermined]
Automatic Piano
Bag Punching by Sadie Leonard
Caught Napping
A Coon Cake Walk
A Country Dance
Dance, Franchonetti Sisters
Day After the Circus
Death of Nancy Sykes
Demonstrating the Action of an Automatic Piano
Finish of the Brooklyn Handicap
First Round: Glove Contest Between the Leonards
Foiled Again
French Acrobatic Dance
Girls' Boarding School
Going to the Post
A Hard Scrabble
Hurdle Race
Lina & Vani
La Petite Adelaide
Plaguing Grandpa
Second Round: Glove Contest Between the Leonards
Six Furlong Handicap
Theatre Hats Off
Willie's Hat

May [day undetermined]
An Affair of Honor
Ancient and Honorable Artillery Parade
Bicycle Girl
Comedy Cake Walk
The Daisy Guard
A Dressing Room Scene
Ferryboat "Winthrop"
Girls Wrestling on the Beach
On the Beach
Pickanninies Dance
The Restless Girl
"Ring Around a Rosie"
Saharet
See Saw
Shooting the Chutes
A "Standard" Picture Animated
Throwing over a Wall
U. S. S. "Massachusetts"

Jun [day undetermined]
Albany Day Boats
The Biggest Fish He Ever Caught
Cornell-Yale-Harvard Boat-Race
Fort Hill Fire Station
Girls Swinging
Harvard Crew
Loading Hay
Observation Train at the Inter-Collegiate Boat-Races
Peeping Tom
The Picnic
Quick Lunch
A Romp
A Rural Courtship
Still Waters Run Deep
A Surprise Party
Three Jolly Girls and the Fun They Had with the Old Swing
The Tramp and the Bather
Trial Scene
The Troubadour
Trout Poachers
Young America

Jul [day undetermined]
The Bad Boy and Poor Old Grandpa
Beach Scene
A Chicken Farm
Expert Driving
Hauling a Scoop Net
In a Chinese Laundry
In the Surf
A Jolly Crowd of Bathers Frolicking on the Beach at Atlantic City
The Junior Republic on Parade
On the Board Walk
Promenading on the Beach
Queen's Jubilee
Quick Dressing
Sprague Electric Train
Vanishing Lady

Aug [day undetermined]
Atlantic City Fire Department
A Busy Corner
Catching a Runaway Team
Fire Boat "Edwin S. Stewart"
Fire Run
A Giant Steam-Shovel
High Diving
Making an Arrest
Mounted Police Drill
Returning from Drill
Rough Riding

Sep [day undetermined]
Aldershot Review
The Coldstream Guards
Dancing Girls Limbering Up
Girls' Acrobatic Feats
Girls Battling for a Hammock
Gordon Highlanders
Pretty Girls and the Rail Fence
Riding on the Merry-Go-Round
Society Girls Playing "Leap Frog"
Threshing Machine at Work

Oct [day undetermined]
The Aerial Slide at Coney Island
Ancient and Honorable Artillery Co.
A Baby Merry-Go-Round
Boston's Subway

The Clarence House Lawn Party
The Crookedest Railroad Yard in the World
Emperor Francis Joseph of Austria
Facial Expressions by Loney Haskell
Fall River Boat "Priscilla"
Fall River Boat Train
Fastest Wrecking Crew in the World
Fatima
A Fishing Schooner
Fun on the Steeple-Chase
Golding Sisters, Champion Swimmers
Hallow-e'en in Coon-town
Harvesting Corn
The Haverstraw Tunnel
Heads, Hats and Faces
His Majesty, King Edward VII
Jordan, Marsh & Co.'s Store
Keith's Theatre
Marshall P. Wilder
A Maxim Gun in Action
A Multicycle Race
New York Elevated Trains
One-Third Mile Bicycle Race
Oriten
A Paced Bicycle Race
Pie-eating Contest
Safety in Four Tracks
Soap Bubbles
Taking on the Pilot
Washing the Baby

Nov [day undetermined]
Arrival of His Majesty, King Edward VII (then Prince of Wales) at the Ascot Races, 1897
Burlesque Cake Walk
The Dancing Skeleton
Diving at Bath Beach
Finish of the English Derby of 1897
German Warship at Spithead
H. M. S. Powerful at Spithead
His Majesty, King Edward VII
Knock-out Drops
Maxim Firing Field Gun
A New Waiter Opening a Fizz
Philadelphia Police on Parade
Sad Sea Waves
Scrub Yacht Race
Sexless Profiles
Tramp in a Millionaire's Bed
A Tramp's Dinner
Wreck of the Schooner "Richmond"

Dec [day undetermined]
The Alarm (Gordon Highlanders)
The "Amphitrite"
At the Top of Brooklyn Bridge
Austrian Mounted Police
The Battery
Battleship "Texas"
Battleships "Maine" and "Iowa"
Battleships "Marblehead" and "Miantonomah"
Bayonet Versus Bayonet
A Camp of Zingari Gypsies
Charge of Hungarian Hussars
Charge of the French Cuirassieurs
A Children's Carnival in Germany
Christmas Eve
Christmas Morning
The Christmas Tree Party
Cruikshank
Emperor William of Germany, and Emperor Franz Josef of Austria
French Cuirassieurs Charging a Field Battery
Girard College Cadets
Girard College Cadets at Double Quick
Girard College Cadets in Review
Gordon Highlanders Marching into Camp
Gymnastic Exercises in the British Army
Her First Corset
The Highland Fling, by the Gordon Highlanders
How a Rat Interrupted an Afternoon Tea
Hungarian Cavalry Charge
The Model
A Mouse in a Girls' Dormitory
Mulberry Bend
Night Before Christmas
Ocean Greyhounds
Only a Rat
Place de la Concorde
Pongo
A Regimental Calisthenic Drill in the British Army
Santa Claus Filling Stockings
Scrambling for Pennies
Side-Walks of New York
A Skipping Rope Dance
"Spike, the Bag-Punching Dog"
Tipping the Cart in Mulberry Bend
Trafalgar Square
Visit of St. Nicholas
The Workers

1898 [month undetermined]
The Armenian Archbishop, Rome
Capuchin Monks, Rome
Corpus Christi Procession, Orvieto
Feeding the Pigs
Gen'l Sir Herbert Kitchener
His Holiness, Leo XIII in the Gardens of the Vatican, Being Photographed by the American Biograph Camera
The Late President Faure of France
Launch of the "Oceanic"
The Mysterious Midgets
President Faure Shooting Pheasants
The Vatican Guards, Rome

Jan [day undetermined]
At the Chorus Girls' Picnic
The Bowery Waiter and the Old Time Ball Player
Charge of the Light Brigade
Clearing a Drift
During the Blizzard
An Early Breakfast
A Fine Day for Sleighing, Boston
Fishing Vessels After the Blizzard
Girls Struggling for a Sofa
Her Morning Exercise
How She Gets Along Without a Maid
An Impromptu Can-can at the Chorus Girls' Picnic
An Interrupted Breakfast
Meeting of Emperor William of Germany and Emperor Franz Josef of Austria
Merry Sleigh Bells
New Year's Carnival
Place de l'Opera
Relieving the Guard at St. James Palace
The See-Saw, at the Chorus Girls' Picnic
Skating
Sleighing Scene
Surf Dashing Against England's Rocky Coast
The Timid Girls and the Terrible Cow
The Tipping Evil
Trinity Church
Unexpected Advent of the School Teacher
What Happened When a Hot Picture Was Taken

Feb [day undetermined]
City Hall
Down in Dixie
Loading a Mississippi Steamboat
Mardi Gras Carnival
The Monitor "Terror"
Pilot Boat "New York"
The Skyscrapers of New York
Spanish Battleship "Viscaya"
They're Not So Warm
A Three Masted Schooner
Torpedo Boat, "Dupont"
"Vizcaya" Under Full Headway
'Way Down South

Mar [day undetermined]
Boston Navy Yard
Brigadier-General Fitz Hugh Lee
Canadian Artillery Marching on Snow Shoes
Canadian Outdoor Sports
Children Coasting
The Christian Herald's Relief Station, Havana
Coasting in Canada
Coasting Scene in Canada
Cruiser "Montgomery"
Cuban Reconcentrados
Divers at Work on the Maine
Feeding the Ducks at Tampa Bay
Fighting Roosters; in Florida
Harbor Defenses
Hockey Match; Quebec
Launch, U. S. Battleship "Kentucky"
Lawn Tennis in Florida
Life Saving; Quebec Fire Department
Quebec Fire Department Drill
A Run of the Havana Fire Department
Scene on the Steamship "Olivette"
The Snow Shoe Club
Spanish Volunteers in Havana
Steamer "Boston"
Steamship "Olivette"
Tampa Bay Hotel, Tampa, Fla.
The Wreck of the "Maine"

Apr [day undetermined]
"Away Aloft"
Bareback Riding, 6th Cavalry, U. S. A.
Battleship "Massachusetts"
Captain Sigsbee
Capture of the "Panama"
Conway Castle
Cruiser "Brooklyn"
Cruiser "Minneapolis"
French Can-Can
Her First Lesson in Dancing
Idle Hours of the English Coast Guards
In Camp, Tampa, Fla.
The "Jennie Deans"
Launching of the "Kearsage"
"Me and My Two Friends"
The Monitor "Amphitrite"
Newport News Ship-Building Co.'s Shipyard
The "Panther"
Pile Drivers; Tampa, Fla.
Practice Warfare
Quebec Fire Department
Quebec Fire Department Drill
Ram "Katahdin"
Red Cross Steamer "Texas"
S. S. "Columbia" Sailing
Sailor Nailing Flag to Mast
The Tenth Battalion
A Terrible Spill
Theodore Roosevelt
Three Men in a Boat
Tossing a Nigger in a Blanket
Troop "A"; N. G. S. N. Y.
A Tug in a Heavy Sea
Twelfth Regiment, N. G. S. N. Y.
Water Polo
What Happened to the Dancing Master's Pupil
With the Army at Tampa
Worthing Life-Saving Station

May [day undetermined]
Battleship "Indiana"
Battleship "Iowa"
Between the Acts
Capture of the "Pedro"
A Country Couple's Visit to an Art Gallery
Cuban Patriots
Effect of a Certain Photograph
Folding Beds Are Tricky
A French Quadrille
Fun in the Barn
Harbor of St. Thomas
How Bridget Served the Salad Undressed
In Front of "Journal" Building
An Interrupted Sitting
Karina
The Kiki Dance
Learning To Do Splits
The "Lorenzo"
Moulin Rouge Dancers
The Old Maid's Picture
One Chair Short
The Sleeping Uncle and the Bad Girls
Some Dudes Can Fight
Spinster's Waterloo
A Swift Chappie

Three Views of the 69th Regiment, N. G. S. N. Y.
The Tramp Trapped
The Unexpected Visit
Warships
What Our Boys Did at Manila
When the Clock Strikes Two in the Tenderloin

Jun [day undetermined]
Anderson Zouaves
"Balancing in the Basket"
Chief Devery at Head of N. Y. Police Parade
Church Temperance League
Countryman and Mischievous Boys
Crossing the Line
Dalgren Post, G. A. R.
The Deserter
A Duel to the Death
The Foragers
Giving the General a Taste of It
The Greased Pig
He Wanted Too Much for His Pies
Hebrew Orphan Asylum Band
How the Ballet Girl Was Smuggled into Camp
Irish Volunteers
John A. Dix Post, G. A. R.
Koltes' Camp, G. A. R.
Military Discipline
N. L. Farnum Post, G. A. R.
Naval Post, G. A. R.
Naval Review Spithead
New York Mounted on Parade
New York Police on Parade
New York Police Parade
The Rainmakers
The Schoolmaster's Surprise
Street Boys at the Seashore
The Teacher's Unexpected Bath
The Tramp and the Giant Firecracker
Uncle Rube's Visit to the Man-o' War
Veteran Zouaves
The Volunteer Fireman

Jul [day undetermined]
Admiral Cervera and Officers of the Spanish Fleet Leaving the "St. Louis"
Admiral McNair, U.S.N.
An Alarm of Fire in a Soubrettes' Boarding House
The Amateur Trapeze Performers
Army Mules
Bathroom Frivolities
Bayonet Charge; by the 2nd Illinois Volunteers
Blind Man's Bluff
A Breezy Day on a Man-o'-War
A Charge by Cavalry
Children's Tea Party
A Chinese Opium Joint
Cholly's First Moustache
The Chorus Girls' Good Samaraitan
Chorus Girl's Revenge
Col. Torrey's "Rough Riders"
Col. Torrey's Rough Riders and Army Mules
Company "C," 1st Regiment, N. J. V.
The Confetti Dance
Cooling Off
Cooling Off a Hot Baby
Cuban Volunteers
Cubans Sharpening their Machetes
The Daughter of the Regiment
Doing Her Big Brother's Tricks on the Bar
Dressing Paper Dolls
An Execution by Hanging
1st Regiment, N. Y. V.
Follow Your Leader
Fun in a Girl's Dormitory
Fun in a Harlem Flat
Gen. Fitzhugh Lee and Staff
Getting a Shape
Girls Imitating Firemen
Going to Jerusalem
Gymnastic Feats After the Bath
Helping a Good Thing Along
Hot Afternoon in a Bachelor Girl's Flat
A Hot Time in a Hammock
How a Bottle of Cocktails Was Smuggled into Camp
How the Athletic Lover Outwitted the Old Man
How the Dressmaker Got Even with a Dead Beat
Imitation of a College Society Girl
The Inquisitive Girls
An Interrupted Kiss
Joe, the Educated Orangoutang
Joe, the Educated Orangoutang, Undressing
Jumping the Rope After Bed Time
Jumping the Stick
The Katzenjammer Kids in School
A Landing Fight
The Landlady Gives Notice to the Barrasing Sisters
Lasso Throwing
The Lazy Girl
A Letter from Her Soldier Lover
Locked Out, but Not Barred Out
The Locomotive Wheel
"London Bridge Is Falling Down"
The Nearsighted School Teacher
"New York Journal's War Issue"
New York Naval Reserves
The Old Maid and the Burglar
An Overloaded Donkey
Playing Horse
Playing Soldiers
Policemen Play No Favorites
Recruits of the 69th Regiment, N. G. S. N. Y.
A Ride on a Switchback
"Riding the Goat"
The Rivals
Rocky Mountain Riders Rough Riding
"Roly Poly"
A Romp in Camp
Roosevelt's Rough Riders
Rough Riding
"Round and Round the Mulberry Bush"
"Rushing the Growler"
Salt Lake City Company of Rocky Mt. Riders
Second Illinois Volunteers at Double Time
Second Illinois Volunteers in Review
A Second Story Man
A Shoe and Stocking Race
Shooting the Chutes at Home
Siamese Twins
69th Regiment Passing in Review
Smoking Her Out
Some Troubles of House Cleaning
The Soubrettes' Wine Dinner
Spanish Sailors on the "St. Louis"
Spanking the Naughty Girl
The Startled Lover
The Stingy Girl and the Box of Candy
The Stolen Stockings
"Teeter Tauter"
The Third Degree
32nd Regiment, Michigan Volunteers
Three Baths for the Price of One
Three Ways of Climbing over a Chair
Tickling the Soles of Her Feet
A Time and Place for Everything
A Tragedy Averted
Train vs. Donovan
The Tramp and the Muscular Cook
The Tramp Caught a Tartar
Tribulations of a Country Schoolmarm
Tribulations of Sleeping in a Hammock
Troop "H," Denver, Col.
Trying to Jump Her Board Bill
Trying to "Skin the Cat"
U. S. Troop-Ships
An Unsuccessful Raid
The Unwelcome Callers
A Very Laughable Mixup
The Washwoman's Daughter
What's the Matter with the Bed
The Wheelbarrow Race
When the Girls Got Frisky
When the Organ Played in Front of the Hotel
Winding the Maypole
A Windy Corner
Wounded Soldiers Embarking in Row Boats
Wreck of the "Vizcaya"

Aug [day undetermined]
The Baldheaded Dutchman
The Bathing Girls Hurdle Race
A Blast at the Solvay Quarries
Boys Stealing Apples
The Coney Island Bikers
The Dude's Experience with a Girl on a Tandem
A Hotel Fire in Paris, and Rescue by Parisian Pompiers
Jumping Net Practice
The Last Round Ended in a Free Fight
"Leapfrog" on the Beach
Little Willie and the Minister
Making Love on the Beach
The Minister's Wooing
Naval Constructor Richmond P. Hobson
101st Regiment, French Infantry
Race Between a Multicycle and a Horse
Ready for the Bath
Seventh Ohio Volunteers
Shooting the Long Sault Rapids
Sixth Pennsylvania Volunteers
65th Regiment, N. Y. V.
65th Regiment at Double Time
A Skirmish Drill
Snap the Whip
Stealing Apples
Steamer "Island Wanderer"
Steamer "New York"
Stolen Sweets
Third Missouri Volunteers
Volley Firing

Sep [day undetermined]
Agoust Family of Jugglers
The Battleship "Oregon"
Behind the Firing Line
A Bigger Fish Than He Could Manage
Broadsword Drill
Capron's Battery
A Catastrophe in a Sailboat
Charge by Rushes
Col. Theodore Roosevelt and Officers of His Staff
Company "H," 3rd N. Y. V.
Crew of the "Yankee"
The Defence of the Flag
18th Pennsylvania Volunteers
Eighth Ohio Volunteers (the President's Own)
The Farmer's Mishap
The Fat Man and the Treacherous Springboard
Fifteenth Minnesota Volunteers
Fifth Massachusetts Volunteers
First Battalion of the 2nd Massachusetts Volunteers
First Maryland Volunteers
First Rhode Island Volunteers
Fourth Infantry, U. S. Regulars
Free Tobacco
A Gallant Charge
The Gallant Young Man
General Wheeler and Secretary of War Alger at Camp Wikoff
He Caught More Than He Was Fishing For
How Farmer Jones Made a Hit at Pleasure Bay
How Uncle Reuben Missed the Fishing Party
In the Trenches
The Last Stand
"Me and Jack"
The Men Behind the Guns
Ninth Regiment, U. S. Regulars
Panoramic View of Camp Wikoff
Peace Jubilee Naval Parade, New York City
A Poor Landing
A Poor Start
A Precarious Position
President McKinley's Inspection of Camp Wikoff
Queer Fish That Swim in the Sea
Rapid Fire, Charge
Rapid Fire Gun Drill
The Red Cross

Second Battalion; 2nd Massachusetts Volunteers
71st Regiment, N. G. S. N. Y. AT CAMP WIKOFF
A Slippery Landing
Tenth Regiment, Ohio Volunteers
They Will Never Do It Again
Thirteenth Infantry, U. S. Regulars
33rd Regiment, Michigan Volunteers
The Tramp's Last Bite
The Treacherous Spring Board
Twenty-Fourth Infantry
22nd Regiment, Kansas Volunteers
U. S. Battleship "Oregon"
"Weary Raggles"

Oct [day undetermined]
Allegorical Floats
Beauseant Commandery of Baltimore
Boston Commandery, Boston, Mass.
Cardinal Gibbons
A Chicago Street
Cleveland Commandery, Cleveland, O.
Coronation of Queen Wilhelmina of Holland
County Democracy
Damascus Commandery, Detroit
Detroit Commandery, No. 1
Famous Battleship Captains—Philadelphia Peace Jubilee Parade
French Soldiers in a Wall-Climbing Drill
Grand Commandery of the State of New York
Hanselmann Commandery, Cincinnati, O.
How the Gobbler Missed the Axe
Hungarian Women Plucking Geese
In the Adirondacks
An Innocent Victim
Launch of the "Illinois"
Louisville Commandery, Louisville, Ky.
Love in a Cornfield
M. H. Pope Leo in Chair
Major-General Nelson A. Miles, and Staff, in the Peace Jubilee Parade
Naval Constructor Richmond P. Hobson and the Crew of the Merrimac
Officers and Crew of the U. S. Cruiser "Brooklyn"
Pea-Hulling Machine
Peace Parade—Chicago
Philadelphia City Troop and a Company of Roosevelt's Rough Riders
Providence Commandery, Providence, R. I.
St. Bernard Commandery, Chicago
St. Vincent's Cadets
South Gate of the Highlands
Stealing a Ham
Street Fight and Arrest
Tancred Commandery, Pittsburg
The Tenth Cavalry
A Texas Steer
Third Pennsylvania Volunteers
Troop "C"
Twenty-Third Regiment, N. G. S. N. Y.
U. S. Marines
Who's Got the Red Ear?

Nov [day undetermined]
Around the Big Swing
The Dance of the Living Picture
A Happy Family
Illinois Central Terminal
A Living Picture Model Posing Before a Mirror
Making an Impression
Mr. B. F. Keith
Gladys Must Be in Bed Before Ten
A Narrow Escape
Pope Leo XIII, No. 31-56
Pope Leo XIII, No. 57-82
Pope Leo XIII and Count Pecci, No. 1
Pope Leo XIII Approaching Garden
Pope Leo XIII Attended by Guard
Pope Leo [XIII] Blessing in the Garden
Pope Leo XIII Giving Blessing from Chair
Pope Leo XIII in Carriage
Pope Leo XIII in Carriage, No. 1
Pope Leo XIII in Sedan Chair, No. 1
Pope Leo XIII in Vatican Garden, No. 1
Pope Leo XIII Passing Through Upper Loggia, No. 1
Pope Leo XIII Preparing To Give Blessing from Chair
Pope Leo XIII Seated in Garden
Pope Leo XIII Walking at Twilight, No. 1
Pope Leo [XIII] Walking in the Garden
The Rivals
"Snapping the Whip"
Socks or Stockings
Underwear Model

Dec [day undetermined]
The Astor Battery
A Boarding School Escape
Country Boarders Locked Out
The Elopement
Ice Yachting
Pope Leo XIII, No. 106
Pope Leo XIII Being Carried in Chair Through Upper Loggia, No. 101
Pope Leo XIII Being Seated Bestowing Blessing Surrounded by Swiss Guards, No. 107
Pope Leo XIII in Canopy Chair, No. 100
Pope Leo XIII in Carriage, No. 102
Pope Leo XIII Leaving Carriage and Being Ushered into Garden, No. 104
Pope Leo XIII Seated in Garden, No. 105
Pope Leo XIII Walking Before Kneeling Guards

1899 [month undetermined]
Armored Train Crossing the Veldt
Beerbohm Tree, the Great English Actor
British Armored Train
Church Parade of the Life Guards
Departure of the Gordon Highlanders
Frere Bridge, as Destroyed by the Boers
General Babbington's Scouts
General Sir Redvers Buller
General Sir Redvers Buller, and Staff, Landing at Cape Town, South Africa
"God Save the Queen"
Her Majesty, Queen Victoria
Her Majesty, Queen Victoria, Reviewing the Honorable Artillery
Her Majesty, Queen Victoria, Reviewing the Household Cavalry at Spital Barracks
Lord Roberts Embarking for South Africa
Lord Wolseley
A Naval Camp
The Prince of Wales (King Edward VII) at the Aldershot Review
Rifle Hill Signal Outpost
Rt. Honorable Cecil Rhodes
Tapping a Blast Furnace
With the British Ammunition Column

Jan [day undetermined]
Fifth Avenue Entrance to Central Park

Mar [day undetermined]
Across Brooklyn Bridge
Around the Big Curves
Around the Big Curves on the Manhattan Elevated R. R.
Bucking the Blizzard
Can-Can in the Klondike
Dance in a Turkish Harem
The Disappointed Old Maid
Fatima, Star of the Orient
Getting Rid of the Surplus
Heavy Sea from Deck of "St. Louis"
Heavy Storm at Sea Taken from S. S. "St. Louis"
A Hot Time in Alaska
How Charlie Got the Dough
In the Grip of the Blizzard
Looking Forward S. S. "St. Louis"
Looking Off S. S. "St. Louis" at Sea
Love in the Kitchen
McKinley Leaving State House, Boston
A Mean Trick on a Sleepy Soubrette
A "Moving" Picture
Niagara Falls in Winter
Over the Bannister
Passengers on Port Side S. S. "St. Louis"
Passing Needles—S. S. "St. Louis"
Queen of the Harem
Rotary Snowplow in Action
Ruins of the Windsor Hotel Fire
A Slide for Life
Storming the Fort
Tommy's Ringing Good Joke on His Dad
What Happened to the Burglar

Apr [day undetermined]
Arrival of Boat, Providence, R. I.
The Artist's Dream
As in a Looking Glass
A Bucking Broncho
Burlesque Queen and Country Photographer
Classic Poses
The Cremation
Cruiser "Raleigh"
A Crusty Old Bachelor
Digging a Trench
The Dusky Serenade
An Easter Parade
Eighth Regiment, Mass. Volunteers
Elevated Railroad and Drawbridge
English Fire Department Run
"Etruria"
Farmer Oatcake Has His Troubles
Ferryboat "St. Louis"
Fire Department Rescue Drill
Frank Gould's Dogs
Going to the Hunt
The Gordon Highlanders
"Graf Waldersee"
Grand National Steeple-Chase
Greater New York
He Thought That He Had 'Em
Her First Pose
High Hurdle Jumping, at Meadowbrook Hunt Club
A High-school Horse
How N. Y. Society Girls Take to the Fad of Tattooing
The Humane Side of Modern Warfare
"It's Unlucky To Pass Under a Ladder"
The Jealous Cook and the Policeman
Johanna's Chase
Liberty Enlightening the World
Little Willie in Mischief Again
Love's Labor Lost
A Marblehead Welcome
Market Square, Providence, R. I.
The Meadowbrook Hunt
"My Ragtime Girl"
Mysterious Disappearance of a Policeman
The Nurse's Joke
Off for China
Oxford and Cambridge University Boat Crews
Oxford-Cambridge Boat-Race
Panoramic View of Windsor Castle
Parade in Providence, R. I.
Patriot's Day Parade
Pole Vaulting at Columbia University
Prize Winning St. Bernards
The Professor's Fall from Grace
Providence Fire Department
Reginald's First High Hat
Review of First Rhode Island Volunteers
Scots Grey
She Wanted to Be a Boy
South Wales Express
The Startled Lover
Stealing a Bride
Symphony in "A" Flat
Teasing the Cook
Third Avenue Elevated Railroad
Tremont Street
A Trip over the Manhattan Elevated Railroad
Under Full Sail
View of Brooklyn Bridge from a Ferryboat

A Welcome Home
Welcoming the Soldier Boys
Why Clara Was Spanked
Why He Resigned from the Lodge
Wreck of the "Norseman"
A Zulu War Dance
Jun [day undetermined]
Finish of the Brooklyn Handicap, 1899
A Football Tackle
Going to the Post
Governor Walcott of Massachusetts
The Suburban
Jul [day undetermined]
Aquatic Sports
Demonstrating the Action of the Cliff-Guibert Hose Reel
Lower Rapids of Niagara Falls
Myopia vs. Dedham
Whirlpool Rapids
Aug [day undetermined]
The X-Ray Mirror
1900 [month undetermined]
Earl Roberts
Earl Roberts and General Baden Powell
Earl Roberts and Staff
John Philip Sousa
Mining Operations
Queen Victoria's Last Visit to Ireland
Razing a Chimney
Jan [day undetermined]
Battle of Colenso
Feb [day undetermined]
Battle of the Upper Tugela
Lord Dundonald's Cavalry Seizing a Kopje in Spion Kop
On to Ladysmith
May [day undetermined]
Bringing in the Wounded During the Battle of Grobler's Kloof
The Queen's Reception to the Heroes of Ladysmith
The Relief of Ladysmith
Jul [day undetermined]
Children of the Royal Family of England
Playing Soldier
Spirit of the Empire
1904
Feb [day undetermined]
Quick Work Behind the Scenes

The American Vending Machine Co.
1909
Oct 16 Life Behind the Bars at Joliet

Anglo-American Films
1909
Jul 24 Territory on Brain
Aug 28 Henpeck's Revolt

Aquila Films
1908
Oct 21 The Voice of the Heart
1909
Mar 22 Living Statue
Two Fathers
May 29 The Emperor
Sep 4 Florian De Lys
Nov 15 The Cursed Cage
1910
Jan 3 The Poem of Life

Aquila-Ottolenghi
1908
Apr 18 The Animated Dummy
May 2 A Mistake in the Dark
A Priest's Conscience
A Story of the 17th Century
May 9 Peasant's Difficulties in Society
The Smokeless Stove
May 16 Lost Pocketbook
May 30 The Castle Ghosts
Remorseful Son
Oct 3 Panic in a Village
Oct 21 A Father's Will
Dec 14 A Fatal Present
Dec 19 Braving Death to Save a Life
Dec 21 In the Nick of Time
1909 [month undetermined]
Peasant and Princess
Mar 22 Hat Making
Apr 24 Artful Art
May 8 First Comes the Fatherland
House Full of Agreeables
May 29 A Piano Lesson
Jun 12 Ski Runners of the Italian Army
Jun 17 The Conjuror
The Girl Heroine
Recompense
Jun 26 Heroine of the Balkans
Jul 3 Bink's Toreador
Jul 24 The Harp Player
Aug 14 A Hero of the Italian Independence
Sep 21 Eleanora
Sep 27 Mother-in-Law's Parrot
Oct 11 The Convict's Wife
1910
Jan 10 The Law of Destiny
Jan 17 A Young Girl's Sacrifice
May 7 Artist's Good Joke
The Sentinel's Romance
Jun 28 Under the Reign of Terror

Armour & Co.
1901 [month undetermined]
Arrival of Train of Cattle
Beef Extract Room
Beef, Sheep and Hog Killing
Branding Hams
Bridge of Sighs
Bull on the Stampede
A Busy Corner at Armour's
Canned Meat Department. No. 1: Filling and Capping
Canned Meat Department. No. 2: Inspecting
Canned Meat Department. No. 5: Vacuum Process
Canned Meat Department. No. 6: Painting and Labeling
Cleaning Pig's Feet
Coming Out of Scraping Machines and Cutting Off Heads
Cutting Beef
Cutting Meat for Sausage (side view)
Cutting Pork
Dressing Beef
Driving Hogs to Slaughter
Drove of Western Cattle
Dumping and Lifting Cattle
Elevated Railroad
Entrance to Union Stock Yards
Export Packing
Feeding Time
Hog Slaughtering. No. 6: Opening and Splitting
Hogs on the Rail
Interior of Armour's Power House
Killing Sheep
Koshering Cattle, (Hebrew Method of Killing)
Labeling Cans
Lard Refinery
Laundry and Sewing Room
Legging Sheep
Loading Cars
Machine and Can Tester
Mince Meat Room
Miscellaneous. No. 6: Panoramic View
Noon Time in Packing Town, (Panoramic)
Noon Time in Packing Town, (Whiskey Point)
Oleo Oil Melting
Oleo Oil Pressing
Pulling Wool
A Ride on the Elevated R. R. (Panoramic)
Sausage Department. No. 2: Chopping
Scalding and Scraping Hogs
Sheep Led to Slaughter by Goat
Shipping Department. No. 2: Loading
Singing Pigs Feet
Skinning Sheep
Slicing Hams and Bacon
Soldering Cans
Square Can Machine
Stamping Tin
Sticking Cattle
Sticking Hogs, (Front View)
Street Sweeping Brigade
Stuffing Cans by Machinery
Stuffing Sausage
Stunning Cattle
Sweating Cans
Testing Cans by Machinery
Testing Hams
Testing Horses
3 Can Testers (side view)
Trimming Room
Weighing Mutton

Atlas Film Co.
1910
Jun 8 The Outlaw's Redemption
Jun 15 Settling a Boundary Dispute
Jun 22 Grandpa's Will
Sheriff's Daughter
Jun 29 The Tenderfoot Parson
Jul 6 Manoeuvers of the New York Police Force
That Little German Band
Jul 13 The Clergyman and His Ward
Jul 20 Levi and Family at Coney Island
Only a Hobo
Jul 27 The Kissing Bug
The Prospector's Treasure
Aug 3 The Rest Cure
Aug 10 The Animated Scare-Crow
The Wrong Bag
Aug 17 Count of Noaccount
Aug 24 A Bully's Waterloo
The Tale of a Hot Dog
Aug 31 Turning the Tables
The Unsophisticated Book Agent
Sep 7 [Jones, the Burglar Catcher]
The Snorer
Sep 14 Animated Powders
Monkeyshines
Sep 21 Trailing the Black Hand
Sep 28 The Laugh's on Father
Levi, the Cop
Oct 5 When Cupid Sleeps
Oct 12 Curing a Grouch
The S. S. Mauretania
Oct 19 The Cat Came Back
Imperfect Perfectos
Oct 26 A Touching Mystery
Nov 2 That Doggone Dog
Turning of the Worm
Nov 9 The King of Beggars
Nov 16 The Hand of Providence
Nov 23 Cast Thy Bread upon the Waters
Nov 30 Saved by a Vision
Dec 7 Nature's Nobleman
Dec 14 Brothers
Dec 21 The Arm of the Law
Dec 28 The Outcast's Salvation

Belcher and Waterson
1907
Feb [day undetermined]
Poor John
Waiting at the Church

The Biograph & Mutoscope Co. for France, Ltd. *see also* **American Mutoscope and Biograph Co.; American Mutoscope Co.; Biograph Co.; British Mutoscope and Biograph Co.; Deutsche Mutoscop and Biograph G.m.b.H.**
1902
Nov [day undetermined]
The Abbe and the Colonel
Allegorical Procession
Arrival of Major Marchand from the Soudan
An Automobile Parade in the Tuilleries Gardens
Beautifyl Beaulieu
The Bon Vivant
Bridge of Alexander III
Captain Dreyfus
The Champs Elysees
The Children of the Czar
A Dance by Kanaka Indians
A Dog's Cemetery
A French Bicycle Corps
French Boxers
From Monte Carlo to Monaco
George J. Marck and His Lions
The Giant Constantin
The India-Rubber Man
Jo Jo, the Dog Faced Boy
King Edward VII at the Birthday Celebration of the King of Denmark
The Longchamps Palace
A Mis-Adventure
Mr. Oldsport's Umbrella
M. Le Comte De Dion

The Old Port of Marseilles
On the Marseilles Tramway
Oom Paul
Paris Exposition
A Parisian Ballet
Prize-Winning Trip of the Santos-Dumont Airship No. 6
Promenade of the Kings
Rulers of Half the World
Ten Minutes at Monte Carlo
The Train to Villefranche
The Valiant Pig
A Water Carnival
"Zip"

Biograph Co. *see also* **American Mutoscope and Biograph Co.; American Mutoscope Co.; The Biograph & Mutoscope Co. for France, Ltd.; British Mutoscope and Biograph Co.; Deutsche Mutoskop und Biograph G.m.b.H.**

1903
Jan 17 The Ascent of Mount Blanc
Aug 1 The Elixir of Life
Dec 12 A Drove of Wild Welsh Mountain Ponies

1909
May 10 The French Duel
May 17 The Jilt
May 20 Resurrection
May 24 Eloping with Aunty
Two Memories
May 27 The Cricket on the Hearth
May 31 What Drink Did
Jun 3 Eradicating Aunty
His Duty
Jun 7 The Violin Maker of Cremona
Jun 10 The Lonely Villa
A New Trick
Jun 14 The Son's Return
Jun 17 The Faded Lillies
Her First Biscuits
Jun 21 Was Justice Served?
Jun 24 The Mexican Sweethearts
The Peachbasket Hat
Jun 28 The Way of Man
Jul 1 The Necklace
Jul 5 The Message
Jul 8 The Country Doctor
Jul 12 The Cardinal's Conspiracy
Jul 15 The Friend of the Family
Tender Hearts
Jul 19 The Renunciation
Jul 22 Jealousy and the Man
Sweet and Twenty
Jul 26 A Convict's Sacrifice
Jul 29 The Slave
Aug 2 A Strange Meeting
Aug 5 The Mended Lute
Aug 9 Jones' Burglar
They Would Elope
Aug 12 The Better Way
Aug 16 With Her Card
Aug 19 His Wife's Visitor
Mrs. Jones' Lover; or, "I Want My Hat"
Aug 23 The Indian Runner's Romance
Aug 26 "Oh, Uncle"
The Seventh Day
Aug 30 The Heart of an Outlaw
The Mills of the Gods
Pranks
Sep 2 The Little Darling
The Sealed Room
Sep 6 "1776" or, The Hessian Renegades
Sep 9 Comata, the Sioux
Sep 13 The Children's Friend
Getting Even
Sep 16 The Broken Locket
Sep 20 In Old Kentucky
Sep 23 A Fair Exchange
Sep 27 Leather Stocking
Sep 30 The Awakening
Wanted, a Child
Oct 4 Pippa Passes; or, The Song of Conscience
Oct 7 Fools of Fate
Oct 11 The Little Teacher
Oct 14 A Change of Heart
Oct 18 His Lost Love
Oct 21 The Expiation
Oct 25 In the Watches of the Night
Oct 28 Lines of White on a Sullen Sea
Nov 1 The Gibson Goddess
What's Your Hurry?
Nov 4 Nursing a Viper
Nov 8 The Restoration
Nov 11 The Light That Came
Nov 15 Two Women and a Man
Nov 18 A Midnight Adventure
Sweet Revenge
Nov 22 The Open Gate
Nov 25 The Mountaineer's Honor
Nov 29 In the Window Recess
The Trick That Failed
Dec 2 The Death Disc: A Story of the Cromwellian Period
Dec 6 Through the Breakers
Dec 9 The Redman's View
Dec 13 A Corner in Wheat
Dec 16 In a Hempen Bag
The Test
Dec 20 A Trap for Santa Claus
Dec 23 In Little Italy
Dec 27 To Save Her Soul
Dec 30 Choosing a Husband
The Day After

1910
Jan 3 The Rocky Road
Jan 6 The Dancing Girl of Butte
Jan 10 Her Terrible Ordeal
Jan 13 All on Account of the Milk
Jan 17 On the Reef
Jan 20 The Call
Jan 24 The Honor of His Family
Jan 27 The Last Deal
Jan 31 The Cloister's Touch
Feb 3 The Woman from Mellon's
Feb 7 The Course of True Love
Feb 10 The Duke's Plan
Feb 14 One Night, and Then —
Feb 17 The Englishman and the Girl
Feb 21 His Last Burglary
Feb 24 Taming a Husband
Feb 28 The Final Settlement
Mar 3 The Newlyweds
Mar 7 The Thread of Destiny
Mar 10 In Old California
Mar 14 The Converts
Mar 17 The Love of Lady Irma
The Man
Mar 21 Faithful
Mar 24 The Twisted Trail
Mar 28 Gold Is Not All
Mar 31 His Last Dollar
The Smoker
Apr 4 As It Is in Life
Apr 7 A Rich Revenge
Apr 11 A Romance of the Western Hills
Apr 14 The Kid
Apr 18 Thou Shalt Not
Apr 21 The Tenderfoot's Triumph
Apr 25 The Way of the World
Apr 28 Up a Tree
May 2 The Gold-Seekers
May 5 The Unchanging Sea
May 9 Love Among the Roses
May 12 The Two Brothers
May 16 Over Silent Paths
May 19 An Affair of Hearts
May 23 Ramona
May 26 A Knot in the Plot
May 30 The Impalement
Jun 2 In the Season of Buds
Jun 6 A Child of the Ghetto
Jun 9 A Victim of Jealousy
Jun 13 In the Border States
Jun 16 The Face at the Window
Jun 20 May and December
Never Again
Jun 23 The Marked Time-Table
Jun 27 A Child's Impulse
Jun 30 Muggsy's First Sweetheart
Jul 4 The Purgation
Jul 7 A Midnight Cupid
Jul 11 What the Daisy Said
Jul 14 A Child's Faith
Jul 18 A Flash of Light
Jul 21 As the Bells Rang Out!
Serious Sixteen
Jul 25 The Call to Arms
Jul 28 Unexpected Help
Aug 1 An Arcadian Maid
Aug 4 Her Father's Pride
Aug 8 The House with Closed Shutters
Aug 11 A Salutary Lesson
Aug 15 The Usurer
Aug 18 An Old Story with a New Ending
When We Were in Our Teens
Aug 22 The Sorrows of the Unfaithful
Aug 25 Wilful Peggy
Aug 29 The Modern Prodigal
Sep 1 The Affair of an Egg
Muggsy Becomes a Hero
Sep 5 A Summer Idyll
Sep 8 Little Angels of Luck
Sep 12 A Mohawk's Way
Sep 15 In Life's Cycle
Sep 19 A Summer Tragedy
Sep 22 The Oath and the Man
Sep 26 Rose O' Salem-Town
Sep 29 Examination Day at School
Oct 3 The Iconoclast
Oct 6 A Gold Necklace
How Hubby Got a Raise
Oct 10 That Chink at Golden Gulch
Oct 13 A Lucky Toothache
The Masher
Oct 17 The Broken Doll
Oct 20 The Banker's Daughters
Oct 24 The Message of the Violin
Oct 27 The Passing of a Grouch
The Proposal
Oct 31 Two Little Waifs
Nov 7 The Fugitive
Waiter No. 5
Nov 10 Simple Charity
Nov 14 Sunshine Sue
Nov 17 Love in Quarantine
The Troublesome Baby
Nov 21 The Song of the Wildwood Flute
Nov 24 His New Lid
Not So Bad as It Seemed
Nov 28 A Plain Song
Dec 1 Effecting a Cure
Dec 5 A Child's Stratagem
Dec 8 Happy Jack, a Hero
Turning the Tables
Dec 12 The Golden Supper
Dec 15 His Sister-in-Law
Dec 19 The Lesson
Dec 22 The Recreation of an Heiress
White Roses
Dec 26 Winning Back His Love
Dec 29 After the Ball
His Wife's Sweethearts

Bison

1909
May 21 Disinherited Son's Loyalty
May 28 Romance of a Fishermaid
Jun 4 "Davy" Crockett in Hearts United
Jun 11 The Squaw's Revenge
Jun 18 A Terrible Attempt
Why Mr. Jones Was Arrested
Jun 25 Cowboy's Narrow Escape
Jul 2 A True Indian's Heart
Jul 9 The Blacksmith's Wife
Jul 16 I Love My Wife, but Oh, You Kid
Jul 23 The Gypsy Artist
Jul 30 My Wife's Gone to the Country
Aug 6 Sailor's Child
Aug 13 Sheltered Under Stars and Stripes
The Yiddisher Cowboy
Aug 20 Half Breed's Treachery
Aug 27 Secret Service Woman
Sep 3 His Two Children
Sep 10 The Paymaster
Sep 17 A Kentucky Planter
Sep 24 A Squaw's Sacrifice
Oct 1 Faithful Wife
Oct 8 Dove Eye's Gratitude
Oct 15 The Gold Seeker's Daughter
Oct 22 Iona, the White Squaw
Oct 29 Mexican's Crime
Nov 5 Young Deer's Bravery
Nov 12 The Ranchman's Wife
Nov 19 An Indian's Bride
Nov 26 Dooley's Thanksgiving Turkey
The Parson's Prayer
Dec 3 The Message of an Arrow
Dec 10 Re-united at the Gallows
Dec 17 The Love of a Savage
Dec 24 An Italian Love Story
Dec 31 The Red Cross Heroine

1910
Jan 7 Red Girl's Romance
Jan 11 A Redman's Devotion
Jan 14 A Forester's Sweetheart
Jan 18 A Cowboy's Reward
Jan 21 Romany Rob's Revenge
Jan 25 A Romance of the Prairie
Jan 28 His Imaginary Crime
Feb 1 The Female Bandit
Feb 4 By His Own Hands
Feb 8 The Ten of Spades; or, A Western Raffle
Feb 11 Young Deer's Gratitude
Feb 15 Government Rations
Feb 18 Dooley's Holiday
The Impostor
Feb 22 For Her Father's Honor
Feb 25 Dooley Referees the Big Fight
Mar 1 The Cowboy and the School Marm
Mar 4 The New Partners
Mar 8 The Indian and the Cowgirl
Mar 11 The Rose of the Ranch
Mar 15 For His Sister's Honor
Mar 18 Mexican's Ward
Mar 22 The Man from Texas
Mar 25 Company "D" to the Rescue
Mar 29 Nannina
Apr 1 A Shot in Time
Apr 5 Romance of a Snake Charmer
Apr 8 Red Wing's Loyalty
Apr 12 Rivalry in the Oil Fields
Apr 15 Red Wing's Constancy
Apr 19 A Husband's Mistake
Apr 22 Adventures of a Cowpuncher
Apr 26 Hazel, the Heart Breaker
Rattlesnakes
Apr 29 The Rescue of the Pioneer's Daughter
May 3 A Sister's Devotion
May 6 Love and Money
May 10 Cupid's Comedy
May 13 Lost for Many Years
May 17 The Feud
May 20 The Mexican's Jealousy
May 24 The Curse of Gambling
May 27 Perils of the Plains
May 31 The Tie That Binds
Jun 3 Married on Horseback
Jun 7 Girls
Jun 10 Saved from the Redmen
Jun 14 An Engineer's Sweetheart
Jun 17 A Cowboy's Race for a Wife
Jun 21 The Sea Wolves
Jun 24 A Mexican Lothario
Jun 28 Her Terrible Peril
Jul 1 A Ranchman's Simple Son
Jul 5 A Sinner's Sacrifice
Jul 8 The Sheriff of Black Gulch
Jul 12 A Mexican Love Affair
Jul 15 Red Fern and the Kid
Jul 19 A Message of the Sea
Jul 22 Black Pete's Reformation
Jul 26 Love in Mexico
Jul 29 In the Wild West
Aug 2 A Miner's Sweetheart
Aug 5 A Cowboy's Generosity
Aug 9 A True Country Heart
Aug 12 The Prairie Post Mistress
Aug 16 A Woman's Better Nature
Aug 19 The Redmen's Persecution
Aug 23 The Mascot of Company "D"
Aug 26 Kit Carson
Aug 30 Dan, the Arizona Scout
Sep 2 The Night Rustlers
Sep 6 Western Justice
Sep 9 A True Indian Brave
Sep 13 A Cowboy's Matrimonial Tangle
Sep 16 For a Western Girl
Sep 20 For the Love of Red Wing
Sep 23 A Cattle Rustler's Daughter
Sep 27 A Cowboy for Love
Sep 30 The Ranch Raiders
Oct 4 Young Deer's Return
Oct 7 The Girl Scout
Oct 11 A Cowboy's Daring Rescue
Oct 14 The Prayer of a Miner's Child
Oct 18 The Lure of Gold
Oct 21 The Wrong Trail
Oct 25 The Girl Cowboy
Oct 28 A Red Girl's Friendship
Nov 1 The Fatal Gold Nugget
Nov 4 Red Wing and the White Girl
Nov 8 The Branded Man
Nov 11 Bud's Triumph
Nov 15 The Flight of Red Wing
Nov 18 An Indian Maiden's Choice
Nov 22 True Western Honor
Nov 25 A Cheyenne's Love for a Sioux
Nov 29 The Ranchman's Personal
Dec 2 A Child of the Wild
Dec 6 A Sioux's Reward
Dec 9 A Brave Western Girl
Dec 13 An Indian's Test
Dec 16 A Girl of the Plains
Dec 20 The Cattle Baron's Daughter
Dec 23 The Pale Faced Princess
Dec 27 An Indian's Elopement
Dec 30 Taming the Terror

Bradenburgh, G. W. *see* **G. W. Bradenburgh**

British and Colonial Kinematograph Co.
1909
Jun 12 The Birth of a Big Gun
Jul 17 Billy's Bugle
Sep 4 Baby's Revenge
1910
May 12 Three Fingered Kate
Jun 21 Drowsy Dick's Dream
Jul 5 The Boy and His Teddy Bear
Jul 12 A Deal in Broken China

British Mutoscope and Biograph Co. *see also* **American Mutoscope and Biograph Co.; American Mutoscope Co,; The Biograph & Mutoscope Co. for France, Ltd.; Biograph Co.; Deutsche Mutoskop und Biograph G.m.b.H.**
1896 [month undetermined]
The Henley Regatta
1897 [month undetermined]
Bath Scene
Burglars in the Pantry
Dutch Fishing Boats
Elephants at the Zoo
A Good Story
"Has He Hit Me?"
He and She
He Kissed the Wrong Girl
Home Life of a Hungarian Family
The Horse Guards
Mr. C. N. Morton
A Panoramic View in the Grand Canal
Panoramic View of Grand Canal
Panoramic View of Venice
Pelicans at the Zoo
A Race for the Gold Cup
The Rocket Coach
Sir Wilfred Laurier and the New South Wales Lancers
"To the Death"
The Zola-Rochefort Duel
Jul [day undetermined]
Queen's Jubilee
Sep [day undetermined]
Aldershot Review
The Coldstream Guards
Gordon Highlanders
Oct [day undetermined]
The Clarence House Lawn Party
Emperor Francis Joseph of Austria
His Majesty, King Edward VII
A Maxim Gun in Action
Nov [day undetermined]
Arrival of His Majesty, King Edward VII (then Prince of Wales) at the Ascot Races, 1897
Finish of the English Derby of 1897
German Warship at Spithead
H. M. S. Powerful at Spithead
His Majesty, King Edward VII
Maxim Firing Field Gun
Dec [day undetermined]
The Alarm (Gordon Highlanders)
Austrian Mounted Police
Bayonet Versus Bayonet
A Camp of Zingari Gypsies
Charge of Hungarian Hussars
Charge of the French Cuirassieurs
A Children's Carnival in Germany
Emperor William of Germany, and Emperor Franz Josef of Austria
French Cuirassieurs Charging a Field Battery
Gordon Highlanders Marching into Camp
Gymnastic Exercises in the British Army
The Highland Fling, by the Gordon Highlanders
Hungarian Cavalry Charge
Place de la Concorde
A Regimental Calisthenic Drill in the British Army
Trafalgar Square
1898 [month undetermined]
The Armenian Archbishop, Rome
Capuchin Monks, Rome
Corpus Christi Procession, Orvieto
Feeding the Pigs
Launch of the "Oceanic"
The Mysterious Midgets
The Vatican Guards, Rome
Jan [day undetermined]
Meeting of Emperor William of Germany and Emperor Franz Josef of Austria
Place de l'Opera
Relieving the Guard at St. James Palace
Surf Dashing Against England's Rocky Coast
Apr [day undetermined]
"Away Aloft"
Conway Castle
Idle Hours of the English Coast Guards
The "Jennie Deans"
"Me and My Two Friends"
A Terrible Spill
Three Men in a Boat
A Tug in a Heavy Sea
Water Polo
Worthing Life-Saving Station
Jun [day undetermined]
Naval Review Spithead
Aug [day undetermined]
A Hotel Fire in Paris, and Rescue by Parisian Pompiers
101st Regiment, French Infantry
Sep [day undetermined]
Agoust Family of Jugglers
Oct [day undetermined]
Coronation of Queen Wilhelmina of Holland
French Soldiers in a Wall-Climbing Drill
Hungarian Women Plucking Geese
Nov [day undetermined]
Pope Leo XIII Approaching Garden
Pope Leo [XIII] Blessing in the Garden
Pope Leo XIII in Carriage
Pope Leo XIII in Carriage, No. 1
Pope Leo XIII in Sedan Chair, No. 1
Pope Leo XIII in Vatican Garden, No. 1
Pope Leo XIII Seated in Garden
Pope Leo XIII Walking at Twilight, No. 1
Pope Leo [XIII] Walking in the Garden
Dec [day undetermined]
Pope Leo XIII Being Seated Bestowing Blessing Surrounded by Swiss Guards, No. 107
Pope Leo XIII in Canopy Chair, No. 100
Pope Leo XIII Leaving Carriage and Being Ushered into Garden, No. 104
Pope Leo XIII Seated in Garden, No. 105
1899 [month undetermined]
Amann
Amann, the Great Impersonator
Armored Train Crossing the Veldt
Beerbohm Tree, the Great English Actor
British Armored Train
Church Parade of the Life Guards
Departure of the Gordon Highlanders
Frere Bridge, as Destroyed by the Boers
General Babbington's Scouts
General Sir Redvers Buller
General Sir Redvers Buller, and Staff, Landing at Cape Town, South Africa
"God Save the Queen"
Her Majesty, Queen Victoria
Her Majesty, Queen Victoria, Reviewing the Honorable Artillery
Her Majesty, Queen Victoria, Reviewing the Household Cavalry at Spital Barracks

Lord Roberts Embarking for South Africa
Lord Wolseley
A Naval Camp
The Prince of Wales (King Edward VII) at the Aldershot Review
Rifle Hill Signal Outpost
Rt. Honorable Cecil Rhodes
Tapping a Blast Furnace
With the British Ammunition Column
Mar [day undetermined]
Grand Military Steeple-Chase
Lockhart's Performing Elephants
Apr [day undetermined]
English Fire Department Run
Fire Department Rescue Drill
The Gordon Highlanders
Grand National Steeple-Chase
The Humane Side of Modern Warfare
Oxford and Cambridge University Boat Crews
Oxford-Cambridge Boat-Race
Panoramic View of Windsor Castle
Scots Grey
South Wales Express
A Zulu War Dance
Jun [day undetermined]
The Derby
Launch of the Porthonstock Life-boat
The Paddock
Wreck of the "Mohican"
Wreck of the S. S. "Paris"
Aug [day undetermined]
"Between the Races"
The Henley Regatta
Stage Coaches Leaving the Hotel Victoria
Sep [day undetermined]
International Collegiate Games
The International Collegiate Games
International Collegiate Games
International Collegiate Games—Half Mile Run
International Collegiate Games—110 Yards Hurdle Race
International Collegiate Games—100 Yards Dash
Launch of the Battleship "Vengeance"
"Man Overboard!"
Polo—A Dash for Goal
Polo—Hurlingham vs. Ranelagh
1900 [month undetermined]
Earl Roberts
Earl Roberts and General Baden Powell
Earl Roberts and Staff
Fight Between Tarantula and Scorpion
John Philip Sousa
Kansas City Fire Department, Winners of the World's Championship at the Paris Exposition
Mining Operations
Oxford-Cambridge Race
Panoramic View of Rome
Paris Exposition
Queen Victoria's Last Visit to Ireland
Razing a Chimney
Speed Trial of the "Albatross"
Jan [day undetermined]
Battle of Colenso
Feb [day undetermined]
Battle of the Upper Tugela
Lord Dundonald's Cavalry Seizing a Kopje in Spion Kop
On to Ladysmith
May [day undetermined]
Bringing in the Wounded During the Battle of Grobler's Kloof
The Queen's Reception to the Heroes of Ladysmith
The Relief of Ladysmith
Trial Speed of H. M. Torpedo Boat Destroyer "Viper"
Jul [day undetermined]
Amateur Athletic Championships
Children of the Royal Family of England
Playing Soldier
Spirit of the Empire
1901 [month undetermined]
Amateur Athletic Association Sports
"Bend Or"
The Builders of Shamrock II
Chamberlain and Balfour
Emar De Flon, the Champion Skater
Launch of Shamrock II
Nabbed by the Nipper
Norway Ski Jumping Contests
Panoramic View of London Streets, Showing Coronation Decorations
Signor Marconi—Wireless Telegraphy
Soot Versus Suds
Spanish Coronation Royal Bull-Fight
Their Majesties the King and Queen
Winter Life in Sweden
Feb [day undetermined]
Departure of Duke and Duchess of Cornwall for Australia
The First Procession in State of H. M. King Edward VII
First Procession in State of H. M. King Edward VII
Queen Victoria's Funeral [Number 1]
Queen Victoria's Funeral [Number 2]
Queen Victoria's Funeral [Number 3]
Jun [day undetermined]
Emperor William's Yacht "Meteor"
English Derby, 1901
International Yacht Races on the Clyde
Panoramic View of the Thames
"Volodyovski"
Aug [day undetermined]
The Henley Regatta, 1901
1902
Sep [day undetermined]
Coronation Parade
Nov [day undetermined]
Dessert at Dan Leno's House
His Morning Bath
Mr. Dan Leno, Assisted by Mr. Herbert Campbell, Editing the "Sun"
The Murderer's Vision
An Obstinate Cork
Rare Fish in the Aquarium
Umbrella Dance, San Toy
1903 [month undetermined]
Brothers of the Misericordia, Rome
1906
May 26 The Olympian Games

Buffalo Bill and Pawnee Bill Film Co.
1910
Sep 15 Buffalo Bill's Wild West and Pawnee Bill's Far East

Bullock, William *see* **William Bullock**

C & J Film Co.
1909
Oct 5 Forgiven at Last
Oct 18 Foolshead's Trousers
Oct 19 Winter Sports in Hungary
Oct 25 The Brigand's Repentance
The Great Lottery
Nov 8 Musical Waiter
1910
Sep 11 Lame Woman

The Capitol Film Co.
1910
May 16 The Heart of Tessa
Jun 18 The Turn of the Tide
Jun 25 Cash on Delivery
Jul 2 Trapped by His Own Mark
Sep 10 The Messenger Boy's Sweetheart
Sep 17 Round Trip $5.98
Sep 24 Bill Mason's Ride
Oct 1 The Adoption of Helen
Oct 8 All's Fair in Love and War
Oct 15 A Shot in the Night
Oct 22 The Locket
Oct 29 Why They Signed the Pledge

Carl F. Messing
1906
May 14 Panoramic View from Alamo Square of San Francisco While Burning
Panoramic View of Market Street San Francisco After the Earthquake and Fire
Panoramic View of San Francisco City Hall, Damaged by Earthquake

Carlo Rossi
1907
Dec 7 A Soldier Must Obey Orders
When Cherries are Ripe
Dec 28 Hunting above the Clouds
1908
Jan 18 The Gay Vagabonds
Mar 14 Electric Sword
Mar 21 The Cook Wins
Good-Hearted Sailor
Apr 11 The Gambling Demon
Nephew's Luck
Apr 18 Butler's Misdeed
May 2 The Accusing Vision
The Baby Strike
Concealed Love
The First Kiss
The First Lottery Prize
Forgotten Ones
Mysterious Stranger
No Divorce Wanted
The Price of a Favor
The Statue of Rocco
Jul 6 The Troublesome Fly
Jul 13 Consoling the Widow
Good Night Clown
Through the Oural Mountains
A Tricky Uncle
The Two Brothers
Jul 25 Transformation with a Hat Rim
Venice and the Lagoon
Aug 1 Peasant and Prince
Aug 29 Pretty Flower Girl
Oct 6 The Chances of Life
A Wedding Under Terror
Oct 7 Manon Lescaut
Oct 10 Boxing Mania
Romance of a School Teacher
Oct 26 The Queen's Lover
Oct 30 The Galley Slave's Return
Dec 5 She Could Be Happy with Either
Dec 12 Timid Dwellers
Dec 14 An Interior Cyclone
Dec 21 The Black Sheep

Carlton Motion Picture Laboratories
1910
Oct 22 In the Gray of the Dawn
Oct 29 The Armorer's Daughter
Nov 5 Where Sea and Shore Doth Meet
Nov 12 Under a Changing Sky
Nov 19 Moulders of Souls
Nov 26 So Runs the Way
Dec 3 When Woman Wills
Dec 10 The Dispensation
Dec 17 The Thin Dark Line
Dec 24 The Refuge
Dec 31 A Sacrifice — And Then

Carson
1909
May 20 With Grant
Jun 1 Wep-Ton-No-Mah, the Indian Mail Carrier
Dec 2 The Lemon Sisters at Muldoon's Picnic
Dec 14 Comrades Under General Grant
Dec 20 The Drunkard's Christmas
1910
Jan 3 The Salted Mine
Feb 3 A Heroine of Chance
Feb 10 A Child of the Prairie
Mar 17 After Four Generations
Mar 24 Adventures of Princess Lovelock
Troublesome Lad
May 7 The Mad Miner Recovers
May 14 The Tramp Organist
Jun 18 A Tragic Evening
Jun 25 Forget Me Not

Centaur Film Co.
1908
Sep 19 A Cowboy Escapade
Nov 16 The Doll Maker's Daughter
Nov 19 The Parson's Thanksgiving Dinner
Nov 23 Circumstantial Evidence; or, Who Ate the Possum Pie
1909
Apr 1 The Sceptical Cowboy
May 8 A Cowboy's Sweetheart
May 15 The Temptation of John Gray
May 22 Johnny and the Indians
May 29 Scrappy Bill
Jun 5 A Nevada Girl
Jun 12 Private Brown
Jun 19 Love Wins
Jun 26 A Cowboy's Romance
Jul 3 The Crystal Ball
Jul 21 A Tale of Texas
Jul 28 Maryland 1777

Aug 11 The Power of Love
Aug 16 The Young Bachelor's Dream
Aug 18 The Lost Letter
Aug 25 The Blacksmith's Daughter
Sep 1 Peaceful Jones
Sep 8 The Diamond Necklace
The Wishing Charm
Sep 15 A White Lie
Sep 22 Dan Blake's Rival
Sep 29 A Close Call
Oct 6 The Sheriff's Girl
Oct 13 His Mexican Bride
Oct 20 Almost a Suicide
The Purse
Oct 27 Brother and Sister
Nov 3 The Lost Years
Dec 11 Santa Claus and the Miner's Child
Dec 18 Beyond the Rockies
Dec 20 Vindicated
Dec 25 The Deceiver
1910
Jan 6 The Nemesis
Jan 13 Forgiven
Mishaps of Bonehead
Jan 27 Bonehead's Second Adventure
The Ordeal
Feb 16 A Daughter's Devotion
Jun 9 Blind Love
Mr. Swell in the Country
Jun 16 Her Lesson
The Old Maid's Picnic
Jun 23 Getting Rid of Uncle
One Good Turn
Jun 30 For Her Son's Sake
She Would Be a Business Man
Jul 7 One Man's Confession
Jul 11 Aviation at Montreal: June 25th to July 5th, 1910
Jul 14 The Badgers
Granddad's Extravagance

Challenge Film
1910 [month undetermined]
Love-Making Under Difficulties
Jan 5 The Wife's Sacrifice
Jan 12 Robert Macaire; or, The Two Vagabonds
Jan 19 The Brothers
Jan 26 An Artist's Inspiration
Feb 2 The Clown's Big Moment
Feb 9 Spike's Battle
Feb 16 The Silent Messenger
Feb 23 The Third Degree
Mar 2 Jack's Return
The Shirtwaist Strike
Mar 9 A Wolf in Sheep's Clothing
Mar 12 Count of Monte Christo
Mar 19 The Parson's Poster
Mar 22 A Winter Romance at Niagara Falls
Mar 29 The End of the Trail
Apr 6 Partners
Apr 13 An Artist's Temptation
Uncle Eph's Dream
Apr 20 Down in Mexico
Apr 27 Baby Has the Colic
Saved by an Indian
May 4 A Soldier's Sweetheart
May 11 Hearts and Home
May 18 Love and a Palette
Love and a Pallette
May 25 Love's Great Tragedy

Champion Film Co.
1910
Jul 13 Abernathy Kids to the Rescue
Jul 20 A Romance of an Anvil
Jul 27 The Cow-Boy and the Squaw
Aug 3 The Spitfire
Aug 10 The Hermit of the Rockies
Aug 17 A Cowboy's Pledge
Aug 24 The Sheriff and His Son
Aug 31 The Cowboy and the Easterner
Sep 7 His Indian Bride
Sep 14 A Wild Goose Chase
Sep 21 The White Princess of the Tribe
Sep 28 A Western Girl's Sacrifice
Oct 5 The Cowboys to the Rescue
Oct 12 How the Tenderfoot Made Good
Oct 19 Stolen by Indians
Oct 26 Doings at the Ranch
Nov 2 Caught by Cowboys
Nov 9 The Ranchman and the Miser
Nov 16 The Way of the West
Nov 23 Let Us Give Thanks
Nov 30 The Indian Land Grab
Dec 7 Hearts of the West
Dec 14 The Sheriff and the Detective
Dec 21 His Mother
Dec 28 The Golden Gates

Charles J. Jones
1905 [month undetermined]
Buffalo Bill Fight
1906 [month undetermined]
Elk
Lion Hunt
Jan [day undetermined]
Whipping Bear

Charles Urban Trading Co.
1903
Sep [day undetermined]
At the Ford, India. Across the Ravi River
The Busy Bee
Coasting in the Alps
A Daring Daylight Burglary
From London to Brighton
The Galloping Tongas
King Edward VII in France
The Llamas of Thibet
A Remarkable Group of Trained Animals
Trained Baby Elephants
Trained Dogs and Elephants
An Unusual Spectacle
The Wise Elephant
1904 [month undetermined]
Arrival and Release of 40,000 Carrying Pigeons at Ambergate, England
The Baby, the Monkey and the Milk Bottle
International Winter Sports
Manoeuvres by British Bluejackets, Afloat and Ashore
The Monkey and the Ice Cream
The Oxford and Cambridge Boat Race
The Russian Army in Manchuria
Jan [day undetermined]
Chameleon Climbing
The Cheese Mites
Pugilistic Toads
The Toad's Luncheon
Feb 23 Jack Sheppard—The Robbery of the Mail Coach
The Salmon Fisheries of Vancouver
Jul [day undetermined]
Dorothy's Dream
Push Ball on Horseback
Aug [day undetermined]
Arrival and Departure of the Ice-Crushing Steamer "Baikal" at Baikal, Siberia
The Arrival of the 1st Siberian Sharpshooters at Harbin
"The Bushranger." Attack and Robbery of a Mail Convoy
Cairo and the Nile
Children Romping on the Lawn
Constantinople and the Bosporus
Curious Sights in Burmah and Cashmere (Section 1)
Curious Sights in Burmah and Cashmere (Section 2)
The Execution (Beheading) of One of the Hunchuses (Chinese Bandits) Outside the Walls of Mukden
Extraordinary Feats of Horsemanship
A Fierce Sword Combat at Tokio
The Great International Automobile Race for the Gordon-Bennett Trophy
"He Won't Be Happy till He Gets It"
The International Congress of the Salvation Army
The Japanese Ogre
The Japanese Standard Bearer
The Military Funeral of the "Standard Bearer of the Yalu"
"A Newspaper in Making"
Nobles Leaving the Kremlin, Moscow, After a Reception by Czar
Piraeus and Athens (Greece). A Visit to Piraeus
Piraeus and Athens (Greece). Athens and the Acropolis
Piraeus and Athens (Greece). Hoisting Cattle on Steamer
Procession of the "Holy Blood"
A Regiment of the Japanese Imperial Guards and Engineer Corps off to the Front
A Trip to Palestine. Jaffa and Its Harbor
A Trip to Palestine. Jerusalem, the Holy City
The War Correspondent and the Two Bear Cubs
1905
Nov [day undetermined]
Among the Snakes
Brick Making Rotifier
By Rail Through Canadian Rockies
Cir. of Blood, Frog's Foot
Cir. of Protoplasm in Waterweed
Convicts' Escape
An English Gymkana
Feeding the Otters
Fresh Water Infusorian
Giant Tortoise Feeding
Head Hunters of Borneo
Hiawatha
The Life Boat
Mr. Martin Duncan
The Newt
An Old Maid's Darling
On a Borneo Railway
Overturning a Mammoth Chimney
Pond Life
The Red Slug Worm
The Red Snow Germs
Roping and Branding Wild Horses
Russian Field Artillery
Russian Kirgis Troops
Russian Mounted Artillery
Snail, Tortoise, Toad
A Snake in the Grass
Stork's Tug of War
Typhoid Fever Germs
White Rat and Young
1907
Jan [day undetermined]
Willie Goodchild Visits His Auntie
Mar [day undetermined]
The Conjuror's Pupil
Conquering the Dolomites
First Snowball
Flashes from Fun City
The Hand of the Artist
His First Camera
Is Marriage a Failure?
Puck's Pranks on Suburbanite
Quaint Holland
Traveling Menagerie
Trip to Borneo
Turkey Raffle
Wonders of Canada
Mar 30 The Arlberg Railway
The Atlantic Voyage
Berlin to Rome
Captain Kidd and His Pirates
A Championship Won on a Foul
Dolomite Towers
The Magic Bottle
Universal Winter Sports
The Yokel's Love Affair
Apr [day undetermined]
Miss Kellerman's Diving Feats
Apr 13 Artist's Model
Baby's Peril
An Early Round with the Milkman
Apr 20 Father! Mother Wants You
Lady Cabby
The Vacuum Cleaner
Apr 27 Great Boxing Contest
A Pig in Society
Servant's Revenge
May 4 The Park Keeper
Sep 7 Hanky Panky Cards
The Warwick Pageant
Nov 4 Accidents Will Happen
Dec [day undetermined]
Diabolo Nightmare
When the Devil Drives
1908
Feb 29 Hackenschmidt-Rodgers Wrestling Match
Mar 14 Student's Joke on the Porter
Mar 21 His Daughter's Voice

Willie's Magic Wand
May 16 Canine Sagacity
May 30 Sammy's Sucker
Jun 20 The Chauffeur's Dream
Jul 13 Two Little Motorists
Aug 29 The Hayseed's Bargain
Sep 12 The Lightning Postcard Artist
Paper Tearing
Oct 20 High Jumping at Hurlingham
Madeira Wicker Chair Industry
Oct 21 Picturesque Switzerland
Oct 23 Over the Hubarthal Railroad
Oct 24 Sunny Madeira
Oct 26 Desperately in Love
The World of Magic
Oct 28 Motor Boat Races
Oct 29 Closed on Sundays
Oct 31 Daisy, the Pretty Typewriter
Nov 2 The Mock Baronets
Nov 17 Champion Globe Trotter
Disappearing Watch
Waterproof Willie

1909

Jan 9 Wright's Aeroplane
Jan 16 South African Gold Fields
Jan 23 Trip on Rhodesian Railway
Feb 1 The Guard's Alarm
Feb 10 Following Mother's Footsteps
Feb 16 The Hand of a Wizard
Feb 24 Polka on Brain
Jun 2 Magic Carpet
Jul 3 Dissolution of Parliament
Jul 14 The Wizard's Walking Stick
Aug 31 Professor Puddenhead's Patents
Nov 17 Workhouse to Mansion
Dec 1 Consul Crosses the Atlantic
Dec 8 Capturing the North Pole; or, How He Cook'ed Peary's Record
Dec 29 Battle in the Clouds

1910

Jan 15 An Absorbing Tale
Jan 26 The Lass Who Loves a Sailor
Mar 2 Baby Bet
May 12 The Invisible Dog
May 18 The Electric Servant
Jun 4 Animated Cotton

Chase, Walter G. *see* **Walter G. Chase**

Cherry Kearton, Ltd.

1910

Apr 18 Roosevelt in Africa

Chicago Film Exchange

1908

Sep 21 Gans-Nelson Fight

1909

Feb 10 A Sign from Heaven
Mar 9 A Providential Chance
Mar 10 Arrival at the Village
For the Motherland
Mar 11 Alcoholic Doctor
Mar 12 Medieval Episode
Mar 13 Grand Maneuvers
The Presidential Inauguration Film
Mar 14 The Summers-Britt Fight Pictures
Mar 20 The Burden of Debt
Mar 27 An Artist's Model's Jealousy
The Beggar's Daughter
Blind Child's Dog
A Convict's Return
A Criminal Invention
Drama in the Forest
Drama in the Village
Episode of War
Fishing by Dynamite
Follow Me and I'll Pay for Dinner
Gadbin, the Refractory Suicide
The Good Vicar
The Heart of a Mother
Hero of the Prussian War
Husband's Vengeance
I Want a Moustache
Indians and Cowboys
Lily Amuses Herself
Love of Travel
Lucia di Lammermoor
Magic Games
Misfortunes of a Cobbler
The New Servant
The Paralytic
The Parricide
The Pirate's Daughter
The Poor Schoolma'am
The Ripe Cheese
The Servant Question Solved
Tracked by a Dog
The Train Robbers
Tubbie's Terrible Troubles
The Unfaithful Cashier
Apr [day undetermined]
A Moroccan Romance
The Over-Eager Heirs
The Troubles of the Pretty School Marm
Apr 17 Automatic Nursing Bottle
The Deacon's Holiday
Nellie's Love Story
Violets
Apr 24 The Deserter
A Heartless Mother
A Lover's Quarrel
Married Under Difficulties
Professor's Anti-Gravitation
The Rival Cyclists
The Stolen Bride
The Unlucky Thief
The Villain's Wooing
May 1 An Unfortunate Bath
May 8 Arrest of the Orderly
Artillery Manoeuvers in the Mountains
Cat in the Pot
Chauffeur Out for a Good Time
Dressed for the Occasion
Filial Devotion
Frolics of Gamins
Glimmeramm
High Art
Husband Goes to Market
Indiscretion of Moving Picture
Jammer-bach
Johnny Is No Longer a Child
The Magic Wand
The Milkman's Wooing
Modern Tramp
Novel Invitation
An Old Man's Honor
Peasant and Photographers
Shark Fishing
Tragedy at the Circus
The Tramp's Luck
Trick Well Played
Tricks of the Photographer
Unlucky Smuggler
Unpleasant Substitution
What William Did
Why the Wedding Didn't Come Off
May 24 Arabian Cavalry
The Artist's Dummy
Berthold in Paris
Blind Farmer
Blind Man's Daughter
Boy's Adventure
Champagne Party
Deserved Punishment
Dr. Clown
Dog and Baby
Dreamer
Flat Hunting
Good People
Grand Stag Hunting
Great Flood in India, September, 1908
Grip in the Family
Happy Artist
Heart of Genevieve
Henry Farman, King of the Air
His First Pants
Home of the Arabians
Hurt
Hypnotism
Innocence
King Edward's Visit to Berlin
Lead and Zinc Mines
Life of a Wood Ant
Little Mother
Masquerade Costume
Military Review
A Miracle
Miracle of Love
Mishaps of a Governess
New Style Airship
The Newlyweds
Only a Dog
Poor Life
Repairing Railroad Tracks
Servant
Sleep Walker
Soldier Manoeuvres in Morocco
Son's Sacrifice
Stronger Than Death
Sweetheart's Bouquet
Sweetheart's Christmas
Telltale Graphophone
Tommy's Tricks
Tragedy in the Family
Tragedy of a Ghost
Troubles of a Fisherman
Useful Young Man
Jun 17 The Conjuror
Cyrano de Bergerac
The Girl Heroine
Officer's Revenge
Recompense

1910

Jun 1 Custer's Last Stand

The Chicago Film Picture Co.

1910

May 16 Johnson Training for His Fight with Jeffries

Clapham, A. J. *see* **A. J. Clapham**

Clarendon Film Co.

1904

Aug [day undetermined]
Attempted Murder in a Train
Off for the Holidays
Sep [day undetermined]
The Pig That Came to Life
The Quarrelsome Washerwoman
Sep 7 Linen Shop
Sep 17 Burglar and Girls
The Convict's Escape
A Kiss and a Tumble
Dec [day undetermined]
Guy Fawkes' Day
Dec 3 Sandy McGregor

1905 [month undetermined]

Fine Feathers Make Fine Birds
Feb 25 Love Letter
Aug [day undetermined]
Blind Man's Bluff
Dangerous Golfers

1906

Sep 20 Rescued in Mid-Air

1908

Jan 18 Anxious Day for Mother
Pied Piper of Hamlin
Jan 20 The Water Babies; or, The Little Chimney Sweep
Feb 17 The Soldier's Wedding
Apr 11 The Captain's Wives
The Downfall of the Burglars' Trust
The Scandalous Boys
May 2 Poor Aunt Matilda
May 9 The Memory of His Mother
Jun 13 Mr. Brown Has a Tile Loose
Three Sportsmen and a Hat
Jul 25 Three Maiden Ladies and a Bull
Aug 1 Follow Your Leader and the Master Follows Last

1909 [month undetermined]

Robin Hood and His Merry Men
Mar 22 Son and Mother-in-law
A Wild Goose Chase
Apr 17 Puritan Maid
Apr 24 Nancy; or, The Burglar's Daughter
May 8 The Cavalier's Wife
Romance of the Crafty Usurper and the Young King
May 22 Favorite Doll
May 29 Lesson in Electricity
Morganatic Marriage
Jul 3 Modern Cinderella
Jul 17 Motor Skates
Sep 23 An Aerial Elopement
Nov 13 The Invaders

1910

Mar 16 Peter's Patent Paint
May 14 Bobby, the Boy Scout
Jun 4 A Drink of Goat's Milk
Jun 24 Lieutenant Rose, R. N.
Jul 1 The Plumber

Clements-Hester Co.
1910
Jun 18 [Welch-Daniels Fight]
Coffroth, J. W. *see* **J. W. Coffroth**
Col. [unidentified abbreviation]
1910
May 9 Saved by Faith
May 12 Wearing of the Green
Columbia-American Films
1909
Aug 14 A Soldier's Wife
Columbia Film Co.
1910
Jun 23 Claim Jumpers
Oct 1 Rip Van Winkle
Oct 8 Jealousy
Oct 15 Tracked across the Sea
Oct 22 Breaking Home Ties
Oct 29 In the Web
Nov 12 The Heroine of 101 Ranch
Nov 19 Oklahoma Bill
Nov 26 Stage Coach Tom
Dec 24 The Cattlemen's Feud
Dec 31 Trapped
Columbia Photograph Co.
1909 [month undetermined]
The American Fleet in Hampton Roads, 1909, After Girdling the Globe
Jul 21 Pennsylvania Monument at Fort Mahone near Petersburg, Va.
Reception of President Taft in Petersburg, Virginia, May 19th, 1909
Comerio
1908
Oct 24 The Revengeful Waiter
The Young Artist
1909
Feb 6 Fatal Wedding
Riding for Love
Feb 13 Circumstantial Evidence
Feb 22 The Galley Slave
Feb 24 Drama Amongst Fishermen
Feb 27 The Shoemaker's Luck
Jun 26 A Painful Joke
Jul 3 Pity and Love
Oct 4 Eve of the Wedding
Oct 12 Noble and Commoner
Oct 18 Berlin Jack the Ripper
Nov 6 The Silk Worm Series
Nov 8 Orange Growing in Palestine
Dec 6 The Electric Safe
Dec 13 The Smuggler's Sweetheart
Dec 20 Lorenzi De Medica
1910
Jan 10 Rudolph of Hapsburg
Jan 17 Arthur's Little Love Affair
The Miners
Jan 20 Martyrs of Pompeii
Jan 26 Angler and the Cyclist
Apr 11 Musical Masterpiece
Spanish Fandalgo
Apr 18 The Queen's Attendant
Apr 26 Grandfather's Story
Apr 27 Bethlehem
Apr 28 Twenty Francs
May 5 Fury of the Waves
Village Beauty
May 12 Two Betrothed
May 17 Child's Doctor
May 19 In the Name of Allah
Jun 4 Battles of Soul
Jun 13 Artist's Dream
Jun 21 Love Is Stronger Than Life
Jun 24 Isis
Jun 30 False Accusation
Jul 4 The Derby
Cosmpolitan
1910
Jan 15 Episode of French Revolution
May 3 The Flood
Crawford Film Exchange Co. *see* **O. T. Crawford Film Exchange Co.**
Crescent Film Co.
1908
Oct 10 A "Skate" on Skates
Troublesome Baby
Young Heroes of the West
Oct 17 Chauncey Proves a Good Detective
What Poverty Leads To
Oct 28 A Desperate Character
Nov 27 Sherlock Holmes in the Great Mystery
Cricks and Martin
1908
Mar 14 For the Baby's Sake
Mar 21 'Twixt Love and Duty; or, A Woman's Heroism
May 2 Freddie's Little Love Affair
The Mission of a Flower
May 9 The Interrupted Bath
Leap Year; or, She Would Be Wed
Professor Bounder's Pills
Jun 6 Hunting Deer
Sep 26 How the Coster Sold the Seeds
Nov 21 The Devil's Bargain
Dec 14 How the Dodger Secured a Meal
1909
Feb 10 Grandfather's Birthday
The Guardian of the Bank
Polly's Excursion
Apr 17 A Traitor to the King
Apr 24 High Game
Jun 12 How Jones Got a New Suit
The Man Housemaid
Jun 26 His Wedding Morn
Jul 3 Lighthouse
Jul 24 Territory on Brain
Aug 7 Butcher Boy
Aug 14 Mr. Isaacs and the Mice
Aug 21 When Jack Gets His Pay
Aug 28 Henpeck's Revolt
Sep 4 Little Jim
Sep 13 Votes for Women
Sep 18 A Tricky Convict
Oct 19 The Phantom Ship
Dec 30 The Motherless Waif
1910
Jan 15 Mind, I Catch You Smoking
Jan 17 Muggins
Mar 30 Robber's Ruse
Apr 5 Boxing Fever
Apr 30 The Sculptor's Dream
May 14 The Convict's Dream
May 18 Wonderful Machine Oil
Jun 4 Adopting a Child
The Last of the Dandies
A Race for a Bride
Jun 29 Fishery in the North
Jul 8 From Gypsy Hands
Jul 15 The Hindoo's Treachery
Cricks and Sharp
1905
Jul [day undetermined]
Fixing the Derby Favorite
Aug [day undetermined]
Lady Barber
Oct [day undetermined]
Pilfered Porker
1906
Jan [day undetermined]
Horse Stealing
1907
Apr 6 Drink and Repentance
Father's Picnic
Foiled by a Woman; or, Falsely Accused
Quarter Day Conjuring
She Would Sing
Slippery Jim, the Burglar
Apr 13 The Tell-Tale Telephone
A Woman's Sacrifice
Jun 1 The Wrong Chimney; or, Every Man His Own Sweep
Jun 29 Bertie's Love Letter
The Comic Duel
Oct 12 Serving a Summons
Oct 19 Cricket Terms Illustrated
Don't Go to the Law
Nov 16 A Drink Cure
Even a Worm Will Turn
Croce et C.
1909
Sep 25 From Portofino to Nervi
Dandy Films see Electragraff - complete overlap
1910
Jun 15 A Message from the East
Jun 22 An Interrupted Courtship
Jun 29 All's Well That Ends Well
Jul 6 No Questions Asked
Jul 13 Among the Breakers
Jul 20 The Power from Above
Defender Film Co.
1910
Jun 10 Russia—The Land of Oppression
Jun 17 Married in Haste
Jun 24 Too Many Girls
Jul 1 Saved from Himself
Jul 8 The Girl Who Dared
Jul 15 A Bridegroom's Mishap
Retribution
Jul 22 Repaid with Interest
Aug 11 Indian Squaw's Sacrifice
Aug 18 Shanghaied
Aug 25 Hazing a New Scholar
Sep 1 Great Marshall Jewel Case
That Letter from Teddy
Sep 8 Cowboy's Courtship
Wanted: An Athletic Instructor
Sep 15 An Attempted Elopement
A Game for Life
Sep 22 The Cattle Thief's Revenge
Sep 29 The School-Marm's Ride for Life
Oct 6 Wild Bill's Defeat
Oct 13 The Tale a Camera Told
Oct 20 The Heart of a Cowboy
Oct 27 A Clause in the Will
Nov 3 Cohen's Generosity
Nov 10 The Last Straw
Nov 17 The Education of Mary Jane
Nov 24 Forgiven
Deloin
1909
Mar 16 Devotion and Its Reward
Kid's Jest
Mar 19 Child's Vision
Tramp's Defense
Mar 23 Cross of Honor
Gift
Deutsche Bioskop
1909
Jun 5 False Piano Professor
Jun 26 Aboard the German Navy
Jul 24 Bachelor's Misfortune
Sep 18 German Spring Parade
Nov 29 Marvelous Shaving Soap
1910
Feb 15 Daring Lion's Bride
Deutsche Mutoskop und Biograph G.m.b.H. *see also* **American Mutoscope and Biograph Co.; American Mutoscope Co.; Biograph Co.; British Mutoscope and Biograph Co.; The Biograph & Mutoscope Co. for France, Ltd.**
1902
Nov [day undetermined]
Aboard the Aegir
The Attack
Banks of the Elbe
Battleship "Odin"
"Be Good Again"
Berlin Fire Department
Between the Decks
Bi-Centennial Jubilee Parade
A Blast in a Gravel Bed
The Bogie Man
Calling the Pigeons
The Children and the Frog
Clever Horsemanship
The Crown Prince of Germany
Dedication of the Alexander Grenadiers' Barracks
The Elephant's Bath
Elevated and Underground
The Emperor and Empress and Crown Prince of Germany
Emperor and Empress of Germany
The Emperor and Empress of Germany
Emperor William II
Emperor William II on Horseback
Emperor William as a Hussar
Emperor William at the Danzig Manoeuvres
Emperor William of Germany on Horseback
Emperor William Returning from Manoeuvres
Empress of Germany at Danzig
Empress of Germany Driving to the Manoeuvres
Field-Marshal Count Von Waldersee
The Flying Train
A Flying Wedge
Fun in a Clothes Basket

Fun on a Sand Hill
Funeral Procession of the Late Empress Frederick
German Artillery in Action
German Cavalry Fording a River
German Cavalry Leaping Hurdles
German Garde Kurassiers
German Lancers
German Military Exercises
German Navy Target Practice
German Railway Service
A German Torpedo Boat Flotilla in Action
The Gourmand
A Hurdle Race
In a German Bath
In the Friedrichstrasse
In the Heart of the Forest
King Albert of Saxony
Launch of the "Koenig Albert"
Launching of the "Kaiser Wilhelm der Grosse"
Marvelous Markmanship
A Mermaid Dance
On Board His Majesty's Battleship "Fuerst Bismark"
On Board His Majesty's Gunboat "Luchs"
On the Elbe
Panorama of Wilhelmshaven
Panoramic View from the Stadtbahn
Panoramic View of the Harbor of Hamburg, Germany
Panoramic View of the Siegesallee
Prince Tsung of China
Rare Fish in an Aquarium
A Rescue at Sea
Return of the German China Fleet
The Rivals
A Run by the Berlin Fire Department, Berlin, Germany
Sailing of Battleship "Wurtemberg"
Torpedo Boat "G-89"
A Tug of War
Unveiling of the Bismarck Monument
An Unwelcome Visitor
Visit of Emperor Francis Josef of Austria to Berlin
When Knighthood Was in Flower
When the Bugle Sounds "Charge!"
Winter in Germany
With Emperor William's Army

1903 [month undetermined]
German Torpedo Boat in Action

1905
Nov [day undetermined]
Drill Under Oars
Torpedo Boat Maneuvering
With the German Fleet
The Wrestling Elephant

1906
Sep [day undetermined]
Trip on Berlin Elevated R. R.
Nov [day undetermined]
On Great Western Railway Ldongotten Station
On Great Western Railway Through Dawhistle

Dial, Eugene *see* **Eugene Dial**
Dickson, William K. L. *see* **William K. L. Dickson**
Dramagraph Co. of America

1910
Aug 11 Beyond Endurance
Sep [day undetermined]
Only a Jew

Duskes, Alfred *see* **Alfred Duskes**
E. Wahlstrom

1907
Dec 27 "King Oscar II's Funeral Films"

Eagle Film Exchange

1909
Sep 29 The Blind Detective
Oct 18 A Drunkard's Son

1910
Feb 3 Foxy Hobo Married for Love
Tom's Last Steeple Chase
Feb 11 Hard Heart
Souvenirs of Paris
Feb 12 False Oath
Nema Lescout
Feb 17 Camargo
Mar 4 Retaliation
Mar 8 Drama on the Britain Coast
Mar 9 Salome
Mar 10 Sacred Fire
We Will Die Together, Love
Mar 11 Mr. Short Sighted
Mar 14 Her First Love
Mar 16 Burglar's Daughter
Loisette
Peter's Patent Paint
Mar 17 After Four Generations
Mar 24 Adventures of Princess Lovelock
Troublesome Lad
Mar 26 Innkeeper's Daughter
Sleeping Pills
Mar 29 Uncle's Will
Mar 30 Inventive Trouser
Robber's Ruse
Apr 1 Pa, Ma and Baby
A Race for Inheritance
Apr 5 Boxing Fever
Love and Art
Apr 6 Honest Little Urchin
Apr 7 Mother Land
Apr 8 New Little Mother
Apr 26 The Penalty of Beauty
Apr 30 Hope of the Village
The Sculptor's Dream
May 2 Safety Suit for Skaters
Scratch
May 3 The Flood
May 4 Hunting Adventure
May 5 Negro's Sacrifice
May 7 Artist's Good Joke
Father's Crime
The Sentinel's Romance
May 9 Beatrice Cenci
Mother's Victory
May 12 The Invisible Dog
Three Fingered Kate
May 14 Bobby, the Boy Scout
The Convict's Dream
Honor of the Alpine Guide
May 18 The Electric Servant
For the Flag
Wonderful Machine Oil
May 21 Mont Blanc
May 23 Good Business
Madness for Love
May 24 Deserter
Kind-Hearted Tramp
May 25 Motherless Child
Reconciled
Jun 2 Gardner at the Convent
Thief
Valgeres Blood
Jun 4 Adopting a Child

Eclair Film Co.

1908
Sep 12 The Daughter of the Gypsy
The Spiteful Groom
Nov 6 Gust of Wind
Pirate's Honor
Dec 2 Devils in the Farm
Every Age Has Its Trouble
Dec 19 Misdeeds of a Tragical Part
Dec 21 My Laundress Inherits

1909
Jan 2 The Corsican's Revenge
Jan 16 The Coiners, or Catching the Counterfeiters
Feb 6 The Banker
The Unwelcome Lover
Feb 27 A Day's Outing
Mar 22 A Borrowed Suit
Brisquet
The Chambermaid and the Dwarf
Chasing the Helmet
Compassion
The Dragonad
Dream of Featart
The Ghost
Main Clues
The Mesmerist
Mother-in-law Too Kindhearted
Lo Piferaro
Pity
The Prophecy
Rifle Bill No. 5
Service of a Friend
Soldier and Witch
State Secret
The Statue
Taming a Husband
United by Misfortune
Apr 24 The Magnetizer
May 1 The Dragoons Under Louis XIV
May 8 Ellen
May 15 Disappointed Heirs
Magic Sack
May 22 Neurasthenique
Perilous Expedition
May 29 Reveler's Dream
Jun 5 Legend of the Erring Jew
Jun 12 Too Clean a Servant
Jun 26 The Buffoon
Police Dogs
Jul 17 The Poisoned Flower
Jul 24 Professor of Dancing
Aug 14 Bouquet Gallantly Offered
A Smart Trick
Aug 21 Honesty Rewarded
Hooligan Against His Will
Aug 28 The Two Friends
Sep 13 The Justifier
Love of Adventures
Sep 18 Calino Objects to Work
For My Children
Man with the Sack in Society
Pietro, the Candy Kid
Pietro, the Mule Driver
Sep 21 Meskal, the Smuggler
Sep 24 Marriage of Yvonne
Nov 2 Honest John, the Coachman
Nov 8 Bandits of the Atlas Gorges
Woes of a Cinematographer
Nov 10 The Necklace of the Holy Virgin
Nov 13 Nana's Mother
Nov 16 Mysterious Luggage
Nov 22 John Farley's Redemption
Legend of the Good Knight
Nov 29 The Painter's Idol
Dec 4 An Unlucky Acquisition
Dec 6 Captain Fracassee
The Heir of Clavencourt Castle
Dec 13 Beethoven
Dec 20 The Prisoner's Strategy
Dec 25 Drama of Villasgne
Pretty Fisher-Woman
Real Brittany
Suicide Club
Dec 31 The Emperor's Staff Officer

1910
Jan 3 A Wall Street Chance
Jan 10 Brave Little Heart
Jan 15 The Double
Jan 17 The Freebooter's Captive
Feb 7 The Child and the Dancing-Jack
Mr. Giddy's Revenge
Feb 12 Vulture of Seine
Feb 14 A Bootblack's Daily Labor in Algiers
The Serum; or, The Antidote
Feb 21 Duty and Conscience
Face to Face
Feb 28 The Castles on the Rhine from Bingen to Coblenz
Nick Carter as Acrobat
Mar 7 The Cage (An Episode in the Adventures of Morgan the Pirate)
Taming Wild Horses at Buenos Aires
Mar 14 Aspirants to the Hand of Helen
The Revenge of Dupont L'Anguille
Mar 21 Honesty, Its Own Reward
The Lover's Embarrassment
Mar 28 The Treasure of Louis
A Trip to Berne
Apr 4 After the Fall of the "Eagle"
The Theater of Phenomenons
Apr 11 The Strength of Duty
Apr 16 Egyptian Village Market
Apr 18 Ascending the Sea of Ice
Love the Conqueror
Apr 25 The Six-Legged Sheep
May 2 The Broken Friendship
My Maid Is Too Slow
May 9 The Prisoner of the Golden Isle
May 16 Barberine
May 23 A Desperate Duel
Juan, the Pelota Player
May 30 Life of the Alpine Shooters in the Frontier Outposts

The Watchmaker's Hat
Jun 6 A Martyr of Love
A Sculptor Who Has Easy Work
Jun 8 The Vivandiera
Jun 13 The Biter Bit
In Love with the Charcoal Woman
Jun 15 The Battle of Legnano; or, Barbarossa
Jun 20 Eugenie Grandet
Jun 23 From Love to Martyrdom
Jun 27 Juliet Wants to Marry an Artist
The Sorceress of the Strand
Jun 30 Faust
Jul 4 The King of the Beggars
Jul 7 Giorgione
Jul 11 John, the Usher
Jul 18 The Nurse's Trunk
To-morrow Is Pay-day
Jul 25 The Silversmith to King Louis XI
Aug 1 She Surveys Her Son-in-Law
The Soldier's Honor
Aug 8 The Buried Man of Tebessa
Competition of the Police and Guard Dogs
Aug 15 The Colonel's Boot
The Monkey Showmen of Djibah
Aug 22 The Firemen of Cairo
Musette's Caprice
Aug 29 Fantastic Furniture
An Unexpected Servant
Sep 5 The Little Blind Girl
The Lost Chance
Sep 11 Lame Woman
Sep 12 Between Duty and Honor
Sep 16 The Sacking of Rome
Sep 19 The Blind Man's Dog
The Falls of the Rhine
Sep 23 Julie Colonna
Tontolini as a Ballet Dancer
Sep 26 The Street Arab of Paris
Sep 30 Giovanni of Medici
Oct 3 Behind the Scenes of the Cinema Stage
Through the Ruins of Carthage
Oct 10 The Carmelite
The Order Is to March
Oct 14 The Mad Lady of Chester
Oct 17 Dr. Geoffrey's Conscience
An Indian Chief's Generosity
Oct 21 The Last of the Savelli
Oct 24 The Absent-Minded Doctor
Saved by Her Dog
Oct 28 The Pretty Dairy Maid
Tontolini Is in Love
Oct 31 The Little Mother
The Manufacture of Cheese at Roquefort
Nov 4 A Wooden Sword
Nov 7 Religious Fetes at Thibet
The Resurrection of Lazarus
Nov 14 The Devil's Billiard Table
Ginhara or Faithful Unto Death
Nov 21 The Exiled Mother
Nov 28 A Difficult Capture
The Wreck
Dec 5 The Laundry Girl's Good Night
The Price of a Sacrifice
Dec 12 The Bowling Craze
Our Dear Uncle from America
Dec 19 The Child of Two Mothers
The Museum of Sovereigns
Dec 26 The Fear of Fire
The Lock-Keeper

Eclipse
1907
Jun 27 The Near-Sighted Cyclist
Dec [day undetermined]
Willing to Oblige
1908
Jul 11 The Organ-Grinder's Daughter
Nov 2 Sold by His Parents
Dec 5 The Country Idyll
1909
Feb 27 Her Daughter's Dowry
Apr 17 Story of a Calf's Head
1910
Nov 2 Crossing the Andes
Tragical Concealment

Edison Mfg. Co. *see also* **Thomas A. Edison; Thomas A. Edison, Inc.**
1893 [month undetermined]
Edison Kinetoscopic Records
1894 [month undetermined]
Imperial Japanese Dance
Leonard—Cushing Fight
Jan [day undetermined]
Edison Kinetoscopic Record of a Sneeze, January 7, 1894
Apr [day undetermined]
Edison Kinetoscopic Records
May [day undetermined]
Souvenir Strip of the Edison Kinetoscope [Sandow, the Modern Hercules]
Nov [day undetermined]
Corbett and Courtney Before the Kinetograph
1895 [month undetermined]
Serpentine Dance—Annabelle
1896 [month undetermined]
The Kiss
Lone Fisherman
Oct [day undetermined]
The Burning Stable
Clark's Thread Mill
East Side Drive, No. 1
East Side Drive, No. 2
Feeding the Doves
A Morning Bath
Park Police Drill Left Wheel and Forward
Park Police Drill Mount and Dismounting
Streets of Cairo
Surf at Long Branch [N.J.]
Wine Garden Scene
Nov [day undetermined]
Charge of West Point Cadets
Fighting the Fire
A Morning Alarm
Mounted Police Charge
The Runaway in the Park
Starting for the Fire
Dec [day undetermined]
American Falls from Above, American Side
American Falls from Bottom of Canadian Shore
American Falls—from Incline R. R.
Black Diamond Express
Buffalo Horse Market
Chicago and Buffalo Express
Cock Fight
Horseshoe Falls—From Luna Isle
Horseshoe Falls from Table Rock, Canadian Side
Hurdle Race—High Jumpers
Rapids at Cave of the Winds
Special Photographing Train
Tally Ho—Arrival
Tally Ho—Departure
Whirlpool Rapids—from Bottom of Canadian Shore
1897 [month undetermined]
Butterfly Dance
The Dolorita Passion Dance
Fire Rescue Scene
Herald Square
Tourist Train Leaving Livingston, Mont.
Jan [day undetermined]
The Farmer's Troubles
The First Sleigh-Ride
Market Square, Harrisburg, Pa.
Parisian Dance
Pennsylvania State Militia, Double Time
Pennsylvania State Militia, Single Time
Police Patrol Wagon
Feb [day undetermined]
Guard Mount, Ft. Myer [Va.]
The Milker's Mishap
Pennsylvania Avenue, Washington, D.C.
Pile Driving, Washington Navy Yard [Washington, D.C.]
Mar [day undetermined]
American and Cuban Flag
Battery A, Light Artillery, U. S. Army
Drum Corps and Militia
Fifth Avenue, New York
McKinley and Cleveland Going to the Capitol
McKinley Taking the Oath
Marines from U. S. Cruiser "New York"
Return of McKinley from the Capitol
71st Regiment, New York
Sleighing in Central Park
Umbrella Brigade
Vice-President Hobart's Escort
Washington Continental Guards
Young Men's Blaine Club of Cincinnati
Apr [day undetermined]
Bareback Hurdle Jumping
Black Diamond Express, No. 1
Black Diamond Express, No. 2
Cavalry Passing in Review
Chas. Werts, Acrobat
The Elopement
Grace Church, New York
Hurdle Jumping and Saddle Vaulting
McKinley Leaving Church
Now I Lay Me Down To Sleep
Panorama of Susquehanna River Taken from the Black Diamond Express
Pennsylvania Avenue, Washington
Receding View, Black Diamond Express
Seminary Girls
The Washwoman's Troubles
May [day undetermined]
Amoskeag Veterans, New Hampshire
Battery B, Governor's Troop, Penna.
Buffalo Bill and Escort
Corcoran Cadets, Washington
General Porter's Oration
Governor Cook and Staff, Connecticut
Governor of Ohio and Staff
Grant Veterans—G. A. R.
Horse Dancing Couchee Couchee
Husking Bee
Making Soap Bubbles
National Lancers of Boston
O'Brien's Trained Horses
Old Guard, New York City
Pillow Fight
President McKinley's Address
7th and 71st Regiment, New York
Sixth U. S. Cavalry
Sun Dance—Annabelle
Tandem Hurdle Jumping
Trick Elephants
Jun [day undetermined]
Boating on the Lake
Chicken Thieves
Children's Toilet
Mr. Edison at Work in His Chemical Laboratory
Jul [day undetermined]
Armour's Electric Trolley
Buffalo Fire Department in Action
Buffalo Police on Parade
Buffalo Stockyards
Cattle Driven to Slaughter
Corner Madison and State Streets, Chicago
Falls of Minnehaha
Free-for-All Race at Charter Oak Park
Giant Coal Dumper
Philadelphia Express, Jersey Central Railway
Racing at Sheepshead Bay
Sheep Run, Chicago Stockyards
Suburban Handicap, 1897
Waterfall in the Catskills
Aug [day undetermined]
Admiral Cigarette
Sep [day undetermined]
Bowery Waltz
Charity Ball
Fisherman's Luck
Sutro Baths, No. 2
Oct [day undetermined]
Ambulance at the Accident
Ambulance Call
Arrest in Chinatown, San Francisco, Cal.
Beach Apparatus—Practice
Boat Wagon and Beach Cart
Boxing for Points
Capsize of Lifeboat
Crissie Sheridan
Cupid and Psyche
Dancing Darkey Boy
Exhibition of Prize Winners

First Avenue, Seattle, Washington, No. 8
Fisherman's Wharf
Fishing Smacks
Horses Loading for Klondike
Hotel Del Monte
Hotel Vendome, San Jose, Cal.
The Jealous Monkey
Judging Tandems
Ladies' Saddle Horses
Launch of Life Boat
Launch of Surf Boat
Leander Sisters
Lick Observatory, Mt. Hamilton, Cal.
Loading Baggage for Klondike
Lurline Baths
Pie Eating Contest
Rainmakers
Rescue—Resuscitation
Return of Lifeboat
S. S. "Coptic" at Dock
S. S. "Coptic" in the Harbor
S. S. "Coptic" Sailing Away
S. S. "Queen" Leaving Dock
S. S. "Queen" Loading
S. S. "Williamette" Leaving for Klondike
The Sea Lions' Home
Single Harness Horses
Southern Pacific Overland Mail
Stanford University, California
Surf at Monterey
Sutro Baths, No. 1
Teams of Horses
Wall Scaling

Nov 27 The Downey and Patterson Fight

Dec [day undetermined]
Fast Mail, Northern Pacific Railroad
Firing by Squad, Gatling Gun
Gatling Gun Crew in Action
Mount and Dismount, Gatling Gun

1898 [month undetermined]
Alciede Capitane
Bathing Scene at Rockaway
Battle of San Juan Hill
Boxing
Boxing Cats
Bucking Broncho
Caciedo
Ghost Dance
Indian War Council
Red Cross at the Front
Sailors Landing Under Fire
Surrender of General Toral

Feb [day undetermined]
Branding Cattle
Buck Dance, Ute Indians
Calf Branding
California Limited, A.T. & S.F.R.R.
California Orange Groves, Panoramic View
Cañon of the Rio Grande
Cattle Fording Stream
Cattle Leaving the Corral
Chinese Procession
Circle Dance, Ute Indians
Coasting
Cripple Creek Float
Decorated Carriages
Denver Fire Brigade
Dogs Playing in the Surf
Eagle Dance, Pueblo Indians
Going Through the Tunnel
Hockey Match on the Ice
Horticultural Floats, No. 9
Indian Day School
Las Viga Canal, Mexico City
Lassoing a Steer
Marching Scene
Market Scene, City of Mexico
Masked Procession
Mexican Fishing Scene
Mexican Rurales Charge
A Mid-Winter Brush
Off for the Rabbit Chase
Ostriches Feeding
Ostriches Running, No. 1
Ostriches Running, No. 2
Parade of Coaches
Picking Oranges
Procession of Mounted Indians and Cowboys
Repairing Streets in Mexico
Royal Gorge
Serving Rations to the Indians, No. 1
Serving Rations to the Indians, No. 2
Snowballing the Coasters
South Spring Street, Los Angeles, Cal.
Spanish Ball Game
Street Scene, San Diego
Sunday Morning in Mexico
Sunset Limited, Southern Pacific Ry.
Surface Transit, Mexico
Train Hour in Durango, Mexico
Wand Dance, Pueblo Indians
Wash Day in Mexico

Feb 19 The Passion Play of Oberammergau

Mar [day undetermined]
Acrobatic Monkey
After Launching
American Flag
Bull Fight, No. 1
Bull Fight, No. 2
Bull Fight, No. 3
Feeding Sea Gulls
Freight Train
Launch of Japanese Man-of-War "Chitosa"
Launching, No. 2
Mexico Street Scene
Mount Tamalpais R. R., No. 1
Mount Tamalpais R. R., No. 2
Mount Taw R. R., No. 3
Native Daughters
Old Glory and Cuban Flag
Parade of Chinese
Procession of Floats
Sea Waves
Union Iron Works
An Unwelcome Visitor

May [day undetermined]
Battery B Pitching Camp

May 20 The Ball Game
Battery B Arriving at Camp
The Burglar
Burial of the "Maine" Victims
Colored Troops Disembarking
Comedy Set-To
Cruiser "Cincinnati"
Cruiser "Detroit"
Cruiser "Marblehead"
Cuban Refugees Waiting for Rations
Cuban Volunteers Marching for Rations
Flagship "New York"
Heaving the Log
Military Camp at Tampa, Taken from Train
Monitor "Terror"
Morro Castle, Havana Harbor
N. Y. Journal Despatch Yacht "Buccaneer"
9th Infantry Boys' Morning Wash
9th U. S. Cavalry Watering Horses
S. S. "Coptic"
S. S. "Coptic" Lying To
S. S. "Coptic" Running Against the Storm
Secretary Long and Captain Sigsbee
See-Saw Scene
Snow Storm
Steamer "Mascotte" Arriving at Tampa
A Street Arab
The Telephone
10th U. S. Infantry Disembarking from Cars
10th U. S. Infantry, 2nd Battalion Leaving Cars
Transport "Whitney" Leaving Dock
U. S. Battleship "Indiana"
U. S. Battleship "Iowa"
U. S. Cavalry Supplies Unloading at Tampa, Florida
U. S. Cruiser "Nashville"
U. S. S. "Castine"
War Correspondents
Wreck of the Battleship "Maine"

Jun [day undetermined]
Afternoon Tea on Board S. S. "Doric"
Arrival of Tokyo Train
Blanket-Tossing a New Recruit
California Volunteers Marching To Embark
Canton River Scene
Canton Steamboat Landing Chinese Passengers
Cuban Volunteers Embarking
14th U. S. Infantry Drilling at the Presidio
Game of Shovel Board on Board S. S. "Doric"
Going to the Yokohama Races
Government House at Hong Kong
Hong Kong Regiment, No. 1
Hong Kong Regiment, No. 2
Hong Kong, Wharf Scene
Honolulu Street Scene
Japanese Sampans
Kanakas Diving for Money [Honolulu], No. 1
Kanakas Diving for Money [Honolulu], No. 2
Landing Wharf at Canton
Loading Horses on Transport
9th and 13th U. S. Infantry at Battalion Drill
Parade of Buffalo Bill's Wild West Show, No. 1
Parade of Buffalo Bill's Wild West Show, No. 2
Railway Station at Yokohama
Returning from the Races
River Scene at Macao, China
Roosevelt's Rough Riders Embarking for Santiago
S. S. "Coptic" Coaling
S. S. "Doric"
S. S. "Doric" in Mid-Ocean
S. S. "Gaelic"
S. S. "Gaelic" at Nagasaki
71st N. Y. Volunteers Embarking for Santiago
Shanghai Police
Shanghai Street Scene No. 1
Shanghai Street Scene No. 2
Sikh Artillery, Hong Kong
Soldiers Washing Dishes
Street Scene in Hong Kong
Street Scene in Yokohama, No. 1
Street Scene in Yokohama, No. 2
Theatre Road, Yokohama
Tourists Starting for Canton
Trained Cavalry Horses
Transport Ships at Port Tampa
Troop Ships for the Philippines
Troops Embarking at San Francisco
Wagon Supply Train en Route
Wharf Scene, Honolulu

Jul [day undetermined]
The Burglar
The Telephone
Tub Race

Aug [day undetermined]
Cuban Ambush
Fake Beggar
Major General Shafter
Mules Swimming Ashore at Daiquiri, Cuba
Pack Mules with Ammunition on the Santiago Trail, Cuba
Packing Ammunition on Mules, Cuba
Shooting Captured Insurgents
U. S. Troops Landing at Daiquiri, Cuba
Victorious Squadron Firing Salute

Sep [day undetermined]
Admiral Sampson on Board the Flagship
Close View of the "Brooklyn," Naval Parade
Excursion Boats, Naval Parade
Farmer Kissing the Lean Girl
The Fleet Steaming Up North River
The "Glen Island," Accompanying Parade
The "Massachusetts," Naval Parade
Merry-Go-Round
Observation Train Following Parade
Police Boats Escorting Naval Parade
Reviewing the "Texas" at Grant's Tomb

Statue of Liberty
The "Texas," Naval Parade
Troops Making Military Road in Front of Santiago
U. S. Battleship "Oregon"
U. S. Cruiser "Brooklyn," Naval Parade
Oct [day undetermined]
Advance Guard, Return of N. J. Troops
Balloon Ascension, Marionettes
Dancing Chinaman, Marionettes
Ella Lola, a la Trilby [Dance]
Parade of Marines, U. S. Cruiser, "Brooklyn"
Return of 2nd Regiment of New Jersey
Return of Troop C, Brooklyn
Skeleton Dance, Marionettes
Turkish Dance, Ella Lola
Nov [day undetermined]
Elopement on Horseback
The Tramp in the Kitchen
Dec [day undetermined]
The Burglar in the Bed Chamber
The Burglar on the Roof
The Cavalier's Dream
The Cop and the Nurse Girl
S. S. "Coptic" Running Before a Gale
Sleighing Scene
Vanishing Lady
What Demoralized the Barber Shop

1899

Jan [day undetermined]
Astor Battery on Parade
Coaches Arriving at Mammoth Hot Springs
Coaches Going to Cinnabar from Yellowstone Park
General Lee's Procession, Havana
Lower Falls, Grand Canyon, Yellowstone Park
Spaniards Evacuating
Tourists Going Round Yellowstone Park
Troops at Evacuation of Havana
Feb [day undetermined]
Jones and His Pal in Trouble
Jones' Interrupted Sleighride
Jones' Return from the Club
Larks Behind the Scene
Panoramic View of Brooklyn Bridge
Poker at Dawson City
Rapids below Suspension Bridge
Willie's First Smoke
Feb 11 The Devil's Laboratory
The Infernal Palace
Mar [day undetermined]
Arabian Gun Twirler
Bicycle Trick Riding, No. 2
Jones Makes a Discovery
Raising Old Glory over Morro Castle
Three Acrobats
Apr [day undetermined]
Casey at the Bat
Morning Colors on U. S. Cruiser "Raleigh"
104th Street Curve, New York, Elevated Railway
Pilot Boats in New York Harbor
Tommy Atkins, Bobby and the Cook
U. S. Cruiser "Raleigh"
A Wringing Good Joke
Apr 10 A Trip to the Moon
May [day undetermined]
Cripple Creek Bar-Room Scene
Jun [day undetermined]
Advance of Kansas Volunteers at Caloocan
The Bibulous Clothier
Capture of Trenches at Candaba [Canda Bar]
A Fair Exchange Is No Robbery
Filipinos Retreat from Trenches
Mesmerist and Country Couple
New York Police Parade, June 1st, 1899
Panoramic View, Horseshoe Curve, From Penna. Ltd.
Rout of the Filipinos
Skirmish of Rough Riders
Strange Adventure of New York Drummer
U. S. Infantry Supported by Rough Riders at El Caney
U. S. Troops and Red Cross in the Trenches Before Caloocan [P. I.]
Jul [day undetermined]
Panoramic View, Horseshoe Curve, Penna. R. R., No. 2
A Ride Through Pack Saddle Mountains, Penna. R.R.
Running through Gallitzen Tunnel, Penna. R.R.
Aug [day undetermined]
The Prentis Trio
Sep [day undetermined]
Admiral Dewey Landing at Gibraltar
The Boston Horseless Fire Department
Colonel Funston Swimming the Baglag River
The Diving Horse
The Early Morning Attack
New Brooklyn to New York via Brooklyn Bridge, No. 1
New Brooklyn to New York via Brooklyn Bridge, No. 2
Shoot the Chutes Series
Oct [day undetermined]
Admiral Dewey and Mayor Van Wyck Going Down Riverside Drive
Admiral Dewey at State House, Boston
Admiral Dewey Leading Land Parade
Admiral Dewey Leading Land Parade, No. 2
Admiral Dewey Leading Land Parade, (Eighth Ave.)
Admiral Dewey Passing Catholic Club Stand
Admiral Dewey Receiving the Washington and New York Committees
Admiral Dewey Taking Leave of Washington Committee on the U. S. Cruiser 'Olympia'
Admiral Dewey's First Step on American Shore
After the Race—Yachts Returning to Anchorage
Battery K Siege Guns
"Columbia" Winning the Cup
Dewey Arch—Troops Passing Under Arch
Dewey Parade, 10th Pennsylvania Volunteers
Flagship Olympia and Cruiser New York in Naval Parade
Governor Roosevelt and Staff
Panorama at Grant's Tomb, Dewey Naval Procession
Panoramic View of Floral Float "Olympia"
Panoramic View of Olympia in New York Harbor
Police Boats and Pleasure Craft on Way to Olympia
Presentation of Loving Cup at City Hall, New York
Presentation of Nation's Sword to Admiral Dewey
Shamrock and Columbia Jockeying for a Start
"Shamrock" and "Columbia" Rounding the Outer Stake Boat
"Shamrock" and "Columbia" Rounding the Outer Stake Boat, No. 2
"Shamrock" and "Columbia" Yacht Race—First Race
"Shamrock" and "Erin" Sailing
West Point Cadets
Nov [day undetermined]
The Astor Tramp
Fun in Camp
Love and War
Pictures Incidental to Yacht Race
2nd Special Service Battalion, Canadian Infantry, Embarking for So. Africa
2nd Special Service Battalion, Canadian Infantry-Parade
"Shamrock" and "Columbia" Yacht Race—1st Race, No. 2
Tenderloin at Night
Trick Bears
U. S. Cruiser "Olympia" Leading Naval Parade
Dec 25 Cinderella

1900

Jan [day undetermined]
Why Jones Discharged His Clerks
Why Mrs. Jones Got a Divorce
Feb [day undetermined]
An Animated Luncheon
Automobile Parade
Ching Ling Foo Outdone
Dick Croker Leaving Tammany Hall
A Dull Razor
Faust and Marguerite
The Magician
Mar [day undetermined]
After the Storm
Annie Oakley
Answering the Alarm
An Artist's Dream
Barroom Scene
Betting Field
Boat Rescue
Bowling Green
British Infantry Marching to Battle
Broadway at Post Office
Carnival Dance
Cissy Fitzgerald
Dancing on the Bowery
A Darktown Dance
Drill of Naval Cadets at Newport
Family Troubles
Fatima's Coochee-Coochee Dance
Foot Ball Game
14th Street and Broadway
Garden Scene
The Girl from Paris
Great Foot Ball Game
Interrupted Lover
Irish Way of Discussing Politics
Jones Gives a Private Supper
Jones Interviews His Wife
Jones' Return from a Masquerade
The Kiss
Little Mischief
The Little Reb
Lucille Sturgis
Military Scenes at Newport, R. I.
Miss Lucy Murray
Mr. and Mrs. Califf at Dinner
Morning Fire Alarm
The Mystic Swing
Opera of Martha
Oriental Dance
Paddle Dance
Panoramic View of the Dewey Arch, New York City
Panoramic View of the Ghetto, New York City
Pat vs. Populist
Paterson Falls
Photographing the Ghost
Pickaninnies
Pluto and the Imp
A Quiet Little Smoke
Race Track Scene
Rosedale
Santa Claus' Visit
Scene on the Bois de Boulogne
Short-Stick Dance
Sidewalks of New York
Silver Dance
Telephone Appointment
The Tramp and the Crap Game
Trial Race Columbia and Defender
Trial Race Columbia and Defender No. 2
Trolley Car Accident
U. S. Marines in Dewey Land Parade
Umbrella Dance
Uncle Josh in a Spooky Hotel
Uncle Josh's Nightmare
Up-to-Date Cake-Walk
View from the Gorge Railroad
A Visit to the Spiritualist
Watermelon Contest
Apr [day undetermined]
Battle of Mafeking
Boer Commissary Train Treking
Boers Bringing in British Prisoners
British Highlanders Exercising
British Troops on Dress Parade
Capture of Boer Battery

The Reversing Sign Painter
A Rough Day on the Ocean
Royal Artillery and English Sailors Marching Through Hyde Park
Royal Exchange, London, England
Scene in Legation Street, Shanghai
Searching the Ruins of the Tarrant Fire
Shooting the Chutes at Providence, Rhode Island
Snowballing Scene in Halifax
Stage Coach Hold-Up in the Days of '49
The Statue of William Tell
Street Scene in Pekin
Such a Headache
Three of a Kind; or, The Pirate's Dream
The Tough Dance
Training a Horse to Jump Hurdles
The Tramp's Miraculous Escape
Two Old Cronies
A Wagon Load of Babies
Washing Down Decks
Why Bridget Stopped Drinking
Wild Bear in Yellowstone Park

Aug [day undetermined]
The "Abbot" and "Cresceus" Race
Aunt Sallie's Wonderful Bustle
The Bad Boy's Joke on the Nurse
Bathing at Atlantic City
Bicycle Paced Race
Canoeing Scene
Circular Panorama of Electric Tower
Circular Panorama of Suspension Bridge and American Falls
Circular Panoramic View of Whirlpool Rapids
Esquimaux Game of Snap-the-Whip
Esquimaux Leap-Frog
The Farmer and the Bad Boys
Panoramic View of Electric Tower from a Balloon
Panoramic View of the Gorge Railroad
Photographing a Country Couple
Professional Handicap Bicycle Race
The Reversible Divers
Sampson-Schley Controversy
Soubrette's Troubles on a Fifth Avenue Stage Coach
Swimming Pool at Coney Island
Tally-Ho Departing for the Races
The Tramp and the Nursing Bottle
"Weary Willie" and the Gardener
What Happened on Twenty-Third Street, New York City

Sep [day undetermined]
Arrival of Funeral Cortege at the City Hall, Buffalo, N. Y.
Complete Funeral Cortege at Canton, Ohio
Faust Family of Acrobats
Life Rescue at Long Branch
Lukens, Novel Gymnast
The Multitude Passing into the City Hall
The Musical Ride
Panoramic View of the Crowd Rushing for the City Hall, Buffalo, to View the Body of President McKinley
Rubes in the Theatre
Sampson and Schley Controversy—Tea Party
Street's Zouaves and Wall Scaling
The Trick Cyclist
What Demoralized the Barber Shop

Sep 21 The Mob Outside the Temple of Music at the Pan-American Exposition [Buffalo]
President McKinley Reviewing the Troops at the Pan-American Exposition
President McKinley's Speech at the Pan-American Exposition

Oct [day undetermined]
Captain Nissen Going Through Whirlpool Rapids, Niagara Falls
Duke and Duchess of Cornwall and York Landing at Queenstown, Ontario
The Duke and Duchess of York Arriving at Quebec
Duke and Duchess of York Leaving the Railroad Station at Montreal, Canada
Duke and Duchess of York Marching Through the Streets of Montreal
The Duke and Duchess of York Presenting Medals to Boer War Veterans at the Unveiling of the Queen's Statue
Duke of York at Montreal and Quebec
Garden Party in Honor of the Duke and Duchess of York
Horse Parade at the Pan-American Exposition
The Lovers, Coal Box, and Fireplace
Panorama, Great Gorge Route over Lewiston Bridge
Spanish Dancers at the Pan-American Exposition
Working the Breeches Buoy

Oct 5 Arrival of McKinley's Funeral Train at Canton, Ohio
Funeral Leaving the President's House and Church at Canton, Ohio
McKinley's Funeral Entering Westlawn Cemetery, Canton [Ohio]
Panoramic View of the President's House at Canton, Ohio
President McKinley's Funeral Cortege at Buffalo, N.Y.
President McKinley's Funeral Cortege at Washington, D. C.
President Roosevelt at the Canton Station
Taking President McKinley's Body from Train at Canton, Ohio

Oct 19 "Columbia" and "Shamrock II": Finishing Second Race
"Columbia" and "Shamrock II": Jockeying and Starting
"Columbia" and "Shamrock II": Start of Second Race
"Columbia" and "Shamrock II": Starting in the Third Race
"Columbia" and "Shamrock II": Turning the Outer Stake Boat
"Columbia" Winning the Cup
The Martyred Presidents
Pan-American Exposition by Night
Panoramic View of the Fleet After Yacht Race
The Yacht Race Fleet Following the Committee Boat "Navigator" Oct. 4th

Oct 26 Little Red Riding Hood

Nov [day undetermined]
Automobile Parade on the Coney Island Boulevard
Catching an Early Train
Panorama of Esplanade by Night
A Phenomenal Contortionist
Royal Train with Duke and Duchess of York, Climbing Mt. Hector
Sham Battle at the Pan-American Exposition
Trapeze Disrobing Act

Nov 16 Execution of Czolgosz, with Panorama of Auburn Prison

Nov 23 A Christmas Dream

Dec [day undetermined]
The Artist's Dilemma
Ascending Mt. Low, California
Building a Harbor at San Pedro
California Oil Wells in Operation
Carrying Out the Snakes
Children Bathing
The Fat and the Lean Wrestling Match
Harry Thompson's Imitations of Sousa
Jeffries Exercising in His Gymnasium
Jeffries Side Stepping and Wrestling
Jeffries Skipping the Rope
Jeffries Sparring with His Brother
Jeffries Throwing the Medicine Ball
Leaping Dogs at Gentry's Circus
Line-Up and Teasing the Snakes
The March of Prayer and Entrance of the Dancers
Moki Snake Dance by Walpapi Indians
The Mysterious Cafe
Ostrich Farms at Pasadena
Panoramic View, Albert Canyon
Panoramic View, Kicking Horse Canyon
Panoramic View, Lower Kicking Horse Canyon
Panoramic View, Lower Kicking Horse Valley
Panoramic View of Boston Subway from an Electric Car
Panoramic View of Moki-Land
Panoramic View of Rubio Canyon, Mt. Low R.R.
Panoramic View, Upper Kicking Horse Canyon
Parade of Snake Dancers before the Dance
Pigeon Farm at Los Angeles, Cal
Prize Winners at the Country Fair
Roeber Wrestling Match
Ruhlin at His Training Quarters
Ruhlin Boxing with "Denver" Ed. Martin
Ruhlin Sparring in His Training Quarters

Dec 14 Jeffries in His Training Quarters
Ruhlin in His Training Quarters

Dec 21 Jeffries and Ruhlin Sparring Contest at San Francisco, Cal., Nov. 15, 1901—Five Rounds

1902 [month undetermined]
Bathing Made Easy
Happy Hooligan Turns Burglar

Jan [day undetermined]
Bird's Eye View of San Francisco, Cal., from a Balloon
A Cable Road in San Francisco, Cal.
Chinese Shaving Scene
Facial Expression
Feeding Geese at Newman's Poultry Farm
Fishing at Faralone Island
New Year's Mummers Parade
Panoramic View Between Palliser and Field, B. C.
Panoramic View near Mt. Golden on the Canadian Pacific R. R.
Panoramic View of Mt. Tamalpais
Panoramic View of Mt. Tamalpais Between Bow Knot and McKinley Cut
Panoramic View of the Canadian Pacific R. R. near Leauchoil, B. C.
Panoramic View of the Golden Gate
Sea Gulls Following Fishing Boats
The Twentieth Century Tramp; or, Happy Hooligan and His Airship
Uncle Josh at the Moving Picture Show
The Weary Hunters and the Magician

Feb [day undetermined]
Arrival of the Governor General, Lord Minto, at Quebec
The Burning of Durland's Riding Academy
Capture of the Biddle Brothers
Christening and Launching Kaiser Wilhelm's Yacht "Meteor"
Circular Panorama of Housing the Ice
Coasting Scene at Montmorency Falls, Canada
Cross-Country Running on Snow Shoes
Cutting and Canaling Ice
The Hindoo Fakir
"Kronprinz Wilhelm" with Prince Henry [of Prussia] on Board Arriving in New York
Loading the Ice on Cars, Conveying It across the Mountains and Loading It into Boats
New York City in a Blizzard
Panorama of the Paterson [N.J.] Fire
Panoramic View of the Hohenzollern
Paterson [N. J.] Fire, Showing the Y. M. C. A. and Library
Prince Henry [of Prussia] Arriving in Washington and Visiting the German Embassy
Ruins of City Hall, Paterson [N. J.]
Skiing in Montreal
Skiing Scene in Quebec
Tobogganing in Canada
Working Rotary Snow Ploughs on Lehigh Valley Railroad

Mar [day undetermined]
"Deutschland" Leaving New York at Full Speed [with Prince Henry of Prussia]
German and American Tableau
Kaiser Wilhelm's Yacht, "Meteor," Entering the Water
Prince Henry [of Prussia] Arriving at West Point
Prince Henry [of Prussia] at Lincoln's Monument, Chicago, Ill.
Prince Henry [of Prussia] at Niagara Falls
Prince Henry [of Prussia] Reviewing the Cadets at West Point
Prince Henry [of Prussia] Visiting Cambridge, Mass. and Harvard University
Sailing of the "Deutschland" with Prince Henry [of Prussia] on Board
Mar 15 Arrival of Prince Henry [of Prussia] and President Roosevelt at Shooter's Island
Apr [day undetermined]
Babies Rolling Eggs
The Bessemer Steel Converter in Operation
The Burlesque Suicide
The Burlesque Suicide, No. 2
Charleston Chain Gang
Circular Panoramic View of Jones and Laughlin's Steel Yard
Egg Rolling at the White House
Feeding the Bear at the Menagerie
Fun in a Bakery Shop
The Golden Chariots
Great Bull Fight
Las Viga Canal, Mexico
Loading a Vessel at Charleston, S. C.
Midway of Charleston Exposition [South Carolina]
Miniature Railway
Moonlight on Lake Maggiore, Italy
New Sunset Limited
Panoramic View from Pittsburgh to Allegheny
Panoramic View of Charleston Exposition [South Carolina]
President Roosevelt Reviewing the Troops at Charleston Exposition [South Carolina]
St. Patrick's Cathedral and Fifth Avenue on Easter Sunday Morning [New York City]
Scrambling for Eggs
The Swimming Ducks at Allentown [Pa.] Duck Farm
Tossing Eggs
May [day undetermined]
The Absent Minded Clerk, Fly Paper and Silk Hat
The Aerial Railway at the Crystal Palace, London, England
Appointment by Telephone
The Baby and the Pet Bird
The Bibulous Wire Walker
A Bowery Five Cent Shave
Building Made Easy; or, How Mechanics Work in the Twentieth Century
The Bull and Bear
The Burglars in the Wine Cellar
Burlesque on Romeo and Juliet
The Burlesque Thieves
Burning of St. Pierre [Martinique]
Carlysle D. Graham Swimming the Whirlpool Rapids
Characteristic Imitations
The Cheese Mites; or, The Lilliputians in a London Restaurant
The Children's Tea Party
The Children's Toys That Came to Life
The Chinese Conjurer and the Devil's Head
A Chinese Mystery
The Clown and His Burlesque Horse
The Clown and His Mysterious Pictures
The Clown and the Automobile
The Clown with the Portable Body
A Country Groceryman's Revenge
The Darktown Comedians Trip to Paris
Deep Water Diving Illustrated
The Devil in the Schoolhouse
The Devil's Kitchen
Devil's Prison
The Devil's Theatre
Dr. Lehwis Automobile Leaving London for a Trip Around the World
The Double Magician and the Magical Head
English Army in the Battlefield
English Cavalry on the Battlefield
English Soldiers Exercising
Entire Series of Yacht Race Pictures with Dissolving Effects
Exploding a Land Mine
Exploding a Submarine Mine
Extraordinary Chinese Magic
The Fat and Lean Comedians
Fire Department of Glasgow, Scotland
The Fisherman's Wonderful Catch
A Gay Old Boy
The Giant and Pygmy
Gibson, the Eccentric American Actor
Going to Bed Under Difficulties
The Great Stag Hunt
The Hair in the Soup
The Haunted Pawnshop
Herrmann, the Great Conjuror
The History of a Crime
The Horrible Nightmare
How the Lover Squared Himself with Papa
How Uncle Josh Defeated the Badgers
The Inexhaustible Wardrobe
Japanese Girl Smoking Cigarettes
Life Rescue Scene at Atlantic City, N. J.
Little Willie's Last Celebration
Magical Changes
The Magical Hen
Magical Sword
The Magician and the Human Pump
The Magician and the Seven Hats
The Mermaid's Ballet
The Mischievous Boys and the Washerwoman
Mt. Pelee in Eruption and Destruction of St. Pierre [Martinique]
Mt. Pelee Smoking Before Eruption [St. Pierre, Martinique]
The Mysterious Doctor
The Mysterious Urn
The Mystic Wreath
The Mystical Burglars
The National Geisha Dance of Japan
Naughty Grandpa and the Field Glass
New Pie Eating Contest
Newsboys and Hokey Pokey Man
The Nurse Maid in the Tunnel
Old Maid Retiring
Ora Pro Nobis Illustrated
The Other Fellow's Laundry
The Pals and the Clothier's Dummy
Panoramic View of New Haven, Conn.
Panoramic View of Switchback, Mauch Chunk
Peasant Children and Their Rocking Horse
The Pioneer Limited
The Puppies and Their Mother
A Railroad Wreck (Imitation)
Rube and the Weighing Machine
Rube's Visit to the Studio
The S. S. "Deutschland" in a Storm
The S. S. "Deutschland" in a Storm, No. 2
The S. S. "Deutschland" in Heavy Sea
The S. S. "Deutschland" Leaving Her Dock in Hoboken
A Schoolroom in the Soudan
Shuffleboard on S. S. "Deutschland"
Sir Thomas Lipton on Board the Erin
The Tight Collar
Tommy Atkins Bathing
Transporting a War Balloon
Trouble in a Barnyard
Troubled Dream
Troubles in a Tenement House
Undressing Under Difficulties
Waves at Dover, England
The Weary Traveller and His Wonderful Dream
What Happened to the Inquisitive Janitor
The Wonderful Baby Incubator
Wonderful Feats of Vivisection
The Wonderful Hair Restorer
Worcester High School Eight-Oared Boat Crews in Action
Jul 15 Jack and the Beanstalk
Aug 30 Crowning of King Edward and Queen Alexandra
The King and Queen Arriving at Westminster Abbey
The King and Queen Leaving Westminster Abbey After the Crowning
King Edward Reviewing Coronation Naval Force at Spithead August 16, 1902
The King's Procession
The New Crowned King and Queen Passing Through Wellington Arch and Down Constitution Hill
Panoramic View of Westminster Abbey and Surroundings
Sep [day undetermined]
Amputating a Leg
Bathing at Kiel, Germany
Bologna Eating Contest
Bowling Alley at a German Picnic
California Naval Reserves
California Naval Reserves Drilling on Board Ship
Ching Ling Foo's Greatest Feats
Circular Panoramic View of St. Pierre from the Lighthouse, Showing Mt. Pelee Smoking in the Distance
Circular Panoramic View of St. Pierre, Showing the Ruins of the Catholic Cathedral and Mt. Pelee Smoking in the Background
Circular Panoramic View of the Market Place at Fort de France, Showing S. S. Korona in the Background
Clearing the Course for the Henley Boat Races, July 10th, 1902
The Columbia-Cornell-Pennsylvania Boat Race at Poughkeepsie
The Cook, Her Lover and the Lady of the House
The Crazy Artist and the Pictures That Came to Life
Crying for His Bottle
The Deonzo Brothers in Their Wonderful Barrel Jumping Act
Departure of the Bride and Groom
A Dutch Soldier's Christmas Box
A Dutchman Shaving
The Dutchman's Interrupted Dinner
German Soldiers Starting for War
The Golf Girls and the Tramp
Graduating Day at West Point Military Academy
Grandma Threading Her Needle
The Haunted Dining Room
His First Dose of Medicine
The Hodcarriers' Ping Pong
Horse Racing in Germany
Ice Racing in Stockholm
Kaiser Wilhelm and Emperor Franz Josef, and Prince Henry Riding Horseback
Kaiser Wilhelm and the Empress of Germany Reviewing Their Troops
Kaiser Wilhelm and the German Cuirrassiers Galloping
Kaiser Wilhelm at Stettin
Kaiser Wilhelm at the Launching of a German Battleship
Kaiser Wilhelm in the Tier Garten, Berlin, Germany
Kaiser Wilhelm Inspecting His Soldiers
Kaiser Wilhelm, of Germany, and Emperor Franz Josef, of Austria
Kaiser Wilhelm's Yacht "Meteor" Under Sail
King Edward VII and Queen Alexandra, of Great Britain

Lightning Facial Changes
Loading Cattle in India
The Lovers and the Donkey
The Lovers and the Egg Merchant
The Magical Dish Mender
Michael Casey and the Steam Roller
Mounted Soldiers Fording a River
Moving Picture Operator on a Drunk
Native Bull Cart at Morne Rouge (A Suburb of St. Pierre)
Native Women of Fort de France at Work
Native Women Washing Clothes at Fort de France
Native Women Washing Clothes at the Gueydon Fountain, Fort de France, Martinique
Natives Unloading a Boat of Fire-Wood at Carbet (A Suburb of St. Pierre)
Natives Unloading a Coaling Vessel at Fort de France, Martinique
An Old Fashioned Way of Pulling a Tooth
The Old Maid's Tea Party
Papa Keeps the Telephone Appointment
A Photographic Contortion
Queen Wilhelmina and Kaiser Wilhelm Riding in the Tier Garten
Queen Wilhelmina Arriving at the Kaiser's Palace
Queen Wilhelmina, of Holland, in Berlin
Sea Sick Excursionists
Selling a Pet Dog
Skate Sailing in Sweden
Skating in Stockholm
Skiing in Stockholm, Sweden
Steeplechasing at the Brooklyn Handicap
Storm at Sea near St. Pierre, Martinique
Street Scene in Cairo
Street Scene in Fort de France, Martinique
Third Trinity, Cambridge, Winning the Race for the Grand Challenge Cup. Taken at Henley on July 10th, 1902
Torpedo Boats Racing off Newport
Tourists Climbing the Alps
Two Germans in a Theatre
The University College of Oxford Winning the Ladies' Challenge Plate
Unveiling the Rochambeau Statue in Washington, D. C.
Unveiling the Rochambeau Statue, Washington, D. C.
Why Papa Reformed, or Setting Back the Clock

Oct [day undetermined]
The Bull and the Picnickers
How They Do Things on the Bowery
The Interrupted Bathers
The Interrupted Picnic
Rock of Ages

Oct 4 A Trip to the Moon

Nov [day undetermined]
Broncho Busting Scene, Championship of the World

Nov 1 Ali Baba and the Forty Thieves

1903

Jan [day undetermined]
Electrocution of an Elephant
Goo Goo Eyes
Life of an American Fireman
The Miller and Chimney Sweep
The Soldier's Return
West Indian Boys Diving for Money

Jan 17 The Ascent of Mount Blanc
Picture Hanging Extraordinary

Jan 31 The Magical Egg
Wonderful Suspension and Evolution

Feb [day undetermined]
Allentown Duck Farm
Annual Circus Parade
Arrival and Departure of President Loubet
Arrival of H.I.M. The German Emperor, at Port Victoria
Arrival of Kaiser Wilhelm in England
Arrival of Lord and Lady Minto at the Barracks, Dawson
Battle Royal
Beauty Show
Before and After
Bootblack and Crossing Sweeper
Broken Trace
Broncho Busting Along the Lines of the Denver & Rio Grande Railway
C. D. Graham Swimming the Lower Rapids
Cadet's First Smoke
Camel Race on the Desert
Canoe Fight
The Canyon of the Grand
Carrying the Crown into Westminster Abbey
Casey's Twins
Cattle Bathing
Chautauqua Aquatic Day. No. 9
Chautauqua Boys' Club. No. 1
Chautauqua Boys' Club. No. 2
Chautauqua Girls' Club. No. 6
Dawson City Fire Department Going to a Fire
Dog Teams Hauling Wood to Dawson City, Up the Yukon
The Dude and the Bootblacks
Extraordinary Black Art
Fat Man's Race
Feeding Brook Trout at the Pennsylvania State Fishery
Feeding the Pigs
Firing the Royal Salute at Dawson City by the Northwest Mounted Police
French Cavalry Evolutions
General Alarm
Gravity Fountain
Great French Cavalry Charge
Great German Cavalry Charge
Harvesting Scene
Herring Fishing in the North Sea
Hooligan's Fourth of July
The Human Fly
The Impossible Feat of Balancing
Jim Post, the Great Facial Comedian, and His Troubles
Juvenile Fire Department
King Edward and Queen Alexandra Passing Through London, England
Life Rescue at Atlantic City
Log-Rolling Contest
Looping the Loop at Coney Island
Lord and Lady Minto with Party, Fording the Rushing Waters of the Klondike on Horseback
The Magic Table
The Magician and the Imp
Market Scene in Cairo, Egypt
Mephistopheles' School of Magic
The Minuet. No. 3
Mrs. Taylor Going over Horseshoe Falls in a Barrel
Mother Goose Nursery Rhymes
Mule Pack Train Taking Gold Dust to Dawson City
North Atlantic Fleet Bombarding Fisher's Island
North Atlantic Fleet Bombarding Fort Adams, Newport Harbor
Oh! Shut Up
An Old Squaw on the Trail
1,000 Mile Ride over the Ice on a Bicycle
Panorama and Bathing Scene of Ostend, Belgium
Panoramic View of the Rocky Mountain on the Rock Island System
Panoramic View of the Streets of Paris, France
Panoramic Views and Scenes at the Garden of the Gods
Paternal Affection
The Peel River Indians with Their Dog Teams and Toboggan Sleighs on the Trail
La Petite Alma, Baby Acrobat
Pike's Peak Cog Wheel Route from Manitou
Policeman and Automobile
Professor Batty's Trained Bears
Race Between Dog Team, Bicycle and Cutter
Reversible Donkey Cart
Sack Race
Santos Dumont's Airship
Scenes on the Short Line
Seattle Fire Department in Action
A Sleigh Load of Squaws
Sluice Mining on Gold Hill in the Klondike, Hutchinson and Johnstone's Claim of No. 6, Eldorado
Smashing a Jersey Mosquito
Smith's Wife Inspects the New Typewriter
Snoqualmie Falls
Sparring Exhibition on Board the U.S.S. "Alabama"
Start of Endurance Run of the Automobile Club of America
Swedish Gymnastics at Chautauqua. No. 8
Team of Horses Hauling Wood to Dawson, Up the Yukon
Trial Run of the Fastest Boat in the World, "The Arrow"
Twentieth Century Conjuring
$25,000 Clean Up on No. 16, Eldorado
United States Mail Leaving Dawson City for White Horse
Up-to-Date Surgery
What Casey Won at the Raffle
Working a Long Tom Rocker on Bonanza Creek
Working the Rocker, Called a Jigger, on Poverty Bar, Fourteen Below Discovery Bonanza Creek

Feb 14 Disagreeable Railroad Passengers
English Barnyard Scene

Mar 7 Robinson Crusoe

Mar 14 Buying a Baby
The Delhi Camp Railway
Logging in Canada
On the Bow River Horse Ranch at Cochrane, North West Territory
Spearing Salmon in the Rivers of the North West Territory

Mar 21 The Little Match Seller
The Workman's Paradise

Apr [day undetermined]
Battle of Confetti at the Nice Carnival
Battle of Flowers at the Nice Carnival
A Japanese Wrestling Match
Launch of Shamrock III
Mary Jane's Mishap; or, Don't Fool with the Parafin
Native Woman Washing a Negro Baby in Nassau, B. I.
Native Women Coaling a Ship and Scrambling for Money [West Indies]
Native Women Coaling a Ship at St. Thomas, D. W. I.
Native Women Washing Clothes at St. Vincent, B. W. I.
Panorama of Morro Castle, Havana, Cuba
Panorama of Willemstadt, Curacao, Taken from the River
Panoramic View of Monte Carlo
Panoramic View of St. Pierre, Martinique
Pilot Leaving "Prinzessen Victoria Luise" at Sandy Hook
Procession of Floats and Masqueraders at Nice Carnival
Railroad Panorama near Spanishtown, Jamaica
Through the Telescope
Tourists Playing Shuffleboard on "Prinzessen Victoria Luise"
West Indian Girls in Native Dance
Wharf Scene and Natives Swimming at St. Thomas, D. W. I.

Apr 11 Acrobatic Sisters Daines

Apr 13 Gulliver's Travels

May [day undetermined]
The Angler
Animated Dolls
Artillery Exercises
Berlin Fire Department at Drill
Chinese National Dance
Coronation Procession Passing Under the Canadian Arch

English and French Boxers
English Soldiers at Gun Drill
Female Contortionist and Acrobatic Dog
Fighting Rams
Fireboat "New Yorker" Answering an Alarm
Fireboat "New Yorker" in Action
Game of Push Ball
Hindoo Street Scene
How the Valet Got into Hot Water
Landing, Sorting and Gutting Fish
Launching Cup Defender "Reliance"
Lehigh Valley Black Diamond Express
London Fire Scene
Market Scene in Hanoi, China
Miniature Prize Fighters
Modern House Furnishing Methods
New Bull Fight
New York City Dumping Wharf
New York City "Ghetto" Fish Market
New York City Police Parade
New York Harbor Police Boat Patrol Capturing Pirates
Oriental Dancers
Pageant of East Indian Princes
Panorama of Blackwell's Island
Panorama of Riker's Island
Panorama Water Front and Brooklyn Bridge from East River
Panoramic View of Geneva, Switzerland
Panoramic View of Herreshoff Works from Bristol Harbor
Panoramic View of the Alps from an Electric Car
Panoramic View of Torpedo Boat "Winslow" and Yacht "Constitution"
Phantom Ride on the Canadian Pacific
Prize Winners at the Dog Show
Procession of Chinamen in Pekin
Procession of Giant Elephants in India
Resourceful Waiter
A Scarecrow Tramp
Skyscrapers of New York City, from the North River
Sorting Refuse at Incinerating Plant, New York City
Spilled Milk
Steamscow "Cinderella" and Ferryboat "Cincinnati"
The Still Alarm
Threshing Outfit at Work
Traders of the East Indian Empire
Training the Hounds
Viceroy of India's Royal Levee
Wheat Harvesting Machines in Operation
White Wings on Review
Window Cleaner's Mishap

May 16 The Gambler's Crime
Smiles and Tears
Spring Cleaning

Jun [day undetermined]
"Africander" Winning the Suburban Handicap, 1903
Arabian Jewish Dance
Crossing the Atlantic
Eating Macaroni in the Streets of Naples
Egyptian Boys in Swimming Race
Egyptian Fakir with Dancing Monkey
Egyptian Market Scene
Excavating Scene at the Pyramids of Sakkarah
Feeding Pigeons in Front of St. Mark's Cathedral, Venice, Italy
Fording the River Nile on Donkeys
Going to Market, Luxor Egypt
Herd of Sheep on the Road to Jerusalem
Jerusalem's Busiest Street, Showing Mt. Zion
A Jewish Dance at Jerusalem
King Edward and President Loubet Reviewing French Troops
King Edward's Visit to Paris
Lake Lucerne, Switzerland
Panorama of Tivoli, Italy, Showing Seven Falls
Panoramic View of an Egyptian Cattle Market
Panoramic View of Beyrouth, Syria, Showing Holiday Festivities
Passengers Embarking from S. S. "Augusta Victoria" at Beyrouth
Primitive Irrigation in Egypt
Shearing a Donkey in Egypt
69th Regiment, N. G. N. Y.
Street Scene at Jaffa
Tourists Embarking at Jaffa
Tourists Landing at Island of Capri, Italy
Tourists Returning on Donkeys from Mizpah
Tourists Starting on Donkeys for the Pyramids of Sakkarah
Tourists Taking Water from the River Jordan
Washing Clothes at Sicily

Jul [day undetermined]
Laplanders at Home
Miniature Railway at Wilmington Springs, Delaware
Policemen's Prank on Their Comrade
Razzle Dazzle
A Scrap in Black and White

Jul 11 Sleeping Beauty

Aug [day undetermined]
Down Where the Wurzburger Flows
The Gay Shoe Clerk
Immigrants Landing at Ellis Island
Little Lillian, Toe Danseuse
Rube and Mandy at Coney Island
Seashore Frolics
Street Car Chivalry
Subub Surprises the Burglar
The Unappreciated Joke

Sep [day undetermined]
Baby Class at Lunch
The Baby Review
The Busy Bee
A Daring Daylight Burglary
Maypole Dance
Miss Jessie Cameron, Champion Child Sword Dancer
Miss Jessie Dogherty, Champion Female Highland Fling Dancer
New York Caledonian Club's Parade
A Norwegian Waterfall
Old Fashioned Scottish Reel
Orphans in the Surf
Reliance and Shamrock III Turning Outer Stake in Second Race
"Reliance" and "Shamrock" III Jockeying and Starting in First Race
"Reliance" Crossing the Line and Winning First Race
Rising Panorama of a Norwegian Waterfall
Rube and the Fender
Sir Thomas Lipton's Yacht Fleet Leaving England
Throwing the Sixteen Pound Hammer
Tub Race
Turning the Tables
Uncle Tom's Cabin

Oct [day undetermined]
Aerial Posing
Ancient and Honourable Artillery of London on Parade
The Ancient and Honourables Homeward Bound
The Animated Poster
Ballet of the Nations
Burglar's Escape
Casey and His Neighbor's Goat
Casey's Nightmare
Chinaman's Acrobatic Guests
Coal Mine
County Fair
Dextrous Hand
A Dope in Difficulties
An East River Novelty
East Side Urchins Bathing in a Fountain
The Enchanted Cup
The Extra Turn
Feeding the Sparrows
Flood Scene in Paterson, N. J.
Following the Hounds
Glimpses of Venice
The Heavenly Twins at Lunch
The Heavenly Twins at Odds
The Impatient Guest
The Irrepressible Burglars
The Julians, Acrobats
King Edward's Visit to Ireland
Leaping Trout
London Zoo
Lovers and the Imp
The Messenger Boy's Mistake
Move On
Neptune's Wife
New York City Public Bath
Performing Dogs
Photographer's Victim
The Physical Culture Girl
Policeman's Interrupted Vision
Pulling Against the Stream
Rattan Slide and General View of Luna Park
The Raw Recruit
Rent Collector
A Romance of the Rail
Rome and the Vatican
Scenes at the Zoo
Serenader's Difficulties
Shooting the Rapids at Luna Park
Soap vs. Blacking
Springfield Fire Department
Street Scene in Hyderabad
Two Chappies in a Box
Washerwomen and Chimney-Sweep

Oct 17 Alice in Wonderland
Oct 31 The Poachers

Nov [day undetermined]
Buster's Joke on Papa
The Great Fire Ruins, Coney Island
Princeton and Yale Football Game
What Happened in the Tunnel

Nov 7 Life of Napoleon
Nov 21 Cruelty on the High Seas
The Deserter
The Ghost in the Graveyard
Letter Came Too Late
Murphy's Wake
The New Cook
A Pugilistic Parson
Quarrelsome Neighbors

Dec [day undetermined]
Buster's Joke on Papa
The Great Train Robbery
How Old Is Ann?
The Office Boy's Revenge
Opening of New East River Bridge, New York
Under the Mistletoe

Dec 12 A Trip to the Giant's Causeway

1904 [month undetermined]
Bull Fight with Matadors Senor Don Luis Mazzantini and Bombita

Jan [day undetermined]
Chameleon Climbing
Chameleons Feeding
The Cheese Mites
Circular Panorama of the Horse Shoe Falls in Winter
Crossing Ice Bridge at Niagara Falls
The Deserter
Elephants at Work
Falling Chimney
Ice Skating in Central Park, N. Y.
Lerfoss Waterfall
Nautical Tournament
Pugilistic Toads
San Francisco Chinese Funeral
Sliding Down Ice Mound at Niagara Falls
The Toad's Luncheon
Treloar and Miss Marshall, Prize Winners at the Physical Culture Show in Madison Square Garden
Trick Bicycle Riding

Jan 2 William Tell
Jan 16 Puss in Boots
Jan 23 Amusing Changes
Charming Enchantment
The Kiddies and the Poultry

Jan 30 Dogs and Rats

Feb [day undetermined]
Animated Painting

Casey's Frightful Dream
Cohen's Advertising Scheme
Halloween Night at the Seminary
Ice Boating on the North Shrewsbury, Red Bank, N. J.
Little German Band
Midnight Intruder
Old Maid and Fortune Teller
Panorama of Ruins from Baltimore and Charles Street
Panorama of Ruins from Lombard and Charles Street
Panorama of Ruins from Water Front
Wifey's Mistake
Feb 6 Devil's Pot
Marie Antoinette
Metamorphosis of the King of Spades
Feb 23 Diving Lucy
Mar [day undetermined]
Buster and Tige Put a Balloon Vendor Out of Business
Buster Brown and the Dude
Buster Makes Room for His Mama at the Bargain Counter
Buster's Dog to the Rescue
Panorama of Ruins from Lombard and Hanover Streets, Baltimore, Md.
Pranks of Buster Brown and His Dog Tige
Section of Buster Brown Series, Showing a Sketch of Buster by Outcault
Sleighing in Central Park, New York
Mar 12 Babe and Dog
Scenes on Every Floor
Apr [day undetermined]
Babe and Puppies
Japanese Acrobats
Apr 9 Living Dummy
Apr 20 After the Siege Tien-Tsin, Native City, China
Battle of Chemulpo Bay
Coal Carriers Chefoo, China
Fashionable Driving on Palace Quay, St. Petersburg
Flower Parade Race Course, Moscow
Japanese Railroad Scene, Kanagarva, Japan
Japanese Sailors Fencing with Capstan Bars
Japs Loading and Firing a Gun on Battleship "Asama"
Japs Loading and Firing a Six Pounder
A Muddy Street, Tien-Tsin, China
Panorama of Railroad Station at Seoul, Korea, from Departing Train
Panorama Russian Battleship "Gronobia"
Polish Fire Brigade Answering an Alarm, Warsaw
Religious Procession, Moscow
Russian Battleship Repulsing Torpedo Attack
Russian Infantry, Warsaw
Russian Outposts Attacked by Japanese
Skirmish Between Russian and Japanese Advance Guards
Warship in Nagasaki Harbor, Japan
Apr 25 At Sea in a Storm
Automobile Ascending Mt. Snowdon
Belated Husband
Building a Lighthouse
Chambermaid's Revenge
The Dear Boys Home for the Holidays
English Lancers at Drill
An Evil Doer's Sad End
Experienced Waiter
Falls of the Clyde
Fantastic Cake Walk
Herding Polo Ponies and Polo Game
Holbein Swimming the English Channel
Homing Pigeons
Inspector's Birthday
A Juggling Contest
The Lady Juggler
Launching the Steamship "Celtic"
Life Guards Responding to Distress Signals
The Living Picture
Moving Pictures While You Wait
Mysterious Performances
No Bathing Allowed
No Room for Dad
Pleasant Breakfast
The Prodigal Son
Robber of the Dead
The Sailor's Rival
Samson and Delilah
The Smugglers
Surf Scene
That Busy Bee
Washerwoman and Buss
What the Window Cleaner Saw
The Wrong Poison
May [day undetermined]
Annual Parade, New York Fire Department
Brush Between Cowboys and Indians
Bucking Broncos
Capsized Boat
The Cop Fools the Sergeant
Cowboys and Indians Fording River in a Wagon
Dog Factory
Driving Cattle to Pasture
Herding Horses across a River
Hold Up in a Country Grocery Store
Rounding Up and Branding Cattle
War Canoe Race
Western Stage Coach Hold Up
May 21 Barnum's Trunk
Jun [day undetermined]
Elephants Shooting the Chutes at Luna Park [Coney Island]
Inter-Collegiate Athletic Association Championships, 1904
Pierrot's Mystification
"Weary Willie" Kidnaps a Child
Jun 4 The Apple Woman
The Cook's Lovers
Jun 18 A Disagreeable Remedy
European Idea of Christopher Columbus Discovering America
Metamorphosis of a Butterfly
A Scandal on the Staircase
Jun 25 Chased by a Dog
Jul [day undetermined]
Acrobat and Pony
All for the Love of a Geisha
Automobile Race at Ballyshannon, Ireland
Barber's Revenge
Bobby and the Automobile
Boxing Horses, Luna Park, Coney Island
Boys Will Be Boys
Bumping Races
Canoeing on the Charles River, Boston, Mass.
Capture and Execution of Spies by Russians
The Chappie at the Well
Children and White Rats
Chutes of Imaha, Finland
A Circus Romance
Cleaning a Stove Pipe
Clown, Tramp and Cop
Coasting Scene in the Alps
College Sports in England
The Coster's Wedding
Courting and Caught
Curate's Love
Dogs Playing Bush Ball
Dorothy's Dream
Driven from Home
Duck Hunt
Dude in an English Railway Coach
Easter Flower Parade in Bois de Boulogne, Paris
Elephants Shooting the Chutes, Luna Park, Coney Island, No. 2
English Locomotive in Shop and on Rail
English Submarine Boat Disaster
Equestrian Bear
Facial Contortions
Foster Parents
Funny Faces
Game of Old Maid
Giovanni and His Trained Parrots
The Gordon Bennett Automobile Trials, Isle of Man
Hauling in the Fish
Haunted Scene Painter
Housemaid's Lovers
Ice Cream Eating Contest Blindfolded
Inter-Collegiate Regatta, Poughkeepsie, N. Y., 1904
Japanese School Children
Japanese State Procession
Japanese Varieties
Kidnapped Child
Landing a "Long Tom" Gun
Launching the Lifeboat
Lion Tamer
London Street Fakirs
Lotto, the Trick Bicyclist
Massachusetts Naval Reserves Leaving the U. S. S. "Alabama"
The Music Hall Manager's Dilemma
Nervous Man Retiring
Night Owl's Return
Obstacle Race, Net and Tank, S. S. "Coptic," Mid-Ocean
Old Maids and the Unfaithful Lovers
Outing, Mystic Shriners, Atlantic City, New Jersey
Parade, Mystic Shriners, Atlantic City, New Jersey
A Parisienne's Bed Time
The Parson's Cooking Lesson
Peeping Frenchman at the German Bathhouse
Pickpocket
Pillow Fight, S. S. "Coptic," Mid-Ocean
"Pollywogs" 71st Regiment, N. G. S. N. Y., Initiating Raw Recruits
Push Ball on Horseback
Rum vs. Cherries
Saturday Afternoon Shopping
Scenes in an Infant Orphan Asylum
Scenes Through a Telescope from Bridge of Russian Battleship
Sick Man's Delirium
Smoked Out
The Snapshot Fiend
Stolen Puppy
Study, Smoke and Soot
Such Is Life
That Impudent Flea
That Terrible Sneeze
Toy Maker and Good Fairy
Tragic Elopement
Troops Landing and Battle Scene
Two Bad Boys in a Church
Two Old Pals at Lunch
Two's Company, Three's None
Voyage of the "Arctic"
What Happened to Jones
Wheelbarrow and Automobile
Zoological Garden
Jul 9 A Disaster in a Colliery
Jul 16 White Star S. S. Baltic Leaving Pier on First Eastern Voyage
Jul 23 Annie's Love Story
Dance Plastiques
Japanese Ambush
The Nest Robbers
Tour in Italy
Aug [day undetermined]
Attempted Murder in a Train
Barber's Tricks
Fire and Flames at Luna Park, Coney Island [An Attraction at Coney Island]
Judge Parker Receiving the Notification of His Nomination for the Presidency
Late for Work
Off for the Holidays
Aug 27 Orla and His Trained Dogs
Sep [day undetermined]
Annual Baby Parade, 1904, Asbury Park, N. J.
Boys' Trick on Grandpa
Burglar, Cop and Barrel
Capture of Yegg Bank Burglars
Children and Rabbits
Defence of Port Arthur
Democratic Presidential Candidate, Judge Parker, and Mayor McClellan, Esopus, N. Y.

Departure 14th Co. Japanese Engineers from Shimbashi Station for Korea
European Rest Cure
Fencing Contest Between Japanese Soldiers, Manchuria
Great Temple Procession, Nikko, Japan
How a French Nobleman Got a Wife Through the New York Herald "Personal" Columns
Japanese Fan Dance
Japanese Flag Dance
Japanese Warriors in Ancient Battle Scene
Military Maneuvers, Manassas, Va.
The Miser's Daughter
President Theodore Roosevelt
Push Ball on Horseback, No. 2
Pussy's Dinner
War Balloon Ascending and Descending
Sep 3 Indians and Cowboys
The Strike
The Wrestling Donkey
Sep 17 Burglar and Girls
Sep 24 Drama in the Air
Fox and Rabbits
Ice Cream Eater
Ruffian's Dance
Oct [day undetermined]
Bobbie's Downfall
Cliffs of Cheddar, England
Death of Robert McCaire and Bertrand
Diving Scene and Reverse
Dwarf's Troubles
Embarking Wood in the Far East
Fisherman, Gendarmes and Bike Thief
Fly Paper Vendors
Impossible to Get a Plunge
Love or Money
Lover's Crime
Love's Dilemma
Maniac Chase
The Market Woman's Mishap
Night Duty
Old Maid's Flirtation
Otter Hunt
Real Warrior
Scenes in a Slate Quarry
Sculptor and Model
Sea Gulls at Newlyn, Cornwall, England
Shooting the Rapids of Killarney
Stop Thief!
Oct 1 Dogs and Cats
The Opera Hat
Park in Barcelona by Moonlight
Oct 8 Fantastic Fishing
Oct 15 Ascending Mount Pilate
Greedy Cat
Oct 29 The Fatal Wig
Trained Hogs
Nov [day undetermined]
City Hall to Harlem in 15 Seconds, via the Subway Route
Coal Heavers
Don't Butt In
Electric Doorbell
Illustrated Songs
Life of a Race Horse
Love Will Find a Way
Miss Lillian Shaffer and Her Dancing Horse
Opening Ceremonies, New York Subway, October 27, 1904
Parsifal
Railroad Smashup
Result Too Much Jealousy
A Rube Couple at a County Fair
Shanghaied by Pirates
"Weary Willie" Kisses the Bride
Wifey's Christmas Gift
Dec [day undetermined]
Bad Boy's Joke on the Nurse
Disturbed Picnic
The Ex-Convict
Great Sea Serpent
Guy Fawkes' Day
Intresting Story
Lady Plumpton's Motor Car
Lion and Lioness
Mining Operations, Pennsylvania Coal Fields
Oh! What a Surprise
Polar Bears at Play with Cubs
Scarecrow Pump
Stowaway
The "Strenuous" Life; or, Anti-Race Suicide
Dec 3 Sandy McGregor

1905

Jan [day undetermined]
Largest Fat Boy in the World
Masher and Oyster Stand
Soldier's Romance
Traction Engine
Tramps in Clover
Feb [day undetermined]
Duel Between Japanese and Russian Soldiers
The Kleptomaniac
Mar [day undetermined]
Awful Donkey
Her First Bicycle Lesson
Inauguration of President Roosevelt. President-Elect Roosevelt, Vice-President-Elect Fairbanks and Escort Going to the Capitol
Inauguration of President Roosevelt. Taking the Oath of Office
Inauguration of President Roosevelt. the Grand Inaugural Parade
President Roosevelt's Inauguration
Too Much for Dad
Apr [day undetermined]
The Seven Ages
Apr 8 Cards and Crime
May [day undetermined]
How Jones Lost His Roll
Kilties' Band
Opening of Belmont Park Race Course
"Play Ball"—Opening Game, National League, N. Y. City, 1905—New York vs. Boston
Start of Ocean Race for Kaiser's Cup
Jun [day undetermined]
Drills and Exercises, Schoolship "St. Mary's"
Jul [day undetermined]
Bishop and Burglar
Blowing Bottles
The Burglar's Slide for Life
Coney Island at Night
Cook and Chimney Sweep
An Eccentric Burglary
Fatal Necklace
Fixing the Derby Favorite
Hippodrome Races, Dreamland, Coney Island
[On] a [Good Ole] 5¢ Trolley Ride
Only Her Brother
The Race for Bed
Raffles, the Dog
Stolen by Gypsies
Torpedo Boats Manoeuvering
The Whole Dam Family and the Dam Dog
Aug [day undetermined]
An Affair of Honor
Aylesbury Ducks
Blind Man's Bluff
Dangerous Golfers
The Electric Mule
Elephant's Tub
Empire State Express, the Second, Taking Water on the Fly
Falsely Accused
His Washing Day
How Jones Saw the Derby
June's Birthday Party
Lady Barber
Masher and Nursemaid
Mystic Shriners' Day, Dreamland, Coney Island
Rehearsing a Play at Home
Robbing His Majesty's Mail
Scenes and Incidents, Russo-Japanese Peace Conference, Portsmouth, N.H.
Terrible Flirt
Whaling
Wide Awake
Won't You Come Home?
Sep [day undetermined]
Always a Gentleman
The Blacksmith's Daughter
The Boarding School Girls
Burglar and Bull Dog
Burglar and Vapor Bath
Chewing Gum
Cigarette Fiend
Cry Baby
Dressing the Baby
Fortune Telling in a Gypsy Camp
Girls and "Barrel of Love"
Girls and Moving Stairway
Girls on the "Bumpety Bumps"
Girls Riding Camels
Girls Riding Steeplechase
Girls Riding "Trolley"
Great Buffalo Chase
The Little Train Robbery
Lucille Mulhall and Trick Horse
Lucille Mulhall Roping and Tying a Steer
Old Maid and Pet Cat
Old Sweethearts
Sneezing
Starting on a Coyote Hunt
Steamboat Travel on Long Island Sound
Western "Bad Man" Shooting Up a Saloon
The White Caps
Oct [day undetermined]
The Czar at Czarkoe Selo
Devil's Dice
Engagement Ring
Firemen's Parade, Scranton, Pa.
He Learned Ju Jitsu, So Did the Missus
Naval Warfare
Pilfered Porker
Scenes in a Police Court
Steel Works
Oct 5 Poor Algy
Oct 24 The Watermelon Patch
Nov [day undetermined]
Digesting a Joke (Jas. T. Powers)
Motor Boat Race at Monaco
Motor Highwayman
Nov 2 Down on the Farm
Nov 6 The Miller's Daughter
Nov 15 Everybody Works but Father
Nov 27 The Train Wreckers
Dec [day undetermined]
Freak Barber
Goaded to Anarchy
Hubby Tries to Keep House
The Night Before Christmas
Dec 5 Desperate Encounter Between Burglar and Police
Life of an American Policeman
A River Tragedy

1906

Jan [day undetermined]
Bicycle Police Chasing Scorching Auto
Horse Stealing
A Misguided Bobby at a Fancy Garden Party
Moose Hunt in Canada
Opium Smoker's Dream
The Peashooter
Shaving by Installments
Two Little Waifs
Feb [day undetermined]
Dream of a Rarebit Fiend
Mar [day undetermined]
Phoebe Snow
Apr [day undetermined]
Runaway in the Park
A Winter Straw Ride
May [day undetermined]
Joke on a Roundsman
Jun [day undetermined]
Bird's Eye View from Hopkins Art Institute
Dynamiting Ruins and Rescuing Soldier Caught in Falling Walls
Earthquake Ruins, New Majestic Theatre and City Hall
Life of a Cowboy
Panorama, City Hall, Van Ness Avenue and College of St. Ignatius
Panorama, Nob Hill and Ruins of Millionaire Residences
Panorama, Notorious "Barbary Coast"

Panorama, Ruins Aristocratic Apartments
Panorama, Russian and Nob Hill from an Automobile
Ruins Bulletin Building, California Theatre and Evening Post
Ruins of Chinatown
The Terrible Kids
Three American Beauties
Vertical Panorama City Hall and Surroundings

Jul [day undetermined]
Fakir and Footpad
House Furnishing Made Easy
Waiting at the Church

Aug [day undetermined]
Arrival Mahukona Express, Kohala, Hawaii
Hauling Sugar Cane, Kohala Plantation, Hawaii
Hawaiians Arriving to Attend a Luau or Native Feast
Hawaiians Departing to Attend a Luau or Native Feast
How the Office Boy Saw the Ball Game
Kathleen Mavoureen
S. S. "Kinau" Landing Passengers, Mahukona, Hawaii
Scenes in Hawaii
Shearing Sheep, Humunla Ranch, Hawaii
Sheep Coming Through Chute, Humunla Ranch, Hawaii
Washing Sheep, Humunla Beach, Hawaii

Oct [day undetermined]
Getting Evidence, Showing the Trials and Tribulations of a Private Detective
Scenes and Incidents U. S. Military Academy, West Point
Vanderbilt Cup 1906

Nov [day undetermined]
The Honeymoon at Niagara Falls
Humuula Sheep Ranch

Dec [day undetermined]
American Falls from Canadian Side, Niagara Falls, N. Y.
American Falls from Goat Island, Niagara Falls, N. Y.
Cave of the Winds
Horseshoe Falls from American Side, Niagara Falls, N. Y.
Horseshoe Falls from Canadian Side Niagara Falls, N. Y.
A Trip on the "Maid in the Mist," Niagara Falls, N. Y.
A Trip on the "Chippewa," Niagara Falls, N. Y.
Whirlpool Rapids

1907

Jan [day undetermined]
Scene at "The Oaks," Portland, Oregon

Feb [day undetermined]
Waiting at the Church

Feb 2 Crowds Returning from the Games, Waikiki, H.I.
The "Float," Waikiki, Honolulu, Hawaiian Islands
Kanaka Fishermen Casting the Throw Net, Hilo, H.I.
Loading Sugar, Kahului, Maui, H.I.
Native Hawaiian Guards in Bayonet Exercises, H.I.
Pa-u Riders, Hawaiian Island
Panoramic View, Crater of Haleakala, H.I.
Panoramic View, Honolulu Harbor, H.I.
Panoramic View, King St. Honolulu, H.I.
Panoramic View, Oahu Railroad, Haleiwa, H.I.
Panoramic View, Oahu Railroad, Pearl Harbor, Hawaiian Islands
Panoramic View of Waikiki Beach, Honolulu, H.I.
Panoramic View, Waikiki, from an Electric Car, H.I.
S. S. "Kinau" Landing Passengers, Laupahoihoi, H.I.
Scenes on a Sugar Plantation, Hawaiian Islands
Shipping Cattle, Hawaihae, Hawaiian Islands
Snapshots, Hawaiian Islands
Surf Board Riders, Waikiki, Honolulu, H.I.
Surf Scene, Laupahoihoi, Hawaiian Island
Surf Scene, Waikiki, Honolulu, H.I.
A Trip Through the Yellowstone Park, U.S.A.
Water Buffalo Wallowing, Hawaiian Island

Mar 2 The Teddy Bears
Apr 6 Daniel Boone; or, Pioneer Days in America
May 11 Fire Run, Colon Fire Department Under Cocoanut Tree
Jamaica Negroes Doing a Two-Step
Jamestown Exposition International Naval Review, Hampton Roads, Virginia
Machete Men Clearing a Jungle [Panama Canal]
Making the Dirt Fly: Scene 1. Steam Shovel in Operation, Culebra Cut
Making the Dirt Fly: Scene 2. Unloading a Dirt Train
Making the Dirt Fly: Scene 3. Dirt Scraper in Operation
Making the Dirt Fly: Scene 4. Railroad Track Lifter in Operation
Making the Dirt Fly: Scene 5. Laborers Lining Up at Mess Tent
Old Market Place, Panama
Panorama from Columbus Point of Atlantic Entrance to the Canal
Panorama La Boca Harbor and Pacific Entrance to Canal
Panorama of Culebra Cut
Panorama Ruins of Old French Machinery
U. S. Sanitary Squad Fumigating a House

May 18 Lost in the Alps
Jun 29 Cohen's Fire Sale
Aug 3 The Nine Lives of a Cat
Aug 31 Stage Struck
Sep 14 Rivals
Sep 28 A Race for Millions
Oct 19 Jack the Kisser
Nov 2 Midnight Ride of Paul Revere
Nov 23 Three American Beauties [No. 2]
The Trainer's Daughter; or, A Race for Love
Dec 7 College Chums
Dec 14 Laughing Gas
Dec 21 The Little Girl Who Did Not Believe in Santa Claus

1908

Jan 18 Rescued from an Eagle's Nest
The Suburbanite's Ingenious Alarm
Feb 1 Fireside Reminiscences
A Yankee Man-o-Warsman's Fight for Love
Feb 15 A Sculptor's Welsh Rabbit Dream
Feb 29 Cupid's Pranks
Mar 7 Playmates
Mar 14 Nellie, the Pretty Typewriter
Mar 21 Animated Snowballs
Stage Memories of an Old Theatrical Trunk
Mar 28 A Country Girl's Seminary Life and Experiences
Apr 11 Tale the Autumn Leaves Told
Apr 12 The Cowboy and the Schoolmarm
Apr 22 Nero and the Burning of Rome
Apr 29 The Merry Widow Waltz Craze
May 6 Bridal Couple Dodging Cameras
May 13 The Gentleman Burglar
May 20 Curious Mr. Curio
May 27 The Painter's Revenge
Jun 3 Skinny's Finish
Jun 10 The Blue and the Gray; or, The Days of '61
Jun 17 Honesty Is the Best Policy
Jun 24 Love Will Find a Way

Jul [day undetermined]
"June Bug" Aeroplane

Jul 1 Pioneers Crossing the Plains in '49
Jul 15 The Boston Tea Party
The Little Coxswain of the Varsity Eight
Jul 22 The Face on the Barroom Floor
Fly Paper
Jul 29 A Dumb Hero
Aug 5 Tales the Searchlight Told
Aug 12 Life's a Game of Cards
Aug 19 Aeroplane Flights by Henry Farman, Coney Island, N. Y., U. S. A.
When Ruben Comes to Town
Aug 26 Romance of a War Nurse
Sep 2 A Comedy in Black and White
Heard over the Phone
Sep 9 The Devil
Sep 15 Wifey's Strategy
Sep 18 Ingomar, the Barbarian
Sep 22 Buying a Title
The Leprechaun—An Irish Fairy Story
Sep 29 Pocahantas — A Child of the Forest
Oct 2 Sandy McPherson's Quiet Fishing Trip
Ten Pickaninnies
Oct 6 The Lover's Guide
Oct 9 A Voice from the Dead
Oct 13 The Bridge of Sighs
Oct 16 Ex-Convict No. 900
Oct 20 Minstrel Mishaps; or, Late for Rehearsal
Oct 23 A Fool for Luck; or, Nearly a Policeman
Oct 27 The Army of Two (An Incident During the American Revolution)
Oct 30 A Football Warrior
Nov 3 Saved by Love
Nov 6 The Jester
Nov 10 The Lovers' Telegraphic Code
Nov 13 "She"
Nov 17 Colonial Virginia
The New Stenographer
Nov 24 The Lady or the Tiger
Nov 27 The King's Pardon
Dec 1 Lord Feathertop
Dec 4 Miss Sherlock Holmes
The Old Maids' Temperance Club
Dec 8 The Tale the Ticker Told
Dec 11 The Angel Child
Dec 15 Cocoa Industry, Trinidad, British West Indies
Dec 18 A Street Waif's Christmas
Dec 22 An Unexpected Santa Claus
Dec 25 Turning over a New Leaf
Dec 29 The Lost New Year's Dinner

1909

Jan 1 A Persistent Suitor
Jan 5 Under Northern Skies
Jan 8 The Worm Will Turn
Jan 12 Where Is My Wandering Boy To-night?
Jan 15 Drawing the Color Line
Jan 19 Pagan and Christian
Jan 22 A Burglar Cupid
Jan 26 A Romance of Old Madrid
Jan 29 A Modest Young Man
Feb 2 The Origin of Beethoven's Moonlight Sonata
Feb 5 The Adventures of an Old Flirt
Feb 9 A Bachelor's Supper
Feb 12 The Saleslady's Matinee Idol
Feb 16 A Daughter of the Sun
Feb 19 The Uplifting of Mr. Barker
Feb 23 The Janitor's Bottle
The Landlady's Portrait
Feb 26 Left Out
Mar 2 Boyhood Dreams
100 Per Cent Jealousy
Mar 5 A Bird in a Gilded Cage
Mar 9 The Colored Stenographer
Mary Jane's Lovers
Mar 12 A Canadian Winter Carnival
Mar 16 Love Is Blind
A Midnight Supper
Mar 19 The Star of Bethlehem
Mar 23 Strolling Players
Mar 26 A Cry from the Wilderness; or, A Tale of the Esquimaux and Midnight Sun
Mar 30 Hard to Beat
Oh! Rats!
Apr 2 On the Western Frontier
Apr 6 Father's First Half-Holiday
Unappreciated Genius
Apr 9 A Cup of Tea and She
Apr 13 The Interrupted Joy Ride

The Other Fellow; or, A Fight for Love
Apr 16 In the Days of Witchcraft
Apr 20 The Wood-Chopper's Child
Apr 23 Who's Who
Apr 27 The Little Shepherd of "Tumbling Run"
Apr 30 Uncle Tom Wins
An Unsuccessul Substitution
May [day undetermined]
Pressing Business
May 4 A Road to Love
May 7 The Doctored Dinner Pail
Fuss and Feathers
May 11 Lunatics in Power
May 14 The Pony Express
See a Pin and Pick It Up, All That Day You'll Have Good Luck
May 18 A Somnambulistic Hero
May 21 Little Miss Moffit and Simian Stone
The Sandman
May 25 Brothers in Arms
May 28 A Child's Prayer
Professor Fix Fixed
Jun 1 The Curfew Bell
Jun 4 The Hold-Up Held Up
A Wife's Ordeal
Jun 8 The Legend of Sterling Keep
Jun 11 The Boots He Couldn't Lose
Buying Manhattan
Jun 15 A Rural Tragedy
Jun 18 Closed on Sunday
How the Tramp Got the Lunch
Jun 22 The Lost Invitation
Jun 25 An Affair of Art
The Whole World Kin
Jun 29 A Man Without a Country
Jul 2 He Wouldn't Go Under a Ladder
Parted on their Honeymoon
Jul 6 Up the Ladder with Tom Bowline
Jul 9 An Absent-Minded Cupid
A Squeedunk Sherlock Holmes
Jul 13 The Secret of the Locket
Jul 16 Caught by the Coupon Craze
The Egyptian Mystery
Jul 20 McGinty's Sudden Rise
The Missionary and the Maid
Jul 23 The Bridegroom's Dilemma
Casey's Jumping Toothache
Jul 27 Mother Goose
Taking His Photograph
Jul 30 Love's Sacrifice
Mulligan's Waterloo
Aug 3 The Prince and the Pauper
Aug 6 Lochinvar
The Tobacco Edict, Old New York, 1648
Aug 10 Apprentice Boys at Newport [R. I.] Naval Training Station
A Coward
Aug 13 Furnished Rooms to Let
The Price of a Soul
Aug 17 Far from the Madding Crowd
A Simple Home Dinner
Aug 20 The Web of Fate: An Incident of the French Revolution
The Wright Brothers Aeroplane
Aug 24 A Child of the Forest
The Patience of Miss Job
Aug 27 A Dash to Death
Aug 31 Suffer Little Children...For of Such Is the Kingdom of Labor
Sep 3 Backward, Turn Backward, O Time, in Your Flight
Ethel's Luncheon
Sep 7 A Dangerous Pair
The Temptation
Sep 10 The Amateur William Tell
The Making of Honey
Sep 14 Little Sister
Sep 17 How the Landlord Collected His Rents
'Tis Now the Very Witching Hour of Night
Sep 21 The Ordeal
Sep 24 A Knight for a Night
Love and War: An Episode of Waterloo
True Love Never Runs Smoothly
Sep 27 Naval Parade of the Hudson-Fulton
Sep 28 Why Girls Leave Home
Oct 1 Two of a Kind
The Wallace Jewels
Oct 5 Laddie
Oct 8 Expert Glass Blowing
The Minister's Daughter
Oct 12 A New Life
Oct 15 Hansel and Gretel
Whitler's Witless Wanderings
Oct 19 Their Social Education
Oct 22 A Great Game
The Lost Handbag
Oct 23 Special Peary Film
Oct 26 The Lie
Oct 29 All's Fair in Love
The Three Kisses
Nov [day undetermined]
The Fox Hunt
Nov 2 Comedy and Tragedy
Nov 5 Bill, the Bill Poster
A Duel in Mid-Air
Nov 9 A Bride and Groom's Visit to the New York Zoological Gardens
Nov 12 His Masterpiece
A Man with Three Wives
Nov 16 The Imp of the Bottle
A Winter's Tale
Nov 19 Three Thanksgivings
Nov 23 A Rose of the Tenderloin
Nov 26 Annual Celebration of School Children at Newark, NJ
Bluebeard
Thanksgiving, Then and Now
Nov 30 Atlanta Automobile Speedway Races
The Heart of a Clown
The Wonderful Electro-Magnet
Dec [day undetermined]
Marie Dressler
Dec 3 The Keeper of the Light
Dec 7 My Lord in Livery
What the Cards Foretold
Dec 10 The House of Cards
Dec 14 Fenton of the 42nd
The New Policeman
Dec 17 A Gift from Santa Claus
Dec 21 A Happy Accident
The Mischievous Elf
Dec 24 Faust
Dec 28 The Cap of Fortune
The Fallen Idol
Tobacco Mania
Dec 31 Fishing Industry at Gloucester, Mass.

1910

Jan 4 Pardners
Jan 7 Ashes
The Engineer's Romance
Jan 11 Bear Hunt in the Rockies
Jan 14 The Parson's Umbrella
Troop "B", 15th U. S. Cavalry Bareback Squad in the Monkey Drill at Fort Myer, Virginia
A Warrior Bold
Jan 18 In the Nick of Time
Jan 21 The Coquette
The Luck of Roaring Camp
Jan 25 A Woman's Strategy
Jan 28 A Georgia Possum Hunt
The Skipper's Yarn
Feb [day undetermined]
New York of Today
Feb 1 A Japanese Peach Boy
Feb 4 The Bad Man from Riley's Gulch
His Just Deserts
The Surprise Party
Feb 8 The Livingston Case
Feb 11 An Equine Hero
A Queen of the Burlesque
Feb 15 The President's Special
Feb 18 The Miniature
A Trip to Mars
Feb 22 A Victim of Bridge
Feb 25 Lost and Regained
That Girl of Dixon's
Mar 1 Ranson's Folly
Mar 4 At the Eleventh Hour
The Man Under the Bed
Mar 8 My Milliner's Bill
The Right Decision
Mar 11 His First Valentine
Love Drops
Mar 15 Fruit Growing, Grand Valley, Colorado (The Results of Irrigation)
A Mountain Blizzard
Mar 18 Frankenstein
Mar 22 The Man with the Weak Heart
A Western Romance
Mar 25 The Suit Case Mystery
Mar 29 Bradford's Claim
The Capture of the Burglar
Apr 1 Michael Strogoff
Apr 5 The Heart of a Rose
It Pays to Advertise
Apr 8 Sandy the Substitute
Apr 12 For Her Sister's Sake
King Cotton
Apr 15 Her First Appearance
Apr 19 A Case of Identity
Apr 22 The Miner and Camille
Ready in a Minute
Apr 26 Gallegher
Apr 29 Drowsy Dick, Officer No. 73
A Yorkshire School
May [day undetermined]
Panoramic Railway View from Front of Train
May 3 The Cigarette Maker of Seville
May 6 Love and Marriage in Poster Land
The Senator and the Suffragettes
May 10 History Repeats Itself
The Stuff That Americans Are Made Of
May 13 Accidents Will Happen
Carminella
May 17 The Princess and the Peasant
May 20 Sisters
May 24 All on Account of a Laundry Mark
Fortune's Fool
May 27 'Mid the Cannon's Roar
May 31 The Mule Driver and the Garrulous Mute
Jun 3 The Piece of Lace
Jun 7 Mr. Bumptious on Birds
The Shyness of Shorty
Jun 10 The Bellringer's Daughter
Jun 14 The House on the Hill
United States Life Saving Drills
Jun 17 A Central American Romance
Jun 21 Bootles' Baby
Jun 24 The Judgment of the Mighty Deep
Jun 28 The Little Fiddler
Jul [day undetermined]
Great Ball Game Between the East and West
St. George and the Dragon
Sea Waves
Jul 1 The Stars and Stripes
Jul 5 Equal to the Emergency
A Tale of Two Coats
Jul 8 A Wireless Romance
Jul 12 Out of the Night
Jul 15 How Bumptious Papered the Parlor
A Vacation in Havana
Jul 19 The Old Loves and the New
Jul 22 A Frontier Hero
Lazy Farmer Brown
Jul 26 Peg Woffington
Jul 29 Bumptious as an Aviator
The Unexpected Reward
Aug [day undetermined]
Carrie de Mar
Pickaninny and the Pup
Aug 2 With Bridges Burned
Aug 5 The Moths and the Flame
U. S. Submarine "Salmon"
Aug 9 The Lady and the Burglar
Aug 12 The Attack on the Mill
Aug 16 His New Family
Aug 19 Bumptious Takes Up Automobiling
How the Squire Was Captured
Aug 23 Love and the Law
Aug 26 The Valet's Vindication
Aug 30 From Tyranny to Liberty
Sep 2 The Man Who Learned
Sep 6 The Big Scoop
Sep 9 Alice's Adventures in Wonderland
Sep 13 The Great Secret
Sep 16 Bumptious as a Fireman
From the Arctics to the Tropics
Sep 20 An Unselfish Love
Sep 23 Almost a Hero
A Jar of Cranberry Sauce; or, The Crime in Room 13
Sep 27 The Footlights or the Farm
Over Mountain Passes
Sep 29 The Stenographer's Friend
Sep 30 Ononko's Vow

Oct 4 More Than His Duty
Oct 7 Bumptious Plays Baseball
The Farmer's Daughter
Oct 11 The Song That Reached His Heart
Oct 14 The Chuncho Indians of the Amazon River, Peru
The Stolen Father
Oct 18 The House of the Seven Gables
Oct 21 A Wedding Trip from Montreal Through Canada to Hong Kong
Oct 25 The Breach of Discipline
Oct 28 The Swiss Guide
Nov 1 The Key of Life
Nov 2 Boy Scouts of America in Camp at Silver Bay, Lake George, N. Y.
Riders of the Plains
Nov 4 The Little Station Agent
Nov 8 The Lassie's Birthday
A Trip over the Rocky and Selkirk Mountains in Canada
Nov 9 The Ship's Husband
Nov 11 The Adoption
Nov 15 Into the Jaws of Death
Nov 16 The Stolen Claim
Nov 18 The Toymaker, the Doll and the Devil
Nov 22 His Mother's Thanksgiving
Nov 23 Through the Clouds
Nov 25 A Daughter of the Mines
Nov 29 The Greater Love
Nov 30 Arms and the Woman
Dec [day undetermined]
Aviation Meet of the Aero Club, St. Louis, Mo.
Dec 2 The Cowpuncher's Glove
Dec 6 The Winning of Miss Langdon
Dec 7 Amateur Night
The Life of a Salmon
Dec 9 The Captain's Bride
Dec 13 A Mountain Maid
An Old Silver Mine in Peru
Dec 14 Pigs Is Pigs
Dec 16 The Red Cross Seal
Dec 20 The Police Force of New York City
Dec 21 The Joke They Played on Bumptious
Dec 23 A Christmas Carol
Dec 27 Eldora, the Fruit Girl
Dec 28 A Family of Vegetarians
Dec 30 The Romance of Hefty Burke

Edison, Thomas A., Inc. *see* **Thomas A. Edison, Inc.**

Edward Daniel MacFee, Jr.

1909 [month undetermined]
The American Fleet in Hampton Roads, 1909, After Girdling the Globe

The Electragraff Co. of Philadelphia

1910
May 22 Proposing Under Difficulties
May 29 Love Your Neighbor as Yourself, but Leave His Wife Alone!
Jun 15 A Message from the East
Jun 22 An Interrupted Courtship
Jun 29 All's Well That Ends Well
Jul 6 No Questions Asked
Jul 13 Among the Breakers
Jul 20 The Power from Above

Empire Film Co.

1908
Oct 21 A Father's Will

1909 [month undetermined]
Peasant and Princess
Feb 10 Grandfather's Birthday
Polly's Excursion
Mar 22 The Duel
Apr 24 The Dog Came Back
May 8 Baby's Chum
The Cavalier's Wife
Earthly Paradise
Ellen
First Comes the Fatherland
Funeral of Joe Petrosino: The American Detective in Merino, Italy
The Gambler's Vow
The Haunted Bridge
House Full of Agreeables
I Will Have a Husband
The Immortal Goose
The Inheritance of Baptiste Durand
Love with Love Is Paid
Romance of the Crafty Usurper and the Young King
Snowball
Sportsmen in Switzerland
Taking Home the Eggs
May 15 Carnival at Nice
The Detective's Ruse
Disappointed Heirs
An Exciting Hunt
Foolshead on the Alps
For a Woman's Sake
For Honor's Sake
Galileo, Inventor of the Pendulum
Humble Heroes
In the Service of the King
Magic Sack
A New Policeman
On the French Littoral
Rosin Industry
The Spoilt Child
Tower of London
Unlucky Bridegroom
Who Has Seen My Head?
May 22 Boys' Holiday
A Clever Detective
Favorite Doll
In Quest of Health
In Sardinia
Longing for Gold
Neurasthenique
Perilous Expedition
Present for Her Husband
River Panorama
Sapho
Scenes in Ceylon
Stratagem Rewarded
Why Father Learned to Ride
You Shall Pay for It
May 29 Apostle of Gaul
The Bear in the Staircase
Count of Monte Cristo
The Emperor
Forester's Son
Frost Bound Nature
His Only Quid
King's Jester
Lesson in Electricity
Mimosa and the Good Prince
Morganatic Marriage
Nantilda
A Piano Lesson
Reveler's Dream
The Suffragist Wants a Husband
Vaccination Against Injuries
Jun 5 Airship Zeppelin
Cat Came Back
Debut of an Alpinist
Dentist's Daughter
Face to Face
False Piano Professor
Gypsy's Child
Italian Artillery
Legend of the Erring Jew
On the Zuider Zee
Resuscitated
Trollhattan in Winter
A True Friend
Jun 12 The Consequences of a Bad Action
Jun 19 The English Derby
Jun 26 Aboard the German Navy
The Buffoon
Bully and Recruit
Chimney Sweep's Debut
Dollar in Each Egg
Foolshead Wrestling
Fratricide
Heroine of the Balkans
His Wedding Morn
Louis the XI
Lover's Mistake
Maddened Players
Misadventures of a Bench
Moonlight on the Thames
The Mother-in-Law Phantasm
Officer's Lodgment
Percy Wanted a Moustache
Police Dogs
Quiet Day at the Cafe
The Shepherd's Dog
Sunshine After Storm
To the Custody of the Father
Winter Horseplay
The Wrong Coat
Jul 3 American Squadron in France
Bee's Eviction
Bink's Toreador
The Dog and the Bone
The Egg Race
Fancy Dress Ball
Infernal Salamandre
A Joke on Teddy
Lighthouse
Lord of Montmorency
Modern Cinderella
A Pair of Truants
Pity and Love
Ski Jumping
The Snow Man
Jul 10 Gaffles, Vice King of Police
The Gambler's Son
Horse to the Rescue
The Interrupted Jollification
The Life of a Pierrot
The Origin of Man
Phonographic Message of Love
Pierrot as a Grocer
Prince of Chalant
The Reason of the Strongest
A Tramp Show Heart
Jul 17 Ballad of the Pumpkin
Brave Little Organ Boy
The Curate of the Races
Expiation
His First Drink
Inexperienced Angler
A Jealous Woman
Miraculous Fluid
Mr. Stubborn
Motor Skates
Mysterious Lodger
Never Gamble for Your Trousers
The Poisoned Flower
The Sacrifice
The Step-Mother
Too Much Lobster for Supper
Tragic Night
Jul 24 Admirer of a Mustache
Bachelor's Misfortune
Columbine's Return
The Good Shepherd
The Harp Player
John Maxwell's Medal
Little Imp
Professor of Dancing
Territory on Brain
Treacherous Policeman
Two Turtle Doves
The Would-Be Acrobats
Jul 31 Game of Nine Pins
Little Gypsy
Missionary
Picturesque Tunis
Three-Wheeled Car
Wine a Gent
Aug 7 Butcher Boy
Clever Horse Hans
The Course of True Love
Double Awakening
Japanese Prince
King of Spain
The Orphan of Messina
Sympathetic Tippler
Troubles of a Coachman
Wonderful Compound
Aug 14 An Amazing Story
Black Hand
Bouquet Gallantly Offered
The Burning Home
Foolshead Sportsman of Love
Her Beautiful Hair
A Hero of the Italian Independence
The Iron Mask
Mr. Isaacs and the Mice
The Mysterious Crime
A Near Tragedy
Nightmare of a Single Man
Race for a Farmer's Cup
Satan's Retreat
A Smart Trick
A Trying Position
Aug 21 False Lunatic
He Preferred to Smoke His Pipe
Honesty Rewarded
Hooligan Against His Will

Madam Lydia's Little Trick
The New General
Niccolo' De' Lapi
Rival Sisters
The Spy
Story of a Picture
When Jack Gets His Pay
Aug 28 Ancestral Treasures
A Cheap Removal
The Farmer's Joke
Foolshead Matrimony
Grandmother's Birthday
Henpeck's Revolt
Little Seller of Cyclamens
Rival Mesmerists
The Spy's Revenge
Squaring the Account
The Two Friends
Sep 4 An Apostle of Temperance
Biskra, Garden of Allah
The Boy and His Kite
The Boy Scouts
Florian De Lys
Foolshead, King of Robbers
How the Bulldog Paid the Rent
How the Page Boy Cured a Flirt
Leap of Alola
Little Jim
Louisa of Lucerne
Love of a Hunchback
Mr. A. Nutt
Mosimilla
Only a Tramp
A Strong Woman's Lover
A Troublesome Malady
Who Laughs Last
Sep 13 Daughter of an Anarchist
Don Carlos
From Millionaire to Porter
Importune Neighbor
The Justifier
Love of Adventures
The Rivals
The Story of a Bad Cigar
Uncle Rube's Visit
Sep 18 Arab Life in South Algeria
The Arithmetic Lesson
A Broken Heart
Calino Objects to Work
A Dream of Paradise
The End of the Terror
For My Children
German Spring Parade
How Money Circulates
If at First You Don't Succeed
Luck of the Cards
Making of a Sailor
Man with the Sack in Society
Pietro, the Candy Kid
Pietro, the Mule Driver
Runaway Model
A Villain's Downfall
Sep 20 His Wife's Troublesome Twitching
Tragical Love
Sep 21 Carlo and the Baby
Eleanora
Meskal, the Smuggler
Sep 22 The Five Divorcees
Sep 23 An Aerial Elopement
Jackson's Last Steeple Chase
A Lucky Man
Sep 24 Marriage of Yvonne
Mrs. Minta's Husband
Sep 25 The Adopted Child
The Eccentric Barber
Father's Beautiful Beard
From Portofino to Nervi
The Little Milliner and the Thief
A Mother's Love
Necessity Is the Mother of Invention
Not Wanted on Voyage
Phaedra
Towards Immortalidated [sic]
Oct 2 Arab Life
Good Cigars
Mady Millicent's Visitor
Mr. Muddlehead's Mistake
The Poacher
Romance of a Pierrot
Oct 9 Napoleon
Oct 18 Berlin Jack the Ripper
Escaped Lunatic
Foolshead's Trousers
Reformation of a Wine-Loving Artist
Oct 19 Man in Pieces
The Phantom Ship
Sardinian Brigand
Winter Sports in Hungary
Oct 25 The Boating Party
The Brigand's Repentance
The Great Lottery
The Indian Phantasy
Love and Vendetta
A Prince's Love
The Strength of Love
The Would-Be Champion
Nov 6 Belgrade, Capital of Servia
Princess and Slave
The Silk Worm Series
Spartacus
Two Brothers
Nov 13 Balloon Trip over Turin
The Cabman's Good Fairy
How Foolshead Paid His Debts
The Invaders
Life for a Life
Mischief of a Big Drum
Nana's Mother
Now Keep Smiling
Romance of Life
The Street Arab
Substitute Pig
Two Little Runaways
Nov 15 Electrified Hunchback
High Treason
Dec 25 The Wonderful Pearl
1910
Jan 10 Rudolph of Hapsburg
Jan 20 Martyrs of Pompeii
Feb 4 Strike Instigator
Winter Days in Sweden
Feb 8 Doctor's Peculiar Treatment
In Winter's Grip
Feb 15 Daring Lion's Bride
Tragedy at Sea
Mar 1 Scenes of the Australian Gold Fields
Mar 2 Electrical Safe
Lines of the Hand
Mar 25 Double Six
Apr 7 Roosevelt at Messina
Roosevelt's Reception
Apr 8 Come to Supper with Me
Motherless Waif
Apr 11 Musical Masterpiece
Spanish Fandalgo
Apr 18 The Queen's Attendant
Apr 26 Among the Snowy Mountains
Grandfather's Story
Apr 27 Bethlehem
Apr 28 The Reservists
Twenty Francs
May 5 Fury of the Waves
Village Beauty
May 10 Mystery of the Cossacks
May 12 Two Betrothed
May 16 Lucretia
May 17 Child's Doctor
May 19 In the Name of Allah
May 20 Cuban War
May 23 Devoted Playmates
May 24 Drive Through Central Park
Sunday Afternoon on Fifth Avenue
Jun 13 Artist's Dream
Views of England
Jun 15 Caught Red-Handed
Rape of the Sabines
Jun 16 Seeing the Real Thing
Spirit of the Sword
Jun 21 Love Is Stronger Than Life
Jun 23 No Smoking
Sea Cave and Cliffs
Jun 24 Isis
Jun 25 Who Owned the Coat
Jun 29 Fishery in the North
Jun 30 False Accusation
Jul 4 The Derby

Empire Films
1909
Sep 4 Love of a Hunchback
1910
Jul 12 Prince of Kyber

Enterprise Optical Co.
1908
Sep 22 Not Guilty
A Tricky Painter's Fate
Sep 29 Buncoed Stage Johnnie
Fun with the Bridal Party
Oct 6 A Grandmother's Story
Oct 17 Honeymoon in a Balloon
Incident from Don Quixote
Oct 27 The Duke's Good Joke
Nov 3 A Love Tragedy in Spain
1909
Oct 13 The Stolen Wireless
Oct 20 For the Cause of Suffrage
Oct 27 Cinderella Up-to-Date
Nov 3 For Sale: A Baby
The Hypnotist's Revenge
Nov 10 A Tumultuous Elopement
Nov 17 The Count's Wooing
Mr. and Mrs. Duff
Nov 24 The Red Star Inn
Dec 1 Fortune Favors the Brave
Seeing Things
Dec 8 The Fatal Ball; or, The Miner's Daughter
Dec 15 The Living Doll

Essanay Film Mfg. Co.
1907
Jul 31 An Awful Skate; or, the Hobo on Rollers
Aug 10 Slow but Sure
Aug 24 Mr. Inquisitive
Sep 7 Life of a Bootblack; or, the Street Urchin
Sep 21 The Dancing Nig
Oct 12 Hey There! Look Out!
99 in the Shade
The Unveiling Ceremonies of the McKinley Memorial, Canton, Ohio, September 30th, 1907
Oct 26 A Free Lunch
The Street Fakir
The Vagabond
Nov 16 The Eleventh Hour
Dec 14 Where Is My Hair?
Dec 20 A Christmas Adoption
1908
Jan 4 The Bell Boy's Revenge
The Football Craze
Jan 11 Jack of All Trades
Jan 18 A Home at Last
Novice on Stilts
Feb 1 The Hoosier Fighter
Feb 8 Babies Will Play
Feb 15 "Louder Please"
Mar 4 All Is Fair in Love and War
Apr 4 Hypnotizing Mother-in-Law
Apr 12 James Boys in Missouri
Apr 15 Michael Strogoff
Apr 22 Sappho
Apr 25 The Dog Cop
Juggler Juggles
A Lord for a Day
Well-Thy Water
May 6 Don't Pull My Leg
Ker-Choo
May 15 Peck's Bad Boy
May 27 An Animated Doll
Jun 13 The Gentle Sex
I Can't Read English
Just Like a Woman
Jun 17 The Little Mad-Cap; or, Oh Splash!
The Tragedian
Jun 20 Younger Brothers
Jul 11 A Plain Clothes Man
Jul 25 The Directoire Gown
Aug 8 A Prodigal Parson
Aug 22 The Checker Fiends
Oh, What Lungs!
Wouldn't It Tire You?
Aug 29 The Baseball Fan
A Disastrous Flirtation
The Escape of the Ape
A Gilded Fool
Sep 5 The Coward
An Enterprising Florist
In the Hands of the Enemy
Lost and Found
Oh! What an Appetite
Stung
Sep 9 Never Again

Romance of a Taxicab
Sep 16 A Wayward Daughter
Sep 23 Hired-Tired-Fired
Sep 30 Beg Pardon
Soul Kiss
Oct 3 Breaking into Society
Oct 7 The Life of Abraham Lincoln
Oct 14 His Own Son
Oct 17 The World's Championship Baseball Series of 1910
Oct 21 The Effect of a Shave
The Impersonator's Jokes
Oct 28 Wrongfully Accused
Nov 4 David Garrick
Nov 11 He Who Laughs Last Laughs Best
If It Don't Concern You, Let It Alone
Nov 18 The Hoodoo Lounge
The Tale of a Thanksgiving Turkey
Nov 25 An All-Wool Garment
Dec 2 An Obstinate Tooth
The Somnambulist
Dec 9 A Christmas Carol
Dec 16 A Battle Royal
The Installment Collector
Dec 23 Bill Jones' New Years Resolution
"Who Is Smoking That Rope?"
Dec 30 In Golden Days

1909

Jan 6 The Haunted Lounge
The Neighbors' Kids
Jan 13 The Actor's Baby Carriage
Professor's Love Tonic
Jan 20 The Old Curiosity Shop
Jan 27 A Cure for Gout
Too Much Dog Biscuit
Feb 3 The Musician's Love Story
Feb 10 Educated Abroad
Feb 17 Bring Me Some Ice
Tag Day
Feb 24 The Tell-Tale Blotter
Mar 3 Shanghaied
Mar 10 The Crazy Barber
An Expensive Sky Piece
Mar 17 The Road Agents
Mar 24 An Energetic Street Cleaner
A Midnight Disturbance
Mar 31 For Love's Sake
Apr 7 A Tale of the West
Apr 14 The Chaperone
The Rubes and the Bunco Men
Apr 21 One Touch of Nature
A Pair of Garters
Apr 28 Old Heidelberg
May 5 A Mexican's Gratitude
May 12 The Bachelor's Wife
Mr. Flip
May 19 The Indian Trailer
May 26 Annie Laurie
Scenes from the World's Largest Pigeon Farm
Jun 2 The Dog and the Sausage
The Sleeping Tonic
Jun 9 Ten Nights in a Bar-room
Jun 16 A Hustling Advertiser
The Little Peacemaker
Jun 23 The Curse of Cocaine
Jun 30 The Policeman's Romance
The Slavey
Jul 7 The Black Sheep
Jul 14 The New Cop
Which Is Which?
Jul 21 The Romance of a Stranded Actress
Jul 28 A Case of Seltzer
The Tramp Story
Aug 4 Much Ado about Nothing
The Mustard Plaster
Aug 11 A Maid of the Mountains
Aug 18 Wonders of Nature
Aug 25 On Another Man's Pass
Sep 1 My Wife's Gone to the Country (Hooray! Hooray!)
Sep 8 Justified
Sleepy Jim
Sep 15 A Case of Tomatoes
Three Reasons for Haste
Sep 20 Taft in Chicago, and at the Ball Game
Sep 22 Gratitude
Sep 29 The Brothers
Oct 6 A Birthday Affair
The Magic Melody
Oct 13 The Twelfth Juror
Oct 20 The Widow
A Woman's Wit
Oct 23 Pittsburgh-Detroit Ball Game
Oct 27 Maud Muller
Nov 3 A Bachelor's Love Affair
Nov 10 The Game
Nov 17 A Mislaid Baby
The Personal Conduct of Henry
Nov 20 The Best Man Wins
Nov 24 A Lady's Purse
On the Wrong Scent
Nov 27 Judgment
Dec 1 Baby Swallows a Nickel
Two Sides to a Story
Dec 4 His Reformation
Dec 8 The Bachelor and the Maid
A Pair of Slippers
Dec 11 The Ranchman's Rival
Dec 15 An Amateur Hold-Up
A Female Reporter
Dec 18 The Spanish Girl
Dec 22 A Kiss in the Dark
Object: Matrimony
Dec 25 The Heart of a Cowboy
Dec 29 Jack's Birthday
The Policeman's Revolver

1910

Jan 1 A Western Maid
Why He Did Not Win Out
Jan 5 The Adventuress
How Hubby Made Good
Jan 8 His Only Child
Jan 12 Electric Insoles
The Old Maid and the Burglar
Jan 15 Review of U. S. Troops—Fort Leavenworth
Jan 19 Flower Parade at Pasadena, California
Won by a Hold-Up
Jan 22 The Confession
Jan 26 The Modern Messenger Boy
Jan 29 An Outlaw's Sacrifice
Feb 2 A Voice from the Fireplace
The Wrong Man
Feb 5 Sensational Logging
Feb 9 The Price of Fame
Feb 12 Bitter-Sweet
Western Chivalry
Feb 16 Aviation at Los Angeles, Calif.
Baby's First Tooth
Feb 19 The Cowboy and the Squaw
Feb 23 Oh, So Sick!
The Winning of Father
Feb 26 The Mexican's Faith
Mar 2 The Egg Trust
Rags, Old Iron!
Mar 5 The Ostrich and the Lady
The Ranch Girl's Legacy
Mar 9 An Interrupted Honeymoon
Mar 12 The Fence on Bar Z Ranch
Mar 16 The Inventor's Model
Method in His Madness
Mar 19 The Girl and the Fugitive
Mar 23 The Hand of Uncle Sam
Mar 26 The Airship Gaze
A Ranchman's Wooing
Mar 30 His Hunting Trip
Apr 2 The Flower of the Ranch
Apr 6 Henry's New Hat
Imagination
Apr 9 A Family Quarrel
The Ranger's Bride
Apr 13 Their Sea Voyage
Apr 16 The Bad Man and the Preacher
The Mistaken Bandit
Apr 20 She Wanted a Bow-Wow
A Wise Guy
Apr 23 The Cowboy's Sweetheart
Apr 27 Flat to Rent
The Latest in Garters
Apr 30 A Vein of Gold
May 4 The Stolen Fortune
May 7 The Sheriff's Sacrifice
May 11 He Stubs His Toe
A Quiet Boarding House
May 14 The Cowpuncher's Ward
May 18 The Danger Line
May 21 The Little Doctor of the Foothills
May 25 Tin Wedding Presents
Where Is Mulcahy?
May 28 The Brother, Sister and Cowpuncher
Jun 1 Henry's Package
Levi's Dilemma
Jun 4 Away Out West
Jun 8 Burly Bill
Jun 11 The Ranchman's Feud
Jun 15 A Honeymoon for Three
Jun 18 The Bandit's Wife
Jun 22 A Victim of Hate
Jun 25 The Forest Ranger
Jun 29 C-H-I-C-K-E-N Spells Chicken
Pat and the 400
Jul 2 The Bad Man's Last Deed
Jul 6 A Darling Confusion
The Other Johnson
Jul 9 The Unknown Claim
Jul 13 An Advertisement Answered
Jul 16 Trailed to the Hills
Jul 20 The Thief
Jul 23 The Desperado
Jul 27 A Fair Exchange
A Personal Matter
Jul 30 Broncho Billy's Redemption
Aug 3 A College Chicken
Mulcahy's Raid
Aug 6 Under Western Skies
Aug 10 Feeding Seals at Catalina Isle
Up-to-Date Servants
Aug 13 The Girl on Triple X
Aug 17 The Count That Counted
Aug 20 The Dumb Half Breed's Defence
Aug 24 Take Me Out to the Ball Game
Aug 27 The Deputy's Love
Aug 31 Who's Who
You Stole My Purse
Sep 3 The Millionaire and the Ranch Girl
Sep 7 A Dog on Business
Sep 10 An Indian Girl's Love
Sep 14 He Met the Champion
Whist
Sep 17 Hank and Lank Joyriding
The Pony Express Rider
Sep 21 A Close Shave
A Flirty Affliction
Sep 24 The Tout's Remembrance
Sep 28 Curing a Masher
Hank and Lank: They Dude Up Some
Oct 1 Patricia of the Plains
Oct 5 All on Account of a Lie
Oct 8 The Bearded Bandit
Oct 12 Hank and Lank: They Get Wise to a New Scheme
Papa's First Outing
Oct 15 The Cowboy's Mother-in-Law
Oct 19 Hank and Lank: Uninvited Guests
Hiring a Gem
Oct 22 Pals of the Range
Oct 26 The Bouquet
Hank and Lank: They Take a Rest
Oct 28 World's Championship Series
Oct 29 The Silent Message
Nov 1 A Fortunate Misfortune
Nov 5 A Westerner's Way
Nov 8 Hank and Lank: Life Savers
The Masquerade Cop
Nov 12 The Marked Trail
Nov 15 Love at First Sight
Nov 19 The Little Prospector
Nov 22 Hank and Lank: as Sandwich Men
That Popular Tune
Nov 26 A Western Woman's Way
Nov 29 The Tie That Binds
Dec 3 Circle "C" Ranch Wedding Present
Dec 6 Love's Awakening
Dec 10 A Cowboy's Vindication
Dec 13 A Tangled Masquerade
Dec 17 The Tenderfoot Messenger
Dec 20 The Greater Call
Hank and Lank
Dec 24 The Bad Man's Christmas Gift
Dec 27 Girls Will Be Boys
Dec 31 A Gambler of the West

Eugene Dial

1905 [month undetermined]
Dial's Girls' Band, Luna Park

The Exclusive American Film Co.

1909

Dec 30 A Romance of the South

1910

Jan 29 Her City Beaux
May 7 The Mad Miner Recovers
May 14 The Tramp Organist
May 23 Devoted Playmates

Exhibitors Film Exchange
1909
Jul 17 Automatic Umbrella Seller
Billy's Bugle
Count Ugolini
Fate and Poverty
Pietro, the Bandit
A Princess' Love Affair
Sep 4 Baby's Revenge
Bad Brother
Bad Day for Lavinsky
By Path of Love
Day After a Spree
Fancy Soldier
Gaffy's King of Detectives
Love and Revenge
Madwoman's Child
Mexican Drama
Sep 20 Blind Against His Will
Oct 25 The False Oath

F. M. Prescott
1894
Nov [day undetermined]
Corbett and Courtney Before the Kinetograph
1897
May [day undetermined]
Husking Bee
Making Soap Bubbles
Pillow Fight
Jun [day undetermined]
Boating on the Lake
Chicken Thieves
Children's Toilet
Mr. Edison at Work in His Chemical Laboratory

Film d'Art
1909
Feb 3 Incriminating Evidence
Feb 17 The Assassination of the Duke of Guise
Mar 20 The Return of Ulysses
Apr 7 The Kiss of Judas
Apr 14 Oliver Cromwell
May 12 The Hunter's Grief
May 22 Cartouche
Jun 9 La Tosca
Jun 16 The Reckoning
Jun 23 The Grandfather
Jun 26 Joan of Arc
Aug 6 The Tragedy of Meudon
Aug 14 The Wild Ass's Skin
Sep 22 The Tower of Nesle
Oct 9 Napoleon
Oct 22 Drink
Nov 5 The Prodigal Son
Nov 14 Rigoletto
Dec 12 La Grande Breteche
1910
Mar 25 No Trifling with Love
Apr 6 The Duchess of Langeais
May 19 Werther
May 26 Don Carlos
Jun 2 Vitellius and Heliogabalus
Jun 4 Macbeth
Jun 9 The Children of Edward IV
Jun 16 The Legend of the Holy Chapel
Jun 23 Oliver Twist
Jun 30 Fort Du Bitche
Jul 6 Love Ye One Another
Jul 7 Jemmy
Jul 14 The End of a Dynasty
Jul 21 Andromache
Mateo Falcone
Jul 28 The Hiding Place
Aug 4 The Eagle and the Eaglet
Aug 11 Charles Le Tremeraire
The Oedipus King
Aug 18 Carmen
Aug 25 In the Time of the First Christians
Sep 1 King of a Day
Sep 8 Conscience of a Child
The Minister's Speech
Sep 15 The Temptation of Sam Bottler

Film d'Arte Italiana
1910
Jan 12 Camille
Feb 16 Carmen
Apr 20 Othello

Film Import and Trading Co.
1908
Sep 12 Antiquary
The Beggar
The Daughter of the Gypsy
Fencing Fiend
Hamlet
Little Walk in Rome
Lottery Ticket
The Model
Root in Mexico
Rose, the Flower Girl
The Spiteful Groom
Strange Inheritance
Who Is It?
Youthful Artist
Sep 19 His Sweetheart's Birthday
In the Time of Rebellion
Sep 26 Duchess of Bracciano
Oct 3 The Ayah's Revenge
My Wife's Dog
Oct 10 Rocanbole
Oct 24 The Revengeful Waiter
The Young Artist
Nov 6 Gust of Wind
Pirate's Honor
Dec 2 Devils in the Farm
Every Age Has Its Trouble
Dec 19 Misdeeds of a Tragical Part
Dec 21 My Laundress Inherits
1909
Jan 2 The Corsican's Revenge
Jan 9 Soldier's Heroism
Jan 16 The Coiners, or Catching the Counterfeiters
Holy Fires
Porcelain of Good Quality
Jan 23 Messina Disaster
Feb 6 The Banker
Fatal Wedding
A Pirate of Turkey
Riding for Love
Feb 13 Circumstantial Evidence
The Showman's Drama
Feb 22 The Galley Slave
Feb 24 Drama Amongst Fishermen
Feb 27 The Shoemaker's Luck
Mar 6 The Ashes of Hercules
The Miner's Wife
The Musician
The Story of a Life
Mar 17 Taming of a Shrew
Mar 20 Western Bill
Mar 27 The Magician
The Reprobate
Apr 3 Life Through a Telescope
Lost in the Snow
Stolen for Spite
Apr 10 Disloyal Lover
Eagle's Prey
Lost in Chinatown
Mishaps of Lover
Apr 12 Give Me a Light
Apr 17 Unforgiving Father
Apr 27 The Bandits
Earthenware Industry
May 1 Misplaced Confidence
May 8 An Awful Toothache
Tribulations of a Lover
May 15 Fishing Industry
May 22 The Attack
Black Coated Brigands
Black's Funeral
Tom's Misfit
Two Pickpockets
Unprofitable Experiment
May 24 The Flirt, a Tale of the Plains
Jun 5 Game of Hearts
Happy Man
Jun 12 Early Days in the West
Episode of Cuban War
Jun 16 Don Juan; or, A War Drama of the Eighteenth Century
Life's Disappointment
Jun 26 A Painful Joke
Jul 10 The Sheriff's Pet
Jul 17 Born for Trouble
A Luckless Nap
An Old Soldier
Jul 28 Maryland 1777
Aug 11 The Power of Love
Aug 18 The Lost Letter
Aug 25 The Blacksmith's Daughter
Sep 1 Peaceful Jones
Sep 8 The Diamond Necklace
The Wishing Charm
Sep 11 Great Airship Flights at Rheims
Sep 15 The Bull Fight
A White Lie
Sep 22 Dan Blake's Rival
Sep 29 A Close Call
Oct 5 Forgiven at Last
Oct 6 The Sheriff's Girl
Oct 13 His Mexican Bride
Oct 20 Almost a Suicide
The Purse
Oct 27 Brother and Sister
Nov 1 Nero; or, The Burning of Rome
Nov 2 Honest John, the Coachman
A Race for the Monkey
Nov 3 The Lost Years
Nov 4 Napoleon and Princess Hatzfeld
Nov 5 A Very Attractive Gentleman
The Witch
Nov 6 Elephant Hunting in Cambodge
The Sack Race
Nov 8 Bandits of the Atlas Gorges
The Bearskin
Boatman of the Riviera
Enthusiastic Hand Ball Player
Father's Holiday
Force of Love
Henry the Third
Lines of the Hand
Miracle of a Necklace
Musical Waiter
Orange Growing in Palestine
Pirates of the Sea
Woes of a Cinematographer
Nov 9 Good for Evil
Nov 10 The Necklace of the Holy Virgin
Nov 11 Bertha's Birthday
Nov 12 The Farmer's Son
Logging in the Italian Alps
Nov 15 The Cursed Cage
Nov 16 Mysterious Luggage
Nov 17 Goddess of the Sea
Nov 18 Julius Caesar
Nov 19 The Love of Little Flora
Nov 20 A Mother's Heart
Nov 22 Ali Bey's Dancing Drops
Honest Little Rag Picker
The Hostage
John Farley's Redemption
Legend of the Good Knight
Napoleon's Game of Chess
Nov 29 The Double Six
Leopard Hunting in Abyssinia
Marvelous Shaving Soap
The Motor Cyclist
The Painter's Idol
Professor Short Sight's Surprise
The Servant of the Actress
Dec 2 The Lemon Sisters at Muldoon's Picnic
Dec 6 An Athlete of a New Kind
Captain Fracassee
The Disguised Bridegroom
The Electric Safe
The Heir of Clavencourt Castle
The Little Vendean
Mr. Sadman's Cure
The Song That Reached Her Heart
Dec 11 Macbeth
Dec 13 Beethoven
The Beggarman's Gratitude
Dr. Lyvenemup's Elixir
Dottynob's Dancing
The Smuggler's Sweetheart
A Trip to the Arctic
Dec 14 Comrades Under General Grant
Dec 20 The Drunkard's Christmas
Explorer's Dream
Granny's Darling
A Little Disagreement
Lorenzi De Medica
Mac Nabb Wants to Get Arrested
Mother-in-Law Must Fly
The Prisoner's Strategy
Dec 27 Admiral Nelson's Son
Dec 28 Foolshead Pays a Visit
Mug Chump's Early Morning Excursion

Dec 29 The Story of My Life
Dec 30 The Rheumatic Bridegroom
Dec 31 A Christmas Legend
The Emperor's Staff Officer
1910
Jan 3 Foolshead's Holiday
A Happy New Year
Madam's Favorite
Patrician and Slave
The Poem of Life
The Salted Mine
Seal and Walrus Hunting
The Strolling Players
A Wall Street Chance
Jan 10 Brave Little Heart
The Garibaldi Boy
Hotstuff Takes on the Champions
The Law of Destiny
Monarchs of All Nations
The Rebel's Fate
The Terrors of the Family
Toes and Teeth
Jan 17 Arthur's Little Love Affair
The Freebooter's Captive
Jealousy, a Bad Counsellor
Mammy's Boy Joins the Army
The Miners
Muggins
Romeo and Juliet at the Seaside
A Young Girl's Sacrifice
Jan 18 Out with It
Jan 26 Angler and the Cyclist
Walkaway's New Boots
Jan 27 Bear Hunting
Feb 3 A Heroine of Chance
Feb 10 A Child of the Prairie

Filmograph Co.
1907
Jul 6 The Human Incubator
Work for Your Grub
Jul 13 Troubles of a Gardener
Aug 10 Young Americans

Frank Graham
1905 [month undetermined]
The Colonel's Friend
Dad's a Gentleman Too

Frieda Klug
1909
Nov 13 A Broken Life

G. A. S. Films
1900
Mar [day undetermined]
Photographing the Ghost
1901
Jun 29 The Inexhaustible Cab
1902
May [day undetermined]
The Absent Minded Clerk, Fly Paper and Silk Hat
Sep [day undetermined]
Grandma Threading Her Needle
1903 [month undetermined]
Two Old Sports
Jan [day undetermined]
The Miller and Chimney Sweep
Feb [day undetermined]
Mother Goose Nursery Rhymes
Apr [day undetermined]
The House That Jack Built
A Kiss in the Tunnel
Mary Jane's Mishap; or, Don't Fool with the Parafin
The Monk in the Monastery Wine Cellar
Pa's Comment on the Morning News
Through the Telescope
Jul 18 The Life of a London Bobby
1904 [month undetermined]
The Baby, the Monkey and the Milk Bottle
Jul [day undetermined]
Dorothy's Dream

G. W. Bradenburgh
1909
Jul 3 The Snow Man
Aug 21 Rival Sisters
Aug 28 Little Seller of Cyclamens
Sep 18 Pietro, the Mule Driver
Sep 29 An Embarrassing Portfolio
Oct 18 A Drunkard's Son
Dec 25 Absorbing Tale
Alberno & Rosamunda
Bath Chair
The Deserter
Drama in the Far West
Drama of Villasgne
Electra
Gypsy Child
Interrupted Rendezvous
The Kidnapped King
Magda
Mule Driver's Bride
Original Sausage Tale
Pork Butcher
Pretty Fisher-Woman
Real Brittany
Reincarnated Mummy
Repentance
Silly Billy
Spring Heeled Jack
Suicide Club
Theodora
Turning Out of Time
Who Seeks Finds
The Wonderful Pearl
1910
Jan 15 An Absorbing Tale
Amorous Minstrel
At the Carnival
Bogus General
Boy Scouts
Church Robber
Consequence of a Lie
The Double
Drama Under Richelieu
Episode of French Revolution
A Father's Love
Follow Me
Forced Treatment
Foster Brothers
Getting Rid of Uncle
Good Tramp
Human Squib
Marvelous Indeed
Mind, I Catch You Smoking
Patent Glue
Rivals
Roast Chicken
Simple Simon
The Twine
Tyrolean Tragedy
May 7 Artist's Good Joke
Father's Crime
The Sentinel's Romance
May 9 Beatrice Cenci
May 12 Three Fingered Kate
May 14 Bobby, the Boy Scout
The Convict's Dream
Honor of the Alpine Guide
May 18 The Electric Servant
For the Flag
Wonderful Machine Oil
Jun 4 Adopting a Child
Am I Mad?
Animated Cotton
Battles of Soul
Boy and Purse
Burglar's Dog
A Drink of Goat's Milk
A Father's Mistake
A Fool's Paradise
Gipsy's Baby
Jane of Montressor
The Last of the Dandies
Negro's Gratitude
Picturesque Sentari
Quarrelsome Man
A Race for a Bride
Scratch as Scratch Can
Servant and Guardian
The Slave's Sacrifice
Teaching a Husband a Lesson
A Trip on the Seine
Two Friends

Gaston Méliès *see also* **Georges Méliès**
1907 [month undetermined]
Bakers in Trouble
Delirium in a Studio
Feb 16 Robert Macaire and Bertrand; or, The Troubles of a Hobo and His Pal, in Paris
Mar 30 The Jota
The Mischievous Sketch
Apr 20 Rogues' Tricks
May 4 The Skipping Cheeses
Jun 15 How Bridget's Lover Escaped
Jun 29 Under the Seas
Jul 13 A New Death Penalty
Jul 27 Tunneling the English Channel
Sep 7 The Bewildering Cabinet
A Drink!
Sep 21 The Eclipse; or, The Courtship of the Sun and the Moon
Oct 12 Chopin's Funeral March, Burlesqued
Oct 19 A Story of Eggs
Oct 26 Hamlet, Prince of Denmark
Nov 2 Shakespeare Writing "Julius Caesar"
Nov 9 Good Glue Sticks
Seek and You Shall Find...Trouble
Nov 16 Sightseeing Through Whiskey
Nov 23 Satan in Prison
Nov 30 A Forester Made King
Dec [day undetermined]
An Angelic Servant
1908
Jan 18 In the Bogie Man's Cave
The Knight of Black Art
Jan 25 The King and the Jester
Feb 8 The Good Luck of a "Souse"
Sep 22 Not Guilty
A Tricky Painter's Fate
Sep 29 Buncoed Stage Johnnie
Fun with the Bridal Party
Oct 6 A Grandmother's Story
Oct 17 Honeymoon in a Balloon
Incident from Don Quixote
Oct 27 The Duke's Good Joke
Nov 3 A Love Tragedy in Spain
1909
Oct 13 The Stolen Wireless
Oct 20 For the Cause of Suffrage
Oct 27 Cinderella Up-to-Date
Nov 3 For Sale: A Baby
The Hypnotist's Revenge
Nov 10 A Tumultuous Elopement
Nov 17 The Count's Wooing
Mr. and Mrs. Duff
Nov 24 The Red Star Inn
Dec 1 Fortune Favors the Brave
Seeing Things
Dec 8 The Fatal Ball; or, The Miner's Daughter
Dec 15 The Living Doll

Gaumont Ltd. *see also* **L. Gaumont and Co.; Société des Etablissements L. Gaumont**
Jun 19 The English Derby

George Scott & Co.
1904 [month undetermined]
The Great Toronto Fire, Toronto, Canada, April 19, 1904

Georges Méliès *see also* **Gaston Méliès**
1899
Feb 11 The Devil's Laboratory
The Infernal Palace
Apr 10 A Trip to the Moon
May 13 The Enchanted Inn
May 20 The Cavern of the Demons
Dec 25 Cinderella
1900
Feb [day undetermined]
Faust and Marguerite
Apr 7 Four Heads Better Than One
Apr 21 X Rays
Jun 30 A Mysterious Portrait
Neptune and Amphitrite
The Power of the Cross
Spanish Inquisition
Wrestling Extraordinary
Nov 11 Joan of Arc
1901
Apr 6 The One Man Orchestra
Jul [day undetermined]
The Mysterious Blackboard
Oh! What a Night; or, The Sultan's Dream
The Statue of William Tell
Oct 26 Little Red Riding Hood
Nov 23 A Christmas Dream
Dec [day undetermined]
The Fat and the Lean Wrestling Match
1902 [month undetermined]
The Man with the Rubber Head
May [day undetermined]

The Burglars in the Wine Cellar
The Clown and the Automobile
The Clown with the Portable Body
The Darktown Comedians Trip to Paris
The Devil in the Schoolhouse
The Double Magician and the Magical Head
Herrmann, the Great Conjuror
The Magician and the Human Pump
Troubles in a Tenement House
Wonderful Feats of Vivisection
May 3 Blue Beard
Oct 4 A Trip to the Moon
1903 [month undetermined]
Beggar's Dream
Black Magic
The Bridegroom's Dilemma
The Cabinet Trick of the Davenport Brothers
Christ Walking on the Water
The Cook's Revenge
The Famous Box Trick
Going to Bed Under Difficulties
The Last Cartridges
The Lightning Change Artist
A Lively Cock Fight
A Maiden's Paradise
A Midnight Episode
The Seven Capital Sins
Summoning the Spirits
The Up-to-Date Spiritualism
Jan [day undetermined]
The Artists Model
Cagliostro's Mirror
Fantastic Dining Room
Jewelry Robbery
The Philosopher's Stone
Pygmalion and Galatea
The Three Bacchantes
What Was Found in a High Hat
Jan 31 The Magical Egg
Wonderful Suspension and Evolution
Feb [day undetermined]
The Human Fly
The Impossible Feat of Balancing
The Magician and the Imp
Mephistopheles' School of Magic
Twentieth Century Conjuring
Up-to-Date Surgery
Mar 7 Robinson Crusoe
Mar 14 Buying a Baby
Apr [day undetermined]
Artist and the Dummy
Bachelor's Paradise
Bewitched Dungeon
The Brahmin and the Butterfly
Conjurer and 100 Tricks
Gigantic Devil
The House of Mystery
How He Missed His Train
The Long and Short of It
Miracles of Brahmin
The Miser
The Sorcerer, Prince and the Good Fairy
What Befell the Inventor's Visitor
Apr 13 Gulliver's Travels
Jun 13 Beelzebub's Daughters
The Cake Walk Infernal
The Enchanted Basket
The Marvelous Wreath
Misfortune Never Comes Alone
The Mysterious Box
The Queen's Musketeers
Jun 27 The Enchanted Well
The Inn where No Man Rests
Jul 25 The Drawing Lesson; or, The Living Statue
The Mystical Flame
The Witch's Revenge
Aug 15 The Melomaniac
The Monster
The Oracle of Delphi
A Spiritualistic Photographer
Sep 5 The Fairyland; or, The Kingdom of the Fairies
Sep 26 The Apothicareric Grotto
The Pigeons, Place St. Marc, Venice
Oct 17 The Apparition
The Infernal Caldron
Nov [day undetermined]
Alcrofrisbas, the Master Magician
Nov 7 Jack Jaggs & Dum Dum
Jupiter's Thunderbolts
10 Ladies in an Umbrella
Nov 21 Bob Kick, the Mischievous Kid
Extraordinary Illusions
Dec 9 The Ballet Master's Dream
Dec 12 The Damnation of Faust
Jack and Jim
Dec 19 The Magic Lantern
1904 [month undetermined]
Algerian Goums in the Desert
Arrival and Release of 40,000 Carrying Pigeons at Ambergate, England
The Baby, the Monkey and the Milk Bottle
Clowns
Cook's Joke
Engineers, French Army
Frivolity
Gavotte
Herring Fishing on French Coast
Highwaymen
International Winter Sports
The Interrupted Couple
Japanese Coaling a Man-of-War
Japanese Infantry Morning Drill
Manoeuvres by British Bluejackets, Afloat and Ashore
The Mischievous Kid, the Duck and the Gendarme
The Monkey and the Ice Cream
Mysterious Clock
The Oxford and Cambridge Boat Race
Panoramic View of Chamonix, Alps
Panoramic View of La Mure, France
Panoramic view of Montreux, Switzerland
The Policeman's Mistake
Preparing the Codfish After the Catch
The Russian Army in Manchuria
Secret Procession of the Algerian Tribes
Toys Competition
Trained Dogs
The Up-to-Date Wizard
View of "La Croisette," Cannes, France
Working in the Charcoal Mines in France
Jan 9 The Terrible Turkish Executioner
Jan 16 A Burlesque Highway Robbery in "Gay Paree"
Jan 23 A Moonlight Serenade; or, The Miser Punished.
Feb 6 Tit for Tat; or, A Good Joke on My Head
Feb 13 Every Man His Own Cigar Lighter
The Invisible Sylvia
A Wager Between Two Magicians; or, Jealous of Myself
Mar 5 The Bewitched Trunk
The Fugitive Apparitions
The Untamable Whiskers
Mar 12 The Clock Maker's Dream
Mar 26 Benvenuto Cellini; or, A Curious Evasion
The Imperceptible Transmutations
A Miracle Under the Inquisition
Apr [day undetermined]
How to Disperse the Crowd
Pierrot, Murderer
Apr 2 Faust and Marguerite
Apr 30 The Jolly Russian Prophets
Tchin-Chao, the Chinese Conjuror
May 7 The Wonderful Living Fan
May 28 Fishing in Newfoundland—French Shore
Our Jolly French Students
The Restive Chicken
Typical Algerian 'Ouled Nails' Muslin Dance
Jun 4 The Cook in Trouble
The Devilish Plank
Jun 18 The Impossible Dinner
The Lyons Mail
Jul 2 The Mermaid
Jul 16 Mischances of a Drunkard
The Providence of the Waves; or, The Dream of a Poor Fisherman
Jul 23 The Barber of Seville
Jul 30 Uncle Rube's Birthday
Aug [day undetermined]
Arrival and Departure of the Ice-Crushing Steamer "Baikal" at Baikal, Siberia
The Arrival of the 1st Siberian Sharpshooters at Harbin
"The Bushranger." Attack and Robbery of a Mail Convoy
Cairo and the Nile
Children Romping on the Lawn
Constantinople and the Bosporus
Curious Sights in Burmah and Cashmere (Section 1)
Curious Sights in Burmah and Cashmere (Section 2)
The Execution (Beheading) of One of the Hunchuses (Chinese Bandits) Outside the Walls of Mukden
Extraordinary Feats of Horsemanship
A Fierce Sword Combat at Tokio
The Great International Automobile Race for the Gordon-Bennett Trophy
"He Won't Be Happy till He Gets It"
The International Congress of the Salvation Army
The Japanese Ogre
The Japanese Standard Bearer
The Military Funeral of the "Standard Bearer of the Yalu"
"A Newspaper in Making"
Nobles Leaving the Kremlin, Moscow, After a Reception by Czar
Piraeus and Athens (Greece). A Visit to Piraeus
Piraeus and Athens (Greece). Athens and the Acropolis
Piraeus and Athens (Greece). Hoisting Cattle on Steamer
Procession of the "Holy Blood"
A Regiment of the Japanese Imperial Guards and Engineer Corps off to the Front
A Trip to Palestine. Jaffa and Its Harbor
A Trip to Palestine. Jerusalem, the Holy City
The War Correspondent and the Two Bear Cubs
Oct [day undetermined]
The Shadowy Lady
A Wedding of Correspondence
Oct 22 The Animated Costumes
Simple Simon's Surprise Party
Oct 29 An Impossible Voyage
Dec [day undetermined]
The Firefall
The Grotto of Surprises
The Wandering Jew
Dec 10 The Astonishing Frame
The Wonderful Rose Tree
Dec 24 Christmas Angel
1905 [month undetermined]
The Angler's Nightmare
Apr 8 The King of Sharpshooters
The Living Playing Cards
Apr 22 The Black Imp
May 13 The Crystal Casket
The Lilliputian Minuet
Jun 17 A Mesmerian Experiment
Jun 24 The Palace of the Arabian Nights
Jul 22 Mr. Dauber and the Whimsical Picture
Aug 5 The Chloroform Fiends
The Venetian Looking-Glass
Aug 19 An Adventurous Automobile Trip
Sep [day undetermined]
Stop Thief!
Sep 23 A Crazy Composer
The Enchanted Sedan-Chair
Oct [day undetermined]
Life Saving Up-to-Date
The Scheming Gambler's Paradise
Oct 28 The Tower of London
Nov 4 The Mysterious Island
Unexpected Fireworks
Nov 25 Rip's Dream
1906 [month undetermined]
Punch and Judy
Feb 24 The Inventor Crazybrains and His Wonderful Airship
Mar 3 Chimney Sweep
Apr 7 The Maestro Do-Mi-Sol-Do
A Mix-Up in the Gallery

Apr 14 Old and New Style Conjurors
May 5 A Desperate Crime
Jun 30 Who Looks, Pays
Jul 14 The Tramp and the Mattress Maker
Jul 21 The Hilarious Posters
Sep 29 A Spiritualistic Meeting
Oct 6 A Road Side Inn
Soap Bubbles
Oct 13 The Merry Frolics of Satan
Nov 24 A Seaside Flirtation
Dec 15 The Mysterious Retort
Dec 20 The Witch

1907 [month undetermined]
Bakers in Trouble
Delirium in a Studio
Feb 16 Robert Macaire and Bertrand; or, The Troubles of a Hobo and His Pal, in Paris
Mar 30 The Jota
The Mischievous Sketch
Apr 20 Rogues' Tricks
May 4 The Skipping Cheeses
Jun 15 How Bridget's Lover Escaped
Jun 29 Under the Seas
Jul 13 A New Death Penalty
Jul 27 Tunneling the English Channel
Sep 7 The Bewildering Cabinet
A Drink!
Sep 21 The Eclipse; or, The Courtship of the Sun and the Moon
Oct 12 Chopin's Funeral March, Burlesqued
Oct 19 A Story of Eggs
Oct 26 Hamlet, Prince of Denmark
Nov 2 Shakespeare Writing "Julius Caesar"
Nov 9 Good Glue Sticks
Seek and You Shall Find...Trouble
Nov 16 Sightseeing Through Whiskey
Nov 23 Satan in Prison
Nov 30 A Forester Made King
Dec [day undetermined]
An Angelic Servant

1908
Jan 18 In the Bogie Man's Cave
The Knight of Black Art
Jan 25 The King and the Jester
Feb 8 The Good Luck of a "Souse"
Mar 14 The Genii of Fire
Mar 21 The Dream of an Opium Fiend
Apr 4 A Night with the Masqueraders in Paris
Apr 12 Why That Actor Was Late
Apr 18 The Prophetess of Thebes
Apr 25 Long Distance Wireless Photography
A Mistaken Identity
May 2 Humanity Through Ages
May 9 In the Barber Shop
A Lover's Hazing
May 23 Catholic Centennial Parade
A Fake Diamond Swindler
Justinian's Human Torches
Jun [day undetermined]
No Trifling with Love
Jun 13 Curiosity Punished
Hunting Teddy Bears
The Miser
Side Show Wrestlers
Up-to-Date Clothes Cleaning
Jun 20 Boston Normal School Pageant
The Little Peace-Maker
Lively Pranks with a Fake Python
Jul [day undetermined]
Love and Molasses
Aug [day undetermined]
French Cops Learning English
Oriental Black Art
Aug 22 The Broken Violin
The Forester's Remedy
His First Job
The Indian Sorcerer
The Magic of Catchy Songs
The Mischances of a Photographer
The Mishaps of the New York-Paris Auto Race
The Mystery of the Garrison
Two Crazy Bugs
The Woes of Roller Skates
Sep 5 The Hotel Mix-Up
Two Talented Vagabonds
Sep 22 Not Guilty
A Tricky Painter's Fate
Sep 29 Buncoed Stage Johnnie
Fun with the Bridal Party
Oct [day undetermined]
A Rude Awakening
Oct 6 A Grandmother's Story
Oct 10 The Helping Hand
The Old Footlight Favorite
Oct 17 Honeymoon in a Balloon
Incident from Don Quixote
Oct 27 The Duke's Good Joke
Nov 3 A Love Tragedy in Spain
Nov 10 The Wonderful Charm

1909
Oct 13 The Stolen Wireless
Oct 20 For the Cause of Suffrage
Oct 27 Cinderella Up-to-Date
Nov 3 For Sale: A Baby
The Hypnotist's Revenge
Nov 10 A Tumultuous Elopement
Nov 17 The Count's Wooing
Mr. and Mrs. Duff
Nov 24 The Red Star Inn
Dec 1 Fortune Favors the Brave
Seeing Things
Dec 8 The End of the Tragedy
The Fatal Ball; or, The Miner's Daughter
Dec 15 The Living Doll

1910
Apr 7 Cyclone Pete's Matrimony
Apr 14 Branding a Thief
Apr 21 The First-Born
Apr 28 The Seal of the Church
May 5 The Debt Repaid
May 12 Speed Versus Death
May 19 A Race for a Bride
A Rough Night on the Bridge
May 26 The Paleface Princess
Jun 2 The Padre's Secret
Jun 9 Love's "C. Q. D."
Jun 16 A Texas Joke
Jun 23 The Stranded Actor
White-Doe's Lover
Jun 30 The Ruling Passion
Jul 7 The Little Preacher
Jul 14 The Golden Secret
Jul 21 A Postal Substitute
Jul 28 The Woman in the Case
Aug 4 Mrs. Bargainday's Baby
Aug 11 The Return of Ta-Wa-Wa
Aug 18 Her Winning Way
Aug 25 The Romance of Circle Ranch
Sep 1 Won in the Fifth
Sep 8 Baseball, That's All
Sep 15 In the Mission Shadows
Sep 22 The Salt on the Bird's Tail
Sep 29 A Plucky American Girl
Oct 6 Billy's Sister
Oct 13 Out for Mischief
Oct 20 Uncle Jim
Oct 27 Under the Stars and Bars
Nov 3 Birthday Cigars
Generous Customers
Nov 10 A Mountain Wife
Nov 17 His Sergeant's Stripes
Nov 24 The Cowboys and the Bachelor Girls
Dec 1 Pals
Dec 8 What Great Bear Learned
Dec 15 Old Norris' Gal
Dec 22 A Western Welcome
Dec 29 In the Tall Grass Country

Globe Film Exchange

1909
Mar 7 Episode in Boer War
A Good Excuse
Mar 8 Hurricane of Lovers
A Widow to Console
Mar 10 Giordono Bruno
Mar 11 Love Letter
Prascovia
Mar 13 The Presidential Inauguration Film
Mar 20 The Burden of Debt
Mar 27 An Artist's Model's Jealousy
The Beggar's Daughter
Blind Child's Dog
A Convict's Return
A Criminal Invention
Drama in the Forest
Drama in the Village
Episode of War
Fishing by Dynamite
Follow Me and I'll Pay for Dinner
Gadbin, the Refractory Suicide
The Good Vicar
The Heart of a Mother
Hero of the Prussian War
Husband's Vengeance
I Want a Moustache
Indians and Cowboys
Lily Amuses Herself
Love of Travel
Lucia di Lammermoor
Magic Games
Misfortunes of a Cobbler
The New Servant
The Paralytic
The Parricide
The Pirate's Daughter
The Poor Schoolma'am
The Ripe Cheese
The Servant Question Solved
Tracked by a Dog
The Train Robbers
Tubbie's Terrible Troubles
The Unfaithful Cashier
Apr [day undetermined]
A Moroccan Romance
The Over-Eager Heirs
The Troubles of the Pretty School Marm
May 24 Dreamer

The Gnome Motion Picture Co.

1911
Jan [day undetermined]
Alice in Funnyland
Alice's New Year's Party
The Birth of the Gnomes

Goodfellow Film Mfg. Co.

1907
Sep 7 Disastrous Flirtation
Sep 28 Getting Even
Goldstein's Luck
It Served Them Right
That Dog Gone Dog
Thursday Is My Jonah Day
Oct 26 Belle of Bald-Head Row
Smuggling Chinese into the U.S.A.
True to Life
Nov 23 Faith's Reward

1908
Feb 29 Coke Industry
Cold Storage Love
Esquimaux of Labrador
Michigan vs. Penn Football game
Miracles of a Pain Pad
Outside Inn
Outwitted
Poor Little Match Girl
Rag Picker's Christmas

Graham, Frank *see* **Frank Graham**

The Graphic Cinematograph Co.

1907
Oct 26 The Lover's Charm

1908
Feb 29 His Sweetheart When a Boy
Mar 7 The Boarder Got the Haddock
The Tricky Twins
May 2 A Sacrifice for Work
May 9 The Gambler's Wife

Great Northern Film Co.

1908
Feb 29 Iceboat Racing on Lake St. Clair
Mar 21 The Hot Temper
The Magic Bag
Apr 4 The Robber's Sweetheart
When the House Rent Was Due
Apr 11 Angelo, Tyrant of Padua
Lion Hunting
Stone Industry in Sweden
Willie's Magic Wand
Apr 25 Ihles & Antonio, Boxers
A Modern Naval-Hero
May 2 The Champagne Bottle
A Misalliance
May 9 Dog Training
When Honor Is Lost Everything Is Lost
May 16 Emperor Nero on the Warpath
Sport from All the World
May 23 The Flight from Seraglio
Winter Manoeuvres of the Norwegian Army
May 30 Mr. Drawee

The Will
Jun 7 Texas Tex
Jun 13 A Chance Shot
The Pupa Changes into a Butterfly
Two Gentlemen
Winter Time in Northern Europe
Aug 29 From Bagdad
Summer in North Europe
Sep 5 The Laplanders
The School of Life
Sep 12 The Hand
The Isle of Bornholm
Sep 19 The Lady with the Camellias
Sep 26 The Codfish Industry
The Magic Rubbers
Oct 3 From the Rococo Times
A Sport at the Music Hall
Oct 10 The Countess' Wedding Day
Oct 28 The Arab Band
Nov [day undetermined]
The Acrobats
Automatic Statue
The Bank Director
The Child and the Gigantic Animal
Cupboard Courtship
The Dance of Death
The Dancing Girl
Little Hannie's Last Dream
The Magic Ring
The Mill
On Roller Skates
The Photographer
Pierrot's Death
The Prima Donna of the Ballet Parody
Rheumatism
Rose That Makes Everybody Dance
Scandanavian North
Supper
The Tinder Box
Nov 1 Bear Hunting in Russia
Nov 4 Clearing the Mountain Track
The Watchmaker's Wedding
Nov 7 The Pillory
The Pilot's Daughter
Nov 14 Blind
Nov 18 Othello
Nov 25 Alexandrian Quadrille
Children of the East
Dec 2 Dummies on the Spree
A Sinner
Dec 9 Sherlock Holmes
Dec 16 The Changing of Souls
The Spring Lock
Dec 23 Count Zeppelin's Aerostat
Hercules the Athlete; or, Love Behind the Scenes
Dec 30 The Quack
The Queen's Love (La Tosca)

1909

Jan 6 "Mafia," the Secret Society; or, Sicilian Family Honor
On Guard at the Powder Magazine
Jan 20 Balloon Races
Jim Smith, the Champion Boxer
Life in Russia
The Stepmother: the Spirit of Unkindness and Jealousy Thwarted
Jan 27 Desert Life
The Gnomes
Feb 3 Moving Furniture
Sultan Abdul Hamid, and the Ladies of His Harem
Summer Sport
Feb 6 Badger Hunt
The Wild Man of Borneo
Feb 17 The Caliph's Adventures
Feb 19 The Barber's Christening
James and Catherine; or, Love on a Farm
Feb 26 Sherlock Holmes II: Raffles Escapes from Prison
Mar 3 The Blind Foundling; or, Alone in the World
The False Superintendent
Four Sweethearts
Sherlock Holmes III: The Detectives Adventure in the Gas Cellar
Mar 6 Two Violins
Mar 8 The Capricious Moment
The Chimney Sweep's Birthday
Round the Lake of Constanz and the Rhine Falls
Mar 9 The Student's Predicament
Mar 14 The Artist's Model's Sweetheart
For Love of a Fisher Girl
From the North Cape
Mar 20 The Grand Procession at the King of Siam Jubilee
Sold to Thieves; or, A Deathbed Confession
A Stage Romance; or, An Actor's Love
Mar 31 The Chauffeur's Adventure
In Ancient Egypt
The Non-Stop Motor Bicycle
William Tell: The Liberator of Switzerland
Apr 5 Nat Pinkerton: The Anarchists Plot
Apr 14 Canals of Copenhagen
A Sailor's Life
Apr 16 Bangkok
Apr 17 The Magic Purse
Apr 21 The Artist's Dream
A Walk Through the Zoo
Apr 24 Modern Egypt
The Viking's Love; or, True to His Chief
Apr 28 Nat Pinkerton [Series II]
May 1 Siamese Actors and Actresses Play a Siamese Drama
Winter Sports and Games at Stockholm, Sweden, 1909
May 5 Boxing Match [by Hallberg of Denmark and Young Joe Gaines "Baltimore Black"]
Hard Working Elephants
May 8 Danish Capitol Under Snow
Neptune's Daughter; or, The Shoemaker's Dream
May 12 The Beggarmaid
Moscow
May 17 Summering in the Austrian Alps
Winter Landscapes Round Stockholm
May 19 The Farmer's Grandson
May 22 The Master Detective; or, The Attack on the Strong Room
May 26 The Human Ape; or, Darwin's Triumph
May 29 The Hasty Tempered Father; or, The Blacksmith's Love
Motherly Love of Animals
Jun 2 Cab Number 519
Jun 9 The Brothers Laurento
The Convict
The General and the Sentry
Street Life in North Siam
Jun 12 The Brave Page Boy
Jun 16 The Wages of Sin
Jun 19 The Art of Fencing
Lesson in Cycling
Jun 23 A Woman of the People
Jul 3 A Mother's Grief
The Mouse
Policeman's Rest
The Prince and the Actor
Jul 10 Herring Fishing
The Persistent Lover
Jul 17 Carnival Merriment in the North
A Shadow of the Past
Jul 24 A Clever Nurse
Off the Coast of Norway
Aug 14 A Soldier's Wife
The Spy
Water Sports
Aug 21 False Alarm
Surroundings of Copenhagen
Aug 28 Cowboys in Argentina
The Shell; or, "A Madman's Revenge"
Sep 4 Cycle Rider and the Witch
The Henpecked Husband
Norrkobing
Sep 11 The Gray Dame
Sep 18 How Dr. Nicola Procured the Chinese CAne
Sep 22 Dr. Cook at Copenhagen
Sep 25 The Great Prize
Life on Board a Training Ship
Oct 2 The Cremation
Heroism Reconciles
Oct 9 Adventures of an Emigrant
Vagabond Life
Oct 16 The Red Domino
Oct 23 The Bracelet
Gotacanal—over Norway's Rockies
A Lunatic's Day Off
Nov 3 Dynamite
Hanson & Co.
Life in Dalerne (Sweden)
Nov 6 The Destiny of Paul Wang
Nov 10 The Short-Sighted Governess
The Suicide Woods
Yachting on the Baltic
Nov 13 A Message to Napoleon; or, An Episode in the Life of the Great Prisoner at Elba
Nov 20 A Girl's Cross Roads
Dec 1 A Boy Hero; or, The Fisherman's Son
Trollhattan
Dec 4 Little Willie's Trip to the North Pole
Wrestling
Dec 8 Gerhardi Mohr
Temptations of the Gold Fields; or, The Two Gold Diggers
Dec 18 The Butcher's Bill
In Southern Sweden
Mother-in-Law Crazy with Music
Dec 25 Father's Busy Papering
An Outcast's Christmas

1910

Jan 1 Refreshing Bath
Vengeance; or, The Forester's Sacrifice
Jan 8 Child as Benefactor
Jan 15 Death of the Brigand Chief
Naughty Boys
Jan 22 Anarchists on Board; or, The Thrilling Episode on the S. S. "Slavonia"
Jan 29 The Mystery of the Lama Convent; or, Dr. Nicola in Thibet
Feb 5 The Foxy Soldiers; or, How Schmidt Got to the Masquerade
A Woman's Destiny
Feb 12 Never Despair; or, From Misery to Happiness
Worried to Death
Feb 19 Ruined by His Son
Feb 26 Doctor's Sacrifice
Mar 5 The Mad Drainpipe
A Pleasant Walk
Mar 12 A Wedding During the French Revolution
Mar 19 A Quiet Honeymoon
The Theft of the Diamonds
Mar 26 Tsing Fu, the Yellow Devil
Apr 2 Madame Sans Gene; or, The Duchess of Danzig
Apr 9 Hustling Mr. Brown
A New Burglar Alarm
Apr 16 The Hidden Treasure
Apr 23 The Conjuror
A Day Off
The Four Seasons
Apr 30 Saved from the Sultan's Sentence
May 7 The Somnambulist
May 14 The Club of the Corpulent
The Marvelous Cure; or, The Wonderful Hair-Growing Fluid
May 21 A Father's Grief
May 28 The Eagle's Egg; or The Rival Lovers
Roosevelt in Denmark
Jun 4 The Carman's Dream
The Jump to Death
Jun 11 The Duel
Jun 18 How Brother Cook Was Taught a Lesson
Lake of Lucerne
Jun 25 The Captain's Wife
The Clown and His Dogs
Jul 2 The Sons of the Minister
Jul 9 The Laughing Machine
The Wonderful Cigar
Jul 16 The Prodigal Son
Jul 23 The Elopement
Fabian Cleaning Chimney
Jul 30 Fabian Arranging Curtain Rods
For the Sake of a Child
Aug 6 Magdalene; or, The Workman's Daughter
Aug 13 The Life Boat
The Stolen Policeman
Aug 27 Fabian's Hollow Tooth
A Society Sinner
Sep 3 Fabian Hunting Rats
The Little Drummer Boy
Sep 10 Robinson Crusoe

Sep 17 Danish Dragoons
Fabian Out for a Picnic
Sep 24 Dr. Jekyll and Mr. Hyde; or, A Strange Case
Oct 1 Bird's Eye View from World's Highest Buildings
The Flight across the Atlantic
Oct 8 The Storms of Life
Oct 15 Saved by Bosco
Willie Visits a Moving Picture Show
Oct 22 The Artist's Luck
Oct 29 Who Is She?
Nov 5 A Fatal Picnic
The Jewel Case
Nov 12 Mother-in-Law Arrives
World's Wrestling Champions
Nov 19 The Diamond Swindler
Nov 26 Kean; or, The Prince and the Actor
Dec 3 The Birthday Present
The Ohami Troupe of Acrobats
Dec 10 The Poacher
Dec 17 A Christmas Letter
Dickey's Courtship
Dec 24 The Necklace of the Dead
Dec 31 Bearhunting
The Scarecrow

The Great Western Film Co.

1910
Jan 22 The Devil Is Loose
Jan 29 The Burglar Trap
The Montana Ranchman
On the Firing Line
Mar 14 Nelson-Wolgast Fight
Apr 15 Sam Langford and John Flynn Fight
May 23 Brotherly Love
May 30 The Squatter's Daughter

Grose

1909
Sep 18 A Broken Heart

Haggar & Sons

1903
Apr [day undetermined]
A Duel with Knives
Oct 31 The Poachers

1904
Jun 4 The Bobby Whitewashed
Dec [day undetermined]
Mary in the Dock

1905
Nov [day undetermined]
Convicts' Escape

1907
Feb [day undetermined]
Message from the Sea

1908
Oct 24 The Red Barn Mystery: A Startling Portrayal of the Great Marie Martin Mystery

Hale's Tour Films

1906
Jun 30 From North to South
From Tacoma to Seattle
Trip over Colorado Midland
Trip over Cripple Creek Short Line
Trip Through Colorado
Trip to Chattanooga and Lookout Mountain
A Trip to Jacksonville, Fla.
A Trip to St. Augustine, Fla.
Trip to Southern Colorado
A Trip to Tampa, Fla.
Ute Pass from a Freight Train

1907
Apr 13 Street in Frankfort

Harstyn, Alfred L. & Co. *see* **Alfred L. Harstyn & Co.**

Hepteroux

1909
Apr 3 De Comtess de Valeria

Hepwix

1909
Feb 25 Holland Cheese
May 1 Farmer Jones Goes to the Market
May 8 The Land of the Pharoah
Sep 4 A Jealous Husband
A Troublesome Malady
Dec 25 The Thames in Winter

Hepworth Mfg. Co.

1902 [month undetermined]
Bathing Made Easy
A Frustrated Elopement
Jul [day undetermined]
Explosion of an Automobile

1903
Feb [day undetermined]
Policeman and Automobile
Reversible Donkey Cart
Sep [day undetermined]
At Brighton Beach
At Terrific Speed
The Devonshire Fair
The Devonshire Hunt
The Diamond Robbery
Start of the Gordon-Bennet Cup Race
A Terrific Race
Oct 17 Alice in Wonderland
Oct 31 Hop Picking
Nov [day undetermined]
The Professor
Nov 21 Animated Picture Studio
Automobile Explosion
Fire and Rescue
Hotel and Bath
Letter Came Too Late
Saturday's Shopping
Dec [day undetermined]
How the Old Woman Caught the Omnibus

1904
Jul [day undetermined]
College Sports in England
The Coster's Wedding
The Parson's Cooking Lesson
Stolen Puppy
Aug [day undetermined]
The Bewitched Traveler
Sep [day undetermined]
Boys' Trick on Grandpa
Oct [day undetermined]
Decoyed
An Englishman's Trip to Paris from London
Lover's Crime
Paris from the Seine
Nov [day undetermined]
Coal Heavers
The Lover's Ruse
Over the Hedge
Petticoat Lane on Sunday
A Race for a Kiss
Dec [day undetermined]
The Honeymoon
Lady Plumpton's Motor Car

1905
Jul [day undetermined]
Only Her Brother
Rescued by Rover
Aug [day undetermined]
Falsely Accused
Rehearsing a Play at Home
Terrible Flirt
Nov [day undetermined]
Elopement
Imp No. 2
In an English Hayfield
Indian Babies' Bath
Japanese Funeral
The London Press
The Naughty Boys and Curate
The Puppies
Ride on Sprinkler Car
The Servant Girl's Dream
The Servant Question
The Three Honeymoons
Two Imps

1907
Mar 30 After the Matinee
Black Beauty
Apr 6 The Busy Man
Apr 27 The Doll's Revenge
A Smart Capture
Jun 1 Fatal Leap
The New Policeman
The Tramp's Dream
Jul 20 A Poet and His Babies
Aug 24 The Doll Maker's Daughter
Hair Restorer
Her Friend, the Enemy
Sep 21 The Ghost Holiday
Oct 12 Drink
Little Meg and the Wonderful Lamp
A Soldier's Jealousy
A Too Devoted Wife
Oct 19 Mischievous Girls
A Modern Don Juan
A Sailor's Lass
A Seaside Girl
Nov 16 Dumb Sagacity
A Tramp's Dream of Wealth
Dec 7 A Letter in the Sand
The Rebellious Schoolgirls
The Sticky Bicycle

1908
Jan 18 The Artful Lovers
The Viking's Bride
Feb 29 Painless Extraction
Mar 14 The Curate's Courtship
May 2 The Greedy Girl
Tell-Tale Cinematograph
May 9 The Doctor's Dodge
May 16 Catching a Burglar
A Faithless Friend
Jun 6 Father's Lesson
Jun 13 The Man and His Bottle
Sep 5 The Hidden Hoard
The Tramp and the Purse
Sep 12 The Burglar and the Clock
Sep 26 The Thief at the Casino
Oct 10 A Den of Thieves
Nov 12 Jack in Letter Box
When Women Rule
Nov 25 Soldier's Love Token
Dec 14 A Free Pardon
Harmless Lunatic's Escape
The Serpent's Tooth
Dec 21 Baby's Playmate
Cabby's Sweetheart

1909
Feb 10 Baby's Exciting Ride
Dog Outwits Kidnapper
A Sign from Heaven
Mar 22 Fairy Sword
Goose Chase
Mail Carrier's Daughter
Master and Servant
Royalist's Wife
Apr 17 A Plucky Little Girl
Apr 24 The Deserter
The Dog Came Back
A Heartless Mother
Last Year's Time Table
A Lover's Quarrel
Married Under Difficulties
Professor's Anti-Gravitation
Runaway Kids
A Thoughtless Beauty
The Unlucky Thief
The Villain's Wooing
May 1 The Anarchist's Sweetheart
The Fickle Husband
An Unfortunate Bath
May 8 The Milkman's Wooing
May 15 The Detective's Ruse
In the Service of the King
The Spoilt Child
Unlucky Bridegroom
May 22 Present for Her Husband
River Panorama
Scenes in Ceylon
Why Father Learned to Ride
May 29 Frost Bound Nature
Jun 5 Cat Came Back
Dentist's Daughter
Gypsy's Child
Jun 12 Cingalese Village Life
Special License
Jun 26 Moonlight on the Thames
The Shepherd's Dog
To the Custody of the Father
The Wrong Coat
Jul 3 The Dog and the Bone
Fancy Dress Ball
A Pair of Truants
Jul 17 The Curate of the Races
Inexperienced Angler
Too Much Lobster for Supper
Jul 24 Treacherous Policeman
Aug 14 Race for a Farmer's Cup
Aug 21 The Spy

Story of a Picture
Aug 28 A Cheap Removal
Rival Mesmerists
Sep 4 Biskra, Garden of Allah
The Boy and His Kite
Only a Tramp
Sep 13 The Rivals
Sep 18 Arab Life in South Algeria
Luck of the Cards
A Villain's Downfall
Sep 25 The Little Milliner and the Thief
Necessity Is the Mother of Invention
Oct 7 The Curse of Money
Oct 11 Invisibility
Mistaken Identity
Oct 12 The New Servant
Oct 18 A Drunkard's Son
Oct 21 Artful Dodger
Nov 13 The Cabman's Good Fairy
The Street Arab
Two Little Runaways
1910
Feb 4 Winter Days in Sweden
Feb 8 In Winter's Grip
Mar 2 Lines of the Hand
Apr 26 The Penalty of Beauty
May 2 Safety Suit for Skaters
May 7 Father's Crime
Jun 4 Adopting a Child
Boy and Purse
A Father's Mistake
Gipsy's Baby
Teaching a Husband a Lesson
Jun 21 Tempered with Mercy
Jul 8 A New Hat for Nothing
Hespano
1909
May 15 Carnival at Nice
Holmes and Depue
1905 [month undetermined]
Accelerated (Crazy) Panorama West Shore, Lake of Garda
Accelerated Panorama from Steamer on the Thames, London
"All Day in the Alps" Panorama from Gorner Grat
Arrival of the Stage at Wawona Hotel, Enroute to Yosemite
Arrival of Train at Oberammergau
Bacchanale Fete of Vevey
Battalion of Seaforth Highlanders at the Dublin Horse Show
Battery of Artillery Crossing Ball's Bridge, Limerick, Ireland
Bears Feeding at the Lake Hotel, Yellowstone Park
Bird Rock, Nordland, Norway
The "Black Growler" Steam Vent, Yellowstone Park
Blasting in the Glory Hole of the Treadwell Mine, Alaska
Brink of the Upper Falls of the Yellowstone River, Wyoming
Brink of the Vernal Fall, Yosemite Valley
Busses Passing Mansion House, London
Camp Life of the Esquimaux at Cape Nome, Alaska
Capt. John Hance Telling about His 14th Wife, Grand Cañon, Arizona
Capt. John Hance Telling His Famous Fish Story, Grand Cañon, Arizona
Carrying Passengers Ashore Davidson Glacier, Alaska
The Castle Geyser, Yellowstone Park
Cavalcade Descending Eagle Peak Trail, Yosemite Valley
Cavalcade Descending the Nevada Trail, Yosemite Valley
Cavalcade Descending Trail into Grand Cañon of Arizona
Cavalcade on Trail into Grand Cañon of Arizona
Children and Carts of Oberammergau
Children Turning Catherine Wheels on Derby Day, Epsom Downs
Chinese Cook at Hance's Camp, Grand Cañon, Arizona
Chutes of Imatra, Finland
Cloud Play on Dolomite Peaks, Tyrol
Coaching Down the Merced Grade into Yosemite Valley
Coaching Down the Merced Grade, Merced Cañon, California
Combined Reaper and Thresher at Merced, San Joaquin Valley, California
Congregation Leaving Trondhjlm Cathedral, Norway
Convent Garden Market, London
Corpus Christi Ceremonies, Botzen, Tyrol
Corpus Christi Cortege, Botzen, Tyrol
The "Crazy" Canal Boat, Norway
"Crazy" Congregation Leaving Church, Cortina, Tyrol
The "Crazy" Ferryboat, San Francisco, California
Crazy (or Accelerated) Panoramic Approach to Taku Glacier, Alaska
The "Crazy" Steamer Yellowstone Park
Crazy Steamers on Lake Lucerne
The "Crazy" Tourists on the Nevada Trail, Yosemite Valley
The "Crazy Tourists" on the Pier at Killisnoo, Alaska
The "Crazy" Tourists Starting for the Trail, Yosemite Valley
Crowds Leaving Theatre, Oberammergau
Dance at Esquimaux Camp, Cape Nome, Alaska
Dance of the Autumn Leaves, Vevey Fete
Deer in Wild Park, Goteborg, Sweden
"Dinner Time" at Camp Curry Yosemite Valley
Dog Teams Dawson City Alaska
Earl of Dudley and Party at the Dublin Horse Show
Embarkation by Crane and Barge at Nome City, Alaska
Empire State Express
Esquimaux Dance, Cape Nome, Alaska
Falls at Hellesylt, Norway
Falls at Trollhattan, Sweden
Fashionable Folks Leaving the Dublin Horse Show
Feeding Mush Dogs, Mulato, Alaska
Fire Brigade, Dawson City, Alaska
Fish Carvers, at Fish Market Bergen Norway
Fishmarket, Bergen, Norway
Fjord Panorama from Moving Ship, Norway
Flap-Jack Lady of the Esquimaux, Cape Nome, Alaska
Floral Parade at the Race Track, Moscow, Russia
Floral Parade Festival of Roses, Pasadena, Cal.
Flying Machine, Earl's Court, London
Fourth of July Celebration, Yosemite California
Fourth of July Parade Yosemite California
Gardener's Dance, Vevey Fete
Garland Dance, Vevey Fete
Girls Dancing on Hampstead Heath
The Great Falls of the Yellowstone
Great Fountain Geyser, Yellowstone Park
Henley Regatta, Three Finishes
Herd of Bison, Yellowstone Park
Horse Fair at Randers, Denmark
Hunters Exercising, Dublin Horse Show
Hunters in Exercising Ring, Dublin Horse Show
Hunters Jumping, Dublin Horse Show
Indian Pony Races, Yosemite Valley, California
Irish Constabulary, Keel, Achill Island, Ireland
Irish Hunters Taking the Stone Wall, Dublin Horse Show
An Irish Jig at Dooagh, Achill Island, Ireland
Irish Kiddies Coming out of School, Achill Island
Jaunting Cars Arriving at Dublin Horse Show
Jaunting Cars in Dublin
Jumping by Irish Hunters, Dublin Horse Show
Kiddies Dancing to Hurdy-Gurdy Music, Soho, London
Landing Passengers at Torghattan Island, Norway
Lang (Andreas) and Son, the Two Davids, Oberammergau
Lang (Anton) and Family, Oberammergau
Lapps at Hammerfest, Norway
London Ladies Looking at Lingerie in Oxford Street Windows, London
Lord Lieutenant of Ireland and Escort, Dublin Horse Show
Market Women Leaving the Railway Station at Galway, Ireland
A Matsuri Procession, Yokohama, Japan
Matsuri Procession, Yokohama, Japan
Meran Fire Brigade Going to a Fire
Minuteman Geyser, Yellowstone Park
Nevada Falls, Yosemite Valley
The Old Boys of Dooagh, Achill Island, Iceland
Old Faithful Geyser, Yellowstone Park
Old Spinning Wheel, Dooagh, Achill Island, Ireland
Old Time Miner Rocking for Gold in the Tailings, Klondike
On the Course, Henley Regatta
Panning Gold on a Claim in the Klondike
Panorama from a Moving Train on White Pass & Yukon Railway, Alaska
Panorama from Car on Mendel Pass Cable Railway
Panorama from Car on Oberammergau Electric Railway
Panorama from Dreisprackenspitz Stelvio Pass
Panorama from Electric Car, Lucerne
Panorama from Gortner Grat
Panorama from Moving Steamer on the River Thames, England
Panorama from Moving Train on Albula Railway, Switzerland
Panorama from Moving Train on Murren Electric Railway, Switzerland
Panorama from Train on Visp-Zermatt Railway
Panorama of a Norwegian Fjord from Alvik to Vik from Moving Ship
Panorama of Eismeer, Switzerland
Panorama of Hammerfest Harbor
Panorama of Stockholm from Steam Ferry
Panorama of the Castle of Chillon, Lake Geneva
Panorama of the Course at Henley Showing a Finish
Panorama of the Folgefond Snowfield, Norway
Panorama of the Norwegian Fjord from Moving Ship
Panorama of the Theatre, Vevey Fete
Panorama of Theatre, Vevey Fete
Parade of Passengers Crossing to North Cape, Norway
Passengers Boarding Busses at Hyde Park Corner, London
Passengers Crossing over Open Car, Balley Bunion Railway
Passing Train, Balleybunion Railway, Ireland
Passing Train, Balleybunion Railway, Ireland No. 2
Passing Train (from above) Balleybunion Railway, Ireland
Playful Bear and Dog, Dawson City, Alaska
Procession of Costumed Characters, Vevey Fete
Procession of Performers at Fete of Vevey
Queen Margherita of Italy Arriving in Oberammergau
Railroad Station at Steinach, Tyrol

Railway Panorama from Moving Train Passing Through Conway Castle, Wales
Rapids of the Silver Apron, Yellowstone Park
Religious Cortege on a Rainy Day, Cortina, Tyrol
Retrogressive Jaunting Car, Reverse Panorama from Moving Train, Dublin, Ireland
Reverse Panorama, Maria Theresian Strasse, Innsbruck
Riverside Geyser, Yellowstone Park
Roman Chariot Race, Pasadena, California
Russian Cavalry Review, St. Petersburg
Scene in Oxford Street, London
Scottish Touring Party enroute to the Romsdale, Norway
Scottish Tourist Party in Stockhaeres, Noes, Norway
Servant's Dance, Lake Hotel, Killarney, Ireland
Shepherd's Dance, Vevey Fete
Shooting the Killarney Rapids, Ireland
Slavonian Miners Running to Dinner, Treadwell Mine, Alaska
Sliding River Craft over Boat Railway, River Thames
Sluicing in the Klondike
Spectators Leaving the Theatre Vevey
The "Spokane's" Passengers Descending the Gangplank at Killisnoo Alaska
Squad of Seaforth Highlanders Leaving Bank of Ireland, Dublin
Stage Coaches, Yellowstone Park
Stage Enroute to Hance's Camp, Grand Cañon of Arizona
Stages Leaving Fountain House, Yellowstone Park
Stages Passing Through Wawona Big Tree, Mariposa Grove, California
Storm Effect, Ampezzo Valley
Sunday "Church Parade" Bergen Norway
Sunrise on the Peak, Tyrol
Sunset and Sunrise over the Eiger & Monk Murren
Sunset Clouds over Monte Rosa, Switzerland
Tourist Party in the Gap of Dunloe, Ireland
Tourists Disembarking at Lucerne
Tourists Enroute to the Cliffs of Moher, Ireland
Tourists Leaving Horgheim in the Romsdale Norway
Tourists on the Road to Hotel Stalheim, Norway
Tourists Party near Kate Kearney's Cottage, Gap of Dunloe, Ireland
Tourists Party on the Axenstrasse Switzerland
Train Arriving at Henley Station
Train on the White Pass & Yukon Railway, Alaska
Trains Arriving at Henley Station with Regatta Visitors
Trains on Rigi Railway, Switzerland
Triumphal Entry of Performers, Vevey Fete
Troop of Horse Guards in St. James Park, London
Turntable of the Ballybunion Railway, Ireland
Tyroler Fest, Steinach, Tyrol
Tyrolese Dance, Innsbruck
Tyrolese Dancers Innsbruck
Unloading Fish, Killisnoo Alaska
Upper Fall of the Yellowstone River
Vernal Falls, Yosemite Valley, California
Voringfos Waterfall Norway
Waterfall from the Road, Stalheim, Norway
Whirlpool Rapids, Niagara, U.S.A.
Wooding Up a River Steamer, Yukon River, Alaska
Working a Scraper on Tailings Klondike

1907 [month undetermined]
Cloud Play at Pulfoss, Norway
Geranger Fjord, Sailing from Merock to Hellisute on a Steamer
Gratli Vand and Tourists Passing, Panorama
Laplander Family, Gratli, Norway
Nord Fjord from Loen to Sandene by Steamer [Norway]
Norway: Crazy Canal Boat on the Telemarken Route
Pulfoss, Norway, Pulfoss Falls
Sailing thro the Sognia Fjord on a Steamer from Ballholm to Gudvangen [Norway]

Imp (Independent Moving Picture Co.)
1909
Oct 25 Hiawatha
Nov 1 Love's Stratagem
Nov 8 Destiny
Nov 15 The Brave (?) Policeman
The Forest Ranger's Daughter
Nov 22 Honor Among Thieves
Levitsky Sees the Parade
Nov 29 Her Generous Way
Dec 6 His Last Game
Dec 13 The Two Sons
Dec 20 Lest We Forget
Dec 27 The Awakening of Bess
1910
Jan 3 The Winning Punch
Jan 10 By Right of Love
Jan 17 The Tide of Fortune
Jan 24 Never Again
A Rose of the Philippines
Jan 31 Coquette's Suitors
Sports in the Snow
Feb 7 Justice in the Far North
Feb 14 The Blind Man's Tact
Brown's Gouty Foot
Feb 21 Jane and the Stranger
Feb 24 The Death of Minnehaha
Feb 28 The Governor's Pardon
Mar 3 The New Minister
Mar 7 Mother Love
Mar 10 The Devotion of Women
Mar 14 The Broken Oath
Mar 17 The Time-Lock Safe
Mar 21 His Sick Friend
Stung!
Mar 24 The Stage Note
Stunts on Skates
Mar 28 Transfusion
Mar 31 Hard Cash
Apr 4 The Miser's Daughter
Apr 7 His Second Wife
Apr 11 The Rosary
Apr 14 The Ace of Hearts
Apr 16 In Africa
Apr 18 In War Time
Apr 21 The Maelstrom
Apr 25 The Power of a Smile
Apr 28 The New Shawl
May 2 Two Men
May 5 Aunt Maria's Substitute
May 9 A Rural Romeo
May 12 The Turn of the Dice
May 16 A Doctor's Perfidy
May 19 Fruit and Flowers
May 23 The Eternal Triangle
May 26 A New Excuse
May 30 A Reno Romance
Jun [day undetermined]
The Funeral of King Edward
Jun 2 A Bachelor's Love
Jun 6 The Nichols on a Vacation
Jun 9 A Discontented Woman
Jun 13 The Way to Win
Jun 16 A Policeman's Son
Jun 20 In the Mesh of the Net
Jun 23 A Self-Made Hero
Jun 27 The Brothers' Feud
Jun 30 A Game for Two
Jul 4 The Fallen Idol
Jul 7 The Call of the Circus
Jul 11 Old Heads and Young Hearts
Jul 14 The Saloon Next Door
Jul 18 Summertime
Jul 21 The Mistake
Jul 25 Two Maids
Jul 28 Bear Ye One Another's Burdens
Aug 1 Irony of Fate
Aug 4 Yankeeanna
Aug 8 Once upon a Time
Aug 11 Hoodoo Alarm Clock
Aug 15 Among the Roses
Aug 18 Senator's Double
Aug 22 The Taming of Jane
Aug 25 For the Sunday Edition
Aug 29 The Widow
Sep 1 The Right Girl
Sep 5 You Saved My Life
Sep 8 A Sister's Sacrifice
Sep 12 The Two Daughters
Sep 15 Dixie
Sep 19 Debt
Sep 22 The New Butler
Sep 26 Pressed Roses
Sep 29 Annie
Oct 3 All the World's a Stage
Oct 6 The Deciding Vote
Oct 10 A Game of Hearts
Jes' Plain Dog
Oct 13 The Garden of Fate
Oct 17 Mother and Child
Oct 20 The Fur Coat
Oct 24 The Count of Montebello
Oct 27 The Hobble Skirt
Mendelssohn's Spring Song
Oct 31 The Idol's Eye
Nov 3 Willie
Nov 7 Keeping His Word
Nov 10 The Model's Redemption
Nov 14 The Double
Nov 17 Fortune's Wheel
Nov 21 Their Day of Thanks
Nov 24 The Country Boarder
Nov 28 The Revolving Doors
Dec 1 A Child's Judgment
Dec 5 The Aspirations of Gerald and Percy
Dec 8 'Twixt Loyalty and Love
Dec 12 A Clever Ruse
Faithful Max
Dec 15 The Poor Student
Dec 19 The Crippled Teddy Bear
Dec 21 The Romance of Count de Beaufort
Dec 22 Little Nell's Tobacco
Dec 26 The Unexpected Honeymoon
Dec 29 Unreasonable Jealousy

The International Film Co. *not related to* **The International Film Mfg. Co.**
1896
Nov [day undetermined]
The Old Pier and Waves
The Street Parade
West Point Cadet Cavalry Charge
West Point Cadet Cavalry Drill

The International Film Mfg. Co. *not related to* **The International Film Co.**
1907
Dec 14 Nervy Nat
Tipsy Tinker

International Projecting and Producing Co.
1908
Sep 26 How the Coster Sold the Seeds
1909 [month undetermined]
Robin Hood and His Merry Men
Mar 22 A Borrowed Suit
Brisquet
The Chambermaid and the Dwarf
Chasi Movement
Chasing the Helmet
Compassion
The Dragonad
Dream of Featart
Duplicate Vases
Fairy Sword
Five Minutes Interview
Foolshead, King of Police
Foolshead Wishes to Commit Suicide
For Honor
The Ghost
Goose Chase
Hat Making
High Game
House of Disagreement
In the Land of the Hindoo
Irritable Woman
Italian Cavalry Maneuvers
Jack Has No Clothes
Living Statue

Who Was the Culprit?
Dec 24 Greediness Spoiled Foolshead's Christmas
In Norway
Dec 29 The Rustic
Dec 31 The Jealous Wife's New Year Day
Norwegian Water Falls

J & J Co.
1910
Jul 6 Jeffries-Johnson World's Championship Boxing Contest, Held at Reno, Nevada, July 4, 1910

J. W. Coffroth
1908
Oct 17 [Moran-Appel Fight]
1909
Oct 24 [Johnson-Ketchel Fight Films]
1910
Dec 24 Owen Moran vs. Battling Nelson

James H. White
1899
Nov [day undetermined]
The Battle of Jeffries and Sharkey for Championship of the World
The Jeffries-Sharkey Contest
Love and War

John B. Rock
1908
Jan 18 In the Bogie Man's Cave
The Knight of Black Art
Jan 25 The King and the Jester
Feb 8 The Good Luck of a "Souse"

Jones, Charles J. *see* **Charles J. Jones**

Kalem Co.
1907
Jun 8 Bowser's House Cleaning
The Dog Snatcher
The Gentleman Farmer
The New Hired Man
The Runaway Sleighbelle
Jun 15 The Pony Express
Jul 15 A Hobo Hero
Jul 31 The Tenderfoot
Aug 5 Off for the Day; or the Parson's Picnic
Aug 17 The Book Agent
The Sea Wolf
Sep 7 Dot Leedle German Band
One-Night Stand
Who'll Do the Washing?
Sep 14 Reggy's Camping Party
Sep 21 The Wooing of Miles Standish
Sep 28 Nature Fakirs
Oct 5 The Amateur Detective
Chinese Slave Smuggling
Oct 14 The Red Man's Way
The Spring Gun
Oct 19 Nathan Hale
Oct 26 The Gold Brick
It Was Mother-in-Law
Nov 2 Bill Butt-in and the Burglars
The Rival Motorists
Nov 9 His Affinity
Troubles of a Tramp
Nov 16 A Dramatic Rehearsal
The Lost Mine
Woman, Cruel Woman
Nov 23 School Days
Dec 7 Ben Hur
Dec 28 The Merry Widow
1908
Jan 4 The Days of '61
Jan 18 Back to the Farm
Dogs of Fashion
Mountaineers
Quack Doctor
Feb 1 Under the Star Spangled Banner
Feb 8 Evangeline
Feb 29 The Banan' Man
College Days
The Stowaway
Mar 7 Captain Kidd
Henry Hudson
Washington at Valley Forge
'Way Down East
Mar 28 Scarlet Letter
Apr 4 The Moonshiner's Daughter
Apr 11 Presidential Possibilities
Apr 25 The Legend of Sleepy Hollow
May 8 Dolly, the Circus Queen
Night Riders
The Under Dog
The White Squaw
With the Fleet in Frisco
May 16 Kidnapped for Hate
Jun 6 An American Soldier
Jun 13 Man Hunt
Sailor in Philippines
Jun 27 Held by Bandits
Jun 28 Lady Audley's Secret
Jul 18 Dynamite Man
Flight of the "June Bug"
Jul 25 The Girl Nihilist
Mrs. Guinness, the Female Bluebeard
The New Hired Girl
The Renegade
The Taft Pictures
Aug 8 A Gypsy Girl's Love
The Walls of Sing Sing
Aug 22 The Padrone
Aug 29 The Frontierman's Bride
Robin Hood
Sep 12 The Great Yellowstone Park Hold-Up
Sep 19 As You Like It
Old Sleuth, the Detective
Sep 26 The Mystery of the Bride, in Black and White
Oct 3 The Girl I Left Behind Me
The Mystery of the Bride in White
Oct 16 Fire at Sea
Oct 25 Caught in the Web
Oct 30 The Half Breed
Nov 2 Humpty-Dumpty Circus
Nov 7 David and Goliath
Jerusalem in the Time of Christ
Nov 13 The Railroad Detective
Nov 20 Hannah Dustin: The Border Wars of New England
Nov 27 A Ragged Hero
Dec 4 For Love of Country: American Patriotism in the Colonial Wars
Dec 11 Maggie, the Dock Rat
Dec 18 The Molly Maguires; or, Labor Wars in the Coal Mines
Dec 25 Red Cloud, the Indian Gambler
1909
Jan 1 The Trial of the White Man
Jan 8 A Florida Feud; or, Love in the Everglades
Jan 15 The Sponge Fishers of Cuba
Jan 22 The Girl at the Old Mill
Jan 29 The Octoroon: The Story of the Turpentine Forest
Feb 5 The Detectives of the Italian Bureau
Feb 12 The High Diver
Feb 19 The Making of a Champion
Sporting Days in the Old South
Feb 26 The New Minister; or, The Drunkard's Daughter
Mar 5 The Old Soldier's Story.
Mar 12 The Seminole's Vengeance; or The Slave Catchers of Florida
Mar 19 The Cracker's Bride
Hungry Hank's Hallucination
Mar 26 The Mysterious Double; or, The Two Girls Who Looked Alike
Apr 2 The Fish Pirates; or, The Game Warden's Test
Apr 6 The Orange Grower's Daughter
Apr 9 Any Port in a Storm
A Trip to the Wonderland of America
Apr 23 The Northern Schoolmaster
Apr 30 The Artist and the Girl
May 7 Love's Triumphs
May 14 Good for Evil
May 15 The Ponce de Leon Fete
May 21 The Girl Spy: An Incident of the Civil War
May 28 A Pig in a Poke
A Poor Wife's Devotion
Jun 4 A Child of the Sea
$5,000 Reward
The Omnibus Taxicab
Jun 11 The Little Angel of Roaring Springs
The Mystic Swing
Jun 18 Mardi Gras in Havana
A Priest of the Wilderness: Father Jogue's Mission to the Iroquois
Jun 25 Famine in the Forest; or, The Trapper's Gratitude
Never Again
Jul 2 The Japanese Invasion
Jul 9 A Soldier of the U. S. Army
Jul 16 The Escape from Andersonville
Jul 23 Tickle Mary
The Tom-Boy
Jul 30 The Factory Girl
Aug 6 Traced by a Kodak
Aug 13 Out of Work
Aug 20 The Dog Circus Rehearsal
Queen of the Quarry
Aug 27 The Conspirators: An Incident of a South American Revolution
The Dyspeptic and His Double
Sep 3 The Pay Car
Sep 10 Hiram's Bride
Sep 17 The Story of a Rose
Winning a Dinner
Sep 24 The Winning Boat
Oct 1 The Mystery of the "Sleeper" Trunk
Oct 8 The Hand-Organ Man
Oct 15 The Man and the Girl
Oct 22 A Brother's Wrong
Oct 24 [Johnson-Ketchel Fight Films]
Oct 29 The Girl Scout; or the Canadian Contingent in the Boer War
Oct 30 [Otto T. Bannard, Republican Candidate for Mayor of New York]
Nov 5 The Cattle Thieves
Nov 12 Dora
Nov 19 The Pale Face's Wooing
Nov 26 The Governor's Daughter
Dec 3 The Geisha Who Saved Japan
Dec 10 The Rally Round the Flag
Dec 17 The Law of the Mountains
Dec 24 The Cardboard Baby
Dec 31 A Slave to Drink
1910
Jan 7 The Deacon's Daughter
Jan 14 The Romance of a Trained Nurse
Jan 21 The Magic Flower
Jan 28 The Man Who Lost
Feb 2 The Step-Mother
Feb 4 The Little Old Men of the Woods
Feb 9 The Confederate Spy
Feb 11 The Feud
Feb 16 The Fisherman's Granddaughter
Feb 18 "That's What They All Say"
The Trapper and the Redskins
Feb 23 The Miser's Child
Feb 25 The Indian Scout's Vengeance
Mar 2 The Court Jester
The Treachery of the Pequots
Mar 4 The Girl Thief
Mar 9 Her Soldier Sweetheart
Mar 11 The Robber Baron
Mar 16 The Seminole's Trust
Mar 18 The Enchanted Castle
Mar 23 The Girl and the Bandit
Mar 25 The Railway Mail Clerk
Mar 30 Lo, the Poor Indian
Red Hawk's Last Raid
Apr 1 The Further Adventures of the Girl Spy
Apr 6 The Uprising of the Utes
Wandering Wilfred's April Fool's Day
Apr 8 The Gipsy Girl's Love
Apr 13 The Old Fiddler
Apr 15 The Forager
Apr 20 Fighting the Iroquois in Canada
Through the Tunnel
Apr 22 The Bravest Girl in the South
Apr 27 The Sacred Turquoise of the Zuni
Apr 29 The Love Romance of the Girl Spy
May 4 Chief Blackfoot's Vindication
May 6 The Egret Hunter
May 11 In the Dark Valley
May 13 Between Love and Duty
May 18 The Aztec Sacrifice
May 20 The Seminole Halfbreeds
May 25 The Cliff Dwellers
May 27 Friends
Jun 1 The Navajo's Bride
Jun 3 The Castaways
Jun 8 The Price of Jealousy
Jun 10 The Exiled Chief
Jun 15 Mistaken Identity
Jun 17 The White Captive of the Sioux
Jun 22 The Wanderers
Jun 24 The Cheyenne Raiders; or, Kit Carson on the Santa Fe Trail
Jun 29 The Miner's Sacrifice
Jul 1 The Colonel's Errand
Jul 6 The Hero Engineer

Jul 8 Attacked by Arapahoes; or, The Gold Seekers and the Indians
Jul 13 Grandmother
Jul 15 Corporal Truman's War Story
Jul 20 Haunted by Conscience
Jul 22 Brave Hearts; or, Saved from the Indians by a Woman's Wit
Jul 27 A Daughter in Dixie
Jul 29 Pure Gold
Aug 3 A Colonial Belle
Aug 5 The Legend of Scar-Face
Aug 10 The Borrowed Baby
Aug 12 The Call of the Blood
Aug 17 The Perversity of Fate
Aug 19 Running Fire
True to His Trust
Aug 24 The Romany Wife
Aug 26 The Canadian Moonshiners
Aug 31 A Game with Fame
Sep 2 White Man's Money, the Indian Curse
Sep 7 Mama's Birthday Present
Sep 9 The Cow Puncher's Sweetheart
Sep 14 The Little Mother
Sep 16 A Leap for Life
Sep 21 The Japanese Spy
Sep 23 The Conspiracy of Pontiac; or, At Fort Detroit in 1763
Sep 28 The Heart of Edna Leslie
Sep 30 Spotted Snake's Schooling
Oct 5 The Engineer's Sweetheart
Oct 7 Big Elk's Turndown
Oct 12 45 Minutes from Broadway
Oct 14 Winona
Oct 19 The Tyranny of the Dark
Oct 21 The Education of Elizabeth
Oct 26 The Strongest Tie
Oct 28 Indian Pete's Gratitude
Nov 2 The Rough Rider's Romance
Nov 4 Silver Cloud's Sacrifice
Nov 9 For a Woman's Honor
Nov 11 The Attack on Fort Ridgely
Nov 16 A Drama of the Present
Nov 18 Jim Bridger's Indian Bride
Nov 19 The Way of Life
Nov 23 The Lad from Old Ireland
Nov 25 The Roses of the Virgin
Nov 30 The Touch of a Child's Hand
Up the Thames to Westminster
Dec 2 Elder Alden's Indian Ward
Dec 7 Rachel
Dec 9 The Rescue of Molly Finney
Dec 14 Seth's Temptation
Dec 16 Her Indian Mother
Dec 21 The Little Spreewald Maiden
Dec 23 When Lovers Part
Dec 28 The Girl Spy Before Vicksburg
Dec 30 The Stranger

Kearton, Cherry, Ltd. *see* **Cherry Kearton, Ltd.**

Kinemacolor Co. of America, Inc.
1910
Jul 15 [Kinemacolor Films]
Dec [day undetermined]
[Artillery Drill at West Point]
Biskra and the Sahara Desert
Farm Yard Friends
Floral Fiends
From Bud to Blossom
[Lake Garda, Northern Italy]
[Liquors and Cigars]
[The London Fire Brigade]
[London Zoological Gardens]
Motor and Yacht Boating in England
[Picking Strawberries]
[Potomac Falls, Virginia]
[The Richmond Horse Show]
Scenes in Algeria
A Visit to the Seaside at Brighton Beach, England
[Washington's Home and Ground at Mount Vernon]

Klank & Herman
1910
Jul 2 Gotch-Zbyszko World's Championship Wrestling Match

Kleine Optical Co.
1898 [month undetermined]
The Armenian Archbishop, Rome
Capuchin Monks, Rome
Corpus Christi Procession, Orvieto
The Mysterious Midgets
The Vatican Guards, Rome
Jan [day undetermined]
Surf Dashing Against England's Rocky Coast
Apr [day undetermined]
"Me and My Two Friends"
Aug [day undetermined]
A Hotel Fire in Paris, and Rescue by Parisian Pompiers
Nov [day undetermined]
Pope Leo XIII in Carriage
Pope Leo XIII in Sedan Chair, No. 1
Pope Leo XIII in Vatican Garden, No. 1
Pope Leo XIII Walking at Twilight, No. 1
Dec [day undetermined]
Pope Leo XIII Being Seated Bestowing Blessing Surrounded by Swiss Guards, No. 107
Pope Leo XIII in Canopy Chair, No. 100
1900 [month undetermined]
Kansas City Fire Department, Winners of the World's Championship at the Paris Exposition
Queen Victoria's Last Visit to Ireland
1902 [month undetermined]
A Frustrated Elopement
May [day undetermined]
Going to Bed Under Difficulties
The Magical Hen
What Happened to the Inquisitive Janitor
Jul [day undetermined]
Explosion of an Automobile
Sep [day undetermined]
A Photographic Contortion
A Telephone Romance
Oct 4 A Trip to the Moon
Nov [day undetermined]
Battleship "Odin"
"Be Good Again"
Berlin Fire Department
Clever Horsemanship
The Elephant's Bath
Emperor William at the Danzig Manoeuvres
The Flying Train
A Flying Wedge
Fun on a Sand Hill
George J. Marck and His Lions
German Cavalry Fording a River
German Railway Service
A German Torpedo Boat Flotilla in Action
The Gourmand
In a German Bath
The Rivals
Rulers of Half the World
A Run by the Berlin Fire Department, Berlin, Germany
Torpedo Boat "G-89"
The Valiant Pig
1903 [month undetermined]
Brothers of the Misericordia, Rome
Jan [day undetermined]
Life of an American Fireman
The Soldier's Return
Jan 17 The Ascent of Mount Blanc
Picture Hanging Extraordinary
Feb [day undetermined]
Battle Royal
Before and After
Oh! Shut Up
Policeman and Automobile
Reversible Donkey Cart
Seattle Fire Department in Action
Smashing a Jersey Mosquito
Up-to-Date Surgery
Feb 14 Disagreeable Railroad Passengers
Mar 7 Robinson Crusoe
Mar 14 The Delhi Camp Railway
Logging in Canada
On the Bow River Horse Ranch at Cochrane, North West Territory
Spearing Salmon in the Rivers of the North West Territory
Mar 21 The Workman's Paradise
Apr [day undetermined]
Ascending a Rock-Chimney on the Grand Charmoz, 11,293 feet
Ascent and Descent of the Aiguilles Des Grandes Charmoz, 11,293 feet
Breaking a Bronco
The Broncho Horse Race
A Gorgeous Pageant of Princes
The Grand Panorama from the Great Schreckhorn, 13,500 feet
A Japanese Wrestling Match
Life and Passion of Christ
Man's Best Friend
Mary Jane's Mishap; or, Don't Fool with the Parafin
Over London Bridge
Panorama of Alpine Peaks
The Pines of the Rockies
Push Ball
Review of Native Chiefs at the Durbar
Review of the Chiefs at the Durbar
Ski Jumping Competition
Apr 11 Acrobatic Sisters Daines
Apr 13 Gulliver's Travels
May [day undetermined]
Animated Dolls
"I Want My Dinner"
Lehigh Valley Black Diamond Express
Life of an English Fireman
Miniature Prize Fighters
Modern House Furnishing Methods
The Still Alarm
Window Cleaner's Mishap
May 16 The Gambler's Crime
Smiles and Tears
Spring Cleaning
Jun [day undetermined]
The Cook Visits the Parlor
Down the Bamboo Slide
The Giddy Dancing Master
Gloomy Gus Gets the Best of It
Happy Hooligan Interferes
How Mike Got the Soap in His Eyes
The Professor of the Drama
Jun 6 Little Tom Thumb
Jul [day undetermined]
The American Soldier in Love and War [Number 1]
The American Soldier in Love and War [Number 2]
The American Soldier in Love and War [Number 3]
Catch-as-Catch-Can Wrestling Bout
The Fate of a Gossip
Happy Hooligan Earns His Dinner
Happy Hooligan in a Trap
How Buttons Got Even with the Butler
Laplanders at Home
Pres. Roosevelt's Fourth of July Oration
The Unfaithful Wife: Murder and Suicide [Part 3]
The Unfaithful Wife: The Fight [Part 2]
The Unfaithful Wife: The Lover [Part 1]
Why Foxy Grandpa Escaped a Ducking
Willie's Camera
Jul 11 Sleeping Beauty
Aug [day undetermined]
The Burglar
The Kidnapper: At Work [Part 1]
The Kidnapper: In the Den [Part 2]
The Kidnapper: The Rescue [Part 3]
A Search for Evidence
Street Car Chivalry
Subub Surprises the Burglar
A Total Accident
The Wages of Sin: A—Murder
The Wages of Sin: B—Retribution
"What Are the Wild Waves Saying Sister?"
The Widow
Aug 1 The Elixir of Life
Sep [day undetermined]
At Brighton Beach
At Terrific Speed
At the Ford, India. Across the Ravi River
Baby Class at Lunch
The Busy Bee
The Camera Fiend
Coasting in the Alps
A Daring Daylight Burglary
The Devonshire Hunt

The Diamond Robbery
From London to Brighton
The Galloping Tongas
How to Get a Wife and Baby
The Insurance Collector
Lady Bountiful Visits the Murphys on Wash Day
The Llamas of Thibet
Love in a Perilous Place
A Norwegian Waterfall
Reproduction of Jeffries-Corbett Contest
Rising Panorama of a Norwegian Waterfall
The Sand Baby
A Terrific Race
Trained Baby Elephants
Trained Dogs and Elephants
The Wise Elephant
Sep 5 The Fairyland; or, The Kingdom of the Fairies
Sep 18 Trailed by Bloodhounds
Oct [day undetermined]
Blessed Is the Peacemaker
Casey's Nightmare
A Catch of Hard Shell Crabs
Happy Hooligan's Interrupted Lunch
Hooligan as a Safe Robber
Hooligan's Roller Skates
Kit Carson
The Pioneers
Rent Collector
Scenes at the Zoo
She Fell Fainting into His Arms
Springfield Fire Department
Toodles and Her Strawberry Tart
Uncle Reuben at the Waldorf
The Wrath of a Jealous Wife
"You Will Send Me to Bed, Eh?"
Oct 17 Alice in Wonderland
Oct 31 Hop Picking
Moses in the Bullrushes
The Poachers
Nov [day undetermined]
Firing the Cook
Next!
Off His Beat
Poor Hooligan, So Hungry Too!
The Professor
What Happened in the Tunnel
Nov 7 Life of Napoleon
Nov 21 Animated Picture Studio
Automobile Explosion
Cruelty on the High Seas
The Deserter
Down Below
Fire and Rescue
The Ghost in the Graveyard
Hotel and Bath
Letter Came Too Late
Murphy's Wake
The New Cook
Nicholas Nickleby
Over the Garden Wall
A Pugilistic Parson
Quarrelsome Neighbors
Saturday's Shopping
A Trip to Southend
Nov 28 Attack on Chinese Mission
The Bather
Bicycle Dive
Jack's Return
Stop Thief
Dec [day undetermined]
Almost a King
Clarence the Cop
The Great Train Robbery
How the Old Woman Caught the Omnibus
The Pickpocket
Waiting for Bill
Dec 12 At Work in a Peat Bog
Cliff Scenery at the Fabbins
A Coach Drive from Glengariffe to Kenmore
A Drove of Wild Welsh Mountain Ponies
Elopement a la Mode
Irish Peasants Bringing Their Milk to a Cooperative Creamery
The Mono-Railway Between Listowel and Ballybunion, Ireland
Panorama of the Lakes of Killarney from Hotel
Polo Match for the Championship at Hurlingham
Scenes in an Irish Bacon Factory
Scenes in an Irish Market Place
Scenes of a New Forest Pony Fair
Scenes of Irish Cottage Life
Scenes on a Welsh Pony Farm
Shooting the Rapids of Killarney
A Trip Through the Gap of Dunloe
A Trip to the Giant's Causeway
Trout Fishing, Landing Three Pounder
Wild Mountain Ponies on Dartmoor

1904

Jan [day undetermined]
The Arbitrator
The Boy Under the Table
Chameleon Climbing
The Cheese Mites
A Drop of Ink
The Easy Chair
The Escaped Lunatic
Love and Jealousy Behind the Scenes
The Power of Authority
Pugilistic Toads
The Story the Biograph Told
Tied to Her Apron Strings
The Toad's Luncheon
What Burglar Bill Found in the Safe
Jan 2 The Somnambulist
William Tell
Jan 16 Puss in Boots
Jan 23 Amusing Changes
Charming Enchantment
The Kiddies and the Poultry
Jan 30 Dogs and Rats
Feb [day undetermined]
A Bucket of Cream Ale
Casey's Frightful Dream
Clarence, the Cop, on the Feed Store Beat
Flour and Feed
An Old Bachelor
Those Troublesome Boys
Feb 6 Devil's Pot
The Little Greedy Beggar
Marie Antoinette
Metamorphosis of the King of Spades
Feb 23 Jack Sheppard—The Robbery of the Mail Coach
The Salmon Fisheries of Vancouver
Mar [day undetermined]
The Battle of the Yalu
Mr. Jack Entertains in His Office
Mar 5 The Untamable Whiskers
Mar 12 Babe and Dog
Scenes on Every Floor
Mar 26 The Passion Play
Wonderful Hair Restorer
Apr [day undetermined]
Nervy Nat
Tracked by Bloodhounds; or, A Lynching at Cripple Creek
The Waif; or, Out in the Street
Apr 2 Faust and Marguerite
Apr 9 The Revolving Table
Apr 20 Battle of Chemulpo Bay
Japanese Sailors Fencing with Capstan Bars
Japs Loading and Firing a Six Pounder
Panorama Russian Battleship "Gronobia"
Russian Outposts Attacked by Japanese
Warship in Nagasaki Harbor, Japan
Apr 25 Falls of the Clyde
The Prodigal Son
The Sailor's Rival
Samson and Delilah
The Smugglers
The Wrong Poison
May [day undetermined]
Igorotte Savages, St. Louis Exposition
Panorama St. Louis Exposition from Launch
Parade of Characters (Asia in America) St. Louis Exposition
May 21 Barnum's Trunk
Jun [day undetermined]
Elephants Shooting the Chutes at Luna Park [Coney Island]
The Eviction
Filipino Scouts, Musical Drill, St. Louis Exposition
The Magic Hat
Military Tactics
"Personal"
Princess Rajah Dance with Chair, St. Louis Exposition
Princess Rajah, Dance Without Chair
Willful Murder
Jun 4 The Apple Woman
The Bobby Whitewashed
The Cook's Lovers
The Coster's Wedding
Jun 18 European Idea of Christopher Columbus Discovering America
Metamorphosis of a Butterfly
A Scandal on the Staircase
Jun 25 Chased by a Dog
The Child Stealers
Naval Attack on Port Arthur
The Office Boy's Revenge
The Postman Whitewashed
Raid on a Coiner's Den
Jul [day undetermined]
Boxing Horses, Luna Park, Coney Island
Capture and Execution of Spies by Russians
College Sports in England
Dorothy's Dream
Equestrian Bear
Giovanni and His Trained Parrots
Hauling in the Fish
Holland Submarine Boat Tests
Japanese Varieties
Outing, Mystic Shriners, Atlantic City, New Jersey
Parade, Mystic Shriners, Atlantic City, New Jersey
"Pollywogs" 71st Regiment, N. G. S. N. Y., Initiating Raw Recruits
President Roosevelt's Home-coming
The Racing Chutes at Dreamland
Scenes in an Infant Orphan Asylum
Speed Test W. K. Vanderbilt, Jr.'s "Tarantula"
Such Is Life
Jul 9 A Disaster in a Colliery
Jul 23 Annie's Love Story
The Barber of Seville
Dance Plastiques
Japanese Ambush
The Nest Robbers
Tour in Italy
Jul 30 Bold Bank Robbery
Aug [day undetermined]
The Bewitched Traveler
The Coney Island Beach Patrol
Fighting the Flames, Dreamland
The Moonshiner
Parade of Floats, St. Louis Exposition
The Widow and the Only Man
Aug 20 Lookout at Port Arthur
Aug 27 A Boar Hunt
Orla and His Trained Dogs
Sep [day undetermined]
Fencing Contest Between Japanese Soldiers, Manchuria
The Hero of Liao Yang
Japanese Fan Dance
Japanese Flag Dance
Japanese Warriors in Ancient Battle Scene
The Miser's Daughter
Panorama from German Building, World's Fair
The Pig That Came to Life
The Quarrelsome Washerwoman
Sep 3 Indians and Cowboys
The Strike
The Wrestling Donkey
Sep 7 Linen Shop
Sep 10 Joseph Sold by His Brothers
Life of an American Soldier
Sep 17 Burglar and Girls
The Convict's Escape
A Kiss and a Tumble
Sep 24 Drama in the Air

The Waterfalls of Glengariffe
White Rat and Young
The White Rats
Winning a Pair of Gloves
With the German Fleet
Wonderful Hat
The Wrestling Elephant
Yantai Episode

1906 [month undetermined]
Army Pack Train Bringing Supplies

Apr [day undetermined]
Aerial Billiard Playing
At Mukden

1907 [month undetermined]
Bakers in Trouble
Delirium in a Studio

Jan [day undetermined]
Beaver Hunt
Cheating Justice
Deer Hunt
Following in Father's Footsteps
The Gardener's Nap
The Little Globe Trotter
Making Champagne
Reformation
The Stepmother
Trial Trip of the Airship "La Patrie"
Whale Fishing
Willie Goodchild Visits His Auntie

Jan 26 Infants at Breakfast
An Officer's Honor
Professor in Difficulties
The Stolen Bride
Stormy Winds Do Blow

Feb [day undetermined]
Animated Stamp Pad
Baby Cries
The Bad Son
Brown Goes to Mother
Burglar and Policeman
Going Away for Holiday
Her First Cake
His First Cigarette
Indian Customs
The Man Monkey
Man Who Hangs Himself
Message from the Sea
The Miner's Daughter
Moonlight on the Ocean
My Master's Coffee Service
My Servant Is a Jewel
My Wife's Birthday
A New Toboggan
Policeman Has an Idea
Skiing in Norway
Snowballing
Soldier to Colonel
Stolen Child
Two Rival Peasants
When Friends Meet
Winter in Switzerland
Wrestling Match, Hackenschmidt

Feb 2 The Artful Dodger
Carnival at Venice
College Boy's First Love
The Double Life
Faces and Grimaces
The Little Rascal's Tricks
Playing a Trick on the Gardener
Playing Truant
Two Cabbies for One Passenger
The Underworld of Paris
Wanted, a Governess
The Zoo at London, Part I
The Zoo at London, Part II

Feb 16 Robert Macaire and Bertrand; or, The Troubles of a Hobo and His Pal, in Paris

Mar [day undetermined]
Cassimir's Night Out
The Conjuror's Pupil
Conquering the Dolomites
Disturbing His Rest
The Electric Belt
First Snowball
Flashes from Fun City
The Hand of the Artist
His First Camera
His First Dinner at Father-in-Law's
Is Marriage a Failure?
Little Lord Mayor
Looking for Lodgings
Mrs. Smithson's Portrait
Moonlight on Lake
Oh! That Molar
Paying Off Scores
Puck's Pranks on Suburbanite
Quaint Holland
The Runaway Van
Traveling Menagerie
Trip to Borneo
Turkey Raffle
Woman Up-to-Date
Wonders of Canada

Mar 2 The Birthday Celebration
A Set of Dishes

Mar 9 The Murderer

Mar 30 The Arlberg Railway
The Atlantic Voyage
Berlin to Rome
Captain Kidd and His Pirates
The Carving Doctor
A Championship Won on a Foul
Curfew Shall Not Ring Tonight
Dolomite Towers
Flirting on the Sands
The Jota
The Magic Bottle
The Mischievous Sketch
Napoleon and Sentry
An Old Coat Story
Parody on Toreador
Take Good Care of Baby
Universal Winter Sports
The Yokel's Love Affair

Apr [day undetermined]
Curious Carriage of Klobenstein
How the World Lives
In a Picture Frame
Miss Kellerman's Diving Feats
Picnic Hampers
Tirolean Dance

Apr 13 Artist's Model
Baby's Peril
An Early Round with the Milkman
Street in Frankfort

Apr 20 Chasing a Sausage
Father! Mother Wants You
Lady Cabby
The Poet's Bid for Fame
Rogues' Tricks
The Terrorist's Remorse
The Vacuum Cleaner

Apr 27 Clowns and Statue
Great Boxing Contest
A Pig in Society
Servant's Revenge
The Smugglers

May 4 The Park Keeper
The Skipping Cheeses

May 11 The Hundred Dollar Bill; or, The Tramp Couldn't Get It Changed

May 18 Barometer of Love
Clever Detective
Cream Eating Contest
Interesting Reading
Kind-Hearted Girl
Robbing a Bird's Nest
Stealing Candies
Trouble at a Wedding

May 25 Beating the Landlord
Buying a Ladder
Catastrophe in the Alps
A Child's Cunning
The Cup and Ball
Dog and the Tramp
Janitor's Tea Party
Nurse Takes a Walk
Rogie Falls and Salmon Fishing
Salome
Sign of the Times
Two Cents Worth of Cheese
The Village Celebration

Jun 1 The Human Clock
An Icy Day
A Perfect Nuisance
A Trip Through the Holy Land
Winter Amusements

Jun 10 The Child Accuser
Dressing in a Hurry
The Faithful Dog; or, True to the End
Saved from the Wreck
The Substitute Drug Clerk

Jun 15 How Bridget's Lover Escaped
Whose Hat Is It?

Jun 22 Moving Under Difficulties
She Won't Pay Her Rent

Jun 24 Comedy Cartoons
Shoeing the Mail Carrier

Jun 25 The Amateur Rider
Mother-in-Law at the White City

Jun 26 The Legless Runner
The Toilet of an Ocean Greyhound

Jun 27 The Near-Sighted Cyclist

Jun 29 Humors of Amateur Golf
The Orange Peel
Under the Seas

Jul 6 Diabolo, the Japanese Top Spinner

Jul 8 Fatality
Scratch My Back
The Soldier's Helmet
Union Workers Spoil the Food

Jul 13 A New Death Penalty

Jul 18 Croker's Horse Winning the Derby

Jul 20 The Dog Acrobats
Don't Pay Rent—Move
Drama in a Spanish Inn
Getting His Change
Prisoner's Escape
Servant's Generosity
Too Stout
Unlucky Interference

Jul 27 Drawing Teacher
Looking for the Medal
The Poacher's Daughter
Tunneling the English Channel

Aug 3 Buying a Donkey

Aug 10 The Dummy
From Cairo to Khartoum
The Gypsies; or, The Abduction
The Helmet
Life Boat Manoeuvres
Life in a South African Gold Mine
Looking at a Balloon
The Magnetized Man
Spring Gardening
Torpedo Attack on H. M. S. Dreadnought

Aug 17 The New Stag Hunt
Poor but Proud

Aug 24 A Big Take of Tunny Fish
The Blacksmith's Strike
The Dervish's Revenge
In an Armchair
Too Many Children
The Tooth Ache
Wandering Willie's Luck

Sep 7 After the Fancy Dress Ball
The Bewildering Cabinet
A Drink!
Hanky Panky Cards
Irish Scenes and Types
Life in a Burmah Teak Forest
The Life of Bee
A Modern Mother
The Motorcyclist
Mount Pilatus Railway
Rail Lying at Crewe
The Strength of Cheese
The Warwick Pageant

Sep 14 The Good Wine
Unlucky Substitution
Who Owns the Pear?

Sep 16 Absent Mindedness
The Amateur Hunter
Art Student's Frivolities
A Baffled Burglar
The Fly
Roumania, Its Citizens and Soldiers
Woodcutter's Daughter

Sep 21 The Eclipse; or, The Courtship of the Sun and the Moon

Sep 23 Amongst the Reptiles
Carl Hagenbeck's Wild Animal Park at Hamburg, Germany
A Chinaman Visits London
Conway to Dublin
Dogs Tracking Burglars
A First Class Restaurant
Glimpses of Erin
Those Boys Again

Uncle's Heritage
Winan's Horses
Wipe Off Your Feet, Please
Sep 26 The Persevering Lover
Sep 30 Coffee Plantation
The Horse That Ate the Baby
How Isaac Won the Cop
Tamer Hopkins
The Undergraduate
Oct 1 A Doctor's Conscience
Fisherman's Luck
The Great Victoria Falls
Oct 5 Late for His Wedding
Returning Good for Evil
Oct 7 The Foster Cabby
The Haunted Bedroom
Madame Goes Shopping
Slavery by Circumstance
Tyrolean Alps in the Winter
A Would Be Champion
Oct 12 Asking His Way
Chopin's Funeral March, Burlesqued
Oct 14 Crazed by a Fad
Farmer Giles' Geese
Rubberneck Reuben
Oct 19 Jealousy Punished
Picturesque Wales
Slate Quarries in North Wales
A Story of Eggs
There Is a Rat in the Room
Oct 26 Brain Storm
Hamlet, Prince of Denmark
Oct 28 The Absent-Minded Professor
The Adventures of a Bath Chair
The Athletic Dude
De Beers Diamond Mines, Kimberly, S.A.
An Episode of the Paris Commune
Floor Polisher
A Four Year Old Heroine
The Glue
The Irresistible Piano
Naval Manoeuvres
Onions Make People Weep
Picturesque Brittany
Smoke Without Fire
The Thieving Umbrella
Through Hong Kong
Towed by an Automobile
Volunteer's Betrothal
Who Has Stolen My Bicycle
Nov 2 Shakespeare Writing "Julius Caesar"
Nov 4 Accidents Will Happen
An Anonymous Letter
A Good Husband
King Edward on H.M.S. Dreadnought
Launch of the British Battleship Bellerophon
The Lost Bass Drum; or, Where Is That Louie?
Raising the Wind
The White Shoes; or, Looking Out for His Banknote
A Wig Made To Order
Nov 9 Good Glue Sticks
Seek and You Shall Find...Trouble
A Shilling Short in Wages
Nov 11 A Rolling Bed
The Stolen Shoes
Nov 14 The Bomb
Grandfather and the Kitten
Turning the Tables
Nov 16 Sightseeing Through Whiskey
Nov 23 Satan in Prison
Nov 30 Bad Boy's Joke
The Colonial Soldier
Comrade Rations
Daughter's Lover in Difficulties
A Forester Made King
French Recruit
Misadventures of a Street Singer
Reedham Boys' Aquatic Sports
Simple-Minded Peasant
Stolen Child's Career
The Tattler
Unlucky Trousers
Dec [day undetermined]
Against the Law
An Angelic Servant
Bulgarian Army
Cabman Mystified
The Cashier
Deaf and Dumb
Diabolo Nightmare
Hatred
Highly Scented Bouquet
Love Levels All Ranks
When the Devil Drives
Willing to Oblige
Youthful Hackenschmidts
Dec 2 Darkest Hour
Harvest Celebration
The Lady Athlete; or, The Jiu Jitsu Downs the Footpads
Tommy's Box of Tools
Wrong Righted
Dec 7 A Soldier Must Obey Orders
When Cherries are Ripe
Dec 9 Notice to Quit
Saving His Country's Flag
Sunday with the Boss
Dec 21 Father Buys a Hand Roller
Dec 23 The Gamekeeper's Dog
Nurse's Travels
A Red Hot Day
The Romance of a Fisherman's Daughter
The Waters of Life
Dec 27 Burns-Moir
Dec 28 Hunting above the Clouds
Dec 30 Cook's Fiancé
False Start
A Tight Fix

1908

Jan 6 The Affianced
Buying a Cow
The Hypnotist's Pranks
The Marvelous Powder
Jan 18 Anxious Day for Mother
The Gay Vagabonds
Girl's Dream
Ingenuity Conquers
Medal Winner
Mr. Sleepy Head
Pied Piper of Hamlin
A Restful Ride
Tenor with Leather Lungs
Valiant Son
Jan 20 The Water Babies; or, The Little Chimney Sweep
Feb 3 Ancient Headgear
Gainsborough Hat
Music Hath Charms
Oh, That Cat
The Scout
Feb 10 The Strenuous War Veteran's Story
Uncle's Clock
Feb 17 An Episode of the French Revolution
Satan's Little Jaunt
The Soldier's Wedding
Feb 29 Hackenschmidt-Rodgers Wrestling Match
Mar 14 Custom Officer's Pull
Electric Sword
Student's Joke on the Porter
Mar 21 The Cook Wins
Good-Hearted Sailor
His Daughter's Voice
Willie's Magic Wand
Apr 11 Antics of Two Spirited Citizens
The Astrologer
Boy and the Coalman
The Captain's Wives
Champion Wrestling Bear
A Contagious Nervousness
The Deserter
A Dislocated Veteran
Doctor's Lunch
The Dog's Scent
The Door-Keeper's Substitute
The Downfall of the Burglars' Trust
The Enchanted Boots
Free Admission
The Gambling Demon
The Half-Moon Tavern
A Lady Who Likes a Moustache
Lion's Tilting Contest
Ma-in-Law Mesmerized
Nephew's Luck
The Novice Tight-Rope Walker
The Professor's Secret
The Scandalous Boys
Trip to Norway
Apr 18 The Accordion
The Animated Dummy
A Bear in the Flat
Butler's Misdeed
The Coal Man's Savings
The Consequences of a Night Out
The Crusaders' Return
The Drama on a Roof
The Enchanted Guitar
False Money
Ice Cream Jack
Improvised Servant
International Illusionist
Just Retribution
Love's Victim
The Miracle
The Misadventures of an Equilibrist
Railway Tragedy
The Shepherd
The Ski-ing Maniac
The Spirit
Tony Has Eaten Garlic
Woman's Forbearance
Youthful Treasure Seekers
May 2 The Accusing Vision
Alone at Last
The Baby Strike
Bad Bargain
Bad Boys
The Best Glue
Biarritz
Cat and Dog Show
Concealed Love
Fiji Islanders
The First Kiss
The First Lottery Prize
Forgotten Ones
Fox Hunting
Frolicsome Powders
Funeral of the Late King of Portugal
Generous Policeman
Greediness Punished
Harvesting
John Is No More a Child
Kidnapped by Gypsies
Life and Customs of Naples
Love's Sacrifice
Marvelous Pacifier
Men and Women
A Mistake in the Dark
Mistaken Identity
Mr. Smith's Difficulties in the Shoe Store
Mrs. Stebbins' Suspicions Unfounded
Modern Hotel
Mysterious Stranger
The Near-Sighted Hunter
No Divorce Wanted
The Outcast Heroine
Oyster Farming
Panorama of Venice
The Pastry Cook
Poor Aunt Matilda
Poor Schoolmistress
The Price of a Favor
A Priest's Conscience
A Ride in a Subway
The Rival Lovers
Rival Sherlock Holmes
Shooting Party
Ski Contest
Soldiers in the Italian Alps
The Statue of Rocco
The Stolen Dagger
A Story of the 17th Century
The Sugar Industry
Tommy the Fireman
Wrongly Charged
May 9 The Bargeman's Son
Bloodless Duel
Bogus Magic Powder
The Boxing Englishman
Country about Rome
Dreams and Realities
Environs of Naples
Excursion to Montreal
Gathering Indian Figs

The Guileless Country Lassie
Indiscreetness of the Kinematograph
The Lover's Tribulation
Manoeuvres of Artillery
The Memory of His Mother
My Cabby Wife
Peasant's Difficulties in Society
Sicily Illustrated
The Smokeless Stove
Tommy Has the Spleen
The Two Guides
The Wand Has Lost Its Magic
May 16 Always Too Late
Australian Sports and Pastimes
Awkward Orderly
The Basket Maker's Daughter
Bertie's Sweetheart
A Bohemian Romance
The Bond
Canine Sagacity
The Carnival at Nice
Chair, If You Please
An Extraordinary Overcoat
Fond of His Paper
A Good Thief
The Little Flower Girl
Lost Pocketbook
Madam Is Capricious
The Magic Powder
Meeting of Kings and Queens
Motoring over the Alps
The Perverse Statues
The Ramming of H. M. S. Gladiator by the St. Paul
A Red Man's Justice
Running for Office
St. Patrick's Day in New York
Schoolboy's Joke
Scotland
Stolen Boots
The Strong Man's Discretion
These Gentlemen Are with Me
Thirty Years After
The Uncle from America
Why Smith Left Home
The Winning Number
The Young Protector
Youthful Samaritan
May 30 Around the Coast of Brittany
Artificial Preparation of the Diamond
Battle of Flowers in Nice
Carnival at Nice
The Castle Ghosts
Expensive Marriage
Hedge Hog Coat
Inventor's Son's Downfall
Magical Suit of Armor
The Marriage of a French Soldier
A Mean Man
The Minstrel's Sacrifice
Mischievous Diabolo
Mr. Farman's Airship
Oxford and Cambridge Boat Race
The Persistent Beggar
Red Man's Revenge
Remorseful Son
River Avon
River in Norway
Rugby Match
Sammy's Sucker
Steel Industry
Student's Predicament
Unlucky Luck
Warsmen at Play
Jun 13 Cast Off by His Father
The Cat's Revenge
Clarinet Solo
The Effective Hair Grower
Faithful Governess Rewarded
Held for Ransom
Magic Dice
Mr. Brown Has a Tile Loose
The Old Actor
The Paralytic's Vengeance
Penniless Poet's Luck
A Poor Knight and the Duke's Daughter
The Saloon-Keeper's Nightmare
Three Sportsmen and a Hat
Usefulness at an End
Jun 20 The Book Agent
The Chauffeur's Dream
Driven by Hunger
The Handy Man at Play
The Matterhorn
Music Which Hath No Charms
The Pony Express
A Russian Bear Hunt
Swiss Peasants' Festival
Tribulations of a Mayor
A Trip on the Venetian Canals
The Viege Zermatt Railway
Jul 4 Ancient Rome
A Bird of Freedom
Blessing the Boats in Arcachon
Bull Fight in Arcachon
The Closing Hour
Constantinople
The Dressmaker's Surprise
A Fine Easter Egg
Fox Hunting
French Dairy Farm
A Gendarme's Tribulations
Heavy Seas
A Love Affair of the Olden Days
Love and Fortune
Mr. Smith, the New Recruit
Niagara Falls in Winter
The Nihilist
Porcelain Industry
Precipitated Removal
Riviera in Motor Car
Scenes in Sicily
Silk Hats Ironed
Swiss Alps
They Want a Divorce
An Unfortunate Mistake
Unrequited Love
Who Owns the Basket?
Jul 6 Artificial Brooding
A Bad Boy
A Costly Coat
Fountains of Rome
Frightened by Burglars
In the Riviera
Keenest of the Two
The Leaking Glue Pot
Lessons in Jiu Jitsu
Love and Hatred
The Mediterranean Fleet
Nothing to Declare; or, Bested by Custom Officials
The Pastry Cook's Misfortune
A Poacher's Trick
Posthumous Jealousy
St. Marc Place
A Second-Hand Camera
The Troublesome Fly
The Two Pickpockets
Views of New York
Wanted: A Colored Servant
Jul 11 The Organ-Grinder's Daughter
The Shipwreckers
The Stone Breaker
A Trip Through Savoy
Jul 13 The Best Remedy
Consoling the Widow
Disappointing Rehearsal
Father Is Late! Go Fetch Him
Good Night Clown
The Grand Canal in Venice
His Girl's Last Wish
The Lady with the Beard; or, Misfortune to Fortune
Sammy's Idea
The Simpleton
The Substitute Automatic Servant
Through the Oural Mountains
A Tricky Uncle
The Triumph of Love
Trying to Get Rid of a Bad Dollar
The Two Brothers
Two Little Motorists
A Walking Tree
Wandering Musician
Jul 25 I Won One Hundred Thousand
Matrimonial Stages
A New Fruit
Obeying Her Mother
Off to Morocco
On the War Path
Physical Phenomena
A Pleasant Evening at the Theatre
Promoted Corporal
The Saw Mill
The Story of the King of Fregola
Sturdy Sailor's Honor
Three Maiden Ladies and a Bull
Too Polite
The Torrent
Transformation with a Hat Rim
The Tyrant Feudal Lord
Venice and the Lagoon
A Wolf in Sheep's Clothing
Aug 1 Baffled Lover
Black Eyed Susan
The Chronic Life-Saver
A Comical Execution
The Dear Little Heart
An Embarrassing Gift
Fishing Boats in the Ocean
Follow Your Leader and the Master Follows Last
His Mother's Melody
An Interesting Conversation
The Killing Remorse
The Learned Dr. Cornelius
Making of Tomato Sauce
The Miraculous Flowers
Out of Patience
Overflowing in Italy
Peasant and Prince
The Policeman and the Cook
The Roses
Secret of Hypnotism
Sensational Duel
The Smuggler Automobilist
Too Hungry to Eat
The Tramp's Daughter
War Episode
Aug 8 The Brigand's Daughter
The Child's Forgiveness
A Country Drama
Flower Fete on the Bois de Boulogne
The French Airship La Republique
German Dragoons Crossing the Elbe
Grand Prix Motor Race at Dieppe
The Gypsy and the Painter
The Gypsy Model
Moscow Under Water
The Rag Pickers' Wedding
Reedham Boys' Festival Drill
Royal Voyage to Canada
The Tempter
Trooping the Colour
Tyrolean Alps Customs
Aug 15 The Cheese Race
Human Vultures
Moscow Under Water
Mother's Darling
Music Hall Agent's Dream
The Picture
The Poor Man, Homeless, Wants to Go to Prison
Undesirable Tenants
Aug 29 The Bewitched Tricycle
The Duck's Finish
The Enchanted Mantle
A False Alarm
The Happy Man's Shirt
The Hayseed's Bargain
Napoleon and the English Sailor
Pretty Flower Girl
Riches, Poverty and Honesty
Yusuf the Pirate
Sep 12 Amateur Brigands
The Asphalters' Dilemma
The Blind Woman's Daughter
The Dover Pageant
The Ever-Laughing Gentleman
Goodwood Races
The Hand-Cart Race
King Edward and the German Emperor at Friedrichshof
The Lightning Postcard Artist
The Marathon Race
Olympic Regatta at Henley
Paper Tearing
Quebec
Quebec to Niagara
The Signalman's Sweetheart

The Son's Crime
A Stern Father
The Swimming Master
Traveling Through Russia
The Wrong Lottery Number
Sep 19 The Luckless Spike
Salome
Oct 3 The Blusterer
Caught Red Handed
Panic in a Village
Romeo and Juliet
Sammy's Saw
Oct 6 The Chances of Life
A Wedding Under Terror
Oct 7 Manon Lescaut
Oct 9 Fantastic Magic
Spending a Holiday
What a Funny Horse
Oct 10 Andalousie
Any Rags
Boxing Mania
Military Swimming Championship
A Mother's Fault
Romance of a School Teacher
A Stiff Neck
Oct 12 Federal Fete of Wrestling, and Alpino Sports
Oct 13 Jerusalem
Political Speeches
Oct 14 Miscalculated Revenge
Oct 16 The Court in Session
The Puppet's Nightmare
Victim of Heroism
Oct 17 Elixir of Youth
Water Bailiff's Daughter
Oct 19 Shadows of Night
A Treasure of a Pig
The Witty Ghost
Oct 20 The Cashier's Romance
High Jumping at Hurlingham
Madeira Wicker Chair Industry
The Puppet Man's Dream
Trials of an Educator
Wheelwright's Daughter
Oct 21 A Father's Will
Picturesque Switzerland
Prince Kin Kin's Malady
Somnambulic (sic) Bell Ringer
The Voice of the Heart
Oct 23 Over the Hubarthal Railroad
Oct 24 The Little Rope Dancer
The Power of Habit
Preparing for Combat
Sunny Madeira
Oct 26 The Convict and the Dove
Desperately in Love
The Queen's Lover
When Pa Went Fishing
The World of Magic
Oct 27 Bald Headed Actor and Fair Lady
He Did Not Know He Was a Monk
Jane Shore
Oct 28 First Love Triumphs
Motor Boat Races
Oct 29 Closed on Sundays
The Flower Thief
Pa and the Girls
Oct 30 The Galley Slave's Return
The Sofa Bed
Oct 31 Cyrano de Bergerac
Daisy, the Pretty Typewriter
Hamlet, Duel Scene with Laertes
In the Barber Shop
The Moon's Gift
Precieuses Ridicules
Thunderbolt on the Mill
What It Might Have Been
With Care
Nov 2 The Automatic Hotel
A Child's Debt
The Fair Young Lady's Telephone Communication
A House of Cards
The Legend of Prometheus
The Mock Baronets
My Daughter Will Only Marry a Strong Man
The Necklace
Sold by His Parents
Thou Shalt Not Love
The Young Tramp
Nov 7 The Four-Legged Thief
Nov 8 Roman Colonel's Bravado
Nov 9 At Night
Feeding a Serpent
The First Servant
The Gorges of the Tarn
The Grandfather's Tobacco
The Lake of Garda, Italy
Looking for the Bald Heads
Monty Buys a Motor
No Race Suicide
Out to Nurse
The Quick Change Mesmerist
The Scare Crow
A Tyrolean Paradise
A Woman's Aid
Nov 14 The Prehistoric Man
Nov 17 Caesar Up-to-Date
Champion Globe Trotter
Disappearing Watch
The Doctor's Wife
Having the Time of Their Lives
The Jester's Daughter
The Prize Camel
A Serious Joke
Tarn Mountains
A Visit to Compiegne and Pierrefond
Waterproof Willie
The Young Poacher
Nov 21 A Love Affair in Toyland
The Swimming Lesson
Dec 1 A Child's Devotion
Jack of All Trades
Looking for the Sea Serpent
Making Home Attractive
Dec 5 The Bewildered Professor
She Could Be Happy with Either
Thompson's Night with the Police
Dec 12 Animated Matches
Fighting for Gold
A Good Watch Dog
The Madman of the Cliff
Timid Dwellers
Dec 14 Christmas: From the Birth of Christ to the Twentieth Century
A Fatal Present
Father and the Kids
An Interior Cyclone
Dec 19 The Angel of Nativity
Braving Death to Save a Life
The Christmas of a Poacher
The Good Playthings
Grimsol, the Mischievous Goblin
Hobo on a Bike
The Little Chimney Sweeps
The Police Band
The Poor Singer Girl
Troubles of an Airship
Dec 21 The Black Sheep
George and Margaret
The Holy Hermit
In Bondage
In the Nick of Time
The Little Marchioness and the Young Shepherdess
Dec 28 Acrobatic Toys
Bobby Has a Pipe Dream
Current News Items
The Devil's Sale
A Heavy Head Piece
Not Guilty

1909

Jan 9 For Baby's Sake
Jan 11 The Bewitched Breton
Converted
A Gypsy's Jealousy
Visions of a Goldsmith
Jan 18 Champion Suffragist
A Hot Remedy
Married Twice
The Persevering Insurance Agent
Troubled Artists
Jan 23 For Mother's Sake
For Their Country's Cause
Messina After the Earthquake
Trip on Rhodesian Railway
Feb 1 Gendarme's Horses
The Guard's Alarm
The Living Wreck
A Mother's Heart
The Nurse's Romance
Feb 9 The Miner's Will
A Sportive Puppet
Feb 10 The Double's Fate
Following Mother's Footsteps
Feb 13 The Ambassador's Dispatch Case
Jones Has Bought a Phonograph
Feb 16 The American Fleet at Sydney, New South Wales
The Hand of a Wizard
Outwitted
Feb 17 Grandfather
A Strong Draught
Feb 20 Bernard Palissy
The Chinamen
Feb 23 An Obstinate Umbrella
Some Milk for Baby
Feb 24 Joel's Wedding
Polka on Brain
Feb 27 The Foxy Husband
The Prince and the Dwarf
Mar 2 The Piano Teacher
Mar 3 An Embarrassing Present
The Sailor's Belt
Mar 6 In Sore Straits
Walking on His Toes
Mar 9 The Blacksmith's Bride
The Postal Clerk
Mar 10 Mother-in-Law's Day in the Country
Rivalry
South American Indians
Mar 13 Buttes Chaumont After a Snow Storm
The Irresolute Man
The Smoking Lamp
Mar 16 Innocent, but Found Guilty
The Musician's Dream
Mar 17 The Celebrated Mountain Climbers
Cremation on the River Ganges
Master Goes Shopping
Mar 20 The Secretary's Revenge
The Survivor's Story
Mar 23 Japanese Magic
Pocket Policeman
Mar 24 I Have Lost Toby
Mr. Pallet Goes Out Landscaping
Mar 27 Across the Border
Mar 30 The Policewoman
The Politician
Mar 31 Arabian Horsemen
Benevolent Employer
Apr 3 Benares
Uncle's Palm Tree
Apr 6 The Prodigal Daughter
The Riviera
Apr 7 Inviting His Boss for Dinner
On the Brink of the Precipice
Apr 10 He Advertised for His Dog
The Tramp at the Masquerade
Apr 13 Charlie Forced to Find a Job
In the Lime Light
Apr 14 Policeman in Action
Under Suspicion
Apr 17 A Bachelor's Persistence
A Plot Foiled
Apr 20 The Poet's Vision
Too Much Advice
Apr 21 Magic Eggs
Sentenced to Death
Apr 24 Found on the Rocks
The Squire and the Noble Lord
Apr 27 The Automatic Monkey
Before and After
How They Propose
Apr 28 An Unwritten Letter
May 1 Dream Spectres
Two Ladies and a Beggar
May 5 Forgotten
The Peddler's Reward
May 8 Four Footed Hawkshaw
New Pain Killer
May 11 The Cyclone Sneezer
An Uneven Keel
May 12 Bamboo Pole Equilibrist
A Timely Apparition
Wilbur Wright and His Majesty King Edward VII
May 15 The Actor's Mother
Free Champagne
May 18 He Couldn't Lose Her

The Policeman Sleeps
The World Upset
May 19 Caught on the Cliffs
Objections Overcome
May 22 A Guest's Predicament
Justice or Mercy
May 25 A Blind Man of Jerusalem
The Glories of Sunset
May 26 How Jones Paid His Debts
Panther Hunting on the Isle of Java
May 29 The Accusing Double
Jun 1 The Cripple's Marriage
The Good Omen
Jun 2 Magic Carpet
Tender Cords
Jun 5 Saved from Conviction
Jun 8 A Mother's Choice
Jun 9 The Race Course
Two Heroes
Jun 12 Historical Fan
A Strong Diet
Jun 15 Hunted to the End
A Paying Business
Jun 16 Modern Algeria
The New Footman
Jun 19 The Cry from the Well
Jun 22 A Good Hearted Policeman
The Troublesome Lamppost
Jun 23 Mrs. Simpson's Attractiveness
Winning a Princess
Jun 26 Stung by a Bee
The Wrong Medicine
Jun 29 No Appetite for Dinner
Saved from the Flames
Jun 30 The Phantom Sirens
Rulers of the World
Jul 3 Dissolution of Parliament
The Hand Bell
The Sunny South of France
Jul 6 The Coin Collector
Raised in the Country
Jul 7 Exciting Steeple-Chase
The Pretty Fisher-Maiden
Jul 10 A Bad Case
Visions of Mother
Jul 13 Only a Dream
A Sure Cure
Jul 14 Conchita, the Spanish Belle
The Wizard's Walking Stick
Jul 17 In the Hands of the Enemy
The Lost Tie
Jul 20 The Man in the Moon
True to His Master
Jul 21 The King's Conspiracy
Jul 24 Brown's Moving Day
The Monk's Mother
Jul 27 The Last Confession
Papa's Hat
Jul 28 His Rival's Hand
Parks in Berlin
Jul 31 An Easy Job
In Hot Water
Aug 3 The Morning After
The Sentinel on Duty
Aug 4 Stripping a Forest in Winter
The Turning Point
Aug 7 Baby Is King
The Hidden Treasure
Aug 10 Cyclist's Horn
Dust in His Eye
Retaliation
Aug 11 Laurels
A Long Reach
Aug 14 The Foxy Farmer
Peddling Shoes
Why She Didn't Marry
Aug 17 The Cobbler and the Millionaire
The Little Drummer of 1792
Aug 18 Building Barrels
The Strikers
Aug 21 The King's Protege
Up the Mountain from Hong Kong
Aug 24 The Frock Coat
Too Gentlemanly
Aug 25 Broken Ties
Sevres Porcelain
Aug 28 A Generous Emperor
Great Event at Podunk
The Horse and the Haystack
Aug 31 The French Battleship "Justice"
Professor Puddenhead's Patents
Sep 1 An Awakened Conscience
Magic Cartoons
Sep 4 In Hot Pursuit
Romantic Italy
Sep 7 First Airships Crossing the English Channel
The Mason's Paradise
Sep 8 Glimpses of Paris
The Stolen Gems
Sep 11 Mozart's Last Requiem
Sep 14 The Fiddle and the Fan
Her Busy Day
The Tricky Dummies
Sep 15 The Fatal Love
Pontine Marshes, Italy
Sep 18 Aeroplane Contests at Rheims
The Farmer's Treasure
Sep 21 Saved from the Quicksands
Taking in a Reef
Sep 22 Dropped from the Clouds
The Legend of the Lighthouse
Sep 25 All for a Nickel
On the Crest of the Waves
Sep 28 Breach of Promise
Wife or Child
Sep 29 Chasing the Ball
Love, the Conqueror
Oct 2 The Masterpiece
Oct 5 Breaking the Bank
The Pill Box
Oct 6 Gambling Passion
Yachting off Cowes
Oct 9 Sleuth and the Wig
Wedding Party in Luna Park
Oct 12 Convicting Evidence
How He Earned His Medal
Oct 13 Liquid Air
Princess of the Sea
Oct 16 Alphonse, the Dead Shot
The Broken Violin
One-Legged Pete and Pat
Oct 19 His Helpmate
Husband's Strategy
Oct 20 Casting Bread upon the Water
Crown Prince of Germany Drilling Battery
Oct 23 Country Life in a Flat
Tickled to Death
Oct 26 The Old Lord of Ventnor
Oct 27 Awakened Memories
Volcanoes of Java
Oct 30 A Barrow Race
The Song of the Cradle
Nov 2 Don Quixote
Mystic Melodies
Nov 3 Tale of the Fiddle
"Ursula," World's Fastest Motor Boat
Nov 6 The Warrior's Sacrifice
Nov 9 A Peace Agitator
The Pigmy World
Telltale Reflections
Nov 10 A Heavy Gale at Biarritz
The Robber Duke
Nov 13 Harlequin's Nightmare
The Rhymester's Ruse
Nov 16 A Convict's Heroism
A Set of Teeth
Nov 17 Fighting Suffragettes
Workhouse to Mansion
Nov 20 Moon for Your Love
Visions of a Nag
Nov 23 Belle of the Harvest
Marriage of Love
Nov 24 A Heart's Devotion
Tulips
Nov 27 Mix-Up at Court
The Village Scare
Nov 30 The Broken Vase
In the Consomme
Dec 1 Consul Crosses the Atlantic
Dec 4 How to Get a City Job
X-Ray Glasses
Dec 7 In a Pickle
Listen
Top-Heavy Mary
Dec 8 Capturing the North Pole; or, How He Cook'ed Peary's Record
The Secret Chamber
Dec 11 Daughters of Poverty
Dec 14 The Life Buoy
Nothing Is Ever Lost
Dec 15 The Red Signal
Switzerland, Conquering the Alps
Dec 18 Cambyses, King of Persia
The Shepherd's Flute
Dec 21 The Stranger
Dec 22 Fiorella, the Bandit's Daughter
From the Fighting Top of a Battleship in Action
Dec 25 The Greek Slave's Passion
Dec 28 A Clever Sleuth
Hush Money
Dec 29 Battle in the Clouds
The Park of Caserta

1910

Jan 1 The Legion of Honor
Jan 4 The Avenging Dentist
The Wreck at Sea
Jan 5 Shanghai of To-day
Tragedy at the Mill
Jan 8 On the Bank of the River
A Seat in the Balcony
Jan 11 Shooting in the Haunted Woods
Towser's New Job
Jan 12 Home of the Gypsies
True to His Oath
Jan 15 Decorated by the Emperor
Railway on the Ice Sea
Jan 18 Fatal Fascination
Getting Square with the Inventor
Jan 19 The Coast Guard
Riva, Austria, and the Lake of Garda
Jan 22 Swallowed by the Deep
Jan 25 The Price of Patriotism
Seaside Adventures at Home
Jan 26 The Lass Who Loves a Sailor
Tommy in Dreamland
Jan 29 The Great Divide
Wild Waves at St. Jean-de-Lux
Feb 1 Ascending the Jura Mountains
The Golden Lily
Feb 2 The Might of the Waters
Sheltered in the Woods
Feb 5 Civil War
Feb 8 Servant from the Country
Settled Out of Court
Feb 9 Coals of Fire
Venetian Isles
Feb 12 A Bag Race
The Gambler's Doom
Feb 15 The Ghost
Pastoral Scenes
Feb 16 The Acrobatic Fly
The Blue Swan Inn
Feb 19 Better Than Gold
The Comedy-Graph
Feb 22 Duped
His Fears Confirmed
Feb 23 The Buried Secret
A Family Outing
Feb 26 Blue Fishing Nets
The Legend of King Midas
Mar 1 The Plucky Suitor
The Vale of Aude
Mar 2 Baby Bet
From Beyond the Seas
Mar 5 The Poet of the Revolution
Mar 8 The Great Scoop
The Legend of Daphne
Mar 9 At the Bar of Justice
The Water-Flyer
Mar 12 The Pirate Airship
Rabelais' Joke
Mar 15 In the Shadow of the Cliffs
The Saraband Dance
Mar 16 The Country Schoolmaster
A Trip Along the Rhine
Mar 19 In the Foothills of Savoy
Little Jack's Letter
Mar 22 The Queen and the Mirror
The Wild Coast of Belle Island
Mar 23 A Maid of the Mountains
Over the Appennines of Italy
Mar 26 The Fall of Babylon
Mar 29 The Diary of a Nurse
Mar 30 Making Sherry Wine at Xeres
The Midnight Escape
Apr 2 Amateur Billiards
The Dreamer
O'er Crag and Torrent
Apr 5 A Drama of the Mountain Pass

Nov 6 Elephant Hunting in Cambodge
The Sack Race
Two Brothers
Nov 17 Goddess of the Sea
Nov 22 Napoleon's Game of Chess
Dec 18 Off to the Wedding
Dec 25 Absorbing Tale
Spring Heeled Jack
Dec 30 The Rheumatic Bridegroom
1910
Jan 15 Consequence of a Lie
Feb 12 The Paris Disaster
Apr 30 Hope of the Village
May 26 Midsummer Night's Dream

London Cinematograph Co.
1910
Jan 15 Boy Scouts
A Father's Love
Forced Treatment
Simple Simon
Tyrolean Tragedy

Lubin Mfg. Co.
1908
Jan 4 Through Darkness to Light
1909
Jan [day undetermined]
In the Land of Upsidedown
A New Old Master
Satan's Fan
Jan 11 When Lips Are Sealed
Jan 14 How Happy Jack Got a Meal
The Troubles of a Stranded Actor
Jan 18 Love's Sweet Melody
Jan 21 The Fighting Parson
The Wrong Burglar
Jan 25 A Suit Case
Who Stole Jones' Wood?
Jan 28 Love Germs
Feb [day undetermined]
A B C's of the U.S.A.
At the Dentist
At the Weser (Song)
Bake That Chicken Pie
Believe Me
The Carnival of Venice
Coon Town Parade
Duet from "Martha" (Flotow)
Katrina's Valentine
Mennett [i. e. Menuett]
The Montebank [sic]
Original Cohens
Il Pagliacci (Leoncavallo)
Peaches and Cream
Smile, Smile, Smile
The Taxidermist's Dream
There Never Was a Girl Like You
Torero Song "Carmen"
Il Trovatore
You've Got to Love Me a Lot
Feb 1 Aunt Emmy's Scrap Book
Messina Earthquake
Feb 4 The Blind Musician
Willie's Water Sprinkler
Feb 8 No. 5874
Feb 11 The Bank Messenger
A Secret
Feb 15 The Silver Dollar
The Unlucky Horseshoe
Feb 18 A Broken Heart
The Pass Key
Feb 22 A Game of Chess
Love Me, Love My Dog
Feb 25 The New Governess
Mar [day undetermined]
Buy Matches, Please
It Might Have Been Worse
The Mill Girl
Mar 1 A Dime Novel Detective
Mar 4 I'll Only Marry a Sport
The Last Call
Mar 8 The Stowaway
Mar 11 The Little Rag Doll
The New Mirror
Which Was the Happiest Time in Your Life?
Mar 15 A Cowboy Argument
Talked to Death
Mar 18 Reforming a Husband
Uncle Reuben's Courtship
Mar 22 The Day of the Dog
Our Ice Supply; or, How'd You Like to Be the Iceman
Mar 25 A Just Reward
Mad Dog
Mar 29 Help! Police!
The Photograph Habit
Apr [day undetermined]
The House That Jack Built
Romance of Engine 999
The Thirteenth at the Table
Through Darkness to Light
Apr 1 The Guarding Angel
Apr 5 The Master of Black Rock
Apr 8 The Escaped Melody
Forecastle Tom
Apr 12 The Curse of Gold
My Friend, Mr. Dummy
Apr 15 After the Bachelors' Ball
Slip-Powder
Apr 19 The Queen of the Ranch
The Yiddisher Boy
Apr 22 A Fatal Flirtation
A School for Lovemaking
Apr 26 Inventions of an Idiot
Why the Mail Was Late
Apr 29 Boys Will Be Boys
The House of Terror
May [day undetermined]
The Conjuror's Outing
An Old Man's Bride
Persistent Jane
May 3 The Falling Arrow
Puzzle Mad
May 6 The Old Hall Clock
May 10 A Golden Lie
May 13 The Right to Labor
May 17 Faded Flowers
The Press Gang
May 20 The Smuggler's Daughter
May 24 Mr. Inquisitive
Officer McCue
May 27 A Bride Won by Bravery
May 31 Father's Glue
The Lost Heiress
Jun [day undetermined]
The Awakening of Mr. Coon
The Fighting Cigar
The Innocent Bystander
Under the Steam Hammer
Jun 3 Are You the Man?
My Friend, the Indian
Jun 7 A Cork Leg Legacy
Saucy Sue
Jun 10 Prof. Wise's Brain Serum Injector
Through Jealousy
Jun 14 Through Shadow to Sunshine
Jun 17 Curing a Jealous Husband
Flossie's New Peach-Basket Hat
Jun 21 The Story of Two Lives
Jun 24 The Hypnotic Cure
Saved by His Sweetheart
Jun 28 Mary Jane Visits Her Country Cousin
The Oysterman's Gold
Jul 1 The Old Army Chest
Jul 5 A Great Wrong Righted
Jul 8 Roommates
The Sideboard Folding Bed
Jul 12 Driven from Home
Jul 15 Two Cousins
Jul 19 A Nugget of Gold
Jul 22 Hiring a Girl
Mexican Bill
Jul 26 A Hot Time at Atlantic City
Jul 29 Mr. Buttinsky
Sporting Blood
Aug 2 When the Flag Falls
Aug 5 His Little Girl
She Would Be an Actress
Aug 9 Drunkard's Child
The Newest Woman
Aug 12 An Unexpected Guest
Aug 16 How Brown Got Married
The Hungry Actor
Aug 19 Measure for Measure
Aug 23 Before the Dawn
Wifey Away, Hubby at Play
Aug 26 The Midnight Sons
Nearsighted Mary
Aug 30 The Doctor's Bride
The Haunted Hat
Sep 2 The Woman Hater
Sep 6 The Call of the Heart
Our Country in Arms
Sep 9 Glimpses of Yellowstone Park
A True Patriot
Sep 13 Her Face Was Her Fortune
Sep 16 All on Account of a Letter
The Fortune Hunters
Sep 20 When Woman Hates
Sep 23 The Conquering Hero
Sep 27 A Fish Story
Old Love Letters
Sep 30 The Judge's Ward
Oct 4 Billiken
Who Discovered the North Pole?
Oct 7 A Blank Check
Oct 11 Out for the Day
Papa's Honeymoon
Oct 14 Sandy, the Poacher
Oct 18 Haps and Mishaps
The Major and the Judge
Oct 21 Aunt Lena's Visit
Mignon
Oct 25 A Buried Secret
A Visit to Uncle
Oct 28 More Precious Than Gold
Nov 1 Brave Women of '76
A Lesson in Palmistry
Nov 4 Let Bygones Be Bygones
Nov 8 For Love's Sweet Sake
Nov 11 The Blue Garter
Found in a Taxi
Nov 15 Children of the Sea
Nov 18 Foiled
Servant's Revenge
Nov 22 The Rubber Man
When Women Win
Nov 25 Finnigan's Initiation
Martyr or Crank?
Nov 29 A Life for a Life
Dec 2 The Cub Reporter
Dec 6 He Wanted a Baby
She Took Mother's Advice
Dec 9 If Love Be True
Dec 13 Jinks the Grouch
When Courage Fled
Dec 16 Romance of the Rocky Coast
Dec 20 A Policeman's Xmas Eve
Three Christmas Dinners
Dec 23 Blissville the Beautiful
Dec 27 The New Chief
The Persistent Poet
Dec 30 Three Fingered Jack
1910
Jan 3 Their Chaperoned Honeymoon
Jan 6 The Tattooed Arm
Jan 10 Glimpses of an Indian Village
Over the Wire
Jan 13 He Joined the Frat
Wild Duck Hunting on Reel Foot Lake
Jan 17 He Got Rid of the Moths
A Slippery Day
Jan 20 The Usurper
Jan 24 Adoring an Ad.
Cupid, D. D. S.
Jan 27 The Flirto-Maniac
Marble Quarrying in Tennessee
Jan 31 Bill's Boots
Too Much Protection
Feb 3 It Might Have Been
Sentimental Sam
Feb 7 The Samaritan's Courtship
Feb 10 Celestial Vengeance
Feb 14 The Hand of the Heiress
Loving Hearts
Feb 17 A Honeymoon Through Snow to Sunshine
Feb 21 The New Marshall at Gila Creek
Feb 24 The District Attorney
Feb 28 The Ranger and the Girl
Mar 3 The Millionaire's Adventure
Mar 7 Marriage in Haste
Mar 10 Hearts Are Trump
Mar 14 The Blunderer
Mamma's Angel Child
Mar 17 The Irish Boy
Mar 21 A Mother's Heart
Mar 24 Two Gentlemen of the Road
Mar 28 His Spanish Wife
Mar 31 The Daughter's Choice
Apr 4 Back to Boarding

The Right House, But —
Apr 7 First Love Is Best
Apr 11 The Fisherman's Luck
Hemlock Hoax, the Detective
Jones' Watch
Apr 14 Western Justice
Apr 18 When the Cat's Away
Apr 21 The Angel of Dawson's Claim
Apr 25 A Child of the Sea
On Time for Business
Apr 28 Indian Blood
May 2 The Master Mechanic
Mrs. Nosey
May 5 The Miner's Sweetheart
May 9 Kidd's Treasure
Rastus in Zululand
May 12 The Cowboy's Devotion
May 16 The Regeneration of Father
May 19 The Indian Girl's Romance
May 23 The Messenger Boy Magician
Winter Bathing in the West Indies
May 26 The Brave Deserve the Fair
The Sisal Industry in the Bahamas
May 30 A Veteran of the G. A. R.
Jun 2 Percy, the Cowboy
Jun 6 Grandfather's Gift
Officer Muldoon's Double
Jun 9 The New Boss of Bar X Ranch
Jun 13 On Panther Creek
The Wild Man of Borneo
Jun 16 Red Eagle's Love Affair
Jun 20 Poetical Jane
The Road to Happiness
Jun 23 The Motion Picture Man
Jun 27 Apache Gold
Jun 30 Faith Lost and Won
Jul 4 His Child's Captive
Jul 7 Ferdie's Vacation
Jul 11 The Almighty Dollar
The Highbinders
Jul 14 The Adopted Daughter
Jul 18 Rosemary for Remembrance
Jul 21 John Graham's Gold
Jul 25 The Step-Daughter
Wifie's Mamma
Jul 28 Three Hearts
Aug 4 Ah Sing and the Greasers
Aug 8 The Heart of a Sioux
Aug 11 A Change of Heart
Aug 15 The District Attorney's Triumph
The Duck Farm
Aug 18 Shorty at the Shore
Aug 22 Cowboy Chivalry
Aug 25 The Anarchistic Grip
The Dream Pill
Aug 29 The Stronger Sex
Sep 1 The Man Who Died
Sep 5 The Healing Faith
Sep 8 Matilda's Winning Ways
Sep 12 The Greenhorn and the Girl
Sep 15 Mrs. Rivington's Pride
Resourceful Robert
Sep 19 Zeb, Zeke and the Widow
Sep 22 Love's Old Sweet Song
Sep 26 The Sheriff's Capture
Sep 29 The Path of Duty
Oct 3 The Baggage Smasher
Oct 6 The Golf Fiend
Woman's Vanity
Oct 10 The Clown and the Minister
Oct 13 Liz's Career
Oct 17 Hearts and Politics
Oct 20 Archie's Archery
Hawkins' Hat
Oct 24 Romance in the Rockies
Oct 27 Edith's Avoirdupois
False Love and True
Oct 31 Brothers
Nov 3 Mike the Housemaid
Nov 7 The Taming of Wild Bill
Nov 10 The Gambler's Charm
The Mystery of the Torn Note
Nov 14 The Street Preacher
Nov 17 Right in Front of Father
Nov 21 Caught by the Camera
Nov 24 Romance of the Lazy K Ranch
Nov 28 Shadows and Sunshine
Dec 1 Spoony Sam
Dec 5 On the Mexican Border
Dec 8 Reggie's Engagement
Dec 12 An Exile's Love
Dec 15 The Musical Ranch
Dec 19 The Dead Letter
Dec 22 An American Count
Dec 26 Making a Man of Him
Dec 29 Blue Horse Mine

Lubin, S. *see* **S. Lubin**

Lubin, Siegmund *see* **Siegmund Lubin**

Lumiere Films

1897 [month undetermined]
Babies Quarrel

1903
Feb [day undetermined]
Santos Dumont's Airship

1909
Oct 13 The Cook's Mistake
The Love Trip
Oct 20 A Good Trick
The Ogress
Oct 27 The Plundered Museum
Sunday at Douarenez
Nov 10 The Haunted Castle
A Serious Error

Lux

1908
Apr 11 The Deserter
The Dog's Scent
Free Admission
Apr 18 The Consequences of a Night Out
The Drama on a Roof
Improvised Servant
International Illusionist
Just Retribution
Love's Victim
Tony Has Eaten Garlic
Woman's Forbearance
May 2 Fox Hunting
Mistaken Identity
May 9 The Bargeman's Son
The Boxing Englishman
Dreams and Realities
Tommy Has the Spleen
May 16 A Good Thief
Madam Is Capricious
The Perverse Statues
The Uncle from America
May 30 Battle of Flowers in Nice
Carnival at Nice
The Marriage of a French Soldier
Mischievous Diabolo
Unlucky Luck
Jun 13 The Cat's Revenge
The Effective Hair Grower
Jul 4 The Closing Hour
A Fine Easter Egg
A Gendarme's Tribulations
Love and Fortune
Precipitated Removal
Riviera in Motor Car
Jul 6 Artificial Brooding
Frightened by Burglars
Keenest of the Two
Lessons in Jiu Jitsu
The Mediterranean Fleet
The Pastry Cook's Misfortune
A Poacher's Trick
Posthumous Jealousy
The Two Pickpockets
Aug 1 A Comical Execution
His Mother's Melody
The Killing Remorse
The Learned Dr. Cornelius
Secret of Hypnotism
The Smuggler Automobilist
The Tramp's Daughter
Aug 29 The Bewitched Tricycle
The Enchanted Mantle
A False Alarm
Oct 3 Caught Red Handed
Oct 9 Fantastic Magic
Spending a Holiday
What a Funny Horse
Oct 10 A Mother's Fault
Oct 14 Miscalculated Revenge
Oct 17 Elixir of Youth
Oct 27 He Did Not Know He Was a Monk
Nov 17 Caesar Up-to-Date
A Serious Joke
Nov 21 The Swimming Lesson
Dec 1 A Child's Devotion
Jack of All Trades
Looking for the Sea Serpent
Making Home Attractive
Dec 12 The Madman of the Cliff
Dec 19 The Angel of Nativity
Grimsol, the Mischievous Goblin
Troubles of an Airship
Dec 28 The Devil's Sale

1909
Mar 13 A Trip to Monte Carlo
Mar 22 Chasi Movement
The Duel
Duplicate Vases
Five Minutes Interview
For Honor
House of Disagreement
Irritable Woman
Louis XVII
Magic French Horn
Marriage in Haste
Maternal Protection
Matrimonial Agency
Norseman
Recommended Servant
Removing
Runaway Dog
The Stolen Inheritance
Apr 24 It Was a Beautiful Dream
May 1 Easter Bells
Removal Under Difficulties
May 8 Earthly Paradise
The Inheritance of Baptiste Durand
Sportsmen in Switzerland
May 15 An Exciting Hunt
For Honor's Sake
May 22 Longing for Gold
May 29 Apostle of Gaul
King's Jester
Nantilda
The Suffragist Wants a Husband
Vaccination Against Injuries
Jun 5 Debut of an Alpinist
Jun 12 The Consequences of a Bad Action
Cyrano de Bergerac's Adventure
Jun 26 Chimney Sweep's Debut
Fratricide
Lover's Mistake
Maddened Players
Misadventures of a Bench
Jul 3 American Squadron in France
Jul 10 Gaffles, Vice King of Police
The Origin of Man
The Reason of the Strongest
A Tramp Show Heart
Jul 17 Ballad of the Pumpkin
A Jealous Woman
Miraculous Fluid
The Sacrifice
Jul 24 Columbine's Return
Jul 31 Little Gypsy
Aug 7 Japanese Prince
Aug 14 Her Beautiful Hair
The Mysterious Crime
A Near Tragedy
Nightmare of a Single Man
A Trying Position
Aug 21 The New General
Rival Sisters
Aug 28 Ancestral Treasures
Sep 4 An Apostle of Temperance
The Crusader's Return
Mexican Drama
A Strong Woman's Lover
Sep 18 The Arithmetic Lesson
Sep 20 Blind Against His Will
Tragical Love
Sep 21 Old Servants
Strike Time in Paris
Sep 23 A Lucky Man
Sep 25 The Adopted Child
Oct 25 The Boating Party
The Indian Phantasy
Love and Vendetta
A Prince's Love
The Strength of Love
Nov 8 The Bearskin
Boatman of the Riviera
Miracle of a Necklace
Nov 13 Mischief of a Big Drum
Nov 15 Electrified Hunchback
Dec 4 Indiscreet Father and Son
Dec 20 The Chemist's Bell

A Persistent Lover
Dec 25 Drama in the Far West
Gypsy Child
Mule Driver's Bride
Original Sausage Tale
Pork Butcher
Reincarnated Mummy
Repentance
Turning Out of Time
Dec 29 The Gold Digger's Son
1910
Jan 5 Drama at Sea
Football Craze
Jan 8 How the Dog Saved the Flag
The Rivals
Jan 12 Broken Happiness
My Aunt's Birthday
Jan 15 Bogus General
Drama Under Richelieu
Follow Me
Foster Brothers
Good Tramp
Roast Chicken
Jan 19 Adventures of a Sandwich Man
The Refugee
Jan 26 He Would Be an Acrobat
Uncle Learns to Hypnotize
Feb 2 Hamlet, Prince of Denmark
Feb 9 The Consequence of a Nod
Pirate's Fiancée
Feb 16 Her Dolly's Revenge
The Man Who Could Not Sit Down
Feb 17 Easy Job
Feb 23 The Fisherman's Honour
The Runaway Stove
Mar 2 The Golf Mania
The Sailor's Dog
Mar 9 A Father's Patriotism
He Knew Best
Mar 16 Life in the Next Century
The Two Brothers
Mar 24 A Family Feud
How a Bad Tempered Man Was Cured
Mar 25 Dwarf Detective
Mar 30 Cured by a Tip
Drama on the Reef
Apr 6 Rico, the Jester
The Snake Man
Apr 13 The Attack upon the Train
Washed Ashore
Apr 20 Grandpa's Darling
A Young Aviator's Dream
Apr 28 Artist's Child
Tommy and the Powder
May 5 The Little Beggar Maid
They Would Roller Skate
May 12 Her Two Suitors
A Mother's Grief
May 19 He Did Not Die
The Lace Maker's Dream
May 25 A Sagacious Animal
Jun 2 A Stray Dog
Jun 3 The Slave's Love
What Happened to a Cinematograph Party
Jun 4 Burglar's Dog
Quarrelsome Man
A Trip on the Seine
Jun 14 A Bitter Enemy
Jun 17 MacNab Visits the Comet
Jun 21 The Devil's Wand
Jun 24 An Exciting Yarn
We Want Your Vote
Jun 28 The Witch's Spectacles
Jul 1 Charles the Fifth
A Quiet Pipe
Jul 8 The Money Lender's Son
Must Be Without Encumbrance
Jul 15 Bill's Serenade
The Greatest of These Is Charity
Jul 22 A Devoted Little Brother
Ma's New Dog
Jul 29 The Bailiff
Aug 25 The Acrobat's Son
The Chemist's Mistake
Sep 15 Aunt Tabitha's Monkey
The Selfish Man's Lesson
Sep 22 The Bobby's Dream
Ma-in-Law as a Statue
Only a Bunch of Flowers
That Typist Again
Sep 29 How Jones Won the Championship
Kindness Abused and Its Results
Oct 6 Auntie in the Fashion
Mother's Portrait
Oct 13 Bill and the Missing Key
Runaway Star
Oct 20 Gilson and Those Boys
The Tyrant
Oct 27 Bewitched
She Required Strength and Got It
Where You Go I Go
Nov 3 Fatty Taking a Bath
Her Diary
Nov 11 Bill as a Boxer
The Truth Revealed
Nov 18 Bill as a Lover
Blopps in Search of the Black Hand
Nov 25 In Friendship's Name
Dec 2 Bill as an Operator
Necessity Is the Mother of Invention
Dec 9 And She Came Back
What Will It Be
Dec 16 Her Favorite Tune
How We Won Her
Dec 23 Bill Plays Bowls
Rosalie's Dowry
Dec 30 Aunt Julia's Portrait
Tim Writes a Poem

MacFee, Edward Daniel, Jr. *see* **Edward Daniel MacFee, Jr.**

Mannegraph Film Co.
1909
Apr 21 Miller's Dream
The Short Circuit House
Apr 28 How Chauncey Became a Champion
May 5 Paza Did It
May 12 Roosevelt in Africa
May 26 The Seventh Clerk
Jun 9 A True Girl from the West

Manufacturer's Film Agency
1909
Dec 25 The Kidnapped King
Silly Billy
1910
Jan 15 Marvelous Indeed

Méliès, Gaston *see* **Gaston Méliès**

Méliès, Georges *see* **Georges Méliès**

Messing, Carl F. *see* **Carl F. Messing**

Messter
1909
May 29 Forester's Son
Jul 17 The Step-Mother
Aug 7 Double Awakening
Oct 12 Winter Sports
Dec 20 Mother-in-Law Must Fly
1910
Jan 17 Romeo and Juliet at the Seaside
Jan 18 Out with It
Feb 8 Doctor's Peculiar Treatment
Feb 15 Tragedy at Sea
Mar 2 Electrical Safe
Jun 23 Sea Cave and Cliffs

Milano Films
1910
Apr 26 Among the Snowy Mountains
Apr 27 Bethlehem
Apr 28 The Reservists

Miles Bros.
1903
Mar [day undetermined]
Blasting the Treadwell Mines
Captain Allard Shooting White Horse Rapids
Dog Baiting and Fighting in Valdez
First Snow Storm of the Season, Valdez
Horses Swimming Copper River
Kalama Railroad Ferry Crossing the Columbia River
Leaving Skagway for the Golden North
Old Method of Mining, No. 11 Eldorado
Operation on the Famous Chechawko Hill
A Pack Train in the Copper River Country
Pack Train Leaving Valdez for Copper Mines
Panorama of Kennicott Glacier Port Hole
Panorama of "Miles Canyon"
Panorama of No. 2 Eldorado
Panorama of Taku Glacier
Panorama of White Horse Rapids
A Rotary Snow Plow in the Great Northwest
Snow-Plow Bucking a 15-foot Snow Slide
Steamer Susie Excursion to Moosehide
Steamer "Yukoner" Leaving Dawson
$35,000 Clean-Up on Eldorado No. 10
Through Cascade Tunnel
Through Miles Canyon on a Cattle Scow
Through Tunnel on the White Pass Route
Through White Horse Rapids
Tunnel Scene of the White Pass Route
Two Miles of the White Pass & Yukon Railroad
Willamette Falls
Winter Sport on Snake River, Nome
1905 [month undetermined]
No Bill Peddlers Allowed
Feb 25 Love Letter
Sep [day undetermined]
Nelson-Britt Prize Fight
Nelson-Britt Prize Fight for Lightweight Championship, San Francisco, September 9th, 1905
1906 [month undetermined]
Gans-Nelson Contest, Goldfield, Nevada, September 3rd, 1906
Head-On Collision at Brighton Beach Race Track, July 4th, 1906
Apr [day undetermined]
A Trip Down Mount Tamalpais
Dec [day undetermined]
O'Brien-Burns Contest, Los Angeles, Cal., Nov. 26th, 1906
1907 [month undetermined]
Jim Jeffries on His California Ranch
Jan 26 Gans-Herman Fight
Mar 30 Indian Basket Weavers
Apr [day undetermined]
Winning a Princess
Apr 20 Anarchist's Mother-in-Law
Auntie's Birthday
The Bad Shilling
Cambridge-Oxford Race
Catch the Kid
A Cheap Skate
Chef's Revenge
The Coroner's Mistake
Eggs
Knight-Errant
Land of Bobby Burns
Life and Customs in India
A Mother's Sin
Murphy's Wake
The Naval Nursery
Polar Bear Hunt
Sailor's Return
True until Death
Village Fire Brigade
Wizard's World
May 4 Boss Away, Choppers Play
The Fatal Hand
Johnny's Run
The Romany's Revenge
Roof to Cellar
Well-Bred
Jun [day undetermined]
Shriners' Conclave at Los Angeles, Cal., May, 1907
Squires, Australian Champion, in His Training Quarters
Jun 15 A Disturbed Dinner
I Never Forget the Wife
The White Slave
A Woman's Duel
Jun 22 The Blackmailer
His Cheap Watch
Revenge
That Awful Tooth
Willie's Dream
Jun 29 Because My Father's Dead
Rummy Robbers
Jul [day undetermined]
Panorama, Crowds at Squires-Burns International Contest, from Center of Ring, Colma, July 4th, 1907

Panorama, Crowds at Squires-Burns International Contest, from Moving Picture Stand, July 4th, 1907
Jul 13 International Contest for the Heavyweight Championship: Squires vs. Burns, Ocean View, Cal., July 4th, 1907
Aug 31 Don Juan
Female Wrestlers
Great Lion Hunt
Happy Bob as a Boxer
Sep 14 For a Woman's Sake
Once Upon a Time There Was...
Sep 21 Arrival of Lusitania
Babes in the Woods
Sep 28 Cheekiest Man on Earth
Invalid's Adventure
Oct 5 His First Topper
The Petticoat Regiment
Nov 9 The Handling of the Fleet

Mitchell & Kenyon
1904
Feb 23 Diving Lucy
Jul [day undetermined]
Driven from Home
Tragic Elopement
Sep [day undetermined]
The Miser's Daughter

Montana Motion Picture Co.
1910
Jun 1 Custer's Last Stand

Motion Picture Distributors and Sales Co.
1910
Jan 20 The Wages of Sin
Jan 27 Bonehead's Second Adventure
The Ordeal
Feb 3 Justice
Feb 9 The Mountaineer
Feb 16 A Daughter's Devotion
The Old Maid and Bonehead
Feb 23 In Arizona
Mar 5 The Vindictive Foreman
Mar 9 On the Little Big Horn
Mar 16 The Silver Lining
Mar 23 The Tenderfoot
Mar 30 The Cowboy Preacher
Apr 6 Frontier Day in the West
Apr 13 At Double Cross Ranch
Apr 20 The Cowboy and the Lieutenant
Apr 25 The Power of a Smile
Apr 27 Days of '49
Apr 28 The New Shawl
May 2 Two Men
May 4 A Daughter of the Mine
May 5 Aunt Maria's Substitute
May 9 A Rural Romeo
May 11 The Indian Princess
May 12 The Turn of the Dice
May 16 A Doctor's Perfidy
May 18 The Fighting Parson
May 19 Fruit and Flowers
Werther
May 23 The Eternal Triangle
May 25 The Red Man's Honor
May 26 Don Carlos
May 30 A Reno Romance
May 31 The Crack Shot
The Tie That Binds
Jun 1 A Just Revenge
The Lily of the Ranch
Prascovia
Jun 2 A Bachelor's Love
Vitellius and Heliogabalus
Jun 3 Married on Horseback
Jun 4 Foolshead as a Porter
Her Portrait
O! That Indian
A Pennyworth of Potatoes
Jun 6 The Nichols on a Vacation
Jun 7 Girls
His Duty
Jun 8 A Jealous Wife
The Outlaw's Redemption
The Shipwrecked Man
Jun 9 The Children of Edward IV
A Discontented Woman
Jun 10 Russia—The Land of Oppression
Saved from the Redmen
Jun 11 Her Romance
Limburger and Love
Linda of Chamouny
Jun 13 The Way to Win
Jun 14 An Engineer's Sweetheart
Wenonah
Jun 15 The Emperor's Message
Jeffries on His Ranch
Settling a Boundary Dispute
Jun 16 The Legend of the Holy Chapel
A Policeman's Son
Jun 17 A Cowboy's Race for a Wife
Married in Haste
Jun 18 Distractions of Foolshead
Her Dad's Pistol
The New Sign of the Globe Hotel
The Phrenologist
Roosevelt's Reception in New York
Jun 20 Hebrew's Gratitude
In the Mesh of the Net
Jun 21 Nevada
The Sea Wolves
Jun 22 Grandpa's Will
Sheriff's Daughter
The Story of Lulu Told by Her Feet
The Tricky Umbrella of Fricot
Jun 23 Oliver Twist
A Self-Made Hero
Jun 24 A Mexican Lothario
Too Many Girls
Jun 25 The Man Suffragette for the Abolition of Work for Women
A Plucky Girl
A White Lie
Why Jones Reformed
Jun 27 The Brothers' Feud
The Heroine of Pawnee Junction
Jun 28 Her Terrible Peril
Mother and Daughter
Jun 29 The Taking of Saragossa
The Tenderfoot Parson
Jun 30 Fort Du Bitche
A Game for Two
Jul 1 A Ranchman's Simple Son
Saved from Himself
Jul 2 Catherine, Duchess of Guisa
The Lady Doctor
The Man Behind the Curtain
Jul 4 The Fallen Idol
The Ghetto Seamstress
Jul 5 On the Border
A Sinner's Sacrifice
Jul 6 Manoeuvers of the New York Police Force
The Tamer; Alfred Schneider and His Lions
That Little German Band
Jul 7 The Call of the Circus
Giorgione
Jemmy
Jul 8 The Girl Who Dared
The Sheriff of Black Gulch
Jul 9 The Abyss
The Burglar and the Baby
Sally's Beaux
Jul 11 The Call of the West
Old Heads and Young Hearts
The Pirate's Dower
Jul 12 A Mexican Love Affair
A Mightier Hand
Jul 13 Abernathy Kids to the Rescue
The Clergyman and His Ward
The Struggle of Two Souls
Tweedle Dum's Aeronautical Adventure
Jul 14 The End of a Dynasty
The Saloon Next Door
Jul 15 A Bridegroom's Mishap
Red Fern and the Kid
Retribution
Jul 16 A Jealous Wife
Mother-in-law, Son-in-law and Tanglefoot
The Tattler
The Voice of the Blood
Jul 18 The Right to Labor
Summertime
Jul 19 A Game of Hearts
A Message of the Sea
Jul 20 Back in the Mountains
Levi and Family at Coney Island
Only a Hobo
The Romance of a Jockey
A Romance of an Anvil
Some Riding Exercises of the Italian Cavalry
Jul 21 Andromache
Mateo Falcone
The Mistake
Jul 22 Black Pete's Reformation
Repaid with Interest
Jul 23 A Cannon Duel
Cohen and Murphy
Let Us Die Together
Our Housemaid
Jul 25 Two Maids
The Ungrateful Daughter-In-Law
Jul 26 Love in Mexico
The Missing Bridegroom
Jul 27 The Cow-Boy and the Squaw
The Kissing Bug
The Prospector's Treasure
The Room of the Secret
A True Pal
Jul 28 Bear Ye One Another's Burdens
The Hiding Place
Jul 29 In the Wild West
Jul 30 A Little Confederate
The Two Bears
The Vixen
Where Can We Hang this Picture?
Aug 1 Irony of Fate
The United States Revenue Detective
Aug 2 Her Private Secretary
Jenk's Day Off
A Miner's Sweetheart
Aug 3 Fricot Drinks a Bottle of Horse Embrocation
The Glove
The Rest Cure
Sons of the West
The Spitfire
Aug 4 The Eagle and the Eaglet
Yankeeanna
Aug 5 A Cowboy's Generosity
The Restoration
Aug 6 Almost a Hero
His Baby's Shirt
Louisa Miller
Magdalene; or, The Workman's Daughter
Aug 8 The Broker's Daughter
Once upon a Time
Aug 9 The Mad Hermit
A Man's Way
A True Country Heart
Aug 10 The Animated Scare-Crow
A Favour Admission to a Play
Hearts of Gold
The Hermit of the Rockies
Truth Beyond Reach of Justice
The Wrong Bag
Aug 11 Beyond Endurance
Charles Le Tremeraire
Hoodoo Alarm Clock
Indian Squaw's Sacrifice
The Oedipus King
Aug 12 Lena Rivers
The Prairie Post Mistress
Aug 13 A Cloud
The Life Boat
Madame Clairo
Papa's Cane
The Stolen Policeman
Winning a Husband
Aug 15 Among the Roses
The Heroic Coward
Aug 16 The Girl Reporter
The Sewing Girl
A Woman's Better Nature
Aug 17 Count of Noaccount
A Cowboy's Pledge
The Hump's Secret
Tweedle Dum Has Missed the Train
Why Dad Was Held Up
Aug 18 Carmen
Senator's Double
Shanghaied
Aug 19 The Redmen's Persecution
She Stoops to Conquer
Aug 20 Agnes Visconti
A Woman's Power
Aug 22 The Firemen of Cairo

The Gang Leader's Reform
Musette's Caprice
The Taming of Jane
Aug 23 A Dainty Politician
The Deceivers
The Gunsmith
The Mascot of Company "D"
Aug 24 A Bully's Waterloo
A Fatal Vengeance
Fricot's Itching Powder
In the Black Hills
The Sheriff and His Son
The Tale of a Hot Dog
Aug 25 The Acrobat's Son
The Chemist's Mistake
For the Sunday Edition
Hazing a New Scholar
In the Time of the First Christians
Aug 26 Kit Carson
The Latchkey
Aug 27 An Enemy of the Dust
Fabian's Hollow Tooth
Foolshead in the Lion's Cage
The Mail Carrier
A Society Sinner
Aug 29 Fantastic Furniture
An Unexpected Servant
Who Killed John Dare?
The Widow
Aug 30 An Assisted Elopement
The Burlesque Queen
Dan, the Arizona Scout
The Horse Shoer's Girl
Aug 31 The Blazed Trail
The Cowboy and the Easterner
The Fisherman's Crime
Turning the Tables
Tweedle Dum's Forged Bank Note
The Unsophisticated Book Agent
Sep [day undetermined]
Only a Jew
Sep 1 Great Marshall Jewel Case
King of a Day
The Right Girl
That Letter from Teddy
Sep 2 A Fresh Start
The Night Rustlers
Sep 3 Fabian Hunting Rats
The Little Drummer Boy
The Matinee Idol
The Vestal
Sep 5 Judge Ye Not in Haste
The Little Blind Girl
The Lost Chance
You Saved My Life
Sep 6 The Girl Next Door
The Inconstant
Mother
Western Justice
Sep 7 The Caprice of a Dame
Fricot Has Lost His Collar Button
His Indian Bride
[Jones, the Burglar Catcher]
The Moonshiner's Daughter
The Snorer
Sep 8 Conscience of a Child
Cowboy's Courtship
The Minister's Speech
A Sister's Sacrifice
Wanted: An Athletic Instructor
Sep 9 The Doctor's Carriage
A True Indian Brave
Sep 10 For the Girl's Sake
The Messenger Boy's Sweetheart
Mr. Coward
Robinson Crusoe
A Thief Well Received
Sep 12 Between Duty and Honor
Captured by Wireless
The Two Daughters
Sep 13 A Cowboy's Matrimonial Tangle
A Day of Pleasure
Tangled Lives
The Tell Tale Perfume
Sep 14 Animated Powders
The Iron Foundry
The Law and the Man
Monkeyshines
A Wild Goose Chase
Sep 15 An Attempted Elopement
Aunt Tabitha's Monkey
Buffalo Bill's Wild West and Pawnee Bill's Far East
Dixie
A Game for Life
The Selfish Man's Lesson
The Temptation of Sam Bottler
Sep 16 For a Western Girl
The Sacking of Rome
The Stolen Invention
Sep 17 Danish Dragoons
Fabian Out for a Picnic
The Falconer
The Pugilist's Child
Round Trip $5.98
World's Championship Motor Races
Sep 19 The Blind Man's Dog
Debt
The Falls of the Rhine
The White Squaw
Sep 20 Aunt Hannah
For the Love of Red Wing
A Husband's Sacrifice
Not Guilty
Sep 21 The Last Friend
Molly at the Regiment—Her Adventures
Strayed from the Range
Trailing the Black Hand
The White Princess of the Tribe
Sep 22 The Bobby's Dream
The Cattle Thief's Revenge
Ma-in-Law as a Statue
The New Butler
Only a Bunch of Flowers
That Typist Again
Sep 23 A Cattle Rustler's Daughter
The Convict
A Husband's Jealous Wife
Julie Colonna
Tontolini as a Ballet Dancer
Sep 24 The Bad Luck of an Old Rake
Bill Mason's Ride
Dr. Jekyll and Mr. Hyde; or, A Strange Case
Foolshead as a Policeman
His Lordship
Sep 26 Pressed Roses
The Street Arab of Paris
The Yankee Girl's Reward
Sep 27 A Cowboy for Love
Home Made Mince Pie
"Oh! You Wives"
The Taming of Buck
Sep 28 The Laugh's on Father
Levi, the Cop
The Virgin of Babylon
A Western Girl's Sacrifice
Where the Sun Sets
Sep 29 Annie
How Jones Won the Championship
Kindness Abused and Its Results
The School-Marm's Ride for Life
Sep 30 Dots and Dashes
Giovanni of Medici
The Ranch Raiders
Oct 1 The Adoption of Helen
Bird's Eye View from World's Highest Buildings
The Flight across the Atlantic
Foolshead Employed in a Bank
Foolshead Has Been Presented with a Foot Ball
The Music Teacher
Rip Van Winkle
Oct 3 All the World's a Stage
Behind the Scenes of the Cinema Stage
Through the Ruins of Carthage
Women of the West
Oct 4 The Beechwood Ghost
Leon of the Table d'Hote
War
Young Deer's Return
Oct 5 The Cowboys to the Rescue
The Golden Hoard
The Pit That Speaks
Tweedledum's Duel
When Cupid Sleeps
Oct 6 Auntie in the Fashion
The Deciding Vote
Mother's Portrait
Wild Bill's Defeat
Oct 7 Avenged
The Girl Scout
Oct 8 All's Fair in Love and War
Foolshead Fisherman
Jealousy
Mrs. Cannon Is Warm
The Storms of Life
Within an Inch of His Life
Oct 10 The Carmelite
A Game of Hearts
Jes' Plain Dog
The Monogrammed Cigarette
The Order Is to March
Oct 11 A Cowboy's Daring Rescue
A Man and a Girl
Pocahontas
Simpson's Skate
Oct 12 The Betrothed's Secret
Curing a Grouch
How the Tenderfoot Made Good
The S. S. Mauretania
Silver Plume Mine
Tweedledum on His First Bicycle
Oct 13 Bill and the Missing Key
The Garden of Fate
Mysteries of Bridge of Sighs at Venice
Runaway Star
The Tale a Camera Told
Oct 14 Delightful Dolly
The Mad Lady of Chester
The Prayer of a Miner's Child
Oct 15 Paid Boots and Stolen Boots
A Pearl of Boy
Saved by Bosco
A Shot in the Night
Tracked across the Sea
Willie Visits a Moving Picture Show
A Woman's Wit
Oct 17 The Copper and the Crook
Dr. Geoffrey's Conscience
An Indian Chief's Generosity
Mother and Child
Oct 18 The Devil
The Lure of Gold
Oh, What a Knight!
Sleepy Jones
Oct 19 The Boys of Topsy-Turvy Ranch
The Cat Came Back
Excursion on the Chain of Mont Blanc
Imperfect Perfectos
Stolen by Indians
Tweedledum's Sleeping Sickness
Oct 20 The Calumny
The Fur Coat
Gilson and Those Boys
The Heart of a Cowboy
The Tyrant
Oct 21 A Child's Sacrifice
The Last of the Savelli
Their Child
The Wrong Trail
Oct 22 The Artist's Luck
Breaking Home Ties
The False Coin
Foolshead Between Two Fires
Hearts of Gold
In the Gray of the Dawn
The Locket
Oct 24 The Absent-Minded Doctor
The Count of Montebello
Saved by Her Dog
Solving the Bond Theft
Oct 25 The Girl Cowboy
The Lord and the Lady
The Plot That Failed
Young Lord Stanley
Oct 26 Doings at the Ranch
Launching the First Italian Dreadnought
Rev. John Wright of Missouri
A Touching Mystery
Tweedledum Wants to be a Jockey
Oct 27 Bewitched
A Clause in the Will
The Hobble Skirt
Mendelssohn's Spring Song
Ruin
She Required Strength and Got It

Where You Go I Go
Oct 28 The Fairies' Hallowe'en
The Pretty Dairy Maid
A Red Girl's Friendship
The Sergeant's Daughter
Tontolini Is in Love
Oct 29 Adventure of a Millionaire
The Armorer's Daughter
An Excursion on the Lake of Garda
Foolshead Volunteer on the Red Cross
In the Web
Who Is She?
Why They Signed the Pledge
Oct 31 The Idol's Eye
The Italian Sherlock Holmes
The Little Mother
The Manufacture of Cheese at Roquefort
Nov 1 The Fatal Gold Nugget
Mental Science
Mistress and Maid
The Sheriff and Miss Jones
Nov 2 Caught by Cowboys
The Girl from the East
The Slave of Carthage
That Doggone Dog
Turning of the Worm
Nov 3 Cohen's Generosity
Fatty Taking a Bath
The Fault of Grandmother
Her Diary
Willie
Nov 4 A Fateful Gift
Red Wing and the White Girl
Ten Nights in a Bar Room
A Wooden Sword
Nov 5 A Fatal Picnic
The Jewel Case
A Russian Romance
A Sufferer of Insomnia
Where Have I Put My Fountain Pen?
Where Sea and Shore Doth Meet
Nov 7 Keeping His Word
Religious Fetes at Thibet
The Resurrection of Lazarus
Spirit of the West
Nov 8 The Branded Man
The Little Fire Chief
Moonshine and Love
When Love Is Young
Nov 9 A Floating Message
The King of Beggars
The Ranchman and the Miser
The Woodsman
Nov 10 The Black Gondola
The Last Straw
The Model's Redemption
A Stormy Seas
Nov 11 The American and the Queen
Bill as a Boxer
Bud's Triumph
The Truth Revealed
A Widow and Her Child
Nov 12 The Coalman's Soap
Foolshead Knows All and Does All
The Heroine of 101 Ranch
Mother-in-Law Arrives
The Ordeal
Under a Changing Sky
World's Wrestling Champions
Nov 14 The Case of the Missing Heir
The Devil's Billiard Table
The Double
Ginhara or Faithful Unto Death
Romantic Redskins
Nov 15 The Flight of Red Wing
How Women Love
Paul and Virginia
That Woman Lawyer
Nov 16 The Hand of Providence
The Mermaid
The Ranchman's Bride
Tweedledum Gets Employed in the Corporation Body
The Way of the West
Nov 17 The Education of Mary Jane
Fortune's Wheel
Judge and Father
The Lure of the City
Nov 18 Bill as a Lover
Blopps in Search of the Black Hand
The City of Her Dreams
Her Father's Sin
An Indian Maiden's Choice
Nov 19 The Diamond Swindler
Foolshead Victim of His Honesty
Moulders of Souls
The New Magdalene
Oklahoma Bill
An Original Palette
Nov 21 The Exiled Mother
Lone Wolf's Trust
Starlight's Devotion
Their Day of Thanks
Nov 22 Absent Minded Arthur
A Thanksgiving Surprise
Thou Shalt Not Kill
True Western Honor
Nov 23 Cast Thy Bread upon the Waters
A Deal in Indians
Gounod's 'Ave Maria'
Let Us Give Thanks
The Story of a Pair of Boots
Nov 24 A Big Joke
The Country Boarder
Forgiven
Nothing but Money
Sacrificed
Nov 25 A Cheyenne's Love for a Sioux
In Friendship's Name
One Touch of Nature
The Wild Flower and the Rose
Nov 26 A Chosen Marksman
Kean; or, The Prince and the Actor
So Runs the Way
A Windy Day
The Woman Hater
Nov 28 A Difficult Capture
The Heart of an Actress
The Regeneration
The Revolving Doors
The Wreck
Nov 29 The Ranchman's Personal
Value—Beyond Price
Wanted—A Baby
Who Wins the Widow?
Nov 30 The Indian Land Grab
The Judas Money; or, An Episode of the War in Vendee
Saved by a Vision
Valley Folks
Dec 1 A Child's Judgment
A Painful Debt
A Touching Affair
Dec 2 Bill as an Operator
A Child of the Wild
John Halifax, Gentleman
Necessity Is the Mother of Invention
Queen of the Nihilists
What Is to Be, Will Be
Dec 3 The Big Drum
The Birthday Present
The Dog Keeper
The Ohami Troupe of Acrobats
When the World Sleeps
When Woman Wills
Dec 5 The Aspirations of Gerald and Percy
In the Czar's Name
The Laundry Girl's Good Night
The Price of a Sacrifice
Vera, the Gypsy Girl
Dec 6 The Medicine Man
The Rehearsal
Rip Van Winkle
A Sioux's Reward
Dec 7 The Conquering Hero
Hearts of the West
Nature's Nobleman
The Tell-Tale Portrait
Tweedledum Learns a Tragical Part
Dec 8 The Soldier of the Cross
'Twixt Loyalty and Love
Two Lucky Jims
Dec 9 And She Came Back
A Brave Western Girl
The Girls He Left Behind Him
The Iron Clad Lover
Lady Betty's Strategy
Western Justice
What Will It Be
Dec 10 The Dispensation
Foolshead Knows How to Take His Precautions
The Good Samaritan
The Poacher
Dec 12 The Bowling Craze
A Clever Ruse
Faithful Max
A Fight for Millions
Our Dear Uncle from America
The Rummage Sale
Dec 13 An Indian's Test
Love and Law
A Plucky Western Kid
The Tramp Bicyclist
Dec 14 Brothers
Dido Forsaken by Aeneas
The Pilgrim
The Sheriff and the Detective
Dec 15 The Binding Shot
The False Accusation
The Poor Student
Dec 16 A Girl of the Plains
Her Favorite Tune
How We Won Her
The Millionaire Milkman
The Old Miner's Doll
Two Suits
Dec 17 A Christmas Letter
Dickey's Courtship
His Gypsy Sweetheart
The Mother's Shadow
Thieves as Quick Change Artists
The Thin Dark Line
Dec 19 The Child of Two Mothers
The Crippled Teddy Bear
Her Fatal Mistake
The Museum of Sovereigns
A Ward of Uncle Sam
Dec 20 The Bachelor's Finish
The Cattle Baron's Daughter
Jack Logan's Dog
Looking Forward
Dec 21 The Arm of the Law
A Desperate Remedy
His Mother
Little Peter's Xmas Day
The Romance of Count de Beaufort
Tweedledum and Frothy Want to Get Married
Dec 22 Her Husband's Deception
Little Nell's Tobacco
Neapolitan Volcanic Islands
A Troublesome Parcel
Who Was the Culprit?
Dec 23 Bill Plays Bowls
The Childhood of Jack Harkaway
The Pale Faced Princess
The Pawnshop
Rosalie's Dowry
The Terror of the Plains
Dec 24 A Father's Love
Greediness Spoiled Foolshead's Christmas
In Norway
The Necklace of the Dead
The Refuge
Dec 26 The Fear of Fire
Girlies
An Insane Heiress
The Lock-Keeper
The Unexpected Honeymoon
Dec 27 Freddie's Courtship
An Indian's Elopement
The Station Agent's Daughter
The Vicar of Wakefield
Dec 28 Drama of the Engine Driver
Elda of the Mountains
The Golden Gates
Grandfather's Pipe
The Outcast's Salvation
Dec 29 The Rustic
The Squaw and the Man
Unreasonable Jealousy
Dec 30 Aunt Julia's Portrait
Hypnotized
The Missing Bridegroom
Mrs. Richard Dare
Taming the Terror
Tim Writes a Poem
Dec 31 Bearhunting

A Daughter of Virginia
The Jealous Wife's New Year Day
Norwegian Water Falls
A Sacrifice — And Then
The Scarecrow

Motograph Co. of America
1910
Jun 15 A Child of the Regiment
Jun 22 Taft for a Day
Jun 29 A Millionaire Tramp

Natural Colour Kinematograph Co.
1910
Jul 15 [Kinemacolor Films]
Dec [day undetermined]
[Liquors and Cigars]
[The London Fire Brigade]
[London Zoological Gardens]
[Picking Strawberries]
[The Richmond Horse Show]
A Visit to the Seaside at Brighton Beach, England

Nestor Co.
1909
Dec 30 The Justice of Solomon
1910
Jan 6 The Nemesis
Jan 13 Forgiven
Mishaps of Bonehead
Jan 20 The Wages of Sin
Jan 27 Bonehead's Second Adventure
The Ordeal
Feb 3 Justice
Feb 9 The Mountaineer
Feb 16 A Daughter's Devotion
The Old Maid and Bonehead
Feb 23 In Arizona
Mar 5 The Vindictive Foreman
Mar 9 On the Little Big Horn
Mar 16 The Silver Lining
Mar 23 The Tenderfoot
Mar 30 The Cowboy Preacher
Apr 6 Frontier Day in the West
Apr 13 At Double Cross Ranch
Apr 20 The Cowboy and the Lieutenant
Apr 27 Days of '49
May 4 A Daughter of the Mine
May 11 The Indian Princess
May 18 The Fighting Parson
May 25 The Red Man's Honor
Jun 1 The Lily of the Ranch
Jun 6 The Bucking Broncho
Jun 13 The Sheriff's Daughter
Jun 20 Boss of Circle E Ranch
Jun 27 The Crooked Trail
Jul 4 A Soldier's Sacrifice
Jul 11 The Call of the West
Jul 20 Back in the Mountains
Jul 27 A True Pal
Aug 3 Sons of the West
Aug 10 Hearts of Gold
Aug 17 Why Dad Was Held Up
Aug 24 In the Black Hills
Aug 31 The Blazed Trail
Sep 7 The Moonshiner's Daughter
Sep 14 The Law and the Man
Sep 21 Strayed from the Range
Sep 28 Where the Sun Sets
Oct 5 The Golden Hoard
Oct 12 Silver Plume Mine
Oct 19 The Boys of Topsy-Turvy Ranch
Oct 26 Rev. John Wright of Missouri
Nov 2 The Girl from the East
Nov 9 The Woodsman
Nov 16 The Ranchman's Bride
Nov 23 A Deal in Indians
Nov 30 Valley Folks
Dec 7 The Conquering Hero
Dec 14 The Pilgrim
Dec 21 A Desperate Remedy
Dec 28 Elda of the Mountains

New York Motion Picture Co.
1909
May 21 Disinherited Son's Loyalty
May 28 Romance of a Fishermaid
Jun 4 "Davy" Crockett in Hearts United
Jun 11 The Squaw's Revenge
Jun 18 A Terrible Attempt
Why Mr. Jones Was Arrested
Jun 25 Cowboy's Narrow Escape
Jul 2 A True Indian's Heart
Jul 9 The Blacksmith's Wife
Jul 16 I Love My Wife, but Oh, You Kid
Jul 23 The Gypsy Artist
Jul 30 My Wife's Gone to the Country
Aug 6 Sailor's Child
Aug 13 Sheltered Under Stars and Stripes
The Yiddisher Cowboy
Aug 20 Half Breed's Treachery
Aug 27 Secret Service Woman
Sep 3 His Two Children
Sep 10 The Paymaster
Sep 17 A Kentucky Planter
Sep 24 A Squaw's Sacrifice
Oct 1 Faithful Wife
Oct 8 Dove Eye's Gratitude
Oct 15 The Gold Seeker's Daughter
Oct 22 Iona, the White Squaw
Oct 29 Mexican's Crime
Nov 5 Young Deer's Bravery
Nov 12 The Ranchman's Wife
Nov 19 An Indian's Bride
Nov 26 Dooley's Thanksgiving Turkey
The Parson's Prayer
Dec 3 The Message of an Arrow
Dec 10 Re-united at the Gallows
Dec 17 The Love of a Savage
Dec 24 An Italian Love Story
Dec 31 The Red Cross Heroine
1910
Jan 7 Red Girl's Romance
Jan 11 A Redman's Devotion
Jan 12 An Episode of Napoleon's War with Spain
Jan 14 A Forester's Sweetheart
Jan 15 The Son of the Wilderness
Jan 18 A Cowboy's Reward
Jan 19 Italian Artillery
Pauli
Jan 21 Romany Rob's Revenge
Jan 22 Football Player
The Tempting Collar
There Are Some Ghosts
Jan 25 A Romance of the Prairie
Jan 26 A Choice Policeman
The Last Keepsake
Jan 28 His Imaginary Crime
Jan 29 A Good Winning
The Timid One
Feb 1 The Female Bandit
Feb 2 Hero and Leander
Feb 4 By His Own Hands
Feb 5 Love and Treason
Feb 8 The Ten of Spades; or, A Western Raffle
Feb 9 The Longing for Gaol
The Strongest
Feb 11 Young Deer's Gratitude
Feb 12 Foolshead Preaches Temperance
Foolshead Receives
Feb 15 Government Rations
Feb 16 I Have Lost My Latch Key
The Silent Piano
Feb 18 Dooley's Holiday
The Impostor
Feb 19 Louise Strozzi
Feb 22 For Her Father's Honor
Feb 23 The Dog of the Cheese Monger
Foolshead at the Ball
Feb 25 Dooley Referees the Big Fight
Feb 26 Why Fricot Was Sent to College
The Witch's Ballad
Mar 1 The Cowboy and the School Marm
Mar 2 The Mysterious Track
The Two Mothers
Mar 4 The New Partners
Mar 5 Supreme Recognition
Mar 8 The Indian and the Cowgirl
Mar 9 Foolshead Chief of the Reporters
The Town Traveler's Revenge
Mar 11 The Rose of the Ranch
Mar 12 Fatal Imprudence
They Have Vanished My Wife
Mar 15 For His Sister's Honor
Mar 16 Insidious Weapons
The Shepherdess
Mar 18 Mexican's Ward
Mar 19 The Betraying Mirror
Mar 22 The Man from Texas
Mar 23 Military Dirigible
The Sea's Vengeance
Mar 25 Company "D" to the Rescue
Mar 26 Foolshead Wishes to Marry the Governor's Daughter
The Rivalry of the Two Guides
Mar 29 Nannina
Mar 30 A Sudden Telephone Call
An Unworthy Fiancé
Apr 1 A Shot in Time
Apr 2 The Servant and the Tutor
Apr 5 Romance of a Snake Charmer
Apr 6 My Life Remembrances of a Dog
An Unpleasant Dream
Apr 8 Red Wing's Loyalty
Apr 9 At the Farm
The Valuable Hat
Apr 12 Rivalry in the Oil Fields
Apr 13 Fricot in College
The Legend of the Cross
Apr 15 Red Wing's Constancy
Apr 16 A Mistake
The Three Brothers
Apr 19 A Husband's Mistake
Apr 20 The Heart of a Vagabond
Petit Jean Louis d'Or & Co.
Apr 22 Adventures of a Cowpuncher
Apr 23 Isabella of Arragon
Apr 26 Hazel, the Heart Breaker
Rattlesnakes
Apr 27 A Doctor's Revenge
Fricot Is Learning a Handicraft
Apr 29 The Rescue of the Pioneer's Daughter
Apr 30 The False Friar
The Fashionable Sport
May 3 A Sister's Devotion
May 4 Blue Jackets' Manoeuvres on a Sailing Vessel
Who Killed Her?
May 6 Love and Money
May 7 How the Great Field Marshall Villars Had an Adopted Daughter
May 10 Cupid's Comedy
May 11 Fricot Gets in a Libertine Mood
The Secret of the Lake
May 13 Lost for Many Years
May 14 Foolshead Learns to Somersault
That Gentleman Has Won a Million
May 17 The Feud
May 18 The Devil on Two Sticks
May 20 The Mexican's Jealousy
May 21 Conquered Again
May 24 The Curse of Gambling
May 25 Estrellita; or, The Invasion of the French Troops in Portugal
May 27 Perils of the Plains
May 28 Foolshead Marries Against His Will
The Knot in the Handkerchief

Nordisk Films Kompagni —DISTRIBUTOR was Great Northern
1907
Apr 20 Anarchist's Mother-in-Law
Auntie's Birthday
Polar Bear Hunt
True until Death
1908
Feb 29 Iceboat Racing on Lake St. Clair
Mar 21 The Hot Temper
The Magic Bag
Apr 4 The Robber's Sweetheart
When the House Rent Was Due
Apr 11 Angelo, Tyrant of Padua
Lion Hunting
Stone Industry in Sweden
Willie's Magic Wand
Apr 25 Ihles & Antonio, Boxers
A Modern Naval-Hero
May 2 The Champagne Bottle
A Misalliance
May 9 Dog Training
When Honor Is Lost Everything Is Lost
May 16 Emperor Nero on the Warpath
Sport from All the World
May 23 The Flight from Seraglio
Winter Manoeuvres of the Norwegian Army
May 30 Mr. Drawee
The Will
Jun 7 Texas Tex
Jun 13 A Chance Shot
The Pupa Changes into a Butterfly
Two Gentlemen
Winter Time in Northern Europe
Aug 29 From Bagdad
Summer in North Europe
Sep 5 The Laplanders

The School of Life
Sep 12 The Hand
The Isle of Bornholm
Sep 19 The Lady with the Camellias
Sep 26 The Codfish Industry
The Magic Rubbers
Oct 3 From the Rococo Times
A Sport at the Music Hall
Oct 10 The Countess' Wedding Day
Oct 28 The Arab Band
Nov [day undetermined]
The Acrobats
Automatic Statue
The Bank Director
The Child and the Gigantic Animal
Cupboard Courtship
The Dance of Death
The Dancing Girl
Little Hannie's Last Dream
The Magic Ring
The Mill
On Roller Skates
The Photographer
Pierrot's Death
The Prima Donna of the Ballet Parody
Rheumatism
Rose That Makes Everybody Dance
Scandanavian North
Supper
The Tinder Box
Nov 1 Bear Hunting in Russia
Nov 4 Clearing the Mountain Track
The Watchmaker's Wedding
Nov 7 The Pillory
The Pilot's Daughter
Nov 14 Blind
Nov 18 Othello
Nov 25 Alexandrian Quadrille
Children of the East
Dec 2 Dummies on the Spree
A Sinner
Dec 9 Sherlock Holmes
Dec 16 The Changing of Souls
The Spring Lock
Dec 23 Count Zeppelin's Aerostat
Hercules the Athlete; or, Love Behind the Scenes
Dec 30 The Quack
The Queen's Love (La Tosca)

1909
Jan 6 "Mafia," the Secret Society; or, Sicilian Family Honor
On Guard at the Powder Magazine
Jan 20 Balloon Races
Jim Smith, the Champion Boxer
Life in Russia
The Stepmother: the Spirit of Unkindness and Jealousy Thwarted
Jan 27 Desert Life
The Gnomes
Feb 3 Moving Furniture
Sultan Abdul Hamid, and the Ladies of His Harem
Summer Sport
Feb 6 Badger Hunt
The Wild Man of Borneo
Feb 17 The Caliph's Adventures
Feb 19 The Barber's Christening
James and Catherine; or, Love on a Farm
Feb 26 Sherlock Holmes II: Raffles Escapes from Prison
Mar 3 The Blind Foundling; or, Alone in the World
The False Superintendent
Four Sweethearts
Sherlock Holmes III: The Detectives Adventure in the Gas Cellar
Mar 6 Two Violins
Mar 8 The Capricious Moment
The Chimney Sweep's Birthday
Round the Lake of Constanz and the Rhine Falls
Mar 9 The Student's Predicament
Mar 14 The Artist's Model's Sweetheart
For Love of a Fisher Girl
From the North Cape
Mar 20 The Grand Procession at the King of Siam Jubilee
Sold to Thieves; or, A Deathbed Confession
A Stage Romance; or, An Actor's Love
Mar 31 The Chauffeur's Adventure
In Ancient Egypt
The Non-Stop Motor Bicycle
William Tell: The Liberator of Switzerland
Apr 5 Nat Pinkerton: The Anarchists Plot
Apr 14 Canals of Copenhagen
A Sailor's Life
Apr 16 Bangkok
Apr 17 The Magic Purse
Apr 21 The Artist's Dream
A Walk Through the Zoo
Apr 24 Modern Egypt
The Viking's Love; or, True to His Chief
Apr 28 Nat Pinkerton [Series II]
May 1 Siamese Actors and Actresses Play a Siamese Drama
Winter Sports and Games at Stockholm, Sweden, 1909
May 5 Boxing Match [by Hallberg of Denmark and Young Joe Gaines "Baltimore Black"]
Hard Working Elephants
May 8 Danish Capitol Under Snow
Neptune's Daughter; or, The Shoemaker's Dream
May 12 The Beggarmaid
Moscow
May 17 Summering in the Austrian Alps
Winter Landscapes Round Stockholm
May 19 The Farmer's Grandson
May 22 The Master Detective; or, The Attack on the Strong Room
May 26 The Human Ape; or, Darwin's Triumph
May 29 The Hasty Tempered Father; or, The Blacksmith's Love
Motherly Love of Animals
Jun 2 Cab Number 519
Jun 9 The Brothers Laurento
The Convict
The General and the Sentry
Street Life in North Siam
Jun 12 The Brave Page Boy
Jun 16 The Wages of Sin
Jun 19 The Art of Fencing
Lesson in Cycling
Jun 23 A Woman of the People
Jul 3 A Mother's Grief
The Mouse
Policeman's Rest
The Prince and the Actor
Jul 10 Herring Fishing
The Persistent Lover
Jul 17 Carnival Merriment in the North
A Shadow of the Past
Jul 24 A Clever Nurse
Off the Coast of Norway
Aug 14 The Spy
Water Sports
Aug 21 False Alarm
Surroundings of Copenhagen
Aug 28 Cowboys in Argentina
The Shell; or, "A Madman's Revenge"
Sep 4 Cycle Rider and the Witch
The Henpecked Husband
Norrkobing
Sep 11 The Gray Dame
Sep 18 How Dr. Nicola Procured the Chinese Cane
Sep 22 Dr. Cook at Copenhagen
Sep 25 The Great Prize
Life on Board a Training Ship
Oct 2 The Cremation
Heroism Reconciles
Oct 9 Adventures of an Emigrant
Vagabond Life
Oct 16 The Red Domino
Oct 23 The Bracelet
Gotacanal—over Norway's Rockies
A Lunatic's Day Off
Nov 3 Dynamite
Hanson & Co.
Life in Dalerne (Sweden)
Nov 6 The Destiny of Paul Wang
Nov 10 The Short-Sighted Governess
The Suicide Woods
Yachting on the Baltic
Nov 13 A Message to Napoleon; or, An Episode in the Life of the Great Prisoner at Elba
Nov 20 A Girl's Cross Roads
Dec 1 A Boy Hero; or, The Fisherman's Son
Trollhattan
Dec 4 Little Willie's Trip to the North Pole
Wrestling
Dec 8 Gerhardi Mohr
Temptations of the Gold Fields; or, The Two Gold Diggers
Dec 18 The Butcher's Bill
In Southern Sweden
Mother-in-Law Crazy with Music
Dec 25 Father's Busy Papering
An Outcast's Christmas

1910
Jan 1 Refreshing Bath
Vengeance; or, The Forester's Sacrifice
Jan 8 Child as Benefactor
Jan 15 Death of the Brigand Chief
Naughty Boys
Jan 22 Anarchists on Board; or, The Thrilling Episode on the S. S. "Slavonia"
Jan 29 The Mystery of the Lama Convent; or, Dr. Nicola in Thibet
Feb 5 The Foxy Soldiers; or, How Schmidt Got to the Masquerade
A Woman's Destiny
Feb 12 Never Despair; or, From Misery to Happiness
Worried to Death
Feb 19 Ruined by His Son
Feb 26 Doctor's Sacrifice
Mar 5 The Mad Drainpipe
A Pleasant Walk
Mar 12 A Wedding During the French Revolution
Mar 19 A Quiet Honeymoon
The Theft of the Diamonds
Mar 26 Tsing Fu, the Yellow Devil
Apr 2 Madame Sans Gene; or, The Duchess of Danzig
Apr 9 Hustling Mr. Brown
A New Burglar Alarm
Apr 16 The Hidden Treasure
Apr 23 The Conjuror
A Day Off
The Four Seasons
Apr 30 Saved from the Sultan's Sentence
May 7 The Somnambulist
May 14 The Club of the Corpulent
The Marvelous Cure; or, The Wonderful Hair-Growing Fluid
May 21 A Father's Grief
May 28 The Eagle's Egg; or The Rival Lovers
Roosevelt in Denmark
Jun 4 The Carman's Dream
The Jump to Death
Jun 11 The Duel
Jun 18 How Brother Cook Was Taught a Lesson
Lake of Lucerne
Jun 25 The Captain's Wife
The Clown and His Dogs
Jul 2 The Sons of the Minister
Jul 9 The Laughing Machine
The Wonderful Cigar
Jul 16 The Prodigal Son
Jul 23 The Elopement
Fabian Cleaning Chimney
Jul 30 Fabian Arranging Curtain Rods
For the Sake of a Child
Aug 6 Magdalene; or, The Workman's Daughter
Aug 13 The Life Boat
The Stolen Policeman
Aug 27 Fabian's Hollow Tooth
A Society Sinner
Sep 3 Fabian Hunting Rats
The Little Drummer Boy
Sep 10 Robinson Crusoe
Sep 17 Danish Dragoons
Fabian Out for a Picnic
Sep 24 Dr. Jekyll and Mr. Hyde; or, A Strange Case
Oct 1 Bird's Eye View from World's Highest Buildings
The Flight across the Atlantic
Oct 8 The Storms of Life
Oct 15 Saved by Bosco
Willie Visits a Moving Picture Show
Oct 22 The Artist's Luck
Oct 29 Who Is She?

Nov 5 A Fatal Picnic
The Jewel Case
Nov 12 Mother-in-Law Arrives
World's Wrestling Champions
Nov 19 The Diamond Swindler
Nov 26 Kean; or, The Prince and the Actor
Dec 3 The Birthday Present
The Ohami Troupe of Acrobats
Dec 10 The Poacher
Dec 17 A Christmas Letter
Dickey's Courtship
Dec 24 The Necklace of the Dead
Dec 31 Bearhunting
The Scarecrow

Norwood
1906
Sep 20 The Dog Detective
1908
Sep 19 His Sweetheart's Birthday
In the Time of Rebellion

O. T. Crawford Film Exchange Co.
1907
Oct 26 International Balloon Races [from the James Gordon Bennett Cup, at St. Louis, Oct. 21, 1907]
Nov 23 The Country Girl

Oklahoma Natural Mutoscene Co.
1908
Dec [day undetermined]
The Bank Robbery
A Round-Up in Oklahoma
The Wolf Hunt

Ottolenghi
1909
Sep 27 The Priest's Niece

Paley and Steiner
1904
Oct [day undetermined]
An Interrupted Flirtation
A Jolly Lawn Party
Just Like a Girl
That Poor Insurance Man
Tramp on a Farm
The Trials and Troubles of an Automobilist
Two Is Company, Three a Crowd
Nov [day undetermined]
Avenging a Crime; or, Burned at the Stake
Willie's Vacation
Dec [day undetermined]
"Champion Pumpkin Eater"
Mischievous Boys
What Happened to a Camera Fiend
1905
Jan [day undetermined]
Around New York in 15 Minutes
Bridget's Troubles
Burlesque Tramp Burglars
Fisherman, Eels or Snakes
He Got His Hat
The Paper Hanger in Trouble
Three Jolly Dutchmen
Tramp and Dump Cart
Mar [day undetermined]
How She Loves Him
Life of the New York Policeman
The Non-Union Bill-Poster
Apr [day undetermined]
The Bigamist
Travels of a Lost Trunk
May [day undetermined]
How Mr. Butt-In Benefits by Chauncey's Mishaps
Jun [day undetermined]
Jack and Jill
Jul [day undetermined]
The Lucky Wishbone
Aug [day undetermined]
Two Strenuous Rubes

Pantograph Corp.
1910
Jan 29 Tale of Colonial Days: An Episode in the Life of Alexander Hamilton and Aaron Burr
Feb 5 His Daughter's Legacy
Feb 12 The Untimely Visit
Feb 18 Hobo's Dream of Wealth
Feb 25 Iron Arm's Remorse
Mar 4 The Electric Bathtub
Mar 11 The Mysterious Armour

Paramount Film Co.
1910
May 9 Saved by Faith
May 12 Wearing of the Green
May 20 Parting His Hair
May 26 Midsummer Night's Dream
May 27 Faust and Marguerite
May 28 Love Amidst Historic Ruins

Parnaland & Ventujol
1904 [month undetermined]
Engineers, French Army
Highwaymen
The Interrupted Couple
Japanese Coaling a Man-of-War
Japanese Infantry Morning Drill
The Mischievous Kid, the Duck and the Gendarme
Panoramic view of Montreux, Switzerland
The Policeman's Mistake
Toys Competition
The Up-to-Date Wizard
View of "La Croisette," Cannes, France

Pasquali & Tempo
1909
Jun 17 Cyrano de Bergerac
Officer's Revenge
Dec 25 Alberno & Rosamunda
The Deserter
Electra
Theodora
1910
Jan 15 The Twine

Pathé Frères
1900
Apr [day undetermined]
Birth of Venus
1902
May [day undetermined]
Gibson, the Eccentric American Actor
Going to Bed Under Difficulties
The History of a Crime
The Magical Hen
What Happened to the Inquisitive Janitor
The Wonderful Hair Restorer
Nov 1 Ali Baba and the Forty Thieves
1903 [month undetermined]
The Infernal Meal
Jan [day undetermined]
Andre at the North Pole
Bathing Horses
Boulevard St. Denis, Paris, France
Bullet vs. Whiskey
Climbing the Greasy Pole
Hunting White Bear
Jolly Monks
Massage Treatment
Quadrille in Drawers
Skating Scene
Snowballing
Spanish Dance
Jan 17 Picture Hanging Extraordinary
Feb [day undetermined]
Cadet's First Smoke
Feb 14 Disagreeable Railroad Passengers
Apr 11 Acrobatic Sisters Daines
May [day undetermined]
The Angler
Animated Dolls
Market Scene in Hanoi, China
Modern House Furnishing Methods
New Bull Fight
Resourceful Waiter
Window Cleaner's Mishap
May 16 The Gambler's Crime
Smiles and Tears
Jun 6 Little Tom Thumb
Jul 11 Sleeping Beauty
Sep 19 Pope Pius X [His Election and the Procession]
Oct [day undetermined]
Ballet of the Nations
Nov 7 Life of Napoleon
1904 [month undetermined]
Bull Fight with Matadors Senor Don Luis Mazzantini and Bombita
Jan 2 William Tell
Jan 16 Puss in Boots
Jan 23 Amusing Changes
Charming Enchantment
Jan 30 Dogs and Rats
Feb 6 Devil's Pot
The Little Greedy Beggar
Marie Antoinette
Metamorphosis of the King of Spades
The Midgets
Mar 12 Babe and Dog
Scenes on Every Floor
Mar 26 The Passion Play
Wonderful Hair Restorer
Apr 9 Living Dummy
The Revolving Table
Apr 25 The Prodigal Son
Samson and Delilah
May 21 Barnum's Trunk
Jun [day undetermined]
The Magic Hat
Pierrot's Mystification
Jun 18 A Disagreeable Remedy
European Idea of Christopher Columbus Discovering America
Metamorphosis of a Butterfly
A Scandal on the Staircase
Jul [day undetermined]
Barber's Revenge
Giovanni and His Trained Parrots
Japanese Varieties
A Parisienne's Bed Time
Jul 2 Don Quixote
Jul 23 Annie's Love Story
Dance Plastiques
Japanese Ambush
The Nest Robbers
Tour in Italy
Aug 20 Lookout at Port Arthur
Aug 27 A Boar Hunt
Orla and His Trained Dogs
Sep 3 Falls of the Rhine
Indians and Cowboys
The Strike
The Wrestling Donkey
Sep 10 Ghezzi and His Circus
Joseph Sold by His Brothers
Sep 24 The Devil's Seven Castles
Drama in the Air
The Fairy of the Spring
Fox and Rabbits
A Gambler's Quarrel
A Good Story
Ice Cream Eater
Quo Vadis
Ruffian's Dance
Oct [day undetermined]
Advance Guard Fight
Alarm
Alcohol and Its Victims
Amphitrite
Arabian Phantasia
Around Port Arthur (No. 2)
Arrival and Departure of a Train
Arrival of a Train
Attack on a Fortress
Attack on a Train
A Bad Rich Man
Battleship Leaving Harbor
The Bear and the Sentinel
The Bird Charmer
Boy's First Smoke
Bride Retiring
The Brothers Laure
Bullocks Swimming
Cakewalk
Capture of a Gun
Cavalry Crossing a River
Cavalry Fording a Stream
Charging Cuirassiers
Charley's Aunt
Cloth Dealer
Convoy of Oxen
Dance of the Sylphs
Death of Robert McCaire and Bertrand
Dranem Salutes the Audience
Drunkard and Statue
Eccentric Tight-rope Walker
Eccentric Waltz
Elephants at Work in India
The Enchanted Wardrobe
Extraordinary Fishing
Fairy of the Black Rocks
Fairy of the Lake

The False Cripple
Fire! Fire!
Flea
Gate Jumping by Unsaddled Horse
Grandma's Glass
Grinning Guillot
A Heavy Sea
Hedge Jumping
Honeymoon Trip
Horse Tied to a Post Jumping
The Illusionist
Impossible to Get a Plunge
Iroquois Theatre Fire in Chicago
Japanese Dance
Japanese Girls at Tea
Jumping Horses
Kickapoo
Kissing in a Tunnel
Ladies of the Court Bathing
Lahury, the Soldier
Living Statues; or, Marble Comes to Life
Looping the Loop
Masks and Faces
Mind! Madame Is Coming
Modern High School Riding
Mysterious Screen
Naval Fight
No Posters Allowed
Outpost Skirmishing
Painter's Misfortune
Passing Trains
Pedestrian Jugglers
Pole Jumping
The Porter's Horrible End
Rolling Bridge in Tunis
Russian Cavalry
Russian Dance
Russian Infantry
Scenes from My Balcony
The Shower Bath
Sisters Barrison
Soap Bubbles
A Sorcerer's Night
Spy's Arrest
Spy's Execution
Startling Pursuit
The Statue Dealer
Street in Canton, China
Street in Tokio
Swimming Horses
Too Hot
Too Late
Up-to-Date Burglars; or, The Mystified Cops
Vision of Art
Water Shoots
Woman's Bath
The Young Farmer Girl

Oct 1 Across the Alps
Dogs and Cats
The Opera Hat
Park in Barcelona by Moonlight
Smoker Too Small

Oct 8 Around Port Arthur
Fantastic Fishing
A Fight on the Yalu

Oct 15 Ascending Mount Pilate
Bathers at Joinville
Greedy Cat

Oct 22 Behind the Lens
The Clever Baker
Disagreeable Five O'Clock
In a Hurry to Catch the Train
Mistake in the Door

Oct 29 Trained Hogs

Nov 12 August, the Monkey
A Princess in Disguise

Nov 19 A Cheeky Traveler

Dec 3 From Christiania to the North Cape
Saluting the Flag

Dec 24 Babies Bathing
Burglars at Work
His First Hunting Day
Louis XIV
Pilgrimage to Lourdes
Solomon's Judgment
The Swing
Vintage

Dec 31 Russian Antisemitic Atrocities

1905 [month undetermined]
Different Hair Dresses
A Little Jules Verne
Love at Each Floor
Out Boating

Jan 14 Big Fountain at Versailles
Christmas, 1904
Wonderful Beehive
Wrestler and Bull

Feb 4 Fireworks
Innocent Flirtation
Prompting Phonograph

Feb 25 Bewitched Lover
From Cairo to the Pyramids
Last Attack on the Hill
Riots in St. Petersburg
Surrender at Port Arthur

Mar 4 Modern Style House Maids

Mar 11 Gluttonous Negro

Mar 25 Assassination of the Grand Duke Serge
The Nihilists in Russia

Apr 1 Winter Sports

Apr 8 The Incendiary
The Sign of the Cross

May 13 The Moon-Lover

May 27 A Father's Honor

Jun 10 In the Mining District

Jun 24 Christian Martyrs

Jul 1 King of Dollars
A Pleasure Trip

Jul 15 The Gun License

Jul 22 The Young Tramps

Jul 29 Great Steeplechase

Aug 5 Mutiny on Man-of-War in Odessa

Aug 19 Modern Brigandage

Aug 26 The Vendetta

Sep 16 Life of Moses

Sep 23 Creusot's Metallurgy

Sep 30 Countryman in Paris
Flower Fairy
Gay Washerwoman
Impatient Customer
Language of Flowers
Loie Fuller
Stunning Creations
Wonderful Album

Oct [day undetermined]
The Cheated Policeman
Chimney Sweep and Pastry Cook

Oct 14 Behind the Stage
A Henpecked Husband
Ill Rewarded Conjuror
The Vicar's Garden Party

Nov [day undetermined]
"Clown Sidney on Stilts"
Defense of a Pagoda
Defense of Port Arthur
"A Frightful Night"
Horses Jumping over a Wall
The King and Queen of Italy in Paris
Pillow Fight
Russian Artillery
A Street in Lourdes
Through the Keyhole
Tight-Rope Walker Undressing
Turkish Atrocities in Macedonia
Yantai Episode

Nov 4 An Impracticable Journey
The Pastry Cook's Practical Jokes
Zoological Garden

Dec 9 The Hen with the Golden Eggs
Love Is Ingenious
The Postman's Christmas Box

Dec 16 Alcoholism Engenders Tuberculosis
Ceylon
Christmas Miracle
A Tragedy at Sea

Dec 23 The Christmas Goose
Disagreeable Mistake
A Great Discovery
The Photographing Bear
The Three Phases of the Moon

Dec 30 Custom House Search
Misadventures of a Hat

1906

Jan 6 The Tramp

Jan 13 The Bicycle Robber
Robbers of Children

Jan 20 Fire Cascades
The Wolf's Trap

Jan 27 The Deserter

Feb 3 Socialism and Nihilism

Feb 10 Beware of My Husband
Tragedy in a Train

Feb 17 Tit-for-Tat
Victims of the Storm

Feb 24 The Heart Governs the Head
The Last Witch

Mar 17 Another's Crime
Ascending Mt. Serrat in Spain
Descending Mt. Serrat in Spain
Engadin in Switzerland
I've Lost My Eyeglasses
Passing Trains
Street in Agra, India
Thibidado
A Trip from Naples to Vesuvius, Showing the Volcano in Action
A Trip Through the Island of Ceylon

Mar 31 A Boarding School Conspiracy

Apr [day undetermined]
The Absent-Minded Shoe Black
Acrobatic Elephant
Aerial Billiard Playing
Apaches in Paris
At Mukden
Baby's Bath
Bad Coffee
Bad Joke
Bad Lodgers
Bath of Sacred Elephants
Bird's Eye View of Paris
Boats on the Nile
Bull Fight
Captain's Inspection
Childish Tricks Baffled
Children's Quarrel
Clown's Revenge
Coal Man's Bath
Compromising Spots
Confession
A Courageous Husband
Dancing Sentry Box
Doorkeeper's Curiosity
Dranem's Dream
Drunkard
The Enchanted Melon
False Alarm
Fantastic Diver
First Night Out
Flying Machine
Frog Fishing
Funny Shave
Gaieties of Divorce
Good Pipe
Great Ballet
Hairdresser's Victim
Haunted House
A Heavy Sea
High Sea Fishing
Improvised Suit
In the Polar Regions
The Indiscreet Bathroom Maid
Indiscreet Mystified
Infernal Cave
Ingenious Dauber
Insolvable Guests
Irascible Fisherman
Jack the Bootblack
Japanese Soldier's Return
Joys of Marriage
Keep It Straight
Kids' Practical Jokes
Lady Undressing
Life on Board Ship
Liliputian Dance
Love Letter
Man with 36 Heads
Martyrs of the Inquisition
Matrimonial Agency
Miniature Theatre
Motor-car and Cripple
Nautical Fancy
Nautical Game
Negro and Policeman
Neighbor's Lamp
Obstacle Jumping by Attached Horses
Obstinate Drunkard
Old Seducer
Pasha's Nightmare
Penny Milk

Phantom's Guard
Phenomenal Hen
Pierrot's Revenge
Practical Conjuror
Prince of Wales in India
Pussy's Breakfast
Remorse
Retaking a Fort
Revolution in Russia
Robbers Robbed
Room, Please
St. Bartholomew's Day
Sardine Fishing
Scenes of Convict Life
Scholar's Breakfast
Schoolboys' Practical Jokes
Ski Running
Sock
Stupendous Jugglers
Surgical Operation
Temptation of St. Anthony
Ten Wives for One Husband
Terrible Anguish
Topsy-Turvy Dance
Touching Pleading
Trained Bears
Transparent Cards
Troublesome Fishbone
Tunisian Dance
Two Drunkards
Unforeseen Meeting
Virtue Rewarded
Voice of Conscience
War of Children
Whence Does He Come?
When the Masters Are Out
Where Is My Horse?
The Wig
Young Apple Thief
Apr 7 The Starvelings
Apr 14 Carnival Night
History of a Pair of Trousers
The Invisible Man
Jewel Robbers Mystified
Living Flowers
Apr 21 Hello! Hello! Grinder
Life in India
Spontaneous Generation
Apr 28 Monte Carlo to Monaco
Playing Truant
May [day undetermined]
Dance of Geishas
May 5 Law of Pardon
May 12 A Shooting Expedition Accident
The Wig Chase
May 19 A Childish Match
May 26 My Hat
Jun 2 Ephemeral Wealth
Escaped from the Cage
Mrs. Brown's Bad Luck
Jun 16 A Detective's Trip Around the World
The Holiday
Three Cent Leeks
The Troubles of a Fireman
Jun 23 The Angler's Dream
I Fetch the Bread
Marriage of Princess Ena and Alphonse XIII, King of Spain
The Olympic Games at Athens, Greece
The Rajah's Casket
The Riderless Bicycle
Jul 7 The Elections
Follower of Women
A Strange Engagement Bouquet
The Target
Jul 14 Butterfly Catching
Corsican Chastisement
Dogs Used as Smugglers
Extraordinary Dislocation
Honor Is Satisfied
The Troublesome Flea
Jul 21 Rival Brothers
Jul 28 Letters Which Speak
Aug [day undetermined]
Pals; or, My Friend, the Dummy
Aug 11 Voyage Around a Star
Sep 8 The Paris Students
Sep 22 The Accordion
Sep 29 The Tenacious Cat
Oct 13 Custom Officials Bewitched
Fun After the Wedding
Ill Rewarded Honesty
Indian's Revenge
Mephisto's Son
New Brother
Nov 3 The Bell Ringer's Daughter
Nov 24 An Artist's Dream
Caught in a Trap
Colonel's Bicycle
The Inexperienced Chauffeur
The Poor Tutor
Travels of a Barrel
Dec 1 The Cab
Cross Country
Day in the Country
Honesty's Strange Reward
The Magic Flute
Man Without Scruple
Marble Industry at Carrara
Old Man's Darling
Poor Mother
The Rebellious Walking Stick
Stealing Tomatoes
The Telescope
The Troubadour
Village Witch
Dec 8 At the Seaside
Child's Revenge
Difficult Problem
Japanese Sports
Love's Thermometer
Magic Roses
Dec 15 Alladin and His Wonder Lamp
Bobby and His Family
Desperate Girl
The Female Spy
In Search of Adventure
The Poacher
1907 [month undetermined]
Botanist's Misadventures
Jan 12 Between Two Fires
Cousin's Visit
Exciting Honeymoon Trip
Fine Birthday Cake
Forbidden Fruit
Friendship Better Than Riches
Gibelot's Hotel
Hot Chestnuts
Hypnotized Police Inspector
Life in Congo
My Wife's Birthday
Niagara Falls
Paris Slums
Pay Day
Saved by a Melon
Scales of Justice
Six Amorous Dragoons
Skating Lessons
Sportsmen and Lion
Strange Mount
Susan Tastes Our Wine
Tragic Wedding
Unexpected Meal
Venetian Tragedy
Wedding on Bicycles
Jan 19 Attempted Suicide
Cabby by the Hour
A Colored Man's Revenge
Crime on the Railroad
Little Blind Girl
Jan 26 Bad Mother
Fan in Japan
The Gypsies
Joined Lips
Misadventures of a Negro King in Paris
Servant's Strike
Wrestler's Wife
Wrestling Matches of 1906
Feb 9 Bobby and His Balloon
The Charmer
Constructed Fishing Boat
Determined Creditor
False Coiners
For Mother's Birthday
Forbidden Sport
In the Cause of Faith
India Rubberman
Julia at the Barracks
Old Mashers
Policeman's Little Run
Spot at the 'Phone
Feb 16 Cavalry School
Difficult Arrest
Phial of Poison
Rat Catching
Sea by Moonlight
Two Little Scamps
Feb 23 The Pork Butcher's Nightmare
Mar 2 The Clever Thief
Little Tich
Mar 16 Ascending Mt. Blanc
Cinderella
Hooligans of the Far West
The Life and Passion of Christ
Suicide Impossible
Tommy at Play
The Yawner
Apr 13 Street in Frankfort
Apr 27 Amateur Photographer
The Baby's First Outing
Boxing Matches in England
From Jealousy to Madness
Golden Beetle
Herring Fishing
Japanese Women
A Military Prison
Picturesque Canada
Pompeii
Tragic Rivalry
Wonderful Flames
Jun 1 Anything to Oblige
Artful Husband
Betrothed's Nightmare
Blind Man's Dog
Brigand Story
Cowboys and Red-skins
Distress
Haunted Kitchen
Horrible Adventure
Julius, the Sandwich Man
Lawyer Enjoys Himself
Looking for Lodgings
Mines and Forge at Decazeville
Modern Burglars
To Tame His Wife
Jun 15 Biker Does the Impossible
Costumes of Different Centuries
Dog Police
Poor Coat
Servant's Vengeance
Straw Hat Factory in Florence
Washings Badly Marked
Weird Fancies
Jun 29 Alps of Chamonix
A Carmen in Danger
Charley Paints
Crime in the Mountains
Frolics of Ding Dong Imps
A Hooligan Idea
Mother-in-Law's Race
Nervous Kitchenmaid
No More Children
Palmistry
A Slave's Love
Struggle for Life
Tragic Moment
Jul 13 Drama on the Riviera
Life's Reality
Quick, I'm on Fire
Seaman's Widow
Woodchopper's Daughter
Jul 20 Harlequin's Story
Magic Drawing Room
Sambo as Footman
Victim of Science
Jul 27 Chasing a Motorist
Diabolo
Dunhard After All
Genevieve of Brabant
Lighthouse Keepers
Sham Beggars
Troubles of a Cook
Vengeance of the Algerine
Window Cleaner
Aug 3 The Express Sculptor
A Kind Grandfather
Ostrich Farm
Poor Little Mites
Aug 10 Angling in Norway
The Dancing Swine

Discipline and Humanity
First Success
From Barrel to Barrel
A Glorious Start
A Lucky Heiress
Aug 17 A Case of Arson
Cock Fight in Seville
The Red Spectre
The Servant Hypnotist
The Smoking Chimney
Aug 24 Chrysanthemums
Nurses' Strike
Robber Robbed
Spanish Views, on Postals
Aug 31 Children's Reformatory
Half Caste's Revenge
I'll Dance the Cakewalk
Lost Umbrella
Modern Painters
Rival Sisters
Three Chatterboxes
Sep 7 Englishman in Harem
Knowing Dogs
The Living Silhouette
Private Atkins Minds the Baby
The Romance of a Singer
Sep 14 At the Colonial Exhibition
Cambodian Customs
A Daring Maid
In Sevilla
The Two Fowls
Sep 21 The Blacksmith's Revenge
Charley's Dream
Dieppe Circuit
The Fortune
Interrupted Card Party
A Pair of Boots, Please
Policeman's Boots
Wood Industry in Canada
Sep 28 The Adventuress
Enchanted Glasses
Indian Idyll
Maniac Juggler
Our Band's Going to the Competition
Poor Pig
Stilt Race
Oct 5 Highwaymen
Riding School
Oct 12 Easter Eggs
The Heart's Bidding
The Japanese Girl
Making Pottery in Japan
The Prodigal Son
William, the Poacher
Oct 19 The Cigar Box
Clever Tailor
A Drama in Seville
Jane Is Furious
Naples to Vesuvius
Save the Pieces
West Africa
Oct 26 Andalusian Dances
Burglary by Motor
A Crime in the Snow
Dog Avenges His Master
Her First Bike Ride
Ice Cutting in Sweden
Magic Lantern
Making Love to the Coalman's Wife
My Mother-in-Law Is an Angel
Pleasant Thoughts
A Quiet Hotel
Red Riding Hood
Satan at Play
Tommy in Society
The Two Orphans
An Unpleasant Legacy
Wonderful Lion Killer
Nov 9 The Elixir of Life
The Mysterious Armor
The Night Watchman
A Pressing Letter
Swedish Sports
Tunny Fisheries in Sicily
Nov 23 Airship Thieves
Ali Baba and the Forty Thieves
Artistic Woodcarver
The Baboon
Chemist's Mistake
Cripple's Duel
The Cupboard
Enchanted Pond
Inexhaustible Barrel
Innkeeper and Wife
The Innkeeper's Wife
Little Conjuror
Mysterious Boudoir
The Pirates
The Plank
Tippler's Race
Nov 30 The Clock-Maker's Secret
Economical Trip
Master in General
Modern Hercules at Work
Ups and Downs of a Hat
Wood Industry in Norway
Your Wife Is Unfaithful to Us
Dec 7 Bobby's Practical Jokes
Doings of a Maniac
An Exciting Ride
The Pearl Fisher
The Poor Old Couple
Dec 14 A Champion After All
Elephants in India
A Mother's Secret
Music, Forward!
Sailor's Practical Joke
A Super's Debut
Up to Date Burglars
Dec 21 The Daily Life of a French Sailor
Madam's Fancies
Manners and Customs of Australia
On the Grass
An Uncle by Marriage
Dec 28 The Bargeman's Child
The Black Witch
Blue Beard
Doings of a Poodle
Elegant Paris
The First Row
The Strong Man
The Talisman or Sheep's Foot
Thieves Caught in Their Own Trap
Thirteen at Table
Unknown Talent
The Witch Kiss
Wonderful Mirrors

1908

Jan 4 Dog and His Various Merits
The Shrimper
The Tulips
Jan 11 Afraid of Microbes
Fatherhood and Drunkenness
Go, Little Cabin Boy
Lovers' Ill Luck
Military Tournament at Saumur
Jan 18 Adventures of an Overcoat
Bewitched Son-in-Law
The Diabolical Itching
First Cigar
Funny Faces Competition
Going to Switzerland
Heavyweight's Race
Kiri-Kis
Lady Doctor's Husband
Man Who Walks on the Water
A Prince's Idea
Red Tapism
Shipowner's Daughter
That Squally Beach
Witch's Secret
Jan 25 Animated Portraits
Charmed Sword
For a Flower
Good Luck for the Coming Year
The Hostage
A Kindhearted Gentleman
Picturesque Smyrna
The Pretty Typist
Skillful Policemen
Slave's Hate
Will He Overtake Them?
Feb 1 Dog's Music Hall
Excursion to Moon
A Gypsy's Revenge
London Streets
A Phlegmatic Gentleman
Soldier's Antics
Feb 8 Artistic Rag-Pickers
Flower of Youth
A Gamble for a Woman
The Runaway Horse
Sandwich Woman
Feb 15 Avenged by the Sea
Cabman's Delusion
Discharging the Maid
Electrocuted
Farman Aeroplane
Fire Maneuvers in Madrid
Forsaken
Incendiary Foreman
Making Charcoal
Man with Calf's Head
Mr. Shortsighted Goes Shrimping
Neapolitan's Revenge
Touaregs in Their Country
Feb 22 Any Barrels to Sell?
I'm Mourning the Loss of Chloe
The Little Cripple
Scullion's Dream
Feb 29 Cruel Joke
Custom Officers Mystified
Hold-Up in Calabria
It Is Not the Cowl That Makes the Friar
Jerusalem
The One-Legged Man
Pierrot's Jealousy
Playing at Chess
Regattas in London
Troubles of a Grass Widower
Unlucky Old Flirt
Up-to-Date Removal
Mar 1 Launching the Roma
What a Razor Can Do
Mar 7 Betrayed by One's Feet
The Explosive Calf
The Mattress
Northern Venice
Only Thoughtlessness
A Statue on a Spree
A Workman's Honor
Mar 8 A Bewitching Woman
The Mummy
A New Way of Traveling
That Mother-in-Law Is a Bore
Mar 14 The Baby Show
Billy Is on Fire
A Briton's Promise
In a Difficult Position
Lost, a Pretty Dog
Mr. and Mrs. Jollygood Go Tandeming
My Watch Is Slow
A Rape Under Louis XVI
Suspicious Husband
Toula's Dream
Mar 15 Angel of the Village
The Frog
Mar 21 Beauty Parlors
The Devil's Three Sins
Engulfed in Quicksands
Gendarme Has a Keen Eye
A Good Joke
I Have Won a Pig
Orderly Jameson
The Vestal
Wedding in Brittany
Whimsical People
Mar 28 Avaricious Father
Different Ways of Smuggling
The Idler
Jim Gets a New Job
A Narrow Escape
Swedish Dances
Transformation of a Horse
Mar 29 A Modern Samson
The Waif
Apr 4 Amateur Acrobat
The Old Maid's Inheritance
What a Good Wine
Apr 5 Black Princess
Military Airship "Ville de Paris"
The Sacrifice
Sleeping Beauty
The Two Brothers
Apr 11 Dynamiters
Shanghai, China
Travels of a Flea
The Videos
Wanted, a Maid
Apr 12 Champagne Industry

The Cossacks
Lottery Ticket
Modern Sculptors
Will Grandfather Forgive?
Apr 18 Cider Industry
Engaged Against His Will
Hunchback Brings Luck
The Nomads
Peggy's Portrait
Thirsty Moving Men
Useful Present for a Child
A Visit to the Public Nursery
Apr 19 Christmas Eve
A Peaceful Inn
Apr 25 A Disastrous Oversight
A French Guard's Bride
Give Me Back My Dummy
Harry, the Country Postman
A Miser's Punishment
The Poacher's Wife
A Poor Man's Romance
Under the Livery
Unwilling Chiropodist
Workman's Revenge
May 2 Clogmaking in Brittany
A Day in the Life of a Suffragette
Diabolical Pickpocket
For Kate's Health
The Hanging Lamp
In the Land of the Gold Mines
Mandrel's Feats
Music Teacher
Sweden
A Useful Beard
May 9 The Bargee's Daughter
Each in His Turn
The False Coin
Female Police Force
Gendarme's Honor
Haunted Castle
In China (Hong Chu Fou)
The Maid's Last Day
Spiritualistic Seance
Students' Jokes
The Two Rivals
May 16 Artist's Inheritance
Japanese Butterflies
Little Chimney Sweep
Locked Up
Mountaineer's Son
Nobleman's Rights
Oscar's Elopement
Pretty Dairymaid
Pretty Flower Girl
Stolen Sausage
May 23 All for a Bird
Blind Woman's Story
End of a Dream
Fashionable Hat
A Good Medicine
Imperial Canal
Legend of a Ghost
Poverty and Probity
Unfortunate Pickpocket
May 30 Anti-Hair Powder
Athletic Woman
Burglar's New Trick
A Complicated Duel
Fire! Fire!
Hide and Seek
In a Submarine
Lucky Accident
An Occasional Porter
Story of a Foundling
Jun 6 Arabian Dagger
Don Juan
Family of Cats
Fish Preserving at Astrakhan
Justice of the Redskin
Lady Barrister
Mrs. Pimpernell's Gown
Tormented by His Mother-in-Law
Weird Symphony
Jun 13 Brazil—The Cascades
Drama in the Tyrol
Dynamite Duel
Joyous Surprise
Messenger's Mistake
Misadventures of a Sheriff
Music and Poetry
The Ragpicker's Daughter
A Tiresome Play
Tracked by the Police Dog
Jun 20 Astrakhan Fisheries
Beatrice Cenci
Double Suicide
Grandfather's Pills
The New Maid
Peculiar People
Poor Pussy
Ruffians Thrashed
Unlucky Artist
Victim of His Honesty
Jun 27 The Fat Baby
For the Sake of a Crown
Magnetic Removal
Mr. Boozer Gets a Fright
Mysterious Flames
Nocturnal Thieves
Our Dog Friends
Troublesome Theft
Walks in Soudan
Jul 4 The Blackmailer
Busy Fiancé
The Country of the "Bogoudens"
The Dreyfus Affair
Husband Wanted
Interrupted Romance
Native Life in Sudan
On Bad Terms with the Janitor
The Specter
Jul 11 The Accuser
The Candidate
Cumbersome Baby
Jealous Fiancé
Latest Style Airship
Noisy Neighbors
The Perjurer
Professor Bric-a-Brac's Inventions
Stockholm
Unsuccessful Flirts
Jul 18 A Bashful Young Man
Bothersome Husband
Contagious Nervous Twitching
The Father Is to Blame
In the Government Service
Korea
Mystery of the Mountains
The Poor Officer
Runaway Mother-in-Law
Russian Review of the Fiftieth Regiment
Jul 25 The Affair of the Select Hotel
Crocodile Turns Thief
Cumbersome First Fight
Hard to Get Arrested
Home Work in China
It Sticks Everything—Even Iron
King Scatterbrain's Troubles
Living Posters
Mr. Softhead Has a Good Time
Story of a Fishermaiden
Aug 1 A Boarding House Acquaintance
Head over Heels in Politics
It Smells of Smoke
The Little Magician
Picturesque Naples
The Secret of the Iron Mask
The Uncle's Fortune
The Vacuum Cleaner
Wanted—A Son-in-Law on Trial
Water Cure
Aug 8 The Boundary
The Curse of Drink
The Improvised Statue
The Inconvenience of Taking Moving Pictures
Jewel of a Servant
The Knowing Birds
The Masque Ball
Miss Hold's Puppets
Susceptible Youth
A Wonderful Fluid
Aug 15 Army Dogs
Dieppe Circuit, 1908
The Dog and the Pipe
A Kind-Hearted Policeman
Lady-Killer Foiled
New York
The Powerful Tenor
Prospective Heirs
The Sailor's Dog
Aug 22 The Blue Bird
Brothers in Arms
Freedom for All
Jim Is Fond of Garlic
A Kindness Never Goes Unrewarded
Manual of a Perfect Gentleman
The Miller, His Son and the Ass
A Trip Through Russia
A Woman's Jealousy
Aug 29 A Country Lad
A Daughter's Honesty
A Good Dinner Badly Digested
The Hapless Hubby
Head-Dresses Worn in Brittany
Mr. Fuzz
Mrs. Toney's Suitors
Troublesome Carbuncle
The Two Models
Sep 1 Samson and Delilah
Sep 5 A Dozen of Fresh Eggs
The Gambler's Fate
The Marathon Race
Olympic Games
Sep 12 The Cabby's Wife
Fighting the Flames
Grotesques
The Mesmerist
Music Hath Its Charms
Tricksy, the Clever Princess
Two Clever Detectives
Sep 19 Beginning of the Game of Diablo
How Glue Is Made
Paris Fire Brigade at Drill
Policeman's Vision
The Shepherdess
Unusual Cooking
Sep 20 Custom Officer's Revenge
Sep 26 The Brahmin's Miracle
Culture of Rice
Fatty's Follies
The Happiest Day of Her Life
Magic Dice
The Magistrate's Conscience
Motor Boat Races, 1908
Oct 3 The Locket
The Sailor's Sweetheart
Spooks Do the Moving
Oct 4 A Basket Party
Palermo and Its Surroundings
The Pardon
Parisian Life in Miniature
A Strong Gale
Oct 10 The Magic Mirror
Making Arabian Pottery
Paris Fire Brigade
Tricked into Giving His Consent
Oct 11 Doll Making
The Fake Doctor
The Innkeeper's Remorse
Two Great Griefs
Oct 17 Crocodile Hunt
For the Sake of the Uniform
Heart of a Gypsy Maid
His First Frock Coat
A Love Affair
The Mind Reader
Result of Eating Horseflesh
An Unselfish Guest (?)
Oct 24 Caught with the Goods
The Fakir's Dream
How Mabel Found a Husband
Hunting for Her Better Half
Mysterious Knight
Pierrette's Talisman
A Sicilian Hermit
Oct 28 The Fortune Hunters
Oct 30 Bear Hunt in Canada
Mabel's Beau in Trouble
Oct 31 Ambulance Dogs
Ideal Policemen
Nov 1 I've Lost My Ball
Troubles of a Coat
Unyielding Parent
Nov 2 How the Pair Butted In
Magic Album
The Penalty of His Crime
Nov 4 Benvenuto Cellini
Don't Fool Your Wife

Maple Sugar
Nov 7 The Peer's Fancy
Push Cart Race
Nov 9 Beauty and the Beast
Hurry Up, Please
Nov 11 Blood Will Tell
Weather Changes at the Smiths
Nov 13 Reception of the American Fleet in Australia
Nov 14 We Close at Noon
Will They Ever Get to Town?
Nov 16 Bicycle Polo
Puss in Boots
Nov 18 Donkey's Skin
Nov 20 Race Prejudice
Wood Floating and Pulp Industry
Nov 21 Cave of the Spooks
Old College Chums
Nov 23 Marie Stewart
Nov 25 L'Arlesienne
Nov 27 Crack Riders of the Russian Cavalry
The Substitute
Nov 28 Merry Widow Waltz
The Vagabond
Nov 30 Her Flowers
The Magic Handkerchief
Dec 2 A Dear Old Grandma
The Nature Fakir Comes to Grief
Dec 4 The Jealous Fisherman
Paris as Seen from a Height of 2600 Feet
Dec 5 Modern Magic
Surprise Package
Dec 7 The Clown's Daughter
Rubber Heels
Dec 9 The Acrobatic Maid
The Deadly Plant
Dec 11 The Miniature Circus
Mother-in-Law Breaks All Records
Dec 12 The Mohammedan at Home
The Quarry Man
Dec 14 No Petticoats for Him
Roman Idyl
Dec 16 The One Best Bet
A Plucky Young Woman
Dec 18 The Bee and the Rose
The Smuggler's Daughter
Dec 19 Electric Hotel
Some Dangerous Members of Bostock's Menagerie
Dec 21 Faithful Little Doggie
The Faun
Too Much Snuff
Dec 23 Antique Wardrobe
An Awkward Habit
Dec 25 The Gallant Guardsman
Silhouettes
Dec 26 Bill Wants to Marry a Toe Dancer
Water Sports
Dec 28 Mr. Soaker at the Seaside
St. Moritz
Dec 30 The Ragtag's Ball
The Sicilian's Revenge

1909

Jan 1 Anonymous Letter
Strasburg
Jan 2 Collection of Stamps
Persistent Suitor
Jan 4 Mysterious Correspondent
Two Very Unlucky Thieves
Jan 6 A Lovely Lass
School Children's Strike
Jan 8 A Drunkard's Dream
The Wooden-Headed Veteran
Jan 9 Burning of Stamboul, Constantinople
Ted and His Little Sister
Jan 11 Duel Under Richeleau
Spanish Blood
Jan 13 A Nervy Thief
The Prehistoric Lid
Stilt Walking
Jan 15 It's Only the Painter
Paper Cock-A-Doodles
Jan 16 The Hunchback
Mr. Pynhead Out for a Good Time
Jan 18 A Pretty Little Milliner
The Sergeant's Stripes
Jan 20 The Stepmother
Wonderful Eggs
Jan 22 Beginning of the Serpentine Dance
Buffin Wins First Prize
Jan 23 Bobby's Sketches
A Fish Story
Lady Cabby's Romance
The Pleasant Side of a Soldier's Life
Jan 25 Sammy Celebrates
The Scar
Jan 27 Calling Day
Nick Carter's Double
Jan 29 Messina
A Put Up Job
Jan 30 On the Zambesi
Saved by His Dog
Feb 1 A Sure 'Nuff Tumbler
The Two Bandboxes
A Village Quarrel
Feb 3 Incriminating Evidence
Feb 5 Choosing a Life Partner
He Can Imitate Anything
Feb 6 The Juggler
Vulture Hunting in Africa
Why They Fell Out
Feb 8 Buster's Revenge
Les Ricochets
Women Chauffeurs
Feb 10 Adventures of a Bag of Coal
Charlotte Corday
Feb 12 Bess and Her Goose
The Laplanders
Feb 13 The Brazilian's Ring
An Evil Day
Palmistry
They Lead the Cops on a Chase
Feb 15 The Hand
Feb 17 The Assassination of the Duke of Guise
Feb 19 Choice of Weapons
His First Flight
How Mother-in-Law Got Even
Feb 20 Exacting Father-in-Law
Now I'm Here, I'll Stay
Feb 22 Grand Canal, Venice
The Miser
Feb 24 A Little Coquette
What a Uniform Will Do
Feb 26 The Jolly Trio's Dream
Mr. Jonah Gets a Little Dust in His Eyes
Topsy-Turvy
Feb 27 Florrie's Birthday
Hypnotic Subject
Mar 1 The Suffragette's Dream
The Test
Mar 3 The Guilty Guardian
The Man Monkey
Mar 5 A Bad Shot
Behind in His Rent
Mar 6 Dr. Wright's Invention
Forced to Play Cop
Mar 8 All's Well That Ends Well
When Love Will
Mar 10 He Can't Lose Wifie's Ma
Little Cyril, the Runaway
Mar 12 Convict's Revenge
Educating the Blind
Mar 13 Sad Awakening
Visit from the "Down Home Folks"
Mar 15 Unusual Elopement
Vampires of the Coast
Mar 17 Jealous Hubby
The Ringleader
Mar 19 Summer Home for the School Children of Paris
Tommy's Own Invention
Mar 20 The Return of Ulysses
Mar 22 The Elixir of Dreams
Mar 24 Chivalrous Beggar
New Cut Roads Up Mt. Blanc
We Must Have a Butler
Mar 26 Jolly Sports
The Maid and the Millionaire
Mar 27 The Electric Belt
Life on a French Training Ship
On the Brink
The Warden's Nightmare
Mar 29 The Child of the Regiment
What Three Tots Saw in the Land of Nod
Mar 31 His Last Illusion Gone
Whale Fishing in Southern Waters
Apr 2 Beware of Evil Companions
Larry, the Limit for Deviltry
Old Aunt Hanna's Cat
Apr 3 Every Lass a Queen
The Martins Leave Home for a Week
Apr 5 The Schoolboy's Revenge
Vercingetorix—Gaul's Hero
Apr 7 The Kiss of Judas
Apr 9 Contemptible Theft
Moscow Clad in Snow
Apr 10 Clarence and His Cigarette
Ponto Runs Away with the Milk Cart
Theodore Yearns to be a Tough
Apr 12 Moonstruck
Pranks of a Mischievous Kid
Apr 14 Oliver Cromwell
Apr 16 The General's Fiancée
The Teamster's Daughter
We're Backing Up
Apr 17 Jack's Successful Bluff
A War Time Tale
Apr 19 The Legend of the Forget-Me-Not
Paul Has Decided to Marry
Apr 21 A Pair of White Gloves
Apr 23 There's No Fool Like an Old Fool
Apr 24 Hungary
Martyrdom of Louis XVII
Apr 26 The Clever Reporter
The Gold Prospectors
Apr 28 The Fairy's Presents
The Love-sick Barber
The Suspicious Fencing Master
Apr 30 Playing Patience
Wilbur Wright's Aeroplane
May 1 The Bohemian Girl
Hunting the Hippopotamus
May 3 Between Love and Honor
Your Turn, Marquis
May 5 Thanksgiving Turkey
Zou-Zou, the Lucky Dog
May 7 A Chinese Wedding
Haunted by the Cops
Instantaneous Nerve Powder
May 8 Eddie Is a Real Live One
The Way to Happiness
May 10 Mirielle's Sincere Love
A Striking Resemblance
May 12 The Hunter's Grief
May 14 A Faithful Old Horse
Manufacturing Steel Rails
May 15 A Distracted Man
The Two Donkeys
A Woman's Heart
May 17 The Beggar's Coin
Fountain of Youth
May 19 Blessings Sometimes Come in Disguise
Père Milon
May 21 Daunted by His First Love
Land of the Midnight Sun
May 22 Cartouche
May 24 The Bondsman's Fate
Cured by Gymnastics
May 26 An Obliging Friend
A Profitable Marriage
May 28 Alphonse Gets in Wrong
Miss Faust
May 29 Bottled Up
A Visit to the London Zoological Gardens
May 31 Advantages of Aviation
An Uninvited Guest
Jun 2 Making Tambourines
Saved by a Waif
Jun 4 A Bruised Heart
Carnival at Nice, 1909
Jun 5 Gambler's Honor
Protector of Animals
A Soldier's Heart
Jun 7 The Blue Legend
The Pulverizer
Jun 9 La Tosca
Jun 11 Snake Skin Industry
A Woman's Intrigue
Jun 12 His Lucky Day
Rapids and Falls of Tannfossen and Rista
Skylight Theater Seat
Jun 14 Cupid's Four Darts
The Dog Detective
Jun 16 The Reckoning
Strenuous Sneezer
Jun 18 Looking for His Umbrella

Mixed in His Dinner Dates
Jun 19 A Good Birthday Present
Making Lace
Poor Little Kiddies
Jun 21 For His Daughter's Sake
Jun 23 The Grandfather
Jun 25 An Affair of Honor
An Assortment of Aeroplanes
Jun 26 Joan of Arc
Jun 28 Broke Again
A Western Hero
Jun 30 Psyche
Jul 2 The Bogey Woman
Fun with a Manikin
Jul 3 Book Taught Hypnotism
Determined Wooer
An Inspiring Sunset
The Sentimental Burglar
Jul 5 A Child's Love
Spanish Army
Jul 7 A Tragic Ending of Shrove Tuesday
Tunisian Industries
Jul 9 The Fan
A Little Detective
Jul 10 Trained Falcon
The Witch's Donkey
Jul 12 Different Rulers of the World
Wood Floating in Morvan
Jul 14 The Evil Spirit in a Girl's Boarding School
True to Her First Love
Jul 16 The Hand of Justice
Jul 17 Automatic Umbrella Seller
The Invisible Thief
A Kind Hearted Tough
The Punch Register
Jul 19 Behind the Mask
Catching Turtles
The Fiddlers
Jul 21 Bewitched Manor House
Little Busybody
Jul 23 A Case of Lumbago
Holding Up the Wedding
Sweet Toothed Dogs
Jul 24 Poor Kid
Jul 26 Champion Heavyweight Lifter
Living Dolls
Sweet Dreams Intermingled with Nightmares
Jul 28 Amazons of Different Periods
The Barber's Revenge
Jul 30 Charity Begins at Home
A Mother's Sorrow
Jul 31 The Gamekeeper's Son
Wonderful Rose Designs
Aug 2 The Butler's Tricks
Fantastic Heads
Aug 4 Thelly's Heart
Aug 6 The Tragedy of Meudon
Aug 7 Arabian Pilgrimage
The Two Pigeons
Aug 9 Charity Rewarded
The Sacrifice
Satan's Smithy
Aug 11 Pompey's Dream
Aug 13 Cigar-Butt Pickers in Paris
A Trip to Jupiter
Aug 14 The Wild Ass's Skin
Aug 16 A Cold Plunge in Moscow
A Heroic Father
Aug 18 Elastic Transformation
Two Lovers and a Coquette
Aug 20 Doomed
Aug 21 Getting Even with Everybody
Rover Turns Santa Claus
Aug 23 Dances of Various Countries
The Hat Juggler
Aug 25 The Eternal Romance
Tennessee Guards
Aug 27 A Billposter's Trials
Manufacturing Bamboo Hats
Aug 28 The Hypnotic Wife
The Professor's Dilemma
Aug 30 The New Mail Carrier
Ralph Benefits by People's Curiosity
Sep 1 The Little Street Singer
Sam Not Wanted in the Family
Sep 3 Show Your License
A Visit to Biskra
Sep 4 A Grave Disappointment
Launching the "Voltaire"
Training Bulls for the Fight
Sep 6 They Robbed the Chief of Police
Versailles
Sep 8 The Little Soldier
Sweden—Gotha Canal
Sep 10 Tom Thumb
Sep 11 Chasing a Sea Lion in the Arctics
How to Tame a Mother-in-Law
Sports in Java
Sep 13 The Amateur Detective
The Child's Prayer
Sep 15 City of Naples
The Pretty Girl of Nice
Sep 17 The Mountebank's Son
Sep 18 Construction of Balloons
The Fresh Kid
Oh, What a Beard!
Sep 20 Aviation Contests at Rheims
Caught in His Own Trap
Sep 22 The Tower of Nesle
Sep 24 Careless Tramp
Caucasian Customs
Sep 25 Servant's Good Joke
Trained Birds
Sep 27 He Learns the Trick of Mesmerism
Suitor's Competition
Sep 29 Jane Is Unwilling to Work
Pierrot, the Fuddler
Oct 1 An Eventful Trip
A Game of Chess
Oct 2 The Garbage of Paris
Vendetta
Oct 4 The Story of a Banknote
Oct 6 Female Sleuth
The Music Lesson
Oct 8 How Jack Helped His Little Sister
Sister Angelica
Oct 9 Anti-Fat Sanitarium
The Dog Pickpocket
Napoleon
Oct 11 The Trappers
Oct 13 A Lucky Husband
A Wonderful Remedy
Oct 15 Blessington's Bonny Babies
The Romance of a Poor Girl
Oct 16 Chums
Physical Culture Fiend
Oct 18 The Belated Wedding
Bob's Electric Theater
Oct 20 A Home Without Children
Hunting Jack Rabbits in Hungary
Oct 22 Drink
Oct 25 The Bogus Heir
Romance in the Andes
Oct 27 The Gambler
Grotesque Make-Up
Oct 29 Buffalo Racing in Madoera
Life Behind the Scenes
Oct 30 Burglar in the Trunk
Mountebank's Watchcase
Nov 1 Across the Island of Ceylon
The Lonely Bachelor
Nov 3 Eat Your Soup
The General's Birthday Present
Nov 5 The Prodigal Son
Nov 6 Cops on a Strike
Malicious Rival
Nov 8 Culture of Tea in Java
Misadventures of a Pair of Trousers
Nov 10 The Flight of Monsieur Valette
Nov 12 Man with the Dolls
Running in Hard Luck
Nov 13 Good Lesson in Charity
Sam's Artistic Beard
Nov 14 Rigoletto
Nov 15 In India, Marriage of the Nephew of the Maharajah of Tagore
Two Chums Looking for Wives
Nov 17 Her Dramatic Career
Nov 19 How French Perfumes Are Made
The Nobleman's Dog
Nov 20 Adonis Is Robbed of His Clothes
The Patient from Punkville
Nov 22 Late for the Recital
Nov 24 A Convenient Lamp-Post
The Sleeper
Nov 26 The Bigamist
Nov 27 Chinese Amusements
The Mixed Letters
Nov 29 A Bunch of Lilacs
Spanish Marriage
Dec 1 Legend of Orpheus
The Wolf Hunt
Dec 3 Forced into Marriage
The Three Neighbors
Dec 4 A Cask of Good Old Wine
The Crocodile Hunt
From the Egg to the Spit
Dec 6 The Lady's Companion
Dec 8 The Evil Philter
Impossible to Get Sleep
Dec 10 Bear Hunt in Russia
Masquerader's Charity
Dec 11 Exploits of a Cowboy
Willyboy Gets His
Dec 12 La Grande Breteche
Dec 13 Repairing the House
The Tramp's Romance
Dec 15 Punch and Judy
The Ugly Girl
Dec 17 The Lucky Number
The Strong Tonic
Dec 18 Hector, the Angel Child
The Honey Industry
Dec 20 The Death of the Duke D'Enghien
Dec 22 Contest for a Handkerchief
The Love Token
Dec 24 Agriculture in Hungary
The Birth of Jesus
Dec 25 The Good Doctor
The Happy Widower
Dec 27 A Bad Bargain
Marvellous Garlands
Dec 29 Oh, You Doggie!
A Well Earned Medal
Dec 31 Corsican Hospitality
A Live Corpse

1910

Jan 1 Tabby's Finish
Trials of a Schoolmaster
Jan 3 The Marriage of the Cook
A Victim of Circumstances
Jan 5 The King's Command
The Overzealous Domestic
Jan 7 An English Boxing Bout
Modern Highwayman
Jan 8 His Opponent's Card
The Last Look
Jan 10 Miss Moneybags Wishes to Wed
Women in India
Jan 12 Camille
Jan 14 The Beggar's Repentance
Story of a Leg
Jan 15 At the Carnival
Church Robber
On a Racket
A Stag Hunt in Java
Jan 17 Testing Their Love
A Visit to Bombay
Jan 19 An Aerial Acrobat
The Bareback Rider
Jan 21 Fickle Fortune
The Painter's Sweetheart
Jan 22 Count Tolstoi
A Russian Heroine
Jan 24 Acrobatic Exercises by the Colibris Dwarfs
The Unlucky Fisherman
Jan 26 Motherless
Jan 28 The Leather Industry
The Scarecrow
Jan 29 Cousin Lou for Mine
The Strong Man
Jan 31 Coffee Culture
Dick's a Winner
Feb 2 The Postmistress
Feb 4 The Model Drama
Roller Skating in Australia
Feb 5 Adam II — Miscellaneous
A Critical Situation
Feb 7 The Bandit
The Two Raffles
Feb 9 Cora, the Contraband's Daughter
In Ancient Greece
Feb 11 Before and After
The Troubadour
Feb 12 The Foot Juggler
The Jockey
Feb 14 Druid Remains in Brittany
The Enterprising Clerk
Feb 16 Carmen

Feb 18 The Little Beggar
A Panicky Picnic
Feb 19 Fate Against Her
Three Queens and a Jack
Feb 21 A Corsican's Revenge
The Gunby's Sojourn in the Country
Feb 23 The Lamp-Post Inspector
Feb 25 The Harry Brothers
Ouchard, the Merchant
Feb 26 Granny's Birthday
In the Gulf of Salerno
Feb 28 Joseph Sold by His Brethren
A Mica Mine, the Ullugura Mountains
Mar 2 The Violin Maker of Cremona
The Wrestling Match
Mar 4 Brittany Lassies
The Door
Mar 5 A Happy Turn
Pierrot
Mar 7 Strenuous Massage
Tragic Idyl
Mar 9 The Arrest of Duchess de Berry
A Tragic Adventure
Mar 11 A Cure for Timidity
A Seaside Flirtation
Mar 12 Sporty Dad
A Tale of a Tenement
Mar 14 Tobacco Culture
Uncle's Money
Mar 16 A Bullfight in Mexico
The Captive
Mar 18 The Exile
Mar 19 Wild Birds in Their Haunts
A Willful Dame
Mar 21 A Woman's Repentance
Mar 23 For the King
The Horseshoe
Mar 25 The Banks of the Ganges
No Trifling with Love
Mar 26 A Conquest
Foxy Ernest
Mar 28 The Little Vixen
The Polar Bear Hunt in the Arctic Seas
Mar 30 Driven to Steal
Out of Sight, Out of Mind
Apr 1 The Rhine Falls at Schaffhausen
A Woman's Caprice
Apr 2 Athletic Sports in India
Lorenzo, the Wolf
Apr 4 Agra
The Good Boss
Apr 6 The Duchess of Langeais
The Vintage
Apr 8 The Hunchbacked Fiddler
Paula Peters and Her Trained Animals
Apr 9 A Hasty Operation
Honest Peggy
Apr 11 Her Sister's Sin
One-Legged Acrobats
Apr 13 Ice Scooters on Lake Ronkonkoma
The Miniature
Apr 15 Johnny's Pictures of the Polar Regions
The Mask Maker
Apr 16 The Bully
The Pillagers
Apr 18 The Greenhorns
Roosevelt in Africa
Simone
Apr 20 Othello
Apr 22 Delhi
The Wreath
Apr 23 The Chivalrous Stranger
The Storm
Apr 25 The Parisian
Venice
Apr 27 The Bagpipe Player
Jim Wants to Get Punched
Apr 29 The Merry Medrano Circus Clowns
The Subterfuge
Apr 30 Bud's Escapade
Deep Sea Fishing
May 2 Only a Faded Flower
The Picturesque Pyrenees
May 4 Diamond Cut Diamond
The Witch of the Ruins
May 6 Customs of the Buddhists in India
A Romantic Girl
May 7 The Cherries
Medium Wanted as Son-in-Law
May 9 Pete Wants a Job
Villainy Defeated
May 11 Cleopatra
May 13 Berlin
The Surgeon's Visit
May 14 The Little Truant
The Wrong Road
May 16 The Girl from Arizona
May 18 The Gold Spider
Who Will Win My Heart?
May 20 A Brave Little Girl
Gee I Am Late
May 21 The Milk Industry in the Alps
A Tempestuous Adventure
May 23 Little Mary and Her Dolly
Romeo Turns Bandit
May 25 Capturing Cub Bears
Max Leads Them a Novel Chase
May 26 Roosevelt in Paris
May 27 A Mirror of the Future
A Prince of Worth
May 28 A Sailor's Friendship
May 30 Down with the Women
Russia, the Caucasian Mountains
Jun 1 Ines de Castro
One Can't Believe One's Eyes
Jun 3 Lillian and Anetta
The Two Portraits
Jun 4 [King Edward's Funeral]
Macbeth
Jun 6 The Flag of Company "H"
Jun 8 The Empty Cradle
Lucy Consults the Oracle
Jun 10 Dmitri Donskoj
24-Hour Automobile Race
Jun 11 Floating to Wealth
An Unexpected Friend
Jun 13 Childish Escapade
Micro-Cinematography: Sleeping Sickness
Jun 15 The Barry Sisters
The Bone-Setter's Daughter
Jun 17 Max Makes a Touch
Poor, but Proud
Jun 18 White Fawn's Devotion
Jun 20 Reconciliation of Foes
Jun 22 Perseverance Rewarded
Riding School in Belgium
Jun 24 Catching Fish with Dynamite
A Curious Invention
Jun 25 The Great Train Hold Up
Jun 27 Caesar in Egypt
Save Us from Our Friends
Jun 29 Napoleon
Jul 1 Inside the Earth
Rebellious Betty
Jul 2 Max Foils the Police
Riding Feats by Cossacks
Jul 4 The Rhine from Cologne to Bingen
The Runaway Dog
Jul 6 Jinks Has the Shooting Mania
Love Ye One Another
Jul 8 Big-Hearted Mary
Colonel Roosevelt Reviewing French Troops
Jul 9 The Champion of the Race
Jul 11 The Faithless Lover
Just for Good Luck
Jul 13 The Overland Coach Robbery
Verona
Jul 15 Please Take One
A Political Discussion
Jul 16 Algerian Stud
A Good Loser
Jul 18 An Awful Symphony
Mistaken Identity
Jul 20 Catching Lobsters
Manon
Jul 22 The Cowboy's Sweetheart and the Bandit
Jul 23 More of Betty's Pranks
Pete Has a Good Time
Jul 25 Breaking Up Ice in Finland
Getting Even with the Lawyer
Jul 27 The Detective's Dream
On the Ethiopian Frontier
Jul 29 Tommy Gets His Sister Married
Jul 30 Cagliostro
Aug 1 Betty as an Errand Girl
Hunting Bats in Sumatra
Aug 3 The Barrel Jumper
Under Both Flags
Aug 5 No Man's Land
No Rest for the Weary
Aug 6 Fiftieth Anniversary of Yokohama
The Latest Fashion in Skirts
Aug 8 Jewish Types in Russia
The Troubles of a Flirt
Aug 10 Her Photograph
The "Ibis"
Aug 12 The Red Girl and the Child
Aug 13 Oliver Twist
Aug 15 Back to Life After 2,000 Years
Max Has to Change
Aug 17 A Cheyenne Brave
Aug 19 The Eriks
A Short-Lived Triumph
Aug 20 A School in New Guinea
The Shepherd's Dog
Aug 22 Butter Making in Normandy
A Miscalculation
Aug 24 Scenes in Norway
The Troubles of a Policeman
Aug 26 The Lovers' Well
Aug 27 The Castaway's Return
How Jack Won His Bride
Aug 29 Kids Will Be Kids
Memento of the Past
Aug 31 Advertising for a Wife
Sep 2 Deer Hunting in Celebes Islands
Saved from Ruin
Sep 3 Maggie Hollihan Gets a Job
Sep 5 Who Is Boss?
Zoological Gardens in Antwerp
Sep 7 The Gambler's Wife
Sep 9 The Belgian Army
Lucy at Boarding School
Sep 10 The Appeal of the Prairie
Sep 12 A Good Glue
Hunting the Panther
Sep 14 The Two Sisters
Sep 16 Unconscious Heroism
Sep 17 The Vagaries of Love
Sep 19 The False Friend
Trip to the Isle of Jersey
Sep 21 An Arizona Romance
Sep 23 Max in a Dilemma
The Mexican Tumblers
Sep 24 A Simple Mistake
Sep 26 Colombo and Its Environs
Max Is Absent-Minded
Sep 28 The Hoodoo
Sep 30 The Sick Baby
Oct 1 Southern Tunis
Who Owns the Rug?
Oct 3 Betty Is Still at Her Old Tricks
Molucca Islands
Oct 5 Different Trades in Bombay
Mirth and Sorrow
Oct 7 A Life for Love
Slippery Jim
Oct 8 An Indian's Gratitude
Oct 10 Betty Is Punished
The Stigma
Oct 12 A Summer Flirtation
Oct 14 Werther
Oct 15 Aeroplanes in Flight and Construction
The Aviation Craze
Oct 17 Jinks Wants to Be an Acrobat
One on Max
Oct 19 Around Pekin
Outwitted
Oct 21 His Life for His Queen
Oct 22 The Mystery of Lonely Gulch
Oct 24 Another's Ghost
Hagenbeck's Menagerie
Oct 26 Bruges, Belgium
The Motor Fiend
Oct 28 Buffalo Fight
Max in the Alps
Oct 29 The Indian and the Maid
Oct 31 Darjiling
Max Has Trouble with His Eyes
New Style Inkwell
Nov 2 Cowboy Justice
The Facori Family
Nov 4 The Woman of Samaria
Nov 5 Abraham Lincoln's Clemency
Nov 7 Micro-Cinematography: Recurrent Fever
Nov 9 A Mexican Legend
Nov 11 A Black Heart

Dutch Types
Nov 12 A Gambler's End
Nov 14 A Shadow of the Past
Nov 16 Love Laughs at Locksmiths
Russian Wolf Hunt
Nov 18 Military Cyclists of Belgium
Phaedra
Nov 19 The Other Way
Nov 21 New South Wales Gold Mine
The Old Longshoreman
Nov 23 How Rastus Gets His Turkey
Wonderful Plates
Nov 25 A Dog's Instinct
Isis
Nov 26 An Eleventh Hour Redemption
Nov 28 A Border Tale
A Freak
Nov 30 Finland—Falls of Imatra
Who Is Nellie?
Dec 2 The Tale the Mirror Told
What a Dinner!
Dec 3 The Maid of Niagara
Dec 5 The Clever Domestic
Dec 7 An Animated Armchair
Cocoanut Plantation
Dec 9 Saved in the Nick of Time
Soap in His Eyes
Dec 10 Her First Husband's Return
Dec 12 In Her Father's Absence
The Julians
Dec 14 Charlie and Kitty in Brussels
Hoboes' Xmas
Dec 16 Little Snowdrop
Dec 17 Saved by Divine Providence
Dec 19 Get Rich Quick
Hunting Sea Lions in Tasmania
Dec 21 Max Goes Skiing
The Runaway Motor Car
Dec 23 Betty's Fireworks
The Lucky Charm
Dec 24 Grand Central Power House Explosion
Sunshine in Poverty Row
Dec 26 The Atonement
The Bowling Fiend
Dec 28 The American Fleet in French Waters
In Full Cry
Running Away from a Fortune
Dec 30 Carnival of Japanese Firemen in Tokio
Catalan, the Minstrel
Dec 31 The Yaqui Girl
1911
Feb 12 Lassoing Wild Animals in Africa
Pathé, Theophile, Cinematograph Compagnie *see* **Theophile Pathé Cinematograph Compagnie**
Paul, Robert W. *see* **Robert W. Paul**
The Penn Motion Picture Co.
1909
Feb 6 The Assassination of Abraham Lincoln
Percival L. Waters
1904
Jun [day undetermined]
Atlantic City Floral Parade
Parade, Fiftieth Anniversary Atlantic City, N. J.
Philadelphia Projector
1909
Jun 26 Percy Wanted a Moustache
Phoenix Film Co.
1909
Jun 1 Wep-Ton-No-Mah, the Indian Mail Carrier
Jun 8 A Conspiracy
Victim of a Crisis
Jun 16 The Brave Girl on the Fifteenth Floor
Jun 17 It Takes Gasoline to Win a Girl
Jun 19 The Bachelor's Dream
The Loyal Indian
A Russian Romance
The Stolen Princess
Jun 26 Egyptian Princess
Jul 1 The Spanish Girl
Jul 5 The Love Plotters
Jul 10 Flirtation Collar
The Salome Craze
Jul 22 Her Favorite Tune
Aug 16 How the Loser Won
The Young Bachelor's Dream
Aug 26 A Strange Reunion
Sep 4 Leap of Alola
Sep 16 The Actor Burglar
Sep 18 A Girl of the Woods
The Railroad Wreck
Sep 23 Nobody Loves a Fat Man
Sep 25 Theodora
Sep 30 The Man and the Law
Oct 7 A Child's Plea
The North Pole Craze
Oct 14 The Telephone Call
Oct 21 A Broken Melody
Oct 28 Dope Head Clancy
The Love Hunter
Nov 4 Actress and Child
The Trouble Kiss
Nov 11 "Hello, Bill"
The Kissing Germ
Nov 18 A Millionaire Bootblack
Nov 25 The Delayed Telegram
Dec 2 The Answered Prayer
Dec 9 A Bad Case of Grip
July 4th, 1910
Dec 16 Her Mother's Mistake
1910
Jan [day undetermined]
A Lucky Knock
Victims of Jealousy
Jan 13 The Celebrated Case (Part I): Convicted by His Own Child
Jan 20 The Celebrated Case (Part II): Saved by His Own Child
May 18 For the Flag
Phono-Ciné-Théâtre
1908
Oct 31 Hamlet, Duel Scene with Laertes
Pineschi
1909
Feb 6 A Pirate of Turkey
Apr 17 Unforgiving Father
May 8 Love with Love Is Paid
May 22 Sapho
Jun 26 The Mother-in-Law Phantasm
Officer's Lodgment
Aug 14 An Amazing Story
Aug 21 Madam Lydia's Little Trick
Sep 4 Louisa of Lucerne
Sep 25 Phaedra
Oct 6 The Devil and the Painter
Nov 6 Spartacus
Nov 8 Enthusiastic Hand Ball Player
Force of Love
Nov 15 High Treason
Polyphos Elektrizitats Gesellschaft, m.b.H.
1910 [month undetermined]
Kinematographic X-Ray Picture of a Human Stomach During Digestion, Taken During One Inspiration
The Powers Co.
1909
Nov 2 Change of Complexion
Nov 9 All for the Love of a Girl
Nov 16 The Gypsy's Secret
Nov 23 A Red Man's Love
Nov 30 Pressing Business
Dec 7 A Run for the Money
Dec 14 Manhood's Reward
Dec 20 Don Quixote
Dec 21 Re-united by Santa Claus
Dec 28 Excelsior
1910
Jan 4 A Frozen Ape
Jan 18 The Little Heroine
Feb 12 The Paris Disaster
Mar 8 Her Cowboy Lover
Mar 15 War Time Pals
Mar 22 John Hardy's Invention
Mar 29 The Man Who Waited
Apr 5 The Actress
Apr 12 His Mother's Letter
Apr 16 [Talking Moving Picture]
Apr 19 Re-Making of a Man
Apr 26 A Newspaper Error
May 3 Legally Dead
May 10 "Salvation" Smith
May 14 The Card Party
The Minister's New Suit
May 17 His Yankee Girl
May 21 On Parole
The Temperance Leader
May 24 The Doctor's Love Story
May 28 The Amateur Hypnotist
His Revenge
May 31 The Crack Shot
Jun 4 Her Portrait
O! That Indian
Jun 7 His Duty
Jun 11 Her Romance
Limburger and Love
Jun 14 Wenonah
Jun 18 Her Dad's Pistol
The Phrenologist
Jun 21 Nevada
Jun 25 A Plucky Girl
Why Jones Reformed
Jun 28 Mother and Daughter
Jul 2 The Lady Doctor
The Man Behind the Curtain
Jul 5 On the Border
Jul 9 The Burglar and the Baby
Sally's Beaux
Jul 12 A Mightier Hand
Jul 16 A Jealous Wife
The Tattler
Jul 19 A Game of Hearts
Jul 23 Cohen and Murphy
Our Housemaid
Jul 26 The Missing Bridegroom
Jul 30 A Little Confederate
The Vixen
Aug 2 Her Private Secretary
Aug 6 Almost a Hero
His Baby's Shirt
Aug 9 A Man's Way
Aug 13 Madame Clairo
Winning a Husband
Aug 16 The Sewing Girl
Aug 20 A Woman's Power
Aug 23 The Deceivers
The Gunsmith
Aug 27 The Mail Carrier
Aug 30 The Burlesque Queen
The Horse Shoer's Girl
Sep 3 The Matinee Idol
Sep 6 The Girl Next Door
The Inconstant
Sep 10 For the Girl's Sake
Sep 13 A Day of Pleasure
The Tell Tale Perfume
Sep 17 The Pugilist's Child
Sep 20 Aunt Hannah
A Husband's Sacrifice
Sep 24 His Lordship
Sep 27 "Oh! You Wives"
The Taming of Buck
Oct 1 The Music Teacher
Oct 4 The Beechwood Ghost
War
Oct 8 Within an Inch of His Life
Oct 11 A Man and a Girl
Simpson's Skate
Oct 15 A Woman's Wit
Oct 18 The Devil
Sleepy Jones
Oct 22 Hearts of Gold
Oct 25 The Lord and the Lady
The Plot That Failed
Oct 29 Adventure of a Millionaire
Nov 1 Mental Science
The Sheriff and Miss Jones
Nov 5 A Russian Romance
Nov 8 Moonshine and Love
When Love Is Young
Nov 12 The Ordeal
Nov 15 How Women Love
That Woman Lawyer
Nov 19 The New Magdalene
Nov 22 Absent Minded Arthur
Thou Shalt Not Kill
Nov 26 The Woman Hater
Nov 29 Wanted—A Baby
Who Wins the Widow?
Dec 3 When the World Sleeps
Dec 6 The Medicine Man
The Rehearsal
Dec 10 A Ride to Death
Dec 13 A Plucky Western Kid
The Tramp Bicyclist
Dec 17 His Gypsy Sweetheart
Dec 20 The Bachelor's Finish
Jack Logan's Dog
Dec 24 A Father's Love
Dec 27 Freddie's Courtship
The Station Agent's Daughter
Dec 31 A Daughter of Virginia

Powhattan
1909
Apr 10 Lost in Chinatown
Apr 12 Give Me a Light
May 1 Misplaced Confidence
May 24 The Flirt, a Tale of the Plains
Jun 12 Early Days in the West
Episode of Cuban War
Hobo's Dream
Jul 10 The Sheriff's Pet
Precision Film Co.
1909
Sep 4 Bad Day for Lavinsky
1910
Jan 15 Rivals
Prescott, F. M. *see* **F. M. Prescott**
Prieur, R. *see* **R. Prieur**
R. Prieur
1909
Dec 29 The Gold Digger's Son
1910
Jan 5 Drama at Sea
Football Craze
Jan 8 How the Dog Saved the Flag
The Rivals
Jan 12 Broken Happiness
My Aunt's Birthday
Jan 19 Adventures of a Sandwich Man
The Refugee
Jan 26 He Would Be an Acrobat
Uncle Learns to Hypnotize
Feb 2 Hamlet, Prince of Denmark
Feb 9 The Consequence of a Nod
Pirate's Fiancée
Feb 16 Her Dolly's Revenge
The Man Who Could Not Sit Down
Feb 17 Easy Job
Feb 23 The Fisherman's Honour
The Runaway Stove
Mar 2 The Golf Mania
The Sailor's Dog
Mar 9 A Father's Patriotism
He Knew Best
Mar 16 Life in the Next Century
The Two Brothers
Mar 24 A Family Feud
How a Bad Tempered Man Was Cured
Mar 25 Dwarf Detective
Mar 30 Cured by a Tip
Drama on the Reef
Apr 6 Rico, the Jester
The Snake Man
Apr 13 The Attack upon the Train
Washed Ashore
Apr 20 Grandpa's Darling
A Young Aviator's Dream
Apr 28 Artist's Child
Tommy and the Powder
May 5 The Little Beggar Maid
They Would Roller Skate
May 12 Her Two Suitors
A Mother's Grief
May 19 He Did Not Die
The Lace Maker's Dream
May 25 A Sagacious Animal
Jun 2 A Stray Dog
Jun 3 The Slave's Love
What Happened to a Cinematograph Party
Jun 14 A Bitter Enemy
Jun 17 MacNab Visits the Comet
Jun 21 The Devil's Wand
Jun 24 An Exciting Yarn
We Want Your Vote
Jun 28 The Witch's Spectacles
Jul 1 Charles the Fifth
A Quiet Pipe
Jul 8 The Money Lender's Son
Must Be Without Encumbrance
Jul 15 Bill's Serenade
The Greatest of These Is Charity
Jul 22 A Devoted Little Brother
Ma's New Dog
Jul 29 The Bailiff
Aug 25 The Acrobat's Son
The Chemist's Mistake
Sep 15 Aunt Tabitha's Monkey
The Selfish Man's Lesson
Sep 22 The Bobby's Dream
Ma-in-Law as a Statue
Only a Bunch of Flowers
That Typist Again
Sep 29 How Jones Won the Championship
Kindness Abused and Its Results
Oct 6 Auntie in the Fashion
Mother's Portrait
Oct 13 Bill and the Missing Key
Runaway Star
Oct 20 Gilson and Those Boys
The Tyrant
Oct 27 Bewitched
She Required Strength and Got It
Where You Go I Go
Nov 3 Fatty Taking a Bath
Her Diary
Nov 11 Bill as a Boxer
The Truth Revealed
Nov 18 Bill as a Lover
Blopps in Search of the Black Hand
Nov 25 In Friendship's Name
Dec 2 Bill as an Operator
Necessity Is the Mother of Invention
Dec 9 And She Came Back
What Will It Be
Dec 16 Her Favorite Tune
How We Won Her
Dec 23 Bill Plays Bowls
Rosalie's Dowry
Dec 30 Aunt Julia's Portrait
Tim Writes a Poem
Radios
1908
Aug 15 Human Vultures
Moscow Under Water
The Picture
Undesirable Tenants
Aug 29 Riches, Poverty and Honesty
Nov 2 A Child's Debt
My Daughter Will Only Marry a Strong Man
The Young Tramp
Nov 17 Tarn Mountains
The Young Poacher
1909
Feb 6 The Delirious Patient
Raleigh and Roberts
1908
Apr 11 Boy and the Coalman
Champion Wrestling Bear
The Door-Keeper's Substitute
Lion's Tilting Contest
May 30 The Minstrel's Sacrifice
Jun 13 Held for Ransom
The Paralytic's Vengeance
Jul 4 Constantinople
Aug 29 Yusuf the Pirate
Oct 10 Andalousie
Oct 12 Federal Fete of Wrestling, and Alpino Sports
Oct 13 Jerusalem
Oct 20 Wheelwright's Daughter
Oct 24 Preparing for Combat
Nov 8 Roman Colonel's Bravado
Dec 21 George and Margaret
1909
Feb 6 The Great Earthquake in Sicily
Mar 22 In the Land of the Hindoo
Procession in Japan
Shooting the Rapids in Japan
Tylda and Her Lions
Where Stormy Winds Do Blow
Zoological Gardens
Apr 3 King for an Hour
Apr 17 The State Secret
Apr 24 Burglary in the Year 2000
The Cabin Boy's Dog
May 1 The Donkey That Was Not an Ass
May 8 The Gambler's Vow
The Haunted Bridge
May 15 On the French Littoral
Jun 5 On the Zuider Zee
Jun 12 A Message from the Sea
Jul 3 The Snow Man
Jul 24 The Good Shepherd
John Maxwell's Medal
Aug 7 Clever Horse Hans
King of Spain
Sympathetic Tippler
Sep 18 Making of a Sailor
Sep 25 Not Wanted on Voyage
Sep 30 Rats
Oct 11 Maneuvers of Ambulance Corps.
Nov 8 Lines of the Hand
Nov 11 Bertha's Birthday
Nov 13 Substitute Pig
Nov 22 Honest Little Rag Picker
Nov 29 The Double Six
The Motor Cyclist
Professor Short Sight's Surprise
Dec 6 The Disguised Bridegroom
Mr. Sadman's Cure
The Song That Reached Her Heart
Dec 13 Dr. Lyvenemup's Elixir
A Trip to the Arctic
Dec 20 Explorer's Dream
Granny's Darling
Mac Nabb Wants to Get Arrested
Dec 28 Mug Chump's Early Morning Excursion
1910
Jan 3 A Happy New Year
Madam's Favorite
Seal and Walrus Hunting
The Strolling Players
Jan 10 Hotstuff Takes on the Champions
Monarchs of All Nations
The Terrors of the Family
Toes and Teeth
Jan 17 Jealousy, a Bad Counsellor
Jan 27 Bear Hunting
Redfern
1904 [month undetermined]
The Monkey and the Ice Cream
Reliance Films Co.
1910
Oct 22 In the Gray of the Dawn
Oct 29 The Armorer's Daughter
Nov 5 Where Sea and Shore Doth Meet
Nov 12 Under a Changing Sky
Nov 19 Moulders of Souls
Nov 26 So Runs the Way
Dec 3 When Woman Wills
Dec 10 The Dispensation
Dec 17 The Thin Dark Line
Dec 24 The Refuge
Dec 31 A Sacrifice — And Then
Revier Motion Picture Co.
1910
Dec 21 Love's Sorrow
Dec 28 Thoughtfulness Remembered by the Ute
Robert W. Paul
1902
May [day undetermined]
The Cheese Mites; or, The Lilliputians in a London Restaurant
The Children's Tea Party
The Children's Toys That Came to Life
The Haunted Pawnshop
Magical Sword
Ora Pro Nobis Illustrated
The Pals and the Clothier's Dummy
A Railroad Wreck (Imitation)
The Tight Collar
Undressing Under Difficulties
The Wonderful Baby Incubator
Sep [day undetermined]
The Deonzo Brothers in Their Wonderful Barrel Jumping Act
The Dutchman's Interrupted Dinner
1903
May [day undetermined]
Miniature Prize Fighters
A Scarecrow Tramp
Jul [day undetermined]
Laplanders at Home
Sep [day undetermined]
How to Get a Wife and Baby
A Norwegian Waterfall
Rising Panorama of a Norwegian Waterfall
Sep 18 Trailed by Bloodhounds
Oct [day undetermined]
Soap vs. Blacking
Washerwomen and Chimney-Sweep
1904
Apr 20 Russian Outposts Attacked by Japanese
Apr 25 What the Window Cleaner Saw
Jul [day undetermined]
All for the Love of a Geisha
Capture and Execution of Spies by Russians

The Chappie at the Well
Haunted Scene Painter
The Music Hall Manager's Dilemma
Rum vs. Cherries
The Snapshot Fiend
Study, Smoke and Soot
That Terrible Sneeze
Toy Maker and Good Fairy
Voyage of the "Arctic"
Aug [day undetermined]
Barber's Tricks
Oct [day undetermined]
Sculptor and Model
1905
Jul [day undetermined]
Cook and Chimney Sweep
Fatal Necklace
The Race for Bed
Oct [day undetermined]
Devil's Dice
He Learned Ju Jitsu, So Did the Missus
Nov [day undetermined]
Father Neptune and Bear
The Midnight Sun at Scalo
Dec [day undetermined]
Freak Barber
Goaded to Anarchy
Hubby Tries to Keep House
1906
Jan [day undetermined]
A Misguided Bobby at a Fancy Garden Party
Opium Smoker's Dream
Shaving by Installments
Jul [day undetermined]
Fakir and Footpad
House Furnishing Made Easy
1907
Apr 6 Signal Man's Son
Apr 20 Chef's Revenge
Knight-Errant
A Mother's Sin
Sailor's Return
Wizard's World
Sep 14 The Cheater's Cheated
Oct 5 His First Topper
1908
Mar 21 The Robbers and the Jew
May 2 The Great Trunk Robbery
Jun 6 The Prodigal Son
1909
May 22 Copenhagen Zoo
Jun 12 Achill's Rocky Shores
Killarney's Lakes
Jul 3 The Egg Race
A Joke on Teddy
Jul 17 Mysterious Lodger
Aug 14 The Burning Home
Sep 25 Father's Beautiful Beard
Oct 18 Lobster Fishing
Rock, John B. *see* **John B. Rock**
Roma Film
1909
Nov 13 A Broken Life
1910
Apr 1 Andrea Chenier
Romo
1910
Feb 17 Camargo
Rosie Films
1909
May 8 What William Did
1910
Jan 15 Getting Rid of Uncle
Rossi, Carlo *see* **Carlo Rossi**
Royal Film Exchange
1909
Mar 9 Story of Every Day
Mar 10 Chances of Life
Scenes of Morocco
Mar 11 Salon in 1820
Mar 12 He Is a Cousin Who Eats Truffle
Love and the Motherland
Mar 13 Father and Son
The Presidential Inauguration Film
Mar 20 The Burden of Debt
Mar 27 An Artist's Model's Jealousy
The Beggar's Daughter
Blind Child's Dog
A Convict's Return
A Criminal Invention
Drama in the Forest
Drama in the Village
Episode of War
Fishing by Dynamite
Follow Me and I'll Pay for Dinner
Gadbin, the Refractory Suicide
The Good Vicar
The Heart of a Mother
Hero of the Prussian War
Husband's Vengeance
I Want a Moustache
Indians and Cowboys
Lily Amuses Herself
Love of Travel
Lucia di Lammermoor
Magic Games
Misfortunes of a Cobbler
The New Servant
The Paralytic
The Parricide
The Pirate's Daughter
The Poor Schoolma'am
The Ripe Cheese
The Servant Question Solved
Tracked by a Dog
The Train Robbers
Tubbie's Terrible Troubles
The Unfaithful Cashier
Apr [day undetermined]
A Moroccan Romance
The Over-Eager Heirs
The Troubles of the Pretty School Marm
May 24 Dreamer
S. Lubin *see also* **Lubin Mfg. Co.; Siegmund Lubin**
1896 [month undetermined]
The Kiss
1897 [month undetermined]
Babies' Dinner
Babies Quarrel
Barnum's Street Parade, Nos. 1, 2, and 3
The Bathers
Battery Park
Board Walk, Atlantic City
The Boardwalk
The Book Agent
Breaking Up Housekeeping
Burglar Caught in the Act
Corbett and Fitzsimmons Fight
Delaware River, Philadelphia
East River, New York
Eighth and Vine St. Philadelphia
5th Avenue, N. Y.
Indian Club Jugglers
Interesting Parlor Scene
Japanese Rope Walker
Japanese Village
Liberty Statue
Life Rescue
Love in a Broker's Office
Making Love in a Hammock
New Pillow Fight
New Watermelon Contest
Reading Flyer
Scene in a Popular Oyster Saloon
Scene in Ike Einstein's Pawn Office
Shooting the Chutes
60 Minute Flyer
Ten Nights in a Barroom
Uninvited Guest
Washington Flyer
Watermelon Contest
Yellow Kid
May [day undetermined]
Unveiling of the Washington Monument
1898 [month undetermined]
After the Battle
American Cavalry Charging with Drawn Swords
American Commissary Wagons Landing on Cuban Soil
Battle of Guantanomo [sic]
Battleship Indiana
Battleship Iowa
The Battleship Maine in the Harbor of Havana
The Battleship Maine Leaving U. S. Harbor for Havana
Battleship Massachusetts
Battleship Oregon
Battleship Texas
The Big Monitor Miantonomah Leaving the Navy Yard
Brave Cubans Firing at Spanish Soldiers
Broadsword Exercise on the Battleship Texas
Can Can
Captain Sigsbee on Deck of the U. S. Battleship Texas
Capture of a Spanish Fort near Santiago
Cleaning and Firing of the Hotchkiss Revolving Cannon on the Battleship Texas
Colored Invincibles
Corbett and Sharkey Fight
Court Martial
Crew of the Battleship Texas
Cruiser Brooklyn
Cruiser Columbia
Cruiser Marblehead
Cruiser New York
Cubans Drilling, Manual of Arms
Dispatch Boat Dolphin
Execution of the Spanish Spy
15,000 Soldiers Reviewed by the President at Camp Alger May 28
Fighting near Santiago
Flag Film [?]
Fun in a Spanish Camp
Fun in the American Camp at Chicamauga
General Miles and Staff
Girls Brigade, of Lansford, Pa.
Governor Hastings and Mounted Police
Grand Army Veterans of Chicago
Grand Army Veterans of New York
Grand Army Veterans of Philadelphia
Hobson and Crew of the Merrimac
Hoisting of the American Flag at Cavite
How the Flag Changed in Cuba
Knights of the Golden Eagle
Launch of the Great Battleship Alabama
Massachusetts Regiment Marching
Mess Call, American Camp at Chicamauga
Mexican Dance
New Couchee Dance
Officers of the War Ships
Outpost Skirmish
Pennsylvania Academy of Fine Arts
Philadelphia Letter Carriers
President McKinley and Cabinet at Camp Alger, May 28, 1898
Return of Our Soldier Boys
Rough Riders
Rough Riders at Guantanamo
71st New York
The Spanish Cruiser Vizcaya
Spanish Infantry Attacking American Soldiers in Camp
State Fencibles, Pennsylvania
Third Regiment Pennsylvania
13th Regiment Pennsylvania Volunteers
Torpedo Boat Winslow
U. S. Battleship Texas
View of Cramp's Shipyard
View of League Island, Philadelphia
Feb [day undetermined]
Battle of San Juan Hill
May 28 Cake Walk
1899 [month undetermined]
Admiral Dewey on the Olympia
Admiral Dewey's Flagship Olympia in Action at Manila
Battle of El Caney
Battle of Santiago
Battleship Oregon in Action
Bicycling Under Difficulties
The Boxing Horse
Capt. Coghlan, One of the Manila Heroes, and Crew of the Raleigh, Reviewed by the President
Capture of Porto Rico
Charge at Las Guasimas, Where Capron and Fish Were Killed

Charge of the Rough Riders at El Caney
Chinese Sailors Placing a Wreath on the Monument
Christmas Morning
The Couchee Couchee Bear
Death of Maceo and His Followers
Destruction of the Spanish Cruiser Maria Theresa
Dewey Arch, New York City
Dewey Land Parade
Dewey Naval Parade
Escort of the President Passing the Monument
Firing the 3 Pounders of the Raleigh
Full View of Brooklyn Bridge
Lady Contortionist
Morelli and Her Leopards
New Lipman Dance
New Umbrella Dance
Plowing Snow in the Park
President McKinley and Wife, Members of His Cabinet and Their Wives and Capt. Coghlan Leaving the Cruiser Raleigh
President McKinley Reviewing the Troops
Raid of a New York Bowery Saloon
Repulse of Spanish Troops at Santiago
Santa Claus
Scaling a Fort at Manila
Schoolship Saratoga
Sev. Regiments Passing the Monument
Sleighing in the Park
Sleighing on Diamond Street
Snowballing After School
The Tramp's Dream
U. S. Cruiser Raleigh
Unveiling of Grant Monument

Feb 11 The Devil's Laboratory
The Infernal Palace

Apr [day undetermined]
The Astronomer's Dream, or the Trip to the Moon

Apr 1 Bear Jumping Hurdles
The Trick Bear
The Wrestling Bear

Apr 29 How Would You Like to Be the Ice Man?

Jun [day undetermined]
Reproduction of the Fitzsimmons-Jeffries Fight in Eleven Rounds Showing the Knock Out

Aug [day undetermined]
American Soldiers Defeating Filipinos Near Manila
The Haunted House
Why Krausemeyer Couldn't Sleep

Sep [day undetermined]
Reproduction of the Jeffries and Sharkey Fight
Reproduction of the Pedlar Palmer and Terry McGovern Fight
Reproduction of the Sharkey and Jeffries Fight
Reproduction of the Terry McGovern and Pedlar Palmer Fight

Sep 30 The Trial of Captain Dreyfus at Rennes, France

Nov [day undetermined]
Battle Flag of the 10th Pennsylvania Volunteers, Carried in the Philippines
Reproduction of the Corbett and Jeffries Fight
Reproduction of the Jeffries and Corbett Fight
Reproduction of the Jeffries and Ruhlin Fight
Reproduction of the Kid McCoy and Peter Maher Fight
Reproduction of the Peter Maher and Kid McCoy Fight
Reproduction of the Ruhlin and Jeffries Fight

Dec [day undetermined]
Fighting in the Transvaal

Dec 23 Pianka and her Lions

Dec 25 Cinderella

1900 [month undetermined]
Alladin and the Wonderful Lamp
Birdseye View of Galveston, Showing Wreckage
Boer War Film
Bull Fight
Burning of the Bremen and Main (another view) [Hoboken]
Burning of the Saale [Hoboken]
Darkey Excursionists Bathing, Atlantic City
Fight Between a Lion and a Bull
Foreign Palaces
Funeral of Chinese Viceroy, Chung Fing Dang, Marching Through the European Quarter at Peking
Grand Palaces
High Diving
Mysterious Acrobat
New Farmer's Mishap
New Sleighing Scene
Niagara Falls in Life Motion Pictures
Old Paris
Palace of Navigation
Panorama of Both Sides of the River Seine
Parade of the Order of Elks in Atlantic City
Paris Exposition
The Republican National Convention
Sapho Kiss
South African War Subjects
Sunken Steamer in Galveston Harbor
Taking the Dead from the Ruins [Galveston]
The Trocadero
Vesper Boat Club
View of City of Galveston from the Waterfront

Jan [day undetermined]
Reproduction of the McGovern and Dixon Fight

Mar [day undetermined]
Irish Way of Discussing Politics
Photographing the Ghost
Reproduction of the Olsen and Roeber Wrestling Match
Reproduction of the Sharkey and Fitzsimmons Fight
Sapho

Mar 10 Feeding Sea Lions

Apr [day undetermined]
Birth of Venus

Apr 7 Clowns Spinning Hats
Four Heads Better Than One
The Inquisitive Clerks
New Life Rescue
New Morning Bath
Two Old Sparks
Visit to a Spiritualist
The Wonder, Ching Ling Foo

Apr 21 X Rays

Jun [day undetermined]
Monte Myro Troupe of Acrobats

Jun 30 A Mysterious Portrait
Neptune and Amphitrite
The Power of the Cross
Spanish Inquisition
Wrestling Extraordinary

Jul [day undetermined]
Burning of the Bremen and Main [Hoboken]
Hoboken Fire
Panoramic View of Burning Wharves and Warehouses [Hoboken]

Aug [day undetermined]
Beheading Chinese Prisoner
Bombarding and Capturing the Taku Forts by the Allied Fleets
Life Motion Photographs of the Fitzsimmons and Ruhlin Fight
Massacre of the Christians by the Chinese
Prisoner in the Chinese Pillory in the Streets of Tien Tsin
Reproduction of the Corbett and McCoy Fight
Reproduction of the Fitzsimmons and Sharkey Fight

Sep 22 The Unexpected Bath

Nov 11 Joan of Arc

1901

Mar [day undetermined]
Fun in a Chinese Laundry

Mar 2 Mrs. Nation & Her Hatchet Brigade

Mar 23 Boxing in Barrels
The Fraudulent Beggar
A Hold-Up
Photographer's Mishap
Two Rubes at the Theatre

Mar 30 The Cook's Revenge
Photographing the Audience

Apr 6 The One Man Orchestra
The Queen's Funeral
The Wonderful Trick Donkey

Apr 20 Barnum and Bailey's Circus

Apr 27 Pie, Tramp and the Bulldog

May [day undetermined]
Lubin's Animated Drop Curtain Announcing Slides

May 18 Affair of Honor

Jun 29 Acrobats in Cairo
Buffalo Street Parade
Couchee Dance on the Midway
Fun at a Children's Party
Going to the Fire and the Rescue
A Good Joke
Grand Entry, Indian Congress
Indians No. 1
The Inexhaustible Cab
Midway Dance
Mounted Police Charge
Panorama of the Exposition, No. 1
Panorama of the Exposition, No. 2
Shad Fishing at Gloucester, N. J.
Tramp's Nap Interrupted
Turkish Dance
Twelve in a Barrel
Wedding Procession in Cairo
You Can't Lose Your Mother-in-Law

Jul [day undetermined]
The Educated Chimpanzee
The Extensive Wardrobe
Mine Explosion and What Followed
The Mysterious Blackboard
Ostrich Farm
The Statue of William Tell
Who Said Chicken?

Jul 9 Esquimaux Village
Panorama of a Philippine Village

Oct 19 The Martyred Presidents

Oct 26 Little Red Riding Hood

Nov 23 A Christmas Dream

Dec [day undetermined]
The Fat and the Lean Wrestling Match

1902 [month undetermined]
All on Account of Eliza
Ballet Rehearsal
Bathing Made Easy
Black and White Hair Dance
Boating in Lakes of Philippine Village
Bostock's Educated Chimpanzee
The Bryn Mawr Horse Show
Buffalo Bill's Wild West Show
Caught in the Act
The Chicken Thief
Collecting the King's Mail
Conture Brothers, Acrobats
Coronation of King Edward VII and Alexandra
Devoy, the Funny Skater
The Dog Caught On
Drawee, the Juggler
The Dull Razor
Eight Japanese Dancing Girls
Electric Tower
The Extensive Wardrobe
Fairmount Park Trolley Panorama
Fire Run, Exposition
The Foot Juggler
Four Hong Kong Sisters
Fu Tschi Dancers
Funeral of the German Empress, Frederick
Geisha Girls
Gen. Otis with His Troops in the Philippines
Gipsies Dancing
Grandma and the Bad Boys
Herald Square, New York
The Hohenzollern
Hu-Ki-Si, Japanese Dancer
Ice Skating
Indians No. 2
Is Ka Trio

Japanese Acrobats
Japanese Bowery
Japanese Dancing Hall
Japanese Yuma Dance
The King and Queen Returning from Westminster
King Edward and Queen Alexandra on Their Way to Westminster
Launch of the Kaiser's Yacht "Meteor"
Life Rescue, Atlantic City
The Lightning Artist
Lohengrin
Loro & Devoy, the Comical Acrobats
Louie Fuliner
Love at 20 and 40 Years After
The Man with the Rubber Head
Martha
The Mechanical Doll
Mikado
The Miniature Railway
Mounted Police
Mysterious Transformation Scene
The New Serpentine and Fire Dance
New Year Shooters
An Obstacle Race
Opening Day Parade No. 1
Opening Day Parade No. 2
Opening Day Parade No. 3
Panorama City of Venice
Panorama of Esplanade from Bridge of Triumph
Panorama of Esquimaux Village
Panorama of Midway
Panorama of Ninth Ave. Elevated R. R.
Panorama of Venice
President and Prince at Washington
Prince Henry at Cramp's Shipyard
Pugilist McKeever and Wife Bag Punching
Reuben Buys a Gold Brick
Rube Waddell and the Champion Playing Ball with the Boston Team
Serving Potatoes, Undressed
The Singing Donkey
Smoking Smokes
Snicklefritz Has a Hot Time
Soldiers in the Strike District
Sowing Seed on the Farm
Street Scene, Tokio
The Stud Farm, No. 1
The Stud Farm, No. 2
The Stud Farm, No. 3
Stud Pony
Target Practice, and What Happened to Widow Flaherty
The Village Blacksmith
Whose Baby Is You?
Why Jones Left Home
Why the Cook Was Fired
Wonderful Magic
Woodside Park Trolley Panorama
Ye Olde Mill

May [day undetermined]
Arrival of Circus Trains
Building Made Easy; or, How Mechanics Work in the Twentieth Century
Camels Eating
Camels in a Tent
Circus Parade No. 1
Circus Parade No. 2
The Devil in the Schoolhouse
The Devil's Kitchen
Elephants in a Tent
Funeral Procession of Admiral Sampson at Washington
Going to Bed Under Difficulties
Magical Changes
The Magical Hen
The Magician and the Human Pump
The Mystic Wreath
Troubles in a Tenement House
What Happened to the Inquisitive Janitor
Wonderful Feats of Vivisection
The Wonderful Hair Restorer

May 3 Blue Beard

Jun [day undetermined]
The Eruption of Mt. Pelee
Panorama of St. Pierre
Taking Out the Dead and Wounded

Jul [day undetermined]
Old Mother Hubbard
Snow White

Jul 15 Jack and the Beanstalk

Aug [day undetermined]
Jeffries-Fitzsimmons Reproduction Prize Fight Films

Sep [day undetermined]
The Farmer's Troubles in a Hotel
Michael Casey and the Steam Roller

Oct [day undetermined]
A Lively Scrimmage
Miners at Work Under Guard of Troops
Troops Leaving Philadelphia for the Coal Regions

Oct 4 A Trip to the Moon
Who Said Watermelon?

Nov 1 Ali Baba and the Forty Thieves

1903 [month undetermined]
Bluejackets Scrubbing Their Hammocks
Dixon-Palmer Fight
German Torpedo Boats
The Hair Dresser
Jack and Jill
Knights Templar Street Parade, Philadelphia
Mephisto's Theatre
The Mysterious Trunk
Reproduction of Fitzsimmons-Gardner Fight
Reproduction of Jeffries-Corbett Fight
A Shocking Incident
Trick Donkey

Jan [day undetermined]
After the Ball
After the Hunt
American Falls from Canadian Side
American Falls from Luna Island
Andre at the North Pole
Animal Parade, Hagenbeck's Circus
The Aquarium
Arabian Acrobats
An Arabian Magician
Arrival of the Bull Fighter
Arrival of the Circus Train, No. 1
Arrival of the Circus Train, No. 2
The Artists Model
At the Grave of Ling Fei Dong
Atlantic City Bathers
Atlantic City Board Walk, Easter Morn
Atlantic City Floral Parade
Aunt Jane's First Lesson in Love
Baby Show Atlantic City
Baby's First Step
Bad Boy and Hod Carrier
Bad Soup
Ballet Scene
Barber Up-to-Date
Bareback Riding
Barnyard Scene
Bathing at Atlantic City
Bathing Horses
Battle of Bladders
Beach at Atlantic City
Beach Scene, Coney Island
Bears Wrestling, Hagenbeck's Circus
The Beauty Show
Behind the Scenes
The Bewildered Astronomer
Bicycle Parade, Philadelphia
Bicyclist and Fisherman
Biddy's Day Off
The Big 4-7 Gun in Action
Birds-eye View of Dawson City on the Yukon River, Alaska
Boat Race
Boer Supply Train Crossing the Veldt
Bostock's Circus Fording a Stream
Bostock's Educated Bears
Boston and New York Express
Boulevard St. Denis, Paris, France
Bowery Street Dancers
Bowling Alley
Boxing Match on Board the U. S. Cruiser Raleigh
Boy Up a Tree; or, Making Love in the Park
Breaker Boys Leaving the Coal Mines
British Troops Leaving for the Transvaal
British, with Music, Leaving for the Transvaal
Buck and Wing Dance
Buck Dance
Bucking Bronchos
Buffalo Bill's Street Parade
Buffaloes Born in the Zoo Gardens
Building the Suez Canal
Bull Fight, No. 1
Bull Fight, No. 2
Bullet vs. Whiskey
Burglar and Fairy
Burglar and Old Maid
Burial of Maine Sailors
Burlesque Cock Fight
Burlesque Lions and Their Tamer, Hagenbeck's Circus
Burning the Rubbish
Butcher Shop No. 1
Butcher Shop No. 2
Cagliostro's Mirror
Cake Walking Horses
Captured
Caravan of Camels
Carlisle's Trained Dogs
Cascade in Switzerland
Cat's Dinner
Chair Dance
Chariot Race
Chicken Thief
Children Saying Their Prayers
A Child's Vision
Chinese Dance
Chinese Laundry
Chinese Silk Mill
Chiquita, the Smallest Woman in the World
Christening Murphy's Baby
Circus Street Parade
City Hall, Philadelphia
Climbing the Greasy Pole
Clog Dance
Clown and Beer-Thief
Clown and Coal Merchant
Clown's Face
Clown's Mixup
Cock Fight
Cock Fight, No. 2
Colored Baby's Morning Bath
Colored Folks Bathing
Colored Sports
Colored Woman Smoking a Pipe
Columbia and Shamrock
Columbia in the Lead
Cossacks
Country Sport and Old Maid
Country Teacher and His Pupils
Courting in Olden Times
Cowboy Fun
Crew of the U. S. Cruiser Raleigh Passing the Grant Monument at Fairmount Park, Philadelphia
Crowd Leaving Athletic Base Ball Grounds
Dance Around the Moon
Dancing for a Chicken
Dancing Skeleton
Darkies' Kiss
Deadly Rivals
Death Curve, New York City
Delaware River Icebound
The Devil's Amusement
The Difficulties of the Manicurist
Digging for Foundation for Large Department Store, Phila.
Disappearing Gun in Action
Doctor's Office
Dolorita
Double-Humped Camels
Driving Cows to Pasture
Drunken Scene
Dutch and Irish Politics
Eating Dinner Under Difficulties
Eating Watermelons for a Prize
Egyptian Sword Dance
Electric Fountain
Electric Treatment
Employees Leaving Fall River Iron Works
The Enchanted Cafe

English Barnyard Scene
Escaped
Essence of Old Virginia
An Evening Chat
Expansion and Contraction
Facial Massage
Fantastic Dining Room
The Farmer and the Old Maid
Farmer Chasing Trespassers
Farmyard Scene
The Fastest Steam Yacht Afloat
Fatima, Couchee Dancer
Feeding Hogs
Feeding the Dogs
Feeding the Elephants
Feeding the Hippopotamus
Feeding the Pigs
Feeding the Swans
Ferris Wheel
Fighting Amazons
Fighting Fifth Northumberland Fusileers
Fire at Triangle Clothing Store, 13th and Ridge Ave., Philadelphia, May 3d, 1899
Fire Dance
Fisherman's Troubles
The Five Acrobats, St. Leons
The Fooled Policeman
Foreign Train Scenes
Fred Poplar and His Pal
French Couchee Dance
A Fresh Bath
Fun in an Opium Joint
Fun on the Beach
Fun on the Ice
Funeral of Lung Fei Dong, the Chinese Mason
A Funny Story (Facial Expression)
Game of Base Ball
Gardener Sprinkling Bad Boy
Gardener's Joke
Georgia Camp Meeting
German Cruisers Bombarding Venezuelan Forts
Ghost Dancers
Giant Wilkins, the Largest Man in the World
Giant Wilkins Walking No. 2
Giddy Old Maid
Gilbert Saroni Preparing for His Act
Girard College Cadets Reviewed by Governor Hastings, at the Dedication of Stephen Girard's Monument
Girls Rolling Down Hill
Going to the Fire
A Good Catch
Grand Entrance into the Hippodrome
Grand Review
Great Gorge R. R., Niagara
Group of Mexicans
Happy Childhood
Hatching Chickens Up-to-Date
Hauling Dirt Up an Incline
He Pulled the Wrong Tooth
Herald Square, New York
Herman the Conjurer
Hey Ding Diddle
Himalayan Bears from India
His Collar Does Not Fit
His First Cigar
His Wife Has Neuralgia
"The Holy City"
Home from the Club
Hon. Wm. Jennings Bryan
Horseshoe Falls from American Side
Horseshoe Falls, from Canadian Side
The House That Jack Built
How a Wife Gets Her Pocket Money
How Murphy Paid His Rent
How Rube Stopped the Trolley Car
The Hungry Countryman
Hunting White Bear
Hurry Up
In the Wrong Room
Indian War Dance
Indians
Inquisitive Models
Introduction of the Rough Riders of the World
The Irate Model
Irish Couple Dancing Breakdown
Irish Reel
James Street, Seattle, Wash.
Japanese Foot Juggler
Japanese Geisha Girls No. 1
Japanese Geisha Girls No. 2
Japanese Sword Fight
Jersey Central Flyer
Jewelry Robbery
Jolly Monks
King Cole
The King's Guardsmen
Kruger and Body Guard Leaving the Volksraad
Kruger Leaving His Residence for the Volksraad
Lafayette Square, Buffalo, N. Y.
L'Argentine Butterfly Dance
L'Argentine Mirror Dance
L'Argentine Silver Dance
Leap Frog
Leaping Tournament over Elephants
Leaving Jerusalem
The Legacy
Lehigh Valley Express "Black Diamond"
Liberty Bell
Lieut. Bagley's Funeral. Escort of Lieut. Bagley's at Raleigh, N. C.
A Lively Night
The Living Posters
Loading a Train with Stone
Loading and Unloading the Chutes at Willow Grove
Lone Fisherman
Loop the Loop
Loro & Devoy, the Comical Acrobats
Love in a Railroad Train
Love Me Little, Love Me Long
Lovers Interrupted
Lovers Interrupted. New
McKinley's Funeral
The Magical Tramp
Magician
Main Street, Buffalo, N. Y.
Main Street, Fall River
Man Couchee Dance
Manning the Yard Arm on the U. S. Cruiser Raleigh
Mary Had a Little Lamb
Massage Treatment
Max Unger, the Strong Man
May Pole Dance
The Mechanical Head
Merry-Go-Round or Carrousel
Mexican Bull Fight
The Miller and Chimney Sweep
Mischievous Boys
Mrs. Schneider's First Pinch of Snuff
Mitchell Day at Wilkes-Barre, Pa.
Morning Exercise on Board the U. S. Cruiser Raleigh
Mules in the Coal Mines
A Narrow Escape
Naval Parade on the Delaware River, Monday, May 1st, in Honor of Admiral Dewey
Never Interfere in Family Troubles
The New Born King
New Chinese Laundry
New Colored Kiss, No. 2
The New Dude and a Market Woman
The New Enchanted Cafe
New Fisherman's Luck
The New Leap Frog
New Passing Train Scene
The New Shooting the Chutes
The New Version of the Two Old Sports
New York's 7th and 71st Regiments
Newell and Chevet, the Famous Acrobats
Nightmare
North American Elk
North American Grey Wolves
Odetta, Chinese Dance
Odetta, Rope Dance No. 1
Odetta, Rope Dance No. 2
Odetta, Spanish Dance
O'Finnegan's Wake
Ohio Colored Troops at Camp Alger
Old Darkey Dancing
Old Maid Courtship
Old Maid's Ballet Dance
Old Maid's First Visit to a Theatre
The Old Maid's Lament
Old Maid's Morning Greeting
On Forbidden Ground
Pacific Avenue, Tacoma, Wash.
Panorama from Elevated Train, New York
Panorama Looking Down Niagara from New Suspension Bridge
Panorama of American Soldiers in Camp
Panorama of Circus Train Unloading Horses
Panorama of City of Venice
Panorama of King's County, N. Y.
Panorama of League Island, Philadelphia
Panorama of New York from Jersey City
Panorama of Schellenen Gorge of Switzerland
Panorama of Thames River
Panorama of the Lehigh Valley Railroad
Panorama of the Menagerie
Panoramic View of Atlantic City Beach
Panoramic View of Haverstraw Tunnel, N. Y.
Parade of the Philadelphia Volunteer Fire Department
Passion Play: Agony in the Garden
Passion Play: Baptism of Jesus
Passion Play: Carrying the Cross
Passion Play: Christ and Disciples Plucking Corn
Passion Play: Christ Before King Herod
Passion Play: Christ Before Pilate and the Condemnation
Passion Play: Christ Before the Two High Priests
Passion Play: Christ Calling Zaccheus from the Tree
Passion Play: Christ Feeding the Multitude
Passion Play: Christ Healing the Sick
Passion Play: Christ in the Carpenter Shop
Passion Play: Christ in the Synagogue
Passion Play: Christ Tempted by the Devil
Passion Play: Flight into Egypt
Passion Play: Herodias Pleads for John the Baptist's Head
Passion Play: Jesus and the Woman of Samaria
Passion Play: Judas' Betrayal and the Messiah's Arrest
Passion Play: Massacre of the Innocents
Passion Play: Placing Jesus in the Tomb
Passion Play: Raising of Lazarus
Passion Play: Shepherds Watching Their Flocks by Night
Passion Play: Suffer Little Children to Come Unto Me
Passion Play: Taking Down the Cross
Passion Play: The Annunciation
Passion Play: The Ascension
Passion Play: The Birth of Christ
Passion Play: The Crucifixion
Passion Play: The Last Supper
Passion Play: The Messiah's Entry into Jerusalem
Passion Play: The Resurrection
Passion Play: The Transfiguration
The Peanut Vendor
Peeping Tom and His Telescope
Performing Elephants
Perkasie Tunnel
Petro in Fairy Land
Philippino War Dance
The Philosopher's Stone
Photographing a Goose
Pie Eating Contest
Pillow Fight, Reversed
Polar Bears

Police Charge on Horseback
Policeman Chasing Bathers
Prairie Emigrant Train Crossing the Plains
President McKinley and His Cabinet on the Reviewing Stand, at Fairmount Park, Phila., May 27, 1899
President Mitchell's Speech
Prince Henry at Washington
Prof. Langtry's Boxing School
Putting Out the Fire
Pygmalion and Galatea
Quadrille in Drawers
Quaker Dance
The Quarrelsome Anglers
Railroad Tunnel Scene
Rapids above American Falls from American Side
Rapids above American Falls from Bridge to Goat Island
Reading a Letter (Facial Expression)
Reading Subway
Rear view of the "Black Diamond Express," Lehigh Valley R. R.
Rear view of the Washington and New York Flyer
Rescue from the Fire
Ricardo Family of Acrobats No. 1
Ricardo Family of Acrobats No. 2
Ricardo Family of Acrobats No. 3
Ricardo Family of Acrobats No. 4
Ricardo Family of Acrobats No. 5
River Drive, Fairmount Park
Riverside Avenue, Spokane, Wash.
Roofs of Paris
Royal Horse Artillery on the March to the Front
The Royal Levee in India [The Delhi 'Durbar']
Rubber Face
Rushing the "Growler"
Sailor's Hornpipe
Scarf Dance
Scene in a Laundry
Scene in Seminary
Scenes of the Wreckage from the Water Front
School Girl's Dance
Scotch Highland Fling
The Sculptor's Studio
Shamrock Placing Her Topsail
Shamrock Rounding Sandy Hook Light Ship
Sharkey-McCoy, 10 Rounds
6th Ave. New York Elevated Railroad
Skating in Fairmount Park
Skating Scene
Skirmish with Boers near Kimberly by a Troop of Cavalry Scouts Attached to Gen. French's Column
Sleigh Riding
Small Boy and Bear, Hagenbeck's Circus
Small Boy and Lion Cub, Hagenbeck's Circus
Snapshot and Its Consequences
Snowballing
Soft Shoe Dance
The Soldier's Return
Spanish Dance
Spokane Falls, Spokane
Squire's Court
Stable on Fire
The Stag Hunt
Station Scene
Stealing Chickens
Steeple Jumping
Submarine Diver
Sunken Vessel in the Harbor
Swimming School
Swiss Training and Breeding Home for St. Bernard Dogs
Taking Out the Dead and Wounded
Teaching Ballet Dancing
Ten Ichi Performing His Wonderful Water Trick
Ten Ichi, the Famous Japanese Magician, with His Troop
10th Pennsylvania Drilling at Manila
There Is No Fool Like an Old Fool
Third Avenue Elevated Train, New York
The Three Bacchantes
Three Bell Sisters in a Fancy Dance
Torpedo Boat in Action
Trained Animals, Hagenbeck's Circus
Trained Bears and Dogs, Hagenbeck's Circus
Trained Goats
The Tramp in the Barber Shop
Tramping on a Rolling Globe
The Tramp's Surprise
Transvaal War Supplies Transported by McKenzie Traction Engines
Trick Dogs, Hagenbeck's Circus
Trick Donkey, No. 2
Trick Donkey, Hagenbeck's Circus
Trick Elephant Bolivar, the Largest Elephant in the World, No. 1
Trick Elephant Bolivar, the Largest Elephant in the World, No. 2
Trick Elephant, Hagenbeck's Circus
Triple Pyramids
Troop Train Conveying the Seaforth Highlanders across the Modder River
Trouble with the Milkmaid
Trouble with the Washerwoman
20th Century Surgeon
24th Chasseurs Steeple Jumping
Two Old Sports
Tyrolienne Dance
U. S. Artillery Drill
U. S. Battleship Indiana
U. S. Monitor Miantonomah Steaming into Key West
U. S. Monitor Terror
Umbrella Dance
Unloading Canal Boat
Unloading the Elephants
An Unpleasant Situation
Upside Down
Vaulting in Saddle and Jumping Hurdle
Venetian Troupe
View of the Residence Section
Volksfest, Philadelphia
Waltz Clog Dance
War Supplies Arriving at Boer Laager by Train of Ox Teams
Washerwoman's Mistake
Washington and New York Flyer
Watering Cavalry Horses
Watermelon Eating Contest
Wedding Procession in a Church at Rome
Western Card Game
What Happened to the Milkman
What Was Found in a High Hat
Whirlpool Rapids
Whitewashing a Colored Baby
Wing Dance
The Wire Walker
Woodside Park Trolley Panorama
A Wringing Good Joke
Yacht Columbia
Yacht Race
Yacht Shamrock
Yachting at Atlantic City

Jan 31 The Magical Egg
Wonderful Suspension and Evolution

Feb [day undetermined]
The Human Fly
The Impossible Feat of Balancing
Smashing a Jersey Mosquito
Up-to-Date Surgery

Feb 14 Disagreeable Railroad Passengers

Mar [day undetermined]
Who Killed Cock Robin?

Mar 7 Robinson Crusoe

Mar 14 Buying a Baby
Logging in Canada
Spearing Salmon in the Rivers of the North West Territory

Apr [day undetermined]
Mary Jane's Mishap; or, Don't Fool with the Parafin
Panorama of Queenstown
Rip Van Winkle
Valentine and Orson

Apr 11 Reproduction of the Corbett-McGovern Fight (San Francisco, Cal, March 31, 1903)

Apr 13 Gulliver's Travels

May [day undetermined]
Animated Dolls
Babes in the Wood
Beauty and the Beast
Goody, Goody Two Shoes
Hickery, Dickery Dock
Little Miss Muffet
Little Snowdrop
Modern House Furnishing Methods
Old Woman Who Lived in a Shoe
Reynard the Fox
Swiss Family Robinson
Three Bears
Three Little Pigs
Tom, Tom the Piper's Son
Uncle Tom's Cabin
Window Cleaner's Mishap

May 16 The Gambler's Crime
Smiles and Tears

Jun 6 Little Tom Thumb

Jun 13 Misfortune Never Comes Alone
The Mysterious Box

Jun 27 The Enchanted Well
The Inn where No Man Rests

Jul 11 Sleeping Beauty

Jul 18 The Life of a London Bobby
Pittsburgh Fire Department in Full Run

Jul 25 The Drawing Lesson; or, The Living Statue
The Mystical Flame
The Witch's Revenge

Aug 1 The Animated Cartoon
DeVoy's Revolving Ladder Act
The Elixir of Life
Fun on Board a Fishing Smack
How to Shut Up a Quarrelsome Wife
Little Tich and His Funny Feet
The Magic Book
Rock of Ages
True Love Never Runs Smooth

Aug 15 The Melomaniac
The Monster
A Spiritualistic Photographer

Sep 5 The Fairyland; or, The Kingdom of the Fairies

Sep 19 Pope Pius X [His Election and the Procession]

Oct [day undetermined]
Ten Nights in a Barroom

Oct 31 The Poachers

Nov 7 Jack Jaggs & Dum Dum
Life of Napoleon
10 Ladies in an Umbrella

Nov 14 The Effects of a Trolley Car Collision
An Episode in the Park
A Shocking Accident
Street Car Chivalry
The Tramp's First Bath
A Visit to the Zoo

Nov 21 The Goose Takes a Trolley Ride

Dec [day undetermined]
How Old Is Ann?
Outcast and Bride

Dec 12 At Work in a Peat Bog
Cliff Scenery at the Fabbins
A Coach Drive from Glengariffe to Kenmore
The Damnation of Faust
Irish Peasants Bringing Their Milk to a Cooperative Creamery
Jack and Jim
The Mono-Railway Between Listowel and Ballybunion, Ireland
Panorama of the Lakes of Killarney from Hotel
Scenes in an Irish Bacon Factory
Scenes in an Irish Market Place
Scenes of Irish Cottage Life
Shooting the Rapids of Killarney
A Trip Through the Gap of Dunloe
A Trip to the Giant's Causeway

Dec 19 Dear Old Stars and Stripes, Goodbye
Discovered Through an Opera Glass
Every Day Is Sunshine When the Heart Beats True
The Magic Lantern
Only a Soldier Boy

1904 [month undetermined]
Ach du Lieber

After Dark
Banjo'Lize
Bull Fight with Matadors Senor Don Luis Mazzantini and Bombita
The Cook Gets Square
Couchee Dance on the Pike
Daisy Donohue
Don't Butt In
Exhibition of the United States Life Saving Crew
From the South
The Funniest Man in the Exposition
Glimpses of Japan
Happy Days in Dixie
The Liberty Bell on Its Way to the Exposition
Life of an American Fireman
Military Serenade
The Missing Link
Our Own Make Polka
Panorama of a Philippine Settlement [Pan-American Exposition]
Trip to the Zoo
The Tunnel Scene
Will He Never Get Undressed
Yum-Yum-Yum

Jan [day undetermined]
Pugilistic Toads

Jan 2 The Somnambulist
William Tell

Jan 9 The Chicago Fire
The Terrible Turkish Executioner

Jan 16 A Burlesque Highway Robbery in "Gay Paree"
Puss in Boots

Jan 23 Russian Cavalry in Corea [sic]

Jan 30 Alligator Farm
Dogs and Rats
The Monkey Bicyclist
Monkey, Dog and Pony Circus

Feb 6 The Automobile Race
Devil's Pot
The Falling Palace
A Ferry in the Far East
Fording a Stream
High Diving and Reverse
Hurdle Jumping
An Intelligent Elephant
The Little Greedy Beggar
Marie Antoinette
Metamorphosis of the King of Spades
The Midgets

Feb 20 The Great Baltimore Fire

Mar 5 The Busy Bee

Mar 12 Babe and Dog
Game of Cards
Hubby to the Rescue
Lovers' Quarrel
Now, You Stop
Scenes on Every Floor

Mar 26 Wonderful Hair Restorer

Apr 9 Bombardment of Port Arthur
Living Dummy
The Revolving Table
Russ-Jap Forces Meeting Near Chemulpo

Apr 25 The Prodigal Son
Samson and Delilah
The Smugglers

May 14 The Fight on the Bridge Between Russians and Japs

May 21 Barnum's Trunk

Jun [day undetermined]
The American Flag, Floating
Art Studies
Barnum & Bailey's Circus Street Parade
Beauty Bathing
Deer Hunting in England
The Devonshire Fair
DeVoy the Wire Walker
Horse-Shoe Curve
The International Yacht Race
The Magic Hat
The Magic Hoop
Pan. of Fifth Ave., Pittsburg, Pa., From a Trolley Car
Pan. of St. Railway Building, Pittsburg, Pa.
The Philadelphia Speedway
Pierrot's Mystification
Pushball Game
Rival Conjurers
Surgical Operation
Surgical Operation by Dr. Hurst
Too Much Mixed Ale
Washing Sheep

Jun 18 A Disagreeable Remedy
European Idea of Christopher Columbus Discovering America
Metamorphosis of a Butterfly
A Scandal on the Staircase

Jun 26 The Great Train Robbery

Jul [day undetermined]
A Circus Romance
A Parisienne's Bed Time

Jul 23 Annie's Love Story
Dance Plastiques
Japanese Ambush
The Nest Robbers

Jul 30 Bold Bank Robbery

Aug 20 Lookout at Port Arthur

Aug 27 A Boar Hunt

Sep 3 Falls of the Rhine
Indians and Cowboys
The Strike

Sep 10 Ghezzi and His Circus
Joseph Sold by His Brothers
Life of an American Soldier

Sep 24 Drama in the Air
The Fairy of the Spring
A Good Story
Ice Cream Eater
Ruffian's Dance

Oct [day undetermined]
Alcohol and Its Victims
Around Port Arthur (No. 2)
Attack on a Train
Bride Retiring
Cakewalk
Charley's Aunt
Cloth Dealer
The False Cripple
An Interrupted Flirtation
Just Like a Girl
Mind! Madame Is Coming
Painter's Misfortune
The Porter's Horrible End
The Shower Bath
Sisters Barrison
Soap Bubbles
Startling Pursuit
That Poor Insurance Man
Too Late
The Trials and Troubles of an Automobilist
The Young Farmer Girl

Oct 1 Dogs and Cats
The Opera Hat
Park in Barcelona by Moonlight
Smoker Too Small

Oct 8 Around Port Arthur
A Fight on the Yalu

Oct 15 Ascending Mount Pilate

Oct 22 Behind the Lens
The Clever Baker
Disagreeable Five O'Clock
Mistake in the Door

Oct 29 An Impossible Voyage

Nov [day undetermined]
Avenging a Crime; or, Burned at the Stake
The Lost Child
Willie's Vacation

Nov 5 Meet Me at the Fountain

Nov 12 August, the Monkey

Nov 19 A Cheeky Traveler

Dec 3 From Christiania to the North Cape
Saluting the Flag

Dec 17 Patrick Street, Cork

Dec 24 Burglars at Work
Solomon's Judgment
The Swing

Dec 31 Russian Antisemitic Atrocities

1905 [month undetermined]
Different Hair Dresses
Love at Each Floor
Out Boating

Jan [day undetermined]
Around New York in 15 Minutes
Tramp and Dump Cart

Jan 14 Wonderful Beehive

Jan 28 Saved from a Watery Grave

Feb 4 Innocent Flirtation
St. Petersburg Massacre

Feb 11 The Counterfeiters

Feb 25 From Cairo to the Pyramids

Mar [day undetermined]
Life of the New York Policeman

Mar 11 President Roosevelt's Inauguration

Apr [day undetermined]
The Bigamist
Evolution of the Japanese
The Pirates
Sins and Sorrows of a Great City
Why the Cook Was Not Fired

Apr 8 The Sign of the Cross

Apr 29 His Master's Breath
His Master's Voice
A Jilted Suitor

May [day undetermined]
Behind the Scenes
The Fake Blind Man
The New Year's Shooters in Philadelphia
Photographed for the Rogue's Gallery
Policeman's Pal
A Sweet Kiss
Tramp's Revenge

May 6 A Catching Story
Good Reason for a Divorce
Policeman's Love Affair
Why Papa Could Not Read

May 13 The Moon-Lover

May 27 A Father's Honor

Jun 3 A Dog Lost, Strayed or Stolen. $25.00 Reward. Apply to Mrs. Brown, 711 Park Ave.

Jun 10 In the Mining District

Jun 24 Christian Martyrs

Jul 1 Highway Robbery
King of Dollars
A Pleasure Trip

Jul 8 I. B. Dam and the Whole Dam Family

Jul 22 Kidnapped Child

Jul 29 Great Steeplechase

Aug 5 Mutiny on Man-of-War in Odessa

Aug 19 Modern Brigandage

Aug 26 On a Vacation Trip
The Vendetta

Sep 16 Impersonation of Britt-Nelson Fight
Life of Moses

Sep 30 Impatient Customer
Language of Flowers
Stunning Creations
Wonderful Album

Oct [day undetermined]
Fire in New York's Bowery
Meet Me Down at Luna, Lena

Oct 14 Behind the Stage
A Henpecked Husband
Ill Rewarded Conjuror

Oct 28 Through the Matrimonial Agency

Nov [day undetermined]
Arrival of the Mail Steamer at Larne
Coaches Starting from Larne and Passing Through Tunnel on the Antrim Coast Road
Getting the Hay
Impersonation of the Fitzsimmons-O'Brien Fight
Market Day at Kenmore
Milking Time: A Kerry Herd
Potters at Work
Railway Panorama Between Green Island and Kilroot
Railway Panorama Between Kilroot and Whitehead
Rock Scene at Ballybunion
A Rough Sea on the Derry Coast
Shooting the Chutes, Cork Exhibition
Through the Keyhole
Through Tunnel on the Antrim Coast
Tourists Leaving the Lake Hotel, Killarney
The Waterfalls of Glengariffe

Nov 4 The Pastry Cook's Practical Jokes

Nov 18 Fun on the Farm

Dec 9 The Hen with the Golden Eggs
The Postman's Christmas Box

Dec 16 A Tragedy at Sea

Dec 23 Disagreeable Mistake
A Great Discovery
Dec 30 Misadventures of a Hat
1906 [month undetermined]
Papa Minds the Baby
Shad Fishing
Wash Day at Casey's
Jan 13 Robbers of Children
Jan 20 The Wolf's Trap
Feb 24 The Wreckers of the Limited Express
Mar [day undetermined]
Nelson-McGovern Fight, 1906
Mar 17 Engadin in Switzerland
Apr [day undetermined]
The Absent-Minded Shoe Black
Baby's Bath
Bad Joke
Bad Lodgers
Childish Tricks Baffled
Compromising Spots
Confession
Doorkeeper's Curiosity
The Enchanted Melon
First Night Out
A Heavy Sea
Improvised Suit
In the Polar Regions
The Indiscreet Bathroom Maid
Jack the Bootblack
Joys of Marriage
Keep It Straight
Kids' Practical Jokes
Martyrs of the Inquisition
Motor-car and Cripple
Phenomenal Hen
Remorse
St. Bartholomew's Day
Scholar's Breakfast
Ski Running
Surgical Operation
Touching Pleading
Transparent Cards
Troublesome Fishbone
War of Children
The Wig
Young Apple Thief
Apr 7 Rescued by Carlo
Apr 14 Cruise of the Steamer Ophir, with Prince and Princess of Wales on Board
Fishing Pictures
Naval Subjects, Merchant Marine, and From All over the World
Railway Panoramas from Every Port of the World
Steamship Panoramas
A Transatlantic Trip of the S. S. Kronprinz Wilhelm, from Bremen to New York
Trip Through Abyssinia
Trip Through America
Trip Through Australia, New Zealand
Trip Through Canada
Trip Through England
Trip Through France
Trip Through Germany
Trip Through India
Trip Through Ireland
Trip Through Italy
Trip Through South Africa
Trip Through Switzerland
Trip Through Transvaal
Turbulent Seas, Waterfalls and Streams
Apr 28 The Clown's Adventures
May 7 Arrival of Refugees at Oakland
City Hall from Market St. and City Hall Ave.
The Doomed City
Effect of Earthquake
Feeding Chinese
The First Trolley Car After the Earthquake
Fun Among the Refugees
Going to the Fire, Showing Chief Sullivan During the Earthquake
The Mission
Panorama from Telegraph Hill
Panorama of Chinatown
Panorama of Market Street before the Fire
Panorama of Nob Hill
Panorama of San Francisco in Smoke and Fire
Panoramas of Market Street, the City Hall, Taken from the Roof of the U. S. Mint
Refugees at the Golden Gate Park
Refugees in Jefferson Square
Refugees on Market St.
St. Francis Hotel
The San Francisco Disaster
Shot for Looting
Thieves in Camp, Golden Gate Park
Waterfront, Refugees Leaving San Francisco
Jun [day undetermined]
Snake Hunting
Jun 23 Blackmailing the Motorists
"A Fresh Bath" or "The Tripper Tripped"
Marriage of Princess Ena and Alphonse XIII, King of Spain
Me and My Two Pals
The Olympic Games at Athens, Greece
Vengeance Is Mine
Jul [day undetermined]
The River Pirates
The Trading Stamp Craze
Jul 14 Anything for Peace and Quietness
A Night Off
Jul 21 The Gambler's Nightmare
Aug [day undetermined]
Impersonation of Gans-Nelson Fight
Aug 4 The Great Mail Robbery
Sep 1 The Secret of Death Valley
Sep 8 Reproduction of Nelson-Gans Fight
Oct [day undetermined]
Wanted: A Husband
The Wishbone
Oct 27 How to Keep Cool or Our Ice Supply
Whale Hunting
Nov 3 The Bank Defaulter
Nov 24 Algy's New Suit
Exmore Stag Hunt
For His Daughter's Honor
Good Night
The Lost Hat: He Got It Alright
Train Collision
Two Seedy Rubes: They Have a Hot Time in the Old Town
Dec [day undetermined]
A Thrilling Detective Story
Dec 1 Honesty's Strange Reward
Marble Industry at Carrara
Tom Moves
Unquenchable Thirst
Dec 15 The Murder of His Seventeen Wives
Dec 29 Cabby's Dream
Disappointed
Furnished on Easy Terms
Kiddies Pets
Tommy's Revenge
Trout Fishing
Weary Willie and His Pal
Won't You Come Home
1907 [month undetermined]
Along the Shore Line of Lake Washington
Botanist's Misadventures
Panorama of Market Street, San Francisco
Passion Play: Baptism by Immersion
Torrents of Zermath
A Trip Up Broadway
Jan [day undetermined]
Base Ball Game
Philadelphia New Year Shooters
Feb [day undetermined]
Her First Cake
Feb 9 Salome "The Dance of the Seven Veils"
Mar 2 The Unwritten Law: A Thrilling Drama Based on the Thaw White Case
Apr 13 The Animated Pill Box
The Borrowed Ladder
Traced by a Laundry Mark
The Vision of a Crime
Apr 20 A Winter Day in the Country
May [day undetermined]
A Little Bit of String
May 4 Too Much Mother-in-Law
May 11 Jamestown Naval Review
May 18 The Anarchists
Father's Washing Day
Life in India
Papa's Letter
The Pirates
Spring Cleaning
The Stolen Bicycle
Wanted, 10,000 Eggs
May 25 And the Dog Came Back
Jun [day undetermined]
Jimmie, the Messenger Boy
Jun 15 When Women Vote
Jun 22 The Enchanted Mattress
The Oyster Industry
Travels of a Lost Trunk
Jun 29 Mother's Dream
Jul [day undetermined]
Among the Igorrotes
Over the Midland Terminal Railroad: Through Cripple Creek District
The Sleepy Cop
Through Yellowstone Park
Jul 13 A Family Outing
Jul 27 Caught with the Goods
Elks' Parade
The Fortune Teller
Gypsy's Revenge
Nervy Jim and the Cop
The New Apprentice
Aug [day undetermined]
An Inquisitive Girl
Aug 3 Albany, N. Y.
Atlantic City
Baltimore
Boston
Brooklyn
Buffalo
Chester, Pa.
Cincinnati
Cleveland
Colorado Springs
Denver
Detroit
Easton
El Paso
Harrisburg
Jersey City
Kansas City
New Haven
New Orleans
New York
Panorama of Court of Honor
Panorama of Market Street Showing the Beautiful Decorations
Paterson, N.J.
Philadelphia
Pittsburg
Reading
San Francisco
Scranton
Toledo
Tyron
Wilmington, Del.
Aug 10 A Misunderstanding
Aug 17 The Actor Annoys the Boarders
Who's Boss of the House?
Aug 24 Are You an Elk?
The Blacksmith's Daughter
Aug 31 Just Married
Sep [day undetermined]
Baxter's Brain Storm
Roasted Chestnuts
Sep 7 Cohen's Bad Luck
Sep 14 The Indian's Friendship
John D. and the Reporter
Sep 21 Grandpa's Vacation
Sep 28 The Amateur Champion
The Scheme That Failed
Oct [day undetermined]
The Cleptomaniac
Miraculous Eggs
A Night at the Gayety
Oct 5 Interrupted Outing
Lucky Jim
Moses Sells a Collar Button
The New Arrival
Oct 12 The First Quarrel
Oct 19 All on Account of a Lost Collar Button
Harbor Pirates
Nov 2 Smuggled into America
Nov 9 The Foundling

Nov 16 How Brown Saw the Baseball Game
Neighbors Who Borrow
Nov 23 A Breeze from the West
Only Kids
The Parson of Hungry Gulch; or, The Right Man in the Right Place May Work Wonders
Nov 30 Bargain Sales
Oh Me! Oh My!
Dec [day undetermined]
An Animated Dummy
Dec 7 The Making of a Modern Newspaper
Dec 14 The Pay Train Robbery
Dec 28 How the Masher Was Punished
1908
Jan [day undetermined]
The Animated Dummy
The Goebel Tragedy
I Rather Two Step Than Waltz
Impossibilities
A Lucky Horseshoe
Pipe Dreams
Jan 4 The Silver King
•Through Darkness to Light
Jan 11 Such a Good Joke, But— Why Don't He Laugh?
Jan 18 Bachelor's Wedding Bells
Have You Seen My Wife?
If Wm. Penn Came to Life
The Ringmaster's Wife
Jan 25 A Gay Old Boy
Feb 1 The Blind Boy
His Week's Wages; or, Where's That Quarter?
The Magnetic Eye
Feb 15 The Count of No Account
Feb 29 Reproduction of Burns-Palmer Fight, London [England], February 10th, 1908
Mar [day undetermined]
The Burglar's Child
A Country Girl in Philadelphia
A Faithful Wife
A Fool and His Money
Julius Caesar
Meet Me at the Station
No Children Wanted
A Persistent Actor
Rube Goes to College
Troubles of Too Ardent Admirers
Mar 7 And a Little Child Shall Lead Them
Mar 14 A New Way to Pay Debts
See the Point?
Mar 21 Easy Money
A Romance of the Fur Country
Mar 28 Do It Now!
The Girl across the Way
Our Own Little Flat
The Pursuit of a Suit
Apr [day undetermined]
The Curse of Gold
The Drink Cure
The Fake Windstorm
The New Breakfast Food
Apr 4 After the Celebration!
The Mountaineers
Apr 13 Neighborly Neighbors
The Parents' Devotion
Apr 16 The Little Easter Fairy
Something on His Mind
Apr 20 The Fatal Card
Apr 23 Willie's Party
The Wrong Overcoat
Apr 27 Acrobatic Pills
The Amateur Hypnotist
Apr 30 Beg Pardon!
Oh, My Feet!
May [day undetermined]
The Stolen Flask
May 4 The Bride's Dream
May 7 The Mysterious Phonograph
Stop That Alarm!
May 11 The Great Jewel Robbery
May 14 The Automatic Laundry
The "Merry Widow" Hats
May 18 The Cause of All the Trouble
May 21 The Circus Boy
The Tale of a Pig
May 25 The Near-Sighted Professor [His Trials and Tribulations]
Why He Signed the Pledge
May 28 A Gallant Knight
Jun [day undetermined]
The Clown
Harlem Flats
Tracked by a Woman
Two Sides of the Wall
Jun 1 The Greed for Gold
Jun 4 The Miner's Daughter
Jun 8 The Hand of Fate
Magnetic Vapor
Jun 11 Robbie's Pet Rat
Two Brothers of the G. A. R.
Jun 15 An Honest Newsboy's Reward
Two Little Dogs
Jun 18 Adventures of Mr. Troubles
Mephisto's Affinity
Jun 22 The Old Maid's Parrot
Romance in a Gypsy Camp
Jun 25 Philadelphia, the Cradle of Liberty
The Student's Prank; or, A Joke on His Parents
Jun 29 Held for Ransom
Jul [day undetermined]
Driven from Home
Jul 2 The New Maid
Outwitted by His Wife
Jul 6 A Western Romance in the Days of '49
Jul 9 Two Little Shoes
Jul 13 The Robbery of the Citizen's Bank
Jul 16 "Captain Molly" or, The Battle of Monmouth
Dr. Curem's Patients
Jul 18 The Dynamite Man
Jul 20 Dick's Sister
Jul 23 A Fatal Likeness
Jul 27 The White Chief
Jul 30 The Woman Who Gambles
Aug [day undetermined]
The Forged Will
Hobo's Revenge
The Rainmaker
Tribulations of a Photographer
Aug 3 A Policeman for an Hour
The Sensational Sheath Gown
Aug 6 The Bogus Lord
Aug 10 The Light in the Window
Aug 13 The Crushed Tragedian
Wanted: An Artist's Model
Aug 17 The King's Diamond
Aug 20 Scenes from the Battlefield of Gettysburg, the Waterloo of the Confederacy
Aug 24 Rivals for a Week
The Wrong Valise
Aug 27 The Midnight Express
Aug 31 Fascinating Fluffy Dimples
Sep [day undetermined]
A Fatal Temptation
The Hat of Fortune
Heating Powder
It's Never Too Late to Mend
Make Yourself at Home
Sep 3 The Pawnbroker
Sep 12 The Dancing Fiend
The Hebrew Fugitive
The Persistent Trombonist
The Washerwoman's Revenge
Sep 13 A Southern Romance of Slavery Days
Sep 21 Hon. William J. Bryan and Hon. John W. Kern
How Rastus Got His Pork Chops
Two Little Breadwinners
Sep 24 In the Nick of Time
The Suicidal Poet
Sep 28 The Criminal's Daughter
The Ticklish Man
Oct [day undetermined]
The Burglar's Ball
The Gondolier's Daughter
Historical Parade
Industrial Parade
The Little Coward
Military Parade, Founders Week Celebration, Philadelphia
Naval Parade
The Woman of 1776
Oct 1 The Masqueraders
Wanted: A Military Man
Oct 5 Redeemed from Sin
Salome and the Devil to Pay
Oct 8 The Saloon Dance
"When Our Ship Comes In"
Oct 12 The Way They Fooled Dad
Oct 15 The Bloodstone
Oct 19 For His Sister's Sake
Oct 22 All on Account of a Butterfly
Hubby's Vacation
Oct 26 Auntie Takes the Children to the Country
How a Pretty Girl Sold Her Hair Restorer
Oct 29 The Mountaineer's Revenge
Nov 2 The Cross Roads
Nov 5 The Key Under the Mat
Lunch Time
Nov 9 The Cotton Industry of the South
Nov 12 The Janitor Falsely Accused
Nov 16 Madam Flirt and Her Adopted Uncle
Through an Orange Grove
Nov 19 The Engineer
Nov 23 The Dirigible Airship
A Pair of Spectacles
Nov 26 Persistency Wins
The Thanksgiving Turkey
Nov 30 The Sexton of Longwyn
Weary Willie's Revenge
Dec [day undetermined]
A Female Fire Department
It Happened at Midnight
The Rain-Dear
The Snowbird
Ten Minutes with Shakespeare
When Ma Goes Shopping
Dec 3 Hobo's Dream
Lady Barbers
Dec 7 The Lighthouse-Keeper's Daughter
Dec 10 Charlie's Ma-in-Law
Dick's Aunt
Dec 14 Button, Button, Where Is the Button?
The Face in the Window
Dec 17 On the Stroke of Twelve
Dec 21 Christmas Eve at Sunset
Dec 24 Restored by Repentance
Dec 28 A New Year
A New Year's Gift
Dec 31 The Forgotten Watch
The House at the Bridge
1909
Jan 4 A Bitter Lesson
The Old Maid's Dream
Jan 7 Leo's Air Rifle
Two Orphans of the G. A. R.
Feb [day undetermined]
•Peaches and Cream

Scott, George, & Co. *see* **George Scott & Co.**

Selig Polyscope Co. *see also* **William N. Selig**
1898 [month undetermined]
The American Flag
Battery Charge
Battle of San Juan Hill
Cavalry Horses Fording a Stream in Santiago de Cuba
Charge at Las Guasimas
Daily March
The Fighting Fifth Cuban Mascot
Infantry Charge
Naval Reserves Returning from the War
Off for the Front
Review of Officers
Sailors Landing Under Fire
Soldiers at Play
Soldiers Firing on Train
Steam Launch of the Olympia
Teaching Cavalry to Ride
Washing the Streets of Porto Rico
Jun [day undetermined]
Blanket-Tossing a New Recruit
Aug [day undetermined]
Fake Beggar
1899
Apr 10 A Trip to the Moon
1900 [month undetermined]
The Parade of Naval Veterans
Mar [day undetermined]
The Mystic Swing
Apr 7 Four Heads Better Than One
Jun 30 A Mysterious Portrait
The Power of the Cross
Wrestling Extraordinary
Oct [day undetermined]
President McKinley Laying Corner Stone

1901 [month undetermined]
Arrival of Train of Cattle
Beef Extract Room
Beef, Sheep and Hog Killing
Branding Hams
Bridge of Sighs
Bull on the Stampede
A Busy Corner at Armour's
Canned Meat Department. No. 1: Filling and Capping
Canned Meat Department. No. 2: Inspecting
Canned Meat Department. No. 5: Vacuum Process
Canned Meat Department. No. 6: Painting and Labeling
Chicago Fat Stock Parade
Chicago Police Parade
Cleaning Pig's Feet
Columbia Post
Coming Out of Scraping Machines and Cutting Off Heads
Cutting Beef
Cutting Meat for Sausage (side view)
Cutting Pork
Dewey Parade
Dressing Beef
Driving Hogs to Slaughter
Drove of Western Cattle
Dumping and Lifting Cattle
Elevated Railroad
Entrance to Union Stock Yards
Export Packing
Feeding Time
Hog Slaughtering. No. 6: Opening and Splitting
Hogs on the Rail
Interior of Armour's Power House
Killing Sheep
Koshering Cattle, (Hebrew Method of Killing)
Labeling Cans
Lafayette Post of New York
Lambs Post of Phila.
Lard Refinery
Laundry and Sewing Room
Legging Sheep
Loading Cars
Machine and Can Tester
Mince Meat Room
Miscellaneous. No. 6: Panoramic View
Noon Time in Packing Town, (Panoramic)
Noon Time in Packing Town, (Whiskey Point)
Oleo Oil Melting
Oleo Oil Pressing
Parade of Horses
Pulling Wool
A Ride on the Elevated R. R. (Panoramic)
Sausage Department. No. 2: Chopping
Scalding and Scraping Hogs
Scenes and Incidents in the G. A. R. Encampment
Sheep Led to Slaughter by Goat
Shipping Department. No. 2: Loading
Singing Pigs Feet
Skinning Sheep
Slicing Hams and Bacon
Soldering Cans
Square Can Machine
Stamping Tin
Sticking Cattle
Sticking Hogs, (Front View)
Street Sweeping Brigade
Stuffing Cans by Machinery
Stuffing Sausage
Stunning Cattle
Sweating Cans
Testing Cans by Machinery
Testing Hams
Testing Horses
3 Can Testers (side view)
Trimming Room
Weighing Mutton
Apr 13 Gans-McGovern Fight
Apr 27 The Life of a Fireman
Pie, Tramp and the Bulldog
Jul [day undetermined]
The Mysterious Blackboard
Aug [day undetermined]
Knight Templars Parade at Louisville, Ky.
Knight Templars Parade Drill
Sep [day undetermined]
President McKinley at the Buffalo Exposition
1902 [month undetermined]
Arrival of Rex
The Continental Guards
Mardi Gras Parade
Panoramic View of the French Market
Turning Keys over to Rex
May [day undetermined]
The Fat and Lean Comedians
Jul [day undetermined]
Black Rock Tunnel on the Rock Island Route
Cavalry Swimming Columbia River
Dancing Skeleton
The DeCarmos
Explosion of an Automobile
Legerdemain Up-to-Date, or the Great Hermann Outdone
The New Pillow Fight
Panorama, Descending Mt. Blanc
Panoramic View of the Alps, Switzerland
The Prodigal Son
Ringling Bros. Circus Parade
Nov [day undetermined]
Arrival on Summit of Pike's Peak
Balloon Ascension
Burlington Flyer
Clear Creek Canyon
Climbing Hagerman Pass
Denver Firemen's Race for Life
Fun in the Glenwood Springs Pool
Horse Toboggan Slide
Hydraulic Giants at Work
Lava Slides in Red Rock Canyon
Leaving the Summit of Pike's Peak
Panorama of Cog Railway
Panorama of the Famous Georgetown Loop
Panorama of the Royal Gorge
Panorama of Ute Pass
Panoramic View of Granite Canon
Panoramic View of Hell Gate
Panoramic View of Seven Castles
Pike's Peak Toboggan Slide
Runaway Stage Coach
Train in Royal Gorge
Trains Leaving Manitou
Ute Pass Express
Where Golden Bars Are Cast
1903 [month undetermined]
Actor's Troubles
The Alarm and Hitch
Arrival of Humpty Dumpty
Auntie and the Bee
Automobile Parade
Babies and Kittens
Babies and Puppies
Baby Lund in Lightning Change Act
Barrel Fighters
Bathers with High Diving
Bathing Horses
Beggar's Dream
Beheading Chinese
Birth of a Fairy
Black Magic
Black Serpentine
Broad Sword Contest
A Brush in the Snow
Bryan at Home
Buffalo Bill's Parade
Business Rivalry
Cake Walk
The California Limited of the Santa Fe Route
Cape Town, South Africa
Chicago Derby Day
Chicago Fire Boats in Action
Chicago Fire Run
La Chimera
Clown and Automaton
The Coke Ovens of Pennsylvania
Colorado Special, Chicago & Northwestern Ry.
Comic Skater
Comrades
Cook County Democracy Parade
Corn Harvesting
The Dance of the Little Texas Magnet
Deadwood Coach
The Dells of Wisconsin
Down the Slide
The Dull Razor
Fancy Drill of the Woodmen of America
Feeding Pigeons in the Streets of Venice
Fire Engines at Work
The Fire, the Leap for Life and the Rescue
Floral Parade
Fool's Parade
Freight Train in the Royal Gorge, Colo.
Fun on the Levee
German Dance
The Girl in Blue
Going to the Fire
Great Diamond Robbery
The Great Whaleback Steamer, Christopher Columbus
Harper's Ferry
The Harvesters
The Hay Mower
Hermann Looked Like Me
The Hold Up
A Hot Time on the Bathing Beach
How Would You Like to Be the Ice Man
Humpty and the Demon
Humpty and the Dude
Humpty and the Piewoman
Humpty Dumpty and the Baby
Humpty's Frolics
Humpty's Troubles with the Policeman
Humpty's Troubles with the Washwoman
The Ice Breaker
Illinois Central Flyer
The Infernal Meal
Interrupted Crap Game
Krousemeyer Kids
LaSavate
Launching a Steamer
Lightning Artist
A Lively Cock Fight
Louis & Nashville Flyer
Louisville Fire Run
Lover's Trouble
The Magician
The Man with the Iron Jaw
The Man with the Many Faces
March of the Post Office Employees
Memphis & Ft. Scott Railway Bridge
Memphis Fire Run
Memphis Water Front
Military Fire Drill
Mississippi River
Murphy and the Midget
Murphy Has Trouble with His Wife
Murphy Returns from a Masquerade
Murphy's Jealousy
Murphy's Troubles with the Photographer
The Mysterious Trunk
New Serpentine Dance
A Night in Blackville
No Place Like Home
Nymph of the Waves
Oriental Dance
Outdoing Ching Ling Foo
Overland Flyer
Parade of Roses
Parade through Chicago Streets
Pennsylvania Limited
Pied Piper of Hamelin
Pioneer Limited
Plowing on the Old Farm
Pres. Krueger
Prince Henry Flyer
The Prince Leaving Chicago
Prize Fight in Coon Town
The Puppies and the Little Tease
The Return to Quarters
Rival Billposters

The Rocky Mountain Limited
Royal Gorge
Shooting Craps
Shooting the Chutes
Snow Fight
Soldier's Dream
Something Good-Negro Kiss
Spanish Bull Fight
Start from the House and the Run
State and Madison Sts., Chicago
Street Scene in Port Huron, Mich.
Streets in Cairo, Egypt
The Stump Speaker
Summoning the Spirits
They're Off
Too Cautious
Train on High Bridge
Trip Around the Union Loop
Troubles of a Country Visitor
Two of a Kind
Two Old Sports
Umbrella Brigade
Uncle Tom's Cabin Parade
The Undelivered Message
Unveiling of Logan's Monument
The Vanishing Burglars
View of State Street
Wash Day in Camp
Washing Elephants
Who Said Watermelon
Willie's First Smoke
Winter Sports on the Lake
The Wrestlers
Young America Celebrating Dewey's Return

Jan [day undetermined]
Fantastic Dining Room
The Philosopher's Stone

Jan 31 S. S. St. Louis
Sensational Hurdle Race

Feb [day undetermined]
Bucking Broncho Contest
Bucking Broncho Contest [Sheridan Contest]
California Limited
Cavalry Parade
Christian Endeavor Greeting
Gallery Gods Watching a Funny Act
Indian Fire Dance
Indian Hideous Dance
Indian Parade
Indians Charging on the Photographer
Santa Fe Colorado Express
Shoshone Indians in Scalp Dance
Stage Hold-Up
Steer Roping Contest at Cheyenne, Wyo.
Ute Indian Snake Dance

May [day undetermined]
Pres. Roosevelt at the Dedication Ceremonies, St. Louis Exposition

Jul 12 Light Heavyweight Championship Contest Between Root and Gardner

1904 [month undetermined]
Bull-Fight at Juarez, Mexico
Chicago Portland Special
Fairbanks
Fish Traps Columbia River
Hauling in a Big Catch
Hauling in Seines and Pulling Seines into Boat
The Little Robin Robbers
Mending Seines on the Columbia River
Panoramic View of Multnomah Falls
Panoramic View of Spokane Falls
Panoramic View of the Columbia River
Roosevelt Dedicating at St. Louis Exposition
Roosevelt Dedication at Lewis and Clark Exposition
A Ruben's Unexpected Bath
Sour Lake Oil Fields
Surf Scene on the Pacific
Unloading Fish at Cannery

Mar [day undetermined]
The Attack on Port Arthur
The Battle of Chemulpo
Torpedo Attack on Port Arthur

Apr [day undetermined]
Tracked by Bloodhounds; or, A Lynching at Cripple Creek

Oct 22 The Girls in the Overalls

1905 [month undetermined]
A Trip Through Samoa and Fiji Islands

Mar 18 Samoa and the Fiji Islands
Apr 29 The Hold-Up of the Leadville Stage
Jul 22 The Serenade
Oct 21 The Gay Deceivers

1906 [month undetermined]
Sights in a Great City
The Tomboys
Trapped by Pinkertons

Jun 30 From North to South
From Tacoma to Seattle
Trip over Colorado Midland
Trip over Cripple Creek Short Line
Trip Through Colorado
A Trip Through the Chicago Stock-Yards
Trip to Chattanooga and Lookout Mountain
A Trip to Jacksonville, Fla.
A Trip to St. Augustine, Fla.
Trip to Southern Colorado
A Trip to Tampa, Fla.
Ute Pass from a Freight Train

Oct 27 Dolly's Papa
The World Series Baseball Games-White Sox and Cubs

Nov 24 The Female Highwayman

1907
Jan 12 Who Is Who?
Jan 26 The Grafter
Feb 9 The Foxy Hoboes
The Tramp Dog
When We Were Boys
Feb 23 A Trip Through Yellowstone Park
Mar 9 The Girl from Montana
Mar 30 His First Ride
Jun 1 One of the Finest
Jun 15 The Masher
Jun 22 Western Justice
Jun 29 The Bandit King
Jul 6 The Book Worm
Jul 20 The Matinee Idol
Jul 27 The Onion Fiend
Aug 3 The Roller Skate Craze
Aug 10 Grand Canyon of Arizona and the Cliff Dwellers
Aug 17 All's Well That Ends Well
Aug 31 Cab 23
Sep 7 A Life for a Life
Sep 21 The Pastry Cook and Musician
Slavery of Children
Oct 12 The Girl and the Judge
Motoring Under Difficulties
Oct 16 Mishaps of a Baby Carriage
Nov 9 A Southern Romance
What a Pipe Did
Nov 16 Wooing and Wedding of a Coon
Nov 30 The Tin Wedding
Dec 7 Mike the Model
Dec 14 What Is Home Without a Mother-in-Law
Dec 21 Burglar and Old Maids
The Eviction
Dec 23 The Two Orphans

1908
Jan 4 The Four-Footed Hero
Jan 18 The Miser's Fate
The Tramp Hypnotist
Jan 25 The Financial Scare
The Irish Blacksmith
The Newlyweds First Meal
Feb 15 Monte Cristo
Feb 28 A Leap Year Proposal
Mar 7 Dr. Jekyll and Mr. Hyde
The Mad Musician [An Escape from an Insane Asylum]
The Squawman's Daughter
Mar 14 The French Spy
Mar 15 Shamus O'Brien
Mar 21 Just His Luck
Mar 28 A Dream of Youth
Friday, the 13th
Swashbuckler
Apr 4 The Mystery of a Diamond Necklace
Apr 11 The Man in the Overalls
The Mishaps of a Bashful Man
Apr 25 The Holy City
May 2 The Blue Bonnet
Rip Van Winkle
May 23 Summer Boarders Taken In
Troubles of a New Drug Clerk
May 31 In the Nick of Time
Jun 6 Damon and Pythias
East Lynne
Not Yet, But Soon
The Shadow of the Law
Jun 20 The Fighting Parson
Jul 11 The Spirit of '76
The Vanishing Tramp
Jul 25 Bobby White in Wonderland
Weary Waggles' Busy Day
Aug 1 The Road to Ruin
Aug 8 The Cowboy's Baby
Aug 22 The Village Gossip
Aug 29 A Pair of Kids
The Power of Labor
Romance of the Old Mill
Sep 12 The Cattle Rustlers
A Hindoo's Ring
The Lion's Bride
Sep 19 Crazed by Jealousy
Sep 21 Gans-Nelson Fight
Sep 26 A Great Wrong Righted
A Magical Tramp
Oct 1 A Daughter of Erin
Oct 3 Bryan in Chicago
Labor Day Parade
Oct 8 The Ranchman's Love
Oct 15 One of the Bravest
Oct 22 The Fisherman's Rival
Oct 29 The Lights and Shadows of Chinatown
Nov 5 The Actor's Child
Nov 12 A Mountain Feud
Nov 19 The Hidden Treasure
Nov 26 On Thanksgiving Day
Dec 3 A Dual Life
The Football Fiend
Dec 10 The Queen of the Arena
Dec 17 A Montana Schoolmarm
Dec 24 The Duke's Motto
Dec 31 In the Shenandoah Valley; or, Sheridan's Ride

1909
Jan 7 Schooldays
The Tenderfoot
The Tyrant's Dream
Jan 14 In Old Arizona
Jan 21 Love and Law
Jan 28 The Prairie Town Romance
Feb 4 Stirring Days in Old Virginia
Feb 18 The King of the Ring
On the Warpath
Feb 25 The Skipper's Daughter
Mar 2 With Taft in Panama
Mar 4 The Mad Miner
Outing Pastimes in Colorado
Mar 11 The Ironworker
Mar 18 Boots and Saddles
Mar 25 Four Wise Men
Infant Terrible
Apr 1 The Settlement Workers
Apr 8 Brother Against Brother
Apr 15 Love Under Spanish Skies
Apr 22 The Dairy Maid's Lovers
A Fighting Chance
Apr 29 Mephisto and the Maiden
May 6 Adventures of a Keg
Chinatown Slavery
May 13 The Bad Lands
May 21 Hunting Big Game in Africa
May 27 A Wartime Sweetheart
Jun 3 Fighting Bob
Jun 10 The Moonstone
Jun 17 In the Sultan's Power
Jun 24 A Country Girl's Peril
Jul 1 Ben's Kid
Jul 3 The Great Automobile Race
Jul 8 The Lion Tamer
Jul 15 The Peasant Prince
Jul 22 Won in the Desert
Jul 29 The Heart of a Race Tout
Aug 5 Before the Mast
Aug 12 The Leopard Queen
Aug 19 The Yellow Jacket Mine
Aug 26 A Royal Outcast
Aug 30 Mrs. Jones' Birthday
Winning a Widow
Sep 2 The Blight of Sin
Sep 6 Spring Has Come

The Stampede
Sep 9 The Engagement Ring
Sep 13 The Freebooters
Sep 16 Crooked Path
Sep 20 The Bachelor's Visit
False Alarm
Sep 23 Stricken Blind
Sep 27 Across the Divide
Sep 30 The Drunkard's Fate
Oct 4 How Binks Butted In
A Trip to Yosemite
Oct 7 Wheels of Justice
Oct 11 Pet of the Big Horn Ranch
Oct 14 Bear and Forbear
Lost in Siberia
Oct 18 A No Man's Land
Oct 21 The Cowboy Millionaire
Oct 25 Briton and Boer
Oct 28 The Senorita
Nov 1 The Witches' Cavern
Nov 4 Sealed Instructions
Villainness Still Pursued Him
Nov 8 The Stage Driver
Nov 11 Across the Isthmus
Nov 15 The Fisherman's Bride
Nov 18 Up San Juan Hill
Nov 22 In Wrong Simms
On the Border
Nov 25 On the Little Big Horn; or, Custer's Last Stand
Nov 29 Brought to Terms
Making It Pleasant for Him
Dec 2 An Indian Wife's Devotion
A Million Dollar Mix-Up
Dec 6 The Engineer's Daughter
Dec 9 The Heroine of Mafeking
Dec 13 Pine Ridge Feud
Dec 16 The Indian
Dec 20 A Modern Dr. Jekyll
Through the Hood River Valley and Along the Columbia in Oregon
Dec 23 The Christian Martyrs
Dec 27 Buried Alive
Dec 30 A Daughter of the Sioux

1910

Jan 3 The Smuggler's Game
Jan 6 Alderman Krautz's Picnic
The Highlander's Defiance
Jan 10 A Tale of the Backwoods
Jan 13 Under the Stars and Stripes
Jan 17 His Vacation
A New Divorce Cure
Jan 20 The Courtship of Miles Standish
Jan 24 An Afternoon Off
The Ranch King's Daughter
Jan 27 The Devil, the Servant, and the Man
Jan 31 Our German Cousin
Shooting an Oil Well
Feb 3 Politics
Feb 7 In the Serpent's Power
Feb 10 In the Shadow of Mt. Shasta
Feb 14 The Roman
Feb 17 The Girls of the Range
Feb 21 Saved from the Tide
Feb 24 Back Among the Old Folks
Feb 28 Industries in Southern California
Mar 3 Samuel of Posen
Mar 7 Told in the Golden West
Mar 10 Across the Plains
Mar 14 A Crowded Hotel
The Dawn of Freedom
Mar 17 In the Frozen North
Mar 21 The Village Inventor
Mar 24 The Wonderful Wizard of Oz
Mar 28 The Treasure Hunters
Mar 31 The Wife of Marcius
Apr 4 The Common Enemy
Apr 7 Hugo, the Hunchback
Apr 11 The Clay Baker
Apr 14 Dorothy and the Scarecrow in Oz
Apr 18 Mr. A. Jonah
The Rival Cooks
Apr 21 Davy Crockett
Apr 25 Mr. Mix at the Mardi Gras
Apr 28 The Angelus
May 2 The Cow-Boy Girls
May 5 Papinta
May 7 The Shriners' Pilgrimage to New Orleans
May 9 The Mulligans Hire Out
7 Days
May 12 Chicken
There, Little Girl, Don't Cry
May 16 The Heart of a Heathen Chinee
May 19 The Land of Oz
May 23 The Unmailed Letter
May 26 In the Great Northwest
May 30 After Many Years
The Trimming of Paradise Gulch
Jun 6 The Barge Man of Old Holland
Jun 9 The Range Riders
Jun 13 Romeo and Juliet in Our Town
Jun 16 Caught in the Rain
Jun 20 Opening an Oyster
A Wasted Effort
Jun 23 Our New Minister
Jun 27 The Long Trail
Jun 30 The Fire Chief's Daughter
Jul 2 Gotch-Zbyszko World's Championship Wrestling Match
Jul 4 Go West, Young Woman, Go West
Jul 7 The Way of the Red Man
Jul 9 Vengeance of Millesaunte
Jul 11 The Hall-Room Boys
Jul 14 A Hunting Story
The Sheriff
Jul 18 The Phoenix
Jul 21 Mazeppa; or, The Wild Horse of Tartary
Jul 25 The Mad Dog Scare
A Sleep Walking Cure
Jul 28 The Cowboy's Stratagem
Jul 31 Ranch Life in the Great South-West
Aug 1 B.P.O.E.
Her First Long Dress
Shrimps
Aug 4 The Law of the West
Aug 8 Forgiven
Aug 11 Lost in the Soudan
Aug 15 Willie
Aug 18 Human Hearts
Aug 22 Dora Thorne
Aug 25 The Indian Raiders
Aug 29 The Emigrant
Aug 30 The Templars Conclave
Sep 1 The Road to Richmond
Sep 5 Led by Little Hands
The New Moving Picture Operator
Sep 8 Jim, the Ranchman
Sep 12 Little Boy
Sep 15 The Schoolmaster of Mariposa
Sep 19 Bertie's Elopement
Big Medicine
Sep 22 The Sergeant
Sep 25 The Ole Swimmin Hole
Sep 29 The Kentucky Pioneer
Oct 3 A Cold Storage Romance
My Friend, the Doctor
Oct 6 For Her Country's Sake
Oct 10 The Sanitarium
Oct 13 In the Golden Harvest Time
Oct 17 The Foreman
Oct 20 Two Boys in Blue
Oct 24 The Ghost in the Oven
Oh You Skeleton
Oct 27 Blasted Hopes
Oct 31 Settled Out of Court
Nov 3 The Early Settlers
Nov 7 The Bachelor
The Lady Barbers
Nov 10 The Vampire
Nov 12 Mexican Centennial
Nov 14 Mr. Four Flush
Nov 17 Gratitude
Nov 21 The Dull Razor
There's No Place Like Home
Nov 24 The Merry Wives of Windsor
Nov 28 The Queen of Hearts
Dec 1 The Stepmother
Dec 5 The Widow of Mill Creek Flat
Dec 8 In the Wilderness
Dec 12 A Tale of the Sea
Dec 15 County Fair
Dec 19 John Dough and the Cherub
Dec 22 Overland to Freemont
Dec 26 The Rustlers
Dec 29 Justinian and Theodora
Dec 31 The Boy City

Selig, William N. *see* **William N. Selig**

Sheffield Photo Co.

1903

Sep [day undetermined]
A Daring Daylight Burglary

1904

Feb 23 Jack Sheppard—The Robbery of the Mail Coach
Jul [day undetermined]
Boys Will Be Boys
Duck Hunt
Aug [day undetermined]
Late for Work
Oct [day undetermined]
Bobbie's Downfall
Fly Paper Vendors
The Market Woman's Mishap
Dec [day undetermined]
Disturbed Picnic

1905

Jan [day undetermined]
Soldier's Romance
Mar [day undetermined]
Awful Donkey
Jul [day undetermined]
An Eccentric Burglary
Aug [day undetermined]
Masher and Nursemaid

1907

May 4 Johnny's Run
The Romany's Revenge
Jun 22 The Blackmailer
His Cheap Watch
Willie's Dream

1908

May 16 Nasty Sticky Stuff

Siegmund Lubin *see also* **Lubin Mfg. Co.; S. Lubin**

1897

May [day undetermined]
Unveiling of the Washington Monument

1898

Feb [day undetermined]
Battle of San Juan Hill

1899

Apr [day undetermined]
The Astronomer's Dream, or the Trip to the Moon
Jun [day undetermined]
Reproduction of the Fitzsimmons-Jeffries Fight in Eleven Rounds Showing the Knock Out
Aug [day undetermined]
American Soldiers Defeating Filipinos Near Manila
The Haunted House
Why Krausemeyer Couldn't Sleep
Sep [day undetermined]
Reproduction of the Jeffries and Sharkey Fight
Reproduction of the Pedlar Palmer and Terry McGovern Fight
Reproduction of the Sharkey and Jeffries Fight
Reproduction of the Terry McGovern and Pedlar Palmer Fight
Sep 30 The Trial of Captain Dreyfus at Rennes, France
Nov [day undetermined]
Battle Flag of the 10th Pennsylvania Volunteers, Carried in the Philippines
Reproduction of the Corbett and Jeffries Fight
Reproduction of the Jeffries and Corbett Fight
Reproduction of the Jeffries and Ruhlin Fight
Reproduction of the Kid McCoy and Peter Maher Fight
Reproduction of the Peter Maher and Kid McCoy Fight
Reproduction of the Ruhlin and Jeffries Fight

1900

Jan [day undetermined]
Reproduction of the McGovern and Dixon Fight
Mar [day undetermined]
Reproduction of the Olsen and Roeber Wrestling Match
Reproduction of the Sharkey and Fitzsimmons Fight

Sapho
Apr 7 The Wonder, Ching Ling Foo
Aug [day undetermined]
Life Motion Photographs of the Fitzsimmons and Ruhlin Fight
Reproduction of the Corbett and McCoy Fight
Reproduction of the Fitzsimmons and Sharkey Fight
1901
Mar [day undetermined]
Fun in a Chinese Laundry
Mar 2 Mrs. Nation & Her Hatchet Brigade
Mar 23 Photographer's Mishap
Two Rubes at the Theatre
Mar 30 The Cook's Revenge
May [day undetermined]
Lubin's Animated Drop Curtain Announcing Slides
May 18 Affair of Honor
Jun 29 A Good Joke
Tramp's Nap Interrupted
Twelve in a Barrel
Jul [day undetermined]
The Educated Chimpanzee
The Extensive Wardrobe
Mine Explosion and What Followed
Ostrich Farm
Who Said Chicken?
Jul 9 Esquimaux Village
Panorama of a Philippine Village
1902
Jul [day undetermined]
Old Mother Hubbard
Snow White
Jul 15 Jack and the Beanstalk
Oct 4 A Trip to the Moon
1903 [month undetermined]
Jack and Jill
Jan [day undetermined]
Mary Had a Little Lamb
Mar [day undetermined]
Who Killed Cock Robin?
Mar 7 Robinson Crusoe
Apr [day undetermined]
Rip Van Winkle
Valentine and Orson
Apr 13 Gulliver's Travels
May [day undetermined]
Babes in the Wood
Beauty and the Beast
Goody, Goody Two Shoes
Hickery, Dickery Dock
Little Miss Muffet
Little Snowdrop
Old Woman Who Lived in a Shoe
Reynard the Fox
Swiss Family Robinson
Three Bears
Three Little Pigs
Tom, Tom the Piper's Son
Uncle Tom's Cabin
May 16 The Gambler's Crime
Jun 6 Little Tom Thumb
Jul 11 Sleeping Beauty
Sep 5 The Fairyland; or, The Kingdom of the Fairies
Oct [day undetermined]
Ten Nights in a Barroom
Dec [day undetermined]
Outcast and Bride
Dec 12 The Damnation of Faust
Dec 19 Dear Old Stars and Stripes, Goodbye
Every Day Is Sunshine When the Heart Beats True
The Magic Lantern
Only a Soldier Boy
1904
Jan 16 Puss in Boots
Jun 26 The Great Train Robbery
Jul [day undetermined]
A Circus Romance
Jul 30 Bold Bank Robbery
Sep 10 Life of an American Soldier
Nov [day undetermined]
The Lost Child
Nov 5 Meet Me at the Fountain
1905
Jan 28 Saved from a Watery Grave
Feb 11 The Counterfeiters
Apr [day undetermined]
Evolution of the Japanese
The Pirates
Sins and Sorrows of a Great City
Why the Cook Was Not Fired
Apr 8 The Sign of the Cross
May [day undetermined]
The Fake Blind Man
Photographed for the Rogue's Gallery
Policeman's Pal
A Sweet Kiss
Tramp's Revenge
Jun 3 A Dog Lost, Strayed or Stolen. $25.00 Reward. Apply to Mrs. Brown, 711 Park Ave.
Jul 1 Highway Robbery
Jul 22 Kidnapped Child
Sep 16 Impersonation of Britt-Nelson Fight
Oct [day undetermined]
Fire in New York's Bowery
Meet Me Down at Luna, Lena
Oct 28 Through the Matrimonial Agency
Nov [day undetermined]
Impersonation of the Fitzsimmons-O'Brien Fight
Nov 18 Fun on the Farm
1906
Feb 24 The Wreckers of the Limited Express
Mar [day undetermined]
Nelson-McGovern Fight, 1906
Apr 7 Rescued by Carlo
Apr 28 The Clown's Adventures
May 7 The San Francisco Disaster
Jun [day undetermined]
Snake Hunting
Jul [day undetermined]
The River Pirates
The Trading Stamp Craze
Jul 14 A Night Off
Aug [day undetermined]
Impersonation of Gans-Nelson Fight
Aug 4 The Great Mail Robbery
Sep 8 Reproduction of Nelson-Gans Fight
Oct [day undetermined]
Wanted: A Husband
The Wishbone
Nov 3 The Bank Defaulter
Nov 24 The Lost Hat: He Got It Alright
Two Seedy Rubes: They Have a Hot Time in the Old Town
Dec [day undetermined]
A Thrilling Detective Story
1907
Jan [day undetermined]
Philadelphia New Year Shooters
Mar 2 The Unwritten Law: A Thrilling Drama Based on the Thaw White Case
Apr 20 A Winter Day in the Country
May 4 Too Much Mother-in-Law
May 11 Jamestown Naval Review
May 25 And the Dog Came Back
Jun [day undetermined]
Jimmie, the Messenger Boy
Jun 15 When Women Vote
Jun 22 The Enchanted Mattress
The Oyster Industry
Jun 29 Mother's Dream
Jul [day undetermined]
The Sleepy Cop
Jul 13 A Family Outing
Jul 27 Caught with the Goods
Elks' Parade
The Fortune Teller
Gypsy's Revenge
Nervy Jim and the Cop
The New Apprentice
Aug [day undetermined]
An Inquisitive Girl
Aug 10 A Misunderstanding
Aug 17 The Actor Annoys the Boarders
Who's Boss of the House?
Aug 24 The Blacksmith's Daughter
Aug 31 Just Married
Sep [day undetermined]
Baxter's Brain Storm
Roasted Chestnuts
Sep 7 Cohen's Bad Luck
Sep 14 The Indian's Friendship
John D. and the Reporter
Sep 28 The Amateur Champion
The Scheme That Failed
Oct [day undetermined]
The Cleptomaniac
Miraculous Eggs
A Night at the Gayety
Oct 5 Interrupted Outing
Lucky Jim
Moses Sells a Collar Button
The New Arrival
Oct 12 The First Quarrel
Nov 2 Smuggled into America
Nov 9 The Foundling
Nov 16 How Brown Saw the Baseball Game
Neighbors Who Borrow
Nov 23 A Breeze from the West
Only Kids
The Parson of Hungry Gulch; or, The Right Man in the Right Place May Work Wonders
Nov 30 Bargain Sales
Oh Me! Oh My!
Dec [day undetermined]
An Animated Dummy
Dec 7 The Making of a Modern Newspaper
Dec 14 The Pay Train Robbery
Dec 28 How the Masher Was Punished
1908
Jan [day undetermined]
The Animated Dummy
The Goebel Tragedy
I Rather Two Step Than Waltz
Impossibilities
A Lucky Horseshoe
Pipe Dreams
Jan 11 Such a Good Joke, But— Why Don't He Laugh?
Jan 18 Bachelor's Wedding Bells
Have You Seen My Wife?
If Wm. Penn Came to Life
The Ringmaster's Wife
Jan 25 A Gay Old Boy
Feb 1 The Blind Boy
His Week's Wages; or, Where's That Quarter?
The Magnetic Eye
Feb 15 The Count of No Account
Feb 29 Reproduction of Burns-Palmer Fight, London [England], February 10th, 1908
Mar [day undetermined]
The Burglar's Child
A Country Girl in Philadelphia
A Faithful Wife
A Fool and His Money
Julius Caesar
Meet Me at the Station
No Children Wanted
A Persistent Actor
Rube Goes to College
Troubles of Too Ardent Admirers
Mar 7 And a Little Child Shall Lead Them
Mar 14 A New Way to Pay Debts
See the Point?
Mar 21 Easy Money
A Romance of the Fur Country
Mar 28 Do It Now!
The Girl across the Way
Our Own Little Flat
The Pursuit of a Suit
Apr [day undetermined]
The Curse of Gold
The Drink Cure
The Fake Windstorm
The New Breakfast Food
Apr 4 The Mountaineers
Apr 13 Neighborly Neighbors
The Parents' Devotion
Apr 16 The Little Easter Fairy
Something on His Mind
Apr 20 The Fatal Card
Apr 23 Willie's Party
The Wrong Overcoat
Apr 27 Acrobatic Pills
The Amateur Hypnotist
Apr 30 Beg Pardon!
Oh, My Feet!
May [day undetermined]
The Stolen Flask
May 4 The Bride's Dream
May 7 The Mysterious Phonograph
Stop That Alarm!
May 11 The Great Jewel Robbery
May 14 The Automatic Laundry

The "Merry Widow" Hats
May 18 The Cause of All the Trouble
May 21 The Circus Boy
The Tale of a Pig
May 25 The Near-Sighted Professor [His Trials and Tribulations]
Why He Signed the Pledge
May 28 A Gallant Knight
Jun [day undetermined]
The Clown
Harlem Flats
Tracked by a Woman
Two Sides of the Wall
Jun 4 The Miner's Daughter
Jun 8 The Hand of Fate
Magnetic Vapor
Jun 11 Robbie's Pet Rat
Two Brothers of the G. A. R.
Jun 15 An Honest Newsboy's Reward
Two Little Dogs
Jun 18 Adventures of Mr. Troubles
Mephisto's Affinity
Jun 22 The Old Maid's Parrot
Romance in a Gypsy Camp
Jun 25 Philadelphia, the Cradle of Liberty
The Student's Prank; or, A Joke on His Parents
Jun 29 Held for Ransom
Jul [day undetermined]
Driven from Home
Jul 2 The New Maid
Outwitted by His Wife
Jul 6 A Western Romance in the Days of '49
Jul 9 Two Little Shoes
Jul 13 The Robbery of the Citizen's Bank
Jul 16 "Captain Molly" or, The Battle of Monmouth
Dr. Curem's Patients
Jul 20 Dick's Sister
Jul 23 A Fatal Likeness
Jul 27 The White Chief
Jul 30 The Woman Who Gambles
Aug [day undetermined]
The Forged Will
Hobo's Revenge
The Rainmaker
Tribulations of a Photographer
Aug 3 A Policeman for an Hour
The Sensational Sheath Gown
Aug 6 The Bogus Lord
Aug 10 The Light in the Window
Aug 13 The Crushed Tragedian
Wanted: An Artist's Model
Aug 17 The King's Diamond
Aug 20 Scenes from the Battlefield of Gettysburg, the Waterloo of the Confederacy
Aug 24 Rivals for a Week
The Wrong Valise
Aug 27 The Midnight Express
Aug 31 Fascinating Fluffy Dimples
Sep [day undetermined]
A Fatal Temptation
The Hat of Fortune
Heating Powder
It's Never Too Late to Mend
Make Yourself at Home
Sep 3 The Pawnbroker
Sep 12 The Dancing Fiend
The Hebrew Fugitive
The Persistent Trombonist
The Washerwoman's Revenge
Sep 13 A Southern Romance of Slavery Days
Sep 21 Hon. William J. Bryan and Hon. John W. Kern
How Rastus Got His Pork Chops
Two Little Breadwinners
Sep 24 In the Nick of Time
The Suicidal Poet
Sep 28 The Criminal's Daughter
The Ticklish Man
Oct [day undetermined]
The Burglar's Ball
The Gondolier's Daughter
Historical Parade
Industrial Parade
The Little Coward
Military Parade, Founders Week Celebration, Philadelphia
Naval Parade
The Woman of 1776
Oct 1 The Masqueraders
Wanted: A Military Man
Oct 5 Redeemed from Sin
Salome and the Devil to Pay
Oct 8 The Saloon Dance
"When Our Ship Comes In"
Oct 12 The Way They Fooled Dad
Oct 15 The Bloodstone
Oct 19 For His Sister's Sake
Oct 22 All on Account of a Butterfly
Hubby's Vacation
Oct 26 Auntie Takes the Children to the Country
How a Pretty Girl Sold Her Hair Restorer
Oct 29 The Mountaineer's Revenge
Nov 2 The Cross Roads
Nov 5 The Key Under the Mat
Lunch Time
Nov 9 The Cotton Industry of the South
Nov 12 The Janitor Falsely Accused
Nov 16 Madam Flirt and Her Adopted Uncle
Nov 19 The Engineer
Nov 23 A Pair of Spectacles
Nov 26 Persistency Wins
Nov 30 The Sexton of Longwyn
Weary Willie's Revenge
Dec [day undetermined]
A Female Fire Department
It Happened at Midnight
The Rain-Dear
The Snowbird
Ten Minutes with Shakespeare
When Ma Goes Shopping
Dec 3 Hobo's Dream
Lady Barbers
Dec 7 The Lighthouse-Keeper's Daughter
Dec 10 Charlie's Ma-in-Law
Dec 14 Button, Button, Where Is the Button?
The Face in the Window
Dec 17 On the Stroke of Twelve
Dec 24 Restored by Repentance
Dec 28 A New Year
A New Year's Gift
Dec 31 The Forgotten Watch
The House at the Bridge

1909
Jan [day undetermined]
In the Land of Upsidedown
A New Old Master
Satan's Fan
Jan 4 A Bitter Lesson
The Old Maid's Dream
Jan 7 Leo's Air Rifle
Two Orphans of the G. A. R.
Jan 11 When Lips Are Sealed
Jan 14 How Happy Jack Got a Meal
The Troubles of a Stranded Actor
Jan 18 Love's Sweet Melody
Jan 21 The Fighting Parson
The Wrong Burglar
Jan 25 A Suit Case
Who Stole Jones' Wood?
Jan 28 Love Germs
Feb [day undetermined]
The Carnival of Venice
The Taxidermist's Dream
Feb 1 Aunt Emmy's Scrap Book
Feb 4 The Blind Musician
Willie's Water Sprinkler
Feb 8 No. 5874
Feb 11 The Bank Messenger
A Secret
Feb 15 The Silver Dollar
The Unlucky Horseshoe
Feb 18 A Broken Heart
The Pass Key
Feb 22 A Game of Chess
Love Me, Love My Dog
Feb 25 The New Governess
Mar 1 A Dime Novel Detective
Mar 4 I'll Only Marry a Sport
The Last Call
Mar 8 The Stowaway
Mar 11 The Little Rag Doll
The New Mirror
Which Was the Happiest Time in Your Life?
Mar 15 Talked to Death
Mar 18 Reforming a Husband
Uncle Reuben's Courtship
Mar 22 The Day of the Dog
Mar 29 The Photograph Habit
Apr [day undetermined]
Through Darkness to Light
Apr 5 The Master of Black Rock
Apr 19 The Yiddisher Boy
Apr 29 The House of Terror
May 17 The Press Gang
Jun 7 Saucy Sue

Società Anonima Ambrosio
1908
Mar 14 Custom Officer's Pull
May 2 Bad Bargain
Bad Boys
The Best Glue
Frolicsome Powders
Generous Policeman
Greediness Punished
Life and Customs of Naples
Modern Hotel
Panorama of Venice
Rival Sherlock Holmes
Shooting Party
Soldiers in the Italian Alps
Wrongly Charged
May 9 Excursion to Montreal
Gathering Indian Figs
Manoeuvres of Artillery
Sicily Illustrated
Jul 4 A Love Affair of the Olden Days
Aug 1 The Dear Little Heart
Making of Tomato Sauce
Overflowing in Italy
The Policeman and the Cook
War Episode
Oct 19 Shadows of Night
Oct 20 The Cashier's Romance
The Puppet Man's Dream
Trials of an Educator
Oct 21 Prince Kin Kin's Malady
Oct 24 The Little Rope Dancer
Nov 17 The Jester's Daughter
1909
Mar 22 Italian Cavalry Maneuvers
Apr 24 A Marvelous Ointment
May 1 Countess Valleria of Issogne
May 8 Artillery Manoeuvers in the Mountains
May 15 Galileo, Inventor of the Pendulum
Humble Heroes
May 22 A Clever Detective
May 29 Count of Monte Cristo
Mimosa and the Good Prince
Jun 5 Italian Artillery
A True Friend
Jun 26 Louis the XI
Jul 10 Phonographic Message of Love
Jul 17 Brave Little Organ Boy
His First Drink
Jul 24 Little Imp
Sep 13 The Story of a Bad Cigar
Sep 20 His Wife's Troublesome Twitching
Sep 23 Jackson's Last Steeple Chase
Oct 2 Mady Millicent's Visitor
Mr. Muddlehead's Mistake
Oct 5 Forgiven at Last
Oct 18 Reformation of a Wine-Loving Artist
Oct 25 The False Oath
Nov 1 Nero; or, The Burning of Rome
Nov 5 A Very Attractive Gentleman
Nov 8 Musical Waiter
Pirates of the Sea
Nov 12 Logging in the Italian Alps
Nov 13 Balloon Trip over Turin
Nov 20 A Mother's Heart
Nov 22 The Hostage
Nov 29 Leopard Hunting in Abyssinia
Dec 6 The Little Vendean
Dec 13 The Beggarman's Gratitude
Dec 29 The Story of My Life
1910
Jan 15 The Son of the Wilderness
Jan 19 Italian Artillery
Pauli
Jan 26 A Choice Policeman
The Last Keepsake
Feb 2 Hero and Leander
Feb 9 The Longing for Gaol
The Strongest
Feb 16 I Have Lost My Latch Key

The Silent Piano
Feb 26 Why Fricot Was Sent to College
The Witch's Ballad
Mar 2 The Mysterious Track
The Two Mothers
Mar 12 Fatal Imprudence
They Have Vanished My Wife
Mar 16 Insidious Weapons
The Shepherdess
Mar 23 Military Dirigible
The Sea's Vengeance
Mar 30 A Sudden Telephone Call
An Unworthy Fiancé
Apr 6 My Life Remembrances of a Dog
An Unpleasant Dream
Apr 7 Roosevelt at Messina
Apr 13 Fricot in College
The Legend of the Cross
Apr 20 The Heart of a Vagabond
Petit Jean Louis d'Or & Co.
Apr 23 Isabella of Arragon
Apr 27 A Doctor's Revenge
Fricot Is Learning a Handicraft
May 4 Blue Jackets' Manoeuvres on a Sailing Vessel
Who Killed Her?
May 11 Fricot Gets in a Libertine Mood
The Secret of the Lake
May 18 The Devil on Two Sticks
May 25 Estrellita; or, The Invasion of the French Troops in Portugal
Jun 1 A Just Revenge
Prascovia
Jun 4 A Fool's Paradise
Jun 8 A Jealous Wife
The Shipwrecked Man
Jun 15 The Emperor's Message
Jun 22 The Story of Lulu Told by Her Feet
The Tricky Umbrella of Fricot
Jun 29 The Taking of Saragossa
Jul 6 The Tamer; Alfred Schneider and His Lions
Jul 13 The Struggle of Two Souls
Tweedle Dum's Aeronautical Adventure
Jul 20 The Romance of a Jockey
Some Riding Exercises of the Italian Cavalry
Jul 27 The Room of the Secret
Aug 3 Fricot Drinks a Bottle of Horse Embrocation
The Glove
Aug 10 A Favour Admission to a Play
Truth Beyond Reach of Justice
Aug 17 The Hump's Secret
Tweedle Dum Has Missed the Train
Aug 24 A Fatal Vengeance
Fricot's Itching Powder
Aug 31 The Fisherman's Crime
Tweedle Dum's Forged Bank Note
Sep 7 The Caprice of a Dame
Fricot Has Lost His Collar Button
Sep 14 The Iron Foundry
Sep 21 The Last Friend
Molly at the Regiment—Her Adventures
Sep 28 The Virgin of Babylon
Oct 5 The Pit That Speaks
Tweedledum's Duel
Oct 12 The Betrothed's Secret
Tweedledum on His First Bicycle
Oct 19 Excursion on the Chain of Mont Blanc
Tweedledum's Sleeping Sickness
Oct 26 Launching the First Italian Dreadnought
Tweedledum Wants to be a Jockey
Nov 2 The Slave of Carthage
Nov 9 A Floating Message
Nov 16 The Mermaid
Tweedledum Gets Employed in the Corporation Body
Nov 23 Gounod's 'Ave Maria'
The Story of a Pair of Boots
Nov 30 The Judas Money; or, An Episode of the War in Vendee
Dec 7 The Tell-Tale Portrait
Tweedledum Learns a Tragical Part
Dec 14 Dido Forsaken by Aeneas
Dec 21 Little Peter's Xmas Day
Tweedledum and Frothy Want to Get Married
Dec 28 Drama of the Engine Driver

Grandfather's Pipe

Società Italiana Cines *see also* **Society Italian Cines**

1907
Aug 14 The Fireman
Fountains of Rome
Kidnapping a Bride
A Modern Youth
The Slavery of Children
Aug 19 The Barber's Daughter
Little Fregoli
Sep 14 Electric Pile
Hunting a Devil
A Modern Samson
Sep 28 Gitana; or, The Gypsy
Oct 12 Monk's Vengeance
Stolen Chickens
Oct 28 Adventures of a Lover
The Sylvan God
Nov 9 Beyond Criticism
Nov 22 In the Dreamland
Where Is My Head
Nov 23 Venetian Baker; or, Drama of Justice
Watchmaker's Secret
Dec 14 The Christmas
Dec 28 Japanese Vaudeville "The Flower Kingdom"

1908
Jan 4 A Brief Story
A Magistrate's Crime
Jan 11 The Farmer
The Rivals: A Love Drama of Pompeii
Jan 18 Adventures of a Countryman
Jan 25 The Butterflies
Feb 15 A Country Drama
Lover and Bicycle
Woman's Army
Feb 29 Othello
Mar [day undetermined]
Comic Serenade
Duel After the Ball
Winning the Gloves
Mar 21 Gaston Visits Museum
The Skull and the Sentinel
Apr 4 A False Accusation
Pulcinella
Apr 6 Romeo and Juliet
Apr 11 The Bad Sister
Basket Mystery or the Traveler's Jest
The Doctor's Monkey
A Dream
The Edily
Judith and Holopherne
A Magician's Love Test
The Mayor's Misfortune
Pierrot and the Devil
Vengeance in Normandy
Apr 22 The Grandmother's Fables
Apr 25 Rejoicing Dreams
Sausage
Tramp's Revenge
Aug 15 A Good Repentance

1909
Jan 9 Soldier's Heroism
Jan 16 Holy Fires
Porcelain of Good Quality
Jan 23 Messina Disaster
Feb 13 The Showman's Drama
May 8 An Awful Toothache
Jul 10 The Life of a Pierrot
Sep 4 Who Laughs Last
Sep 13 Don Carlos
Importune Neighbor
Sep 18 How Money Circulates
Oct 2 Arab Life
Romance of a Pierrot
Oct 4 Careless Life
Love and Sacrifice
Oct 6 Deputy
Oct 11 Love Stronger Than Revenge
Dec 6 An Athlete of a New Kind
Dec 11 Macbeth
Dec 25 A Surprising Powder
Who Seeks Finds
The Wonderful Pearl

1910
Jan 3 Patrician and Slave
Jan 10 The Garibaldi Boy
The Rebel's Fate
Jan 15 Amorous Minstrel
Jan 17 Mammy's Boy Joins the Army
Jan 26 Walkaway's New Boots
Feb 4 Strike Instigator
Mar 25 Double Six
Apr 8 Come to Supper with Me
Motherless Waif
May 9 Beatrice Cenci
Jun 4 Jane of Montressor
The Slave's Sacrifice
Two Friends
Jun 8 The Vivandiera
Jun 15 The Battle of Legnano; or, Barbarossa
Jun 23 From Love to Martyrdom
Jun 30 Faust
Jul 7 Giorgione
Aug 27 The Cantiniere
Sep 16 The Sacking of Rome
Sep 23 Julie Colonna
Tontolini as a Ballet Dancer
Sep 30 Giovanni of Medici
Oct 14 The Mad Lady of Chester
Oct 21 The Last of the Savelli
Oct 28 The Pretty Dairy Maid
Tontolini Is in Love
Nov 4 A Wooden Sword

Société des Etablissements L. Gaumont *see also* **Gaumont Ltd.; L. Gaumont and Co.**

1903
Mar 14 Buying a Baby
May 23 Railway Ride in the Alps
Sep [day undetermined]
Rip Van Winkle
Sep 26 The Apothicareric Grotto
The Pigeons, Place St. Marc, Venice
Oct [day undetermined]
Dextrous Hand
Photographer's Victim
Oct 31 Moses in the Bullrushes
The Poachers
Nov 21 Cruelty on the High Seas
The Ghost in the Graveyard
Murphy's Wake
The New Cook
Nicholas Nickleby
A Pugilistic Parson
Dec [day undetermined]
The Pickpocket
Dec 12 Elopement a la Mode

1904 [month undetermined]
Algerian Goums in the Desert
Clowns
Cook's Joke
Frivolity
Gavotte
Herring Fishing on French Coast
Mysterious Clock
Panoramic View of Chamonix, Alps
Panoramic View of La Mure, France
Preparing the Codfish After the Catch
Secret Procession of the Algerian Tribes
Trained Dogs
Working in the Charcoal Mines in France
Jan 2 The Somnambulist
Apr [day undetermined]
How to Disperse the Crowd
Pierrot, Murderer
Apr 25 Falls of the Clyde
Inspector's Birthday
Life Guards Responding to Distress Signals
No Room for Dad
Pleasant Breakfast
The Sailor's Rival
That Busy Bee
May 28 Fishing in Newfoundland—French Shore
Our Jolly French Students
The Restive Chicken
Typical Algerian 'Ouled Nails' Muslin Dance
Jun [day undetermined]
The Eviction
Military Tactics
Willful Murder
Jun 4 The Apple Woman
The Bobby Whitewashed
The Cook's Lovers
The Coster's Wedding
Jun 18 The Lyons Mail
Jun 25 Chased by a Dog
The Child Stealers
Naval Attack on Port Arthur

The Office Boy's Revenge
The Postman Whitewashed
Raid on a Coiner's Den
Jul [day undetermined]
Old Maids and the Unfaithful Lovers
Such Is Life
Jul 9 A Disaster in a Colliery
Oct [day undetermined]
Cruelty to Horses
Kissing the Blarney Stone
The Masher's Dilemma
Mixed Bathing
Night Duty
Putting Up the Swing
Revenge!
Shooting the Rapids of Killarney
Oct 15 A Railway Tragedy
Oct 17 A Little Boy Called "Taps"
Oct 29 The Fatal Wig
Three Little Maids
Nov [day undetermined]
Electric Doorbell
Dec [day undetermined]
The Amorous Militiaman
At Brighton
Dunloe Women
Mary in the Dock
Dec 3 Life of a Race Horse
1905
May [day undetermined]
Behind the Scenes
Sep [day undetermined]
The Blacksmith's Daughter
Nov [day undetermined]
The Baby Show
Fiscal Problem
Over in Jersey
A Smart Captive
Wonderful Hat
1906
Jan [day undetermined]
The Peashooter
Jan 27 A False Alarm
The Opium Smoker's Dream
May 26 The Lost Leg of Mutton
The Olympian Games
Aug 18 Fayet-Chamonix: Trip on the New Trolley Line from Le Fayet-St. Gervais to Chamonix
From Menton to Nice
Les Gorges du Fier
Perefitte to Luz
Aug 25 The Henly Regatta
The Paris-Bordeaux Auto Race
Playmates
Sep 20 The Dog Detective
Rescued in Mid-Air
Dec [day undetermined]
The Drunken Mattress
A Modern Diogenes
1907
Jan [day undetermined]
Cheating Justice
The Gardener's Nap
The Little Globe Trotter
Reformation
The Stepmother
Jan 5 Life of Christ
Jan 26 Professor in Difficulties
The Stolen Bride
Stormy Winds Do Blow
Feb [day undetermined]
Animated Stamp Pad
Baby Cries
The Bad Son
Brown Goes to Mother
Burglar and Policeman
Going Away for Holiday
Her First Cake
His First Cigarette
The Man Monkey
Man Who Hangs Himself
Message from the Sea
The Miner's Daughter
Moonlight on the Ocean
My Servant Is a Jewel
A New Toboggan
Policeman Has an Idea
Soldier to Colonel
Stolen Child
When Friends Meet
Winter in Switzerland
Feb 2 The Artful Dodger
The Double Life
Playing a Trick on the Gardener
Playing Truant
The Underworld of Paris
The Zoo at London, Part I
The Zoo at London, Part II
Mar [day undetermined]
Cassimir's Night Out
Disturbing His Rest
The Electric Belt
Little Lord Mayor
Looking for Lodgings
Mrs. Smithson's Portrait
Moonlight on Lake
Oh! That Molar
Paying Off Scores
The Runaway Van
Woman Up-to-Date
Mar 2 The Birthday Celebration
A Set of Dishes
Mar 9 The Murderer
Mar 30 The Carving Doctor
Curfew Shall Not Ring Tonight
An Old Coat Story
Parody on Toreador
Take Good Care of Baby
Apr [day undetermined]
In a Picture Frame
Picnic Hampers
Apr 20 Cambridge-Oxford Race
Catch the Kid
Chasing a Sausage
Land of Bobby Burns
The Poet's Bid for Fame
The Terrorist's Remorse
Village Fire Brigade
Apr 27 Clowns and Statue
The Smugglers
May 11 The Hundred Dollar Bill; or, The Tramp Couldn't Get It Changed
May 25 Buying a Ladder
A Child's Cunning
The Cup and Ball
Dog and the Tramp
Janitor's Tea Party
Nurse Takes a Walk
Salome
Sign of the Times
Two Cents Worth of Cheese
The Village Celebration
Jun 1 The Human Clock
An Icy Day
A Perfect Nuisance
Jun 10 The Child Accuser
Dressing in a Hurry
Saved from the Wreck
The Substitute Drug Clerk
Jun 15 Whose Hat Is It?
Jun 22 She Won't Pay Her Rent
Jun 24 Shoeing the Mail Carrier
Jun 25 The Amateur Rider
Mother-in-Law at the White City
Jun 26 The Legless Runner
Jun 29 The Orange Peel
Jul 8 Fatality
Scratch My Back
The Soldier's Helmet
Union Workers Spoil the Food
Jul 18 Croker's Horse Winning the Derby
Jul 20 The Dog Acrobats
Don't Pay Rent—Move
Drama in a Spanish Inn
Getting His Change
Prisoner's Escape
Servant's Generosity
Unlucky Interference
Jul 27 Drawing Teacher
Looking for the Medal
Aug 3 Buying a Donkey
Aug 10 The Dummy
The Helmet
Looking at a Balloon
The Magnetized Man
Spring Gardening
Aug 24 The Dervish's Revenge
In an Armchair
Sep 7 After the Fancy Dress Ball
A Modern Mother
The Motorcyclist
Sep 14 The Good Wine
Sep 23 A Chinaman Visits London
A First Class Restaurant
Those Boys Again
Uncle's Heritage
Winan's Horses
Wipe Off Your Feet, Please
Sep 26 The Persevering Lover
Sep 30 Coffee Plantation
The Horse That Ate the Baby
How Isaac Won the Cop
Tamer Hopkins
The Undergraduate
Oct 5 Late for His Wedding
Returning Good for Evil
Oct 12 Asking His Way
Oct 19 Jealousy Punished
Oct 28 The Absent-Minded Professor
The Adventures of a Bath Chair
The Athletic Dude
An Episode of the Paris Commune
Floor Polisher
A Four Year Old Heroine
The Glue
The Irresistible Piano
Naval Manoeuvres
Onions Make People Weep
Smoke Without Fire
The Thieving Umbrella
Towed by an Automobile
Volunteer's Betrothal
Who Has Stolen My Bicycle
Nov 4 A Good Husband
The Lost Bass Drum; or, Where Is That Louie?
Raising the Wind
The White Shoes; or, Looking Out for His Banknote
A Wig Made To Order
Nov 9 A Shilling Short in Wages
Nov 11 A Rolling Bed
The Stolen Shoes
Nov 14 The Bomb
Grandfather and the Kitten
Turning the Tables
Nov 30 The Colonial Soldier
Dec 2 Darkest Hour
Harvest Celebration
The Lady Athlete; or, The Jiu Jitsu Downs the Footpads
Tommy's Box of Tools
Wrong Righted
Dec 9 Notice to Quit
Saving His Country's Flag
Sunday with the Boss
Dec 21 Father Buys a Hand Roller
Dec 23 The Gamekeeper's Dog
Nurse's Travels
A Red Hot Day
The Romance of a Fisherman's Daughter
The Waters of Life
Dec 30 Cook's Fiancé
False Start
A Tight Fix
1908
Jan 6 The Affianced
Buying a Cow
The Hypnotist's Pranks
The Marvelous Powder
Jan 18 Anxious Day for Mother
Girl's Dream
Ingenuity Conquers
Medal Winner
Pied Piper of Hamlin
A Restful Ride
Tenor with Leather Lungs
Valiant Son
Jan 20 The Water Babies; or, The Little Chimney Sweep
Feb 3 Ancient Headgear
Gainsborough Hat
Music Hath Charms
Oh, That Cat
The Scout
Feb 10 The Strenuous War Veteran's Story
Uncle's Clock
Feb 17 An Episode of the French Revolution
Satan's Little Jaunt

The Soldier's Wedding
Apr 11 The Astrologer
The Captain's Wives
A Contagious Nervousness
A Dislocated Veteran
The Downfall of the Burglars' Trust
The Enchanted Boots
A Lady Who Likes a Moustache
Ma-in-Law Mesmerized
The Novice Tight-Rope Walker
The Professor's Secret
The Scandalous Boys
Trip to Norway
Apr 18 The Accordion
A Bear in the Flat
The Coal Man's Savings
The Crusaders' Return
The Enchanted Guitar
False Money
Ice Cream Jack
The Miracle
The Misadventures of an Equilibrist
Railway Tragedy
The Shepherd
The Ski-ing Maniac
The Spirit
Youthful Treasure Seekers
May 2 Alone at Last
Biarritz
Funeral of the Late King of Portugal
Men and Women
Poor Aunt Matilda
Ski Contest
The Stolen Dagger
The Sugar Industry
Tommy the Fireman
May 9 The Guileless Country Lassie
The Lover's Tribulation
The Memory of His Mother
The Two Guides
May 16 Awkward Orderly
An Extraordinary Overcoat
Fond of His Paper
Running for Office
Thirty Years After
May 30 Expensive Marriage
Hedge Hog Coat
Magical Suit of Armor
Mr. Farman's Airship
Oxford and Cambridge Boat Race
The Persistent Beggar
Steel Industry
Jun 13 Cast Off by His Father
Clarinet Solo
Magic Dice
Penniless Poet's Luck
A Poor Knight and the Duke's Daughter
The Saloon-Keeper's Nightmare
Usefulness at an End
Jul 4 Blessing the Boats in Arcachon
Bull Fight in Arcachon
The Dressmaker's Surprise
Fox Hunting
French Dairy Farm
Mr. Smith, the New Recruit
Niagara Falls in Winter
They Want a Divorce
Unrequited Love
Jul 13 Father Is Late! Go Fetch Him
His Girl's Last Wish
The Lady with the Beard; or, Misfortune to Fortune
The Simpleton
Trying to Get Rid of a Bad Dollar
A Walking Tree
Wandering Musician
Jul 25 I Won One Hundred Thousand
A New Fruit
Obeying Her Mother
Off to Morocco
On the War Path
A Pleasant Evening at the Theatre
Promoted Corporal
The Saw Mill
The Story of the King of Fregola
Sturdy Sailor's Honor
Too Polite
The Torrent
The Tyrant Feudal Lord

A Wolf in Sheep's Clothing
Aug 1 Baffled Lover
Black Eyed Susan
The Chronic Life-Saver
Fishing Boats in the Ocean
An Interesting Conversation
Out of Patience
The Roses
Aug 15 The Cheese Race
Mother's Darling
Music Hall Agent's Dream
The Poor Man, Homeless, Wants to Go to Prison
Aug 29 The Duck's Finish
The Happy Man's Shirt
Napoleon and the English Sailor
Sep 19 The Luckless Spike
Salome
Oct 3 The Blusterer
Romeo and Juliet
Sammy's Saw
Oct 10 Any Rags
Deep Down within the Cellar
Down in Jungle Town
Harrigan
I Want What I Want When I Want It
I Would Like to Marry You
I'm Sorry
I've Taken Quite a Fancy to You
Just Some One
L-A-Z-Y
A Lemon in the Garden of Love
Lincoln's Speech at Gettysburg
Make Believe
A Stiff Neck
Stupid Mr. Cupid
A Talk on Trousers
Whistle It
Wouldn't You Like to Have Me for a Sweetheart
You Got to Love Me a Lot
Oct 13 Political Speeches
Oct 16 The Court in Session
The Puppet's Nightmare
Victim of Heroism
Oct 17 Water Bailiff's Daughter
Oct 19 A Treasure of a Pig
The Witty Ghost
Oct 21 Somnambulic (sic) Bell Ringer
Oct 24 The Power of Habit
Oct 26 The Convict and the Dove
When Pa Went Fishing
Oct 27 Bald Headed Actor and Fair Lady
Jane Shore
Oct 28 First Love Triumphs
Oct 29 The Flower Thief
Pa and the Girls
Oct 30 The Sofa Bed
Oct 31 Cuddle Up a Little Closer
Don't You Think It's Time to Marry
Hep Yo' Self, Peck-a-Boo
The Honeybees' Honeymoon
I'm Afraid to Come Home in the Dark
I'm Going on the War Path
In the Barber Shop
The Moon's Gift
Thunderbolt on the Mill
Tipperary
Under Any Old Flag at All
What It Might Have Been
Who? Me?
With Care
Wouldn't You Like to Flirt with me
Nov 2 The Automatic Hotel
The Fair Young Lady's Telephone Communication
A House of Cards
The Legend of Prometheus
The Necklace
Thou Shalt Not Love
Nov 7 The Four-Legged Thief
Nov 9 Feeding a Serpent
The First Servant
The Grandfather's Tobacco
Looking for the Bald Heads
No Race Suicide
Out to Nurse
A Woman's Aid
Nov 17 The Doctor's Wife
Having the Time of Their Lives

The Prize Camel
Nov 21 A Love Affair in Toyland
Dec 5 The Bewildered Professor
Thompson's Night with the Police
Dec 12 Animated Matches
A Good Watch Dog
Dec 14 Father and the Kids
Dec 19 The Christmas of a Poacher
The Good Playthings
The Little Chimney Sweeps
The Police Band
The Poor Singer Girl
Dec 21 The Holy Hermit
In Bondage
The Little Marchioness and the Young Shepherdess
Dec 28 Acrobatic Toys
Bobby Has a Pipe Dream
Current News Items
A Heavy Head Piece
Not Guilty

1909

Jan 9 For Baby's Sake
Jan 11 The Bewitched Breton
Converted
Visions of a Goldsmith
Jan 16 An Unprofitable Call
Jan 18 Champion Suffragist
A Hot Remedy
Married Twice
The Persevering Insurance Agent
Jan 23 For Mother's Sake
For Their Country's Cause
Messina After the Earthquake
Jan 30 The Frolic of Youth
Feb 1 Gendarme's Horses
A Mother's Heart
The Nurse's Romance
Feb 9 The Miner's Will
A Sportive Puppet
Feb 13 The Ambassador's Dispatch Case
Jones Has Bought a Phonograph
Feb 17 Grandfather
A Strong Draught
Feb 20 Bernard Palissy
The Chinamen
Feb 23 An Obstinate Umbrella
Some Milk for Baby
Feb 27 The Foxy Husband
The Prince and the Dwarf
Mar 2 The Piano Teacher
Mar 6 In Sore Straits
Walking on His Toes
Mar 9 The Blacksmith's Bride
The Postal Clerk
Mar 13 Buttes Chaumont After a Snow Storm
The Irresolute Man
The Smoking Lamp
Mar 16 Innocent, but Found Guilty
The Musician's Dream
Mar 20 The Secretary's Revenge
The Survivor's Story
Mar 23 Japanese Magic
Pocket Policeman
Mar 27 Across the Border
Mar 30 The Policewoman
The Politician
Apr 3 Benares
Uncle's Palm Tree
Apr 6 The Prodigal Daughter
The Riviera
Apr 10 He Advertised for His Dog
The Tramp at the Masquerade
Apr 13 Charlie Forced to Find a Job
In the Lime Light
Apr 14 Policeman in Action
Under Suspicion
Apr 20 The Poet's Vision
Too Much Advice
Apr 21 Magic Eggs
Sentenced to Death
Apr 24 The Magic of Music
Apr 27 The Automatic Monkey
Before and After
How They Propose
Apr 28 An Unwritten Letter
May 1 Dream Spectres
Two Ladies and a Beggar
May 8 Four Footed Hawkshaw
New Pain Killer
May 11 The Cyclone Sneezer

An Uneven Keel
May 15 The Actor's Mother
Free Champagne
May 18 He Couldn't Lose Her
The Policeman Sleeps
The World Upset
May 22 A Guest's Predicament
Justice or Mercy
May 25 A Blind Man of Jerusalem
The Glories of Sunset
May 29 The Accusing Double
Jun 1 The Cripple's Marriage
The Good Omen
Jun 5 Saved from Conviction
Jun 8 A Mother's Choice
Jun 12 Historical Fan
A Strong Diet
Jun 15 Hunted to the End
A Paying Business
Jun 19 The Cry from the Well
Jun 22 A Good Hearted Policeman
The Troublesome Lamppost
Jun 26 Stung by a Bee
The Wrong Medicine
Jun 29 No Appetite for Dinner
Saved from the Flames
Jul 3 The Hand Bell
The Sunny South of France
Jul 6 The Coin Collector
Raised in the Country
Jul 10 A Bad Case
Visions of Mother
Jul 13 Only a Dream
A Sure Cure
Jul 17 In the Hands of the Enemy
The Lost Tie
Jul 20 The Man in the Moon
True to His Master
Jul 24 Admirer of a Mustache
Brown's Moving Day
The Monk's Mother
Jul 27 The Last Confession
Papa's Hat
Jul 31 An Easy Job
In Hot Water
Missionary
Aug 3 The Morning After
The Sentinel on Duty
Aug 7 The Orphan of Messina
Aug 10 Cyclist's Horn
Dust in His Eye
Retaliation
Aug 11 Laurels
A Long Reach
Aug 14 The Foxy Farmer
Peddling Shoes
Why She Didn't Marry
Aug 17 The Cobbler and the Millionaire
The Little Drummer of 1792
Aug 24 The Frock Coat
Too Gentlemanly
Aug 25 Broken Ties
Sevres Porcelain
Aug 28 A Generous Emperor
Great Event at Podunk
The Horse and the Haystack
The Spy's Revenge
Sep 1 An Awakened Conscience
Magic Cartoons
Sep 7 First Airships Crossing the English Channel
The Mason's Paradise
Sep 8 Glimpses of Paris
The Stolen Gems
Sep 11 Mozart's Last Requiem
Sep 14 The Fiddle and the Fan
Her Busy Day
The Tricky Dummies
Sep 21 Saved from the Quicksands
Taking in a Reef
Sep 22 Dropped from the Clouds
The Legend of the Lighthouse
Sep 25 All for a Nickel
On the Crest of the Waves
Oct 2 The Masterpiece
Oct 5 Breaking the Bank
The Pill Box
Oct 9 Sleuth and the Wig
Wedding Party in Luna Park
Oct 12 Convicting Evidence
How He Earned His Medal
Oct 13 Liquid Air
Princess of the Sea
Oct 16 Alphonse, the Dead Shot
The Broken Violin
One-Legged Pete and Pat
Oct 19 His Helpmate
Husband's Strategy
Oct 23 Country Life in a Flat
Tickled to Death
Oct 26 Ambulance Ventilators
The Old Lord of Ventnor
Oct 30 A Barrow Race
The Song of the Cradle
Nov 2 Don Quixote
Mystic Melodies
Nov 6 The Warrior's Sacrifice
Nov 9 A Peace Agitator
The Pigmy World
Telltale Reflections
Nov 13 Harlequin's Nightmare
The Rhymester's Ruse
Nov 16 A Convict's Heroism
A Set of Teeth
Nov 20 Moon for Your Love
Visions of a Nag
Nov 24 A Heart's Devotion
Tulips
Nov 27 Mix-Up at Court
The Village Scare
Nov 30 The Broken Vase
In the Consomme
Dec 4 How to Get a City Job
X-Ray Glasses
Dec 7 In a Pickle
Listen
Top-Heavy Mary
Dec 11 Daughters of Poverty
Dec 14 The Life Buoy
Nothing Is Ever Lost
Dec 18 Cambyses, King of Persia
The Shepherd's Flute
Dec 21 The Stranger
Dec 25 The Greek Slave's Passion
Dec 28 A Clever Sleuth
Hush Money

1910

Jan 1 The Legion of Honor
Jan 4 The Avenging Dentist
The Wreck at Sea
Jan 8 On the Bank of the River
A Seat in the Balcony
Jan 11 Shooting in the Haunted Woods
Towser's New Job
Jan 15 Decorated by the Emperor
Human Squib
Railway on the Ice Sea
Jan 18 Fatal Fascination
Getting Square with the Inventor
Jan 22 Swallowed by the Deep
Jan 25 The Price of Patriotism
Seaside Adventures at Home
Jan 29 The Great Divide
Wild Waves at St. Jean-de-Lux
Feb 1 Ascending the Jura Mountains
The Golden Lily
Feb 5 Civil War
Feb 8 Servant from the Country
Settled Out of Court
Feb 12 A Bag Race
The Gambler's Doom
Feb 15 The Ghost
Pastoral Scenes
Feb 19 Better Than Gold
The Comedy-Graph
Feb 22 Duped
His Fears Confirmed
Feb 26 Blue Fishing Nets
The Legend of King Midas
Mar 1 The Plucky Suitor
The Vale of Aude
Mar 5 The Poet of the Revolution
Mar 8 The Great Scoop
The Legend of Daphne
Mar 12 The Pirate Airship
Rabelais' Joke
Mar 15 In the Shadow of the Cliffs
The Saraband Dance
Mar 19 In the Foothills of Savoy
Little Jack's Letter
Mar 22 The Queen and the Mirror
The Wild Coast of Belle Island
Mar 26 The Fall of Babylon
Mar 29 The Diary of a Nurse
Apr 2 Amateur Billiards
The Dreamer
O'er Crag and Torrent
Apr 5 A Drama of the Mountain Pass
Poetry of the Waters
Apr 9 The Kiss Was Mightier Than the Sword
O'er Hill and Vale
Apr 12 The Stubborn Lover
Vintage in Lanquedoc
The Volcano of Chinyero
Apr 16 Mephisto at a Masquerade
Touring the Canary Islands
Apr 19 A Penitent of Florence
Apr 23 Judith and Holofernes
Apr 26 Paying Attention
The Potter's Wheel
Solving the Puzzle
Apr 30 The Captain of the Guard
The Cheese Box
May 3 The Banks of the Danube
The Money Bag
May 7 The Call of the Forest
Gigantic Waves
May 10 A Little Vagrant
A Sea of Clouds
May 14 Christopher Columbus
May 17 Marvellous Waters
Racing for a Bride
May 21 The Centenarian
The Masher's Delirium
May 24 Floral Studies
Over the Cliffs
May 28 The Messenger's Dog
Pete Has Nine Lives
May 31 Jarnac's Treacherous Blow
The Little German Band
Won and Lost
Jun 4 Beneath the Walls of Notre Dame
The Office Seeker
Jun 7 The Monastery in the Forest
A Night on the Coast
Jun 11 Lerin's Abbey on St. Honorat's Island
The Marriage of Esther
Jun 14 At the Dawning; or, The Fear of the Comet
Jun 18 Esther and Mordecai
The Spanish Frontier
Jun 21 Hercules and the Big Stick
Princess and Pigeon
Jun 25 Does Nephew Get the Cash?
Lakes at Eventide
Jun 28 The Elder Sister
The Unlimited Train
Jul 2 Motoring Among the Cliffs and Gorges of France
On the Threshold
Jul 5 The Clink of Gold
Life in Senegal, Africa
Jul 9 The Invincible Sword
Ruins of Mediaeval Fortifications in France
Jul 12 A Hidden Serpent
In the Realm of the Czar
Jul 16 The Jolly Whirl
Jupiter Smitten
Jul 19 The Failure of Success
Jul 23 The Foxy Lawyer
The Princess and the Fishbone
Jul 26 An Angler's Dream
The Beautiful Margaret
Making Wooden Shoes
Jul 30 The Forbidden Novel; or, Don't Do as I Do, Do as I Say
The Sculptor's Ideal
Aug 2 The Ace of Hearts
An Ancient Mariner
Aug 6 The Lord's Prayer
Teneriffe, the Gem of the Canaries
Aug 9 Picturesque Waters of Italy
The Water Cure
Aug 13 Drifts of Snow in Chamonix Valley
Entombed Alive
Aug 16 Across Russian Poland
The Estrangement
Aug 20 Buying a Mother-in-Law
Refusing a Mansion
Aug 23 Four Little Tailors

Neighbors; or, Yvonne's Daughter
Aug 27 In the Pyrenees
The Vow, or, Jephthah's Daughter
Aug 30 Ancient Castles of Austria
The Shepherd and the Maid
Sep 3 Calino Takes New Lodgings
Unrequited Love
Sep 6 The Way of the Transgressor Is Hard
Sep 10 Robert the Devil
Sep 13 An Easy Winner
A Powerful Voice
Sep 17 A Dummy in Disguise
Poems in Pictures
Sep 20 Sunset
Tactics of Cupid
Sep 24 The Reserved Shot
The Times Are Out of Joint
Sep 27 The Sunken Submarine
Too Much Water
Oct 1 The Diver's Honor
A High-Speed Biker
Oct 4 Her Fiancé and the Dog
The Little Acrobat
Oct 8 The Dunce Cap
A Skier Training
Oct 11 The Lovers' Mill
The Three Friends
Oct 15 The Romance of a Necklace
Oct 18 Grandmother's Plot
Phantom Ride from Aix-les-Bains
Oct 22 The Cheat
Oct 25 The Amazon
The First Gray Hair
Oct 29 The Life of Molière
Nov 1 Both Were Stung
Picturesque Majorca
Nov 5 The Fishing Smack
Nov 8 Pharoah; or, Israel in Egypt
Nov 12 Faithful until Death
A Trip to the Blue Grotto, Capri, Italy
Nov 15 Nebuchadnezzar's Pride
Nov 19 Lisbon, Before and During the Revolution
Spanish Loyalty
Nov 22 Cast into the Flames
A Woman's Wit
Nov 26 Calino Travels as a Prince
Samson's Betrayal
Nov 29 The Flat Next Door
Tarascon on the Rhone
Dec 3 Lured by a Phantom; or, The King of Thule
Nancy's Wedding Trip
Dec 6 A Man of Honor
Professor's Hat
Dec 10 The Revolt
Dec 13 Closed Gate
The Phantom Rider
Dec 17 Herod and the New Born King
Dec 20 His Cinderella Girl
The Kingdom of Flowers
Dec 24 Cain and Abel
The Old Home
Dec 27 The Adventuress
Dec 31 The Doctor's Secretary

Society Italian Cines *see also* **Società Italiana Cines**

1907

Aug 14 The Fireman
Fountains of Rome
Kidnapping a Bride
A Modern Youth
The Slavery of Children
Aug 19 The Barber's Daughter
Little Fregoli
Sep 14 Electric Pile
Hunting a Devil
A Modern Samson
Sep 28 Gitana; or, The Gypsy
Oct 12 Monk's Vengeance
Stolen Chickens
Oct 28 Adventures of a Lover
The Sylvan God
Nov 9 Beyond Criticism
Nov 22 In the Dreamland
Where Is My Head
Nov 23 Venetian Baker; or, Drama of Justice
Watchmaker's Secret
Dec 14 The Christmas
Dec 28 Japanese Vaudeville "The Flower Kingdom"

1908

Jan 4 A Brief Story
A Magistrate's Crime
Jan 11 The Farmer
The Rivals: A Love Drama of Pompeii
Jan 18 Adventures of a Countryman
Jan 25 The Butterflies
Feb 15 A Country Drama
Lover and Bicycle
Woman's Army
Feb 29 Othello
Mar 21 Gaston Visits Museum
The Skull and the Sentinel
Apr 4 A False Accusation
Pulcinella
Apr 6 Romeo and Juliet
Apr 11 The Bad Sister
Basket Mystery or the Traveler's Jest
The Doctor's Monkey
A Dream
The Edily
Judith and Holopherne
A Magician's Love Test
The Mayor's Misfortune
Pierrot and the Devil
Vengeance in Normandy
Apr 22 The Grandmother's Fables
Apr 25 Rejoicing Dreams
Sausage
Tramp's Revenge

Solax Co.

1910

Oct 21 A Child's Sacrifice
Oct 28 The Sergeant's Daughter
Nov 4 A Fateful Gift
Nov 11 A Widow and Her Child
Nov 18 Her Father's Sin
Nov 25 One Touch of Nature
Dec 2 What Is to Be, Will Be
Dec 9 Lady Betty's Strategy
Dec 16 Two Suits
Dec 23 The Pawnshop
Dec 30 Mrs. Richard Dare

Sports Picture Co.

1910

Jul 8 Reproduction of Jeffries-Johnson Championship Contest
Aug 18 Knights Templars Conclave

Stella

1909

Jun 12 Drama at Messina
Man with the Cut Throat
Jun 26 Dollar in Each Egg
Jul 10 Pierrot as a Grocer
Aug 14 Black Hand
Aug 21 He Preferred to Smoke His Pipe
Aug 28 Grandmother's Birthday
Oct 25 The Brigand's Repentance
The Would-Be Champion
Nov 13 Now Keep Smiling

Thanhouser Film Corp.

1910

Mar 15 The Actor's Children
Mar 22 St. Elmo
Mar 29 She's Done It Again
Apr 5 Daddy's Double
Apr 15 The Old Shoe Came Back
A 29-Cent Robbery
Apr 22 Her Battle for Existence
Sand Man's Cure
Apr 29 The Cigars His Wife Bought
She Wanted to Marry a Hero
May 6 Jane Eyre
May 13 The Best Man Wins
May 20 Cupid at the Circus
May 27 The Winter's Tale
Jun 3 The Girl of the Northern Woods
Jun 7 The Two Roses
Jun 10 The Writing on the Wall
Jun 14 The Woman Hater
Jun 17 The Little Hero of Holland
Jun 18 Roosevelt's Return
Jun 21 Thelma
Jun 24 The Governor's Daughter
Jun 28 Tempest and Sunshine
Jul 1 The Flag of His Country
Jul 5 Booming Business
Gone to Coney Island
Jul 8 The Girl Strike Leader
Jul 12 The Lucky Shot
Jul 15 The Converted Deacon
Jul 19 The Girls of the Ghetto
Jul 22 The Playwright's Love
Jul 26 Uncle Tom's Cabin
Jul 29 The Mermaid
Aug 2 Jenk's Day Off
Aug 5 The Restoration
Aug 9 The Mad Hermit
Aug 12 Lena Rivers
Aug 16 The Girl Reporter
Aug 19 She Stoops to Conquer
Aug 23 A Dainty Politician
Aug 26 The Latchkey
Aug 30 An Assisted Elopement
Sep 2 A Fresh Start
Sep 6 Mother
Sep 9 The Doctor's Carriage
Sep 13 Tangled Lives
Sep 16 The Stolen Invention
Sep 20 Not Guilty
Sep 23 The Convict
A Husband's Jealous Wife
Sep 27 Home Made Mince Pie
Sep 30 Dots and Dashes
Oct 4 Leon of the Table d'Hote
Oct 7 Avenged
Oct 11 Pocahontas
Oct 14 Delightful Dolly
Oct 18 Oh, What a Knight!
Oct 21 Their Child
Oct 25 Young Lord Stanley
Oct 28 The Fairies' Hallowe'en
Nov 1 Mistress and Maid
Nov 4 Ten Nights in a Bar Room
Nov 8 The Little Fire Chief
Nov 11 The American and the Queen
Nov 15 Paul and Virginia
Nov 18 The City of Her Dreams
Nov 22 A Thanksgiving Surprise
Nov 25 The Wild Flower and the Rose
Nov 29 Value—Beyond Price
Dec 2 John Halifax, Gentleman
Dec 6 Rip Van Winkle
Dec 9 The Girls He Left Behind Him
The Iron Clad Lover
Dec 13 Love and Law
Dec 16 The Millionaire Milkman
Dec 20 Looking Forward
Dec 23 The Childhood of Jack Harkaway
Dec 27 The Vicar of Wakefield
Dec 30 Hypnotized

Theatro

1910

Jun 4 Picturesque Sentari

Theophile Pathé Cinematograph Compagnie

1907

Jan 26 Infants at Breakfast
An Officer's Honor
Feb 2 College Boy's First Love
Faces and Grimaces
The Little Rascal's Tricks
Two Cabbies for One Passenger
Wanted, a Governess
May 18 Barometer of Love
Clever Detective
Cream Eating Contest
Interesting Reading
Kind-Hearted Girl
Robbing a Bird's Nest
Stealing Candies
Trouble at a Wedding
Aug 24 The Blacksmith's Strike
Too Many Children
Sep 14 Unlucky Substitution
Who Owns the Pear?
Oct 26 Brain Storm

1908

May 2 John Is No More a Child
Love's Sacrifice
The Near-Sighted Hunter
The Pastry Cook
Poor Schoolmistress
May 9 Bloodless Duel
Indiscreetness of the Kinematograph
The Wand Has Lost Its Magic
May 30 Around the Coast of Brittany
Artificial Preparation of the Diamond
Jul 6 A Costly Coat
The Leaking Glue Pot
Nothing to Declare; or, Bested by Custom Officials

A Second-Hand Camera
Jul 13 Disappointing Rehearsal
1909
Nov 10 The Haunted Castle
A Serious Error
Dec 4 Punishment of an Athlete
Dec 18 The Forced Loan
Reformed Thief
Dec 25 The Sailor's Son
Thomas A. Edison *see also* **Edison Mfg. Co.; Thomas A. Edison, Inc.**
1895 [month undetermined]
Serpentine Dance—Annabelle
1896
Oct [day undetermined]
The Burning Stable
Clark's Thread Mill
East Side Drive, No. 1
East Side Drive, No. 2
Feeding the Doves
A Morning Bath
Park Police Drill Left Wheel and Forward
Park Police Drill Mount and Dismounting
Streets of Cairo
Surf at Long Branch [N.J.]
Wine Garden Scene
Nov [day undetermined]
Charge of West Point Cadets
Fighting the Fire
A Morning Alarm
Mounted Police Charge
The Runaway in the Park
Starting for the Fire
Dec [day undetermined]
American Falls from Above, American Side
American Falls from Bottom of Canadian Shore
American Falls—from Incline R. R.
Black Diamond Express
Buffalo Horse Market
Chicago and Buffalo Express
Cock Fight
Horseshoe Falls—From Luna Isle
Horseshoe Falls from Table Rock, Canadian Side
Hurdle Race—High Jumpers
Rapids at Cave of the Winds
Special Photographing Train
Tally Ho—Arrival
Tally Ho—Departure
Whirlpool Rapids—from Bottom of Canadian Shore
1897
Jan [day undetermined]
The Farmer's Troubles
The First Sleigh-Ride
Market Square, Harrisburg, Pa.
Parisian Dance
Pennsylvania State Militia, Double Time
Pennsylvania State Militia, Single Time
Police Patrol Wagon
Feb [day undetermined]
Guard Mount, Ft. Myer [Va.]
The Milker's Mishap
Pennsylvania Avenue, Washington, D.C.
Pile Driving, Washington Navy Yard [Washington, D.C.]
Mar [day undetermined]
American and Cuban Flag
Battery A, Light Artillery, U. S. Army
Drum Corps and Militia
Fifth Avenue, New York
McKinley and Cleveland Going to the Capitol
McKinley Taking the Oath
Marines from U. S. Cruiser "New York"
Return of McKinley from the Capitol
71st Regiment, New York
Sleighing in Central Park
Umbrella Brigade
Vice-President Hobart's Escort
Washington Continental Guards
Young Men's Blaine Club of Cincinnati
Apr [day undetermined]
Bareback Hurdle Jumping
Black Diamond Express, No. 1
Black Diamond Express, No. 2
Cavalry Passing in Review
Chas. Werts, Acrobat
The Elopement
Grace Church, New York
Hurdle Jumping and Saddle Vaulting
McKinley Leaving Church
Now I Lay Me Down To Sleep
Panorama of Susquehanna River Taken from the Black Diamond Express
Pennsylvania Avenue, Washington
Receding View, Black Diamond Express
Seminary Girls
The Washwoman's Troubles
May [day undetermined]
Amoskeag Veterans, New Hampshire
Battery B, Governor's Troop, Penna.
Buffalo Bill and Escort
Corcoran Cadets, Washington
General Porter's Oration
Governor Cook and Staff, Connecticut
Governor of Ohio and Staff
Grant Veterans—G. A. R.
Horse Dancing Couchee Couchee
Husking Bee
Making Soap Bubbles
National Lancers of Boston
O'Brien's Trained Horses
Old Guard, New York City
Pillow Fight
President McKinley's Address
7th and 71st Regiment, New York
Sixth U. S. Cavalry
Sun Dance—Annabelle
Tandem Hurdle Jumping
Trick Elephants
Jun [day undetermined]
Boating on the Lake
Chicken Thieves
Children's Toilet
Mr. Edison at Work in His Chemical Laboratory
Jul [day undetermined]
Armour's Electric Trolley
Buffalo Fire Department in Action
Buffalo Police on Parade
Buffalo Stockyards
Cattle Driven to Slaughter
Corner Madison and State Streets, Chicago
Falls of Minnehaha
Free-for-All Race at Charter Oak Park
Giant Coal Dumper
Philadelphia Express, Jersey Central Railway
Racing at Sheepshead Bay
Sheep Run, Chicago Stockyards
Suburban Handicap, 1897
Waterfall in the Catskills
Aug [day undetermined]
Admiral Cigarette
Sep [day undetermined]
Bowery Waltz
Charity Ball
Fisherman's Luck
Sutro Baths, No. 2
Oct [day undetermined]
Ambulance at the Accident
Ambulance Call
Arrest in Chinatown, San Francisco, Cal.
Beach Apparatus—Practice
Boat Wagon and Beach Cart
Boxing for Points
Capsize of Lifeboat
Crissie Sheridan
Cupid and Psyche
Dancing Darkey Boy
Exhibition of Prize Winners
First Avenue, Seattle, Washington, No. 8
Fisherman's Wharf
Fishing Smacks
Horses Loading for Klondike
Hotel Del Monte
Hotel Vendome, San Jose, Cal.
The Jealous Monkey
Judging Tandems
Ladies' Saddle Horses
Launch of Life Boat
Launch of Surf Boat
Leander Sisters
Lick Observatory, Mt. Hamilton, Cal.
Loading Baggage for Klondike
Lurline Baths
Pie Eating Contest
Rainmakers
Rescue—Resuscitation
Return of Lifeboat
S. S. "Coptic" at Dock
S. S. "Coptic" in the Harbor
S. S. "Coptic" Sailing Away
S. S. "Queen" Leaving Dock
S. S. "Queen" Loading
S. S. "Williamette" Leaving for Klondike
The Sea Lions' Home
Single Harness Horses
Southern Pacific Overland Mail
Stanford University, California
Surf at Monterey
Sutro Baths, No. 1
Teams of Horses
Wall Scaling
Dec [day undetermined]
Fast Mail, Northern Pacific Railroad
Firing by Squad, Gatling Gun
Gatling Gun Crew in Action
Mount and Dismount, Gatling Gun
1898
Feb [day undetermined]
Branding Cattle
Buck Dance, Ute Indians
Calf Branding
California Limited, A.T. & S.F.R.R.
California Orange Groves, Panoramic View
Cañon of the Rio Grande
Cattle Fording Stream
Cattle Leaving the Corral
Chinese Procession
Circle Dance, Ute Indians
Coasting
Cripple Creek Float
Decorated Carriages
Denver Fire Brigade
Dogs Playing in the Surf
Eagle Dance, Pueblo Indians
Going Through the Tunnel
Hockey Match on the Ice
Horticultural Floats, No. 9
Indian Day School
Las Viga Canal, Mexico City
Lassoing a Steer
Marching Scene
Market Scene, City of Mexico
Masked Procession
Mexican Fishing Scene
Mexican Rurales Charge
A Mid-Winter Brush
Off for the Rabbit Chase
Ostriches Feeding
Ostriches Running, No. 1
Ostriches Running, No. 2
Parade of Coaches
Picking Oranges
Procession of Mounted Indians and Cowboys
Repairing Streets in Mexico
Royal Gorge
Serving Rations to the Indians, No. 1
Serving Rations to the Indians, No. 2
Snowballing the Coasters
South Spring Street, Los Angeles, Cal.
Spanish Ball Game
Street Scene, San Diego
Sunday Morning in Mexico
Sunset Limited, Southern Pacific Ry.
Surface Transit, Mexico
Train Hour in Durango, Mexico
Wand Dance, Pueblo Indians
Wash Day in Mexico
Mar [day undetermined]
Acrobatic Monkey
After Launching
American Flag
Bull Fight, No. 1
Bull Fight, No. 2
Bull Fight, No. 3
Feeding Sea Gulls
Freight Train

Launch of Japanese Man-of-War "Chitosa"
Launching, No. 2
Mexico Street Scene
Mount Tamalpais R. R., No. 1
Mount Tamalpais R. R., No. 2
Mount Taw R. R., No. 3
Native Daughters
Old Glory and Cuban Flag
Parade of Chinese
Procession of Floats
Sea Waves
Union Iron Works
An Unwelcome Visitor

May [day undetermined]
Battery B Pitching Camp

May 20 The Ball Game
Battery B Arriving at Camp
The Burglar
Burial of the "Maine" Victims
Colored Troops Disembarking
Comedy Set-To
Cruiser "Cincinnati"
Cruiser "Detroit"
Cruiser "Marblehead"
Cuban Refugees Waiting for Rations
Cuban Volunteers Marching for Rations
Flagship "New York"
Heaving the Log
Military Camp at Tampa, Taken from Train
Monitor "Terror"
Morro Castle, Havana Harbor
N. Y. Journal Despatch Yacht "Buccaneer"
9th Infantry Boys' Morning Wash
9th U. S. Cavalry Watering Horses
S. S. "Coptic"
S. S. "Coptic" Lying To
S. S. "Coptic" Running Against the Storm
Secretary Long and Captain Sigsbee
See-Saw Scene
Snow Storm
Steamer "Mascotte" Arriving at Tampa
A Street Arab
The Telephone
10th U. S. Infantry Disembarking from Cars
10th U. S. Infantry, 2nd Battalion Leaving Cars
Transport "Whitney" Leaving Dock
U. S. Battleship "Indiana"
U. S. Battleship "Iowa"
U. S. Cavalry Supplies Unloading at Tampa, Florida
U. S. Cruiser "Nashville"
U. S. S. "Castine"
War Correspondents
Wreck of the Battleship "Maine"

Jun [day undetermined]
Afternoon Tea on Board S. S. "Doric"
Arrival of Tokyo Train
Blanket-Tossing a New Recruit
California Volunteers Marching To Embark
Canton River Scene
Canton Steamboat Landing Chinese Passengers
Cuban Volunteers Embarking
14th U. S. Infantry Drilling at the Presidio
Game of Shovel Board on Board S. S. "Doric"
Going to the Yokohama Races
Government House at Hong Kong
Hong Kong Regiment, No. 1
Hong Kong Regiment, No. 2
Hong Kong, Wharf Scene
Honolulu Street Scene
Japanese Sampans
Kanakas Diving for Money [Honolulu], No. 1
Kanakas Diving for Money [Honolulu], No. 2
Landing Wharf at Canton
Loading Horses on Transport
9th and 13th U. S. Infantry at Battalion Drill
Parade of Buffalo Bill's Wild West Show, No. 1
Parade of Buffalo Bill's Wild West Show, No. 2
Railway Station at Yokohama
Returning from the Races
River Scene at Macao, China
Roosevelt's Rough Riders Embarking for Santiago
S. S. "Coptic" Coaling
S. S. "Doric"
S. S. "Doric" in Mid-Ocean
S. S. "Gaelic"
S. S. "Gaelic" at Nagasaki
71st N. Y. Volunteers Embarking for Santiago
Shanghai Police
Shanghai Street Scene No. 1
Shanghai Street Scene No. 2
Sikh Artillery, Hong Kong
Soldiers Washing Dishes
Street Scene in Hong Kong
Street Scene in Yokohama, No. 1
Street Scene in Yokohama, No. 2
Theatre Road, Yokohama
Tourists Starting for Canton
Trained Cavalry Horses
Transport Ships at Port Tampa
Troop Ships for the Philippines
Troops Embarking at San Francisco
Wagon Supply Train en Route
Wharf Scene, Honolulu

Jul [day undetermined]
The Burglar
The Telephone

Aug [day undetermined]
Cuban Ambush
Fake Beggar
Major General Shafter
Mules Swimming Ashore at Daiquiri, Cuba
Pack Mules with Ammunition on the Santiago Trail, Cuba
Packing Ammunition on Mules, Cuba
Shooting Captured Insurgents
U. S. Troops Landing at Daiquiri, Cuba
Victorious Squadron Firing Salute

Sep [day undetermined]
Admiral Sampson on Board the Flagship
Close View of the "Brooklyn," Naval Parade
Excursion Boats, Naval Parade
Farmer Kissing the Lean Girl
The Fleet Steaming Up North River
The "Glen Island," Accompanying Parade
The "Massachusetts," Naval Parade
Merry-Go-Round
Observation Train Following Parade
Police Boats Escorting Naval Parade
Reviewing the "Texas" at Grant's Tomb
Statue of Liberty
The "Texas," Naval Parade
Troops Making Military Road in Front of Santiago
U. S. Battleship "Oregon"
U. S. Cruiser "Brooklyn," Naval Parade

Oct [day undetermined]
Advance Guard, Return of N. J. Troops
Balloon Ascension, Marionettes
Dancing Chinaman, Marionettes
Ella Lola, a la Trilby [Dance]
Parade of Marines, U. S. Cruiser, "Brooklyn"
Return of 2nd Regiment of New Jersey
Return of Troop C, Brooklyn
Skeleton Dance, Marionettes
Turkish Dance, Ella Lola

Nov [day undetermined]
Elopement on Horseback
The Tramp in the Kitchen

Dec [day undetermined]
The Burglar in the Bed Chamber
The Burglar on the Roof
The Cavalier's Dream
The Cop and the Nurse Girl
S. S. "Coptic" Running Before a Gale
Sleighing Scene
Vanishing Lady
What Demoralized the Barber Shop

1899

Jan [day undetermined]
Astor Battery on Parade
Coaches Arriving at Mammoth Hot Springs
Coaches Going to Cinnabar from Yellowstone Park
General Lee's Procession, Havana
Lower Falls, Grand Canyon, Yellowstone Park
Tourists Going Round Yellowstone Park
Troops at Evacuation of Havana

Feb [day undetermined]
Jones and His Pal in Trouble
Jones' Interrupted Sleighride
Jones' Return from the Club
Larks Behind the Scene
Panoramic View of Brooklyn Bridge
Poker at Dawson City
Rapids below Suspension Bridge
Willie's First Smoke

Mar [day undetermined]
Arabian Gun Twirler
Bicycle Trick Riding, No. 2
Jones Makes a Discovery
Raising Old Glory over Morro Castle
Three Acrobats

Apr [day undetermined]
Casey at the Bat
Morning Colors on U. S. Cruiser "Raleigh"
104th Street Curve, New York, Elevated Railway
Pilot Boats in New York Harbor
Tommy Atkins, Bobby and the Cook
U. S. Cruiser "Raleigh"
A Wringing Good Joke

May [day undetermined]
Cripple Creek Bar-Room Scene

Jun [day undetermined]
Advance of Kansas Volunteers at Caloocan
The Bibulous Clothier
Capture of Trenches at Candaba [Canda Bar]
A Fair Exchange Is No Robbery
Filipinos Retreat from Trenches
Mesmerist and Country Couple
New York Police Parade, June 1st, 1899
Panoramic View, Horseshoe Curve, From Penna. Ltd.
Rout of the Filipinos
Skirmish of Rough Riders
Strange Adventure of New York Drummer
U. S. Infantry Supported by Rough Riders at El Caney
U. S. Troops and Red Cross in the Trenches Before Caloocan [P. I.]

Jul [day undetermined]
Panoramic View, Horseshoe Curve, Penna. R. R., No. 2
A Ride Through Pack Saddle Mountains, Penna. R.R.
Running through Gallitzen Tunnel, Penna. R.R.

Aug [day undetermined]
The Prentis Trio

Sep [day undetermined]
Admiral Dewey Landing at Gibraltar
The Boston Horseless Fire Department
Colonel Funston Swimming the Baglag River
The Diving Horse
The Early Morning Attack
New Brooklyn to New York via Brooklyn Bridge, No. 1
New Brooklyn to New York via Brooklyn Bridge, No. 2
Shoot the Chutes Series

Oct [day undetermined]
Admiral Dewey at State House, Boston
Admiral Dewey Leading Land Parade
Admiral Dewey Leading Land Parade, No. 2
Admiral Dewey Passing Catholic Club Stand
Admiral Dewey Receiving the Washington and New York Committees

Admiral Dewey Taking Leave of Washington Committee on the U. S. Cruiser 'Olympia'
After the Race—Yachts Returning to Anchorage
Battery K Siege Guns
"Columbia" Winning the Cup
Dewey Arch—Troops Passing Under Arch
Dewey Parade, 10th Pennsylvania Volunteers
Governor Roosevelt and Staff
Panorama at Grant's Tomb, Dewey Naval Procession
Panoramic View of Floral Float "Olympia"
"Shamrock" and "Columbia" Rounding the Outer Stake Boat
"Shamrock" and "Columbia" Rounding the Outer Stake Boat, No. 2
"Shamrock" and "Columbia" Yacht Race—First Race
"Shamrock" and "Erin" Sailing
West Point Cadets

Nov [day undetermined]
The Astor Tramp
Fun in Camp
Pictures Incidental to Yacht Race
2nd Special Service Battalion, Canadian Infantry, Embarking for So. Africa
2nd Special Service Battalion, Canadian Infantry-Parade
"Shamrock" and "Columbia" Yacht Race—1st Race, No. 2
Tenderloin at Night
Trick Bears
U. S. Cruiser "Olympia" Leading Naval Parade

1900

Jan [day undetermined]
Why Jones Discharged His Clerks
Why Mrs. Jones Got a Divorce

Feb [day undetermined]
An Animated Luncheon
Automobile Parade
Ching Ling Foo Outdone
Dick Croker Leaving Tammany Hall
A Dull Razor
Faust and Marguerite
The Magician

Mar [day undetermined]
An Artist's Dream
The Kiss
The Mystic Swing
Uncle Josh in a Spooky Hotel
Uncle Josh's Nightmare

Apr [day undetermined]
Battle of Mafeking
Boer Commissary Train Treking
Boers Bringing in British Prisoners
Capture of Boer Battery
Capture of Boer Battery by British
Charge of Boer Cavalry
English Lancers Charging
Overland Express Arriving at Helena, Mont.
Red Cross Ambulance on Battlefield
White Horse Rapids

May [day undetermined]
Discharging a Whitehead Torpedo
Exploding a Whitehead Torpedo
New Black Diamond Express
Panorama of Gorge Railway
Panoramic View of Newport [R. I.]
Torpedo Boat "Morris" Running

Jun [day undetermined]
High Diving by A. C. Holden
Watermelon Contest

Jul [day undetermined]
Burning of the Standard Oil Co. 's Tanks, Bayonne, N.J.

Aug [day undetermined]
Bombardment of Taku Forts, by the Allied Fleets
Breaking of the Crowd at Military Review at Longchamps
Champs de Mars
Champs Elysees
Eiffel Tower from Trocadero Palace
Esplanade des Invalides
Palace of Electricity
Panorama from the Moving Boardwalk
Panorama of Eiffel Tower
Panorama of Place De L'Opera
Panorama of the Moving Boardwalk
Panorama of the Paris Exposition, from the Seine
Panoramic View of the Champs Elysees
Panoramic View of the Place de la Concorde
Scene from the Elevator Ascending Eiffel Tower
Scene in the Swiss Village at Paris Exposition
A Storm at Sea
Swiss Village, No. 2

Sep [day undetermined]
Bird's-Eye View of Dock Front, Galveston
Launching a Stranded Schooner from the Docks
Panorama of East Galveston
Panorama of Galveston Power House
Panorama of Orphans' Home, Galveston
Panorama of Wreckage of Water Front
Panoramic View of Tremont Hotel, Galveston
Searching Ruins on Broadway, Galveston, for Dead Bodies

Nov [day undetermined]
The Clown and the Alchemist
Congress of Nations
The Enchanted Drawing
Gun Drill by Naval Cadets at Newport [R.I., Naval] Training School
Gymnasium Exercises and Drill at Newport [R.I., Naval] Training School
Hooligan Assists the Magician
Maude's Naughty Little Brother
Naval Apprentices at Sail Drill on Historic Ship "Constellation"
Naval Sham Battle at Newport

Dec [day undetermined]
Grandma and the Bad Boys
A Wringing Good Joke

1901

Jan [day undetermined]
Love in a Hammock

Feb 23 Ice-Boat Racing at Redbank, N.J.
Terrible Teddy, the Grizzly King

Mar [day undetermined]
The Automatic Weather Prophet
The Old Maid in the Horsecar

Mar 2 The Finish of Bridget McKeen
Follow the Leader
A Joke on Grandma

Mar 9 The Old Maid Having Her Picture Taken
Why Mr. Nation Wants a Divorce

Mar 16 The Kansas Saloon Smashers
President McKinley and Escort Going to the Capitol
President McKinley Taking the Oath

Mar 23 The Donkey Party
Love by the Light of the Moon
Montreal Fire Department on Runners

Apr 13 Happy Hooligan April-Fooled
Happy Hooligan Surprised

Apr 27 The Gordon Sisters Boxing
Laura Comstock's Bag-Punching Dog
Pie, Tramp and the Bulldog
The Tramp's Dream

May [day undetermined]
Another Job for the Undertaker
A Day at the Circus
Fun in a Butcher Shop
How the Dutch Beat the Irish
Old Faithful Geyser
Packers on the Trail
Panoramic View of the White Pass Railroad
Riverside Geyser, Yellowstone Park
The Tramp's Strategy That Failed
The Tramp's Unexpected Skate

May 4 Burro Pack Train on the Chilcoot Pass
Miles Canyon Tramway
Rocking Gold in the Klondike
Upper Falls of the Yellowstone
Washing Gold on 20 above Hunker, Klondike

Jun 8 Opening of the Pan-American Exposition showing Vice President Roosevelt Leading the Procession
'Varsity Crew Race on Cayuga Lake, on Decoration Day, Lehigh Valley Observation Train Following the Race, Showing Cornell Crew Finishing First, Columbia Second, University of Pennsylvania Third Ithaca, N. Y., Showing Lehigh Valley Observation Train

Jun 22 A Trip Around the Pan-American Exposition

Jul [day undetermined]
The Educated Chimpanzee
The Esquimaux Village
Japanese Village
The Photographer's Mishap
The Tramp's Miraculous Escape

Aug [day undetermined]
The "Abbot" and "Cresceus" Race
Aunt Sallie's Wonderful Bustle
The Bad Boy's Joke on the Nurse
Bathing at Atlantic City
Bicycle Paced Race
Canoeing Scene
Circular Panorama of Electric Tower
Circular Panorama of Suspension Bridge and American Falls
Circular Panoramic View of Whirlpool Rapids
Esquimaux Game of Snap-the-Whip
Esquimaux Leap-Frog
The Farmer and the Bad Boys
Panoramic View of Electric Tower from a Balloon
Panoramic View of the Gorge Railroad
Photographing a Country Couple
Professional Handicap Bicycle Race
The Reversible Divers
Sampson-Schley Controversy
Soubrette's Troubles on a Fifth Avenue Stage Coach
Swimming Pool at Coney Island
Tally-Ho Departing for the Races
The Tramp and the Nursing Bottle
"Weary Willie" and the Gardener
What Happened on Twenty-Third Street, New York City

Sep [day undetermined]
Faust Family of Acrobats
Life Rescue at Long Branch
Lukens, Novel Gymnast
The Musical Ride
Rubes in the Theatre
Sampson and Schley Controversy—Tea Party
Street's Zouaves and Wall Scaling
The Trick Cyclist
What Demoralized the Barber Shop

Sep 21 The Mob Outside the Temple of Music at the Pan-American Exposition [Buffalo]
President McKinley Reviewing the Troops at the Pan-American Exposition
President McKinley's Speech at the Pan-American Exposition

Oct [day undetermined]
Captain Nissen Going Through Whirlpool Rapids, Niagara Falls
Duke and Duchess of Cornwall and York Landing at Queenstown, Ontario
Duke of York at Montreal and Quebec
Horse Parade at the Pan-American Exposition
The Lovers, Coal Box, and Fireplace
Panorama, Great Gorge Route over Lewiston Bridge
Spanish Dancers at the Pan-American Exposition
Working the Breeches Buoy

Oct 5 Arrival of McKinley's Funeral Train at Canton, Ohio
Funeral Leaving the President's House and Church at Canton, Ohio
McKinley's Funeral Entering Westlawn Cemetery, Canton [Ohio]
Panoramic View of the President's House at Canton, Ohio

President McKinley's Funeral Cortege at Buffalo, N.Y.
President McKinley's Funeral Cortege at Washington, D. C.
President Roosevelt at the Canton Station
Taking President McKinley's Body from Train at Canton, Ohio

Oct 19 "Columbia" and "Shamrock II": Finishing Second Race
"Columbia" and "Shamrock II": Jockeying and Starting
"Columbia" and "Shamrock II": Start of Second Race
"Columbia" and "Shamrock II": Starting in the Third Race
"Columbia" and "Shamrock II": Turning the Outer Stake Boat
"Columbia" Winning the Cup
The Martyred Presidents
Pan-American Exposition by Night
Panoramic View of the Fleet After Yacht Race
The Yacht Race Fleet Following the Committee Boat "Navigator" Oct. 4th

Nov [day undetermined]
Automobile Parade on the Coney Island Boulevard
Catching an Early Train
Panorama of Esplanade by Night
A Phenomenal Contortionist
Royal Train with Duke and Duchess of York, Climbing Mt. Hector
Sham Battle at the Pan-American Exposition
Trapeze Disrobing Act

Nov 16 Execution of Czolgosz, with Panorama of Auburn Prison

Dec [day undetermined]
The Artist's Dilemma
Ascending Mt. Low, California
Building a Harbor at San Pedro
California Oil Wells in Operation
Carrying Out the Snakes
Children Bathing
The Fat and the Lean Wrestling Match
Harry Thompson's Imitations of Sousa
Leaping Dogs at Gentry's Circus
Line-Up and Teasing the Snakes
The March of Prayer and Entrance of the Dancers
Moki Snake Dance by Walpapi Indians
The Mysterious Cafe
Ostrich Farms at Pasadena
Panoramic View, Albert Canyon
Panoramic View, Kicking Horse Canyon
Panoramic View, Lower Kicking Horse Canyon
Panoramic View, Lower Kicking Horse Valley
Panoramic View of Boston Subway from an Electric Car
Panoramic View of Moki-Land
Panoramic View of Rubio Canyon, Mt. Low R.R.
Panoramic View, Upper Kicking Horse Canyon
Parade of Snake Dancers before the Dance
Pigeon Farm at Los Angeles, Cal
Prize Winners at the Country Fair
Roeber Wrestling Match

Dec 14 Jeffries in His Training Quarters
Ruhlin in His Training Quarters

Dec 21 Jeffries and Ruhlin Sparring Contest at San Francisco, Cal., Nov. 15, 1901—Five Rounds

1902 [month undetermined]
Happy Hooligan Turns Burglar

Jan [day undetermined]
Bird's Eye View of San Francisco, Cal., from a Balloon
A Cable Road in San Francisco, Cal.
Chinese Shaving Scene
Facial Expression
Feeding Geese at Newman's Poultry Farm
Fishing at Faralone Island
New Year's Mummers Parade
Panoramic View Between Palliser and Field, B. C.
Panoramic View near Mt. Golden on the Canadian Pacific R. R.
Panoramic View of Mt. Tamalpais
Panoramic View of Mt. Tamalpais Between Bow Knot and McKinley Cut
Panoramic View of the Canadian Pacific R. R. near Leauchoil, B. C.
Panoramic View of the Golden Gate
Sea Gulls Following Fishing Boats
The Twentieth Century Tramp; or, Happy Hooligan and His Airship
Uncle Josh at the Moving Picture Show
The Weary Hunters and the Magician

Feb [day undetermined]
Arrival of the Governor General, Lord Minto, at Quebec
The Burning of Durland's Riding Academy
Capture of the Biddle Brothers
Christening and Launching Kaiser Wilhelm's Yacht "Meteor"
Circular Panorama of Housing the Ice
Coasting Scene at Montmorency Falls, Canada
Cross-Country Running on Snow Shoes
Cutting and Canaling Ice
The Hindoo Fakir
"Kronprinz Wilhelm" with Prince Henry [of Prussia] on Board Arriving in New York
Loading the Ice on Cars, Conveying It across the Mountains and Loading It into Boats
New York City in a Blizzard
Panorama of the Paterson [N.J.] Fire
Panoramic View of the Hohenzollern
Paterson [N. J.] Fire, Showing the Y. M. C. A. and Library
Prince Henry [of Prussia] Arriving in Washington and Visiting the German Embassy
Ruins of City Hall, Paterson [N. J.]
Skiing in Montreal
Skiing Scene in Quebec
Tobogganing in Canada
Working Rotary Snow Ploughs on Lehigh Valley Railroad

Mar [day undetermined]
"Deutschland" Leaving New York at Full Speed [with Prince Henry of Prussia]
German and American Tableau
Kaiser Wilhelm's Yacht, "Meteor," Entering the Water
Prince Henry [of Prussia] Arriving at West Point
Prince Henry [of Prussia] at Lincoln's Monument, Chicago, Ill.
Prince Henry [of Prussia] at Niagara Falls
Prince Henry [of Prussia] Reviewing the Cadets at West Point
Prince Henry [of Prussia] Visiting Cambridge, Mass. and Harvard University
Sailing of the "Deutschland" with Prince Henry [of Prussia] on Board

Mar 15 Arrival of Prince Henry [of Prussia] and President Roosevelt at Shooter's Island

Apr [day undetermined]
Babies Rolling Eggs
The Bessemer Steel Converter in Operation
The Burlesque Suicide
Charleston Chain Gang
Circular Panoramic View of Jones and Laughlin's Steel Yard
Feeding the Bear at the Menagerie
Fun in a Bakery Shop
The Golden Chariots
Great Bull Fight
Las Viga Canal, Mexico
Loading a Vessel at Charleston, S. C.
Midway of Charleston Exposition [South Carolina]
Miniature Railway
Moonlight on Lake Maggiore, Italy
New Sunset Limited
Panoramic View from Pittsburgh to Allegheny
Panoramic View of Charleston Exposition [South Carolina]
President Roosevelt Reviewing the Troops at Charleston Exposition [South Carolina]
St. Patrick's Cathedral and Fifth Avenue on Easter Sunday Morning [New York City]
Scrambling for Eggs
The Swimming Ducks at Allentown [Pa.] Duck Farm
Tossing Eggs

May [day undetermined]
Appointment by Telephone
Burning of St. Pierre [Martinique]
Mt. Pelee in Eruption and Destruction of St. Pierre [Martinique]
Mt. Pelee Smoking Before Eruption [St. Pierre, Martinique]
The S. S. "Deutschland" in a Storm
The S. S. "Deutschland" in a Storm, No. 2
The S. S. "Deutschland" in Heavy Sea
The S. S. "Deutschland" Leaving Her Dock in Hoboken
Shuffleboard on S. S. "Deutschland"

Oct [day undetermined]
The Bull and the Picnickers
How They Do Things on the Bowery
The Interrupted Bathers
The Interrupted Picnic
Rock of Ages

Nov [day undetermined]
Broncho Busting Scene, Championship of the World

1903

Jan [day undetermined]
Electrocution of an Elephant
Goo Goo Eyes
Life of an American Fireman
West Indian Boys Diving for Money

Feb [day undetermined]
Market Scene in Cairo, Egypt

Apr [day undetermined]
Battle of Confetti at the Nice Carnival
Battle of Flowers at the Nice Carnival
Native Woman Washing a Negro Baby in Nassau, B. I.
Native Women Coaling a Ship and Scrambling for Money [West Indies]
Native Women Coaling a Ship at St. Thomas, D. W. I.
Native Women Washing Clothes at St. Vincent, B. W. I.
Panorama of Morro Castle, Havana, Cuba
Panorama of Willemstadt, Curacao, Taken from the River
Panoramic View of Monte Carlo
Panoramic View of St. Pierre, Martinique
Pilot Leaving "Prinzessen Victoria Luise" at Sandy Hook
Procession of Floats and Masqueraders at Nice Carnival
Railroad Panorama near Spanishtown, Jamaica
Tourists Playing Shuffleboard on "Prinzessen Victoria Luise"
West Indian Girls in Native Dance
Wharf Scene and Natives Swimming at St. Thomas, D. W. I.

May [day undetermined]
Fireboat "New Yorker" Answering an Alarm
Fireboat "New Yorker" in Action
Lehigh Valley Black Diamond Express
New York City Dumping Wharf
New York City "Ghetto" Fish Market
New York City Police Parade
New York Harbor Police Boat Patrol Capturing Pirates
Panorama of Blackwell's Island
Panorama of Riker's Island
Panorama Water Front and Brooklyn Bridge from East River

Skyscrapers of New York City, from the North River
Sorting Refuse at Incinerating Plant, New York City
Steamscow "Cinderella" and Ferryboat "Cincinnati"
The Still Alarm
White Wings on Review

Jun [day undetermined]
"Africander" Winning the Suburban Handicap, 1903
Arabian Jewish Dance
Crossing the Atlantic
Eating Macaroni in the Streets of Naples
Egyptian Boys in Swimming Race
Egyptian Fakir with Dancing Monkey
Egyptian Market Scene
Excavating Scene at the Pyramids of Sakkarah
Feeding Pigeons in Front of St. Mark's Cathedral, Venice, Italy
Fording the River Nile on Donkeys
Going to Market, Luxor Egypt
Herd of Sheep on the Road to Jerusalem
Jerusalem's Busiest Street, Showing Mt. Zion
A Jewish Dance at Jerusalem
King Edward and President Loubet Reviewing French Troops
King Edward's Visit to Paris
Lake Lucerne, Switzerland
Panorama of Tivoli, Italy, Showing Seven Falls
Panoramic View of an Egyptian Cattle Market
Panoramic View of Beyrouth, Syria, Showing Holiday Festivities
Passengers Embarking from S. S. "Augusta Victoria" at Beyrouth
Primitive Irrigation in Egypt
Shearing a Donkey in Egypt
69th Regiment, N. G. N. Y.
Street Scene at Jaffa
Tourists Embarking at Jaffa
Tourists Landing at Island of Capri, Italy
Tourists Returning on Donkeys from Mizpah
Tourists Starting on Donkeys for the Pyramids of Sakkarah
Tourists Taking Water from the River Jordan
Washing Clothes at Sicily

Jul [day undetermined]
Miniature Railway at Wilmington Springs, Delaware
Policemen's Prank on Their Comrade
Razzle Dazzle
A Scrap in Black and White

Aug [day undetermined]
Down Where the Wurzburger Flows
The Gay Shoe Clerk
Immigrants Landing at Ellis Island
Little Lillian, Toe Danseuse
Rube and Mandy at Coney Island
Seashore Frolics
Street Car Chivalry
Subub Surprises the Burglar
The Unappreciated Joke

Sep [day undetermined]
Baby Class at Lunch
The Baby Review
Maypole Dance
Miss Jessie Cameron, Champion Child Sword Dancer
Miss Jessie Dogherty, Champion Female Highland Fling Dancer
New York Caledonian Club's Parade
Old Fashioned Scottish Reel
Orphans in the Surf
"Reliance" and "Shamrock" III Jockeying and Starting in First Race
"Reliance" Crossing the Line and Winning First Race
Rube and the Fender
Throwing the Sixteen Pound Hammer
Tub Race
Turning the Tables
Uncle Tom's Cabin

Oct [day undetermined]
Ancient and Honourable Artillery of London on Parade
The Ancient and Honourables Homeward Bound
The Animated Poster
Casey and His Neighbor's Goat
An East River Novelty
East Side Urchins Bathing in a Fountain
The Extra Turn
Flood Scene in Paterson, N. J.
The Heavenly Twins at Lunch
The Heavenly Twins at Odds
The Messenger Boy's Mistake
Move On
New York City Public Bath
The Physical Culture Girl
A Romance of the Rail
Two Chappies in a Box

Nov [day undetermined]
Buster's Joke on Papa
The Great Fire Ruins, Coney Island
Princeton and Yale Football Game
What Happened in the Tunnel

Dec [day undetermined]
Buster's Joke on Papa
The Great Train Robbery
How Old Is Ann?
The Office Boy's Revenge
Opening of New East River Bridge, New York
Under the Mistletoe

1904

Jan [day undetermined]
Circular Panorama of the Horse Shoe Falls in Winter
Crossing Ice Bridge at Niagara Falls
Ice Skating in Central Park, N. Y.
Sliding Down Ice Mound at Niagara Falls
Treloar and Miss Marshall, Prize Winners at the Physical Culture Show in Madison Square Garden

Feb [day undetermined]
Animated Painting
Casey's Frightful Dream
Cohen's Advertising Scheme
Halloween Night at the Seminary
Ice Boating on the North Shrewsbury, Red Bank, N. J.
Little German Band
Midnight Intruder
Old Maid and Fortune Teller
Panorama of Ruins from Baltimore and Charles Street
Panorama of Ruins from Lombard and Charles Street
Panorama of Ruins from Water Front
Wifey's Mistake

Mar [day undetermined]
Buster and Tige Put a Balloon Vendor Out of Business
Buster Brown and the Dude
Buster Makes Room for His Mama at the Bargain Counter
Buster's Dog to the Rescue
Panorama of Ruins from Lombard and Hanover Streets, Baltimore, Md.
Pranks of Buster Brown and His Dog Tige
Section of Buster Brown Series, Showing a Sketch of Buster by Outcault
Sleighing in Central Park, New York

Apr [day undetermined]
Babe and Puppies
Japanese Acrobats

Apr 20 Battle of Chemulpo Bay
Skirmish Between Russian and Japanese Advance Guards

May [day undetermined]
Annual Parade, New York Fire Department
Brush Between Cowboys and Indians
Bucking Broncos
Capsized Boat
The Cop Fools the Sergeant
Cowboys and Indians Fording River in a Wagon
Dog Factory
Driving Cattle to Pasture
Herding Horses across a River
Hold Up in a Country Grocery Store
Rounding Up and Branding Cattle
War Canoe Race
Western Stage Coach Hold Up

Jun [day undetermined]
Elephants Shooting the Chutes at Luna Park [Coney Island]
Inter-Collegiate Athletic Association Championships, 1904
"Weary Willie" Kidnaps a Child

Jul [day undetermined]
Boxing Horses, Luna Park, Coney Island
Canoeing on the Charles River, Boston, Mass.
Elephants Shooting the Chutes, Luna Park, Coney Island, No. 2
Inter-Collegiate Regatta, Poughkeepsie, N. Y., 1904
Outing, Mystic Shriners, Atlantic City, New Jersey
Parade, Mystic Shriners, Atlantic City, New Jersey
"Pollywogs" 71st Regiment, N. G. S. N. Y., Initiating Raw Recruits
Scenes in an Infant Orphan Asylum

Jul 16 White Star S. S. Baltic Leaving Pier on First Eastern Voyage

Aug [day undetermined]
Fire and Flames at Luna Park, Coney Island [An Attraction at Coney Island]
Judge Parker Receiving the Notification of His Nomination for the Presidency

Sep [day undetermined]
Annual Baby Parade, 1904, Asbury Park, N. J.
Capture of Yegg Bank Burglars
European Rest Cure
How a French Nobleman Got a Wife Through the New York Herald "Personal" Columns
Military Maneuvers, Manassas, Va.

Oct [day undetermined]
Maniac Chase

Nov [day undetermined]
City Hall to Harlem in 15 Seconds, via the Subway Route
Miss Lillian Shaffer and Her Dancing Horse
Opening Ceremonies, New York Subway, October 27, 1904
Parsifal
Railroad Smashup
A Rube Couple at a County Fair
"Weary Willie" Kisses the Bride

Dec [day undetermined]
Bad Boy's Joke on the Nurse
The Ex-Convict
Mining Operations, Pennsylvania Coal Fields
Scarecrow Pump
The "Strenuous" Life; or, Anti-Race Suicide

1905

Feb [day undetermined]
The Kleptomaniac

Mar [day undetermined]
President Roosevelt's Inauguration

Apr [day undetermined]
The Seven Ages

May [day undetermined]
How Jones Lost His Roll
Opening of Belmont Park Race Course
Start of Ocean Race for Kaiser's Cup

Jun [day undetermined]
Drills and Exercises, Schoolship "St. Mary's"

Jul [day undetermined]
The Burglar's Slide for Life
Coney Island at Night
Hippodrome Races, Dreamland, Coney Island
[On] a [Good Ole] 5¢ Trolley Ride
Raffles, the Dog
Stolen by Gypsies
The Whole Dam Family and the Dam Dog

Aug [day undetermined]
The Electric Mule
Empire State Express, the Second, Taking Water on the Fly
June's Birthday Party
Mystic Shriners' Day, Dreamland, Coney Island
Scenes and Incidents, Russo-Japanese Peace Conference, Portsmouth, N.H.
Sep [day undetermined]
The Boarding School Girls
The Little Train Robbery
The White Caps
Oct 5 Poor Algy
Oct 24 The Watermelon Patch
Nov 2 Down on the Farm
Nov 6 The Miller's Daughter
Nov 15 Everybody Works but Father
Nov 27 The Train Wreckers
Dec [day undetermined]
The Night Before Christmas
Dec 5 Life of an American Policeman
1906
Feb [day undetermined]
Dream of a Rarebit Fiend
Mar [day undetermined]
Phoebe Snow
Apr [day undetermined]
A Winter Straw Ride
Jun [day undetermined]
Life of a Cowboy
The Terrible Kids
Three American Beauties
Jul [day undetermined]
Waiting at the Church
Aug [day undetermined]
Arrival Mahukona Express, Kohala, Hawaii
Hauling Sugar Cane, Kohala Plantation, Hawaii
Hawaiians Arriving to Attend a Luau or Native Feast
Hawaiians Departing to Attend a Luau or Native Feast
How the Office Boy Saw the Ball Game
Kathleen Mavoureen
S. S. "Kinau" Landing Passengers, Mahukona, Hawaii
Shearing Sheep, Humunla Ranch, Hawaii
Sheep Coming Through Chute, Humunla Ranch, Hawaii
Washing Sheep, Humunla Beach, Hawaii
Oct [day undetermined]
Getting Evidence, Showing the Trials and Tribulations of a Private Detective
Nov [day undetermined]
The Honeymoon at Niagara Falls
1907
Feb 2 Crowds Returning from the Games, Waikiki, H.I.
The "Float," Waikiki, Honolulu, Hawaiian Islands
Kanaka Fishermen Casting the Throw Net, Hilo, H.I.
Loading Sugar, Kahului, Maui, H.I.
Native Hawaiian Guards in Bayonet Exercises, H.I.
Pa-u Riders, Hawaiian Island
Panoramic View, Crater of Haleakala, H.I.
Panoramic View, Honolulu Harbor, H.I.
Panoramic View, King St. Honolulu, H.I.
Panoramic View, Oahu Railroad, Haleiwa, H.I.
Panoramic View, Oahu Railroad, Pearl Harbor, Hawaiian Islands
Panoramic View of Waikiki Beach, Honolulu, H.I.
Panoramic View, Waikiki, from an Electric Car, H.I.
S. S. "Kinau" Landing Passengers, Laupahoihoi, H.I.
Scenes on a Sugar Plantation, Hawaiian Islands
Shipping Cattle, Hawaihae, Hawaiian Islands
Snapshots, Hawaiian Islands
Surf Board Riders, Waikiki, Honolulu, H.I.
Surf Scene, Laupahoihoi, Hawaiian Island
Surf Scene, Waikiki, Honolulu, H.I.
A Trip Through the Yellowstone Park, U.S.A.
Water Buffalo Wallowing, Hawaiian Island
Mar 2 The Teddy Bears
Apr 6 Daniel Boone; or, Pioneer Days in America
May 11 Fire Run, Colon Fire Department Under Cocoanut Tree
Jamaica Negroes Doing a Two-Step
Machete Men Clearing a Jungle [Panama Canal]
Making the Dirt Fly: Scene 1. Steam Shovel in Operation, Culebra Cut
Making the Dirt Fly: Scene 2. Unloading a Dirt Train
Making the Dirt Fly: Scene 3. Dirt Scraper in Operation
Making the Dirt Fly: Scene 4. Railroad Track Lifter in Operation
Making the Dirt Fly: Scene 5. Laborers Lining Up at Mess Tent
Old Market Place, Panama
Panorama from Columbus Point of Atlantic Entrance to the Canal
Panorama La Boca Harbor and Pacific Entrance to Canal
Panorama of Culebra Cut
Panorama Ruins of Old French Machinery
U. S. Sanitary Squad Fumigating a House
May 18 Lost in the Alps
Jun 29 Cohen's Fire Sale
Aug 3 The Nine Lives of a Cat
Aug 31 Stage Struck
Sep 14 Rivals
Sep 28 A Race for Millions
Oct 19 Jack the Kisser
Nov 23 Three American Beauties [No. 2]
Thomas A. Edison, Inc. *see also* **Edison Mfg. Co.; Thomas A. Edison**
1901 [month undetermined]
Fire Department of Albany, N. Y.
Jul [day undetermined]
The Fire Department of Chelsea, Mass.
1902 [month undetermined]
Skidoo-23
1903 [month undetermined]
Chicago—Michigan Football Game
1904 [month undetermined]
Convention of Red Men, Lancaster, Pa.
Apr 20 Camel Caravan, Pekin, China
Jun [day undetermined]
Atlantic City Floral Parade
Parade, Fiftieth Anniversary Atlantic City, N. J.
1905 [month undetermined]
[Launching the Ferryboat Richmond—Staten Island]
Sep [day undetermined]
Odd Fellows Parade, Philadelphia, Pa.
Dec [day undetermined]
Spectacular Scenes During a New York City Fire
1906 [month undetermined]
Army Pack Train Bringing Supplies
Exploded Gas Tanks, U. S. Mint, Emporium and Spreckels' Bld'g.
Yale Harvard Boat Race, New London, Conn., 1906
Jun [day undetermined]
Floral Fiesta, Los Angeles, Cal.
1907 [month undetermined]
[Launching of the Salem at the Fore River Shipyards—Quincy, Mass.—July 27, 1907]
Feb [day undetermined]
Poor John
1910 [month undetermined]
The Comet
Tiger
1909
Jun 8 A Conspiracy
Victim of a Crisis
Jun 19 The Loyal Indian
A Russian Romance
The Stolen Princess
Jul 5 The Love Plotters
The Tournament Film Co.
1910
Sep 17 Cowboy and Indian Frontier Celebration
Tournament Picture Co.
1909
Oct 8 United States Military Tournament
Tyler, Walter *see* **Walter Tyler**
U. S. Film Mfg. Co.
1909
Sep 4 The Life of a Red Man
United States Film Mfg. Co. *see* **U. S. Film Mfg. Co.**
Urban, Charles, Trading Co. *see* **Charles Urban Trading Co.**
Urban-Eclipse
1907
Jan [day undetermined]
Beaver Hunt
Deer Hunt
Following in Father's Footsteps
Making Champagne
Trial Trip of the Airship "La Patrie"
Whale Fishing
Feb [day undetermined]
Indian Customs
My Master's Coffee Service
My Wife's Birthday
Skiing in Norway
Snowballing
Two Rival Peasants
Wrestling Match, Hackenschmidt
Feb 2 Carnival at Venice
Mar [day undetermined]
His First Dinner at Father-in-Law's
Mar 30 Flirting on the Sands
Napoleon and Sentry
Parody on Toreador
Apr [day undetermined]
Curious Carriage of Klobenstein
How the World Lives
Tirolean Dance
May 25 Beating the Landlord
Catastrophe in the Alps
Rogie Falls and Salmon Fishing
Jun 1 A Trip Through the Holy Land
Winter Amusements
Jun 10 The Faithful Dog; or, True to the End
Jun 22 Moving Under Difficulties
Jun 24 Comedy Cartoons
Jun 26 The Toilet of an Ocean Greyhound
Jun 29 Humors of Amateur Golf
Jul 6 Diabolo, the Japanese Top Spinner
Jul 20 Too Stout
Jul 27 The Poacher's Daughter
Aug 10 From Cairo to Khartoum
The Gypsies; or, The Abduction
Life Boat Manoeuvres
Life in a South African Gold Mine
Torpedo Attack on H. M. S. Dreadnought
Aug 17 The New Stag Hunt
Poor but Proud
Aug 24 A Big Take of Tunny Fish
The Tooth Ache
Wandering Willie's Luck
Sep 7 Irish Scenes and Types
Life in a Burmah Teak Forest
The Life of Bee
Mount Pilatus Railway
Rail Lying at Crewe
The Strength of Cheese
Sep 16 Absent Mindedness
The Amateur Hunter
Art Student's Frivolities
A Baffled Burglar
The Fly
Roumania, Its Citizens and Soldiers
Woodcutter's Daughter
Sep 23 Amongst the Reptiles
Carl Hagenbeck's Wild Animal Park at Hamburg, Germany
Conway to Dublin
Dogs Tracking Burglars
Glimpses of Erin
Oct 1 A Doctor's Conscience
Fisherman's Luck

The Great Victoria Falls
Oct 7 The Foster Cabby
The Haunted Bedroom
Madame Goes Shopping
Slavery by Circumstance
Tyrolean Alps in the Winter
A Would Be Champion
Oct 14 Crazed by a Fad
Farmer Giles' Geese
Rubberneck Reuben
Oct 19 Picturesque Wales
Slate Quarries in North Wales
There Is a Rat in the Room
Oct 28 De Beers Diamond Mines, Kimberly, S.A.
Picturesque Brittany
Through Hong Kong
Nov 4 An Anonymous Letter
King Edward on H.M.S. Dreadnought
Launch of the British Battleship Bellerophon
Nov 30 Bad Boy's Joke
Comrade Rations
Daughter's Lover in Difficulties
French Recruit
Misadventures of a Street Singer
Reedham Boys' Aquatic Sports
Simple-Minded Peasant
Stolen Child's Career
The Tattler
Unlucky Trousers
Dec [day undetermined]
Against the Law
Bulgarian Army
Cabman Mystified
The Cashier
Deaf and Dumb
Hatred
Highly Scented Bouquet
Love Levels All Ranks
Youthful Hackenschmidts
Dec 27 Burns-Moir

1908

Jan 18 Mr. Sleepy Head
Apr 11 Antics of Two Spirited Citizens
Doctor's Lunch
The Half-Moon Tavern
May 2 Cat and Dog Show
Fiji Islanders
Harvesting
Kidnapped by Gypsies
Marvelous Pacifier
Mr. Smith's Difficulties in the Shoe Store
Mrs. Stebbins' Suspicions Unfounded
The Outcast Heroine
Oyster Farming
A Ride in a Subway
The Rival Lovers
May 9 Bogus Magic Powder
Country about Rome
Environs of Naples
My Cabby Wife
May 16 Always Too Late
Australian Sports and Pastimes
The Basket Maker's Daughter
Bertie's Sweetheart
A Bohemian Romance
The Bond
The Carnival at Nice
Chair, If You Please
The Little Flower Girl
The Magic Powder
Meeting of Kings and Queens
Motoring over the Alps
A Red Man's Justice
St. Patrick's Day in New York
Schoolboy's Joke
Scotland
Stolen Boots
The Strong Man's Discretion
These Gentlemen Are with Me
Why Smith Left Home
The Winning Number
The Young Protector
Youthful Samaritan
May 30 Inventor's Son's Downfall
A Mean Man
Red Man's Revenge
River Avon
River in Norway
Rugby Match
Student's Predicament
Warsmen at Play
Jun 13 Faithful Governess Rewarded
The Old Actor
Jun 20 The Book Agent
Driven by Hunger
The Handy Man at Play
The Matterhorn
Music Which Hath No Charms
The Pony Express
A Russian Bear Hunt
Swiss Peasants' Festival
Tribulations of a Mayor
A Trip on the Venetian Canals
The Viege Zermatt Railway
Jul 4 Ancient Rome
A Bird of Freedom
Heavy Seas
The Nihilist
Scenes in Sicily
Silk Hats Ironed
Swiss Alps
An Unfortunate Mistake
Who Owns the Basket?
Jul 6 A Bad Boy
Fountains of Rome
In the Riviera
Love and Hatred
St. Marc Place
Views of New York
Jul 11 The Shipwreckers
The Stone Breaker
A Trip Through Savoy
Jul 13 The Best Remedy
The Grand Canal in Venice
Sammy's Idea
The Substitute Automatic Servant
The Triumph of Love
Jul 25 Matrimonial Stages
Physical Phenomena
Aug 1 An Embarrassing Gift
The Miraculous Flowers
Sensational Duel
Too Hungry to Eat
Aug 8 The Brigand's Daughter
The Child's Forgiveness
A Country Drama
Flower Fete on the Bois de Boulogne
The French Airship La Republique
German Dragoons Crossing the Elbe
Grand Prix Motor Race at Dieppe
The Gypsy and the Painter
The Gypsy Model
Moscow Under Water
The Rag Pickers' Wedding
Reedham Boys' Festival Drill
Royal Voyage to Canada
The Tempter
Trooping the Colour
Tyrolean Alps Customs
Sep 12 Amateur Brigands
The Asphalters' Dilemma
The Blind Woman's Daughter
The Dover Pageant
The Ever-Laughing Gentleman
Goodwood Races
The Hand-Cart Race
King Edward and the German Emperor at Friedrichshof
The Marathon Race
Olympic Regatta at Henley
Quebec
Quebec to Niagara
The Signalman's Sweetheart
The Son's Crime
A Stern Father
The Swimming Master
Traveling Through Russia
The Wrong Lottery Number
Oct 10 Military Swimming Championship
Nov 9 The Gorges of the Tarn
The Lake of Garda, Italy
Monty Buys a Motor
The Quick Change Mesmerist
The Scare Crow
A Tyrolean Paradise
Nov 14 The Prehistoric Man
Nov 17 A Visit to Compiegne and Pierrefond
Dec 19 Hobo on a Bike

1909

Jan 11 A Gypsy's Jealousy
Jan 16 The Captain's Love
Jan 18 Troubled Artists
Feb 1 The Living Wreck
Feb 10 The Double's Fate
Feb 16 The American Fleet at Sydney, New South Wales
Outwitted
Feb 24 Joel's Wedding
Mar 3 An Embarrassing Present
The Sailor's Belt
Mar 10 Mother-in-Law's Day in the Country
Rivalry
South American Indians
Mar 17 The Celebrated Mountain Climbers
Cremation on the River Ganges
Master Goes Shopping
Mar 24 I Have Lost Toby
Mr. Pallet Goes Out Landscaping
Mar 31 Arabian Horsemen
Benevolent Employer
Apr 7 Inviting His Boss for Dinner
On the Brink of the Precipice
Apr 17 A Bachelor's Persistence
A Plot Foiled
Apr 24 Found on the Rocks
The Squire and the Noble Lord
May 5 Forgotten
The Peddler's Reward
May 12 Bamboo Pole Equilibrist
A Timely Apparition
Wilbur Wright and His Majesty King Edward VII
May 19 Caught on the Cliffs
Objections Overcome
May 26 How Jones Paid His Debts
Panther Hunting on the Isle of Java
Jun 2 Tender Cords
Jun 9 The Race Course
Two Heroes
Jun 16 Modern Algeria
The New Footman
Jun 23 Mrs. Simpson's Attractiveness
Winning a Princess
Jun 30 The Phantom Sirens
Rulers of the World
Jul 7 Exciting Steeple-Chase
The Pretty Fisher-Maiden
Jul 14 Conchita, the Spanish Belle
Jul 21 The King's Conspiracy
Jul 28 His Rival's Hand
Parks in Berlin
Aug 4 Stripping a Forest in Winter
The Turning Point
Aug 7 Baby Is King
The Hidden Treasure
Aug 18 Building Barrels
The Strikers
Aug 21 The King's Protege
Up the Mountain from Hong Kong
Aug 31 The French Battleship "Justice"
Sep 4 In Hot Pursuit
Romantic Italy
Sep 15 The Fatal Love
Pontine Marshes, Italy
Sep 18 Aeroplane Contests at Rheims
The Farmer's Treasure
Sep 28 Breach of Promise
Wife or Child
Sep 29 Chasing the Ball
Love, the Conqueror
Oct 6 Gambling Passion
Yachting off Cowes
Oct 20 Casting Bread upon the Water
Crown Prince of Germany Drilling Battery
Oct 27 Awakened Memories
Volcanoes of Java
Nov 3 Tale of the Fiddle
"Ursula," World's Fastest Motor Boat
Nov 10 A Heavy Gale at Biarritz
The Robber Duke
Nov 17 Fighting Suffragettes
Nov 23 Belle of the Harvest
Marriage of Love
Dec 8 The Secret Chamber
Dec 15 The Red Signal
Switzerland, Conquering the Alps
Dec 22 Fiorella, the Bandit's Daughter

From the Fighting Top of a Battleship in Action
Dec 29 The Park of Caserta
1910
Jan 5 Shanghai of To-day
Tragedy at the Mill
Jan 12 Home of the Gypsies
True to His Oath
Jan 19 The Coast Guard
Riva, Austria, and the Lake of Garda
Jan 26 Tommy in Dreamland
Feb 2 The Might of the Waters
Sheltered in the Woods
Feb 9 Coals of Fire
Venetian Isles
Feb 16 The Acrobatic Fly
The Blue Swan Inn
Feb 23 The Buried Secret
A Family Outing
Mar 2 From Beyond the Seas
Mar 9 At the Bar of Justice
The Water-Flyer
Mar 16 The Country Schoolmaster
A Trip Along the Rhine
Mar 23 A Maid of the Mountains
Over the Appennines of Italy
Mar 30 Making Sherry Wine at Xeres
The Midnight Escape
Apr 6 The Fly Pest
Her Father's Choice
Apr 13 The Lookout; or, Saved from the Sea
A Ramble Through the Isle of Sumatra
Apr 20 The Lover's Oracle
Trawler Fishing in a Hurricane
Apr 27 The Rival Miners
Volcanic Eruptions of Mt. Aetna
May 4 Called to the Sea
Immigrants' Progress in Canada
May 11 Purged by Fire
Roosevelt in Cairo
May 18 The Girl Conscript
Modern Railway Construction
May 25 His Wife's Testimony
Jun 1 Her Life for Her Love
Making Salt
Jun 8 The Mountain Lake
The Nightmare
Jun 15 The Gum-Shoe Kid
A Trip to Brazil
Jun 22 A Child of the Squadron
An Excursion into Wales
Jun 29 St. Paul and the Centurion
Jul 6 A Russian Spy
Tropical Java of the South Sea Islands
Jul 13 The Moonlight Flitting
The Wicked Baron and the Page
Jul 20 Pekin, the Walled City
Through the Enemy's Line
Jul 27 The Art Lover's Strategy
Mexican Domain
Aug 3 Camel and Horse Racing in Egypt
The Witch of Carabosse
Aug 10 On the Banks of the Zuyder Zee, Holland
The Silent Witness
Aug 17 Paris Viewed from the Eiffel Tower
The Rival Serenaders
Aug 24 Escape of the Royalists
Shipbuilders of Toulon
Aug 31 Buying a Bear
A Cruise in the Mediterranean
Sep 7 Ingratitude; or, The Justice of Providence
Military Kite Flying at Rheims
Sep 14 The Artisan
The Tramps
Sep 21 A Corsican Vendetta
Scenes in the Celestial Empire
Sep 28 The Quarrel
Reedham's Orphanage Festival, 1910
Oct 5 City of the Hundred Mosques, Broussa, Asia Minor
The Dishonest Steward
Oct 12 Foiled by a Cigarette; or, The Stolen Plans of the Fortress
Oct 19 In the Shadow of the Night
Tunny Fishing off Palermo, Italy
Oct 26 In the Spreewald
The Signet Ring
Nov 9 Secret of the Cellar
A Trip Through Scotland
Nov 16 An Alpine Retreat
The Rival Barons
Nov 23 Behind a Mask
Nantes and Its Surroundings
Nov 30 Ramble Through Ceylon
The Return at Midnight
Dec 7 The Death of Admiral Coligny
Dec 14 The Little Matchseller's Christmas
Scenes in British India
Dec 21 A Chamois Hunt
The Tyrant of Florence
Dec 28 Coaching in Devonshire, England
A Mexican Romance

Vesuvio Films
1910
Apr 5 Love and Art

Vitagraph Co. of America
1903
Jan [day undetermined]
The Soldier's Return
Mar 21 Life of a London Fireman
The Workman's Paradise
1905
Sep 23 Raffles, the Amateur Cracksman
Sep 30 The Servant Girl Problem
Oct 14 The Adventures of Sherlock Holmes; or, Held for a Ransom
License No. 13; or, The Hoodoo Automobile
Oct 21 Vanderbilt Auto Race
Oct 28 Black and White; or, The Mystery of a Brooklyn Baby Carriage
Nov 4 The Escape from Sing Sing
Nov 18 Burglar Bill
Nov 25 Moving Day; or, No Children Allowed
Dec 2 The Green Goods Man; or, Josiah and Samanthy's Experience with the Original "American Confidence Game"
Monsieur Beaucaire, the Adventures of a Gentleman of France
The Newsboy
Oh! You Dirty Boy!
Dec 30 Man Wanted
1906 [month undetermined]
Circular Panorama of Market St. and Stockton
General Circular Panorama of the Burned Business District
Great Railroad Panorama Through Colorado
Juvenile Chicken Thieves
Military Feeding Starving and Destitute Refugees in Golden Gate Park
Panorama of Market Street, San Francisco
Panoramic View of Van Ness Ave.
Park Lodge, Golden Gate Park
A Strenuous Wedding
Wealthy but Homeless Citizens of San Francisco Cooking Their Meals in the Open Air at Jefferson Sq.
Wrecked Mansions Along Van Ness Avenue
Jan [day undetermined]
Flags and Faces of All Races
Post No Bills
Feb [day undetermined]
The Flat Dwellers
The Man with the Ladder and the Hose
The Modern Oliver Twist; or, The Life of a Pickpocket'
Mar [day undetermined]
The Lost Collar Button; or, A Strenuous Search
Please Help the Blind; or, A Game of Graft
Stop Thief
Apr [day undetermined]
Humorous Phases of Funny Faces
Nobody Works Like Father
May [day undetermined]
Dynamiting Ruins and Pulling Down Walls in San Francisco
Love vs. Title; or, An Up-to-Date Elopement
Oh! That Limburger, the Story of a Piece of Cheese
Jun [day undetermined]
All Aboard! or, Funny Episodes in a Street Car
The Jail Bird and How He Flew, a Farce Comedy Escape
The Prospectors, a Romance of the Gold Fields
Jul [day undetermined]
The Acrobatic Burglars
The 100 to 1 Shot; or, A Run of Luck
The Snapshot Fiend; or, Willie's New Camera
Aug [day undetermined]
Pals; or, My Friend, the Dummy
Secret Service; or, The Diamond Smugglers
Sep [day undetermined]
The Automobile Thieves
Great Naval Review
The Indian's Revenge; or, Osceola, the Last of the Seminoles
William Jennings Bryan
Oct [day undetermined]
Mother-in-Law, a Domestic Comedy
A Race for a Wife
Nov [day undetermined]
And the Villain Still Pursued Her; or, The Author's Dream
Dec [day undetermined]
A Mid-winter Night's Dream; or, Little Joe's Luck
1907
Jan [day undetermined]
Foul Play; or, A False Friend
Jan 19 The Mechanical Statue and the Ingenious Servant
Feb 2 The Bad Man: A Tale of the West
Feb 9 Fun in a Fotograf Gallery
Feb 23 The Haunted Hotel; or, The Strange Adventures of a Traveler
Mar 9 The Spy, a Romantic Story of the Civil War
Mar 16 A Curious Dream
Mar 30 The Belle of the Ball
Retribution; or, The Brand of Cain
Apr 6 The Hero
Apr 13 Amateur Night; or, Get the Hook
Apr 27 The Flat Dwellers; or, The House of Too Much Trouble
On the Stage; or, Melodrama from the Bowery
May 4 The Pirates' Treasure; or, A Sailor's Love Story
May 18 The Stolen Pig
May 25 A Horse of Another Color
A Square Deal; or, The End of a Bad Man
Jun 1 Forty Winks; or, A Strenuous Dream
One Man Baseball
Jun 8 The Bunco Steerers; and, How They Were Caught
How to Cure a Cold
Jun 15 The Slave, a Story of the South Before the War
Jun 22 The Awkward Man; or, Oh! So Clumsy
Jun 29 The Bandits; or, A Story of Sunny Italy
Jul 6 The Wrong Flat; or, A Comedy of Errors
Jul 13 Lost in an Arizona Desert
Oliver Twist
The Window Demonstration
Jul 20 Father's Quiet Sunday
Jul 27 Elks' Convention Parade
Elks' Convention Parade: "Spirit of '76" and Views of the Grand Stand
Lightning Sketches
Aug 3 Athletic American Girls
The Boy, the Bust and the Bath
Aug 10 The Bargain Fiend; or, Shopping a la Mode
A Double-Barreled Suicide
The Easterner, or, A Tale of the West
White Man's First Smoke; or, Puritan Days in America
Aug 13 The Baby Elephant
Aug 17 The Starving Artist, or, Realism in Art
Aug 24 Man, Hat and Cocktail, a New Drink, but an Old Joke
Two Thousand Miles Without a Dollar
Aug 31 Bathing Under Difficulties
Sep 7 The Fountain of Youth
Liquid Electricity; or, The Inventor's Galvanic Fluid
Sep 14 Cast Up by the Sea

The Ghost Story
Sep 21 The Disintegrated Convict
Sep 28 The Burglar; or, A Midnight Surprise
The Mill Girl, a Story of Factory Life
Purchasing an Automobile
Oct 5 The Gypsy's Warning
Oct 12 The Piker's Dream, a Race Track Fantasy
Oct 19 The Masquerade Party
Oct 26 The Inquisitive Boy; or, Uncle's Present
The Veiled Beauty; or, Anticipation and Realization
Nov 2 The Kitchen Maid's Dream
The Soldier's Dream
Nov 9 A Little Hero
The Twin Brother's Joke
Nov 16 A Crazy Quilt
A Fish Story
Nov 23 The Despatch Bearer; or, Through the Enemy's Lines
Nov 30 The Burglar and the Baby
Under False Colors
Dec [day undetermined]
Lost, Strayed or Stolen
The Shaughraun, an Irish Romance
Dec 7 Laughing Gas
The Need of Gold
Dec 14 A Tale of the Sea
Dec 21 A Clown's Love Story
A Night in Dreamland
Dec 28 The Miser's Hoard
Work Made Easy

1908

Jan 4 An Indian Love Story
The Jealous Wife
Jan 18 The Last Cartridge, an Incident of the Sepoy Rebellion in India
Feb 1 Caught, a Detective Story
A Cowboy Elopement
The Intermittent Alarm Clock
Sold Again
The Thieving Hand
Feb 8 Francesca da Rimini; or, The Two Brothers
Galvanic Fluid; or, More Fun with Liquid Electricity
Feb 15 A Comedy of Errors
Feb 29 The Deceiver
The Farmer's Daughter; or, The Wages of Sin
House to Let; or, The New Tenants
Mashing the Masher
Mar 1 Too Much Champagne
Mar 8 The Story of Treasure Island
Mar 15 At the Stage Door; or, Bridget's Romance
A Child's Prayer; or, The Good Samaritan
For He's a Jolly Good Fellow
Mar 21 The Money Lender
Mar 28 The Tale of a Shirt
Mar 29 Cupid's Realm; or, A Game of Hearts
Apr [day undetermined]
The Dancing Legs
Dora: A Rustic Idyll
Apr 4 A Mexican Love Story
Apr 5 The Fresh-Air Fiend; or, How He Was Cured
Apr 12 After Midnight; or, A Burglar's Daughter
Jealousy
Troubles of a Flirt
Who Needed the Dough?
Apr 19 Macbeth, Shakespeare's Sublime Tragedy
Apr 25 The Airship; or, 100 Years Hence
True Hearts Are More Than Coronets
May 2 The Drummer's Day Off
Indian Bitters; or, The Patent Medicine Man
Parlez Vous Francais? (Do You Speak French?)
Turning the Tables; or, Waiting on the Waiter
What One Small Boy Can Do
A Wife's Devotion
May 9 The Flower Girl
A Mother's Crime
She Wanted to Be an Actress
Tit for Tat; or, Outwitted by Wit
May 16 The Gambler
A Good Boy
Nellie, the Beautiful Housemaid
An Odd Pair of Limbs
May 23 Bill, the Bill Poster, and Pete, the Paperhanger
He Got Soap in His Eyes
A Lover's Ruse; or, The Miser's Daughter
The Orphan; or, A Mountain Romance
May 30 A Fool and His Money Are Soon Parted; or, The Prodigal Son
Up-to-Date
A Husband's Revenge; or, The Poisoned Pills
The Salt Did It; or, If You Want To Catch a Bird, Put Salt on It's [sic] Tail
Jun [day undetermined]
East Lynne; or, Led Astray
Jun 6 The Braggart; or, What He Said He Would Do and What He Really Did
Romeo and Juliet, a Romantic Story of the Ancient Feud Between the Italian Houses of Montague and Capulet
The Two Traveling Bags; or, The Adventures of Percy White and Pauline Wells
Jun 13 Circumstantial Evidence, or, An Innocent Victim
Gratitude
A Noble Jester; or, Faint Heart Never Won Fair Lady
When Casey Joined the Lodge
Jun 20 A Bachelor's Baby; or, A General Misunderstanding
The Determined Lovers; or, Where There's a Will, There's a Way
The Reprieve, an Episode in the Life of Abraham Lincoln
The Selfish Man
Jun 27 Avenged; or, The Two Sisters
Leap Year Proposals of an Old Maid
The Patriot; or, The Horrors of War
The Story the Boots Told
Jul 4 The Chorus Girl
Mother-in-Law and the Artist's Model
A Rustic Heroine; or, In the Days of King George
A Tragedy of Japan
Jul 11 Get Me a Stepladder
The Guilty Conscience
John's New Suit; or, Why He Didn't Go to Church
'Twixt Love and Duty
Jul 18 The Chieftain's Revenge; or, A Tragedy in the Highlands of Scotland
The Mourners; or, A Clever Undertaking
Stricken Blind; or, To Forgive Is Divine
The Wish Bone
Jul 25 Lady Jane's Flight, a 17th Century Romance
Levitsky's Insurance Policy; or, When Thief Meets Thief
A Policeman's Dream
The Press Gang; or, A Romance in the Time of King George III
Aug [day undetermined]
H. R. H. The Prince of Wales Decorating the Monument of Champlain and Receiving Addresses of Welcome from the Mayor of Quebec, the Governor General of Canada and Vice-President Fairbanks, Representative of the United States
H. R. H. The Prince of Wales Viewing the Grand Military Review on the Plains of Abraham, Quebec
Aug 1 Captured by Telephone
The Female Politician, Mrs. Bell, Is Nominated for Mayor
Love Laughs at Locksmiths, an 18th Century Romance
The Viking's Daughter, the Story of the Ancient Norsemen
Aug 8 An Indian's Honor
The Little Detective
The Promise! Henri Promises Never to Gamble Again
The Water Sprite, a Legend of the Rhine
Aug 15 Buried Alive; or, Frolics on the Beach at Coney Island
The Gypsy's Revenge
The Kind-Hearted Bootblack; or Generosity Rewarded
The Poisoned Bouquet, an Italian Tragedy of the XV Century
Tercentenary Celebrations to Commemorate the 300th Anniversary of the Founding of Quebec by Champlain
Aug 22 Just Plain Folks, the Story of a Simple Country Girl
The Merry Widower; or, The Rejuvenation of a Fossil
Aug 29 Biscuits Like Mother Used to Make
The Discoverers, a Grand Historical Pageant Picturing the Discovery and Founding of New France, Canada
How Simpkins Discovered the North Pole
Lonely Gentleman; or, Incompatibility of Temper
Salome; or, The Dance of the Seven Veils
Sep [day undetermined]
The Mardi Gras Parade at Coney Island
Reception for the Victorious Olympic Team of American Athletes at City Hall, New York
Sep 5 The Clown's Christmas Eve
The Dumb Witness
In the Days of the Pilgrims, a Romance of the 15th Century in America
Western Courtship, a Love Story of Arizona
Sep 12 By a Woman's Wit
The Wages of Sin, an Italian Tragedy
A Workingman's Dream
Sep 19 Bathing; or, Charlie and Mary in the Country
The Stolen Plans; or, The Boy Detective
A Tale of a Harem: The Caliph and the Pirate
Willie's Fall from Grace
Sep 26 Her Newsboy Friend
Sep 28 Richard III, a Shakespearian Tragedy
Oct 3 Duty Versus Revenge
The Professor's Trip to the Country; or, A Case of Mistaken Identity
Oct 4 The Gambler and the Devil
A Romance of the Alps
Oct 10 Leah, the Forsaken
Oct 11 The Naughty Little Princess
Two Broken Hearts, the Story of a Worthless Husband and a Faithful Dog
Oct 17 An Auto Heroine; or, The Race for the Vitagraph Cup and How It Was Won
A Spanish Romance
Two's Company, Three's a Crowd
Oct 24 A Dearly Paid for Kiss
The Merry Widow Hat
A Night Out; or, He Couldn't Go Home until Morning
The Witch
Oct 27 House Cleaning Days; or, No Rest for the Weary
The Mummer's Daughter
Oct 31 The Renunciation
Nov 1 The Stage-Struck Daughter
Nov 3 Antony and Cleopatra, the Love Story of the Noblest Roman and the Most Beautiful Egyptian
Nov 7 Barbara Fritchie, the Story of a Patriotic American Woman
Yens Yensen, The Swedish Butcher Boy; or, Mistaken for a Burglar
Nov 10 The Right of the Seigneur
Two Affinities; or, A Domestic Reunion
Nov 14 The Inn of Death, an Adventure in the Pyrenees Mountains
The Jealous Old Maid; or, No One to Love Her
Nov 17 The Elf King, a Norwegian Fairy Tale
Nov 21 The Shoemaker of Coepenick
A Tale of the Crusades
Nov 24 A Lover's Stratagems
The Peasant Girl's Loyalty
Nov 28 Charity Begins at Home, a Story of the South During the Civil War

The Miner's Daughter
Dec 1 Julius Caesar, an Historical Tragedy
Dec 5 How Jones Saw the Carnival
A Summer Idyl
Dec 8 Making Moving Pictures
Dec 12 Christmas in Paradise Alley
Slippery Jim's Repentance
Dec 15 Sheridan's Ride
Slumberland
Dec 19 The Dancer and the King, a Romantic Story of Spain
Weary's Christmas Dinner
Dec 22 The Merchant of Venice
Dec 26 The Flower Girl of Paris
The Hazers
Dec 29 A Dream of Wealth, a Tale of the Gold Seekers of '49
Monkeyland, a Jungle Romance

1909

Jan 2 Cure for Bashfulness
A Sister's Love, a Tale of the Franco-Prussian War
Jan 5 The Bride of Lammermoor, a Tragedy of Bonnie Scotland
The Painting
Jan 9 He Went to See the Devil Play
A Telepathic Warning, the Story of a Child's Love for Her Father
Jan 12 The Castaways
The Heroine of the Forge
Jan 16 The Bride of Tabaiva
The Two Sons
Jan 19 Ruy Blas
Jan 23 A Case of Spirits; or, All's Well That Ends Well
A Colonial Romance
Jan 26 The Love of the Pasha's Son, a Turkish Romance
The Treasure; or, The House Next Door
Jan 30 Cleopatra's Lover; or, A Night of Enchantment
Feb 2 The Deacon's Love Letter
The Marathon Race; or, How Tom Paid Off the Mortgage
Feb 6 The Great Earthquake in Sicily
Virginius
Feb 9 A Clever Trick
Jessie, the Stolen Child
Feb 13 An Irish Hero
Lost in a Folding Bed
Feb 16 The Honor of the Slums
How the Kids Got Even
Feb 20 C. Q. D.; or, Saved by Wireless, a True Story of "The Wreck of the Republic"
Feb 23 The Perpetual Proposal; or, An Ardent Wooer
The Poor Musician
Feb 27 Saul and David: The Biblical Story of the Shepherd Boy Who Became King of the Israelites
Mar 2 And His Coat Came Back
Mogg Megone, an Indian Romance
Mar 6 A Day in Washington, the Capital of the United States, Showing Many Points of Interest
Inauguration of President William H. Taft
Mar 9 Adventures of a Drummer Boy
Parted, but United Again
Mar 13 Kenilworth
Mar 16 A Cure for Rheumatism
A Home at Last
Mar 20 A Brave Irish Lass, the Story of an Eviction in Ireland
A Friend in the Enemy's Camp
Mar 23 Cohen at Coney Island
Cohen's Dream of Coney Island
Mar 27 King Lear
Mar 30 Children of the Plains, an Episode of Pioneer Days
The Wooden Indian
Apr 3 The Auto Maniac
The Shepherd's Daughter
Apr 6 The Life Drama of Napoleon Bonaparte and Empress Josephine of France
Apr 10 Napoleon: the Man of Destiny
Apr 13 A Marriage of Convenience
A Tax on Bachelors
Apr 17 Forgiven; or, Father and Son
Student Days
Apr 20 The Dynamite Waistcoat
Outcast, or Heroine
Apr 24 A Faithful Fool
The Lost Sheep
Apr 27 A Belated Meal
His First Girl
May 1 The Marathon Craze
The Sculptor's Love
May 4 Grin and Win; or, Converted by a Billiken
Plain Mame; or, All That Glitters Is Not Gold
May 8 Where There's a Will There's a Way
May 11 For Her Country's Sake
The Infernal Machine
May 15 Dime Novel Dan
A False Accusation, a Story of Paternal Devotion
May 18 Bridget on Strike
Teddy in Jungleland
May 22 Jepthah's Daughter, a Biblical Tragedy
The Judgment of Solomon
May 25 Cigarette Making: From Plantation to Consumer
Old Sweethearts of Mine, a Phantasy in Smoke
May 29 The Empty Sleeve; or, Memories of By-Gone Days
He Couldn't Dance, but He Learned
Jun 1 Oliver Twist
Jun 5 The Oriental Mystic
The Truer Lover
Jun 8 A Friend in Need Is a Friend Indeed
Mr. Physical Culture's Surprise Party
Jun 12 Caught at Last
A Romance of Old Mexico
Jun 15 The Foundling—A Dressing Room Waif
Jun 19 A Maker of Diamonds
The Plot That Failed
Jun 22 The Duke's Jester; or, A Fool's Revenge
Jun 26 The Old Organ
The Troubles of an Amateur Detective
Jun 29 Washington under the British Flag
Jul 3 Washington Under the American Flag
Jul 6 The Dramatist's Dream
Led Astray
Jul 10 Mine at Last
Wearybones Seeks Rest, and Gets It
Jul 13 The Cobbler and the Caliph
Ski-ing at Ispheming, Mich.
Jul 17 The Birth and Adventures of a Fountain Pen
The Magic Fountain Pen
Jul 20 The Adventures of Fifine
Instruction by Correspondence
Jul 24 The Sword and the King
Jul 27 The Little Orphan; or, All Roads Lead to Rome
Midwinter Sports
Jul 31 The Artist's Revenge
A Georgia Wedding
Aug 3 The Bugle Call
The Truant; or, How Willie Fixed His Father
Aug 7 A Woman's Way
Aug 10 For Her Sweetheart's Sake
Princess Nicotine; or, The Smoke Fairy
Aug 14 The Gift of Youth, a Fairy Story
The Obdurate Father
Aug 17 The Judge's Whiskers and the Magic Hair Restorer
Liberty for an Hour; or, An Act of Unselfishness
Aug 21 The Way of the Cross, the Story of Ancient Rome
Aug 24 Borrowed Clothes; or, Fine Feathers Make Fine Birds
Judge Not That Ye Be Not Judged
Aug 28 The Evil That Men Do
Aug 31 The Hunchback
Niagara in Winter Dress
Sep 4 The Galley Slave
Sep 7 The Fisherman; or, Men Must Work and Women Must Weep
He Tried on Hand Cuffs
Sep 11 An Alpine Echo; or, The Symphony of a Swiss Music Box
Sep 14 The Little Father; or, The Dressmaker's Loyal Son
The Wealthy Rival; or A Summer Story That Needs No Explanation
Sep 18 The Marble Heart; or, The Sculptor's Dream
Sep 21 The Siren's Necklace
The Unspoken Goodbye
Sep 25 Fantine; or, A Mother's Love
Sep 27 Grand Naval Parade
Sep 28 Onawanda; or, An Indian's Devotion
The Romance of an Umbrella
Sep 30 Historic Parade
Oct 2 The Scales of Justice
Oct 4 Commander R. E. Peary
Military Parade
Oct 5 Betty's Choice
Never Eat Green Apples
Oct 9 For Her Sake; or, Two Sailors and a Girl
Oct 12 Red Wing's Gratitude
Too Many on the Job
Oct 16 The Diver's Remorse
Oct 19 A Dull Knife
The Mexican's Revenge
Oct 23 Cosette
Oct 26 He Fell in Love with His Wife
The Two Mr. Whites
Oct 30 Entombed Alive
[Judge Gaynor and Hon. John H. McCooey]
Nov 2 Adele's Wash Day
Miss Annette Kellerman
Nov 6 From Cabin Boy to King
Nov 9 Into the Shadow
A Sticky Proposition
Nov 13 Launcelot and Elaine
Nov 16 Benedict Arnold
Indian Basket Making
Nov 20 The Sins of the Fathers
Nov 23 Why They Married
Nov 27 Jean Valjean
Nov 30 The Bridegroom's Joke
Dirigible Balloons at St. Louis
Dec 4 The Life of Moses
Dec 7 A Day with Our Soldier Boys
A Lesson in Domestic Economy
Dec 11 Gambling with Death
Dec 14 A Merry Christmas and a Happy New Year
The Professor and the Thomas Cats
Dec 18 Two Christmas Tides
Dec 21 The Cook Makes Madeira Sauce
The Forgotten Watch
Dec 25 A Midsummer Night's Dream
Dec 28 The Power of the Press

1910

Jan 1 Cupid and the Motor Boat
Jan 4 Forty Years in the Land of Midian [The Life of Moses Part II]
Jan 8 Richelieu; or, The Conspiracy
Jan 11 The Call Boy's Vengeance
The Old Maid's Valentine
Jan 15 A Sister's Sacrifice
Jan 18 The Toymaker's Secret
Jan 22 Five Minutes to Twelve
A Pair of Schemers; or, My Wife and My Uncle
Jan 25 The Plagues of Egypt and the Deliverance of the Hebrew [The Life of Moses Part III]
Jan 29 The Girl and the Judge; or A Terrible Temptation
Feb 1 Caught in His Own Trap
The Skeleton
Feb 5 Twelfth Night
Feb 8 The Passing Shadow
Feb 12 The Victory of Israel [The Life of Moses Part IV]
Feb 14 [Paris Flood Pictures]
Feb 15 The Wayside Shrine
Feb 18 Muriel's Stratagem
Trip Through North of England
Feb 19 The Promised Land [The Life of Moses Part V]
Feb 22 Paid in Full
Feb 25 A Lesson by the Sea
Feb 26 The Soul of Venice
Mar 1 An Eye for an Eye
Mar 4 On the Border Line
Mar 5 The Beautiful Snow
The History of a Sardine Sandwich
Mar 8 A Brother's Devotion

Mar 11 "Conscience;" or, The Baker Boy
Mar 12 Taming a Grandfather
Mar 15 Victims of Fate
Mar 18 The Mystery of Temple Court
Mar 19 The Courting of the Merry Widow
Mar 22 Capital vs. Labor
Mar 25 The Hand of Fate
Mar 26 The Broken Spell
Mar 29 The Indiscretion of Betty
Apr 1 The Tongue of Scandal
Apr 2 The Fruits of Vengeance
Apr 5 From Shadow to Sunshine
Apr 8 Elektra
Apr 9 The Conqueror
Apr 12 The Girl in the Barracks
Apr 15 The Call of the Heart
Apr 16 The Merry Widow Takes Another Partner
Apr 19 Love's Awakening
Apr 22 Her Sweet Revenge
Apr 23 St. Elmo
Apr 26 Through the Darkness
Apr 29 The Portrait
Apr 30 The Minotaur
May 3 The Lost Trail
May 6 One of the Finest
May 7 Mario's Swan Song
May 10 The Three Wishes
May 13 The Closed Door
May 14 The Special Agent
May 17 A Funny Story
Music Hath Charms
May 20 Out of the Past
May 21 The Wings of Love
May 24 Convict No. 796
May 27 Auntie at the Boat Race
May 28 King Edward's Funeral
The Love of Chrysanthemum
May 31 The Peacemaker
Jun 3 Davy Jones' Parrot
Jun 4 The Majesty of the Law
Jun 7 A Modern Cinderella
Jun 10 Over the Garden Wall
Jun 11 The Altar of Love
Jun 14 The Russian Lion
Jun 15 How Championships Are Won—and Lost
Jun 17 Davy Jones' Landladies
Jun 18 Col. Theodore Roosevelt's Reception
Ito, the Beggar Boy
Jun 21 The Little Mother at the Baby Show
Jun 24 A Family Feud
Jun 25 By the Faith of a Child
Jun 28 When Old New York Was Young
Jul 1 Saved by the Flag
Wilson's Wife's Countenance
Jul 2 Old Glory
Jul 5 A Boarding School Romance
Jul 6 Jeffries-Johnson World's Championship Boxing Contest, Held at Reno, Nevada, July 4, 1910
Jul 8 Between Love and Honor
Jul 9 Becket
Jul 12 Nellie's Farm
Jul 15 Her Uncle's Will
Jul 16 A Broken Symphony
Jul 19 Twa Hieland Lads
Jul 22 Davy Jones and Captain Bragg
Jul 23 Hako's Sacrifice
Jul 26 Uncle Tom's Cabin, Part 1
Jul 29 Uncle Tom's Cabin, Part 2
Jul 30 Uncle Tom's Cabin, Part 3
Aug 2 An Unfair Game
Aug 5 The Wooing O't
Aug 6 Her Mother's Wedding Gown
Aug 9 The Death of Michael Grady
Aug 12 Mrs. Barrington's House Party
Aug 13 The Turn of the Balance
Aug 16 Daisies
Aug 19 Back to Nature
Aug 20 Under the Old Apple Tree
Aug 23 The Three Cherry Pits; or, The Veteran's Honor
Aug 26 The Men Hater's Club
Aug 27 Rose Leaves
Aug 30 Jean and the Calico Doll
Sep 2 A Life for a Life
Sep 3 The Wrong Box
Sep 6 Chew-Chew Land; or, The Adventures of Dolly and Jim
A Rough Weather Courtship
Sep 9 How She Won Him
Sep 10 The Three of Them
Sep 13 The Sepoy's Wife
Sep 16 Two Waifs and a Stray
Sep 17 A Lunatic at Large
Sep 20 Jean the Matchmaker
Sep 23 A Modern Knight Errant
Sep 24 Renunciation
Sep 27 Her Adopted Parents
Sep 30 A Home Melody
Oct 1 The Bachelor and the Baby
Oct 4 Ransomed; or, A Prisoner of War
Oct 7 The Last of the Saxons
Oct 8 The Sage, the Cherub and the Widow
Oct 11 Actors' Fund Field Day
Brother Man
Oct 14 On Her Doorsteps
Oct 15 The Legacy
Oct 18 Auld Robin Grey
Oct 21 Davy Jones' Domestic Troubles
Oct 22 Clothes Make the Man
Oct 25 Jean Goes Foraging
Oct 28 Captain Barnacle's Chaperone
Oct 29 A Day on the French Battleship "Justice"
The Telephone
Nov 1 A Double Elopement
Nov 4 The Children's Revolt
Nov 5 In the Mountains of Kentucky
Nov 8 A Tale of a Hat
Nov 11 The Nine of Diamonds
Nov 12 Jean Goes Fishing
Nov 15 Drumsticks
Nov 18 The Bum and the Bomb
A Modern Courtship
Nov 19 Francesca Da Rimini
Nov 22 Suspicion
Nov 25 A Four-Footed Pest
The Statue Dog
Nov 26 Love, Luck and Gasoline
Nov 29 A Woman's Love
Dec 2 Jack Fat and Jim Slim at Coney Island
Dec 3 The Preacher's Wife
Dec 6 A Tin-Type Romance
Dec 9 He Who Laughs Last
Dec 10 The Color Sergeant's Horse
Dec 13 The Law and the Man
Dec 15 The Renowned International Aviation Meet
Dec 16 The International Motor Boat Races
Playing at Divorce
Dec 17 A Dixie Mother
Dec 20 The Light in the Window
Dec 23 Clancy
Dec 24 Jean and the Waif
Dec 27 In Neighboring Kingdoms
Dec 30 Crazy Apples
Dec 31 Where the Winds Blow

W. W. Wittig

1908

Apr 11 Gotch-Hackenschmidt Wrestling Match

Wahlstrom, E. *see* **E. Wahlstrom**

Walter G. Chase

1905 [month undetermined]
Epileptic Seizure

1906 [month undetermined]
Epileptic Seizure No. 8
Epileptic Seizure, No. 9

Walter Tyler

1908

Nov 25 Kind Old Lady

1909

Sep 18 A Tricky Convict
Sep 25 The Eccentric Barber

Walturdaw Co. Ltd.

1907

Apr 13 The Animated Pill Box
The Borrowed Ladder
Apr 20 The Bad Shilling
Eggs
Life and Customs in India
Murphy's Wake
The Naval Nursery
May [day undetermined]
A Little Bit of String
May 4 The Fatal Hand
May 18 Father's Washing Day
Papa's Letter
Spring Cleaning
The Stolen Bicycle
Jul 20 The Matinee Idol
Sep 21 The Pastry Cook and Musician
Slavery of Children

1908

Oct 10 I Would Like to Marry You

1909

May 22 Boys' Holiday
In Quest of Health
May 29 His Only Quid
Jun 5 Trollhattan in Winter
Jun 12 A False Friend
Only a Dart
Oct 5 Hot Time in Cold Quarters
Oct 7 Was It a Snake Bite?
Oct 19 Winter Sports in Hungary
Nov 6 Belgrade, Capital of Servia

Warwick Trading Co.

1899 [month undetermined]
Ritchie, the Tramp Bicyclist

1902

Sep [day undetermined]
Reproduction, Coronation Ceremonies—King Edward VII

1903

Jan 17 The Ascent of Mount Blanc
Mar 14 The Delhi Camp Railway
Logging in Canada
On the Bow River Horse Ranch at Cochrane, North West Territory
Spearing Salmon in the Rivers of the North West Territory
Apr [day undetermined]
Acquatic Sports
Ascending a Rock-Chimney on the Grand Charmoz, 11,293 feet
Ascent and Descent of the Aiguilles Des Grandes Charmoz, 11,293 feet
Breaking a Bronco
The Broncho Horse Race
Coaching in Ireland
Coaching Through the Tunnel on the Kenmere Road
Coster Sports
"The Devil of the Deep" and the Sea Urchins
A Devonshire Fair
A Duel with Knives
England's Colonial Troops
An English Prize-Fight
A Gorgeous Pageant of Princes
The Grand Canal, Venice
The Grand Panorama from the Great Schreckhorn, 13,500 feet
The House That Jack Built
A Japanese Wrestling Match
A Kennel Club Parade
A Kiss in the Tunnel
Landing Guns
Launch of Shamrock III
Life and Passion of Christ
Looping the Loop
A Majestic Stag
Man's Best Friend
Mary Jane's Mishap; or, Don't Fool with the Parafin
The Monk in the Monastery Wine Cellar
Mountain Torrents
On Horseback, Killarney
On the Grand Canal, Venice
Over London Bridge
Panorama of Alpine Peaks
Panorama of Grindelwald
Panorama of Lucerne Lake
Panorama of Queenstown
Panorama on the St. Gothard Railway
A Paper Chase
Pa's Comment on the Morning News
The Pines of the Rockies
Push Ball
Review of Native Chiefs at the Durbar
Review of the Chiefs at the Durbar
The River Shannon
Ski Jumping Competition
Spanish Bull Fight
Stag Hunting in England
A Swiss Carnival
Through the Telescope
A Triple Balloon Ascent
A Two Handed Sword Contest

Don't Go to the Law
Just in Time
Mischievous Girls
A Modern Don Juan
A Sailor's Lass
A Seaside Girl
Wild Animals
Oct 26 The Lover's Charm
Nov 16 A Drink Cure
Dumb Sagacity
Even a Worm Will Turn
Testing of a Lifeboat
A Tramp's Dream of Wealth
Nov 23 The Collar'd Herring
Dec 7 A Letter in the Sand
The Rebellious Schoolgirls
The Sticky Bicycle
1908
Jan 18 The Artful Lovers
The Viking's Bride
Feb 29 His Sweetheart When a Boy
Jealous Husband
Painless Extraction
Mar 7 The Boarder Got the Haddock
The Tricky Twins
Mar 14 The Curate's Courtship
For the Baby's Sake
The Inquisitive Fly and the Bald Head
Mar 21 The Robbers and the Jew
'Twixt Love and Duty; or, A Woman's Heroism
May 2 Freddie's Little Love Affair
The Great Trunk Robbery
The Greedy Girl
Lazy Jim's Luck
The Mission of a Flower
Portland Stone Industry
A Sacrifice for Work
Tell-Tale Cinematograph
May 9 The Doctor's Dodge
The Gambler's Wife
The Interrupted Bath
Leap Year; or, She Would Be Wed
Professor Bounder's Pills
May 16 Catching a Burglar
A Faithless Friend
Nasty Sticky Stuff
Jun 6 Father's Lesson
Hunting Deer
The Prodigal Son
Jun 13 The Man and His Bottle
Sep 5 The Hidden Hoard
The Tramp and the Purse
Sep 12 The Burglar and the Clock
Sep 26 The Thief at the Casino
Oct 10 A Den of Thieves
Oct 24 If I Catch You I Will
The Red Barn Mystery: A Startling Portrayal of the Great Marie Martin Mystery
Nov 12 Jack in Letter Box
When Women Rule
Nov 21 The Devil's Bargain
Grandpa's Pension Day
Nov 25 Kind Old Lady
Soldier's Love Token
Dec 14 A Free Pardon
Harmless Lunatic's Escape
How the Dodger Secured a Meal
The Serpent's Tooth
Dec 21 The Baby and the Loafer
Baby's Playmate
Cabby's Sweetheart
Spoof and His Monkey
1909
Apr [day undetermined]
Henpecked
Sep 18 A Tricky Convict

Williamson & Co.
1902
Sep [day undetermined]
The Hodcarriers' Ping Pong
A Photographic Contortion
A Telephone Romance
1903
Jan [day undetermined]
The Soldier's Return
Mar 21 Life of a London Fireman
The Little Match Seller
The Workman's Paradise
May 16 Spring Cleaning
Aug 1 The Elixir of Life
Nov 21 The Deserter
Down Below
Over the Garden Wall
Quarrelsome Neighbors
A Trip to Southend
Nov 28 Attack on Chinese Mission
The Bather
Bicycle Dive
Jack's Return
Stop Thief
1904
Feb [day undetermined]
Those Troublesome Boys
Apr 25 The Dear Boys Home for the Holidays
An Evil Doer's Sad End
The Wrong Poison
Dec [day undetermined]
Great Sea Serpent
Intresting Story
Oh! What a Surprise
Stowaway
1905
Aug [day undetermined]
An Affair of Honor
Nov [day undetermined]
Cake-Walk in Our Alley
Magic Cone
Magic Hair Restorer
Police Raid on a Club
Sambo
Winning a Pair of Gloves
1906
Jan [day undetermined]
Two Little Waifs
1907
Oct 12 A Day of His Own
The Sham Sword Swallower
Oct 19 Just in Time
1908
Jan 25 Pa Takes Up Physical Culture
Why the Wedding Was Put Off
Feb 8 Gabriel Grub
Home for the Holidays
Feb 15 Bobby's Birthday
Rival Barbers
The Story of an Egg
Mar 7 Duchess' Crime
Sad Awakening
Mar 14 Our New Errand Boy
Remorse
Mar 21 Poor Pa's Folly
When Our Sailor Son Comes Home
Apr 4 Big Bow Mystery
Boats
Brigand's Daughter
Getting Rid of His Dog
Moonbeams
The Orphans
The Soul Kiss
Starvelings
Struck
Terrors of the Deep
Apr 11 £100 Reward
Oct 3 The Ayah's Revenge
My Wife's Dog
1909
Apr 24 The Rival Cyclists
May 15 Tower of London
Jun 26 Bully and Recruit
Sunshine After Storm
Aug 28 Squaring the Account
Sep 4 The Boy Scouts
Sep 13 The Boy and the Convict
1910
Jun 4 Scratch as Scratch Can

The Winthrop Moving Picture Co.
1907 [month undetermined]
Dancing Boxing Match, Montgomery and Stone
The Dutch Kiddies: Montgomery and Stone
Goodbye John
Grant's Tomb
Marceline, the World-Renowned Clown of the N.Y. Hippodrome
Jul 17 Christy Mathewson, N. Y. National League Baseball Team

Winthrop Press
1906 [month undetermined]
The Auto-Somnambulist
Before the Ball
Chest and Neck Development
Clown Juggler
Deep Breathing and Chest Expansion
Developing Muscles of Back and Chest
Developing Muscles of Chest and Back
Everybody Works but Mother
Game of Chess
Good Night
Have a Light, Sir
Here's to the Prettiest
Irish Reel
It Was Coming to Him
Kisses Sweet
Mr. Butt-in-Sky
New Year's Toast
Poker in the West
She Was Good to Him
Substitute for Smoking
Taking His Medicine
Three of a Kind
Trying It on His Dog
You Won't Cut Any Ice with Me

Wittig, W. *see* **W. Wittig**

World Film Mfg. Co.
1908
Sep 19 The Amateur Bicyclist
Brother Lieutenants
Buying a Hat
The Man with the Big Mouth
A New Electrical Discovery and Its Uses
The New Houseman's Idea
The Umatilla Indians
Oct 10 The Dynamiter
Oct 19 A Desperate Chance
1909
May 17 The Intruder
Jun 7 Two Frolicking Youths
Jun 14 Ingratitude
Jun 21 The Red Man
Jun 28 The Great Rose Festival of Portland
Jul 12 The Aborigine's Devotion
Jul 31 A Game for a Life
Nov 18 The Cost of Forgetfulness
An Hour of Terror
Nov 25 President Taft in the Far West

Wrench Film Co.
1909
Mar 22 Phantom Games
May 22 Stratagem Rewarded
Jun 12 Weary Willie Wheeling
Jun 26 Winter Horseplay
Jul 10 The Interrupted Jollification
Aug 28 The Farmer's Joke
Sep 18 A Dream of Paradise
Sep 21 Carlo and the Baby
Oct 6 The Mysterious Motor
Nov 8 Father's Holiday
1910
Jul 1 The Fresh Air Fiend

Yankee Film Co.
1910
Jun 15 Jeffries on His Ranch
Jun 20 Hebrew's Gratitude
Jun 27 The Heroine of Pawnee Junction
Jul 4 The Ghetto Seamstress
Jul 11 The Pirate's Dower
Jul 18 The Right to Labor
Jul 25 The Ungrateful Daughter-In-Law
Aug 1 The United States Revenue Detective
Aug 8 The Broker's Daughter
Aug 15 The Heroic Coward
Aug 22 The Gang Leader's Reform
Aug 29 Who Killed John Dare?
Sep 5 Judge Ye Not in Haste
Sep 12 Captured by Wireless
Sep 19 The White Squaw
Sep 26 The Yankee Girl's Reward
Oct 3 Women of the West
Oct 10 The Monogrammed Cigarette
Oct 17 The Copper and the Crook
Oct 24 Solving the Bond Theft
Oct 31 The Italian Sherlock Holmes
Nov 7 Spirit of the West
Nov 14 The Case of the Missing Heir
Nov 21 Lone Wolf's Trust
Nov 28 The Heart of an Actress

Dec 2 Queen of the Nihilists
Dec 5 In the Czar's Name
Dec 9 Western Justice
Dec 12 A Fight for Millions
Dec 16 The Old Miner's Doll
Dec 19 A Ward of Uncle Sam
Dec 23 The Terror of the Plains
Dec 26 An Insane Heiress
Dec 30 The Missing Bridegroom

KEYWORD INDEX

★ The Keyword Index provides limited subject access to films based on significant words in the film titles. As many of the titles are, in fact, descriptions of content, a keyword index provides an appropriate alternative to full subject cataloguing, which will not be possible until the films have been fully cataloged. Translations of original and alternate foreign-language titles have also been used to create keyword headings, as some of the foreign-language titles contain significant words not found in their English-language release titles. In such cases, the foreign-language title from which the keyword was derived is given in parentheses following the English-language release title. Actual historical persons and geographic locations are included in the Keyword Index, as are literary works and fictional characters if they were included in film titles.

In creating the Keyword Index, no effort has been made to make value judgements concerning the significance of words other than articles, conjunctions, connectives, interjections, prepositions and pronouns, which have been eliminated. Words based on the same root, such as **Saw, See, Seeing** and **Seen**, have been grouped together under one heading (in this case **Seeing**), and where appropriate, cross-references have been created. In certain instances, readers are directed to related terms (*rt*), such as **Alcoholism** and **Drink**, which will expand the number of film titles that may be pertinent to a particular topic. When words seemed to make better sense as part of a multi-word phrase, such as **New York City**, the multi-word phrase has been used. In many cases, an attempt has been made to use separate entries for distinct meanings of terms such as **Brooklyn (New York City)** and **Brooklyn (Ship)**. Terms for geographic locations have been changed to reflect current usage; thus **Beyrouth (Syria)** is listed as **Beirut (Lebanon)**. For more complete geographic listings, readers should also consult the Geographic Index. Unlike other *Film Beginnings* indexes, the film titles in the Keyword Index are arranged alphabetically within each year of release, rather than within individual dates of release.

KEYWORD INDEX

1910 Acrobatic Exercises by the Colibris Dwarfs
The Acrobatic Fly
The Acrobat's Son
An Aerial Acrobat
He Would Be an Acrobat
Jinks Wants to Be an Acrobat
The Little Acrobat
Nick Carter as Acrobat
The Ohami Troupe of Acrobats
One-Legged Acrobats

Acropolis (Greece)
1904 Piraeus and Athens (Greece). Athens and the Acropolis

Action
1897 Buffalo Fire Department in Action
Demonstrating the Action of an Automatic Piano
Gatling Gun Crew in Action
A Maxim Gun in Action
1899 Admiral Dewey's Flagship Olympia in Action at Manila
Battleship Oregon in Action
Demonstrating the Action of a Patent Street Sprinkler of the American Car Sprinkler Co. of Worcester, Mass
Demonstrating the Action of the Cliff-Guibert Hose Reel
Demonstrating the Action of the Northrop Looms
Rotary Snowplow in Action
1900 Demonstrating the Action of Pneumatic Shell Riveters on the Underside of the Hull of a Steel Vessel. Taken for the Chicago Pneumatic Tool Co.
Demonstrating the Action of the Brown Hoisting and Conveying Machine in Unloading a Schooner of Iron Ore, and Loading the Material on the Cars
Demonstrating the Action of the Chicago Pneumatic Tool Co.'s Deck Machine
Going into Action
1901 The Boston Fire Boat in Action
Breslau Fire Department in Action
General Quarters for Action
1902 Demonstrating the Action of a Mergenthaler-Horton Basket Making Machine
Demonstrating the Action of an Agnew Mailing Machine
Demonstrating the Action of an Altman-Taylor Clover Huller
Demonstrating the Action of an Altman-Taylor Threshing Machine
German Artillery in Action
A German Torpedo Boat Flotilla in Action
Worcester High School Eight-Oared Boat Crews in Action
1903 Battleship "Indiana" in Action
The Big 4-7 Gun in Action
Chicago Fire Boats in Action
Disappearing Gun in Action
Fireboat "New Yorker" in Action
German Torpedo Boat in Action
Seattle Fire Department in Action
Torpedo Boat in Action
1905 German Torpedo Boat in Action
1906 Hoe Printing Press in Action
A Trip from Naples to Vesuvius, Showing the Volcano in Action
1909 The Consequences of a Bad Action
From the Fighting Top of a Battleship in Action
Policeman in Action

Actors and actresses
1899 Beerbohm Tree, the Great English Actor
1902 Gibson, the Eccentric American Actor
1903 Actor's Troubles
1907 The Actor Annoys the Boarders
1908 The Actor's Child
Bald Headed Actor and Fair Lady
The Old Actor
A Persistent Actor
She Wanted to Be an Actress
Why That Actor Was Late
1909 The Actor Burglar
The Actor's Baby Carriage
The Actor's Mother
Actress and Child
The Hungry Actor
The Prince and the Actor
The Romance of a Stranded Actress
The Servant of the Actress
She Would Be an Actress
Siamese Actors and Actresses Play a Siamese Drama
A Stage Romance; or, An Actor's Love
The Troubles of a Stranded Actor
1910 The Actor's Children
Actors' Fund Field Day
The Actress
The Heart of an Actress
Kean; or, The Prince and the Actor
The Stranded Actor

Acts
1897 Burglar Caught in the Act
The Pretty Typewriter; or, "Caught in the Act"
1898 Between the Acts
1900 A Four-Horse Circus Act
1901 Trapeze Disrobing Act
1902 Caught in the Act
The Deonzo Brothers in Their Wonderful Barrel Jumping Act
1903 Arab Act, Luna Park
Baby Lund in Lightning Change Act
DeVoy's Revolving Ladder Act
Double Ring Act, Luna Park
Gallery Gods Watching a Funny Act
Gilbert Saroni Preparing for His Act
1905 Latina, Dislocation Act
1909 Liberty for an Hour; or, An Act of Unselfishness

Adam
1910 Adam II — Miscellaneous

Adams Express Co.
1904 Fire, Adams Express Co.

Addresses
1897 President McKinley's Address
1903 President Roosevelt Addressing Crew of "Kearsarge"
1904 Sec'y Taft's Address & Panorama
1908 H. R. H. The Prince of Wales Decorating the Monument of Champlain and Receiving Addresses of Welcome from the Mayor of Quebec, the Governor General of Canada and Vice-President Fairbanks, Representative of the United States

Adelaide
1897 La Petite Adelaide

Adele
1909 Adele's Wash Day

Adirondacks
1898 In the Adirondacks
1900 Eccentricities of an Adirondack Canoe
A Launch Party in the Adirondacks

Adjustable
1905 The Adjustable Chair

Admiral
1897 Admiral Cigarette
1898 Admiral Cervera and Officers of the Spanish Fleet Leaving the "St. Louis"
Admiral McNair, U.S.N.
Admiral Sampson on Board the Flagship
1899 Admiral Dewey
Admiral Dewey and Mayor Van Wyck Going Down Riverside Drive
Admiral Dewey at State House, Boston
Admiral Dewey Landing at Gibraltar
Admiral Dewey Leading Land Parade
Admiral Dewey Leading Land Parade, No. 2
Admiral Dewey Leading Land Parade, (Eighth Ave.)
Admiral Dewey on the Olympia
Admiral Dewey Passing Catholic Club Stand
Admiral Dewey Receiving His Mail
Admiral Dewey Receiving the Washington and New York Committees
Admiral Dewey Taking Leave of Washington Committee on the U.S. Cruiser 'Olympia'
Admiral Dewey's Dog, "Bob"
Admiral Dewey's First Step on American Shore
Admiral Dewey's Flagship Olympia in Action at Manila
Presentation of Nation's Sword to Admiral Dewey
"Sagasta" Admiral Dewey's Pet Pig
1902 Funeral Procession of Admiral Sampson at Washington
1903 Naval Parade on the Delaware River, Monday, May 1st, in Honor of Admiral Dewey
President Roosevelt's Visit to Admiral Barker
1909 Admiral Nelson's Son
1910 The Death of Admiral Coligny

Admirers
1908 Troubles of Too Ardent Admirers
1909 Admirer of a Mustache

Admission
1908 Free Admission
1910 A Favour Admission to a Play

Ado
1909 Much Ado About Nothing

Adonis
1909 Adonis Is Robbed of His Clothes

Adoption
1907 A Christmas Adoption
1908 Madam Flirt and Her Adopted Uncle
1909 The Adopted Child
1910 The Adopted Daughter
Adopting a Child
The Adoption
The Adoption of Helen
Her Adopted Parents
How the Great Field Marshall Villars Had an Adopted Daughter

Adoration
1904 The Passion Play (L'adoration des Mages)
1910 Adoring an Ad.

Advance
1898 Advance Guard, Return of N.J. Troops
1899 Advance of Kansas Volunteers at Caloocan
1900 An Advance by Rushes
On the Advance of Gen. Wheaton
1904 Advance Guard Fight
Skirmish Between Russian and Japanese Advance Guards

Advantages
1909 Advantages of Aviation

Advent
1898 Unexpected Advent of the School Teacher

Adventures
1899 Strange Adventure of New York Drummer
1903 Robinson Crusoe (Les aventures de Robinson Crusoë)
1904 Don Quixote (Aventures de Don Quichotte)
1905 The Adventures of Sherlock Holmes; or, Held for a Ransom
An Adventurous Automobile Trip
The Curate's Adventures
Monsieur Beaucaire, the Adventures of a Gentleman of France
1906 The Clown's Adventures
In Search of Adventure
1907 The Adventures of a Bath Chair
Adventures of a Lover
The Haunted Hotel; or, The Strange Adventures of a Traveler
Horrible Adventure
Invalid's Adventure
1908 Adventures of a Beggar
Adventures of a Countryman
Adventures of an Overcoat
The Adventures of Dollie
Adventures of Mr. Troubles
Her First Adventure [Kidnapped with the Aid of a Street Piano]
The Inn of Death, an Adventure in the Pyrenees Mountains
The Two Traveling Bags; or, The Adventures of Percy White and Pauline Wells
Incident from Don Quixote (Aventures de Don Quichotte)
1909 Adventures of a Bag of Coal
Adventures of a Drummer Boy
Adventures of a Keg
Adventures of an Emigrant
The Adventures of an Old Flirt
The Adventures of Fifine
The Birth and Adventures of a Fountain Pen
Boy's Adventure
The Caliph's Adventures
The Chauffeur's Adventure
Cyrano de Bergerac's Adventure
Love of Adventures
A Midnight Adventure
Sherlock Holmes III: The Detectives Adventure in the Gas Cellar
1910 Adventure of a Millionaire
Adventures of a Cowpuncher
Adventures of a Sandwich Man
Adventures of Princess Lovelock
Alice's Adventures in Wonderland
Bonehead's Second Adventure

1900 Answering the Alarm
The Last Alarm
Morning Fire Alarm
1903 The Alarm and Hitch
A False Alarm in the Dressing Room
Fireboat "New Yorker" Answering an Alarm
General Alarm
The Still Alarm
1904 Alarm
Polish Fire Brigade Answering an Alarm, Warsaw
1906 A False Alarm
False Alarm
1908 A False Alarm
The Intermittent Alarm Clock
A Night Alarm
Stop That Alarm!
The Suburbanite's Ingenious Alarm
1909 False Alarm
The Guard's Alarm
1910 Hoodoo Alarm Clock
A New Burglar Alarm

Alaska
1899 A Hot Time in Alaska
1903 Birds-eye View of Dawson City on the Yukon River, Alaska
1905 Blasting in the Glory Hole of the Treadwell Mine, Alaska
Camp Life of the Esquimaux at Cape Nome, Alaska
Carrying Passengers Ashore Davidson Glacier, Alaska
Crazy (or Accelerated) Panoramic Approach to Taku Glacier, Alaska
The "Crazy Tourists" on the Pier at Killisnoo, Alaska
Dance at Esquimaux Camp, Cape Nome, Alaska
Dog Teams Dawson City Alaska
Embarkation by Crane and Barge at Nome City, Alaska
Esquimaux Dance, Cape Nome, Alaska
Feeding Mush Dogs, Mulato, Alaska
Fire Brigade, Dawson City, Alaska
Flap-Jack Lady of the Esquimaux, Cape Nome, Alaska
Panorama from a Moving Train on White Pass & Yukon Railway, Alaska
Playful Bear and Dog, Dawson City, Alaska
Slavonian Miners Running to Dinner, Treadwell Mine, Alaska
The "Spokane's" Passengers Descending the Gangplank at Killisnoo Alaska
Train on the White Pass & Yukon Railway, Alaska
Unloading Fish, Killisnoo Alaska
Wooding Up a River Steamer, Yukon River, Alaska

Albany (New York)
1897 Albany Day Boats
1901 Fire Department of Albany, N.Y.
1907 Albany, N.Y.

Albatross (Boat)
1900 Speed Trial of the "Albatross"

Alberno
1909 Alberno & Rosamunda

Albert Canyon, British Columbia (Canada)
1901 Panoramic View, Albert Canyon

Albert, King of Saxony
1902 King Albert of Saxony

Albula Railway (Switzerland)
1905 Panorama from Moving Train on Albula Railway, Switzerland

Album
1905 Wonderful Album
1908 Magic Album

Albuquerque (New Mexico)
1903 Carpenter Work, Albuquerque School
Fire Drill: Albuquerque Indian School
Girls' Department, Albuquerque School
Indian Boys, Albuquerque School

Alchemist
1900 The Clown and the Alchemist
1906 The Mysterious Retort (L'alchimiste Parafaragamus ou la cornue infernale)

Alcoholism
rt **Drink**
1903 What Befell the Inventor's Visitor (Le pochard et l'inventor)
1904 Alcohol and Its Victims
Drunkard and Statue
Mischances of a Drunkard
1905 Alcoholism Engenders Tuberculosis
1906 Drunkard
Obstinate Drunkard
Two Drunkards
1907 A Drink! (Le delirium tremens ou la fin d'un alcoolique)
1908 Fatherhood and Drunkenness
1909 Alcoholic Doctor
Drunkard's Child
The Drunkard's Christmas
A Drunkard's Dream
The Drunkard's Fate
A Drunkard's Reformation
A Drunkard's Son
The New Minister; or, The Drunkard's Daughter

Alcrofrisbas
1903 Alcrofrisbas, the Master Magician

Alden, Elder
1910 Elder Alden's Indian Ward

Aldershot (England)
1897 Aldershot Review
1899 The Prince of Wales (King Edward VII) at the Aldershot Review

Ale
1902 A Little Mix-Up in a Mixed Ale Joint
1904 A Bucket of Cream Ale
Too Much Mixed Ale

Alexander Grenadiers
1902 Dedication of the Alexander Grenadiers' Barracks

Alexander III
1902 Bridge of Alexander III

Alexandra, Queen consort of Great Britain
1902 Coronation of King Edward VII and Alexandra
Crowning of King Edward and Queen Alexandra
King Edward VII and Queen Alexandra, of Great Britain
King Edward and Queen Alexandra on Their Way to Westminster
1903 King Edward and Queen Alexandra Passing Through London, England

Alexandrian
1908 Alexandrian Quadrille

Alfalfa
1903 U.S. Interior Dept.: Irrigation of Alfalfa Lands

Alger, Russell Alexander
1898 General Wheeler and Secretary of War Alger at Camp Wikoff

Algeria
1904 Algerian Goums in the Desert
Secret Procession of the Algerian Tribes
Typical Algerian 'Ouled Nails' Muslin Dance
1907 Vengeance of the Algerine
1909 Arab Life in South Algeria
Modern Algeria
1910 Algerian Stud
Scenes in Algeria

Algiers (Algeria)
1906 A Spiritualistic Meeting (Le fantome d'Alger)
1910 A Bootblack's Daily Labor in Algiers

Algy
1901 Little Algy's Glorious Fourth of July
1905 Poor Algy
1906 Algy's New Suit

Ali Baba
1902 Ali Baba and the Forty Thieves
Ali Baba and the Forty Thieves (Ali Baba et les quarante voleurs)
1907 Ali Baba and the Forty Thieves

Ali Barbouyou
1907 Delirium in a Studio (Ali Barbouyou et Ali Bouf à l'huile)

Ali Bey
1909 Ali Bey's Dancing Drops

Ali Bouf
1907 Delirium in a Studio (Ali Barbouyou et Ali Bouf à l'huile)

Alice
1903 Alice in Wonderland
1910 Alice's Adventures in Wonderland
1911 Alice in Funnyland
Alice's New Year's Party

Alighting
1903 Passengers Alighting and Drinking Shasta Water

Alike
1909 The Mysterious Double; or, The Two Girls Who Looked Alike

Alive
1908 Buried Alive; or, Frolics on the Beach at Coney Island
1909 Buried Alive
Entombed Alive
1910 Entombed Alive

All-wool
1908 An All-Wool Garment

Allabad
1900 Allabad, the Arabian Wizard

Alladin
1900 Alladin and the Wonderful Lamp
1906 Alladin and His Wonder Lamp

Allah
1909 Biskra, Garden of Allah
1910 In the Name of Allah

Allard, Captain
1903 Captain Allard Shooting White Horse Rapids

Allegheny (Pennsylvania)
1902 Panoramic View from Pittsburgh to Allegheny

Allegorical
1898 Allegorical Floats
1902 Allegorical Procession

Allentown (Pennsylvania)
1902 The Swimming Ducks at Allentown [Pa.] Duck Farm
1903 Allentown Duck Farm

Alley
1900 Trouble in Hogan's Alley
1902 Bowling Alley at a German Picnic
1903 Bowling Alley
1905 Cake-Walk in Our Alley
1908 Christmas in Paradise Alley

Alliance
1899 The International Alliance

Allied Fleets
1900 Bombarding and Capturing the Taku Forts by the Allied Fleets
Bombardment of Taku Forts, by the Allied Fleets

Alligator
1900 Alligator Bait
The 'Gator and the Pickaninny
1904 Alligator Farm

Allowed
1904 No Bathing Allowed
No Posters Allowed
1905 Moving Day; or, No Children Allowed
No Bill Peddlers Allowed

Alma
1903 La Petite Alma, Baby Acrobat

Alma, M'lle
1900 M'lle Alma

Almighty
1910 The Almighty Dollar

Aloft
1898 "Away Aloft"

Alola
1909 Leap of Alola

Alone
1903 Misfortune Never Comes Alone
1904 Alone
1908 Alone at Last
If It Don't Concern You, Let It Alone
1909 The Blind Foundling; or, Alone in the World
1910 Love Your Neighbor as Yourself, but Leave His Wife Alone!

Alphonse
1902 Alphonse and Gaston
1903 Alphonse and Gaston 3
Alphonse and Gaston and the Burglar (Thumb Book)
Alphonse and Gaston Balcony Scene (Thumb Book)
Alphonse and Gaston (Journal Thumb Book)
Alphonse and Gaston Target Practice (Thumb Book)
1909 Alphonse Gets in Wrong
Alphonse, the Dead Shot

Alphonse XIII, King of Spain
1906 Marriage of Princess Ena and Alphonse XIII, King of Spain

The Russian Army in Manchuria
1906 Army Pack Train Bringing Supplies
7th Regiment at 69th Army Dedication
1907 Bulgarian Army
1908 Army Dogs
The Army of Two (An Incident During the American Revolution)
Winter Manoeuvres of the Norwegian Army
Woman's Army
1909 The Old Army Chest
The Salvation Army Lass
Ski Runners of the Italian Army
A Soldier of the U.S. Army
Spanish Army
1910 The Belgian Army
Mammy's Boy Joins the Army

Army-Navy football game
1901 President Roosevelt at the Army-Navy Game
President Roosevelt Entering Grounds at Army-Navy Football Game

Arnold, Benedict
1909 Benedict Arnold

Arranging
1910 Fabian Arranging Curtain Rods

Arrest
1896 An Arrest at New Haven, Conn.
1897 Arrest in Chinatown, San Francisco, Cal.
Making an Arrest
1898 Street Fight and Arrest
1900 Arrest of a Shoplifter
1903 Passion Play: Judas' Betrayal and the Messiah's Arrest
1904 Spy's Arrest
The Passion Play (Le baiser de Judas—l'arrestation)
1907 Difficult Arrest
1908 Hard to Get Arrested
1909 Arrest of the Orderly
Mac Nabb Wants to Get Arrested
Trying to Get Arrested
Why Mr. Jones Was Arrested
1910 The Arrest of Duchess de Berry

Arrival
1896 Tally Ho—Arrival
1897 Arrival of His Majesty, King Edward VII (then Prince of Wales) at the Ascot Races, 1897
1898 Arrival of Tokyo Train
Battery B Arriving at Camp
Steamer "Mascotte" Arriving at Tampa
1899 Arrival of Boat, Providence, R.I.
Coaches Arriving at Mammoth Hot Springs
1900 Arrival of Train at Muskoka Wharf
Arrival of Train at Paris Exposition
Overland Express Arriving at Helena, Mont.
1901 Ammunition Wagons Arriving on the Battlefield
Arrival at Falls View Station
Arrival of Funeral Cortege at St. George's Chapel
Arrival of Funeral Cortege at the City Hall, Buffalo, N.Y.
Arrival of McKinley's Funeral Train at Canton, Ohio
Arrival of Tongkin Train
Arrival of Train at Station
Arrival of Train of Cattle
The Duke and Duchess of York Arriving at Quebec
The Funeral Arriving at Hyde Park
The Funeral Cortege Arriving at Trinity Pier
1902 Arrival of Circus Trains
Arrival of Major Marchand from the Soudan
Arrival of Prince Henry [of Prussia] and President Roosevelt at Shooter's Island
Arrival of Rex
Arrival of the Governor General, Lord Minto, at Quebec
Arrival on Summit of Pike's Peak
The King and Queen Arriving at Westminster Abbey
"Kronprinz Wilhelm" with Prince Henry [of Prussia] on Board Arriving in New York
Prince Henry [of Prussia] Arriving at West Point
Prince Henry [of Prussia] Arriving in Washington and Visiting the German Embassy
Queen Wilhelmina Arriving at the Kaiser's Palace
1903 Arrival and Departure of President Loubet
Arrival of H.I.M. The German Emperor, at Port Victoria
Arrival of Humpty Dumpty
Arrival of Kaiser Wilhelm in England
Arrival of Lord and Lady Minto at the Barracks, Dawson
Arrival of the Bull Fighter
Arrival of the Circus Train, No. 1
Arrival of the Circus Train, No. 2
Arrival of Tourists at the Hotel in Yellowstone Park
Arrival of Train at Gardner
Mr. Chalmers and Mr. Gibbs Arrive at Club, National Cash Register Co.
Mr. Patterson and Mr. Mark Arriving, National Cash Register Co.
President Roosevelt's Arrival at "Kearsarge"
War Supplies Arriving at Boer Laager by Train of Ox Teams
1904 Arrival and Departure of a Train
Arrival and Departure of the Ice-Crushing Steamer "Baikal" at Baikal, Siberia
Arrival and Release of 40,000 Carrying Pigeons at Ambergate, England
Arrival of a Train
The Arrival of the 1st Siberian Sharpshooters at Harbin
1905 Arrival of the Mail Steamer at Larne
Arrival of the Stage at Wawona Hotel, Enroute to Yosemite
Arrival of Train at Oberammergau
Jaunting Cars Arriving at Dublin Horse Show
Panorama of the Sultan of Morocco's Troop Forming a Square Awaiting the Arrival of H. M. S.
Queen Margherita of Italy Arriving in Oberammergau
Train Arriving at Henley Station
Trains Arriving at Henley Station with Regatta Visitors
1906 Arrival Mahukona Express, Kohala, Hawaii
Arrival of Immigrants, Ellis Island
Arrival of Refugees at Oakland
Hawaiians Arriving to Attend a Luau or Native Feast
1907 Arrival of Lusitania
The New Arrival
1909 Arrival at the Village
1910 Mother-in-Law Arrives

Arrow
1909 The Falling Arrow
The Message of an Arrow

Arrow (Boat)
1903 Trial Run of the Fastest Boat in the World, "The Arrow"

Arson
1907 A Case of Arson

Art and artists
1898 A Country Couple's Visit to an Art Gallery
Pennsylvania Academy of Fine Arts
1899 The Artist's Dream
A Cold Day for Art
1900 The Art of "Making Up"
"Art Studies"
An Artist's Dream
Confounding the Art Critic
How the Artist Captured the Chinese Boxers
1901 The Artist's Dilemma
Artist's Point
Jiu Jitsu, the Japanese Art of Self-Defense
1902 The Crazy Artist and the Pictures That Came to Life
The Lightning Artist
1903 Artist and the Dummy
The Artists Model
The Artist's Studio
Extraordinary Black Art
The Fate of the Artist's Model
Lightning Artist
The Lightning Change Artist
U.S. Interior Dept.: Panorama from Artist's Point
1904 Art Studies
The Committee on Art
Vision of Art
1906 An Artist's Dream
Bird's Eye View from Hopkins Art Institute
1907 Art Student's Frivolities
Artistic Woodcarver
Artist's Model
The Hand of the Artist
The Starving Artist, or, Realism in Art
1908 Artistic Rag-Pickers
Artist's Inheritance
The Artist's Nightmare
The Knight of Black Art
The Lightning Postcard Artist
Mother-in-Law and the Artist's Model
Oriental Black Art
Unlucky Artist
Wanted: An Artist's Model
The Young Artist
Youthful Artist
1909 An Affair of Art
The Art of Fencing
Artful Art
The Artist and the Girl
The Artist's Dream
The Artist's Dummy
An Artist's Model's Jealousy
The Artist's Model's Sweetheart
The Artist's Revenge
The Gypsy Artist
Happy Artist
High Art
Reformation of a Wine-Loving Artist
Sam's Artistic Beard
Troubled Artists
1910 The Art Lover's Strategy
Artist's Child
Artist's Dream
Artist's Good Joke
An Artist's Inspiration
The Artist's Luck
An Artist's Temptation
Juliet Wants to Marry an Artist
Love and Art
Thieves as Quick Change Artists

Artesian
1899 Shooting an Artesian Well

Artful
1907 The Artful Dodger
Artful Husband
1908 The Artful Lovers
Mr. Simpson's Artful Ruse
1909 Artful Art
Artful Dodger

Arthur
1910 Absent Minded Arthur
Arthur's Little Love Affair

Artificial
1908 Artificial Brooding
Artificial Preparation of the Diamond

Artillery
1897 Ancient and Honorable Artillery Co.
Ancient and Honorable Artillery Parade
Battery A, Light Artillery, U.S. Army
Review of Artillery
U.S. Cavalry and Artillery
1898 Canadian Artillery Marching on Snow Shoes
Sikh Artillery, Hong Kong
1899 First Heavy Artillery
Her Majesty, Queen Victoria, Reviewing the Honorable Artillery
Mounted Artillery
1901 Artillery Drill at Annapolis
Japanese Artillery
Review of Russian Artillery
Royal Artillery and English Sailors Marching Through Hyde Park
The War in China—British Light Artillery
1902 German Artillery in Action
1903 Ancient and Honourable Artillery of London on Parade
Artillery Exercises
The Honourable Artillery Company of London
The Providence Light Artillery
Royal Horse Artillery on the March to the Front
U.S. Artillery Drill
1904 Battery "A," Rhode Island Light Artillery
1905 Battery of Artillery Crossing Ball's Bridge, Limerick, Ireland
Russian Artillery
Russian Field Artillery
Russian Mounted Artillery
1908 Manoeuvres of Artillery
1909 Artillery Manoeuvers in the Mountains
Italian Artillery

Russian Outposts Attacked by Japanese
Torpedo Attack
Torpedo Attack on Port Arthur
1905 Last Attack on the Hill
1906 Attack on Fort Boonesboro
1907 Attack on Emigrant Train
Torpedo Attack on H. M. S. Dreadnought
1909 The Attack
The Master Detective; or, The Attack on the Strong Room
Bandits of the Atlas Gorges (Dans les gorges de l'Atlas (attaque d'une diligence))
1910 The Attack on Fort Ridgely
The Attack on the Mill
The Attack upon the Train
Attacked by Arapahoes; or, The Gold Seekers and the Indians

Attell, Abe
1908 [Moran-Attell Fight]

Attempt
1899 An Attempt to Escape
1904 Attempted Murder in a Train
1907 Attempted Suicide
1909 A Terrible Attempt
1910 An Attempted Elopement

Attend
1898 Pope Leo XIII Attended by Guard
1906 Hawaiians Arriving to Attend a Luau or Native Feast
Hawaiians Departing to Attend a Luau or Native Feast
1910 The Queen's Attendant

Attention
1910 Paying Attention

Attraction
1904 Fighting the Flames [An Attraction at Coney Island]
Fire and Flames at Luna Park, Coney Island [An Attraction at Coney Island]

Attractiveness
1908 Making Home Attractive
1909 Mrs. Simpson's Attractiveness
A Very Attractive Gentleman

Auburn Prison (New York)
1901 Execution of Czolgosz, with Panorama of Auburn Prison

Auction
1904 Auction of Deserters' Effects

Aude (France)
1910 The Vale of Aude

Audience
1901 Photographing the Audience
1904 Dranem Salutes the Audience

Audley, Lady
1908 Lady Audley's Secret

August (Monkey)
1904 August, the Monkey

August (Month)
1902 King Edward Reviewing Coronation Naval Force at Spithead August 16, 1902
1903 Finish of the First Race, Aug. 22
Finish of Yacht Race, Aug. 25th
Jockeying and Start of Yacht[s] Aug. 25th
Jockeying for the Start Aug. 20
Jockeying for the Start Aug. 22
Reliance Rounding Turn, August 20th
"Reliance" vs. "Shamrock" III, Aug. 20
Start of the First Race, Aug. 22

Augusta Victoria (Boat)
1903 Passengers Embarking from S.S. "Augusta Victoria" at Beyrouth

Auld Robin Grey
1910 Auld Robin Grey

Aunt
1900 Aunt Jane's Experience with Tabasco Sauce
1901 Aunt Sallie's Wonderful Bustle
1902 Aunt Jane and the Tobasco Sauce
1903 Aunt Jane's First Lesson in Love
Auntie and the Bee
1904 Charley's Aunt
1907 Auntie's Birthday
Willie Goodchild Visits His Auntie
1908 Auntie Takes the Children to the Country
Dick's Aunt
Poor Aunt Matilda
1909 Aunt Emmy's Scrap Book
Aunt Lena's Visit
Eloping with Aunty
Eradicating Aunty
Old Aunt Hanna's Cat
1910 Aunt Hannah
Aunt Julia's Portrait
Aunt Maria's Substitute
Aunt Tabitha's Monkey
Auntie at the Boat Race
Auntie in the Fashion
My Aunt's Birthday

Austin Glen (New York)
1906 Through Austin Glen, Catskill Railway

Australia
1897 Sir Wilfred Laurier and the New South Wales Lancers
1901 Departure of Duke and Duchess of Cornwall for Australia
1904 Convoy of Oxen (Convoi de boeufs en Australie)
1906 Trip Through Australia, New Zealand
1907 Manners and Customs of Australia
Squires, Australian Champion, in His Training Quarters
1908 Australian Sports and Pastimes
Reception of the American Fleet in Australia
1910 New South Wales Gold Mine
Roller Skating in Australia
Scenes of the Australian Gold Fields

Austria
1897 Austrian Mounted Police
Emperor Francis Joseph of Austria
Emperor William of Germany, and Emperor Franz Josef of Austria
1898 Meeting of Emperor William of Germany and Emperor Franz Josef of Austria
1902 Kaiser Wilhelm, of Germany, and Emperor Franz Josef, of Austria
Visit of Emperor Francis Josef of Austria to Berlin
1909 Summering in the Austrian Alps
1910 Ancient Castles of Austria
Riva, Austria, and the Lake of Garda

Author
1906 And the Villain Still Pursued Her; or, The Author's Dream

Authority
1904 The Power of Authority

Auto boat
1904 Auto Boat Race on the Hudson River
1905 Speed Trial of Auto Boat Challenger, Lake Worth, Fla.

Auto-somnambulist
1906 The Auto-Somnambulist

Automatic
1897 Automatic Piano
Demonstrating the Action of an Automatic Piano
1899 The Automatic Prize Fight
1901 The Automatic Weather Prophet
1908 The Automatic Hotel
The Automatic Laundry
The Automatic Nurse
Automatic Statue
The Substitute Automatic Servant
1909 The Automatic Monkey
Automatic Nursing Bottle
Automatic Umbrella Seller

Automaton
1903 Clown and Automaton

Automobile
1899 Hipwood-Barrett Car Fender
1900 Automobile Parade
1901 Automobile Parade on the Coney Island Boulevard
1902 An Automobile Parade in the Tuilleries Gardens
The Clown and the Automobile
Dr. Lehwis Automobile Leaving London for a Trip Around the World
Explosion of an Automobile
1903 Automobile Explosion
Automobile Parade
Eclipse Car Fender Test
Over Route of Roosevelt Parade in an Automobile
Panorama of Factory from Automobile, National Cash Register Co.
Policeman and Automobile
1904 Automobile Ascending Mt. Snowdon
The Automobile Race
Automobile Race at Ballyshannon, Ireland
Automobile Race for the Vanderbilt Cup
Automobiling Among the Clouds
Bobby and the Automobile
The Great International Automobile Race for the Gordon-Bennett Trophy
Lady Plumpton's Motor Car
The Trials and Troubles of an Automobilist
Wheelbarrow and Automobile
1905 An Adventurous Automobile Trip
Automobile Races at Ormond, Fla.
License No. 13; or, The Hoodoo Automobile
Vanderbilt Auto Race
1906 The Automobile Thieves
Bicycle Police Chasing Scorching Auto
Motor-car and Cripple
Panorama, Russian and Nob Hill from an Automobile
The Paris-Bordeaux Auto Race
1907 Man Being Run Over by Automobile
Purchasing an Automobile
Towed by an Automobile
The Skipping Cheeses (Les fromages automobiles)
1908 An Auto Heroine; or, The Race for the Vitagraph Cup and How It Was Won
Briarcliff Auto Race
Buying an Automobile
The Mishaps of the New York-Paris Auto Race
Riviera in Motor Car
The Smuggler Automobilist
Starting of Around the World Automobile Race
1909 Atlanta Automobile Speedway Races
The Auto Maniac
The Great Automobile Race
1910 Bumptious Takes Up Automobiling
The Runaway Motor Car
24-Hour Automobile Race

Automobile Club of America
1903 Start of Endurance Run of the Automobile Club of America

Autumn
1905 Dance of the Autumn Leaves, Vevey Fete
1908 Tale the Autumn Leaves Told

Avaricious
1908 Avaricious Father

Ave Maria
1910 Gounod's 'Ave Maria'

Avenge
1904 Avenging a Crime; or, Burned at the Stake
1907 Dog Avenges His Master
1908 Avenged by the Sea
Avenged; or, The Two Sisters
1910 Avenged
The Avenging Dentist

Avenues
1896 Li Hung Chang, 5th Avenue & 55th Street, N.Y.
Union Square and Fourth Avenue
1897 5th Avenue, N.Y.
Fifth Avenue, New York
First Avenue, Seattle, Washington, No. 8
Pennsylvania Avenue, Washington
Pennsylvania Avenue, Washington, D.C.
1899 Admiral Dewey Leading Land Parade, (Eighth Ave.)
Fifth Avenue Entrance to Central Park
Third Avenue Elevated Railroad
1901 Soubrette's Troubles on a Fifth Avenue Stage Coach
1902 Panorama of Ninth Ave. Elevated R.R.
Park Avenue Explosion
St. Patrick's Cathedral and Fifth Avenue on Easter Sunday Morning [New York City]
1903 Fire at Triangle Clothing Store, 13th and Ridge Ave., Philadelphia, May 3d, 1899
Pacific Avenue, Tacoma, Wash.
Riverside Avenue, Spokane, Wash.
6th Ave. New York Elevated Railroad
Third Avenue Elevated Train, New York
1904 Pan. of Fifth Ave., Pittsburg, Pa., From a Trolley Car
1905 A Dog Lost, Strayed or Stolen. $25.00 Reward. Apply to Mrs. Brown, 711 Park Ave.
1906 City Hall from Market St. and City Hall Ave.
Panorama, City Hall, Van Ness Avenue and College of St. Ignatius
Panoramic View of Van Ness Ave.
Wrecked Mansions Along Van Ness Avenue
1910 Sunday Afternoon on Fifth Avenue

The Bad Sister
On Bad Terms with the Janitor
Peck's Bad Boy
Trying to Get Rid of a Bad Dollar
1909 A Bad Bargain
Bad Brother
A Bad Case
A Bad Case of Grip
Bad Day for Lavinsky
The Bad Lands
A Bad Shot
The Consequences of a Bad Action
The Story of a Bad Cigar
1910 The Bad Luck of an Old Rake
How a Bad Tempered Man Was Cured
Jealousy, a Bad Counsellor
Not So Bad as It Seemed

Bad Lands
1909 The Bad Lands

Baden-Powell, General
1900 Earl Roberts and General Baden Powell

Badger game
1905 The Badger Game

Badgers
1902 How Uncle Josh Defeated the Badgers
1909 Badger Hunt
1910 The Badgers

Badmen
1905 Western "Bad Man" Shooting Up a Saloon
1907 The Bad Man: A Tale of the West
A Square Deal; or, The End of a Bad Man
1910 The Bad Man and the Preacher
The Bad Man from Riley's Gulch
The Bad Man's Christmas Gift
The Bad Man's Last Deed

Baffled
1900 Sherlock Holmes Baffled
1906 Childish Tricks Baffled
1907 A Baffled Burglar
1908 Baffled Lover

Bag catcher
1903 Inside Car, Showing Bag Catcher [U.S.P.O.]

Bag punching
1897 Bag Punching by Sadie Leonard
"Spike, the Bag-Punching Dog"
1901 Laura Comstock's Bag-Punching Dog
Moline Bag Punching Platform
1902 Pugilist McKeever and Wife Bag Punching
1903 Expert Bag Punching

Bagdad (Iraq)
1908 From Bagdad

Baggage
1897 Loading Baggage for Klondike
1900 How the Dude Got the Soubrette's Baggage
1910 The Baggage Smasher

Baglag River
1899 Colonel Funston Swimming the Baglag River

Bagley, Lt.
1903 Lieut. Bagley's Funeral. Escort of Lieut. Bagley's at Raleigh, N. C.

Bagpipe
1910 The Bagpipe Player

Bags
1903 Clerks Casing Mail for Bags, U.S.P.O.
Clerks Tying Bags, U.S.P.O.
Clerks Tying Up for Bags, U.S.P.O.
Throwing Mail into Bags, U.S.P.O.
Train Taking Up Mail Bag, U.S.P.O.
Tying Up Bags for Train, U.S.P.O.
1904 Bag Inspection
1908 The Magic Bag
The Two Traveling Bags; or, The Adventures of Percy White and Pauline Wells
1909 Adventures of a Bag of Coal
In a Hempen Bag
1910 A Bag Race
The Money Bag
The Wrong Bag

Bahamas
1910 The Sisal Industry in the Bahamas

Baikal (Siberia)
1904 Arrival and Departure of the Ice-Crushing Steamer "Baikal" at Baikal, Siberia

Bailiff
1908 Water Bailiff's Daughter
1909 Bailiff Makes a Seizure
1910 The Bailiff

Bait
1900 Alligator Bait

Baiting
1903 Dog Baiting and Fighting in Valdez

Baker Family
1899 Miss Jewett and the Baker Family

Bakers
1904 The Clever Baker
1907 Bakers in Trouble
Venetian Baker; or, Drama of Justice
1909 Bake That Chicken Pie
1910 The Clay Baker
"Conscience;" or, The Baker Boy

Bakery
1902 Fun in a Bakery Shop

Baking powder
1902 Good Luck Baking Powder Train No. 1
Good Luck Baking Powder Train No. 2

Balance
1898 "Balancing in the Basket"
1903 The Impossible Feat of Balancing
1910 The Turn of the Balance

Balcony
1903 Alphonse and Gaston Balcony Scene (Thumb Book)
1904 Scenes from My Balcony
1910 A Seat in the Balcony

Bald Mountain
1903 Indians Leaving Bald Mountain
Trappers Crossing Bald Mountain

Bald-head Row
1907 Belle of Bald-Head Row

Bald-headedness
1898 The Baldheaded Dutchman
1908 Bald Headed Actor and Fair Lady
The Inquisitive Fly and the Bald Head
Looking for the Bald Heads

Balfour, Arthur James, 1st Earl of Balfour
1901 Chamberlain and Balfour

Balkans
1909 Heroine of the Balkans

Balked
1908 Balked at the Altar

Ball
1903 Window Display Revolving Balls, National Cash Register Co.
1907 The Cup and Ball
1908 I've Lost My Ball
1909 Chasing the Ball

Ball (Game)
rt **Baseball**
Basketball
1901 Children Playing Ball
1906 Play Ball on the Beach

Ball's Bridge, Limerick (Ireland)
1905 Battery of Artillery Crossing Ball's Bridge, Limerick, Ireland

Ballad
1909 Ballad of the Pumpkin
1910 The Witch's Ballad

Ballet
1898 How the Ballet Girl Was Smuggled into Camp
1899 Ballet of the Ghosts
1902 Ballet Rehearsal
The Mermaid's Ballet
A Parisian Ballet
1903 The Ballet Master's Dream
Ballet of the Nations
The Ballet Rehearsal
Ballet Scene
Old Maid's Ballet Dance
Teaching Ballet Dancing
Spanish Dance (Ballet espagnol)
1904 Dance of the Sylphs (Ballet des Slyphides)
Russian Dance (Ballet ruse)
1906 Great Ballet
1908 The Prima Donna of the Ballet Parody
1910 Tontolini as a Ballet Dancer

Ballholm (Norway)
1907 Sailing thro the Sognia Fjord on a Steamer from Ballholm to Gudvangen [Norway]

Balloon
1898 Balloon Ascension, Marionettes
1901 Panoramic View of Electric Tower from a Balloon
1902 Balloon Ascension
Bird's Eye View of San Francisco, Cal., from a Balloon
Transporting a War Balloon
1903 Balloon Race
A Triple Balloon Ascent
Andre at the North Pole (Le ballon d'Andrée au pole nord)
Andre at the North Pole (Une scène dans les régions glaciales—le ballon d'Andrée)
1904 Buster and Tige Put a Balloon Vendor Out of Business
War Balloon Ascending and Descending
1906 Society Ballooning
1907 Bobby and His Balloon
International Balloon Races [from the James Gordon Bennett Cup, at St. Louis, Oct. 21, 1907]
Looking at a Balloon
1908 Honeymoon in a Balloon
1909 Balloon Races
Balloon Trip over Turin
Construction of Balloons
Dirigible Balloons at St. Louis
1910 Tweedle Dum's Aeronautical Adventure (Osservazioni di Robinet sul ballo)

Ballroom
1905 A Ballroom Tragedy

Balls (Parties)
1897 Charity Ball
1899 After the Ball
Four A.M. at the French Ball
A Lark at the French Ball
1900 Why Mrs. McCarthy Went to the Ball
1902 A Ball on a Battleship
1903 After the Ball
1904 A Joke at the French Ball
1906 Before the Ball
1907 After the Fancy Dress Ball
The Belle of the Ball
The Deaf-Mutes' Ball
Fitznoodle's Last Ball
1908 At the French Ball
The Burglar's Ball
Duel After the Ball
The Masque Ball
Mr. Jones at the Ball
The Ragtag's Ball
1909 After the Bachelors' Ball
Fancy Dress Ball
The Fatal Ball; or, The Miner's Daughter
1910 After the Ball
Foolshead at the Ball

Bally-Hoo
1901 Bally-Hoo Cake Walk

Ballybunion (Ireland)
1905 Rock Scene at Ballybunion

Ballybunion Railway (Ireland)
1903 The Mono-Railway Between Listowel and Ballybunion, Ireland
1905 Passengers Crossing over Open Car, Balley Bunion Railway
Passing Train, Balleybunion Railway, Ireland
Passing Train, Balleybunion Railway, Ireland No. 2
Passing Train (from Above) Balleybunion Railway, Ireland
Turntable of the Ballybunion Railway, Ireland

Ballyshannon (Ireland)
1904 Automobile Race at Ballyshannon, Ireland

Baltic
1904 The Baltic Fleet and the North Sea Trawlers
1909 Yachting on the Baltic

Baltic (Boat)
1904 White Star S.S. Baltic Leaving Pier on First Eastern Voyage

Baltimore (Maryland)
1898 Beauseant Commandery of Baltimore
1904 The Great Baltimore Fire
Panorama of Ruins from Baltimore and Charles Street
Panorama of Ruins from Lombard and Hanover Streets, Baltimore, Md.
1907 Baltimore

"Baltimore Black"
1909 Boxing Match [by Hallberg of Denmark and Young Joe Gaines "Baltimore Black"]

Bamboo
1903 Down the Bamboo Slide
1905 Under the Bamboo Tree
1909 Bamboo Pole Equilibrist
Manufacturing Bamboo Hats

Barton, Bessie
1908 The Courtship of Bessie Barton

Base
1901 Circular Panorama of the Base of the Electric Tower, Ending Looking Down the Mall

Baseball
1898 The Ball Game
The Bowery Waiter and the Old Time Ball Player
Spanish Ball Game
1899 Casey at the Bat
1902 Rube Waddell and the Champion Playing Ball with the Boston Team
1903 Crowd Leaving Athletic Base Ball Grounds
Game of Base Ball
1904 Kindergarten Ball Game, Missouri Commission
1905 "Play Ball"—Opening Game, National League, N.Y. City, 1905—New York vs. Boston
1906 How the Office Boy Saw the Ball Game
The World Series Baseball Games-White Sox and Cubs
1907 Base Ball Game
Christy Mathewson, N.Y. National League Baseball Team
How Brown Saw the Baseball Game
One Man Baseball
1908 Baseball
The Baseball Fan
The World's Championship Baseball Series of 1910
1909 Pittsburgh-Detroit Ball Game
Taft in Chicago, and at the Ball Game
1910 Baseball, That's All
Bumptious Plays Baseball
Great Ball Game Between the East and West
Take Me Out to the Ball Game

Bashful
1908 A Bashful Young Man
The Mishaps of a Bashful Man
1909 Cure for Bashfulness

Basins
1901 Fountain, Tower, and Basins—Pan-American Exposition

Basket
1898 "Balancing in the Basket"
1902 Demonstrating the Action of a Mergenthaler-Horton Basket Making Machine
Fun in a Clothes Basket
1903 The Enchanted Basket
1907 Indian Basket Weavers
1908 The Basket Maker's Daughter
Basket Mystery or the Traveler's Jest
A Basket Party
Who Owns the Basket?
1909 The Burglar in a Basket
Indian Basket Making

Basketball
1901 Basket Ball
1903 U.S. Interior Dept.: Basket Ball, Indian School
1904 Basket ball, Missouri Valley College

Bass drums
1907 The Lost Bass Drum; or, Where Is That Louie?

Bass fishing
1901 Bass Fishing

Bastille (Paris)
1906 Bird's Eye View of Paris (Ce que l'on voit de la Bastille)

Bath Beach, Long Island (New York)
1897 Diving at Bath Beach

Bath chairs
1907 The Adventures of a Bath Chair
1909 Bath Chair

Bathhouses
1904 Peeping Frenchman at the German Bathhouse
1905 He Got into the Wrong Bath House

Bathing
1896 Atlantic City Bathers
Bathers and Lifeboat, Atlantic City
Boys Bathing, Leapfrog—Atlantic City
A Morning Bath
Pussy's Bath
Showing Group of Bathers, Atlantic City Beach
1897 Bath Scene
The Bathers
A Jolly Crowd of Bathers Frolicking on the Beach at Atlantic City
Lurline Baths
Sutro Baths, No. 1
Sutro Baths, No. 2
The Tramp and the Bather
1898 The Bathing Girls Hurdle Race
Bathing Scene at Rockaway
Gymnastic Feats After the Bath
Ready for the Bath
The Teacher's Unexpected Bath
Three Baths for the Price of One
1899 Baby's Bath
The Bather's Lunch
How Bill the Burglar Got a Bath
The Way French Bathing Girls Bathe
1900 Darkey Excursionists Bathing, Atlantic City
New Morning Bath
The Unexpected Bath
What the Bathing Girls Did to the Kodak Fiend
1901 Bathing at Atlantic City
Boys Entering Free Bath
Boys Free Public Baths
Children Bathing
The Fisherman and the Bathers
Hooligan Takes His Annual Bath
Ladies Day at the Public Baths
Saturday at the Free Baths
Women of the Ghetto Bathing
1902 Bathing at Kiel, Germany
Bathing Made Easy
The Elephant's Bath
His Morning Bath
In a German Bath
The Interrupted Bathers
Rex's Bath
St. John's Guild. Bathing in Surf and Leaving Water
St. John's Guild. Going to Salt-water Bath Room
Tommy Atkins Bathing
1903 Atlantic City Bathers
The Bather
Bathers with High Diving
Bathing at Atlantic City
Bathing Horses
Bathing in Samoa
Cattle Bathing
Colored Baby's Morning Bath
Colored Folks Bathing
East Side Urchins Bathing in a Fountain
A Fresh Bath
A Hot Time on the Bathing Beach
Hotel and Bath
New York City Public Bath
Panorama and Bathing Scene of Ostend, Belgium
Policeman Chasing Bathers
The Tramp's First Bath
1904 Babies Bathing
Bathers at Joinville
Beauty Bathing
The Homemade Turkish Bath
Ladies of the Court Bathing
Mixed Bathing
No Bathing Allowed
A Ruben's Unexpected Bath
The Shower Bath
Woman's Bath
1905 Bathing in the Ice at the L Street Bath, Boston
Indian Babies' Bath
1906 Baby's Bath
Bath of Sacred Elephants
Coal Man's Bath
"A Fresh Bath" or "The Tripper Tripped"
1907 Bathing Under Difficulties
The Boy, the Bust and the Bath
Wrong Bath
1908 Bathing; or, Charlie and Mary in the Country
The Interrupted Bath
1909 An Unfortunate Bath
1910 Fatty Taking a Bath
Refreshing Bath
Winter Bathing in the West Indies

Bathroom
1898 Bathroom Frivolities
1905 The Boarding House Bathroom
1906 The Indiscreet Bathroom Maid

Bathtub
1910 The Electric Bathtub

Bats
1910 Hunting Bats in Sumatra

Battalion
1898 First Battalion of the 2nd Massachusetts Volunteers
9th and 13th U.S. Infantry at Battalion Drill
Second Battalion; 2nd Massachusetts Volunteers
The Tenth Battalion
10th U.S. Infantry, 2nd Battalion Leaving Cars
1899 Second Battalion, 1st Regiment, N. G. of Pennsylvania
2nd Battalion, 3rd New York Provisional Regiment, Rochester and Syracuse, Separate Companies
2nd Special Service Battalion, Canadian Infantry, Embarking for So. Africa
2nd Special Service Battalion, Canadian Infantry-Parade
1901 Band and Battalion of the U.S. Indian School
1905 Battalion of Seaforth Highlanders at the Dublin Horse Show

Battery
1897 Battery A, Light Artillery, U.S. Army
Battery B, Governor's Troop, Penna.
French Cuirassieurs Charging a Field Battery
1898 The Astor Battery
Battery B Arriving at Camp
Battery B Pitching Camp
Battery Charge
Capron's Battery
1899 Astor Battery on Parade
Battery K Siege Guns
1900 Capture of Boer Battery
Capture of Boer Battery by British
1901 Capt. Reilly's Battery, Bombardment of Pekin
Capt. Reilly's Battery Limbering
Reilly's Light Battery F
1904 Battery "A," Rhode Island Light Artillery
1905 Battery of Artillery Crossing Ball's Bridge, Limerick, Ireland
1909 Crown Prince of Germany Drilling Battery

Battery (New York City)
1897 The Battery
Battery Park
1901 New York Sky-Line from East River and Battery

Battlefield
1900 Red Cross Ambulance on Battlefield
1901 Ammunition Wagons Arriving on the Battlefield
Red Cross of the German Army on the Battlefield
1902 English Army in the Battlefield
English Cavalry on the Battlefield
1908 Scenes from the Battlefield of Gettysburg, the Waterloo of the Confederacy

Battles
1897 Girls Battling for a Hammock
1898 After the Battle
Battle of Guantanomo [sic]
Battle of San Juan Hill
1899 Battle Flag of the 10th Pennsylvania Volunteers, Carried in the Philippines
Battle of El Caney
The Battle of Jeffries and Sharkey for Championship of the World
Battle of Santiago
1900 Battle of Colenso
Battle of Mafeking
The Battle of Mt. Ariat
Battle of the Upper Tugela
Bringing in the Wounded During the Battle of Grobler's Kloof
British Infantry Marching to Battle
Naval Sham Battle at Newport
Sham Battle on Land by Cadets at Newport Naval Training School
1901 Sham Battle at the Pan-American Exposition
1903 Battle Flags of the 9th U.S. Infantry
Battle of Bladders
Battle of Confetti at the Nice Carnival
Battle of Flowers at the Nice Carnival
Battle Royal
1904 The Battle of Chemulpo
Battle of Chemulpo Bay

Beauty and the Beast
Beauty Parlors
Nellie, the Beautiful Housemaid
Sleeping Beauty
1909 Blissville the Beautiful
Father's Beautiful Beard
Her Beautiful Hair
It Was a Beautiful Dream
A Thoughtless Beauty
1910 The Beautiful Margaret
The Beautiful Snow
The Penalty of Beauty
Village Beauty

Beaux
1907 Lena and the Beaux
1908 Mabel's Beau in Trouble
1910 Her City Beaux
Sally's Beaux

Beaver
1903 Beaver Show Case
1907 Beaver Hunt

Becket
1910 Becket

Bed
1897 Tramp in a Millionaire's Bed
1898 The Burglar in the Bed Chamber
Folding Beds Are Tricky
Jumping the Rope After Bed Time
Gladys Must Be in Bed Before Ten
What's the Matter with the Bed
1900 The Burglar-Proof Bed
Found a Man Under the Bed
1902 A Blast in a Gravel Bed
Going to Bed Under Difficulties
1903 Going to Bed Under Difficulties
Pulling Off the Bed Clothes
"You Will Send Me to Bed, Eh?"
A Midnight Episode (Un bon lit)
The Bridegroom's Dilemma (Le coucher de la mariée ou triste nuit de noces)
1904 A Parisienne's Bed Time
1905 The Race for Bed
1907 A Rolling Bed
1908 Man Under the Bed
The Sofa Bed
Too Many in Bed
1909 Lost in a Folding Bed
The Sideboard Folding Bed
1910 The Man Under the Bed

Bedelia
1905 Bedelia and the Witch

Bedroom
1907 The Haunted Bedroom

Bee
1897 Husking Bee
1903 Auntie and the Bee
The Busy Bee
1904 The Busy Bee
That Busy Bee
1907 The Life of Bee
1908 The Bee and the Rose
1909 Bee's Eviction
Stung by a Bee

Beechwood
1910 The Beechwood Ghost

Beef
1901 Beef Extract Room
Beef, Sheep and Hog Killing
Cutting Beef
Dressing Beef

Beehive
1905 Wonderful Beehive

Beelzebub
1903 Beelzebub's Daughters

Beer
1900 "Ein Bier"
A Champion Beer Drinker
The Champion Beer Drinker
1903 Clown and Beer-Thief

Beethoven, Ludwig van
1909 Beethoven
The Origin of Beethoven's Moonlight Sonata

Beetle
1907 Golden Beetle

Beggars
1898 Fake Beggar
1901 The Fraudulent Beggar
1903 Beggar's Dream
1904 The Little Greedy Beggar
1907 Sham Beggars
1908 Adventures of a Beggar
The Beggar
The Persistent Beggar
1909 The Beggarmaid
The Beggarman's Gratitude
The Beggar's Coin
The Beggar's Daughter
Chivalrous Beggar
Two Ladies and a Beggar
1910 The Beggar's Repentance
Ito, the Beggar Boy
The King of Beggars
The King of the Beggars
The Little Beggar
The Little Beggar Maid

Beheading
1900 Beheading Chinese Prisoner
1903 Beheading Chinese
1904 The Execution (Beheading) of One of the Hunchuses (Chinese Bandits) Outside the Walls of Mukden

Beirut (Lebanon)
1903 Panoramic View of Beyrouth, Syria, Showing Holiday Festivities
Passengers Embarking from S.S. "Augusta Victoria" at Beyrouth

Belated
1904 Belated Husband
1909 A Belated Meal
The Belated Wedding

Belgium
1903 Panorama and Bathing Scene of Ostend, Belgium
1910 The Belgian Army
Bruges, Belgium
Military Cyclists of Belgium
Riding School in Belgium

Belgrade (Serbia)
1909 Belgrade, Capital of Servia

Believe
1907 The Little Girl Who Did Not Believe in Santa Claus
1909 Believe Me
1910 One Can't Believe One's Eyes

Bell, Mrs.
1908 The Female Politician, Mrs. Bell, Is Nominated for Mayor

Bell, Franklin, Brigadier-General
1900 Brigadier-General Franklin Bell and Staff

Bell Sisters
1903 Three Bell Sisters in a Fancy Dance

Belle
1902 Belles of the Beach
1907 Belle of Bald-Head Row
The Belle of the Ball
1909 Belle of the Harvest
Conchita, the Spanish Belle
1910 A Colonial Belle
The Wild Coast of Belle Island

Bellerophon (Battleship)
1907 Launch of the British Battleship Bellerophon

Bells
1897 Ye Merry Sleigh Bells
1898 Merry Sleigh Bells
1900 General Bell's Expedition
Those Wedding Bells Shall Not Ring Out
1903 Liberty Bell
1904 The Liberty Bell on Its Way to the Exposition
West Point Cadets Escorting Liberty Bell, St. Louis Exposition
1906 The Bell Ringer's Daughter
No Wedding Bells for Him
1908 Bachelor's Wedding Bells
The Bell Boy's Revenge
Somnambulic (sic) Bell Ringer
1909 The Chemist's Bell
The Curfew Bell
Easter Bells
The Hand Bell
1910 As the Bells Rang Out!
The Bellringer's Daughter

Belly dance
1906 Tunisian Dance (Danse du ventre: 1. danse tunisienne)

Belmont Park Race Course (New York)
1905 Opening of Belmont Park Race Course

Belt
1907 The Electric Belt
1909 The Electric Belt
The Sailor's Belt

Ben
1901 "Laughing Ben"
1909 Ben's Kid

Ben Bolt (Horse)
1899 Champion High Jumpers, "Chappie" and "Ben Bolt"

Ben Hur
1907 Ben Hur

Benares (India)
1909 Benares

Benches
1901 On the Benches in the Park
1904 The Bench in the Park
1907 The Girl on Park Bench
1909 Misadventures of a Bench

Bend
1897 Mulberry Bend
Tipping the Cart in Mulberry Bend

Bend Or (Horse)
1901 "Bend Or"

Benediction
1907 The Benediction of the Sea

Benefactor
1908 The Youthful Benefactor
1910 Child as Benefactor

Benefits
1905 How Mr. Butt-In Benefits by Chauncey's Mishaps
1909 Ralph Benefits by People's Curiosity

Benevolent
1909 Benevolent Employer

Bengal Lancers
1901 The Bengal Lancers
Charge by 1st Bengal Lancers
First Bengal Lancers
First Bengal Lancers, Distant View
The War in China—First Bengal Lancers

Bennett, James Gordon
1907 International Balloon Races [from the James Gordon Bennett Cup, at St. Louis, Oct. 21, 1907]

Bergen (Norway)
1905 Fish Carvers, at Fish Market Bergen Norway
Fishmarket, Bergen, Norway
Sunday "Church Parade" Bergen Norway

Bergerac, Cyrano de
1908 Cyrano de Bergerac
1909 Cyrano de Bergerac
Cyrano de Bergerac's Adventure

Berkeley (California)
1906 A Trip to Berkeley, Cal.

Berlin (Germany)
1902 Berlin Fire Department
Kaiser Wilhelm in the Tier Garten, Berlin, Germany
Queen Wilhelmina, of Holland, in Berlin
A Run by the Berlin Fire Department, Berlin, Germany
Visit of Emperor Francis Josef of Austria to Berlin
1903 Berlin Fire Department at Drill
1906 Trip on Berlin Elevated R.R.
1907 Berlin to Rome
1909 King Edward's Visit to Berlin
Parks in Berlin
1910 Berlin

Berlin Jack the Ripper
1909 Berlin Jack the Ripper

Bernard le bucheron
1907 A Forester Made King (Bernard le bucheron ou le miracle de Saint Hubert)

Berne (Switzerland)
1910 A Trip to Berne

Berry, Duchess de
1910 The Arrest of Duchess de Berry

Bertha
1909 Bertha's Birthday

Berthold
1909 Berthold in Paris

Bertie
1907 Bertie's Love Letter
1908 Bertie's Sweetheart
1910 Bertie's Elopement

Bertrand
1904 Death of Robert McCaire and Bertrand
1907 Robert Macaire and Bertrand; or, The Troubles of a Hobo and His Pal, in Paris

Bird Rock, Nordland (Norway)
1905 Bird Rock, Nordland, Norway

Bird's-eye views
1900 Bird's-Eye View of Dock Front, Galveston
Birdseye View of Galveston, Showing Wreckage
1902 Bird's Eye View of San Francisco, Cal., from a Balloon
1903 Birds-eye View of Dawson City on the Yukon River, Alaska
1905 Panoramic Bird's Eye View of Montreal, Canada
1906 Bird's Eye View from Hopkins Art Institute
Bird's Eye View of Paris
1910 Bird's Eye View from World's Highest Buildings

Birth
1900 Birth of Venus
1901 "Birth of the Pearl"
1903 Birth of a Fairy
Passion Play: The Birth of Christ
1908 Christmas: From the Birth of Christ to the Twentieth Century
1909 The Birth and Adventures of a Fountain Pen
The Birth of a Big Gun
The Birth of Jesus
1911 The Birth of the Gnomes

Birthday
1899 The Soubrette's Birthday
1902 King Edward VII at the Birthday Celebration of the King of Denmark
1904 Inspector's Birthday
Uncle Rube's Birthday
1905 June's Birthday Party
1907 Auntie's Birthday
The Birthday Celebration
Fine Birthday Cake
For Mother's Birthday
My Wife's Birthday
1908 Bobby's Birthday
His Sweetheart's Birthday
1909 Bertha's Birthday
A Birthday Affair
The Chimney Sweep's Birthday
Florrie's Birthday
The General's Birthday Present
A Good Birthday Present
Grandfather's Birthday
Grandmother's Birthday
Jack's Birthday
Mrs. Jones' Birthday
1910 Birthday Cigars
The Birthday Present
Granny's Birthday
The Lassie's Birthday
Mama's Birthday Present
My Aunt's Birthday

Biscuit
1904 Shredded Wheat Biscuit
Shredded Wheat Biscuit No. 1
Shredded Wheat Biscuit No. 2
1908 Biscuits Like Mother Used to Make
1909 Her First Biscuits
Too Much Dog Biscuit

Bishop
1905 Bishop and Burglar

Biskra (Algeria)
1909 Biskra, Garden of Allah
A Visit to Biskra
1910 Biskra and the Sahara Desert

Bismarck Monument, Berlin (Germany)
1902 Unveiling of the Bismarck Monument

Bismarck Museum, Friedrichsruh (Germany)
1901 Opening of Bismarck's Museum

Bismark (Boat)
1901 Steamship "Bismark"

Bison
1905 Herd of Bison, Yellowstone Park

Bitche (France)
1910 Fort Du Bitche

Bite
1898 The Tramp's Last Bite
1909 Was It a Snake Bite?

Biter bit
1910 The Biter Bit

Bitter
1908 In Bitter Rivalry
1909 A Bitter Lesson
1910 A Bitter Enemy

Bitters
1908 Indian Bitters; or, The Patent Medicine Man

Bittersweet
1910 Bitter-Sweet

Black
1900 The Black Storm
1902 Black and White Hair Dance
1903 Black Serpentine
Extraordinary Black Art
A Scrap in Black and White
1904 Fairy of the Black Rocks
1905 Black and White; or, The Mystery of a Brooklyn Baby Carriage
The Black Imp
In the Mining District (Au pays noir)
1907 Black-White
The Black Witch
1908 Black Princess
The Black Sheep
The Black Viper
A Comedy in Black and White
The Knight of Black Art
The Mystery of the Bride, in Black and White
Oriental Black Art
Under the Black Flag
1909 Black Coated Brigands
The Black Sheep
Black's Funeral
The Master of Black Rock
1910 The Black Gondola
A Black Heart

Black Beauty
1907 Black Beauty

Black Diamond Express
1896 Black Diamond Express
1897 Black Diamond Express, No. 1
Black Diamond Express, No. 2
Panorama of Susquehanna River Taken from the Black Diamond Express
Receding View, Black Diamond Express
1900 New Black Diamond Express
1903 Lehigh Valley Black Diamond Express
Lehigh Valley Express "Black Diamond"
Rear View of the "Black Diamond Express," Lehigh Valley R.R.

"Black Growler" Steam Vent
1905 The "Black Growler" Steam Vent, Yellowstone Park

Black Gulch
1910 The Sheriff of Black Gulch

Black Hand
1906 The Black Hand
1909 Black Hand
1910 Blopps in Search of the Black Hand
Trailing the Black Hand

Black Hills
1910 In the Black Hills

Black magic
1903 Black Magic

Black Pete
1910 Black Pete's Reformation

Black Rock Tunnel
1902 Black Rock Tunnel on the Rock Island Route

Black-eyed Susan
1908 Black Eyed Susan

Blackboard
1901 The Mysterious Blackboard

Blackface
1905 Everybody Works But Father (Blackface)

Blackfoot, Chief
1910 Chief Blackfoot's Vindication

Blacking
1903 Soap vs. Blacking

Blackmail
1905 Blackmail
1906 Blackmailing the Motorists
1907 The Blackmailer
1908 The Blackmailer

Blacks
rt **Octoroons**
1896 Dancing Darkies
1897 A Coon Cake Walk
Dancing Darkey Boy
Hallow-e'en in Coon-town
Pickanninies Dance
1898 Colored Invincibles
Colored Troops Disembarking
Tossing a Nigger in a Blanket
1899 The Dusky Serenade
1900 Darkey Excursionists Bathing, Atlantic City
A Darktown Dance
The 'Gator and the Pickaninny
The Mail-Man in Coon Town
Pickaninnies
1902 The Darktown Comedians Trip to Paris
1903 Colored Baby's Morning Bath
Colored Folks Bathing
Colored Sports
Colored Woman Smoking a Pipe
Darkies' Kiss
Native Woman Washing a Negro Baby in Nassau, B. I.
New Colored Kiss, No. 2
Ohio Colored Troops at Camp Alger
Old Darkey Dancing
Prize Fight in Coon Town
Something Good-Negro Kiss
Whitewashing a Colored Baby
1904 A Nigger in the Woodpile
1905 Gluttonous Negro
1906 Negro and Policeman
1907 A Colored Man's Revenge
The Dancing Nig
Jamaica Negroes Doing a Two-Step
Misadventures of a Negro King in Paris
Wooing and Wedding of a Coon
1908 Colored Maid Getting Rid of a Suitor
Coon in Red
Ten Pickaninnies
Wanted: A Colored Servant
1909 The Awakening of Mr. Coon
The Colored Stenographer
Coon Town Parade
1910 Negro's Gratitude
Negro's Sacrifice
Pickaninny and the Pup

Blacksmith
1902 The Village Blacksmith
1905 The Blacksmith's Daughter
1907 The Blacksmith's Daughter
The Blacksmith's Revenge
The Blacksmith's Strike
1908 The Irish Blacksmith
1909 The Blacksmith's Bride
The Blacksmith's Daughter
The Blacksmith's Wife
The Hasty Tempered Father; or, The Blacksmith's Love

Blackville
1903 A Night in Blackville

Blackwell's Island (New York)
1903 Panorama of Blackwell's Island

Bladders
1903 Battle of Bladders

Blaine Club of Cincinnati
1897 Young Men's Blaine Club of Cincinnati
1900 Blaine Club of Cincinnati

Blake, Dan
1909 Dan Blake's Rival

Blame
1908 The Father Is to Blame

Blanco Bridge, Manila (Philippines)
1899 Blanco Bridge

Blank
1909 A Blank Check

Blanket
1897 13th Infantry, U.S. Army—Blanket Court Martial, Governors Island
1898 Blanket-Tossing a New Recruit
Tossing a Nigger in a Blanket
1903 Navajo Squaw Weaving Blanket

Blarney Stone
1904 Kissing the Blarney Stone

Blas, Ruy
1909 Ruy Blas

Blast
1898 A Blast at the Solvay Quarries
1901 The Finish of Michael Casey; or, Blasting Rocks in Harlem
1902 A Blast in a Gravel Bed
1903 Blasting the Treadwell Mines
1905 Blasting in the Glory Hole of the Treadwell Mine, Alaska
1906 Brannigan Sets Off the Blast

Blast furnaces
1899 Tapping a Blast Furnace

Blaze
1902 A Big Blaze
1903 A Midwinter Blaze
1910 The Blazed Trail

Torpedo Boats Racing off Newport
Worcester High School Eight-Oared Boat Crews in Action
1903 Boat Race
Boat Race No. 2
Chicago Fire Boats in Action
German Torpedo Boat in Action
German Torpedo Boats
New York Harbor Police Boat Patrol Capturing Pirates
Panorama of Excursion Boats
Panoramic View of Torpedo Boat "Winslow" and Yacht "Constitution"
Stake Boat with Stake ("John Scully")
Torpedo Boat in Action
Trial Run of the Fastest Boat in the World, "The Arrow"
Unloading Canal Boat
1904 Auto Boat Race on the Hudson River
Capsized Boat
English Submarine Boat Disaster
Hauling in Seines and Pulling Seines into Boat
Holland Submarine Boat Tests
Ice Boating on the North Shrewsbury, Red Bank, N.J.
The Oxford and Cambridge Boat Race
1905 Boating Carnival, Palm Beach, Fla.
The "Crazy" Canal Boat, Norway
German Torpedo Boat in Action
The Life Boat
Motor Boat Race at Monaco
Out Boating
Sliding River Craft over Boat Railway, River Thames
Speed Trial of Auto Boat Challenger, Lake Worth, Fla.
Torpedo Boat Maneuvering
Torpedo Boats Manoeuvering
1906 Boats on the Nile
Maneuvering a Small Motor Boat
White Fox Motor Boat
Yale Harvard Boat Race, New London, Conn., 1906
1907 Constructed Fishing Boat
Life Boat Manoeuvres
Norway: Crazy Canal Boat on the Telemarken Route
1908 Blessing the Boats in Arcachon
Boats
Fishing Boats in the Ocean
Motor Boat Races
Motor Boat Races, 1908
Oxford and Cambridge Boat Race
The Yale-Harvard Boat Race
1909 The Boating Party
Boatman of the Riviera
"Ursula," World's Fastest Motor Boat
The Winning Boat
1910 Auntie at the Boat Race
Cupid and the Motor Boat
The International Motor Boat Races
The Life Boat
Motor and Yacht Boating in England

Bob
1899 Admiral Dewey's Dog, "Bob"
1906 Miniature Theatre (Le théâtre de Bob)
1909 Bob's Electric Theater
Fighting Bob

Bobbie
1904 Bobbie's Downfall

Bobbies
use **Police**

Bobby
1899 Tommy Atkins, Bobby and the Cook
1904 Bobby and the Automobile
1906 Bobby and His Family
1907 Bobby and His Balloon
Bobby's Practical Jokes
1908 Bobby Has a Pipe Dream
Bobby's Birthday
Bobby's Kodak
1909 Bobby's Sketches
1910 Bobby, the Boy Scout

Body
1900 Bringing General Lawton's Body Back to Manila
Searching Ruins on Broadway, Galveston, for Dead Bodies
1901 Panoramic View of the Crowd Rushing for the City Hall, Buffalo, to View the Body of President McKinley
Taking President McKinley's Body from Train at Canton, Ohio
1902 The Clown with the Portable Body
1903 Discovery of Bodies
1910 Tweedledum Gets Employed in the Corporation Body

Bodyguard
1903 Kruger and Body Guard Leaving the Volksraad

Boer
1899 Frere Bridge, as Destroyed by the Boers
1900 Boer Commissary Train Treking
Boer War Film
Boers Bringing in British Prisoners
Capture of Boer Battery
Capture of Boer Battery by British
Charge of Boer Cavalry
Off for the Boer War
1901 The Duke and Duchess of York Presenting Medals to Boer War Veterans at the Unveiling of the Queen's Statue
1903 Boer Supply Train Crossing the Veldt
Skirmish with Boers near Kimberly by a Troop of Cavalry Scouts Attached to Gen. French's Column
War Supplies Arriving at Boer Laager by Train of Ox Teams
1904 Spy's Arrest (Arrestation d'un espion boer (no. 1))
1905 The Boer War
1909 Briton and Boer
Episode in Boer War
The Girl Scout; or the Canadian Contingent in the Boer War

Boer Laager (South Africa)
1903 War Supplies Arriving at Boer Laager by Train of Ox Teams

Bog
1903 At Work in a Peat Bog

Bogey
1909 The Bogey Woman

Bogieman
1902 The Bogie Man
1908 In the Bogie Man's Cave

Bogoudens
1908 The Country of the "Bogoudens"

Bogus
1908 The Bogus Lord
Bogus Magic Powder
1909 The Bogus Heir
1910 Bogus General

Bohemian
1908 A Bohemian Romance
1909 The Bohemian Girl

Boiling water
1907 Rogues' Tricks (La douche d'eau bouillante)

Bois de Boulogne, Paris (France)
1900 Scene on the Bois de Boulogne
1904 Easter Flower Parade in Bois de Boulogne, Paris
1908 Flower Fete on the Bois de Boulogne

Bold
1904 Bold Bank Robbery
The Bold Soger Boy
1908 When Knights Were Bold
1910 A Warrior Bold

Boleyn, Anne
1905 The Tower of London (La Tour de Londres et les dernières moments d'Anne Boleyn)

Bolivar (Elephant)
1903 Trick Elephant Bolivar, the Largest Elephant in the World, No. 1
Trick Elephant Bolivar, the Largest Elephant in the World, No. 2

Bologna
1902 Bologna Eating Contest

Bolster
1901 Bolster Sparring

Bomb
1907 The Bomb
1910 The Bum and the Bomb

Bombard
1900 Bombarding and Capturing the Taku Forts by the Allied Fleets
Bombardment of Taku Forts, by the Allied Fleets
1901 Capt. Reilly's Battery, Bombardment of Pekin
1902 Bombardment of Newport
1903 German Cruisers Bombarding Venezuelan Forts
North Atlantic Fleet Bombarding Fisher's Island
North Atlantic Fleet Bombarding Fort Adams, Newport Harbor
1904 Bombardment of Port Arthur

Bombay (India)
1910 Different Trades in Bombay
A Visit to Bombay

Bombay Cavalry
1901 The War in China—Bombay Cavalry

Bombita
1904 Bull Fight with Matadors Senor Don Luis Mazzantini and Bombita

Bon vivant
1902 The Bon Vivant

Bonanza Creek (Alaska)
1903 Working a Long Tom Rocker on Bonanza Creek
Working the Rocker, Called a Jigger, on Poverty Bar, Fourteen Below Discovery Bonanza Creek

Bonaparte, Napoleon
1909 The Life Drama of Napoleon Bonaparte and Empress Josephine of France

Bond
1908 The Bond
1910 Solving the Bond Theft

Bondage
1908 In Bondage

Bonding
1900 Demonstrating the Operation of the Harrington Rail Bonding System on the Line of the Coney Island and Brooklyn Railroad Co.

Bondsman
1909 The Bondsman's Fate

Bone
1908 The Wish Bone
1909 The Dog and the Bone
1910 The Bone-Setter's Daughter

Bonehead
1910 Bonehead's Second Adventure
Mishaps of Bonehead
The Old Maid and Bonehead

Bonnet
1908 The Blue Bonnet

Bonnie
1909 The Bride of Lammermoor, a Tragedy of Bonnie Scotland

Bonny
1909 Blessington's Bonny Babies

Book
1897 The Book Agent
1900 The Downward Path: The Fresh Book Agent [Part 1]
1903 Alphonse and Gaston and the Burglar (Thumb Book)
Alphonse and Gaston Balcony Scene (Thumb Book)
Alphonse and Gaston (Journal Thumb Book)
Alphonse and Gaston Target Practice (Thumb Book)
Foxy Grandpa [Thumb Book]
Hooligan and Dogs (Journal Thumb Book)
Hooligan's Thanksgiving Dinner (Thumb Book)
Katzenjammer Kids (Journal Thumb Book)
The Magic Book
Toodles' Christmas (Thumb Book)
Toodles Recites a Recitation (Thumb Book)
Toodles' Strawberry Tart (Journal Thumb Book)
Toodles' Tea Party (Thumb Book)
1907 The Book Agent
The Book Worm
1908 The Book Agent
1909 Aunt Emmy's Scrap Book
Book Taught Hypnotism
Jones and the Lady Book Agent
1910 The Unsophisticated Book Agent

Boomerang
1900 The Boomerang

Booming
1910 Booming Business

Boone, Daniel
1907 Daniel Boone; or, Pioneer Days in America

Boonesboro (Fort), Louisville (Kentucky)
1906 Attack on Fort Boonesboro

Bootblack
1903 Bootblack and Crossing Sweeper
The Dude and the Bootblacks
1906 Jack the Bootblack
1907 Life of a Bootblack; or, the Street Urchin
1908 The Kind-Hearted Bootblack; or Generosity Rewarded
1909 A Millionaire Bootblack
1910 A Bootblack's Daily Labor in Algiers
Booth, William, General
1902 General Booth
Bootles
1910 Bootles' Baby
Boots
1904 Puss in Boots
1907 A Pair of Boots, Please
Policeman's Boots
1908 The Enchanted Boots
Puss in Boots
Stolen Boots
The Story the Boots Told
1909 Boots and Saddles
The Boots He Couldn't Lose
1910 Bill's Boots
The Colonel's Boot
Paid Boots and Stolen Boots
The Story of a Pair of Boots
Walkaway's New Boots
Boozer, Mr.
1908 Mr. Boozer Gets a Fright
Boozy
1907 How the Lovers Got Rid of Boozy Pa
Bordeauz (France)
1906 The Paris-Bordeaux Auto Race
Border
1908 Hannah Dustin: The Border Wars of New England
1909 Across the Border
On the Border
1910 A Border Tale
In the Border States
On the Border
On the Border Line
On the Mexican Border
Bore
1908 That Mother-in-Law Is a Bore
Born
1903 Buffaloes Born in the Zoo Gardens
1909 Born for Trouble
Borneo
1905 Head Hunters of Borneo
On a Borneo Railway
1907 Trip to Borneo
1909 The Wild Man of Borneo
1910 The Wild Man of Borneo
Bornholm (Denmark)
1908 The Isle of Bornholm
Borrowing
1904 The Borrowing Girl
The Borrowing Girl and the Atomizer
1907 The Borrowed Ladder
Neighbors Who Borrow
1909 Borrowed Clothes; or, Fine Feathers Make Fine Birds
A Borrowed Suit
1910 The Borrowed Baby
Bosco
1910 Saved by Bosco
Bosporus
1904 Constantinople and the Bosporus
Boss
1907 Boss Away, Choppers Play
Sunday with the Boss
Who's Boss of the House?
1909 Inviting His Boss for Dinner
1910 Boss of Circle E Ranch
The Good Boss
The New Boss of Bar X Ranch
Who Is Boss?
Bostock Circus
1902 Bostock's Educated Chimpanzee
1903 Bostock's Circus Fording a Stream
Bostock's Educated Bears
1908 Some Dangerous Members of Bostock's Menagerie
Boston (Massachusetts)
1897 Boston's Subway
National Lancers of Boston
1898 Boston Commandery, Boston, Mass.
Boston Navy Yard
A Fine Day for Sleighing, Boston
Steamer "Boston"
1899 Admiral Dewey at State House, Boston
The Boston Horseless Fire Department
First Boston School Regiment
McKinley Leaving State House, Boston
Second Boston School Regiment
Third Boston School Regiment
1901 The Boston Fire Boat in Action
Panoramic View of Boston Subway from an Electric Car
1902 Rube Waddell and the Champion Playing Ball with the Boston Team
1903 Boston and New York Express
1904 Canoeing on the Charles River, Boston, Mass.
1905 Bathing in the Ice at the L Street Bath, Boston
"Play Ball"—Opening Game, National League, N.Y. City, 1905—New York vs. Boston
1906 Seeing Boston
1907 Boston
1908 Boston Normal School Pageant
The Boston Tea Party
Boston and New York Express
1903 Boston and New York Express
Botanist
1907 Botanist's Misadventures
Bothersome
1908 Bothersome Husband
Bottle
1898 How a Bottle of Cocktails Was Smuggled into Camp
1901 The Tramp and the Nursing Bottle
1902 Crying for His Bottle
1904 The Baby, the Monkey and the Milk Bottle
Mellin's Food Baby and Bottle
The Two Bottle Babies
1905 Blowing Bottles
1907 The Magic Bottle
1908 The Champagne Bottle
The Man and His Bottle
1909 Automatic Nursing Bottle
Bottled Up
The Imp of the Bottle
The Janitor's Bottle
The Medicine Bottle
1910 Fricot Drinks a Bottle of Horse Embrocation
Bottler, Sam
1910 The Temptation of Sam Bottler
Bottom
1896 American Falls from Bottom of Canadian Shore
Whirlpool Rapids—from Bottom of Canadian Shore
Botzen, Tyrol (Austria)
1905 Corpus Christi Ceremonies, Botzen, Tyrol
Corpus Christi Cortege, Botzen, Tyrol
Boudoir
1903 In My Lady's Boudoir
1907 Mysterious Boudoir
Boulevard
1896 On the Boulevard
View on Boulevard, New York City
1900 Scene on the Boulevard DeCapucines
1901 Automobile Parade on the Coney Island Boulevard
1903 Boulevard St. Denis, Paris, France
Boulevard DeCapucines, Paris (France)
1900 Scene on the Boulevard DeCapucines
Boulevard St. Denis, Paris (France)
1903 Boulevard St. Denis, Paris, France
Bouncing
1902 "Bouncing"
Bound
1897 Steamship "St. Paul" Outward Bound
1900 The "St. Paul" Outward Bound
1903 The Ancient and Honourables Homeward Bound
1909 Frost Bound Nature
Boundary
1908 The Boundary
1910 Settling a Boundary Dispute
Bounder, Professor
1908 Professor Bounder's Pills
Bountiful, Lady
1903 Lady Bountiful Visits the Murphys on Wash Day
Bouquet
1906 A Strange Engagement Bouquet
1907 Highly Scented Bouquet
1908 The Poisoned Bouquet, an Italian Tragedy of the XV Century
1909 Bouquet Gallantly Offered
Sweetheart's Bouquet
1910 The Bouquet
Bout
1903 Catch-as-Catch-Can Wrestling Bout
1910 An English Boxing Bout
Bow
1903 Sea Washing over the Bow of Kearsage
1908 Big Bow Mystery
Bow Knot (California)
1902 Panoramic View of Mt. Tamalpais Between Bow Knot and McKinley Cut
Bow River, Alberta (Canada)
1903 On the Bow River Horse Ranch at Cochrane, North West Territory
Bowery
1897 A Bowery Cafe
Bowery Waltz
1898 The Bowery Waiter and the Old Time Ball Player
1899 Raid of a New York Bowery Saloon
1900 Dancing on the Bowery
Knock-out Drops on the Bowery
1901 The Bowery Kiss
1902 A Bowery Five Cent Shave
The Bowery Kiss
How They Do Things on the Bowery
Japanese Bowery
1903 Bowery Street Dancers
1905 Fire in New York's Bowery
1907 On the Stage; or, Melodrama from the Bowery
Bowline, Tom
1909 Up the Ladder with Tom Bowline
Bowling
1902 Bowling Alley at a German Picnic
1903 Bowling Alley
1910 The Bowling Craze
The Bowling Fiend
Bowling Green (New York City)
1900 Bowling Green
Bowls
1910 Bill Plays Bowls
Bowser
1907 Bowser's House Cleaning
Box
1898 The Stingy Girl and the Box of Candy
1901 The Lovers, Coal Box, and Fireplace
1902 A Dutch Soldier's Christmas Box
1903 The Famous Box Trick
The Mysterious Box
Two Chappies in a Box
1904 Casting a Guide Box, Westinghouse Works
1905 The Postman's Christmas Box
1906 Dancing Sentry Box
1907 The Animated Pill Box
The Cigar Box
Tommy's Box of Tools
1908 Jack in Letter Box
The Man in the Box
The Tinder Box
1909 An Alpine Echo; or, The Symphony of a Swiss Music Box
The Pill Box
1910 The Cheese Box
The Wrong Box
Boxer Rebellion
use **China—History—Boxer Rebellion, 1899-1901**
Boxers and boxing
rt **Prizefight**
1897 Boxing for Points
1898 Boxing
Boxing Cats
1899 Boxing Dogs
The Boxing Horse
Jeffries and Brother Boxing
Jeffries Boxing with Tommy Ryan
1901 Boxing in Barrels
The Gordon Sisters Boxing
Ruhlin Boxing with "Denver" Ed. Martin
1902 French Boxers
Pugilist McKeever and Wife Bag Punching
1903 Boxing Match on Board the U.S. Cruiser Raleigh
English and French Boxers
Prof. Langtry's Boxing School
A Pugilistic Parson
1904 Boxing Horses, Luna Park, Coney Island
Pugilistic Toads

1907 Boxing Matches in England
Dancing Boxing Match, Montgomery and Stone
Great Boxing Contest
Happy Bob as a Boxer
1908 The Boxing Englishman
Boxing Mania
The Girls Boxing Match
Ihles & Antonio, Boxers
1909 Boxing Match [by Hallberg of Denmark and Young Joe Gaines "Baltimore Black"]
Jim Smith, the Champion Boxer
1910 Bill as a Boxer
Boxing Fever
An English Boxing Bout
Jeffries-Johnson World's Championship Boxing Contest, Held at Reno, Nevada, July 4, 1910
The Pugilist's Child

Boy
1896 Boys Bathing, Leapfrog—Atlantic City
1897 The Bad Boy and Poor Old Grandpa
"Boys Will Be Boys"
Dancing Darkey Boy
1898 Boys Stealing Apples
Countryman and Mischievous Boys
9th Infantry Boys' Morning Wash
Return of Our Soldier Boys
Street Boys at the Seashore
What Our Boys Did at Manila
1899 A Gay Old Boy
She Wanted to Be a Boy
Welcoming the Soldier Boys
1900 Grandma and the Bad Boys
1901 The Bad Boy's Joke on the Nurse
Boys Diving
Boys Entering Free Bath
Boys Free Public Baths
The Farmer and the Bad Boys
"You Dirty Boy"
1902 The Boys Help Themselves to Foxy Grandpa's Cigars
The Boys, Still Determined, Try It Again on Foxy Grandpa, with the Same Result
The Boys Think They Have One on Foxy Grandpa, but He Fools Them
The Boys Try to Put One Up on Foxy Grandpa
Foxy Grandpa Shows the Boys a Trick or Two with the Tramp
Foxy Grandpa Tells the Boys a Funny Story
A Gay Old Boy
Grandma and the Bad Boys
Jo Jo, the Dog Faced Boy
The Mischievous Boys and the Washerwoman
1903 Bad Boy and Hod Carrier
The Boy in the Barrel
Boy Up a Tree; or, Making Love in the Park
Breaker Boys Leaving the Coal Mines
Chautauqua Boys' Club. No. 1
Chautauqua Boys' Club. No. 2
Egyptian Boys in Swimming Race
Gardener Sprinkling Bad Boy
Indian Boys, Albuquerque School
The Messenger Boy's Mistake
Mischievous Boys
The Office Boy's Revenge
Only a Soldier Boy
Signal Boys Wig-Wagging
Small Boy and Bear, Hagenback's Circus
Small Boy and Lion Cub, Hagenback's Circus
West Indian Boys Diving for Money
1904 Bad Boy's Joke on the Nurse
The Bold Soger Boy
The Boy Under the Table
Boy's First Smoke
Boys' Trick on Grandpa
Boys Will Be Boys
The Dear Boys Home for the Holidays
A Little Boy Called "Taps"
Mischievous Boys
The Office Boy's Revenge
Those Troublesome Boys
Two Bad Boys in a Church
1905 The Bad Boy and the Grocery Man
Largest Fat Boy in the World
The Naughty Boys and Curate
Oh! You Dirty Boy!
The Old Boys of Dooagh, Achill Island, Iceland
1906 How the Office Boy Saw the Ball Game
1907 Bad Boy's Joke
The Boy, the Bust and the Bath
College Boy's First Love
The Inquisitive Boy; or, Uncle's Present
Jimmie, the Messenger Boy
Reedham Boys' Aquatic Sports
Those Boys Again
When We Were Boys
1908 A Bad Boy
Bad Boys
The Bell Boy's Revenge
The Blind Boy
Boy and the Coalman
The Boy Detective; or, The Abductors Foiled
The Circus Boy
A Gay Old Boy
Go, Little Cabin Boy
A Good Boy
The Hallroom Boys Received Queer Freight
His Sweetheart When a Boy
James Boys in Missouri
Our New Errand Boy
Peck's Bad Boy
Reedham Boys' Festival Drill
The Scandalous Boys
The Stolen Plans; or, The Boy Detective
What One Small Boy Can Do
Yens Yensen, The Swedish Butcher Boy; or, Mistaken for a Burglar
First Cigar (Le premier cigare d'un collégien)
1909 Adventures of a Drummer Boy
Apprentice Boys at Newport [R.I.] Naval Training Station
The Boy and His Kite
The Boy and the Convict
A Boy Hero; or, The Fisherman's Son
The Boy Scouts
Boyhood Dreams
Boy's Adventure
Boys' Holiday
Boys Will Be Boys
Brave Little Organ Boy
The Brave Page Boy
Butcher Boy
The Cabin Boy's Dog
A Day with Our Soldier Boys
From Cabin Boy to King
How the Page Boy Cured a Flirt
Saul and David: The Biblical Story of the Shepherd Boy Who Became King of the Israelites
Boy
Where Is My Wandering Boy To-night?
The Yiddisher Boy
1910 Bobby, the Boy Scout
The Boy and His Teddy Bear
Boy and Purse
The Boy City
Boy Scouts
The Boys of Topsy-Turvy Ranch
The Call Boy's Vengeance
"Conscience;" or, The Baker Boy
The Garibaldi Boy
Gilson and Those Boys
Girls Will Be Boys
The Hall-Room Boys
The Irish Boy
Ito, the Beggar Boy
A Japanese Peach Boy
Little Boy
The Little Drummer Boy
Mammy's Boy Joins the Army
The Messenger Boy Magician
The Messenger Boy's Sweetheart
The Modern Messenger Boy
Naughty Boys
A Pearl of Boy
Two Boys in Blue

Boy Scouts of America
rt **Scouts**
Boy Scouts of America in Camp at Silver Bay, Lake George, N.Y.

Boycotting
1903 Unfair House, Butchers Boycotting, San Francisco

Boynton, Capt.
1900 Capt. Boynton Feeding His Pets

Boynton, Paul, Capt.
1899 Prof. Paul Boynton Feeding His Sea Lions
1900 Capt. Boynton Feeding His Pets

Boyville
1902 Boyville Fire Brigade

Brabant
1907 Genevieve of Brabant

Bracciano
1908 Duchess of Bracciano

Bracelet
1909 The Bracelet

Bradford
1910 Bradford's Claim

Bragg, Captain
1910 Davy Jones and Captain Bragg

Braggart
1908 The Braggart; or, What He Said He Would Do and What He Really Did

Brahma
1909 The Brahma Diamond

Brahmin
1903 The Brahmin and the Butterfly
Miracles of Brahmin
1908 The Brahmin's Miracle

Brain
1907 Baxter's Brain Storm
Brain Storm
1909 Polka on Brain
Prof. Wise's Brain Serum Injector
Territory on Brain

Brake
1904 Westinghouse Air Brake Co., Casting Machine
Westinghouse Air Brake Co. Westinghouse Works

Branch
1903 Rural Wagon Giving Mail to Branch, U.S.P.O.

Brand
1898 Branding Cattle
Calf Branding
1901 Branding Hams
1904 Rounding Up and Branding Cattle
1905 Roping and Branding Wild Horses
1907 Retribution; or, The Brand of Cain
1910 The Branded Man
Branding a Thief

Brannigan
1906 Brannigan Sets Off the Blast

Bravado
1908 Roman Colonel's Bravado

Bravery
1898 Brave Cubans Firing at Spanish Soldiers
1907 Presentation of Firemen's Bravery Medals by Mayor McClellan
1908 Braving Death to Save a Life
One of the Bravest
1909 The Brave Girl on the Fifteenth Floor
A Brave Irish Lass, the Story of an Eviction in Ireland
Brave Little Organ Boy
The Brave Page Boy
The Brave (?) Policeman
Brave Women of '76
A Bride Won by Bravery
Fortune Favors the Brave
Young Deer's Bravery
1910 The Brave Deserve the Fair
Brave Hearts; or, Saved from the Indians by a Woman's Wit
A Brave Little Girl
Brave Little Heart
A Brave Western Girl
The Bravest Girl in the South

Braves
1910 A Cheyenne Brave
A True Indian Brave

Brazil
1908 Brazil—The Cascades
1909 The Brazilian's Ring
1910 A Trip to Brazil

Breach
1909 Breach of Promise
1910 The Breach of Discipline

Bread
1904 The Passion Play (La multiplication des pains)
1906 I Fetch the Bread
1909 Casting Bread upon the Water
1910 Cast Thy Bread upon the Waters

Bring
1899 Bringing a Friend Home for Dinner
1900 Boers Bringing in British Prisoners
Bringing General Lawton's Body Back to Manila
Bringing in the Wounded During the Battle of Grobler's Kloof
1903 Irish Peasants Bringing Their Milk to a Cooperative Creamery
1905 Bringing Up a Girl in the Way She Should Go [No. 1]
Bringing Up a Girl in the Way She Should Go [No. 2]
1906 Army Pack Train Bringing Supplies
1908 Hunchback Brings Luck
1909 Bring Me Some Ice
Brought to Terms

Brink
1905 Brink of the Upper Falls of the Yellowstone River, Wyoming
Brink of the Vernal Fall, Yosemite Valley
1909 On the Brink
On the Brink of the Precipice

Brisquet
1909 Brisquet

Bristol Harbor
1903 Panoramic View of Herreshoff Works from Bristol Harbor

British
use **England and the English**

British Columbia
1902 Panoramic View Between Palliser and Field, B. C.
Panoramic View of the Canadian Pacific R.R. near Leauchoil, B. C.

British India
1910 Scenes in British India

British West Indies
1903 Native Women Washing Clothes at St. Vincent, B. W. I.
1908 Cocoa Industry, Trinidad, British West Indies

Britt, Jimmy
1905 Impersonation of Britt-Nelson Fight
Nelson-Britt Prize Fight
1909 The Summers-Britt Fight Pictures

Brittany (France)
1907 Picturesque Brittany
1908 Around the Coast of Brittany
Clogmaking in Brittany
Head-Dresses Worn in Brittany
Wedding in Brittany
1909 Real Brittany
1910 Brittany Lassies
Druid Remains in Brittany

Broadjumping
1899 Yale Athletes Broad Jumping

Broadsword
bt **Sword**
1898 Broadsword Drill
Broadsword Exercise on the Battleship Texas
1903 Broad Sword Contest

Broadway (New York City)
1896 Broadway & Park Row, Front of U.S. Post Office, N.Y.
Li Hung Chang Driving Through 4th St. and Broadway [New York City]
1897 Broadway, New York, at Madison Square
1900 Broadway at Post Office
14th Street and Broadway
1901 Broadway and Fourteenth St.
Experimental
1902 Broadway & Union Square, New York
Scene on Lower Broadway
1905 The Broadway Massage Parlor
1907 A Trip Up Broadway
1910 45 Minutes from Broadway

Broadway, Galveston (Texas)
1900 Searching Ruins on Broadway, Galveston, for Dead Bodies

Broke
1909 Broke Again

Broken
1903 Broken Trace
1908 The Broken Heart
The Broken Violin
Two Broken Hearts, the Story of a Worthless Husband and a Faithful Dog
1909 A Broken Heart
A Broken Life
The Broken Locket
A Broken Melody
Broken Ties
The Broken Vase
The Broken Violin
1910 The Broken Doll
The Broken Friendship
Broken Happiness
The Broken Oath
The Broken Spell
A Broken Symphony
A Deal in Broken China

Broker
1897 Love in a Broker's Office
1905 The Broker's Athletic Typewriter
1910 The Broker's Daughter

Broncho
1898 Bucking Broncho
1899 A Bucking Broncho
1902 Broncho Busting Scene, Championship of the World
1903 Breaking a Bronco
Broncho Busting Along the Lines of the Denver & Rio Grande Railway
The Broncho Horse Race
Bucking Broncho Contest
Bucking Broncho Contest [Sheridan Contest]
Bucking Bronchos
1904 Bucking Broncos
1910 The Bucking Broncho

Broncho Billy
1910 Broncho Billy's Redemption

Brooding
1908 Artificial Brooding

Brook trout
1900 Brook Trout Fishing
1903 Feeding Brook Trout at the Pennsylvania State Fishery

Brooklyn (New York City)
1898 Return of Troop C, Brooklyn
1899 New Brooklyn to New York via Brooklyn Bridge, No. 1
New Brooklyn to New York via Brooklyn Bridge, No. 2
1900 Brooklyn Lodge, No. 22, B.P.O. Elks
1903 Burning of the Academy of Music, Brooklyn
Fusion, On to Brooklyn!
1905 Black and White; or, The Mystery of a Brooklyn Baby Carriage
1907 Brooklyn

Brooklyn (Ship)
1898 Close View of the "Brooklyn," Naval Parade
Cruiser Brooklyn
Cruiser "Brooklyn"
Officers and Crew of the U.S. Cruiser "Brooklyn"
Parade of Marines, U.S. Cruiser, "Brooklyn"
U.S. Cruiser "Brooklyn," Naval Parade

Brooklyn Bridge (New York City)
1897 At the Top of Brooklyn Bridge
1899 Across Brooklyn Bridge
Full View of Brooklyn Bridge
New Brooklyn to New York via Brooklyn Bridge, No. 1
New Brooklyn to New York via Brooklyn Bridge, No. 2
Panoramic View of Brooklyn Bridge
View of Brooklyn Bridge from a Ferryboat
1901 Panorama of Brooklyn Bridge, River Front, and Tall Buildings from the East River
1903 Battleship "Illinois" Passing Under Brooklyn Bridge
Panorama Water Front and Brooklyn Bridge from East River

Brooklyn Handicap
1897 Finish of the Brooklyn Handicap
1899 Finish of the Brooklyn Handicap, 1899
1902 Steeplechasing at the Brooklyn Handicap
1904 The Brooklyn Handicap, 1904

Brother
1898 Doing Her Big Brother's Tricks on the Bar
1899 Jeffries and Brother Boxing
1900 Maude's Naughty Little Brother
1901 Jeffries Sparring with His Brother
1902 Capture of the Biddle Brothers
Conture Brothers, Acrobats
The Deonzo Brothers in Their Wonderful Barrel Jumping Act
1903 Brother
The Cabinet Trick of the Davenport Brothers
1904 The Brothers Laure
Joseph Sold by His Brothers
1905 Only Her Brother
1906 New Brother
Rival Brothers
1907 Brother Willie's Revenge
The Twin Brother's Joke
1908 Brother Lieutenants
Brothers in Arms
Brother
Brothers in Arms
The Two Brothers
Two Brothers of the G.A.R.
Younger Brothers
Acrobatic Toys (Exercices des frères bouts-de-bois)
1909 Bad Brother
Brother Against Brother
Brother and Sister
The Brothers
Brothers in Arms
The Brothers Laurento
A Brother's Wrong
Twin Brothers
Two Brothers
The Wright Brothers Aeroplane
1910 Brother Man
The Brother, Sister and Cowpuncher
Brotherly Love
Brothers
The Brothers
A Brother's Devotion
The Brothers' Feud
A Devoted Little Brother
Foster Brothers
The Harry Brothers
How Brother Cook Was Taught a Lesson
Joseph Sold by His Brethren
The Three Brothers
The Two Brothers

Broussa
1910 City of the Hundred Mosques, Broussa, Asia Minor

Brown
1907 Brown Goes to Mother
How Brown Saw the Baseball Game
1909 Brown's Moving Day
How Brown Got Married
1910 Brown's Gouty Foot

Brown, Farmer
1910 Lazy Farmer Brown

Brown, Mr.
1908 Mr. Brown Has a Tile Loose
1910 Hustling Mr. Brown

Brown, Mrs.
1905 A Dog Lost, Strayed or Stolen. $25.00 Reward. Apply to Mrs. Brown, 711 Park Ave.
1906 Mrs. Brown's Bad Luck

Brown, Private
1909 Private Brown

Brown, Rube
1907 Rube Brown in Town

Brown Hoisting and Conveying Machine
1900 Demonstrating the Action of the Brown Hoisting and Conveying Machine in Unloading a Schooner of Iron Ore, and Loading the Material on the Cars

Bruges (Belgium)
1910 Bruges, Belgium

Bruised
1909 A Bruised Heart

Bruno, Giordono
1909 Giordono Bruno

Brush
1898 A Mid-Winter Brush
1900 A Brush on the Speedway
1903 A Brush in the Snow
1904 Brush Between Cowboys and Indians

Brussels (Belgium)
1908 'Round Brussels in Ten Minutes
1910 Charlie and Kitty in Brussels

Bryan, William Jennings
1900 William J. Bryan in the Biograph
1903 Bryan at Home
Hon. Wm. Jennings Bryan
1906 Bryan
William Jennings Bryan
1908 Bryan in Chicago
Bryan's Reception in New York
Hon. William J. Bryan and Hon. John W. Kern

Bryn Mawr (Pennsylvania)
1900 Bryn Mawr Horse Show
1902 The Bryn Mawr Horse Show

Bubbles
1897 Making Soap Bubbles
Soap Bubbles
1904 Bubbles!
Soap Bubbles
1906 Soap Bubbles

Buccaneer (Ship)
1898 N.Y. Journal Despatch Yacht "Buccaneer"

Buck
1910 The Taming of Buck

Buck dance
1898 Buck Dance, Ute Indians
1903 Buck and Wing Dance
Buck Dance

Bucket
1904 A Bucket of Cream Ale

Bucking
1898 Bucking Broncho
1899 A Bucking Broncho
Bucking the Blizzard
1903 Bucking Broncho Contest
Bucking Broncho Contest [Sheridan Contest]
Bucking Bronchos
Snow-Plow Bucking a 15-foot Snow Slide
1904 Bucking Broncos
1910 The Bucking Broncho

Bud
1910 Bud's Escapade
Bud's Triumph

Buddhists
1910 Customs of the Buddhists in India

Buds
1910 From Bud to Blossom
In the Season of Buds

Buenos Aires (Argentina)
1910 Taming Wild Horses at Buenos Aires

Buff
1904 Blind Man's Buff

Buffalo
1903 Buffaloes Born in the Zoo Gardens
1905 Great Buffalo Chase
1907 Buffalo Hunt
1909 Buffalo Racing in Madoera
1910 Buffalo Fight

Buffalo (New York)
1896 Buffalo Horse Market
1897 Buffalo Fire Department in Action
Buffalo Police on Parade
Buffalo Stockyards
1899 Buffalo Fire Department
1901 Arrival of Funeral Cortege at the City Hall, Buffalo, N.Y.
Buffalo Street Parade
Chapin Post of Buffalo
The Mob Outside the Temple of Music at the Pan-American Exposition [Buffalo]
Panoramic View of the Crowd Rushing for the City Hall, Buffalo, to View the Body of President McKinley
President McKinley at the Buffalo Exposition
President McKinley's Funeral Cortege at Buffalo, N.Y.
1903 Lafayette Square, Buffalo, N.Y.
Main Street, Buffalo, N.Y.
1907 Buffalo

Buffalo Bill
1897 Buffalo Bill and Escort
1899 Home of Buffalo Bill
1905 Buffalo Bill Fight

Buffalo Bill's Wild West Show
1898 Parade of Buffalo Bill's Wild West Show, No. 1
Parade of Buffalo Bill's Wild West Show, No. 2
1900 Buffalo Bill's Wild West Parade
Buffalo Bill's Wild West Show
1901 Buffalo Bill's Wild West Parade
1902 Buffalo Bill's Wild West Show
1903 Buffalo Bill's Parade
Buffalo Bill's Street Parade
1910 Buffalo Bill's Wild West and Pawnee Bill's Far East

Buffin
1909 Buffin Wins First Prize

Buffoon
1909 The Buffoon

Bug
1908 Two Crazy Bugs
1910 The Kissing Bug

Bugle
1902 When the Bugle Sounds "Charge!"
1909 Billy's Bugle
The Bugle Call

Building
1898 In Front of "Journal" Building
1901 The Builders of Shamrock II
Building a Harbor at San Pedro
A Composite Picture of the Principal Buildings in Washington, D.C.
Demolishing and Building Up the Star Theatre
The Horticultural Building
Panorama of Brooklyn Bridge, River Front, and Tall Buildings from the East River
Panoramic View Gov't Building, Pan. Am. Exp.
1902 Building Made Easy; or, How Mechanics Work in the Twentieth Century
Pontoon Bridge Building
1903 Building the Suez Canal
Carriers Leaving Building, U.S.P.O.
The House That Jack Built
A Windy Day at the Flatiron Building
1904 Building a Lighthouse
Panorama from German Building, World's Fair
Pan. of St. Railway Building, Pittsburg, Pa.
1905 Panorama from the Roof of the Times Building, New York
1906 Exploded Gas Tanks, U.S. Mint, Emporium and Spreckels' Bld'g.
Ruins Bulletin Building, California Theatre and Evening Post
Singer Building Foundation Co.
1907 Bill Butt-in and the Burglars
[Building a Railroad in Africa]
1909 Building Barrels
The House That Jack Built
1910 Bird's Eye View from World's Highest Buildings

Bulgarian
1907 Bulgarian Army

Bull
1900 Fight Between a Lion and a Bull
1901 Bull on the Stampede
1902 The Bull and Bear
The Bull and the Picnickers
1905 Wrestler and Bull
1908 Three Maiden Ladies and a Bull
Uncle Bill's Bull
1909 Training Bulls for the Fight

Bull cart
1902 Native Bull Cart at Morne Rouge (A Suburb of St. Pierre)

Bulldog
1901 Pie, Tramp and the Bulldog
1905 The British Bull Dog
Burglar and Bull Dog
1909 How the Bulldog Paid the Rent

Buller, Redvers, General Sir
1899 General Sir Redvers Buller
General Sir Redvers Buller, and Staff, Landing at Cape Town, South Africa

Bullet
1903 Bullet vs. Whiskey

Bulletin
1906 Ruins Bulletin Building, California Theatre and Evening Post

Bullfight
1898 Bull Fight, No. 1
Bull Fight, No. 2
Bull Fight, No. 3
1900 Bull Fight
1901 Spanish Coronation Royal Bull-Fight
1902 Great Bull Fight
1903 Arrival of the Bull Fighter
Bull Fight, No. 1
Bull Fight, No. 2
Mexican Bull Fight
New Bull Fight
Spanish Bull Fight
1904 Bull-Fight at Juarez, Mexico
Bull Fight with Matadors Senor Don Luis Mazzantini and Bombita
1906 Bull Fight
1908 Bull Fight in Arcachon
1909 The Bull Fight
The Bull Fight of Oran
1910 A Bullfight in Mexico

Bullocks
1904 Bullocks Swimming

Bullrushes
1903 Moses in the Bullrushes

Bully
1909 Bully and Recruit
1910 The Bully
A Bully's Waterloo

Bum
1900 How They Fired the Bum
One on the Bum
1907 What the Bum Did to the Dude
1910 The Bum and the Bomb

Bumpety Bumps
1905 Girls on the "Bumpety Bumps"

Bumping
1902 "What Ho, She Bumps!"
1904 Bumping Races

Bumptious
1910 Bumptious as a Fireman
Bumptious as an Aviator
Bumptious Plays Baseball
Bumptious Takes Up Automobiling
How Bumptious Papered the Parlor
The Joke They Played on Bumptious
Mr. Bumptious on Birds

Bunch
1907 Casey on a Souse—Gives the Bunch a Douse
1909 A Bunch of Lilacs
1910 Only a Bunch of Flowers

Bunco
1899 Bunco on the Seashore
1900 How the Farmer Was Buncoed
1907 The Bunco Steerers; and, How They Were Caught
1908 Buncoed Stage Johnnie
1909 The Rubes and the Bunco Men

Bund
1901 The Bund, Shanghai

Bundle
1899 The Burglar and the Bundle

Bungling
1897 The Bungling Waiter

Buoy
1899 The Breeches Buoy
1901 Working the Breeches Buoy
1909 The Life Buoy

Burden
1909 The Burden of Debt
1910 Bear Ye One Another's Burdens

Bureau
1909 The Detectives of the Italian Bureau

Burglar
1897 Burglar Caught in the Act
Burglars in the Pantry
1898 The Burglar
The Burglar in the Bed Chamber
The Burglar on the Roof
The Old Maid and the Burglar
1899 The Burglar and the Bundle
How Bill the Burglar Got a Bath
Little Willie and the Burglar
What Happened to the Burglar
1900 The Burglar-Proof Bed
The Tramp and the Burglar
1901 How the Professor Fooled the Burglars
1902 The Burglars in the Wine Cellar
A Gentleman Burglar
Happy Hooligan Turns Burglar
The Mystical Burglars
1903 Alphonse and Gaston and the Burglar (Thumb Book)
The Burglar
Burglar and Fairy
Burglar and Old Maid
Burglar's Escape
A Daring Daylight Burglary
The Dude and the Burglars
The Irrepressible Burglars
Subub Surprises the Burglar
The Vanishing Burglars
1904 Burglar and Girls
Burglar, Cop and Barrel
Burglars at Work
Capture of Yegg Bank Burglars
The Girls and the Burglar
A Novel Way of Catching a Burglar
Up-to-Date Burglars; or, The Mystified Cops
What Burglar Bill Found in the Safe

1905 The Athletic Girl and the Burglar
Bishop and Burglar
Burglar and Bull Dog
Burglar and Vapor Bath
Burglar Bill
The Burglar's Slide for Life
Burlesque Tramp Burglars
Desperate Encounter Between Burglar and Police
An Eccentric Burglary
The Girls, the Burglar, and the Rat
1906 The Acrobatic Burglars
1907 A Baffled Burglar
Burglar and Old Maids
Burglar and Policeman
The Burglar and the Baby
The Burglar; or, A Midnight Surprise
Burglary by Motor
Dogs Tracking Burglars
Modern Burglars
Slippery Jim, the Burglar
Up to Date Burglars
1908 After Midnight; or, A Burglar's Daughter
The Bifton Burglar
The Burglar and the Clock
The Burglar's Ball
The Burglar's Child
Burglar's New Trick
A Calamitous Elopement: How It Proved a Windfall for Burglar Bill
Catching a Burglar
The Christmas Burglars
Concealing a Burglar
The Downfall of the Burglars' Trust
Frightened by Burglars
The Gentleman Burglar
Yens Yensen, The Swedish Butcher Boy; or, Mistaken for a Burglar
1909 The Actor Burglar
A Burglar Cupid
The Burglar in a Basket
Burglar in the Trunk
A Burglar's Mistake
Burglary in the Year 2000
Jones' Burglar
Nancy; or, The Burglar's Daughter
The Sentimental Burglar
The Welcome Burglar
The Wrong Burglar
1910 The Burglar and the Baby
The Burglar Trap
Burglar's Daughter
Burglar's Dog
The Capture of the Burglar
His Last Burglary
[Jones, the Burglar Catcher]
The Lady and the Burglar
A New Burglar Alarm
The Old Maid and the Burglar

Burglar Bill
1904 What Burglar Bill Found in the Safe
1905 Burglar Bill
1908 A Calamitous Elopement: How It Proved a Windfall for Burglar Bill

Buried
1898 Burial of the "Maine" Victims
1903 Burial of Maine Sailors
1908 Buried Alive; or, Frolics on the Beach at Coney Island
1909 Buried Alive
A Buried Secret
1910 The Buried Man of Tebessa
The Buried Secret

Burke, Hefty
1910 The Romance of Hefty Burke

Burlesque
1897 Burlesque Cake Walk
1899 A Burlesque Queen
Burlesque Queen and a Country Photographer
Burlesque Queen and Country Photographer
1902 Burlesque on Romeo and Juliet
The Burlesque Suicide
The Burlesque Suicide, No. 2
The Burlesque Thieves
The Clown and His Burlesque Horse
1903 Burlesque Cock Fight
Burlesque Lions and Their Tamer, Hagenback's Circus
From Show Girl to Burlesque Queen
1904 A Burlesque Highway Robbery in "Gay Paree"
A Fire in a Burlesque Theatre
The Troubles of a Manager of a Burlesque Show
1905 Burlesque Tramp Burglars
1907 Chopin's Funeral March, Burlesqued
1910 The Burlesque Queen
A Queen of the Burlesque

Burlington Flyer
1902 Burlington Flyer

Burly
1910 Burly Bill

Burma
1904 Curious Sights in Burmah and Cashmere (Section 1)
Curious Sights in Burmah and Cashmere (Section 2)
1907 Life in a Burmah Teak Forest

Burn
1896 The Burning Stable
1900 Burning of the Bremen and Main [Hoboken]
Burning of the Bremen and Main (Another view) [Hoboken]
Burning of the Saale [Hoboken]
Burning of the Standard Oil Co.'s Tanks, Bayonne, N.J.
Burning of the Standard Oil Tanks
Panoramic View of Burning Wharves and Warehouses [Hoboken]
1902 The Burning of Durland's Riding Academy
Burning of St. Pierre [Martinique]
1903 Burning of the Academy of Music, Brooklyn
Burning the Rubbish
1904 Avenging a Crime; or, Burned at the Stake
1906 General Circular Panorama of the Burned Business District
Panoramic View from Alamo Square of San Francisco While Burning
1907 Colonial Virginia and Burning of Jamestown
1908 Nero and the Burning of Rome
1909 The Burning Home
Burning of Stamboul, Constantinople
Nero; or, The Burning of Rome
1910 With Bridges Burned

Burns, Bobby
1907 Land of Bobby Burns

Burns, Tommy
1906 O'Brien-Burns Contest, Los Angeles, Cal., Nov. 26th, 1906
1907 Burns-Moir
International Contest for the Heavyweight Championship: Squires vs. Burns, Ocean View, Cal., July 4th, 1907
Panorama, Crowds at Squires-Burns International Contest, from Center of Ring, Colma, July 4th, 1907
Panorama, Crowds at Squires-Burns International Contest, from Moving Picture Stand, July 4th, 1907
1908 Reproduction of Burns-Palmer Fight, London [England], February 10th, 1908
1909 World's Heavyweight Championship Pictures Between Tommy Burns and Jack Johnson

Burr, Aaron
1910 Tale of Colonial Days: An Episode in the Life of Alexander Hamilton and Aaron Burr

Burro
1901 Burro Pack Train on Main Street, Dawson City
Burro Pack Train on the Chilcoot Pass

Bush
1898 "Round and Round the Mulberry Bush"
1902 Around the Mulberry Bush

Bushnell, Governor
1897 Governor Bushnell of Ohio, and Staff

Bushranger
1904 "The Bushranger." Attack and Robbery of a Mail Convoy

Business
1903 Business Rivalry
1904 Buster and Tige Put a Balloon Vendor Out of Business
1905 Monkey Business
1906 General Circular Panorama of the Burned Business District
1909 A Paying Business
Pressing Business
1910 Booming Business
A Dog on Business
Good Business
On Time for Business
She Would Be a Business Man

Buss
1904 Washerwoman and Buss

Busses
1896 Busses Leaving R.R. Depot, Atlantic City
1905 Busses Passing Mansion House, London
Passengers Boarding Busses at Hyde Park Corner, London

Bust
1907 The Boy, the Bust and the Bath

Buster
1903 Buster's Joke on Papa
1904 Buster and Tige Put a Balloon Vendor Out of Business
Buster Makes Room for His Mama at the Bargain Counter
Buster's Dog to the Rescue
Section of Buster Brown Series, Showing a Sketch of Buster by Outcault
1909 Buster's Revenge

Buster Brown
1904 Buster Brown and the Dude
Pranks of Buster Brown and His Dog Tige
Section of Buster Brown Series, Showing a Sketch of Buster by Outcault

Busting
1902 Broncho Busting Scene, Championship of the World
1903 Broncho Busting Along the Lines of the Denver & Rio Grande Railway

Bustle
1901 Aunt Sallie's Wonderful Bustle
1904 The Bustle in the Narrow Door

Busy
1897 A Busy Corner
1899 In Busy 'Frisco
1901 A Busy Corner at Armour's
1903 The Busy Bee
Jerusalem's Busiest Street, Showing Mt. Zion
1904 The Busy Bee
A Busy Day for the Corset Model
That Busy Bee
1907 Busy Lizzie Loses Her Clothes
The Busy Man
1908 Busy Fiancé
Weary Waggles' Busy Day
1909 Father's Busy Papering
Her Busy Day
One Busy Hour

Busybody
1909 Little Busybody

Butcher
1901 Fun in a Butcher Shop
1903 Butcher Shop No. 1
Butcher Shop No. 2
Butchering and Cleaning Tables U.S.F.C.
Unfair House, Butchers Boycotting, San Francisco
1907 The Pork Butcher's Nightmare
1908 Yens Yensen, The Swedish Butcher Boy; or, Mistaken for a Burglar
1909 Butcher Boy
The Butcher's Bill
Pork Butcher

Butler
1903 How Buttons Got Even with the Butler
1908 Butler's Misdeed
1909 The Butler's Tricks
We Must Have a Butler
1910 The New Butler

Butler, Nicholas Murray
1902 Installation Ceremonies of President Butler

Butt
1904 Don't Butt In
1908 How the Pair Butted In
1909 How Binks Butted In

Butt, McCroskey, Gen.
1899 Gen. McCrosky Butt and Staff

Butt's Manual
1904 Butt's Manual, St. John's School

Butt-In, Mr.
1905 How Mr. Butt-In Benefits by Chauncey's Mishaps
1906 Mr. Butt-In

Butt-In, Bill
1907 Bill Butt-in and the Burglars

Butte (Montana)
1910 The Dancing Girl of Butte

Butter
1910 Butter Making in Normandy

Butterfly
1896 Butterfly Dance
1897 Butterfly Dance
1903 The Brahmin and the Butterfly
L'Argentine Butterfly Dance
1904 Metamorphosis of a Butterfly
1906 Butterfly Catching
1908 All on Account of a Butterfly
The Butterflies
Japanese Butterflies
The Pupa Changes into a Butterfly

Buttes Chaumont
1909 Buttes Chaumont After a Snow Storm

Buttinsky, Mr.
1906 Mr. Butt-in-Sky
1909 Mr. Buttinsky

Button
1903 How Buttons Got Even with the Butler
1906 The Lost Collar Button; or, A Strenuous Search
1907 All on Account of a Lost Collar Button
Moses Sells a Collar Button
1908 Button, Button, Where Is the Button?
The Button of Invisibility
1910 Fricot Has Lost His Collar Button

Buy
1902 Reuben Buys a Gold Brick
1903 Buying a Baby
Buying Stamps from Rural Wagon, U.S.P.O.
1907 Buying a Donkey
Buying a Ladder
Father Buys a Hand Roller
1908 Buying a Cow
Buying a Hat
Buying a Title
Buying an Automobile
Monty Buys a Motor
1909 Buy Matches, Please
Buying Manhattan
Jones Has Bought a Phonograph
1910 Buying a Bear
Buying a Mother-in-Law
The Cigars His Wife Bought

Bygone
1909 The Empty Sleeve; or, Memories of By-Gone Days
Let Bygones Be Bygones

Bystander
1909 The Innocent Bystander

Byzantium
1909 Theodora (Teodora imperatrice di Bisanzio)

C.Q.D.
1909 C.Q.D.; or, Saved by Wireless, a True Story of "The Wreck of the Republic"
1910 Love's "C.Q.D."

Cabin
1899 Founder's Log Cabin
1903 Firing the Cabin
Uncle Tom's Cabin
Uncle Tom's Cabin Parade
1908 Go, Little Cabin Boy
1909 The Cabin Boy's Dog
From Cabin Boy to King
1910 Uncle Tom's Cabin
Uncle Tom's Cabin, Part 1
Uncle Tom's Cabin, Part 2
Uncle Tom's Cabin, Part 3

Cabinet
1898 President McKinley and Cabinet at Camp Alger, May 28, 1898
1899 President McKinley and Wife, Members of His Cabinet and Their Wives and Capt. Coghlan Leaving the Cruiser Raleigh
1903 The Cabinet Trick of the Davenport Brothers
President McKinley and His Cabinet on the Reviewing Stand, at Fairmount Park, Phila., May 27, 1899
1907 The Bewildering Cabinet

Cable
1902 A Cable Road in San Francisco, Cal.
1905 Panorama from Car on Mendel Pass Cable Railway

Cable car
1905 Panorama from Car on Mendel Pass Cable Railway

Caciedo
1898 Caciedo

Cadets
1896 Charge of West Point Cadets
Parade, Elkins Cadets, Canton, O.
West Point Cadet Cavalry
West Point Cadet Cavalry Charge
West Point Cadet Cavalry Drill
West Point Cadet Drill
1897 Corcoran Cadets, Washington
First Corps Cadets; Mass. National Guard
Girard College Cadets
Girard College Cadets at Double Quick
Girard College Cadets in Review
West Point Cadets
1898 St. Vincent's Cadets
1899 Girard College Cadets
West Point Cadets
The West Point Cadets and Band
1900 A Cadet Cavalry Charge
Dress Parade of the Woodward High School Cadets
Drill of Naval Cadets at Newport
Gun Drill by Naval Cadets at Newport [R.I., Naval] Training School
Orchard Lake Cadets
Sham Battle on Land by Cadets at Newport Naval Training School
Walnut Hill Cadets
1901 The High School Cadets
U.S. Naval Cadets Marching in Review
1902 Prince Henry [of Prussia] Reviewing the Cadets at West Point
Review of Cadets at West Point
Review of Cadets, West Point
1903 Cadet's First Smoke
Girard College Cadets Reviewed by Governor Hastings, at the Dedication of Stephen Girard's Monument
1904 West Point Cadets Escorting Liberty Bell, St. Louis Exposition
1907 Pres. Roosevelt Reviewing West Point Cadets

Cadillac, Sieur de
1901 Landing of Cadillac

Caesar, Julius
1907 Shakespeare Writing "Julius Caesar"
1908 Caesar Up-to-Date
Julius Caesar
Julius Caesar, an Historical Tragedy
1909 Julius Caesar
1910 Caesar in Egypt

Cafe
1897 A Bowery Cafe
1901 The Mysterious Cafe
1903 The Enchanted Cafe
The New Enchanted Cafe
1909 Quiet Day at the Cafe
1910 The Masher's Delirium (Le rêve du garçon de café)
The Masher's Delirium (Le songe du garçon de café)

Cage
1906 Escaped from the Cage
1909 A Bird in a Gilded Cage
The Cursed Cage
1910 The Cage (An Episode in the Adventures of Morgan the Pirate)
Foolshead in the Lion's Cage

Cagliostro
1903 Cagliostro's Mirror
1910 Cagliostro

Cain
1907 Retribution; or, The Brand of Cain
1910 Cain and Abel

Cairo (Egypt)
1896 Streets of Cairo
1901 Acrobats in Cairo
Wedding Procession in Cairo
1902 Street Scene in Cairo
1903 Market Scene in Cairo, Egypt
Streets in Cairo, Egypt
1904 Cairo and the Nile
1905 From Cairo to the Pyramids
1907 From Cairo to Khartoum
1910 The Firemen of Cairo
Roosevelt in Cairo

Cake
1900 For Ice Cream and Cake
1905 The Stolen Cake
1907 Fine Birthday Cake
Her First Cake

Cakewalk
1897 Burlesque Cake Walk
Comedy Cake Walk
A Coon Cake Walk
1898 Cake Walk
1900 Up-to-Date Cake-Walk
1901 Bally-Hoo Cake Walk
1903 Cake Walk
The Cake Walk Infernal
Cake Walking Horses
1904 Cakewalk
Fantastic Cake Walk
A Seaside Cakewalk
The Midgets (Le cake-walk chez les nains)
1905 Cake-Walk in Our Alley
1907 I'll Dance the Cakewalk

Calabria (Italy)
1908 Hold-Up in Calabria

Calamitous
1908 A Calamitous Elopement: How It Proved a Windfall for Burglar Bill

Caldron
1903 The Infernal Caldron

Caledonian Club (New York City)
1903 New York Caledonian Club's Parade

Calf
1898 Calf Branding
1908 The Explosive Calf
Man with Calf's Head
1909 Story of a Calf's Head

Calico
1910 Jean and the Calico Doll

Califf, Mr. and Mrs.
1900 Mr. and Mrs. Califf at Dinner

California
1897 Arrest in Chinatown, San Francisco, Cal.
Lick Observatory, Mt. Hamilton, Cal.
Stanford University, California
1898 California Limited, A.T. & S.F.R.R.
California Orange Groves, Panoramic View
California Volunteers Marching To Embark
South Spring Street, Los Angeles, Cal.
1901 Ascending Mt. Low, California
California Oil Wells in Operation
Jeffries and Ruhlin Sparring Contest at San Francisco, Cal., Nov. 15, 1901—Five Rounds
Launching of the New Battleship "Ohio" at San Francisco, Cal. When President McKinley Was There
Pigeon Farm at Los Angeles, Cal
1902 Bird's Eye View of San Francisco, Cal., from a Balloon
A Cable Road in San Francisco, Cal.
California Naval Reserves
California Naval Reserves Drilling on Board Ship
1903 California Limited
The California Limited of the Santa Fe Route
Oil Fields, Tanks and Lakes of Oil; Kern Co., Cal.
Panorama of Cal. Oil Fields
Past Shasta Spring, California
Reproduction of the Corbett-McGovern Fight (San Francisco, Cal, March 31, 1903)
Sacramento Valley, Cal. from Pilot of Engine
1905 Coaching Down the Merced Grade, Merced Cañon, California
Combined Reaper and Thresher at Merced, San Joaquin Valley, California
The "Crazy" Ferryboat, San Francisco, California
Floral Parade Festival of Roses, Pasadena, Cal.
Fourth of July Celebration, Yosemite California
Fourth of July Parade Yosemite California
Indian Pony Races, Yosemite Valley, California
Roman Chariot Race, Pasadena, California
Stages Passing Through Wawona Big Tree, Mariposa Grove, California
Vernal Falls, Yosemite Valley, California
1906 A Daring Hold-Up in Southern California
Floral Fiesta, Los Angeles, Cal.
O'Brien-Burns Contest, Los Angeles, Cal., Nov. 26th, 1906
Railroad Collision at Los Angeles, Calif.
Ruins Bulletin Building, California Theatre and Evening Post
A Trip to Berkeley, Cal.
1907 Floral Parade at Pasadena, Calif.
International Contest for the Heavyweight Championship: Squires vs. Burns, Ocean View, Cal., July 4th, 1907

Jim Jeffries on His California Ranch
1910 Aviation at Los Angeles, Calif.
Flower Parade at Pasadena, California
In Old California
Industries in Southern California

Calino
1909 Calino Objects to Work
1910 Calino Takes New Lodgings
Calino Travels as a Prince

Caliph
1908 A Tale of a Harem: The Caliph and the Pirate
1909 The Caliph's Adventures
The Cobbler and the Caliph

Calisthenics
1897 A Regimental Calisthenic Drill in the British Army
1901 Calisthenic Drill
1903 Musical Calisthenics
1904 Central High School, Calisthenics, Missouri Commission
Emerson School, Calisthenics, Missouri Commission
Lathrop School, Calisthenics, Missouri Commission
Linwood School, Calisthenics, Missouri Commission
Whittier School, Calisthenics, Missouri Commission

Call
1897 Ambulance Call
1898 Mess Call, American Camp at Chicamauga
The Unwelcome Callers
1899 Phillis Was Not Dressed to Receive Callers
1900 The Call to Arms!
1901 A Close Call
1902 Calling the Pigeons
1903 Passion Play: Christ Calling Zaccheus from the Tree
1908 The Call of the Wild
1909 The Bugle Call
The Call of the Heart
Calling Day
A Close Call
The Last Call
The Telephone Call
An Unprofitable Call
1910 The Call
The Call of the Blood
The Call of the Circus
The Call of the Forest
The Call of the Heart
The Call of the West
The Call to Arms
The Greater Call
A Sudden Telephone Call

Call boy
1910 The Call Boy's Vengeance

Caloocan (Philippines)
1899 Advance of Kansas Volunteers at Caloocan
U.S. Troops and Red Cross in the Trenches Before Caloocan [P. I.]

Calumny
1910 The Calumny

Calypso
1905 The Mysterious Island (L'île de Calypso. Ulysse et le géant polypheme)

Camargo
1910 Camargo

Cambodge
1909 Elephant Hunting in Cambodge

Cambodian
1907 Cambodian Customs

Cambridge (Massachusetts)
1902 Prince Henry [of Prussia] Visiting Cambridge, Mass. and Harvard University

Cambridge University (England)
1899 Oxford and Cambridge University Boat Crews
Oxford-Cambridge Boat-Race
1900 Oxford-Cambridge Race
1901 International Field Sports—Oxford-Cambridge vs. Harvard-Yale
1902 Third Trinity, Cambridge, Winning the Race for the Grand Challenge Cup. Taken at Henley on July 10th, 1902
1904 The Oxford and Cambridge Boat Race
1907 Cambridge-Oxford Race
1908 Oxford and Cambridge Boat Race

Cambyses
1909 Cambyses, King of Persia

Camellias
1908 The Lady with the Camellias

Camels
1902 Camels Eating
Camels in a Tent
1903 Camel Race on the Desert
Caravan of Camels
Double-Humped Camels
"Holy Moses" the Camel
1904 Camel Caravan, Pekin, China
1905 Girls Riding Camels
1908 The Prize Camel
1910 Camel and Horse Racing in Egypt

Camera
1898 His Holiness, Leo XIII in the Gardens of the Vatican, Being Photographed by the American Biograph Camera
1900 Experimental—Handcamera
1903 The Camera Fiend
The Camera Fiend, No. 2
Willie's Camera
1904 What Happened to a Camera Fiend
1906 Deer Stalking with a Camera
The Snapshot Fiend; or, Willie's New Camera
1907 His First Camera
1908 Bridal Couple Dodging Cameras
Nellie's Camera
A Second-Hand Camera
1910 Caught by the Camera
The Tale a Camera Told

Cameron, Jessie, Miss
1903 Miss Jessie Cameron, Champion Child Sword Dancer

Camille
1910 Camille
The Miner and Camille

Camp
1897 A Camp of Zingari Gypsies
Gordon Highlanders Marching into Camp
1898 Battery B Arriving at Camp
Battery B Pitching Camp
15,000 Soldiers Reviewed by the President at Camp Alger May 28
Fun in a Spanish Camp
Fun in the American Camp at Chicamauga
General Wheeler and Secretary of War Alger at Camp Wikoff
How a Bottle of Cocktails Was Smuggled into Camp
How the Ballet Girl Was Smuggled into Camp
In Camp, Tampa, Fla.
Koltes' Camp, G.A.R.
Mess Call, American Camp at Chicamauga
Military Camp at Tampa, Taken from Train
Panoramic View of Camp Wikoff
President McKinley and Cabinet at Camp Alger, May 28, 1898
President McKinley's Inspection of Camp Wikoff
A Romp in Camp
71st Regiment, N.G.S.N.Y. at Camp Wikoff
Spanish Infantry Attacking American Soldiers in Camp
1899 Fun in Camp
A Naval Camp
1901 In the Gypsy Camp
1903 Georgia Camp Meeting
Ohio Colored Troops at Camp Alger
Panorama of American Soldiers in Camp
Wash Day in Camp
1905 Camp Life of the Esquimaux at Cape Nome, Alaska
Chinese Cook at Hance's Camp, Grand Cañon, Arizona
Dance at Esquimaux Camp, Cape Nome, Alaska
"Dinner Time" at Camp Curry Yosemite Valley
Fortune Telling in a Gypsy Camp
Stage Enroute to Hance's Camp, Grand Cañon of Arizona
1906 Thieves in Camp, Golden Gate Park
1907 Reggy's Camping Party
1908 Romance in a Gypsy Camp
1909 A Friend in the Enemy's Camp
1910 Boy Scouts of America in Camp at Silver Bay, Lake George, N.Y.
The Luck of Roaring Camp

Camp Alger (Virginia)
1898 15,000 Soldiers Reviewed by the President at Camp Alger May 28
President McKinley and Cabinet at Camp Alger, May 28, 1898
1903 Ohio Colored Troops at Camp Alger

Camp Curry, Yosemite Valley (California)
1905 "Dinner Time" at Camp Curry Yosemite Valley

Camp Wikoff, Montauk Point, Long Island (New York)
1898 General Wheeler and Secretary of War Alger at Camp Wikoff
Panoramic View of Camp Wikoff
President McKinley's Inspection of Camp Wikoff
71st Regiment, N.G.S.N.Y. at Camp Wikoff

Campbell, Herbert
1902 Mr. Dan Leno, Assisted by Mr. Herbert Campbell, Editing the "Sun"

Campus
1901 The Campus Martius

Cana
1904 The Passion Play (Les noces de Cana)

Canada
1896 American Falls from Bottom of Canadian Shore
Horseshoe Falls from Table Rock, Canadian Side
Whirlpool Rapids—from Bottom of Canadian Shore
1898 Canadian Artillery Marching on Snow Shoes
Canadian Outdoor Sports
Coasting in Canada
Coasting Scene in Canada
1899 43rd Rifles; Royal Canadian Infantry
2nd Special Service Battalion, Canadian Infantry, Embarking for So. Africa
2nd Special Service Battalion, Canadian Infantry-Parade
1900 Canadian Mounted Rifles on the March
1901 American Falls from Top of Canadian Shore
Duke and Duchess of York Leaving the Railroad Station at Montreal, Canada
Hockey Match on the Ice at Montreal, Canada
1902 Coasting Scene at Montmorency Falls, Canada
Tobogganing in Canada
1903 American Falls from Canadian Side
Coronation Procession Passing Under the Canadian Arch
Horseshoe Falls, from Canadian Side
Logging in Canada
1904 The Great Toronto Fire, Toronto, Canada, April 19, 1904
1905 Panoramic Bird's Eye View of Montreal, Canada
1906 American Falls from Canadian Side, Niagara Falls, N.Y.
Horseshoe Falls from Canadian Side Niagara Falls, N.Y.
Moose Hunt in Canada
Trip Through Canada
1907 Hunting in Canadian Woods
Picturesque Canada
Wonders of Canada
Wood Industry in Canada
1908 Bear Hunt in Canada
The Discoverers, a Grand Historical Pageant Picturing the Discovery and Founding of New France, Canada
H. R. H. The Prince of Wales Decorating the Monument of Champlain and Receiving Addresses of Welcome from the Mayor of Quebec, the Governor General of Canada and Vice-President Fairbanks, Representative of the United States
Royal Voyage to Canada
1909 A Canadian Winter Carnival
1910 The Canadian Moonshiners
Fighting the Iroquois in Canada
Immigrants' Progress in Canada
A Trip over the Rocky and Selkirk Mountains in Canada
A Wedding Trip from Montreal Through Canada to Hong Kong

Captains
1898 Famous Battleship Captains—Philadelphia Peace Jubilee Parade
1899 The Trial of Captain Dreyfus at Rennes, France
Trial of Captain Dreyfus
1901 Captain Nissen Going Through Whirlpool Rapids, Niagara Falls
Capt. Reilly's Battery, Bombardment of Pekin
Capt. Reilly's Battery Limbering
1906 Captain's Inspection
1907 Captain Kidd and His Pirates
[Picture Taken for Capt. Lovelace]
1908 Captain Kidd
"Captain Molly" or, The Battle of Monmouth
The Captain's Wives
1909 The Captain's Love
1910 The Captain of the Guard
The Captain's Bride
The Captain's Wife

Captive
1905 A Smart Captive
1910 The Captive
The Freebooter's Captive
His Child's Captive
The White Captive of the Sioux

Capture
1898 Capture of a Spanish Fort near Santiago
Capture of the "Panama"
Capture of the "Pedro"
Shooting Captured Insurgents
1899 Capture of Porto Rico
Capture of Trenches at Candaba [Canda Bar]
1900 Bombarding and Capturing the Taku Forts by the Allied Fleets
Capture of Boer Battery
Capture of Boer Battery by British
How the Artist Captured the Chinese Boxers
1902 Capture of the Biddle Brothers
1903 Captured
New York Harbor Police Boat Patrol Capturing Pirates
1904 Capture and Execution of Spies by Russians
Capture of a Gun
Capture of Yegg Bank Burglars
1907 A Smart Capture
1908 Captured by Telephone
1909 Capturing the North Pole; or, How He Cook'ed Peary's Record
1910 The Capture of the Burglar
Captured by Wireless
Capturing Cub Bears
A Difficult Capture
How the Squire Was Captured
The Sheriff's Capture

Capuchin Monks
1898 Capuchin Monks, Rome

Capulet
1908 Romeo and Juliet, a Romantic Story of the Ancient Feud Between the Italian Houses of Montague and Capulet

Car
use **Automobile**

Carabosse
1906 The Witch (La fée carabosse ou le poignard fatal)
1910 The Witch of Carabosse

Caravan
1903 Caravan of Camels
1904 Camel Caravan, Pekin, China

Carbet (Martinique)
1902 Natives Unloading a Boat of Fire-Wood at Carbet (A Suburb of St. Pierre)

Carbuncle
1908 Troublesome Carbuncle

Cardboard
1909 The Cardboard Baby

Cardinal
1898 Cardinal Gibbons
1909 The Cardinal's Conspiracy

Cards
1903 Western Card Game
1904 Game of Cards
1905 Cards and Crime
The Living Playing Cards
Unlucky at Cards, Lucky at Love
1906 Transparent Cards
1907 Hanky Panky Cards
Interrupted Card Party
1908 The Fatal Card
A House of Cards
Life's a Game of Cards
1909 The House of Cards
Luck of the Cards
Mr. Jones Has a Card Party
What the Cards Foretold
With Her Card
1910 The Card Party
His Opponent's Card

Care
1907 Take Good Care of Baby
1908 With Care

Career
1900 A Career of Crime, No. 1: Start in Life
A Career of Crime, No. 2: Going the Pace
A Career of Crime, No. 3: Robbery & Murder
A Career of Crime, No. 4: In the Toils
A Career of Crime, No. 5: The Death Chair
1907 Stolen Child's Career
1909 Her Dramatic Career
1910 Liz's Career

Careless
1909 Careless Life
Careless Tramp

Caribou
1907 A Caribou Hunt

Caribou Bridge (Canada)
1899 Caribou Bridge

Carlisle
1903 Carlisle's Trained Dogs

Carlisle Indian School (Pennsylvania)
1901 Club Swinging, Carlisle Indian School

Carlo
1906 Rescued by Carlo
1909 Carlo and the Baby

Carman
1910 The Carman's Dream

Carmelite
1910 The Carmelite

Carmen
1907 Carmen
A Carmen in Danger
1909 Torero Song "Carmen"
1910 Carmen

Carminella
1910 Carminella

Carney, Mr.
1903 Mr. Carney and Friend, National Cash Register Co.

Carnival
1897 A Children's Carnival in Germany
1898 Mardi Gras Carnival
New Year's Carnival
1900 Carnival Dance
1902 A Water Carnival
1903 Battle of Confetti at the Nice Carnival
Battle of Flowers at the Nice Carnival
Procession of Floats and Masqueraders at Nice Carnival
A Swiss Carnival
A Water Carnival
1905 Boating Carnival, Palm Beach, Fla.
1906 Carnival Night
1907 Carnival at Venice
1908 The Carnival at Nice
Carnival at Nice
How Jones Saw the Carnival
1909 A Canadian Winter Carnival
Carnival at Nice
Carnival at Nice, 1909
Carnival Merriment in the North
The Carnival of Venice
1910 At the Carnival
Carnival of Japanese Firemen in Tokio

Carpenter
1903 Carpenter Work, Albuquerque School
Passion Play: Christ in the Carpenter Shop

Carpet
1909 Magic Carpet

Carrara (Italy)
1906 Marble Industry at Carrara

Carriage
1896 Parade at Canton O., Showing Major McKinley in Carriage
1897 McKinley and Others in Carriage
Ten Inch Disappearing Carriage Gun Loading and Firing, Sandy Hook
1898 Decorated Carriages
Pope Leo XIII in Carriage
Pope Leo XIII in Carriage, No. 1
Pope Leo XIII in Carriage, No. 102
Pope Leo XIII Leaving Carriage and Being Ushered into Garden, No. 104
1903 Pope [Leo XIII] in His Carriage
The President's Carriage
1905 Black and White; or, The Mystery of a Brooklyn Baby Carriage
1907 Curious Carriage of Klobenstein
Mishaps of a Baby Carriage
1909 The Actor's Baby Carriage
1910 The Doctor's Carriage

Carriers
1898 Pope Leo XIII Being Carried in Chair Through Upper Loggia, No. 101
1899 Battle Flag of the 10th Pennsylvania Volunteers, Carried in the Philippines
"Shamrock" After Carrying Away Topsail
1901 Carrying Out the Snakes
The Hod Carrier's Revenge
1903 Bad Boy and Hod Carrier
Carrying the Crown into Westminster Abbey
Passion Play: Carrying the Cross
1904 Coal Carriers Chefoo, China
1905 Carrying Passengers Ashore Davidson Glacier, Alaska

Carroll, Mr.
1903 Mr. Carroll and Assistant, National Cash Register Co.

Carrousels
1900 Annual French Military Carousal
1903 Merry-Go-Round or Carrousel

Carrying pigeons
1904 Arrival and Release of 40,000 Carrying Pigeons at Ambergate, England

Cars
1898 10th U.S. Infantry Disembarking from Cars
10th U.S. Infantry, 2nd Battalion Leaving Cars
1900 Demonstrating the Action of the Brown Hoisting and Conveying Machine in Unloading a Schooner of Iron Ore, and Loading the Material on the Cars
Showing a Giant Crane Dumping a 40-Ton Car
1901 Loading Cars
1902 Loading the Ice on Cars, Conveying It Across the Mountains and Loading It into Boats
1905 Gen'l Elec. No. 3 Handling Cars at the Barn
Jaunting Cars Arriving at Dublin Horse Show
Jaunting Cars in Dublin
Retrogressive Jaunting Car, Reverse Panorama from Moving Train, Dublin, Ireland
Ride on Sprinkler Car
1909 The Pay Car
Three-Wheeled Car

Carson, Kit
1903 Kit Carson
Kit Carson #6: Panorama
1910 The Cheyenne Raiders; or, Kit Carson on the Santa Fe Trail
Kit Carson

Carter, Nick
1909 Nick Carter's Double
The Coiners, or Catching the Counterfeiters (Nick carter: les faux-monnayeurs)
1910 Nick Carter as Acrobat

Carthage
1910 The Slave of Carthage
Through the Ruins of Carthage

Cartoons
1900 Homer Davenport, the Cartoonist
1903 The Animated Cartoon
1907 Comedy Cartoons
1909 Magic Cartoons

Cartouche
1909 Cartouche

Cartridges
1903 The Last Cartridges
1908 The Last Cartridge, an Incident of the Sepoy Rebellion in India

Carts
1897 Boat Wagon and Beach Cart
Tipping the Cart in Mulberry Bend
1901 Ox Carts
1902 Native Bull Cart at Morne Rouge (A Suburb of St. Pierre)

Catskills (New York)
1897 Waterfall in the Catskills
1906 The Gateway to the Catskills
In the Heart of the Catskills
Through Austin Glen, Catskill Railway

Cattle
1897 Cattle Driven to Slaughter
1898 Branding Cattle
Cattle Fording Stream
Cattle Leaving the Corral
The Timid Girls and the Terrible Cow
1901 Arrival of Train of Cattle
Drove of Western Cattle
Dumping and Lifting Cattle
Herd of Cattle
Koshering Cattle, (Hebrew Method of Killing)
Sticking Cattle
Stunning Cattle
1902 The Accomodating Cow
Loading Cattle in India
1903 Cattle Bathing
Driving Cows to Pasture
Panoramic View of an Egyptian Cattle Market
Through Miles Canyon on a Cattle Scow
1904 Driving Cattle to Pasture
Piraeus and Athens (Greece). Hoisting Cattle on Steamer
Rounding Up and Branding Cattle
1907 Shipping Cattle, Hawaihae, Hawaiian Islands
1908 Buying a Cow
The Cattle Rustlers
1909 The Cattle Thieves
1910 The Cattle Baron's Daughter
A Cattle Rustler's Daughter
The Cattle Thief's Revenge

Cattlemen
1910 The Cattlemen's Feud

Caucasian
1909 Caucasian Customs
1910 Russia, the Caucasian Mountains

Cauliflower
1901 Cutting Cucumbers and Cauliflower, Heinz

Causes
1899 A Just Cause for Divorce
1901 Hooligan Causes a Sensation
1907 In the Cause of Faith
1908 The Cause of All the Trouble
1909 For the Cause of Suffrage
For Their Country's Cause

Causeway
1903 A Trip to the Giant's Causeway

Cautious
1903 Too Cautious

Cavalcade
1905 Cavalcade Descending Eagle Peak Trail, Yosemite Valley
Cavalcade Descending the Nevada Trail, Yosemite Valley
Cavalcade Descending Trail into Grand Cañon of Arizona
Cavalcade on Trail into Grand Cañon of Arizona

Cavaliers
1898 The Cavalier's Dream
1905 Three Cavaliers of the Road
Horses Jumping over a Wall (Sauts de mur et de haie par le comte de Turin et ses cavaliers)
1909 The Cavalier's Wife

Cavalry
1896 West Point Cadet Cavalry
West Point Cadet Cavalry Charge
West Point Cadet Cavalry Drill
1897 Cavalry Charge
Cavalry Horses at Play
Cavalry Musical Drill
Cavalry Passing in Review
Hungarian Cavalry Charge
Musical Drill; Troop A., Third Cavalry
Sixth U.S. Cavalry
U.S. Cavalry and Artillery
Wrestling, Bareback; 3rd Cavalry
1898 American Cavalry Charging with Drawn Swords
Bareback Riding, 6th Cavalry, U.S.A.
Cavalry Horses Fording a Stream in Santiago de Cuba
A Charge by Cavalry
9th U.S. Cavalry Watering Horses
Teaching Cavalry to Ride
The Tenth Cavalry
Trained Cavalry Horses
U.S. Cavalry Supplies Unloading at Tampa, Florida
1899 Her Majesty, Queen Victoria, Reviewing the Household Cavalry at Spital Barracks
Troop "F," 3rd Cavalry
1900 A Cadet Cavalry Charge
Charge of Boer Cavalry
The 4th Cavalry
Lord Dundonald's Cavalry Seizing a Kopje in Spion Kop
1901 A Cavalry Manoeuvre
Charge of Cossack Cavalry
Cossack Cavalry
Great Cavalry Charge
Second Squad, Sixth U.S. Cavalry
6th Cavalry Assaulting South Gate of Pekin
Sixth U.S. Cavalry Charging
Sixth U.S. Cavalry, Skirmish Line
The War in China—Bombay Cavalry
1902 Cavalry Swimming Columbia River
English Cavalry on the Battlefield
German Cavalry Fording a River
German Cavalry Leaping Hurdles
1903 Cavalry Parade
French Cavalry Evolutions
Great French Cavalry Charge
Great German Cavalry Charge
Skirmish with Boers near Kimberly by a Troop of Cavalry Scouts Attached to Gen. French's Column
Watering Cavalry Horses
1904 Cavalry Crossing a River
Cavalry Fording a Stream
Russian Cavalry
Russian Cavalry in Corea [sic]
1905 Russian Cavalry Review, St. Petersburg
1907 Cavalry School
1908 Crack Riders of the Russian Cavalry
1909 Arabian Cavalry
Italian Cavalry Maneuvers
1910 Some Riding Exercises of the Italian Cavalry
Troop "B", 15th U.S. Cavalry Bareback Squad in the Monkey Drill at Fort Myer, Virginia

Cave
1896 Rapids at Cave of the Winds
1906 Cave of the Winds
Infernal Cave
1908 Cave of the Spooks
In the Bogie Man's Cave
1910 Sea Cave and Cliffs

Cavern
1899 The Cavern of the Demons
1909 The Witches' Cavern

Cavite (Philippines)
1898 Hoisting of the American Flag at Cavite

Cayuga Lake (New York)
1901 'Varsity Crew Race on Cayuga Lake, on Decoration Day, Lehigh Valley Observation Train Following the Race, Showing Cornell Crew Finishing First, Columbia Second, University of Pennsylvania Third Ithaca, N.Y., Showing Lehigh Valley Observation Train

Celebes Islands (Indonesia)
1910 Deer Hunting in Celebes Islands

Celebrations
1902 King Edward VII at the Birthday Celebration of the King of Denmark
Little Willie's Last Celebration
1903 Young America Celebrating Dewey's Return
1905 Fourth of July Celebration, Yosemite California
1907 The Birthday Celebration
Harvest Celebration
The Village Celebration
1908 After the Celebration!
Military Parade, Founders Week Celebration, Philadelphia
Tercentenary Celebrations to Commemorate the 300th Anniversary of the Founding of Quebec by Champlain
1909 Annual Celebration of School Children at Newark, NJ
The Celebrated Mountain Climbers
Sammy Celebrates
1910 The Celebrated Case (Part I): Convicted by His Own Child
The Celebrated Case (Part II): Saved by His Own Child
Cowboy and Indian Frontier Celebration

Celestial
1910 Celestial Vengeance
Scenes in the Celestial Empire

Cellar
1902 The Burglars in the Wine Cellar
1903 The Monk in the Monastery Wine Cellar
1907 Roof to Cellar
1908 Deep Down within the Cellar
1909 Sherlock Holmes III: The Detectives Adventure in the Gas Cellar
1910 Secret of the Cellar

Cellini, Benvenuto
1904 Benvenuto Cellini; or, A Curious Evasion
1908 Benvenuto Cellini

Celtic (Steamship)
1904 Launching the Steamship "Celtic"

Cemetery
1901 McKinley's Funeral Entering Westlawn Cemetery, Canton [Ohio]
U.S. National Cemetery
1902 A Dog's Cemetery

Cenci, Beatrice
1908 Beatrice Cenci
1910 Beatrice Cenci

Census
1900 The Census on Cherry Hill

Centenarian
1910 The Centenarian

Centennial
1901 Centennial Parade
1908 Catholic Centennial Parade
1910 Mexican Centennial

Center
1907 Panorama, Crowds at Squires-Burns International Contest, from Center of Ring, Colma, July 4th, 1907

Central America
1910 A Central American Romance

Central High School (Missouri)
1904 Central High School, Calisthenics, Missouri Commission

Central Park (New York City)
1897 Sleighing in Central Park
1899 Fifth Avenue Entrance to Central Park
1900 After Dark in Central Park
In Central Park
Skating in Central Park
1901 Hooligan Visits Central Park
1904 Ice Skating in Central Park, N.Y.
Sleighing in Central Park, New York
1910 Drive Through Central Park

Cents
1902 A Bowery Five Cent Shave
1906 Three Cent Leeks
1907 Two Cents Worth of Cheese
1909 He Was 25 Cents Short of His Salary

Centuries
1907 Costumes of Different Centuries

Centurion
1910 St. Paul and the Centurion

Ceremonies
1902 Installation Ceremonies, Columbia University
Installation Ceremonies of President Butler
Reproduction, Coronation Ceremonies—King Edward VII
1903 Pres. Roosevelt at the Dedication Ceremonies, St. Louis Exposition
1904 Opening Ceremonies, New York Subway, October 27, 1904
Opening Ceremonies, St. Louis Exposition
1905 Corpus Christi Ceremonies, Botzen, Tyrol
1906 John Paul Jones Ceremonies
1907 The Unveiling Ceremonies of the McKinley Memorial, Canton, Ohio, September 30th, 1907

Cervera y Topete, Pascual, Admiral
1898 Admiral Cervera and Officers of the Spanish Fleet Leaving the "St. Louis"

Ceylon
1905 Ceylon
1906 A Trip Through the Island of Ceylon
1909 Across the Island of Ceylon
Scenes in Ceylon
1910 Ramble Through Ceylon

Ch-ien-men Gate, Peking (China)
1901 The Ch-ien-men Gate, Pekin
Chagrin
1903 Bullet Vs. Whiskey (Chagrin d'amour)
Chain
1910 Excursion on the Chain of Mont Blanc
Chain gang
1902 Charleston Chain Gang
Chair
1898 M. H. Pope Leo in Chair
One Chair Short
Pope Leo XIII Being Carried in Chair Through Upper Loggia, No. 101
Pope Leo XIII Giving Blessing from Chair
Pope Leo XIII in Canopy Chair, No. 100
Pope Leo XIII in Sedan Chair, No. 1
Pope Leo XIII Preparing To Give Blessing from Chair
Three Ways of Climbing over a Chair
1900 A Career of Crime, No. 5: The Death Chair
1901 Unveiling Chair of Justice
1902 Floral Chair Parade
Mischievous Willie's Rocking Chair Motor
1903 Chair Dance
H. H. Pope Leo [XIII] in Chair
Visitors in Wheeling Chairs, National Cash Register Co.
1904 The Easy Chair
Princess Rajah Dance with Chair, St. Louis Exposition
Princess Rajah, Dance Without Chair
1905 The Adjustable Chair
The Enchanted Sedan-Chair
1907 The Adventures of a Bath Chair
1908 Chair, If You Please
Madeira Wicker Chair Industry
1909 Bath Chair
Chalant
1909 Prince of Chalant
Challenge plate
1902 The University College of Oxford Winning the Ladies' Challenge Plate
Challenger
1905 Speed Trial of Auto Boat Challenger, Lake Worth, Fla.
Chalmers, Mr.
1903 Mr. Chalmers and Mr. Gibbs Arrive at Club, National Cash Register Co.
Mr. Chalmers Going to Officers' Club, National Cash Register Co.
Chamber
1898 The Burglar in the Bed Chamber
1905 The Bridal Chamber
1909 The Secret Chamber
Chamberlain, Arthur Neville
1901 Chamberlain and Balfour
Chambermaid
1904 Chambermaid's Revenge
1909 The Chambermaid and the Dwarf
Chameleons
1904 Chameleon Climbing
Chameleons Feeding
Chamois
1910 A Chamois Hunt
Chamonix (France)
1904 Panoramic View of Chamonix, Alps
1906 Fayet-Chamonix: Trip on the New Trolley Line from Le Fayet-St. Gervais to Chamonix
1907 Alps of Chamonix
1910 Drifts of Snow in Chamonix Valley
Chamouny
1910 Linda of Chamouny
Champagne
1907 Making Champagne
1908 The Champagne Bottle
Champagne Industry
Too Much Champagne
1909 Champagne Party
Free Champagne
Champions and championships
1897 Champion Rolla O. Heikes, Breaking the Record at Flying Targets with Winchester Shotgun
Golding Sisters, Champion Swimmers
1899 The Battle of Jeffries and Sharkey for Championship of the World
Champion High Jumpers, "Chappie" and "Ben Bolt"
"Sampson" Champion High Stepper
Some Future Champions
1900 Amateur Athletic Championships
A Champion Beer Drinker
The Champion Beer Drinker
Champion Polo Players
Kansas City Fire Department, Winners of the World's Championship at the Paris Exposition
Stallion Championship
1901 Emar De Flon, the Champion Skater
1902 Broncho Busting Scene, Championship of the World
Rube Waddell and the Champion Playing Ball with the Boston Team
1903 Light Heavyweight Championship Contest Between Root and Gardner
Miss Jessie Cameron, Champion Child Sword Dancer
Miss Jessie Dogherty, Champion Female Highland Fling Dancer
Polo Match for the Championship at Hurlingham
1904 "Champion Pumpkin Eater"
Inter-Collegiate Athletic Association Championships, 1904
1905 Nelson-Britt Prize Fight for Lightweight Championship, San Francisco, September 9th, 1905
1907 The Amateur Champion
A Champion After All
A Championship Won on a Foul
International Contest for the Heavyweight Championship: Squires vs. Burns, Ocean View, Cal., July 4th, 1907
Squires, Australian Champion, in His Training Quarters
A Would Be Champion
Wrestling Matches of 1906 (Championnat de lutte 1906)
1908 Champion Globe Trotter
Champion Wrestling Bear
Military Swimming Championship
The World's Championship Baseball Series of 1910
1909 Champion Heavyweight Lifter
Champion Suffragist
How Chauncey Became a Champion
Jim Smith, the Champion Boxer
The Making of a Champion
World's Heavyweight Championship Pictures Between Tommy Burns and Jack Johnson
The Would-Be Champion
Police Dogs (Championnat du monde des chiens de police)
1910 The Champion of the Race
Gotch-Zbyszko World's Championship Wrestling Match
He Met the Champion
Hotstuff Takes on the Champions
How Championships Are Won—and Lost
How Jones Won the Championship
Jeffries-Johnson World's Championship Boxing Contest, Held at Reno, Nevada, July 4, 1910
Reproduction of Jeffries-Johnson Championship Contest
World's Championship Motor Races
World's Championship Series
World's Wrestling Champions
Solving the Puzzle (Le champion du jeu à la mode)
Champlain, Samuel de
1908 H. R. H. The Prince of Wales Decorating the Monument of Champlain and Receiving Addresses of Welcome from the Mayor of Quebec, the Governor General of Canada and Vice-President Fairbanks, Representative of the United States
Tercentenary Celebrations to Commemorate the 300th Anniversary of the Founding of Quebec by Champlain
Champs de Mars, Paris (France)
1900 Champs de Mars
Champs Elysses, Paris (France)
1900 Champs Elysees
Panoramic View of the Champs Elysees
1902 The Champs Elysees
Chance
1908 A Chance Shot
The Chances of Life
A Desperate Chance
1909 Chances of Life
A Fighting Chance
A Providential Chance
1910 A Heroine of Chance
The Lost Chance
A Wall Street Chance
Chang, Li Hung
1896 Li Hung Chang at Grant's Tomb
Li Hung Chang Driving Through 4th St. and Broadway [New York City]
Li Hung Chang, 5th Avenue & 55th Street, N.Y.
1901 Li Hung Chang
Change
1898 How the Flag Changed in Cuba
1902 Lightning Facial Changes
Magical Changes
1903 Baby Lund in Lightning Change Act
Changing Horses at Glen
Changing Horses at Linden
The Lightning Change Artist
U.S. Interior Dept.: Changing Coaches, Raymond Coach
1904 Amusing Changes
1905 Gen'l Elec. No. 2 Trolley Changing from Di. to Alter. Cur.
1907 Getting His Change
The Hundred Dollar Bill; or, The Tramp Couldn't Get It Changed
1908 The Changing of Souls
The Pupa Changes into a Butterfly
The Quick Change Mesmerist
Weather Changes at the Smiths
1909 Change of Complexion
A Change of Heart
1910 A Change of Heart
Max Has to Change
Thieves as Quick Change Artists
Under a Changing Sky
Channel
1904 Holbein Swimming the English Channel
1907 Tunneling the English Channel
1909 First Airships Crossing the English Channel
Chapel
1901 Arrival of Funeral Cortege at St. George's Chapel
1910 The Legend of the Holy Chapel
Chaperone
1909 The Chaperone
1910 Captain Barnacle's Chaperone
Their Chaperoned Honeymoon
Chapin Post of Buffalo (New York)
1901 Chapin Post of Buffalo
Chappie
1898 A Swift Chappie
1903 Two Chappies in a Box
1904 The Chappie at the Well
Chappie (Horse)
1899 Champion High Jumpers, "Chappie" and "Ben Bolt"
Characteristic
1902 Characteristic Imitations
Characters
1904 Parade of Characters (Asia in America) St. Louis Exposition
1905 Procession of Costumed Characters, Vevey Fete
1908 A Desperate Character
Charcoal
1904 Working in the Charcoal Mines in France
1908 Making Charcoal
1910 In Love with the Charcoal Woman
Charges
1896 Charge of West Point Cadets
Mounted Police Charge
West Point Cadet Cavalry Charge
1897 Cavalry Charge
Charge of Hungarian Hussars
Charge of the French Cuirassieurs
Charge, Through Intervals of Skirmishes
French Cuirassieurs Charging a Field Battery
Hungarian Cavalry Charge
1898 American Cavalry Charging with Drawn Swords
Battery Charge
Bayonet Charge; by the 2nd Illinois Volunteers
Charge at Las Guasimas
A Charge by Cavalry
Charge by Rushes
Charge of the Light Brigade
A Gallant Charge
Infantry Charge
Mexican Rurales Charge
Rapid Fire, Charge

1899 Charge at Las Guasimas, Where Capron and Fish Were Killed
Charge of the Rough Riders at El Caney
1900 A Charge of the Insurgents
A Cadet Cavalry Charge
Charge of Boer Cavalry
English Lancers Charging
1901 Charge by 1st Bengal Lancers
Charge of Cossack Cavalry
Great Cavalry Charge
Mounted Police Charge
Sixth U.S. Cavalry Charging
1902 When the Bugle Sounds "Charge!"
1903 Great French Cavalry Charge
Great German Cavalry Charge
Indians Charging on the Photographer
Police Charge on Horseback
1904 Charging Cuirassiers
1908 Wrongly Charged

Chariots
1902 The Golden Chariots
1903 Chariot Race
1905 Roman Chariot Race, Pasadena, California

Charity
1897 Charity Ball
1904 Christmas Angel (Detresse et charite)
1908 Charity Begins at Home, a Story of the South During the Civil War
1909 Charity Begins at Home
Charity Rewarded
Good Lesson in Charity
Masquerader's Charity
1910 The Greatest of These Is Charity
Simple Charity

Charles River, Boston (Massachusetts)
1904 Canoeing on the Charles River, Boston, Mass.

Charles Street, Baltimore (Maryland)
1904 Panorama of Ruins from Baltimore and Charles Street
Panorama of Ruins from Lombard and Charles Street

Charles V
1910 Charles the Fifth

Charleston (South Carolina)
1902 Charleston Chain Gang
Loading a Vessel at Charleston, S. C.
Midway of Charleston Exposition [South Carolina]
Panoramic View of Charleston Exposition [South Carolina]
President Roosevelt Reviewing the Troops at Charleston Exposition [South Carolina]

Charley
1904 Charley's Aunt
1907 Charley Paints
Charley's Dream

Charlie
1899 Charlie Wanted the Earth
How Charlie Got the Dough
1900 How Charlie Lost the Heiress
1908 Bathing; or, Charlie and Mary in the Country
Charlie's Ma-in-Law
1909 Charlie Forced to Find a Job
1910 Charlie and Kitty in Brussels

Charm
1904 The Bird Charmer
Charming Enchantment
1907 The Charmer
The Lover's Charm
1908 Charmed Sword
Music Hath Charms
Music Hath Its Charms
Music Which Hath No Charms
The Wonderful Charm
1909 The Wishing Charm
1910 The Gambler's Charm
The Lucky Charm
Music Hath Charms
Romance of a Snake Charmer

Charter Oak Park, Hartford (Connecticut)
1897 Free-for-All Race at Charter Oak Park

Chases
1898 Off for the Rabbit Chase
1899 Johanna's Chase
1900 Chasing the Cherry Pickers
1902 A Stern Chase
1903 Farmer Chasing Trespassers
A Paper Chase
Policeman Chasing Bathers
1904 Chased by a Dog
Maniac Chase
The Passion Play (Jésus chassant les vendeurs du temple)
1905 Great Buffalo Chase
1906 Bicycle Police Chasing Scorching Auto
The Wig Chase
1907 Chasing a Motorist
Chasing a Sausage
1908 A Bike Chase
1909 Chasing a Sea Lion in the Arctics
Chasing the Ball
Chasing the Helmet
Goose Chase
They Lead the Cops on a Chase
A Wild Goose Chase
1910 Max Leads Them a Novel Chase
A Wild Goose Chase

Chasi
1909 Chasi Movement

Chasseurs
1903 24th Chasseurs Steeple Jumping

Chastisement
1906 Corsican Chastisement

Chat
1903 An Evening Chat

Chattanooga (Tennessee)
1906 Trip to Chattanooga and Lookout Mountain

Chatterboxes
1907 Three Chatterboxes

Chauffeurs
1906 The Inexperienced Chauffeur
1908 The Chauffeur's Dream
1909 Chauffeur Out for a Good Time
The Chauffeur's Adventure
Women Chauffeurs

Chauncey
1905 Chauncey Explains
How Mr. Butt-In Benefits by Chauncey's Mishaps
1908 Chauncey Proves a Good Detective
1909 How Chauncey Became a Champion

Chautauqua (New York)
1903 Chautauqua Aquatic Day. No. 9
Chautauqua Boys' Club. No. 1
Chautauqua Boys' Club. No. 2
Chautauqua Girls' Club. No. 6
Swedish Gymnastics at Chautauqua. No. 8

Cheap
1907 A Cheap Skate
His Cheap Watch
1909 A Cheap Removal

Cheat
1905 The Cheated Policeman
1907 The Cheater's Cheated
Cheating Justice
1910 The Cheat

Chechawko Hill (Alaska)
1903 Operation on the Famous Chechawko Hill

Check
1904 Girls Taking Time Checks, Westinghouse Works
1909 A Blank Check

Checker
1908 The Checker Fiends

Cheddar (England)
1904 Cliffs of Cheddar, England

Cheeky
1904 A Cheeky Traveler
1907 Cheekiest Man on Earth

Cheese
1902 The Cheese Mites; or, The Lilliputians in a London Restaurant
1904 The Cheese Mites
1906 Oh! That Limburger, the Story of a Piece of Cheese
1907 The Skipping Cheeses
The Strength of Cheese
Two Cents Worth of Cheese
1908 The Cheese Race
1909 Holland Cheese
The Ripe Cheese
1910 The Cheese Box
The Dog of the Cheese Monger
The Manufacture of Cheese at Roquefort

Chef
1907 Chef's Revenge

Chefoo (China)
1904 Coal Carriers Chefoo, China
1905 Yantai Episode

Chelsea (Massachusetts)
1901 The Fire Department of Chelsea, Mass.

Chemistry
1897 Mr. Edison at Work in His Chemical Laboratory
1907 Chemist's Mistake
1908 His First Experiment in Chemistry
1909 The Chemist's Bell
1910 The Chemist's Mistake

Chemulpo (South Korea)
1904 The Battle of Chemulpo
Battle of Chemulpo Bay
Russ-Jap Forces Meeting Near Chemulpo

Chenier, Andrea
1910 Andrea Chenier

Cherries
1900 Chasing the Cherry Pickers
1904 Rum vs. Cherries
1907 When Cherries Are Ripe
1910 The Cherries
The Three Cherry Pits; or, The Veteran's Honor

Cherry Hill
1900 The Census on Cherry Hill

Cherub
1910 John Dough and the Cherub
The Sage, the Cherub and the Widow

Chess
1906 Game of Chess
1908 Playing at Chess
1909 A Game of Chess
Napoleon's Game of Chess

Chest
1906 Chest and Neck Development
Deep Breathing and Chest Expansion
Developing Muscles of Back and Chest
Developing Muscles of Chest and Back
1909 The Old Army Chest

Chester
1910 The Mad Lady of Chester

Chester (Pennsylvania)
1907 Chester, Pa.

Chestnuts
1907 Hot Chestnuts
Roasted Chestnuts

Chevalier
1901 The Mysterious Blackboard (Le chevalier mystère)
1905 The Chloroform Fiends (Les chevaliers du chloroforme)

Chevet
1903 Newell and Chevet, the Famous Acrobats

Chew-Chew Land
1910 Chew-Chew Land; or, The Adventures of Dolly and Jim

Chewing
1905 Chewing Gum

Cheyenne (Wyoming)
1903 Steer Roping Contest at Cheyenne, Wyo.

Cheyenne Indians
1910 A Cheyenne Brave
The Cheyenne Raiders; or, Kit Carson on the Santa Fe Trail
A Cheyenne's Love for a Sioux

Chicago (Illinois)
1897 Corner Madison and State Streets, Chicago
Sheep Run, Chicago Stockyards
1898 A Chicago Street
Grand Army Veterans of Chicago
Peace Parade—Chicago
St. Bernard Commandery, Chicago
1900 How They Rob Men in Chicago
1901 Chicago Fat Stock Parade
Chicago Police Parade
1902 Prince Henry [of Prussia] at Lincoln's Monument, Chicago, Ill.
1903 Chicago Derby Day
Chicago Fire Boats in Action
Chicago Fire Run
Chicago—Michigan Football Game
Parade Through Chicago Streets
The Prince Leaving Chicago
State and Madison Sts., Chicago
1904 The Chicago Fire
Iroquois Theatre Fire in Chicago
1906 A Trip Through the Chicago Stock-Yards
1908 Bryan in Chicago
1909 Taft in Chicago, and at the Ball Game

Chicago and Buffalo Express
1896 Chicago and Buffalo Express
Chicago and Northwestern Railway
1903 Colorado Special, Chicago & Northwestern Ry.
Chicago Cubs (Baseball team)
1906 The World Series Baseball Games-White Sox and Cubs
Chicago Fast Mail
1896 Chicago Fast Mail NYC. R.R.
Chicago Pneumatic Tool Company
1900 Demonstrating the Action of Pneumatic Shell Riveters on the Underside of the Hull of a Steel Vessel. Taken for the Chicago Pneumatic Tool Co.
Demonstrating the Action of the Chicago Pneumatic Tool Co.'s Deck Machine
Chicago White Sox (Baseball team)
1906 The World Series Baseball Games-White Sox and Cubs
Chicago—Portland Special
1904 Chicago Portland Special
Chickamauga (Georgia)
1898 Fun in the American Camp at Chicamauga
Mess Call, American Camp at Chicamauga
Chicken
1897 A Chicken Farm
Chicken Thieves
1899 Chickens Coming Out of the Shell
1900 Who Said Chicken?
1901 Who Said Chicken?
1902 The Chicken Thief
1903 Chicken Thief
Dancing for a Chicken
Hatching Chickens Up-to-Date
Stealing Chickens
U.S. Interior Dept.: Laguna Indian Chicken-Pulling Race
1904 The Chicken Thief
The Restive Chicken
1906 Juvenile Chicken Thieves
1907 Stolen Chickens
1909 Bake That Chicken Pie
1910 C-H-I-C-K-E-N Spells Chicken
Chicken
A College Chicken
Roast Chicken
Chiefs
1898 Chief Devery at Head of N.Y. Police Parade
1899 Chief Devery and Staff
1903 Review of Native Chiefs at the Durbar
Review of the Chiefs at the Durbar
1906 Going to the Fire, Showing Chief Sullivan During the Earthquake
1908 The White Chief
1909 The New Chief
They Robbed the Chief of Police
The Viking's Love; or, True to His Chief
1910 Chief Blackfoot's Vindication
Death of the Brigand Chief
The Exiled Chief
Foolshead Chief of the Reporters
An Indian Chief's Generosity
Chieftain
1908 The Chieftain's Revenge; or, A Tragedy in the Highlands of Scotland
Chilcoot Pass (Canada)
1901 Burro Pack Train on the Chilcoot Pass
Children
rt **Kids**
1897 Children Playing with Fish
A Children's Carnival in Germany
Children's Toilet
1898 Children Coasting
Children's Tea Party
1899 Childhood's Happy Days
Children Feeding Ducklings
Jeffries and a Child at Play
1900 Childhood's Vows
Children of the Royal Family of England
Children Rolling Down Hill
1901 Children Bathing
Children Playing Ball
Fun at a Children's Party
"The Sleeping Child"
1902 The Children and the Frog
The Children of the Czar
Children Playing with Lion Cubs
The Children's Tea Party
The Children's Toys That Came to Life
Peasant Children and Their Rocking Horse
St. John's Guild. Crippled Children to and from Wagon
1903 Child Eating
Children Coasting
Children Saying Their Prayers
A Child's Vision
Happy Childhood
Miss Jessie Cameron, Champion Child Sword Dancer
Passion Play: Suffer Little Children to Come Unto Me
Patterson Children in Pony Wagon, National Cash Register Co.
Patterson Children Leaving Home, National Cash Register Co.
Patterson Children on Horseback, National Cash Register Co.
President Reviewing School Children
Rescue of Child from Indians
1904 The Child Stealers
Children and Rabbits
Children and White Rats
The Children in the Surf
Children Romping on the Lawn
Japanese School Children
Kidnapped Child
The Lost Child
Orphan Children on the Beach at Coney Island
"Weary Willie" Kidnaps a Child
1905 Children and Carts of Oberammergau
Children Turning Catherine Wheels on Derby Day, Epsom Downs
Children's Hour on the Farm
Kidnapped Child
Mother's Angel Child
Moving Day; or, No Children Allowed
1906 A Childish Match
Childish Tricks Baffled
Children's Quarrel
Child's Revenge
Robbers of Children
War of Children
A Boarding School Conspiracy (L'enfant terrible au pensionnat)
1907 The Bargeman's Child
The Child Accuser
Children's Reformatory
A Child's Cunning
His Second Childhood
No More Children
The Slavery of Children
Slavery of Children
Stolen Child
Stolen Child's Career
Too Many Children
1908 The Actor's Child
And a Little Child Shall Lead Them
The Angel Child
Auntie Takes the Children to the Country
The Burglar's Child
The Child and the Gigantic Animal
Child Slave Freed
Children of the East
A Child's Debt
A Child's Devotion
The Child's Forgiveness
A Child's Prayer; or, The Good Samaritan
John Is No More a Child
No Children Wanted
Pocahantas — A Child of the Forest
The Redman and the Child
Rescue of Children by Dogs
Useful Present for a Child
A Grandmother's Story (Conte de la grand'mère et rêve de l'enfant)
1909 Actress and Child
The Adopted Child
And a Little Child Shall Lead Them
Annual Celebration of School Children at Newark, NJ
Blind Child's Dog
A Child of the Forest
The Child of the Regiment
A Child of the Sea
Children of the Plains, an Episode of Pioneer Days
Children of the Sea
The Children's Friend
A Child's Love
A Child's Plea
A Child's Prayer
The Child's Prayer
Child's Vision
Drunkard's Child
For My Children
Gypsy Child
Gypsy's Child
Hector, the Angel Child
His Two Children
A Home Without Children
Jessie, the Stolen Child
Johnny Is No Longer a Child
Madwoman's Child
Sailor's Child
Santa Claus and the Miner's Child
School Children's Strike
The Spoilt Child
Suffer Little Children...For of Such Is the Kingdom of Labor
Summer Home for the School Children of Paris
A Telepathic Warning, the Story of a Child's Love for Her Father
Wanted, a Child
What Three Tots Saw in the Land of Nod
Wife or Child
The Wood-Chopper's Child
1910 The Actor's Children
Adopting a Child
Artist's Child
By the Faith of a Child
The Celebrated Case (Part I): Convicted by His Own Child
The Celebrated Case (Part II): Saved by His Own Child
The Child and the Dancing-Jack
Child as Benefactor
A Child of the Ghetto
A Child of the Prairie
A Child of the Regiment
A Child of the Sea
A Child of the Squadron
A Child of the Wild
The Child of Two Mothers
The Childhood of Jack Harkaway
Childish Escapade
The Children of Edward IV
The Children's Revolt
Child's Doctor
A Child's Faith
A Child's Impulse
A Child's Judgment
A Child's Sacrifice
A Child's Stratagem
Conscience of a Child
For the Sake of a Child
His Child's Captive
His Only Child
Mamma's Angel Child
The Miser's Child
Mother and Child
Motherless Child
The Prayer of a Miner's Child
The Pugilist's Child
The Red Girl and the Child
Their Child
The Touch of a Child's Hand
A Widow and Her Child
Chillon, Castle of, Lake Geneva (Switzerland)
1905 Panorama of the Castle of Chillon, Lake Geneva
Chimera
1903 La Chimera
Chimney
1900 Razing a Chimney
1903 Ascending a Rock-Chimney on the Grand Charmoz, 11,293 feet
1904 Falling Chimney
1905 Overturning a Mammoth Chimney
1907 The Smoking Chimney
The Wrong Chimney; or, Every Man His Own Sweep
1910 Fabian Cleaning Chimney
Chimney sweep
1900 The Chimney Sweep and the Miller
1903 The Miller and Chimney Sweep
Washerwomen and Chimney-Sweep
1905 Chimney Sweep and Pastry Cook
Cook and Chimney Sweep
1906 Chimney Sweep
1907 The Wrong Chimney; or, Every Man His Own Sweep
1908 The Chimney Sweeper
Little Chimney Sweep
The Little Chimney Sweeps
The Water Babies; or, The Little Chimney Sweep
1909 The Chimney Sweep's Birthday
Chimney Sweep's Debut

Panoramas of Market Street, the City Hall, Taken from the Roof of the U.S. Mint
Panoramic View of San Francisco City Hall, Damaged by Earthquake
Vertical Panorama City Hall and Surroundings

Civil War
1907 The Spy, a Romantic Story of the Civil War
1908 Charity Begins at Home, a Story of the South During the Civil War
1909 The Girl Spy: An Incident of the Civil War
1910 Civil War

Clad
1909 Moscow Clad in Snow
1910 The Iron Clad Lover

Claiche, Bertha
1905 Bertha Claiche

Claim
1903 Sluice Mining on Gold Hill in the Klondike, Hutchinson and Johnstone's Claim of No. 6, Eldorado
1905 Panning Gold on a Claim in the Klondike
1910 The Angel of Dawson's Claim
Bradford's Claim
Claim Jumpers
The Stolen Claim
The Unknown Claim

Clairo, Madame
1910 Madame Clairo

Clancy
1910 Clancy

Clancy, Dope Head
1909 Dope Head Clancy

Clara
1899 Why Clara Was Spanked

Clarence
1897 The Clarence House Lawn Party
1903 Clarence the Cop
1904 Clarence, the Cop, on the Feed Store Beat
1909 Clarence and His Cigarette

Clarinet
1908 Clarinet Solo

Clark
1896 Clark's Thread Mill

Class
1903 Baby Class at Lunch
1904 Fencing Class, Missouri Valley College
Hyde Park School Graduating Class, Missouri Commission
Panorama of Harvard Class Day
The Swimming Class
1907 A First Class Restaurant

Classic
1899 Classic Poses

Classmates
1908 Classmates

Clause
1910 A Clause in the Will

Clavencourt Castle
1909 The Heir of Clavencourt Castle

Clay
1910 The Clay Baker

Clean-up
1903 $35,000 Clean-Up on Eldorado No. 10
$25,000 Clean Up on No. 16, Eldorado

Cleaners and cleaning
1898 Cleaning and Firing of the Hotchkiss Revolving Cannon on the Battleship Texas
Some Troubles of House Cleaning
1901 Cleaning Pig's Feet
1903 Butchering and Cleaning Tables U.S.F.C.
Spring Cleaning
Window Cleaner's Mishap
1904 Cleaning a Stove Pipe
What the Window Cleaner Saw
1907 Bowser's House Cleaning
Spring Cleaning
The Vacuum Cleaner
Window Cleaner
1908 House Cleaning Days; or, No Rest for the Weary
Up-to-Date Clothes Cleaning
The Vacuum Cleaner
1909 An Energetic Street Cleaner
Too Clean a Servant
1910 Fabian Cleaning Chimney

Clear Creek Canyon (Colorado)
1902 Clear Creek Canyon

Clearing
1898 Clearing a Drift
1901 Squad of Men Clearing the Road
1902 Clearing the Course for the Henley Boat Races, July 10th, 1902
1907 Machete Men Clearing a Jungle [Panama Canal]
1908 Clearing the Mountain Track

Clemency
1910 Abraham Lincoln's Clemency

Cleopatra
1908 Antony and Cleopatra, the Love Story of the Noblest Roman and the Most Beautiful Egyptian
1909 Cleopatra's Lover; or, A Night of Enchantment
1910 Cleopatra

Cleptomaniac
1907 The Cleptomaniac

Clergyman
1910 The Clergyman and His Ward

Clerks
1900 The Inquisitive Clerks
Why Jones Discharged His Clerks
1901 The Mischievous Clerks; or, How the Office was Wrecked
1902 The Absent Minded Clerk, Fly Paper and Silk Hat
1903 Clerks Casing Mail for Bags, U.S.P.O.
Clerks Tying Bags, U.S.P.O.
Clerks Tying Up for Bags, U.S.P.O.
The Gay Shoe Clerk
1907 The Substitute Drug Clerk
1908 Troubles of a New Drug Clerk
1909 The Postal Clerk
The Seventh Clerk
1910 The Enterprising Clerk
The Railway Mail Clerk

Cleveland, Grover
1897 McKinley and Cleveland Going to the Capitol
President Cleveland and President McKinley

Cleveland (Ohio)
1897 Troop "A" of Cleveland, O.
1898 Cleveland Commandery, Cleveland, O.
1899 5th Ohio Volunteers of Cleveland
1900 Public Square, Cleveland
1901 Panorama, Public Square, Cleveland, O.
1907 Cleveland

Cleveland and Eastern Railway
1900 On the Cleveland and Eastern Railway

Clever
1902 Clever Horsemanship
1904 The Clever Baker
1907 Clever Detective
Clever Tailor
The Clever Thief
1908 The Mourners; or, A Clever Undertaking
Tricksy, the Clever Princess
Two Clever Detectives
1909 A Clever Detective
Clever Horse Hans
A Clever Nurse
The Clever Reporter
A Clever Sleuth
A Clever Trick
1910 The Clever Domestic
A Clever Ruse

Cliff House, San Francisco (California)
1903 Panorama of Beach and Cliff House

Cliff-Guibert
1899 Demonstrating the Action of the Cliff-Guibert Hose Reel
1900 Another Demonstration of the Cliff-Guibert Fire Hose Reel, Showing a Young Girl Coming from an Office, Detaching the Hose, Running with It 60 Feet, and Playing a Stream, All Inside of 30 Seconds

Cliffs
1896 Pa. R.R. Cliffs, Jersey City
1903 Cliff Scenery at the Fabbins
Panorama of Beach and Cliff House
1904 Cliffs of Cheddar, England
1905 Tourists Enroute to the Cliffs of Moher, Ireland
1907 Grand Canyon of Arizona and the Cliff Dwellers
1908 The Madman of the Cliff
1909 Caught on the Cliffs
1910 The Cliff Dwellers
In the Shadow of the Cliffs
Motoring Among the Cliffs and Gorges of France
Over the Cliffs
Sea Cave and Cliffs

Climbing
1898 French Soldiers in a Wall-Climbing Drill
Three Ways of Climbing over a Chair
1899 Climbing Jacob's Ladder
1901 Royal Train with Duke and Duchess of York, Climbing Mt. Hector
1902 Climbing Hagerman Pass
Tourists Climbing the Alps
1903 Climbing the Greasy Pole
1904 Chameleon Climbing
1905 Climbing the American Alps
1909 The Celebrated Mountain Climbers

Clink
1910 The Clink of Gold

Clock
1898 When the Clock Strikes Two in the Tenderloin
1902 Why Papa Reformed, or Setting Back the Clock
1904 Mysterious Clock
1907 The Human Clock
1908 Animated Clock
The Burglar and the Clock
The Intermittent Alarm Clock
Uncle's Clock
1909 The Old Hall Clock
1910 Hoodoo Alarm Clock

Clockmakers
1904 The Clock Maker's Dream
1907 The Clock-Maker's Secret

Clog
1903 Clog Dance
Waltz Clog Dance
1908 Clogmaking in Brittany

Cloister
1910 The Cloister's Touch

Close
1898 Close View of the "Brooklyn," Naval Parade
1899 A Close Finish
"Columbia" Close to the Wind
1900 A Close Finish
1901 A Close Call
A Close Shave
1908 The Closing Hour
Cuddle Up a Little Closer
We Close at Noon
1909 A Close Call
1910 A Close Shave

Closed
1908 Closed on Sundays
1909 Closed on Sunday
1910 The Closed Door
Closed Gate
The House with Closed Shutters

Cloth
1904 Cloth Dealer

Clothes
1899 The Bibulous Clothier
1902 Fun in a Clothes Basket
Native Women Washing Clothes at Fort de France
Native Women Washing Clothes at the Gueydon Fountain, Fort de France, Martinique
The Pals and the Clothier's Dummy
1903 Fire at Triangle Clothing Store, 13th and Ridge Ave., Philadelphia, May 3d, 1899
Native Women Washing Clothes at St. Vincent, B. W. I.
Piping Down. Wash Clothes. Scrambling for Clothes
Pulling Off the Bed Clothes
Washing Clothes at Sicily
1904 Scrubbing Clothes
1907 Busy Lizzie Loses Her Clothes
1908 Up-to-Date Clothes Cleaning
A Wolf in Sheep's Clothing
A Fake Diamond Swindler (L'habit ne fait pas le moine)
1909 Adonis Is Robbed of His Clothes
Borrowed Clothes; or, Fine Feathers Make Fine Birds
Jack Has No Clothes
1910 Clothes Make the Man
A Wolf in Sheep's Clothing

1904 Preparing the Codfish After the Catch
1908 The Codfish Industry

Coffee
1906 Bad Coffee
1907 Coffee Plantation
My Master's Coffee Service
1910 Coffee Culture

Cog
1902 Panorama of Cog Railway
1903 Pike's Peak Cog Wheel Route from Manitou

Coghlan, Capt.
1899 Capt. Coghlan, One of the Manila Heroes, and Crew of the Raleigh, Reviewed by the President
President McKinley and Wife, Members of His Cabinet and Their Wives and Capt. Cohlan Leaving the Cruiser Raleigh

Cohen
1903 Levi & Cohen, The Irish Comedians
1904 Cohen's Advertising Scheme
1907 Cohen's Bad Luck
Cohen's Fire Sale
1909 Cohen at Coney Island
Cohen's Dream of Coney Island
Original Cohens
1910 Cohen and Murphy
Cohen's Generosity

Coil
1904 Coil Winding Machines, Westinghouse Works
Coil Winding Section E, Westinghouse Works
Taping Coils, Westinghouse Works

Coin
1908 The False Coin
The Lost Coin
1909 The Beggar's Coin
The Coin Collector
1910 The False Coin

Coiners
1904 Raid on a Coiner's Den
1907 False Coiners
1909 The Coiners, or Catching the Counterfeiters

Coke
1903 The Coke Ovens of Pennsylvania
1908 Coke Industry

Cold
1899 A Cold Day for Art
A Warm Baby with a Cold Deck
When Their Love Grew Cold
1900 A Cold Water Cure
1907 How to Cure a Cold
1908 Cold Storage Love
1909 A Cold Plunge in Moscow
Hot Time in Cold Quarters
1910 A Cold Storage Romance

Coldstream
1897 The Coldstream Guards

Cole, King
1903 King Cole

Colenso (South Africa)
1900 Battle of Colenso

Colibris Dwarfs
1910 Acrobatic Exercises by the Colibris Dwarfs

Colic
1910 Baby Has the Colic

Coligny, Gaspard II de, Admiral
1910 The Death of Admiral Coligny

Collar
1902 The Tight Collar
1903 His Collar Does Not Fit
1906 The Lost Collar Button; or, A Strenuous Search
1907 All on Account of a Lost Collar Button
The Collar'd Herring
Moses Sells a Collar Button
1909 Flirtation Collar
1910 Fricot Has Lost His Collar Button
The Tempting Collar

Collecting
1902 Collecting the King's Mail
1903 Collecting Mail, U.S.P.O.
The Insurance Collector
Rent Collector
1908 The Installment Collector
1909 The Coin Collector
Collection of Stamps
How the Landlord Collected His Rents

College
1897 Girard College Cadets
Girard College Cadets at Double Quick
Girard College Cadets in Review
1898 Imitation of a College Society Girl
1899 Girard College Cadets
International Collegiate Games
The International Collegiate Games
International Collegiate Games
International Collegiate Games—Half Mile Run
International Collegiate Games—110 Yards Hurdle Race
International Collegiate Games—100 Yards Dash
1902 The University College of Oxford Winning the Ladies' Challenge Plate
1903 Girard College Cadets Reviewed by Governor Hastings, at the Dedication of Stephen Girard's Monument
1904 Basket ball, Missouri Valley College
College Sports in England
Dance of the College Women's Club
Fencing Class, Missouri Valley College
Minuet and Dance—College Women's Club
1906 A College Girl's Affair of Honor
College Life at Amherst
Panorama, City Hall, Van Ness Avenue and College of St. Ignatius
1907 College Boy's First Love
College Chums
1908 College Days
Old College Chums
Rube Goes to College
1910 A College Chicken
Fricot in College
Why Fricot Was Sent to College

Colliery
1904 A Disaster in a Colliery

Collinwood (Ohio)
1908 The Collinwood [Ohio] School Fire
The Collinwood [Ohio] School Fire Funeral

Collision
1903 The Effects of a Trolley Car Collision
1906 Head-On Collision at Brighton Beach Race Track, July 4th, 1906
Railroad Collision at Los Angeles, Calif.
Train Collision
1907 The Great Brighton Beach Head-On Locomotive Collision

Colma
1907 Panorama, Crowds at Squires-Burns International Contest, from Center of Ring, Colma, July 4th, 1907

Cologne (Germany)
1910 The Rhine from Cologne to Bingen

Colombo (Sri Lanka)
1910 Colombo and Its Environs

Colon (Panama)
1907 Colon to Panama Canal Picture
Fire Run, Colon Fire Department Under Cocoanut Tree

Colonel
1898 Col. Torrey's "Rough Riders"
Col. Torrey's Rough Riders and Army Mules
1902 The Abbe and the Colonel
1905 The Colonel's Friend
1906 Colonel's Bicycle
1907 Soldier to Colonel
1908 Roman Colonel's Bravado
1910 The Colonel's Boot
The Colonel's Errand

Colonial
1903 England's Colonial Troops
1907 At the Colonial Exhibition
The Colonial Soldier
Colonial Virginia and Burning of Jamestown
1908 Colonial Virginia
For Love of Country: American Patriotism in the Colonial Wars
1909 A Colonial Romance
1910 A Colonial Belle
Tale of Colonial Days: An Episode in the Life of Alexander Hamilton and Aaron Burr

Colonna, Julie
1910 Julie Colonna

Color
1899 Morning Colors on U.S. Cruiser "Raleigh"
1903 Raising Colors, Battleship "Indiana"
1907 A Horse of Another Color
Under False Colors
1908 Trooping the Colour
1909 Drawing the Color Line
1910 The Color Sergeant's Horse

Colorado
1903 Freight Train in the Royal Gorge, Colo.
Santa Fe Colorado Express
1906 Great Railroad Panorama Through Colorado
Trip over Colorado Midland
Trip Through Colorado
Trip to Southern Colorado
1909 Outing Pastimes in Colorado
1910 Fruit Growing, Grand Valley, Colorado (The Results of Irrigation)

Colorado Special, Chicago & Northwestern Ry.
1903 Colorado Special, Chicago & Northwestern Ry.

Colorado Springs (Colorado)
1907 Colorado Springs

Colored
use **Blacks**

Columbia (Boat)
1898 Cruiser Columbia
S.S. "Columbia" Sailing
1899 "Columbia"
"Columbia" and "Defender" Rounding Stake-Boat
"Columbia" Close to the Wind
"Columbia" vs. "Defender"
"Columbia" Winning the Cup
Mrs. C. Oliver Iselin and Crew of Columbia
Running Up the Topsail on the "Columbia"
"Shamrock" and "Columbia"
Shamrock and Columbia Jockeying for a Start
"Shamrock" and "Columbia" Rounding the Outer Stake Boat
"Shamrock" and "Columbia" Rounding the Outer Stake Boat, No. 2
"Shamrock" and "Columbia" Yacht Race—First Race
"Shamrock" and "Columbia" Yacht Race—1st Race, No. 2
Start of Race Between "Columbia" and "Shamrock"
Turning Stake Boat; "Columbia" and "Shamrock"
1900 Trial Race Columbia and Defender
Trial Race Columbia and Defender No. 2
1901 "Columbia" and "Shamrock II": Finishing Second Race
"Columbia" and "Shamrock II": Jockeying and Starting
"Columbia" and "Shamrock II": Start of Second Race
"Columbia" and "Shamrock II": Starting in the Third Race
"Columbia" and "Shamrock II": Turning the Outer Stake Boat
"Columbia" Winning the Cup
Hail Columbia!
International Yacht Races—Columbia vs. Shamrock
1903 Columbia and Shamrock
Columbia in the Lead
Yacht Columbia

Columbia bicycle factory, Hartford (Connecticut)
1897 Columbia Bicycle Factory

Columbia Post
1901 Columbia Post

Columbia River
1902 Cavalry Swimming Columbia River
1903 Kalama Railroad Ferry Crossing the Columbia River
Salmon Seining on Columbia River U.S.F.C.
1904 Fish Traps Columbia River
Mending Seines on the Columbia River
Panoramic View of the Columbia River
1909 Through the Hood River Valley and Along the Columbia in Oregon

Columbia School (New York City)
1897 Columbia School Girls

Columbia University (New York City)
1899 Pole Vaulting at Columbia University

1901 Panoramic View of London Streets, Showing Coronation Decorations
Spanish Coronation Royal Bull-Fight
1902 Coronation of King Edward VII and Alexandra
Coronation Parade
King Edward Reviewing Coronation Naval Force at Spithead August 16, 1902
Reproduction, Coronation Ceremonies—King Edward VII
1903 Coronation Procession Passing Under the Canadian Arch

Coroner
1907 The Coroner's Mistake

Coronets
1908 True Hearts Are More Than Coronets

Corporal
1908 Promoted Corporal

Corporation
1910 Tweedledum Gets Employed in the Corporation Body

Corps
1897 Drum Corps and Militia
First Corps Cadets; Mass. National Guard
1899 Ambulance Corps Drill
1902 A French Bicycle Corps
1904 A Regiment of the Japanese Imperial Guards and Engineer Corps off to the Front
1909 Maneuvers of Ambulance Corps.

Corpse
1909 A Live Corpse

Corpulent
1910 The Club of the Corpulent

Corpus Christi
1898 Corpus Christi Procession, Orvieto
1901 The Great Corpus Christi Procession in Breslau
1905 Corpus Christi Ceremonies, Botzen, Tyrol
Corpus Christi Cortege, Botzen, Tyrol

Corral
1898 Cattle Leaving the Corral

Correction
1899 Female Prisoners: Detroit House of Correction

Correspondence
1904 A Wedding of Correspondence
1909 Instruction by Correspondence

Correspondents
1898 War Correspondents
1904 The War Correspondent and the Two Bear Cubs
1909 Mysterious Correspondent

Corridor
1903 Down the Hotel Corridor

Corsair (Boat)
1899 The "Corsair"
"Corsair" in Wake of Tugboat

Corsets
1897 Her First Corset
1899 The Corset Model
1904 A Busy Day for the Corset Model
The Way to Sell Corsets
1905 Airy Fairy Lillian Tries on Her New Corsets
1908 Fluffy's New Corsets

Corsican
1906 Corsican Chastisement
1909 Corsican Hospitality
The Corsican's Revenge
1910 A Corsican Vendetta
A Corsican's Revenge

Cortege
1901 Arrival of Funeral Cortege at St. George's Chapel
Arrival of Funeral Cortege at the City Hall, Buffalo, N.Y.
Complete Funeral Cortege at Canton, Ohio
The Complete Funeral Cortege Passing Through Windsor
The Funeral Cortege Arriving at Trinity Pier
President McKinley's Funeral Cortege at Buffalo, N.Y.
President McKinley's Funeral Cortege at Washington, D.C.
1905 Corpus Christi Cortege, Botzen, Tyrol
Religious Cortege on a Rainy Day, Cortina, Tyrol

Cortina (Italy)
1905 "Crazy" Congregation Leaving Church, Cortina, Tyrol
Religious Cortege on a Rainy Day, Cortina, Tyrol

Cosette
1909 Cosette

Cossacks
1901 Charge of Cossack Cavalry
Cossack Cavalry
Von Waldersee Reviewing Cossacks
1903 Cossacks
1908 The Cossacks
1910 Mystery of the Cossacks
Riding Feats by Cossacks

Cost
1908 A Costly Coat
1909 The Cost of Forgetfulness

Coster
1903 Coster Sports
1904 The Coster's Wedding
1908 How the Coster Sold the Seeds

Costumes
1904 The Animated Costumes
1905 Procession of Costumed Characters, Vevey Fete
1907 Costumes of Different Centuries
1909 Masquerade Costume

Cosy
1903 Cosy Corner Dance

Cottage
1903 Scenes of Irish Cottage Life
1905 Tourists Party near Kate Kearney's Cottage, Gap of Dunloe, Ireland

Cotton
1908 The Cotton Industry of the South
1910 Animated Cotton
King Cotton

Couchee dance
1897 Horse Dancing Couchee Couchee
1898 New Couchee Dance
1899 The Couchee Couchee Bear
1900 Fatima's Coochee-Coochee Dance
1901 Couchee Dance on the Midway
1903 Fatima, Couchee Dancer
French Couchee Dance
Man Couchee Dance
1904 Couchee Dance on the Pike

Coughdrop
1899 How Tottie Coughdrop's Summer Suit Was Spoiled

Council
1898 Indian War Council

Council Bluffs (Nebraska)
1900 From Council Bluffs to Omaha

Counsellor
1910 Jealousy, a Bad Counsellor

Count
1898 Pope Leo XIII and Count Pecci, No. 1
1902 M. Le Comte De Dion
1904 Cavalry Fording a Stream (Passage d'un torrent par le comte de Turin et son etat-major)
1905 Horses Jumping over a Wall (Sauts de mur et de haie par le comte de Turin et ses cavaliers)
1908 The Count of No Account
1909 Count of Monte Cristo
The Count's Wooing
1910 An American Count
Count of Monte Christo
The Count of Montebello
Count of Noaccount
The Count That Counted
The Romance of Count de Beaufort

Countenance
1910 Wilson's Wife's Countenance

Counter
1904 Buster Makes Room for His Mama at the Bargain Counter

Counterfeiters
1900 A Raid on "Dago" Counterfeiters
1905 The Counterfeiters
1909 The Coiners, or Catching the Counterfeiters

Countess
1908 The Countess' Wedding Day
1909 De Comtess de Valeria

Country
1897 A Country Dance
1898 Country Boarders Locked Out
A Country Couple's Visit to an Art Gallery
Tribulations of a Country Schoolmarm
1899 Burlesque Queen and a Country Photographer
Burlesque Queen and Country Photographer
Mesmerist and Country Couple
1901 Photographing a Country Couple
Prize Winners at the Country Fair
1902 A Country Groceryman's Revenge
"A Sweet Little Home in the Country"
1903 Country Sport and Old Maid
Country Teacher and His Pupils
A Pack Train in the Copper River Country
Troubles of a Country Visitor
1904 Hold Up in a Country Grocery Store
1905 A Country Courtship
1906 The Country Schoolmaster
Day in the Country
1907 The Country Girl
Saving His Country's Flag
A Winter Day in the Country
1908 Auntie Takes the Children to the Country
Bathing; or, Charlie and Mary in the Country
Country About Rome
A Country Drama
A Country Girl in Philadelphia
A Country Girl's Seminary Life and Experiences
The Country Idyll
A Country Lad
The Country of the "Bogoudens"
For Love of Country: American Patriotism in the Colonial Wars
The Guileless Country Lassie
Harry, the Country Postman
Just Plain Folks, the Story of a Simple Country Girl
The Professor's Trip to the Country; or, A Case of Mistaken Identity
A Romance of the Fur Country
Touaregs in Their Country
1909 The Country Doctor
A Country Girl's Peril
Country Life in a Flat
Dances of Various Countries
For Her Country's Sake
For Their Country's Cause
A Man Without a Country
Mary Jane Visits Her Country Cousin
Mother-in-Law's Day in the Country
My Wife's Gone to the Country
My Wife's Gone to the Country (Hooray! Hooray!)
Our Country in Arms
Raised in the Country
1910 The Country Boarder
The Country Schoolmaster
The Flag of His Country
For Her Country's Sake
The Gunby's Sojourn in the Country
In the Tall Grass Country
Mr. Swell in the Country
Servant from the Country
A True Country Heart

Countryman
1898 Countryman and Mischievous Boys
1903 The Hungry Countryman
1905 Countryman in Paris
1906 Love Letter (Lettre à la payse)
1908 Adventures of a Countryman

County
1898 County Democracy

County fair
1903 County Fair
1904 A Rube Couple at a County Fair
1910 County Fair

Couple
1898 A Country Couple's Visit to an Art Gallery
1899 Mesmerist and Country Couple
1901 Photographing a Country Couple
1903 Irish Couple Dancing Breakdown
1904 A Couple of Lightweights at Coney Island
The Interrupted Couple
A Rube Couple at a County Fair
1907 The Poor Old Couple
1908 Bridal Couple Dodging Cameras

Coupon
1909 Caught by the Coupon Craze

Courage
1906 A Courageous Husband
1909 When Courage Fled

1904 Tracked by Bloodhounds; or, A Lynching at Cripple Creek
1906 Trip over Cripple Creek Short Line
1907 Over the Midland Terminal Railroad: Through Cripple Creek District
1910 The New Marshall at Gila Creek
On Panther Creek
The Widow of Mill Creek Flat

Cremation
1899 The Cremation
1900 Spanish Inquisition (La crémation)
1909 The Cremation
Cremation on the River Ganges

Cremona (Italy)
1909 The Violin Maker of Cremona
1910 The Violin Maker of Cremona

Cresceus (Boat)
1901 The "Abbot" and "Cresceus" Race

Crest
1909 On the Crest of the Waves

Cretinetti
1909 How Foolshead Paid His Debts (Come Cretinetti paga i debiti)
Foolshead Looks for a Duel (Cretinetti cerca un duello)
Foolshead's Trousers (Cretinetti e i pantaloni)
Foolshead Pays a Visit (Cretinetti in visita)
Foolshead Wrestling (Cretinetti lottatore)
How Foolshead Paid His Debts (Cretinetti paga i debiti)
Foolshead, King of Police (Cretinetti re dei poliziotti)
Foolshead Sportsman of Love (Cretinetti sportivo per amore)
Foolshead Wishes to Commit Suicide (Cretinetti suicida)
Foolshead on the Alps (Cretinetti sulle alpi)
1910 Greediness Spoiled Foolshead's Christmas (Come fu che l'ingordigia rovino' il natale a Cretinetti)
Foolshead at the Ball (Cretinetti al ballo)
Distractions of Foolshead (Cretinetti distratto)
Foolshead As a Porter (Cretinetti facchino)
Foolshead Between Two Fires (Cretinetti fra i fuochi)
Foolshead Learns to Somersault (Cretinetti impara il salto mortale)
Foolshead in the Lion's Cage (Cretinetti nella gabbia dei leoni)
Foolshead Fisherman (Cretinetti pescatore)
Foolshead As a Policeman (Cretinetti poliziotto)
Foolshead Chief of the Reporters (Cretinetti re dei giornalisti)
Foolshead Receives (Cretinetti riceve)
Foolshead Knows How to Take His Precautions (Cretinetti sa prendere le sue precauzioni)
Foolshead Marries Against His Will (Cretinetti sposo suo malgrado)
Foolshead Victim of His Honesty (Cretinetti vittima della sua onesta')
Foolshead Volunteer on the Red Cross (Cretinetti volontario alla croce rossa)
Foolshead Wishes to Marry the Governor's Daughter (Cretinetti vuol sposare la figlia del padrone)

Creusot
1905 Creusot's Metallurgy

Crew
1897 Fastest Wrecking Crew in the World
Gatling Gun Crew in Action
Harvard Crew
1898 Crew of the Battleship Texas
Crew of the "Yankee"
Hobson and Crew of the Merrimac
Naval Constructor Richmond P. Hobson and the Crew of the Merrimac
Officers and Crew of the U.S. Cruiser "Brooklyn"
1899 Capt. Coghlan, One of the Manila Heroes, and Crew of the Raleigh, Reviewed by the President
Crew of the "Shamrock"
Crew of the "Shamrock," at Work
Crew of the U.S. Cruiser "Raleigh"
Gen. Snowden and Staff, and Crew of the U.S.S. "Raleigh"
Mrs. C. Oliver Iselin and Crew of Columbia
Oxford and Cambridge University Boat Crews
The Yale Crew
1901 Crew of a Pacific Liner
'Varsity Crew Race on Cayuga Lake, on Decoration Day, Lehigh Valley Observation Train Following the Race, Showing Cornell Crew Finishing First, Columbia Second, University of Pennsylvania Third Ithaca, N.Y., Showing Lehigh Valley Observation Train
1902 Worcester High School Eight-Oared Boat Crews in Action
1903 Crew of the U.S. Cruiser Raleigh Passing the Grant Monument at Fairmount Park, Philadelphia
President Roosevelt Addressing Crew of "Kearsarge"
1904 Exhibition of the United States Life Saving Crew
1905 New York Athletic Club Crew at Phila., Pa.

Crewe (England)
1907 Rail Lying at Crewe

Cricket
1907 Cricket Terms Illustrated
1909 The Cricket on the Hearth

Crime
1900 A Career of Crime, No. 1: Start in Life
A Career of Crime, No. 2: Going the Pace
A Career of Crime, No. 3: Robbery & Murder
A Career of Crime, No. 4: In the Toils
A Career of Crime, No. 5: The Death Chair
1902 The History of a Crime
1903 The Gambler's Crime
1904 Avenging a Crime; or, Burned at the Stake
Lover's Crime
1905 Cards and Crime
1906 Another's Crime
A Desperate Crime
1907 Crime in the Mountains
A Crime in the Snow
Crime on the Railroad
Crime Wave
The Vision of a Crime
1908 The Criminal's Daughter
Duchess' Crime
A Magistrate's Crime
A Mother's Crime
The Penalty of His Crime
The Son's Crime
Curiosity Punished (Le crime de la rue de cherche-midi à quartorze heures)
1909 The Criminal Hypnotist
A Criminal Invention
Mexican's Crime
The Mysterious Crime
1910 Father's Crime
The Fisherman's Crime
His Imaginary Crime
A Jar of Cranberry Sauce; or, The Crime in Room 13

Cripple
1902 St. John's Guild. Crippled Children to and from Wagon
1904 The False Cripple
1906 Motor-car and Cripple
1907 Cripple's Duel
1908 The Little Cripple
1909 The Cripple's Marriage
1910 The Crippled Teddy Bear

Cripple Creek (Colorado)
1898 Cripple Creek Float
1899 Cripple Creek Bar-Room Scene
1904 Tracked by Bloodhounds; or, A Lynching at Cripple Creek
1906 Trip over Cripple Creek Short Line
1907 Over the Midland Terminal Railroad: Through Cripple Creek District

Crisis
1909 Victim of a Crisis

Critic
1900 Confounding the Art Critic
1906 The Critic
1907 Beyond Criticism

Critical
1910 A Critical Situation

Crockett, Davy
1909 "Davy" Crockett in Hearts United
1910 Davy Crockett

Crocodile
1908 Crocodile Hunt
Crocodile Turns Thief
1909 The Crocodile Hunt

Croker, Richard
1900 Dick Croker Leaving Tammany Hall
1907 Croker's Horse Winning the Derby

Cromwell, Oliver
1909 Oliver Cromwell

Cromwellian period
1909 The Death Disc: A Story of the Cromwellian Period

Cronies
1900 Two Old Cronies
1901 Two Old Cronies

Cronje, Piet Arnoldus, General
1905 General Cronje & Mystic Shriners

Cronk, Hiram
1905 Funeral of Hiram Cronk

Crook
1904 Photographing a Female Crook
1905 Female Crook and Her Easy Victim
1910 The Copper and the Crook

Crooked
1897 The Crookedest Railroad Yard in the World
1907 Crooked Dog
1909 Crooked Path
1910 The Crooked Trail

Cross
1900 The Power of the Cross
1903 Passion Play: Carrying the Cross
Passion Play: Taking Down the Cross
1904 The Passion Play (La descente de croix)
The Passion Play (Jésus succombe sous sa croix)
1905 The Sign of the Cross
1909 Cross of Honor
The Way of the Cross, the Story of Ancient Rome
1910 At Double Cross Ranch
The Legend of the Cross
The Soldier of the Cross

Cross-country
1902 Cross-Country Running on Snow Shoes
1905 Intercollegiate Cross Country Run
1906 Cross Country

Crossing
1898 Crossing the Line
1899 Armored Train Crossing the Veldt
1901 Train Crossing Dale Creek Fill
1903 Boer Supply Train Crossing the Veldt
Bootblack and Crossing Sweeper
Crossing the Atlantic
Kalama Railroad Ferry Crossing the Columbia River
Prairie Emigrant Train Crossing the Plains
"Reliance" Crossing the Line and Winning First Race
Trappers Crossing Bald Mountain
1904 Cavalry Crossing a River
Crossing Ice Bridge at Niagara Falls
1905 Battery of Artillery Crossing Ball's Bridge, Limerick, Ireland
Parade of Passengers Crossing to North Cape, Norway
Passengers Crossing over Open Car, Balley Bunion Railway
1908 German Dragoons Crossing the Elbe
Pioneers Crossing the Plains in '49
1909 Consul Crosses the Atlantic
First Airships Crossing the English Channel
1910 Crossing the Andes

Crossroads
1908 At the Crossroads of Life
The Cross Roads
1909 A Girl's Cross Roads

Croton Dam (New York)
1900 The Croton Dam Strike

Crow
1902 From the Crow's Nest

Crow Indians
1903 Crow Indian Festival Dance
Crow Indian War Dance
Crow Indians Harvesting

Crowds
1897 A Jolly Crowd of Bathers Frolicking on the Beach at Atlantic City
1900 Breaking of the Crowd at Military Review at Longchamps
1901 Panoramic View of the Crowd Rushing for the City Hall, Buffalo, to View the Body of President McKinley

How a Bad Tempered Man Was Cured
The Marvelous Cure; or, The Wonderful Hair-Growing Fluid
A New Divorce Cure
The Rest Cure
Sand Man's Cure
A Sleep Walking Cure
The Water Cure

Curem, Dr.
1908 Dr. Curem's Patients

Curfew
1900 Why Curfew Did Not Ring Last Night
1907 Curfew Shall Not Ring Tonight
1909 The Curfew Bell

Curio, Mr.
1908 Curious Mr. Curio

Curious
1904 Benvenuto Cellini; or, A Curious Evasion
Curious Sights in Burmah and Cashmere (Section 1)
Curious Sights in Burmah and Cashmere (Section 2)
1906 Doorkeeper's Curiosity
1907 Curious Carriage of Klobenstein
A Curious Dream
1908 Curiosity Punished
Curious Mr. Curio
1909 The Old Curiosity Shop
Ralph Benefits by People's Curiosity
1910 A Curious Invention

Current
1908 Current News Items

Curse
1908 The Curse of Drink
The Curse of Gold
1909 The Curse of Cocaine
The Curse of Gold
The Curse of Money
The Cursed Cage
1910 The Curse of Gambling
White Man's Money, the Indian Curse

Curtain
1901 Lubin's Animated Drop Curtain Announcing Slides
1904 As Seen on the Curtain
Pull Down the Curtain, Susie
1908 Oh That Curtain
1909 The Curtain Pole
1910 Fabian Arranging Curtain Rods
The Man Behind the Curtain

Curtis, M. B.
1899 M. B. Curtis

Curve
1899 Around the Big Curves
Around the Big Curves on the Manhattan Elevated R.R.
Around Tynsborough Curve
104th Street Curve, New York, Elevated Railway
Panoramic View, Horseshoe Curve, From Penna. Ltd.
Panoramic View, Horseshoe Curve, Penna. R.R., No. 2
1903 Death Curve, New York City
1904 Horse-Shoe Curve

Cushing, Jack
1894 Leonard—Cushing Fight

Custer, George Armstrong
1909 On the Little Big Horn; or, Custer's Last Stand
1910 Custer's Last Stand

Custody
1909 To the Custody of the Father

Customers
1900 The Barber's Queer Customer
A Customer Drops In
1905 Impatient Customer
1910 Generous Customers

Customs
1900 Scandal in the Custom House
1905 Custom House Search
1906 Custom Officials Bewitched
1907 Cambodian Customs
Indian Customs
Life and Customs in India
Manners and Customs of Australia
1908 Custom Officers Mystified
Custom Officer's Pull
Custom Officer's Revenge
Life and Customs of Naples
Nothing to Declare; or, Bested by Custom Officials
Tyrolean Alps Customs
1909 Caucasian Customs
1910 Customs of the Buddhists in India

Cut
1901 Coming Out of Scraping Machines and Cutting Off Heads
Cutting Beef
Cutting Cucumbers and Cauliflower, Heinz
Cutting Meat for Sausage (side view)
Cutting Pork
Cutting Sugar Cane
Fish Cut
1902 Cutting and Canaling Ice
Panoramic View of Mt. Tamalpais Between Bow Knot and McKinley Cut
1906 You Won't Cut Any Ice with Me
1907 Ice Cutting in Sweden
1909 Man with the Cut Throat
New Cut Roads Up Mt. Blanc
1910 Diamond Cut Diamond

Cut-out
1904 Mellin's Food Cut-Out

Cut-up
1906 The Village Cut-Up

Cutter
1901 Schooner "Idler" and Revenue Cutter "Gresham"
1903 Race Between Dog Team, Bicycle and Cutter

Cuyahoga Gorge (Ohio)
1901 Cuyahoga Gorge

Cyclamens
1909 Little Seller of Cyclamens

Cycle
1910 In Life's Cycle

Cyclists
1901 The Trick Cyclist
1907 The Near-Sighted Cyclist
1909 Cycle Rider and the Witch
Cyclist's Horn
Lesson in Cycling
The Motor Cyclist
The Rival Cyclists
1910 Angler and the Cyclist
Military Cyclists of Belgium

Cyclone
1908 An Interior Cyclone
1909 The Cyclone Sneezer
1910 Cyclone Pete's Matrimony

Cyril
1909 Little Cyril, the Runaway

Czar
1902 The Children of the Czar
1904 Nobles Leaving the Kremlin, Moscow, After a Reception by Czar
1905 The Czar at Czarkoe Selo
1908 The Slaves of the Czar
1910 In the Czar's Name
In the Realm of the Czar

Czarkoe Selo
1905 The Czar at Czarkoe Selo

Czolgosz, Leon F.
1901 Execution of Czolgosz, with Panorama of Auburn Prison

Dad
use **Father**

Dagger
1906 The Witch (La fée carabosse ou le poignard fatal)
1908 Arabian Dagger
The Stolen Dagger
1909 The Hindoo Dagger

"Dago"
use **Italy and Italians**

Dahlias
1904 Dance Plastiques (Les dahlias 1. Danses plastiques)
Ruffian's Dance (Les dahlias 2. Danse des apaches)

Daily
1898 Daily March
1907 The Daily Life of a French Sailor
1910 A Bootblack's Daily Labor in Algiers

Daines
1903 Acrobatic Sisters Daines

Dainty
1910 A Dainty Politician

Daiquiri (Cuba)
1898 Mules Swimming Ashore at Daiquiri, Cuba
U.S. Troops Landing at Daiquiri, Cuba

Dairy
1899 The Dairy Maid's Revenge
1908 French Dairy Farm
Pretty Dairymaid
1909 The Dairy Maid's Lovers
Romance of a Dairy Maid
1910 The Pretty Dairy Maid

Daisy
1897 The Daisy Guard
1908 Daisy, the Pretty Typewriter
1910 Daisies
What the Daisy Said

Dale Creek Valley (Wyoming)
1901 Train Crossing Dale Creek Fill

Dalerne (Sweden)
1909 Life in Dalerne (Sweden)

Dalgren
1898 Dalgren Post, G.A.R.

Daly, Charles D.
1902 Daly, of West Point

Daly's Grade (Canada)
1899 Bridge No. 804, and Daly's Grade

Dam, I. B.
1905 I. B. Dam and the Whole Dam Family

Dam Family
1905 I. B. Dam and the Whole Dam Family
The Whole Dam Family and the Dam Dog

Damaged
1906 Panoramic View of San Francisco City Hall, Damaged by Earthquake

Damascus Commandery (Detroit)
1898 Damascus Commandery, Detroit

Dame
1909 The Gray Dame
1910 The Caprice of a Dame
A Willful Dame

Damnation
1903 The Damnation of Faust
1904 Faust and Marguerite (Damnation du docteur Faust)

Damon
1908 Damon and Pythias

Dan
1909 Dime Novel Dan
1910 Dan, the Arizona Scout

Dance
1894 Imperial Japanese Dance
1895 Serpentine Dance—Annabelle
1896 Annabelle in Flag Dance
Butterfly Dance
Dancing Darkies
Serpentine Dance by Annabelle
Tambourine Dance—by Annabelle
1897 Butterfly Dance
A Country Dance
Dance, Franchonetti Sisters
Dancing Darkey Boy
Dancing Girls Limbering Up
The Dancing Skeleton
The Dolorita Passion Dance
French Acrobatic Dance
Gaiety Dance
Horse Dancing Couchee Couchee
Parisian Dance
Pickanninies Dance
A Skipping Rope Dance
Sun Dance—Annabelle
1898 Buck Dance, Ute Indians
Circle Dance, Ute Indians
The Confetti Dance
The Dance of the Living Picture
Dancing Chinaman, Marionettes
Eagle Dance, Pueblo Indians
Ella Lola, a la Trilby [Dance]
Ghost Dance
Her First Lesson in Dancing
The Kiki Dance
Mexican Dance
Moulin Rouge Dancers
New Couchee Dance
Skeleton Dance, Marionettes
Turkish Dance, Ella Lola
Wand Dance, Pueblo Indians
What Happened to the Dancing Master's Pupil
1899 Dance in a Turkish Harem
New Lipman Dance
New Umbrella Dance
Wonderful Dancing Girls
A Zulu War Dance
1900 Carnival Dance
Dancing on the Bowery
A Darktown Dance

In Golden Days
In the Days of the Pilgrims, a Romance of the 15th Century in America
Labor Day Parade
A Lord for a Day
A Love Affair of the Olden Days
The Maid's Last Day
On Thanksgiving Day
A Rustic Heroine; or, In the Days of King George
A Southern Romance of Slavery Days
Weary Waggles' Busy Day
A Western Romance in the Days of '49
1909 Adele's Wash Day
Bad Day for Lavinsky
Brown's Moving Day
Calling Day
Children of the Plains, an Episode of Pioneer Days
The Day After
Day After a Spree
A Day in Washington, the Capital of the United States, Showing Many Points of Interest
The Day of the Dog
A Day with Our Soldier Boys
A Day's Outing
Early Days in the West
The Empty Sleeve; or, Memories of By-Gone Days
An Evil Day
Frontier Days
Her Busy Day
His Lucky Day
In the Days of Witchcraft
A Lunatic's Day Off
Mother-in-Law's Day in the Country
Out for the Day
Quiet Day at the Cafe
See a Pin and Pick It Up, All That Day You'll Have Good Luck
The Seventh Day
Sporting Days in the Old South
Stirring Days in Old Virginia
Story of Every Day
Student Days
Tag Day
1910 Actors' Fund Field Day
A Day of Pleasure
A Day Off
A Day on the French Battleship "Justice"
Days of '49
Examination Day at School
Frontier Day in the West
The Jealous Wife's New Year Day
Jenk's Day Off
King of a Day
Little Peter's Xmas Day
7 Days
A Slippery Day
Taft for a Day
Tale of Colonial Days: An Episode in the Life of Alexander Hamilton and Aaron Burr
Their Day of Thanks
To-morrow Is Pay-day
Wandering Wilfred's April Fool's Day
A Windy Day
Winter Days in Sweden

Dazzle
1903 Razzle Dazzle

Deacon
1909 The Deacon's Holiday
The Deacon's Love Letter
1910 The Converted Deacon
The Deacon's Daughter

Dead
use **Death**

Dead letters
1910 The Dead Letter

Dead shots
1909 Alphonse, the Dead Shot

Deadbeats
1898 How the Dressmaker Got Even with a Dead Beat

Deadwood
1903 Deadwood Coach
1905 The Deadwood Sleeper

Deaf-mutes
1901 Deaf Mute Recitation
Star Spangled Banner by a Deaf Mute
1904 Our Deaf Friend, Fogarty
1907 Deaf and Dumb
The Deaf-Mutes' Ball

Deal
1904 Cloth Dealer
The Statue Dealer
1907 A Square Deal; or, The End of a Bad Man
1910 A Deal in Broken China
A Deal in Indians
The Last Deal

Dear
1903 Dear Old Stars and Stripes, Goodbye
1904 The Dear Boys Home for the Holidays
1907 Dear Little Sister
1908 The Dear Little Heart
A Dear Old Grandma
A Dearly Paid for Kiss
The Rain-Dear
1910 Our Dear Uncle from America

Death
1897 Death of Nancy Sykes
13th Infantry, U.S. Army—Scaling Walls with Wounded and Dying, Governors Island
"To the Death"
1898 A Duel to the Death
1899 Death of Maceo and His Followers
1900 A Career of Crime, No. 5: The Death Chair
Searching Ruins on Broadway, Galveston, for Dead Bodies
Taking the Dead from the Ruins [Galveston]
1901 Ten Nights in a Bar-Room: Death of Little Mary
Ten Nights in a Bar-Room: Death of Slade
1902 Taking Out the Dead and Wounded
1903 Deadly Rivals
Death Curve, New York City
Taking Out the Dead and Wounded
1904 Death of Robert McCaire and Bertrand
Robber of the Dead
The Passion Play (Jésus succombe sous sa croix)
The Passion Play (La mort du Christ)
1905 Reading the Death Sentence
1906 The Secret of Death Valley
The Starvelings (Les meurt de faim)
1907 Because My Father's Dead
A New Death Penalty
True Until Death
Shakespeare Writing "Julius Caesar" (Shakespeare. La mort de Jules César)
1908 Braving Death to Save a Life
The Dance of Death
The Deadly Plant
The Inn of Death, an Adventure in the Pyrenees Mountains
Pierrot's Death
A Voice from the Dead
1909 A Dash to Death
The Death Disc: A Story of the Cromwellian Period
The Death of the Duke D'Enghien
Gambling with Death
Sentenced to Death
Sold to Thieves; or, A Deathbed Confession
Stronger Than Death
Talked to Death
Tickled to Death
Mozart's Last Requiem (La mort de Mozart)
1910 The Death of Admiral Coligny
The Death of Michael Grady
The Death of Minnehaha
Death of the Brigand Chief
Faithful Until Death
Ginhara or Faithful Unto Death
He Did Not Die
Into the Jaws of Death
The Jump to Death
Legally Dead
Let Us Die Together
The Man Who Died
The Necklace of the Dead
A Ride to Death
Speed Versus Death
We Will Die Together, Love
Worried to Death

De Beers
1907 De Beers Diamond Mines, Kimberly, S.A.

Debt
1908 A Child's Debt
A New Way to Pay Debts
1909 The Burden of Debt
How Foolshead Paid His Debts
How Jones Paid His Debts
1910 Debt
The Debt Repaid
A Painful Debt

Debut
1906 The Inexperienced Chauffeur (Les débuts d'un chauffeur)
1907 A Super's Debut
1909 Chimney Sweep's Debut
Debut of an Alpinist

DeCarmos
1902 The DeCarmos

Decazeville (France)
1907 Mines and Forge at Decazeville

December
1910 May and December

Deception
1905 The Gay Deceivers
1908 Deceived Slumming Party
The Deceiver
1909 The Deceiver
The Deception
1910 The Deceivers
Her Husband's Deception

Decision
1909 Paul Has Decided to Marry
1910 The Deciding Vote
The Right Decision

Deck
1898 Captain Sigsbee on Deck of the U.S. Battleship Texas
1899 Heavy Sea from Deck of "St. Louis"
A Warm Baby with a Cold Deck
1900 Demonstrating the Action of the Chicago Pneumatic Tool Co.'s Deck Machine
1901 Washing Down Decks
1902 Between the Decks
St. John's Guild. Plank to Deck, Floating Hospital

Declare
1908 Nothing to Declare; or, Bested by Custom Officials

Decorate
1898 Decorated Carriages
1901 Panoramic View of London Streets, Showing Coronation Decorations
1907 Panorama of Market Street Showing the Beautiful Decorations
1908 H. R. H. The Prince of Wales Decorating the Monument of Champlain and Receiving Addresses of Welcome from the Mayor of Quebec, the Governor General of Canada and Vice-President Fairbanks, Representative of the United States
1910 Decorated by the Emperor

Decoration Day
1901 'Varsity Crew Race on Cayuga Lake, on Decoration Day, Lehigh Valley Observation Train Following the Race, Showing Cornell Crew Finishing First, Columbia Second, University of Pennsylvania Third Ithaca, N.Y., Showing Lehigh Valley Observation Train

Decoyed
1904 Decoyed

Dedham (Boston polo team)
1899 Myopia vs. Dedham
1900 Polo Game: Myopia vs. Dedham

Dedication
1902 Dedication of the Alexander Grenadiers' Barracks
1903 Girard College Cadets Reviewed by Governor Hastings, at the Dedication of Stephen Girard's Monument
Pres. Roosevelt at the Dedication Ceremonies, St. Louis Exposition
1904 Roosevelt Dedicating at St. Louis Exposition
Roosevelt Dedication at Lewis and Clark Exposition
1906 7th Regiment at 69th Army Dedication

De Dion, M. Le Comte
1902 M. Le Comte De Dion

Deed
1910 The Bad Man's Last Deed

Deep
1897 Still Waters Run Deep
1900 Deep Sea Fishing
1902 Deep Water Diving Illustrated
1903 "The Devil of the Deep" and the Sea Urchins

1906 Deep Breathing and Chest Expansion
1908 Deep Down within the Cellar
Terrors of the Deep
1910 Deep Sea Fishing
The Judgment of the Mighty Deep
Swallowed by the Deep
Deer
1902 Deer in Park
1904 Deer Hunting in England
1905 Deer in Wild Park, Goteborg, Sweden
1906 Deer Stalking with a Camera
1907 Deer Hunt
1908 Hunting Deer
1910 Deer Hunting in Celebes Islands
Defaulting
1906 The Bank Defaulter
1909 The Defaulting Solicitor
Defeat
1899 American Soldiers Defeating Filipinos Near Manila
1902 How Uncle Josh Defeated the Badgers
1904 Dinah's Defeat
1910 Villainy Defeated
Wild Bill's Defeat
Defender (Boat)
1899 "Columbia" and "Defender" Rounding Stake-Boat
"Columbia" vs. "Defender"
1900 Trial Race Columbia and Defender
Trial Race Columbia and Defender No. 2
1903 Launching Cup Defender "Reliance"
Defense
1898 The Defence of the Flag
Harbor Defenses
1904 Defence of Port Arthur
1905 Defense of a Pagoda
Defense of Port Arthur
1909 Tramp's Defense
1910 The Dumb Half Breed's Defence
Defiance
1910 The Highlander's Defiance
De Flon, Emar
1901 Emar De Flon, the Champion Skater
De' Lapi, Niccolo'
1909 Niccolo' De' Lapi
Delaware
1903 Miniature Railway at Wilmington Springs, Delaware
1907 Wilmington, Del.
Delaware River, Philadelphia (Pennsylvania)
1897 Delaware River, Philadelphia
1903 Delaware River Icebound
Naval Parade on the Delaware River, Monday, May 1st, in Honor of Admiral Dewey
Delayed
1909 The Delayed Telegram
Delhi (India)
1903 The Delhi Camp Railway
The Royal Levee in India [The Delhi 'Durbar']
1910 Delhi
Delight
1905 The Barber's Dee-Light
1910 Delightful Dolly
Delilah
1904 Samson and Delilah
1908 Samson and Delilah
Delirium
1904 Sick Man's Delirium
1907 Delirium in a Studio
1909 The Delirious Patient
1910 The Masher's Delirium
Delirium tremens
1907 A Drink! (Le delirium tremens ou la fin d'un alcoolique)
Deliver
1902 St. John's Guild. Launch Delivering Patients to F. H.
1903 Delivering Mail from Sub-Station [U.S.P.O.]
Post Man Delivering Mail, U.S.P.O.
Rural Wagon Delivering Mail, U.S.P.O.
Special Delivery Messenger, U.S.P.O.
1910 Cash on Delivery
The Plagues of Egypt and the Deliverance of the Hebrew [The Life of Moses Part III]
Dell
1899 "Ding, Dong, Dell, Johnny's in the Well"
Dells (Wisconsin)
1903 The Dells of Wisconsin
Delphi (Greece)
1903 The Oracle of Delphi
Delusion
1902 A Delusion
1908 Cabman's Delusion
De Lys, Florian
1909 Florian De Lys
Democracy
1898 County Democracy
1903 Cook County Democracy Parade
Democratic Party
1904 Democratic National Committee at Esopus
Democratic Presidential Candidate, Judge Parker, and Mayor McClellan, Esopus, N.Y.
Demolishing
1901 Demolishing and Building Up the Star Theatre
Demon
1899 The Cavern of the Demons
The Demon Barber
1903 Humpty and the Demon
1908 The Gambling Demon
Demonstrate
1897 Demonstrating the Action of an Automatic Piano
1899 Demonstrating the Action of a Patent Street Sprinkler of the American Car Sprinkler Co. of Worcester, Mass
Demonstrating the Action of the Cliff-Guibert Hose Reel
Demonstrating the Action of the Northrop Looms
1900 Another Demonstration of the Cliff-Guibert Fire Hose Reel, Showing a Young Girl Coming from an Office, Detaching the Hose, Running with It 60 Feet, and Playing a Stream, All Inside of 30 Seconds
Another Picture Showing Demonstration of a Pneumatic Shell Riveter
Demonstrating the Action of Pneumatic Shell Riveters on the Underside of the Hull of a Steel Vessel. Taken for the Chicago Pneumatic Tool Co.
Demonstrating the Action of the Brown Hoisting and Conveying Machine in Unloading a Schooner of Iron Ore, and Loading the Material on the Cars
Demonstrating the Action of the Chicago Pneumatic Tool Co.'s Deck Machine
Demonstrating the Operation of the Harrington Rail Bonding System on the Line of the Coney Island and Brooklyn Railroad Co.
1902 Demonstrating the Action of a Mergenthaler-Horton Basket Making Machine
Demonstrating the Action of an Agnew Mailing Machine
Demonstrating the Action of an Altman-Taylor Clover Huller
Demonstrating the Action of an Altman-Taylor Threshing Machine
1907 The Window Demonstration
Demoralized
1898 What Demoralized the Barber Shop
1901 What Demoralized the Barber Shop
Den
1903 The Kidnapper: In the Den [Part 2]
1904 Raid on a Coiner's Den
1908 A Den of Thieves
D'Enghien, Duke
1909 The Death of the Duke D'Enghien
Denmark
1902 King Edward VII at the Birthday Celebration of the King of Denmark
1905 Horse Fair at Randers, Denmark
1907 Hamlet, Prince of Denmark
1909 Boxing Match [by Hallberg of Denmark and Young Joe Gaines "Baltimore Black"]
Danish Capitol Under Snow
1910 Danish Dragoons
Hamlet, Prince of Denmark
Roosevelt in Denmark
Dentist
1908 The Doctor's Monkey (La scimmia dentiste)
1909 At the Dentist
Dentist's Daughter
An Awful Toothache (La trovata del dentista)
1910 The Avenging Dentist
Denver & Rio Grande Railway
1903 Broncho Busting Along the Lines of the Denver & Rio Grande Railway
Denver (Colorado)
1898 Denver Fire Brigade
Troop "H," Denver, Col.
1902 Denver Firemen's Race for Life
1907 Denver
Deonzo Brothers
1902 The Deonzo Brothers in Their Wonderful Barrel Jumping Act
Department
1901 Canned Meat Department. No. 1: Filling and Capping
Canned Meat Department. No. 2: Inspecting
Canned Meat Department. No. 5: Vacuum Process
Canned Meat Department. No. 6: Painting and Labeling
Sausage Department. No. 2: Chopping
Shipping Department. No. 2: Loading
1903 Digging for Foundation for Large Department Store, Phila.
Girls' Department, Albuquerque School
U.S. Interior Dept.: Basket Ball, Indian School
U.S. Interior Dept.: Bridal Veil Falls
U.S. Interior Dept.: Changing Coaches, Raymond Coach
U.S. Interior Dept.: Irrigation of Alfalfa Lands
U.S. Interior Dept.: Laguna Indian Chicken-Pulling Race
U.S. Interior Dept.: Laguna Indian Foot Race
U.S. Interior Dept.: Laguna Indian Horse Race
U.S. Interior Dept.: Mail Coach Yosemite Valley
U.S. Interior Dept.: Panorama from Artist's Point
U.S. Interior Dept.: Panorama of Grand Canyon
U.S. Interior Dept.: Santa Fe Coach
U.S. Interior Dept.: Vernal Falls
U.S.P.O. Dept. Santa Fe Mail Train
1907 Post Office Department Picture
Post Office Dept. Picture
Departure
1896 Tally Ho—Departure
1899 Departure of the Gordon Highlanders
1900 Departure of Boats from Muskoka Wharf
Departure of the Second Canadian Contingent
1901 Departure of Duke and Duchess of Cornwall for Australia
Tally-Ho Departing for the Races
1902 Departure of the Bride and Groom
1903 Arrival and Departure of President Loubet
President Roosevelt's Departure from "Kearsarge"
1904 Arrival and Departure of a Train
Arrival and Departure of the Ice-Crushing Steamer "Baikal" at Baikal, Siberia
Departure 14th Co. Japanese Engineers from Shimbashi Station for Korea
Panorama of Railroad Station at Seoul, Korea, from Departing Train
1905 Departure of Peary for the North Pole
1906 Hawaiians Departing to Attend a Luau or Native Feast
Depot
1896 Busses Leaving R.R. Depot, Atlantic City
Deputy
1909 Deputy
1910 The Deputy's Love
Derby
1897 Finish of the English Derby of 1897
1899 The Derby
1901 English Derby, 1901
1903 Chicago Derby Day
1905 Children Turning Catherine Wheels on Derby Day, Epsom Downs
Fixing the Derby Favorite
How Jones Saw the Derby
1907 Croker's Horse Winning the Derby
1909 The English Derby
1910 The Derby

Admiral Dewey's Flagship Olympia in Action at Manila
Dewey Land Parade
Dewey Naval Parade
Dewey Parade, 10th Pennsylvania Volunteers
Fourth Connecticut Volunteers, Dewey Parade
Panorama at Grant's Tomb, Dewey Naval Procession
Presentation of Nation's Sword to Admiral Dewey
"Sagasta" Admiral Dewey's Pet Pig
1900 Dewey Land Parade, Detroit
U.S. Marines in Dewey Land Parade
1901 Dewey Parade
1903 Naval Parade on the Delaware River, Monday, May 1st, in Honor of Admiral Dewey
Young America Celebrating Dewey's Return

Dewey Arch (New York City)
1899 The Dewey Arch
Dewey Arch, New York City
Dewey Arch—Troops Passing Under Arch
1900 Panoramic View of the Dewey Arch, New York City

Dextrous
1903 Dextrous Hand

Deyo
1897 Deyo
1907 Deyo

Diablo
1908 Beginning of the Game of Diablo

Diabolical
1905 Mr. Dauber and the Whimsical Picture (Le peintre Barbouillard et le tableau diabolique)
1908 The Diabolical Itching
Diabolical Pickpocket

Diabolo
1907 Diabolo
Diabolo Nightmare
Diabolo, the Japanese Top Spinner
1908 Mischievous Diabolo

Dial's Girls' Band
1905 Dial's Girls' Band, Luna Park

Diamond
1903 The Diamond Robbery
Great Diamond Robbery
1906 Secret Service; or, The Diamond Smugglers
1907 De Beers Diamond Mines, Kimberly, S.A.
1908 Artificial Preparation of the Diamond
The Diamond Thieves
A Fake Diamond Swindler
The King's Diamond
The Mystery of a Diamond Necklace
1909 The Brahma Diamond
The Diamond Necklace
A Maker of Diamonds
1910 Diamond Cut Diamond
The Diamond Swindler
The Nine of Diamonds
The Theft of the Diamonds

Diamond Street
1899 Sleighing on Diamond Street

Diary
1910 The Diary of a Nurse
Her Diary

Dice
1905 Devil's Dice
1908 Magic Dice
1910 The Turn of the Dice

Dick
1908 Dick's Aunt
Dick's Sister
1910 Dick's a Winner

Dickey
1910 Dickey's Courtship

Diddle
1903 Hey Ding Diddle

Dido
1910 Dido Forsaken by Aeneas

Die
use **Death**

Dieppe (France)
1907 Dieppe Circuit
1908 Dieppe Circuit, 1908
Grand Prix Motor Race at Dieppe

Diet
1902 On a Milk Diet
1909 A Strong Diet

Different
1905 Different Hair Dresses
1907 Costumes of Different Centuries
1908 Different Ways of Smuggling
1909 Amazons of Different Periods
Different Rulers of the World
1910 Different Trades in Bombay

Difficulties
1899 Bicycling Under Difficulties
1902 Going to Bed Under Difficulties
Undressing Under Difficulties
1903 The Difficulties of the Manicurist
A Dope in Difficulties
Eating Dinner Under Difficulties
Going to Bed Under Difficulties
Serenader's Difficulties
1906 Difficult Problem
1907 Bathing Under Difficulties
Daughter's Lover in Difficulties
Difficult Arrest
Motoring Under Difficulties
Moving Under Difficulties
Professor in Difficulties
1908 In a Difficult Position
Mr. Smith's Difficulties in the Shoe Store
Peasant's Difficulties in Society
1909 Married Under Difficulties
Removal Under Difficulties
1910 A Difficult Capture
Love-Making Under Difficulties
Proposing Under Difficulties

Dig
1899 Digging a Trench
1903 Digging for Foundation for Large Department Store, Phila.
1909 The Gold Digger's Son
Temptations of the Gold Fields; or, The Two Gold Diggers

Digest
1905 Digesting a Joke (Jas. T. Powers)
1908 A Good Dinner Badly Digested
1910 Kinematographic X-Ray Picture of a Human Stomach During Digestion, Taken During One Inspiration

Dilemma
1901 The Artist's Dilemma
1903 The Bridegroom's Dilemma
1904 Love's Dilemma
The Masher's Dilemma
The Music Hall Manager's Dilemma
1908 The Asphalters' Dilemma
1909 The Bridegroom's Dilemma
The Professor's Dilemma
1910 Levi's Dilemma
Max in a Dilemma

Dime
1900 A Strike in a Dime Museum
1909 Dime Novel Dan
A Dime Novel Detective

Dimples
1908 Fascinating Fluffy Dimples

Dinah
1904 Dinah's Defeat

Ding
1899 "Ding, Dong, Dell, Johnny's in the Well"
1903 Hey Ding Diddle
1907 Frolics of Ding Dong Imps

Dining room
1902 The Haunted Dining Room
1903 Danger of Dining in Private Dining Rooms
Fantastic Dining Room
1905 Women Employee's Dining Room

Dinner
1897 Babies' Dinner
A Tramp's Dinner
1898 The Soubrettes' Wine Dinner
1899 Bringing a Friend Home for Dinner
How the Tramp Lost His Dinner
Male Prisoners Marching to Dinner
Stealing a Dinner
1900 Mr. and Mrs. Califf at Dinner
1902 The Dutchman's Interrupted Dinner
1903 Cat's Dinner
Eating Dinner Under Difficulties
Happy Hooligan Earns His Dinner
Hooligan's Thanksgiving Dinner (Thumb Book)
"I Want My Dinner"
1904 The Impossible Dinner
Pussy's Dinner
1905 "Dinner Time" at Camp Curry Yosemite Valley
Slavonian Miners Running to Dinner, Treadwell Mine, Alaska
1907 A Disturbed Dinner
His First Dinner at Father-in-Law's
1908 A Good Dinner Badly Digested
The Lost New Year's Dinner
The Parson's Thanksgiving Dinner
Weary's Christmas Dinner
1909 The Doctored Dinner Pail
Follow Me and I'll Pay for Dinner
Inviting His Boss for Dinner
Mixed in His Dinner Dates
No Appetite for Dinner
A Simple Home Dinner
Three Christmas Dinners
Winning a Dinner
1910 What a Dinner!

Diogenes
1906 A Modern Diogenes

Dip
1899 A Dip in the Mediterranean
Her Morning Dip

Dippy, Dr.
1906 Dr. Dippy's Sanitarium

Directoire
1908 The Directoire Gown

Director
1908 The Bank Director

Dirigible
1908 The Dirigible Airship
1909 Dirigible Balloons at St. Louis
1910 Military Dirigible

Dirt
1901 "You Dirty Boy"
1903 Hauling Dirt Up an Incline
1905 Oh! You Dirty Boy!
1907 Making the Dirt Fly: Scene 1. Steam Shovel in Operation, Culebra Cut
Making the Dirt Fly: Scene 2. Unloading a Dirt Train
Making the Dirt Fly: Scene 3. Dirt Scraper in Operation
Making the Dirt Fly: Scene 4. Railroad Track Lifter in Operation
Making the Dirt Fly: Scene 5. Laborers Lining Up at Mess Tent

Disagree
1903 Disagreeable Railroad Passengers
1904 Disagreeable Five O'Clock
A Disagreeable Remedy
1905 Disagreeable Mistake
1909 House of Disagreement
A Little Disagreement

Disappear
1897 Projectile from Ten Inch Disappearing Gun Striking Water, Sandy Hook
Ten Inch Disappearing Carriage Gun Loading and Firing, Sandy Hook
1899 Mysterious Disappearance of a Policeman
1903 Disappearing Gun in Action
1908 Disappearing Watch

Disappoint
1899 The Disappointed Old Maid
1906 Disappointed
1908 Disappointing Rehearsal
1909 Disappointed Heirs
A Grave Disappointment
Life's Disappointment

Disaster
1900 Galveston Disaster
The Galveston Disaster
1904 A Disaster in a Colliery
English Submarine Boat Disaster
The Slocum Disaster
1906 The San Francisco Disaster
1907 Disastrous Flirtation
1908 A Disastrous Flirtation
A Disastrous Oversight
Comic Serenade (Serenata disastrosa)
1909 Messina Disaster
1910 The Paris Disaster

Disc
1909 The Death Disc: A Story of the Cromwellian Period

Discharge
1900 Discharging a Whitehead Torpedo
Why Jones Discharged His Clerks
1908 Discharged by the Foreman
Discharging the Maid

Dodge, Grenville Mellen, Major-General
1897 Major-General Dodge and Staff

Doggone
1910 That Doggone Dog

Dogherty, Jessie, Miss
1903 Miss Jessie Dogherty, Champion Female Highland Fling Dancer

Dogs and puppies
1897 "Spike, the Bag-Punching Dog"
1898 Dogs Playing in the Surf
1899 Admiral Dewey's Dog, "Bob"
Boxing Dogs
Frank Gould's Dogs
Hurdle Jumping; by Trained Dogs
1900 A Dog Fight
1901 Laura Comstock's Bag-Punching Dog
Leaping Dogs at Gentry's Circus
1902 The Dog Caught On
Dog Sleighing
A Dog's Cemetery
A Husky Dog Team
Jo Jo, the Dog Faced Boy
The Puppies and Their Mother
Selling a Pet Dog
1903 Babies and Puppies
Carlisle's Trained Dogs
Dog Baiting and Fighting in Valdez
Dog Teams Hauling Wood to Dawson City, Up the Yukon
Feeding the Dogs
Female Contortionist and Acrobatic Dog
Hooligan and Dogs (Journal Thumb Book)
"Love Me, Love My Dog"
The Peel River Indians with Their Dog Teams and Toboggan Sleighs on the Trail
Performing Dogs
Prize Winners at the Dog Show
The Puppies and the Little Tease
Race Between Dog Team, Bicycle and Cutter
Snarleyow the Dog Fiend
Swiss Training and Breeding Home for St. Bernard Dogs
Trained Bears and Dogs, Hagenback's Circus
Trained Dogs and Elephants
Trick Dogs, Hagenback's Circus
A Yard of Puppies
Disagreeable Railroad Passengers (Le chien et le pipe)
1904 Babe and Dog
Babe and Puppies
The Baby and the Puppies
Buster's Dog to the Rescue
Chased by a Dog
The Dog and the Baby
Dog Factory
Dogs and Cats
Dogs and Rats
Dogs Playing Bush Ball
Monkey, Dog and Pony Circus
Orla and His Trained Dogs
Pranks of Buster Brown and His Dog Tige
Stolen Puppy
Trained Dogs
1905 The British Bull Dog
Burglar and Bull Dog
A Dog Lost, Strayed or Stolen. $25.00 Reward. Apply to Mrs. Brown, 711 Park Ave.
Dog Teams Dawson City Alaska
Feeding Mush Dogs, Mulato, Alaska
Playful Bear and Dog, Dawson City, Alaska
The Puppies
Raffles, the Dog
Wanted: A Dog
The Whole Dam Family and the Dam Dog
1906 The Dog Detective
Dogs Used as Smugglers
Police Raid at a Dog Fight
Trying It on His Dog
1907 And the Dog Came Back
Blind Man's Dog
Crooked Dog
The Dog Acrobats
Dog and the Tramp
Dog Avenges His Master
Dog Police
The Dog Snatcher
Dogs Tracking Burglars
The Faithful Dog; or, True to the End
The Gamekeeper's Dog
Knowing Dogs
That Dog Gone Dog
The Tramp Dog
Rat Catching (Chiens et rats)
1908 Ambulance Dogs
Army Dogs
Cat and Dog Show
Dog and His Various Merits
The Dog and the Pipe
The Dog Cop
Dog Training
Dog's Music Hall
Dogs of Fashion
The Dog's Scent
Faithful Little Doggie
Getting Rid of His Dog
A Good Watch Dog
Lost, a Pretty Dog
My Wife's Dog
Our Dog Friends
A Pretty Little Dog
Rescue of Children by Dogs
The Sailor's Dog
Tracked by the Police Dog
Two Broken Hearts, the Story of a Worthless Husband and a Faithful Dog
Two Little Dogs
1909 Blind Child's Dog
The Cabin Boy's Dog
The Day of the Dog
Dog and Baby
The Dog and the Bone
The Dog and the Sausage
The Dog Came Back
The Dog Circus Rehearsal
The Dog Detective
Dog Outwits Kidnapper
The Dog Pickpocket
He Advertised for His Dog
Love Me, Love My Dog
Mad Dog
The Nobleman's Dog
Oh, You Doggie!
Only a Dog
Police Dogs
Runaway Dog
Saved by His Dog
The Shepherd's Dog
Sweet Toothed Dogs
Too Much Dog Biscuit
Tracked by a Dog
Zou-Zou, the Lucky Dog
1910 The Blind Man's Dog
Burglar's Dog
The Clown and His Dogs
Competition of the Police and Guard Dogs
The Dog Keeper
The Dog of the Cheese Monger
A Dog on Business
A Dog's Instinct
Her Fiancé and the Dog
How the Dog Saved the Flag
The Invisible Dog
Jack Logan's Dog
Jes' Plain Dog
The Mad Dog Scare
Ma's New Dog
The Messenger's Dog
My Life Remembrances of a Dog
The Runaway Dog
The Sailor's Dog
Saved by Her Dog
She Wanted a Bow-Wow
The Shepherd's Dog
The Statue Dog
A Stray Dog
The Tale of a Hot Dog
That Doggone Dog

Doings
1907 Doings of a Maniac
Doings of a Poodle
1910 Doings at the Ranch

Doll
1898 Dressing Paper Dolls
1901 The Mechanical Doll
1902 The Mechanical Doll
1903 Animated Dolls
1907 The Doll Maker's Daughter
Dolls in Dreamland
The Doll's Revenge
1908 An Animated Doll
The Doll Maker's Daughter
Doll Making
1909 Favorite Doll
The Little Rag Doll
The Living Doll
Living Dolls
Man with the Dolls
1910 The Broken Doll
Jean and the Calico Doll
The Old Miner's Doll
The Toymaker, the Doll and the Devil

Dollar
1905 King of Dollars
1907 Two Thousand Miles Without a Dollar
1908 Trying to Get Rid of a Bad Dollar
1909 Dollar in Each Egg
The Silver Dollar
1910 The Almighty Dollar
His Last Dollar

Dollie
1908 The Adventures of Dollie

Dolly
1906 Dolly's Papa
1908 Dolly, the Circus Queen
1910 Chew-Chew Land; or, The Adventures of Dolly and Jim
Delightful Dolly
Her Dolly's Revenge
Little Mary and Her Dolly

Dolomites (Italy)
1905 Cloud Play on Dolomite Peaks, Tyrol
1907 Conquering the Dolomites
Dolomite Towers

Dolorita
1897 The Dolorita Passion Dance
1903 Dolorita

Dolphin (Boat)
1898 Dispatch Boat Dolphin

Domain
1910 Mexican Domain

Domestic
1906 Mother-in-Law, a Domestic Comedy
When the Masters Are Out (Nos bons domestiques)
1908 Two Affinities; or, A Domestic Reunion
1909 A Lesson in Domestic Economy
1910 The Clever Domestic
Davy Jones' Domestic Troubles
The Overzealous Domestic

Domino
1909 The Red Domino

Don Carlos
1909 Don Carlos
1910 Don Carlos

Don Juan
1907 Don Juan
A Modern Don Juan
1908 Don Juan
1909 Don Juan; or, A War Drama of the Eighteenth Century

Don Quixote
1904 Don Quixote
1908 Incident from Don Quixote
1909 Don Quixote

Dong
1899 "Ding, Dong, Dell, Johnny's in the Well"
1907 Frolics of Ding Dong Imps

Dong, Lung Fei
1903 At the Grave of Ling Fei Dong
Funeral of Lung Fei Dong, the Chinese Mason

Donkey
1898 An Overloaded Donkey
1901 The Donkey Party
The War in China—A British Donkey Train
The Wonderful Trick Donkey
1902 The Lovers and the Donkey
The Singing Donkey
1903 A Donkey Party
Fording the River Nile on Donkeys
Reversible Donkey Cart
Shearing a Donkey in Egypt
Tourists Returning on Donkeys from Mizpah
Tourists Starting on Donkeys for the Pyramids of Sakkarah
Trick Donkey
Trick Donkey, No. 2
Trick Donkey, Hagenback's Circus
1904 The Wrestling Donkey
A Princess in Disguise (Peau d'ane)
1905 Awful Donkey
1907 Buying a Donkey
1908 Donkey's Skin
1909 The Donkey That Was Not an Ass
The Two Donkeys
The Witch's Donkey

Mother's Dream
A Night in Dreamland
The Piker's Dream, a Race Track Fantasy
The Soldier's Dream
The Tired Tailor's Dream
The Tramp's Dream
A Tramp's Dream of Wealth
Willie's Dream
1908 Bobby Has a Pipe Dream
The Bride's Dream
The Chauffeur's Dream
A Dream
The Dream of an Opium Fiend
A Dream of Wealth, a Tale of the Gold Seekers of '49
A Dream of Youth
Dreams and Realities
End of a Dream
The Fakir's Dream
Girl's Dream
Hobo's Dream
Little Hannie's Last Dream
Music Hall Agent's Dream
Pipe Dreams
A Policeman's Dream
The Puppet Man's Dream
Rejoicing Dreams
Scullion's Dream
A Sculptor's Welsh Rabbit Dream
Toula's Dream
A Workingman's Dream
1909 The Artist's Dream
The Bachelor's Dream
Boyhood Dreams
Cohen's Dream of Coney Island
The Dramatist's Dream
Dream of a Fisherman
Dream of Featart
A Dream of Paradise
Dream Spectres
Dreamer
A Drunkard's Dream
The Elixir of Dreams
Explorer's Dream
Hobo's Dream
It Was a Beautiful Dream
The Jolly Trio's Dream
The Marble Heart; or, The Sculptor's Dream
A Midsummer Night's Dream
Miller's Dream
The Musician's Dream
Neptune's Daughter; or, The Shoemaker's Dream
The Old Maid's Dream
Only a Dream
Pompey's Dream
Reveler's Dream
The Suffragette's Dream
Sweet Dreams Intermingled with Nightmares
The Taxidermist's Dream
The Tyrant's Dream
The Young Bachelor's Dream
1910 An Angler's Dream
Artist's Dream
The Bobby's Dream
The Carman's Dream
The City of Her Dreams
The Convict's Dream
The Detective's Dream
The Dream Pill
The Dreamer
Drowsy Dick's Dream
Hobo's Dream of Wealth
The Lace Maker's Dream
Midsummer Night's Dream
The Sculptor's Dream
Tommy in Dreamland
Uncle Eph's Dream
An Unpleasant Dream
A Young Aviator's Dream
The Masher's Delirium (Le songe du garçon de café)

Dreamland, Coney Island (New York)
1904 Fighting the Flames, Dreamland
The Racing Chutes at Dreamland
1905 Hippodrome Races, Dreamland, Coney Island
Mystic Shriners' Day, Dreamland, Coney Island
1907 Mystic Shriners at Dreamland

Dreisprackenspitz Stelvio Pass, Ortler Mountains
1905 Panorama from Dreisprackenspitz Stelvio Pass

Dress
1897 Quick Dressing
13th Infantry, U.S. Army—Full Dress Parade and Manoeuvering, Governors Island
13th Infantry, U.S. Army—Full Dress Parade, Governors Island
1899 Phillis Was Not Dressed to Receive Callers
1900 British Troops on Dress Parade
Dress Parade of the Woodward High School Cadets
1901 Dressing Beef
1904 Dress Parade of the Filipino Scouts, St. Louis Exposition
Dress Parade, St. John's Academy
1905 Dressing the Baby
1907 After the Fancy Dress Ball
Dressing in a Hurry
1909 Dressed for the Occasion
Fancy Dress Ball
Niagara in Winter Dress
1910 Her First Long Dress

Dressing room
1897 A Dressing Room Scene
1900 A Hot Time in the Dressing Room
Jealousy in the Dressing Room
1903 A False Alarm in the Dressing Room
In the Dressing Room
1904 Mr. Jack Is Caught in the Dressing Room
Mr. Jack Visits the Dressing Room
A Scrap in the Dressing Room
1905 Peeping Tom in the Dressing Room
1908 Scene in a Dressing Room
What the Dude Lost in the Dressing Room
1909 The Foundling—A Dressing Room Waif

Dressler, Marie
1909 Marie Dressler

Dressmaker
1898 How the Dressmaker Got Even with a Dead Beat
1901 Dressmaking
1903 At the Dressmaker's
The Dressmaker's Accident
1908 The Dressmaker's Surprise
1909 The Little Father; or, The Dressmaker's Loyal Son

Dreyfus, Alfred
1899 Dreyfus Receiving His Sentence
The Trial of Captain Dreyfus at Rennes, France
Trial of Captain Dreyfus
1902 Captain Dreyfus
1908 The Dreyfus Affair

Drift
1898 Clearing a Drift
1910 Drifts of Snow in Chamonix Valley

Drill
1896 Park Police Drill Left Wheel and Forward
Park Police Drill Mount and Dismounting
West Point Cadet Cavalry Drill
West Point Cadet Drill
1897 Cavalry Musical Drill
Mounted Police Drill
Musical Drill; Troop A., Third Cavalry
A Regimental Calisthenic Drill in the British Army
Returning from Drill
13th Infantry, U.S. Army—Musical Drill, Governors Island
1898 Broadsword Drill
Cubans Drilling, Manual of Arms
14th U.S. Infantry Drilling at the Presidio
French Soldiers in a Wall-Climbing Drill
9th and 13th U.S. Infantry at Battalion Drill
Quebec Fire Department Drill
Rapid Fire Gun Drill
A Skirmish Drill
1899 Ambulance Corps Drill
Fire Department Rescue Drill
Fire Drill at the Factory of Parke, Davis & Co.
Police Drill
1900 Drill of Naval Cadets at Newport
"Drill, Ye Tarriers, Drill"
Gatling Gun Drill
Gun Drill by Naval Cadets at Newport [R.I., Naval] Training School
Gymnasium Exercises and Drill at Newport [R.I., Naval] Training School
Mounted Rifles at Drill
Naval Apprentices at Sail Drill on Historic Ship "Constellation"
School Fire Drill
Shelter Tent Drill
1901 Artillery Drill at Annapolis
Boat Drill in Mid-Ocean
Calisthenic Drill
Energizing Drill
Fire Drills at Breslau, Germany
Girls Dumbbell Drill
Knight Templars Parade Drill
1902 California Naval Reserves Drilling on Board Ship
1903 Berlin Fire Department at Drill
Drill by Providence Police
English Soldiers at Gun Drill
Fancy Drill of the Woodmen of America
Fire Drill: Albuquerque Indian School
Girls Flag Drill, Moqui School
Military Fire Drill
Musical Drill with Arms
Rock Drill at Work in Subway
Shelter Tent Drill
10th Pennsylvania Drilling at Manila
U.S. Artillery Drill
1904 Company Drill, St. John's Military Academy
Drill
English Lancers at Drill
Exhibition Fire Drill, Union Square, N.Y.
Filipino Scouts, Musical Drill, St. Louis Exposition
Gun Drill St. John's Academy
Japanese Infantry Morning Drill
1905 Drill Under Oars
Drills and Exercises, Schoolship "St. Mary's"
1908 Paris Fire Brigade at Drill
Reedham Boys' Festival Drill
1909 Crown Prince of Germany Drilling Battery
1910 [Artillery Drill at West Point]
Troop "B", 15th U.S. Cavalry Bareback Squad in the Monkey Drill at Fort Myer, Virginia
United States Life Saving Drills

Drink
rt **Alcoholism**
1896 The Drunken Acrobat
1897 Smoking, Eating, and Drinking Scene
1900 A Champion Beer Drinker
The Champion Beer Drinker
1901 Why Bridget Stopped Drinking
1902 Moving Picture Operator on a Drunk
1903 Drunken Scene
Passengers Alighting and Drinking Shasta Water
"Who Pays for the Drinks?"
1906 The Drunken Mattress
1907 A Drink!
Drink
Drink and Repentance
A Drink Cure
Man, Hat and Cocktail, a New Drink, but an Old Joke
1908 All That Trouble for a Drink
The Curse of Drink
The Drink Cure
1909 Drink
His First Drink
A Slave to Drink
What Drink Did
1910 A Drink of Goat's Milk
Fricot Drinks a Bottle of Horse Embrocation

Drive
1896 East Side Drive, No. 1
East Side Drive, No. 2
Li Hung Chang Driving Through 4th St. and Broadway [New York City]
1897 Cattle Driven to Slaughter
Expert Driving
1899 Admiral Dewey and Mayor Van Wyck Going Down Riverside Drive
1901 Driving Hogs to Slaughter
Expert Driving
1902 Empress of Germany Driving to the Manoeuvres
1903 A Coach Drive from Glengariffe to Kenmore
Driving Cows to Pasture
River Drive, Fairmount Park
1904 Driven from Home
Driving Cattle to Pasture
Fashionable Driving on Palace Quay, St. Petersburg

Durland's Academy (New York City)
1902 The Burning of Durland's Riding Academy
Fire at Durland's Academy, N.Y. City
"Dusky"
use **Blacks**
Dust
1902 The Gold Dust Twins
Let the Gold Dust Twins Do Your Work
1903 Gold Dust Twins
Mule Pack Train Taking Gold Dust to Dawson City
1909 Dust in His Eye
Mr. Jonah Gets a Little Dust in His Eyes
1910 An Enemy of the Dust
Dustin, Hannah
1908 Hannah Dustin: The Border Wars of New England
Dutch
use **Netherlands**
Dutch West Indies
1903 Native Women Coaling a Ship at St. Thomas, D.W.I.
Wharf Scene and Natives Swimming at St. Thomas, D.W.I.
Duty
1904 Night Duty
1908 Duty Versus Revenge
'Twixt Love and Duty
'Twixt Love and Duty; or, A Woman's Heroism
1909 His Duty
The Sentinel on Duty
1910 Between Duty and Honor
Between Love and Duty
Duty and Conscience
His Duty
More Than His Duty
The Path of Duty
The Strength of Duty
Dwarf
1896 Exit of Rip and the Dwarf
Rip Meeting the Dwarf
1903 The Long and Short of It (Nain et géant)
1904 Dwarf's Troubles
1909 The Chambermaid and the Dwarf
The Prince and the Dwarf
1910 Acrobatic Exercises by the Colibris Dwarfs
Dwarf Detective
Dwellers
1906 The Flat Dwellers
1907 The Flat Dwellers; or, The House of Too Much Trouble
Grand Canyon of Arizona and the Cliff Dwellers
1908 Timid Dwellers
1910 The Cliff Dwellers
Dying
use **Death**
Dynamite
1906 Dynamiting Ruins and Pulling Down Walls in San Francisco
Dynamiting Ruins and Rescuing Soldier Caught in Falling Walls
1908 Dynamite Duel
Dynamite Man
The Dynamite Man
The Dynamiter
Dynamiters
1909 Dynamite
The Dynamite Waistcoat
Fishing by Dynamite
1910 Catching Fish with Dynamite
Dynasty
1910 The End of a Dynasty
Dyspeptic
1909 The Dyspeptic and His Double
Eagle
1898 Knights of the Golden Eagle
1903 Parade of Eagles, New York
1908 Rescued from an Eagle's Nest
1909 Eagle's Prey
1910 After the Fall of the "Eagle"
The Eagle and the Eaglet
The Eagle's Egg; or The Rival Lovers
Eagle Dance
1898 Eagle Dance, Pueblo Indians
Eagle Peak Trail, Yosemite Valley (California)
1905 Cavalcade Descending Eagle Peak Trail, Yosemite Valley
Ear
1898 Who's Got the Red Ear?
Earl
1900 Earl Roberts
Earl Roberts and General Baden Powell
1905 Earl of Dudley and Party at the Dublin Horse Show
Earl's Court, London (England)
1905 Flying Machine, Earl's Court, London
Early
1898 An Early Breakfast
1899 The Early Morning Attack
1901 Catching an Early Train
1907 An Early Round with the Milkman
1909 Early Days in the West
Mug Chump's Early Morning Excursion
1910 The Early Settlers
Earn
1903 Happy Hooligan Earns His Dinner
1909 How He Earned His Medal
A Well Earned Medal
Earth
1899 Charlie Wanted the Earth
1907 Cheekiest Man on Earth
1909 Earthly Paradise
1910 Inside the Earth
Earthenware
1909 Earthenware Industry
Earthquake
1906 Earthquake Ruins, New Majestic Theatre and City Hall
Effect of Earthquake
The First Trolley Car After the Earthquake
Going to the Fire, Showing Chief Sullivan During the Earthquake
Panoramic View of Market Street San Francisco After the Earthquake and Fire
Panoramic View of San Francisco City Hall, Damaged by Earthquake
1909 The Great Earthquake in Sicily
Messina After the Earthquake
Messina Earthquake
East
1908 Children of the East
'Way Down East
1910 The Girl from the East
Great Ball Game Between the East and West
A Message from the East
East Galveston (Texas)
1900 Panorama of East Galveston
East Indian
1903 Pageant of East Indian Princes
Traders of the East Indian Empire
East Lynne
1908 East Lynne
East Lynne; or, Led Astray
East River (New York City)
1897 East River, New York
1901 New York Sky-Line from East River and Battery
Panorama of Brooklyn Bridge, River Front, and Tall Buildings from the East River
1903 An East River Novelty
Opening of New East River Bridge, New York
Panorama Water Front and Brooklyn Bridge from East River
East Side (New York City)
1903 East Side Urchins Bathing in a Fountain
East Side Drive, Central Park (New York City)
1896 East Side Drive, No. 1
East Side Drive, No. 2
Easter
1899 An Easter Parade
1902 St. Patrick's Cathedral and Fifth Avenue on Easter Sunday Morning [New York City]
1903 Atlantic City Board Walk, Easter Morn
1904 Easter Flower Parade in Bois de Boulogne, Paris
1907 Easter Eggs
1908 A Fine Easter Egg
The Little Easter Fairy
Orphan's Easter Eggs
1909 Easter Bells
Eastern
1899 The Eastern Slope of the Rockies, Passing Anthracite Station
Passing Steamboat and Great Eastern Rocks
1900 On the Cleveland and Eastern Railway
1904 White Star S.S. Baltic Leaving Pier on First Eastern Voyage
1907 The Easterner, or, A Tale of the West
1910 The Cowboy and the Easterner
Easton
1907 Easton
Easy
1902 Bathing Made Easy
Building Made Easy; or, How Mechanics Work in the Twentieth Century
1904 The Easy Chair
The Furnished Room House—Taking Life Easy
1905 Female Crook and Her Easy Victim
1906 Furnished on Easy Terms
House Furnishing Made Easy
1907 Work Made Easy
1908 Easy Money
1909 An Easy Job
1910 Easy Job
An Easy Winner
A Sculptor Who Has Easy Work
Easy mark
1903 Mr. Easy Mark
1907 Mr. Easy Mark
Eat
1897 Pie Eating Contest
Pie-eating Contest
Smoking, Eating, and Drinking Scene
1902 Bologna Eating Contest
Camels Eating
New Pie Eating Contest
1903 Child Eating
Eating Dinner Under Difficulties
Eating Macaroni in the Streets of Naples
Eating Watermelons for a Prize
Pie Eating Contest
Watermelon Eating Contest
1904 "Champion Pumpkin Eater"
Ice Cream Eater
Ice Cream Eating Contest Blindfolded
1907 Cream Eating Contest
The Horse That Ate the Baby
1908 Circumstantial Evidence; or, Who Ate the Possum Pie
Result of Eating Horseflesh
Tony Has Eaten Garlic
Too Hungry to Eat
1909 Eat Your Soup
He Is a Cousin Who Eats Truffle
Never Eat Green Apples
Eavesdropper
1909 The Eavesdropper
Eccentric
1900 Eccentricities of an Adirondack Canoe
1902 Gibson, the Eccentric American Actor
1904 Eccentric Tight-rope Walker
Eccentric Waltz
1905 An Eccentric Burglary
1909 The Eccentric Barber
Echo
1909 An Alpine Echo; or, The Symphony of a Swiss Music Box
Echo (Town)
1899 By Pulpit Rock and Through the Town of Echo
Eclipse
1900 How He Saw the Eclipse
1903 Eclipse Car Fender Test
1906 Eclipse of Sun
1907 The Eclipse; or, The Courtship of the Sun and the Moon
Economy
1907 Economical Trip
1909 A Lesson in Domestic Economy
Eddie
1909 Eddie Is a Real Live One
Edgar
1909 Edgar and Lucy
Edict
1909 The Tobacco Edict, Old New York, 1648
Edily
1908 The Edily
Edison, Thomas Alva
1897 Mr. Edison at Work in His Chemical Laboratory
Edison Kinetoscope
1893 Edison Kinetoscopic Records
1894 Edison Kinetoscopic Record of a Sneeze, January 7, 1894
Edison Kinetoscopic Records
Souvenir Strip of the Edison Kinetoscope [Sandow, the Modern Hercules]

Electrocution
1903 Electrocution of an Elephant
1908 Electrocuted
Electromagnet
1909 The Wonderful Electro-Magnet
Elegant
1907 Elegant Paris
Elektra
use **Electra**
Elephant
1897 Elephants at the Zoo
Trick Elephants
1899 Elephants in a Circus Parade
Frank Melville's Trick Elephant
Lockhart's Performing Elephants
1902 The Elephant's Bath
Elephants in a Tent
1903 Electrocution of an Elephant
Feeding the Elephants
A Juvenile Elephant Trainer
Leaping Tournament over Elephants
Performing Elephants
Procession of Giant Elephants in India
Trained Baby Elephants
Trained Dogs and Elephants
Trick Elephant Bolivar, the Largest Elephant in the World, No. 1
Trick Elephant Bolivar, the Largest Elephant in the World, No. 2
Trick Elephant, Hagenback's Circus
Unloading the Elephants
Washing Elephants
The Wise Elephant
1904 Elephants at Work
Elephants at Work in India
Elephants Shooting the Chutes at Luna Park [Coney Island]
Elephants Shooting the Chutes, Luna Park, Coney Island, No. 2
An Intelligent Elephant
1905 Elephant's Tub
The Wrestling Elephant
1906 Acrobatic Elephant
Bath of Sacred Elephants
1907 The Baby Elephant
Elephants in India
1909 Elephant Hunting in Cambodge
Hard Working Elephants
Elevated railroad
1897 New York Elevated Trains
1899 Around the Big Curves on the Manhattan Elevated R.R.
Elevated Railroad and Drawbridge
104th Street Curve, New York, Elevated Railway
Third Avenue Elevated Railroad
A Trip over the Manhattan Elevated Railroad
1901 Elevated Railroad
A Ride on the Elevated R.R. (Panoramic)
1902 Elevated and Underground
Panorama of Ninth Ave. Elevated R.R.
1903 Panorama from Elevated Train, New York
6th Ave. New York Elevated Railroad
Third Avenue Elevated Train, New York
1906 Trip on Berlin Elevated R.R.
Elevator
1900 Scene from the Elevator Ascending Eiffel Tower
Eleven
1899 Reproduction of the Fitzsimmons-Jeffries Fight in Eleven Rounds Showing the Knock Out
Eleventh hour
1907 The Eleventh Hour
1910 At the Eleventh Hour
An Eleventh Hour Redemption
Elf
1908 The Elf King, a Norwegian Fairy Tale
1909 The Mischievous Elf
Elgin (Illinois)
1910 Elgin National Trophy Races
Elixir
1903 The Elixir of Life
1907 The Elixir of Life
1908 Elixir of Youth
1909 Dr. Lyvenemup's Elixir
The Elixir of Dreams
Eliza
1902 All on Account of Eliza
Elizabeth
1910 The Education of Elizabeth
Elk
1903 North American Elk
1906 Elk
Elkins Cadets, Canton (Ohio)
1896 Parade, Elkins Cadets, Canton, O.
Elks
1900 Atlantic City Lodge, 276, B.P.O. Elks
Brooklyn Lodge, No. 22, B.P.O. Elks
Parade of the Order of Elks in Atlantic City
Philadelphia Lodge, No. 2, B.P.O. Elks
Washington Lodge, No. 15, B.P.O. Elks
1907 Are You an Elk?
Elks' Convention Parade
Elks' Convention Parade: "Spirit of '76" and Views of the Grand Stand
Elks' Parade
1910 B.P.O.E.
Ellen
1909 Ellen
Ellis Island (New York City)
1903 Immigrants Landing at Ellis Island
1906 Arrival of Immigrants, Ellis Island
Elopement
1897 The Elopement
1898 The Elopement
Elopement on Horseback
1902 A Frustrated Elopement
1903 The Elopement
Elopement a la Mode
1904 The Elopers Who Didn't Elope
Tragic Elopement
1905 Elopement
1906 Love vs. Title; or, An Up-to-Date Elopement
1907 An Acadian Elopement
The Elopement
1908 A Calamitous Elopement: How It Proved a Windfall for Burglar Bill
A Cowboy Elopement
Oscar's Elopement
1909 An Aerial Elopement
Eloping with Aunty
A Rural Elopement
They Would Elope
A Tumultuous Elopement
Unusual Elopement
1910 An Assisted Elopement
An Attempted Elopement
Bertie's Elopement
A Double Elopement
The Elopement
An Indian's Elopement
Embark
1898 California Volunteers Marching To Embark
Cuban Volunteers Embarking
Roosevelt's Rough Riders Embarking for Santiago
71st N.Y. Volunteers Embarking for Santiago
Troops Embarking at San Francisco
Wounded Soldiers Embarking in Row Boats
1899 Lord Roberts Embarking for South Africa
2nd Special Service Battalion, Canadian Infantry, Embarking for So. Africa
1903 Passengers Embarking from S.S. "Augusta Victoria" at Beyrouth
Tourists Embarking at Jaffa
1904 Embarking Wood in the Far East
Recruits Embarking
1905 Embarkation by Crane and Barge at Nome City, Alaska
Embarrassment
1900 Four Heads Better Than One (Le homme de têtes ou les quatres têtes embarrassantes)
1908 An Embarrassing Gift
1909 An Embarrassing Portfolio
An Embarrassing Present
1910 The Lover's Embarrassment
Embassy
1902 Prince Henry [of Prussia] Arriving in Washington and Visiting the German Embassy
Embrocation
1910 Fricot Drinks a Bottle of Horse Embrocation
Emergency
1910 Equal to the Emergency
Emerie
1903 Silveon and Emerie "On the Web"
Emerson School, Kansas City (Missouri)
1904 Emerson School, Calisthenics, Missouri Commission
Emigrant
1903 Prairie Emigrant Train Crossing the Plains
1907 Attack on Emigrant Train
1909 Adventures of an Emigrant
1910 The Emigrant
Emmy, Aunt
1909 Aunt Emmy's Scrap Book
Emperor
1897 Emperor Francis Joseph of Austria
Emperor William of Germany, and Emperor Franz Josef of Austria
1898 Meeting of Emperor William of Germany and Emperor Franz Josef of Austria
1901 Emperor William's Yacht "Meteor"
1902 The Emperor and Empress and Crown Prince of Germany
Emperor and Empress of Germany
The Emperor and Empress of Germany
Emperor William II
Emperor William II on Horseback
Emperor William as a Hussar
Emperor William at the Danzig Manoeuvres
Emperor William of Germany on Horseback
Emperor William Returning from Manoeuvres
Kaiser Wilhelm and Emperor Franz Josef, and Prince Henry Riding Horseback
Kaiser Wilhelm, of Germany, and Emperor Franz Josef, of Austria
Visit of Emperor Francis Josef of Austria to Berlin
With Emperor William's Army
1903 Arrival of H.I.M. The German Emperor, at Port Victoria
1908 Emperor Nero on the Warpath
King Edward and the German Emperor at Friedrichshof
1909 The Emperor
The Emperor's Staff Officer
A Generous Emperor
1910 Decorated by the Emperor
The Emperor's Message
Empire
1900 Spirit of the Empire
1901 The Empire Theatre
1903 Traders of the East Indian Empire
Life of Napoleon (L'empire)
1910 Scenes in the Celestial Empire
Empire State Express
1896 Empire State Express
Empire State Express No. 2
Empire State Express, N.Y. Central R.R.
1905 Empire State Express
Empire State Express, the Second, Taking Water on the Fly
Employees and employers
1899 Employes of Bausch, Lomb & Co.
Parke Davis' Employees
1900 Employees of Wolfson's Spice Mills, Toledo
1903 Employees Leaving Fall River Iron Works
March of the Post Office Employees
1904 Parade of National Cash Register Co.'s Employees, St. Louis Exposition
Westinghouse Employees Boarding Train
Westinghouse Employees, Westinghouse Works
1905 Employees Leaving Office
Gen'l Elec. No. 1 Employees Leaving Work
Women Employee's Dining Room
1909 Benevolent Employer
1910 Foolshead Employed in a Bank
Tweedledum Gets Employed in the Corporation Body
Emporium
1906 Exploded Gas Tanks, U.S. Mint, Emporium and Spreckels' Bld'g.
Empress
1902 The Emperor and Empress and Crown Prince of Germany
Emperor and Empress of Germany
The Emperor and Empress of Germany
Empress of Germany at Danzig
Empress of Germany Driving to the Manoeuvres

Enthusiastic
1909 Enthusiastic Hand Ball Player

Entire
1902 Entire Series of Yacht Race Pictures with Dissolving Effects

Entombed
1909 Entombed Alive
1910 Entombed Alive

Entrance
1899 Fifth Avenue Entrance to Central Park
The Gap, Entrance to the Rocky Mountains
West of Peterson; Entrance to Weber Canyon
1901 Entrance to Union Stock Yards
Grand Entry, Indian Congress
Main Entrance to Pan-American Exp.
The March of Prayer and Entrance of the Dancers
1903 Grand Entrance into the Hippodrome
Passion Play: The Messiah's Entry into Jerusalem
1904 The Passion Play (L'entrée à Jérusalem)
1905 Triumphal Entry of Performers, Vevey Fete
1907 Panorama from Columbus Point of Atlantic Entrance to the Canal
Panorama La Boca Harbor and Pacific Entrance to Canal

Envelope
1903 Envelope Folder and Sealer, National Cash Register Co.

Environs
1908 Environs of Naples
1910 Colombo and Its Environs

Envoys
1905 Peace Envoys at Portsmouth, N.H.

Eph, Uncle
1910 Uncle Eph's Dream

Ephemeral
1906 Ephemeral Wealth

Epileptic
1905 Epileptic Seizure
1906 Epileptic Seizure No. 8
Epileptic Seizure, No. 9

Episode
1900 A Hair-Raising Episode
1903 An Episode in the Park
A Midnight Episode
1905 Yantai Episode
1906 All Aboard! or, Funny Episodes in a Street Car
1907 An Episode of the Paris Commune
1908 An Episode of the French Revolution
The Reprieve, an Episode in the Life of Abraham Lincoln
War Episode
1909 Children of the Plains, an Episode of Pioneer Days
Episode in Boer War
Episode of Cuban War
Episode of War
Love and War: An Episode of Waterloo
Medieval Episode
A Message to Napoleon; or, An Episode in the Life of the Great Prisoner at Elba
1910 Anarchists on Board; or, The Thrilling Episode on the S.S. "Slavonia"
The Cage (An Episode in the Adventures of Morgan the Pirate)
Episode of French Revolution
An Episode of Napoleon's War with Spain
The Judas Money; or, An Episode of the War in Vendee
Tale of Colonial Days: An Episode in the Life of Alexander Hamilton and Aaron Burr

Epsom Downs (England)
1905 Children Turning Catherine Wheels on Derby Day, Epsom Downs

Equal
1910 Equal to the Emergency

Equestrian
1904 Equestrian Bear

Equilibrist
1906 Stupendous Jugglers (Equilibristes stupéfiants)
1908 The Misadventures of an Equilibrist
1909 Bamboo Pole Equilibrist

Equine
1910 An Equine Hero

Eradicating
1909 Eradicating Aunty

Erie Railroad
1896 Niagara Gorge from Erie R.R.

Eriks
1910 The Eriks

Erin
use **Ireland**

Erin (Boat)
1899 The "Erin"
"Shamrock" and "Erin" Sailing
Sir Thomas Lipton and Party on "Erin's" Launch
Sir Thomas Lipton's Steam Yacht "Erin"
1902 Sir Thomas Lipton on Board the Erin

Ernest
1910 Foxy Ernest

Errand
1908 Our New Errand Boy
1910 Betty as an Errand Girl
The Colonel's Errand

Errant
1910 A Modern Knight Errant

Erring
1909 Legend of the Erring Jew

Error
1907 The Wrong Flat; or, A Comedy of Errors
1908 A Comedy of Errors
1909 A Serious Error
1910 A Newspaper Error

Eruption
1902 The Eruption of Mt. Pelee
Mt. Pelee in Eruption and Destruction of St. Pierre [Martinique]
Mt. Pelee Smoking Before Eruption [St. Pierre, Martinique]
1906 Eruption of Mt. Vesuvius
1908 The Eruption of Mt. Vesuvius
1910 Volcanic Eruptions of Mt. Aetna

Escapade
1908 A Cowboy Escapade
1909 Lady Helen's Escapade
1910 Bud's Escapade
Childish Escapade

Escape
1898 A Boarding School Escape
A Narrow Escape
1899 An Attempt to Escape
1900 Escape from Sing Sing
1901 Hooligan's Narrow Escape
The Tramp's Miraculous Escape
The Wages of Sin—The Assassin's Escape
1903 Burglar's Escape
Escaped
A Narrow Escape
Why Foxy Grandpa Escaped a Ducking
1904 The Convict's Escape
An Escape from the Flames
The Escaped Lunatic
1905 Convicts' Escape
The Escape from Sing Sing
1906 Escaped from the Cage
The Jail Bird and How He Flew, a Farce Comedy Escape
1907 How Bridget's Lover Escaped
Prisoner's Escape
1908 The Escape of the Ape
A Famous Escape
Harmless Lunatic's Escape
The Mad Musician [An Escape from an Insane Asylum]
A Narrow Escape
1909 Cowboy's Narrow Escape
The Escape from Andersonville
Escaped Lunatic
The Escaped Melody
Sherlock Holmes II: Raffles Escapes from Prison
1910 Escape of the Royalists
The Midnight Escape

Escolta
1899 The Escolta

Escort
1897 Buffalo Bill and Escort
Vice-President Hobart's Escort
1898 Police Boats Escorting Naval Parade
1899 Escort of the President Passing the Monument
1900 Under Armed Escort
1901 President McKinley and Escort Going to the Capitol
1903 Lieut. Bagley's Funeral. Escort of Lieut. Bagley's at Raleigh, N. C.
1904 West Point Cadets Escorting Liberty Bell, St. Louis Exposition
1905 Inauguration of President Roosevelt. President-Elect Roosevelt, Vice-President-Elect Fairbanks and Escort Going to the Capitol
Lord Lieutenant of Ireland and Escort, Dublin Horse Show

Eskimos
1901 Esquimaux Dance
An Esquimaux Game
Esquimaux Game of Snap-the-Whip
Esquimaux Leap-Frog
The Esquimaux Village
Esquimaux Village
The Esquimaux Village
1902 Panorama of Esquimaux Village
1905 Camp Life of the Esquimaux at Cape Nome, Alaska
Dance at Esquimaux Camp, Cape Nome, Alaska
Esquimaux Dance, Cape Nome, Alaska
Flap-Jack Lady of the Esquimaux, Cape Nome, Alaska
1908 Esquimaux of Labrador
1909 A Cry from the Wilderness; or, A Tale of the Esquimaux and Midnight Sun

Esopus (New York)
1904 Democratic National Committee at Esopus
Democratic Presidential Candidate, Judge Parker, and Mayor McClellan, Esopus, N.Y.
Judge Parker & Mayor McClellan at Esopus
1906 The Valley of Esopus

Esplanade des Invalides, Paris Exposition
1900 Esplanade des Invalides

Esplanade, Pan American Exposition, Buffalo (New York)
1901 Circular Panorama of the Esplanade with the Electric Tower in the Background
Circular Panorama of the Esplanade and Forecourt
Panorama of Esplanade by Night
Panoramic View of the Temple of Music and Esplanade
1902 Panorama of Esplanade from Bridge of Triumph

Essence
1903 Essence of Old Virginia

Esther
1910 Esther and Mordecai
The Marriage of Esther

Estrangement
1910 The Estrangement

Estrellita
1910 Estrellita; or, The Invasion of the French Troops in Portugal

Eternal
1909 The Eternal Romance
1910 The Eternal Triangle

Ethel
1909 Ethel's Luncheon

Ethiopian
1910 On the Ethiopian Frontier

Etna (Mountain), Sicily (Italy)
1910 Volcanic Eruptions of Mt. Aetna

Etruria (Boat)
1899 "Etruria"

Europe
1908 Summer in North Europe
Winter Time in Northern Europe

European
1900 Funeral of Chinese Viceroy, Chung Fing Dang, Marching Through the European Quarter at Peking
1904 European Idea of Christopher Columbus Discovering America
European Rest Cure

Evacuation
1899 Spaniards Evacuating
Troops at Evacuation of Havana
1901 The War in China—The Evacuation of Pekin

Evangeline
1908 Evangeline

Evasion
1904 Benvenuto Cellini; or, A Curious Evasion

Even
1898 How the Dressmaker Got Even with a Dead Beat
1903 How Buttons Got Even with the Butler

1907 Even a Worm Will Turn
Getting Even
1908 It Sticks Everything—Even Iron
1909 Getting Even
Getting Even with Everybody
How Mother-in-Law Got Even
How the Kids Got Even
1910 Getting Even with the Lawyer

Evening
1903 An Evening Chat
1906 Ruins Bulletin Building, California Theatre and Evening Post
1908 Christmas Eve
Christmas Eve at Sunset
The Clown's Christmas Eve
A Pleasant Evening at the Theatre
1909 Eve of the Wedding
A Policeman's Xmas Eve
1910 A Tragic Evening

Event
1909 An Eventful Trip
Great Event at Podunk

Eventide
1910 Lakes at Eventide

Everglades (Florida)
1909 A Florida Feud; or, Love in the Everglades

Eviction
1904 The Eviction
1907 The Eviction
1909 Bee's Eviction
A Brave Irish Lass, the Story of an Eviction in Ireland

Evidence
1900 The Evidence Was Against Him
1903 The Divorce: The Evidence Secured [Part 3]
A Search for Evidence
A Victim of Circumstantial Evidence
1906 Getting Evidence, Showing the Trials and Tribulations of a Private Detective
1908 Circumstantial Evidence, or, An Innocent Victim
Circumstantial Evidence; or, Who Ate the Possum Pie
1909 Circumstantial Evidence
Convicting Evidence
Incriminating Evidence

Evil
1898 The Tipping Evil
1904 An Evil Doer's Sad End
1907 Returning Good for Evil
1909 Beware of Evil Companions
An Evil Day
The Evil Philter
The Evil Spirit in a Girl's Boarding School
The Evil That Men Do
Good for Evil

Evolution
1903 French Cavalry Evolutions
Wonderful Suspension and Evolution
1905 Evolution of the Japanese

Ex-convict
1904 The Ex-Convict
1908 Ex-Convict No. 900

Exacting
1909 Exacting Father-in-Law

Examination
1902 St. John's Guild. Examination of Patients
1904 Physical Examinations
1907 Examining a Recruit U.S.N.
1910 Examination Day at School

Excavation
1903 Excavating Scene at the Pyramids of Sakkarah
1905 Pennsylvania Tunnel Excavation

Excelsior
1902 The Magician and the Human Pump (Excelsior!)
1909 Excelsior

Exchange
1899 A Fair Exchange Is No Robbery
1901 Royal Exchange, London, England
1903 Exchange of Mail at Rural P.O., U.S.P.O.
1904 A Fair Exchange No Robbery
1909 A Fair Exchange
1910 A Fair Exchange

Exciting
1899 An Exciting Finish
1907 Exciting Honeymoon Trip
Exciting Night of Their Honeymoon
An Exciting Ride
1909 Baby's Exciting Ride
An Exciting Hunt
Exciting Steeple-Chase
1910 An Exciting Yarn

Excursion
1898 Excursion Boats, Naval Parade
1900 Darkey Excursionists Bathing, Atlantic City
1902 Sea Sick Excursionists
1903 Panorama of Excursion Boats
Steamer Susie Excursion to Moosehide
1907 Niagara Falls (Excursion aux chutes du Niagara)
1908 Excursion to Montreal
Excursion to Moon
1909 Mug Chump's Early Morning Excursion
Polly's Excursion
1910 An Excursion into Wales
Excursion on the Chain of Mont Blanc
An Excursion on the Lake of Garda

Excuse
1909 A Good Excuse
1910 A New Excuse

Execution
1898 An Execution by Hanging
Execution of the Spanish Spy
1900 Execution of a Spy
1901 Execution of Czolgosz, with Panorama of Auburn Prison
1904 Capture and Execution of Spies by Russians
The Execution (Beheading) of One of the Hunchuses (Chinese Bandits) Outside the Walls of Mukden
Spy's Execution
The Terrible Turkish Executioner
1905 An Execution by Hanging
1908 A Comical Execution

Exempt
1903 Parade of "Exempt" Firemen

Exercise
1897 Gymnastic Exercises in the British Army
13th Infantry, U.S. Army—Bayonet Exercise, Governors Island
1898 Broadsword Exercise on the Battleship Texas
Her Morning Exercise
1900 British Highlanders Exercising
Gymnasium Exercises and Drill at Newport [R.I., Naval] Training School
1901 Jeffries Exercising in His Gymnasium
1902 English Soldiers Exercising
German Military Exercises
1903 Artillery Exercises
Bayonet Exercises
Men in Physical Exercise, National Cash Register Co.
Morning Exercise on Board the U.S. Cruiser Raleigh
1904 High School Field Exercises, Missouri Commission
1905 Al Treloar in Muscle Exercises
Drills and Exercises, Schoolship "St. Mary's"
Hunters Exercising, Dublin Horse Show
Hunters in Exercising Ring, Dublin Horse Show
1907 Native Hawaiian Guards in Bayonet Exercises, H.I.
1910 Acrobatic Exercises by the Colibris Dwarfs
Some Riding Exercises of the Italian Cavalry

Exhibition
1897 Exhibition of Prize Winners
1903 Sparring Exhibition on Board the U.S.S. "Alabama"
1904 Exhibition Fire Drill, Union Square, N.Y.
Exhibition of the United States Life Saving Crew
1905 Shooting the Chutes, Cork Exhibition
1907 At the Colonial Exhibition

Exile
1910 The Exile
The Exiled Chief
The Exiled Mother
An Exile's Love

Existence
1910 Her Battle for Existence

Exit
1896 Exit of Rip and the Dwarf

Exmore
1906 Exmore Stag Hunt

Exodus
1902 The Summer Exodus

Expansion
1903 Expansion and Contraction
1906 Deep Breathing and Chest Expansion

Expedition
1900 General Bell's Expedition
1906 A Shooting Expedition Accident
1909 Perilous Expedition

Expensive
1908 Expensive Marriage
1909 An Expensive Sky Piece

Experience
1898 The Dude's Experience with a Girl on a Tandem
1900 Aunt Jane's Experience with Tabasco Sauce
Uncle Si's Experience in a Concert Hall
1901 The Hayseed's Experience at Washington Monument
1903 Santos Dumont's Airship (Expérience du ballon dirigeable de M. Santos Dumont)
Santos Dumont's Airship (Expérience du dirigeable de Santos Dumont)
1904 Experienced Waiter
1905 The Green Goods Man; or, Josiah and Samanthy's Experience with the Original "American Confidence Game"
1908 A Country Girl's Seminary Life and Experiences

Experiment
1900 Experimental—Handcamera
1901 Broadway and Fourteenth St. Experimental
Experimental
Finish of Race Sheepshead Bay, Experimental
Mr. H. Casler and Baby. Experimental
1902 Experimental. Moving Picture Machine
Experimental. Southwestern Limited Train
1903 Experimental
Experiment
Railroad View—Experimental
1905 A Mesmerian Experiment
1908 His First Experiment in Chemistry
1909 Unprofitable Experiment

Expert
1897 Expert Driving
1901 Expert Driving
1903 Expert Bag Punching
1909 Expert Glass Blowing

Expiation
1909 Expiation
The Expiation

Explanation
1905 Chauncey Explains
1909 The Wealthy Rival; or A Summer Story That Needs No Explanation

Exploits
1909 Exploits of a Cowboy

Explorer
1909 Explorer's Dream

Explosion
1900 Exploding a Whitehead Torpedo
1901 The Falling Walls at the Tarrant Explosion
A Good Test of High Explosives
Mine Explosion and What Followed
1902 Exploding a Land Mine
Exploding a Submarine Mine
Explosion of an Automobile
The Lamp Explodes
Park Avenue Explosion
1903 Automobile Explosion
1906 Exploded Gas Tanks, U.S. Mint, Emporium and Spreckels' Bld'g.
1908 The Explosive Calf
1910 Grand Central Power House Explosion

Export
1899 A Flock of Export Sheep
1901 Export Packing

Exposed
1900 The Exposed Seance
1907 How Fritz's Pipe Exposed Him to the Maid

Exposition
1900 Arrival of Train at Paris Exposition
Kansas City Fire Department, Winners of the World's Championship at the Paris Exposition
Pan-American Exposition
Panorama of the Paris Exposition, from the Seine

Paris Exposition
Scene in the Swiss Village at Paris Exposition
1901 The Bridge of Sighs—Pan-American Exposition
The Court of Fountains—Pan-American Exposition
Fair Japan—Pan-American Exposition
Fountain, Tower, and Basins—Pan-American Exposition
Horse Parade at the Pan-American Exposition
The Mob Outside the Temple of Music at the Pan-American Exposition [Buffalo]
On the Midway—Pan-American Exposition
Opening of the Pan-American Exposition Showing Vice President Roosevelt Leading the Procession
Pan-American Exposition by Night
Panorama of Midway—Pan-American Exposition
Panorama of the Exposition, No. 1
Panorama of the Exposition, No. 2
Panoramic View Gov't Building, Pan. Am. Exp.
President McKinley at the Buffalo Exposition
President McKinley Reviewing the Troops at the Pan-American Exposition
President McKinley's Speech at the Pan-American Exposition
Propylaea and North End of Plaza, Pan. Am. Exp.
Scene in Beautiful Orient—Pan-American Exposition
Sevillenas Dance—Pan-American Exposition
Sham Battle at the Pan-American Exposition
Spanish Dancers at the Pan-American Exposition
A Trip Around the Pan-American Exposition
Triumphal Bridge, Pan-American Exposition
1902 Fire Run, Exposition
Midway of Charleston Exposition [South Carolina]
Panoramic View of Charleston Exposition [South Carolina]
Paris Exposition
President Roosevelt Reviewing the Troops at Charleston Exposition [South Carolina]
1903 Pres. Roosevelt at the Dedication Ceremonies, St. Louis Exposition
1904 Dress Parade of the Filipino Scouts, St. Louis Exposition
Filipino Scouts, Musical Drill, St. Louis Exposition
The Funniest Man in the Exposition
Igorotte Savages, St. Louis Exposition
Imitation Naval Battle—St. Louis Exposition
The Liberty Bell on Its Way to the Exposition
Opening Ceremonies, St. Louis Exposition
Panorama from St. Louis Plaza, St. Louis Exposition
Panorama of a Philippine Settlement [Pan-American Exposition]
Panorama of St. Louis Exposition from Wireless Tower
Panorama St. Louis Exposition from Launch
Parade of Characters (Asia in America) St. Louis Exposition
Parade of Floats, St. Louis Exposition
Parade of Military, St. Louis Exposition
Parade of National Cash Register Co.'s Employees, St. Louis Exposition
Parade of the Pikers, St. Louis Exposition
Princess Rajah Dance with Chair, St. Louis Exposition
Roosevelt Dedicating at St. Louis Exposition
Roosevelt Dedication at Lewis and Clark Exposition
Twenty Mule Team, St. Louis Exposition
West Point Cadets Escorting Liberty Bell, St. Louis Exposition
1907 Jamestown Exposition
Jamestown Exposition International Naval Review, Hampton Roads, Virginia

Express
1896 Chicago and Buffalo Express
Empire State Express
Empire State Express No. 2
Empire State Express, N.Y. Central R.R.
The Pennsylvania Limited Express
1897 Keystone Express
Philadelphia Express, Jersey Central Railway
1899 South Wales Express
1900 Overland Express Arriving at Helena, Mont.
1902 Ute Pass Express
1903 Boston and New York Express
Santa Fe Colorado Express
Modern House Furnishing Methods (Emménagement express)
1905 Empire State Express
Empire State Express, the Second, Taking Water on the Fly
1906 Arrival Mahukona Express, Kohala, Hawaii
Hold-Up of the Rocky Mt. Express
The Wreckers of the Limited Express
1907 The Express Sculptor
The Pony Express
1908 The Midnight Express
The Pony Express
1909 The Pony Express
1910 The Pony Express Rider

Expression
1897 Facial Expressions by Loney Haskell
1902 Facial Expression
1903 A Funny Story (Facial Expression)
Reading a Letter (Facial Expression)

Extensive
1901 The Extensive Wardrobe
1902 The Extensive Wardrobe

Exterior
1904 Panorama Exterior Westinghouse Works

Extra
1899 Distributing a War Extra
1903 The Extra Turn

Extract
1901 Beef Extract Room
1908 Painless Extraction

Extraordinary
1900 Wrestling Extraordinary
1902 Extraordinary Chinese Magic
1903 Extraordinary Black Art
Extraordinary Illusions
Picture Hanging Extraordinary
1904 Extraordinary Feats of Horsemanship
Extraordinary Fishing
1906 Extraordinary Dislocation
1908 An Extraordinary Overcoat

Extravagance
1901 The Fat and the Lean Wrestling Match (Nouvelles luttes extravagantes)
1910 Granddad's Extravagance

Eye
1903 Goo Goo Eyes
How Mike Got the Soap in His Eyes
1904 Eye Tests, etc., Recruiting
1908 Gendarme Has a Keen Eye
He Got Soap in His Eyes
The Magnetic Eye
1909 Dove Eye's Gratitude
Dust in His Eye
Mr. Jonah Gets a Little Dust in His Eyes
1910 An Eye for an Eye
The Idol's Eye
Max Has Trouble with His Eyes
One Can't Believe One's Eyes
Soap in His Eyes

Eyeglasses
use **Glass**

Eyre, Jane
1910 Jane Eyre

Fabbins (Ireland)
1903 Cliff Scenery at the Fabbins

Fabian
1910 Fabian Arranging Curtain Rods
Fabian Cleaning Chimney
Fabian Hunting Rats
Fabian Out for a Picnic
Fabian's Hollow Tooth

Fables
1908 The Grandmother's Fables

Face
1897 Facial Expressions by Loney Haskell
Heads, Hats and Faces
1902 Facial Expression
Jo Jo, the Dog Faced Boy
Lightning Facial Changes
1903 Clown's Face
Facial Massage
A Funny Story (Facial Expression)
Jim Post, the Great Facial Comedian, and His Troubles
The Man with the Many Faces
Reading a Letter (Facial Expression)
Rubber Face
1904 Facial Contortions
Funny Faces
Masks and Faces
1906 Flags and Faces of All Races
Humorous Phases of Funny Faces
1907 Faces and Grimaces
1908 The Face in the Window
The Face on the Barroom Floor
Funny Faces Competition
1909 Face to Face
Her Face Was Her Fortune
1910 The Face at the Window
Face to Face

Facetious
1904 Barber's Revenge (Le barbier facétieux)

Facori
1910 The Facori Family

Factory
1896 Winchester Arms Factory at Noon Time
1897 Columbia Bicycle Factory
1899 Fire Drill at the Factory of Parke, Davis & Co.
1903 Men Leaving Factory, National Cash Register Co.
Panorama of Factory from Automobile, National Cash Register Co.
Scenes in an Irish Bacon Factory
1904 Dog Factory
1907 The Mill Girl, a Story of Factory Life
Straw Hat Factory in Florence
1909 The Factory Girl

Fad
1899 How N.Y. Society Girls Take to the Fad of Tattooing
1907 Crazed by a Fad

Faded
1909 Faded Flowers
The Faded Lillies
1910 Only a Faded Flower

Fail
1901 The Tramp's Strategy That Failed
1902 The Light That Didn't Fail
1907 Is Marriage a Failure?
The Scheme That Failed
1909 The Plot That Failed
The Trick That Failed
1910 The Failure of Success
The Plot That Failed

Faint
1903 She Fell Fainting into His Arms
1908 A Noble Jester; or, Faint Heart Never Won Fair Lady

Fair
1899 A Fair Exchange Is No Robbery
1901 Fair Japan—Pan-American Exposition
1904 A Fair Exchange No Robbery
In Fair Japan
1907 Dreams of Fair Women
1908 All Is Fair in Love and War
Bald Headed Actor and Fair Lady
The Fair Young Lady's Telephone Communication
A Noble Jester; or, Faint Heart Never Won Fair Lady
1909 All's Fair in Love
A Fair Exchange
1910 All's Fair in Love and War
The Brave Deserve the Fair
A Fair Exchange

Fairbanks
1904 Fairbanks

Fairbanks, Charles Warren, Vice-President
1905 Inauguration of President Roosevelt. President-Elect Roosevelt, Vice-President-Elect Fairbanks and Escort Going to the Capitol
1908 H. R. H. The Prince of Wales Decorating the Monument of Champlain and Receiving Addresses of Welcome from the Mayor of Quebec, the Governor General of Canada and Vice-President Fairbanks, Representative of the United States

1910 Fantastic Furniture
Fantasy
1899 A Midnight Fantasy
1907 The Piker's Dream, a Race Track Fantasy
1909 The Indian Phantasy
Old Sweethearts of Mine, a Phantasy in Smoke
Fantine
1909 Fantine; or, A Mother's Love
Far East
1904 Embarking Wood in the Far East
A Ferry in the Far East
1910 Buffalo Bill's Wild West and Pawnee Bill's Far East
Far North
1910 Justice in the Far North
Far West
1907 Hooligans of the Far West
1909 Drama in the Far West
President Taft in the Far West
Farallon Islands (California)
1902 Fishing at Faralone Island
Farce
1905 The Pastry Cook's Practical Jokes (Les farces de Toto Gâte-sauce)
1906 The Jail Bird and How He Flew, a Farce Comedy Escape
The Merry Frolics of Satan (Les 400 farces du diable)
Farley, John
1909 John Farley's Redemption
Farman, Henri
1908 Aeroplane Flights by Henry Farman, Coney Island, N.Y., U.S.A.
Farman Aeroplane
Mr. Farman's Airship
1909 Henry Farman, King of the Air
Farms and farmers
1897 A Chicken Farm
The Farmer's Troubles
1898 Farmer Kissing the Lean Girl
The Farmer's Mishap
How Farmer Jones Made a Hit at Pleasure Bay
1899 Farmer Oatcake Has His Troubles
Farmer Wayback Entertains
1900 The Farmer and the Trolley Car
A Farmer Who Could Not Let Go
A Farmer's Imitation of Ching Ling Foo
How the Farmer Was Buncoed
New Farmer's Mishap
1901 The Farmer and the Bad Boys
Ostrich Farm
The Ostrich Farm—On the Midway
Ostrich Farms at Pasadena
Pigeon Farm at Los Angeles, Cal
1902 The Farmer's Troubles in a Hotel
Feeding Geese at Newman's Poultry Farm
Milking Time on the Farm
Sowing Seed on the Farm
The Stud Farm, No. 1
The Stud Farm, No. 2
The Stud Farm, No. 3
The Swimming Ducks at Allentown [Pa.] Duck Farm
1903 Allentown Duck Farm
The Farmer and the Old Maid
Farmer Chasing Trespassers
Farmyard Scene
Plowing on the Old Farm
Scenes on a Welsh Pony Farm
1904 Alligator Farm
Tramp on a Farm
The Young Farmer Girl
1905 Children's Hour on the Farm
Down on the Farm
Fun on the Farm
High Jumping Horses—Sidney Holloway's Farm
1906 Ostrich Farm
Pigeon Farm
1907 Farmer Giles' Geese
The Gentleman Farmer
Ostrich Farm
1908 Back to the Farm
Devils in the Farm
The Farmer
Farmer Greene's Summer Boarders
The Farmer's Daughter; or, The Wages of Sin
French Dairy Farm
Oyster Farming
1909 Blind Farmer
Farmer Jones Goes to the Market
The Farmer's Grandson
The Farmer's Joke
The Farmer's Son
The Farmer's Treasure
The Foxy Farmer
James and Catherine; or, Love on a Farm
Race for a Farmer's Cup
Scenes from the World's Largest Pigeon Farm
1910 At the Farm
The Duck Farm
Farm Yard Friends
The Farmer's Daughter
The Footlights or the Farm
Lazy Farmer Brown
Nellie's Farm
Farnum, N. L.
1898 N. L. Farnum Post, G.A.R.
Farragut Naval Post (Ohio)
1901 Farragut Naval Post, Ohio State
Fascination
1908 Fascinating Fluffy Dimples
1909 The Fascinating Mrs. Francis
1910 Fatal Fascination
Fashion
1902 An Old Fashioned Way of Pulling a Tooth
1903 Old Fashioned Scottish Reel
1904 Fashionable Driving on Palace Quay, St. Petersburg
1905 Fashionable Folks Leaving the Dublin Horse Show
1908 Dogs of Fashion
Fashionable Hat
1910 Auntie in the Fashion
The Fashionable Sport
The Latest Fashion in Skirts
Fast
1896 Chicago Fast Mail NYC. R.R.
1897 Fast Mail, Northern Pacific Railroad
Fastest Wrecking Crew in the World
1900 Union Pacific Fast Mail
1903 The Fastest Steam Yacht Afloat
Trial Run of the Fastest Boat in the World, "The Arrow"
1908 The Fast Train
1909 "Ursula," World's Fastest Motor Boat
Fat
1898 The Fat Man and the Treacherous Springboard
1900 Pierrot's Problem, or How To Make a Fat Wife Out of Two Lean Ones
1901 Chicago Fat Stock Parade
The Fat and the Lean Wrestling Match
1902 The Fat and Lean Comedians
1903 Fat Man's Race
1905 The Fat Girl's Love Affair
Largest Fat Boy in the World
1908 The Fat Baby
1909 Nobody Loves a Fat Man
1910 Jack Fat and Jim Slim at Coney Island
Fatal
1901 Ten Nights in a Bar-Room: The Fatal Blow
The Wages of Sin—The Fatal Choice
1904 The Fatal Wig
1905 Fatal Necklace
1906 The Witch (La fée carabosse ou le poignard fatal)
1907 The Fatal Hand
Fatal Leap
Fatality
1908 The Fatal Card
The Fatal Hour
A Fatal Likeness
A Fatal Present
A Fatal Temptation
1909 The Fatal Ball; or, The Miner's Daughter
A Fatal Flirtation
The Fatal Love
Fatal Wedding
1910 Fatal Fascination
The Fatal Gold Nugget
Fatal Imprudence
A Fatal Picnic
A Fatal Vengeance
Her Fatal Mistake
Fate
1903 The Fate of a Gossip
The Fate of the Artist's Model
1908 The Gambler's Fate
The Hand of Fate
The Miser's Fate
A Tricky Painter's Fate
1909 The Bondsman's Fate
The Double's Fate
The Drunkard's Fate
Fate and Poverty
Fools of Fate
The Web of Fate: An Incident of the French Revolution
1910 Fate Against Her
A Fateful Gift
The Garden of Fate
The Hand of Fate
Irony of Fate
The Perversity of Fate
The Rebel's Fate
Victims of Fate
Father
1896 Why Papa Cannot Sleep
1899 How Little Willie Put a Head on His Pa
How Papa Set Off the Fireworks
Tommy's Ringing Good Joke on His Dad
1900 His Dad Caught Him Smoking
1902 How the Lover Squared Himself with Papa
Papa Keeps the Telephone Appointment
Why Papa Reformed, or Setting Back the Clock
1903 Buster's Joke on Papa
Pa's Comment on the Morning News
1904 No Room for Dad
Uncle Rube's Birthday (La fête au Père Mathieu)
1905 Dad's a Gentleman Too
Everybody Works but Father
Everybody Works But Father (Blackface)
Everybody Works But Father (Whiteface)
Father Neptune and Bear
A Father's Honor
"Osler"-ising Papa
Too Much for Dad
Why Papa Could Not Read
1906 Dolly's Papa
Nobody Works Like Father
Papa Minds the Baby
1907 Because My Father's Dead
Father Buys a Hand Roller
Father! Mother Wants You
Father's Picnic
Father's Quiet Sunday
Father's Washing Day
Following in Father's Footsteps
Fussy Father Fooled
How the Lovers Got Rid of Boozy Pa
Papa's Letter
Gibelot's Hotel (L'auberge de Père Gibelotte)
1908 Avaricious Father
Cast Off by His Father
Father and the Kids
Father Gets in the Game
Father Is Late! Go Fetch Him
The Father Is to Blame
Fatherhood and Drunkenness
Father's Lesson
A Father's Will
Pa and the Girls
Pa Takes Up Physical Culture
Poor Pa's Folly
A Stern Father
The Way They Fooled Dad
When Pa Went Fishing
1909 Father and Son
Father's Beautiful Beard
Father's Busy Papering
Father's First Half-Holiday
Father's Glue
Father's Holiday
Forgiven; or, Father and Son
The Girls and Daddy
The Hasty Tempered Father; or, The Blacksmith's Love
A Heroic Father
Indiscreet Father and Son
The Little Father; or, The Dressmaker's Loyal Son
The Obdurate Father
Papa's Hat
Papa's Honeymoon
A Priest of the Wilderness: Father Jogue's Mission to the Iroquois
The Sins of the Fathers
A Telepathic Warning, the Story of a Child's Love for Her Father
To the Custody of the Father
The Truant; or, How Willie Fixed His Father

Feudal
1908 The Tyrant Feudal Lord

Fever
1905 Typhoid Fever Germs
1910 Boxing Fever
Micro-Cinematography: Recurrent Fever

Fiancés and fiancées
1907 Cook's Fiancé
1908 Busy Fiancé
Jealous Fiancé
1909 The General's Fiancée
1910 Her Fiancé and the Dog
Pirate's Fiancée
An Unworthy Fiancé

Fickle
1909 The Fickle Husband
1910 Fickle Fortune

Fiddle
1909 The Fiddle and the Fan
The Fiddlers
Tale of the Fiddle
1910 The Hunchbacked Fiddler
The Little Fiddler
The Old Fiddler

Fido
1903 Poor Old Fido!

Field
1900 Betting Field
In the Field
1903 Oil Fields, Tanks and Lakes of Oil; Kern Co., Cal.
Panorama of Cal. Oil Fields
1904 High School Field Exercises, Missouri Commission
Mining Operations, Pennsylvania Coal Fields
Sour Lake Oil Fields
1906 The Prospectors, a Romance of the Gold Fields
1909 South African Gold Fields
Temptations of the Gold Fields; or, The Two Gold Diggers
1910 Rivalry in the Oil Fields
Scenes of the Australian Gold Fields

Field artillery
1905 Russian Field Artillery

Field battery
1897 French Cuirassieurs Charging a Field Battery

Field day
1910 Actors' Fund Field Day

Field glass
1902 Naughty Grandpa and the Field Glass

Field gun
1897 Maxim Firing Field Gun

Field Marshals
1902 Field-Marshal Count Von Waldersee
1910 How the Great Field Marshall Villars Had an Adopted Daughter

Field sports
1901 International Field Sports
International Field Sports—Oxford-Cambridge vs. Harvard-Yale

Field Street, St. Joseph (Missouri)
1904 Panorama of Field St., St. Joseph, Mo., Missouri Commission

Field, British Columbia (Canada)
1899 Under the Shadow of Mt. Stephen, Passing Field's Station in the Rocky Mountains
1902 Panoramic View Between Palliser and Field, B. C.

Fiend
1900 What the Bathing Girls Did to the Kodak Fiend
1903 The Camera Fiend
The Camera Fiend, No. 2
Snarleyow the Dog Fiend
1904 The Snapshot Fiend
What Happened to a Camera Fiend
1905 The Chloroform Fiends
Cigarette Fiend
Dream of the Race Track Fiend
1906 Dream of a Rarebit Fiend
The Snapshot Fiend; or, Willie's New Camera
1907 The Bargain Fiend; or, Shopping a la Mode
The Onion Fiend
1908 The Checker Fiends
The Dancing Fiend
The Dream of an Opium Fiend
Fencing Fiend
The Football Fiend
The Fresh-Air Fiend; or, How He Was Cured
1909 Physical Culture Fiend
1910 The Bowling Fiend
Floral Fiends
The Fresh Air Fiend
The Golf Fiend
The Motor Fiend

Fier River (France)
1906 Les Gorges du Fier

Fierce
1904 A Fierce Sword Combat at Tokio

Fiesta
use **Festival**

Fife
1903 Fife Getting Instructions from Committee

Fifine
1909 The Adventures of Fifine

Fifteenth
1898 Fifteenth Minnesota Volunteers
1900 15th Infantry
1909 The Brave Girl on the Fifteenth Floor
1910 Troop "B", 15th U.S. Cavalry Bareback Squad in the Monkey Drill at Fort Myer, Virginia

Fifteenth century
1908 In the Days of the Pilgrims, a Romance of the 15th Century in America
The Poisoned Bouquet, an Italian Tragedy of the XV Century

Fifth
1898 Fifth Massachusetts Volunteers
The Fighting Fifth Cuban Mascot
1899 The Dandy Fifth
5th Ohio Volunteers of Cleveland
1903 Fighting Fifth Northumberland Fusileers
1910 Won in the Fifth

Fifth Avenue (New York City)
1896 Li Hung Chang, 5th Avenue & 55th Street, N.Y.
1897 Fifth Avenue, New York
5th Avenue, N.Y.
1899 Fifth Avenue Entrance to Central Park
1901 Soubrette's Troubles on a Fifth Avenue Stage Coach
1902 St. Patrick's Cathedral and Fifth Avenue on Easter Sunday Morning [New York City]
1910 Sunday Afternoon on Fifth Avenue

Fifth Avenue (Pittsburg, Pennsylvania)
1904 Pan. of Fifth Ave., Pittsburg, Pa., From a Trolley Car

Fiftieth
1904 Parade, Fiftieth Anniversary Atlantic City, N.J.
1908 The 50th Regiment Jubilee
Russian Review of the Fiftieth Regiment
1910 Fiftieth Anniversary of Yokohama

55th Street (New York City)
1896 Li Hung Chang, 5th Avenue & 55th Street, N.Y.

Fifty-five
1900 Love at 55

Fight
1894 Leonard—Cushing Fight
1896 Fighting the Fire
1897 Corbett and Fitzsimmons Fight
The Downey and Patterson Fight
New Pillow Fight
Pillow Fight
A Pillow Fight
1898 Corbett and Sharkey Fight
The Fighting Fifth Cuban Mascot
Fighting near Santiago
Fighting Roosters; in Florida
A Landing Fight
The Last Round Ended in a Free Fight
Some Dudes Can Fight
Street Fight and Arrest
1899 The Automatic Prize Fight
Barrel Fight
Fighting in the Transvaal
In Fighting Trim
Reproduction of the Corbett and Jeffries Fight
Reproduction of the Fitzsimmons-Jeffries Fight in Eleven Rounds Showing the Knock Out
Reproduction of the Jeffries and Corbett Fight
Reproduction of the Jeffries and Ruhlin Fight
Reproduction of the Jeffries and Sharkey Fight
Reproduction of the Kid McCoy and Peter Maher Fight
Reproduction of the Pedlar Palmer and Terry McGovern Fight
Reproduction of the Peter Maher and Kid McCoy Fight
Reproduction of the Ruhlin and Jeffries Fight
Reproduction of the Sharkey and Jeffries Fight
Reproduction of the Terry McGovern and Pedlar Palmer Fight
1900 A Dog Fight
Fight Between a Lion and a Bull
Fight Between Tarantula and Scorpion
The Fighting 36th
A Gesture Fight in Hester Street
Life Motion Photographs of the Fitzsimmons and Ruhlin Fight
Reproduction of the Corbett and McCoy Fight
Reproduction of the Fitzsimmons and Sharkey Fight
Reproduction of the McGovern and Dixon Fight
Reproduction of the Sharkey and Fitzsimmons Fight
1901 Firemen Fighting the Tarrant Fire
Gans-McGovern Fight
1902 Jeffries-Fitzsimmons Reproduction Prize Fight Films
The New Pillow Fight
1903 Barrel Fighters
Canoe Fight
Dixon-Palmer Fight
Dog Baiting and Fighting in Valdez
Fighting Amazons
Fighting Fifth Northumberland Fusileers
Fighting Rams
Japanese Sword Fight
Miniature Prize Fighters
Pillow Fight, Reversed
Prize Fight in Coon Town
Reproduction of Corbett-McGovern Fight
Reproduction of Fitzsimmons-Gardner Fight
Reproduction of Jeffries-Corbett Fight
Reproduction of the Corbett-McGovern Fight (San Francisco, Cal, March 31, 1903)
Snow Fight
The Unfaithful Wife: The Fight [Part 2]
1904 Advance Guard Fight
A Fight in the Dormitory
The Fight on the Bridge Between Russians and Japs
A Fight on the Yalu
Fighting the Flames [An Attraction at Coney Island]
Fighting the Flames, Dreamland
How the Japs Fought at Port Arthur
Naval Fight
Pillow Fight, S.S. "Coptic," Mid-Ocean
1905 Buffalo Bill Fight
A Fight for a Bride
Impersonation of Britt-Nelson Fight
Impersonation of the Fitzsimmons-O'Brien Fight
Nelson-Britt Prize Fight
Nelson-Britt Prize Fight for Lightweight Championship, San Francisco, September 9th, 1905
Pillow Fight
The Pillow Fight, No. 2
1906 Impersonation of Gans-Nelson Fight
Nelson-McGovern Fight, 1906
Police Raid at a Dog Fight
Reproduction of Nelson-Gans Fight
1907 Fights of Nations
Gans-Herman Fight
Light-Fight-White
1908 Cumbersome First Fight
The Fight for Freedom
Fighting for Gold
The Fighting Parson
Fighting the Flames
Gans-Nelson Fight
The Hoosier Fighter
[Moran-Attell Fight]
Reproduction of Burns-Palmer Fight, London [England], February 10th, 1908
A Yankee Man-o-Warsman's Fight for Love

1899 Marines of the Atlantic Fleet
Sailors of the Atlantic Fleet
1900 Bombarding and Capturing the Taku Forts by the Allied Fleets
Bombardment of Taku Forts, by the Allied Fleets
1901 Panoramic View of the Fleet After Yacht Race
The Yacht Race Fleet Following the Committee Boat "Navigator" Oct. 4th
1902 Return of the German China Fleet
1903 North Atlantic Fleet Bombarding Fisher's Island
North Atlantic Fleet Bombarding Fort Adams, Newport Harbor
Sir Thomas Lipton's Yacht Fleet Leaving England
1904 The Baltic Fleet and the North Sea Trawlers
1905 Reception of British Fleet
With the German Fleet
1907 The Handling of the Fleet
1908 The Mediterranean Fleet
Reception of the American Fleet in Australia
With the Fleet in Frisco
1909 The American Fleet at Sydney, New South Wales
The American Fleet in Hampton Roads, 1909, After Girdling the Globe
1910 The American Fleet in French Waters

Flight
1903 Passion Play: Flight into Egypt
1906 The Jail Bird and How He Flew, a Farce Comedy Escape
1908 The Flight from Seraglio
Lady Jane's Flight, a 17th Century Romance
1909 Backward, Turn Backward, O Time, in Your Flight
The Flight of Monsieur Valette
When Courage Fled
1910 The Flight of Red Wing

Flight to Egypt
1904 The Passion Play (La fuite en Egypte)

Fling
1897 The Highland Fling, by the Gordon Highlanders
1903 Miss Jessie Dogherty, Champion Female Highland Fling Dancer
Scotch Highland Fling

Flip, Mr.
1909 Mr. Flip

Flip-Flap Railroad (Coney Island)
1900 Around the Flip-Flap Railroad
1901 Flip-Flap Railway

Flip-Rip-Zip
1907 Flip-Rip-Zip

Flirtation
1900 A Flirtation
1903 A Flirtation in Silhouette
A Frontier Flirtation; or, "How the Tenderfoot Won Out"
1904 An Interrupted Flirtation
Old Maid's Flirtation
Honeymoon Trip (Flirt en chemin de fer)
1905 Innocent Flirtation
Terrible Flirt
1906 A Seaside Flirtation
1907 Disastrous Flirtation
Flirting on the Sands
Flirty Fan
Flirty Fred
1908 A Disastrous Flirtation
Madam Flirt and Her Adopted Uncle
Troubles of a Flirt
Unlucky Old Flirt
Unsuccessful Flirts
Wouldn't You Like to Flirt with me
1909 The Adventures of an Old Flirt
A Fatal Flirtation
The Flirt, a Tale of the Plains
Flirtation Collar
How the Page Boy Cured a Flirt
1910 A Flirty Affliction
A Seaside Flirtation
A Summer Flirtation
The Troubles of a Flirt

Flirto-Maniac
1910 The Flirto-Maniac

Flitting
1910 The Moonlight Flitting

Floating
1902 St. John's Guild. Dispensary Scene, Floating Hospital
St. John's Guild. Plank to Deck, Floating Hospital
1903 Wonderful Suspension and Evolution (La femme volante)
1904 The American Flag, Floating
1908 Wood Floating and Pulp Industry
1909 Wood Floating in Morvan
1910 A Floating Message
Floating to Wealth

Floats
1898 Allegorical Floats
Cripple Creek Float
Horticultural Floats, No. 9
Procession of Floats
1899 Panoramic View of Floral Float "Olympia"
1901 Industrial Floats
1903 Procession of Floats and Masqueraders at Nice Carnival
1904 Parade of Floats, St. Louis Exposition
1907 The "Float," Waikiki, Honolulu, Hawaiian Islands

Flock
1899 A Flock of Export Sheep
A Flock of Sheep
1901 Flock of Sheep
1903 Passion Play: Shepherds Watching Their Flocks by Night

Flood
1903 Flood Scene in Paterson, N.J.
1909 Great Flood in India, September, 1908
1910 The Flood
Paris Flood
[Paris Flood Pictures]

Floor
1904 Scenes on Every Floor
1905 Love at Each Floor
1906 A Mix-up in the Gallery (Une chute de cinq étages)
1907 Floor Polisher
1908 The Face on the Barroom Floor
1909 The Brave Girl on the Fifteenth Floor

Flora
1909 The Love of Little Flora

Floral
rt **Flower**
1899 Panoramic View of Floral Float "Olympia"
1902 Floral Chair Parade
1903 Atlantic City Floral Parade
Floral Parade
1904 Atlantic City Floral Parade
1905 Floral Parade at the Race Track, Moscow, Russia
Floral Parade Festival of Roses, Pasadena, Cal.
1906 Floral Fiesta, Los Angeles, Cal.
1907 Floral Parade at Pasadena, Calif.
1910 Floral Fiends
Floral Studies

Florence (Italy)
1907 Straw Hat Factory in Florence
1910 A Penitent of Florence
The Tyrant of Florence

Florida
1898 Fighting Roosters; in Florida
In Camp, Tampa, Fla.
Lawn Tennis in Florida
Pile Drivers; Tampa, Fla.
Tampa Bay Hotel, Tampa, Fla.
U.S. Cavalry Supplies Unloading at Tampa, Florida
1905 Automobile Races at Ormond, Fla.
Boating Carnival, Palm Beach, Fla.
In the Swimming Pool, Palm Beach, Fla.
Speed Trial of Auto Boat Challenger, Lake Worth, Fla.
1906 A Trip to Jacksonville, Fla.
A Trip to St. Augustine, Fla.
A Trip to Tampa, Fla.
1909 A Florida Feud; or, Love in the Everglades
The Seminole's Vengeance; or The Slave Catchers of Florida

Florist
use **Flower**

Florrie
1909 Florrie's Birthday

Flossie
1909 Flossie's New Peach-Basket Hat

Flotilla
1902 A German Torpedo Boat Flotilla in Action

Flotow
1909 Duet from "Martha" (Flotow)

Flour
1904 Flour and Feed

Flower
rt **Floral**
1901 A Flower Parade
1902 When Knighthood Was in Flower
1903 Battle of Flowers at the Nice Carnival
1904 Easter Flower Parade in Bois de Boulogne, Paris
Flower Parade Race Course, Moscow
1905 Flower Fairy
Language of Flowers
1906 Living Flowers
1907 Japanese Vaudeville "The Flower Kingdom"
1908 Battle of Flowers in Nice
An Enterprising Florist
Flower Fete on the Bois de Boulogne
Flower of Youth
The Flower Thief
For a Flower
Her Flowers
The Miraculous Flowers
The Mission of a Flower
1909 Faded Flowers
The Poisoned Flower
1910 The Flower of the Ranch
Flower Parade at Pasadena, California
Fruit and Flowers
The Kingdom of Flowers
The Magic Flower
Only a Bunch of Flowers
Only a Faded Flower
The Wild Flower and the Rose

Flower girl
1908 The Flower Girl
The Flower Girl of Paris
The Little Flower Girl
Pretty Flower Girl
Rose, the Flower Girl

Flows
1903 Down Where the Wurzburger Flows

Fluffy
1908 Fascinating Fluffy Dimples
Fluffy's New Corsets

Fluid
1907 Liquid Electricity; or, The Inventor's Galvanic Fluid
1908 Galvanic Fluid; or, More Fun with Liquid Electricity
The Invisible Fluid
A Wonderful Fluid
1909 Miraculous Fluid
1910 The Marvelous Cure; or, The Wonderful Hair-Growing Fluid

Flume
1899 The Flume

Flute
1906 The Magic Flute
1908 The Magic Flute
1909 The Shepherd's Flute
1910 The Song of the Wildwood Flute

Fly
1899 The Spider and the Fly
1900 "Shoo Fly"
The Troublesome Fly
1903 The Human Fly
1905 Empire State Express, the Second, Taking Water on the Fly
1907 The Fly
Making the Dirt Fly: Scene 1. Steam Shovel in Operation, Culebra Cut
Making the Dirt Fly: Scene 2. Unloading a Dirt Train
Making the Dirt Fly: Scene 3. Dirt Scraper in Operation
Making the Dirt Fly: Scene 4. Railroad Track Lifter in Operation
Making the Dirt Fly: Scene 5. Laborers Lining Up at Mess Tent
She Seemed Shy but She Was Fly
1908 The Inquisitive Fly and the Bald Head
The Troublesome Fly
1909 Mother-in-Law Must Fly
1910 The Acrobatic Fly
The Fly Pest

1903 At the Ford, India. Across the Ravi River
Bostock's Circus Fording a Stream
Fording the River Nile on Donkeys
Lord and Lady Minto with Party, Fording the Rushing Waters of the Klondike on Horseback
Old Mail Coach at Ford, U.S.P.O.
1904 Cavalry Fording a Stream
Cowboys and Indians Fording River in a Wagon
Fording a Stream

Fore
1901 Shamrock to the Fore

Fore River (Massachusetts)
1907 [Launching of the Salem at the Fore River Shipyards—Quincy, Mass.—July 27, 1907]

Forecastle
1903 The Forecastle of the "Kearsage" in a Heavy Sea
1909 Forecastle Tom

Forecourt
1901 Circular Panorama of the Esplanade and Forecourt

Foreign
1900 Foreign Palaces
1903 Foreign Train Scenes

Foreman
1908 Discharged by the Foreman
Incendiary Foreman
1910 The Foreman
The Vindictive Foreman

Forests and foresters
1901 Oh! What a Night; or, the Sultan's Dream (La rêve du rajah ou la forêt enchantée)
1902 In the Heart of the Forest
1903 Scenes of a New Forest Pony Fair
1906 E. Forest Fish Gun Assn.
1907 A Forester Made King
Life in a Burmah Teak Forest
1908 The Forester's Remedy
Pocahantas — A Child of the Forest
1909 A Child of the Forest
Drama in the Forest
Famine in the Forest; or, The Trapper's Gratitude
The Forest Ranger's Daughter
Forester's Son
The Octoroon: The Story of the Turpentine Forest
Stripping a Forest in Winter
1910 The Call of the Forest
The Forest Ranger
A Forester's Sweetheart
The Monastery in the Forest
Vengeance; or, The Forester's Sacrifice

Foretold
1909 What the Cards Foretold

Forge
1901 Forging
1907 Mines and Forge at Decazeville
1909 The Heroine of the Forge

Forgery
1908 The Forged Will
1910 Tweedle Dum's Forged Bank Note

Forget
1901 He Forgot His Umbrella
1907 I Never Forget the Wife
1908 Forgotten Ones
The Forgotten Watch
They Forgot the Messenger
1909 The Cost of Forgetfulness
Forgotten
The Forgotten Watch
Lest We Forget

Forget-me-not
1909 The Legend of the Forget-Me-Not
1910 Forget Me Not

Forgive
1908 The Child's Forgiveness
Stricken Blind; or, To Forgive Is Divine
Will Grandfather Forgive?
1909 Forgiven at Last
Forgiven; or, Father and Son
1910 Forgiven

Forgot
use **Forget**

Forming
1905 Panorama of the Sultan of Morocco's Troop Forming a Square Awaiting the Arrival of H. M. S.

Forsaken
1908 Forsaken
Leah, the Forsaken
1910 Dido Forsaken by Aeneas

Fort Adams, Newport Harbor
1903 North Atlantic Fleet Bombarding Fort Adams, Newport Harbor

Fort de France (Martinique)
1902 Circular Panoramic View of the Market Place at Fort de France, Showing S.S. Korona in the Background
Native Women of Fort de France at Work
Native Women Washing Clothes at Fort de France
Native Women Washing Clothes at the Gueydon Fountain, Fort de France, Martinique
Natives Unloading a Coaling Vessel at Fort de France, Martinique
Street Scene in Fort de France, Martinique

Fort Leavenworth (Kansas)
1910 Review of U.S. Troops—Fort Leavenworth

Fort Mahone (Virginia)
1909 Pennsylvania Monument at Fort Mahone near Petersburg, Va.

Fort Myer (Virginia)
1897 Guard Mount, Ft. Myer [Va.]
1910 Troop "B", 15th U.S. Cavalry Bareback Squad in the Monkey Drill at Fort Myer, Virginia

Fort Ridgely
1910 The Attack on Fort Ridgely

Fort Scott (Kansas)
1903 Memphis & Ft. Scott Railway Bridge

Forts
1897 Fort Hill Fire Station
Guard Mount, Ft. Myer [Va.]
1898 Capture of a Spanish Fort near Santiago
1899 Scaling a Fort at Manila
Storming the Fort
1900 Bombarding and Capturing the Taku Forts by the Allied Fleets
Bombardment of Taku Forts, by the Allied Fleets
1901 Indian Fort, Sherman Hill Tunnel
1902 Circular Panoramic View of the Market Place at Fort de France, Showing S.S. Korona in the Background
Native Women of Fort de France at Work
Native Women Washing Clothes at Fort de France
Native Women Washing Clothes at the Gueydon Fountain, Fort de France, Martinique
Natives Unloading a Coaling Vessel at Fort de France, Martinique
Street Scene in Fort de France, Martinique
1903 German Cruisers Bombarding Venezuelan Forts
North Atlantic Fleet Bombarding Fort Adams, Newport Harbor
The Sand Fort
1904 Attack on a Fortress
1906 Attack on Fort Boonesboro
Retaking a Fort
1909 Pennsylvania Monument at Fort Mahone near Petersburg, Va.
1910 The Attack on Fort Ridgely
The Conspiracy of Pontiac; or, At Fort Detroit in 1763
Foiled by a Cigarette; or, The Stolen Plans of the Fortress
Fort Du Bitche
Review of U.S. Troops—Fort Leavenworth
Ruins of Mediaeval Fortifications in France
Troop "B", 15th U.S. Cavalry Bareback Squad in the Monkey Drill at Fort Myer, Virginia

Fortune
1907 The Fortune
1908 The Fortune Hunters
The Hat of Fortune
The Lady with the Beard; or, Misfortune to Fortune
Love and Fortune
The Uncle's Fortune
1909 The Cap of Fortune
Fortune Favors the Brave
The Fortune Hunters
Her Face Was Her Fortune
1910 Fickle Fortune
A Fortunate Misfortune
Fortune's Fool
Fortune's Wheel
Running Away from a Fortune
The Stolen Fortune
The Tide of Fortune

Fortune-teller
1904 Old Maid and Fortune Teller
1905 Fortune Telling in a Gypsy Camp
1907 The Fortune Teller

Forty
1900 Showing a Giant Crane Dumping a 40-Ton Car
1902 Ali Baba and the Forty Thieves
Love at 20 and 40 Years After
1907 Ali Baba and the Forty Thieves
Forty Winks; or, A Strenuous Dream
1910 Forty Years in the Land of Midian [The Life of Moses Part II]

Forty-eighth
1902 48th Highlanders Regiment

Forty-five
1910 45 Minutes from Broadway

Forty-second
1909 Fenton of the 42nd

42nd Street (New York City)
1905 Interior N.Y. Subway, 14th St. to 42nd St.

Forty-third
1899 43rd Rifles; Royal Canadian Infantry

Forward
1896 Park Police Drill Left Wheel and Forward
1899 Looking Forward S.S. "St. Louis"
1901 "Forward"
1907 Music, Forward!
1910 Looking Forward

Fossil
1908 The Merry Widower; or, The Rejuvenation of a Fossil

Foster
1899 The Foster Mother
1904 Foster Parents
1907 The Foster Cabby
1910 Foster Brothers

Fougere
1899 Fougere

Foul
1907 A Championship Won on a Foul

Foul play
1907 Foul Play; or, A False Friend

Found
use **Find**

Foundation
1903 Digging for Foundation for Large Department Store, Phila.
Lifting a Wagon from a New York Foundation
1906 Singer Building Foundation Co.

Founding
1899 Founder's Log Cabin
1908 The Discoverers, a Grand Historical Pageant Picturing the Discovery and Founding of New France, Canada
Military Parade, Founders Week Celebration, Philadelphia
Tercentenary Celebrations to Commemorate the 300th Anniversary of the Founding of Quebec by Champlain

Foundling
1907 The Foundling
1908 Story of a Foundling
1909 The Blind Foundling; or, Alone in the World
The Foundling—A Dressing Room Waif

Foundry
1910 The Iron Foundry

Fountain
1901 The Court of Fountains—Pan-American Exposition
Fountain, Tower, and Basins—Pan-American Exposition
1902 At the Fountain
Native Women Washing Clothes at the Gueydon Fountain, Fort de France, Martinique
1903 East Side Urchins Bathing in a Fountain
Electric Fountain
Fountain Geyser
Gravity Fountain
1904 Meet Me at the Fountain
1905 Big Fountain at Versailles
Great Fountain Geyser, Yellowstone Park
Stages Leaving Fountain House, Yellowstone Park
1907 The Fountain of Youth
Fountains of Rome

Frankfort (Germany)
1907 Street in Frankfort
Frankfurters
1900 A Yard of Frankfurters
1910 The Tale of a Hot Dog
Frat
1910 He Joined the Frat
Fratricide
1909 Fratricide
Fraudulent
1901 The Fraudulent Beggar
Frazer Canyon, British Columbia (Canada)
1899 Frazer Canyon, East of Yale
Freak
1905 Freak Barber
1910 A Freak
Fred
1907 Flirty Fred
Freddie
1908 Freddie's Little Love Affair
1910 Freddie's Courtship
Frederick, German Empress
1902 Funeral of the German Empress, Frederick
Funeral Procession of the Late Empress Frederick
Free
1898 Free Tobacco
The Last Round Ended in a Free Fight
1901 Boys Entering Free Bath
Boys Free Public Baths
Saturday at the Free Baths
1904 Free Arm Movement, All Schools, Missouri Commission
1906 Free Show on the Beach
1907 A Free Lunch
1908 Free Admission
A Free Pardon
The Free Pass
1909 Free Champagne
Free-for-all
1897 Free-for-All Race at Charter Oak Park
1899 The Great Free-for-All Pacing Race
Freebooter
1909 The Freebooters
1910 The Freebooter's Captive
Freedom
1905 A Break for Freedom
1908 A Bird of Freedom
Child Slave Freed
The Fight for Freedom
Freedom for All
1910 The Dawn of Freedom
Freemont
1910 Overland to Freemont
Fregola
1908 The Story of the King of Fregola
Fregoli
1907 Little Fregoli
Freight
1898 Freight Train
1903 Freight Train in the Royal Gorge, Colo.
1905 General Electric Engine Hauling Freight
1906 Ute Pass from a Freight Train
1908 The Hallroom Boys Received Queer Freight
French, George Arthur, General
1903 Skirmish with Boers near Kimberly by a Troop of Cavalry Scouts Attached to Gen. French's Column
French horn
1909 Magic French Horn
French language
1908 Parlez Vous Francais? (Do You Speak French?)
Frere Bridge (South Africa)
1899 Frere Bridge, as Destroyed by the Boers
Fresh
1899 The Finish of Mr. Fresh
1900 The Downward Path: The Fresh Book Agent [Part 1]
What Happened to a Fresh Johnnie
1901 The Fresh Lover
1903 A Fresh Bath
Strictly Fresh Eggs
1905 Fresh Water Infusorian
1906 "A Fresh Bath" or "The Tripper Tripped"
1908 A Dozen of Fresh Eggs
1909 The Fresh Kid
1910 A Fresh Start
Fresh air
1908 The Fresh-Air Fiend; or, How He Was Cured
1910 The Fresh Air Fiend
Freshman
1899 Hazing a Freshman
Friar
1908 It Is Not the Cowl That Makes the Friar
1910 The False Friar
Fricot
1910 Fricot Drinks a Bottle of Horse Embrocation
Fricot Gets in a Libertine Mood
Fricot Has Lost His Collar Button
Fricot in College
Fricot Is Learning a Handicraft
Fricot's Itching Powder
The Tricky Umbrella of Fricot
Why Fricot Was Sent to College
Friday the 13th
1908 Friday, the 13th
Friedrichshof
1908 King Edward and the German Emperor at Friedrichshof
Friedrichstrasse, Berlin (Germany)
1902 In the Friedrichstrasse
Friend
1898 "Me and My Two Friends"
1899 Bringing a Friend Home for Dinner
1903 Jack's Four Footed Friend. Mike the Ship's Mascot
Man's Best Friend
Mr. Carney and Friend, National Cash Register Co.
1904 Our Deaf Friend, Fogarty
1905 The Colonel's Friend
1906 A Friend in Need Is a Friend Indeed
Pals; or, My Friend, the Dummy
1907 Foul Play; or, A False Friend
Friendship Better Than Riches
Her Friend, the Enemy
The Indian's Friendship
Vanishing Friends
When Friends Meet
1908 A Faithless Friend
Her Newsboy Friend
Our Dog Friends
The Test of Friendship
1909 The Children's Friend
A False Friend
A Friend in Need Is a Friend Indeed
A Friend in the Enemy's Camp
The Friend of the Family
My Friend, Mr. Dummy
My Friend, the Indian
An Obliging Friend
Service of a Friend
A True Friend
The Two Friends
1910 The Broken Friendship
The False Friend
Farm Yard Friends
Friends
His Sick Friend
In Friendship's Name
The Last Friend
My Friend, the Doctor
A Red Girl's Friendship
A Sailor's Friendship
Save Us from Our Friends
The Stenographer's Friend
The Three Friends
Two Friends
An Unexpected Friend
Fright
1904 Casey's Frightful Dream
1905 "A Frightful Night"
1908 Frightened by Burglars
Mr. Boozer Gets a Fright
Frisky
1898 When the Girls Got Frisky
Fritchie, Barbara
1908 Barbara Fritchie, the Story of a Patriotic American Woman
Fritz
1907 How Fritz's Pipe Exposed Him to the Maid
Frivolity
1898 Bathroom Frivolities
1904 Frivolity
1907 Art Student's Frivolities
Frock
1908 His First Frock Coat
1909 The Frock Coat
Frog
1902 The Children and the Frog
1905 Cir. of Blood, Frog's Foot
1906 Frog Fishing
1908 The Frog
Frolic
1897 A Jolly Crowd of Bathers Frolicking on the Beach at Atlantic City
1901 Girl's Frolic at the Lake
1903 Humpty's Frolics
Seashore Frolics
1906 The Merry Frolics of Satan
1907 Frolics of Ding Dong Imps
1908 Buried Alive; or, Frolics on the Beach at Coney Island
Frolicsome Powders
1909 The Frolic of Youth
Frolics of Gamins
Two Frolicking Youths
Front
1896 Broadway & Park Row, Front of U.S. Post Office, N.Y.
1898 In Front of "Journal" Building
Troops Making Military Road in Front of Santiago
When the Organ Played in Front of the Hotel
1900 Bird's-Eye View of Dock Front, Galveston
1901 Sticking Hogs, (Front View)
1903 Feeding Pigeons in Front of St. Mark's Cathedral, Venice, Italy
1910 Panoramic Railway View from Front of Train
Right in Front of Father
The Front (War)
1898 Off for the Front
Red Cross at the Front
1903 Royal Horse Artillery on the March to the Front
1904 A Regiment of the Japanese Imperial Guards and Engineer Corps off to the Front
Frontier
1903 A Frontier Flirtation; or, "How the Tenderfoot Won Out"
1908 The Frontierman's Bride
A Trapper on the Frontier
1909 Frontier Days
On the Western Frontier
1910 Cowboy and Indian Frontier Celebration
Frontier Day in the West
A Frontier Hero
Life of the Alpine Shooters in the Frontier Outposts
On the Ethiopian Frontier
The Spanish Frontier
Frost
1909 Frost Bound Nature
Frothy
1910 Tweedledum and Frothy Want to Get Married
Frowsy
1907 Frowsy Lizzie Knocks Them Dizzy
Frozen
1910 A Frozen Ape
In the Frozen North
Fruit
1907 Forbidden Fruit
1908 A New Fruit
1910 Eldora, the Fruit Girl
Fruit and Flowers
Fruit Growing, Grand Valley, Colorado (The Results of Irrigation)
The Fruits of Vengeance
Frustrated
1902 A Frustrated Elopement
Fu Tschi
1902 Fu Tschi Dancers
Fuddler
1909 Pierrot, the Fuddler
Fuerst Bismark (Battleship)
1902 On Board His Majesty's Battleship "Fuerst Bismark"
Fugitive
1904 The Fugitive Apparitions
1908 The Hebrew Fugitive
1910 The Fugitive
The Girl and the Fugitive

Panorama of Galveston Power House
Panorama of Orphans' Home, Galveston
Panoramic View of Tremont Hotel, Galveston
Panoramic View, Rescue Work, Galveston
Panoramic View, Wreckage Along Shore, Galveston
Searching Ruins on Broadway, Galveston, for Dead Bodies
Sunken Steamer in Galveston Harbor
Taking the Dead from the Ruins [Galveston]
View of City of Galveston from the Waterfront

Galway (Ireland)
1905 Market Women Leaving the Railway Station at Galway, Ireland

Gamble
1903 The Gambler's Crime
1904 A Gambler's Quarrel
1905 The Scheming Gambler's Paradise
1906 The Gambler's Nightmare
1908 A Gamble for a Woman
The Gambler
The Gambler and the Devil
The Gambler's Fate
The Gambler's Wife
The Gambling Demon
The Promise! Henri Promises Never to Gamble Again
Red Cloud, the Indian Gambler
The Woman Who Gambles
1909 The Gambler
Gambler's Honor
The Gambler's Son
The Gambler's Vow
Gambling Passion
Gambling with Death
Never Gamble for Your Trousers
1910 The Curse of Gambling
A Gambler of the West
The Gambler's Charm
The Gambler's Doom
A Gambler's End
The Gambler's Wife

Game
1898 The Ball Game
Game of Shovel Board on Board S.S. "Doric"
Spanish Ball Game
1899 International Collegiate Games
The International Collegiate Games
International Collegiate Games
International Collegiate Games—Half Mile Run
International Collegiate Games—110 Yards Hurdle Race
International Collegiate Games—100 Yards Dash
An Interrupted Crap Game
1900 Foot Ball Game
Great Foot Ball Game
Polo Game: Myopia vs. Dedham
The Tramp and the Crap Game
1901 An Esquimaux Game
Esquimaux Game of Snap-the-Whip
Football Game: West Point vs. Annapolis
President Roosevelt at the Army-Navy Game
President Roosevelt Entering Grounds at Army-Navy Football Game
1903 Chicago—Michigan Football Game
Game of Base Ball
Game of Push Ball
Harvard-Pennsylvania Football Game
Interrupted Crap Game
One of Jack's Games Aboard a Man o' War
Princeton and Yale Football Game
Western Card Game
1904 Game of Cards
Game of Old Maid
Herding Polo Ponies and Polo Game
Kindergarten Ball Game, Missouri Commission
Pushball Game
1905 The Badger Game
The Green Goods Man; or, Josiah and Samanthy's Experience with the Original "American Confidence Game"
"Play Ball"—Opening Game, National League, N.Y. City, 1905—New York vs. Boston
1906 Game of Chess
How the Office Boy Saw the Ball Game
Nautical Game
The Olympian Games
The Olympic Games at Athens, Greece
Please Help the Blind; or, A Game of Graft
The World Series Baseball Games-White Sox and Cubs
1907 Base Ball Game
Crowds Returning from the Games, Waikiki, H.I.
How Brown Saw the Baseball Game
1908 Beginning of the Game of Diablo
Cupid's Realm; or, A Game of Hearts
Father Gets in the Game
Life's a Game of Cards
Michigan vs. Penn Football game
Olympic Games
1909 The Fish Pirates; or, The Game Warden's Test
The Game
A Game for a Life
A Game of Chess
Game of Hearts
Game of Nine Pins
The Game of Pallone
A Great Game
High Game
His Last Game
Hunting Big Game in Africa
Magic Games
Napoleon's Game of Chess
Phantom Games
Pittsburgh-Detroit Ball Game
Taft in Chicago, and at the Ball Game
Winter Sports and Games at Stockholm, Sweden, 1909
1910 A Game for Life
A Game for Two
A Game of Hearts
A Game with Fame
Great Ball Game Between the East and West
The Smuggler's Game
Take Me Out to the Ball Game
An Unfair Game

Gamekeeper
1907 The Gamekeeper's Dog
1909 Gamekeeper's Bride
The Gamekeeper's Son

Gamins
1909 Frolics of Gamins

Gang
1900 The Growler Gang Catches a Tartar
1908 The Press Gang; or, A Romance in the Time of King George III
1909 The Press Gang
1910 The Gang Leader's Reform

Ganges River (India)
1909 Cremation on the River Ganges
1910 The Banks of the Ganges

Gangplank
1905 The "Spokane's" Passengers Descending the Gangplank at Killisnoo Alaska

Gans, Joe
1901 Gans-McGovern Fight
1906 Gans-Nelson Contest, Goldfield, Nevada, September 3rd, 1906
Impersonation of Gans-Nelson Fight
Reproduction of Nelson-Gans Fight
1907 Gans-Herman Fight
1908 Gans-Nelson Fight

Ganswindt
1902 Ganswindt's Flying Machine

Gap
1899 The Gap, Entrance to the Rocky Mountains
1903 A Trip Through the Gap of Dunloe
1905 Tourist Party in the Gap of Dunloe, Ireland
Tourists Party near Kate Kearney's Cottage, Gap of Dunloe, Ireland

Garbage
1909 The Garbage of Paris

Garda (Lake), Italy
1905 Accelerated (Crazy) Panorama West Shore, Lake of Garda
1908 The Lake of Garda, Italy
1910 An Excursion on the Lake of Garda
[Lake Garda, Northern Italy]
Riva, Austria, and the Lake of Garda

Garden
1896 Wine Garden Scene
1898 His Holiness, Leo XIII in the Gardens of the Vatican, Being Photographed by the American Biograph Camera
Pope Leo XIII Approaching Garden
Pope Leo [XIII] Blessing in the Garden
Pope Leo XIII in Vatican Garden, No. 1
Pope Leo XIII Leaving Carriage and Being Ushered into Garden, No. 104
Pope Leo XIII Seated in Garden
Pope Leo XIII Seated in Garden, No. 105
Pope Leo [XIII] Walking in the Garden
1900 Garden Scene
1901 Garden Party in Honor of the Duke and Duchess of York
"Weary Willie" and the Gardener
1902 An Automobile Parade in the Tuilleries Gardens
1903 Buffaloes Born in the Zoo Gardens
Gardener Sprinkling Bad Boy
Gardener's Joke
Over the Garden Wall
Panoramic Views and Scenes at the Garden of the Gods
Passion Play: Agony in the Garden
1904 Treloar and Miss Marshall, Prize Winners at the Physical Culture Show in Madison Square Garden
Zoological Garden
1905 Convent Garden Market, London
Gardener's Dance, Vevey Fete
The Vicar's Garden Party
Zoological Garden
1906 A Misguided Bobby at a Fancy Garden Party
1907 The Gardener's Nap
Playing a Trick on the Gardener
Spring Gardening
Troubles of a Gardener
1908 A Lemon in the Garden of Love
1909 Biskra, Garden of Allah
A Bride and Groom's Visit to the New York Zoological Gardens
A Visit to the London Zoological Gardens
Zoological Gardens
1910 The Garden of Fate
[London Zoological Gardens]
Over the Garden Wall
Zoological Gardens in Antwerp

Garden of the Gods (Colorado)
1903 Panoramic Views and Scenes at the Garden of the Gods

Gardiner (Montana)
1903 Arrival of Train at Gardner

Gardner
1910 Gardner at the Convent

Gardner, George
1903 Light Heavyweight Championship Contest Between Root and Gardner
Reproduction of Fitzsimmons-Gardner Fight

Garibaldi
1910 The Garibaldi Boy

Garland
1905 Garland Dance, Vevey Fete
1909 Marvellous Garlands

Garlic
1908 Jim Is Fond of Garlic
Tony Has Eaten Garlic

Garment
1908 An All-Wool Garment

Garrick, David
1908 David Garrick

Garrison
1908 The Mystery of the Garrison

Garrulous
1910 The Mule Driver and the Garrulous Mute

Garters
1909 The Blue Garter
A Pair of Garters
1910 The Latest in Garters

Gas
1904 Testing Gas Engine, Westinghouse Works
1906 Exploded Gas Tanks, U.S. Mint, Emporium and Spreckels' Bld'g.
1907 Laughing Gas
1909 It Takes Gasoline to Win a Girl
Sherlock Holmes III: The Detectives Adventure in the Gas Cellar
1910 Love, Luck and Gasoline

German Lancers
German Military Exercises
German Navy Target Practice
German Railway Service
German Soldiers Starting for War
A German Torpedo Boat Flotilla in Action
Horse Racing in Germany
In a German Bath
Kaiser Wilhelm and the Empress of Germany Reviewing Their Troops
Kaiser Wilhelm and the German Cuirrassiers Galloping
Kaiser Wilhelm at the Launching of a German Battleship
Kaiser Wilhelm in the Tier Garten, Berlin, Germany
Kaiser Wilhelm, of Germany, and Emperor Franz Josef, of Austria
Panoramic View of the Harbor of Hamburg, Germany
Prince Henry of Germany
Prince Henry [of Prussia] Arriving in Washington and Visiting the German Embassy
Return of the German China Fleet
A Run by the Berlin Fire Department, Berlin, Germany
Two Germans in a Theatre
Winter in Germany
1903 Arrival of H.I.M. The German Emperor, at Port Victoria
German Cruisers Bombarding Venezuelan Forts
German Dance
German Flag Afloat, National Cash Register Co.
German Torpedo Boat in Action
German Torpedo Boats
Great German Cavalry Charge
1904 Little German Band
Panorama from German Building, World's Fair
Peeping Frenchman at the German Bathhouse
1905 German Torpedo Boat in Action
A German Warship in a Heavy Sea
With the German Fleet
1906 Trip Through Germany
1907 Carl Hagenbeck's Wild Animal Park at Hamburg, Germany
Dot Leedle German Band
1908 German Dragoons Crossing the Elbe
King Edward and the German Emperor at Friedrichshof
1909 Aboard the German Navy
Crown Prince of Germany Drilling Battery
German Spring Parade
1910 The Little German Band
Our German Cousin
That Little German Band

Germs
1905 The Red Snow Germs
Typhoid Fever Germs
1909 The Kissing Germ
Love Germs

Gerry Society
1903 The Gerry Society's Mistake

Gesture
1900 A Gesture Fight in Hester Street

Getting
1896 Getting Off Trolley at Atlantic City
1898 Getting a Shape
How She Gets Along Without a Maid
How the Dressmaker Got Even with a Dead Beat
When the Girls Got Frisky
Who's Got the Red Ear?
1899 Getting Rid of the Surplus
Getting Up in the World
How Bill the Burglar Got a Bath
How Charlie Got the Dough
1900 Getting Ready for the Seashore
How the Dude Got the Soubrette's Baggage
How the Magician Got the Best of the Installment Man
How the Old Maid Got a Husband
How the Young Man Got Stuck at Ocean Beach
How They Got Rid of Mamma
The Tramp Gets Whitewashed
Why Mrs. Jones Got a Divorce
1903 "Don't Get Gay with Your Manicure!"
Fife Getting Instructions from Committee
Girls Getting on Trolley, National Cash Register Co.
Gloomy Gus Gets the Best of It
How a Wife Gets Her Pocket Money
How Buttons Got Even with the Butler
How Mike Got the Soap in His Eyes
How the Valet Got into Hot Water
How to Get a Wife and Baby
How Tommy Got a Pull on His Grandpa
Men Getting on Trolley, National Cash Register Co.
1904 The Cook Gets Square
Getting Strong; or, The Soubrette's Home Gymnasium
"He Won't Be Happy till He Gets It"
How a French Nobleman Got a Wife Through the New York Herald "Personal" Columns
Impossible to Get a Plunge
Will He Never Get Undressed
1905 Getting the Hay
He Got His Hat
He Got into the Wrong Bath House
How Willie Got the Eggs
1906 Getting Evidence, Showing the Trials and Tribulations of a Private Detective
The Lost Hat: He Got It Alright
1907 Amateur Night; or, Get the Hook
Bachelor Gets a Baby and Other Things He Don't Want
Getting Even
Getting His Change
How the Lovers Got Rid of Boozy Pa
The Hundred Dollar Bill; or, The Tramp Couldn't Get It Changed
1908 The Boarder Got the Haddock
Colored Maid Getting Rid of a Suitor
Father Gets in the Game
Get Me a Stepladder
Getting Rid of His Dog
Hard to Get Arrested
He Got Soap in His Eyes
How Rastus Got His Pork Chops
Jim Gets a New Job
Mr. Boozer Gets a Fright
Time to Get Married
Trying to Get Rid of a Bad Dollar
Will They Ever Get to Town?
You Got to Love Me a Lot
1909 Alphonse Gets in Wrong
Getting Even
Getting Even with Everybody
How Brown Got Married
How Happy Jack Got a Meal
How Jones Got a New Suit
How Mother-in-Law Got Even
How the Kids Got Even
How the Tramp Got the Lunch
How to Get a City Job
Impossible to Get Sleep
Mac Nabb Wants to Get Arrested
Mr. Jonah Gets a Little Dust in His Eyes
Trying to Get Arrested
Wearybones Seeks Rest, and Gets It
When Jack Gets His Pay
Willyboy Gets His
You've Got to Love Me a Lot
1910 Does Nephew Get the Cash?
The Foxy Soldiers; or, How Schmidt Got to the Masquerade
Fricot Gets in a Libertine Mood
Get Rich Quick
Getting Even with the Lawyer
Getting Rid of Uncle
Getting Square with the Inventor
Hank and Lank: They Get Wise to a New Scheme
He Got Rid of the Moths
How Hubby Got a Raise
How Rastus Gets His Turkey
Jim Wants to Get Punched
Maggie Hollihan Gets a Job
She Required Strength and Got It
Tommy Gets His Sister Married
Tweedledum and Frothy Want to Get Married
Tweedledum Gets Employed in the Corporation Body

Gettysburg (Pennsylvania)
1908 Lincoln's Speech at Gettysburg
Scenes from the Battlefield of Gettysburg, the Waterloo of the Confederacy

Geyser
1901 Old Faithful Geyser
Riverside Geyser, Yellowstone Park
1903 Fountain Geyser
1905 The Castle Geyser, Yellowstone Park
Great Fountain Geyser, Yellowstone Park
Minuteman Geyser, Yellowstone Park
Old Faithful Geyser, Yellowstone Park
Riverside Geyser, Yellowstone Park

Ghetto
1900 Panoramic View of the Ghetto, New York City
1901 Women of the Ghetto Bathing
1903 New York City "Ghetto" Fish Market
1910 A Child of the Ghetto
The Ghetto Seamstress
The Girls of the Ghetto

Ghezzi
1904 Ghezzi and His Circus

Ghorkhas
1901 The Fourth Ghorkhas

Ghost
1898 Ghost Dance
1899 Ballet of the Ghosts
What Julia Did to the Ghosts
1900 Ghosts in a Chinese Laundry
Photographing the Ghost
1901 The Ghost Train
1903 Ghost Dancers
The Ghost in the Graveyard
1907 The Ghost Holiday
The Ghost Story
Pat's Ghost
1908 The Castle Ghosts
Legend of a Ghost
The Witty Ghost
1909 The Ghost
Tragedy of a Ghost
1910 Another's Ghost
The Beechwood Ghost
The Ghost
The Ghost in the Oven
There Are Some Ghosts

Giant
1897 Giant Coal Dumper
A Giant Steam-Shovel
1898 The Tramp and the Giant Firecracker
1900 Showing a Giant Crane Dumping a 40-Ton Car
1902 The Giant and Pygmy
The Giant Constantin
Hydraulic Giants at Work
1903 Giant Wilkins, the Largest Man in the World
Giant Wilkins Walking No. 2
Procession of Giant Elephants in India
A Trip to the Giant's Causeway
Gulliver's Travels (Le voyage de Gulliver à Lilliput et chez les géants)
1905 Giant Tortoise Feeding
The Mysterious Island (L'île de Calypso. Ulysse et le géant polypheme)
1908 The Giant Baby

Gibbons, James, Cardinal
1898 Cardinal Gibbons

Gibbs
1903 Mr. Chalmers and Mr. Gibbs Arrive at Club, National Cash Register Co.

Gibbs, F. S.
1901 F. S. Gibbs and Family

Gibelot
1907 Gibelot's Hotel

Gibraltar (British colony)
1899 Admiral Dewey Landing at Gibraltar

Gibraltar Dale Creek Fill (Wyoming)
1901 Through Gibraltar

Gibson
1909 The Gibson Goddess

Gibson, W.
1902 Gibson, the Eccentric American Actor

Giddy
1903 The Giddy Dancing Master
Giddy Old Maid
1904 What a Mechanical Toy Did To Some Giddy Girls
1910 Mr. Giddy's Revenge

Gift
1904 Wifey's Christmas Gift
1908 An Embarrassing Gift
The Moon's Gift
A New Year's Gift
1909 Gift
A Gift from Santa Claus
The Gift of Youth, a Fairy Story
1910 The Bad Man's Christmas Gift
A Fateful Gift
Grandfather's Gift

Eldora, the Fruit Girl
The Englishman and the Girl
For a Western Girl
For the Girl's Sake
The Further Adventures of the Girl Spy
The Gipsy Girl's Love
The Girl and the Bandit
The Girl and the Fugitive
The Girl and the Judge; or A Terrible Temptation
The Girl Conscript
The Girl Cowboy
The Girl from Arizona
The Girl from the East
The Girl in the Barracks
The Girl Next Door
The Girl of the Northern Woods
A Girl of the Plains
The Girl on Triple X
The Girl Reporter
The Girl Scout
The Girl Spy Before Vicksburg
The Girl Strike Leader
The Girl Thief
The Girl Who Dared
Girlies
Girls
The Girls He Left Behind Him
The Girls of the Ghetto
The Girls of the Range
Girls Will Be Boys
The Greenhorn and the Girl
His Cinderella Girl
His Yankee Girl
The Horse Shoer's Girl
An Indian Girl's Love
The Indian Girl's Romance
The Laundry Girl's Good Night
The Little Blind Girl
The Love Romance of the Girl Spy
A Man and a Girl
The Millionaire and the Ranch Girl
A Plucky American Girl
A Plucky Girl
The Ranch Girl's Legacy
The Ranger and the Girl
The Red Girl and the Child
A Red Girl's Friendship
Red Girl's Romance
Red Wing and the White Girl
The Right Girl
A Romantic Girl
The Sewing Girl
That Girl of Dixon's
There, Little Girl, Don't Cry
Too Many Girls
Vera, the Gypsy Girl
A Western Girl's Sacrifice
The Yankee Girl's Reward
The Yaqui Girl
A Young Girl's Sacrifice

Girl scouts
use **Scouts**

Gitana
1907 Gitana; or, The Gypsy

Giving
1898 Giving the General a Taste of It
The Landlady Gives Notice to the Barrasing Sisters
Pope Leo XIII Giving Blessing from Chair
Pope Leo XIII Preparing To Give Blessing from Chair
1900 Jones Gives a Private Supper
1903 Rural Wagon Giving Mail to Branch, U.S.P.O.
1907 Casey on a Souse—Gives the Bunch a Douse
1908 Give Me Back My Dummy
Tricked into Giving His Consent
1909 Give Me a Light
1910 Let Us Give Thanks

Glacier
1903 Panorama of Kennicott Glacier Port Hole
Panorama of Taku Glacier
1905 Carrying Passengers Ashore Davidson Glacier, Alaska
Crazy (or Accelerated) Panoramic Approach to Taku Glacier, Alaska
1908 The Glacier's Victim

H.M.S. Gladiator
1908 The Ramming of H. M. S. Gladiator by the St. Paul

Gladioli
1901 Gathering Gladioli

Gladys
1898 Gladys Must Be in Bed Before Ten
1906 The Cruise of the Gladys

Glasgow (Scotland)
1902 Fire Department of Glasgow, Scotland

Glass
1899 As in a Looking Glass
1902 Grandpa's Reading Glass
Naughty Grandpa and the Field Glass
1903 Discovered Through an Opera Glass
1904 Grandma's Glass
1906 I've Lost My Eyeglasses
1907 Enchanted Glasses
1908 A Pair of Spectacles
1909 Expert Glass Blowing
X-Ray Glasses
1910 The Witch's Spectacles

Glen
1899 Glen House Stage
1903 Changing Horses at Glen

Glen Island
1898 The "Glen Island," Accompanying Parade

Glengariff (Ireland)
1903 A Coach Drive from Glengariffe to Kenmore
1905 The Waterfalls of Glengariffe

Glenwood Springs (Colorado)
1902 Fun in the Glenwood Springs Pool

Glimmeramm
1909 Glimmeramm

Glimpses
1897 Glimpses of the Grant Parade
1903 Glimpses of Venice
1904 Glimpses of Japan
1907 Glimpses of Erin
1909 Glimpses of Paris
Glimpses of Yellowstone Park
1910 Glimpses of an Indian Village

Glitters
1908 Behind the Scenes: Where All Is Not Gold That Glitters
1909 Plain Mame; or, All That Glitters Is Not Gold

Globe
1903 Tramping on a Rolling Globe
1907 The Little Globe Trotter
1908 Champion Globe Trotter
1909 The American Fleet in Hampton Roads, 1909, After Girdling the Globe
1910 The New Sign of the Globe Hotel

Gloomy
1903 Gloomy Gus Gets the Best of It

Glory
1901 Little Algy's Glorious Fourth of July
1905 Blasting in the Glory Hole of the Treadwell Mine, Alaska
1907 A Glorious Start
1909 The Glories of Sunset

Gloucester (Massachusetts)
1909 Fishing Industry at Gloucester, Mass.

Gloucester (New Jersey)
1901 Shad Fishing at Gloucester, N.J.

Glove
1897 First Round: Glove Contest Between the Leonards
Second Round: Glove Contest Between the Leonards
1905 Winning a Pair of Gloves
1908 Winning the Gloves
1909 A Pair of White Gloves
1910 The Cowpuncher's Glove
The Glove

Glue
1907 The Glue
Good Glue Sticks
1908 The Best Glue
How Glue Is Made
The Leaking Glue Pot
1909 Father's Glue
1910 A Good Glue
Patent Glue

Gluttonous
1905 Gluttonous Negro

Gnomes
1909 The Gnomes
1911 The Birth of the Gnomes

Go
1897 Going to the Post
McKinley and Cleveland Going to the Capitol
1898 Going Through the Tunnel
Going to Jerusalem
Going to the Yokohama Races
1899 Admiral Dewey and Mayor Van Wyck Going Down Riverside Drive
Coaches Going to Cinnabar from Yellowstone Park
Going to the Firing Line
Going to the Hunt
Going to the Post
Tourists Going Round Yellowstone Park
1900 A Career of Crime, No. 2: Going the Pace
A Farmer Who Could Not Let Go
Going into Action
"A Gone Goose"
1901 Captain Nissen Going Through Whirlpool Rapids, Niagara Falls
Going to the Fire and the Rescue
President McKinley and Escort Going to the Capitol
1902 Going to Bed Under Difficulties
St. John's Guild. Going in Water.
St. John's Guild. Going to Salt-water Bath Room
1903 Dawson City Fire Department Going to a Fire
Girls Going to Lunch. National Cash Register Co.
Going to Bed Under Difficulties
Going to Market, Luxor Egypt
Going to the Fire
Mr. Chalmers Going to Officers' Club, National Cash Register Co.
Mrs. Taylor Going over Horseshoe Falls in a Barrel
1905 Bringing Up a Girl in the Way She Should Go [No. 1]
Bringing Up a Girl in the Way She Should Go [No. 2]
Inauguration of President Roosevelt. President-Elect Roosevelt, Vice-President-Elect Fairbanks and Escort Going to the Capitol
Meran Fire Brigade Going to a Fire
1906 Going to the Fire, Showing Chief Sullivan During the Earthquake
1907 Brown Goes to Mother
Don't Go to the Law
Going Away for Holiday
Madame Goes Shopping
Our Band's Going to the Competition
That Dog Gone Dog
1908 Archie Goes Shopping with the girls
Father Is Late! Go Fetch Him
Go, Little Cabin Boy
Going to Switzerland
I'm Going on the War Path
John's New Suit; or, Why He Didn't Go to Church
A Kindness Never Goes Unrewarded
Mr. and Mrs. Jollygood Go Tandeming
Mr. Shortsighted Goes Shrimping
A Night Out; or, He Couldn't Go Home Until Morning
The Poor Man, Homeless, Wants to Go to Prison
Rube Goes to College
When Ma Goes Shopping
1909 Farmer Jones Goes to the Market
Going Home to Mother
He Wouldn't Go Under a Ladder
His Last Illusion Gone
Husband Goes to Market
Master Goes Shopping
Mr. Pallet Goes Out Landscaping
My Wife's Gone to the Country
My Wife's Gone to the Country (Hooray! Hooray!)
1910 Go West, Young Woman, Go West
Gone to Coney Island
Jean Goes Fishing
Jean Goes Foraging
Max Goes Skiing
Where You Go I Go

Goaded
1905 Goaded to Anarchy

Goal
use **Jail**
1899 Polo—A Dash for Goal

Goat
1898 "Riding the Goat"
1901 Sheep Led to Slaughter by Goat
1903 Casey and His Neighbor's Goat
Trained Goats

1910 A Drink of Goat's Milk

Goat Island (New York)
1896 American Falls, Goat Island
1903 American Falls, Goat Island
Rapids Above American Falls from Bridge to Goat Island
1906 American Falls from Goat Island, Niagara Falls, N.Y.

Gobbler
1898 How the Gobbler Missed the Axe

Goblin
1908 Grimsol, the Mischievous Goblin

God
1899 "God Save the Queen"
1901 God Save the King

Goddess
1909 The Gibson Goddess
Goddess of the Sea

Gods
1907 The Sylvan God
1909 The Mills of the Gods

Goebel
1908 The Goebel Tragedy

Goes
use **Go**

Going
use **Go**

Gold
1897 A Race for the Gold Cup
1901 Rocking Gold in the Klondike
Washing Gold on 20 Above Hunker, Klondike
1902 The Gold Dust Twins
Let the Gold Dust Twins Do Your Work
Reuben Buys a Gold Brick
1903 Gold Dust Twins
Mule Pack Train Taking Gold Dust to Dawson City
Sluice Mining on Gold Hill in the Klondike, Hutchinson and Johnstone's Claim of No. 6, Eldorado
The Miser (Le songe d'or de l'avare)
1905 Old Time Miner Rocking for Gold in the Tailings, Klondike
Panning Gold on a Claim in the Klondike
1906 The Prospectors, a Romance of the Gold Fields
1907 The Gold Brick
Life in a South African Gold Mine
The Need of Gold
1908 Behind the Scenes: Where All Is Not Gold That Glitters
The Curse of Gold
A Dream of Wealth, a Tale of the Gold Seekers of '49
Fighting for Gold
For Love of Gold
Gold-Buys
The Greed for Gold
In the Land of the Gold Mines
The Pirate's Gold
1909 The Curse of Gold
The Gold Digger's Son
The Gold Prospectors
The Gold Seeker's Daughter
Longing for Gold
More Precious Than Gold
A Nugget of Gold
The Oysterman's Gold
Plain Mame; or, All That Glitters Is Not Gold
South African Gold Fields
Temptations of the Gold Fields; or, The Two Gold Diggers
1910 Apache Gold
Attacked by Arapahoes; or, The Gold Seekers and the Indians
Better Than Gold
The Clink of Gold
The Fatal Gold Nugget
Gold Is Not All
A Gold Necklace
The Gold-Seekers
The Gold Spider
Hearts of Gold
John Graham's Gold
The Lure of Gold
New South Wales Gold Mine
Pure Gold
Scenes of the Australian Gold Fields
A Vein of Gold

Golden
1898 Knights of the Golden Eagle
1902 The Golden Chariots
Where Golden Bars Are Cast
1903 Leaving Skagway for the Golden North
1905 The Hen with the Golden Eggs
1907 Golden Beetle
1908 In Golden Days
1909 A Golden Lie
The Golden Louis
1910 The Golden Gates
The Golden Hoard
The Golden Lily
The Golden Secret
The Golden Supper
In the Golden Harvest Time
The Prisoner of the Golden Isle
That Chink at Golden Gulch
Told in the Golden West

Golden (Mountain), Canada
1902 Panoramic View near Mt. Golden on the Canadian Pacific R.R.

Golden Gate, San Francisco (California)
1901 Panorama, Golden Gate
1902 Panoramic View of the Golden Gate

Golden Gate Park, San Francisco (California)
1906 Military Feeding Starving and Destitute Refugees in Golden Gate Park
Park Lodge, Golden Gate Park
Refugees at the Golden Gate Park
Thieves in Camp, Golden Gate Park

Goldfield (Nevada)
1906 Gans-Nelson Contest, Goldfield, Nevada, September 3rd, 1906

Golding
1897 Golding Sisters, Champion Swimmers
1899 The Golding Family

Goldsmith
1909 Visions of a Goldsmith

Goldstein
1907 Goldstein's Luck

Golf
1902 The Golf Girls and the Tramp
1905 Dangerous Golfers
1907 Humors of Amateur Golf
1910 The Golf Fiend
The Golf Mania

Goliath
1908 David and Goliath

Gondola
1904 Tour in Italy (Venise en gondole)
1908 The Gondolier's Daughter
1910 The Black Gondola

Gone
use **Go**

Goo goo eyes
1903 Goo Goo Eyes

Good
1897 A Good Story
1898 Helping a Good Thing Along
1899 A Good Shot
Tommy's Ringing Good Joke on His Dad
A Wringing Good Joke
1900 Too Much of a Good Thing
A Wringing Good Joke
1901 A Good Joke
A Good Test of High Explosives
1902 "Be Good Again"
1903 Be Good
A Good Catch
Something Good-Negro Kiss
A Wringing Good Joke
1904 A Good Story
Tit for Tat; or, A Good Joke on My Head
1905 Good Reason for a Divorce
[On] a [Good Ole] 5¢ Trolley Ride
1906 Good Pipe
She Was Good to Him
1907 Good Glue Sticks
A Good Husband
The Good Wine
Returning Good for Evil
Take Good Care of Baby
1908 Chauncey Proves a Good Detective
The Duke's Good Joke
For He's a Jolly Good Fellow
A Good Boy
A Good Dinner Badly Digested
A Good Joke
A Good Medicine
The Good Playthings
A Good Repentance
Good Resolutions
A Good Thief
A Good Watch Dog
Such a Good Joke, But— Why Don't He Laugh?
What a Good Wine
1909 A Cask of Good Old Wine
A Good Birthday Present
Good Cigars
The Good Doctor
A Good Excuse
Good for Evil
Good for Nothing Nephew
Good Lesson in Charity
The Good Omen
Good People
The Good Shepherd
A Good Trick
The Good Vicar
Legend of the Good Knight
Mimosa and the Good Prince
Porcelain of Good Quality
Servant's Good Joke
'Tis an Ill Wind That Blows No Good
1910 Artist's Good Joke
The Good Boss
Good Business
A Good Glue
A Good Loser
Good Tramp
A Good Winning
How Hubby Made Good
How the Tenderfoot Made Good
One Good Turn

Good fairy
1903 The Sorcerer, Prince and the Good Fairy
1904 Toy Maker and Good Fairy
1909 The Cabman's Good Fairy

Good luck
1908 Good Luck for the Coming Year
The Good Luck of a "Souse"
1909 See a Pin and Pick It Up, All That Day You'll Have Good Luck
1910 Just for Good Luck

Good Luck Baking Powder
1902 Good Luck Baking Powder Train No. 1
Good Luck Baking Powder Train No. 2

Good night
1906 Good Night
1908 Good Night Clown
1910 The Laundry Girl's Good Night

Good Samaritan
1898 The Chorus Girls' Good Samaraitan
1908 A Child's Prayer; or, The Good Samaritan
1909 The Good Samaritan
1910 The Good Samaritan

Good time
1900 A Good Time Behind the Scenes
A Good Time with the Organ Grinder
1908 Mr. Softhead Has a Good Time
1909 Chauffeur Out for a Good Time
Mr. Pynhead Out for a Good Time
1910 Pete Has a Good Time

Good-hearted
1908 Good-Hearted Sailor
1909 A Good Hearted Policeman

Goodbye
1903 Dear Old Stars and Stripes, Goodbye
1907 Goodbye John
1909 The Unspoken Goodbye

Goodchild, Willie
1907 Willie Goodchild Visits His Auntie

Goods
1907 Caught with the Goods
1908 Caught with the Goods

Goodwood
1908 Goodwood Races

Goody two shoes
1903 Goody, Goody Two Shoes

Goorkhas
1901 The War in China—The Fourth Goorkhas

Goose
1898 Hungarian Women Plucking Geese
1900 "A Gone Goose"
1902 Feeding Geese at Newman's Poultry Farm
1903 The Goose Takes a Trolley Ride
Mother Goose Nursery Rhymes
Photographing a Goose
1905 The Christmas Goose
1907 Farmer Giles' Geese
1909 Bess and Her Goose
Goose Chase
The Immortal Goose
Mother Goose

Gordon Highlanders
1897 The Alarm (Gordon Highlanders)
Gordon Highlanders
Gordon Highlanders Marching into Camp
The Highland Fling, by the Gordon Highlanders
1899 Departure of the Gordon Highlanders
The Gordon Highlanders
Gordon Sisters
1901 The Gordon Sisters Boxing
Gordon-Bennett Cup Race
1903 Start of the Gordon-Bennet Cup Race
1904 The Gordon Bennett Automobile Trials, Isle of Man
The Great International Automobile Race for the Gordon-Bennett Trophy
Gorge
1896 Niagara Gorge from Erie R.R.
Pointing Down Gorge, Niagara Falls
Taken from Trolley in Gorge, Niagara Falls
1898 Royal Gorge
1900 Panorama of Gorge Railway
View from the Gorge Railroad
1901 Cuyahoga Gorge
Panorama, Great Gorge Route over Lewiston Bridge
Panoramic View of the Gorge Railroad
1902 Panorama of the Royal Gorge
Train in Royal Gorge
1903 Freight Train in the Royal Gorge, Colo.
Great Gorge R.R., Niagara
Panorama of Schellenen Gorge of Switzerland
Royal Gorge
1906 Les Gorges du Fier
1908 The Gorges of the Tarn
1909 Bandits of the Atlas Gorges
1910 Motoring Among the Cliffs and Gorges of France
Gorgeous
1903 A Gorgeous Pageant of Princes
Gorner Grat (Switzerland)
1905 "All Day in the Alps" Panorama from Gorner Grat
Panorama from Gortner Grat
Gossip
1903 The Fate of a Gossip
1906 The Gossipers
1908 The Girl and the Gossip
The Village Gossip
Got
use **Getting**
Gotacanal (Norway)
1909 Gotacanal—over Norway's Rockies
Gotch, Frank
1908 Gotch-Hackenschmidt Wrestling Match
1910 Gotch-Zbyszko World's Championship Wrestling Match
Goteborg (Sweden)
1905 Deer in Wild Park, Goteborg, Sweden
Gotha Canal (Sweden)
1909 Sweden—Gotha Canal
Gotham
use **New York**
Gould, Frank
1899 Frank Gould's Dogs
Goums
1904 Algerian Goums in the Desert
Gounod, Charles-François
1910 Gounod's 'Ave Maria'
Gourmand
1902 The Gourmand
Gout
1909 A Cure for Gout
1910 Brown's Gouty Foot
Governess
1907 Wanted, a Governess
1908 Faithful Governess Rewarded
1909 Mishaps of a Governess
The New Governess
The Short-Sighted Governess
Government
1898 Government House at Hong Kong
1901 Panoramic View Gov't Building, Pan. Am. Exp.
United States Government Gun Test
1908 In the Government Service
1910 Government Rations
Governor
1897 Battery B, Governor's Troop, Penna.
Governor Bushnell of Ohio, and Staff
Governor Cook and Staff, Connecticut
Gov. John A. Tanner, of Virginia, and Staff
Governor of Ohio and Staff
1898 Governor Hastings and Mounted Police
1899 Governor Roosevelt and Staff
Governor Walcott of Massachusetts
2nd Company Governor's Footguards, Conn.
1900 Governor Nash of Ohio
1903 Girard College Cadets Reviewed by Governor Hastings, at the Dedication of Stephen Girard's Monument
1905 Gov. Wm. L. Douglas, of Mass.
1909 The Governor's Daughter
1910 Foolshead Wishes to Marry the Governor's Daughter
The Governor's Daughter
The Governor's Pardon
Governor General of Canada
1902 Arrival of the Governor General, Lord Minto, at Quebec
1908 H. R. H. The Prince of Wales Decorating the Monument of Champlain and Receiving Addresses of Welcome from the Mayor of Quebec, the Governor General of Canada and Vice-President Fairbanks, Representative of the United States
Governors Island (New York)
1897 Ferryboat and Tug Passing Governors Island, New York Harbor
Outbound Vessel Passing Governors Island, N.Y. Harbor
13th Infantry, U.S. Army—Bayonet Exercise, Governors Island
13th Infantry, U.S. Army—Blanket Court Martial, Governors Island
13th Infantry, U.S. Army—Full Dress Parade and Manoeuvering, Governors Island
13th Infantry, U.S. Army—Full Dress Parade, Governors Island
13th Infantry, U.S. Army, in Heavy Marching Order, Double-Time, Governors Island
13th Infantry, U.S. Army—Manual of Arms, Governors Island
13th Infantry, U.S. Army—Marching and Counter Marching (Band and Troops), Governors Island
13th Infantry, U.S. Army Marching Through Sallyport, Governors Island
13th Infantry, U.S. Army—Musical Drill, Governors Island
13th Infantry, U.S. Army—Scaling Walls in Retreat, Governors Island
13th Infantry, U.S. Army—Scaling Walls with Wounded and Dying, Governors Island
1907 Governor's Island Taken U.S.N.
Governs
1906 The Heart Governs the Head
Gown
1903 Having Her Gown Fitted
1908 The Directoire Gown
Mrs. Pimpernell's Gown
The Sensational Sheath Gown
1909 The Lure of the Gown
1910 Her Mother's Wedding Gown
Grab
1910 The Indian Land Grab
Grace
1899 The Professor's Fall from Grace
1908 Willie's Fall from Grace
Grace Church (New York)
1897 Grace Church, New York
Grade
1899 Bridge No. 804, and Daly's Grade
Up the Big Grade in the Valley of the Kicking Horse
1905 Coaching Down the Merced Grade into Yosemite Valley
Coaching Down the Merced Grade, Merced Cañon, California
Graduate
1899 The Sweet Girl Graduate
1902 Graduating Day at West Point Military Academy
1904 Hyde Park School Graduating Class, Missouri Commission
Grady, Michael
1910 The Death of Michael Grady
Graf Waldersee (Steamship)
1899 "Graf Waldersee"
1901 Steamship "Graf Waldersee"
Graft
1906 Please Help the Blind; or, A Game of Graft
1907 The Grafter
Graham, Carlysle D.
1902 Carlysle D. Graham Swimming the Whirlpool Rapids
1903 C. D. Graham Swimming the Lower Rapids
Graham, John
1910 John Graham's Gold
Grand
1899 Grand Military Steeple-Chase
Grand National Steeple-Chase
Grand Trunk R.R. Bridge over Whirlpool
1900 Grand Palaces
1901 Grand Entry, Indian Congress
1903 Grand Entrance into the Hippodrome
The Grand Panorama from the Great Schreckhorn, 13,500 feet
Grand Review
1905 Inauguration of President Roosevelt. the Grand Inaugural Parade
1908 The Discoverers, a Grand Historical Pageant Picturing the Discovery and Founding of New France, Canada
H. R. H. The Prince of Wales Viewing the Grand Military Review on the Plains of Abraham, Quebec
1909 Grand Maneuvers
Grand Naval Parade
The Grand Procession at the King of Siam Jubilee
Grand Stag Hunting
Grand Army
1898 Grand Army Veterans of Chicago
Grand Army Veterans of New York
Grand Army Veterans of Philadelphia
Grand Canal (Venice, Italy)
1897 A Panoramic View in the Grand Canal
Panoramic View of Grand Canal
1903 The Grand Canal, Venice
On the Grand Canal, Venice
1908 The Grand Canal in Venice
1909 Grand Canal, Venice
Grand Canyon (Arizona)
1903 U.S. Interior Dept.: Panorama of Grand Canyon
1905 Capt. John Hance Telling About His 14th Wife, Grand Cañon, Arizona
Capt. John Hance Telling His Famous Fish Story, Grand Cañon, Arizona
Cavalcade Descending Trail into Grand Cañon of Arizona
Cavalcade on Trail into Grand Cañon of Arizona
Chinese Cook at Hance's Camp, Grand Cañon, Arizona
Stage Enroute to Hance's Camp, Grand Cañon of Arizona
1907 Grand Canyon of Arizona and the Cliff Dwellers
Grand Canyon (Colorado)
1903 The Canyon of the Grand
Grand Canyon, Yellowstone Park (Wyoming)
1899 Lower Falls, Grand Canyon, Yellowstone Park
Grand Central Station (New York City)
1910 Grand Central Power House Explosion
Grand Challenge Cup
1902 Third Trinity, Cambridge, Winning the Race for the Grand Challenge Cup. Taken at Henley on July 10th, 1902
Grand Charmoz
1903 Ascending a Rock-Chimney on the Grand Charmoz, 11,293 feet
Ascent and Descent of the Aiguilles Des Grandes Charmoz, 11,293 feet
Grand Commandery
1898 Grand Commandery of the State of New York
Grand Duke
1905 Assassination of the Grand Duke Serge
Grand Hotel
1906 Grand Hotel to Big Indian

Great Schreckhorn (Switzerland)
1903 The Grand Panorama from the Great Schreckhorn, 13,500 feet
Great Western Railway
1906 On Great Western Railway Ldongotten Station
On Great Western Railway Through Dawhistle
Greece
1904 Piraeus and Athens (Greece). A Visit to Piraeus
Piraeus and Athens (Greece). Athens and the Acropolis
Piraeus and Athens (Greece). Hoisting Cattle on Steamer
1906 The Olympic Games at Athens, Greece
1909 The Greek Slave's Passion
1910 In Ancient Greece
Greed
1904 Greedy Cat
The Little Greedy Beggar
1908 The Greed for Gold
Greediness Punished
The Greedy Girl
1910 Greediness Spoiled Foolshead's Christmas
Green
1909 Never Eat Green Apples
1910 Wearing of the Green
Green goods man
1905 The Green Goods Man; or, Josiah and Samanthy's Experience with the Original "American Confidence Game"
Green Island
1905 Railway Panorama Between Green Island and Kilroot
Green River (Utah)
1899 Toll Gate and Castle Rock near Green River
Greene, Farmer
1908 Farmer Greene's Summer Boarders
Greenhorn
1910 The Greenhorn and the Girl
The Greenhorns
Greeting
1903 Christian Endeavor Greeting
Old Maid's Morning Greeting
Grenadiers
1902 Dedication of the Alexander Grenadiers' Barracks
Gresham (Boat)
1901 Schooner "Idler" and Revenue Cutter "Gresham"
Gretel
1909 Hansel and Gretel
Grey
use **Gray**
Greyhound
1897 Ocean Greyhounds
1907 The Toilet of an Ocean Greyhound
Grief
1901 The Wages of Sin—A Mother's Grief
1908 The Nature Fakir Comes to Grief
Two Great Griefs
1909 The Hunter's Grief
A Mother's Grief
1910 A Father's Grief
A Mother's Grief
Grimaces
1907 Faces and Grimaces
Grimsol
1908 Grimsol, the Mischievous Goblin
Grin
1904 Grinning Guillot
1909 Grin and Win; or, Converted by a Billiken
Grindelwald (Switzerland)
1903 Panorama of Grindelwald
Grinder
1906 Hello! Hello! Grinder
Grip
1899 In the Grip of the Blizzard
1909 A Bad Case of Grip
Grip in the Family
1910 The Anarchistic Grip
In Winter's Grip
Grizzly
1901 Terrible Teddy, the Grizzly King
Grobler's Kloof, Battle of
1900 Bringing in the Wounded During the Battle of Grobler's Kloof

Grocer
1902 A Country Groceryman's Revenge
1904 Hold Up in a Country Grocery Store
1905 The Bad Boy and the Grocery Man
1908 The Grocer's Show
1909 Pierrot as a Grocer
Gronobia (Battleship)
1904 Panorama Russian Battleship "Gronobia"
Groom
1902 Departure of the Bride and Groom
1908 The Spiteful Groom
1909 A Bride and Groom's Visit to the New York Zoological Gardens
Grotesque
1908 Grotesques
1909 Grotesque Make-Up
Grotto
1903 The Apothicareric Grotto
1904 The Grotto of Surprises
1910 A Trip to the Blue Grotto, Capri, Italy
Grouch
1909 Jinks the Grouch
1910 Curing a Grouch
The Passing of a Grouch
Ground
1901 President Roosevelt Entering Grounds at Army-Navy Football Game
U.S. Proving Grounds, Sandy Hook
1903 Crowd Leaving Athletic Base Ball Grounds
On Forbidden Ground
1908 Jerusalem (En terre sainte.—Jérusalem)
1910 [Washington's Home and Ground at Mount Vernon]
Group
1896 Showing Group of Bathers, Atlantic City Beach
1903 Group of Mexicans
A Remarkable Group of Trained Animals
Groves
1898 California Orange Groves, Panoramic View
1903 Loading and Unloading the Chutes at Willow Grove
1905 Stages Passing Through Wawona Big Tree, Mariposa Grove, California
1908 Through an Orange Grove
Growing
1899 When Their Love Grew Cold
1908 The Effective Hair Grower
1909 The Orange Grower's Daughter
Orange Growing in Palestine
1910 Fruit Growing, Grand Valley, Colorado (The Results of Irrigation)
Growler
1898 "Rushing the Growler"
1900 The Growler Gang Catches a Tartar
1903 Rushing the "Growler"
Grub
1907 Work for Your Grub
Grub, Gabriel
1908 Gabriel Grub
Grumbler
1909 The Old Grumbler at the Magicians
Guantanamo (Cuba)
1898 Battle of Guantanomo [sic]
Rough Riders at Guantanamo
Guards
1897 The Coldstream Guards
The Daisy Guard
Guard Mount, Ft. Myer [Va.]
The Horse Guards
Washington Continental Guards
1898 Advance Guard, Return of N.J. Troops
Idle Hours of the English Coast Guards
Pope Leo XIII Attended by Guard
Pope Leo XIII Being Seated Bestowing Blessing Surrounded by Swiss Guards, No. 107
Pope Leo XIII Walking Before Kneeling Guards
Relieving the Guard at St. James Palace
The Vatican Guards, Rome
1899 Guardians of the Peace
Michigan Naval Reserves and the Detroit Light Guards
1902 The Continental Guards
German Garde Kurassiers
Miners at Work Under Guard of Troops
1903 A Guardian of the Peace
The King's Guardsmen
1904 Advance Guard Fight
A Regiment of the Japanese Imperial Guards and Engineer Corps off to the Front
Skirmish Between Russian and Japanese Advance Guards
1905 Troop of Horse Guards in St. James Park, London
1906 Phantom's Guard
1907 Native Hawaiian Guards in Bayonet Exercises, H.I.
1908 A French Guard's Bride
The Gallant Guardsman
1909 The Guardian of the Bank
The Guarding Angel
The Guard's Alarm
The Guilty Guardian
On Guard at the Powder Magazine
Tennessee Guards
1910 The Captain of the Guard
Competition of the Police and Guard Dogs
Servant and Guardian
Gudvangen (Norway)
1907 Sailing thro the Sognia Fjord on a Steamer from Ballholm to Gudvangen [Norway]
Guerrilla
1908 The Guerrilla
Guests
1897 Uninvited Guest
1903 Chinaman's Acrobatic Guests
The Impatient Guest
1904 Simple Simon's Surprise Party (Les invités de M. Latourte)
1906 Insolvable Guests
1908 An Unselfish Guest (?)
1909 A Guest's Predicament
An Unexpected Guest
An Uninvited Guest
1910 Hank and Lank: Uninvited Guests
Gueydon Fountain, Fort de France (Martinique)
1902 Native Women Washing Clothes at the Gueydon Fountain, Fort de France, Martinique
Gugusse
1906 Clown's Revenge (La revanche de Gugusse)
Guide
1904 Casting a Guide Box, Westinghouse Works
1908 The Lover's Guide
The Two Guides
1910 Honor of the Alpine Guide
The Rivalry of the Two Guides
The Swiss Guide
Guignol
1906 Punch and Judy (L'arnarchie chez Guignol)
Guild
1902 St. John's Guild. Bathing in Surf and Leaving Water
St. John's Guild. Crippled Children to and from Wagon
St. John's Guild. Dispensary Scene, Floating Hospital
St. John's Guild. Dock to Plank, 35th St.
St. John's Guild. Examination of Patients
St. John's Guild. From Launch to Dock
St. John's Guild. Going in Water.
St. John's Guild. Going to Salt-water Bath Room
St. John's Guild. Julliard and Tug in Narrows
St. John's Guild. Julliard Passing; Fire-Hose Playing
St. John's Guild. Launch Approaching Dock
St. John's Guild. Launch Delivering Patients to F. H.
St. John's Guild. Patients Down Bridge. S.S.H.
St. John's Guild. Plank to Deck, Floating Hospital
Guileless
1908 The Guileless Country Lassie
Guillot
1904 Grinning Guillot
Guilt
1908 The Guilty Conscience
Not Guilty
1909 The Guilty Guardian
Innocent, but Found Guilty
1910 Not Guilty
Guinness, Mrs.
1908 Mrs. Guinness, the Female Bluebeard
Guise (France)
1909 The Assassination of the Duke of Guise
1910 Catherine, Duchess of Guisa

Hard-shelled crabs
1903 A Catch of Hard Shell Crabs
Hardhearted
1910 Hard Heart
Hardworking
1909 Hard Working Elephants
Hardy, John
1910 John Hardy's Invention
Harem
1899 Dance in a Turkish Harem
An Intrigue in the Harem
Queen of the Harem
1900 Rescue from a Harem
1907 Englishman in Harem
1908 A Tale of a Harem: The Caliph and the Pirate
1909 Sultan Abdul Hamid, and the Ladies of His Harem
Harkaway, Jack
1910 The Childhood of Jack Harkaway
Harlem (New York City)
1898 Fun in a Harlem Flat
1901 The Finish of Michael Casey; or, Blasting Rocks in Harlem
1904 City Hall to Harlem in 15 Seconds, via the Subway Route
1908 Harlem Flats
Harlequin
1907 Harlequin's Story
1909 Harlequin's Nightmare
Harmless
1908 Harmless Lunatic's Escape
Harness
1897 Single Harness Horses
1899 High Steppers in Harness
Harp
1909 The Harp Player
Harper's Ferry (West Virginia)
1903 Harper's Ferry
Harrigan
1908 Harrigan
Harrington Rail Bonding System
1900 Demonstrating the Operation of the Harrington Rail Bonding System on the Line of the Coney Island and Brooklyn Railroad Co.
Harris Training Tower
1900 Harris Training Tower
Harrisburg
1907 Harrisburg
Harrisburg (Pennsylvania)
1897 Market Square, Harrisburg, Pa.
Harry
1908 Harry, the Country Postman
Harry Brothers
1910 The Harry Brothers
Harvard University, Cambridge (Massachusetts)
1897 Cornell-Yale-Harvard Boat-Race
Harvard Crew
1901 International Field Sports—Oxford-Cambridge vs. Harvard-Yale
1902 Prince Henry [of Prussia] Visiting Cambridge, Mass. and Harvard University
1903 Harvard-Pennsylvania Football Game
1904 Panorama of Harvard Class Day
1905 Kicking Football—Harvard
1906 Yale Harvard Boat Race, New London, Conn., 1906
1908 The Yale-Harvard Boat Race
Harvest
1897 Harvesting Corn
1903 Corn Harvesting
Crow Indians Harvesting
The Harvesters
Harvesting Scene
Wheat Harvesting Machines in Operation
1907 Harvest Celebration
1908 Harvesting
1909 Belle of the Harvest
1910 In the Golden Harvest Time
Haskell, Loney
1897 Facial Expressions by Loney Haskell
Haste
1909 The Hasty Tempered Father; or, The Blacksmith's Love
Marriage in Haste
Three Reasons for Haste
1910 A Hasty Operation
Judge Ye Not in Haste
Marriage in Haste
Married in Haste
Hastings, Governor
1898 Governor Hastings and Mounted Police
1903 Girard College Cadets Reviewed by Governor Hastings, at the Dedication of Stephen Girard's Monument
Hatchet
1901 Mrs. Nation & Her Hatchet Brigade
Hatching
1899 Eggs Hatching
Two Hours After Hatching
1903 Hatching Chickens Up-to-Date
Hate
1907 Hatred
1908 Kidnapped for Hate
Love and Hatred
Slave's Hate
1909 When Woman Hates
The Woman Hater
1910 The Men Hater's Club
A Victim of Hate
The Woman Hater
Hats
1897 Heads, Hats and Faces
Theatre Hat
Theatre Hats Off
Willie's Hat
1899 Reginald's First High Hat
1900 Clowns Spinning Hats
1902 The Absent Minded Clerk, Fly Paper and Silk Hat
The Magician and the Seven Hats
1903 The Minister's Hat
What Was Found in a High Hat
1904 A Crushed Hat
The Magic Hat
The Opera Hat
1905 He Got His Hat
Misadventures of a Hat
Wonderful Hat
1906 The Lost Hat: He Got It Alright
My Hat
1907 Man, Hat and Cocktail, a New Drink, but an Old Joke
Straw Hat Factory in Florence
Ups and Downs of a Hat
Whose Hat Is It?
1908 Buying a Hat
Enchanted Hat
Fashionable Hat
Gainsborough Hat
The Hat of Fortune
The Merry Widow Hat
The "Merry Widow" Hats
Silk Hats Ironed
A Tale of a Hat
Three Sportsmen and a Hat
Transformation with a Hat Rim
1909 Flossie's New Peach-Basket Hat
The Hat Juggler
Hat Making
The Haunted Hat
Manufacturing Bamboo Hats
Mrs. Jones' Lover; or, "I Want My Hat"
Papa's Hat
The Peachbasket Hat
Those Awful Hats
1910 Hawkins' Hat
Henry's New Hat
A New Hat for Nothing
Professor's Hat
A Tale of a Hat
The Valuable Hat
The Watchmaker's Hat
Hatzfeld, Princess
1909 Napoleon and Princess Hatzfeld
Haul
1897 Hauling a Scoop Net
1901 Hauling a Shad Net
A Large Haul of Fish
1903 Dog Teams Hauling Wood to Dawson City, Up the Yukon
Hauling Dirt Up an Incline
Team of Horses Hauling Wood to Dawson, Up the Yukon
1904 Hauling in a Big Catch
Hauling in Seines and Pulling Seines into Boat
Hauling in the Fish
1905 General Electric Engine Hauling Freight
1906 Hauling Sugar Cane, Kohala Plantation, Hawaii
Haunt
1899 The Haunted House
1900 Tramp in the Haunted House
1902 The Haunted Dining Room
The Haunted Pawnshop
1904 Haunted Scene Painter
1906 Haunted House
In the Haunts of Rip Van Winkle
1907 The Haunted Bedroom
The Haunted Hotel; or, The Strange Adventures of a Traveler
Haunted Kitchen
1908 Haunted Castle
1909 The Haunted Bridge
Haunted by the Cops
The Haunted Castle
The Haunted Hat
The Haunted Lounge
1910 Haunted by Conscience
Shooting in the Haunted Woods
Wild Birds in Their Haunts
Havana (Boat)
1899 The "Havana"
Havana (Cuba)
1898 The Battleship Maine in the Harbor of Havana
The Battleship Maine Leaving U.S. Harbor for Havana
The Christian Herald's Relief Station, Havana
Morro Castle, Havana Harbor
A Run of the Havana Fire Department
Spanish Volunteers in Havana
1899 General Lee's Procession, Havana
Troops at Evacuation of Havana
1903 Panorama of Morro Castle, Havana, Cuba
1909 Mardi Gras in Havana
1910 A Vacation in Havana
Haverstraw (New York)
1897 The Haverstraw Tunnel
1903 From Haverstraw to Newburg
Panoramic View of Haverstraw Tunnel, N.Y.
Hawaihae (Hawaii)
1907 Shipping Cattle, Hawaihae, Hawaiian Islands
Hawaii
1906 Arrival Mahukona Express, Kohala, Hawaii
Hauling Sugar Cane, Kohala Plantation, Hawaii
Hawaiians Arriving to Attend a Luau or Native Feast
Hawaiians Departing to Attend a Luau or Native Feast
S.S. "Kinau" Landing Passengers, Mahukona, Hawaii
Scenes in Hawaii
Shearing Sheep, Humunla Ranch, Hawaii
Sheep Coming Through Chute, Humunla Ranch, Hawaii
Washing Sheep, Humunla Beach, Hawaii
1907 Crowds Returning from the Games, Waikiki, H.I.
The "Float," Waikiki, Honolulu, Hawaiian Islands
Kanaka Fishermen Casting the Throw Net, Hilo, H.I.
Loading Sugar, Kahului, Maui, H.I.
Native Hawaiian Guards in Bayonet Exercises, H.I.
Pa-u Riders, Hawaiian Island
Panoramic View, Crater of Haleakala, H.I.
Panoramic View, Honolulu Harbor, H.I.
Panoramic View, King St. Honolulu, H.I.
Panoramic View, Oahu Railroad, Haleiwa, H.I.
Panoramic View, Oahu Railroad, Pearl Harbor, Hawaiian Islands
Panoramic View of Waikiki Beach, Honolulu, H.I.
Panoramic View, Waikiki, from an Electric Car, H.I.
S.S. "Kinau" Landing Passengers, Laupahoihoi, H.I.
Scenes on a Sugar Plantation, Hawaiian Islands
Shipping Cattle, Hawaihae, Hawaiian Islands
Snapshots, Hawaiian Islands
Surf Board Riders, Waikiki, Honolulu, H.I.
Surf Scene, Laupahoihoi, Hawaiian Island
Surf Scene, Waikiki, Honolulu, H.I.
Water Buffalo Wallowing, Hawaiian Island

Hawkins
1910 Hawkins' Hat
Hawkshaw
1909 Four Footed Hawkshaw
Hay
1897 Loading Hay
1903 The Hay Mower
1905 Getting the Hay
In an English Hayfield
1908 Fun in the Hay
1909 The Horse and the Haystack
Haymarket (Dance hall), New York City
1903 The Haymarket
Hayrick, Senator
1908 Hon. Senator Hayrick
Hayseed
1901 The Hayseed's Experience at Washington Monument
1908 The Hayseed's Bargain
Hazel
1910 Hazel, the Heart Breaker
Hazing
1899 Hazing a Freshman
Hazing Affair in a Girls' Boarding School
1908 The Hazers
A Lover's Hazing
1910 Hazing a New Scholar
Head
1897 Heads, Hats and Faces
1898 Chief Devery at Head of N.Y. Police Parade
1899 How Little Willie Put a Head on His Pa
1900 Four Heads Better Than One
1901 Coming Out of Scraping Machines and Cutting Off Heads
1902 The Chinese Conjurer and the Devil's Head
The Double Magician and the Magical Head
The Man with the Rubber Head
1903 The Mechanical Head
Passion Play: Herodias Pleads for John the Baptist's Head
1904 Tit for Tat; or, A Good Joke on My Head
1906 The Heart Governs the Head
Man with 36 Heads
1907 Where Is My Head
1908 Ancient Headgear
Bald Headed Actor and Fair Lady
A Heavy Head Piece
The Inquisitive Fly and the Bald Head
Looking for the Bald Heads
Man with Calf's Head
1909 Fantastic Heads
Story of a Calf's Head
Who Has Seen My Head?
1910 Old Heads and Young Hearts
Head-on collisions
1906 Head-On Collision at Brighton Beach Race Track, July 4th, 1906
1907 The Great Brighton Beach Head-On Locomotive Collision
Head over heels
1908 Head over Heels in Politics
Headache
1901 Such a Headache
Headdresses
1908 Head-Dresses Worn in Brittany
Headhunters
1905 Head Hunters of Borneo
Headquarters
1901 Headquarters, Staff and Band, Ohio State
Headway
1898 "Vizcaya" Under Full Headway
Healing
1903 Passion Play: Christ Healing the Sick
1910 The Healing Faith
Health
1908 For Kate's Health
1909 In Quest of Health
Heard
1908 Heard over the Phone
Heart
1901 The Heart of New York
1902 In the Heart of the Forest
1903 Every Day Is Sunshine When the Heart Beats True
1906 The Heart Governs the Head
In the Heart of the Catskills
1907 The Heart's Bidding
1908 The Broken Heart
Cupid's Realm; or, A Game of Hearts
The Dear Little Heart
Heart of a Gypsy Maid
The Heart of O Yama
A Noble Jester; or, Faint Heart Never Won Fair Lady
True Hearts Are More Than Coronets
Two Broken Hearts, the Story of a Worthless Husband and a Faithful Dog
The Voice of the Heart
The Zulu's Heart
1909 A Broken Heart
A Bruised Heart
The Call of the Heart
A Change of Heart
"Davy" Crockett in Hearts United
Game of Hearts
A Good Hearted Policeman
The Heart of a Clown
The Heart of a Cowboy
The Heart of a Mother
The Heart of a Race Tout
The Heart of an Outlaw
Heart of Genevieve
A Heart's Devotion
A Kind Hearted Tough
The Marble Heart; or, The Sculptor's Dream
A Mother's Heart
The Road to the Heart
The Roue's Heart
A Soldier's Heart
The Song That Reached Her Heart
Tender Hearts
Thelly's Heart
A Tramp Show Heart
A True Indian's Heart
A Woman's Heart
1910 The Ace of Hearts
An Affair of Hearts
A Black Heart
Brave Hearts; or, Saved from the Indians by a Woman's Wit
Brave Little Heart
The Call of the Heart
A Change of Heart
A Game of Hearts
Hazel, the Heart Breaker
The Heart of a Cowboy
The Heart of a Heathen Chinee
The Heart of a Rose
The Heart of a Sioux
The Heart of a Vagabond
The Heart of an Actress
The Heart of Edna Leslie
The Heart of Tessa
Hearts and Home
Hearts and Politics
Hearts Are Trump
Hearts of Gold
Hearts of the West
Human Hearts
Loving Hearts
The Man with the Weak Heart
A Mother's Heart
Old Heads and Young Hearts
The Queen of Hearts
The Song That Reached His Heart
Three Hearts
A True Country Heart
Who Will Win My Heart?
Heartbreaker
1910 Hazel, the Heart Breaker
Hearth
1909 The Cricket on the Hearth
Heartless
1909 A Heartless Mother
Heath
1905 Girls Dancing on Hampstead Heath
Heathen
1904 The Heathen Chinese and the Sunday School Teachers
1910 The Heart of a Heathen Chinee
Heating
1908 Heating Powder
Heaven
1903 The Heavenly Twins at Lunch
The Heavenly Twins at Odds
1909 A Sign from Heaven
Heaving
1898 Heaving the Log
1904 Coal Heavers
Heavy
1897 13th Infantry, U.S. Army, in Heavy Marching Order, Double-Time, Governors Island
1898 A Tug in a Heavy Sea
1899 First Heavy Artillery
Heavy Sea from Deck of "St. Louis"
Heavy Storm at Sea Taken from S.S. "St. Louis"
1901 Heavy Gymnastics
1902 A Heavy Surf at Atlantic City
The S.S. "Deutschland" in Heavy Sea
1903 The Forecastle of the "Kearsage" in a Heavy Sea
1904 A Heavy Sea
1905 A German Warship in a Heavy Sea
1906 A Heavy Sea
1908 A Heavy Head Piece
Heavy Seas
1909 A Heavy Gale at Biarritz
Heavyweight
1907 International Contest for the Heavyweight Championship: Squires vs. Burns, Ocean View, Cal., July 4th, 1907
1908 Heavyweight's Race
1909 Champion Heavyweight Lifter
World's Heavyweight Championship Pictures Between Tommy Burns and Jack Johnson
Hebrew
use **Jews**
Hector
1909 Hector, the Angel Child
Hector (Mountain), Alberta (Canada)
1901 Royal Train with Duke and Duchess of York, Climbing Mt. Hector
Hedge
1904 Hedge Jumping
Over the Hedge
Hedgehog
1908 Hedge Hog Coat
Heel
1908 Rubber Heels
1909 Spring Heeled Jack
Heidelberg (Germany)
1909 Old Heidelberg
Height
1908 Paris as Seen from a Height of 2600 Feet
Heikes, Rolla O.
1897 Champion Rolla O. Heikes, Breaking the Record at Flying Targets with Winchester Shotgun
Heinz
1901 Cutting Cucumbers and Cauliflower, Heinz
Packing Pickle Jars, Heinz
Heirs and heiresses
1900 How Charlie Lost the Heiress
1907 A Lucky Heiress
1908 Prospective Heirs
1909 The Bogus Heir
Disappointed Heirs
The Heir of Clavencourt Castle
The Lost Heiress
The Over-Eager Heirs
1910 The Case of the Missing Heir
The Hand of the Heiress
An Insane Heiress
The Recreation of an Heiress
Held
use **Hold**
Held, Anna
1901 Anna Held
Helen
1910 The Adoption of Helen
Aspirants to the Hand of Helen
Helen, Lady
1909 Lady Helen's Escapade
Helena (Montana)
1900 Overland Express Arriving at Helena, Mont.
Heliogabalus
1910 Vitellius and Heliogabalus
Hell
1903 The Damnation of Faust (Faust aux enfers)
Hell Gate (Colorado)
1902 Panoramic View of Hell Gate
Hell Gate, East River (New York City)
1902 Thro' Hell Gate
Hell's Kitchen
1900 A Wake in "Hell's Kitchen"
Heller
1902 A Private Supper at Heller's

1901 The High School Cadets
1902 Worcester High School Eight-Oared Boat Crews in Action
1904 Central High School, Calisthenics, Missouri Commission
High School Field Exercises, Missouri Commission
Modern High School Riding

High seas
1903 Cruelty on the High Seas
1906 High Sea Fishing
1907 Lighthouse Keepers (Gardiens de phare de haute-mer)

High-speed
1910 A High-Speed Biker

High steppers
1899 High Steppers in Harness
"Sampson" Champion High Stepper

High treason
1909 High Treason

Highbinders
1910 The Highbinders

Highland Fling
1897 The Highland Fling, by the Gordon Highlanders
1903 Miss Jessie Dogherty, Champion Female Highland Fling Dancer
Scotch Highland Fling

Highlander
1897 The Highland Fling, by the Gordon Highlanders
1900 British Highlanders Exercising
1902 48th Highlanders Regiment
1903 Troop Train Conveying the Seaforth Highlanders Across the Modder River
1905 Battalion of Seaforth Highlanders at the Dublin Horse Show
Squad of Seaforth Highlanders Leaving Bank of Ireland, Dublin
1910 The Highlander's Defiance

Highlands
1898 South Gate of the Highlands
1908 The Chieftain's Revenge; or, A Tragedy in the Highlands of Scotland

Highway
1901 An Oriental Highway
1904 A Burlesque Highway Robbery in "Gay Paree"
1905 Highway Robbery

Highwayman
1904 Highwaymen
1905 The Gentlemen Highwaymen
Motor Highwayman
1906 The Female Highwayman
The Lone Highwayman
1907 Highwaymen
1908 The Highwayman
1910 Modern Highwayman

Hilarious
1902 Foxy Grandpa and Polly in a Little Hilarity
1906 The Hilarious Posters

Hill
1897 Fort Hill Fire Station
1898 Battle of San Juan Hill
1899 Rifle Hill Signal Outpost
1900 The Census on Cherry Hill
Children Rolling Down Hill
Walnut Hill Cadets
1901 Indian Fort, Sherman Hill Tunnel
1902 Fun on a Sand Hill
The New Crowned King and Queen Passing Through Wellington Arch and Down Constitution Hill
1903 Girls Rolling Down Hill
Operation on the Famous Chechawko Hill
Sluice Mining on Gold Hill in the Klondike, Hutchinson and Johnstone's Claim of No. 6, Eldorado
1904 Turning Panorama from Hill, Westinghouse Works
1905 Last Attack on the Hill
1906 Panorama from Telegraph Hill
Panorama, Nob Hill and Ruins of Millionaire Residences
Panorama of Nob Hill
Panorama, Russian and Nob Hill from an Automobile
1908 Over the Hills to the Poor House
1909 Up San Juan Hill
1910 The House on the Hill
In the Black Hills
O'er Hill and Vale
A Romance of the Western Hills
Trailed to the Hills

Hilo (Hawaii)
1901 Steamboat Leaving for Hilo
1907 Kanaka Fishermen Casting the Throw Net, Hilo, H.I.

Himalayan
1903 Himalayan Bears from India

Hindoo
1902 The Hindoo Fakir
1903 Hindoo Street Scene
1908 A Hindoo's Ring
1909 The Hindoo Dagger
In the Land of the Hindoo
1910 The Hindoo's Treachery

Hippodrome (New York City)
1903 Grand Entrance into the Hippodrome
1905 Hippodrome Races, Dreamland, Coney Island
1907 Marceline, the World-Renowned Clown of the N.Y. Hippodrome

Hippopotamus
1899 Hippopotamus "Babe"
1903 Feeding the Hippopotamus
1909 Hunting the Hippopotamus

Hipwood-Barrett
1899 Hipwood-Barrett Car Fender

Hiram
1909 Hiram's Bride

Hire
1907 The New Hired Man
1908 Hired-Tired-Fired
The New Hired Girl
1909 Hiring a Girl
1910 Hiring a Gem
The Mulligans Hire Out

History
1900 An Historic Feat
Naval Apprentices at Sail Drill on Historic Ship "Constellation"
1902 The History of a Crime
1904 Charley's Aunt (Histoire grivoise racontée par une concierge)
1906 History of a Pair of Trousers
A Desperate Crime (Histoire d'un crime)
1908 The Discoverers, a Grand Historical Pageant Picturing the Discovery and Founding of New France, Canada
Historical Parade
Julius Caesar, an Historical Tragedy
1909 Historic Parade
Historical Fan
1910 The History of a Sardine Sandwich
History Repeats Itself
Love Amidst Historic Ruins

Hit
1897 "Has He Hit Me?"
1898 How Farmer Jones Made a Hit at Pleasure Bay

Hitch
1901 A Quick Hitch
1903 The Alarm and Hitch

Hoard
1907 The Miser's Hoard
1908 The Hidden Hoard
1910 The Golden Hoard

Hoax, Hemlock
1910 Hemlock Hoax, the Detective

Hobart, Garret Augustus
1897 Vice-President Hobart's Escort

Hobble
1910 The Hobble Skirt

Hobo
1907 An Awful Skate; or, the Hobo on Rollers
The Foxy Hoboes
A Hobo Hero
Robert Macaire and Bertrand; or, The Troubles of a Hobo and His Pal, in Paris
1908 Hobo on a Bike
Hobo's Dream
Hobo's Revenge
1909 Hobo's Dream
1910 Foxy Hobo Married for Love
Hoboes' Xmas
Hobo's Dream of Wealth
Only a Hobo

Hoboken (New Jersey)
1900 Burning of the Bremen and Main [Hoboken]
Burning of the Bremen and Main (Another view) [Hoboken]
Burning of the Saale [Hoboken]
Hoboken Fire
The Hoboken Holocaust
Panoramic View of Burning Wharves and Warehouses [Hoboken]
1902 The S.S. "Deutschland" Leaving Her Dock in Hoboken

Hobson, Richmond P.
1898 Hobson and Crew of the Merrimac
Naval Constructor Richmond P. Hobson
Naval Constructor Richmond P. Hobson and the Crew of the Merrimac

Hockey
1898 Hockey Match on the Ice
Hockey Match; Quebec
1901 Hockey Match on the Ice at Montreal, Canada

Hod carrier
1901 The Hod Carrier's Revenge
1902 The Hodcarriers' Ping Pong
1903 Bad Boy and Hod Carrier

Hoe
1906 Hoe Printing Press in Action

Hogan
1900 Trouble in Hogan's Alley

Hogs
1901 Beef, Sheep and Hog Killing
Driving Hogs to Slaughter
Hog Slaughtering. No. 6: Opening and Splitting
Hogs on the Rail
Scalding and Scraping Hogs
Sticking Hogs, (Front View)
1903 Feeding Hogs
1904 Trained Hogs

Hohenzollern (Germany)
1902 The Hohenzollern
The "Hohenzollern"
Panoramic View of the Hohenzollern

Hoisting
1898 Hoisting of the American Flag at Cavite
1904 Piraeus and Athens (Greece). Hoisting Cattle on Steamer

Hokey pokey man
1902 Newsboys and Hokey Pokey Man

Holbein
1904 Holbein Swimming the English Channel

Hold
1905 The Adventures of Sherlock Holmes; or, Held for a Ransom
1908 Held by Bandits
Held for Ransom
Our Village Club Holds a Marathon Race
1909 The Hold-Up Held Up
Holding Up the Wedding
1910 Jeffries-Johnson World's Championship Boxing Contest, Held at Reno, Nevada, July 4, 1910

Hold, Miss
1908 Miss Hold's Puppets

Holden, A. C.
1900 High Diving by A. C. Holden

Holdups
1901 A Hold-Up
A Legal Hold-Up
Stage Coach Hold-Up in the Days of '49
1903 The Hold Up
Stage Hold-Up
1904 Hold Up in a Country Grocery Store
Western Stage Coach Hold Up
1905 The Hold-Up of the Leadville Stage
1906 A Daring Hold-Up in Southern California
Hold-Up of the Rocky Mt. Express
1908 The Great Yellowstone Park Hold-Up
Hold-Up in Calabria
1909 An Amateur Hold-Up
The Hold-Up Held Up
1910 The Great Train Hold Up
Why Dad Was Held Up
Won by a Hold-Up

Hole
1903 Panorama of Kennicott Glacier Port Hole
1905 Blasting in the Glory Hole of the Treadwell Mine, Alaska
1906 The Old Swimming Hole
1910 The Ole Swimmin Hole

Holiday
1903 Panoramic View of Beyrouth, Syria, Showing Holiday Festivities
1904 The Dear Boys Home for the Holidays
Off for the Holidays
1906 The Holiday
1907 The Ghost Holiday
Going Away for Holiday

1908 Hon. Senator Hayrick
Hon. William J. Bryan and Hon. John W. Kern
1909 [Judge Gaynor and Hon. John H. McCooey]
Hood River Valley (Oregon)
1909 Through the Hood River Valley and Along the Columbia in Oregon
Hoodoo
1905 License No. 13; or, The Hoodoo Automobile
1908 The Hoodoo Lounge
1910 The Hoodoo
Hoodoo Alarm Clock
Hook
1907 Amateur Night; or, Get the Hook
Hooksett Falls (Massachusetts)
1899 Hooksett Falls Bridge
Hooligan
rt **Happy Hooligan**
1900 Hooligan Assists the Magician
1901 Happy Hooligan April-Fooled
Happy Hooligan Has Troubles with the Cook
Happy Hooligan Surprised
Hooligan and the Summer Girls
Hooligan at the Seashore
Hooligan Causes a Sensation
Hooligan Takes His Annual Bath
Hooligan Visits Central Park
Hooligan's Narrow Escape
1902 Happy Hooligan Turns Burglar
The Twentieth Century Tramp; or, Happy Hooligan and His Airship
1903 Happy Hooligan Earns His Dinner
Happy Hooligan in a Trap
Happy Hooligan Interferes
Happy Hooligan's Interrupted Lunch
Hooligan and Dogs (Journal Thumb Book)
Hooligan as a Safe Robber
Hooligan in Jail
Hooligan to the Rescue
Hooligan's Christmas Dream
Hooligan's Fourth of July
Hooligan's Roller Skates
Hooligan's Thanksgiving Dinner (Thumb Book)
Poor Hooligan, So Hungry Too!
1907 A Hooligan Idea
Hooligans of the Far West
1909 Hooligan Against His Will
Hoop
1904 The Hoop and the Lovers
The Magic Hoop
Hooray
1909 My Wife's Gone to the Country (Hooray! Hooray!)
Hoosier
1908 The Hoosier Fighter
Hop
1903 Hop Picking
Hope
1910 Blasted Hopes
Hope of the Village
Hope Webbing Company
1903 Noon Hour at Hope Webbing Company
Hopkins
1907 Tamer Hopkins
Hopkins Art Institute, San Francisco (California)
1906 Bird's Eye View from Hopkins Art Institute
Horgheim (Norway)
1905 Tourists Leaving Horgheim in the Romsdale Norway
Horn
1909 Cyclist's Horn
Magic French Horn
Hornpipe
1903 Sailor's Hornpipe
Horrible
1902 The Horrible Nightmare
1904 The Porter's Horrible End
1907 Horrible Adventure
Horrors
1908 The Patriot; or, The Horrors of War
Horse Shoe Falls, Niagara Falls (New York)
1904 Circular Panorama of the Horse Shoe Falls in Winter
Horsecar
1901 The Old Maid in the Horsecar
Horseflesh
1908 Result of Eating Horseflesh
Horseless
1897 Jumbo, Horseless Fire-Engine
1899 The Boston Horseless Fire Department
Horsemen
1902 Clever Horsemanship
1903 Indian Horsemanship
1904 Extraordinary Feats of Horsemanship
1909 Arabian Horsemen
Horseplay
1909 Winter Horseplay
Horses
1896 Buffalo Horse Market
1897 Cavalry Horses at Play
Fencing on Horseback
Horse Dancing Couchee Couchee
The Horse Guards
Horses Loading for Klondike
Ladies' Saddle Horses
O'Brien's Trained Horses
Single Harness Horses
Teams of Horses
1898 Cavalry Horses Fording a Stream in Santiago de Cuba
Elopement on Horseback
Loading Horses on Transport
9th U.S. Cavalry Watering Horses
Playing Horse
Race Between a Multicycle and a Horse
Trained Cavalry Horses
1899 The Boxing Horse
The Diving Horse
A High-school Horse
"King" and "Queen," the Great High Diving Horses
Judging Ladies' Saddle Horses
1900 Bryn Mawr Horse Show
A Somersault on Horseback
White Horse Rapids
1901 Horse Parade at the Pan-American Exposition
Horses Jumping Water Jump
Parade of Horses
Testing Horses
Training a Horse to Jump Hurdles
1902 The Bryn Mawr Horse Show
The Clown and His Burlesque Horse
Emperor William II on Horseback
Emperor William of Germany on Horseback
The Horse Market
Horse Racing in Germany
Horse Toboggan Slide
Kaiser Wilhelm and Emperor Franz Josef, and Prince Henry Riding Horseback
Peasant Children and Their Rocking Horse
1903 Bathing Horses
The Broncho Horse Race
Cake Walking Horses
Captain Allard Shooting White Horse Rapids
Changing Horses at Glen
Changing Horses at Linden
Horses Drawing in Seine
Horses Drawing Salmon Seine
Horses Swimming Copper River
Lord and Lady Minto with Party, Fording the Rushing Waters of the Klondike on Horseback
Navajo Indian Horse Race
On Horseback, Killarney
On the Bow River Horse Ranch at Cochrane, North West Territory
Panorama of Circus Train Unloading Horses
Panorama of White Horse Rapids
Patterson Children on Horseback, National Cash Register Co.
Police Charge on Horseback
Royal Horse Artillery on the March to the Front
Team of Horses Hauling Wood to Dawson, Up the Yukon
Through White Horse Rapids
U.S. Interior Dept.: Laguna Indian Horse Race
United States Mail Leaving Dawson City for White Horse
Watering Cavalry Horses
1904 Boxing Horses, Luna Park, Coney Island
Circular Panorama of the Horse Shoe Falls in Winter
Cruelty to Horses
Gate Jumping by Unsaddled Horse
Herding Horses Across a River
Horse Tied to a Post Jumping
Jumping Horses
Life of a Race Horse
Miss Lillian Shaffer and Her Dancing Horse
Push Ball on Horseback
Push Ball on Horseback, No. 2
Swimming Horses
1905 Battalion of Seaforth Highlanders at the Dublin Horse Show
Earl of Dudley and Party at the Dublin Horse Show
Fashionable Folks Leaving the Dublin Horse Show
High Jumping Horses—Sidney Holloway's Farm
Horse Fair at Randers, Denmark
The Horse-Thief
Horses Jumping over a Wall
Hunters Exercising, Dublin Horse Show
Hunters in Exercising Ring, Dublin Horse Show
Hunters Jumping, Dublin Horse Show
Irish Hunters Taking the Stone Wall, Dublin Horse Show
Jaunting Cars Arriving at Dublin Horse Show
Jumping by Irish Hunters, Dublin Horse Show
Lord Lieutenant of Ireland and Escort, Dublin Horse Show
Lucille Mulhall and Trick Horse
Roping and Branding Wild Horses
Troop of Horse Guards in St. James Park, London
1906 Horse Stealing
Obstacle Jumping by Attached Horses
Where Is My Horse?
1907 Croker's Horse Winning the Derby
A Horse of Another Color
The Horse That Ate the Baby
The Punishment of the Horse Thief
Winan's Horses
1908 The International Horse Show
The Runaway Horse
Transformation of a Horse
What a Funny Horse
1909 Clever Horse Hans
A Faithful Old Horse
Gendarme's Horses
The Horse and the Haystack
Horse to the Rescue
1910 Blue Horse Mine
Camel and Horse Racing in Egypt
The Color Sergeant's Horse
Fricot Drinks a Bottle of Horse Embrocation
The Horse Shoer's Girl
Married on Horseback
Mazeppa; or, The Wild Horse of Tartary
[The Richmond Horse Show]
Taming Wild Horses at Buenos Aires
Horseshoe
1908 A Lucky Horseshoe
1909 The Unlucky Horseshoe
1910 The Horseshoe
Horseshoe Curve (Pennsylvania)
1899 Panoramic View, Horseshoe Curve, From Penna. Ltd.
Panoramic View, Horseshoe Curve, Penna. R.R., No. 2
1904 Horse-Shoe Curve
Horseshoe Falls, Niagara Falls
1896 Horseshoe Falls—From Luna Isle
Horseshoe Falls from Table Rock, Canadian Side
1903 Horseshoe Falls from American Side
Horseshoe Falls, from Canadian Side
Mrs. Taylor Going over Horseshoe Falls in a Barrel
1906 Horseshoe Falls from American Side, Niagara Falls, N.Y.
Horseshoe Falls from Canadian Side Niagara Falls, N.Y.
Horsewhipping
1900 Horsewhipping an Editor
Horticultural
1898 Horticultural Floats, No. 9
1901 The Horticultural Building
Hose
1899 Demonstrating the Action of the Cliff-Guibert Hose Reel

1908 Human Vultures
Justinian's Human Torches
1909 The Human Ape; or, Darwin's Triumph
1910 Human Hearts
Human Squib
Kinematographic X-Ray Picture of a Human Stomach During Digestion, Taken During One Inspiration
The Jolly Whirl (Singeries humaines)

Humane
1899 The Humane Side of Modern Warfare

Humanity
1907 Discipline and Humanity
1908 Humanity Through Ages

Humble
1909 Humble Heroes

Humor
1906 Humorous Phases of Funny Faces
1907 Humors of Amateur Golf

Hump
1903 Double-Humped Camels
1910 The Hump's Secret

Humpty
1903 Humpty and the Demon
Humpty and the Dude
Humpty and the Piewoman
Humpty's Frolics
Humpty's Troubles with the Policeman
Humpty's Troubles with the Washwoman

Humpty Dumpty
1903 Arrival of Humpty Dumpty
Humpty Dumpty and the Baby
1908 Humpty-Dumpty Circus

Humunla (Hawaii)
1906 Humuula Sheep Ranch
Shearing Sheep, Humunla Ranch, Hawaii
Sheep Coming Through Chute, Humunla Ranch, Hawaii
Washing Sheep, Humunla Beach, Hawaii

Hunchback
1908 Hunchback Brings Luck
1909 Electrified Hunchback
The Hunchback
Love of a Hunchback
1910 Hugo, the Hunchback
The Hunchbacked Fiddler
The Betrothed's Secret (Il segreto del gobbo)

Hunchuses
1904 The Execution (Beheading) of One of the Hunchuses (Chinese Bandits) Outside the Walls of Mukden

Hundred
1910 City of the Hundred Mosques, Broussa, Asia Minor

Hundred dollar bill
1907 The Hundred Dollar Bill; or, The Tramp Couldn't Get It Changed

Hungary and Hungarians
1897 Charge of Hungarian Hussars
Home Life of a Hungarian Family
Hungarian Cavalry Charge
1898 Hungarian Women Plucking Geese
1909 Agriculture in Hungary
Hungary
Hunting Jack Rabbits in Hungary
Winter Sports in Hungary

Hunger
1903 The Hungry Countryman
Poor Hooligan, So Hungry Too!
1906 Ingenious Dauber (La faim justife les moyens)
1907 The Parson of Hungry Gulch; or, The Right Man in the Right Place May Work Wonders
1908 Driven by Hunger
Too Hungry to Eat
1909 The Hungry Actor
Hungry Hank's Hallucination

Hunker
1901 Washing Gold on 20 Above Hunker, Klondike

Hunting and hunters
1899 Going to the Hunt
High Hurdle Jumping, at Meadowbrook Hunt Club
The Meadowbrook Hunt
Schooling Hunters
1901 The Fox Hunt
1902 The Great Stag Hunt
The Weary Hunters and the Magician
1903 After the Hunt
The Devonshire Hunt
Hunting White Bear
The Stag Hunt
Stag Hunting in England
1904 A Boar Hunt
Deer Hunting in England
Duck Hunt
His First Hunting Day
Otter Hunt
1905 Head Hunters of Borneo
Hunters Exercising, Dublin Horse Show
Hunters in Exercising Ring, Dublin Horse Show
Hunters Jumping, Dublin Horse Show
Irish Hunters Taking the Stone Wall, Dublin Horse Show
Jumping by Irish Hunters, Dublin Horse Show
Starting on a Coyote Hunt
1906 Exmore Stag Hunt
The Fox-Hunt
Lion Hunt
Moose Hunt in Canada
Moose Hunt in New Brunswick
Snake Hunting
Turkey Hunt at Pinehurst
Whale Hunting
1907 The Amateur Hunter
Beaver Hunt
Buffalo Hunt
A Caribou Hunt
Deer Hunt
Great Lion Hunt
Hunters Dream
Hunting a Devil
Hunting Above the Clouds
Hunting in Canadian Woods
The New Stag Hunt
Polar Bear Hunt
1908 Bear Hunt in Canada
Bear Hunting in Russia
Crocodile Hunt
A Day in the Life of a Hunt
The Fortune Hunters
Fox Hunting
Hunting Deer
Hunting for Her Better Half
Hunting Teddy Bears
Lion Hunting
Man Hunt
The Near-Sighted Hunter
A Russian Bear Hunt
The Wolf Hunt
1909 Badger Hunt
Bear Hunt in Russia
The Crocodile Hunt
Elephant Hunting in Cambodge
An Exciting Hunt
Flat Hunting
The Fortune Hunters
The Fox Hunt
Grand Stag Hunting
Hunted to the End
The Hunter's Grief
Hunting Big Game in Africa
Hunting Jack Rabbits in Hungary
Hunting the Hippopotamus
Leopard Hunting in Abyssinia
The Love Hunter
Panther Hunting on the Isle of Java
Vulture Hunting in Africa
The Wolf Hunt
1910 Bear Hunt in the Rockies
Bear Hunting
A Chamois Hunt
Deer Hunting in Celebes Islands
The Egret Hunter
Fabian Hunting Rats
A Georgia Possum Hunt
His Hunting Trip
Hunting Adventure
Hunting Bats in Sumatra
Hunting Sea Lions in Tasmania
A Hunting Story
Hunting the Panther
The Polar Bear Hunt in the Arctic Seas
Russian Wolf Hunt
Seal and Walrus Hunting
A Stag Hunt in Java
The Treasure Hunters
Wild Duck Hunting on Reel Foot Lake

Hurdle
1896 Hurdle Race—High Jumpers
1897 Bareback Hurdle Jumping
Hurdle Jumping and Saddle Vaulting
Hurdle Race
Jumping Hurdles
Tandem Hurdle Jumping
Troopers Hurdling
1898 The Bathing Girls Hurdle Race
1899 Bear Jumping Hurdles
High Hurdle Jumping, at Meadowbrook Hunt Club
Hurdle Jumping
Hurdle Jumping; by Trained Dogs
International Collegiate Games—110 Yards Hurdle Race
Running the Hurdles
1901 Jumping Hurdles
Training a Horse to Jump Hurdles
1902 German Cavalry Leaping Hurdles
A Hurdle Race
1903 Sensational Hurdle Race
Vaulting in Saddle and Jumping Hurdle
1904 Hurdle Jumping

Hurdy-gurdy
1905 Kiddies Dancing to Hurdy-Gurdy Music, Soho, London

Hurlingham (England)
1899 Polo—Hurlingham vs. Ranelagh
1903 Polo Match for the Championship at Hurlingham
1905 Military Display at Hurlingham
1908 High Jumping at Hurlingham

Hurricane
1909 Hurricane of Lovers
1910 Trawler Fishing in a Hurricane

Hurry
1903 Hurry Up
1904 In a Hurry to Catch the Train
1907 Dressing in a Hurry
Mr. Hurry-Up
1908 Hurry Up, Please
1909 What's Your Hurry?

Hurst, Dr.
1904 Surgical Operation by Dr. Hurst

Hurt
1909 Hurt

Husband
1897 Waiting for Hubby
1900 How the Old Maid Got a Husband
They Led Her Husband Astray
1904 Belated Husband
Hubby to the Rescue
1905 A Henpecked Husband
Hubby Tries to Keep House
1906 Beware of My Husband
A Courageous Husband
The Henpecked Husband
Ten Wives for One Husband
Wanted: A Husband
1907 Artful Husband
A Good Husband
1908 Bothersome Husband
The Hapless Hubby
How Mabel Found a Husband
Hubby's Vacation
Husband Wanted
A Husband's Revenge; or, The Poisoned Pills
Jealous Husband
Lady Doctor's Husband
A Smoked Husband
Suspicious Husband
Troublesome Husband
Two Broken Hearts, the Story of a Worthless Husband and a Faithful Dog
1909 Choosing a Husband
Curing a Jealous Husband
The Fickle Husband
The Foxy Husband
The Henpecked Husband
Husband Goes to Market
Husband's Strategy
Husband's Vengeance
I Will Have a Husband
Jealous Hubby
A Jealous Husband
A Lucky Husband
Mrs. Minta's Husband
Present for Her Husband
Reforming a Husband
The Suffragist Wants a Husband
Taming a Husband
Wifey Away, Hubby at Play
1910 Her First Husband's Return
Her Husband's Deception
How Hubby Got a Raise
How Hubby Made Good
A Husband's Jealous Wife

Imperceptible
1904 The Imperceptible Transmutations
Imperfect
1910 Imperfect Perfectos
Imperial
1894 Imperial Japanese Dance
1904 A Regiment of the Japanese Imperial Guards and Engineer Corps off to the Front
Imperial Canal
1908 Imperial Canal
Imperial Limited
1899 The Imperial Limited
"Imperial Limited." Canadian Pacific R.R.
1900 A Hand Car and the Imperial Limited
The Imperial Limited
Imperial Limited
Impersonation
1899 Amann, the Great Impersonator
1905 Impersonation of Britt-Nelson Fight
Impersonation of the Fitzsimmons-O'Brien Fight
1906 Impersonation of Gans-Nelson Fight
1908 The Impersonator's Jokes
Importune
1909 Importune Neighbor
Impossible
1903 The Impossible Feat of Balancing
1904 The Impossible Dinner
Impossible to Get a Plunge
An Impossible Voyage
1906 The Impossible Convicts
1907 Biker Does the Impossible
Suicide Impossible
1908 Impossibilities
1909 Impossible to Get Sleep
Impostor
1910 The Impostor
Impracticable
1905 An Impracticable Journey
Impression
1898 Making an Impression
Impromptu
1898 An Impromptu Can-can at the Chorus Girls' Picnic
1900 An Impromptu Hairdresser
Improved
1902 Biograph's Improved Incubator
Improvised
1906 Improvised Suit
1908 Improvised Servant
The Improvised Statue
Imprudence
1910 Fatal Imprudence
Impudent
1904 That Impudent Flea
Impulse
1910 A Child's Impulse
Inauguration
1897 Bicyclers in Inaugural Parade
A Part of Inaugural Parade, Washington
Troop "A" in Inaugural Parade
1901 The Second Inauguration
1905 The Inauguration of President Roosevelt
Inauguration of President Roosevelt. Leaving the Capitol
Inauguration of President Roosevelt. President-Elect Roosevelt, Vice-President-Elect Fairbanks and Escort Going to the Capitol
Inauguration of President Roosevelt. Taking the Oath of Office
Inauguration of President Roosevelt. the Grand Inaugural Parade
President Roosevelt's Inauguration
1909 Inauguration of President William H. Taft
Inauguration of Taft
The Presidential Inauguration Film
Incendiary
1905 The Incendiary
1906 A Desperate Crime (Les incendiaires)
1908 Incendiary Foreman
Inch
1897 Projectile from Ten Inch Disappearing Gun Striking Water, Sandy Hook
Ten Inch Disappearing Carriage Gun Loading and Firing, Sandy Hook
1910 Within an Inch of His Life
Incident
1899 Pictures Incidental to Yacht Race
1901 Scenes and Incidents in the G.A.R. Encampment
1903 A Shocking Incident
1905 Scenes and Incidents, Russo-Japanese Peace Conference, Portsmouth, N.H.
1906 Scenes and Incidents U.S. Military Academy, West Point
1908 The Army of Two (An Incident During the American Revolution)
Incident from Don Quixote
The Last Cartridge, an Incident of the Sepoy Rebellion in India
1909 The Conspirators: An Incident of a South American Revolution
The Girl Spy: An Incident of the Civil War
The Web of Fate: An Incident of the French Revolution
Incinerating
1903 Sorting Refuse at Incinerating Plant, New York City
Incline
1896 American Falls—from Incline R.R.
1903 Hauling Dirt Up an Incline
Incompatibility
1908 Lonely Gentleman; or, Incompatibility of Temper
Inconstant
1910 The Inconstant
Inconvenience
1908 The Inconvenience of Taking Moving Pictures
Incriminating
1909 Incriminating Evidence
Incubator
1902 Biograph's Improved Incubator
The Wonderful Baby Incubator
1907 The Human Incubator
Independence
1909 A Hero of the Italian Independence
India
1902 Loading Cattle in India
1903 At the Ford, India. Across the Ravi River
Himalayan Bears from India
Pageant of East Indian Princes
Procession of Giant Elephants in India
The Royal Levee in India [The Delhi 'Durbar']
Traders of the East Indian Empire
Viceroy of India's Royal Levee
1904 Elephants at Work in India
1906 Life in India
Prince of Wales in India
Street in Agra, India
Trip Through India
1907 Elephants in India
India Rubberman
Life and Customs in India
Life in India
1908 The Last Cartridge, an Incident of the Sepoy Rebellion in India
1909 Great Flood in India, September, 1908
In India, Marriage of the Nephew of the Maharajah of Tagore
1910 Athletic Sports in India
Customs of the Buddhists in India
Scenes in British India
Women in India
India-Rubber
1902 The India-Rubber Man
Indiana
1900 Indiana Whitecaps
Indiana (Battleship)
1898 Battleship Indiana
Battleship "Indiana"
U.S. Battleship "Indiana"
1903 Battleship "Indiana" in Action
Inspection Aboard Battleship "Indiana"
Man Overboard! "INDIANA"
Raising Colors, Battleship "Indiana"
U.S. Battleship Indiana
Indians of North America
1897 Indian Club Jugglers
1898 Buck Dance, Ute Indians
Circle Dance, Ute Indians
Eagle Dance, Pueblo Indians
Indian Day School
Indian War Council
Procession of Mounted Indians and Cowboys
Serving Rations to the Indians, No. 1
Serving Rations to the Indians, No. 2
Wand Dance, Pueblo Indians
1901 The Assembly in the Indian Village
Band and Battalion of the U.S. Indian School
Club Swinging, Carlisle Indian School
Grand Entry, Indian Congress
The Indian Congress
Indian Fort, Sherman Hill Tunnel
Indians No. 1
Moki Snake Dance by Walpapi Indians
1902 A Dance by Kanaka Indians
Indians No. 2
1903 Crow Indian Festival Dance
Crow Indian War Dance
Crow Indians Harvesting
Fire Drill: Albuquerque Indian School
Indian Boys, Albuquerque School
Indian Fire Dance
Indian Hideous Dance
Indian Horsemanship
Indian Parade
Indian War Dance
Indians
Indians Charging on the Photographer
Indians Leaving Bald Mountain
Moqui Indian Rain Dance
Navajo Indian Foot Race
Navajo Indian Horse Race
Navajo Indian Tug-of-War
Navajo Indians Wrestling
The Peel River Indians with Their Dog Teams and Toboggan Sleighs on the Trail
Rescue of Child from Indians
Shoshone Indians in Scalp Dance
U.S. Interior Dept.: Basket Ball, Indian School
U.S. Interior Dept.: Laguna Indian Chicken-Pulling Race
U.S. Interior Dept.: Laguna Indian Foot Race
U.S. Interior Dept.: Laguna Indian Horse Race
Ute Indian Snake Dance
1904 Brush Between Cowboys and Indians
Convention of Red Men, Lancaster, Pa.
Cowboys and Indians Fording River in a Wagon
Indians and Cowboys
1905 Indian Babies' Bath
Indian Pony Races, Yosemite Valley, California
1906 Grand Hotel to Big Indian
Indian's Revenge
The Indian's Revenge; or, Osceola, the Last of the Seminoles
1907 Cowboys and Red-skins
Indian Basket Weavers
Indian Customs
Indian Idyll
The Indian's Friendship
The Red Man's Way
1908 Gathering Indian Figs
Indian Bitters; or, The Patent Medicine Man
An Indian Love Story
The Indian Sorcerer
The Indian's Gratitude
An Indian's Honor
Justice of the Redskin
Red Cloud, the Indian Gambler
The Red Girl
A Red Man's Justice
Red Man's Revenge
The Redman and the Child
The Umatilla Indians
1909 The Indian
Indian Basket Making
The Indian Phantasy
The Indian Runner's Romance
The Indian Trailer
An Indian Wife's Devotion
Indians and Cowboys
An Indian's Bride
Johnny and the Indians
The Life of a Red Man
The Loyal Indian
Mogg Megone, an Indian Romance
My Friend, the Indian
Onawanda; or, An Indian's Devotion
The Red Man
A Red Man's Love
The Redman's View
A True Indian's Heart
Wep-Ton-No-Mah, the Indian Mail Carrier
The Wooden Indian
1910 Attacked by Arapahoes; or, The Gold Seekers and the Indians

Brave Hearts; or, Saved from the Indians by a Woman's Wit
Cowboy and Indian Frontier Celebration
A Deal in Indians
Elder Alden's Indian Ward
Glimpses of an Indian Village
Her Indian Mother
His Indian Bride
The Indian and the Cowgirl
The Indian and the Maid
Indian Blood
An Indian Chief's Generosity
An Indian Girl's Love
The Indian Girl's Romance
The Indian Land Grab
An Indian Maiden's Choice
Indian Pete's Gratitude
The Indian Princess
The Indian Raiders
The Indian Scout's Vengeance
Indian Squaw's Sacrifice
An Indian's Elopement
An Indian's Gratitude
An Indian's Test
Jim Bridger's Indian Bride
Lo, the Poor Indian
O! That Indian
The Red Girl and the Child
A Red Girl's Friendship
Red Girl's Romance
The Red Man's Honor
A Redman's Devotion
The Redmen's Persecution
Romantic Redskins
Saved by an Indian
Saved from the Redmen
Stolen by Indians
The Trapper and the Redskins
A True Indian Brave
The Way of the Red Man
White Man's Money, the Indian Curse

Indians of South America
1909 South American Indians
1910 The Chuncho Indians of the Amazon River, Peru

Indians—Mixed blood
1908 The Half Breed
1909 Half Breed's Treachery
1910 The Dumb Half Breed's Defence
The Seminole Halfbreeds

Indiscretion
1906 The Indiscreet Bathroom Maid
Indiscreet Mystified
1908 Indiscreetness of the Kinematograph
1909 Indiscreet Father and Son
Indiscretion of Moving Picture
1910 The Indiscretion of Betty

Industry
1901 Industrial Floats
Industrial Parade of the Cincinnati Fall Festival
1906 Marble Industry at Carrara
1907 The Fishing Industry
The Oyster Industry
Wood Industry in Canada
Wood Industry in Norway
Fan in Japan (Industrie des éventails au Japon)
1908 Champagne Industry
Cider Industry
Cocoa Industry, Trinidad, British West Indies
The Codfish Industry
Coke Industry
The Cotton Industry of the South
Industrial Parade
Madeira Wicker Chair Industry
Porcelain Industry
Portland Stone Industry
Steel Industry
Stone Industry in Sweden
The Sugar Industry
Wood Floating and Pulp Industry
1909 Earthenware Industry
Fishing Industry
Fishing Industry at Gloucester, Mass.
The Honey Industry
Rosin Industry
Snake Skin Industry
Tunisian Industries
1910 Industries in Southern California
The Leather Industry
The Milk Industry in the Alps
The Sisal Industry in the Bahamas

Inexhaustible
1901 The Inexhaustible Cab
1902 The Inexhaustible Wardrobe
1907 Inexhaustible Barrel

Inexperienced
1906 The Inexperienced Chauffeur
1909 Inexperienced Angler

Infant
1904 Scenes in an Infant Orphan Asylum
1907 Infants at Breakfast
1909 Infant Terrible

Infantry
1897 13th Infantry, U.S. Army—Bayonet Exercise, Governors Island
13th Infantry, U.S. Army—Blanket Court Martial, Governors Island
13th Infantry, U.S. Army—Full Dress Parade and Manoeuvering, Governors Island
13th Infantry, U.S. Army—Full Dress Parade, Governors Island
13th Infantry, U.S. Army, in Heavy Marching Order, Double-Time, Governors Island
13th Infantry, U.S. Army—Manual of Arms, Governors Island
13th Infantry, U.S. Army—Marching and Counter Marching (Band and Troops), Governors Island
13th Infantry, U.S. Army Marching Through Sallyport, Governors Island
13th Infantry, U.S. Army—Musical Drill, Governors Island
13th Infantry, U.S. Army—Scaling Walls in Retreat, Governors Island
13th Infantry, U.S. Army—Scaling Walls with Wounded and Dying, Governors Island
1898 14th U.S. Infantry Drilling at the Presidio
Fourth Infantry, U.S. Regulars
Infantry Charge
9th and 13th U.S. Infantry at Battalion Drill
9th Infantry Boys' Morning Wash
101st Regiment, French Infantry
Spanish Infantry Attacking American Soldiers in Camp
10th U.S. Infantry Disembarking from Cars
10th U.S. Infantry, 2nd Battalion Leaving Cars
Thirteenth Infantry, U.S. Regulars
Twenty-Fourth Infantry
1899 43rd Rifles; Royal Canadian Infantry
2nd Special Service Battalion, Canadian Infantry, Embarking for So. Africa
2nd Special Service Battalion, Canadian Infantry-Parade
33rd Infantry, U.S.A.
U.S. Infantry Supported by Rough Riders at El Caney
1900 British Infantry Marching to Battle
15th Infantry
The 17th Infantry, U.S.A.
25th Infantry
1901 Japanese Infantry on the March
The 9th Infantry, U.S.A.
The War in China—Japanese Infantry
1903 Battle Flags of the 9th U.S. Infantry
1904 Japanese Infantry Morning Drill
Russian Infantry
Russian Infantry, Warsaw

Infernal
1899 The Infernal Palace
1903 The Cake Walk Infernal
The Infernal Caldron
The Infernal Meal
1906 Infernal Cave
The Mysterious Retort (L'alchimiste Parafaragamus ou la cornue infernale)
1907 The Bewildering Cabinet (Le placard infernal)
1909 The Infernal Machine
Infernal Salamandre

Infusorian
1905 Fresh Water Infusorian

Ingenious
1905 Love Is Ingenious
1906 Ingenious Dauber
1907 The Mechanical Statue and the Ingenious Servant
1908 Love Is Ingenious
The Suburbanite's Ingenious Alarm

Ingenuity
1908 Ingenuity Conquers

Ingomar
1908 The Barbarian Ingomar
Ingomar, the Barbarian

Ingratitude
1908 The Ingrate
1909 Ingratitude
1910 Ingratitude; or, The Justice of Providence

Inheritance
1908 Artist's Inheritance
My Laundress Inherits
The Old Maid's Inheritance
Strange Inheritance
1909 The Inheritance of Baptiste Durand
The Stolen Inheritance
1910 A Race for Inheritance

Initiation
1904 "Pollywogs" 71st Regiment, N.G.S.N.Y., Initiating Raw Recruits
1909 Finnigan's Initiation

Injector
1909 Prof. Wise's Brain Serum Injector

Injury
1904 First Aid to the Injured
1909 Vaccination Against Injuries

Ink
1904 A Drop of Ink
1910 New Style Inkwell

Inn
1899 The Enchanted Inn
1903 The Inn Where No Man Rests
1906 A Road Side Inn
1907 Drama in a Spanish Inn
Innkeeper and Wife
The Innkeeper's Wife
1908 The Inn of Death, an Adventure in the Pyrenees Mountains
The Innkeeper's Remorse
Outside Inn
A Peaceful Inn
1909 The Red Star Inn
1910 The Blue Swan Inn
Innkeeper's Daughter

Innocence
1898 An Innocent Victim
1903 An Innocent Conspirator
Passion Play: Massacre of the Innocents
1905 Innocent Flirtation
1908 Circumstantial Evidence, or, An Innocent Victim
1909 Innocence
Innocent, but Found Guilty
The Innocent Bystander

Innsbruck (Austria)
1905 Reverse Panorama, Maria Theresian Strasse, Innsbruck
Tyrolese Dance, Innsbruck
Tyrolese Dancers Innsbruck

Inquisition
1900 Spanish Inquisition
1904 A Miracle Under the Inquisition
1906 Martyrs of the Inquisition

Inquisitive
1898 The Inquisitive Girls
1900 The Inquisitive Clerks
1902 What Happened to the Inquisitive Janitor
1903 Inquisitive Models
1907 The Inquisitive Boy; or, Uncle's Present
An Inquisitive Girl
Mr. Inquisitive
1908 The Inquisitive Fly and the Bald Head
1909 Mr. Inquisitive

Insane
1908 The Mad Musician [An Escape from an Insane Asylum]
1910 An Insane Heiress

Insidious
1910 Insidious Weapons

Insoles
1910 Electric Insoles

Insolvable
1906 Insolvable Guests

Insomnia
1910 A Sufferer of Insomnia

Inspection
1898 President McKinley's Inspection of Camp Wikoff
1900 A Military Inspection
1901 Canned Meat Department. No. 2: Inspecting
1902 Kaiser Wilhelm Inspecting His Soldiers

1903 Inspection Aboard Battleship "Indiana"
Smith's Wife Inspects the New Typewriter
1904 Bag Inspection
Inspector's Birthday
1906 Captain's Inspection
1907 Hypnotized Police Inspector
1910 The Lamp-Post Inspector

Inspiration
1909 An Inspiring Sunset
1910 An Artist's Inspiration
Kinematographic X-Ray Picture of a Human Stomach During Digestion, Taken During One Inspiration

Installation
1902 Installation Ceremonies, Columbia University
Installation Ceremonies of President Butler

Installment
1900 How the Magician Got the Best of the Installment Man
1906 Shaving by Installments
1908 The Installment Collector

Instantaneous
1909 Instantaneous Nerve Powder

Instigator
1910 Strike Instigator

Instinct
1910 A Dog's Instinct

Institute
1906 Bird's Eye View from Hopkins Art Institute

Instruction
1903 Fife Getting Instructions from Committee
1909 Instruction by Correspondence
Sealed Instructions
1910 Wanted: An Athletic Instructor

Insurance
1900 Insured Against Loss
1903 The Insurance Collector
1904 That Poor Insurance Man
1905 N.Y. Life Insurance Co. Pres. McCall & Officers
1906 The Insurance Solicitor; or, A Story of a Blasted Ambition
1908 Levitsky's Insurance Policy; or, When Thief Meets Thief
1909 The Persevering Insurance Agent

Insurgents
1898 Shooting Captured Insurgents
1900 A Charge of the Insurgents

Intelligent
1904 An Intelligent Elephant

Intercollegiate
1897 Observation Train at the Inter-Collegiate Boat-Races
1904 Inter-Collegiate Athletic Association Championships, 1904
Inter-Collegiate Regatta, Poughkeepsie, N.Y., 1904
1905 Intercollegiate Cross Country Run

Interest
1897 Interesting Parlor Scene
1904 Intresting Story
1907 Interesting Reading
1908 An Interesting Conversation
1909 A Day in Washington, the Capital of the United States, Showing Many Points of Interest
1910 Repaid with Interest

Interfere
1903 Happy Hooligan Interferes
Never Interfere in Family Troubles
1907 Unlucky Interference

Interior
1899 Interior Coney Island Club House, No. 1-4
1901 Interior of Armour's Power House
1905 Interior N.Y. Subway, 14th St. to 42nd St.
1908 An Interior Cyclone

Interior Dept.
use **United States. Interior Dept.**

Intermingled
1909 Sweet Dreams Intermingled with Nightmares

Intermittent
1908 The Intermittent Alarm Clock

Internal
1903 Transporting Internal Rev. Stamps, U.S.P.O.

International
1899 The International Alliance
International Collegiate Games
The International Collegiate Games
International Collegiate Games
International Collegiate Games—Half Mile Run
International Collegiate Games—110 Yards Hurdle Race
International Collegiate Games—100 Yards Dash
1901 International Field Sports
International Field Sports—Oxford-Cambridge vs. Harvard-Yale
International Track Athletic Meeting—Start and Finish of the One Mile Run
International Yacht Races—Columbia vs. Shamrock
International Yacht Races on the Clyde
1904 The Great International Automobile Race for the Gordon-Bennett Trophy
The International Congress of the Salvation Army
International Winter Sports
The International Yacht Race
1906 Cross Country (Great international cross-country)
1907 International Balloon Races [from the James Gordon Bennett Cup, at St. Louis, Oct. 21, 1907]
International Contest for the Heavyweight Championship: Squires vs. Burns, Ocean View, Cal., July 4th, 1907
Jamestown Exposition International Naval Review, Hampton Roads, Virginia
Panorama, Crowds at Squires-Burns International Contest, from Center of Ring, Colma, July 4th, 1907
Panorama, Crowds at Squires-Burns International Contest, from Moving Picture Stand, July 4th, 1907
1908 The International Horse Show
International Illusionist
1910 The International Motor Boat Races
The Renowned International Aviation Meet

Interrupted
1897 How a Rat Interrupted an Afternoon Tea
1898 An Interrupted Breakfast
An Interrupted Kiss
An Interrupted Sitting
1899 An Interrupted Crap Game
Jones' Interrupted Sleighride
1900 Interrupted Lover
1901 Tramp's Nap Interrupted
1902 The Dutchman's Interrupted Dinner
The Interrupted Bathers
The Interrupted Picnic
1903 Happy Hooligan's Interrupted Lunch
Interrupted Crap Game
Lovers Interrupted
Lovers Interrupted. New
Policeman's Interrupted Vision
1904 The Interrupted Couple
An Interrupted Flirtation
1907 Interrupted Card Party
Interrupted Outing
1908 The Interrupted Bath
Interrupted Romance
1909 The Interrupted Jollification
The Interrupted Joy Ride
Interrupted Rendezvous
1910 An Interrupted Courtship
An Interrupted Honeymoon

Intervals
1897 Charge, Through Intervals of Skirmishes

Interview
1900 Jones Interviews His Wife
1909 Five Minutes Interview

Intrigue
1899 An Intrigue in the Harem
1909 A Woman's Intrigue

Introduction
1903 Introduction of the Rough Riders of the World

Intruder
1904 Midnight Intruder
1905 The Intruders
1909 The Intruder

Invading
1900 Wifie Invades the Studio
1909 The Invaders
The Japanese Invasion
1910 Estrellita; or, The Invasion of the French Troops in Portugal

Invalid
1907 Invalid's Adventure

Inventions and inventors
1903 What Befell the Inventor's Visitor
1906 The Inventor Crazybrains and His Wonderful Airship
1907 Liquid Electricity; or, The Inventor's Galvanic Fluid
1908 Inventor's Son's Downfall
Professor Bric-a-Brac's Inventions
1909 A Criminal Invention
Dr. Wright's Invention
Galileo, Inventor of the Pendulum
Inventions of an Idiot
Necessity Is the Mother of Invention
Tommy's Own Invention
1910 A Curious Invention
Getting Square with the Inventor
Inventive Trouser
The Inventor's Model
John Hardy's Invention
Necessity Is the Mother of Invention
The Stolen Invention
The Village Inventor

Invincible
1898 Colored Invincibles
1910 The Invincible Sword

Invisible
1904 The Invisible Sylvia
1906 The Invisible Man
1908 The Button of Invisibility
The Invisible Fluid
The Invisible Men
1909 Invisibility
The Invisible Thief
1910 The Invisible Dog

Invitation
1909 Inviting His Boss for Dinner
The Lost Invitation
Novel Invitation

Iona
1909 Iona, the White Squaw

Iowa (Battleship)
1897 Battleships "Maine" and "Iowa"
1898 Battleship Iowa
Battleship "Iowa"
U.S. Battleship "Iowa"

Irascible
1906 Irascible Fisherman

Irate
1903 The Irate Model

Ireland and the Irish
1898 Irish Volunteers
1900 Irish Way of Discussing Politics
Queen Victoria's Last Visit to Ireland
1901 How the Dutch Beat the Irish
1903 Coaching in Ireland
Dutch and Irish Politics
Irish Couple Dancing Breakdown
Irish Peasants Bringing Their Milk to a Cooperative Creamery
Irish Reel
King Edward's Visit to Ireland
Levi & Cohen, The Irish Comedians
The Mono-Railway Between Listowel and Ballybunion, Ireland
Scenes in an Irish Bacon Factory
Scenes in an Irish Market Place
Scenes of Irish Cottage Life
1904 Automobile Race at Ballyshannon, Ireland
1905 Battery of Artillery Crossing Ball's Bridge, Limerick, Ireland
Irish Constabulary, Keel, Achill Island, Ireland
Irish Hunters Taking the Stone Wall, Dublin Horse Show
An Irish Jig at Dooagh, Achill Island, Ireland
Irish Kiddies Coming out of School, Achill Island
Jumping by Irish Hunters, Dublin Horse Show
Lord Lieutenant of Ireland and Escort, Dublin Horse Show
Market Women Leaving the Railway Station at Galway, Ireland
Old Spinning Wheel, Dooagh, Achill Island, Ireland
Passing Train, Balleybunion Railway, Ireland
Passing Train, Balleybunion Railway, Ireland No. 2
Passing Train (from Above) Balleybunion Railway, Ireland

1906 Trip Through Italy
1907 The Bandits; or, A Story of Sunny Italy
1908 The Lake of Garda, Italy
Overflowing in Italy
The Poisoned Bouquet, an Italian Tragedy of the XV Century
Romeo and Juliet, a Romantic Story of the Ancient Feud Between the Italian Houses of Montague and Capulet
Soldiers in the Italian Alps
The Wages of Sin, an Italian Tragedy
1909 The Detectives of the Italian Bureau
Funeral of Joe Petrosino: The American Detective in Merino, Italy
A Hero of the Italian Independence
In Little Italy
Italian Artillery
Italian Cavalry Maneuvers
An Italian Love Story
Logging in the Italian Alps
Pontine Marshes, Italy
Romantic Italy
Ski Runners of the Italian Army
1910 Italian Artillery
The Italian Sherlock Holmes
[Lake Garda, Northern Italy]
Launching the First Italian Dreadnought
Over the Appennines of Italy
Picturesque Waters of Italy
Some Riding Exercises of the Italian Cavalry
A Trip to the Blue Grotto, Capri, Italy
Tunny Fishing off Palermo, Italy

Itching
1908 The Diabolical Itching
1910 Fricot's Itching Powder

Items
1908 Current News Items

Ithaca (New York)
1901 'Varsity Crew Race on Cayuga Lake, on Decoration Day, Lehigh Valley Observation Train Following the Race, Showing Cornell Crew Finishing First, Columbia Second, University of Pennsylvania Third Ithaca, N.Y., Showing Lehigh Valley Observation Train

Ito
1910 Ito, the Beggar Boy

Jack
1898 "Me and Jack"
1899 Jack Tars Ashore
1902 Jack and the Beanstalk
1903 The House That Jack Built
Jack and Jill
Jack and Jim
Jack Jaggs & Dum Dum
Jack's Four Footed Friend. Mike the Ship's Mascot
Jack's Return
One of Jack's Games Aboard a Man o' War
1904 Mr. Jack Entertains in His Office
Mr. Jack Is Caught in the Dressing Room
Mr. Jack Visits the Dressing Room
1905 Jack and Jill
1906 Jack the Bootblack
Chimney Sweep (Jack le ramoneur)
1907 Jack the Kisser
1908 Ice Cream Jack
Jack in Letter Box
Jack of All Trades
1909 The House That Jack Built
How Happy Jack Got a Meal
How Jack Helped His Little Sister
Hunting Jack Rabbits in Hungary
Jack Has No Clothes
Jack's Birthday
Jack's Successful Bluff
Spring Heeled Jack
Three Fingered Jack
When Jack Gets His Pay
1910 Happy Jack, a Hero
How Jack Won His Bride
Jack Fat and Jim Slim at Coney Island
Jack's Return
Little Jack's Letter
Three Queens and a Jack

Jack the Ripper
1909 Berlin Jack the Ripper

Jackies
1904 Japanese Jackies

Jacks
1903 Testing Jacks, National Cash Register Co.

Jackson
1909 Jackson's Last Steeple Chase

Jacksonville (Florida)
1906 A Trip to Jacksonville, Fla.

Jacob's ladder
1899 Climbing Jacob's Ladder

Jaffa (Israel)
1903 Street Scene at Jaffa
Tourists Embarking at Jaffa
1904 A Trip to Palestine. Jaffa and Its Harbor

Jag
1907 Mags Jag

Jaggs, Jack
1903 Jack Jaggs & Dum Dum

Jail
1903 Hooligan in Jail
1906 The Jail Bird and How He Flew, a Farce Comedy Escape
1910 The Longing for Gaol

Jamaica
1903 Railroad Panorama near Spanishtown, Jamaica
1907 Jamaica Negroes Doing a Two-Step

James
1904 Pedestrian Jugglers (Miss Anna et James)
1909 James and Catherine; or, Love on a Farm

James boys
1908 James Boys in Missouri

James Gordon Bennett Cup
1907 International Balloon Races [from the James Gordon Bennett Cup, at St. Louis, Oct. 21, 1907]

James Street, Seattle (Washington)
1903 James Street, Seattle, Wash.

Jameson
1908 Orderly Jameson

Jamestown (Virginia)
1907 Colonial Virginia and Burning of Jamestown
Jamestown Exposition
Jamestown Exposition International Naval Review, Hampton Roads, Virginia
Jamestown Naval Review

Jammer-bach
1909 Jammer-bach

Jane
1907 Jane Is Furious
1909 Jane Is Unwilling to Work
Persistent Jane
1910 Jane and the Stranger
Jane of Montressor
Poetical Jane
The Taming of Jane

Jane, Aunt
1900 Aunt Jane's Experience with Tabasco Sauce
1902 Aunt Jane and the Tobasco Sauce
1903 Aunt Jane's First Lesson in Love

Jane, Lady
1908 Lady Jane's Flight, a 17th Century Romance

Janitor
1902 What Happened to the Inquisitive Janitor
1907 Janitor's Tea Party
1908 The Janitor Falsely Accused
On Bad Terms with the Janitor
1909 The Janitor's Bottle

January
1894 Edison Kinetoscopic Record of a Sneeze, January 7, 1894

Japan and the Japanese
1894 Imperial Japanese Dance
1897 Japanese Rope Walker
Japanese Village
1898 Japanese Sampans
Launch of Japanese Man-of-War "Chitosa"
1901 Coaling a Steamer, Nagasaki Bay, Japan
Fair Japan—Pan-American Exposition
In a Japanese Tattooing Parlor
Japanese Artillery
Japanese Fencing
Japanese Infantry on the March
A Japanese Railway Train
Japanese Soldiers on the Taku Road
Japanese Village
Japanese Wrestling
Jiu Jitsu, the Japanese Art of Self-Defense
Panorama of Kobe Harbor, Japan
Rickshaw Parade, Japan
Street Scene, Tokio, Japan
The War in China—Japanese Infantry
1902 Eight Japanese Dancing Girls
Hu-Ki-Si, Japanese Dancer
Japanese Acrobats
Japanese Bowery
Japanese Dancing Hall
Japanese Girl Smoking Cigarettes
Japanese Yuma Dance
The National Geisha Dance of Japan
1903 Japanese Foot Juggler
Japanese Geisha Girls No. 1
Japanese Geisha Girls No. 2
Japanese Sword Fight
A Japanese Wrestling Match
Ten Ichi, the Famous Japanese Magician, with His Troop
1904 Departure 14th Co. Japanese Engineers from Shimbashi Station for Korea
Fencing Contest Between Japanese Soldiers, Manchuria
The Fight on the Bridge Between Russians and Japs
Glimpses of Japan
Great Temple Procession, Nikko, Japan
How the Japs Fought at Port Arthur
In Fair Japan
The Jap Behind the Guns
Japanese Acrobats
Japanese Ambush
Japanese Coaling a Man-of-War
Japanese Dance
Japanese Fan Dance
Japanese Flag Dance
Japanese Girls at Tea
Japanese Infantry Morning Drill
Japanese Jackies
The Japanese Ogre
Japanese Railroad Scene, Kanagarva, Japan
Japanese Sailors Fencing with Capstan Bars
Japanese School Children
The Japanese Standard Bearer
Japanese State Procession
Japanese Varieties
Japanese Warriors in Ancient Battle Scene
Japs Loading and Firing a Gun on Battleship "Asama"
Japs Loading and Firing a Six Pounder
A Regiment of the Japanese Imperial Guards and Engineer Corps off to the Front
Russ-Jap Forces Meeting Near Chemulpo
Russian Outposts Attacked by Japanese
Skirmish Between Russian and Japanese Advance Guards
Warship in Nagasaki Harbor, Japan
1905 Duel Between Japanese and Russian Soldiers
Evolution of the Japanese
Japanese Funeral
A Matsuri Procession, Yokohama, Japan
Matsuri Procession, Yokohama, Japan
Scenes and Incidents, Russo-Japanese Peace Conference, Portsmouth, N.H.
1906 Japanese Soldier's Return
Japanese Sports
1907 Diabolo, the Japanese Top Spinner
Fan in Japan
The Japanese Girl
Japanese Vaudeville "The Flower Kingdom"
Japanese Women
Making Pottery in Japan
1908 Jap Sports
Jap Women
Japanese Butterflies
A Tragedy of Japan
1909 The Geisha Who Saved Japan
The Japanese Invasion
Japanese Magic
Japanese Prince
Procession in Japan
Shooting the Rapids in Japan
1910 Carnival of Japanese Firemen in Tokio
A Japanese Peach Boy
The Japanese Spy

Jarnac
1910 Jarnac's Treacherous Blow

Jars
1901 Packing Pickle Jars, Heinz
1910 A Jar of Cranberry Sauce; or, The Crime in Room 13

Jim
1903 Jack and Jim
1907 Lucky Jim
Nervy Jim and the Cop
Slippery Jim, the Burglar
1908 Jim Gets a New Job
Jim Is Fond of Garlic
Lazy Jim's Luck
Slippery Jim's Repentance
1909 Little Jim
Lucky Jim
Sleepy Jim
1910 Chew-Chew Land; or, The Adventures of Dolly and Jim
Jack Fat and Jim Slim at Coney Island
Jim, the Ranchman
Jim Wants to Get Punched
Slippery Jim
Two Lucky Jims
Uncle Jim
Jimjams
1900 The Man in the Jimjams
Jimmie
1907 Jimmie, the Messenger Boy
Jink, Dr.
1908 Doctor Jink's Liquid Life Restorer
Jinks
1909 Jinks the Grouch
1910 Jinks Has the Shooting Mania
Jinks Wants to Be an Acrobat
Jo Jo
1902 Jo Jo, the Dog Faced Boy
Joan of Arc
1900 Joan of Arc
1909 Joan of Arc
Job
1901 Another Job for the Undertaker
1908 His First Job
Jim Gets a New Job
1909 Charlie Forced to Find a Job
An Easy Job
How to Get a City Job
A Put Up Job
Too Many on the Job
1910 Easy Job
Maggie Hollihan Gets a Job
Pete Wants a Job
Towser's New Job
Job, Miss
1909 The Patience of Miss Job
Jockey
1910 The Jockey
The Romance of a Jockey
Tweedledum Wants to be a Jockey
Jockeying
1899 Shamrock and Columbia Jockeying for a Start
1901 "Columbia" and "Shamrock II":' ALL Jockeying and Starting
1903 Jockeying and Start of Yacht[s] Aug. 25th
Jockeying for the Start Aug. 20
Jockeying for the Start Aug. 22
"Reliance" and "Shamrock" III Jockeying and Starting in First Race
Jocko
1909 The Automatic Monkey (Les beaux-arts de Jocko)
Joe
1898 Joe, the Educated Orangoutang
Joe, the Educated Orangoutang, Undressing
1906 A Mid-winter Night's Dream; or, Little Joe's Luck
1908 'Ostler Joe
Joel
1909 Joel's Wedding
Jogue, Father
1909 A Priest of the Wilderness: Father Jogue's Mission to the Iroquois
Johanna
1899 Johanna's Chase
John
1907 Goodbye John
John D. and the Reporter
Poor John
Sightseeing Through Whiskey (Pauvre John ou les aventures d'un buveur de whiskey)
1908 John Is No More a Child
John's New Suit; or, Why He Didn't Go to Church
1909 Honest John, the Coachman
1910 John, the Usher
John A. Dix Post, G.A.R.
1898 John A. Dix Post, G.A.R.
John M. Hutchinson (Fire boat)
1900 Fire Boat "John M. Hutchinson"
John Scully (Boat)
1903 Stake Boat with Stake ("John Scully")
John the Baptist
1903 Passion Play: Herodias Pleads for John the Baptist's Head
Johnnie
1900 What Happened to a Fresh Johnnie
1903 The Johnnie and the Telephone
1908 Buncoed Stage Johnnie
Johnny
1899 "Ding, Dong, Dell, Johnny's in the Well"
1907 Johnny's Run
1909 Johnny and the Indians
Johnny Is No Longer a Child
1910 Johnny's Pictures of the Polar Regions
Johnson
1910 The Other Johnson
Johnson, Jack
1909 [Johnson-Ketchel Fight Films]
World's Heavyweight Championship Pictures Between Tommy Burns and Jack Johnson
1910 [Jack Johnson's Own Story of the Big Fight]
Jeffries-Johnson World's Championship Boxing Contest, Held at Reno, Nevada, July 4, 1910
Johnson Training for His Fight with Jeffries
Reproduction of Jeffries-Johnson Championship Contest
Johnstone
1903 Sluice Mining on Gold Hill in the Klondike, Hutchinson and Johnstone's Claim of No. 6, Eldorado
Join
1907 Joined Lips
1908 When Casey Joined the Lodge
1910 He Joined the Frat
Mammy's Boy Joins the Army
Joint
1898 A Chinese Opium Joint
1900 A Raid on a Chinese Opium Joint
1902 A Little Mix-Up in a Mixed Ale Joint
1903 Fun in an Opium Joint
1905 Reuben in the Opium Joint
1910 The Times Are Out of Joint
Joinville (France)
1904 Bathers at Joinville
Joke
1899 A Bare Skin Joke
The Nurse's Joke
Tommy's Ringing Good Joke on His Dad
A Wringing Good Joke
1900 A Joke on the Old Maid
A Wringing Good Joke
1901 An April Fool Joke
The Bad Boy's Joke on the Nurse
A Good Joke
A Joke on Grandma
A Joke on Whom?
1903 Buster's Joke on Papa
Gardener's Joke
The Unappreciated Joke
A Wringing Good Joke
1904 Bad Boy's Joke on the Nurse
Cook's Joke
A Joke at the French Ball
Tit for Tat; or, A Good Joke on My Head
1905 Digesting a Joke (Jas. T. Powers)
The Pastry Cook's Practical Jokes
1906 Bad Joke
Joke on a Roundsman
Kids' Practical Jokes
Schoolboys' Practical Jokes
1907 Bad Boy's Joke
Bobby's Practical Jokes
Man, Hat and Cocktail, a New Drink, but an Old Joke
Sailor's Practical Joke
The Twin Brother's Joke
1908 Cruel Joke
The Duke's Good Joke
A Good Joke
The Impersonator's Jokes
Schoolboy's Joke
A Serious Joke
Student's Joke on the Porter
Students' Jokes
The Student's Prank; or, A Joke on His Parents
Such a Good Joke, But— Why Don't He Laugh?
1909 The Bridegroom's Joke
The Farmer's Joke
A Joke on Teddy
A Painful Joke
Servant's Good Joke
1910 Artist's Good Joke
A Big Joke
The Joke They Played on Bumptious
Rabelais' Joke
A Texas Joke
Joliet (Illinois)
1909 Life Behind the Bars at Joliet
Jolly
1897 A Jolly Crowd of Bathers Frolicking on the Beach at Atlantic City
Three Jolly Girls and the Fun They Had with the Old Swing
1903 Jolly Monks
1904 The Jolly Bill-Posters
A Jolly Lawn Party
The Jolly Russian Prophets
Our Jolly French Students
1905 Three Jolly Dutchmen
1906 The Jolly Monks of Malabar
1908 For He's a Jolly Good Fellow
1909 The Interrupted Jollification
Jolly Sports
The Jolly Trio's Dream
1910 The Jolly Whirl
Jollygood
1908 Mr. and Mrs. Jollygood Go Tandeming
Jonah
1907 Thursday Is My Jonah Day
1909 Mr. Jonah Gets a Little Dust in His Eyes
Jonah, A., Mr.
1910 Mr. A. Jonah
Jones
1898 How Farmer Jones Made a Hit at Pleasure Bay
1899 Jones and His Pal in Trouble
Jones' Interrupted Sleighride
Jones Makes a Discovery
Jones' Return from the Club
1900 Jones Gives a Private Supper
Jones Interviews His Wife
Jones' Return from a Masquerade
Why Jones Discharged His Clerks
Why Mrs. Jones Got a Divorce
1902 Circular Panoramic View of Jones and Laughlin's Steel Yard
Why Jones Left Home
1904 What Happened to Jones
1905 How Jones Lost His Roll
How Jones Saw the Derby
1908 How Jones Saw the Carnival
Mr. Jones at the Ball
1909 Farmer Jones Goes to the Market
How Jones Got a New Suit
How Jones Paid His Debts
Jones and His New Neighbors
Jones and the Lady Book Agent
Jones' Burglar
Jones Has Bought a Phonograph
The Joneses Have Amateur Theatricals
Mr. Jones Has a Card Party
Mrs. Jones' Birthday
Mrs. Jones Entertains
Mrs. Jones' Lover; or, "I Want My Hat"
Peaceful Jones
Who Stole Jones' Wood?
Why Mr. Jones Was Arrested
1910 How Jones Won the Championship
[Jones, the Burglar Catcher]
Jones' Watch
Sleepy Jones
Why Jones Reformed
Jones, Miss
1910 The Sheriff and Miss Jones
Jones, Bill
1908 Bill Jones' New Years Resolution
Jones, Davy
1900 Davy Jones' Locker
1910 Davy Jones and Captain Bragg
Davy Jones' Domestic Troubles
Davy Jones' Landladies
Davy Jones' Parrot

A Just Reward
The Justice of Solomon
Justice or Mercy
Justified
The Justifier
The Scales of Justice
Was Justice Served?
Wheels of Justice
1910 At the Bar of Justice
Cowboy Justice
A Day on the French Battleship "Justice"
His Just Deserts
Ingratitude; or, The Justice of Providence
A Just Revenge
Justice
Justice in the Far North
Truth Beyond Reach of Justice
Western Justice

Justinian
1908 Justinian's Human Torches
1910 Justinian and Theodora

Juvenile
1903 A Juvenile Elephant Trainer
Juvenile Fire Department
Juvenile Stakes
1906 Juvenile Chicken Thieves

Kahului (Hawaii)
1907 Loading Sugar, Kahului, Maui, H.I.

Kaiser
1902 Christening and Launching Kaiser Wilhelm's Yacht "Meteor"
Kaiser Wilhelm and Emperor Franz Josef, and Prince Henry Riding Horseback
Kaiser Wilhelm and the Empress of Germany Reviewing Their Troops
Kaiser Wilhelm and the German Cuirrassiers Galloping
Kaiser Wilhelm at Stettin
Kaiser Wilhelm at the Launching of a German Battleship
Kaiser Wilhelm in the Tier Garten, Berlin, Germany
Kaiser Wilhelm Inspecting His Soldiers
Kaiser Wilhelm, of Germany, and Emperor Franz Josef, of Austria
Kaiser Wilhelm's Yacht, "Meteor," Entering the Water
Kaiser Wilhelm's Yacht "Meteor" Under Sail
Launch of the Kaiser's Yacht "Meteor"
Queen Wilhelmina and Kaiser Wilhelm Riding in the Tier Garten
Queen Wilhelmina Arriving at the Kaiser's Palace
1903 Arrival of Kaiser Wilhelm in England
1905 Start of Ocean Race for Kaiser's Cup

Kaiser Wilhelm der Grosse (Boat)
1902 Launching of the "Kaiser Wilhelm der Grosse"

Kalama Railroad Ferry, Benecia (California)
1903 Kalama Railroad Ferry Crossing the Columbia River

Kanagarva (Japan)
1904 Japanese Railroad Scene, Kanagarva, Japan

Kanaka Indians
1898 Kanakas Diving for Money [Honolulu], No. 1
Kanakas Diving for Money [Honolulu], No. 2
1902 A Dance by Kanaka Indians
1907 Kanaka Fishermen Casting the Throw Net, Hilo, H.I.

Kansas
1898 22nd Regiment, Kansas Volunteers
1899 Advance of Kansas Volunteers at Caloocan
1901 The Kansas Saloon Smashers

Kansas City (Missouri)
1900 Kansas City Fire Department, Winners of the World's Championship at the Paris Exposition
1907 Kansas City

Karina
1898 Karina

Kashmir (India)
1904 Curious Sights in Burmah and Cashmere (Section 1)
Curious Sights in Burmah and Cashmere (Section 2)

Kate
1908 For Kate's Health
1910 Three Fingered Kate

Katrina
1909 Katrina's Valentine

Katzenjammer Kids
1898 The Katzenjammer Kids in School
1900 The Katzenjammer Kids Have a Love Affair
1903 Katzenjammer Kids (Journal Thumb Book)

Kean, Edmund
1910 Kean; or, The Prince and the Actor

Kearney, Kate
1905 Tourists Party near Kate Kearney's Cottage, Gap of Dunloe, Ireland

Kearsarge (Boat)
1898 Launching of the "Kearsage"
1903 The Forecastle of the "Kearsage" in a Heavy Sea
President Roosevelt Addressing Crew of "Kearsarge"
President Roosevelt's Arrival at "Kearsarge"
President Roosevelt's Departure from "Kearsarge"
Pres. Roosevelt's Sunday Visit to Kearsage
Sea Washing over the Bow of Kearsage
Sparring Match on the "Kearsarge"

Keel
1909 An Uneven Keel

Keel, Achill Island (Ireland)
1905 Irish Constabulary, Keel, Achill Island, Ireland

Keen
1908 Gendarme Has a Keen Eye
Keenest of the Two

Keep
1902 Papa Keeps the Telephone Appointment
1905 Hubby Tries to Keep House
1906 How to Keep Cool or Our Ice Supply
Keep It Straight
1907 Lighthouse Keepers
The Park Keeper
1909 The Keeper of the Light
The Legend of Sterling Keep
Now Keep Smiling
1910 The Dog Keeper
Keeping His Word

Keepsake
1910 The Last Keepsake

Keg
1909 Adventures of a Keg

Keith, B. F.
1898 Mr. B. F. Keith
1902 B. F. Keith's New Million Dollar Theatre

Keith's Theatre, Boston (Massachusetts)
1897 Keith's Theatre

Keith's Theatre, London (England)
1900 Keith's Theater, London

Kellerman, Annette
1907 Miss Kellerman's Diving Feats
1909 Miss Annette Kellerman

Kenilworth
1909 Kenilworth

Kenmare (Ireland)
1903 A Coach Drive from Glengariffe to Kenmore
Coaching Through the Tunnel on the Kenmere Road
1905 Market Day at Kenmore

Kennel
1903 A Kennel Club Parade

Kennicott Glacier (Alaska)
1903 Panorama of Kennicott Glacier Port Hole

Kent House
1902 Kent House Slide

Kentucky
1898 Louisville Commandery, Louisville, Ky.
1900 Scene from "Old Kentucky"
1901 Knight Templars Parade at Louisville, Ky.
1904 The Kentucky Squire
1905 A Kentucky Feud
1908 The Kentuckian
1909 In Old Kentucky
A Kentucky Planter
1910 In the Mountains of Kentucky
The Kentucky Pioneer

Kentucky (Battleship)
1898 Launch, U.S. Battleship "Kentucky"

Ker-Choo
1908 Ker-Choo

Kern, John W.
1908 Hon. William J. Bryan and Hon. John W. Kern

Kern County (California)
1903 Oil Fields, Tanks and Lakes of Oil; Kern Co., Cal.

Kerry (Ireland)
1905 Milking Time: A Kerry Herd

Ketchel, Stanley
1909 [Johnson-Ketchel Fight Films]

Key
1902 Turning Keys over to Rex
1908 The Key Under the Mat
1909 The Pass Key
1910 Bill and the Missing Key
I Have Lost My Latch Key
The Key of Life

Key West (Florida)
1903 U.S. Monitor Miantonomah Steaming into Key West

Keyhole
1900 Through the Key-Hole in the Door
1902 What Happened to the Inquisitive Janitor (Par le trou de la serrure)
1905 Through the Keyhole

Keystone Express
1897 Keystone Express

Khartoum (Sudan)
1907 From Cairo to Khartoum

Kick
1900 Uncle Reuben Lands a Kick
1904 She Kicked on the Cooking
1905 Kicking Football—Harvard

Kick, Bob
1903 Bob Kick, the Mischievous Kid

Kickapoo
1904 Kickapoo

Kicking Horse Canyon, British Columbia (Canada)
1899 Down the Western Slope of the Canadian Rockies Through Kicking Horse Pass
Up the Big Grade in the Valley of the Kicking Horse
1901 Panoramic View, Kicking Horse Canyon
Panoramic View, Lower Kicking Horse Canyon
Panoramic View, Lower Kicking Horse Valley
Panoramic View, Upper Kicking Horse Canyon

Kidd, William
1907 Captain Kidd and His Pirates
1908 Captain Kidd
1910 Kidd's Treasure

Kidnapped
1903 The Kidnapper: At Work [Part 1]
The Kidnapper: In the Den [Part 2]
The Kidnapper: The Rescue [Part 3]
1904 Kidnapped Child
"Weary Willie" Kidnaps a Child
1905 Kidnapped Child
1907 Kidnapping a Bride
1908 Her First Adventure [Kidnapped with the Aid of a Street Piano]
Kidnapped by Gypsies
Kidnapped for Hate
1909 Dog Outwits Kidnapper
The Kidnapped King

Kids
rt **Children**
1897 Yellow Kid
1898 The Katzenjammer Kids in School
1900 The Katzenjammer Kids Have a Love Affair
The Tough Kid's Waterloo
1903 Bob Kick, the Mischievous Kid
Katzenjammer Kids (Journal Thumb Book)
Krousemeyer Kids
1904 The Kiddies and the Poultry
The Mischievous Kid, the Duck and the Gendarme
1905 Irish Kiddies Coming out of School, Achill Island
Kiddies Dancing to Hurdy-Gurdy Music, Soho, London
1906 Kiddies Pets
Kids' Practical Jokes
Pierce Kids
The Terrible Kids
1907 Catch the Kid
The Dutch Kiddies: Montgomery and Stone
Only Kids

1901 The Bowery Kiss
1902 The Bowery Kiss
1903 Darkies' Kiss
A Kiss in the Tunnel
New Colored Kiss, No. 2
Something Good-Negro Kiss
1904 A Kiss and a Tumble
A Kiss in the Dark
Kiss Me!
Kissing in a Tunnel
Kissing the Blarney Stone
The Misdirected Kiss
A Race for a Kiss
"Weary Willie" Kisses the Bride
1905 A Sweet Kiss
1906 Kisses Sweet
1907 Dream Kisses
Jack the Kisser
Kissers Caught
The Witch Kiss
1908 A Dearly Paid for Kiss
The First Kiss
Soul Kiss
The Soul Kiss
1909 A Kiss in the Dark
The Kiss of Judas
The Kissing Germ
The Three Kisses
The Trouble Kiss
1910 The Kiss Was Mightier Than the Sword
The Kissing Bug

Kitchen
1898 The Tramp in the Kitchen
1899 Love in the Kitchen
Spirits in the Kitchen
1900 A Wake in "Hell's Kitchen"
1902 The Devil's Kitchen
1907 Haunted Kitchen
The Kitchen Maid's Dream
The Kitchen Terror
Nervous Kitchenmaid
1908 In the Bogie Man's Cave (La cuisine de l'ogre)

Kitchener, Horatio Herbert
1898 Gen'l Sir Herbert Kitchener

Kite
1909 The Boy and His Kite
1910 Military Kite Flying at Rheims

Kittens
use **Cats and kittens**

Kitty
1910 Charlie and Kitty in Brussels

Kleptomaniacs
1900 "The Kleptomaniacs"
1905 The Kleptomaniac

Klobenstein
1907 Curious Carriage of Klobenstein

Klondike, Yukon Territory (Canada)
1897 Horses Loading for Klondike
Loading Baggage for Klondike
S.S. "Williamette" Leaving for Klondike
1899 Can-Can in the Klondike
1900 A Gun Play in the Klondike
1901 Rocking Gold in the Klondike
Washing Gold on 20 Above Hunker, Klondike
1903 Lord and Lady Minto with Party, Fording the Rushing Waters of the Klondike on Horseback
Sluice Mining on Gold Hill in the Klondike, Hutchinson and Johnstone's Claim of No. 6, Eldorado
1905 Old Time Miner Rocking for Gold in the Tailings, Klondike
Panning Gold on a Claim in the Klondike
Sluicing in the Klondike
Working a Scraper on Tailings Klondike

Kneeling
1898 Pope Leo XIII Walking Before Kneeling Guards

Knife
1903 A Duel with Knives
1909 A Dull Knife

Knight
1898 Knights of the Golden Eagle
1899 A Bad (K)Night
1902 When Knighthood Was in Flower
1907 Knight-Errant
1908 A Gallant Knight
The Knight of Black Art
Mysterious Knight
A Poor Knight and the Duke's Daughter
When Knights Were Bold
1909 A Knight for a Night
Legend of the Good Knight
1910 A Modern Knight Errant
Oh, What a Knight!

Knights Templar
1901 Knight Templars Parade at Louisville, Ky.
Knight Templars Parade Drill
1903 Knights Templar Street Parade, Philadelphia
1910 Knights Templars Conclave
The Templars Conclave

Knock
1907 Frowsy Lizzie Knocks Them Dizzy
1910 A Lucky Knock

Knockout
1897 Knock-out Drops
1899 Reproduction of the Fitzsimmons-Jeffries Fight in Eleven Rounds Showing the Knock Out
1900 Knock-out Drops on the Bowery
1901 An Unexpected Knockout

Knot
1902 The Lovers' Knot
Panoramic View of Mt. Tamalpais Between Bow Knot and McKinley Cut
1910 The Knot in the Handkerchief
A Knot in the Plot

Know
1907 Knowing Dogs
1908 He Did Not Know He Was a Monk
The Knowing Birds
1909 The Man Who Knows How to Whistle
1910 Foolshead Knows All and Does All
Foolshead Knows How to Take His Precautions
He Knew Best

Kobe Harbor (Japan)
1901 Panorama of Kobe Harbor, Japan

Kodak
1899 The Makers of the Kodak
1900 What the Bathing Girls Did to the Kodak Fiend
1908 Bobby's Kodak
1909 Traced by a Kodak

Koenig Albert (Boat)
1902 Launch of the "Koenig Albert"

Kohala (Hawaii)
1906 Arrival Mahukona Express, Kohala, Hawaii
Hauling Sugar Cane, Kohala Plantation, Hawaii

Koltes
1898 Koltes' Camp, G.A.R.

Kopje
1900 Lord Dundonald's Cavalry Seizing a Kopje in Spion Kop

Korea
1904 Departure 14th Co. Japanese Engineers from Shimbashi Station for Korea
Panorama of Railroad Station at Seoul, Korea, from Departing Train
Russian Cavalry in Corea [sic]
1908 Korea

Korona (Boat)
1902 Circular Panoramic View of the Market Place at Fort de France, Showing S.S. Korona in the Background

Koshering
1901 Koshering Cattle, (Hebrew Method of Killing)

Krausemeyer
1899 Why Krausemeyer Couldn't Sleep

Krautz, Alderman
1910 Alderman Krautz's Picnic

Kremlin (Moscow)
1904 Nobles Leaving the Kremlin, Moscow, After a Reception by Czar

Kronprinz Wilhelm (Boat)
1902 "Kronprinz Wilhelm" with Prince Henry [of Prussia] on Board Arriving in New York
1906 A Transatlantic Trip of the S.S. Kronprinz Wilhelm, from Bremen to New York

Krousemeyer Kids
1903 Krousemeyer Kids

Kruger, Paul
1902 Oom Paul
1903 Kruger and Body Guard Leaving the Volksraad
Kruger Leaving His Residence for the Volksraad
Pres. Krueger

Kurassiers
1902 German Garde Kurassiers

Kyber
1910 Prince of Kyber

L Street, Boston (Massachusetts)
1905 Bathing in the Ice at the L Street Bath, Boston

Lab
1908 The Runaway Lab

Labeling
1901 Canned Meat Department. No. 6: Painting and Labeling
Labeling Cans

La Boca Harbor (Panama Canal Zone)
1907 Panorama La Boca Harbor and Pacific Entrance to Canal

Labor
1899 Love's Labor Lost
1907 Making the Dirt Fly: Scene 5. Laborers Lining Up at Mess Tent
1908 The Molly Maguires; or, Labor Wars in the Coal Mines
The Power of Labor
1909 The Right to Labor
Suffer Little Children...For of Such Is the Kingdom of Labor
1910 A Bootblack's Daily Labor in Algiers
Capital vs. Labor
The Right to Labor

Labor Day
1908 Labor Day Parade

Laboratory
1897 Mr. Edison at Work in His Chemical Laboratory
1899 The Devil's Laboratory
1900 Marvin and Casler's Laboratory
1901 Laboratory Study

Labors
1910 Hercules and the Big Stick (Les douze travaux d'Hercule)

Labrador (Canada)
1908 Esquimaux of Labrador

Lace
1900 Where the Female Smuggler Hid the Lace
1909 Making Lace
1910 The Lace Maker's Dream
The Piece of Lace

La Croisette, Cannes (France)
1904 View of "La Croisette," Cannes, France

Lad
1908 A Country Lad
1910 The Lad from Old Ireland
Troublesome Lad
Twa Hieland Lads

Ladder
1899 Climbing Jacob's Ladder
"It's Unlucky To Pass Under a Ladder"
1903 DeVoy's Revolving Ladder Act
1906 The Man with the Ladder and the Hose
1907 The Borrowed Ladder
Buying a Ladder
1909 He Wouldn't Go Under a Ladder
Up the Ladder with Tom Bowline

Laddie
1909 Laddie

Ladies
use **Women**

Ladies day
1901 Ladies Day at the Public Baths

Lady (Title)
1899 Lord and Lady Minto
1903 Arrival of Lord and Lady Minto at the Barracks, Dawson
Lady Bountiful Visits the Murphys on Wash Day
Lord and Lady Minto with Party, Fording the Rushing Waters of the Klondike on Horseback
1904 Lady Plumpton's Motor Car
1908 Lady Jane's Flight, a 17th Century Romance
1909 Lady Helen's Escapade
1910 Lady Betty's Strategy
The Lord and the Lady
The Love of Lady Irma

Lady-killer
1908 Lady-Killer Foiled

Ladysmith (South Africa)
1900 On to Ladysmith
The Queen's Reception to the Heroes of Ladysmith
The Relief of Ladysmith

Hank and Lank: They Take a Rest
Hank and Lank: Uninvited Guests

Lanquedoc (France)
1910 Vintage in Lanquedoc

Lansford (Pennslyvania)
1898 Girls Brigade, of Lansford, Pa.

La Patrie
1907 Trial Trip of the Airship "La Patrie"

Laplander
1903 Laplanders at Home
1905 Lapps at Hammerfest, Norway
1907 Laplander Family, Gratli, Norway
1908 The Laplanders
1909 The Laplanders

Larchmont Regatta
1900 Larchmont Regatta

Lard
1901 Lard Refinery

Large
1901 A Large Haul of Fish
1903 Digging for Foundation for Large Department Store, Phila.
Giant Wilkins, the Largest Man in the World
Trick Elephant Bolivar, the Largest Elephant in the World, No. 1
Trick Elephant Bolivar, the Largest Elephant in the World, No. 2
1904 Testing Large Turbines, Westinghouse Co. Works
1905 Largest Fat Boy in the World
1909 Scenes from the World's Largest Pigeon Farm
1910 A Lunatic at Large

Lark
1899 A Lark at the French Ball
Larks Behind the Scene

Larne (Northern Ireland)
1905 Arrival of the Mail Steamer at Larne
Coaches Starting from Larne and Passing Through Tunnel on the Antrim Coast Road

Larry
1909 Larry, the Limit for Deviltry

Las Guásimas (Cuba)
1898 Charge at Las Guasimas
1899 Charge at Las Guasimas, Where Capron and Fish Were Killed

Las Viga Canal, Mexico City (Mexico)
1898 Las Viga Canal, Mexico City
1902 Las Viga Canal, Mexico

LaSavate
1903 LaSavate

Lass
1903 The Chorus Girl and the Salvation Army Lassie
1907 A Sailor's Lass
1908 The Guileless Country Lassie
1909 A Brave Irish Lass, the Story of an Eviction in Ireland
Every Lass a Queen
A Lovely Lass
The Salvation Army Lass
1910 Brittany Lassies
The Lass Who Loves a Sailor
The Lassie's Birthday

Lassoing
1898 Lasso Throwing
Lassoing a Steer
1911 Lassoing Wild Animals in Africa

Last
1898 The Last Round Ended in a Free Fight
The Last Stand
The Tramp's Last Bite
1900 The Last Alarm
Queen Victoria's Last Visit to Ireland
Why Curfew Did Not Ring Last Night
1902 Little Willie's Last Celebration
1903 The Last Cartridges
1905 Last Attack on the Hill
The Tower of London (La Tour de Londres et les dernières moments d'Anne Boleyn)
1906 The Indian's Revenge; or, Osceola, the Last of the Seminoles
The Last Witch
1907 Fitznoodle's Last Ball
1908 Alone at Last
Follow Your Leader and the Master Follows Last
He Who Laughs Last Laughs Best
His Girl's Last Wish
A Home at Last
The Last Cartridge, an Incident of the Sepoy Rebellion in India
Little Hannie's Last Dream
The Maid's Last Day
1909 Caught at Last
Forgiven at Last
His Last Game
His Last Illusion Gone
A Home at Last
Jackson's Last Steeple Chase
The Last Call
The Last Confession
Last Year's Time Table
Mine at Last
Mozart's Last Requiem
On the Little Big Horn; or, Custer's Last Stand
Who Laughs Last
1910 The Bad Man's Last Deed
Custer's Last Stand
He Who Laughs Last
His Last Burglary
His Last Dollar
The Last Deal
The Last Friend
The Last Keepsake
The Last Look
The Last of the Dandies
The Last of the Savelli
The Last of the Saxons
The Last Straw
Red Hawk's Last Raid
Tom's Last Steeple Chase

Last Supper
1903 Passion Play: The Last Supper
1904 The Passion Play (La cène)

Latchkey
1910 I Have Lost My Latch Key
The Latchkey

Late
1898 The Late President Faure of France
1902 Funeral Procession of the Late Empress Frederick
1903 Letter Came Too Late
1904 Late for Work
The Late Senator Mark Hanna
Too Late
1907 Late for His Wedding
1908 Always Too Late
Father Is Late! Go Fetch Him
Funeral of the Late King of Portugal
It's Never Too Late to Mend
Latest Style Airship
Minstrel Mishaps; or, Late for Rehearsal
Why That Actor Was Late
1909 Late for the Recital
Why the Mail Was Late
1910 Gee I Am Late
The Latest Fashion in Skirts
The Latest in Garters

Lathrop School, Kansas City (Missouri)
1904 Lathrop School, Calisthenics, Missouri Commission

Latina
1905 Latina, Contortionist
Latina, Dislocation Act
Latina, Physical Culture Poses [No. 1]
Latina, Physical Culture Poses [No. 2]

Latourte, Monsieur
1904 Simple Simon's Surprise Party (Les invités de m. Latourte)

Laugh
1898 A Very Laughable Mixup
1901 "Laughing Ben"
1907 Laughing Gas
1908 The Ever-Laughing Gentleman
He Who Laughs Last Laughs Best
Love Laughs at Locksmiths, an 18th Century Romance
Such a Good Joke, But— Why Don't He Laugh?
1909 Who Laughs Last
1910 He Who Laughs Last
The Laughing Machine
The Laugh's on Father
Love Laughs at Locksmiths

Laughlin
1902 Circular Panoramic View of Jones and Laughlin's Steel Yard

Launcelot
1909 Launcelot and Elaine

Launch
1897 Launch of Life Boat
Launch of Surf Boat
1898 After Launching
Launch of Japanese Man-of-War "Chitosa"
Launch of the Great Battleship Alabama
Launch of the "Illinois"
Launch of the "Oceanic"
Launch, U.S. Battleship "Kentucky"
Launching, No. 2
Launching of the "Kearsage"
Steam Launch of the Olympia
1899 Launch of the Battleship "Vengeance"
Launch of the Porthonstock Life-boat
Launching the Lifeboat
Sir Thomas Lipton and Party on "Erin's" Launch
1900 A Launch Party in the Adirondacks
Launching a Stranded Schooner from the Docks
1901 Launch
Launch of Shamrock II
Launch of the "Saturn"
Launching of the New Battleship "Ohio" at San Francisco, Cal. When President McKinley Was There
Shanghai from a Launch
1902 Christening and Launching Kaiser Wilhelm's Yacht "Meteor"
Kaiser Wilhelm at the Launching of a German Battleship
Launch of Meteor III
Launch of the Kaiser's Yacht "Meteor"
Launch of the "Koenig Albert"
Launching of the "Kaiser Wilhelm der Grosse"
St. John's Guild. From Launch to Dock
St. John's Guild. Launch Approaching Dock
St. John's Guild. Launch Delivering Patients to F. H.
1903 Launch of Shamrock III
Launching a Steamer
Launching Cup Defender "Reliance"
1904 Launching of the U.S.S. Battleship "Connecticut"
Launching the Lifeboat
Launching the Steamship "Celtic"
Panorama St. Louis Exposition from Launch
1905 [Launching the Ferryboat Richmond—Staten Island]
1907 Launch of the British Battleship Bellerophon
[Launching of the Salem at the Fore River Shipyards—Quincy, Mass.—July 27, 1907]
1908 Launching the Roma
1909 Launching the "Voltaire"
1910 Launching the First Italian Dreadnought

Laundry
1897 In a Chinese Laundry
1900 Ghosts in a Chinese Laundry
1901 Fun in a Chinese Laundry
Laundry and Sewing Room
1902 The Other Fellow's Laundry
1903 Chinese Laundry
New Chinese Laundry
Scene in a Laundry
1907 Traced by a Laundry Mark
Yale Laundry
1908 The Automatic Laundry
My Laundress Inherits
1910 All on Account of a Laundry Mark
The Laundry Girl's Good Night

Laupahoihoi (Hawaii)
1907 S.S. "Kinau" Landing Passengers, Laupahoihoi, H.I.
Surf Scene, Laupahoihoi, Hawaiian Island

Laure
1904 The Brothers Laure

Laurels
1909 Laurels

Laurento
1909 The Brothers Laurento

Laurier, Wilfred, Sir
1897 Sir Wilfred Laurier and the New South Wales Lancers

Lava
1902 Lava Slides in Red Rock Canyon

Spectators Leaving the Theatre Vevey
Squad of Seaforth Highlanders Leaving Bank of Ireland, Dublin
Stages Leaving Fountain House, Yellowstone Park
Tourists Leaving Horgheim in the Romsdale Norway
Tourists Leaving the Lake Hotel, Killarney
1906 Waterfront, Refugees Leaving San Francisco
1908 The Girl I Left Behind Me
Why Smith Left Home
1909 Left Out
The Martins Leave Home for a Week
Why Girls Leave Home
1910 The Girls He Left Behind Him
Love Your Neighbor as Yourself, but Leave His Wife Alone!

Lebanon
1903 Panoramic View of Beyrouth, Syria, Showing Holiday Festivities

Lee, Fitzhugh, General
1898 Brigadier-General Fitz Hugh Lee
Gen. Fitzhugh Lee and Staff
1899 General Lee's Procession, Havana

Leedle, Dot
1907 Dot Leedle German Band

Leeks
1906 Three Cent Leeks

Le Fayet (France)
1906 Fayet-Chamonix: Trip on the New Trolley Line from Le Fayet-St. Gervais to Chamonix

Leg
1899 How Mamie Had Her Leg Pulled
1902 Amputating a Leg
1904 Four Beautiful Pairs of Legs
1906 The Lost Leg of Mutton
1908 The Dancing Legs
Don't Pull My Leg
1909 A Cork Leg Legacy
The Wooden Leg
1910 The Six-Legged Sheep
Story of a Leg

Legacy
1903 The Legacy
1907 An Unpleasant Legacy
1909 A Cork Leg Legacy
1910 His Daughter's Legacy
The Legacy
The Ranch Girl's Legacy

Legal
1901 A Legal Hold-Up
1910 Legally Dead

Legation Street, Shanghai (China)
1901 Scene in Legation Street, Shanghai

Legend
1908 Legend of a Ghost
The Legend of Prometheus
The Legend of Sleepy Hollow
The Legend of Stars
The Water Sprite, a Legend of the Rhine
1909 The Blue Legend
A Christmas Legend
Legend of Orpheus
The Legend of Sterling Keep
Legend of the Erring Jew
The Legend of the Forget-Me-Not
Legend of the Good Knight
The Legend of the Lighthouse
1910 The Legend of Daphne
The Legend of King Midas
The Legend of Scar-Face
The Legend of the Cross
The Legend of the Holy Chapel
A Mexican Legend

Legerdemain
1902 Legerdemain Up-to-Date, or the Great Hermann Outdone

Legging
1901 Legging Sheep

Legion
1910 The Legion of Honor

Legless
1907 The Legless Runner

Legnano (Italy)
1910 The Battle of Legnano; or, Barbarossa

Lehigh Valley Railroad
1901 'Varsity Crew Race on Cayuga Lake, on Decoration Day, Lehigh Valley Observation Train Following the Race, Showing Cornell Crew Finishing First, Columbia Second, University of Pennsylvania Third Ithaca, N.Y., Showing Lehigh Valley Observation Train
1902 Working Rotary Snow Ploughs on Lehigh Valley Railroad
1903 Lehigh Valley Black Diamond Express
Lehigh Valley Express "Black Diamond"
Panorama of the Lehigh Valley Railroad
Rear View of the "Black Diamond Express," Lehigh Valley R.R.

Lehwis, Dr.
1902 Dr. Lehwis Automobile Leaving London for a Trip Around the World

Leinster
1900 The Royal Leinster Regiment
Royal Leinster Regiment on Parade
Royal Leinsters on Review

Lemon
1908 A Lemon in the Garden of Love

Lemon Sisters
1909 The Lemon Sisters at Muldoon's Picnic

Lena
1905 Meet Me Down at Luna, Lena
1907 Lena and the Beaux
1909 Aunt Lena's Visit

Lender
1908 The Money Lender
1910 The Money Lender's Son

Leno, Dan
1902 Dessert at Dan Leno's House
Mr. Dan Leno, Assisted by Mr. Herbert Campbell, Editing the "Sun"

Lens
1904 Behind the Lens

Leo
1909 Leo's Air Rifle

Leo XIII, Pope
1898 His Holiness, Leo XIII in the Gardens of the Vatican, Being Photographed by the American Biograph Camera
M. H. Pope Leo in Chair
Pope Leo XIII, No. 31-56
Pope Leo XIII, No. 57-82
Pope Leo XIII, No. 106
Pope Leo XIII and Count Pecci, No. 1
Pope Leo XIII Approaching Garden
Pope Leo XIII Attended by Guard
Pope Leo XIII Being Carried in Chair Through Upper Loggia, No. 101
Pope Leo XIII Being Seated Bestowing Blessing Surrounded by Swiss Guards, No. 107
Pope Leo [XIII] Blessing in the Garden
Pope Leo XIII Giving Blessing from Chair
Pope Leo XIII in Canopy Chair, No. 100
Pope Leo XIII in Carriage
Pope Leo XIII in Carriage, No. 1
Pope Leo XIII in Carriage, No. 102
Pope Leo XIII in Sedan Chair, No. 1
Pope Leo XIII in Vatican Garden, No. 1
Pope Leo XIII Leaving Carriage and Being Ushered into Garden, No. 104
Pope Leo XIII Passing Through Upper Loggia, No. 1
Pope Leo XIII Preparing To Give Blessing from Chair
Pope Leo XIII Seated in Garden
Pope Leo XIII Seated in Garden, No. 105
Pope Leo XIII Walking at Twilight, No. 1
Pope Leo XIII Walking Before Kneeling Guards
Pope Leo [XIII] Walking in the Garden
1903 H. H. Pope Leo [XIII] in Chair
Pope [Leo XIII] in His Carriage
Pope [Leo XIII] Passing Through Upper Loggia

Leon, Casper
1906 Dixon-Chester Leon Contest

Leon of the Table d'Hote
1910 Leon of the Table d'Hote

Leonard, Mike
1894 Leonard—Cushing Fight
1897 First Round: Glove Contest Between the Leonards
Second Round: Glove Contest Between the Leonards

Leonard, Sadie
1897 Bag Punching by Sadie Leonard
First Round: Glove Contest Between the Leonards
Second Round: Glove Contest Between the Leonards

Leoncavallo, Ruggero
1909 Il Pagliacci (Leoncavallo)

Leopard
1899 Morelli and Her Leopards
1909 Leopard Hunting in Abyssinia
The Leopard Queen

Leprechaun
1908 The Leprechaun—An Irish Fairy Story

Lerfoss Waterfall (Norway)
1904 Lerfoss Waterfall

Lerin, Iles de (France)
1910 Lerin's Abbey on St. Honorat's Island

Lescaut, Manon
1908 Manon Lescaut

Lescout, Nema
1910 Nema Lescout

Leslie, Edna
1910 The Heart of Edna Leslie

Lesson
1898 Her First Lesson in Dancing
1901 A Language Lesson
A Muffin Lesson
1903 Aunt Jane's First Lesson in Love
The Drawing Lesson; or, The Living Statue
1904 The Parson's Cooking Lesson
1905 Her First Bicycle Lesson
1906 Physical Culture Lesson
1907 Skating Lessons
1908 Father's Lesson
Lessons in Jiu Jitsu
The Swimming Lesson
1909 The Arithmetic Lesson
A Bitter Lesson
Good Lesson in Charity
Lesson in Cycling
A Lesson in Domestic Economy
Lesson in Electricity
A Lesson in Palmistry
The Music Lesson
A Piano Lesson
1910 Her Lesson
How Brother Cook Was Taught a Lesson
The Lesson
A Lesson by the Sea
A Salutary Lesson
The Selfish Man's Lesson
Teaching a Husband a Lesson

Lest
1909 Lest We Forget

Let
1900 A Farmer Who Could Not Let Go
1902 Let the Gold Dust Twins Do Your Work
1904 Let Uncle Ruben Show You How
1908 House to Let; or, The New Tenants
If It Don't Concern You, Let It Alone
1909 Furnished Rooms to Let
Let Bygones Be Bygones
1910 Let Us Die Together
Let Us Give Thanks

Le Tremeraire, Charles
1910 Charles Le Tremeraire

Letter
1898 A Letter from Her Soldier Lover
1903 Letter Came Too Late
Reading a Letter (Facial Expression)
1906 Letters Which Speak
1907 An Anonymous Letter
A Letter in the Sand
Papa's Letter
A Pressing Letter
1908 Jack in Letter Box
Scarlet Letter
1909 All on Account of a Letter
Anonymous Letter
The Lost Letter
The Mixed Letters
Old Love Letters
An Unwritten Letter
1910 A Christmas Letter
The Dead Letter
His Mother's Letter
Little Jack's Letter
That Letter from Teddy
The Unmailed Letter

Levee
1903 Fun on the Levee
The Royal Levee in India [The Delhi 'Durbar']
Viceroy of India's Royal Levee

Lifeline
1899 Shooting the Life Line
Lift
1899 A Roll Lift Draw Bridge
1901 Dumping and Lifting Cattle
1903 Lifting a Wagon from a New York Foundation
Lifting Salmon Trap
1905 Lifting the Lid
1907 Making the Dirt Fly: Scene 4. Railroad Track Lifter in Operation
1909 Champion Heavyweight Lifter
Light
1897 Battery A, Light Artillery, U.S. Army
1898 Charge of the Light Brigade
1899 Michigan Naval Reserves and the Detroit Light Guards
1901 Love by the Light of the Moon
Reilly's Light Battery F
The War in China—British Light Artillery
1902 General Electric Flash Light
The Light That Didn't Fail
1903 The Providence Light Artillery
Shamrock Rounding Sandy Hook Light Ship
Tying the Red Light on the Tiger's Tail
1904 Battery "A," Rhode Island Light Artillery
1906 Have a Light, Sir
1907 Light-Fight-White
1908 The Light in the Window
The Lights and Shadows of Chinatown
Through Darkness to Light
1909 Give Me a Light
In the Lime Light
The Keeper of the Light
The Light That Came
Through Darkness to Light
1910 A Flash of Light
The Light in the Window
Light heavyweight
1903 Light Heavyweight Championship Contest Between Root and Gardner
Lighter
1900 Unloading Lighters, Manila
1904 Every Man His Own Cigar Lighter
Lighthouse
1902 Circular Panoramic View of St. Pierre from the Lighthouse, Showing Mt. Pelee Smoking in the Distance
1904 Building a Lighthouse
1907 The Lighthouse
Lighthouse Keepers
1908 The Lighthouse-Keeper's Daughter
1909 The Legend of the Lighthouse
Lighthouse
Lightning
1902 The Lightning Artist
Lightning Facial Changes
1903 Baby Lund in Lightning Change Act
Lightning Artist
The Lightning Change Artist
1907 Lightning Sketches
1908 The Lightning Postcard Artist
Lightweight
1904 A Couple of Lightweights at Coney Island
1905 Nelson-Britt Prize Fight for Lightweight Championship, San Francisco, September 9th, 1905
Like
1899 How Would You Like to Be the Ice Man?
1900 "How'd You Like To Be the Iceman?"
1903 How Would You Like to Be the Ice Man
1908 As You Like It
I Would Like to Marry You
A Lady Who Likes a Moustache
Wouldn't You Like to Flirt with me
Wouldn't You Like to Have Me for a Sweetheart
1909 Our Ice Supply; or, How'd You Like to Be the Iceman
Likeness
1903 Hermann Looked Like Me
1908 A Fatal Likeness
Lilacs
1909 A Bunch of Lilacs
Lillian
1903 Little Lillian, Toe Danseuse
1905 Airy Fairy Lillian Tries on Her New Corsets
1910 Lillian and Anetta
Lillies
1909 The Faded Lillies
Lilliputian
1902 The Cheese Mites; or, The Lilliputians in a London Restaurant
1903 Gulliver's Travels (Le voyage de Gulliver à Lilliput et chez les géants)
1905 The Lilliputian Minuet
1906 Liliputian Dance
Lily
1909 Lily Amuses Herself
1910 The Golden Lily
The Lily of the Ranch
Limbering
1897 Dancing Girls Limbering Up
1901 Capt. Reilly's Battery Limbering
Limbs
1908 An Odd Pair of Limbs
Limburger
1906 Oh! That Limburger, the Story of a Piece of Cheese
1910 Limburger and Love
Limelight
1909 In the Lime Light
Limerick (Ireland)
1905 Battery of Artillery Crossing Ball's Bridge, Limerick, Ireland
Limit
1900 "Above the Limit"
1909 Larry, the Limit for Deviltry
Limited
1896 The Pennsylvania Limited Express
1898 California Limited, A.T. & S.F.R.R.
Sunset Limited, Southern Pacific Ry.
1899 The Imperial Limited
"Imperial Limited." Canadian Pacific R.R.
Overland Limited
The "Overland Limited" Passing Witch Rocks
Panoramic View, Horseshoe Curve, From Penna. Ltd.
The Saratoga Limited
1900 A Hand Car and the Imperial Limited
The Imperial Limited
Imperial Limited
1901 The Overland Limited
A Race with the Overland Limited
1902 Experimental. Southwestern Limited Train
New Sunset Limited
The Pioneer Limited
1903 California Limited
The California Limited of the Santa Fe Route
Pennsylvania Limited
Pioneer Limited
The Rocky Mountain Limited
1906 The Wreckers of the Limited Express
Lina
1897 Lina & Vani
Lincoln, Abraham
1908 The Life of Abraham Lincoln
Lincoln's Speech at Gettysburg
The Reprieve, an Episode in the Life of Abraham Lincoln
1909 The Assassination of Abraham Lincoln
1910 Abraham Lincoln's Clemency
Lincoln Park, Chicago (Illinois)
1900 Lincoln Park
Lincoln's Monument, Chicago (Illinois)
1902 Prince Henry [of Prussia] at Lincoln's Monument, Chicago, Ill.
Linda of Chamouny
1910 Linda of Chamouny
Linden (New Jersey)
1903 Changing Horses at Linden
Line
1898 Behind the Firing Line
Crossing the Line
1899 Going to the Firing Line
Shooting the Life Line
1900 Demonstrating the Operation of the Harrington Rail Bonding System on the Line of the Coney Island and Brooklyn Railroad Co.
1901 Sixth U.S. Cavalry, Skirmish Line
1903 Broncho Busting Along the Lines of the Denver & Rio Grande Railway
"Reliance" Crossing the Line and Winning First Race
Scenes on the Short Line
The Angler (Le pêcheur à la ligne)
1904 Beyond the Danger Line
1905 Fun on the Joy Line
1906 Fayet-Chamonix: Trip on the New Trolley Line from Le Fayet-St. Gervais to Chamonix
Trip over Cripple Creek Short Line
1907 Along the Shore Line of Lake Washington
The Despatch Bearer; or, Through the Enemy's Lines
Making the Dirt Fly: Scene 5. Laborers Lining Up at Mess Tent
Angling in Norway (Pêche à la ligne sous la glace)
1909 Drawing the Color Line
Lines of the Hand
Lines of White on a Sullen Sea
1910 The Danger Line
Lines of the Hand
On the Border Line
On the Firing Line
The Thin Dark Line
Through the Enemy's Line
Linen
1904 Linen Shop
Liner
1901 Crew of a Pacific Liner
Sampans Racing Toward Liner
1902 Docking a Liner
Lineup
1901 Line-Up and Teasing the Snakes
Lingerie
1905 London Ladies Looking at Lingerie in Oxford Street Windows, London
Lining
1910 The Silver Lining
Link
1904 The Missing Link
Linwood School, Kansas City (Missouri)
1904 Linwood School, Calisthenics, Missouri Commission
Lion
1899 Pianka and her Lions
1900 Fight Between a Lion and a Bull
1902 Children Playing with Lion Cubs
George J. Marck and His Lions
1903 Burlesque Lions and Their Tamer, Hagenback's Circus
Small Boy and Lion Cub, Hagenback's Circus
1904 Lion and Lioness
Lion Tamer
1906 Lion Hunt
1907 Great Lion Hunt
Sportsmen and Lion
Wonderful Lion Killer
1908 Lion Hunting
The Lion's Bride
Lion's Tilting Contest
1909 The Lion Tamer
Tylda and Her Lions
The Vengeance of the Lion Tamer
1910 Daring Lion's Bride
Foolshead in the Lion's Cage
The Russian Lion
The Tamer; Alfred Schneider and His Lions
Lipman Dance
1899 New Lipman Dance
Lips
1907 Joined Lips
1908 When Other Lips
1909 When Lips Are Sealed
Lipton, Thomas, Sir
1899 Sir Thomas Lipton and Party on "Erin's" Launch
Sir Thomas Lipton's Steam Yacht "Erin"
1902 Sir Thomas Lipton on Board the Erin
1903 Sir Thomas Lipton's Yacht Fleet Leaving England
Liquid
1907 Liquid Electricity; or, The Inventor's Galvanic Fluid
1908 Doctor Jink's Liquid Life Restorer
Galvanic Fluid; or, More Fun with Liquid Electricity
1909 Liquid Air
Liquors
1910 [Liquors and Cigars]
Lisbon (Portugal)
1910 Lisbon, Before and During the Revolution
Listen
1909 Listen

Hulda's Lovers
An Indian Love Story
The Jealous Old Maid; or, No One to Love Her
A Lemon in the Garden of Love
A Love Affair
A Love Affair in Toyland
A Love Affair of the Olden Days
Love and Fortune
Love and Hatred
Love and Molasses
Love in 20 Minutes
Love Is Ingenious
Love Laughs at Locksmiths, an 18th Century Romance
A Love Tragedy in Spain
Love Will Find a Way
Lover and Bicycle
The Lover's Guide
A Lover's Hazing
Lovers' Ill Luck
A Lover's Ruse; or, The Miser's Daughter
A Lover's Stratagems
The Lovers' Telegraphic Code
The Lover's Tribulation
Love's Sacrifice
Love's Victim
A Magician's Love Test
A Mexican Love Story
No Trifling with Love
The Queen's Love (La Tosca)
The Queen's Lover
The Ranchman's Love
The Rival Lovers
The Rivals: A Love Drama of Pompeii
Saved by Love
Soldier's Love Token
Thou Shalt Not Love
The Triumph of Love
'Twixt Love and Duty
'Twixt Love and Duty; or, A Woman's Heroism
Unrequited Love
Western Courtship, a Love Story of Arizona
A Yankee Man-o-Warsman's Fight for Love
You Got to Love Me a Lot

1909 All for the Love of a Girl
All's Fair in Love
A Bachelor's Love Affair
Between Love and Honor
By Path of Love
The Captain's Love
A Child's Love
Cleopatra's Lover; or, A Night of Enchantment
The Course of True Love
The Dairy Maid's Lovers
Daunted by His First Love
Disloyal Lover
Fantine; or, A Mother's Love
The Fatal Love
A Florida Feud; or, Love in the Everglades
Foolshead Sportsman of Love
For Love of a Fisher Girl
For Love's Sake
For Love's Sweet Sake
Force of Love
The Hasty Tempered Father; or, The Blacksmith's Love
He Fell in Love with His Wife
His Lost Love
His Ward's Love
Hurricane of Lovers
I Love My Wife, but Oh, You Kid
If Love Be True
An Italian Love Story
James and Catherine; or, Love on a Farm
Love and Law
Love and Revenge
Love and Sacrifice
Love and the Motherland
Love and Vendetta
Love and War: An Episode of Waterloo
Love Finds a Way
Love Germs
The Love Hunter
Love Is Blind
Love Me, Love My Dog
Love of a Hunchback
The Love of a Savage
Love of Adventures
The Love of Little Flora
The Love of the Pasha's Son, a Turkish Romance
Love of Travel
The Love Plotters
The Love-sick Barber
Love Stronger Than Revenge
Love, the Conqueror
The Love Token
The Love Trip
Love Under Spanish Skies
Love Wins
Love with Love Is Paid
Lover's Mistake
A Lover's Quarrel
Love's Sacrifice
Love's Stratagem
Love's Sweet Melody
Love's Triumphs
Marriage of Love
Mary Jane's Lovers
Miracle of Love
Mirielle's Sincere Love
Mishaps of Lover
Mrs. Jones' Lover; or, "I Want My Hat"
Moon for Your Love
Motherly Love of Animals
A Mother's Love
The Musician's Love Story
Nellie's Love Story
Nobody Loves a Fat Man
The Other Fellow; or, A Fight for Love
A Persistent Lover
The Persistent Lover
Phonographic Message of Love
Pity and Love
The Politician's Love Story
The Power of Love
A Prince's Love
A Princess' Love Affair
Professor's Love Tonic
A Red Man's Love
Riding for Love
A Road to Love
A School for Lovemaking
The Sculptor's Love
A Sister's Love, a Tale of the Franco-Prussian War
A Stage Romance; or, An Actor's Love
The Strength of Love
A Strong Woman's Lover
A Telepathic Warning, the Story of a Child's Love for Her Father
Tragic Love
Tragical Love
Tribulations of a Lover
True Love Never Runs Smoothly
True to Her First Love
The Truer Lover
Two Lovers and a Coquette
The Unwelcome Lover
The Viking's Love; or, True to His Chief
When Love Will
You've Got to Love Me a Lot
Nero; or, the Burning of Rome (Nerone, ossia amore di Schivia)

1910 All's Fair in Love and War
The Altar of Love
The Art Lover's Strategy
Arthur's Little Love Affair
A Bachelor's Love
Between Love and Duty
Between Love and Honor
Bill as a Lover
Blind Love
Brotherly Love
By Right of Love
A Cheyenne's Love for a Sioux
The Course of True Love
A Cowboy for Love
The Deputy's Love
The Doctor's Love Story
The Eagle's Egg; or The Rival Lovers
An Exile's Love
The Faithless Lover
False Love and True
A Father's Love
First Love Is Best
For the Love of Red Wing
Foxy Hobo Married for Love
From Love to Martyrdom
The Gipsy Girl's Love
The Greater Love
Her Cowboy Lover
Her First Love
Her Life for Her Love
How Women Love
In Love with the Charcoal Woman
An Indian Girl's Love
The Iron Clad Lover
The Lass Who Loves a Sailor
A Life for Love
Limburger and Love
Love Amidst Historic Ruins
Love Among the Roses
Love and a Palette
Love and a Pallette
Love and Art
Love and Law
Love and Marriage in Poster Land
Love and Money
Love and the Law
Love and Treason
Love at First Sight
Love Drops
Love in Mexico
Love in Quarantine
Love Is Stronger Than Life
Love Laughs at Locksmiths
Love, Luck and Gasoline
Love-Making Under Difficulties
The Love of Chrysanthemum
The Love of Lady Irma
The Love Romance of the Girl Spy
Love the Conqueror
Love Ye One Another
Love Your Neighbor as Yourself, but Leave His Wife Alone!
The Lover's Embarrassment
The Lovers' Mill
The Lover's Oracle
The Lovers' Well
Love's Awakening
Love's "C.Q.D."
Love's Great Tragedy
Love's Old Sweet Song
Love's Sorrow
Loving Hearts
Madness for Love
A Martyr of Love
A Mexican Love Affair
Moonshine and Love
Mother Love
No Trifling with Love
The Old Loves and the New
The Playwright's Love
Red Eagle's Love Affair
The Slave's Love
The Stubborn Lover
Testing Their Love
Tontolini Is in Love
'Twixt Loyalty and Love
Unrequited Love
An Unselfish Love
The Vagaries of Love
We Will Die Together, Love
When Love Is Young
When Lovers Part
White-Doe's Lover
The Wings of Love
Winning Back His Love
A Woman's Love

Love letter

1905 Love Letter
1906 Love Letter
1907 Bertie's Love Letter
1909 The Deacon's Love Letter
Love Letter
Old Love Letters

Lovelace, Capt.

1907 [Picture Taken for Capt. Lovelace]

Lovelock, Princess

1910 Adventures of Princess Lovelock

Lovely

1909 A Lovely Lass

Loving Cup

1899 Presentation of Loving Cup at City Hall, New York

Lowe (Mountain), California

1901 Ascending Mt. Low, California
Panoramic View of Rubio Canyon, Mt. Low R.R.
1906 Ascent of Mount Lowe

Loyalty

1908 The Peasant Girl's Loyalty
1909 Disinherited Son's Loyalty
The Little Father; or, The Dressmaker's Loyal Son
The Loyal Indian
1910 Red Wing's Loyalty
Spanish Loyalty

1899 Scrubbem's Washing Machine
1900 Demonstrating the Action of the Chicago Pneumatic Tool Co.'s Deck Machine
1901 Coming Out of Scraping Machines and Cutting Off Heads
Machine and Can Tester
Square Can Machine
Stuffing Cans by Machinery
Testing Cans by Machinery
1902 Demonstrating the Action of a Mergenthaler-Horton Basket Making Machine
Demonstrating the Action of an Agnew Mailing Machine
Demonstrating the Action of an Altman-Taylor Threshing Machine
Experimental. Moving Picture Machine
Ganswindt's Flying Machine
Rube and the Weighing Machine
1903 Cancelling Machine, U.S.P.O.
Wheat Harvesting Machines in Operation
1904 Coil Winding Machines, Westinghouse Works
Panorama of Machine Co. Aisle, Westinghouse Co. Works
Westinghouse Air Brake Co., Casting Machine
Westinghouse Co., No. 3, Moulding Machine
1905 Flying Machine, Earl's Court, London
1906 Flying Machine
1907 Panorama Ruins of Old French Machinery
1909 The Infernal Machine
1910 The Laughing Machine
Wonderful Machine Oil

McKeen, Bridget
1901 The Finish of Bridget McKeen

McKeever
1902 Pugilist McKeever and Wife Bag Punching

McKenzie Traction Engines
1903 Transvaal War Supplies Transported by McKenzie Traction Engines

Mackerel
1901 Unloading a Mackerel Schooner

McKinley, William
1896 McKinley at Home, Canton, Ohio
Parade at Canton O., Showing Major McKinley in Carriage
1897 McKinley and Cleveland Going to the Capitol
McKinley and Others in Carriage
McKinley Leaving Church
McKinley Taking the Oath
McKinley Train, Penn. R.R.
President Cleveland and President McKinley
President McKinley's Address
Return of McKinley from the Capitol
1898 President McKinley and Cabinet at Camp Alger, May 28, 1898
President McKinley's Inspection of Camp Wikoff
1899 McKinley Leaving State House, Boston
Mrs. U.S. Grant and President McKinley
President and Mrs. McKinley
President McKinley
President McKinley and Mayor Ashbridge of Philadelphia
President McKinley and Wife, Members of His Cabinet and Their Wives and Capt. Coghlan Leaving the Cruiser Raleigh
President McKinley Reviewing the Troops
1900 President McKinley Laying Corner Stone
1901 Arrival of McKinley's Funeral Train at Canton, Ohio
Funeral of President McKinley
Launching of the New Battleship "Ohio" at San Francisco, Cal. When President McKinley Was There
McKinley Funeral—In Solemn State
McKinley's Funeral Entering Westlawn Cemetery, Canton [Ohio]
Panoramic View of the Crowd Rushing for the City Hall, Buffalo, to View the Body of President McKinley
President McKinley and Escort Going to the Capitol
President McKinley at the Buffalo Exposition
President McKinley Leaving the White House for the Capitol
President McKinley Reviewing the Troops at the Pan-American Exposition
President McKinley Taking the Oath
President McKinley's Funeral
President McKinley's Funeral Cortege at Buffalo, N.Y.
President McKinley's Funeral Cortege at Washington, D.C.
President McKinley's Speech at the Pan-American Exposition
Taking President McKinley's Body from Train at Canton, Ohio
1903 McKinley's Funeral
President McKinley and His Cabinet on the Reviewing Stand, at Fairmount Park, Phila., May 27, 1899

McKinley, William, Mrs.
1899 President McKinley and Wife, Members of His Cabinet and Their Wives and Capt. Coghlan Leaving the Cruiser Raleigh

McKinley Cut, Mount Tamalpais (California)
1902 Panoramic View of Mt. Tamalpais Between Bow Knot and McKinley Cut

McKinley Homestead, Canton (Ohio)
1901 Panoramic View of the McKinley Homestead

McKinley Memorial
1907 The Unveiling Ceremonies of the McKinley Memorial, Canton, Ohio, September 30th, 1907

MacNab
1910 MacNab Visits the Comet

MacNabb
1909 Mac Nabb Wants to Get Arrested

McNair, Admiral
1898 Admiral McNair, U.S.N.

McPherson, Sandy
1908 Sandy McPherson's Quiet Fishing Trip

Mad
1908 The Mad Musician [An Escape from an Insane Asylum]
Money Mad
1909 Mad Dog
The Mad Miner
Puzzle Mad
1910 Am I Mad?
The Mad Dog Scare
The Mad Drainpipe
The Mad Hermit
The Mad Lady of Chester
The Mad Miner Recovers

Madam
1907 Madam's Fancies
1908 Madam Flirt and Her Adopted Uncle
Madam Is Capricious
1909 Madam Lydia's Little Trick
1910 Madam's Favorite

Madame
1904 Mind! Madame Is Coming
In a Hurry to Catch the Train (Monsieur et madame sont pressés)
1907 Madame Goes Shopping
1910 Madame Clairo

Madcap
1908 The Little Mad-Cap; or, Oh Splash!

Maddened
1909 Maddened Players

Madding
1909 Far from the Madding Crowd

Madeira
1908 Madeira Wicker Chair Industry
Sunny Madeira
1909 The Cook Makes Madeira Sauce

Madison Square (New York City)
1897 Broadway, New York, at Madison Square
1902 Madison Square, New York City
1903 Madison Square, New York

Madison Square Garden (New York City)
1904 Treloar and Miss Marshall, Prize Winners at the Physical Culture Show in Madison Square Garden

Madison Street (Chicago)
1897 Corner Madison and State Streets, Chicago
1903 State and Madison Sts., Chicago

Madman
1908 The Madman of the Cliff
1909 The Shell; or, "A Madman's Revenge"

Madness
1907 From Jealousy to Madness
1910 Madness for Love
Method in His Madness

Madoera (Java)
1909 Buffalo Racing in Madoera

Madonna
1903 Gigantic Devil (Le diable géant ou le miracle de la Madonne)

Madrid (Spain)
1908 Fire Maneuvers in Madrid
1909 A Romance of Old Madrid

Madwoman
1909 Madwoman's Child

Maelstrom
1910 The Maelstrom

Maestro
1906 The Maestro Do-Mi-Sol-Do

Mafeking (South Africa)
1900 Battle of Mafeking
1909 The Heroine of Mafeking

Mafia
1909 "Mafia," the Secret Society; or, Sicilian Family Honor

Magalang (Philippines)
1900 The Attack on Magalang

Magazine
1909 On Guard at the Powder Magazine

Magda
1909 Magda

Magdalene
1910 Magdalene; or, The Workman's Daughter
The New Magdalene

Maggie
1908 Maggie, the Dock Rat

Maggiore (Lake), Italy
1902 Moonlight on Lake Maggiore, Italy

Magi
1904 The Passion Play (L'adoration des Mages)

Magic and magicians
1899 Merlin, the Magician
1900 Hooligan Assists the Magician
How the Magician Got the Best of the Installment Man
The Magic Picture
The Magician
1902 The Double Magician and the Magical Head
Extraordinary Chinese Magic
Magical Changes
The Magical Dish Mender
The Magical Hen
Magical Sword
The Magician and the Human Pump
The Magician and the Seven Hats
The Weary Hunters and the Magician
Wonderful Magic
1903 Alcrofrisbas, the Master Magician
An Arabian Magician
Black Magic
The Magic Book
The Magic Table
The Magical Egg
The Magical Tramp
The Magician
Magician
The Magician and the Imp
Mephistopheles' School of Magic
Ten Ichi, the Famous Japanese Magician, with His Troop
1904 The Magic Hat
The Magic Hoop
A Wager Between Two Magicians; or, Jealous of Myself
1905 Magic Cone
Magic Hair Restorer
1906 The Magic Flute
Magic Roses
1907 The Magic Bottle
Magic Drawing Room
1908 Bogus Magic Powder
Fantastic Magic
The Little Magician
Magic Album
The Magic Bag
Magic Dice
The Magic Flute
The Magic Handkerchief
The Magic Mirror
The Magic of Catchy Songs
The Magic Powder
The Magic Ring
The Magic Rubbers
Magical Suit of Armor
A Magical Tramp
A Magician's Love Test
Modern Magic
The Wand Has Lost Its Magic
Willie's Magic Wand

The Violin Maker of Cremona

Makeup
1899 The "Make-Up" Thief
1904 The Untamable Whiskers (Le roi du maquillage)
1909 Grotesque Make-Up

Making
1897 Making an Arrest
Making Love in a Hammock
Making Soap Bubbles
1898 Making an Impression
Making Love on the Beach
Troops Making Military Road in Front of Santiago
1899 Jones Makes a Discovery
1900 The Art of "Making Up"
How Bridget Made the Fire
Making Manila Rope
Pierrot's Problem, or How To Make a Fat Wife Out of Two Lean Ones
1902 Demonstrating the Action of a Mergenthaler-Horton Basket Making Machine
1903 Boy Up a Tree; or, Making Love in the Park
Making a Welch Rabbit
1904 Buster Makes Room for His Mama at the Bargain Counter
How the Cook Made Her Mark
"A Newspaper in Making"
1905 Brick Making Rotifier
A Poor Place for Love Making
1907 Making Champagne
Making Love to the Coalman's Wife
The Making of a Modern Newspaper
Making Pottery in Japan
Making the Dirt Fly: Scene 1. Steam Shovel in Operation, Culebra Cut
Making the Dirt Fly: Scene 2. Unloading a Dirt Train
Making the Dirt Fly: Scene 3. Dirt Scraper in Operation
Making the Dirt Fly: Scene 4. Railroad Track Lifter in Operation
Making the Dirt Fly: Scene 5. Laborers Lining Up at Mess Tent
A Wig Made To Order
1908 Biscuits Like Mother Used to Make
Doll Making
How Glue Is Made
Making a Sale
Making Arabian Pottery
Making Charcoal
Making Home Attractive
Making Moving Pictures
Making of Tomato Sauce
Rose That Makes Everybody Dance
Sabot Making
1909 Bailiff Makes a Seizure
Cigarette Making: From Plantation to Consumer
The Cook Makes Madeira Sauce
Hat Making
How French Perfumes Are Made
Indian Basket Making
Making It Pleasant for Him
Making Lace
The Making of a Champion
Making of a Sailor
The Making of Honey
Making Tambourines
1910 Butter Making in Normandy
Clothes Make the Man
How Hubby Made Good
How the Tenderfoot Made Good
Making a Man of Him
Making Salt
Making Sherry Wine at Xeres
Making Wooden Shoes
Max Makes a Touch

Malabar (India)
1906 The Jolly Monks of Malabar

Malady
1908 Prince Kin Kin's Malady
1909 A Troublesome Malady

Malice
1903 The Mysterious Box (La boîte à malice)
1909 Malicious Rival

Mall
1901 Circular Panorama of the Base of the Electric Tower, Ending Looking Down the Mall

Mama
use **Mother**

Mame
1909 Plain Mame; or, All That Glitters Is Not Gold

Mamie
1899 How Mamie Had Her Leg Pulled
Why Mamie Missed the Masquerade

Mamma
use **Mother**

Mammoth
1905 Overturning a Mammoth Chimney

Mammoth Hot Springs, Yellowstone National Park (Wyoming)
1899 Coaches Arriving at Mammoth Hot Springs

Mammouth Paint Pot, Yosemite Valley (California)
1903 Mammouth Paint Pot, Yosemite Valley

Mammy
1910 Mammy's Boy Joins the Army

Man
1896 Wrestling Pony and Man
1898 The Men Behind the Guns
Three Men in a Boat
1899 Male Prisoners Marching to Dinner
"Man Overboard!"
1900 Found a Man Under the Bed
How They Rob Men in Chicago
The Man in the Jimjams
Not a Man in Sight
Not the Man She Waited for
What they Do to Respectable Men in the Tenderloin
Four Heads Better Than One (Un homme de tête)
Four Heads Better Than One (Le homme de têtes ou les quatres têtes embarrassantes)
1901 Firemen Rescuing Men and Women
Squad of Men Clearing the Road
1902 A Little Man
1903 Giant Wilkins, the Largest Man in the World
The Inn Where No Man Rests
Man Couchee Dance
Man Overboard! "INDIANA"
The Man with the Iron Jaw
The Man with the Many Faces
Man's Best Friend
Men Getting on Trolley, National Cash Register Co.
Men in Physical Exercise, National Cash Register Co.
Men Leaving Factory, National Cash Register Co.
Men Taking Fish from Salmon Seine
Conjurer and 100 Tricks (L'homme aux cent trucs)
The Lightning Change Artist (L'homme protée)
1904 Every Man His Own Cigar Lighter
The Funniest Man in the Exposition
Nervous Man Retiring
Sick Man's Delirium
The Widow and the Only Man
1905 Man Wanted
1906 The Man with the Ladder and the Hose
Man with 36 Heads
Man Without Scruple
1907 The Awkward Man; or, Oh! So Clumsy
The Busy Man
Cheekiest Man on Earth
The Magnetized Man
Man Being Run Over by Automobile
Man, Hat and Cocktail, a New Drink, but an Old Joke
Man Who Hangs Himself
The Parson of Hungry Gulch; or, The Right Man in the Right Place May Work Wonders
Wanted a Man Badly
The Wrong Chimney; or, Every Man His Own Sweep
1908 The Happy Man's Shirt
The Invisible Men
The Man and His Bottle
The Man and the Woman
Man Hunt
The Man in the Box
The Man in the Overalls
Man Under the Bed
Man Who Walks on the Water
Man with Calf's Head
The Man with the Big Mouth
A Mean Man
Men and Women
The Mishaps of a Bashful Man
The Selfish Man
The Ticklish Man
1909 Are You the Man?
A Distracted Man
The Evil That Men Do
The Fisherman; or, Men Must Work and Women Must Weep
Happy Man
The Irresolute Man
Jealousy and the Man
A Lucky Man
The Man and the Girl
The Man and the Law
The Man Housemaid
Man in Pieces
The Man Who Knows How to Whistle
Man with the Cut Throat
Man with the Dolls
Man with the Sack in Society
A Man with Three Wives
A Man Without a Country
Napoleon: the Man of Destiny
On Another Man's Pass
The Origin of Man
Two Women and a Man
The Way of Man
A Pair of White Gloves (L'homme aux gants blancs)
The Invisible Thief (L'homme invisible)
1910 The Branded Man
Brother Man
The Buried Man of Tebessa
Clothes Make the Man
The Devil, the Servant, and the Man
How a Bad Tempered Man Was Cured
The Law and the Man
Making a Man of Him
The Man
A Man and a Girl
The Man Behind the Curtain
The Man from Texas
A Man of Honor
The Man Suffragette for the Abolition of Work for Women
The Man Under the Bed
The Man Who Could Not Sit Down
The Man Who Died
The Man Who Learned
The Man Who Lost
The Man Who Waited
The Man with the Weak Heart
A Man's Way
The Oath and the Man
One Man's Confession
Quarrelsome Man
Re-Making of a Man
The Selfish Man's Lesson
The Shipwrecked Man
The Squaw and the Man
Two Men
The Wrong Man

Man-haters
1910 The Men Hater's Club

Man in the moon
1899 A Trip to the Moon (L'homme dans la lune)
1909 The Man in the Moon

Man-monkey
1907 The Man Monkey
1909 The Man Monkey

Man-of-war
1898 A Breezy Day on a Man-o'-War
Launch of Japanese Man-of-War "Chitosa"
Uncle Rube's Visit to the Man-o' War
1903 One of Jack's Games Aboard a Man o' War
1904 Japanese Coaling a Man-of-War
1905 Mutiny on Man-of-War in Odessa
1908 A Yankee Man-o-Warsman's Fight for Love

Manage
1898 A Bigger Fish Than He Could Manage

Manager
1904 The Music Hall Manager's Dilemma
The Troubles of a Manager of a Burlesque Show

Manassas (Virginia)
1904 Military Maneuvers, Manassas, Va.

Market Scene in Cairo, Egypt
Market Scene in Hanoi, China
The New Dude and a Market Woman
New York City "Ghetto" Fish Market
Panoramic View of an Egyptian Cattle Market
Scenes in an Irish Market Place
1904 The Market Woman's Mishap
1905 Convent Garden Market, London
Fish Carvers, at Fish Market Bergen Norway
Market Day at Kenmore
Market Women Leaving the Railway Station at Galway, Ireland
1907 Old Market Place, Panama
1909 Farmer Jones Goes to the Market
Husband Goes to Market
1910 Egyptian Village Market

Market Square, Harrisburg (Pennsylvania)
1897 Market Square, Harrisburg, Pa.

Market Square, Providence (Rhode Island)
1899 Market Square, Providence, R.I.

Market Street
1907 Panorama of Market Street Showing the Beautiful Decorations

Market Street, San Francisco (California)
1899 Market Street
1903 Fourth and Market Sts., San Francisco
Market Street Before Parade
1906 Circular Panorama of Market St. and Stockton
City Hall from Market St. and City Hall Ave.
Panorama of Market Street Before the Fire
Panorama of Market Street, San Francisco
Panoramas of Market Street, the City Hall, Taken from the Roof of the U.S. Mint
Panoramic View of Market Street San Francisco After the Earthquake and Fire
Refugees on Market St.
1907 Panorama of Market Street, San Francisco

Marksmanship
1902 Marvelous Markmanship
1910 A Chosen Marksman

Marquis
1909 Your Turn, Marquis

Marriage
1902 Will He Marry the Girl?
1906 Joys of Marriage
Marriage of Princess Ena and Alphonse XIII, King of Spain
Married for Millions
A Childish Match (Mariage enfantin)
1907 Is Marriage a Failure?
Just Married
Trial Marriages
An Uncle by Marriage
How Bridget's Lover Escaped (Le mariage de Victoire)
How Bridget's Lover Escaped (Le mariage de Victorine)
1908 Bill Wants to Marry a Toe Dancer
Don't You Think It's Time to Marry
Expensive Marriage
I Would Like to Marry You
The Marriage of a French Soldier
My Daughter Will Only Marry a Strong Man
Time to Get Married
A Lover's Hazing (Mariage de raison et mariage d'amour)
1909 The Cripple's Marriage
Forced into Marriage
How Brown Got Married
I'll Only Marry a Sport
In India, Marriage of the Nephew of the Maharajah of Tagore
Marriage in Haste
A Marriage of Convenience
Marriage of Love
Marriage of Yvonne
Married Twice
Married Under Difficulties
Morganatic Marriage
Paul Has Decided to Marry
A Profitable Marriage
Spanish Marriage
Why She Didn't Marry
Why They Married
1910 Foolshead Marries Against His Will
Foolshead Wishes to Marry the Governor's Daughter
Foxy Hobo Married for Love
Juliet Wants to Marry an Artist
Love and Marriage in Poster Land
Marriage in Haste
The Marriage of Esther
The Marriage of the Cook
Married in Haste
Married on Horseback
She Wanted to Marry a Hero
Tommy Gets His Sister Married
Tweedledum and Frothy Want to Get Married

Mars
1910 A Trip to Mars

Marseilles (France)
1902 The Old Port of Marseilles
On the Marseilles Tramway

Marshall
1910 Great Marshall Jewel Case

Marshall, Miss
1904 Treloar and Miss Marshall, Prize Winners at the Physical Culture Show in Madison Square Garden

Marshals
1910 The New Marshall at Gila Creek

Marshes
1909 Pontine Marshes, Italy

Martha
1902 Martha

Martha (Opera)
1900 Opera of Martha
1909 Duet from "Martha" (Flotow)

Martin
1909 The Martins Leave Home for a Week

Martin, "Denver" Ed
1901 Ruhlin Boxing with "Denver" Ed. Martin

Martin, Marie
1908 The Red Barn Mystery: A Startling Portrayal of the Great Marie Martin Mystery

Martinique
1902 Burning of St. Pierre [Martinique]
Mt. Pelee in Eruption and Destruction of St. Pierre [Martinique]
Mt. Pelee Smoking Before Eruption [St. Pierre, Martinique]
Native Women Washing Clothes at the Gueydon Fountain, Fort de France, Martinique
Natives Unloading a Coaling Vessel at Fort de France, Martinique
Storm at Sea near St. Pierre, Martinique
Street Scene in Fort de France, Martinique
1903 Panoramic View of St. Pierre, Martinique

Martius
1901 The Campus Martius

Martyrs
1901 The Martyred Presidents
1905 Christian Martyrs
1906 Martyrs of the Inquisition
1909 The Christian Martyrs
Martyr or Crank?
Martyrdom of Louis XVII
1910 From Love to Martyrdom
A Martyr of Love
Martyrs of Pompeii

Marvelous
1902 Marvelous Markmanship
1903 The Marvelous Wreath
1908 Marvelous Pacifier
The Marvelous Powder
1909 Marvellous Garlands
A Marvelous Ointment
Marvelous Shaving Soap
1910 Marvellous Waters
The Marvelous Cure; or, The Wonderful Hair-Growing Fluid
Marvelous Indeed

Marvin
1900 Marvin and Casler's Laboratory

Marvin, H. N.
1900 H. N. Marvin's Family

Mary
1901 Ten Nights in a Bar-Room: Death of Little Mary
Ten Nights in a Bar-Room: Vision of Mary
1903 Mary Had a Little Lamb
1904 Mary in the Dock
1908 Bathing; or, Charlie and Mary in the Country
1909 Nearsighted Mary
Tickle Mary
Top-Heavy Mary
1910 Big-Hearted Mary
Little Mary and Her Dolly

Mary Jane
1903 Mary Jane's Mishap; or, Don't Fool with the Parafin
1909 Mary Jane Visits Her Country Cousin
Mary Jane's Lovers
1910 The Education of Mary Jane

Maryland
1898 First Maryland Volunteers
1904 Panorama of Ruins from Lombard and Hanover Streets, Baltimore, Md.
1909 Maryland 1777

Mascot
1898 The Fighting Fifth Cuban Mascot
1903 Jack's Four Footed Friend. Mike the Ship's Mascot
1910 The Mascot of Company "D"

Mascotte (Steamer)
1898 Steamer "Mascotte" Arriving at Tampa

Mash
1907 A Mash a Smash a Splash

Masher
1900 The Masher's Waterloo
1904 The Masher's Dilemma
1905 Masher and Nursemaid
Masher and Oyster Stand
1907 How the Masher Was Punished
The Masher
Old Mashers
1908 Mashing the Masher
1910 Curing a Masher
The Masher
The Masher's Delirium

Mask
1898 Masked Procession
1904 Masks and Faces
1908 Masked Policeman
The Secret of the Iron Mask
1909 Behind the Mask
The Iron Mask
1910 Behind a Mask
The Mask Maker

Mason
1903 Funeral of Lung Fei Dong, the Chinese Mason
1909 The Mason's Paradise

Mason, Bill
1910 Bill Mason's Ride

Masquerade
1899 Why Mamie Missed the Masquerade
1900 Jones' Return from a Masquerade
1903 Murphy Returns from a Masquerade
Procession of Floats and Masqueraders at Nice Carnival
1906 The Masqueraders
1907 The Masquerade Party
1908 The Masque Ball
The Masqueraders
A Night with the Masqueraders in Paris
1909 Masquerade Costume
Masquerader's Charity
The Tramp at the Masquerade
1910 The Foxy Soldiers; or, How Schmidt Got to the Masquerade
The Masquerade Cop
Mephisto at a Masquerade
A Tangled Masquerade

Massachusetts
1897 First Corps Cadets; Mass. National Guard
1898 Boston Commandery, Boston, Mass.
Fifth Massachusetts Volunteers
First Battalion of the 2nd Massachusetts Volunteers
Massachusetts Regiment Marching
Second Battalion; 2nd Massachusetts Volunteers
1899 Demonstrating the Action of a Patent Street Sprinkler of the American Car Sprinkler Co. of Worcester, Mass
Eighth Regiment, Mass. Volunteers
Governor Walcott of Massachusetts
1901 The Fire Department of Chelsea, Mass.
1902 Prince Henry [of Prussia] Visiting Cambridge, Mass. and Harvard University
1904 Massachusetts Naval Reserves Leaving the U.S.S. "Alabama"
1905 Gov. Wm. L. Douglas, of Mass.
Mobilization of the Massachusetts State Troops
1906 The 9th Mass. Vol. Militia

The Military Funeral of the "Standard Bearer of the Yalu"
Military Maneuvers, Manassas, Va.
Military Serenade
Military Tactics
Parade of Military, St. Louis Exposition
1905 Military Display at Hurlingham
1906 Military Feeding Starving and Destitute Refugees in Golden Gate Park
Scenes and Incidents U.S. Military Academy, West Point
1907 A Military Prison
1908 H. R. H. The Prince of Wales Viewing the Grand Military Review on the Plains of Abraham, Quebec
Military Airship "Ville de Paris"
Military Parade, Founders Week Celebration, Philadelphia
Military Swimming Championship
Military Tournament at Saumur
Wanted: A Military Man
1909 Military Parade
Military Review
United States Military Tournament
1910 Military Cyclists of Belgium
Military Dirigible
Military Kite Flying at Rheims

Militia
1897 Drum Corps and Militia
Pennsylvania State Militia, Double Time
Pennsylvania State Militia, Single Time
1899 New York Naval Militia
1900 U.S. Naval Militia
1904 The Amorous Militiaman
1906 The 9th Mass. Vol. Militia

Milk
1897 The Milker's Mishap
1902 Milking Time on the Farm
On a Milk Diet
1903 Irish Peasants Bringing Their Milk to a Cooperative Creamery
Spilled Milk
Spilt Milk
Trouble with the Milkmaid
What Happened to the Milkman
1904 The Baby, the Monkey and the Milk Bottle
1905 Milking Time: A Kerry Herd
1906 Penny Milk
1907 An Early Round with the Milkman
1909 The Milkman's Wooing
Ponto Runs Away with the Milk Cart
Some Milk for Baby
1910 All on Account of the Milk
A Drink of Goat's Milk
The Milk Industry in the Alps
The Millionaire Milkman

Mill Creek
1910 The Widow of Mill Creek Flat

Miller
1900 The Chimney Sweep and the Miller
1903 The Miller and Chimney Sweep
1905 The Miller's Daughter
1908 The Miller, His Son and the Ass
1909 Miller's Dream

Miller, Louisa
1910 Louisa Miller

Miller Bros.
1907 Scenes from Miller Bros.

Millesaunte
1910 Vengeance of Millesaunte

Millicent, Mady
1909 Mady Millicent's Visitor

Milliner
1909 The Little Milliner and the Thief
A Pretty Little Milliner
1910 My Milliner's Bill

Million
1902 B. F. Keith's New Million Dollar Theatre
1906 Married for Millions
1907 A Race for Millions
1909 A Million Dollar Mix-Up
1910 A Fight for Millions
That Gentleman Has Won a Million

Millionaire
1897 Tramp in a Millionaire's Bed
1905 How Millionaires Sometimes Entertain Aboard Their Yachts
1906 Panorama, Nob Hill and Ruins of Millionaire Residences
1909 The Cobbler and the Millionaire
The Cowboy Millionaire
From Millionaire to Porter
The Maid and the Millionaire
A Millionaire Bootblack
1910 Adventure of a Millionaire
The Millionaire and the Ranch Girl
The Millionaire Milkman
A Millionaire Tramp
The Millionaire's Adventure

Mills
1896 Clark's Thread Mill
1900 Employees of Wolfson's Spice Mills, Toledo
Mill Hands
1902 Ye Olde Mill
1903 Chinese Silk Mill
Wiring Pike in a Mill Stream
1907 The Mill Girl, a Story of Factory Life
1908 The Mill
Romance of the Old Mill
The Saw Mill
Thunderbolt on the Mill
1909 The Girl at the Old Mill
The Mill Girl
The Mills of the Gods
The Poet and the Maid at the Mill
1910 The Attack on the Mill
The Lovers' Mill
Tragedy at the Mill

Milon, Père
1909 Père Milon

Mimosa
1909 Mimosa and the Good Prince

Mince
1901 Mince Meat Room
1910 Home Made Mince Pie

Mind
1908 Something on His Mind
1910 Out of Sight, Out of Mind

Mind reader
1908 The Mind Reader

Minding
1904 Mind! Madame Is Coming
1906 Papa Minds the Baby
1907 Private Atkins Minds the Baby
1910 Mind, I Catch You Smoking

Mines, miners and mining
1900 Mining Operations
1901 Mine Explosion and What Followed
1902 Exploding a Land Mine
Exploding a Submarine Mine
Miners at Work Under Guard of Troops
1903 Blasting the Treadwell Mines
Breaker Boys Leaving the Coal Mines
Coal Mine
Hydraulic Mining in Oregon
Mules in the Coal Mines
Old Method of Mining, No. 11 Eldorado
Pack Train Leaving Valdez for Copper Mines
Sluice Mining on Gold Hill in the Klondike, Hutchinson and Johnstone's Claim of No. 6, Eldorado
1904 Mining Operations, Pennsylvania Coal Fields
Working in the Charcoal Mines in France
1905 Blasting in the Glory Hole of the Treadwell Mine, Alaska
In the Mining District
Old Time Miner Rocking for Gold in the Tailings, Klondike
Slavonian Miners Running to Dinner, Treadwell Mine, Alaska
1907 De Beers Diamond Mines, Kimberly, S.A.
Life in a South African Gold Mine
The Lost Mine
The Miner's Daughter
Mines and Forge at Decazeville
1908 In the Land of the Gold Mines
The Miner's Daughter
The Molly Maguires; or, Labor Wars in the Coal Mines
1909 The Fatal Ball; or, The Miner's Daughter
Lead and Zinc Mines
The Mad Miner
The Miner's Wife
The Miner's Will
Santa Claus and the Miner's Child
The Yellow Jacket Mine
1910 Blue Horse Mine
A Daughter of the Mine
A Daughter of the Mines
The Mad Miner Recovers
A Mica Mine, the Ullugura Mountains
The Miner and Camille
The Miners
The Miner's Sacrifice
A Miner's Sweetheart
The Miner's Sweetheart
New South Wales Gold Mine
The Old Miner's Doll
An Old Silver Mine in Peru
The Prayer of a Miner's Child
The Rival Miners
The Salted Mine
Silver Plume Mine

Miniature
1901 Miniature Railway
1902 Miniature Railway
The Miniature Railway
1903 Miniature Prize Fighters
Miniature Railway at Wilmington Springs, Delaware
1906 Miniature Theatre
1908 The Miniature Circus
Parisian Life in Miniature
1910 The Miniature

Minister
1898 Little Willie and the Minister
The Minister's Wooing
1903 The Minister's Hat
1909 The Minister's Daughter
The New Minister; or, The Drunkard's Daughter
1910 The Clown and the Minister
The Minister's New Suit
The Minister's Speech
The New Minister
Our New Minister
The Sons of the Minister

Minneapolis (Ship)
1898 Cruiser "Minneapolis"

Minnehaha
1897 Falls of Minnehaha
1910 The Death of Minnehaha

Minnesota
1898 Fifteenth Minnesota Volunteers

Minotaur
1910 The Minotaur

Minstrel
1905 A Moorish Street Minstrel Performing at Morocco City
1908 Minstrel Mishaps; or, Late for Rehearsal
The Minstrel's Sacrifice
1910 Amorous Minstrel
Catalan, the Minstrel

Mint
1906 Exploded Gas Tanks, U.S. Mint, Emporium and Spreckels' Bld'g.
Panoramas of Market Street, the City Hall, Taken from the Roof of the U.S. Mint

Minta, Mrs.
1909 Mrs. Minta's Husband

Minto, Lady
1899 Lord and Lady Minto
1903 Arrival of Lord and Lady Minto at the Barracks, Dawson
Lord and Lady Minto with Party, Fording the Rushing Waters of the Klondike on Horseback

Minto, Lord
1899 Lord and Lady Minto
1902 Arrival of the Governor General, Lord Minto, at Quebec
1903 Arrival of Lord and Lady Minto at the Barracks, Dawson
Lord and Lady Minto with Party, Fording the Rushing Waters of the Klondike on Horseback

Minuet
1903 The Minuet. No. 3
1904 Minuet and Dance—College Women's Club

Minuteman Geyser, Yellowstone Park
1905 Minuteman Geyser, Yellowstone Park

Minutes
1897 60 Minute Flyer
1901 Five Minutes to Train Time
1902 A Mile a Minute on an Ice Yacht
Ten Minutes at Monte Carlo
1905 Around New York in 15 Minutes
1908 Love in 20 Minutes
'Round Brussels in Ten Minutes
Ten Minutes with Shakespeare
1909 Five Minutes Interview
1910 Five Minutes to Twelve
45 Minutes from Broadway
Ready in a Minute

Mixed
1902 A Little Mix-Up in a Mixed Ale Joint
1904 Mixed Bathing
Too Much Mixed Ale
1908 Mixed Babies
1909 Mixed in His Dinner Dates
The Mixed Letters

Mix-up
1898 A Very Laughable Mixup
1902 A Little Mix-Up in a Mixed Ale Joint
1903 Clown's Mixup
1906 A Mix-Up in the Gallery
1908 The Hotel Mix-Up
1909 A Million Dollar Mix-Up
Mix-Up at Court

Mizpah (Jordan)
1903 Tourists Returning on Donkeys from Mizpah

Mob
1901 The Mob Outside the Temple of Music at the Pan-American Exposition [Buffalo]

Mobilization
1905 Mobilization of the Massachusetts State Troops

Mock
1908 The Mock Baronets

Modder River (South Africa)
1903 Troop Train Conveying the Seaforth Highlanders Across the Modder River

Model
1897 The Model
1898 A Living Picture Model Posing Before a Mirror
Underwear Model
1899 The Corset Model
The Jealous Model
1901 "The Pouting Model"
1902 The Draped Model
1903 The Artists Model
The Fate of the Artist's Model
Inquisitive Models
The Irate Model
1904 A Busy Day for the Corset Model
The Model That Didn't Pose
The Rival Models
Sculptor and Model
1907 Artist's Model
Mike the Model
The Model's Ma
Bakers in Trouble (La boulangerie modèle)
1908 The Fisherman's Model
The Gypsy Model
The Model
Mother-in-Law and the Artist's Model
Selling a Model
The Two Models
Wanted: An Artist's Model
1909 An Artist's Model's Jealousy
The Artist's Model's Sweetheart
Runaway Model
1910 The Inventor's Model
The Model Drama
The Model's Redemption

Modern
1894 Souvenir Strip of the Edison Kinetoscope [Sandow, the Modern Hercules]
1899 The Humane Side of Modern Warfare
1903 Modern House Furnishing Methods
1904 Modern High School Riding
1905 Modern Brigandage
A Modern Sappho
Modern Style House Maids
1906 A Modern Diogenes
The Modern Oliver Twist; or, The Life of a Pickpocket'
1907 The Making of a Modern Newspaper
Modern Burglars
A Modern Don Juan
Modern Hercules at Work
A Modern Mother
Modern Painters
A Modern Samson
A Modern Youth
1908 Modern Hotel
Modern Magic
A Modern Naval-Hero
A Modern Samson
Modern Sculptors
1909 Modern Algeria
Modern Cinderella
A Modern Dr. Jekyll
Modern Egypt
Modern Tramp
1910 A Modern Cinderella
A Modern Courtship
Modern Highwayman
A Modern Knight Errant
The Modern Messenger Boy
The Modern Prodigal
Modern Railway Construction

Modest
1909 A Modest Young Man

Mohammedan
1908 The Mohammedan at Home

Mohawk Indians
1910 A Mohawk's Way

Moher (Ireland)
1905 Tourists Enroute to the Cliffs of Moher, Ireland

Mohican (Ship)
1899 Wreck of the "Mohican"

Mohr, Gerhardi
1909 Gerhardi Mohr

Moir, Gunner
1907 Burns-Moir

Moki Snake Dance
1901 Moki Snake Dance by Walpapi Indians

Moki-Land (Arizona)
1901 Panoramic View of Moki-Land

Molar
1907 Oh! That Molar

Molasses
1908 Love and Molasses

Molière
1910 The Life of Molière

Moline
1901 Moline Bag Punching Platform

Molly
1910 Molly at the Regiment—Her Adventures

Molly Maguires
1908 The Molly Maguires; or, Labor Wars in the Coal Mines

Molucca Islands (Indonesia)
1910 Molucca Islands

Moment
1905 The Tower of London (La Tour de Londres et les dernières moments d'Anne Boleyn)
1907 Tragic Moment
1908 An Awful Moment
1909 The Capricious Moment
1910 The Clown's Big Moment

Monaco
1902 From Monte Carlo to Monaco
1905 Motor Boat Race at Monaco
1906 Monte Carlo to Monaco

Monaghan
1897 Downey-Monaghan (Round 1)
Downey vs. Monaghan

Monarchs
1910 Monarchs of All Nations

Monastery
1903 The Monk in the Monastery Wine Cellar
1910 The Monastery in the Forest

Monday
1903 Naval Parade on the Delaware River, Monday, May 1st, in Honor of Admiral Dewey
1908 Monday Morning in a Coney Island Police Court

Money
1896 Parade, Sound Money Club, Canton, O.
The Sound Money Parade
Sound Money Parade
1898 Kanakas Diving for Money [Honolulu], No. 1
Kanakas Diving for Money [Honolulu], No. 2
1903 How a Wife Gets Her Pocket Money
Native Women Coaling a Ship and Scrambling for Money [West Indies]
West Indian Boys Diving for Money
1904 Love or Money
1905 It's a Shame To Take the Money
1908 Easy Money
False Money
A Fool and His Money
A Fool and His Money Are Soon Parted; or, The Prodigal Son Up-to-Date
Money Mad
1909 The Curse of Money
How Money Circulates
Hush Money
A Run for the Money
1910 The Judas Money; or, An Episode of the War in Vendee
Love and Money
The Money Bag
Nothing but Money
Uncle's Money
White Man's Money, the Indian Curse

Moneybags, Miss
1910 Miss Moneybags Wishes to Wed

Moneylender
1908 The Money Lender
1910 The Money Lender's Son

Moneyweight
1904 Moneyweight Salesmen

Monger
1910 The Dog of the Cheese Monger

Monitor
1898 The Big Monitor Miantonomah Leaving the Navy Yard
The Monitor "Amphitrite"
Monitor "Terror"
The Monitor "Terror"
1903 U.S. Monitor Miantonomah Steaming into Key West
U.S. Monitor Terror

Monk Murren (Switzerland)
1905 Sunset and Sunrise over the Eiger & Monk Murren

Monkey
1896 The Monkey's Feast
1897 The Jealous Monkey
The Mischievous Monkey
1898 Acrobatic Monkey
1903 Egyptian Fakir with Dancing Monkey
1904 August, the Monkey
The Baby, the Monkey and the Milk Bottle
The Monkey and the Ice Cream
The Monkey Bicyclist
Monkey, Dog and Pony Circus
1905 Monkey Business
1907 At the Monkey House
The Man Monkey
1908 The Doctor's Monkey
Spoof and His Monkey
1909 The Automatic Monkey
The Man Monkey
A Race for the Monkey
1910 Aunt Tabitha's Monkey
The Monkey Showmen of Djibah
Troop "B", 15th U.S. Cavalry Bareback Squad in the Monkey Drill at Fort Myer, Virginia

Monkeyland
1908 Monkeyland, a Jungle Romance

Monkeyshines
1910 Monkeyshines

Monks
1898 Capuchin Monks, Rome
1903 Jolly Monks
The Monk in the Monastery Wine Cellar
1906 The Jolly Monks of Malabar
1907 Monk's Vengeance
1908 He Did Not Know He Was a Monk
A Fake Diamond Swindler (L'habit ne fait pas le moine)
1909 The Monk's Mother

Monmouth, Battle of
1908 "Captain Molly" or, The Battle of Monmouth

Monogrammed
1910 The Monogrammed Cigarette

Mono-Railway
1903 The Mono-Railway Between Listowel and Ballybunion, Ireland

Monsieur
1903 How He Missed His Train (Le réveil d'un monsieur pressé)
1904 In a Hurry to Catch the Train (Monsieur et madame sont pressés)
1906 Follower of Women (Un monsieur qui suit les femmes)

Monster
1903 The Monster

Mont Blanc (France)
1902 Panorama, Descending Mt. Blanc
1903 The Ascent of Mount Blanc
1907 Ascending Mt. Blanc
1909 New Cut Roads Up Mt. Blanc
1910 Excursion on the Chain of Mont Blanc
Mont Blanc

1906 Everybody Works but Mother
Everybody Works But Mother
Poor Mother
1907 Bad Mother
Brown Goes to Mother
Father! Mother Wants You
For Mother's Birthday
The Model's Ma
A Modern Mother
Mother's Dream
A Mother's Secret
A Mother's Sin
1908 Anxious Day for Mother
Biscuits Like Mother Used to Make
His Mother's Melody
The Memory of His Mother
A Mother's Crime
Mother's Darling
A Mother's Fault
Obeying Her Mother
Oh Mama
When Ma Goes Shopping
1909 The Actor's Mother
Fantine; or, A Mother's Love
Following Mother's Footsteps
For Mother's Sake
Going Home to Mother
He Can't Lose Wifie's Ma
The Heart of a Mother
A Heartless Mother
Her Mother's Mistake
His Wife's Mother
I Did It, Mamma
Little Mother
The Monk's Mother
Motherly Love of Animals
A Mother's Choice
A Mother's Grief
A Mother's Heart
A Mother's Love
A Mother's Sorrow
Nana's Mother
Necessity Is the Mother of Invention
She Took Mother's Advice
Visions of Mother
1910 The Child of Two Mothers
A Dixie Mother
The Exiled Mother
Her Indian Mother
Her Mother's Wedding Gown
His Mother
His Mother's Letter
His Mother's Thanksgiving
The Little Mother
The Little Mother at the Baby Show
Mama's Birthday Present
Mamma's Angel Child
Ma's New Dog
Mother
Mother and Child
Mother and Daughter
Mother Land
Mother Love
A Mother's Grief
A Mother's Heart
Mother's Portrait
The Mother's Shadow
Mother's Victory
Necessity Is the Mother of Invention
New Little Mother
Pa, Ma and Baby
The Two Mothers
Wifie's Mamma

Mother Goose
1903 Mother Goose Nursery Rhymes
1909 Mother Goose

Mother Hubbard
1902 Old Mother Hubbard

Mother-in-law
1901 You Can't Lose Your Mother-in-Law
1906 Mother-in-Law, a Domestic Comedy
1907 Anarchist's Mother-in-Law
It Was Mother-in-Law
Mother-in-Law at the White City
Mother-in-Law's Race
My Mother-in-Law Is an Angel
Too Much Mother-in-Law
What Is Home Without a Mother-in-Law
1908 Charlie's Ma-in-Law
Hypnotizing Mother-in-Law
Ma-in-Law Mesmerized
Mother-in-Law and the Artist's Model
Mother-in-Law Breaks All Records
Runaway Mother-in-Law
That Mother-in-Law Is a Bore
Tormented by His Mother-in-Law
1909 How Mother-in-Law Got Even
How to Tame a Mother-in-Law
Mother-in-Law Crazy with Music
Mother-in-Law Must Fly
The Mother-in-Law Phantasm
Mother-in-law Too Kindhearted
Mother-in-Law's Day in the Country
Mother-in-Law's Parrot
Son and Mother-in-law
1910 Buying a Mother-in-Law
The Cowboy's Mother-in-Law
Ma-in-Law as a Statue
Mother-in-Law Arrives
Mother-in-law, Son-in-law and Tanglefoot

Motherland
1909 For the Motherland
Love and the Motherland

Motherless
1909 The Motherless Waif
1910 Motherless
Motherless Child
Motherless Waif

Moths
1910 He Got Rid of the Moths
The Moths and the Flame

Motion pictures
rt **Pictures**
1894 Corbett and Courtney Before the Kinetograph
1898 Flag Film [?]
1899 A "Moving" Picture
1900 Boer War Film
Life Motion Photographs of the Fitzsimmons and Ruhlin Fight
Niagara Falls in Life Motion Pictures
1902 Experimental. Moving Picture Machine
Jeffries-Fitzsimmons Reproduction Prize Fight Films
Moving Picture Operator on a Drunk
Uncle Josh at the Moving Picture Show
1904 Moving Pictures While You Wait
1907 "King Oscar II's Funeral Films"
The Moving Picture Man
Panorama, Crowds at Squires-Burns International Contest, from Moving Picture Stand, July 4th, 1907
1908 The Inconvenience of Taking Moving Pictures
Indiscreetness of the Kinematograph
Making Moving Pictures
Tell-Tale Cinematograph
1909 Indiscretion of Moving Picture
[Johnson-Ketchel Fight Films]
The Presidential Inauguration Film
Special Peary Film
Woes of a Cinematographer
1910 Behind the Scenes of the Cinema Stage
[Kinemacolor Films]
Kinematographic X-Ray Picture of a Human Stomach During Digestion, Taken During One Inspiration
Micro-Cinematography: Recurrent Fever
Micro-Cinematography: Sleeping Sickness
The Motion Picture Man
The New Moving Picture Operator
[Talking Moving Picture]
What Happened to a Cinematograph Party
Willie Visits a Moving Picture Show

Motor
1902 Mischievous Willie's Rocking Chair Motor
1904 Panorama Motor Room, Westinghouse Works
1905 Motor Highwayman
1906 Motor Race
1907 Burglary by Motor
1908 Grand Prix Motor Race at Dieppe
Monty Buys a Motor
1909 The Motor Cyclist
Motor Skates
The Mysterious Motor
The Non-Stop Motor Bicycle
1910 The Motor Fiend
World's Championship Motor Races

Motorboats
1905 Motor Boat Race at Monaco
1906 Maneuvering a Small Motor Boat
White Fox Motor Boat
1908 Motor Boat Races
Motor Boat Races, 1908
1909 "Ursula," World's Fastest Motor Boat
1910 Cupid and the Motor Boat
The International Motor Boat Races
Motor and Yacht Boating in England

Motor-car
use **Automobile**

Motorcyclist
1907 The Motorcyclist

Motorists
1906 Blackmailing the Motorists
1907 Chasing a Motorist
Motoring Under Difficulties
The Rival Motorists
1908 Motoring Around the World
Motoring over the Alps
Two Little Motorists
1910 Motoring Among the Cliffs and Gorges of France

Motto
1908 The Duke's Motto

Moulding
1904 Westinghouse Co., No. 3, Moulding Machine
1910 Moulders of Souls

Moulin Rouge, Paris (France)
1898 Moulin Rouge Dancers
1903 Quadrille in Drawers (Quadrille dansé par les etoiles du Moulin-Rouge. 1. En jupon)

Mound
1904 Sliding Down Ice Mound at Niagara Falls

Mount
1896 Park Police Drill Mount and Dismounting
1897 Guard Mount, Ft. Myer [Va.]
Mount and Dismount, Gatling Gun
1907 Strange Mount

Mount of Olives
1904 The Passion Play (Jésus au jardin des oliviers)

Mount Pilatus (Switzerland)
1907 Mount Pilatus Railway

Mount Vernon (Virginia)
1910 [Washington's Home and Ground at Mount Vernon]

Mountaineers
1908 Mountaineers
The Mountaineers
The Mountaineer's Revenge
Mountaineer's Son
1909 The Mountaineer's Honor
1910 The Mountaineer

Mountains
1896 Rip Passing over the Mountain
1897 Lick Observatory, Mt. Hamilton, Cal.
1898 Mount Tamalpais R.R., No. 1
Mount Tamalpais R.R., No. 2
Mount Taw R.R., No. 3
Rocky Mountain Riders Rough Riding
Salt Lake City Company of Rocky Mt. Riders
1899 Down Mount Tom
The Gap, Entrance to the Rocky Mountains
A Ride Through Pack Saddle Mountains, Penna. R.R.
Sliding Down Mount Washington
Summit of Mt. Washington
Under the Shadow of Mt. Stephen, Passing Field's Station in the Rocky Mountains
1900 The Battle of Mt. Ariat
1901 Ascending Mt. Low, California
Panoramic View of Rubio Canyon, Mt. Low R.R.
Royal Train with Duke and Duchess of York, Climbing Mt. Hector
1902 Circular Panoramic View of St. Pierre from the Lighthouse, Showing Mt. Pelee Smoking in the Distance
Circular Panoramic View of St. Pierre, Showing the Ruins of the Catholic Cathedral and Mt. Pelee Smoking in the Background
Down the Mountain Side
The Eruption of Mt. Pelee
Loading the Ice on Cars, Conveying It Across the Mountains and Loading It into Boats
Mt. Pelee in Eruption and Destruction of St. Pierre [Martinique]
Mt. Pelee Smoking Before Eruption [St. Pierre, Martinique]
Panorama, Descending Mt. Blanc
Panoramic View near Mt. Golden on the Canadian Pacific R.R.
Panoramic View of Mt. Tamalpais
Panoramic View of Mt. Tamalpais Between Bow Knot and McKinley Cut
Turning Panorama of Mt. Beacon

1910 The Museum of Sovereigns

Mush dogs
1905 Feeding Mush Dogs, Mulato, Alaska

Music and musicians
1897 Cavalry Musical Drill
Musical Drill; Troop A., Third Cavalry
13th Infantry, U.S. Army—Musical Drill, Governors Island
1901 The Mob Outside the Temple of Music at the Pan-American Exposition [Buffalo]
The Musical Ride
Panoramic View of the Temple of Music and Esplanade
1903 British, with Music, Leaving for the Transvaal
Burning of the Academy of Music, Brooklyn
Musical Calisthenics
Musical Drill with Arms
1904 Filipino Scouts, Musical Drill, St. Louis Exposition
1905 Kiddies Dancing to Hurdy-Gurdy Music, Soho, London
1907 Music, Forward!
The Pastry Cook and Musician
1908 The Mad Musician [An Escape from an Insane Asylum]
Music and Poetry
Music Hath Charms
Music Hath Its Charms
The Music Master
Music Which Hath No Charms
Wandering Musician
1909 The Blind Musician
The Magic of Music
Mother-in-Law Crazy with Music
The Music Lesson
Musical Waiter
The Musician
The Musician's Dream
The Musician's Love Story
The Poor Musician
1910 Music Hath Charms
Musical Masterpiece
The Musical Ranch

Music box
1909 An Alpine Echo; or, The Symphony of a Swiss Music Box

Music halls
1904 The Music Hall Manager's Dilemma
1908 Dog's Music Hall
Music Hall Agent's Dream
A Sport at the Music Hall

Music teachers
1908 Music Teacher
1910 The Music Teacher

Musketeers
1903 The Queen's Musketeers

Muskoka, Ontario (Canada)
1900 Arrival of Train at Muskoka Wharf
Departure of Boats from Muskoka Wharf

Muslin
1904 Typical Algerian 'Ouled Nails' Muslin Dance

Mustache
use **Moustache**

Mustard plaster
1909 The Mustard Plaster

Mute
1910 The Mule Driver and the Garrulous Mute

Mutiny
1905 Mutiny on Man-of-War in Odessa
The Mutiny on the Potemkin

Muto
1908 Special Muto Reel Mellin's Food Co.

Mutton
1901 Hot Mutton Pies
Weighing Mutton
1906 The Lost Leg of Mutton

Myopia (Boston polo team)
1899 Myopia vs. Dedham
1900 Polo Game: Myopia vs. Dedham

Mystery
1898 The Mysterious Midgets
1899 Baxter Street Mystery
Mysterious Disappearance of a Policeman
1900 Mysterious Acrobat
A Mysterious Portrait
1901 The Mysterious Blackboard
The Mysterious Cafe
1902 A Chinese Mystery
The Clown and His Mysterious Pictures
The Mysterious Doctor
Mysterious Transformation Scene
The Mysterious Urn
The Clown with the Portable Body (Dislocations mystérieuse—vue étonnante)
The Clown with the Portable Body (Dislocations mystérieuses)
1903 The House of Mystery
The Mysterious Box
The Mysterious Trunk
1904 Mysterious Clock
Mysterious Performances
Mysterious Screen
The Passion Play (L'etoile mystérieuse)
1905 Black and White; or, The Mystery of a Brooklyn Baby Carriage
The Great Jewel Mystery
The Mysterious Island
1906 The Mysterious Retort
1907 The Mysterious Armor
Mysterious Boudoir
1908 Basket Mystery or the Traveler's Jest
Big Bow Mystery
Mysterious Flames
Mysterious Knight
The Mysterious Phonograph
Mysterious Stranger
The Mystery of a Diamond Necklace
The Mystery of the Bride, in Black and White
The Mystery of the Bride in White
The Mystery of the Garrison
Mystery of the Mountains
The Red Barn Mystery: A Startling Portrayal of the Great Marie Martin Mystery
Sherlock Holmes in the Great Mystery
1909 The Egyptian Mystery
Mysterious Correspondent
The Mysterious Crime
The Mysterious Double; or, The Two Girls Who Looked Alike
Mysterious Lodger
Mysterious Luggage
The Mysterious Motor
The Mystery of the "Sleeper" Trunk
1910 Mysteries of Bridge of Sighs at Venice
The Mysterious Armour
The Mysterious Track
The Mystery of Lonely Gulch
The Mystery of Temple Court
Mystery of the Cossacks
The Mystery of the Lama Convent; or, Dr. Nicola in Thibet
The Mystery of the Torn Note
The Suit Case Mystery
A Touching Mystery

Mystic
1900 The Mystic Swing
1901 A Mystic Re-Incarnation
1902 The Mystic Wreath
The Mystical Burglars
1903 The Mystical Flame
1909 Mystic Melodies
The Mystic Swing
The Oriental Mystic

Mystic Shriners
1904 Outing, Mystic Shriners, Atlantic City, New Jersey
Parade, Mystic Shriners, Atlantic City, New Jersey
Parade of Mystic Shriners, Luna Park, Coney Island
1905 General Cronje & Mystic Shriners
Mystic Shriners' Day, Dreamland, Coney Island
1907 Mystic Shriners at Dreamland

Mystification
1904 Pierrot's Mystification
Up-to-Date Burglars; or, The Mystified Cops
1906 Indiscreet Mystified
Jewel Robbers Mystified
1907 Cabman Mystified
1908 Custom Officers Mystified

Nabbed
1901 Nabbed by the Nipper

Nag
1909 Visions of a Nag

Nagasaki (Japan)
1898 S.S. "Gaelic" at Nagasaki
1901 Coaling a Steamer, Nagasaki Bay, Japan
1904 Warship in Nagasaki Harbor, Japan

Nailing
1898 Sailor Nailing Flag to Mast

Name
1900 His Name Was Mud
1906 Her Name Was Maude
1910 In Friendship's Name
In the Czar's Name
In the Name of Allah

Nana
1909 Nana's Mother

Nancy
1909 Nancy; or, The Burglar's Daughter
1910 Nancy's Wedding Trip

Nannina
1910 Nannina

Nantes (France)
1910 Nantes and Its Surroundings

Nantilda
1909 Nantilda

Nap
1897 Caught Napping
1901 Tramp's Nap Interrupted
1907 The Gardener's Nap
1909 A Luckless Nap

Naples (Italy)
1903 Eating Macaroni in the Streets of Naples
1904 Tour in Italy (De Naples au Vésuve)
1906 A Trip from Naples to Vesuvius, Showing the Volcano in Action
1907 Naples to Vesuvius
1908 Environs of Naples
Life and Customs of Naples
Neapolitan's Revenge
Picturesque Naples
1909 City of Naples
1910 Neapolitan Volcanic Islands

Napoleon
1903 Life of Napoleon
1907 Napoleon and Sentry
1908 Napoleon and the English Sailor
1909 A Message to Napoleon; or, An Episode in the Life of the Great Prisoner at Elba
Napoleon
Napoleon and Princess Hatzfeld
Napoleon: the Man of Destiny
Napoleon's Game of Chess
1910 An Episode of Napoleon's War with Spain
Napoleon

Narrow
1898 A Narrow Escape
1901 Hooligan's Narrow Escape
1903 A Narrow Escape
1904 The Bustle in the Narrow Door
1908 A Narrow Escape
1909 Cowboy's Narrow Escape

Narrows
1900 The Narrows
Steamer "Stowell" Running the Narrows
1902 St. John's Guild. Julliard and Tug in Narrows

Nash, George K.
1900 Governor Nash of Ohio

Nashville (Boat)
1898 U.S. Cruiser "Nashville"

Nashville (Louis &) Flyer
1903 Louis & Nashville Flyer

Nassau (Bahama Islands)
1903 Native Woman Washing a Negro Baby in Nassau, B. I.

Nasty
1908 Nasty Sticky Stuff

Nat
1904 Nervy Nat
1907 Nervy Nat

Nation, Carrie
1901 Carrie Nation Smashing a Saloon
Mrs. Nation & Her Hatchet Brigade
Why Mr. Nation Wants a Divorce

National
1897 National Lancers of Boston
1899 Grand National Steeple-Chase
1900 Republican National Committee of 1900
The Republican National Convention
1901 U.S. National Cemetery
1902 The National Geisha Dance of Japan
1903 Chinese National Dance
1904 Democratic National Committee at Esopus
1910 Elgin National Trophy Races

National Cash Register Co.
1902 Officers of National Cash Register Co. Leaving Club House

1910 A Gold Necklace
The Necklace of the Dead
The Romance of a Necklace

Necromancer
1903 The Necromancer

Need
1906 A Friend in Need Is a Friend Indeed
1907 The Need of Gold
1908 Who Needed the Dough?
1909 A Friend in Need Is a Friend Indeed
The Wealthy Rival; or A Summer Story That Needs No Explanation
1910 In Need of a Painter

Needle
1899 Passing Needles—S.S. "St. Louis"
1902 Grandma Threading Her Needle

Negroes
use **Blacks**

Neighbor
1903 Casey and His Neighbor's Goat
Quarrelsome Neighbors
1906 Neighbor's Lamp
1907 Neighbors
Neighbors Who Borrow
1908 Neighborly Neighbors
Noisy Neighbors
1909 Importune Neighbor
Jones and His New Neighbors
The Neighbors' Kids
The Three Neighbors
1910 In Neighboring Kingdoms
Love Your Neighbor as Yourself, but Leave His Wife Alone!
Neighbors; or, Yvonne's Daughter

Nell
1910 Little Nell's Tobacco

Nellie
1908 Nellie, the Beautiful Housemaid
Nellie, the Pretty Typewriter
Nellie's Camera
1909 Nellie's Love Story
1910 Nellie's Farm
Who Is Nellie?

Nelson, Battling
1905 Impersonation of Britt-Nelson Fight
Nelson-Britt Prize Fight
Nelson-Britt Prize Fight for Lightweight Championship, San Francisco, September 9th, 1905
1906 Impersonation of Gans-Nelson Fight
Nelson-McGovern Fight, 1906
Reproduction of Nelson-Gans Fight
1908 Gans-Nelson Fight
1909 [Nelson-Hyland Fight Pictures]
1910 Nelson-Wolgast Fight
Owen Moran vs. Battling Nelson

Nelson, Horatio, Admiral
1909 Admiral Nelson's Son

Nemesis
1910 The Nemesis

Nephew
1908 Nephew's Luck
1909 Good for Nothing Nephew
In India, Marriage of the Nephew of the Maharajah of Tagore
1910 Does Nephew Get the Cash?

Neptune
1900 Neptune and Amphitrite
Neptune's Daughters
1903 Neptune's Wife
1905 Father Neptune and Bear
1909 Neptune's Daughter; or, The Shoemaker's Dream

Nero
1908 Emperor Nero on the Warpath
Nero and the Burning of Rome
1909 Nero; or, The Burning of Rome

Nerve
1909 Instantaneous Nerve Powder

Nervi (Italy)
1909 From Portofino to Nervi

Nervous
1904 Nervous Man Retiring
1907 Nervous Kitchenmaid
1908 Contagious Nervous Twitching
A Contagious Nervousness

Nervy
1904 Nervy Nat
1907 Nervy Jim and the Cop
Nervy Nat
1909 A Nervy Thief

Nesle (France)
1909 The Tower of Nesle

Nest
1902 From the Crow's Nest
1904 The Nest Robbers
1907 Robbing a Bird's Nest
1908 Rescued from an Eagle's Nest

Net
1897 Hauling a Scoop Net
1898 Jumping Net Practice
1901 Hauling a Shad Net
1904 Obstacle Race, Net and Tank, S.S. "Coptic," Mid-Ocean
1907 Kanaka Fishermen Casting the Throw Net, Hilo, H.I.
1910 Blue Fishing Nets
In the Mesh of the Net

Netherlands and the Dutch
1897 Dutch Fishing Boats
1898 The Baldheaded Dutchman
Coronation of Queen Wilhelmina of Holland
1901 How the Dutch Beat the Irish
1902 A Dutch Soldier's Christmas Box
A Dutchman Shaving
The Dutchman's Interrupted Dinner
Queen Wilhelmina, of Holland, in Berlin
1903 Dutch and Irish Politics
1904 Holland Submarine Boat Tests
1905 Three Jolly Dutchmen
1907 The Dutch Kiddies: Montgomery and Stone
Quaint Holland
1909 Holland Cheese
1910 The Barge Man of Old Holland
Dutch Types
The Little Hero of Holland
On the Banks of the Zuyder Zee, Holland

Neuralgia
1903 His Wife Has Neuralgia

Neurasthenic
1909 Neurasthenique

Nevada
1906 Gans-Nelson Contest, Goldfield, Nevada, September 3rd, 1906
1909 A Nevada Girl
1910 Jeffries-Johnson World's Championship Boxing Contest, Held at Reno, Nevada, July 4, 1910
Nevada

Nevada Falls, Yosemite Valley (California)
1901 Nevada Falls
1905 Nevada Falls, Yosemite Valley

Nevada Trail, Yosemite Valley (California)
1905 Cavalcade Descending the Nevada Trail, Yosemite Valley
The "Crazy" Tourists on the Nevada Trail, Yosemite Valley

Never
1898 They Will Never Do It Again
1903 Misfortune Never Comes Alone
Never Interfere in Family Troubles
"Never Touched Him!"
True Love Never Runs Smooth
1904 Will He Never Get Undressed
1907 I Never Forget the Wife
1908 It's Never Too Late to Mend
A Kindness Never Goes Unrewarded
Never Again
A Noble Jester; or, Faint Heart Never Won Fair Lady
The Promise! Henri Promises Never to Gamble Again
1909 Never Again
Never Eat Green Apples
Never Gamble for Your Trousers
There Never Was a Girl Like You
True Love Never Runs Smoothly
1910 Never Again
Never Despair; or, From Misery to Happiness

New
1897 New Pillow Fight
A New Waiter Opening a Fizz
New Watermelon Contest
1898 Blanket-Tossing a New Recruit
New Couchee Dance
1899 New Lipman Dance
New Umbrella Dance
1900 The Downward Path: The New Soubrette [Part 4]
New Black Diamond Express
New Farmer's Mishap
New Life Rescue
New Morning Bath
New Sleighing Scene
1901 Launching of the New Battleship "Ohio" at San Francisco, Cal. When President McKinley Was There
The New Maid
The Fat and the Lean Wrestling Match (Nouvelles luttes extravagantes)
1902 B. F. Keith's New Million Dollar Theatre
The New Crowned King and Queen Passing Through Wellington Arch and Down Constitution Hill
New Pie Eating Contest
The New Pillow Fight
The New Serpentine and Fire Dance
New Sunset Limited
1903 Lovers Interrupted. New
New Bull Fight
New Chinese Laundry
New Colored Kiss, No. 2
The New Cook
The New Dude and a Market Woman
The New Enchanted Cafe
New Fisherman's Luck
The New Leap Frog
New Passing Train Scene
New Serpentine Dance
The New Shooting the Chutes
The New Version of the Two Old Sports
Panorama Looking Down Niagara from New Suspension Bridge
Scenes of a New Forest Pony Fair
Smith's Wife Inspects the New Typewriter
1904 Looping the Loop (Nouveau sport)
1905 Airy Fairy Lillian Tries on Her New Corsets
1906 Algy's New Suit
Fayet-Chamonix: Trip on the New Trolley Line from Le Fayet-St. Gervais to Chamonix
New Brother
Old and New Style Conjurors
The Snapshot Fiend; or, Willie's New Camera
1907 Man, Hat and Cocktail, a New Drink, but an Old Joke
The New Apprentice
The New Arrival
A New Death Penalty
The New Hired Man
The New Policeman
The New Stag Hunt
A New Toboggan
1908 Burglar's New Trick
Fluffy's New Corsets
House to Let; or, The New Tenants
Jim Gets a New Job
John's New Suit; or, Why He Didn't Go to Church
Mr. Smith, the New Recruit
The New Breakfast Food
A New Electrical Discovery and Its Uses
A New Fruit
The New Hired Girl
The New Houseman's Idea
The New Maid
The New Stenographer
A New Way of Traveling
A New Way to Pay Debts
Our New Errand Boy
Troubles of a New Drug Clerk
Turning over a New Leaf
1909 An Athlete of a New Kind
Flossie's New Peach-Basket Hat
How Jones Got a New Suit
Jones and His New Neighbors
The New Chief
The New Cop
New Cut Roads Up Mt. Blanc
The New Footman
The New General
The New Governess
A New Life
The New Mail Carrier
The New Minister; or, The Drunkard's Daughter
The New Mirror
A New Old Master
New Pain Killer
The New Policeman
A New Policeman
The New Servant
New Style Airship
A New Trick
The Newest Woman

A Sweep Across New York
Third Avenue Elevated Train, New York
1904 Annual Parade, New York Fire Department
Democratic Presidential Candidate, Judge Parker, and Mayor McClellan, Esopus, N.Y.
Electric Locomotive Tests and Races, Schenectady, N.Y.
Exhibition Fire Drill, Union Square, N.Y.
Ice Skating in Central Park, N.Y.
Inter-Collegiate Regatta, Poughkeepsie, N.Y., 1904
Opening Ceremonies, New York Subway, October 27, 1904
"Pollywogs" 71st Regiment, N.G.S.N.Y., Initiating Raw Recruits
Sleighing in Central Park, New York
1905 Across the New Viaduct of New York
Around New York in 15 Minutes
Bargain Day on 14th Street, New York
Fire in New York's Bowery
Interior N.Y. Subway, 14th St. to 42nd St.
Life of the New York Policeman
New York Athletic Club Crew at Phila., Pa.
New York City Fire Department on Parade
N.Y. Life Insurance Co. Pres. McCall & Officers
N.Y. Police Parade, 1905
Panorama from the Roof of the Times Building, New York
"Play Ball"—Opening Game, National League, N.Y. City, 1905—New York vs. Boston
Rough House in a New York Honky-Tonk
A Saturday Afternoon at Travers' Island with the New York Athletic Club
Spectacular Scenes During a New York City Fire
1906 American Falls from Canadian Side, Niagara Falls, N.Y.
American Falls from Goat Island, Niagara Falls, N.Y.
Horseshoe Falls from American Side, Niagara Falls, N.Y.
Horseshoe Falls from Canadian Side Niagara Falls, N.Y.
The Streets of New York
A Transatlantic Trip of the S.S. Kronprinz Wilhelm, from Bremen to New York
A Trip on the "Maid in the Mist," Niagara Falls, N.Y.
A Trip on the "Chippewa," Niagara Falls, N.Y.
1907 Albany, N.Y.
Christy Mathewson, N.Y. National League Baseball Team
Marceline, the World-Renowned Clown of the N.Y. Hippodrome
New York
Skating on N.Y. Theatre Roof
Unloading Mail at Pier 13, N. R., N.Y.
1908 Aeroplane Flights by Henry Farman, Coney Island, N.Y., U.S.A.
Bryan's Reception in New York
The Mishaps of the New York-Paris Auto Race
New York
Reception for the Victorious Olympic Team of American Athletes at City Hall, New York
St. Patrick's Day in New York
Views of New York
1909 A Bride and Groom's Visit to the New York Zoological Gardens
[Otto T. Bannard, Republican Candidate for Mayor of New York]
The Tobacco Edict, Old New York, 1648
1910 Boy Scouts of America in Camp at Silver Bay, Lake George, N.Y.
Manoeuvers of the New York Police Force
New York of Today
The Police Force of New York City
Roosevelt's Reception in New York
When Old New York Was Young

New York Athletic Club
1905 Sparring at the N.Y.A.C.
Wrestling at the N.Y.A.C.
1906 Fencing N.Y.A.C.

New York Central Railroad
1896 Empire State Express, N.Y. Central R.R.
Train Taking Water, N.Y. Central R.R.

New York City Railroad
1896 Chicago Fast Mail NYC. R.R.

New York Herald
1904 How a French Nobleman Got a Wife Through the New York Herald "Personal" Columns

New York Journal
1898 In Front of "Journal" Building
N.Y. Journal Despatch Yacht "Buccaneer"
"New York Journal's War Issue"

New York Times
1905 Panorama from the Roof of the Times Building, New York

New Yorker (Boat)
1899 The Fire Boat "New Yorker"
1903 Fireboat "New Yorker" Answering an Alarm
Fireboat "New Yorker" in Action

New Zealand
1906 Trip Through Australia, New Zealand

Newark (New Jersey)
1901 Great Newark Fire
1909 Annual Celebration of School Children at Newark, NJ

Newborn
1903 The New Born King
1910 Herod and the New Born King

Newburgh (New York)
1903 From Haverstraw to Newburg

Newell
1903 Newell and Chevet, the Famous Acrobats

Newfoundland (Canada)
1904 Fishing in Newfoundland—French Shore
1908 Newfoundland Fisherman

Newlyn (England)
1904 Sea Gulls at Newlyn, Cornwall, England

Newlyweds
1908 The Newlyweds First Meal
1909 The Newlyweds
1910 The Newlyweds

Newman's Poultry Farm, Long Island (New York)
1902 Feeding Geese at Newman's Poultry Farm

Newport (Rhode Island)
1900 Drill of Naval Cadets at Newport
Gun Drill by Naval Cadets at Newport [R.I., Naval] Training School
Gymnasium Exercises and Drill at Newport [R.I., Naval] Training School
Military Scenes at Newport, R.I.
Naval Sham Battle at Newport
Panoramic View of Newport [R.I.]
Sham Battle on Land by Cadets at Newport Naval Training School
1902 Bombardment of Newport
Torpedo Boats Racing off Newport
1903 North Atlantic Fleet Bombarding Fort Adams, Newport Harbor
1909 Apprentice Boys at Newport [R.I.] Naval Training Station

Newport News (Virginia)
1898 Newport News Ship-Building Co.'s Shipyard

Newsboys
1897 A Newsboys' Scrap
1902 Newsboys and Hokey Pokey Man
1905 The Newsboy
1908 Her Newsboy Friend
An Honest Newsboy's Reward

Newspaper
1903 Pa's Comment on the Morning News
1904 "A Newspaper in Making"
1907 The Making of a Modern Newspaper
1908 Current News Items
1910 A Newspaper Error

Newt
1905 The Newt

Next
1903 Next!
1909 The Treasure; or, The House Next Door
1910 The Flat Next Door
The Girl Next Door
The Saloon Next Door

Niagara (Boat)
1899 The "Niagara"

Niagara Falls
1896 Lower Rapids, Niagara Falls
Niagara Gorge from Erie R.R.
Pointing Down Gorge, Niagara Falls
Taken from Trolley in Gorge, Niagara Falls
1899 The Approach to Niagara
Lower Rapids of Niagara Falls
Niagara Falls in Winter
Niagara Falls Station
Panoramic View of Niagara Falls
1900 Niagara Falls in Life Motion Pictures
1901 Captain Nissen Going Through Whirlpool Rapids, Niagara Falls
Circular Panorama of Niagara Falls
1902 Prince Henry [of Prussia] at Niagara Falls
1903 Great Gorge R.R., Niagara
Panorama Looking Down Niagara from New Suspension Bridge
1904 Crossing Ice Bridge at Niagara Falls
Sliding Down Ice Mound at Niagara Falls
1905 Whirlpool Rapids, Niagara, U.S.A.
1906 American Falls from Canadian Side, Niagara Falls, N.Y.
American Falls from Goat Island, Niagara Falls, N.Y.
The Honeymoon at Niagara Falls
Horseshoe Falls from American Side, Niagara Falls, N.Y.
Horseshoe Falls from Canadian Side Niagara Falls, N.Y.
A Trip on the "Maid in the Mist," Niagara Falls, N.Y.
A Trip on the "Chippewa," Niagara Falls, N.Y.
1907 Niagara Falls
1908 Niagara Falls in Winter
Quebec to Niagara
1909 Niagara in Winter Dress
1910 The Maid of Niagara
A Winter Romance at Niagara Falls

Niccolo' De' Lapi
1909 Niccolo' De' Lapi

Nice (France)
1903 Battle of Confetti at the Nice Carnival
Battle of Flowers at the Nice Carnival
Procession of Floats and Masqueraders at Nice Carnival
1906 From Menton to Nice
1907 Ostrich Farm (La ferme d'autruches de Nice)
1908 Battle of Flowers in Nice
The Carnival at Nice
Carnival at Nice
1909 Carnival at Nice
Carnival at Nice, 1909
The Pretty Girl of Nice

Nichols
1910 The Nichols on a Vacation

Nick
1908 In the Nick of Time
1910 In the Nick of Time
Saved in the Nick of Time

Nickel
1909 All for a Nickel
Baby Swallows a Nickel

Nickleby, Nicholas
1903 Nicholas Nickleby

Nicola, Dr.
1909 How Dr. Nicola Procured the Chinese Cane
1910 The Mystery of the Lama Convent; or, Dr. Nicola in Thibet

Nicotine
1909 Princess Nicotine; or, The Smoke Fairy

Niece
1909 The Priest's Niece

"Nigger"
use **Blacks**

Nightmare
1900 Uncle Josh's Nightmare
1902 The Horrible Nightmare
1903 Casey's Nightmare
Nightmare
1905 The Angler's Nightmare
1906 The Gambler's Nightmare
Pasha's Nightmare
The Inventor Crazybrains and His Wonderful Airship (Le dirigeable fantastique ou le cauchemar d'un inventeur)
1907 Betrothed's Nightmare
Diabolo Nightmare
The Pork Butcher's Nightmare
Under the Seas (Deux cent mille lieues sous les mers; ou le cauchemar d'un pêcheur)
Tunneling the English Channel (Le tunnel sous la manche ou le cauchemar franco-anglais)
1908 The Artist's Nightmare
The Puppet's Nightmare

The Saloon-Keeper's Nightmare
The Sculptor's Nightmare
1909 The Betrothed's Nightmare
Harlequin's Nightmare
Nightmare of a Single Man
Sweet Dreams Intermingled with Nightmares
The Warden's Nightmare
1910 The Nightmare

Nights
1897 Night Before Christmas
Ten Nights in a Barroom
1899 Tenderloin at Night
1900 Seeing Things at Night
A Terrible Night
Why Curfew Did Not Ring Last Night
1901 Oh! What a Night; or, The Sultan's Dream
Pan-American Exposition by Night
Panorama of Esplanade by Night
Ten Nights in a Bar-Room: Death of Little Mary
Ten Nights in a Bar-Room: Death of Slade
Ten Nights in a Bar-Room: Murder of Willie
Ten Nights in a Bar-Room: The Fatal Blow
Ten Nights in a Bar-Room: Vision of Mary
1903 A Lively Night
A Night in Blackville
Passion Play: Shepherds Watching Their Flocks by Night
Poor Girl, It Was a Hot Night and the Mosquitos Were Thick
Ten Nights in a Barroom
The Bridegroom's Dilemma (Le coucher de la mariée ou triste nuit de noces)
Animated Dolls (Nuit de noel)
1904 Halloween Night at the Seminary
Night Duty
Night Owl's Return
A Sorcerer's Night
1905 Coney Island at Night
"A Frightful Night"
The Night Before Christmas
The Palace of the Arabian Nights
1906 Carnival Night
First Night Out
Good Night
A Mid-winter Night's Dream; or, Little Joe's Luck
Night of the Party
A Night Off
1907 Amateur Night; or, Get the Hook
Cassimir's Night Out
Exciting Night of Their Honeymoon
A Night at the Gayety
A Night in Dreamland
The Night Watchman
1908 At Night
The Consequences of a Night Out
Good Night Clown
A Night Alarm
A Night of Terror
A Night Out; or, He Couldn't Go Home Until Morning
Night Riders
A Night with the Masqueraders in Paris
Shadows of Night
Thompson's Night Out
Thompson's Night with the Police
1909 Cleopatra's Lover; or, A Night of Enchantment
In the Watches of the Night
A Knight for a Night
A Midsummer Night's Dream
Ten Nights in a Bar-room
'Tis Now the Very Witching Hour of Night
Tragic Night
1910 Amateur Night
In the Shadow of the Night
The Laundry Girl's Good Night
Midsummer Night's Dream
A Night on the Coast
The Night Rustlers
One Night, and Then ——
Out of the Night
A Rough Night on the Bridge
A Shot in the Night
Ten Nights in a Bar Room
Twelfth Night

Nihilism
1905 The Nihilists
The Nihilists in Russia
1906 Socialism and Nihilism
1908 The Girl Nihilist
The Nihilist
1910 Queen of the Nihilists

Nikko (Japan)
1904 Great Temple Procession, Nikko, Japan

Nile River
1903 Fording the River Nile on Donkeys
1904 Cairo and the Nile
1906 Boats on the Nile
1909 A Moonlight Trip on the Nile

Nine
1907 The Nine Lives of a Cat
1909 Game of Nine Pins
1910 The Nine of Diamonds
Pete Has Nine Lives

99
1907 99 in the Shade

Ninth
1898 9th and 13th U.S. Infantry at Battalion Drill
9th Infantry Boys' Morning Wash
Ninth Regiment, U.S. Regulars
9th U.S. Cavalry Watering Horses
1899 Ninth Regiment, N.G.S.N.Y.
1901 The 9th Infantry, U.S.A.
1903 Battle Flags of the 9th U.S. Infantry
1906 The 9th Mass. Vol. Militia

Ninth Avenue (New York City)
1902 Panorama of Ninth Ave. Elevated R.R.

Nipper
1901 Nabbed by the Nipper

Nissen, N. P., Captain
1901 Captain Nissen Going Through Whirlpool Rapids, Niagara Falls

No-man's-land
1909 A No Man's Land
1910 No Man's Land

Noaccount
1910 Count of Noaccount

Nob Hill, San Francisco (California)
1906 Panorama, Nob Hill and Ruins of Millionaire Residences
Panorama of Nob Hill
Panorama, Russian and Nob Hill from an Automobile

Noble
1904 How a French Nobleman Got a Wife Through the New York Herald "Personal" Columns
Nobles Leaving the Kremlin, Moscow, After a Reception by Czar
1908 Antony and Cleopatra, the Love Story of the Noblest Roman and the Most Beautiful Egyptian
A Noble Jester; or, Faint Heart Never Won Fair Lady
Nobleman's Rights
1909 Noble and Commoner
The Nobleman's Dog
The Squire and the Noble Lord
1910 Nature's Nobleman

Nocturnal
1908 Nocturnal Thieves

Nod
1909 What Three Tots Saw in the Land of Nod
1910 The Consequence of a Nod

Noes (Norway)
1905 Scottish Tourist Party in Stockhaeres, Noes, Norway

Noisy
1908 Noisy Neighbors

Nomads
1908 The Nomads

Nome (Alaska)
1903 Winter Sport on Snake River, Nome
1905 Camp Life of the Esquimaux at Cape Nome, Alaska
Dance at Esquimaux Camp, Cape Nome, Alaska
Embarkation by Crane and Barge at Nome City, Alaska
Esquimaux Dance, Cape Nome, Alaska
Flap-Jack Lady of the Esquimaux, Cape Nome, Alaska

Nomination
1904 Judge Parker Receiving the Notification of His Nomination for the Presidency
1908 The Female Politician, Mrs. Bell, Is Nominated for Mayor

Non-stop
1909 The Non-Stop Motor Bicycle

Non-Union
1901 A Non-Union Paper Hanger
1905 The Non-Union Bill-Poster

Noon
1896 Winchester Arms Factory at Noon Time
1901 Noon Time in Packing Town, (Panoramic)
Noon Time in Packing Town, (Whiskey Point)
1903 Noon Hour at Hope Webbing Company
1908 We Close at Noon

Nora
1901 Nora's 4th of July

Nord Fjord (Norway)
1907 Nord Fjord from Loen to Sandene by Steamer [Norway]

Nordland (Norway)
1905 Bird Rock, Nordland, Norway

Normal school
1908 Boston Normal School Pageant

Normandy (France)
1908 Vengeance in Normandy
1910 Butter Making in Normandy

Norris
1910 Old Norris' Gal

Norrköping (Sweden)
1909 Norrkobing

Norseman
1908 The Viking's Daughter, the Story of the Ancient Norsemen
1909 Norseman

Norseman (Boat)
1899 Wreck of the "Norseman"

North
1901 Propylaea and North End of Plaza, Pan. Am. Exp.
1903 Leaving Skagway for the Golden North
1906 From North to South
1908 Northern Venice
Scandanavian North
Winter Time in Northern Europe
1909 Carnival Merriment in the North
The Northern Schoolmaster
Under Northern Skies
1910 Fishery in the North
The Girl of the Northern Woods
In the Frozen North
Justice in the Far North
[Lake Garda, Northern Italy]
Trip Through North of England

North American elk
1903 North American Elk

North American grey wolves
1903 North American Grey Wolves

North Atlantic Fleet
1903 North Atlantic Fleet Bombarding Fisher's Island
North Atlantic Fleet Bombarding Fort Adams, Newport Harbor

North Cape (Norway)
1904 From Christiania to the North Cape
1905 Parade of Passengers Crossing to North Cape, Norway
1909 From the North Cape

North Carolina
1901 Panoramic View, Asheville, N. C.
1903 Lieut. Bagley's Funeral. Escort of Lieut. Bagley's at Raleigh, N. C.

North Europe
1908 Summer in North Europe

North Pole
1903 Andre at the North Pole
1905 Departure of Peary for the North Pole
1908 How Simpkins Discovered the North Pole
1909 Capturing the North Pole; or, How He Cook'ed Peary's Record
Little Willie's Trip to the North Pole
The North Pole Craze
Who Discovered the North Pole?

North River (New York)
1898 The Fleet Steaming Up North River
1901 New York Sky-Line from the North River
1903 Skyscrapers of New York City, from the North River

North Sea
1903 Herring Fishing in the North Sea
1904 The Baltic Fleet and the North Sea Trawlers

North Shrewsbury River (New Jersey)
1904 Ice Boating on the North Shrewsbury, Red Bank, N.J.
North Siam
1909 Street Life in North Siam
North Wales
1907 Slate Quarries in North Wales
Northern Pacific Railroad
1897 Fast Mail, Northern Pacific Railroad
Northland (Boat)
1899 Steamship "Northland"
Northrop Looms
1899 Demonstrating the Action of the Northrop Looms
Northumberland Fusileers
1903 Fighting Fifth Northumberland Fusileers
Northwest
1903 A Rotary Snow Plow in the Great Northwest
1908 The Great Northwest
1910 In the Great Northwest
Northwest Mounted Police
1903 Firing the Royal Salute at Dawson City by the Northwest Mounted Police
Northwest Territories (Canada)
1903 On the Bow River Horse Ranch at Cochrane, North West Territory
Spearing Salmon in the Rivers of the North West Territory
Northwestern
1900 Northwestern Mounted Rifles
Norway
1901 Norway Ski Jumping Contests
1903 A Norwegian Waterfall
Rising Panorama of a Norwegian Waterfall
1904 From Christiania to the North Cape
1905 Bird Rock, Nordland, Norway
Congregation Leaving Trondhjlm Cathedral, Norway
The "Crazy" Canal Boat, Norway
Falls at Hellesylt, Norway
Fish Carvers, at Fish Market Bergen Norway
Fishmarket, Bergen, Norway
Fjord Panorama from Moving Ship, Norway
Landing Passengers at Torghattan Island, Norway
Lapps at Hammerfest, Norway
Panorama of a Norwegian Fjord from Alvik to Vik from Moving Ship
Panorama of the Folgefond Snowfield, Norway
Panorama of the Norwegian Fjord from Moving Ship
Parade of Passengers Crossing to North Cape, Norway
Scottish Touring Party Enroute to the Romsdale, Norway
Scottish Tourist Party in Stockhaeres, Noes, Norway
Sunday "Church Parade" Bergen Norway
Tourists Leaving Horgheim in the Romsdale Norway
Tourists on the Road to Hotel Stalheim, Norway
Voringfos Waterfall Norway
Waterfall from the Road, Stalheim, Norway
1907 Angling in Norway
Cloud Play at Pulfoss, Norway
Laplander Family, Gratli, Norway
Nord Fjord from Loen to Sandene by Steamer [Norway]
Norway: Crazy Canal Boat on the Telemarken Route
Pulfoss, Norway, Pulfoss Falls
Sailing thro the Sognia Fjord on a Steamer from Ballholm to Gudvangen [Norway]
Skiing in Norway
Wood Industry in Norway
1908 The Elf King, a Norwegian Fairy Tale
On the Coast of Norway
River in Norway
Trip to Norway
Winter Manoeuvres of the Norwegian Army
1909 From the North Cape
Gotacanal—over Norway's Rockies
Off the Coast of Norway
1910 In Norway
Norwegian Water Falls
Scenes in Norway

Nosey, Mrs.
1910 Mrs. Nosey
Notch
1899 Crawford Notch
Note
1903 A Discordant Note
1909 The Note in the Shoe
1910 The Mystery of the Torn Note
The Stage Note
Tweedle Dum's Forged Bank Note
Nothing
1908 Nothing to Declare; or, Bested by Custom Officials
1909 Good for Nothing Nephew
Much Ado About Nothing
Nothing Is Ever Lost
1910 A New Hat for Nothing
Nothing but Money
Notification
1898 The Landlady Gives Notice to the Barrasing Sisters
1904 Judge Parker Receiving the Notification of His Nomination for the Presidency
1907 Notice to Quit
Notorious
1906 Panorama, Notorious "Barbary Coast"
Notre Dame, Paris (France)
1910 Beneath the Walls of Notre Dame
Notre-dame des flots
1904 The Providence of the Waves; or, the Dream of a Poor Fisherman (La providence de Notre-dame des flots)
Novel
1909 Dime Novel Dan
A Dime Novel Detective
1910 The Forbidden Novel; or, Don't Do as I Do, Do as I Say
Novelty
1901 Lukens, Novel Gymnast
1903 An East River Novelty
1904 A Novel Way of Catching a Burglar
1909 Novel Invitation
1910 Max Leads Them a Novel Chase
November
1901 Jeffries and Ruhlin Sparring Contest at San Francisco, Cal., Nov. 15, 1901—Five Rounds
1906 O'Brien-Burns Contest, Los Angeles, Cal., Nov. 26th, 1906
Novice
1908 Novice on Stilts
The Novice Tight-Rope Walker
Now
1897 Now I Lay Me Down To Sleep
1904 Now, You Stop
1905 "Gee, If Me Mudder Could Only See Me Now"
1908 Do It Now!
1909 Now I'm Here, I'll Stay
Now Keep Smiling
Thanksgiving, Then and Now
'Tis Now the Very Witching Hour of Night
Nugget
1909 A Nugget of Gold
1910 The Fatal Gold Nugget
Nuisance
1907 A Perfect Nuisance
Number
1897 Barnum's Street Parade, Nos. 1, 2, and 3
1901 Queen Victoria's Funeral [Number 1]
Queen Victoria's Funeral [Number 2]
Queen Victoria's Funeral [Number 3]
1903 The American Soldier in Love and War [Number 1]
The American Soldier in Love and War [Number 2]
The American Soldier in Love and War [Number 3]
1908 The Winning Number
The Wrong Lottery Number
1909 Cab Number 519
The Lucky Number
Nurse
1898 The Cop and the Nurse Girl
1899 The Nurse's Joke
1901 The Bad Boy's Joke on the Nurse
The Tramp and the Nursing Bottle
1902 The Nurse Maid in the Tunnel
1904 Bad Boy's Joke on the Nurse
1906 Wanted—A Nurse
1907 Nurse Takes a Walk
Nurses' Strike
Nurse's Travels
1908 The Automatic Nurse
Out to Nurse
Romance of a War Nurse
1909 Automatic Nursing Bottle
A Clever Nurse
The Nurse's Romance
Nursing a Viper
1910 The Diary of a Nurse
The Nurse's Trunk
The Romance of a Trained Nurse
Nursemaid
1905 Masher and Nursemaid
Nursery
1903 Mother Goose Nursery Rhymes
1907 The Naval Nursery
1908 A Visit to the Public Nursery
Nutt, A., Mr.
1909 Mr. A. Nutt
Nymph
1900 A Nymph of the Waves
1902 Water Nymphs
1903 Nymph of the Waves
O Yama
1908 The Heart of O Yama
Oahu (Hawaii)
1907 Panoramic View, Oahu Railroad, Haleiwa, H.I.
Panoramic View, Oahu Railroad, Pearl Harbor, Hawaiian Islands
Oakland (California)
1906 Arrival of Refugees at Oakland
Oakley, Annie
1900 Annie Oakley
The Oaks, Portland (Oregon)
1907 Scene at "The Oaks," Portland, Oregon
Oars
1901 Boats Under Oars
1902 Worcester High School Eight-Oared Boat Crews in Action
1905 Drill Under Oars
Oatcake
1899 Farmer Oatcake Has His Troubles
Oath
1897 McKinley Taking the Oath
1901 President McKinley Taking the Oath
1905 Inauguration of President Roosevelt. Taking the Oath of Office
1909 The False Oath
1910 The Broken Oath
False Oath
The Oath and the Man
True to His Oath
Obdurate
1909 The Obdurate Father
Oberammergau (Germany)
1898 The Passion Play of Oberammergau
1905 Arrival of Train at Oberammergau
Children and Carts of Oberammergau
Crowds Leaving Theatre, Oberammergau
Lang (Andreas) and Son, the Two Davids, Oberammergau
Lang (Anton) and Family, Oberammergau
Panorama from Car on Oberammergau Electric Railway
Queen Margherita of Italy Arriving in Oberammergau
Obey
1907 A Soldier Must Obey Orders
1908 Obeying Her Mother
Object
1909 Object: Matrimony
Objections
1909 Calino Objects to Work
Objections Overcome
Oblige
1907 Anything to Oblige
Willing to Oblige
1909 An Obliging Friend
O'Brien
1897 O'Brien's Trained Horses
O'Brien, Philadelphia Jack
1905 Impersonation of the Fitzsimmons-O'Brien Fight
1906 O'Brien-Burns Contest, Los Angeles, Cal., Nov. 26th, 1906
O'Brien, Shamus
1908 Shamus O'Brien

1906 Old and New Style Conjurors
Old Seducer
The Old Swimming Hole
Two Seedy Rubes: They Have a Hot Time in the Old Town
1907 A Four Year Old Heroine
Man, Hat and Cocktail, a New Drink, but an Old Joke
An Old Coat Story
Old Mashers
Panorama Ruins of Old French Machinery
The Poor Old Couple
Under the Old Apple Tree
1908 A Dear Old Grandma
A Gay Old Boy
Kind Old Lady
A Love Affair of the Olden Days
The Old Actor
Old College Chums
The Old Footlight Favorite
Old Isaacs, the Pawnbroker
Old Sleuth, the Detective
The Old Story
Romance of the Old Mill
Stage Memories of an Old Theatrical Trunk
Under Any Old Flag at All
Unlucky Old Flirt
1909 The Adventures of an Old Flirt
A Cask of Good Old Wine
A Faithful Old Horse
The Girl at the Old Mill
In Old Arizona
In Old Kentucky
A New Old Master
The Old Army Chest
Old Aunt Hanna's Cat
The Old Curiosity Shop
The Old Grumbler at the Magicians
The Old Hall Clock
Old Heidelberg
The Old Lord of Ventnor
Old Love Letters
The Old Organ
The Old Schoolmaster
Old Servants
An Old Soldier
The Old Soldier's Story.
Old Sweethearts of Mine, a Phantasy in Smoke
A Romance of Old Madrid
A Romance of Old Mexico
Sporting Days in the Old South
Stirring Days in Old Virginia
There's No Fool Like an Old Fool
The Tobacco Edict, Old New York, 1648
1910 Back Among the Old Folks
The Bad Luck of an Old Rake
The Barge Man of Old Holland
Betty Is Still at Her Old Tricks
In Old California
The Lad from Old Ireland
Love's Old Sweet Song
The Old Fiddler
Old Heads and Young Hearts
The Old Home
The Old Longshoreman
The Old Loves and the New
The Old Miner's Doll
Old Norris' Gal
The Old Shoe Came Back
An Old Silver Mine in Peru
An Old Story with a New Ending
Rags, Old Iron!
Under the Old Apple Tree
When Old New York Was Young

Old Faithful Geyser, Yosemite Valley (California)
1901 Old Faithful Geyser
1903 "Old Faithful," Yosemite Valley
1905 Old Faithful Geyser, Yellowstone Park

Old Glory
1898 Old Glory and Cuban Flag
1899 Raising Old Glory over Morro Castle
1910 Old Glory

Old guard
1897 Old Guard, New York City
The Old Guard of New York

Old maids
1898 The Old Maid and the Burglar
The Old Maid's Picture
1899 The Disappointed Old Maid
1900 How the Old Maid Got a Husband
A Joke on the Old Maid
Tramps in the Old Maid's Orchard
1901 The Old Maid Having Her Picture Taken
The Old Maid in the Horsecar
1902 Old Maid Retiring
The Old Maid's Tea Party
1903 Burglar and Old Maid
Country Sport and Old Maid
The Farmer and the Old Maid
Giddy Old Maid
Old Maid Courtship
Old Maid's Ballet Dance
Old Maid's First Visit to a Theatre
The Old Maid's Lament
Old Maid's Morning Greeting
1904 Game of Old Maid
Old Maid and Fortune Teller
Old Maids and the Unfaithful Lovers
Old Maid's Flirtation
1905 Old Maid and Pet Cat
An Old Maid's Darling
1907 Burglar and Old Maids
1908 The Jealous Old Maid; or, No One to Love Her
Leap Year Proposals of an Old Maid
The Old Maid's Inheritance
The Old Maid's Parrot
The Old Maids' Temperance Club
1909 The Old Maid's Dream
1910 The Old Maid and Bonehead
The Old Maid and the Burglar
The Old Maid's Picnic
The Old Maid's Valentine

Old man
1898 How the Athletic Lover Outwitted the Old Man
1906 Old Man's Darling
1909 An Old Man's Bride
An Old Man's Honor
1910 The Little Old Men of the Woods

Oldsport
1902 Mr. Oldsport's Umbrella

Ole
1905 [On] a [Good Ole] 5¢ Trolley Ride
1910 The Ole Swimmin Hole

Oleo
1901 Oleo Oil Melting
Oleo Oil Pressing

Olivette (Boat)
1898 Scene on the Steamship "Olivette"
Steamship "Olivette"

Olsen
1900 Reproduction of the Olsen and Roeber Wrestling Match

Olympia (Boat)
1898 Steam Launch of the Olympia
1899 Admiral Dewey on the Olympia
Admiral Dewey Taking Leave of Washington Committee on the U.S. Cruiser 'Olympia'
Admiral Dewey's Flagship Olympia in Action at Manila
Flagship Olympia and Cruiser New York in Naval Parade
Officers of the "Olympia"
Panoramic View of Floral Float "Olympia"
Panoramic View of Olympia in New York Harbor
Police Boats and Pleasure Craft on Way to Olympia
U.S. Cruiser "Olympia" Leading Naval Parade

Olympics
1906 The Olympian Games
The Olympic Games at Athens, Greece
1908 Olympic Games
Olympic Regatta at Henley
Reception for the Victorious Olympic Team of American Athletes at City Hall, New York

Omaha (Nebraska)
1900 From Council Bluffs to Omaha

Omen
1909 The Good Omen

Omnibus
1902 The Darktown Comedians Trip to Paris (L'omnibus des toqués)
1903 How the Old Woman Caught the Omnibus
1909 The Omnibus Taxicab

Onawanda
1909 Onawanda; or, An Indian's Devotion

Once
1907 Once Upon a Time There Was...
1910 Once upon a Time

One
1898 One Chair Short
Three Baths for the Price of One
1899 Capt. Coghlan, One of the Manila Heroes, and Crew of the Raleigh, Reviewed by the President
1900 Four Heads Better Than One
One on the Bum
1902 The Boys Think They Have One on Foxy Grandpa, but He Fools Them
The Boys Try to Put One Up on Foxy Grandpa
1904 The Execution (Beheading) of One of the Hunchuses (Chinese Bandits) Outside the Walls of Mukden
One Way of Taking a Girl's Picture
1905 Always Room for One More
1906 Ten Wives for One Husband
1907 One of the Finest
Two Cabbies for One Passenger
1908 Betrayed by One's Feet
The One Best Bet
One of the Bravest
What One Small Boy Can Do
1909 Eddie Is a Real Live One
One Busy Hour
One Touch of Nature
1910 Kinematographic X-Ray Picture of a Human Stomach During Digestion, Taken During One Inspiration
One Can't Believe One's Eyes
One Good Turn
One Night, and Then —
One of the Finest
One on Max
One Touch of Nature
Please Take One
The Timid One

One another
1910 Bear Ye One Another's Burdens
Love Ye One Another

One Hundred Fourth Street (New York City)
1899 104th Street Curve, New York, Elevated Railway

One hundred thousand
1908 I Won One Hundred Thousand

100 to 1
1906 The 100 to 1 Shot; or, A Run of Luck

100 tricks
1903 Conjurer and 100 Tricks

100-yard dash
1899 International Collegiate Games—100 Yards Dash

One hundred years
1908 The Airship; or, 100 Years Hence

One-legged
1908 The One-Legged Man
1909 One-Legged Pete and Pat
1910 One-Legged Acrobats

One-man
1901 The One Man Orchestra
1907 One Man Baseball
1908 A One Man Band

One mile
1899 One Mile Dash
1901 International Track Athletic Meeting—Start and Finish of the One Mile Run

One-night stand
1907 One-Night Stand

One third
1897 One-Third Mile Bicycle Race

One thousand
1899 One Thousand Mile Tree, Weber Canyon
1903 1,000 Mile Ride over the Ice on a Bicycle

Ones
1900 Pierrot's Problem, or How To Make a Fat Wife Out of Two Lean Ones
"Three Ones"
1908 Forgotten Ones

Ong, Chin
1899 Chuck Connors vs. Chin Ong

Onion
1907 The Onion Fiend
Onions Make People Weep

Only
1897 Only a Rat
1903 Only a Soldier Boy
1904 The Widow and the Only Man

Othello
1908 Othello
1910 Othello
Otis, Harrison Gray
1902 Gen. Otis with His Troops in the Philippines
Ottawa (Canada)
1900 The Great Ottawa Fire
Otter
1904 Otter Hunt
1905 Feeding the Otters
Ouchard
1910 Ouchard, the Merchant
Ouled-Naïl Mountains (Algeria)
1904 Typical Algerian 'Ouled Nails' Muslin Dance
Oural Mountains
1908 Through the Oural Mountains
Outbound
1897 Outbound Vessel Passing Governors Island, N.Y. Harbor
Outcast
1903 Outcast and Bride
1908 The Outcast Heroine
1909 Outcast, or Heroine
An Outcast's Christmas
A Royal Outcast
1910 The Outcast's Salvation
Outcault, Richard Felton
1904 Section of Buster Brown Series, Showing a Sketch of Buster by Outcault
Outdoing
1900 Ching Ling Foo Outdone
1902 Legerdemain Up-to-Date, or the Great Hermann Outdone
1903 Outdoing Ching Ling Foo
Outdoor
1898 Canadian Outdoor Sports
Outer
1899 "Shamrock" and "Columbia" Rounding the Outer Stake Boat
"Shamrock" and "Columbia" Rounding the Outer Stake Boat, No. 2
1901 "Columbia" and "Shamrock II": Turning the Outer Stake Boat
1903 Reliance and Shamrock III Turning Outer Stake in Second Race
Outfit
1903 Threshing Outfit at Work
1904 Serving Outfits to Recruits
Outing
1904 Outing, Mystic Shriners, Atlantic City, New Jersey
1907 The Baby's First Outing
A Family Outing
Interrupted Outing
1909 The Conjuror's Outing
A Day's Outing
Outing Pastimes in Colorado
1910 A Family Outing
Papa's First Outing
Outlaw
1908 The Girl and the Outlaw
The Outlaw
1909 The Heart of an Outlaw
1910 The Outlaw's Redemption
An Outlaw's Sacrifice
Outposts
1898 Outpost Skirmish
1899 Rifle Hill Signal Outpost
1904 Outpost Skirmishing
Russian Outposts Attacked by Japanese
1910 Life of the Alpine Shooters in the Frontier Outposts
Outward
1897 Steamship "St. Paul" Outward Bound
1900 The "St. Paul" Outward Bound
Outwit
1898 How the Athletic Lover Outwitted the Old Man
1908 The Bandit's Waterloo: The Outwitting of an Andalusian Brigand by a Pretty Senora
The Cobbler Outwitted
Outwitted
Outwitted by His Wife
Tit for Tat; or, Outwitted by Wit
1909 Dog Outwits Kidnapper
Outwitted
1910 Outwitted

Ovens
1903 The Coke Ovens of Pennsylvania
1910 The Ghost in the Oven
Overalls
1904 The Girls in the Overalls
1908 The Man in the Overalls
Overanxious
1903 The Over-Anxious Waiter
Overboard
1899 "Man Overboard!"
1903 Man Overboard! "INDIANA"
Overcoat
1908 Adventures of an Overcoat
An Extraordinary Overcoat
The Wrong Overcoat
Overcome
1909 Objections Overcome
Overeager
1909 The Over-Eager Heirs
Overflowing
1908 Overflowing in Italy
Overland
1897 Southern Pacific Overland Mail
1899 Overland Limited
The "Overland Limited" Passing Witch Rocks
1900 Overland Express Arriving at Helena, Mont.
1901 The Overland Limited
A Race with the Overland Limited
1903 Overland Flyer
1910 The Overland Coach Robbery
Overland to Freemont
Overloaded
1898 An Overloaded Donkey
Oversight
1908 A Disastrous Oversight
Overtake
1908 Will He Overtake Them?
Overturning
1905 Overturning a Mammoth Chimney
Overzealous
1910 The Overzealous Domestic
Owl
1904 Night Owl's Return
Oxen
1901 Ox Carts
1903 War Supplies Arriving at Boer Laager by Train of Ox Teams
1904 Convoy of Oxen
Oxford Street, London (England)
1905 London Ladies Looking at Lingerie in Oxford Street Windows, London
Scene in Oxford Street, London
Oxford University (England)
1899 Oxford and Cambridge University Boat Crews
Oxford-Cambridge Boat-Race
1900 Oxford-Cambridge Race
1901 International Field Sports—Oxford-Cambridge vs. Harvard-Yale
1902 The University College of Oxford Winning the Ladies' Challenge Plate
1904 The Oxford and Cambridge Boat Race
1907 Cambridge-Oxford Race
1908 Oxford and Cambridge Boat Race
Oyster
1897 Scene in a Popular Oyster Saloon
1905 Masher and Oyster Stand
1907 The Oyster Industry
1908 Oyster Farming
1909 The Oysterman's Gold
1910 Opening an Oyster
Oz
1910 Dorothy and the Scarecrow in Oz
The Land of Oz
The Wonderful Wizard of Oz
Pa-u
1907 Pa-u Riders, Hawaiian Island
Pace
1897 A Paced Bicycle Race
1899 The Great Free-for-All Pacing Race
1900 A Career of Crime, No. 2: Going the Pace
1901 Bicycle Paced Race
Pacific
1901 Crew of a Pacific Liner
1904 Surf Scene on the Pacific
1907 Panorama La Boca Harbor and Pacific Entrance to Canal

Pacific Avenue (Tacoma, Washington)
1903 Pacific Avenue, Tacoma, Wash.
Pacifier
1908 Marvelous Pacifier
Pack mules
1898 Pack Mules with Ammunition on the Santiago Trail, Cuba
Packing Ammunition on Mules, Cuba
Pack Saddle Mountains (Pennsylvania)
1899 A Ride Through Pack Saddle Mountains, Penna. R.R.
Pack train
1901 Burro Pack Train on Main Street, Dawson City
Burro Pack Train on the Chilcoot Pass
1903 Mule Pack Train Taking Gold Dust to Dawson City
A Pack Train in the Copper River Country
Pack Train Leaving Valdez for Copper Mines
1906 Army Pack Train Bringing Supplies
Package
1908 Surprise Package
1910 Henry's Package
Packing
1901 Export Packing
Noon Time in Packing Town, (Panoramic)
Noon Time in Packing Town, (Whiskey Point)
Packers on the Trail
Packing Pickle Jars, Heinz
Pad
1907 Animated Stamp Pad
1908 Miracles of a Pain Pad
Paddle
1900 Paddle Dance
Paddock
1899 The Paddock
Padre
1910 The Padre's Secret
Padrone
1908 The Padrone
Padua (Italy)
1908 Angelo, Tyrant of Padua
Pagan
1909 Pagan and Christian
Page
1909 The Brave Page Boy
How the Page Boy Cured a Flirt
1910 The Wicked Baron and the Page
Pageant
1903 A Gorgeous Pageant of Princes
Pageant of East Indian Princes
1907 The Warwick Pageant
1908 Boston Normal School Pageant
The Discoverers, a Grand Historical Pageant Picturing the Discovery and Founding of New France, Canada
The Dover Pageant
Pagliacci
1909 Il Pagliacci (Leoncavallo)
Pagoda
1905 Defense of a Pagoda
Pail
1909 The Doctored Dinner Pail
Pain
1902 Pain's Fireworks
1908 Miracles of a Pain Pad
1909 New Pain Killer
A Painful Joke
1910 A Painful Debt
Painless
1908 Painless Extraction
Paint
1901 Canned Meat Department. No. 6: Painting and Labeling
The Reversing Sign Painter
1904 Animated Painting
Haunted Scene Painter
Painter's Misfortune
1907 Charley Paints
Modern Painters
1908 The Gypsy and the Painter
The Painter's Revenge
A Tricky Painter's Fate
1909 The Devil and the Painter
It's Only the Painter
The Painter's Idol
The Painting
1910 In Need of a Painter
The Painter's Sweetheart
Peter's Patent Paint

Pair
1903 A Pair of Queens
1904 Four Beautiful Pairs of Legs
1905 Winning a Pair of Gloves
1906 History of a Pair of Trousers
1907 A Pair of Boots, Please
1908 How the Pair Butted In
An Odd Pair of Limbs
A Pair of Kids
A Pair of Spectacles
1909 A Dangerous Pair
Misadventures of a Pair of Trousers
A Pair of Garters
A Pair of Slippers
A Pair of Truants
A Pair of White Gloves
1910 A Pair of Schemers; or, My Wife and My Uncle
The Story of a Pair of Boots

Pajama
1900 Boarding School Girls' Pajama Parade
1903 The Pajama Dance
The Pajama Girl
The Pajama Statue Girls

Pal
1899 Jones and His Pal in Trouble
1902 The Pals and the Clothier's Dummy
1903 Fred Poplar and His Pal
1904 Two Old Pals at Lunch
1905 Policeman's Pal
1906 Me and My Two Pals
Pals; or, My Friend, the Dummy
Weary Willie and His Pal
1907 Robert Macaire and Bertrand; or, The Troubles of a Hobo and His Pal, in Paris
1910 Pals
Pals of the Range
A True Pal
War Time Pals

Palace
1898 Relieving the Guard at St. James Palace
1899 The Infernal Palace
1900 Eiffel Tower from Trocadero Palace
Foreign Palaces
Grand Palaces
Palace of Electricity
Palace of Navigation
1901 Reading the Proclamation at St. James Palace
1902 The Aerial Railway at the Crystal Palace, London, England
The Longchamps Palace
Queen Wilhelmina Arriving at the Kaiser's Palace
1904 The Falling Palace
Fashionable Driving on Palace Quay, St. Petersburg
1905 The Palace of the Arabian Nights

Paleface
1909 The Pale Face's Wooing
1910 The Pale Faced Princess
The Paleface Princess

Palermo (Italy)
1908 Palermo and Its Surroundings
1910 Tunny Fishing off Palermo, Italy

Palestine
1904 A Trip to Palestine. Jaffa and Its Harbor
A Trip to Palestine. Jerusalem, the Holy City
1909 Orange Growing in Palestine

Palette
1910 Love and a Palette
Love and a Pallette
An Original Palette

Palissy, Bernard
1909 Bernard Palissy

Pallet
1909 Mr. Pallet Goes Out Landscaping

Palliser, British Columbia (Canada)
1902 Panoramic View Between Palliser and Field, B. C.

Pallone
1909 The Game of Pallone

Palm
1909 Uncle's Palm Tree

Palm Beach (Florida)
1905 Boating Carnival, Palm Beach, Fla.
In the Swimming Pool, Palm Beach, Fla.

Palmer, Pedlar
1899 Reproduction of the Pedlar Palmer and Terry McGovern Fight
Reproduction of the Terry McGovern and Pedlar Palmer Fight
1903 Dixon-Palmer Fight
1908 Reproduction of Burns-Palmer Fight, London [England], February 10th, 1908

Palmistry
1905 The Society Palmist
1907 Palmistry
1909 A Lesson in Palmistry
Palmistry

Pan-American Exposition
1900 Pan-American Exposition
1901 The Bridge of Sighs—Pan-American Exposition
The Court of Fountains—Pan-American Exposition
Fair Japan—Pan-American Exposition
Fountain, Tower, and Basins—Pan-American Exposition
Horse Parade at the Pan-American Exposition
Main Entrance to Pan-American Exp.
The Mob Outside the Temple of Music at the Pan-American Exposition [Buffalo]
On the Midway—Pan-American Exposition
Opening of the Pan-American Exposition Showing Vice President Roosevelt Leading the Procession
Pan-American Exposition by Night
Panorama of Midway—Pan-American Exposition
Panoramic View Gov't Building, Pan. Am. Exp.
President McKinley Reviewing the Troops at the Pan-American Exposition
President McKinley's Speech at the Pan-American Exposition
Propylaea and North End of Plaza, Pan. Am. Exp.
Scene in Beautiful Orient—Pan-American Exposition
Sevillenas Dance—Pan-American Exposition
Sham Battle at the Pan-American Exposition
Spanish Dancers at the Pan-American Exposition
A Trip Around the Pan-American Exposition
Triumphal Bridge, Pan-American Exposition
1904 Panorama of a Philippine Settlement [Pan-American Exposition]

Panama
1907 Old Market Place, Panama
1909 With Taft in Panama

Panama (Boat)
1898 Capture of the "Panama"

Panama Canal
1907 Colon to Panama Canal Picture
Machete Men Clearing a Jungle [Panama Canal]
Panorama from Columbus Point of Atlantic Entrance to the Canal
Panorama La Boca Harbor and Pacific Entrance to Canal

Panic
1908 Panic in a Village
1910 A Panicky Picnic

Panning
1905 Panning Gold on a Claim in the Klondike

Panorama
1896 Canadian Falls—Panoramic [View] from Michigan Central R.R.
Panorama of American & Canadian Falls—Taken Opposite American Falls
Panoramic View from Trolley, Atlantic City
1897 Panorama of Susquehanna River Taken from the Black Diamond Express
A Panoramic View in the Grand Canal
Panoramic View of Grand Canal
Panoramic View of Venice
1898 California Orange Groves, Panoramic View
Panoramic View of Camp Wikoff
1899 Panorama at Grant's Tomb, Dewey Naval Procession
Panoramic View, Horseshoe Curve, From Penna. Ltd.
Panoramic View, Horseshoe Curve, Penna. R.R., No. 2
Panoramic View of Brooklyn Bridge
Panoramic View of Floral Float "Olympia"
Panoramic View of Manila Harbor
Panoramic View of Niagara Falls
Panoramic View of Olympia in New York Harbor
Panoramic View of Windsor Castle
1900 Panorama from the Moving Boardwalk
Panorama of Both Sides of the River Seine
Panorama of East Galveston
Panorama of Eiffel Tower
Panorama of Galveston Power House
Panorama of Gorge Railway
Panorama of Orphans' Home, Galveston
Panorama of Place De L'Opera
Panorama of the Moving Boardwalk
Panorama of the Paris Exposition, from the Seine
Panorama of Wreckage of Water Front
Panoramic View of Burning Wharves and Warehouses [Hoboken]
Panoramic View of Newport [R.I.]
Panoramic View of Rome
Panoramic View of the Champs Elysees
Panoramic View of the Dewey Arch, New York City
Panoramic View of the Ghetto, New York City
Panoramic View of the Place de la Concorde
Panoramic View of Tremont Hotel, Galveston
Panoramic View, Rescue Work, Galveston
Panoramic View, Wreckage Along Shore, Galveston
1901 Circular Panorama of Atlantic City, N.J.
Circular Panorama of Electric Tower
Circular Panorama of Mauch Chunk, Penna.
Circular Panorama of Niagara Falls
Circular Panorama of Suspension Bridge and American Falls
Circular Panorama of the American Falls
Circular Panorama of the Base of the Electric Tower, Ending Looking Down the Mall
Circular Panorama of the Electric Tower and Pond
Circular Panorama of the Esplanade with the Electric Tower in the Background
Circular Panorama of the Esplanade and Forecourt
Circular Panorama of the Midway
Circular Panoramic View of Whirlpool Rapids
Execution of Czolgosz, with Panorama of Auburn Prison
Miscellaneous. No. 6: Panoramic View
Noon Time in Packing Town, (Panoramic)
Panorama, Golden Gate
Panorama, Great Gorge Route over Lewiston Bridge
Panorama of a Philippine Village
Panorama of Brooklyn Bridge, River Front, and Tall Buildings from the East River
Panorama of Esplanade by Night
Panorama of Kobe Harbor, Japan
Panorama of Midway—Pan-American Exposition
Panorama of the Exposition, No. 1
Panorama of the Exposition, No. 2
Panorama of Water Front
Panorama, Public Square, Cleveland, O.
Panoramic View, Albert Canyon
Panoramic View, Asheville, N. C.
Panoramic View Gov't Building, Pan. Am. Exp.
Panoramic View, Kicking Horse Canyon
Panoramic View, Lower Kicking Horse Canyon
Panoramic View, Lower Kicking Horse Valley
Panoramic View of Boston Subway from an Electric Car
Panoramic View of Electric Tower from a Balloon
Panoramic View of London Streets, Showing Coronation Decorations
Panoramic View of Moki-Land
Panoramic View of Rubio Canyon, Mt. Low R.R.
Panoramic View of the Bay of Fundy
Panoramic View of the Capitol, Washington, D.C.
Panoramic View of the Crowd Rushing for the City Hall, Buffalo, to View the Body of President McKinley

Panoramic View of the Fleet After Yacht Race
Panoramic View of the Gorge Railroad
Panoramic View of the McKinley Homestead
Panoramic View of the President's House at Canton, Ohio
Panoramic View of the Temple of Music and Esplanade
Panoramic View of the Thames
Panoramic View of the White House, Washington, D.C.
Panoramic View of the White Pass Railroad
Panoramic View, Upper Kicking Horse Canyon
A Ride on the Elevated R.R. (Panoramic)
1902 Circular Panorama of Housing the Ice
Circular Panoramic View of Jones and Laughlin's Steel Yard
Circular Panoramic View of St. Pierre from the Lighthouse, Showing Mt. Pelee Smoking in the Distance
Circular Panoramic View of St. Pierre, Showing the Ruins of the Catholic Cathedral and Mt. Pelee Smoking in the Background
Circular Panoramic View of the Market Place at Fort de France, Showing S.S. Korona in the Background
Fairmount Park Trolley Panorama
Panorama City of Venice
Panorama, Descending Mt. Blanc
Panorama of Cog Railway
Panorama of Esplanade from Bridge of Triumph
Panorama of Esquimaux Village
Panorama of Lower New York
Panorama of Midway
Panorama of Ninth Ave. Elevated R.R.
Panorama of St. Pierre
Panorama of the Famous Georgetown Loop
Panorama of the Paterson [N.J.] Fire
Panorama of the Royal Gorge
Panorama of Ute Pass
Panorama of Venice
Panorama of Wilhelmshaven
Panoramic View Between Palliser and Field, B. C.
Panoramic View from Pittsburgh to Allegheny
Panoramic View from the Stadtbahn
Panoramic View near Mt. Golden on the Canadian Pacific R.R.
Panoramic View of Charleston Exposition [South Carolina]
Panoramic View of Granite Canon
Panoramic View of Hell Gate
Panoramic View of Mt. Tamalpais
Panoramic View of Mt. Tamalpais Between Bow Knot and McKinley Cut
Panoramic View of New Haven, Conn.
Panoramic View of Seven Castles
Panoramic View of Switchback, Mauch Chunk
Panoramic View of the Alps, Switzerland
Panoramic View of the Canadian Pacific R.R. near Leauchoil, B. C.
Panoramic View of the French Market
Panoramic View of the Golden Gate
Panoramic View of the Harbor of Hamburg, Germany
Panoramic View of the Hohenzollern
Panoramic View of the Siegesallee
Panoramic View of Westminster Abbey and Surroundings
Turning Panorama of Mt. Beacon
Woodside Park Trolley Panorama
1903 The Grand Panorama from the Great Schreckhorn, 13,500 feet
Kit Carson #6: Panorama
Panorama and Bathing Scene of Ostend, Belgium
Panorama from Canoe, No. 6
Panorama from Elevated Train, New York
Panorama Looking Down Niagara from New Suspension Bridge
Panorama of Alpine Peaks
Panorama of American Soldiers in Camp
Panorama of Beach and Cliff House
Panorama of Blackwell's Island
Panorama of Cal. Oil Fields
Panorama of Circus Train Unloading Horses
Panorama of City of Venice
Panorama of Excursion Boats
Panorama of Factory from Automobile, National Cash Register Co.
Panorama of Grindelwald
Panorama of Kennicott Glacier Port Hole
Panorama of King's County, N.Y.
Panorama of League Island, Philadelphia
Panorama of Lucerne Lake
Panorama of "Miles Canyon"
Panorama of Morro Castle, Havana, Cuba
Panorama of New York from Jersey City
Panorama of No. 2 Eldorado
Panorama of Queenstown
Panorama of Riker's Island
Panorama of Schellenen Gorge of Switzerland
Panorama of Taku Glacier
Panorama of Thames River
Panorama of the Lakes of Killarney from Hotel
Panorama of the Lehigh Valley Railroad
Panorama of the Menagerie
Panorama of Tivoli, Italy, Showing Seven Falls
Panorama of White Horse Rapids
Panorama of Willemstadt, Curacao, Taken from the River
Panorama of Yellowstone Lake
Panorama on the St. Gothard Railway
Panorama, Union Square, San Francisco
Panorama Water Front and Brooklyn Bridge from East River
Panoramic View of an Egyptian Cattle Market
Panoramic View of Atlantic City Beach
Panoramic View of Beyrouth, Syria, Showing Holiday Festivities
Panoramic View of Geneva, Switzerland
Panoramic View of Haverstraw Tunnel, N.Y.
Panoramic View of Herreshoff Works from Bristol Harbor
Panoramic View of Hot Springs, Yellowstone Park
Panoramic View of Monte Carlo
Panoramic View of St. Pierre, Martinique
Panoramic View of the Alps from an Electric Car
Panoramic View of the Rocky Mountain on the Rock Island System
Panoramic View of the Streets of Paris, France
Panoramic View of Torpedo Boat "Winslow" and Yacht "Constitution"
Panoramic Views and Scenes at the Garden of the Gods
Railroad Panorama near Spanishtown, Jamaica
Rising Panorama of a Norwegian Waterfall
U.S. Interior Dept.: Panorama from Artist's Point
U.S. Interior Dept.: Panorama of Grand Canyon
Woodside Park Trolley Panorama
1904 Circular Panorama of the Horse Shoe Falls in Winter
Panorama Exterior Westinghouse Works
Panorama from German Building, World's Fair
Panorama from St. Louis Plaza, St. Louis Exposition
Panorama Motor Room, Westinghouse Works
Panorama of a Philippine Settlement [Pan-American Exposition]
Panorama of Field St., St. Joseph, Mo., Missouri Commission
Pan. of Fifth Ave., Pittsburg, Pa., From a Trolley Car
Panorama of 4th St., St. Joseph, Mo., Missouri Commission
Panorama of Harvard Class Day
Panorama of Machine Co. Aisle, Westinghouse Co. Works
Panorama of Race Track Crowd, St. Louis
Panorama of Railroad Station at Seoul, Korea, from Departing Train
Panorama of Ruins from Baltimore and Charles Street
Panorama of Ruins from Lombard and Charles Street
Panorama of Ruins from Lombard and Hanover Streets, Baltimore, Md.
Panorama of Ruins from Water Front
Panorama of St. Louis Exposition from Wireless Tower
Pan. of St. Railway Building, Pittsburg, Pa.
Panorama of 3rd Street, St. Joseph, Mo., Missouri Commission
Panorama Russian Battleship "Gronobia"
Panorama St. Louis Exposition from Launch
Panoramic View Aisle B., Westinghouse Works
Panoramic View of Chamonix, Alps
Panoramic View of La Mure, France
Panoramic View of Montreux, Switzerland
Panoramic View of Multnomah Falls
Panoramic View of Spokane Falls
Panoramic View of the Columbia River
Railroad Panorama, Pittsburg to Stewart, Westinghouse Works
Sec'y Taft's Address & Panorama
Turning Panorama from Hill, Westinghouse Works
1905 Accelerated (Crazy) Panorama West Shore, Lake of Garda
Accelerated Panorama from Steamer on the Thames, London
"All Day in the Alps" Panorama from Gorner Grat
Crazy (or Accelerated) Panoramic Approach to Taku Glacier, Alaska
Fjord Panorama from Moving Ship, Norway
Panorama from a Moving Train on White Pass & Yukon Railway, Alaska
Panorama from Car on Mendel Pass Cable Railway
Panorama from Car on Oberammergau Electric Railway
Panorama from Dreisprackenspitz Stelvio Pass
Panorama from Electric Car, Lucerne
Panorama from Gortner Grat
Panorama from Moving Steamer on the River Thames, England
Panorama from Moving Train on Albula Railway, Switzerland
Panorama from Moving Train on Murren Electric Railway, Switzerland
Panorama from the Roof of the Times Building, New York
Panorama from Train on Visp-Zermatt Railway
Panorama of a Norwegian Fjord from Alvik to Vik from Moving Ship
Panorama of Eismeer, Switzerland
Panorama of Hammerfest Harbor
Panorama of Stockholm from Steam Ferry
Panorama of the Castle of Chillon, Lake Geneva
Panorama of the Course at Henley Showing a Finish
Panorama of the Folgefond Snowfield, Norway
Panorama of the Norwegian Fjord from Moving Ship
Panorama of the Sultan of Morocco's Troop Forming a Square Awaiting the Arrival of H. M. S.
Panorama of the Theatre, Vevey Fete
Panorama of Theatre, Vevey Fete
Panoramic Bird's Eye View of Montreal, Canada
Railway Panorama Between Green Island and Kilroot
Railway Panorama Between Kilroot and Whitehead
Railway Panorama from Moving Train Passing Through Conway Castle, Wales
Retrogressive Jaunting Car, Reverse Panorama from Moving Train, Dublin, Ireland
Reverse Panorama, Maria Theresian Strasse, Innsbruck
1906 Circular Panorama of Market St. and Stockton
General Circular Panorama of the Burned Business District
Great Railroad Panorama Through Colorado
Panorama, City Hall, Van Ness Avenue and College of St. Ignatius
Panorama from Telegraph Hill
Panorama, Nob Hill and Ruins of Millionaire Residences

Panorama, Notorious "Barbary Coast"
Panorama of Chinatown
Panorama of Market Street Before the Fire
Panorama of Market Street, San Francisco
Panorama of Nob Hill
Panorama of San Francisco in Smoke and Fire
Panorama, Ruins Aristocratic Apartments
Panorama, Russian and Nob Hill from an Automobile
Panoramas of Market Street, the City Hall, Taken from the Roof of the U.S. Mint
Panoramic View from Alamo Square of San Francisco While Burning
Panoramic View of Market Street San Francisco After the Earthquake and Fire
Panoramic View of San Francisco City Hall, Damaged by Earthquake
Panoramic View of Van Ness Ave.
Railway Panoramas from Every Port of the World
Steamship Panoramas
Vertical Panorama City Hall and Surroundings
Thibidado (Panorama de Thibidabo (Espagne))

1907 Gratli Vand and Tourists Passing, Panorama
Panorama, Crowds at Squires-Burns International Contest, from Center of Ring, Colma, July 4th, 1907
Panorama, Crowds at Squires-Burns International Contest, from Moving Picture Stand, July 4th, 1907
Panorama from Columbus Point of Atlantic Entrance to the Canal
Panorama La Boca Harbor and Pacific Entrance to Canal
Panorama of Court of Honor
Panorama of Culebra Cut
Panorama of Market Street, San Francisco
Panorama of Market Street Showing the Beautiful Decorations
Panorama Ruins of Old French Machinery
Panoramic View, Crater of Haleakala, H.I.
Panoramic View, Honolulu Harbor, H.I.
Panoramic View, King St. Honolulu, H.I.
Panoramic View, Oahu Railroad, Haleiwa, H.I.
Panoramic View, Oahu Railroad, Pearl Harbor, Hawaiian Islands
Panoramic View of Waikiki Beach, Honolulu, H.I.
Panoramic View, Waikiki, from an Electric Car, H.I.

1908 Panorama of Venice

1909 River Panorama

1910 Panoramic Railway View from Front of Train

Panther

1909 Panther Hunting on the Isle of Java

1910 Hunting the Panther
On Panther Creek

Panther (Boat)

1898 The "Panther"

Pantry

1897 Burglars in the Pantry

Pants

1909 His First Pants

Papanaguaz

1906 A Seaside Flirtation (Le rastaquouère Rodriguez y Papanaguaz)

Paper

1899 Diving Through Paper Screens

1902 The Absent Minded Clerk, Fly Paper and Silk Hat

1903 A Paper Chase

1904 Fly Paper Vendors

1908 Fly Paper
Fond of His Paper
Paper Tearing

1909 Father's Busy Papering
Paper Cock-A-Doodles

1910 How Bumptious Papered the Parlor

Paper dolls

1898 Dressing Paper Dolls

Paperhanger

1901 A Non-Union Paper Hanger

1905 The Paper Hanger in Trouble

1908 Bill, the Bill Poster, and Pete, the Paperhanger

Papinta

1910 Papinta

Parade

1896 Parade, Americus Club, Canton Ohio
Parade at Canton O., Showing Major McKinley in Carriage
Parade, Elkins Cadets, Canton, O.
Parade, First Brigade
Parade, Sound Money Club, Canton, O.
The Sound Money Parade
Sound Money Parade
The Street Parade

1897 Ancient and Honorable Artillery Parade
Barnum's Street Parade, Nos. 1, 2, and 3
Bicyclers in Inaugural Parade
Buffalo Police on Parade
Glimpses of the Grant Parade
The Junior Republic on Parade
A Part of Inaugural Parade, Washington
Philadelphia Police on Parade
13th Infantry, U.S. Army—Full Dress Parade and Manoeuvering, Governors Island
13th Infantry, U.S. Army—Full Dress Parade, Governors Island
Troop "A" in Inaugural Parade

1898 Chief Devery at Head of N.Y. Police Parade
Close View of the "Brooklyn," Naval Parade
Excursion Boats, Naval Parade
Famous Battleship Captains—Philadelphia Peace Jubilee Parade
The "Glen Island," Accompanying Parade
Major-General Nelson A. Miles, and Staff, in the Peace Jubilee Parade
The "Massachusetts," Naval Parade
New York Mounted on Parade
New York Police on Parade
New York Police Parade
Observation Train Following Parade
Parade of Buffalo Bill's Wild West Show, No. 1
Parade of Buffalo Bill's Wild West Show, No. 2
Parade of Chinese
Parade of Coaches
Parade of Marines, U.S. Cruiser, "Brooklyn"
Peace Jubilee Naval Parade, New York City
Peace Parade—Chicago
Police Boats Escorting Naval Parade
The "Texas," Naval Parade
U.S. Cruiser "Brooklyn," Naval Parade

1899 Admiral Dewey Leading Land Parade
Admiral Dewey Leading Land Parade, No. 2
Admiral Dewey Leading Land Parade, (Eighth Ave.)
Astor Battery on Parade
Church Parade of the Life Guards
Dewey Land Parade
Dewey Naval Parade
Dewey Parade, 10th Pennsylvania Volunteers
An Easter Parade
Elephants in a Circus Parade
Flagship Olympia and Cruiser New York in Naval Parade
Fourth Connecticut Volunteers, Dewey Parade
New York Police Parade, June 1st, 1899
Odd Fellows Parade
Parade in Providence, R.I.
Patriot's Day Parade
2nd Special Service Battalion, Canadian Infantry-Parade
Sunday School Parade
U.S. Cruiser "Olympia" Leading Naval Parade

1900 Automobile Parade
Boarding School Girls' Pajama Parade
British Troops on Dress Parade
Buffalo Bill's Wild West Parade
Dewey Land Parade, Detroit
Dress Parade of the Woodward High School Cadets
May Day Parade
The Parade of Naval Veterans
Parade of the Order of Elks in Atlantic City
Royal Leinster Regiment on Parade
A Speedway Parade
U.S. Marines in Dewey Land Parade

1901 Automobile Parade on the Coney Island Boulevard
Buffalo Bill's Wild West Parade
Buffalo Street Parade
Centennial Parade
Chicago Fat Stock Parade
Chicago Police Parade
Dewey Parade
A Flower Parade
Horse Parade at the Pan-American Exposition
Industrial Parade of the Cincinnati Fall Festival
Knight Templars Parade at Louisville, Ky.
Knight Templars Parade Drill
Parade of Horses
Parade of Snake Dancers Before the Dance
Parade on the Speedway
Parade to the Post
Rickshaw Parade, Japan

1902 An Automobile Parade in the Tuilleries Gardens
Baby Parade
Bi-Centennial Jubilee Parade
Circus Parade No. 1
Circus Parade No. 2
Coronation Parade
Floral Chair Parade
Mardi Gras Parade
New Year's Mummers Parade
Opening Day Parade No. 1
Opening Day Parade No. 2
Opening Day Parade No. 3
Ringling Bros. Circus Parade
The Speedway Parade

1903 Ancient and Honourable Artillery of London on Parade
Animal Parade, Hagenback's Circus
Annual Circus Parade
Atlantic City Floral Parade
Automobile Parade
Bicycle Parade, Philadelphia
Buffalo Bill's Parade
Buffalo Bill's Street Parade
Cavalry Parade
Circus Street Parade
Cook County Democracy Parade
Floral Parade
Fool's Parade
Indian Parade
A Kennel Club Parade
Knights Templar Street Parade, Philadelphia
Market Street Before Parade
Naval Parade on the Delaware River, Monday, May 1st, in Honor of Admiral Dewey
New York Caledonian Club's Parade
New York City Police Parade
Over Route of Roosevelt Parade in an Automobile
Parade of Eagles, New York
Parade of "Exempt" Firemen
Parade of Roses
Parade of the Philadelphia Volunteer Fire Department
Parade Through Chicago Streets
Porters in Parade, National Cash Register Co.
Uncle Tom's Cabin Parade

1904 Annual Baby Parade, 1904, Asbury Park, N.J.
Annual Parade, New York Fire Department
Atlantic City Floral Parade
Barnum & Bailey's Circus Street Parade
Brewers' Parade, Philadelphia, Pa.
Dress Parade of the Filipino Scouts, St. Louis Exposition
Dress Parade, St. John's Academy
Easter Flower Parade in Bois de Boulogne, Paris
Flower Parade Race Course, Moscow
Parade, Fiftieth Anniversary Atlantic City, N.J.
Parade, Mystic Shriners, Atlantic City, New Jersey
Parade of Characters (Asia in America) St. Louis Exposition
Parade of Floats, St. Louis Exposition
Parade of Military, St. Louis Exposition
Parade of Mystic Shriners, Luna Park, Coney Island
Parade of National Cash Register Co.'s Employees, St. Louis Exposition

Parade of the Pikers, St. Louis Exposition
Russian Infantry (Défilé d'infanterie russe)
Russian Cavalry (Défilé de cavalerie russe)
1905 Firemen's Parade, Scranton, Pa.
Floral Parade at the Race Track, Moscow, Russia
Floral Parade Festival of Roses, Pasadena, Cal.
Fourth of July Parade Yosemite California
Inauguration of President Roosevelt. the Grand Inaugural Parade
New Year's Day Parade, Philadelphia
New York City Fire Department on Parade
N.Y. Police Parade, 1905
Odd Fellows Parade, Philadelphia, Pa.
Parade of Passengers Crossing to North Cape, Norway
Sunday "Church Parade" Bergen Norway
Russian Artillery (Défilé d'artillerie russe)
1906 Volunteer Fire Department Parade
1907 Elks' Convention Parade
Elks' Convention Parade: "Spirit of '76" and Views of the Grand Stand
Elks' Parade
Floral Parade at Pasadena, Calif.
1908 Catholic Centennial Parade
Historical Parade
Industrial Parade
Labor Day Parade
The Mardi Gras Parade at Coney Island
Military Parade, Founders Week Celebration, Philadelphia
Naval Parade
1909 Coon Town Parade
German Spring Parade
Grand Naval Parade
Historic Parade
Levitsky Sees the Parade
Military Parade
Naval Parade of the Hudson-Fulton
1910 Flower Parade at Pasadena, California

Paradise
1903 Bachelor's Paradise
A Maiden's Paradise
The Workman's Paradise
1905 The Scheming Gambler's Paradise
1908 Christmas in Paradise Alley
A Tyrolean Paradise
1909 A Dream of Paradise
Earthly Paradise
The Mason's Paradise
From Portofino to Nervi (Il paradiso d'Italia da Portofino a Nervi)
1910 A Fool's Paradise
The Trimming of Paradise Gulch

Parafaragamus
1906 The Mysterious Retort (L'alchimiste Parafaragamus ou la cornue infernale)

Parafin
1903 Mary Jane's Mishap; or, Don't Fool with the Parafin

Paralytic
1908 The Paralytic's Vengeance
1909 The Paralytic

Parcel
1910 A Troublesome Parcel

Pardners
1910 Pardners

Pardon
1906 Law of Pardon
1908 Beg Pardon
Beg Pardon!
A Free Pardon
The King's Pardon
The Pardon
1910 The Governor's Pardon

Parent
1904 Foster Parents
1908 The Parents' Devotion
Sold by His Parents
The Student's Prank; or, A Joke on His Parents
Unyielding Parent
1910 Her Adopted Parents

Paris (Boat)
1899 Wreck of the S.S. "Paris"

Paris (France)
1897 Parisian Dance
Les Parisiennes
1898 A Hotel Fire in Paris, and Rescue by Parisian Pompiers
1900 Arrival of Train at Paris Exposition
The Girl from Paris
Kansas City Fire Department, Winners of the World's Championship at the Paris Exposition
Old Paris
Panorama of the Paris Exposition, from the Seine
Paris Exposition
Scene in the Swiss Village at Paris Exposition
The Shah's Return from Paris
Street Scene at Place de la Concorde, Paris, France
1902 The Darktown Comedians Trip to Paris
Paris Exposition
A Parisian Ballet
1903 Boulevard St. Denis, Paris, France
King Edward's Visit to Paris
Panoramic View of the Streets of Paris, France
Roofs of Paris
1904 A Burlesque Highway Robbery in "Gay Paree"
Easter Flower Parade in Bois de Boulogne, Paris
An Englishman's Trip to Paris from London
Paris from the Seine
A Parisienne's Bed Time
1905 Countryman in Paris
The King and Queen of Italy in Paris
An Adventurous Automobile Trip (Le raid Paris-Monte Carlo en deux heures)
An Adventurous Automobile Trip (Le voyage automobile Paris-Monte Carlo en deux heures)
1906 Apaches in Paris
Bird's Eye View of Paris
The Paris-Bordeaux Auto Race
The Paris Students
1907 Elegant Paris
An Episode of the Paris Commune
Misadventures of a Negro King in Paris
Paris Slums
Robert Macaire and Bertrand; or, The Troubles of a Hobo and His Pal, in Paris
The Underworld of Paris
1908 The Flower Girl of Paris
The Mishaps of the New York-Paris Auto Race
A Night with the Masqueraders in Paris
Paris as Seen from a Height of 2600 Feet
Paris Fire Brigade
Paris Fire Brigade at Drill
Parisian Life in Miniature
1909 Berthold in Paris
Cigar-Butt Pickers in Paris
The Garbage of Paris
Glimpses of Paris
Strike Time in Paris
Summer Home for the School Children of Paris
1910 The Paris Disaster
Paris Flood
[Paris Flood Pictures]
Paris Viewed from the Eiffel Tower
The Parisian
Roosevelt in Paris
Souvenirs of Paris
The Street Arab of Paris
Submarines in Paris

Park
1896 Park Police Drill Left Wheel and Forward
Park Police Drill Mount and Dismounting
The Runaway in the Park
1897 Battery Park
Free-for-All Race at Charter Oak Park
Sleighing in Central Park
1899 Coaches Going to Cinnabar from Yellowstone Park
Fifth Avenue Entrance to Central Park
Lower Falls, Grand Canyon, Yellowstone Park
Plowing Snow in the Park
Sleighing in the Park
Tourists Going Round Yellowstone Park
1900 After Dark in Central Park
In Central Park
Lincoln Park
A Scene in Fairmount Park, Phila.
Skating in Central Park
1901 The Funeral Arriving at Hyde Park
Hooligan Visits Central Park
On the Benches in the Park
Riverside Geyser, Yellowstone Park
Royal Artillery and English Sailors Marching Through Hyde Park
Springtime in the Park
Wild Bear in Yellowstone Park
1902 Deer in Park
Fairmount Park Trolley Panorama
Woodside Park Trolley Panorama
1903 Arab Act, Luna Park
Arrival of Tourists at the Hotel in Yellowstone Park
Boy Up a Tree; or, Making Love in the Park
Crew of the U.S. Cruiser Raleigh Passing the Grant Monument at Fairmount Park, Philadelphia
Double Ring Act, Luna Park
An Episode in the Park
Panoramic View of Hot Springs, Yellowstone Park
President McKinley and His Cabinet on the Reviewing Stand, at Fairmount Park, Phila., May 27, 1899
Rattan Slide and General View of Luna Park
River Drive, Fairmount Park
Shooting the Chutes, Luna Park
Shooting the Rapids at Luna Park
Skating in Fairmount Park
Slide for Life, Luna Park
United States Troops in Yellowstone Park
The Vaidis Sisters, Luna Park
Woodside Park Trolley Panorama
1904 The Bench in the Park
Boxing Horses, Luna Park, Coney Island
Elephants Shooting the Chutes at Luna Park [Coney Island]
Elephants Shooting the Chutes, Luna Park, Coney Island, No. 2
Fire and Flames at Luna Park, Coney Island [An Attraction at Coney Island]
Hyde Park School Graduating Class, Missouri Commission
Hyde Park School Room 2, Missouri Commission
Ice Skating in Central Park, N.Y.
Parade of Mystic Shriners, Luna Park, Coney Island
Park in Barcelona by Moonlight
Sleighing in Central Park, New York
"While Strolling in the Park"
1905 Bears Feeding at the Lake Hotel, Yellowstone Park
The "Black Growler" Steam Vent, Yellowstone Park
The Castle Geyser, Yellowstone Park
The "Crazy" Steamer Yellowstone Park
Deer in Wild Park, Goteborg, Sweden
Dial's Girls' Band, Luna Park
Great Fountain Geyser, Yellowstone Park
Herd of Bison, Yellowstone Park
Minuteman Geyser, Yellowstone Park
Old Faithful Geyser, Yellowstone Park
Passengers Boarding Busses at Hyde Park Corner, London
Rapids of the Silver Apron, Yellowstone Park
Riverside Geyser, Yellowstone Park
Stage Coaches, Yellowstone Park
Stages Leaving Fountain House, Yellowstone Park
Troop of Horse Guards in St. James Park, London
1906 Military Feeding Starving and Destitute Refugees in Golden Gate Park
Park Lodge, Golden Gate Park
Refugees at the Golden Gate Park
Runaway in the Park
Thieves in Camp, Golden Gate Park
1907 Carl Hagenbeck's Wild Animal Park at Hamburg, Germany
The Girl on Park Bench
The Park Keeper
Scenes from Luna Park
Through Yellowstone Park
A Trip Through the Yellowstone Park, U.S.A.
A Trip Through Yellowstone Park
1908 The Great Yellowstone Park Hold-Up
1909 Glimpses of Yellowstone Park
The Park of Caserta
Parks in Berlin
Wedding Party in Luna Park
1910 Drive Through Central Park

Passion Play: Christ Feeding the Multitude
Passion Play: Christ Healing the Sick
Passion Play: Christ in the Carpenter Shop
Passion Play: Christ in the Synagogue
Passion Play: Christ Tempted by the Devil
Passion Play: Flight into Egypt
Passion Play: Herodias Pleads for John the Baptist's Head
Passion Play: Jesus and the Woman of Samaria
Passion Play: Judas' Betrayal and the Messiah's Arrest
Passion Play: Massacre of the Innocents
Passion Play: Placing Jesus in the Tomb
Passion Play: Raising of Lazarus
Passion Play: Shepherds Watching Their Flocks by Night
Passion Play: Suffer Little Children to Come Unto Me
Passion Play: Taking Down the Cross
Passion Play: The Annunciation
Passion Play: The Ascension
Passion Play: The Birth of Christ
Passion Play: The Crucifixion
Passion Play: The Last Supper
Passion Play: The Messiah's Entry into Jerusalem
Passion Play: The Resurrection
Passion Play: The Transfiguration
1904 The Passion Play
1907 Passion Play: Baptism by Immersion

Passkey
1909 The Pass Key

Past
1903 Past Shasta Spring, California
1909 A Shadow of the Past
1910 Memento of the Past
Out of the Past
A Shadow of the Past

Pastimes
1908 Australian Sports and Pastimes
Cowboy Sports and Pastimes
1909 Outing Pastimes in Colorado

Pastoral
1910 Pastoral Scenes

Pastry
1905 Chimney Sweep and Pastry Cook
The Pastry Cook's Practical Jokes
1907 The Pastry Cook and Musician
1908 The Pastry Cook
The Pastry Cook's Misfortune

Pasture
1903 Driving Cows to Pasture
1904 Driving Cattle to Pasture

Pat
1900 Pat vs. Populist
1904 And Pat Took Him at His Word
1907 Pat's Ghost
1909 One-Legged Pete and Pat
1910 Pat and the 400

Patch
1903 Jack Tar Sewing a Patch on the Seat of His Trousers
1905 The Watermelon Patch

Patent
1899 Demonstrating the Action of a Patent Street Sprinkler of the American Car Sprinkler Co. of Worcester, Mass
1909 Professor Puddenhead's Patents
1910 Patent Glue
Peter's Patent Paint

Patent medicine
1908 Indian Bitters; or, The Patent Medicine Man

Paternal
1903 Paternal Affection
1909 A False Accusation, a Story of Paternal Devotion

Paterson, Nan
1905 Reproduction, Nan Paterson's Trial

Paterson (New Jersey)
1900 Paterson Falls
1902 Panorama of the Paterson [N.J.] Fire
The Paterson Fire
Paterson [N.J.] Fire, Showing the Y.M.C.A. and Library
Ruins of City Hall, Paterson [N.J.]
1903 Flood Scene in Paterson, N.J.
1907 Paterson, N.J.

Path
1900 The Downward Path: She Ran Away [Part 2]
The Downward Path: The Fresh Book Agent [Part 1]
The Downward Path: The Girl Who Went Astray [Part 3]
The Downward Path: The New Soubrette [Part 4]
The Downward Path: The Suicide [Part 5]
1908 I'm Going on the War Path
On the War Path
1909 By Path of Love
Crooked Path
1910 Over Silent Paths
The Path of Duty

Patience
1901 A Patient Sufferer
1908 Out of Patience
1909 The Patience of Miss Job
Playing Patience

Patient
1902 St. John's Guild. Examination of Patients
St. John's Guild. Launch Delivering Patients to F. H.
St. John's Guild. Patients Down Bridge. S.S.H.
1903 The Doctor's Favorite Patient
1905 The Barber's Pretty Patient
1908 Dr. Curem's Patients
1909 The Delirious Patient
The Patient from Punkville

Patricia
1910 Patricia of the Plains

Patrician
1910 Patrician and Slave

Patrick Street, Cork (Ireland)
1904 Patrick Street, Cork

Patriotism
1898 Cuban Patriots
1908 Barbara Fritchie, the Story of a Patriotic American Woman
For Love of Country: American Patriotism in the Colonial Wars
The Patriot; or, The Horrors of War
1909 A True Patriot
1910 A Father's Patriotism
The Price of Patriotism

Patriot's Day
1899 Patriot's Day Parade

Patrol
1897 Police Patrol Wagon
1899 Arabis Patrol
1903 New York Harbor Police Boat Patrol Capturing Pirates
1904 The Coney Island Beach Patrol

Patron
1908 Unappreciated Patron

Patsey, Scrappy
1907 The Finish of Scrappy Patsey

Patterson (Boxer)
1897 The Downey and Patterson Fight

Patterson Family
1903 Mr. Patterson and Mr. Mark Arriving, National Cash Register Co.
Patterson Children in Pony Wagon, National Cash Register Co.
Patterson Children Leaving Home, National Cash Register Co.
Patterson Children on Horseback, National Cash Register Co.

Paul
1909 Paul Has Decided to Marry
1910 Paul and Virginia

Pauli
1910 Pauli

Pauper
1909 The Prince and the Pauper

Pavonia (Steamship)
1899 Steamship "Pavonia"

Pawnbrokers and pawnshops
1897 Scene in Ike Einstein's Pawn Office
1902 The Haunted Pawnshop
1908 Old Isaacs, the Pawnbroker
The Pawnbroker
1910 The Pawnshop

Pawnee Bill's Far East Show
1910 Buffalo Bill's Wild West and Pawnee Bill's Far East

Pawnee Junction
1910 The Heroine of Pawnee Junction

Pawtucket (Rhode Island)
1903 Run of Pawtucket Fire Dept.

Pay
1903 How Murphy Paid His Rent
"Who Pays for the Drinks?"
1906 Who Looks, Pays
1907 Don't Pay Rent—Move
Pay Day
The Pay Train Robbery
Paying Off Scores
She Won't Pay Her Rent
1908 A Dearly Paid for Kiss
A New Way to Pay Debts
Salome and the Devil to Pay
1909 Follow Me and I'll Pay for Dinner
Foolshead Pays a Visit
How Foolshead Paid His Debts
How Jones Paid His Debts
How the Bulldog Paid the Rent
Love with Love Is Paid
The Marathon Race; or, How Tom Paid Off the Mortgage
The Pay Car
A Paying Business
When Jack Gets His Pay
You Shall Pay for It
1910 It Pays to Advertise
Paid Boots and Stolen Boots
Paid in Full
Paying Attention
To-morrow Is Pay-day

Paymaster
1906 The Paymaster
1909 The Paymaster

Paza
1909 Paza Did It

Pea-hulling
1898 Pea-Hulling Machine

Peace
1898 Famous Battleship Captains—Philadelphia Peace Jubilee Parade
Major-General Nelson A. Miles, and Staff, in the Peace Jubilee Parade
Peace Jubilee Naval Parade, New York City
Peace Parade—Chicago
1899 Guardians of the Peace
1903 Blessed Is the Peacemaker
A Guardian of the Peace
1905 Peace Envoys at Portsmouth, N.H.
Scenes and Incidents, Russo-Japanese Peace Conference, Portsmouth, N.H.
1906 Anything for Peace and Quietness
1908 The Little Peace-Maker
A Peaceful Inn
1909 The Little Peacemaker
A Peace Agitator
Peaceful Jones
1910 The Peacemaker

Peach
1909 Peaches and Cream
1910 A Japanese Peach Boy

Peachbasket
1909 Flossie's New Peach-Basket Hat
The Peachbasket Hat

Peak
1902 Arrival on Summit of Pike's Peak
Leaving the Summit of Pike's Peak
Pike's Peak Toboggan Slide
1903 Panorama of Alpine Peaks
Pike's Peak Cog Wheel Route from Manitou
1905 Cavalcade Descending Eagle Peak Trail, Yosemite Valley
Cloud Play on Dolomite Peaks, Tyrol
Sunrise on the Peak, Tyrol
1906 Neighbor's Lamp (Le piton de suspension)

Peanut
1903 The Peanut Vendor
1907 Peanuts

Pear
1907 Who Owns the Pear?

Pearl
1901 "Birth of the Pearl"
1907 The Pearl Fisher
An Angelic Servant (La perle des savants)
1909 The Wonderful Pearl
1910 A Pearl of Boy

Pearl Harbor (Hawaii)
1907 Panoramic View, Oahu Railroad, Pearl Harbor, Hawaiian Islands

Peary, Robert E.
1905 Departure of Peary for the North Pole
1909 Capturing the North Pole; or, How He Cook'ed Peary's Record
Commander R. E. Peary
Special Peary Film

Peru
1910 The Chuncho Indians of the Amazon River, Peru
An Old Silver Mine in Peru
Perverse
1908 The Perverse Statues
1910 The Perversity of Fate
Pest
1910 The Fly Pest
A Four-Footed Pest
Pete
1908 Bill, the Bill Poster, and Pete, the Paperhanger
1909 One-Legged Pete and Pat
1910 Cyclone Pete's Matrimony
Indian Pete's Gratitude
Pete Has a Good Time
Pete Has Nine Lives
Pete Wants a Job
Peter
1910 Little Peter's Xmas Day
Peter's Patent Paint
Peters, Paula
1910 Paula Peters and Her Trained Animals
Petersburg (Virginia)
1909 Pennsylvania Monument at Fort Mahone near Petersburg, Va.
Reception of President Taft in Petersburg, Virginia, May 19th, 1909
Peterson (Utah)
1899 West of Peterson; Entrance to Weber Canyon
Petit Jean Louis d'Or & Co.
1910 Petit Jean Louis d'Or & Co.
Petite
1897 La Petite Adelaide
1903 La Petite Alma, Baby Acrobat
Petro
1903 Petro in Fairy Land
Petrosino, Joe
1909 Funeral of Joe Petrosino: The American Detective in Merino, Italy
Pets
1899 Baby Lund and Her Pets
"Sagasta" Admiral Dewey's Pet Pig
1900 Capt. Boynton Feeding His Pets
1902 The Baby and the Pet Bird
Selling a Pet Dog
1905 Old Maid and Pet Cat
1906 Kiddies Pets
1908 Robbie's Pet Rat
1909 Pet of the Big Horn Ranch
The Sheriff's Pet
Petticoat
1907 The Petticoat Regiment
1908 No Petticoats for Him
Petticoat Lane, London (England)
1904 Petticoat Lane on Sunday
Phaedra
1909 Phaedra
1910 Phaedra
Phantasia
1904 Arabian Phantasia
Phantasm
1909 The Mother-in-Law Phantasm
Phantasy
use **Fantasy**
Phantom
1903 Phantom Ride on the Canadian Pacific
1906 Phantom's Guard
1909 Phantom Games
The Phantom Ship
The Phantom Sirens
1910 Lured by a Phantom; or, The King of Thule
Phantom Ride from Aix-les-Bains
The Phantom Rider
Pharoah
1909 The Land of the Pharoah
1910 Pharoah; or, Israel in Egypt
Phases
1905 The Three Phases of the Moon
1906 Humorous Phases of Funny Faces
Pheasants
1898 President Faure Shooting Pheasants
Phenomenal
1901 A Phenomenal Contortionist
1906 Phenomenal Hen
Phenomenon
1908 Physical Phenomena
1910 The Theater of Phenomenons

Phial
1907 Phial of Poison
Philadelphia (Pennsylvania)
1896 Pa. R.R. Train near Phila.
Train Coming out of Station, Philadelphia, Pa.
1897 Delaware River, Philadelphia
Eighth and Vine St. Philadelphia
Philadelphia Police on Parade
1898 Famous Battleship Captains—Philadelphia Peace Jubilee Parade
Grand Army Veterans of Philadelphia
Philadelphia City Troop and a Company of Roosevelt's Rough Riders
Philadelphia Letter Carriers
View of League Island, Philadelphia
1899 First City Troop of Philadelphia
1st Penn' Volunteers of Philadelphia
President McKinley and Mayor Ashbridge of Philadelphia
1900 Philadelphia Lodge, No. 2, B.P.O. Elks
Philadelphia's Pride
A Scene in Fairmount Park, Phila.
1901 Capt. Schuyler Post of Philadelphia
Lambs Post of Phila.
1902 Prince Henry at Philadelphia
Troops Leaving Philadelphia for the Coal Regions
1903 Bicycle Parade, Philadelphia
City Hall, Philadelphia
Crew of the U.S. Cruiser Raleigh Passing the Grant Monument at Fairmount Park, Philadelphia
Digging for Foundation for Large Department Store, Phila.
Fire at Triangle Clothing Store, 13th and Ridge Ave., Philadelphia, May 3d, 1899
Knights Templar Street Parade, Philadelphia
Panorama of League Island, Philadelphia
Parade of the Philadelphia Volunteer Fire Department
President McKinley and His Cabinet on the Reviewing Stand, at Fairmount Park, Phila., May 27, 1899
Volksfest, Philadelphia
1904 Brewers' Parade, Philadelphia, Pa.
The Philadelphia Speedway
1905 New Year's Day Parade, Philadelphia
The New Year's Shooters in Philadelphia
New York Athletic Club Crew at Phila., Pa.
Odd Fellows Parade, Philadelphia, Pa.
1907 Philadelphia
Philadelphia New Year Shooters
1908 A Country Girl in Philadelphia
Military Parade, Founders Week Celebration, Philadelphia
Philadelphia, the Cradle of Liberty
Philadelphia Express
1897 Philadelphia Express, Jersey Central Railway
Philippines and Filipinos
1898 Troop Ships for the Philippines
1899 American Soldiers Defeating Filipinos Near Manila
Battle Flag of the 10th Pennsylvania Volunteers, Carried in the Philippines
Filipinos Retreat from Trenches
Rout of the Filipinos
1900 A Filipino Town Surprised
1901 A Filipino Cock Fight
Panorama of a Philippine Village
1902 Boating in Lakes of Philippine Village
Gen. Otis with His Troops in the Philippines
1903 Philippino War Dance
1904 Dress Parade of the Filipino Scouts, St. Louis Exposition
Filipino Scouts, Musical Drill, St. Louis Exposition
Panorama of a Philippine Settlement [Pan-American Exposition]
1908 Sailor in Philippines
1910 A Rose of the Philippines
Phillis
1899 Phillis Was Not Dressed to Receive Callers
Philosopher
1903 The Philosopher's Stone
Philter
1909 The Evil Philter

Phlegmatic
1908 A Phlegmatic Gentleman
Phoenix
1905 The Crystal Casket (Le phênix ou le coffret de cristal)
1910 The Phoenix
Phonograph
1905 Prompting Phonograph
1908 The Mysterious Phonograph
1909 Jones Has Bought a Phonograph
Phonographic Message of Love
Photography
1896 Special Photographing Train
1898 Effect of a Certain Photograph
His Holiness, Leo XIII in the Gardens of the Vatican, Being Photographed by the American Biograph Camera
1899 Burlesque Queen and a Country Photographer
Burlesque Queen and Country Photographer
1900 Fun in a Photograph Gallery
Life Motion Photographs of the Fitzsimmons and Ruhlin Fight
Photographing the Ghost
The Tribulations of an Amateur Photographer
1901 Photographer's Mishap
The Photographer's Mishap
Photographing a Country Couple
Photographing the Audience
1902 Biograph Snapshots at the President
The Photographer's Fourth of July
A Photographic Contortion
1903 Indians Charging on the Photographer
Murphy's Troubles with the Photographer
Photographer's Victim
Photographing a Goose
Snapshot and Its Consequences
A Spiritualistic Photographer
1904 Photographing a Female Crook
The Picture the Photographer Took
The Snapshot Fiend
1905 Photographed for the Rogue's Gallery
The Photographing Bear
1906 The Snapshot Fiend; or, Willie's New Camera
1907 Amateur Photographer
Fun in a Fotograf Gallery
Snapshots, Hawaiian Islands
1908 Long Distance Wireless Photography
The Mischances of a Photographer
The Photographer
Tribulations of a Photographer
1909 Peasant and Photographers
The Photograph Habit
Taking His Photograph
Tricks of the Photographer
1910 Her Photograph
Phrenologist
1910 The Phrenologist
Phrosine
1900 Phrosine and Meledore
Physical
1901 Physical Training
1903 Men in Physical Exercise, National Cash Register Co.
1904 Physical Examinations
1908 Physical Phenomena
Physical culture
1903 Girls in Physical Culture, National Cash Register Co.
The Physical Culture Girl
The Physical Culture Girl, No. 1
The Physical Culture Girl, No. 2
The Physical Culture Girl, No. 3
1904 Physical Culture, Kirksville, Mo.
Treloar and Miss Marshall, Prize Winners at the Physical Culture Show in Madison Square Garden
1905 Latina, Physical Culture Poses [No. 1]
Latina, Physical Culture Poses [No. 2]
Physical Culture Poses
1906 Physical Culture Lesson
1908 Pa Takes Up Physical Culture
1909 Mr. Physical Culture's Surprise Party
Physical Culture Fiend
Pianka
1899 Pianka and her Lions
Piano
1897 Automatic Piano
Demonstrating the Action of an Automatic Piano

1908 The Pillory
Pillow
1897 New Pillow Fight
Pillow Fight
A Pillow Fight
1902 The New Pillow Fight
1903 Pillow Fight, Reversed
1904 Pillow Fight, S.S. "Coptic," Mid-Ocean
1905 Pillow Fight
The Pillow Fight, No. 2
Pills
1908 Acrobatic Pills
Grandfather's Pills
A Husband's Revenge; or, The Poisoned Pills
Poisoned Pills
Professor Bounder's Pills
1910 The Dream Pill
Sleeping Pills
Pilot
1897 Taking on the Pilot
1903 Pilot Leaving "Prinzessen Victoria Luise" at Sandy Hook
Sacramento Valley, Cal. from Pilot of Engine
1908 The Pilot's Daughter
Pilot boat
1898 Pilot Boat "New York"
1899 Pilot Boats in New York Harbor
Pimpernell
1908 Mrs. Pimpernell's Gown
Pinch
1903 Mrs. Schneider's First Pinch of Snuff
Pine Ridge
1909 Pine Ridge Feud
Pine Ridge Bluffs, Laramie (Wyoming)
1901 Pine Ridge Bluffs
Pinehurst (North Carolina)
1906 Quail Shooting at Pinehurst
Turkey Hunt at Pinehurst
Pines
1903 The Pines of the Rockies
Ping pong
1902 The Hodcarriers' Ping Pong
Pinkerton, Nat
1909 Nat Pinkerton [Series II]
Nat Pinkerton: The Anarchists Plot
Pinkertons
1906 Trapped by Pinkertons
Pins
1909 Game of Nine Pins
See a Pin and Pick It Up, All That Day You'll Have Good Luck
Pioneer
1902 The Pioneer Limited
1903 Pioneer Limited
The Pioneers
1907 Daniel Boone; or, Pioneer Days in America
1908 Pioneers Crossing the Plains in '49
1909 Children of the Plains, an Episode of Pioneer Days
1910 The Kentucky Pioneer
The Rescue of the Pioneer's Daughter
Pipe
1902 A Pipe Story of the Fourth
1903 Colored Woman Smoking a Pipe
Disagreeable Railroad Passengers (Le chien et le pipe)
1904 Cleaning a Stove Pipe
1906 Good Pipe
1907 How Fritz's Pipe Exposed Him to the Maid
What a Pipe Did
1908 The Dog and the Pipe
1909 He Preferred to Smoke His Pipe
1910 Grandfather's Pipe
A Quiet Pipe
Pipe dream
1905 A Pipe Dream
1908 Bobby Has a Pipe Dream
Pipe Dreams
Piper
1903 Pied Piper of Hamelin
Tom, Tom the Piper's Son
1905 Tom, Tom, the Piper's Son
1908 Pied Piper of Hamlin
Piping
1903 Piping Down. Wash Clothes. Scrambling for Clothes

Pippa
1909 Pippa Passes; or, The Song of Conscience
Pirate
1901 Three of a Kind; or, The Pirate's Dream
1903 New York Harbor Police Boat Patrol Capturing Pirates
1904 Shanghaied by Pirates
1905 The Pirates
The River Pirates
1906 The River Pirates
1907 Captain Kidd and His Pirates
Harbor Pirates
The Pirates
The Pirates' Treasure; or, A Sailor's Love Story
1908 The Pirates
The Pirate's Gold
Pirate's Honor
A Tale of a Harem: The Caliph and the Pirate
Yusuf the Pirate
1909 The Fish Pirates; or, The Game Warden's Test
A Pirate of Turkey
The Pirate's Daughter
Pirates of the Sea
The Prophecy (Morgan le Pirate: la propheti)
1910 The Cage (An Episode in the Adventures of Morgan the Pirate)
The Pirate Airship
The Pirate's Dower
Pirate's Fiancée
Piraeus (Greece)
1904 Piraeus and Athens (Greece). A Visit to Piraeus
Piraeus and Athens (Greece). Athens and the Acropolis
Piraeus and Athens (Greece). Hoisting Cattle on Steamer
Pistol
1910 Her Dad's Pistol
Pit
1906 Scene in a Rat Pit
1910 The Pit That Speaks
The Three Cherry Pits; or, The Veteran's Honor
Pitcher, Molly
1908 "Captain Molly" or, The Battle of Monmouth
Pitching
1898 Battery B Pitching Camp
Pittsburgh (Pennsylvania)
1898 Tancred Commandery, Pittsburg
1902 Panoramic View from Pittsburgh to Allegheny
1903 Pittsburgh Fire Department in Full Run
1904 Pan. of Fifth Ave., Pittsburg, Pa., From a Trolley Car
Pan. of St. Railway Building, Pittsburg, Pa.
Railroad Panorama, Pittsburg to Stewart, Westinghouse Works
1907 Pittsburg
1909 Pittsburgh-Detroit Ball Game
Pity
1899 Pity the Blind
1904 Pity the Blind, No. 2
1909 Pity
Pity and Love
Pius X, Pope
1903 Pope Pius X [His Election and the Procession]
Place
1898 A Time and Place for Everything
1900 Market Place
Panorama of Place De L'Opera
1902 Circular Panoramic View of the Market Place at Fort de France, Showing S.S. Korona in the Background
1903 Love in a Perilous Place
No Place Like Home
Scenes in an Irish Market Place
1905 A Poor Place for Love Making
1907 The Parson of Hungry Gulch; or, The Right Man in the Right Place May Work Wonders
1910 The Hiding Place
There's No Place Like Home
Place de l'Opera, Paris (France)
1898 Place de l'Opera
1900 Panorama of Place De L'Opera

Place de la Concorde, Paris (France)
1897 Place de la Concorde
1900 Panoramic View of the Place de la Concorde
Street Scene at Place de la Concorde, Paris, France
Placing
1899 Chinese Sailors Placing a Wreath on the Monument
1903 Passion Play: Placing Jesus in the Tomb
Shamrock Placing Her Topsail
Plague
1897 Plaguing Grandpa
1910 The Plagues of Egypt and the Deliverance of the Hebrew [The Life of Moses Part III]
Plain
1908 Just Plain Folks, the Story of a Simple Country Girl
1909 Plain Mame; or, All That Glitters Is Not Gold
1910 Jes' Plain Dog
A Plain Song
Plainclothes man
1908 A Plain Clothes Man
Plains
1903 Prairie Emigrant Train Crossing the Plains
1908 H. R. H. The Prince of Wales Viewing the Grand Military Review on the Plains of Abraham, Quebec
Pioneers Crossing the Plains in '49
1909 Children of the Plains, an Episode of Pioneer Days
The Flirt, a Tale of the Plains
1910 Across the Plains
A Girl of the Plains
Patricia of the Plains
Perils of the Plains
Riders of the Plains
The Terror of the Plains
Plank
1902 St. John's Guild. Dock to Plank, 35th St.
St. John's Guild. Plank to Deck, Floating Hospital
1904 The Devilish Plank
1907 The Plank
Plans
1908 The Stolen Plans; or, The Boy Detective
1910 The Duke's Plan
Foiled by a Cigarette; or, The Stolen Plans of the Fortress
Plant
1903 Sorting Refuse at Incinerating Plant, New York City
Plantation
1901 On the Old Plantation
1906 Hauling Sugar Cane, Kohala Plantation, Hawaii
1907 Coffee Plantation
Scenes on a Sugar Plantation, Hawaiian Islands
1909 Cigarette Making: From Plantation to Consumer
1910 Cocoanut Plantation
Planter
1908 The Planter's Wife
1909 A Kentucky Planter
Plants and planting
1905 The King Planting a Tree at the Royal Agricultural Society's Show Yard
1908 The Deadly Plant
Plaster
1903 The Porous Plaster
Plastiques
1904 Dance Plastiques
Plate
1899 A Plate of Ice Cream and Two Spoons
1902 The University College of Oxford Winning the Ladies' Challenge Plate
1910 Wonderful Plates
Platform
1901 Moline Bag Punching Platform
1903 Mailing Platform, U.S.P.O.
Player
1899 The Violin Player
1900 Champion Polo Players
1909 Enthusiastic Hand Ball Player
The Harp Player
Maddened Players
Strolling Players
1910 The Bagpipe Player
Football Player
Juan, the Pelota Player

Poison
1904 The Wrong Poison
1907 Phial of Poison
1908 A Husband's Revenge; or, The Poisoned Pills
The Poisoned Bouquet, an Italian Tragedy of the XV Century
Poisoned Pills
1909 The Poisoned Flower

Poke
1909 A Pig in a Poke

Poker
1899 Poker at Dawson City
1906 Poker in the West

Poland
1904 Polish Fire Brigade Answering an Alarm, Warsaw
1910 Across Russian Poland

Polar bear
1903 Polar Bears
1904 Polar Bears at Play with Cubs
1907 Polar Bear Hunt
1910 The Polar Bear Hunt in the Arctic Seas

Polar regions
1903 Andre at the North Pole
1905 Departure of Peary for the North Pole
1906 In the Polar Regions
1908 How Simpkins Discovered the North Pole
1909 Capturing the North Pole; or, How He Cook'ed Peary's Record
Little Willie's Trip to the North Pole
The North Pole Craze
Who Discovered the North Pole?
1910 Johnny's Pictures of the Polar Regions

Pole
1903 Climbing the Greasy Pole
May Pole Dance
1909 Bamboo Pole Equilibrist
The Curtain Pole

Pole vaulting
1899 Pole Vaulting at Columbia University
1901 Pole Vaulting
1904 Pole Jumping

Police
1896 Mounted Police Charge
Park Police Drill Left Wheel and Forward
Park Police Drill Mount and Dismounting
1897 Austrian Mounted Police
Buffalo Police on Parade
Mounted Police Drill
Philadelphia Police on Parade
Police Patrol Wagon
1898 Chief Devery at Head of N.Y. Police Parade
The Cop and the Nurse Girl
Governor Hastings and Mounted Police
New York Police on Parade
New York Police Parade
Police Boats Escorting Naval Parade
Policemen Play No Favorites
Shanghai Police
1899 The Jealous Cook and the Policeman
Mysterious Disappearance of a Policeman
New York Mounted Police
New York Police
New York Police Parade, June 1st, 1899
Police Boats and Pleasure Craft on Way to Olympia
Police Drill
1900 Bribing the Police
1901 Chicago Police Parade
Mounted Police Charge
1902 Mounted Police
1903 Clarence the Cop
Drill by Providence Police
Firing the Royal Salute at Dawson City by the Northwest Mounted Police
The Fooled Policeman
Humpty's Troubles with the Policeman
The Life of a London Bobby
New York City Police Parade
New York Harbor Police Boat Patrol Capturing Pirates
Police Charge on Horseback
Policeman and Automobile
Policeman Chasing Bathers
Policeman's Interrupted Vision
Policemen's Prank on Their Comrade
Weary Willie and the Policeman
1904 The Bobby Whitewashed
Burglar, Cop and Barrel
Clarence, the Cop, on the Feed Store Beat
Clown, Tramp and Cop
The Cop Fools the Sergeant
The Policeman's Mistake
A Trick on the Cop
Up-to-Date Burglars; or, The Mystified Cops
1905 The Cheated Policeman
Desperate Encounter Between Burglar and Police
Life of an American Policeman
Life of the New York Policeman
N.Y. Police Parade, 1905
Police Raid on a Club
Policeman's Love Affair
Policeman's Pal
Scenes in a Police Court
1906 Bicycle Police Chasing Scorching Auto
A Misguided Bobby at a Fancy Garden Party
Negro and Policeman
Police Raid at a Dog Fight
1907 Burglar and Policeman
Dog Police
How Isaac Won the Cop
Hypnotized Police Inspector
Nervy Jim and the Cop
The New Policeman
Policeman Has an Idea
Policeman's Boots
Policeman's Little Run
The Sleepy Cop
1908 The Dog Cop
Female Police Force
A Fool for Luck; or, Nearly a Policeman
French Cops Learning English
Generous Policeman
Ideal Policemen
A Kind-Hearted Policeman
Masked Policeman
Monday Morning in a Coney Island Police Court
The Police Band
The Policeman and the Cook
A Policeman for an Hour
A Policeman's Dream
Policeman's Vision
Skillful Policemen
Thompson's Night with the Police
Tracked by the Police Dog
What the Copper Saw
1909 The Brave (?) Policeman
Cops on a Strike
Foolshead, King of Police
Forced to Play Cop
Gaffles, Vice King of Police
A Good Hearted Policeman
Haunted by the Cops
Help! Police!
Mishaps of a Policeman
The New Cop
The New Policeman
A New Policeman
Pocket Policeman
Police Dogs
Policeman in Action
The Policeman Sleeps
Policeman's Rest
The Policeman's Revolver
The Policeman's Romance
A Policeman's Xmas Eve
The Policewoman
They Lead the Cops on a Chase
They Robbed the Chief of Police
Treacherous Policeman
1910 The Bobby's Dream
A Choice Policeman
Competition of the Police and Guard Dogs
The Copper and the Crook
Foolshead as a Policeman
Levi, the Cop
Manoeuvers of the New York Police Force
The Masquerade Cop
Max Foils the Police
The Police Force of New York City
A Policeman's Son
The Stolen Policeman
The Troubles of a Policeman

Policy
1908 Honesty Is the Best Policy
Levitsky's Insurance Policy; or, When Thief Meets Thief

Polisher
1907 Floor Polisher

Polite
1902 The Polite Frenchman
1908 Too Polite

Politics
1900 Irish Way of Discussing Politics
A Political Discussion
1903 Dutch and Irish Politics
1908 The Female Politician, Mrs. Bell, Is Nominated for Mayor
Head over Heels in Politics
Political Speeches
1909 The Politician
The Politician's Love Story
1910 A Dainty Politician
Hearts and Politics
A Political Discussion
Politics

Polka
1904 Our Own Make Polka
1909 Polka on Brain

Polly
1902 Foxy Grandpa and Polly in a Little Hilarity
1909 Polly's Excursion

Pollywogs
1904 "Pollywogs" 71st Regiment, N.G.S.N.Y., Initiating Raw Recruits

Polo
1898 Water Polo
1899 Polo—A Dash for Goal
Polo—Hurlingham vs. Ranelagh
1900 Champion Polo Players
Polo Game: Myopia vs. Dedham
1903 Polo Match for the Championship at Hurlingham
1904 Herding Polo Ponies and Polo Game
1908 Bicycle Polo

Polypheme
1905 The Mysterious Island (L'île de Calypso. Ulysse et le géant polypheme)

Pompeii (Italy)
1907 Pompeii
1908 The Rivals: A Love Drama of Pompeii
1910 Martyrs of Pompeii

Pompey
1905 Pompey's Honey Girl
1909 Pompey's Dream

Pompiers
1898 A Hotel Fire in Paris, and Rescue by Parisian Pompiers

Ponce de León, Juan
1909 The Ponce de Leon Fete

Pond
1901 Circular Panorama of the Electric Tower and Pond
1905 Pond Life
1907 Enchanted Pond

Pongo
1897 Pongo

Pontiac
1910 The Conspiracy of Pontiac; or, At Fort Detroit in 1763

Pontine Marshes (Italy)
1909 Pontine Marshes, Italy

Ponto
1909 Ponto Runs Away with the Milk Cart

Pontoon bridge
1902 Pontoon Bridge Building

Pony
1896 Wrestling Ponies
Wrestling Pony and Man
1902 Stud Pony
1903 A Drove of Wild Welsh Mountain Ponies
Patterson Children in Pony Wagon, National Cash Register Co.
Scenes of a New Forest Pony Fair
Scenes on a Welsh Pony Farm
Wild Mountain Ponies on Dartmoor
1904 Acrobat and Pony
Herding Polo Ponies and Polo Game
Monkey, Dog and Pony Circus
1905 Indian Pony Races, Yosemite Valley, California

Pony express
1907 The Pony Express
1908 The Pony Express
1909 The Pony Express
1910 The Pony Express Rider

Poodle
1907 Doings of a Poodle

Pool
1901 Swimming Pool at Coney Island
1902 Fun in the Glenwood Springs Pool
1905 In the Swimming Pool, Palm Beach, Fla.

Quebec (Canada)
1898 Hockey Match; Quebec
Life Saving; Quebec Fire Department
Quebec Fire Department
Quebec Fire Department Drill
1901 The Duke and Duchess of York Arriving at Quebec
Duke of York at Montreal and Quebec
1902 Arrival of the Governor General, Lord Minto, at Quebec
Quebec Fire Department on Sleds
Skiing Scene in Quebec
1906 Salmon Fishing in Quebec
1908 H. R. H. The Prince of Wales Decorating the Monument of Champlain and Receiving Addresses of Welcome from the Mayor of Quebec, the Governor General of Canada and Vice-President Fairbanks, Representative of the United States
H. R. H. The Prince of Wales Viewing the Grand Military Review on the Plains of Abraham, Quebec
Quebec
Quebec to Niagara
Tercentenary Celebrations to Commemorate the 300th Anniversary of the Founding of Quebec by Champlain

Queen
1897 Queen's Jubilee
1898 Coronation of Queen Wilhelmina of Holland
1899 A Burlesque Queen
Burlesque Queen and a Country Photographer
Burlesque Queen and Country Photographer
"God Save the Queen"
Her Majesty, Queen Victoria
Her Majesty, Queen Victoria, Reviewing the Honorable Artillery
Her Majesty, Queen Victoria, Reviewing the Household Cavalry at Spital Barracks
"King" and "Queen," the Great High Diving Horses
Queen of the Harem
1900 Queen Victoria's Last Visit to Ireland
The Queen's Reception to the Heroes of Ladysmith
1901 The Duke and Duchess of York Presenting Medals to Boer War Veterans at the Unveiling of the Queen's Statue
Queen Victoria's Funeral [Number 1]
Queen Victoria's Funeral [Number 2]
Queen Victoria's Funeral [Number 3]
The Queen's Funeral
The Queen's Road
Second Queen's Rajputs
Their Majesties the King and Queen
1902 Crowning of King Edward and Queen Alexandra
The King and Queen Arriving at Westminster Abbey
The King and Queen Leaving Westminster Abbey After the Crowning
The King and Queen Returning from Westminster
King Edward VII and Queen Alexandra, of Great Britain
King Edward and Queen Alexandra on Their Way to Westminster
The New Crowned King and Queen Passing Through Wellington Arch and Down Constitution Hill
Queen Wilhelmina and Kaiser Wilhelm Riding in the Tier Garten
Queen Wilhelmina Arriving at the Kaiser's Palace
Queen Wilhelmina, of Holland, in Berlin
1903 From Show Girl to Burlesque Queen
King Edward and Queen Alexandra Passing Through London, England
A Pair of Queens
The Queen's Musketeers
Steamer Queen on Ice
1905 The King and Queen of Italy in Paris
Queen Margherita of Italy Arriving in Oberammergau
1908 Dolly, the Circus Queen
Meeting of Kings and Queens
The Queen of the Arena
The Queen's Love (La Tosca)
The Queen's Lover
1909 Every Lass a Queen
The Leopard Queen
Queen of the Quarry
The Queen of the Ranch
1910 The American and the Queen
The Burlesque Queen
His Life for His Queen
The Queen and the Mirror
The Queen of Hearts
A Queen of the Burlesque
Queen of the Nihilists
The Queen's Attendant
Three Queens and a Jack

Queen (Boat)
1897 S.S. "Queen" Leaving Dock
S.S. "Queen" Loading

Queenstown (Ireland)
1903 Panorama of Queenstown

Queenstown, Ontario (Canada)
1901 Duke and Duchess of Cornwall and York Landing at Queenstown, Ontario

Queer
1898 Queer Fish That Swim in the Sea
1900 The Barber's Queer Customer
1908 The Hallroom Boys Received Queer Freight

Quest
1909 In Quest of Health

Question
1905 The Servant Question
1909 The Servant Question Solved
1910 No Questions Asked

Quick
1897 Girard College Cadets at Double Quick
Quick Dressing
Quick Lunch
1901 A Quick Hitch
A Quick Recovery
1904 Quick Work Behind the Scenes
Quick Work for the Soubrettes
A Railroad Quick Lunch
1907 Quick, I'm on Fire
1910 Get Rich Quick

Quick-change
1908 The Quick Change Mesmerist
1910 Thieves as Quick Change Artists

Quicksands
1908 Engulfed in Quicksands
1909 Saved from the Quicksands

Quid
1909 His Only Quid

Quiet
1900 A Quiet Little Smoke
Such a Quiet Girl, Too!
1906 Anything for Peace and Quietness
1907 Father's Quiet Sunday
A Quiet Hotel
1908 Sandy McPherson's Quiet Fishing Trip
1909 Quiet Day at the Cafe
1910 A Quiet Boarding House
A Quiet Honeymoon
A Quiet Pipe

Quilt
1907 A Crazy Quilt

Quincy (Massachusetts)
1907 [Launching of the Salem at the Fore River Shipyards—Quincy, Mass.—July 27, 1907]

Quit
1907 Notice to Quit

Quite
1908 I've Taken Quite a Fancy to You

Quo Vadis
1904 Quo Vadis

Rabbit
1896 Imro Fox Rabbit Trick
1898 Off for the Rabbit Chase
1901 Nature Study, the Rabbit
1903 Making a Welch Rabbit
A Welsh Rabbit
1904 Children and Rabbits
Fox and Rabbits
1908 A Sculptor's Welsh Rabbit Dream
1909 Hunting Jack Rabbits in Hungary

Rabelais, François
1910 Rabelais' Joke

Race
1896 Hurdle Race—High Jumpers
Sack Race
1897 Arrival of His Majesty, King Edward VII (then Prince of Wales) at the Ascot Races, 1897
Cornell-Yale-Harvard Boat-Race
Free-for-All Race at Charter Oak Park
Hurdle Race
A Multicycle Race
Observation Train at the Inter-Collegiate Boat-Races
One-Third Mile Bicycle Race
A Paced Bicycle Race
A Race for the Gold Cup
Racing at Sheepshead Bay
Scrub Yacht Race
1898 The Bathing Girls Hurdle Race
Going to the Yokohama Races
Race Between a Multicycle and a Horse
Returning from the Races
A Shoe and Stocking Race
Tub Race
The Wheelbarrow Race
1899 After the Race—Yachts Returning to Anchorage
"Between the Races"
The Great Free-for-All Pacing Race
International Collegiate Games—110 Yards Hurdle Race
Oxford-Cambridge Boat-Race
Pictures Incidental to Yacht Race
"Shamrock" and "Columbia" Yacht Race—First Race
"Shamrock" and "Columbia" Yacht Race—1st Race, No. 2
Start of Race Between "Columbia" and "Shamrock"
Start of Second Cup Race
Start of the Second Cup Race
Start of Third Day's Race
Torpedo Boats at the Yacht Race
A Unique Race
Yacht Race—Finish
1900 Oxford-Cambridge Race
Trial Race Columbia and Defender
Trial Race Columbia and Defender No. 2
1901 The "Abbot" and "Cresceus" Race
Bicycle Paced Race
"Columbia" and "Shamrock II": Finishing Second Race
"Columbia" and "Shamrock II": Start of Second Race
"Columbia" and "Shamrock II": Starting in the Third Race
Finish of Race Sheepshead Bay, Experimental
Finish of the Third Cup Race
Ice-Boat Racing at Redbank, N.J.
International Yacht Races—Columbia vs. Shamrock
International Yacht Races on the Clyde
Match Race, Endurance by Right vs. Heno
Panoramic View of the Fleet After Yacht Race
Professional Handicap Bicycle Race
A Race with the Overland Limited
Sampans Racing Toward Liner
Start of the Third Cup Race
Tally-Ho Departing for the Races
'Varsity Crew Race on Cayuga Lake, on Decoration Day, Lehigh Valley Observation Train Following the Race, Showing Cornell Crew Finishing First, Columbia Second, University of Pennsylvania Third Ithaca, N.Y., Showing Lehigh Valley Observation Train
The Yacht Race Fleet Following the Committee Boat "Navigator" Oct. 4th
1902 Clearing the Course for the Henley Boat Races, July 10th, 1902
The Columbia-Cornell-Pennsylvania Boat Race at Poughkeepsie
Denver Firemen's Race for Life
Entire Series of Yacht Race Pictures with Dissolving Effects
Horse Racing in Germany
A Hurdle Race
Ice Racing in Stockholm
Ice Yacht Racing
An Obstacle Race
Third Trinity, Cambridge, Winning the Race for the Grand Challenge Cup. Taken at Henley on July 10th, 1902
Torpedo Boats Racing off Newport
A Tub Race
1903 Balloon Race
Boat Race
Boat Race No. 2
The Broncho Horse Race
Camel Race on the Desert

Railroad View—Experimental
Rear View of the "Black Diamond Express," Lehigh Valley R.R.
6th Ave. New York Elevated Railroad
Two Miles of the White Pass & Yukon Railroad
1904 Japanese Railroad Scene, Kanagarva, Japan
Panorama of Railroad Station at Seoul, Korea, from Departing Train
Railroad Panorama, Pittsburg to Stewart, Westinghouse Works
A Railroad Quick Lunch
Railroad Smashup
1905 Railroad Station at Steinach, Tyrol
1906 Great Railroad Panorama Through Colorado
Railroad Collision at Los Angeles, Calif.
Trip on Berlin Elevated R.R.
1907 [Building a Railroad in Africa]
Crime on the Railroad
Making the Dirt Fly: Scene 4. Railroad Track Lifter in Operation
Over the Midland Terminal Railroad: Through Cripple Creek District
Panoramic View, Oahu Railroad, Haleiwa, H.I.
Panoramic View, Oahu Railroad, Pearl Harbor, Hawaiian Islands
1908 Over the Hubarthal Railroad
The Railroad Detective
1909 The Railroad Wreck
Repairing Railroad Tracks

Railway
rt **Railroad**
1897 Philadelphia Express, Jersey Central Railway
1898 Railway Station at Yokohama
1899 104th Street Curve, New York, Elevated Railway
1900 On the Cleveland and Eastern Railway
Panorama of Gorge Railway
1901 Flip-Flap Railway
A Japanese Railway Train
Miniature Railway
1902 The Aerial Railway at the Crystal Palace, London, England
German Railway Service
Miniature Railway
The Miniature Railway
Panorama of Cog Railway
1903 Broncho Busting Along the Lines of the Denver & Rio Grande Railway
The Delhi Camp Railway
Inside Car, Showing Bag Catcher [U.S.P.O.]
Memphis & Ft. Scott Railway Bridge
Miniature Railway at Wilmington Springs, Delaware
Panorama on the St. Gothard Railway
Railway Ride in the Alps
1904 Dude in an English Railway Coach
Pan. of St. Railway Building, Pittsburg, Pa.
A Railway Tragedy
Honeymoon Trip (Flirt en chemin de fer)
1905 Leap Frog Railway, Coney Island
Market Women Leaving the Railway Station at Galway, Ireland
On a Borneo Railway
Panorama from a Moving Train on White Pass & Yukon Railway, Alaska
Panorama from Car on Mendel Pass Cable Railway
Panorama from Car on Oberammergau Electric Railway
Panorama from Moving Train on Albula Railway, Switzerland
Panorama from Moving Train on Murren Electric Railway, Switzerland
Panorama from Train on Visp-Zermatt Railway
Passengers Crossing over Open Car, Balley Bunion Railway
Passing Train, Balleybunion Railway, Ireland
Passing Train, Balleybunion Railway, Ireland No. 2
Passing Train (from Above) Balleybunion Railway, Ireland
Railway Panorama Between Green Island and Kilroot
Railway Panorama Between Kilroot and Whitehead
Railway Panorama from Moving Train Passing Through Conway Castle, Wales
Sliding River Craft over Boat Railway, River Thames
Train on the White Pass & Yukon Railway, Alaska
Trains on Rigi Railway, Switzerland
Turntable of the Ballybunion Railway, Ireland
1906 On Great Western Railway Ldongotten Station
On Great Western Railway Through Dawhistle
Railway Panoramas from Every Port of the World
Through Austin Glen, Catskill Railway
1907 The Arlberg Railway
Mount Pilatus Railway
1908 Railway Tragedy
The Viege Zermatt Railway
1909 Trip on Rhodesian Railway
1910 Modern Railway Construction
Panoramic Railway View from Front of Train
The Railway Mail Clerk
Railway on the Ice Sea

Rain
1899 A Ray of Sunshine After the Rain
1905 Religious Cortege on a Rainy Day, Cortina, Tyrol
1908 The Rain-Dear
1910 Caught in the Rain

Rain dance
1903 Moqui Indian Rain Dance
Rain Dance at Orabi

Raines
1905 In a Raines Law Hotel

Rainmaker
1897 Rainmakers
1898 The Rainmakers
1908 The Rainmaker

Raise
1910 How Hubby Got a Raise

Raised
1909 Raised in the Country

Raising
1899 Raising Old Glory over Morro Castle
1903 Passion Play: Raising of Lazarus
Raising Colors, Battleship "Indiana"
Raising Salmon Trap U.S.F.C.
1907 Raising the Wind

Rajah
1904 Princess Rajah Dance with Chair, St. Louis Exposition
Princess Rajah, Dance Without Chair
1906 The Rajah's Casket

Rajputs
1901 Second Queen's Rajputs
The War in China—British Rajputs

Rake
1910 The Bad Luck of an Old Rake

Raleigh (North Carolina)
1903 Lieut. Bagley's Funeral. Escort of Lieut. Bagley's at Raleigh, N. C.

Raleigh (Ship)
1899 Capt. Coghlan, One of the Manila Heroes, and Crew of the Raleigh, Reviewed by the President
Crew of the U.S. Cruiser "Raleigh"
Cruiser "Raleigh"
Firing the 3 Pounders of the Raleigh
Gen. Snowden and Staff, and Crew of the U.S.S. "Raleigh"
Morning Colors on U.S. Cruiser "Raleigh"
President McKinley and Wife, Members of His Cabinet and Their Wives and Capt. Coghlan Leaving the Cruiser Raleigh
U.S. Cruiser "Raleigh"
U.S. Cruiser Raleigh
1903 Boxing Match on Board the U.S. Cruiser Raleigh
Crew of the U.S. Cruiser Raleigh Passing the Grant Monument at Fairmount Park, Philadelphia
Manning the Yard Arm on the U.S. Cruiser Raleigh
Morning Exercise on Board the U.S. Cruiser Raleigh

Rally
1909 The Rally Round the Flag

Ralph
1909 Ralph Benefits by People's Curiosity

Ram Katahdin (Boat)
1898 Ram "Katahdin"

Ramble
1910 Ramble Through Ceylon
A Ramble Through the Isle of Sumatra

Ramming
1908 The Ramming of H. M. S. Gladiator by the St. Paul

Ramona
1910 Ramona

Rams
1903 Fighting Rams

Ranch
1903 On the Bow River Horse Ranch at Cochrane, North West Territory
1906 Humuula Sheep Ranch
Shearing Sheep, Humunla Ranch, Hawaii
Sheep Coming Through Chute, Humunla Ranch, Hawaii
1907 Jim Jeffries on His California Ranch
[Ranch 101]
1909 Pet of the Big Horn Ranch
The Queen of the Ranch
1910 At Double Cross Ranch
Boss of Circle E Ranch
The Boys of Topsy-Turvy Ranch
Circle "C" Ranch Wedding Present
Doings at the Ranch
The Fence on Bar Z Ranch
The Flower of the Ranch
The Heroine of 101 Ranch
Jeffries on His Ranch
The Lily of the Ranch
The Millionaire and the Ranch Girl
The Musical Ranch
The New Boss of Bar X Ranch
The Ranch Girl's Legacy
The Ranch King's Daughter
Ranch Life in the Great South-West
The Ranch Raiders
The Romance of Circle Ranch
Romance of the Lazy K Ranch
The Rose of the Ranch

Ranch 101
1907 [Ranch 101]
1910 The Heroine of 101 Ranch

Ranchman
1908 The Ranchman's Love
1909 The Ranchman's Rival
The Ranchman's Wife
1910 Jim, the Ranchman
The Montana Ranchman
The Ranchman and the Miser
The Ranchman's Bride
The Ranchman's Feud
The Ranchman's Personal
A Ranchman's Simple Son
A Ranchman's Wooing

Randers (Denmark)
1905 Horse Fair at Randers, Denmark

Ranelagh
1899 Polo—Hurlingham vs. Ranelagh

Range
1910 The Girls of the Range
Pals of the Range
The Range Riders
Strayed from the Range

Rangeley Lakes (Maine)
1906 Trout Fishing in Rangeley Lakes

Ranger
1909 The Forest Ranger's Daughter
1910 The Forest Ranger
The Ranger and the Girl
The Ranger's Bride

Ranks
1907 Love Levels All Ranks

Ransom
1905 The Adventures of Sherlock Holmes; or, Held for a Ransom
1908 Held for Ransom
1910 Ransomed; or, A Prisoner of War

Ranson
1910 Ranson's Folly

Rape
1908 A Rape Under Louis XVI
1910 Rape of the Sabines

Rapid fire
1898 Rapid Fire, Charge
Rapid Fire Gun Drill

The Red Star Inn

Red Bank (New Jersey)
1901 Ice-Boat Racing at Redbank, N.J.
1904 Ice Boating on the North Shrewsbury, Red Bank, N.J.

Red Cloud
1908 Red Cloud, the Indian Gambler

Red Cross
1898 The Red Cross
Red Cross at the Front
Red Cross Steamer "Texas"
1899 U.S. Troops and Red Cross in the Trenches Before Caloocan [P. I.]
1900 Red Cross Ambulance on Battlefield
1901 Red Cross of the German Army on the Battlefield
1909 The Red Cross Heroine
1910 Foolshead Volunteer on the Red Cross
The Red Cross Seal

Red Eagle
1910 Red Eagle's Love Affair

Red Fern
1910 Red Fern and the Kid

Red girl; Red man; Redskins
use **Indians of North America**

Red-handed
1908 Caught Red Handed
1910 Caught Red-Handed

Red Hawk
1910 Red Hawk's Last Raid

Red-hot
1907 A Red Hot Day

Red Riding Hood
1901 Little Red Riding Hood
1907 Red Riding Hood

Red Rock Canyon (Colorado)
1902 Lava Slides in Red Rock Canyon

Red tape
1908 Red Tapism

Red Wing
1909 Red Wing's Gratitude
1910 The Flight of Red Wing
For the Love of Red Wing
Red Wing and the White Girl
Red Wing's Constancy
Red Wing's Loyalty

Redemption
1908 Redeemed from Sin
1909 John Farley's Redemption
1910 Broncho Billy's Redemption
An Eleventh Hour Redemption
The Model's Redemption
The Outlaw's Redemption

Reedham
1907 Reedham Boys' Aquatic Sports
1908 Reedham Boys' Festival Drill
1910 Reedham's Orphanage Festival, 1910

Reef
1909 Taking in a Reef
1910 Drama on the Reef
On the Reef

Reel
1899 Demonstrating the Action of the Cliff-Guibert Hose Reel
1900 Another Demonstration of the Cliff-Guibert Fire Hose Reel, Showing a Young Girl Coming from an Office, Detaching the Hose, Running with It 60 Feet, and Playing a Stream, All Inside of 30 Seconds
1903 Irish Reel
Old Fashioned Scottish Reel
1906 Irish Reel
1908 Special Muto Reel Mellin's Food Co.
1910 Wild Duck Hunting on Reel Foot Lake

Referees
1910 Dooley Referees the Big Fight

Refinery
1901 Lard Refinery

Reflections
1909 Telltale Reflections

Reform
1902 Why Papa Reformed, or Setting Back the Clock
1907 Children's Reformatory
Reformation
1909 A Drunkard's Reformation
His Reformation
Reformation of a Wine-Loving Artist
Reformed Thief
Reforming a Husband
1910 Black Pete's Reformation
The Gang Leader's Reform
Why Jones Reformed

Refractory
1909 Gadbin, the Refractory Suicide

Refreshing
1910 Refreshing Bath

Refuge
1910 The Refuge

Refugee
1898 Cuban Refugees Waiting for Rations
1906 Arrival of Refugees at Oakland
Fun Among the Refugees
Military Feeding Starving and Destitute Refugees in Golden Gate Park
Refugees at the Golden Gate Park
Refugees in Jefferson Square
Refugees on Market St.
Waterfront, Refugees Leaving San Francisco
1910 The Refugee

Refuse
1903 Sorting Refuse at Incinerating Plant, New York City

Refusing
1910 Refusing a Mansion

Regained
1910 Lost and Regained

Regatta
1896 The Henley Regatta
1899 The Henley Regatta
1900 Larchmont Regatta
1901 The Henley Regatta, 1901
1904 Inter-Collegiate Regatta, Poughkeepsie, N.Y., 1904
1905 Henley Regatta, Three Finishes
On the Course, Henley Regatta
Trains Arriving at Henley Station with Regatta Visitors
1906 The Henly Regatta
Poughkeepsie Regatta
1908 Olympic Regatta at Henley
Regattas in London

Regeneration
1910 The Regeneration
The Regeneration of Father

Reggie
1910 Reggie's Engagement

Reggy
1907 Reggy's Camping Party

Regiment
1897 A Regimental Calisthenic Drill in the British Army
7th and 71st Regiment, New York
7th Regiment, N.G.S.N.Y.
71st Regiment, N.G.S.N.Y.
71st Regiment, New York
1898 Company "C," 1st Regiment, N.J.V.
The Daughter of the Regiment
1st Regiment, N.Y.V.
Hong Kong Regiment, No. 1
Hong Kong Regiment, No. 2
Massachusetts Regiment Marching
Ninth Regiment, U.S. Regulars
101st Regiment, French Infantry
Recruits of the 69th Regiment, N.G.S.N.Y.
Return of 2nd Regiment of New Jersey
71st Regiment, N.G.S.N.Y. at Camp Wikoff
65th Regiment, N.Y.V.
65th Regiment at Double Time
69th Regiment Passing in Review
Tenth Regiment, Ohio Volunteers
Third Regiment Pennsylvania
13th Regiment Pennsylvania Volunteers
32nd Regiment, Michigan Volunteers
33rd Regiment, Michigan Volunteers
Three Views of the 69th Regiment, N.G.S.N.Y.
Twelfth Regiment, N.G.S.N.Y.
22nd Regiment, Kansas Volunteers
Twenty-Third Regiment, N.G.S.N.Y.
1899 Eighth Regiment, Mass. Volunteers
Eighth Regiment, N.G.S.N.Y.
First Boston School Regiment
Ninth Regiment, N.G.S.N.Y.
Second Battalion, 1st Regiment, N. G. of Pennsylvania
2nd Battalion, 3rd New York Provisional Regiment, Rochester and Syracuse, Separate Companies
Second Boston School Regiment
Sev. Regiments Passing the Monument
7th Regiment, New York City
Third Boston School Regiment
Twenty-Second Regiment, N.G.S.N.Y.
1900 The Royal Leinster Regiment
Royal Leinster Regiment on Parade
1901 A German Cuirassier Regiment
1902 48th Highlanders Regiment
1903 New York's 7th and 71st Regiments
69th Regiment, N.G.N.Y.
1904 "Pollywogs" 71st Regiment, N.G.S.N.Y., Initiating Raw Recruits
A Regiment of the Japanese Imperial Guards and Engineer Corps off to the Front
1906 7th Regiment at 69th Army Dedication
1907 The Petticoat Regiment
1908 The 50th Regiment Jubilee
Russian Review of the Fiftieth Regiment
1909 The Child of the Regiment
The Regimental Barber
1910 A Child of the Regiment
Molly at the Regiment—Her Adventures

Reginald
1899 Reginald's First High Hat

Regions
1902 Troops Leaving Philadelphia for the Coal Regions
1906 In the Polar Regions
1910 Johnny's Pictures of the Polar Regions

Register
1909 The Punch Register

Regulars
1898 Fourth Infantry, U.S. Regulars
Ninth Regiment, U.S. Regulars
Thirteenth Infantry, U.S. Regulars
1907 Pres. Roosevelt Reviewing U.S. Regulars

Rehearsal
1902 Ballet Rehearsal
1903 The Ballet Rehearsal
The Rehearsal
1905 Rehearsing a Play at Home
1907 A Dramatic Rehearsal
1908 Disappointing Rehearsal
Minstrel Mishaps; or, Late for Rehearsal
1909 The Dog Circus Rehearsal
1910 The Rehearsal

Reign
1910 Under the Reign of Terror

Reilly, Capt.
1901 Capt. Reilly's Battery, Bombardment of Pekin
Capt. Reilly's Battery Limbering
Reilly's Light Battery F

Reincarnation
1901 A Mystic Re-Incarnation
1909 Reincarnated Mummy

Rejected
1908 Uncle's Rejected Present

Rejoicing
1908 Rejoicing Dreams

Rejuvenation
1908 The Merry Widower; or, The Rejuvenation of a Fossil

Release
1904 Arrival and Release of 40,000 Carrying Pigeons at Ambergate, England

Reliance (Boat)
1903 Launching Cup Defender "Reliance"
Reliance and Shamrock III Turning Outer Stake in Second Race
"Reliance" and "Shamrock" III Jockeying and Starting in First Race
"Reliance" Crossing the Line and Winning First Race
Reliance Rounding Turn, August 20th
"Reliance" vs. "Shamrock" III, Aug. 20
Start of Race—"Reliance" Ahead

Relief
1898 The Christian Herald's Relief Station, Havana
1900 The Relief of Ladysmith

Relieving
1898 Relieving the Guard at St. James Palace

Religious
1904 Religious Procession, Moscow
1905 Religious Cortege on a Rainy Day, Cortina, Tyrol
1910 Religious Fetes at Thibet

Remains
1910 Druid Remains in Brittany

Restaurant
1900 In a Chinese Restaurant
1902 The Cheese Mites; or, The Lilliputians in a London Restaurant
1907 A First Class Restaurant

Restive
1904 The Restive Chicken

Restless
1897 The Restless Girl

Restoration
1908 Doctor Jink's Liquid Life Restorer
Restored by Repentance
1909 The Restoration
1910 The Restoration

Result
1902 The Boys, Still Determined, Try It Again on Foxy Grandpa, with the Same Result
1904 Result Too Much Jealousy
1908 Result of Eating Horseflesh
1910 Fruit Growing, Grand Valley, Colorado (The Results of Irrigation)
Kindness Abused and Its Results

Resurrection
1903 Passion Play: The Resurrection
1909 Resurrection
1910 The Resurrection of Lazarus

Resuscitation
1897 Rescue—Resuscitation
1909 Resuscitated

Retaking
1906 Retaking a Fort

Retaliation
1909 Retaliation
1910 Retaliation

Retiring
1902 Old Maid Retiring
1904 Bride Retiring
Nervous Man Retiring

Retort
1906 The Mysterious Retort

Retreat
1897 13th Infantry, U.S. Army—Scaling Walls in Retreat, Governors Island
1899 Filipinos Retreat from Trenches
1909 Satan's Retreat
1910 An Alpine Retreat

Retribution
1903 The Wages of Sin: B—Retribution
1907 Retribution; or, The Brand of Cain
1908 Just Retribution
1910 Retribution

Retrogressive
1905 Retrogressive Jaunting Car, Reverse Panorama from Moving Train, Dublin, Ireland

Return
1896 The Prodigal's Return; 3 A.M.
1897 Return of Lifeboat
Return of McKinley from the Capitol
Returning from Drill
1898 Advance Guard, Return of N.J. Troops
Naval Reserves Returning from the War
Return of Our Soldier Boys
Return of 2nd Regiment of New Jersey
Return of Troop C, Brooklyn
Returning from the Races
1899 After the Race—Yachts Returning to Anchorage
Chinamen Returning to China
Jones' Return from the Club
1900 Jones' Return from a Masquerade
Return of the Canadian Contingent
The Shah's Return from Paris
1902 Emperor William Returning from Manoeuvres
The King and Queen Returning from Westminster
Return of the German China Fleet
1903 Jack's Return
Murphy Returns from a Masquerade
N.Y. Fire Department Returning
The Return to Quarters
The Soldier's Return
Tourists Returning on Donkeys from Mizpah
Young America Celebrating Dewey's Return
1904 Night Owl's Return
1906 Japanese Soldier's Return
1907 Crowds Returning from the Games, Waikiki, H.I.
Returning Good for Evil
Sailor's Return
1908 The Crusaders' Return
The Galley Slave's Return
Wanderer's Return
1909 Columbine's Return
A Convict's Return
The Crusader's Return
The Return of Ulysses
The Son's Return
1910 The Castaway's Return
Her First Husband's Return
Jack's Return
The Return at Midnight
The Return of Ta-Wa-Wa
Roosevelt's Return
Young Deer's Return

Reuben
1898 How Uncle Reuben Missed the Fishing Party
1900 Uncle Reuben Lands a Kick
1902 Reuben Buys a Gold Brick
1903 Uncle Reuben at the Waldorf
1905 Reuben in the Opium Joint
Reuben in the Subway
1907 Rubberneck Reuben
1909 Uncle Reuben's Courtship

Reunion
1908 Two Affinities; or, A Domestic Reunion
1909 Re-united at the Gallows
Re-united by Santa Claus
A Strange Reunion

Revealed
1910 The Truth Revealed

Reveler
1909 Reveler's Dream

Revenge
1898 Chorus Girl's Revenge
1899 The Dairy Maid's Revenge
1901 The Cook's Revenge
The Hod Carrier's Revenge
1902 A Country Groceryman's Revenge
A Poet's Revenge
1903 The Cook's Revenge
The Office Boy's Revenge
The Witch's Revenge
1904 Barber's Revenge
Chambermaid's Revenge
The Office Boy's Revenge
Revenge!
1905 Tramp's Revenge
1906 Child's Revenge
Clown's Revenge
Indian's Revenge
The Indian's Revenge; or, Osceola, the Last of the Seminoles
Pierrot's Revenge
Tommy's Revenge
1907 The Blacksmith's Revenge
Brother Willie's Revenge
Chef's Revenge
A Colored Man's Revenge
The Dervish's Revenge
The Doll's Revenge
Gypsy's Revenge
Half Caste's Revenge
The Hypnotist's Revenge
Revenge
The Romany's Revenge
Servant's Revenge
1908 The Ayah's Revenge
The Bell Boy's Revenge
The Cat's Revenge
The Chieftain's Revenge; or, A Tragedy in the Highlands of Scotland
The Chorus Man's Revenge
Custom Officer's Revenge
Duty Versus Revenge
A Gypsy's Revenge
The Gypsy's Revenge
Hobo's Revenge
A Husband's Revenge; or, The Poisoned Pills
A Jilted Woman's Revenge
Miscalculated Revenge
The Mountaineer's Revenge
Neapolitan's Revenge
The Painter's Revenge
Red Man's Revenge
The Revengeful Waiter
The Sicilian's Revenge
Tramp's Revenge
The Washerwoman's Revenge
Weary Willie's Revenge
Workman's Revenge
1909 The Artist's Revenge
Baby's Revenge
The Barber's Revenge
Buster's Revenge
Convict's Revenge
The Corsican's Revenge
The Duke's Jester; or, A Fool's Revenge
A Fool's Revenge
The Hypnotist's Revenge
Love and Revenge
Love Stronger Than Revenge
The Mexican's Revenge
Officer's Revenge
The Schoolboy's Revenge
The Secretary's Revenge
Servant's Revenge
The Shell; or, "A Madman's Revenge"
The Spy's Revenge
The Squaw's Revenge
Sweet Revenge
1910 The Cattle Thief's Revenge
A Corsican's Revenge
A Doctor's Revenge
Her Dolly's Revenge
Her Sweet Revenge
His Revenge
A Just Revenge
Mr. Giddy's Revenge
The Revenge of Dupont L'Anguille
A Rich Revenge
Romany Rob's Revenge
The Town Traveler's Revenge

Revenue
1901 Schooner "Idler" and Revenue Cutter "Gresham"
1910 The United States Revenue Detective

Revere, Paul
1907 Midnight Ride of Paul Revere

Reverse
1901 The Reversible Divers
The Reversing Sign Painter
1903 Pillow Fight, Reversed
Reversible Donkey Cart
1904 Diving Scene and Reverse
High Diving and Reverse
1905 Retrogressive Jaunting Car, Reverse Panorama from Moving Train, Dublin, Ireland
Reverse Panorama, Maria Theresian Strasse, Innsbruck

Review
1897 Aldershot Review
Cavalry Passing in Review
Girard College Cadets in Review
Review of Artillery
1898 15,000 Soldiers Reviewed by the President at Camp Alger May 28
Naval Review Spithead
Review of Officers
Reviewing the "Texas" at Grant's Tomb
Second Illinois Volunteers in Review
69th Regiment Passing in Review
1899 Capt. Coghlan, One of the Manila Heroes, and Crew of the Raleigh, Reviewed by the President
Her Majesty, Queen Victoria, Reviewing the Honorable Artillery
Her Majesty, Queen Victoria, Reviewing the Household Cavalry at Spital Barracks
President McKinley Reviewing the Troops
The Prince of Wales (King Edward VII) at the Aldershot Review
Review of First Rhode Island Volunteers
1900 Breaking of the Crowd at Military Review at Longchamps
Royal Leinsters on Review
1901 President McKinley Reviewing the Troops at the Pan-American Exposition
Review of Russian Artillery
U.S. Naval Cadets Marching in Review
Von Waldersee Reviewing Cossacks
The War in China—Review of German Troops
The War in China—Von Waldersee's Review
1902 Kaiser Wilhelm and the Empress of Germany Reviewing Their Troops
King Edward Reviewing Coronation Naval Force at Spithead August 16, 1902
President Roosevelt Reviewing the Troops at Charleston Exposition [South Carolina]
Prince Henry [of Prussia] Reviewing the Cadets at West Point
Review of Cadets at West Point
Review of Cadets, West Point

1901 Little Red Riding Hood
1902 The Burning of Durland's Riding Academy
Kaiser Wilhelm and Emperor Franz Josef, and Prince Henry Riding Horseback
Queen Wilhelmina and Kaiser Wilhelm Riding in the Tier Garten
1903 Bareback Riding
Sleigh Riding
1904 Modern High School Riding
Trick Bicycle Riding
1905 Girls Riding Camels
Girls Riding Steeplechase
Girls Riding "Trolley"
1907 Riding School
1909 Riding for Love
1910 Riding Feats by Cossacks
Riding School in Belgium
Some Riding Exercises of the Italian Cavalry

Rifle Bill
1909 Rifle Bill No. 5

Rifle Hill
1899 Rifle Hill Signal Outpost

Rifles
1899 43rd Rifles; Royal Canadian Infantry
1900 Canadian Mounted Rifles on the March
Mounted Rifles at Drill
Northwestern Mounted Rifles
Toronto Mounted Rifles
1909 Leo's Air Rifle

Rigged
1899 Full Rigged Ship at Sea

Right
1904 Duel Scene, "By Right of Sword"
1907 It Served Them Right
The Parson of Hungry Gulch; or, The Right Man in the Right Place May Work Wonders
1908 It Serves Him Right
The Right of the Seigneur
1909 The Right to Labor
1910 By Right of Love
The Right Decision
The Right Girl
The Right House, But —
Right in Front of Father
The Right to Labor

Right (Jockey)
1901 Match Race, Endurance by Right vs. Heno

Righted
1907 Wrong Righted
1908 A Great Wrong Righted
1909 A Great Wrong Righted

Rights
1908 Nobleman's Rights

Rigi (Switzerland)
1905 Trains on Rigi Railway, Switzerland

Rigoletto
1909 Rigoletto

Riker's Island (New York City)
1903 Panorama of Riker's Island

Riley
1907 Row at Rileys

Riley's Gulch
1910 The Bad Man from Riley's Gulch

Rim
1908 Transformation with a Hat Rim

Ringing
1899 Tommy's Ringing Good Joke on His Dad
1900 Those Wedding Bells Shall Not Ring Out
Why Curfew Did Not Ring Last Night
1906 The Bell Ringer's Daughter
1907 Curfew Shall Not Ring Tonight
1908 Somnambulic (sic) Bell Ringer
1910 As the Bells Rang Out!

Ringleader
1909 The Ringleader

Ringling Bros. Circus
1902 Ringling Bros. Circus Parade

Ringmaster
1908 The Ringmaster's Wife

Rings
1897 "Ring Around a Rosie"
1903 Double Ring Act, Luna Park
On the Flying Rings
1905 Hunters in Exercising Ring, Dublin Horse Show

Rings (Boxing)
1907 Panorama, Crowds at Squires-Burns International Contest, from Center of Ring, Colma, July 4th, 1907
1909 The King of the Ring

Rings (Jewelry)
1904 Welding Big Ring
1905 Engagement Ring
1908 A Hindoo's Ring
The Magic Ring
1909 The Brazilian's Ring
The Engagement Ring
1910 The Signet Ring

Rio Grande
1898 Cañon of the Rio Grande
1903 Broncho Busting Along the Lines of the Denver & Rio Grande Railway

Riots
1905 Riots in St. Petersburg

Rip Van Winkle
1896 Awakening of Rip
Exit of Rip and the Dwarf
Rip Leaving Sleepy Hollow
Rip Meeting the Dwarf
Rip Passing over the Mountain
Rip's Toast
Rip's Toast to Hudson
Rip's Twenty Years' Sleep
1903 Rip Van Winkle
1905 Rip's Dream
1906 In the Haunts of Rip Van Winkle
1908 Rip Van Winkle
1910 Rip Van Winkle

Ripe
1907 When Cherries Are Ripe
1909 The Ripe Cheese

Rise
1903 Rising Panorama of a Norwegian Waterfall
1904 A Girl Who Wanted to Rise in the World
1909 McGinty's Sudden Rise

Rista
1909 Rapids and Falls of Tannfossen and Rista

Ritchie
1899 Ritchie, the Tramp Bicyclist

Riva (Austria)
1910 Riva, Austria, and the Lake of Garda

Rivalry
1898 The Rivals
1902 The Rivals
1903 Business Rivalry
Deadly Rivals
Rival Billposters
1904 Rival Conjurers
The Rival Models
The Sailor's Rival
1906 Rival Brothers
1907 The Rival Motorists
Rival Sisters
Rivals
Tragic Rivalry
Two Rival Peasants
1908 The Fisherman's Rival
In Bitter Rivalry
Rival Barbers
The Rival Lovers
Rival Sherlock Holmes
The Rivals: A Love Drama of Pompeii
Rivals for a Week
The Two Rivals
1909 Dan Blake's Rival
His Rival's Hand
Malicious Rival
The Ranchman's Rival
The Rival Cyclists
Rival Mesmerists
Rival Sisters
Rivalry
The Rivals
The Wealthy Rival; or A Summer Story That Needs No Explanation
1910 The Eagle's Egg; or The Rival Lovers
The Rival Barons
The Rival Cooks
The Rival Miners
The Rival Serenaders
Rivalry in the Oil Fields
The Rivalry of the Two Guides
The Rivals
Rivals

River
1897 Delaware River, Philadelphia
East River, New York
Fall River Boat "Priscilla"
Fall River Boat Train
Panorama of Susquehanna River Taken from the Black Diamond Express
1898 Canton River Scene
The Fleet Steaming Up North River
River Scene at Macao, China
1899 Colonel Funston Swimming the Baglag River
Toll Gate and Castle Rock near Green River
1900 Panorama of Both Sides of the River Seine
1901 New York Sky-Line from East River and Battery
New York Sky-Line from the North River
Panorama of Brooklyn Bridge, River Front, and Tall Buildings from the East River
1902 Cavalry Swimming Columbia River
German Cavalry Fording a River
Mounted Soldiers Fording a River
1903 At the Ford, India. Across the Ravi River
Birds-eye View of Dawson City on the Yukon River, Alaska
Delaware River Icebound
An East River Novelty
Employees Leaving Fall River Iron Works
Fording the River Nile on Donkeys
Horses Swimming Copper River
Kalama Railroad Ferry Crossing the Columbia River
Main Street, Fall River
Mississippi River
Naval Parade on the Delaware River, Monday, May 1st, in Honor of Admiral Dewey
On the Bow River Horse Ranch at Cochrane, North West Territory
Opening of New East River Bridge, New York
A Pack Train in the Copper River Country
Panorama of Thames River
Panorama of Willemstadt, Curacao, Taken from the River
Panorama Water Front and Brooklyn Bridge from East River
The Peel River Indians with Their Dog Teams and Toboggan Sleighs on the Trail
The River Shannon
Salmon Seining on Columbia River U.S.F.C.
Skyscrapers of New York City, from the North River
Spearing Salmon in the Rivers of the North West Territory
Tourists Taking Water from the River Jordan
Troop Train Conveying the Seaforth Highlanders Across the Modder River
Winter Sport on Snake River, Nome
1904 Auto Boat Race on the Hudson River
Canoeing on the Charles River, Boston, Mass.
Cavalry Crossing a River
Cowboys and Indians Fording River in a Wagon
Fish Traps Columbia River
Herding Horses Across a River
Mending Seines on the Columbia River
Panoramic View of the Columbia River
1905 Brink of the Upper Falls of the Yellowstone River, Wyoming
Panorama from Moving Steamer on the River Thames, England
The River Pirates
A River Tragedy
Sliding River Craft over Boat Railway, River Thames
Upper Fall of the Yellowstone River
Wooding Up a River Steamer, Yukon River, Alaska
1906 The River Pirates
1907 [Launching of the Salem at the Fore River Shipyards—Quincy, Mass.—July 27, 1907]
1908 River Avon
River in Norway
1909 Cremation on the River Ganges
River Panorama
Through the Hood River Valley and Along the Columbia in Oregon
1910 The Chuncho Indians of the Amazon River, Peru
On the Bank of the River

River Drive, Fairmount Park, Philadelphia (Pennsylvania)
1903 River Drive, Fairmount Park

1903 Girls Rolling Down Hill
Tramping on a Rolling Globe
1904 Rolling Bridge in Tunis
1907 A Rolling Bed

Roly-poly
1898 "Roly Poly"

Roma (Boat)
1908 Launching the Roma

Romance
1902 A Telephone Romance
1903 A Romance of the Rail
1904 A Circus Romance
1905 Soldier's Romance
1906 The Prospectors, a Romance of the Gold Fields
1907 The Romance of a Fisherman's Daughter
The Romance of a Singer
The Shaughraun, an Irish Romance
A Southern Romance
The Spy, a Romantic Story of the Civil War
1908 At the Stage Door; or, Bridget's Romance
A Bohemian Romance
The Cashier's Romance
The Dancer and the King, a Romantic Story of Spain
In the Days of the Pilgrims, a Romance of the 15th Century in America
Interrupted Romance
Lady Jane's Flight, a 17th Century Romance
Love Laughs at Locksmiths, an 18th Century Romance
Monkeyland, a Jungle Romance
The Orphan; or, A Mountain Romance
A Poor Man's Romance
The Press Gang; or, A Romance in the Time of King George III
Romance in a Gypsy Camp
Romance of a Jewess
Romance of a School Teacher
Romance of a Taxicab
Romance of a War Nurse
The Romance of an Egg
A Romance of the Alps
A Romance of the Fur Country
Romance of the Old Mill
Romeo and Juliet, a Romantic Story of the Ancient Feud Between the Italian Houses of Montague and Capulet
A Southern Romance of Slavery Days
A Spanish Romance
A Western Romance in the Days of '49
1909 A Colonial Romance
A Cowboy's Romance
The Eternal Romance
The Indian Runner's Romance
Lady Cabby's Romance
The Love of the Pasha's Son, a Turkish Romance
Mogg Megone, an Indian Romance
A Moroccan Romance
The Nurse's Romance
The Policeman's Romance
The Prairie Town Romance
Romance in the Andes
Romance of a Dairy Maid
Romance of a Fishermaid
Romance of a Pierrot
The Romance of a Poor Girl
The Romance of a Stranded Actress
The Romance of an Umbrella
Romance of Engine 999
Romance of Life
A Romance of Old Madrid
A Romance of Old Mexico
Romance of the Crafty Usurper and the Young King
Romance of the Rocky Coast
A Romance of the South
Romantic Italy
A Russian Romance
A Stage Romance; or, An Actor's Love
The Tramp's Romance
1910 An Arizona Romance
A Boarding School Romance
A Central American Romance
A Cold Storage Romance
The Engineer's Romance
Her Romance
The Indian Girl's Romance
The Love Romance of the Girl Spy
A Mexican Romance
Red Girl's Romance
A Reno Romance
Romance in the Rockies
The Romance of a Jockey
The Romance of a Necklace
Romance of a Snake Charmer
The Romance of a Trained Nurse
A Romance of an Anvil
The Romance of Circle Ranch
The Romance of Count de Beaufort
The Romance of Hefty Burke
Romance of the Lazy K Ranch
A Romance of the Prairie
A Romance of the Western Hills
A Romantic Girl
Romantic Redskins
The Rough Rider's Romance
A Russian Romance
The Sentinel's Romance
A Tin-Type Romance
A Western Romance
A Winter Romance at Niagara Falls
A Wireless Romance

Romany
1907 The Romany's Revenge
1910 Romany Rob's Revenge
The Romany Wife

Romany Rob
1910 Romany Rob's Revenge

Rome and Romans
1898 The Armenian Archbishop, Rome
Capuchin Monks, Rome
The Vatican Guards, Rome
1900 Panoramic View of Rome
1903 Brothers of the Misericordia, Rome
Rome and the Vatican
Wedding Procession in a Church at Rome
1904 Tour in Italy (Rome antique et moderne)
1905 Roman Chariot Race, Pasadena, California
1907 Berlin to Rome
Fountains of Rome
1908 Ancient Rome
Antony and Cleopatra, the Love Story of the Noblest Roman and the Most Beautiful Egyptian
Country About Rome
Fountains of Rome
Little Walk in Rome
Nero and the Burning of Rome
Roman Colonel's Bravado
Roman Idyl
1909 The Little Orphan; or, All Roads Lead to Rome
Nero; or, The Burning of Rome
The Way of the Cross, the Story of Ancient Rome
1910 The Roman
The Sacking of Rome

Romeo
1902 Burlesque on Romeo and Juliet
1908 Romeo and Juliet
Romeo and Juliet, a Romantic Story of the Ancient Feud Between the Italian Houses of Montague and Capulet
1910 Romeo and Juliet at the Seaside
Romeo and Juliet in Our Town
Romeo Turns Bandit
A Rural Romeo

Romp
1897 A Romp
1898 A Romp in Camp
1902 A Romp on the Lawn
1904 Children Romping on the Lawn

Romsdale (Norway)
1905 Scottish Touring Party Enroute to the Romsdale, Norway
Tourists Leaving Horgheim in the Romsdale Norway

Ronkonkoma (Lake), New York
1910 Ice Scooters on Lake Ronkonkoma

Roof
1898 The Burglar on the Roof
1903 Roofs of Paris
1904 A Windy Day on the Roof
1905 Panorama from the Roof of the Times Building, New York
1906 Panoramas of Market Street, the City Hall, Taken from the Roof of the U.S. Mint
1907 Roof to Cellar
Skating on N.Y. Theatre Roof
1908 The Drama on a Roof

Roommates
1909 Roommates

Rooms
1901 Beef Extract Room
Laundry and Sewing Room
Mince Meat Room
Trimming Room
1902 A Corner in the Play Room
The Haunted Dining Room
St. John's Guild. Going to Salt-water Bath Room
1903 Danger of Dining in Private Dining Rooms
Fantastic Dining Room
In the Wrong Room
1904 Buster Makes Room for His Mama at the Bargain Counter
The Furnished Room House—Taking Life Easy
Hyde Park School Room 2, Missouri Commission
No Room for Dad
Panorama Motor Room, Westinghouse Works
The Wrong Room
1905 Always Room for One More
Rooms for Gentlemen Only
Women Employee's Dining Room
1906 Room, Please
1907 Magic Drawing Room
There Is a Rat in the Room
1909 Furnished Rooms to Let
The Master Detective; or, The Attack on the Strong Room
The Sealed Room
1910 A Jar of Cranberry Sauce; or, The Crime in Room 13
The Room of the Secret
Ten Nights in a Bar Room

Roosevelt, Theodore
1898 Col. Theodore Roosevelt and Officers of His Staff
Philadelphia City Troop and a Company of Roosevelt's Rough Riders
Roosevelt's Rough Riders
Roosevelt's Rough Riders Embarking for Santiago
Theodore Roosevelt
1899 Governor Roosevelt and Staff
1901 Opening of the Pan-American Exposition Showing Vice President Roosevelt Leading the Procession
President Roosevelt at the Army-Navy Game
President Roosevelt at the Canton Station
President Roosevelt Entering Grounds at Army-Navy Football Game
1902 Arrival of Prince Henry [of Prussia] and President Roosevelt at Shooter's Island
President Roosevelt Reviewing the Troops at Charleston Exposition [South Carolina]
1903 Over Route of Roosevelt Parade in an Automobile
President Roosevelt Addressing Crew of "Kearsarge"
Pres. Roosevelt at the Dedication Ceremonies, St. Louis Exposition
Pres. Roosevelt Leaving the Flagship
President Roosevelt's Arrival at "Kearsarge"
President Roosevelt's Departure from "Kearsarge"
Pres. Roosevelt's Fourth of July Oration
Pres. Roosevelt's Sunday Visit to Kearsage
President Roosevelt's Visit to Admiral Barker
1904 President Roosevelt's Home-coming
President Theodore Roosevelt
Roosevelt Dedicating at St. Louis Exposition
Roosevelt Dedication at Lewis and Clark Exposition
1905 The Inauguration of President Roosevelt
Inauguration of President Roosevelt. Leaving the Capitol
Inauguration of President Roosevelt. President-Elect Roosevelt, Vice-President-Elect Fairbanks and Escort Going to the Capitol
Inauguration of President Roosevelt. Taking the Oath of Office
Inauguration of President Roosevelt. the Grand Inaugural Parade
President Roosevelt at Portland
President Roosevelt at Seattle
President Roosevelt at Tacoma
President Roosevelt at Walla Walla

Rude
1908 A Rude Awakening
1909 A Rude Hostess
Rudolph
1910 Rudolph of Hapsburg
Ruffians
1904 Ruffian's Dance
1908 Ruffians Thrashed
Rug
1910 Who Owns the Rug?
Rugby
1908 Rugby Match
Ruhlin, Gus
1899 Reproduction of the Jeffries and Ruhlin Fight
Reproduction of the Ruhlin and Jeffries Fight
1900 Life Motion Photographs of the Fitzsimmons and Ruhlin Fight
1901 Jeffries and Ruhlin Sparring Contest at San Francisco, Cal., Nov. 15, 1901—Five Rounds
Ruhlin at His Training Quarters
Ruhlin Boxing with "Denver" Ed. Martin
Ruhlin in His Training Quarters
Ruhlin Sparring in His Training Quarters
Ruin
1908 The Road to Ruin
1910 Ruin
Ruined by His Son
Saved from Ruin
Ruins
1899 Ruins of the Windsor Hotel Fire
1900 Searching Ruins on Broadway, Galveston, for Dead Bodies
Taking the Dead from the Ruins [Galveston]
1901 Searching the Ruins of the Tarrant Fire
The War in China—Ruins of Tien-Tsin
1902 Circular Panoramic View of St. Pierre, Showing the Ruins of the Catholic Cathedral and Mt. Pelee Smoking in the Background
Ruins of City Hall, Paterson [N.J.]
1903 The Great Fire Ruins, Coney Island
1904 Panorama of Ruins from Baltimore and Charles Street
Panorama of Ruins from Lombard and Charles Street
Panorama of Ruins from Lombard and Hanover Streets, Baltimore, Md.
Panorama of Ruins from Water Front
1906 Dynamiting Ruins and Pulling Down Walls in San Francisco
Dynamiting Ruins and Rescuing Soldier Caught in Falling Walls
Earthquake Ruins, New Majestic Theatre and City Hall
Panorama, Nob Hill and Ruins of Millionaire Residences
Panorama, Ruins Aristocratic Apartments
Ruins Bulletin Building, California Theatre and Evening Post
Ruins of Chinatown
1907 Panorama Ruins of Old French Machinery
1910 Love Amidst Historic Ruins
Ruins of Mediaeval Fortifications in France
Through the Ruins of Carthage
The Witch of the Ruins
Rule
1902 Rulers of Half the World
1908 When Women Rule
1909 Different Rulers of the World
Rulers of the World
1910 The Ruling Passion
Rum
1904 Rum vs. Cherries
Rummage
1910 The Rummage Sale
Rummy
1907 Rummy Robbers
Run
1897 Fire Run
Sheep Run, Chicago Stockyards
Still Waters Run Deep
1898 Ostriches Running, No. 1
Ostriches Running, No. 2
A Run of the Havana Fire Department
S.S. "Coptic" Running Against the Storm
S.S. "Coptic" Running Before a Gale
1899 English Fire Department Run
International Collegiate Games—Half Mile Run
Jeffries Running with His Trainers
Running the Hurdles
Running Through Gallitzen Tunnel, Penna. R.R.
Running Up the Topsail on the "Columbia"
1900 Another Demonstration of the Cliff-Guibert Fire Hose Reel, Showing a Young Girl Coming from an Office, Detaching the Hose, Running with It 60 Feet, and Playing a Stream, All Inside of 30 Seconds
Steamer "Stowell" Running the Narrows
Torpedo Boat "Morris" Running
Trial Run of the Battleship "Alabama"
1901 International Track Athletic Meeting—Start and Finish of the One Mile Run
Montreal Fire Department on Runners
Run of the Worcester Fire Department
1902 Cross-Country Running on Snow Shoes
Fire Run, Exposition
A Run by the Berlin Fire Department, Berlin, Germany
Run of a Snow Shoe Club
1903 Chicago Fire Run
Louisville Fire Run
Memphis Fire Run
Pittsburgh Fire Department in Full Run
Run of N.Y. Fire Department
Run of Pawtucket Fire Dept.
Start from the House and the Run
Start of Endurance Run of the Automobile Club of America
Trial Run of the Fastest Boat in the World, "The Arrow"
True Love Never Runs Smooth
1905 Intercollegiate Cross Country Run
Slavonian Miners Running to Dinner, Treadwell Mine, Alaska
1906 The 100 to 1 Shot; or, A Run of Luck
Ski Running
1907 Fire Run, Colon Fire Department Under Cocoanut Tree
Johnny's Run
The Legless Runner
Man Being Run Over by Automobile
Policeman's Little Run
1908 Running for Office
1909 The Indian Runner's Romance
The Little Shepherd of "Tumbling Run"
Ponto Runs Away with the Milk Cart
A Run for the Money
Running Away from Home
Running in Hard Luck
Ski Runners of the Italian Army
True Love Never Runs Smoothly
1910 Running Away from a Fortune
Running Fire
So Runs the Way
Runaway
1896 The Runaway in the Park
1897 Catching a Runaway Team
1900 The Downward Path: She Ran Away [Part 2]
1902 Runaway Stage Coach
1906 Runaway in the Park
1907 The Runaway Sleighbelle
The Runaway Van
1908 The Runaway Horse
The Runaway Lab
Runaway Mother-in-Law
1909 Little Cyril, the Runaway
Runaway Dog
Runaway Kids
Runaway Model
Two Little Runaways
1910 The Runaway Dog
The Runaway Motor Car
Runaway Star
The Runaway Stove
Rural
1897 A Rural Courtship
1903 Buying Stamps from Rural Wagon, U.S.P.O.
Coach at Rural Post Office, U.S.P.O.
Exchange of Mail at Rural P.O., U.S.P.O.
Rural Wagon Delivering Mail, U.S.P.O.
Rural Wagon Giving Mail to Branch, U.S.P.O.
1909 A Rural Elopement
A Rural Tragedy
1910 A Rural Romeo
Rurales
1898 Mexican Rurales Charge
Ruse
1904 The Lover's Ruse
1908 A Lover's Ruse; or, The Miser's Daughter
Mr. Simpson's Artful Ruse
1909 The Detective's Ruse
The Rhymester's Ruse
1910 A Clever Ruse
Robber's Ruse
Rushes
1898 Charge by Rushes
1900 An Advance by Rushes
Rushing
1898 "Rushing the Growler"
1901 Panoramic View of the Crowd Rushing for the City Hall, Buffalo, to View the Body of President McKinley
1903 Lord and Lady Minto with Party, Fording the Rushing Waters of the Klondike on Horseback
Rushing the "Growler"
Russell, Lillian
1906 Lillian Russell
Russia and Russians
1901 Review of Russian Artillery
Russian Sharp Shooters
1903 Feeding the Russian Bear
1904 Capture and Execution of Spies by Russians
The Fight on the Bridge Between Russians and Japs
The Jolly Russian Prophets
Panorama Russian Battleship "Gronobia"
Russ-Jap Forces Meeting Near Chemulpo
Russian Antisemitic Atrocities
The Russian Army in Manchuria
Russian Battleship Repulsing Torpedo Attack
Russian Cavalry
Russian Cavalry in Corea [sic]
Russian Dance
Russian Infantry
Russian Infantry, Warsaw
Russian Outposts Attacked by Japanese
Scenes Through a Telescope from Bridge of Russian Battleship
Skirmish Between Russian and Japanese Advance Guards
Water Shoots (Montagnes russes nautiques)
1905 Duel Between Japanese and Russian Soldiers
Floral Parade at the Race Track, Moscow, Russia
The Nihilists in Russia
Russian Artillery
Russian Cavalry Review, St. Petersburg
Russian Field Artillery
Russian Kirgis Troops
Russian Mounted Artillery
Scenes and Incidents, Russo-Japanese Peace Conference, Portsmouth, N.H.
Mutiny on Man-of-war in Odessa (La révolution en Russie)
1906 Panorama, Russian and Nob Hill from an Automobile
Revolution in Russia
1908 Bear Hunting in Russia
Crack Riders of the Russian Cavalry
A Russian Bear Hunt
Russian Review of the Fiftieth Regiment
Traveling Through Russia
A Trip Through Russia
1909 Bear Hunt in Russia
Life in Russia
A Russian Romance
1910 Across Russian Poland
Jewish Types in Russia
Russia, the Caucasian Mountains
Russia—The Land of Oppression
A Russian Heroine
The Russian Lion
A Russian Romance
A Russian Spy
Russian Wolf Hunt
Russo-Japanese War, 1904-1905
1904 Naval Fight (Combat naval russo-japonais)
1905 Defense of Port Arthur (Guerre russo-japonaise no. 4)
Rustic
1908 Dora: A Rustic Idyll
A Rustic Heroine; or, In the Days of King George

1904 Battleship Leaving Harbor (Les croiseurs cuirassés "St-Louis" et "Gaulois")

St. Louis (Missouri)
1904 Panorama of Race Track Crowd, St. Louis
1907 International Balloon Races [from the James Gordon Bennett Cup, at St. Louis, Oct. 21, 1907]
1909 Dirigible Balloons at St. Louis
1910 Aviation Meet of the Aero Club, St. Louis, Mo.

St. Louis Exposition
1903 Pres. Roosevelt at the Dedication Ceremonies, St. Louis Exposition
1904 Dress Parade of the Filipino Scouts, St. Louis Exposition
Filipino Scouts, Musical Drill, St. Louis Exposition
Igorotte Savages, St. Louis Exposition
Imitation Naval Battle—St. Louis Exposition
Opening Ceremonies, St. Louis Exposition
Panorama from St. Louis Plaza, St. Louis Exposition
Panorama of St. Louis Exposition from Wireless Tower
Panorama St. Louis Exposition from Launch
Parade of Characters (Asia in America) St. Louis Exposition
Parade of Floats, St. Louis Exposition
Parade of Military, St. Louis Exposition
Parade of National Cash Register Co.'s Employees, St. Louis Exposition
Parade of the Pikers, St. Louis Exposition
Princess Rajah Dance with Chair, St. Louis Exposition
Roosevelt Dedicating at St. Louis Exposition
Twenty Mule Team, St. Louis Exposition
West Point Cadets Escorting Liberty Bell, St. Louis Exposition

St. Mary's (Schoolship)
1905 Drills and Exercises, Schoolship "St. Mary's"

St. Mary's Church, Fall River (Massachusetts)
1900 St. Mary's Congregation

Saint-Moritz (Switzerland)
1908 St. Moritz

St. Nicholas
1897 Visit of St. Nicholas

St. Patrick's Cathedral (New York City)
1902 St. Patrick's Cathedral and Fifth Avenue on Easter Sunday Morning [New York City]

St. Patrick's Day
1908 St. Patrick's Day in New York

St. Paul
1910 St. Paul and the Centurion

St. Paul (Boat)
1897 Steamship "St. Paul" Outward Bound
1900 The "St. Paul" Outward Bound
1908 The Ramming of H. M. S. Gladiator by the St. Paul

St. Petersburg (Russia)
1904 Fashionable Driving on Palace Quay, St. Petersburg
1905 Riots in St. Petersburg
Russian Cavalry Review, St. Petersburg
St. Petersburg Massacre

St. Pierre (Martinique)
1902 Burning of St. Pierre [Martinique]
Circular Panoramic View of St. Pierre from the Lighthouse, Showing Mt. Pelee Smoking in the Distance
Circular Panoramic View of St. Pierre, Showing the Ruins of the Catholic Cathedral and Mt. Pelee Smoking in the Background
Mt. Pelee in Eruption and Destruction of St. Pierre [Martinique]
Mt. Pelee Smoking Before Eruption [St. Pierre, Martinique]
Native Bull Cart at Morne Rouge (A Suburb of St. Pierre)
Natives Unloading a Boat of Fire-Wood at Carbet (A Suburb of St. Pierre)
Panorama of St. Pierre
Storm at Sea near St. Pierre, Martinique
1903 Panoramic View of St. Pierre, Martinique

St. Thomas (Virgin Islands)
1898 Harbor of St. Thomas
1903 Native Women Coaling a Ship at St. Thomas, D.W.I.
Wharf Scene and Natives Swimming at St. Thomas, D.W.I.

Saint Véronique
1904 The Passion Play (Le miracle de Sainte Véronique)

St. Vincent (Virgin Islands)
1903 Native Women Washing Clothes at St. Vincent, B. W. I.

St. Vincent's, Philadelphia (Pennsylvania)
1898 St. Vincent's Cadets

Sainte Anne (Canada)
1900 From Vaudreuil to St. Anne's

Saints
1897 Visit of St. Nicholas
1900 Temptation of St. Anthony
1904 The Passion Play (Le miracle de Sainte Véronique)
1906 Temptation of St. Anthony
1907 A Forester Made King (Bernard le bucheron ou le miracle de saint hubert)
1909 The Heroes of St. Bernard
1910 St. Elmo
St. George and the Dragon
St. Paul and the Centurion

Sake
1907 For a Woman's Sake
1908 For His Sister's Sake
For the Baby's Sake
For the Sake of a Crown
For the Sake of the Uniform
1909 For a Woman's Sake
For Baby's Sake
For Her Country's Sake
For Her Sake; or, Two Sailors and a Girl
For Her Sweetheart's Sake
For His Daughter's Sake
For Honor's Sake
For Love's Sake
For Love's Sweet Sake
For Mother's Sake
1910 For Her Country's Sake
For Her Sister's Sake
For Her Son's Sake
For the Girl's Sake
For the Sake of a Child

Sakkarah (Egypt)
1903 Excavating Scene at the Pyramids of Sakkarah
Tourists Starting on Donkeys for the Pyramids of Sakkarah

Salad
1898 How Bridget Served the Salad Undressed

Salamandre
1909 Infernal Salamandre

Salary
1909 He Was 25 Cents Short of His Salary

Salem (Boat)
1907 [Launching of the Salem at the Fore River Shipyards—Quincy, Mass.—July 27, 1907]

Salem (Massachusetts)
1910 Rose O' Salem-Town

Salerno, Gulf of (Italy)
1910 In the Gulf of Salerno

Sales
1904 Moneyweight Salesmen
1907 Bargain Sales
Cohen's Fire Sale
1908 The Devil's Sale
Making a Sale
1909 For Sale: A Baby
The Saleslady's Matinee Idol
1910 The Rummage Sale

Sallie, Aunt
1901 Aunt Sallie's Wonderful Bustle

Sally
1910 Sally's Beaux

Sallyport, Governors Island (New York)
1897 13th Infantry, U.S. Army Marching Through Sallyport, Governors Island

Salmon
1903 Horses Drawing Salmon Seine
Lifting Salmon Trap
Men Taking Fish from Salmon Seine
Raising Salmon Trap U.S.F.C.
Salmon Seining on Columbia River U.S.F.C.
Spearing Salmon in the Rivers of the North West Territory
1904 The Salmon Fisheries of Vancouver
1906 Salmon Fishing in Quebec
1907 Rogie Falls and Salmon Fishing
1910 The Life of a Salmon
U.S. Submarine "Salmon"

Salome
1907 Salome
Salome "The Dance of the Seven Veils"
1908 Salome
Salome and the Devil to Pay
Salome; or, The Dance of the Seven Veils
1909 The Salome Craze
1910 Salome

Salon
1909 Salon in 1820

Saloon
1897 Scene in a Popular Oyster Saloon
1899 Raid of a New York Bowery Saloon
1901 Carrie Nation Smashing a Saloon
The Kansas Saloon Smashers
1905 Western "Bad Man" Shooting Up a Saloon
1908 The Saloon Dance
The Saloon-Keeper's Nightmare
1910 The Saloon Next Door

Salt
1908 The Salt Did It; or, If You Want To Catch a Bird, Put Salt on It's [sic] Tail
1910 Making Salt
The Salt on the Bird's Tail
The Salted Mine

Salt Lake City (Utah)
1898 Salt Lake City Company of Rocky Mt. Riders
1905 A Trip to Salt Lake City
1910 [Salt Lake City]

Saltwater
1902 St. John's Guild. Going to Salt-water Bath Room

Salutary
1910 A Salutary Lesson

Salute
1898 Victorious Squadron Firing Salute
1902 The Royal Salute
1903 Firing the Royal Salute at Dawson City by the Northwest Mounted Police
1904 Dranem Salutes the Audience
Saluting the Flag

Salvation
1903 The Chorus Girl and the Salvation Army Lassie
1904 The International Congress of the Salvation Army
1909 The Salvation Army Lass
1910 The Outcast's Salvation
"Salvation" Smith

Sam
1909 Sam Not Wanted in the Family
Sam's Artistic Beard
1910 Sentimental Sam
Spoony Sam

Samanthy
1905 The Green Goods Man; or, Josiah and Samanthy's Experience with the Original "American Confidence Game"

Samaria
1903 Passion Play: Jesus and the Woman of Samaria
1910 The Woman of Samaria

Samaritan
1904 The Passion Play (Jésus et la Samaritaine)
1908 Youthful Samaritan
1910 The Samaritan's Courtship

Sambo
1905 Sambo
1907 Sambo as Footman

Sammy
1907 Mischievous Sammy
1908 Sammy's Idea
Sammy's Saw
Sammy's Sucker
1909 Sammy Celebrates

Samoa
1903 Bathing in Samoa
1905 Samoa and the Fiji Islands
A Trip Through Samoa and Fiji Islands

Sampans
1898 Japanese Sampans
1901 Sampans Racing Toward Liner

Sampson
1899 "Sampson" Champion High Stepper

Sampson, Willaim Thomas, Admiral
1898 Admiral Sampson on Board the Flagship
1901 Sampson and Schley Controversy—Tea Party
Sampson-Schley Controversy

Saved by an Indian
Saved by Bosco
Saved by Divine Providence
Saved by Faith
Saved by Her Dog
Saved by the Flag
Saved from Himself
Saved from Ruin
Saved from the Redmen
Saved from the Sultan's Sentence
Saved from the Tide
Saved in the Nick of Time
United States Life Saving Drills
You Saved My Life

Savoy (France)
1908 A Trip Through Savoy
1910 In the Foothills of Savoy

Saw
use **Seeing**

Saw mills
1908 The Saw Mill

Sawing
1896 Sawing Wood

Saws
1908 Sammy's Saw

Saxons
1910 The Last of the Saxons

Saxony (Germany)
1902 King Albert of Saxony

Say
1900 Who Said Chicken?
1901 Who Said Chicken?
1902 Who Said Watermelon?
1903 Children Saying Their Prayers
"What Are the Wild Waves Saying Sister?"
Who Said Watermelon
1908 The Braggart; or, What He Said He Would Do and What He Really Did
1910 The Forbidden Novel; or, Don't Do as I Do, Do as I Say
"That's What They All Say"
What the Daisy Said

Scaffold
1905 A Reprieve from the Scaffold

Scalding
1901 Scalding and Scraping Hogs

Scales
1907 Scales of Justice
1909 The Scales of Justice

Scaling
1897 13th Infantry, U.S. Army—Scaling Walls in Retreat, Governors Island
13th Infantry, U.S. Army—Scaling Walls with Wounded and Dying, Governors Island
Wall Scaling
1899 Scaling a Fort at Manila
1901 Street's Zouaves and Wall Scaling

Scalo
1905 The Midnight Sun at Scalo

Scalp
1903 Shoshone Indians in Scalp Dance

Scamps
1907 Two Little Scamps

Scandal
1899 A Scandalous Proceeding
1900 Scandal in the Custom House
1904 A Scandal on the Staircase
1908 The Scandalous Boys
1910 The Tongue of Scandal

Scandanavian
1908 Scandanavian North

Scar
1909 The Scar

Scar-Face
1910 The Legend of Scar-Face

Scare
1908 The Financial Scare
1909 The Village Scare
1910 The Mad Dog Scare

Scarecrow
1903 A Scarecrow Tramp
1904 Scarecrow Pump
1908 The Scare Crow
1910 The Animated Scare-Crow
Dorothy and the Scarecrow in Oz
The Scarecrow

Scarf
1903 Scarf Dance

Scarlet
1908 Scarlet Letter

Scatterbrain
1908 King Scatterbrain's Troubles

Scenery
1903 Cliff Scenery at the Fabbins

Scenes
1896 Sea Scene
Wine Garden Scene
1897 Bath Scene
Beach Scene
A Dressing Room Scene
Fire Rescue Scene
Interesting Parlor Scene
New England Church Scene
Scene in a Popular Oyster Saloon
Scene in Ike Einstein's Pawn Office
Smoking, Eating, and Drinking Scene
Trial Scene
1898 Bathing Scene at Rockaway
Canton River Scene
Coasting Scene in Canada
Hong Kong, Wharf Scene
Honolulu Street Scene
Marching Scene
Market Scene, City of Mexico
Mexican Fishing Scene
Mexico Street Scene
River Scene at Macao, China
Scene on the Steamship "Olivette"
See-Saw Scene
Shanghai Street Scene No. 1
Shanghai Street Scene No. 2
Sleighing Scene
Street Scene in Hong Kong
Street Scene in Yokohama, No. 1
Street Scene in Yokohama, No. 2
Street Scene, San Diego
Wharf Scene, Honolulu
1899 Cripple Creek Bar-Room Scene
Larks Behind the Scene
1900 Barroom Scene
Garden Scene
A Good Time Behind the Scenes
Military Scenes at Newport, R.I.
New Sleighing Scene
Race Track Scene
Scene from "Old Kentucky"
Scene from the Elevator Ascending Eiffel Tower
Scene in Chinatown
A Scene in Fairmount Park, Phila.
Scene in the Swiss Village at Paris Exposition
Scene on the Bois de Boulogne
Scene on the Boulevard DeCapucines
The Stocking Scene from "Naughty Anthony"
Street Scene at Place de la Concorde, Paris, France
1901 Canoeing Scene
Scene in Beautiful Orient—Pan-American Exposition
Scene in Legation Street, Shanghai
Scenes and Incidents in the G.A.R. Encampment
Snowballing Scene in Halifax
Street Scene in Pekin
Street Scene in Shanghai
Street Scene, Shanghai
Street Scene, Tientsin [China]
Street Scene, Tokio, Japan
1902 Broncho Busting Scene, Championship of the World
Chinese Shaving Scene
Coasting Scene at Montmorency Falls, Canada
Life Rescue Scene at Atlantic City, N.J.
Mysterious Transformation Scene
St. John's Guild. Dispensary Scene, Floating Hospital
Scene on Lower Broadway
Skiing Scene in Quebec
Street Scene
Street Scene in Cairo
Street Scene in Fort de France, Martinique
Street Scene, Tokio
1903 Alphonse and Gaston Balcony Scene (Thumb Book)
Ballet Scene
Barnyard Scene
Beach Scene, Coney Island
Behind the Scenes
Drunken Scene
Egyptian Market Scene
English Barnyard Scene
Excavating Scene at the Pyramids of Sakkarah
Farmyard Scene
Flood Scene in Paterson, N.J.
Foreign Train Scenes
Hammock Scene—(Abandoned)
Harvesting Scene
Hindoo Street Scene
London Fire Scene
Market Scene in Cairo, Egypt
Market Scene in Hanoi, China
Murder Scene from "King of the Detectives"
New Passing Train Scene
Panorama and Bathing Scene of Ostend, Belgium
Panoramic Views and Scenes at the Garden of the Gods
Railroad Tunnel Scene
Scene in a Laundry
Scene in Seminary
Scenes at the Zoo
Scenes in an Irish Bacon Factory
Scenes in an Irish Market Place
Scenes of a New Forest Pony Fair
Scenes of Irish Cottage Life
Scenes of the Wreckage from the Water Front
Scenes on a Welsh Pony Farm
Scenes on the Short Line
Skating Scene
Station Scene
Street Scene at Jaffa
Street Scene in Hyderabad
Street Scene in Port Huron, Mich.
Tunnel Scene of the White Pass Route
Wharf Scene and Natives Swimming at St. Thomas, D.W.I.
Andre at the North Pole (Une scène dans les régions glaciales—le ballon d'Andrée)
1904 Coasting Scene in the Alps
Diving Scene and Reverse
Duel Scene, "By Right of Sword"
Haunted Scene Painter
Japanese Railroad Scene, Kanagarva, Japan
Japanese Warriors in Ancient Battle Scene
Love and Jealousy Behind the Scenes
Quick Work Behind the Scenes
The Scene Behind the Scenes
Scenes from My Balcony
Scenes in a Slate Quarry
Scenes in an Infant Orphan Asylum
Scenes on Every Floor
Scenes Through a Telescope from Bridge of Russian Battleship
Surf Scene
Surf Scene on the Pacific
Troops Landing and Battle Scene
The Tunnel Scene
1905 Behind the Scenes
Duel Scene from "Macbeth"
Rock Scene at Ballybunion
Scene in Oxford Street, London
Scenes and Incidents, Russo-Japanese Peace Conference, Portsmouth, N.H.
Scenes at the Zoo
Scenes in a Police Court
Spectacular Scenes During a New York City Fire
Threshing Scene
1906 Scene in a Rat Pit
Scenes and Incidents U.S. Military Academy, West Point
Scenes in Hawaii
Scenes in San Francisco
Scenes of Convict Life
Scenes Washington, D.C.
1907 Irish Scenes and Types
Making the Dirt Fly: Scene 1. Steam Shovel in Operation, Culebra Cut
Making the Dirt Fly: Scene 2. Unloading a Dirt Train
Making the Dirt Fly: Scene 3. Dirt Scraper in Operation
Making the Dirt Fly: Scene 4. Railroad Track Lifter in Operation
Making the Dirt Fly: Scene 5. Laborers Lining Up at Mess Tent
Scene at "The Oaks," Portland, Oregon
Scenes from Luna Park
Scenes from Miller Bros.
Scenes on a Sugar Plantation, Hawaiian Islands

Scow
1903 Through Miles Canyon on a Cattle Scow
Scrabble
1897 A Hard Scrabble
Scrambling
1897 Scrambling for Pennies
1902 Scrambling for Eggs
1903 Native Women Coaling a Ship and Scrambling for Money [West Indies]
Piping Down. Wash Clothes. Scrambling for Clothes
Scranton (Pennsylvania)
1905 Firemen's Parade, Scranton, Pa.
1907 Scranton
Scrap
1897 A Newsboys' Scrap
1903 A Scrap in Black and White
1904 A Scrap in the Dressing Room
Scrapbook
1909 Aunt Emmy's Scrap Book
Scraping
1901 Coming Out of Scraping Machines and Cutting Off Heads
Scalding and Scraping Hogs
1905 Working a Scraper on Tailings Klondike
1907 Making the Dirt Fly: Scene 3. Dirt Scraper in Operation
Scrappy
1907 The Finish of Scrappy Patsey
1909 Scrappy Bill
Scratch
1907 Scratch My Back
1910 Scratch
Scratch as Scratch Can
Screens
1899 Diving Through Paper Screens
1904 Behind the Screen
Mysterious Screen
Scrimmage
1901 Yale Football, Practice Scrimmage
1902 A Lively Scrimmage
Scrub
1897 Scrub Yacht Race
Scrubbem
1899 Scrubbem's Washing Machine
Scrubbing
1903 Bluejackets Scrubbing Their Hammocks
1904 Scrubbing Clothes
Scruple
1906 Man Without Scruple
Scullion
1908 Scullion's Dream
Sculptor
1903 The Sculptor's Studio
1904 Sculptor and Model
1907 The Express Sculptor
1908 Modern Sculptors
The Sculptor's Nightmare
A Sculptor's Welsh Rabbit Dream
1909 The Marble Heart; or, The Sculptor's Dream
The Sculptor's Love
1910 A Sculptor Who Has Easy Work
The Sculptor's Dream
The Sculptor's Ideal
Sea
1896 Sea Scene
1897 Sad Sea Waves
1898 Queer Fish That Swim in the Sea
Sea Waves
A Tug in a Heavy Sea
1899 Full Rigged Ship at Sea
Heavy Sea from Deck of "St. Louis"
Heavy Storm at Sea Taken from S.S. "St. Louis"
Looking Off S.S. "St. Louis" at Sea
1900 Deep Sea Fishing
A Storm at Sea
1901 After a Rescue at Sea
1902 A Rescue at Sea
The S.S. "Deutschland" in Heavy Sea
Storm at Sea near St. Pierre, Martinique
1903 Cruelty on the High Seas
The Forecastle of the "Kearsage" in a Heavy Sea
Sea Washing over the Bow of Kearsage
1904 At Sea in a Storm
A Heavy Sea
1905 A German Warship in a Heavy Sea
A Rough Sea on the Derry Coast
A Tragedy at Sea
1906 A Heavy Sea
High Sea Fishing
Turbulent Seas, Waterfalls and Streams
1907 The Benediction of the Sea
Cast Up by the Sea
Message from the Sea
Sea by Moonlight
The Sea Wolf
A Tale of the Sea
Under the Seas
1908 Avenged by the Sea
Fire at Sea
Heavy Seas
Under the Sea in a Submarine
1909 A Child of the Sea
Children of the Sea
Goddess of the Sea
Lines of White on a Sullen Sea
A Message from the Sea
Pirates of the Sea
Poetry of the Sea
Princess of the Sea
A Stormy Sea
1910 Ascending the Sea of Ice
Called to the Sea
A Child of the Sea
Deep Sea Fishing
Drama at Sea
From Beyond the Seas
A Lesson by the Sea
The Lookout; or, Saved from the Sea
A Message of the Sea
The Polar Bear Hunt in the Arctic Seas
Railway on the Ice Sea
Sea Cave and Cliffs
A Sea of Clouds
Sea Waves
The Sea Wolves
The Sea's Vengeance
A Stormy Seas
A Tale of the Sea
Their Sea Voyage
Tracked Across the Sea
Tragedy at Sea
The Unchanging Sea
Where Sea and Shore Doth Meet
The Wreck at Sea
Sea gulls
1898 Feeding Sea Gulls
1901 Sea Gulls
1902 Sea Gulls Following Fishing Boats
1904 Sea Gulls at Newlyn, Cornwall, England
Sea lions
1897 The Sea Lions' Home
1899 Prof. Paul Boynton Feeding His Sea Lions
1900 Feeding Sea Lions
1909 Chasing a Sea Lion in the Arctics
1910 Hunting Sea Lions in Tasmania
Sea serpent
1904 Great Sea Serpent
1908 Looking for the Sea Serpent
Sea urchins
1903 "The Devil of the Deep" and the Sea Urchins
Seaforth Highlanders
1903 Troop Train Conveying the Seaforth Highlanders Across the Modder River
1905 Battalion of Seaforth Highlanders at the Dublin Horse Show
Squad of Seaforth Highlanders Leaving Bank of Ireland, Dublin
Seal
1903 Envelope Folder and Sealer, National Cash Register Co.
1909 Sealed Instructions
The Sealed Room
When Lips Are Sealed
1910 The Red Cross Seal
The Seal of the Church
Seals
1910 Feeding Seals at Catalina Isle
Seal and Walrus Hunting
Seaman
1907 Seaman's Widow
Seamstress
1910 The Ghetto Seamstress
Seance
1900 The Exposed Seance
1908 Spiritualistic Seance
Search
1900 Searching Ruins on Broadway, Galveston, for Dead Bodies
1901 Searching the Ruins of the Tarrant Fire
1903 A Search for Evidence
1905 Custom House Search
1906 In Search of Adventure
The Lost Collar Button; or, A Strenuous Search
1910 Blopps in Search of the Black Hand
Searchlight
1908 Tales the Searchlight Told
Seashore
1898 Street Boys at the Seashore
1899 Bunco on the Seashore
1900 Getting Ready for the Seashore
1901 Hooligan at the Seashore
1902 A Seashore Gymkana
1903 Seashore Frolics
1904 The Seashore Baby
1908 A Day at the Sea Shore
Seasickness
1902 Sea Sick Excursionists
Seaside
1904 A Seaside Cakewalk
1906 At the Seaside
A Seaside Flirtation
1907 A Seaside Girl
1908 Mr. Soaker at the Seaside
1910 Romeo and Juliet at the Seaside
Seaside Adventures at Home
A Seaside Flirtation
A Visit to the Seaside at Brighton Beach, England
Seasons
1903 First Snow Storm of the Season, Valdez
1904 The Four Seasons
1910 The Four Seasons
In the Season of Buds
Seat
1903 Jack Tar Sewing a Patch on the Seat of His Trousers
1909 Skylight Theater Seat
1910 A Seat in the Balcony
Seated
1898 Pope Leo XIII Being Seated Bestowing Blessing Surrounded by Swiss Guards, No. 107
Pope Leo XIII Seated in Garden
Pope Leo XIII Seated in Garden, No. 105
Seattle (Washington)
1897 First Avenue, Seattle, Washington, No. 8
1903 James Street, Seattle, Wash.
Seattle Fire Department in Action
1905 President Roosevelt at Seattle
1906 From Tacoma to Seattle
Second
1897 Second Round: Glove Contest Between the Leonards
1898 Bayonet Charge; by the 2nd Illinois Volunteers
First Battalion of the 2nd Massachusetts Volunteers
Return of 2nd Regiment of New Jersey
Second Battalion; 2nd Massachusetts Volunteers
Second Illinois Volunteers at Double Time
Second Illinois Volunteers in Review
10th U.S. Infantry, 2nd Battalion Leaving Cars
1899 "Langton Performer 2nd"
Second Battalion, 1st Regiment, N. G. of Pennsylvania
2nd Battalion, 3rd New York Provisional Regiment, Rochester and Syracuse, Separate Companies
Second Boston School Regiment
Second City Troop
2nd Company Governor's Footguards, Conn.
2nd Special Service Battalion, Canadian Infantry, Embarking for So. Africa
2nd Special Service Battalion, Canadian Infantry-Parade
Start of Second Cup Race
Start of the Second Cup Race
1900 Departure of the Second Canadian Contingent
1901 "Columbia" and "Shamrock II": Finishing Second Race
"Columbia" and "Shamrock II": Start of Second Race
The Second Inauguration
Second Queen's Rajputs
Second Squad, Sixth U.S. Cavalry
'Varsity Crew Race on Cayuga Lake, on Decoration Day, Lehigh Valley Observation Train Following the Race, Showing Cornell Crew Finishing First, Columbia Second, University of Pennsylvania Third Ithaca, N.Y., Showing Lehigh Valley Observation Train

Serenade
1899 The Dusky Serenade
The Serenaders
1903 Serenader's Difficulties
1904 Military Serenade
A Moonlight Serenade; or, The Miser Punished.
1905 The Serenade
1908 Comic Serenade
1910 Bill's Serenade
The Rival Serenaders

Serge, Grand Duke
1905 Assassination of the Grand Duke Serge

Sergeant
1904 The Cop Fools the Sergeant
1909 The Sergeant's Stripes
The Two Sergeants
1910 The Color Sergeant's Horse
His Sergeant's Stripes
The Sergeant
The Sergeant's Daughter

Series
1899 Shoot the Chutes Series
1902 Entire Series of Yacht Race Pictures with Dissolving Effects
1904 Around Port Arthur (Autour de Port-Arthur (1e serie))
Around Port Arthur (No. 2) (Autour de Port-Arthur (2e serie))
1906 The World Series Baseball Games-White Sox and Cubs
1908 The World's Championship Baseball Series of 1910
1909 Nat Pinkerton [Series II]
The Silk Worm Series
Rifle Bill No. 5 (Rifle-Bill (5eme serie))
1910 World's Championship Series

Serious
1908 A Serious Joke
1909 A Serious Error
1910 Serious Sixteen

Serpent
1908 Feeding a Serpent
The Serpent's Tooth
1910 A Hidden Serpent
In the Serpent's Power

Serpentine dance
1895 Serpentine Dance—Annabelle
1896 Serpentine Dance by Annabelle
1902 The New Serpentine and Fire Dance
1903 Black Serpentine
New Serpentine Dance
1909 Beginning of the Serpentine Dance

Serrat (Mountain), Spain
1906 Ascending Mt. Serrat in Spain
Descending Mt. Serrat in Spain

Serum
1909 Prof. Wise's Brain Serum Injector
1910 The Serum; or, The Antidote

Servant
1905 The Servant Girl Problem
The Servant Girl's Dream
The Servant Question
Servant's Dance, Lake Hotel, Killarney, Ireland
1907 An Angelic Servant
The Mechanical Statue and the Ingenious Servant
My Servant Is a Jewel
The Servant Hypnotist
Servant's Generosity
Servant's Revenge
Servant's Strike
Servant's Vengeance
1908 The First Servant
Improvised Servant
Jewel of a Servant
The Substitute Automatic Servant
Wanted: A Colored Servant
1909 Master and Servant
The New Servant
Old Servants
Recommended Servant
Servant
The Servant of the Actress
The Servant Question Solved
Servant's Good Joke
Servant's Revenge
Too Clean a Servant
1910 The Devil, the Servant, and the Man
The Electric Servant
Servant and Guardian
The Servant and the Tutor
Servant from the Country
An Unexpected Servant
Up-to-Date Servants

Serve
1898 How Bridget Served the Salad Undressed
Serving Rations to the Indians, No. 1
Serving Rations to the Indians, No. 2
1902 Serving Potatoes, Undressed
1904 Serving Outfits to Recruits
1906 The Subpoena Server
1907 It Served Them Right
Serving a Summons
1908 It Serves Him Right
1909 Was Justice Served?

Service
1899 2nd Special Service Battalion, Canadian Infantry, Embarking for So. Africa
2nd Special Service Battalion, Canadian Infantry-Parade
1902 After the Service
German Railway Service
1906 Secret Service; or, The Diamond Smugglers
1907 My Master's Coffee Service
1908 In the Government Service
1909 In the Service of the King
Secret Service Woman
Service of a Friend

Session
1908 The Court in Session

Set-to
1898 Comedy Set-To

Seth
1910 Seth's Temptation

Sets
1907 A Set of Dishes
1908 The Village Set
1909 A Set of Teeth

Setting
1899 How Papa Set Off the Fireworks
1901 At the Setting of the Sun
1902 Why Papa Reformed, or Setting Back the Clock
1906 Brannigan Sets Off the Blast
1910 Where the Sun Sets

Settlement
1904 Panorama of a Philippine Settlement [Pan-American Exposition]
1909 The Settlement Workers
1910 The Final Settlement

Settler
1903 Settler's Home Life
1910 The Early Settlers

Settling
1910 Settled Out of Court
Settling a Boundary Dispute

Seven
1902 The Magician and the Seven Hats
Panoramic View of Seven Castles
1903 Panorama of Tivoli, Italy, Showing Seven Falls
The Seven Capital Sins
1904 The Devil's Seven Castles
1905 The Seven Ages
1907 Salome "The Dance of the Seven Veils"
1908 Salome; or, The Dance of the Seven Veils
1910 The House of the Seven Gables
7 Days

Seventeen
1906 The Murder of His Seventeen Wives

Seventeenth
1900 The 17th Infantry, U.S.A.

Seventeenth century
1908 Lady Jane's Flight, a 17th Century Romance
A Story of the 17th Century

Seventh
1897 7th and 71st Regiment, New York
7th Regiment, N.G.S.N.Y.
1898 Seventh Ohio Volunteers
1899 7th Regiment, New York City
1903 New York's 7th and 71st Regiments
1906 7th Regiment at 69th Army Dedication
1909 The Seventh Clerk
The Seventh Day

Seventy-first
1897 7th and 71st Regiment, New York
71st Regiment, N.G.S.N.Y.
71st Regiment, New York
1898 71st New York
71st N.Y. Volunteers Embarking for Santiago
1903 New York's 7th and 71st Regiments
1904 "Pollywogs" 71st Regiment, N.G.S.N.Y., Initiating Raw Recruits

Seville (Spain)
1901 Sevillenas Dance—Pan-American Exposition
1904 The Barber of Seville
1907 Cock Fight in Seville
A Drama in Seville
In Sevilla
1910 The Cigarette Maker of Seville

Sevres (France)
1909 Sevres Porcelain

Sewing
1901 Laundry and Sewing Room
1903 Jack Tar Sewing a Patch on the Seat of His Trousers
1910 The Sewing Girl

Sex
1908 The Gentle Sex
1910 The Stronger Sex

Sexless
1897 Sexless Profiles

Sexton
1908 The Sexton of Longwyn

Shad
1901 Hauling a Shad Net
Shad Fishing at Gloucester, N.J.
1903 Stripping Shad U.S.F.C.
1906 Shad Fishing

Shade
1904 On the Window Shade
1907 99 in the Shade

Shadow
1899 Under the Shadow of Mt. Stephen, Passing Field's Station in the Rocky Mountains
1904 The Shadowy Lady
1908 The Lights and Shadows of Chinatown
The Shadow of the Law
Shadows of Night
1909 Into the Shadow
A Shadow of the Past
Through Shadow to Sunshine
1910 From Shadow to Sunshine
In the Mission Shadows
In the Shadow of Mt. Shasta
In the Shadow of the Cliffs
In the Shadow of the Night
The Mother's Shadow
The Passing Shadow
A Shadow of the Past
Shadows and Sunshine

Shaffer, Lillian
1904 Miss Lillian Shaffer and Her Dancing Horse

Shafter, William Rufus, Major General
1898 Major General Shafter

Shah
1900 The Shah's Return from Paris

Shakespeare, William
1907 Shakespeare Writing "Julius Caesar"
1908 Macbeth, Shakespeare's Sublime Tragedy
Richard III, a Shakespearian Tragedy
Ten Minutes with Shakespeare

Sham
1900 Naval Sham Battle at Newport
Sham Battle on Land by Cadets at Newport Naval Training School
1901 Sham Battle at the Pan-American Exposition
1907 Sham Beggars
The Sham Sword Swallower

Shame
1905 It's a Shame To Take the Money

Shamrock (Boat)
1899 Crew of the "Shamrock"
Crew of the "Shamrock," at Work
"Shamrock"
"Shamrock I"
"Shamrock" After Carrying Away Topsail
"Shamrock" and "Columbia"
Shamrock and Columbia Jockeying for a Start
"Shamrock" and "Columbia" Rounding the Outer Stake Boat
"Shamrock" and "Columbia" Rounding the Outer Stake Boat, No. 2
"Shamrock" and "Columbia" Yacht Race—First Race
"Shamrock" and "Columbia" Yacht Race—1st Race, No. 2
"Shamrock" and "Erin" Sailing
Shamrock Starting on Trial Trip
Start of Race Between "Columbia" and "Shamrock"

Shoemaker
1908 The Shoemaker of Coepenick
1909 Neptune's Daughter; or, The Shoemaker's Dream
The Shoemaker's Luck

Shoes
1898 Canadian Artillery Marching on Snow Shoes
A Shoe and Stocking Race
The Snow Shoe Club
1902 Cross-Country Running on Snow Shoes
Run of a Snow Shoe Club
1903 The Gay Shoe Clerk
Goody, Goody Two Shoes
Old Woman Who Lived in a Shoe
Soft Shoe Dance
1907 The Stolen Shoes
The White Shoes; or, Looking Out for His Banknote
1908 Mr. Smith's Difficulties in the Shoe Store
Two Little Shoes
1909 A Baby's Shoe
The Note in the Shoe
Peddling Shoes
1910 The Horse Shoer's Girl
Making Wooden Shoes
The Old Shoe Came Back
The Story of a Shoe

Shoo
1900 "Shoo Fly"

Shooters
1901 Russian Sharp Shooters
1902 New Year Shooters
1905 The New Year's Shooters in Philadelphia
1907 Philadelphia New Year Shooters
1910 Life of the Alpine Shooters in the Frontier Outposts

Shooters Island (New York)
1902 Arrival of Prince Henry [of Prussia] and President Roosevelt at Shooter's Island

Shooting
1896 "Shooting the Chutes"
1897 Shooting the Chutes
1898 President Faure Shooting Pheasants
Shooting Captured Insurgents
Shooting the Chutes at Home
Shooting the Long Sault Rapids
1899 Shoot the Chutes Series
Shooting an Artesian Well
Shooting the Life Line
1901 Shooting the Chutes at Providence, Rhode Island
1903 Captain Allard Shooting White Horse Rapids
The New Shooting the Chutes
Shooting Craps
Shooting the Chutes
Shooting the Chutes, Luna Park
Shooting the Rapids at Luna Park
Shooting the Rapids of Killarney
1904 Elephants Shooting the Chutes at Luna Park [Coney Island]
Elephants Shooting the Chutes, Luna Park, Coney Island, No. 2
Shooting the Rapids of Killarney
Water Shoots
1905 Shooting the Chutes, Cork Exhibition
Shooting the Killarney Rapids, Ireland
Western "Bad Man" Shooting Up a Saloon
1906 Quail Shooting at Pinehurst
A Shooting Expedition Accident
1907 Trap Pigeon Shooting
1908 Shooting Party
1909 Shooting the Rapids in Japan
1910 Jinks Has the Shooting Mania
Shooting an Oil Well
Shooting in the Haunted Woods

Shoplifter
1900 Arrest of a Shoplifter

Shopping
1903 Saturday's Shopping
1904 Saturday Afternoon Shopping
1907 The Bargain Fiend; or, Shopping a la Mode
Madame Goes Shopping
1908 Archie Goes Shopping with the girls
When Ma Goes Shopping
1909 Master Goes Shopping

Shops
1898 What Demoralized the Barber Shop
1901 Fun in a Butcher Shop
What Demoralized the Barber Shop
1902 Fun in a Bakery Shop
1903 Butcher Shop No. 1
Butcher Shop No. 2
Passion Play: Christ in the Carpenter Shop
The Tramp in the Barber Shop
1904 English Locomotive in Shop and on Rail
Linen Shop
1908 In the Barber Shop
1909 The Old Curiosity Shop

Shore
1896 American Falls from Bottom of Canadian Shore
Whirlpool Rapids—from Bottom of Canadian Shore
1899 Admiral Dewey's First Step on American Shore
1900 Panoramic View, Wreckage Along Shore, Galveston
1901 American Falls from Top of Canadian Shore
1904 Fishing in Newfoundland—French Shore
1905 Accelerated (Crazy) Panorama West Shore, Lake of Garda
1907 Along the Shore Line of Lake Washington
1909 Achill's Rocky Shores
1910 Shorty at the Shore
Where Sea and Shore Doth Meet

Shore, Jane
1908 Jane Shore

Short
1898 One Chair Short
1903 The Long and Short of It
1907 A Shilling Short in Wages
1909 He Was 25 Cents Short of His Salary

Short-circuit
1909 The Short Circuit House

Short Line, Cripple Creek (Colorado)
1903 Scenes on the Short Line
1906 Trip over Cripple Creek Short Line

Short Sight, Professor
1909 Professor Short Sight's Surprise

Short-stick
1900 Short-Stick Dance

Shortening
1901 Middies Shortening Sails

Short-lived
1910 A Short-Lived Triumph

Shortsighted
1908 Mr. Shortsighted Goes Shrimping
1909 The Short-Sighted Governess
1910 Mr. Short Sighted

Shorty
1910 Shorty at the Shore
The Shyness of Shorty

Shoshone Indians
1903 Shoshone Indians in Scalp Dance

Shot
1899 A Good Shot
1906 The 100 to 1 Shot; or, A Run of Luck
Shot for Looting
1908 A Chance Shot
1909 Alphonse, the Dead Shot
A Bad Shot
1910 The Binding Shot
The Crack Shot
The Lucky Shot
The Reserved Shot
A Shot in the Night
A Shot in Time

Shotgun
1897 Champion Rolla O. Heikes, Breaking the Record at Flying Targets with Winchester Shotgun

Shovel
1907 Making the Dirt Fly: Scene 1. Steam Shovel in Operation, Culebra Cut

Show girls
1903 From Show Girl to Burlesque Queen

Showcase
1903 Beaver Show Case

Shower bath
1904 The Shower Bath
1907 Rogues' Tricks (La douche d'eau bouillante)

Showing
1896 Parade at Canton O., Showing Major McKinley in Carriage
Showing Group of Bathers, Atlantic City Beach
1899 Reproduction of the Fitzsimmons-Jeffries Fight in Eleven Rounds Showing the Knock Out
1900 Another Demonstration of the Cliff-Guibert Fire Hose Reel, Showing a Young Girl Coming from an Office, Detaching the Hose, Running with It 60 Feet, and Playing a Stream, All Inside of 30 Seconds
Another Picture Showing Demonstration of a Pneumatic Shell Riveter
Birdseye View of Galveston, Showing Wreckage
Showing a Giant Crane Dumping a 40-Ton Car
1901 Opening of the Pan-American Exposition Showing Vice President Roosevelt Leading the Procession
Panoramic View of London Streets, Showing Coronation Decorations
'Varsity Crew Race on Cayuga Lake, on Decoration Day, Lehigh Valley Observation Train Following the Race, Showing Cornell Crew Finishing First, Columbia Second, University of Pennsylvania Third Ithaca, N.Y., Showing Lehigh Valley Observation Train
1902 Circular Panoramic View of St. Pierre from the Lighthouse, Showing Mt. Pelee Smoking in the Distance
Circular Panoramic View of St. Pierre, Showing the Ruins of the Catholic Cathedral and Mt. Pelee Smoking in the Background
Circular Panoramic View of the Market Place at Fort de France, Showing S.S. Korona in the Background
Foxy Grandpa Shows the Boys a Trick or Two with the Tramp
1903 Inside Car, Showing Bag Catcher [U.S.P.O.]
Jerusalem's Busiest Street, Showing Mt. Zion
Panorama of Tivoli, Italy, Showing Seven Falls
Panoramic View of Beyrouth, Syria, Showing Holiday Festivities
1904 Let Uncle Ruben Show You How
Section of Buster Brown Series, Showing a Sketch of Buster by Outcault
1905 Panorama of the Course at Henley Showing a Finish
1906 Getting Evidence, Showing the Trials and Tribulations of a Private Detective
Going to the Fire, Showing Chief Sullivan During the Earthquake
A Trip from Naples to Vesuvius, Showing the Volcano in Action
1907 Panorama of Market Street Showing the Beautiful Decorations
1909 A Day in Washington, the Capital of the United States, Showing Many Points of Interest
Show Your License

Showman
1909 The Showman's Drama
1910 The Monkey Showmen of Djibah

Shows
1898 Parade of Buffalo Bill's Wild West Show, No. 1
Parade of Buffalo Bill's Wild West Show, No. 2
1900 Bryn Mawr Horse Show
Buffalo Bill's Wild West Show
1902 The Bryn Mawr Horse Show
Buffalo Bill's Wild West Show
Uncle Josh at the Moving Picture Show
1903 Baby Show Atlantic City
The Beauty Show
Beauty Show
Prize Winners at the Dog Show
1904 Treloar and Miss Marshall, Prize Winners at the Physical Culture Show in Madison Square Garden
The Troubles of a Manager of a Burlesque Show
1905 The Baby Show
Battalion of Seaforth Highlanders at the Dublin Horse Show
Earl of Dudley and Party at the Dublin Horse Show
Fashionable Folks Leaving the Dublin Horse Show
Hunters Exercising, Dublin Horse Show
Hunters in Exercising Ring, Dublin Horse Show
Hunters Jumping, Dublin Horse Show

Singapore
1908 The Indian Sorcerer (Le fakir de Singapour)
Singer Building (New York City)
1906 Singer Building Foundation Co.
Singing
1901 Singing Pigs Feet
1902 The Singing Donkey
1907 Misadventures of a Street Singer
The Romance of a Singer
She Would Sing
1908 The Poor Singer Girl
1909 The Little Street Singer
Single
1897 Pennsylvania State Militia, Single Time
Single Harness Horses
1909 Nightmare of a Single Man
Sins and sinners
1901 The Wages of Sin—A Mother's Grief
The Wages of Sin—The Assassin's Escape
The Wages of Sin—The Fatal Choice
The Wages of Sin—The Murder of Bess
1903 The Seven Capital Sins
The Wages of Sin: A—Murder
The Wages of Sin: B—Retribution
1905 Sins and Sorrows of a Great City
1907 A Mother's Sin
1908 The Devil's Three Sins
The Farmer's Daughter; or, The Wages of Sin
Redeemed from Sin
A Sinner
The Wages of Sin, an Italian Tragedy
1909 The Blight of Sin
The Sins of the Fathers
The Wages of Sin
1910 Her Father's Sin
Her Sister's Sin
A Sinner's Sacrifice
A Society Sinner
The Wages of Sin
Sioux Indians
1909 Comata, the Sioux
A Daughter of the Sioux
1910 A Cheyenne's Love for a Sioux
The Heart of a Sioux
A Sioux's Reward
The White Captive of the Sioux
Sir
1897 Sir Wilfred Laurier and the New South Wales Lancers
1898 Gen'l Sir Herbert Kitchener
1899 Sir Thomas Lipton and Party on "Erin's" Launch
Sir Thomas Lipton's Steam Yacht "Erin"
1902 Sir Thomas Lipton on Board the Erin
1903 Sir Thomas Lipton's Yacht Fleet Leaving England
1906 Have a Light, Sir
Siren
1909 The Phantom Sirens
The Siren's Necklace
Sisal
1910 The Sisal Industry in the Bahamas
Sister-in-law
1910 His Sister-in-Law
Sisters
1897 Dance, Franchonetti Sisters
Golding Sisters, Champion Swimmers
Leander Sisters
1898 The Landlady Gives Notice to the Barrasing Sisters
1899 The Wicked Sister and the Lobster
1900 Little Sister
1901 The Gordon Sisters Boxing
1902 Four Hong Kong Sisters
1903 Acrobatic Sisters Daines
Three Bell Sisters in a Fancy Dance
The Two Sisters!
The Vaidis Sisters, Luna Park
"What Are the Wild Waves Saying Sister?"
1904 Sisters Barrison
1907 Dear Little Sister
Rival Sisters
1908 Avenged; or, The Two Sisters
The Bad Sister
Dick's Sister
For His Sister's Sake
1909 Brother and Sister
How Jack Helped His Little Sister
The Lemon Sisters at Muldoon's Picnic
Little Sister
Rival Sisters
A Sister's Love, a Tale of the Franco-Prussian War
Ted and His Little Sister
1910 The Barry Sisters
Billy's Sister
The Brother, Sister and Cowpuncher
The Elder Sister
For Her Sister's Sake
For His Sister's Honor
Her Sister's Sin
Sisters
A Sister's Devotion
A Sister's Sacrifice
Tommy Gets His Sister Married
The Two Sisters
Sit
1898 An Interrupted Sitting
1910 The Man Who Could Not Sit Down
Situation
1903 An Unpleasant Situation
1910 A Critical Situation
Siva
1904 The Invisible Sylvia (Siva l'invisible)
Six
1897 Six Furlong Handicap
1903 Acrobatic Sisters Daines (Les six soeurs Dainef)
1904 Japs Loading and Firing a Six Pounder
1907 Six Amorous Dragoons
1909 The Double Six
1910 Double Six
The Six-Legged Sheep
Sixteen
1903 Throwing the Sixteen Pound Hammer
1910 Serious Sixteen
Sixth
1897 Sixth U.S. Cavalry
1898 Bareback Riding, 6th Cavalry, U.S.A.
Sixth Pennsylvania Volunteers
1901 Second Squad, Sixth U.S. Cavalry
6th Cavalry Assaulting South Gate of Pekin
Sixth U.S. Cavalry Charging
Sixth U.S. Cavalry, Skirmish Line
1904 Scenes from My Balcony (Ce que je vois de mon sixieme)
Sixth Avenue (New York City)
1903 6th Ave. New York Elevated Railroad
Sixty-fifth
1898 65th Regiment, N.Y.V.
65th Regiment at Double Time
Sixty minute
1897 60 Minute Flyer
Sixty-ninth
1898 Recruits of the 69th Regiment, N.G.S.N.Y.
69th Regiment Passing in Review
Three Views of the 69th Regiment, N.G.S.N.Y.
1903 69th Regiment, N.G.N.Y.
1906 7th Regiment at 69th Army Dedication
Skagway (Alaska)
1903 Leaving Skagway for the Golden North
Skating and skaters
1898 Skating
1900 Skating in Central Park
1901 Emar De Flon, the Champion Skater
The Tramp's Unexpected Skate
1902 Devoy, the Funny Skater
Ice Skating
Skate Sailing in Sweden
Skating in Stockholm
1903 Comic Skater
Hooligan's Roller Skates
Skating in Fairmount Park
Skating Scene
1904 Ice Skating in Central Park, N.Y.
1907 An Awful Skate; or, the Hobo on Rollers
A Cheap Skate
The Roller Skate Craze
Skating Lessons
Skating on N.Y. Theatre Roof
1908 On Roller Skates
A "Skate" on Skates
The Woes of Roller Skates
1909 Motor Skates
1910 Roller Skating in Australia
Safety Suit for Skaters
Simpson's Skate
Stunts on Skates
They Would Roller Skate
Skeeter
1900 A Jersey Skeeter
Skeleton
1897 The Dancing Skeleton
1898 Skeleton Dance, Marionettes
1899 The Skeleton at the Feast
1902 Dancing Skeleton
1903 Dancing Skeleton
1910 Oh You Skeleton
The Skeleton
Sketch
1904 Section of Buster Brown Series, Showing a Sketch of Buster by Outcault
1907 Lightning Sketches
The Mischievous Sketch
1909 Bobby's Sketches
Ski
1901 Norway Ski Jumping Contests
1902 Amateur Ski Jumpers
Skiing in Montreal
Skiing in Stockholm, Sweden
Skiing Scene in Quebec
1903 Ski Jumping Competition
1906 Ski Running
1907 Skiing in Norway
1908 Ski Contest
The Ski-ing Maniac
1909 Ski-ing at Ispheming, Mich.
Ski Jumping
Ski Runners of the Italian Army
1910 Max Goes Skiing
A Skier Training
Skidoo-23
1902 Skidoo-23
Skies
1909 An Expensive Sky Piece
Love Under Spanish Skies
Under Northern Skies
1910 Under a Changing Sky
Under Western Skies
Skillful
1908 Skillful Policemen
Skimmer
1902 An Unsinkable Skimmer
Skin
1898 Trying to "Skin the Cat"
1899 A Bare Skin Joke
1901 Skinning Sheep
1904 A Princess in Disguise (Peau d'ane)
1908 Donkey's Skin
1909 Snake Skin Industry
The Wild Ass's Skin
Skinny
1908 Skinny's Finish
Skinum, Dr.
1907 Dr. Skinum
Skipper
1909 The Skipper's Daughter
1910 The Skipper's Yarn
Skipping
1897 A Skipping Rope Dance
1901 Jeffries Skipping the Rope
1907 The Skipping Cheeses
Skirmish
1897 Charge, Through Intervals of Skirmishes
1898 Outpost Skirmish
A Skirmish Drill
1899 Skirmish of Rough Riders
1901 Sixth U.S. Cavalry, Skirmish Line
1903 Skirmish with Boers near Kimberly by a Troop of Cavalry Scouts Attached to Gen. French's Column
1904 Outpost Skirmishing
Skirmish Between Russian and Japanese Advance Guards
Skirt
1910 The Hobble Skirt
The Latest Fashion in Skirts
Skull
1908 The Skull and the Sentinel
Skylight
1909 Skylight Theater Seat
Skyline
1901 New York Sky-Line from East River and Battery
New York Sky-Line from the North River
Skyscraper
1898 The Skyscrapers of New York
1902 Starting a Skyscraper
1903 Skyscrapers of New York City, from the North River
1906 Skyscrapers

Slabs
1903 Disposition of Slabs and Waste at Pt. Blakeley

Slade
1901 Ten Nights in a Bar-Room: Death of Slade

Slate
1904 Scenes in a Slate Quarry
1907 Slate Quarries in North Wales

Slaughter
1897 Cattle Driven to Slaughter
1901 Driving Hogs to Slaughter
Hog Slaughtering. No. 6: Opening and Splitting
Sheep Led to Slaughter by Goat

Slaves
1900 The Slave Market
1907 Chinese Slave Smuggling
The Slave, a Story of the South Before the War
Slavery by Circumstance
The Slavery of Children
Slavery of Children
A Slave's Love
The White Slave
1908 Child Slave Freed
The Galley Slave's Return
Slave's Hate
The Slaves of the Czar
A Southern Romance of Slavery Days
1909 Chinatown Slavery
The Galley Slave
The Greek Slave's Passion
Princess and Slave
The Seminole's Vengeance; or The Slave Catchers of Florida
The Slave
A Slave to Drink
The Slavey
1910 Patrician and Slave
The Slave of Carthage
The Slave's Love
The Slave's Sacrifice

Slavonia (Boat)
1910 Anarchists on Board; or, The Thrilling Episode on the S.S. "Slavonia"

Slavonian
1905 Slavonian Miners Running to Dinner, Treadwell Mine, Alaska

Sled
use **Sleigh**

Sleep
1896 Rip's Twenty Years' Sleep
Why Papa Cannot Sleep
1897 Now I Lay Me Down To Sleep
1898 The Sleeping Uncle and the Bad Girls
Tribulations of Sleeping in a Hammock
1899 A Mean Trick on a Sleepy Soubrette
Why Krausemeyer Couldn't Sleep
1901 "The Sleeping Child"
1902 The Sleeper
1903 Sleeping Beauty
1905 The Sleepy Soubrette
1907 The Sleepy Cop
1908 Sleeping Beauty
Beauty and the Beast (La belle au bois dormant)
1909 Impossible to Get Sleep
The Policeman Sleeps
Sleep Walker
The Sleeper
The Sleeping Tonic
Sleepy Jim
A Sound Sleeper
1910 Micro-Cinematography: Sleeping Sickness
A Sleep Walking Cure
Sleeping Pills
Sleepy Jones
Tweedledum's Sleeping Sickness
When Cupid Sleeps
When the World Sleeps

Sleeper
1905 The Deadwood Sleeper

Sleeper trunk
1909 The Mystery of the "Sleeper" Trunk

Sleepy Head, Mr.
1908 Mr. Sleepy Head

Sleepy Hollow
1896 Rip Leaving Sleepy Hollow
1908 The Legend of Sleepy Hollow

Sleeve
1909 The Empty Sleeve; or, Memories of By-Gone Days

Sleigh
1897 The First Sleigh-Ride
Sleighing in Central Park
Ye Merry Sleigh Bells
1898 A Fine Day for Sleighing, Boston
Merry Sleigh Bells
Sleighing Scene
1899 Jones' Interrupted Sleighride
Sleighing in the Park
Sleighing on Diamond Street
1900 New Sleighing Scene
1902 Dog Sleighing
Quebec Fire Department on Sleds
1903 The Peel River Indians with Their Dog Teams and Toboggan Sleighs on the Trail
A Sleigh Load of Squaws
Sleigh Riding
1904 Sleighing in Central Park, New York
1905 Winter Sports (Sports d'hiver: partie de traineaux)
1907 The Runaway Sleighbelle

Sleuth
1908 Old Sleuth, the Detective
1909 A Clever Sleuth
Female Sleuth
Sleuth and the Wig

Slicing
1901 Slicing Hams and Bacon

Slide
1897 The Aerial Slide at Coney Island
1899 Devil's Slide
A Slide for Life
Sliding Down Mount Washington
1901 Lubin's Animated Drop Curtain Announcing Slides
The Slippery Slide
1902 Horse Toboggan Slide
Kent House Slide
Lava Slides in Red Rock Canyon
Pike's Peak Toboggan Slide
Toboggan Slide
1903 Down the Bamboo Slide
Down the Slide
Rattan Slide and General View of Luna Park
Slide for Life, Luna Park
Snow-Plow Bucking a 15-foot Snow Slide
1904 Sliding Down Ice Mound at Niagara Falls
The Soubrette's Slide
1905 The Burglar's Slide for Life
Sliding River Craft over Boat Railway, River Thames

Slim
1910 Jack Fat and Jim Slim at Coney Island

Slip
1902 Ferryboat Entering Slip

Slip-Powder
1909 Slip-Powder

Slippers
1907 Cinderella (Cendrillon ou la pantoufle merveilleuse)
1909 A Pair of Slippers

Slippery
1898 A Slippery Landing
1901 The Slippery Slide
1907 Slippery Jim, the Burglar
1908 Slippery Jim's Repentance
1910 A Slippery Day
Slippery Jim

Slocum (Boat)
1904 The Slocum Disaster

Slope
1899 Down the Western Slope of the Canadian Rockies Through Kicking Horse Pass
The Eastern Slope of the Rockies, Passing Anthracite Station

Slow
1900 Slow but Sure
1907 Slow but Sure
1908 My Watch Is Slow
1910 My Maid Is Too Slow

Slug
1905 The Red Slug Worm

Sluice
1903 Sluice Mining on Gold Hill in the Klondike, Hutchinson and Johnstone's Claim of No. 6, Eldorado
1905 Sluicing in the Klondike

Slumberland
1908 Slumberland

Slumming
1908 Deceived Slumming Party

Slums
1907 Paris Slums
1909 The Honor of the Slums

Smack
1897 Fishing Smacks
1903 Fun on Board a Fishing Smack
1910 The Fishing Smack

Small
1899 Smallest Train in the World
1903 Chiquita, the Smallest Woman in the World
Small Boy and Bear, Hagenback's Circus
Small Boy and Lion Cub, Hagenback's Circus
1904 Smoker Too Small
1906 Maneuvering a Small Motor Boat
1908 What One Small Boy Can Do

Smart
1905 A Smart Captive
1907 A Smart Capture
1909 A Smart Trick

Smash
1901 Carrie Nation Smashing a Saloon
The Kansas Saloon Smashers
1903 Smashing a Jersey Mosquito
1904 Railroad Smashup
1907 A Mash a Smash a Splash
1910 The Baggage Smasher

Smells
1908 It Smells of Smoke

Smile
1903 Smiles and Tears
1909 Now Keep Smiling
Smile, Smile, Smile
1910 The Power of a Smile

Smith
1903 Smith's Wife Inspects the New Typewriter
1908 Mr. Smith, the New Recruit
Mr. Smith's Difficulties in the Shoe Store
Weather Changes at the Smiths
Why Smith Left Home
1910 "Salvation" Smith

Smith, Jim
1909 Jim Smith, the Champion Boxer

Smith, John
1906 Looking for John Smith

Smithers
1907 Mrs. Smithers' Boarding-School

Smithson
1907 Mrs. Smithson's Portrait

Smithy
1909 Satan's Smithy

Smitten
1910 Jupiter Smitten

Smoke
1897 His First Smoke
Smoking, Eating, and Drinking Scene
1898 Smoking Her Out
1899 Willie's First Smoke
1900 His Dad Caught Him Smoking
A Quiet Little Smoke
1902 Circular Panoramic View of St. Pierre from the Lighthouse, Showing Mt. Pelee Smoking in the Distance
Circular Panoramic View of St. Pierre, Showing the Ruins of the Catholic Cathedral and Mt. Pelee Smoking in the Background
Japanese Girl Smoking Cigarettes
Mt. Pelee Smoking Before Eruption [St. Pierre, Martinique]
Smoking Smokes
1903 Cadet's First Smoke
Colored Woman Smoking a Pipe
The Smoky Stove
Willie's First Smoke
1904 Boy's First Smoke
Smoked Out
Smoker Too Small
Study, Smoke and Soot
1906 The Opium Smoker's Dream
Opium Smoker's Dream
Panorama of San Francisco in Smoke and Fire
Substitute for Smoking
1907 Smoke Without Fire
The Smoking Chimney
Smoking Up
White Man's First Smoke; or, Puritan Days in America

1908 It Smells of Smoke
A Smoked Husband
The Smokeless Stove
"Who Is Smoking That Rope?"
1909 He Preferred to Smoke His Pipe
Old Sweethearts of Mine, a Phantasy in Smoke
Princess Nicotine; or, The Smoke Fairy
The Smoking Lamp
1910 Mind, I Catch You Smoking
No Smoking
The Smoker

Smooth
1903 True Love Never Runs Smooth
1909 True Love Never Runs Smoothly

Smuggle
1898 How a Bottle of Cocktails Was Smuggled into Camp
How the Ballet Girl Was Smuggled into Camp
1900 Where the Female Smuggler Hid the Lace
1904 The Smugglers
1906 Dogs Used as Smugglers
Secret Service; or, The Diamond Smugglers
1907 Chinese Slave Smuggling
Smuggled into America
The Smugglers
Smuggling Chinese into the U.S.A.
1908 Different Ways of Smuggling
The Smuggler Automobilist
The Smuggler's Daughter
1909 Meskal, the Smuggler
The Smuggler's Sweetheart
The Smuggler's Daughter
Unlucky Smuggler
1910 The Smuggler's Game

Smyrna (Turkey)
1908 Picturesque Smyrna

Snail
1905 Snail, Tortoise, Toad

Snake
1901 Carrying Out the Snakes
Line-Up and Teasing the Snakes
Moki Snake Dance by Walpapi Indians
Parade of Snake Dancers Before the Dance
1903 Ute Indian Snake Dance
Winter Sport on Snake River, Nome
1905 Among the Snakes
Fisherman, Eels or Snakes
A Snake in the Grass
1906 Snake Hunting
1909 Snake Skin Industry
Was It a Snake Bite?
1910 Romance of a Snake Charmer
The Snake Man
Spotted Snake's Schooling

Snap-the-whip
1898 Snap the Whip
"Snapping the Whip"
1901 Esquimaux Game of Snap-the-Whip

Snapshot
use **Photography**

Snare
1904 A Snare for Lovers

Snarleyow
1903 Snarleyow the Dog Fiend

Snatcher
1907 The Dog Snatcher

Sneeze
1894 Edison Kinetoscopic Record of a Sneeze, January 7, 1894
1904 That Terrible Sneeze
1905 Sneezing
1909 The Cyclone Sneezer
Strenuous Sneezer

Snicklefritz
1902 Snicklefritz Has a Hot Time

Snoqualmie Falls (Washington)
1903 Snoqualmie Falls

Snorer
1910 The Snorer

Snow
1898 Snow Storm
1899 Plowing Snow in the Park
1901 Duel in the Snow
1902 After the First Snow
Working Rotary Snow Ploughs on Lehigh Valley Railroad
1903 A Brush in the Snow
First Snow Storm of the Season, Valdez
A Rotary Snow Plow in the Great Northwest
Snow Fight
Snow-Plow Bucking a 15-foot Snow Slide
1905 The Red Snow Germs
1907 A Crime in the Snow
1909 Buttes Chaumont After a Snow Storm
Danish Capitol Under Snow
Lost in the Snow
Moscow Clad in Snow
1910 The Beautiful Snow
Drifts of Snow in Chamonix Valley
A Honeymoon Through Snow to Sunshine
Sports in the Snow

Snow, Phoebe
1906 Phoebe Snow

Snow White
1902 Snow White

Snowball
1898 Snowballing the Coasters
1899 Snowballing After School
1901 Snowballing Scene in Halifax
1903 Snowballing
1907 First Snowball
Snowballing
1908 Animated Snowballs
1909 Snowball

Snowbird
1908 The Snowbird

Snowden, General
1899 Gen. Snowden and Staff, and Crew of the U.S.S. "Raleigh"

Snowdon (Mountain), Wales
1904 Automobile Ascending Mt. Snowdon

Snowdrop
1903 Little Snowdrop
1910 Little Snowdrop

Snowfield
1905 Panorama of the Folgefond Snowfield, Norway

Snowman
1896 Snow Men
1908 The Snowman
1909 The Snow Man

Snowplow
1899 Rotary Snowplow in Action
1903 Snow-Plow Bucking a 15-foot Snow Slide

Snowshoes
1898 Canadian Artillery Marching on Snow Shoes
The Snow Shoe Club
1902 Cross-Country Running on Snow Shoes
Run of a Snow Shoe Club

Snowy Mountains
1910 Among the Snowy Mountains

Snuff
1903 Mrs. Schneider's First Pinch of Snuff
1908 Too Much Snuff

Soaker
1908 Mr. Soaker at the Seaside

Soap
1897 Making Soap Bubbles
Soap Bubbles
1903 How Mike Got the Soap in His Eyes
Soap vs. Blacking
1904 Soap Bubbles
1906 Soap Bubbles
1908 He Got Soap in His Eyes
1909 Marvelous Shaving Soap
1910 The Coalman's Soap
Soap in His Eyes

Social
1909 Their Social Education

Socialism
1906 Socialism and Nihilism

Society
1897 Society Girls Playing "Leap Frog"
1898 Imitation of a College Society Girl
1899 How N.Y. Society Girls Take to the Fad of Tattooing
1903 The Gerry Society's Mistake
1905 The King Planting a Tree at the Royal Agricultural Society's Show Yard
The Society Palmist
The Society Raffles
1906 Society Ballooning
1907 Congested Street Society
A Pig in Society
Tommy in Society
1908 Breaking into Society
Crowded Street-Congested Street Society
Peasant's Difficulties in Society
1909 "Mafia," the Secret Society; or, Sicilian Family Honor
Man with the Sack in Society
1910 A Society Sinner

Sock
1898 Socks or Stockings
1906 Sock

Sofa
1898 Girls Struggling for a Sofa
1908 The Sofa Bed

Softhead
1908 Mr. Softhead Has a Good Time

Soft-shoe
1903 Soft Shoe Dance

Soger
1904 The Bold Soger Boy

Sognia Fjord (Norway)
1907 Sailing thro the Sognia Fjord on a Steamer from Ballholm to Gudvangen [Norway]

Soho, London (England)
1905 Kiddies Dancing to Hurdy-Gurdy Music, Soho, London

Soil
1898 American Commissary Wagons Landing on Cuban Soil

Sojourn
1910 The Gunby's Sojourn in the Country

Soldering
1901 Soldering Cans

Soldier
1898 Brave Cubans Firing at Spanish Soldiers
15,000 Soldiers Reviewed by the President at Camp Alger May 28
French Soldiers in a Wall-Climbing Drill
A Letter from Her Soldier Lover
Playing Soldiers
Return of Our Soldier Boys
Soldiers at Play
Soldiers Firing on Train
Soldiers Washing Dishes
Spanish Infantry Attacking American Soldiers in Camp
Wounded Soldiers Embarking in Row Boats
1899 American Soldiers Defeating Filipinos Near Manila
How the Porto Rican Girls Entertain Uncle Sam's Soldiers
Soldiers of the Future
Welcoming the Soldier Boys
1900 Playing Soldier
Soldiers of Greater Britain
1901 Japanese Soldiers on the Taku Road
1902 A Dutch Soldier's Christmas Box
English Soldiers Exercising
German Soldiers Starting for War
Kaiser Wilhelm Inspecting His Soldiers
Mounted Soldiers Fording a River
Soldiers in the Strike District
1903 The American Soldier in Love and War
The American Soldier in Love and War [Number 1]
The American Soldier in Love and War [Number 2]
The American Soldier in Love and War [Number 3]
English Soldiers at Gun Drill
Only a Soldier Boy
Panorama of American Soldiers in Camp
Soldier's Dream
The Soldier's Return
1904 Fencing Contest Between Japanese Soldiers, Manchuria
Lahury, the Soldier
Life of an American Soldier
1905 Duel Between Japanese and Russian Soldiers
Soldier's Romance
1906 Dynamiting Ruins and Rescuing Soldier Caught in Falling Walls
Japanese Soldier's Return
1907 The Colonial Soldier
Roumania, Its Citizens and Soldiers
A Soldier Must Obey Orders
Soldier to Colonel
The Soldier's Dream
The Soldier's Helmet
A Soldier's Jealousy
1908 An American Soldier
The Amorous Soldier
The Marriage of a French Soldier
Soldier's Antics
Soldiers in the Italian Alps
Soldier's Love Token
The Soldier's Wedding
1909 A Day with Our Soldier Boys
Fancy Soldier

Southern Tunis
1910 Southern Tunis
Southwest
1910 Ranch Life in the Great South-West
Southwestern Limited
1902 Experimental. Southwestern Limited Train
Souvenir
1894 Souvenir Strip of the Edison Kinetoscope [Sandow, the Modern Hercules]
1910 Souvenirs of Paris
Sovereigns
1910 The Museum of Sovereigns
Sowing
1902 Sowing Seed on the Farm
Spades
1904 Metamorphosis of the King of Spades
1910 The Ten of Spades; or, A Western Raffle
Spain and Spaniards
1898 Admiral Cervera and Officers of the Spanish Fleet Leaving the "St. Louis"
Brave Cubans Firing at Spanish Soldiers
Capture of a Spanish Fort near Santiago
Execution of the Spanish Spy
Fun in a Spanish Camp
Spanish Ball Game
Spanish Battleship "Viscaya"
The Spanish Cruiser Vizcaya
Spanish Infantry Attacking American Soldiers in Camp
Spanish Sailors on the "St. Louis"
Spanish Volunteers in Havana
1899 Destruction of the Spanish Cruiser Maria Theresa
Repulse of Spanish Troops at Santiago
Spaniards Evacuating
1900 Bridge of Spain
Spanish Inquisition
1901 Spanish Coronation Royal Bull-Fight
Spanish Dancers at the Pan-American Exposition
1903 Odetta, Spanish Dance
Spanish Bull Fight
Spanish Dance
1906 Ascending Mt. Serrat in Spain
Descending Mt. Serrat in Spain
Marriage of Princess Ena and Alphonse XIII, King of Spain
Spanish Barbecue
Thibidado (Panorama de Thibidabo (Espagne))
1907 Drama in a Spanish Inn
The Spanish Lovers
Spanish Views, on Postals
1908 The Dancer and the King, a Romantic Story of Spain
A Love Tragedy in Spain
A Spanish Romance
1909 Conchita, the Spanish Belle
King of Spain
Love Under Spanish Skies
Spanish Army
Spanish Blood
The Spanish Girl
Spanish Marriage
The Man in the Moon (Clair de lune espagnol)
1910 An Episode of Napoleon's War with Spain
His Spanish Wife
Spanish Fandalgo
The Spanish Frontier
Spanish Loyalty
Spangled
1901 Star Spangled Banner by a Deaf Mute
1908 Under the Star Spangled Banner
Spanish-American War
1899 Col. John Jacob Astor, Staff and Veterans of the Spanish-American War
Spanishtown (Jamaica)
1903 Railroad Panorama near Spanishtown, Jamaica
Spanking
1898 Spanking the Naughty Girl
1899 Why Clara Was Spanked
Sparks
1900 Two Old Sparks
Sparring
1896 Sparring Contest, Canastota, N.Y.
1901 Bolster Sparring
Jeffries and Ruhlin Sparring Contest at San Francisco, Cal., Nov. 15, 1901—Five Rounds
Jeffries Sparring with His Brother
Ruhlin Sparring in His Training Quarters
1903 Sparring Exhibition on Board the U.S.S. "Alabama"
Sparring Match on the "Kearsarge"
1905 Sparring at the N.Y.A.C.
Sparrows
1903 Feeding the Sparrows
Spartacus
1909 Spartacus
Speak
1906 Letters Which Speak
1908 Parlez Vous Francais? (Do You Speak French?)
1910 The Pit That Speaks
Spearing
1903 Spearing Salmon in the Rivers of the North West Territory
Special
1896 Special Photographing Train
1899 2nd Special Service Battalion, Canadian Infantry, Embarking for So. Africa
2nd Special Service Battalion, Canadian Infantry-Parade
1903 Special Delivery Messenger, U.S.P.O.
1908 Special Muto Reel Mellin's Food Co.
1909 Special License
Special Peary Film
1910 The President's Special
The Special Agent
Spectacle
1903 An Unusual Spectacle
Spectacles
use **Glass**
Spectacular
1899 A Spectacular Start
1905 Spectacular Scenes During a New York City Fire
Spectators
1905 Spectators Leaving the Theatre Vevey
Specter
1903 Jewelry Robbery (Le spectre)
1907 The Red Spectre
1908 The Specter
1909 Dream Spectres
Speeches
1901 President McKinley's Speech at the Pan-American Exposition
1903 President Mitchell's Speech
The Stump Speaker
1904 Speech by President Francis, World's Fair
1908 Lincoln's Speech at Gettysburg
Political Speeches
1910 The Minister's Speech
Speed
1900 At Break-Neck Speed
Speed Trial of the "Albatross"
Trial Speed of H. M. Torpedo Boat Destroyer "Viper"
1902 "Deutschland" Leaving New York at Full Speed [with Prince Henry of Prussia]
1903 At Terrific Speed
1904 Speed Test W. K. Vanderbilt, Jr.'s "Tarantula"
1905 Speed Trial of Auto Boat Challenger, Lake Worth, Fla.
1910 Speed Versus Death
Speedway
1900 Above the Speedway
A Brush on the Speedway
A Speedway Parade
1901 Parade on the Speedway
Washington Bridge and Speedway
1902 On the Speedway
The Speedway Parade
1904 The Philadelphia Speedway
1909 Atlanta Automobile Speedway Races
Spelling
1910 C-H-I-C-K-E-N Spells Chicken
Spells
1910 The Broken Spell
Spending
1908 Spending a Holiday
Spice
1900 Employees of Wolfson's Spice Mills, Toledo
Spider
1899 The Spider and the Fly
1910 The Gold Spider
Spike
1897 "Spike, the Bag-Punching Dog"
1908 The Luckless Spike
1910 Spike's Battle
Spill
1898 A Terrible Spill
1902 A Spill
A Spill from an Ice Yacht
1903 Spilled Milk
Spilt Milk
Spinkles
1903 Old Gentleman Spinkles
Spinning
1900 Clowns Spinning Hats
1905 Old Spinning Wheel, Dooagh, Achill Island, Ireland
1907 Diabolo, the Japanese Top Spinner
Spinster
1898 Spinster's Waterloo
Spion Kop (South Africa)
1900 Lord Dundonald's Cavalry Seizing a Kopje in Spion Kop
Spirit
1899 Spirits in the Kitchen
The Wizard and the Spirit of the Tree
1900 Spirit of the Empire
1903 Summoning the Spirits
The House of Mystery (L'antre des esprits)
1905 Spirit of '76
1907 Elks' Convention Parade: "Spirit of '76" and Views of the Grand Stand
1908 Antics of Two Spirited Citizens
The Spirit
The Spirit of '76
1909 A Case of Spirits; or, All's Well That Ends Well
The Evil Spirit in a Girl's Boarding School
The Stepmother: the Spirit of Unkindness and Jealousy Thwarted
1910 Spirit of the Sword
Spirit of the West
Spiritualism
1900 Visit to a Spiritualist
A Visit to the Spiritualist
1903 A Spiritualistic Photographer
The Up-to-Date Spiritualism
1906 A Spiritualistic Meeting
1908 Spiritualistic Seance
Spit
1909 From the Egg to the Spit
Spital Barracks
1899 Her Majesty, Queen Victoria, Reviewing the Household Cavalry at Spital Barracks
Spite
1908 The Spiteful Groom
1909 Stolen for Spite
Spitfire
1910 The Spitfire
Spithead (England)
1897 German Warship at Spithead
H. M. S. Powerful at Spithead
1898 Naval Review Spithead
1902 King Edward Reviewing Coronation Naval Force at Spithead August 16, 1902
Splash
1907 A Mash a Smash a Splash
1908 The Little Mad-Cap; or, Oh Splash!
Spleen
1908 Tommy Has the Spleen
Splits
1898 Learning To Do Splits
Splitting
1901 Hog Slaughtering. No. 6: Opening and Splitting
Spoil
1899 How Tottie Coughdrop's Summer Suit Was Spoiled
1907 Union Workers Spoil the Food
1908 [The Spoilers]
1909 The Spoilt Child
1910 Greediness Spoiled Foolshead's Christmas
Spokane (Boat)
1905 The "Spokane's" Passengers Descending the Gangplank at Killisnoo Alaska
Spokane (Washington)
1903 Riverside Avenue, Spokane, Wash.
Spokane Falls, Spokane
1904 Panoramic View of Spokane Falls
Sponge
1909 The Sponge Fishers of Cuba
Spontaneous
1904 Amusing Changes (Transformations spontanées)

Earl Roberts and Staff
Major-General Arthur MacArthur and Staff
1901 Headquarters, Staff and Band, Ohio State
The War in China—Von Waldersee and Staff
1909 The Emperor's Staff Officer

Stag
1902 The Great Stag Hunt
1903 A Majestic Stag
The Stag Hunt
Stag Hunting in England
With the Stag Hounds
1906 Exmore Stag Hunt
1907 The New Stag Hunt
1909 Grand Stag Hunting
1910 A Stag Hunt in Java

Stage
1905 Behind the Stage
1907 On the Stage; or, Melodrama from the Bowery
Stage Struck
1908 At the Stage Door; or, Bridget's Romance
Buncoed Stage Johnnie
Stage Memories of an Old Theatrical Trunk
1909 A Stage Romance; or, An Actor's Love
1910 All the World's a Stage
Behind the Scenes of the Cinema Stage
The Stage Note

Stagecoaches
rt **Coaches**
Mail coaches
1899 Glen House Stage
Stage Coaches Leaving the Hotel Victoria
1901 Soubrette's Troubles on a Fifth Avenue Stage Coach
Stage Coach Hold-Up in the Days of '49
1902 Runaway Stage Coach
1903 Stage Hold-Up
1904 Western Stage Coach Hold Up
1905 Arrival of the Stage at Wawona Hotel, Enroute to Yosemite
The Hold-Up of the Leadville Stage
Stage Coaches, Yellowstone Park
Stage Enroute to Hance's Camp, Grand Cañon of Arizona
Stages Leaving Fountain House, Yellowstone Park
Stages Passing Through Wawona Big Tree, Mariposa Grove, California
1908 The Stage Rustler
1909 The Stage Driver
Bandits of the Atlas Gorges (Dans les gorges de l'atlas (attaque d'une diligence))
1910 Stage Coach Tom

Stages
1908 Matrimonial Stages

Stagestruck
1908 The Stage-Struck Daughter

Stairs
1904 A Scandal on the Staircase
1905 Girls and Moving Stairway
1909 The Bear in the Staircase

Stake
1901 Finish of Flatbush Stakes, Gravesend Track
The Matron Stakes
1903 Juvenile Stakes
Reliance and Shamrock III Turning Outer Stake in Second Race
1904 Avenging a Crime; or, Burned at the Stake

Stake boat
1899 "Columbia" and "Defender" Rounding Stake-Boat
"Shamrock" and "Columbia" Rounding the Outer Stake Boat
"Shamrock" and "Columbia" Rounding the Outer Stake Boat, No. 2
Turning Stake Boat; "Columbia" and "Shamrock"
1901 "Columbia" and "Shamrock II": Turning the Outer Stake Boat
1903 Stake Boat with Stake ("John Scully")

Stalheim (Norway)
1905 Tourists on the Road to Hotel Stalheim, Norway
Waterfall from the Road, Stalheim, Norway

Stalking
1906 Deer Stalking with a Camera

Stallion
1900 Stallion Championship

Stamboul, Istanbul (Turkey)
1909 Burning of Stamboul, Constantinople

Stamp
1903 Buying Stamps from Rural Wagon, U.S.P.O.
Transporting Internal Rev. Stamps, U.S.P.O.
1906 The Trading Stamp Craze
1907 Animated Stamp Pad
1909 Collection of Stamps

Stampede
1901 Bull on the Stampede
1909 The Stampede

Stamping
1901 Stamping Tin

Stand
1897 Standing in Stirrups
1898 The Last Stand
1899 Admiral Dewey Passing Catholic Club Stand
1903 President McKinley and His Cabinet on the Reviewing Stand, at Fairmount Park, Phila., May 27, 1899
1905 Masher and Oyster Stand
1907 One-Night Stand
Panorama, Crowds at Squires-Burns International Contest, from Moving Picture Stand, July 4th, 1907
1909 On the Little Big Horn; or, Custer's Last Stand
1910 Custer's Last Stand

Standard
1897 A "Standard" Picture Animated
1900 Burning of the Standard Oil Co.'s Tanks, Bayonne, N.J.
Burning of the Standard Oil Tanks
1904 The Japanese Standard Bearer
The Military Funeral of the "Standard Bearer of the Yalu"
1908 The Standard Bearer

Standish, Miles
1907 The Wooing of Miles Standish
1910 The Courtship of Miles Standish

Stanford University (California)
1897 Stanford University, California

Stanley, Lord
1910 Young Lord Stanley

Star Spangled Banner
1901 Star Spangled Banner by a Deaf Mute
1908 Under the Star Spangled Banner

Star Theatre (New York City)
1901 Demolishing and Building Up the Star Theatre

Stars
1899 Fatima, Star of the Orient
1903 Quadrille in Drawers (Quadrille dansé par les etoiles du Moulin-Rouge. 1. En jupon)
1904 White Star S.S. Baltic Leaving Pier on First Eastern Voyage
The Passion Play (L'etoile mystérieuse)
Vision of Art (La fée aux etoiles)
1906 Voyage Around a Star
1908 The Legend of Stars
1909 The Red Star Inn
The Star of Bethlehem
1910 Runaway Star
Starlight's Devotion

Stars and Stripes
1903 Dear Old Stars and Stripes, Goodbye
1909 Sheltered Under Stars and Stripes
1910 The Stars and Stripes
Under the Stars and Bars
Under the Stars and Stripes

Start
1896 Starting for the Fire
1898 A Poor Start
Tourists Starting for Canton
1899 Shamrock and Columbia Jockeying for a Start
Shamrock Starting on Trial Trip
A Spectacular Start
Start of Race Between "Columbia" and "Shamrock"
Start of Second Cup Race
Start of the Second Cup Race
Start of Third Day's Race
1900 A Career of Crime, No. 1: Start in Life
1901 "Columbia" and "Shamrock II": Jockeying and Starting
"Columbia" and "Shamrock II": Start of Second Race
"Columbia" and "Shamrock II": Starting in the Third Race
International Track Athletic Meeting—Start and Finish of the One Mile Run
Shamrock's Start
Start of the Third Cup Race
1902 German Soldiers Starting for War
Starting a Skyscraper
1903 Jockeying and Start of Yacht[s] Aug. 25th
Jockeying for the Start Aug. 20
Jockeying for the Start Aug. 22
"Reliance" and "Shamrock" III Jockeying and Starting in First Race
Start from the House and the Run
Start of Endurance Run of the Automobile Club of America
Start of Race—"Reliance" Ahead
Start of the First Race, Aug. 22
Start of the Gordon-Bennet Cup Race
Tourists Starting on Donkeys for the Pyramids of Sakkarah
1905 Coaches Starting from Larne and Passing Through Tunnel on the Antrim Coast Road
The "Crazy" Tourists Starting for the Trail, Yosemite Valley
Start of Ocean Race for Kaiser's Cup
Starting on a Coyote Hunt
1907 False Start
A Glorious Start
1908 Starting of Around the World Automobile Race
1910 A Fresh Start

Startle
1898 The Startled Lover
1899 The Startled Lover
1904 Startling Pursuit
1908 The Red Barn Mystery: A Startling Portrayal of the Great Marie Martin Mystery

Starving
1906 Military Feeding Starving and Destitute Refugees in Golden Gate Park
The Starvelings
1907 The Starving Artist, or, Realism in Art
1908 Starvelings

State
1896 Empire State Express No. 2
1897 Pennsylvania State Militia, Double Time
Pennsylvania State Militia, Single Time
1898 Grand Commandery of the State of New York
State Fencibles, Pennsylvania
1899 State Fencibles
1901 Farragut Naval Post, Ohio State
The First Procession in State of H. M. King Edward VII
First Procession in State of H. M. King Edward VII
Headquarters, Staff and Band, Ohio State
McKinley Funeral—In Solemn State
1903 Feeding Brook Trout at the Pennsylvania State Fishery
View of State Street
1904 Japanese State Procession
Pan. of St. Railway Building, Pittsburg, Pa.
1905 Mobilization of the Massachusetts State Troops
1909 State Secret
The State Secret

State fair
1910 [Roosevelt at the Arkansas State Fair]

State House, Boston (Massachusetts)
1899 Admiral Dewey at State House, Boston
McKinley Leaving State House, Boston

State Street, Chicago (Illinois)
1897 Corner Madison and State Streets, Chicago
1903 State and Madison Sts., Chicago

Staten Island (New York City)
1905 [Launching the Ferryboat Richmond—Staten Island]

Station
1896 Train Coming out of Station, Philadelphia, Pa.
1897 Fort Hill Fire Station
1898 The Christian Herald's Relief Station, Havana
Railway Station at Yokohama
Worthing Life-Saving Station
1899 The Eastern Slope of the Rockies, Passing Anthracite Station

1909 Strenuous Sneezer
1910 Strenuous Massage

Stretcher
1904 Stretcher Race over Obstacles

Stricken
1908 Stricken Blind; or, To Forgive Is Divine
1909 Stricken Blind

Strictly
1903 Strictly Fresh Eggs

Strikes
1900 The Croton Dam Strike
A Strike in a Dime Museum
1902 Soldiers in the Strike District
1904 The Strike
1906 A Coal Strike
1907 The Blacksmith's Strike
Nurses' Strike
Servant's Strike
1908 The Baby Strike
1909 Bridget on Strike
Cops on a Strike
School Children's Strike
Strike Time in Paris
The Strikers
1910 The Girl Strike Leader
The Shirtwaist Strike
Strike Instigator

Striking
1897 Projectile from Ten Inch Disappearing Gun Striking Water, Sandy Hook
1898 When the Clock Strikes Two in the Tenderloin
1909 A Striking Resemblance

String
1901 A Little Piece of String
1904 Tied to Her Apron Strings
1907 A Little Bit of String

Strip
1894 Souvenir Strip of the Edison Kinetoscope [Sandow, the Modern Hercules]

Stripes
1903 Dear Old Stars and Stripes, Goodbye
1909 The Sergeant's Stripes
Sheltered Under Stars and Stripes
1910 His Sergeant's Stripes
The Stars and Stripes
Under the Stars and Stripes

Stripping
1903 Stripping Pike Perch U.S.F.C.
Stripping Shad U.S.F.C.
1907 Stripped-Stripped
1909 Stripping a Forest in Winter

Strogoff, Michael
1908 Michael Strogoff
1910 Michael Strogoff

Stroke
1908 On the Stroke of Twelve

Strolling
1904 "While Strolling in the Park"
1909 Strolling Players
1910 The Strolling Players

Strong
1904 Getting Strong; or, The Soubrette's Home Gymnasium
1907 The Strength of Cheese
1908 A Strong Gale
1909 Love Stronger Than Revenge
The Master Detective; or, The Attack on the Strong Room
The Reason of the Strongest
The Strength of Love
A Strong Diet
A Strong Draught
The Strong Tonic
A Strong Woman's Lover
Stronger Than Death
1910 Love Is Stronger Than Life
She Required Strength and Got It
The Strength of Duty
The Stronger Sex
The Strongest
The Strongest Tie

Strongmen
1903 Max Unger, the Strong Man
1907 The Strong Man
1908 My Daughter Will Only Marry a Strong Man
The Strong Man's Discretion
1910 The Strong Man

Strozzi, Louise
1910 Louise Strozzi

Struck
1907 Stage Struck
1908 Struck

Struggle
1898 Girls Struggling for a Sofa
1907 Struggle for Life
1910 The Struggle of Two Souls

Stubborn
1909 Mr. Stubborn
1910 The Stubborn Lover

Stubs
1910 He Stubs His Toe

Stuck
use **Stick**

Stud
1902 The Stud Farm, No. 1
The Stud Farm, No. 2
The Stud Farm, No. 3
Stud Pony
1910 Algerian Stud

Student
1904 Our Jolly French Students
1906 The Paris Students
1907 Art Student's Frivolities
1908 Student's Joke on the Porter
Students' Jokes
The Student's Prank; or, A Joke on His Parents
Student's Predicament
1909 Student Days
The Student's Predicament
1910 The Poor Student

Studio
1899 Lunch Time in the Studio
1900 What the Jay Saw in the Studio
Wifie Invades the Studio
1902 Rube's Visit to the Studio
1903 Animated Picture Studio
The Artist's Studio
The Sculptor's Studio
1907 Delirium in a Studio

Study
1900 "Art Studies"
1901 Laboratory Study
Nature Study, the Rabbit
1902 A Study in Openwork
1904 Art Studies
Study, Smoke and Soot
1905 A Study in Feet
1910 Floral Studies

Stuff
1908 Nasty Sticky Stuff
1910 The Stuff That Americans Are Made Of

Stuffing
1901 Stuffing Cans by Machinery
Stuffing Sausage

Stump
1903 The Stump Speaker

Stung
1908 Stung
1909 Stung by a Bee
1910 Both Were Stung
Stung!

Stunning
1901 Stunning Cattle
1905 Stunning Creations

Stunts
1910 Stunts on Skates

Stupendous
1906 Stupendous Jugglers

Stupid
1908 Stupid Mr. Cupid

Sturdy
1908 Sturdy Sailor's Honor

Sturgis, Lucille
1900 Lucille Sturgis

Style
1905 Modern Style House Maids
1906 Old and New Style Conjurors
1908 Latest Style Airship
1909 New Style Airship
1910 New Style Inkwell

Subjects
1900 South African War Subjects
1904 A Subject for the Rogue's Gallery
1906 Naval Subjects, Merchant Marine, and From All over the World
1909 Hypnotic Subject

Sublime
1908 Macbeth, Shakespeare's Sublime Tragedy

Submarine
1902 Exploding a Submarine Mine
1903 Submarine Diver
1904 English Submarine Boat Disaster
Holland Submarine Boat Tests
1908 In a Submarine
Under the Sea in a Submarine
1910 Submarines in Paris
The Sunken Submarine
U.S. Submarine "Salmon"

Subpoena
1906 The Subpoena Server

Substation
1903 Delivering Mail from Sub-Station [U.S.P.O.]

Substitute
1906 Substitute for Smoking
1907 The Substitute Drug Clerk
Unlucky Substitution
1908 The Door-Keeper's Substitute
The Substitute
The Substitute Automatic Servant
1909 Substitute Pig
Unpleasant Substitution
An Unsuccessful Substitution
1910 Aunt Maria's Substitute
A Postal Substitute
Sandy the Substitute

Subterfuge
1910 The Subterfuge

Subub
1903 Subub Surprises the Burglar

Suburbs
1897 Suburban Handicap, 1897
1899 The Suburban
1900 Love in the Suburbs
The Suburban of 1900
1902 Native Bull Cart at Morne Rouge (A Suburb of St. Pierre)
Natives Unloading a Boat of Fire-Wood at Carbet (A Suburb of St. Pierre)
The Suburban of 1902
1903 "Africander" Winning the Suburban Handicap, 1903
1904 The Suburbanite
1907 Puck's Pranks on Suburbanite
1908 The Suburbanite's Ingenious Alarm

Subway
1897 Boston's Subway
1901 Panoramic View of Boston Subway from an Electric Car
1902 New York's New Subway
1903 Reading Subway
Rock Drill at Work in Subway
1904 City Hall to Harlem in 15 Seconds, via the Subway Route
Opening Ceremonies, New York Subway, October 27, 1904
1905 Interior N.Y. Subway, 14th St. to 42nd St.
Reuben in the Subway
2 A.M. in the Subway
1908 A Ride in a Subway

Success
1907 First Success
1909 If at First You Don't Succeed
Jack's Successful Bluff
1910 The Failure of Success

Sucker
1908 Sammy's Sucker

Suckling
1899 Suckling Pigs

Sudan
1902 Arrival of Major Marchand from the Soudan
A Schoolroom in the Soudan
1908 Native Life in Sudan
Walks in Soudan
1910 Lost in the Soudan

Sudden
1901 Love's Ardor Suddenly Cooled
1909 McGinty's Sudden Rise
1910 A Sudden Telephone Call

Suds
1901 Soot Versus Suds

Sue
1909 Saucy Sue
1910 Sunshine Sue

Suez Canal
1903 Building the Suez Canal

Suffer
1901 A Patient Sufferer
1903 Passion Play: Suffer Little Children to Come Unto Me

Surrender
1898 Surrender of General Toral
1905 Surrender at Port Arthur
Surrounded
1898 Pope Leo XIII Being Seated Bestowing Blessing Surrounded by Swiss Guards, No. 107
Surroundings
1902 Panoramic View of Westminster Abbey and Surroundings
1906 Vertical Panorama City Hall and Surroundings
1908 Palermo and Its Surroundings
1909 Surroundings of Copenhagen
1910 Nantes and Its Surroundings
Surveys
1910 She Surveys Her Son-in-Law
Survivor
1909 The Survivor's Story
Susan
1907 Susan Tastes Our Wine
Susceptible
1908 Susceptible Youth
Susie
1904 Pull Down the Curtain, Susie
Susie (Boat)
1903 Steamer Susie Excursion to Moosehide
Suspension
1899 Rapids below Suspension Bridge
1901 Circular Panorama of Suspension Bridge and American Falls
1903 Panorama Looking Down Niagara from New Suspension Bridge
Wonderful Suspension and Evolution
Suspicion
1908 Mrs. Stebbins' Suspicions Unfounded
Suspicious Husband
1909 The Suspicious Fencing Master
Under Suspicion
1910 Suspicion
Susquehanna River
1897 Panorama of Susquehanna River Taken from the Black Diamond Express
Sutro
1897 Sutro Baths, No. 1
Sutro Baths, No. 2
Swallow
1907 The Sham Sword Swallower
1909 Baby Swallows a Nickel
1910 Swallowed by the Deep
Swan song
1910 Mario's Swan Song
Swans
1903 Feeding the Swans
1910 The Blue Swan Inn
Swashbuckler
1908 Swashbuckler
Swearing
1904 Swearing in Recruits
Sweating
1901 Sweating Cans
Sweden and Swedes
1901 Winter Life in Sweden
1902 Skate Sailing in Sweden
Skiing in Stockholm, Sweden
1903 Swedish Gymnastics at Chautauqua. No. 8
1905 Deer in Wild Park, Goteborg, Sweden
Falls at Trollhattan, Sweden
1907 Ice Cutting in Sweden
Swedish Sports
1908 Stone Industry in Sweden
Sweden
Swedish Dances
Yens Yensen, The Swedish Butcher Boy; or, Mistaken for a Burglar
1909 In Southern Sweden
Life in Dalerne (Sweden)
Sweden—Gotha Canal
Winter Sports and Games at Stockholm, Sweden, 1909
1910 Winter Days in Sweden
Sweep
1901 Street Sweeping Brigade
1903 Bootblack and Crossing Sweeper
A Sweep Across New York
Sweet
1899 The Sweet Girl Graduate
1902 "A Sweet Little Home in the Country"
1903 Sweets for the Sweet
1905 A Sweet Kiss
1906 Kisses Sweet
1909 For Love's Sweet Sake
Love's Sweet Melody
Sweet and Twenty
Sweet Dreams Intermingled with Nightmares
Sweet Revenge
Sweet Toothed Dogs
1910 Her Sweet Revenge
Love's Old Sweet Song
Sweetheart
1902 Sweethearts
1905 Old Sweethearts
1908 Bertie's Sweetheart
Cabby's Sweetheart
His Sweetheart When a Boy
His Sweetheart's Birthday
The Robber's Sweetheart
The Sailor's Sweetheart
The Signalman's Sweetheart
Wouldn't You Like to Have Me for a Sweetheart
1909 The Anarchist's Sweetheart
The Artist's Model's Sweetheart
A Cowboy's Sweetheart
For Her Sweetheart's Sake
Four Sweethearts
The Mexican Sweethearts
Old Sweethearts of Mine, a Phantasy in Smoke
Saved by His Sweetheart
The Smuggler's Sweetheart
Sweetheart's Bouquet
Sweetheart's Christmas
A Wartime Sweetheart
1910 The Cow Puncher's Sweetheart
The Cowboy's Sweetheart
The Cowboy's Sweetheart and the Bandit
An Engineer's Sweetheart
The Engineer's Sweetheart
A Forester's Sweetheart
Her Soldier Sweetheart
His Gypsy Sweetheart
His Wife's Sweethearts
The Messenger Boy's Sweetheart
A Miner's Sweetheart
The Miner's Sweetheart
Muggsy's First Sweetheart
The Painter's Sweetheart
A Soldier's Sweetheart
Sweets
1898 Stolen Sweets
1903 Sweets for the Sweet
Swell
1907 A Swell Time
1910 Mr. Swell in the Country
Swift
1898 A Swift Chappie
Swim
1897 Golding Sisters, Champion Swimmers
1898 Mules Swimming Ashore at Daiquiri, Cuba
Queer Fish That Swim in the Sea
1899 Colonel Funston Swimming the Baglag River
Professor Billy Opperman's Swimming School
1901 Swimming Pool at Coney Island
1902 Carlysle D. Graham Swimming the Whirlpool Rapids
Cavalry Swimming Columbia River
The Swimming Ducks at Allentown [Pa.] Duck Farm
1903 C. D. Graham Swimming the Lower Rapids
Egyptian Boys in Swimming Race
Horses Swimming Copper River
Swimming School
Wharf Scene and Natives Swimming at St. Thomas, D.W.I.
1904 Bullocks Swimming
Holbein Swimming the English Channel
The Swimming Class
Swimming Horses
A Swimming Race at Coney Island
1905 In the Swimming Pool, Palm Beach, Fla.
1906 The Old Swimming Hole
1908 Military Swimming Championship
The Swimming Lesson
The Swimming Master
1910 The Ole Swimmin Hole
Swindler
1908 A Fake Diamond Swindler
1910 The Diamond Swindler
Swine
1907 The Dancing Swine
Swing
1897 Girls Swinging
Three Jolly Girls and the Fun They Had with the Old Swing
1898 Around the Big Swing
1900 The Mystic Swing
1901 Club Swinging, Carlisle Indian School
1904 Putting Up the Swing
The Swing
1905 The Angler's Nightmare (Le cauchemar du pêcheur ou l'escarpolette fantastique)
1909 The Mystic Swing
Swiss Family Robinson
1903 Swiss Family Robinson
Switchback
1898 A Ride on a Switchback
1902 Panoramic View of Switchback, Mauch Chunk
Switzerland and the Swiss
1898 Pope Leo XIII Being Seated Bestowing Blessing Surrounded by Swiss Guards, No. 107
1900 Scene in the Swiss Village at Paris Exposition
Swiss Village, No. 2
1901 Great Waterfall of the Rhein at Schaffhausen, Switzerland
1902 Panoramic View of the Alps, Switzerland
1903 Cascade in Switzerland
Lake Lucerne, Switzerland
Panorama of Schellenen Gorge of Switzerland
Panoramic View of Geneva, Switzerland
A Swiss Carnival
Swiss Family Robinson
Swiss Training and Breeding Home for St. Bernard Dogs
1904 Panoramic View of Montreux, Switzerland
1905 Panorama from Moving Train on Albula Railway, Switzerland
Panorama from Moving Train on Murren Electric Railway, Switzerland
Panorama of Eismeer, Switzerland
Sunset Clouds over Monte Rosa, Switzerland
Tourists Party on the Axenstrasse Switzerland
Trains on Rigi Railway, Switzerland
1906 Engadin in Switzerland
Trip Through Switzerland
1907 Winter in Switzerland
1908 Ascending Mt. Pilatus in Switzerland
Going to Switzerland
Picturesque Switzerland
Swiss Alps
Swiss Peasants' Festival
1909 An Alpine Echo; or, The Symphony of a Swiss Music Box
Sportsmen in Switzerland
Switzerland, Conquering the Alps
William Tell: The Liberator of Switzerland
1910 The Swiss Guide
Sword
nt **Broadsword**
1898 American Cavalry Charging with Drawn Swords
1899 Presentation of Nation's Sword to Admiral Dewey
1902 Magical Sword
1903 Broad Sword Contest
Egyptian Sword Dance
Japanese Sword Fight
Miss Jessie Cameron, Champion Child Sword Dancer
A Two Handed Sword Contest
1904 Duel Scene, "By Right of Sword"
A Fierce Sword Combat at Tokio
1907 The Sham Sword Swallower
1908 Charmed Sword
Electric Sword
1909 Fairy Sword
The Sword and the King
1910 The Invincible Sword
The Kiss Was Mightier Than the Sword
Spirit of the Sword
A Wooden Sword
Sydney (Australia)
1909 The American Fleet at Sydney, New South Wales

Terror (Boat)
1898 Monitor "Terror"
The Monitor "Terror"
1903 U.S. Monitor Terror
Tessa
1910 The Heart of Tessa
Testimony
1910 His Wife's Testimony
Tests
1899 Test. Coney Island Athletic Club
1901 A Good Test of High Explosives
Machine and Can Tester
Testing Cans by Machinery
Testing Hams
Testing Horses
3 Can Testers (side view)
United States Government Gun Test
1903 Eclipse Car Fender Test
Testing Jacks, National Cash Register Co.
1904 Assembling and Testing Turbines, Westinghouse Works
Electric Locomotive Tests and Races, Schenectady, N.Y.
Eye Tests, etc., Recruiting
Holland Submarine Boat Tests
Speed Test W. K. Vanderbilt, Jr.'s "Tarantula"
Testing a Rotary, Westinghouse Works
Testing Gas Engine, Westinghouse Works
Testing Large Turbines, Westinghouse Co. Works
Testing Steam Engine, Westinghouse Works
1907 Testing of a Lifeboat
1908 Faithful to the Test
A Magician's Love Test
The Test of Friendship
1909 The Fish Pirates; or, The Game Warden's Test
The Test
1910 An Indian's Test
Testing Their Love
Tex
1908 Texas Tex
Texas
1898 A Texas Steer
1903 The Dance of the Little Texas Magnet
1908 Texas Tex
1909 A Tale of Texas
1910 The Man from Texas
A Texas Joke
Texas (Boat)
1897 Battleship "Texas"
1898 Battleship Texas
Broadsword Exercise on the Battleship Texas
Captain Sigsbee on Deck of the U.S. Battleship Texas
Cleaning and Firing of the Hotchkiss Revolving Cannon on the Battleship Texas
Crew of the Battleship Texas
Red Cross Steamer "Texas"
Reviewing the "Texas" at Grant's Tomb
The "Texas," Naval Parade
U.S. Battleship Texas
Thailand and the Thai
1909 The Grand Procession at the King of Siam Jubilee
Siamese Actors and Actresses Play a Siamese Drama
Street Life in North Siam
Thames River (England)
1901 Panoramic View of the Thames
1903 Panorama of Thames River
1905 Accelerated Panorama from Steamer on the Thames, London
Panorama from Moving Steamer on the River Thames, England
Sliding River Craft over Boat Railway, River Thames
1909 Moonlight on the Thames
The Thames in Winter
1910 Up the Thames to Westminster
Thanks
1910 Let Us Give Thanks
Their Day of Thanks
Thanksgiving
1903 Hooligan's Thanksgiving Dinner (Thumb Book)
1908 On Thanksgiving Day
The Parson's Thanksgiving Dinner
The Tale of a Thanksgiving Turkey
The Thanksgiving Turkey
1909 Dooley's Thanksgiving Turkey
Thanksgiving, Then and Now
Thanksgiving Turkey
Three Thanksgivings
1910 His Mother's Thanksgiving
A Thanksgiving Surprise
Thaw, Harry
1906 Thaw-White Tragedy
1907 The Unwritten Law: A Thrilling Drama Based on the Thaw White Case
Theater
1897 Keith's Theatre
Theatre Hat
Theatre Hats Off
1898 Theatre Road, Yokohama
1899 Orpheum Theatre, San Francisco
1900 Keith's Theater, London
Orpheum Theatre
1901 Demolishing and Building Up the Star Theatre
The Empire Theatre
Rubes in the Theatre
Two Rubes at the Theatre
1902 B. F. Keith's New Million Dollar Theatre
The Devil's Theatre
Two Germans in a Theatre
1903 Mephisto's Theatre
Old Maid's First Visit to a Theatre
1904 A Fire in a Burlesque Theatre
Iroquois Theatre Fire in Chicago
1905 Crowds Leaving Theatre, Oberammergau
Panorama of the Theatre, Vevey Fete
Panorama of Theatre, Vevey Fete
Spectators Leaving the Theatre Vevey
1906 Earthquake Ruins, New Majestic Theatre and City Hall
Miniature Theatre
Ruins Bulletin Building, California Theatre and Evening Post
1907 Skating on N.Y. Theatre Roof
1908 A Pleasant Evening at the Theatre
Stage Memories of an Old Theatrical Trunk
1909 Bob's Electric Theater
The Joneses Have Amateur Theatricals
Skylight Theater Seat
1910 The Theater of Phenomenons
Thebes
1908 The Prophetess of Thebes
Theft
use **Thieves**
Thelly
1909 Thelly's Heart
Thelma
1910 Thelma
Theodora
1909 Theodora
1910 Justinian and Theodora
Theodore
1909 Theodore Yearns to be a Tough
Thermometer
1906 Love's Thermometer
Thibet
use **Tibet**
Thibidado (Spain)
1906 Thibidado
Thick
1903 Poor Girl, It Was a Hot Night and the Mosquitos Were Thick
Thieves
1897 Chicken Thieves
1899 The "Make-Up" Thief
1900 "Stop Thief!"
The Thief and the Pie Woman
A Thief in a Soubrette's Boarding House
1902 Ali Baba and the Forty Thieves
The Burlesque Thieves
The Chicken Thief
1903 Chicken Thief
Clown and Beer-Thief
Stop Thief
1904 The Chicken Thief
Fisherman, Gendarmes and Bike Thief
Stop Thief!
1905 The Horse-Thief
Stop Thief!
1906 The Automobile Thieves
Juvenile Chicken Thieves
Stop Thief
Thieves in Camp, Golden Gate Park
Young Apple Thief
1907 Airship Thieves
Ali Baba and the Forty Thieves
The Clever Thief
The Punishment of the Horse Thief
Thieves Caught in Their Own Trap
The Thieving Umbrella
1908 Crocodile Turns Thief
A Den of Thieves
The Diamond Thieves
The Flower Thief
The Four-Legged Thief
A Good Thief
Levitsky's Insurance Policy; or, When Thief Meets Thief
Nocturnal Thieves
The Thief at the Casino
The Thieving Hand
Troublesome Theft
1909 The Cattle Thieves
Contemptible Theft
Honor Among Thieves
The Honor of Thieves
The Invisible Thief
The Little Milliner and the Thief
A Nervy Thief
Reformed Thief
Sold to Thieves; or, A Deathbed Confession
Two Very Unlucky Thieves
The Unlucky Thief
1910 Branding a Thief
The Cattle Thief's Revenge
The Girl Thief
Solving the Bond Theft
The Theft of the Diamonds
The Thief
Thief
A Thief Well Received
Thieves as Quick Change Artists
Thin
1910 The Thin Dark Line
Thing
1898 Helping a Good Thing Along
1900 Seeing Things at Night
Too Much of a Good Thing
1902 How They Do Things on the Bowery
1907 Bachelor Gets a Baby and Other Things He Don't Want
1909 Seeing Things
1910 Seeing the Real Thing
Think
1899 He Thought That He Had 'Em
1902 The Boys Think They Have One on Foxy Grandpa, but He Fools Them
1907 Pleasant Thoughts
1908 Don't You Think It's Time to Marry
Third
1897 Musical Drill; Troop A., Third Cavalry
Wrestling, Bareback; 3rd Cavalry
1898 Company "H," 3rd N.Y.V.
Third Missouri Volunteers
Third Pennsylvania Volunteers
Third Regiment Pennsylvania
1899 2nd Battalion, 3rd New York Provisional Regiment, Rochester and Syracuse, Separate Companies
Start of Third Day's Race
Third Boston School Regiment
Troop "F," 3rd Cavalry
1901 "Columbia" and "Shamrock II": Starting in the Third Race
Finish of the Third Cup Race
Start of the Third Cup Race
'Varsity Crew Race on Cayuga Lake, on Decoration Day, Lehigh Valley Observation Train Following the Race, Showing Cornell Crew Finishing First, Columbia Second, University of Pennsylvania Third Ithaca, N.Y., Showing Lehigh Valley Observation Train
1902 Third Trinity, Cambridge, Winning the Race for the Grand Challenge Cup. Taken at Henley on July 10th, 1902
1909 Henry the Third
Third Avenue (New York City)
1899 Third Avenue Elevated Railroad
1903 Third Avenue Elevated Train, New York
Third degree
1898 The Third Degree
1908 The Third Degree
1910 The Third Degree
3rd Street, St. Joseph (Missouri)
1904 Panorama of 3rd Street, St. Joseph, Mo., Missouri Commission

Tightrope walkers
1904 Eccentric Tight-rope Walker
1905 Tight-Rope Walker Undressing
1908 The Novice Tight-Rope Walker
Tile
1908 Mr. Brown Has a Tile Loose
Tilley, Vesta
1906 Vesta Tilley
Tilting
1908 Lion's Tilting Contest
Tim
1910 Tim Writes a Poem
Time
1896 Winchester Arms Factory at Noon Time
1897 Pennsylvania State Militia, Double Time
Pennsylvania State Militia, Single Time
1898 The Bowery Waiter and the Old Time Ball Player
Jumping the Rope After Bed Time
Second Illinois Volunteers at Double Time
65th Regiment at Double Time
A Time and Place for Everything
1899 Lunch Time in the Studio
1900 A Good Time Behind the Scenes
A Good Time with the Organ Grinder
1901 Feeding Time
Five Minutes to Train Time
Noon Time in Packing Town, (Panoramic)
Noon Time in Packing Town, (Whiskey Point)
1902 Milking Time on the Farm
Rag Time Dance
1903 Courting in Olden Times
1904 Girls Taking Time Checks, Westinghouse Works
A Parisienne's Bed Time
A Heavy Sea (Gros temps en mer)
1905 "Dinner Time" at Camp Curry Yosemite Valley
Milking Time: A Kerry Herd
Old Time Miner Rocking for Gold in the Tailings, Klondike
1907 Just in Time
Once Upon a Time There Was...
Sign of the Times
A Swell Time
1908 Don't You Think It's Time to Marry
From the Rococo Times
Having the Time of Their Lives
In the Nick of Time
In the Time of Rebellion
Jerusalem in the Time of Christ
Lunch Time
Mr. Softhead Has a Good Time
The Press Gang; or, A Romance in the Time of King George III
Time to Get Married
Winter Time in Northern Europe
1909 Backward, Turn Backward, O Time, in Your Flight
Chauffeur Out for a Good Time
Mr. Pynhead Out for a Good Time
Strike Time in Paris
A Timely Apparition
Turning Out of Time
A War Time Tale
Which Was the Happiest Time in Your Life?
A Wreath in Time
1910 In the Golden Harvest Time
In the Nick of Time
In the Time of the First Christians
In War Time
On Time for Business
Once upon a Time
Pete Has a Good Time
Saved in the Nick of Time
A Shot in Time
The Times Are Out of Joint
War Time Pals
Time lock
1910 The Time-Lock Safe
Timetable
1909 Last Year's Time Table
1910 The Marked Time-Table
Timid
1898 The Timid Girls and the Terrible Cow
1908 Timid Dwellers
1910 A Cure for Timidity
The Timid One
Tin
1901 Stamping Tin
1907 The Tin Wedding
1910 Tin Wedding Presents
Tinder
1908 The Tinder Box
Tinker
1907 Tipsy Tinker
Tintype
1910 A Tin-Type Romance
Tip
1897 Tipping the Cart in Mulberry Bend
1898 The Tipping Evil
1910 Cured by a Tip
Tipperary (Ireland)
1908 Tipperary
Tippler
1907 Tippler's Race
1909 Sympathetic Tippler
Tipsy
1907 Tipsy Tinker
Tired
1907 The Tired Tailor's Dream
1908 Hired-Tired-Fired
A Tiresome Play
Wouldn't It Tire You?
Tirolean
1907 Tirolean Dance
Tit for tat
1904 Tit for Tat; or, A Good Joke on My Head
1906 Tit-for-Tat
1908 Tit for Tat; or, Outwitted by Wit
1909 Tit for Tat
Title
1906 Love vs. Title; or, An Up-to-Date Elopement
1908 Buying a Title
Tivoli (Italy)
1903 Panorama of Tivoli, Italy, Showing Seven Falls
Toad
1904 Pugilistic Toads
The Toad's Luncheon
1905 Snail, Tortoise, Toad
Toast
1896 Rip's Toast
Rip's Toast to Hudson
1906 New Year's Toast
Tobacco
1898 Free Tobacco
1908 The Grandfather's Tobacco
1909 The Tobacco Edict, Old New York, 1648
Tobacco Mania
1910 Little Nell's Tobacco
Tobacco Culture
Tobasco
1902 Aunt Jane and the Tobasco Sauce
Toboggan
1902 Horse Toboggan Slide
Pike's Peak Toboggan Slide
Toboggan Slide
Tobogganing in Canada
1903 The Peel River Indians with Their Dog Teams and Toboggan Sleighs on the Trail
1905 Winter Sports (Sports d'hiver: le tobogan)
1907 A New Toboggan
Toby
1909 I Have Lost Toby
Today
1910 New York of Today
Shanghai of To-day
Toe
1903 Little Lillian, Toe Danseuse
1908 Bill Wants to Marry a Toe Dancer
1909 Walking on His Toes
1910 He Stubs His Toe
Toes and Teeth
Together
1910 Let Us Die Together
We Will Die Together, Love
Toilet
1897 Children's Toilet
1907 The Toilet of an Ocean Greyhound
Toils
1900 A Career of Crime, No. 4: In the Toils
Token
1908 Soldier's Love Token
1909 The Love Token
Tokyo (Japan)
1898 Arrival of Tokyo Train
1901 Street Scene, Tokio, Japan
1902 Street Scene, Tokio
1904 A Fierce Sword Combat at Tokio
Street in Tokio
1910 Carnival of Japanese Firemen in Tokio
Told
use **Telling**
Toledo (Ohio)
1900 Employees of Wolfson's Spice Mills, Toledo
1907 Toledo
Toll
1899 Toll Gate and Castle Rock near Green River
Tolstoy, Leo
1910 Count Tolstoi
Tom
1897 Peeping Tom
1903 Peeping Tom and His Telescope
Tom, Tom the Piper's Son
Uncle Tom's Cabin
Uncle Tom's Cabin Parade
Working a Long Tom Rocker on Bonanza Creek
1904 Landing a "Long Tom" Gun
1905 Peeping Tom in the Dressing Room
Tom, Tom, the Piper's Son
1906 Tom Moves
1909 Forecastle Tom
The Marathon Race; or, How Tom Paid Off the Mortgage
Tom's Misfit
Uncle Tom Wins
1910 Stage Coach Tom
Tom's Last Steeple Chase
Uncle Tom's Cabin
Uncle Tom's Cabin, Part 1
Uncle Tom's Cabin, Part 2
Uncle Tom's Cabin, Part 3
Tom (Mountain), Massachusetts
1899 Down Mount Tom
Tom Thumb
1903 Little Tom Thumb
1909 Tom Thumb
Tom Tight
1903 Jack Jaggs & Dum Dum (Tom Tight et Dum-Dum)
Tomato
1906 Stealing Tomatoes
1908 Making of Tomato Sauce
1909 A Case of Tomatoes
Tomboys
1906 The Tomboys
1909 The Tom-Boy
Tombs
1896 Li Hung Chang at Grant's Tomb
1898 Reviewing the "Texas" at Grant's Tomb
1899 Panorama at Grant's Tomb, Dewey Naval Procession
1903 Passion Play: Placing Jesus in the Tomb
1904 The Passion Play (La mise au tombeau)
1906 In the Tombs
1907 Grant's Tomb
Tommy
1899 Tommy's Ringing Good Joke on His Dad
1900 Tommy's Trick on Grandpa
1903 How Tommy Got a Pull on His Grandpa
1906 Tommy's Revenge
1907 Tommy at Play
Tommy in Society
Tommy's Box of Tools
1908 Tommy Has the Spleen
Tommy the Fireman
1909 Tommy's Own Invention
Tommy's Tricks
1910 Tommy and the Powder
Tommy Gets His Sister Married
Tommy in Dreamland
Tomorrow
1910 To-morrow Is Pay-day
Toney
1908 Mrs. Toney's Suitors
Tongas
1903 The Galloping Tongas
Tongkin Train (China)
1901 Arrival of Tongkin Train
Tongue
1910 The Tongue of Scandal
Tonic
1909 Professor's Love Tonic
The Sleeping Tonic
The Strong Tonic
Tonight
1907 Curfew Shall Not Ring Tonight
1909 Where Is My Wandering Boy To-night?

Towser
1910 Towser's New Job

Toys
1902 The Children's Toys That Came to Life
1904 Toy Maker and Good Fairy
Toys Competition
What a Mechanical Toy Did To Some Giddy Girls
1908 Acrobatic Toys
A Love Affair in Toyland
A Grandmother's Story (Au pays des jouets)
1910 The Toymaker, the Doll and the Devil
The Toymaker's Secret

Trace
1903 Broken Trace
1907 Traced by a Laundry Mark
1909 Traced by a Kodak

Track
1897 Safety in Four Tracks
1900 Race Track Scene
1901 Finish of Flatbush Stakes, Gravesend Track
International Track Athletic Meeting—Start and Finish of the One Mile Run
1904 Panorama of Race Track Crowd, St. Louis
Tracked by Bloodhounds; or, A Lynching at Cripple Creek
1905 Dream of the Race Track Fiend
Floral Parade at the Race Track, Moscow, Russia
1906 Head-On Collision at Brighton Beach Race Track, July 4th, 1906
May's Mechanical Race Track
1907 Dogs Tracking Burglars
Making the Dirt Fly: Scene 4. Railroad Track Lifter in Operation
The Piker's Dream, a Race Track Fantasy
1908 Clearing the Mountain Track
Tracked by a Woman
Tracked by the Police Dog
1909 Repairing Railroad Tracks
Tracked by a Dog
1910 The Mysterious Track
Tracked Across the Sea

Traction
1903 Transvaal War Supplies Transported by McKenzie Traction Engines
1905 Traction Engine

Trade
1899 Board of Trade
1903 Traders of the East Indian Empire
1906 The Trading Stamp Craze
1908 Jack of All Trades
1910 Different Trades in Bombay

Trafalgar Square, London (England)
1897 Trafalgar Square

Traffic
1901 Bridge Traffic, Manila

Tragedian
1908 The Crushed Tragedian
The Tragedian

Tragedy
1898 A Tragedy Averted
1904 A Railway Tragedy
1905 A Ballroom Tragedy
A River Tragedy
A Tragedy at Sea
1906 Thaw-White Tragedy
Tragedy in a Train
1907 A Tenderloin Tragedy
Venetian Tragedy
1908 The Chieftain's Revenge; or, A Tragedy in the Highlands of Scotland
The Goebel Tragedy
Julius Caesar, an Historical Tragedy
A Love Tragedy in Spain
Macbeth, Shakespeare's Sublime Tragedy
The Poisoned Bouquet, an Italian Tragedy of the XV Century
Railway Tragedy
Richard III, a Shakespearian Tragedy
A Tragedy of Japan
The Wages of Sin, an Italian Tragedy
1909 The Bride of Lammermoor, a Tragedy of Bonnie Scotland
Comedy and Tragedy
The End of the Tragedy
Jepthah's Daughter, a Biblical Tragedy
A Near Tragedy
A Rural Tragedy
Tragedy at the Circus
Tragedy in the Family
Tragedy of a Ghost
The Tragedy of Meudon
1910 Love's Great Tragedy
A Summer Tragedy
Tragedy at Sea
Tragedy at the Mill
Tyrolean Tragedy

Tragic
1904 Tragic Elopement
1907 Tragic Moment
Tragic Rivalry
Tragic Wedding
1908 Misdeeds of a Tragical Part
1909 A Tragic Ending of Shrove Tuesday
Tragic Love
Tragic Night
Tragical Love
1910 A Tragic Adventure
A Tragic Evening
Tragic Idyl
Tragical Concealment
Tweedledum Learns a Tragical Part

Trail
1898 Pack Mules with Ammunition on the Santiago Trail, Cuba
1901 Packers on the Trail
1903 The Divorce: On the Trail [Part 2]
Down the Bright Angel Trail
An Old Squaw on the Trail
The Peel River Indians with Their Dog Teams and Toboggan Sleighs on the Trail
Trailed by Bloodhounds
1905 Cavalcade Descending Eagle Peak Trail, Yosemite Valley
Cavalcade Descending the Nevada Trail, Yosemite Valley
Cavalcade Descending Trail into Grand Cañon of Arizona
Cavalcade on Trail into Grand Cañon of Arizona
The "Crazy" Tourists on the Nevada Trail, Yosemite Valley
The "Crazy" Tourists Starting for the Trail, Yosemite Valley
1909 The Indian Trailer
1910 The Blazed Trail
The Cheyenne Raiders; or, Kit Carson on the Santa Fe Trail
The Crooked Trail
The End of the Trail
The Long Trail
The Lost Trail
The Marked Trail
Trailed to the Hills
Trailing the Black Hand
The Twisted Trail
The Wrong Trail

Train
rt **Railroad**
1896 Pa. R.R. Train near Phila.
Special Photographing Train
Train Coming out of Station, Philadelphia, Pa.
Train Taking Water, N.Y. Central R.R.
1897 Fall River Boat Train
McKinley Train, Penn. R.R.
New York Elevated Trains
Observation Train at the Inter-Collegiate Boat-Races
Sprague Electric Train
Tourist Train Leaving Livingston, Mont.
1898 Arrival of Tokyo Train
Freight Train
Military Camp at Tampa, Taken from Train
Observation Train Following Parade
Soldiers Firing on Train
Train Hour in Durango, Mexico
Wagon Supply Train en Route
1899 Armored Train Crossing the Veldt
British Armored Train
Smallest Train in the World
1900 Arrival of Train at Muskoka Wharf
Arrival of Train at Paris Exposition
Boer Commissary Train Treking
The Train for Angeles
1901 Arrival of McKinley's Funeral Train at Canton, Ohio
Arrival of Tongkin Train
Arrival of Train at Station
Arrival of Train of Cattle
Burro Pack Train on Main Street, Dawson City
Burro Pack Train on the Chilcoot Pass
Catching an Early Train
Five Minutes to Train Time
The Ghost Train
A Japanese Railway Train
Royal Train with Duke and Duchess of York, Climbing Mt. Hector
Taking President McKinley's Body from Train at Canton, Ohio
Train Crossing Dale Creek Fill
Train of Sugar Cane on Way to Crusher
'Varsity Crew Race on Cayuga Lake, on Decoration Day, Lehigh Valley Observation Train Following the Race, Showing Cornell Crew Finishing First, Columbia Second, University of Pennsylvania Third Ithaca, N.Y., Showing Lehigh Valley Observation Train
The War in China—A British Donkey Train
The War in China—An Army Transport Train
1902 Arrival of Circus Trains
Experimental. Southwestern Limited Train
The Flying Train
Good Luck Baking Powder Train No. 1
Good Luck Baking Powder Train No. 2
Train in Royal Gorge
The Train to Villefranche
Trains Leaving Manitou
1903 Arrival of the Circus Train, No. 1
Arrival of the Circus Train, No. 2
Arrival of Train at Gardner
Boer Supply Train Crossing the Veldt
Foreign Train Scenes
Freight Train in the Royal Gorge, Colo.
The Great Train Robbery
How He Missed His Train
Loading a Train with Stone
Love in a Railroad Train
Mule Pack Train Taking Gold Dust to Dawson City
New Passing Train Scene
A Pack Train in the Copper River Country
Pack Train Leaving Valdez for Copper Mines
Panorama from Elevated Train, New York
Panorama of Circus Train Unloading Horses
Prairie Emigrant Train Crossing the Plains
Third Avenue Elevated Train, New York
Train on High Bridge
Train Taking Up Mail Bag, U.S.P.O.
Troop Train Conveying the Seaforth Highlanders Across the Modder River
Tying Up Bags for Train, U.S.P.O.
U.S.P.O. Dept. Santa Fe Mail Train
War Supplies Arriving at Boer Laager by Train of Ox Teams
1904 Arrival and Departure of a Train
Arrival of a Train
Attack on a Train
Attempted Murder in a Train
The Great Train Robbery
In a Hurry to Catch the Train
Panorama of Railroad Station at Seoul, Korea, from Departing Train
Passing Trains
Westinghouse Employees Boarding Train
1905 Arrival of Train at Oberammergau
The Little Train Robbery
Panorama from a Moving Train on White Pass & Yukon Railway, Alaska
Panorama from Moving Train on Albula Railway, Switzerland
Panorama from Moving Train on Murren Electric Railway, Switzerland
Panorama from Train on Visp-Zermatt Railway
Passing Train, Balleybunion Railway, Ireland
Passing Train, Balleybunion Railway, Ireland No. 2
Passing Train (from Above) Balleybunion Railway, Ireland
Railway Panorama from Moving Train Passing Through Conway Castle, Wales
Retrogressive Jaunting Car, Reverse Panorama from Moving Train, Dublin, Ireland
Train Arriving at Henley Station
Train on the White Pass & Yukon Railway, Alaska
The Train Wreckers
Trains Arriving at Henley Station with Regatta Visitors

1910 Trawler Fishing in a Hurricane

Treachery
1898 The Fat Man and the Treacherous Springboard
The Treacherous Spring Board
1909 Half Breed's Treachery
Treacherous Policeman
1910 The Hindoo's Treachery
Jarnac's Treacherous Blow
The Treachery of the Pequots

Treadwell Mine (Alaska)
1903 Blasting the Treadwell Mines
1905 Blasting in the Glory Hole of the Treadwell Mine, Alaska
Slavonian Miners Running to Dinner, Treadwell Mine, Alaska

Treason
1909 High Treason
1910 Love and Treason

Treasure
1903 Mephistopheles' School of Magic (Les trésors de Satan)
1907 The Pirates' Treasure; or, A Sailor's Love Story
1908 The Hidden Treasure
The Story of Treasure Island
A Treasure of a Pig
Youthful Treasure Seekers
1909 Ancestral Treasures
The Farmer's Treasure
The Hidden Treasure
The Treasure; or, The House Next Door
1910 The Hidden Treasure
Kidd's Treasure
The Prospector's Treasure
The Treasure Hunters
The Treasure of Louis

Treatment
1903 Electric Treatment
Massage Treatment
1910 Doctor's Peculiar Treatment
Forced Treatment

Tree
1897 The Christmas Tree Party
1899 One Thousand Mile Tree, Weber Canyon
The Wizard and the Spirit of the Tree
1901 Wawona, Big Tree
1903 Boy Up a Tree; or, Making Love in the Park
Passion Play: Christ Calling Zaccheus from the Tree
1904 Under the Tree
The Wonderful Rose Tree
1905 The King Planting a Tree at the Royal Agricultural Society's Show Yard
Stages Passing Through Wawona Big Tree, Mariposa Grove, California
Under the Bamboo Tree
1907 Fire Run, Colon Fire Department Under Cocoanut Tree
Under the Old Apple Tree
1908 A Walking Tree
1909 Uncle's Palm Tree
1910 Under the Old Apple Tree
Up a Tree

Tree, Beerbohm
1899 Beerbohm Tree, the Great English Actor

Treking
1900 Boer Commissary Train Treking

Treloar, Al
1904 Treloar and Miss Marshall, Prize Winners at the Physical Culture Show in Madison Square Garden
1905 Al Treloar in Muscle Exercises

Tremont Hotel, Galveston (Texas)
1900 Panoramic View of Tremont Hotel, Galveston

Tremont Street, Boston (Massachusetts)
1899 Tremont Street

Trenches
1898 In the Trenches
1899 Capture of Trenches at Candaba [Canda Bar]
Digging a Trench
Filipinos Retreat from Trenches
U.S. Troops and Red Cross in the Trenches Before Caloocan [P. I.]

Trespassers
1903 Farmer Chasing Trespassers

Trestle
1899 The Frankenstein Trestle

Trial
1897 Trial Scene
1899 Shamrock Starting on Trial Trip
The Trial of Captain Dreyfus at Rennes, France
Trial of Captain Dreyfus
1900 Speed Trial of the "Albatross"
Trial Race Columbia and Defender
Trial Race Columbia and Defender No. 2
Trial Run of the Battleship "Alabama"
Trial Speed of H. M. Torpedo Boat Destroyer "Viper"
1902 Trial Trip of "Meteor"
1903 Trial Run of the Fastest Boat in the World, "The Arrow"
1904 The Gordon Bennett Automobile Trials, Isle of Man
The Trials and Troubles of an Automobilist
1905 The Bigamist's Trial
Reproduction, Nan Paterson's Trial
Speed Trial of Auto Boat Challenger, Lake Worth, Fla.
1906 Getting Evidence, Showing the Trials and Tribulations of a Private Detective
1907 Trial Marriages
Trial Trip of the Airship "La Patrie"
1908 The Caleb Powers Trial
The Near-Sighted Professor [His Trials and Tribulations]
Trials of an Educator
Wanted—A Son-in-Law on Trial
1909 A Billposter's Trials
The Trial of the White Man
1910 Trials of a Schoolmaster

Triangle
1910 The Eternal Triangle

Triangle Clothing Store, Philadelphia (Pennsylvania)
1903 Fire at Triangle Clothing Store, 13th and Ridge Ave., Philadelphia, May 3d, 1899

Tribe
1904 Secret Procession of the Algerian Tribes
1910 The White Princess of the Tribe

Triboulet
1908 The King and the Jester (François Ier et Triboulet)

Tribulation
1898 Tribulations of a Country Schoolmarm
Tribulations of Sleeping in a Hammock
1900 The Tribulations of an Amateur Photographer
1906 Getting Evidence, Showing the Trials and Tribulations of a Private Detective
1908 A Gendarme's Tribulations
The Lover's Tribulation
The Near-Sighted Professor [His Trials and Tribulations]
Tribulations of a Mayor
Tribulations of a Photographer
1909 Tribulations of a Lover

Trick
1896 Imro Fox Rabbit Trick
1897 Trick Elephants
1898 Doing Her Big Brother's Tricks on the Bar
1899 Bicycle Trick Riding, No. 2
Frank Melville's Trick Elephant
A Mean Trick on a Sleepy Soubrette
The Trick Bear
Trick Bears
1900 Tommy's Trick on Grandpa
1901 The Trick Cyclist
The Wonderful Trick Donkey
1902 Foxy Grandpa Shows the Boys a Trick or Two with the Tramp
1903 The Cabinet Trick of the Davenport Brothers
Conjurer and 100 Tricks
The Famous Box Trick
Ten Ichi Performing His Wonderful Water Trick
Trick Dogs, Hagenback's Circus
Trick Donkey
Trick Donkey, No. 2
Trick Donkey, Hagenback's Circus
Trick Elephant Bolivar, the Largest Elephant in the World, No. 1
Trick Elephant Bolivar, the Largest Elephant in the World, No. 2
Trick Elephant, Hagenback's Circus
1904 Barber's Tricks
Boys' Trick on Grandpa
Lotto, the Trick Bicyclist
Trick Bicycle Riding
A Trick on the Cop
1905 Lucille Mulhall and Trick Horse
1906 Childish Tricks Baffled
1907 The Little Rascal's Tricks
Playing a Trick on the Gardener
Rogues' Tricks
1908 Burglar's New Trick
A Poacher's Trick
Tricked into Giving His Consent
1909 The Butler's Tricks
A Clever Trick
A Good Trick
He Learns the Trick of Mesmerism
Madam Lydia's Little Trick
A New Trick
A Smart Trick
Tommy's Tricks
The Trick That Failed
Trick Well Played
Tricks of the Photographer
1910 Betty Is Still at Her Old Tricks

Tricksy
1908 Tricksy, the Clever Princess

Tricky
1898 Folding Beds Are Tricky
1908 A Tricky Painter's Fate
The Tricky Twins
A Tricky Uncle
1909 A Tricky Convict
The Tricky Dummies
1910 The Tricky Umbrella of Fricot

Tricycle
1906 Water Tricycle
1908 The Bewitched Tricycle

Trifling
1908 No Trifling with Love
1910 No Trifling with Love

Trilby
1896 Trilby and Little Billee
1898 Ella Lola, a la Trilby [Dance]

Trim
1899 In Fighting Trim
1901 Trimming Room
1910 The Trimming of Paradise Gulch

Trinidad
1908 Cocoa Industry, Trinidad, British West Indies

Trinity
1902 Third Trinity, Cambridge, Winning the Race for the Grand Challenge Cup. Taken at Henley on July 10th, 1902

Trinity Church, Boston (Massachusetts)
1898 Trinity Church

Trinity Pier, London (England)
1901 The Funeral Cortege Arriving at Trinity Pier

Trio
1899 The Prentis Trio
1902 Is Ka Trio
1909 The Jolly Trio's Dream

Trip
rt **Touring and tourists**
Travel
1899 The Astronomer's Dream, or the Trip to the Moon
Shamrock Starting on Trial Trip
A Trip over the Manhattan Elevated Railroad
A Trip to the Moon
1901 A Trip Around the Pan-American Exposition
1902 The Darktown Comedians Trip to Paris
Dr. Lehwis Automobile Leaving London for a Trip Around the World
Prize-Winning Trip of the Santos-Dumont Airship No. 6
Trial Trip of "Meteor"
A Trip to the Moon
1903 Trip Around the Union Loop
A Trip Through the Gap of Dunloe
A Trip to Southend
A Trip to the Giant's Causeway
Bewitched Dungeon (La tour maudite)
1904 An Englishman's Trip to Paris from London
Honeymoon Trip
A Trip to Palestine. Jaffa and Its Harbor
A Trip to Palestine. Jerusalem, the Holy City
Trip to the Zoo
1905 An Adventurous Automobile Trip
On a Vacation Trip
A Pleasure Trip
A Trip Through Samoa and Fiji Islands
A Trip to Salt Lake City

Troubles of a Country Visitor
1904 The Cook in Trouble
Dwarf's Troubles
Those Troublesome Boys
The Trials and Troubles of an Automobilist
The Troubles of a Manager of a Burlesque Show
1905 Bridget's Troubles
The Paper Hanger in Trouble
1906 The Troubles of a Fireman
Troublesome Fishbone
The Troublesome Flea
1907 Bakers in Trouble
The Flat Dwellers; or, The House of Too Much Trouble
Robert Macaire and Bertrand; or, The Troubles of a Hobo and His Pal, in Paris
Seek and You Shall Find...Trouble
Trouble at a Wedding
Troubles of a Cook
Troubles of a Gardener
Troubles of a Tramp
1908 Adventures of Mr. Troubles
All That Trouble for a Drink
The Cause of All the Trouble
Every Age Has Its Trouble
King Scatterbrain's Troubles
Mabel's Beau in Trouble
Mrs. Trouble
Troubles of a Coat
Troubles of a Flirt
Troubles of a Grass Widower
Troubles of a New Drug Clerk
Troubles of an Airship
Troubles of Too Ardent Admirers
Troublesome Baby
Troublesome Carbuncle
The Troublesome Fly
Troublesome Husband
Troublesome Theft
1909 Born for Trouble
His Wife's Troublesome Twitching
The Trouble Kiss
Troubled Artists
Troubles of a Coachman
Troubles of a Fisherman
The Troubles of a Stranded Actor
The Troubles of an Amateur Detective
The Troubles of the Pretty School Marm
The Troublesome Lamppost
A Troublesome Malady
A Troublesome Satchel
Tubbie's Terrible Troubles
1910 Davy Jones' Domestic Troubles
Max Has Trouble with His Eyes
The Troubles of a Flirt
The Troubles of a Policeman
The Troublesome Baby
Troublesome Lad
A Troublesome Parcel

Troupe
1900 Monte Myro Troupe of Acrobats
1903 Venetian Troupe
1910 The Ohami Troupe of Acrobats

Trousers
1903 Jack Tar Sewing a Patch on the Seat of His Trousers
1906 History of a Pair of Trousers
1907 Unlucky Trousers
1908 A Talk on Trousers
1909 Foolshead's Trousers
Misadventures of a Pair of Trousers
Never Gamble for Your Trousers
1910 Inventive Trouser

Trousseau
1899 The Bride's Trousseau

Trout
1897 Trout Poachers
1900 Brook Trout Fishing
1903 Feeding Brook Trout at the Pennsylvania State Fishery
Leaping Trout
Trout Fishing, Landing Three Pounder
1906 Trout Fishing
Trout Fishing in Rangeley Lakes

Il Trovatore
1909 Il Trovatore

Truant
1906 Playing Truant
1907 Playing Truant
The Truants
1909 A Pair of Truants
The Truant; or, How Willie Fixed His Father
1910 The Little Truant

True
1903 Every Day Is Sunshine When the Heart Beats True
True Love Never Runs Smooth
1905 The Course of True Love
1907 The Faithful Dog; or, True to the End
True to Life
True Until Death
1908 True Hearts Are More Than Coronets
1909 C.Q.D.; or, Saved by Wireless, a True Story of "The Wreck of the Republic"
The Course of True Love
If Love Be True
A True Friend
A True Girl from the West
A True Indian's Heart
True Love Never Runs Smoothly
A True Patriot
True to Her First Love
True to His Master
The Truer Lover
The Viking's Love; or, True to His Chief
1910 The Course of True Love
False Love and True
A True Country Heart
A True Indian Brave
A True Pal
True to His Oath
True to His Trust
True Western Honor
Truth Beyond Reach of Justice
The Truth Revealed

Truffle
1909 He Is a Cousin Who Eats Truffle

Truman, Corporal
1910 Corporal Truman's War Story

Trump
1910 Hearts Are Trump

Trunk
1899 Grand Trunk R.R. Bridge over Whirlpool
1903 The Mysterious Trunk
1904 Barnum's Trunk
The Bewitched Trunk
1905 Travels of a Lost Trunk
1907 Travels of a Lost Trunk
1908 The Great Trunk Robbery
Stage Memories of an Old Theatrical Trunk
1909 Burglar in the Trunk
The Mystery of the "Sleeper" Trunk
1910 The Nurse's Trunk

Trust
1908 The Downfall of the Burglars' Trust
1910 The Egg Trust
Lone Wolf's Trust
The Seminole's Trust
True to His Trust

Truth
use **True**

Try
1898 Trying to Jump Her Board Bill
Trying to "Skin the Cat"
1902 The Boys, Still Determined, Try It Again on Foxy Grandpa, with the Same Result
The Boys Try to Put One Up on Foxy Grandpa
1905 Airy Fairy Lillian Tries on Her New Corsets
Hubby Tries to Keep House
1906 Trying It on His Dog
1908 Trying to Get Rid of a Bad Dollar
1909 He Tried on Hand Cuffs
A Trying Position
Trying to Get Arrested

Tsing Fu
1910 Tsing Fu, the Yellow Devil

Tsung, Prince
1902 Prince Tsung of China

Tub
1898 Tub Race
1902 A Tub Race
1903 Tub Race
1905 Elephant's Tub

Tubbie
1909 Tubbie's Terrible Troubles

Tuberculosis
1905 Alcoholism Engenders Tuberculosis

Tuesday
1909 A Tragic Ending of Shrove Tuesday

Tug
1897 Ferryboat and Tug Passing Governors Island, New York Harbor
1898 A Tug in a Heavy Sea
1899 "Corsair" in Wake of Tugboat
1902 St. John's Guild. Julliard and Tug in Narrows

Tug-of-war
1900 Tug-o-War on Board an Ocean Steamer
1902 A Tug of War
1903 Navajo Indian Tug-of-War
1905 Stork's Tug of War

Tugela River (South Africa)
1900 Battle of the Upper Tugela

Tuilleries Gardens, Paris (France)
1902 An Automobile Parade in the Tuilleries Gardens

Tulips
1908 The Tulips
1909 Tulips

Tumble
1901 A Mighty Tumble
1904 A Kiss and a Tumble
1909 A Sure 'Nuff Tumbler
1910 The Mexican Tumblers

Tumbling Run
1909 The Little Shepherd of "Tumbling Run"

Tumultuous
1909 A Tumultuous Elopement

Tune
1909 Her Favorite Tune
1910 Her Favorite Tune
That Popular Tune

Tunisia
1904 Rolling Bridge in Tunis
1906 Tunisian Dance
1909 Picturesque Tunis
Tunisian Industries
1910 Southern Tunis

Tunnel
1897 The Haverstraw Tunnel
1898 Going Through the Tunnel
1899 Port Huron; West End of St. Clair Tunnel
Running Through Gallitzen Tunnel, Penna. R.R.
St. Clair Tunnel
Tunnel "No. Three"
West Side St. Clair Tunnel
1900 Opening of the Rapid Transit Tunnel
St. Clair Tunnel
1901 Indian Fort, Sherman Hill Tunnel
1902 Black Rock Tunnel on the Rock Island Route
The Nurse Maid in the Tunnel
1903 Coaching Through the Tunnel on the Kenmere Road
In the Rapid-Transit Tunnel
A Kiss in the Tunnel
Panoramic View of Haverstraw Tunnel, N.Y.
Perkasie Tunnel
Railroad Tunnel Scene
Through Cascade Tunnel
Through Tunnel on the White Pass Route
Tunnel Scene of the White Pass Route
What Happened in the Tunnel
1904 Kissing in a Tunnel
The Tunnel Scene
1905 Coaches Starting from Larne and Passing Through Tunnel on the Antrim Coast Road
Pennsylvania Tunnel Excavation
Through Tunnel on the Antrim Coast
1906 The Tunnel Workers
1907 Tunneling the English Channel
1910 Through the Tunnel

Tunny
1907 A Big Take of Tunny Fish
Tunny Fisheries in Sicily
1910 Tunny Fishing off Palermo, Italy

Turbines
1904 Assembling and Testing Turbines, Westinghouse Works
Testing Large Turbines, Westinghouse Co. Works

Turbulent
1906 Turbulent Seas, Waterfalls and Streams

Turin (Italy)
1904 Cavalry Fording a Stream (Passage d'un torrent par le comte de Turin et son etat-major)

The Mysterious Double; or, The Two Girls Who Looked Alike
The Story of Two Lives
Temptations of the Gold Fields; or, The Two Gold Diggers
The Two Bandboxes
Two Brothers
Two Christmas Tides
Two Chums Looking for Wives
Two Cousins
The Two Donkeys
Two Fathers
The Two Friends
Two Frolicking Youths
Two Heroes
Two Ladies and a Beggar
Two Little Runaways
Two Lovers and a Coquette
Two Memories
The Two Mr. Whites
Two of a Kind
Two Orphans of the G.A.R.
Two Pickpockets
The Two Pigeons
The Two Sergeants
Two Sides to a Story
The Two Sons
Two Turtle Doves
Two Very Unlucky Thieves
Two Violins
Two Women and a Man
1910 The Child of Two Mothers
The Devil on Two Sticks
Foolshead Between Two Fires
A Game for Two
Her Two Suitors
The Rivalry of the Two Guides
Robert Macaire; or, The Two Vagabonds
The Struggle of Two Souls
A Tale of Two Coats
Twa Hieland Lads
The Two Bears
Two Betrothed
Two Boys in Blue
The Two Brothers
The Two Daughters
Two Friends
Two Gentlemen of the Road
Two Little Waifs
Two Lucky Jims
Two Maids
Two Men
The Two Mothers
The Two Portraits
The Two Raffles
The Two Roses
The Two Sisters
Two Suits
Two Waifs and a Stray

2 A.M.
1905 2 A.M. in the Subway

Two hundred thousand
1907 Under the Seas (Deux cent mille lieues sous les mers; ou le cauchemar d'un pêcheur)

Two-step
1907 Jamaica Negroes Doing a Two-Step

Two thousand
1907 Two Thousand Miles Without a Dollar

2000 Years
1910 Back to Life After 2,000 Years

Tying
1903 Clerks Tying Bags, U.S.P.O.
Clerks Tying Up for Bags, U.S.P.O.
Tying the Red Light on the Tiger's Tail
Tying Up Bags for Train, U.S.P.O.
1905 Lucille Mulhall Roping and Tying a Steer

Tylda
1909 Tylda and Her Lions

Tyngsborough (Massachusetts)
1899 Around Tynsborough Curve

Types
1907 Irish Scenes and Types
1910 Dutch Types
Jewish Types in Russia

Typewriter
1897 The Pretty Typewriter; or, "Caught in the Act"
1900 Necessary Qualifications of a Typewriter
1903 Smith's Wife Inspects the New Typewriter
1905 The Broker's Athletic Typewriter
1908 Daisy, the Pretty Typewriter
Nellie, the Pretty Typewriter
The Pretty Typist
1910 That Typist Again

Typhoid
1905 Typhoid Fever Germs

Typical
1904 Typical Algerian 'Ouled Nails' Muslin Dance

Tyranny
1910 From Tyranny to Liberty
The Tyranny of the Dark

Tyrant
1908 Angelo, Tyrant of Padua
The Tyrant Feudal Lord
1909 The Tyrant's Dream
1910 The Tyrant
The Tyrant of Florence

Tyrol
1903 Tyrolienne Dance
1905 Cloud Play on Dolomite Peaks, Tyrol
Corpus Christi Ceremonies, Botzen, Tyrol
Corpus Christi Cortege, Botzen, Tyrol
"Crazy" Congregation Leaving Church, Cortina, Tyrol
Railroad Station at Steinach, Tyrol
Religious Cortege on a Rainy Day, Cortina, Tyrol
Sunrise on the Peak, Tyrol
Tyroler Fest, Steinach, Tyrol
Tyrolese Dance, Innsbruck
Tyrolese Dancers Innsbruck
1907 Tyrolean Alps in the Winter
1908 Drama in the Tyrol
Tyrolean Alps Customs
A Tyrolean Paradise
1910 Tyrolean Tragedy

Tyron
1907 Tyron

Ugly
1900 The Ugly Tempered Tramp
1909 The Ugly Girl

Ugolini, Count
1909 Count Ugolini

Uintah (Wyoming)
1899 East of Uintah in Weber Canyon

Ullugura Mountains
1910 A Mica Mine, the Ullugura Mountains

Ulysses
1905 The Mysterious Island (L'île de Calypso. Ulysse et le géant polypheme)
1909 The Return of Ulysses

Umatilla Indians
1908 The Umatilla Indians

Umbrella
1897 Umbrella Brigade
1899 New Umbrella Dance
1900 Umbrella Dance
1901 He Forgot His Umbrella
1902 Mr. Oldsport's Umbrella
Umbrella Dance, San Toy
1903 Umbrella Brigade
Umbrella Dance
1907 Lost Umbrella
The Thieving Umbrella
1909 Automatic Umbrella Seller
Looking for His Umbrella
An Obstinate Umbrella
The Romance of an Umbrella
1910 The Parson's Umbrella
The Tricky Umbrella of Fricot

Unappreciated
1903 The Unappreciated Joke
1908 Unappreciated Patron
1909 Unappreciated Genius

Unchanging
1910 The Unchanging Sea

Uncle
1898 How Uncle Reuben Missed the Fishing Party
The Sleeping Uncle and the Bad Girls
Uncle Rube's Visit to the Man-o' War
1900 Uncle Josh in a Spooky Hotel
Uncle Josh's Nightmare
Uncle Reuben Lands a Kick
Uncle Si's Experience in a Concert Hall
1902 How Uncle Josh Defeated the Badgers
Uncle Josh at the Moving Picture Show
1903 Uncle Reuben at the Waldorf
1904 Let Uncle Ruben Show You How
Uncle Rube's Birthday
1907 The Inquisitive Boy; or, Uncle's Present
An Uncle by Marriage
Uncle's Heritage
1908 Madam Flirt and Her Adopted Uncle
A Tricky Uncle
The Uncle from America
Uncle's Clock
The Uncle's Fortune
Uncle's Rejected Present
1909 "Oh, Uncle"
Uncle Reuben's Courtship
Uncle Rube's Visit
Uncle Tom Wins
Uncle's Palm Tree
A Visit to Uncle
1910 Getting Rid of Uncle
Her Uncle's Will
Our Dear Uncle from America
A Pair of Schemers; or, My Wife and My Uncle
Uncle Eph's Dream
Uncle Jim
Uncle Learns to Hypnotize
Uncle's Money
Uncle's Will

Uncle Sam
1899 How the Porto Rican Girls Entertain Uncle Sam's Soldiers
1910 The Hand of Uncle Sam
A Ward of Uncle Sam

Uncle Tom's Cabin
1903 Uncle Tom's Cabin
Uncle Tom's Cabin Parade
1910 Uncle Tom's Cabin
Uncle Tom's Cabin, Part 1
Uncle Tom's Cabin, Part 2
Uncle Tom's Cabin, Part 3

Unconscious
1910 Unconscious Heroism

Undelivered
1903 The Undelivered Message

Underdog
1908 The Under Dog

Undergraduate
1907 The Undergraduate

Underground
1902 Elevated and Underground

Underside
1900 Demonstrating the Action of Pneumatic Shell Riveters on the Underside of the Hull of a Steel Vessel. Taken for the Chicago Pneumatic Tool Co.

Understudy
1905 The Prima Donna's Understudy

Undertaker
1901 Another Job for the Undertaker

Undertaking
1908 The Mourners; or, A Clever Undertaking

Undertow
1902 Caught in the Undertow

Underwear
1898 Underwear Model

Underworld
1907 The Underworld of Paris

Undesirable
1908 Undesirable Tenants

Undone
1907 Undone by a Suit Case

Undress
1898 How Bridget Served the Salad Undressed
Joe, the Educated Orangoutang, Undressing
1902 Serving Potatoes, Undressed
Undressing Under Difficulties
1903 Going to Bed Under Difficulties (Le déshabillage impossible)
1904 Will He Never Get Undressed
The Enchanted Wardrobe (Un déshabillé désopilant)
1905 Tight-Rope Walker Undressing
1906 Lady Undressing

Uneven
1909 An Uneven Keel

Unexpected
1898 The Teacher's Unexpected Bath
Unexpected Advent of the School Teacher
The Unexpected Visit
1900 The Unexpected Bath
1901 The Tramp's Unexpected Skate
An Unexpected Knockout
1903 The Teacher's Unexpected Ducking
Resourceful Waiter (Restitution inattendue)
1904 A Ruben's Unexpected Bath
1905 Unexpected Fireworks
1907 Unexpected Meal
Sportsmen and Lion (Gibier inattendu)

Crew of the U.S. Cruiser "Raleigh"
Gen. Snowden and Staff, and Crew of the U.S.S. "Raleigh"
Morning Colors on U.S. Cruiser "Raleigh"
U.S. Cruiser "Olympia" Leading Naval Parade
U.S. Cruiser "Raleigh"
U.S. Cruiser Raleigh
1903 Boxing Match on Board the U.S. Cruiser Raleigh
Crew of the U.S. Cruiser Raleigh Passing the Grant Monument at Fairmount Park, Philadelphia
Manning the Yard Arm on the U.S. Cruiser Raleigh
Morning Exercise on Board the U.S. Cruiser Raleigh
U.S. Battleship Indiana
U.S. Monitor Miantonomah Steaming into Key West
U.S. Monitor Terror
1904 Launching of the U.S.S. Battleship "Connecticut"
Massachusetts Naval Reserves Leaving the U.S.S. "Alabama"
1910 U.S. Submarine "Salmon"

Universal
1907 Universal Winter Sports
Good Glue Sticks (La colle universelle)

University
1897 Stanford University, California
1899 Oxford and Cambridge University Boat Crews
Pole Vaulting at Columbia University
1901 'Varsity Crew Race on Cayuga Lake, on Decoration Day, Lehigh Valley Observation Train Following the Race, Showing Cornell Crew Finishing First, Columbia Second, University of Pennsylvania Third Ithaca, N.Y., Showing Lehigh Valley Observation Train
1902 Installation Ceremonies, Columbia University
Prince Henry [of Prussia] Visiting Cambridge, Mass. and Harvard University
The University College of Oxford Winning the Ladies' Challenge Plate
1904 University of Pennsylvania Football Team

University of Pennsylvania
1901 'Varsity Crew Race on Cayuga Lake, on Decoration Day, Lehigh Valley Observation Train Following the Race, Showing Cornell Crew Finishing First, Columbia Second, University of Pennsylvania Third Ithaca, N.Y., Showing Lehigh Valley Observation Train
1903 Harvard-Pennsylvania Football Game
1904 University of Pennsylvania Football Team

Unkindness
1909 The Stepmother: the Spirit of Unkindness and Jealousy Thwarted

Unknown
1907 Unknown Talent
1910 The Unknown Claim

Unlimited
1910 The Unlimited Train

Unloading
1898 U.S. Cavalry Supplies Unloading at Tampa, Florida
1900 Demonstrating the Action of the Brown Hoisting and Conveying Machine in Unloading a Schooner of Iron Ore, and Loading the Material on the Cars
Unloading Lighters, Manila
1901 Unloading a Mackerel Schooner
Unloading Cod
Unloading Halibut
1902 Natives Unloading a Boat of Fire-Wood at Carbet (A Suburb of St. Pierre)
Natives Unloading a Coaling Vessel at Fort de France, Martinique
1903 Loading and Unloading the Chutes at Willow Grove
Panorama of Circus Train Unloading Horses
Unloading Canal Boat
Unloading the Elephants
1904 Unloading Fish at Cannery
1905 Unloading Fish, Killisnoo Alaska
1907 Making the Dirt Fly: Scene 2. Unloading a Dirt Train
Unloading Mail at Pier 13, N. R., N.Y.

Unlucky
1899 "It's Unlucky To Pass Under a Ladder"
1901 An Unlucky Lover
1905 Unlucky at Cards, Lucky at Love
1907 Unlucky Interference
Unlucky Substitution
Unlucky Trousers
1908 Unlucky Artist
Unlucky Luck
Unlucky Old Flirt
1909 Two Very Unlucky Thieves
An Unlucky Acquisition
Unlucky Bridegroom
The Unlucky Horseshoe
Unlucky Smuggler
The Unlucky Thief
1910 The Unlucky Fisherman

Unmailed
1910 The Unmailed Letter

Unpleasant
1903 An Unpleasant Situation
1907 An Unpleasant Legacy
1909 Unpleasant Substitution
1910 An Unpleasant Dream

Unprofitable
1909 An Unprofitable Call
Unprofitable Experiment

Unprotected
1903 An Unprotected Female

Unquenchable
1906 Unquenchable Thirst

Unreasonable
1910 Unreasonable Jealousy

Unrequited
1908 Unrequited Love
1910 Unrequited Love

Unrewarded
1908 A Kindness Never Goes Unrewarded

Unsaddled
1904 Gate Jumping by Unsaddled Horse

Unselfishness
1908 An Unselfish Guest (?)
1909 Liberty for an Hour; or, An Act of Unselfishness
1910 An Unselfish Love

Unsinkable
1902 An Unsinkable Skimmer

Unsophisticated
1910 The Unsophisticated Book Agent

Unspoken
1909 The Unspoken Goodbye

Unsuccessful
1898 An Unsuccessful Raid
1908 Unsuccessful Flirts
1909 An Unsuccessful Substitution

Untamable
1904 The Untamable Whiskers

Untimely
1910 The Untimely Visit

Unusual
1903 An Unusual Spectacle
1908 Unusual Cooking
1909 Unusual Elopement

Unveiling
1897 Unveiling of the Washington Monument
1899 Unveiling of Grant Monument
Unveiling the Statue of Gen. U.S. Grant
1901 The Duke and Duchess of York Presenting Medals to Boer War Veterans at the Unveiling of the Queen's Statue
Unveiling Chair of Justice
1902 Unveiling of the Bismarck Monument
Unveiling the Rochambeau Statue in Washington, D.C.
Unveiling the Rochambeau Statue, Washington, D.C.
1903 Unveiling of Logan's Monument
1907 The Unveiling Ceremonies of the McKinley Memorial, Canton, Ohio, September 30th, 1907

Unwelcome
1898 The Unwelcome Callers
An Unwelcome Visitor
1902 An Unwelcome Visitor
1909 The Unwelcome Lover

Unwilling
1908 Unwilling Chiropodist
1909 Jane Is Unwilling to Work

Unworthy
1910 An Unworthy Fiancé

Unwritten
1907 The Unwritten Law: A Thrilling Drama Based on the Thaw White Case
1909 An Unwritten Letter

Unyielding
1908 Unyielding Parent

Up-to-date
1899 An Up-to-date Female Drummer
1900 Up-to-date Cake-Walk
1902 Legerdemain Up-to-date, or the Great Hermann Outdone
1903 Barber Up-to-date
Hatching Chickens Up-to-date
The Up-to-date Spiritualism
Up-to-date Surgery
1904 Up-to-date Burglars; or, The Mystified Cops
The Up-to-date Wizard
1905 Life Saving Up-to-date
1906 Love vs. Title; or, An Up-to-date Elopement
1907 Woman Up-to-date
1908 Caesar Up-to-date
A Fool and His Money Are Soon Parted; or, The Prodigal Son Up-to-date
Up-to-date Clothes Cleaning
Up-to-date Removal
1909 Cinderella Up-to-date
1910 Up-to-date Servants

Uplifting
1909 The Uplifting of Mr. Barker

Upper Falls, Yellowstone River (Wyoming)
1901 Upper Falls of the Yellowstone
1905 Brink of the Upper Falls of the Yellowstone River, Wyoming
Upper Fall of the Yellowstone River

Upper Kicking Horse Canyon (Canada)
1901 Panoramic View, Upper Kicking Horse Canyon

Upper Rapids, Niagara Falls (New York)
1896 Upper Rapids, from Bridge

Upper Tugela (South Africa)
1900 Battle of the Upper Tugela

Uprising
1910 The Uprising of the Utes

Upset
1907 Upset by a Cigarette
1909 The World Upset

Upside down
1903 Upside Down
1909 In the Land of Upsidedown

Urchins
1903 East Side Urchins Bathing in a Fountain
1907 Life of a Bootblack; or, the Street Urchin
1910 Honest Little Urchin

Urn
1902 The Mysterious Urn

Ursula (Boat)
1909 "Ursula," World's Fastest Motor Boat

Ursus
1905 Wrestler and Bull (Ursus et son taureau lutteur)

Use
1902 Mr. Grauman. For Private Use
1906 Dogs Used as Smugglers
1908 A New Electrical Discovery and Its Uses
A Useful Beard
Useful Present for a Child
Usefulness at an End
1909 Useful Young Man

Usher
1898 Pope Leo XIII Leaving Carriage and Being Ushered into Garden, No. 104
1910 John, the Usher

Usurer
1910 The Usurer

Usurper
1909 Romance of the Crafty Usurper and the Young King
1910 The Usurper

Ute Indians
1898 Buck Dance, Ute Indians
Circle Dance, Ute Indians
1903 Ute Indian Snake Dance
1910 Thoughtfulness Remembered by the Ute
The Uprising of the Utes

Ute Pass (Colorado)
1902 Panorama of Ute Pass
Ute Pass Express

Venetian Tragedy
1908 The Grand Canal in Venice
The Merchant of Venice
Northern Venice
Panorama of Venice
A Trip on the Venetian Canals
Venice and the Lagoon
1909 The Carnival of Venice
Grand Canal, Venice
1910 Mysteries of Bridge of Sighs at Venice
The Soul of Venice
Venetian Isles
Venice

Vent
1905 The "Black Growler" Steam Vent, Yellowstone Park

Ventilators
1909 Ambulance Ventilators

Ventnor (England)
1909 The Old Lord of Ventnor

Venus
1900 Birth of Venus

Vera
1910 Vera, the Gypsy Girl

Vercingetorix
1909 Vercingetorix—Gaul's Hero

Vernal Falls, Yosemite Valley (California)
1903 U.S. Interior Dept.: Vernal Falls
1905 Brink of the Vernal Fall, Yosemite Valley
Vernal Falls, Yosemite Valley, California

Verne, Jules
1905 A Little Jules Verne

Verona (Italy)
1910 Verona

Versailles (France)
1905 Big Fountain at Versailles
1909 Versailles

Version
1903 The New Version of the Two Old Sports

Versus
1897 Bayonet Versus Bayonet
Downey vs. Monaghan
1898 Train vs. Donovan
1899 Armor vs. Amour
Chuck Connors vs. Chin Ong
"Columbia" vs. "Defender"
Myopia vs. Dedham
Polo—Hurlingham vs. Ranelagh
1900 Pat vs. Populist
Polo Game: Myopia vs. Dedham
1901 Football Game: West Point vs. Annapolis
International Field Sports—Oxford-Cambridge vs. Harvard-Yale
International Yacht Races—Columbia vs. Shamrock
Match Race, Endurance by Right vs. Heno
Soot Versus Suds
1903 Bullet vs. Whiskey
"Reliance" vs. "Shamrock" III, Aug. 20
Soap vs. Blacking
1904 Rum vs. Cherries
1905 "Play Ball"—Opening Game, National League, N.Y. City, 1905—New York vs. Boston
1906 Love vs. Title; or, An Up-to-Date Elopement
Terrier vs. Wild Cat
1908 Duty Versus Revenge
Michigan vs. Penn Football game
1910 Capital vs. Labor
Owen Moran vs. Battling Nelson
Speed Versus Death

Vertical
1906 Vertical Panorama City Hall and Surroundings

Vesper Boat Club, Philadelphia (Pennsylvania)
1900 Vesper Boat Club

Vessel
1897 Outbound Vessel Passing Governors Island, N.Y. Harbor
1898 Fishing Vessels After the Blizzard
1900 Demonstrating the Action of Pneumatic Shell Riveters on the Underside of the Hull of a Steel Vessel. Taken for the Chicago Pneumatic Tool Co.
1902 Loading a Vessel at Charleston, S. C.
Natives Unloading a Coaling Vessel at Fort de France, Martinique
1903 Sunken Vessel in the Harbor
1904 An Ice Covered Vessel
1910 Blue Jackets' Manoeuvres on a Sailing Vessel

Vestal
1908 The Vestal
1910 The Vestal

Vesuvius (Italy)
1904 Tour in Italy (De Naples au Vésuve)
1906 A Trip from Naples to Vesuvius, Showing the Volcano in Action
1907 Naples to Vesuvius

Vesuvius (Mountain), Italy
1906 Eruption of Mt. Vesuvius
1908 The Eruption of Mt. Vesuvius

Veteran
1897 Amoskeag Veterans, New Hampshire
Grant Veterans—G.A.R.
1898 Grand Army Veterans of Chicago
Grand Army Veterans of New York
Grand Army Veterans of Philadelphia
Veteran Zouaves
1899 Col. John Jacob Astor, Staff and Veterans of the Spanish-American War
1900 The Parade of Naval Veterans
1901 The Duke and Duchess of York Presenting Medals to Boer War Veterans at the Unveiling of the Queen's Statue
1908 A Dislocated Veteran
The Strenuous War Veteran's Story
1909 The Wooden-Headed Veteran
1910 The Three Cherry Pits; or, The Veteran's Honor
A Veteran of the G.A.R.

Vevey (Switzerland)
1905 Bacchanale Fete of Vevey
Dance of the Autumn Leaves, Vevey Fete
Gardener's Dance, Vevey Fete
Garland Dance, Vevey Fete
Panorama of the Theatre, Vevey Fete
Panorama of Theatre, Vevey Fete
Procession of Costumed Characters, Vevey Fete
Procession of Performers at Fete of Vevey
Shepherd's Dance, Vevey Fete
Spectators Leaving the Theatre Vevey
Triumphal Entry of Performers, Vevey Fete

Viaduct
1905 Across the New Viaduct of New York

Vicar
1905 The Vicar's Garden Party
1909 The Good Vicar
1910 The Vicar of Wakefield

Vice
1909 Gaffles, Vice King of Police

Vice-President
1897 Vice-President Hobart's Escort
1901 Opening of the Pan-American Exposition Showing Vice President Roosevelt Leading the Procession
1905 Inauguration of President Roosevelt. President-Elect Roosevelt, Vice-President-Elect Fairbanks and Escort Going to the Capitol
1908 H. R. H. The Prince of Wales Decorating the Monument of Champlain and Receiving Addresses of Welcome from the Mayor of Quebec, the Governor General of Canada and Vice-President Fairbanks, Representative of the United States

Viceroy
1900 Funeral of Chinese Viceroy, Chung Fing Dang, Marching Through the European Quarter at Peking
1903 Viceroy of India's Royal Levee

Vicksburg (Mississippi)
1910 The Girl Spy Before Vicksburg

Victim
1898 Burial of the "Maine" Victims
An Innocent Victim
1903 Photographer's Victim
A Victim of Circumstantial Evidence
1904 Alcohol and Its Victims
1905 Female Crook and Her Easy Victim
1906 Hairdresser's Victim
Victims of the Storm
1907 Victim of Science
1908 Circumstantial Evidence, or, An Innocent Victim
The Glacier's Victim
Love's Victim
Victim of Heroism
Victim of His Honesty
1909 Victim of a Crisis
1910 Foolshead Victim of His Honesty
A Victim of Bridge
A Victim of Circumstances
A Victim of Hate
A Victim of Jealousy
Victims of Fate
Victims of Jealousy

Victoire
1907 How Bridget's Lover Escaped (Le mariage de Victoire)

Victoria Falls (Africa)
1907 The Great Victoria Falls

Victoria Jubilee Bridge, Montreal (Canada)
1900 Victoria Jubilee Bridge

Victoria, Hotel, London (England)
1899 Stage Coaches Leaving the Hotel Victoria

Victoria, Port
1903 Arrival of H.I.M. The German Emperor, at Port Victoria

Victoria, Queen of England, 1819-1901
1899 Her Majesty, Queen Victoria
Her Majesty, Queen Victoria, Reviewing the Honorable Artillery
Her Majesty, Queen Victoria, Reviewing the Household Cavalry at Spital Barracks
1900 Queen Victoria's Last Visit to Ireland
1901 Queen Victoria's Funeral [Number 1]
Queen Victoria's Funeral [Number 2]
Queen Victoria's Funeral [Number 3]

Victorine
1907 How Bridget's Lover Escaped (Le mariage de Victorine)

Victory
1898 Victorious Squadron Firing Salute
1908 Reception for the Victorious Olympic Team of American Athletes at City Hall, New York
1910 Mother's Victory
The Victory of Israel [The Life of Moses Part IV]

Videos
1908 The Videos

Viege Zermatt Railway
1908 The Viege Zermatt Railway

View
1896 Canadian Falls—Panoramic [View] from Michigan Central R.R.
Panoramic View from Trolley, Atlantic City
View on Boulevard, New York City
1897 A Panoramic View in the Grand Canal
Panoramic View of Grand Canal
Panoramic View of Venice
Receding View, Black Diamond Express
1898 California Orange Groves, Panoramic View
Close View of the "Brooklyn," Naval Parade
Panoramic View of Camp Wikoff
Three Views of the 69th Regiment, N.G.S.N.Y.
View of Cramp's Shipyard
View of League Island, Philadelphia
1899 Full View of Brooklyn Bridge
Panoramic View, Horseshoe Curve, From Penna. Ltd.
Panoramic View, Horseshoe Curve, Penna. R.R., No. 2
Panoramic View of Brooklyn Bridge
Panoramic View of Floral Float "Olympia"
Panoramic View of Manila Harbor
Panoramic View of Niagara Falls
Panoramic View of Olympia in New York Harbor
Panoramic View of Windsor Castle
View of Brooklyn Bridge from a Ferryboat
1900 Bird's-Eye View of Dock Front, Galveston
Birdseye View of Galveston, Showing Wreckage
Panoramic View of Burning Wharves and Warehouses [Hoboken]
Panoramic View of Newport [R.I.]
Panoramic View of Rome
Panoramic View of the Champs Elysees
Panoramic View of the Dewey Arch, New York City
Panoramic View of the Ghetto, New York City
Panoramic View of the Place de la Concorde
Panoramic View of Tremont Hotel, Galveston
Panoramic View, Rescue Work, Galveston
Panoramic View, Wreckage Along Shore, Galveston

Virginia (State)
1897 Gov. John A. Tanner, of Virginia, and Staff
Guard Mount, Ft. Myer [Va.]
1903 Essence of Old Virginia
1904 Military Maneuvers, Manassas, Va.
1907 Colonial Virginia and Burning of Jamestown
Jamestown Exposition International Naval Review, Hampton Roads, Virginia
1908 Colonial Virginia
1909 Pennsylvania Monument at Fort Mahone near Petersburg, Va.
Reception of President Taft in Petersburg, Virginia, May 19th, 1909
Stirring Days in Old Virginia
1910 A Daughter of Virginia
[Potomac Falls, Virginia]
Troop "B", 15th U.S. Cavalry Bareback Squad in the Monkey Drill at Fort Myer, Virginia

Virginius
1909 Virginius

Virtue
1906 Virtue Rewarded

Viscaya (Boat)
1898 Spanish Battleship "Viscaya"

Visconti, Agnes
1910 Agnes Visconti

Vision
1901 Ten Nights in a Bar-Room: Vision of Mary
1902 The Murderer's Vision
1903 A Child's Vision
Policeman's Interrupted Vision
1904 Vision of Art
1907 The Vision of a Crime
1908 The Accusing Vision
Policeman's Vision
1909 Child's Vision
The Poet's Vision
Visions of a Goldsmith
Visions of a Nag
Visions of Mother
1910 Saved by a Vision

Visit
1897 Visit of St. Nicholas
1898 A Country Couple's Visit to an Art Gallery
Uncle Rube's Visit to the Man-o' War
The Unexpected Visit
An Unwelcome Visitor
1900 Queen Victoria's Last Visit to Ireland
Santa Claus' Visit
Visit to a Spiritualist
A Visit to Baby Roger
A Visit to the Spiritualist
1901 Hooligan Visits Central Park
1902 Prince Henry [of Prussia] Arriving in Washington and Visiting the German Embassy
Prince Henry [of Prussia] Visiting Cambridge, Mass. and Harvard University
Rube's Visit to the Studio
An Unwelcome Visitor
Visit of Emperor Francis Josef of Austria to Berlin
1903 The Cook Visits the Parlor
King Edward's Visit to Ireland
King Edward's Visit to Paris
Lady Bountiful Visits the Murphys on Wash Day
Old Maid's First Visit to a Theatre
Pres. Roosevelt's Sunday Visit to Kearsage
President Roosevelt's Visit to Admiral Barker
Troubles of a Country Visitor
A Visit to the London Zoo
A Visit to the Zoo
Visitors in Wheeling Chairs, National Cash Register Co.
What Befell the Inventor's Visitor
1904 Mr. Jack Visits the Dressing Room
Piraeus and Athens (Greece). A Visit to Piraeus
1905 Trains Arriving at Henley Station with Regatta Visitors
Custom House Search (Visite de la douane)
1907 A Chinaman Visits London
Cousin's Visit
Willie Goodchild Visits His Auntie
1908 Gaston Visits Museum
A Visit to Compiegne and Pierrefond
A Visit to the Public Nursery
1909 Aunt Lena's Visit
The Bachelor's Visit
A Bride and Groom's Visit to the New York Zoological Gardens
Foolshead Pays a Visit
His Wife's Visitor
King Edward's Visit to Berlin
Mady Millicent's Visitor
Mary Jane Visits Her Country Cousin
Uncle Rube's Visit
Visit from the "Down Home Folks"
A Visit to Biskra
A Visit to the London Zoological Gardens
A Visit to Uncle
1910 MacNab Visits the Comet
The Surgeon's Visit
The Untimely Visit
A Visit to Bombay
A Visit to the Seaside at Brighton Beach, England
Willie Visits a Moving Picture Show

Visp-Zermatt Railway
1905 Panorama from Train on Visp-Zermatt Railway

Vitagraph Cup
1908 An Auto Heroine; or, The Race for the Vitagraph Cup and How It Was Won

Vitellius
1910 Vitellius and Heliogabalus

Vivandiera
1910 The Vivandiera

Vivant
1902 The Bon Vivant

Vivisection
1902 Wonderful Feats of Vivisection

Vixen
1910 The Little Vixen
The Vixen

Vizcaya (Boat)
1898 The Spanish Cruiser Vizcaya
"Vizcaya" Under Full Headway
Wreck of the "Vizcaya"

Voice
1905 His Master's Voice
1906 Voice of Conscience
1907 What His Girl's Voice Did
1908 His Daughter's Voice
A Voice from the Dead
The Voice of the Heart
1909 The Voice of the Violin
1910 A Powerful Voice
A Voice from the Fireplace
The Voice of the Blood

Volcano
1906 A Trip from Naples to Vesuvius, Showing the Volcano in Action
1909 Volcanoes of Java
1910 Neapolitan Volcanic Islands
Volcanic Eruptions of Mt. Aetna
The Volcano of Chinyero

Volksfest
1903 Volksfest, Philadelphia

Volksraad
1903 Kruger and Body Guard Leaving the Volksraad
Kruger Leaving His Residence for the Volksraad

Volley
1898 Volley Firing

Volodyovski (Horse)
1901 "Volodyovski"

Voltaire (Boat)
1909 Launching the "Voltaire"

Volunteer
1898 Bayonet Charge; by the 2nd Illinois Volunteers
California Volunteers Marching To Embark
Company "C," 1st Regiment, N.J.V.
Company "H," 3rd N.Y.V.
Cuban Volunteers
Cuban Volunteers Embarking
Cuban Volunteers Marching for Rations
18th Pennsylvania Volunteers
Eighth Ohio Volunteers (the President's Own)
Fifteenth Minnesota Volunteers
Fifth Massachusetts Volunteers
First Battalion of the 2nd Massachusetts Volunteers
First Maryland Volunteers
1st Regiment, N.Y.V.
First Rhode Island Volunteers
Irish Volunteers
Second Battalion; 2nd Massachusetts Volunteers
Second Illinois Volunteers at Double Time
Second Illinois Volunteers in Review
Seventh Ohio Volunteers
71st N.Y. Volunteers Embarking for Santiago
Sixth Pennsylvania Volunteers
65th Regiment, N.Y.V.
Spanish Volunteers in Havana
Tenth Regiment, Ohio Volunteers
Third Missouri Volunteers
Third Pennsylvania Volunteers
13th Regiment Pennsylvania Volunteers
32nd Regiment, Michigan Volunteers
33rd Regiment, Michigan Volunteers
22nd Regiment, Kansas Volunteers
The Volunteer Fireman
1899 Advance of Kansas Volunteers at Caloocan
Battle Flag of the 10th Pennsylvania Volunteers, Carried in the Philippines
Dewey Parade, 10th Pennsylvania Volunteers
Eighth Regiment, Mass. Volunteers
5th Ohio Volunteers of Cleveland
1st Penn' Volunteers of Philadelphia
Fourth Connecticut Volunteers, Dewey Parade
Review of First Rhode Island Volunteers
10th Penn'a Volunteers
A Volunteer Fire Company
1902 Old Volunteer Fire Dept.
1903 Parade of the Philadelphia Volunteer Fire Department
1906 The 9th Mass. Vol. Militia
Volunteer Fire Department Parade
1907 Volunteer's Betrothal
1910 Foolshead Volunteer on the Red Cross

Voringfos Waterfall (Norway)
1905 Voringfos Waterfall Norway

Vote
1907 When Women Vote
1908 Votes for Women
1909 Votes for Women
1910 The Deciding Vote
We Want Your Vote

Vow
1900 Childhood's Vows
1908 The Vaquero's Vow
1909 The Gambler's Vow
1910 Ononko's Vow
The Vow, or, Jephthah's Daughter

Voyage
1904 An Impossible Voyage
Voyage of the "Arctic"
White Star S.S. Baltic Leaving Pier on First Eastern Voyage
1906 Voyage Around a Star
A Road Side Inn (L'hotel des voyageurs de commerce)
Engadin in Switzerland (Voyage en Suisse—l'Engadine)
1907 The Atlantic Voyage
A Rolling Bed (Le lit voyageur)
1908 Royal Voyage to Canada
1909 Not Wanted on Voyage
1910 Their Sea Voyage

Vulture
1908 Human Vultures
1909 Vulture Hunting in Africa
1910 Vulture of Seine

Waddell, Rube
1902 Rube Waddell and the Champion Playing Ball with the Boston Team

Waders
1903 The Waders

Wager
1904 A Wager Between Two Magicians; or, Jealous of Myself

Wages
1901 The Wages of Sin—A Mother's Grief
The Wages of Sin—The Assassin's Escape
The Wages of Sin—The Fatal Choice
The Wages of Sin—The Murder of Bess
1903 The Wages of Sin: A—Murder
The Wages of Sin: B—Retribution
1907 A Shilling Short in Wages
1908 The Farmer's Daughter; or, The Wages of Sin
His Week's Wages; or, Where's That Quarter?

War
1898 Indian War Council
Naval Reserves Returning from the War
"New York Journal's War Issue"
Practice Warfare
1899 Col. John Jacob Astor, Staff and Veterans of the Spanish-American War
Distributing a War Extra
The Humane Side of Modern Warfare
Love and War
1900 Boer War Film
Off for the Boer War
South African War Subjects
1901 The Duke and Duchess of York Presenting Medals to Boer War Veterans at the Unveiling of the Queen's Statue
The War in China
The War in China—A British Donkey Train
The War in China—An Army Transport Train
The War in China—Bombay Cavalry
The War in China—British Light Artillery
The War in China—British Rajputs
The War in China—Coolies at Work
The War in China—First Bengal Lancers
The War in China—Japanese Infantry
The War in China
The War in China—Review of German Troops
The War in China—Ruins of Tien-Tsin
The War in China—The Evacuation of Pekin
The War in China—The Fourth Goorkhas
The War in China—The German Contingent
The War in China—Von Waldersee and Staff
The War in China—Von Waldersee's Review
1902 German Soldiers Starting for War
Transporting a War Balloon
1903 The American Soldier in Love and War
The American Soldier in Love and War [Number 1]
The American Soldier in Love and War [Number 2]
The American Soldier in Love and War [Number 3]
Transvaal War Supplies Transported by McKenzie Traction Engines
War Supplies Arriving at Boer Laager by Train of Ox Teams
1904 War Balloon Ascending and Descending
War Canoe Race
1905 The Boer War
Naval Warfare
Defense of Port Arthur (Guerre russo-japonaise no. 4)
1906 War of Children
1907 The Slave, a Story of the South Before the War
The Spy, a Romantic Story of the Civil War
1908 All Is Fair in Love and War
Charity Begins at Home, a Story of the South During the Civil War
For Love of Country: American Patriotism in the Colonial Wars
Hannah Dustin: The Border Wars of New England
The Molly Maguires; or, Labor Wars in the Coal Mines
The Patriot; or, The Horrors of War
Romance of a War Nurse
The Strenuous War Veteran's Story
War Episode
1909 Don Juan; or, A War Drama of the Eighteenth Century
Episode in Boer War
Episode of Cuban War
Episode of War
The Girl Scout; or the Canadian Contingent in the Boer War
The Girl Spy: An Incident of the Civil War
Hero of the Prussian War
Love and War: An Episode of Waterloo
A Sister's Love, a Tale of the Franco-Prussian War
A War Time Tale
A Wartime Sweetheart
1910 All's Fair in Love and War
Civil War
Corporal Truman's War Story
Cuban War
An Episode of Napoleon's War with Spain
In War Time
The Judas Money; or, An Episode of the War in Vendee
Ransomed; or, A Prisoner of War
War
War Time Pals

War correspondents
1898 War Correspondents
1904 The War Correspondent and the Two Bear Cubs

War dance
1899 A Zulu War Dance
1903 Crow Indian War Dance
Indian War Dance
Philippino War Dance

Ward
1909 His Ward's Love
The Judge's Ward
1910 The Clergyman and His Ward
The Cowpuncher's Ward
Elder Alden's Indian Ward
Mexican's Ward
A Ward of Uncle Sam

Warden
1909 The Fish Pirates; or, The Game Warden's Test
The Warden's Nightmare

Wardrobe
1901 The Extensive Wardrobe
1902 The Extensive Wardrobe
The Inexhaustible Wardrobe
1904 The Enchanted Wardrobe
1908 Antique Wardrobe

Warehouses
1900 Panoramic View of Burning Wharves and Warehouses [Hoboken]

Warm
1898 They're Not So Warm
1899 A Warm Baby with a Cold Deck
1904 A Warm Occasion
1910 Mrs. Cannon Is Warm

Warning
1907 The Gypsy's Warning
1908 Gypsy's Warning
1909 A Telepathic Warning, the Story of a Child's Love for Her Father

Warpath
1908 Emperor Nero on the Warpath
I'm Going on the War Path
On the War Path
1909 On the Warpath

Warrior
1904 Japanese Warriors in Ancient Battle Scene
Real Warrior
1908 A Football Warrior
1909 The Warrior's Sacrifice
1910 A Warrior Bold

Warsaw (Poland)
1904 Polish Fire Brigade Answering an Alarm, Warsaw
Russian Infantry, Warsaw

Warship
1897 German Warship at Spithead
1898 Officers of the War Ships
Warships
1904 Warship in Nagasaki Harbor, Japan
1905 A German Warship in a Heavy Sea

Warsmen
1908 Warsmen at Play

Warwick (England)
1907 The Warwick Pageant

Wash
1896 A Hard Wash
1897 Washing the Baby
1898 9th Infantry Boys' Morning Wash
Soldiers Washing Dishes
Wash Day in Mexico
Washing the Streets of Porto Rico
1901 Washing Down Decks
Washing Gold on 20 Above Hunker, Klondike
1902 Native Women Washing Clothes at Fort de France
Native Women Washing Clothes at the Gueydon Fountain, Fort de France, Martinique
Wash Day
1903 Lady Bountiful Visits the Murphys on Wash Day
Native Woman Washing a Negro Baby in Nassau, B. I.
Native Women Washing Clothes at St. Vincent, B. W. I.
Piping Down. Wash Clothes. Scrambling for Clothes
Sea Washing over the Bow of Kearsage
Wash Day in Camp
Washing Clothes at Sicily
Washing Elephants
1904 Washing Sheep
1905 His Washing Day
1906 Wash Day at Casey's
Washing Sheep, Humunla Beach, Hawaii
1907 Father's Washing Day
Washings Badly Marked
Who'll Do the Washing?
1909 Adele's Wash Day
Mr. Jenkins Washes Up
1910 Washed Ashore

Washerwoman
1897 The Washwoman's Troubles
1898 The Washwoman's Daughter
1902 The Mischievous Boys and the Washerwoman
1903 Humpty's Troubles with the Washwoman
Trouble with the Washerwoman
Washerwoman's Mistake
Washerwomen and Chimney-Sweep
1904 The Quarrelsome Washerwoman
Washerwoman and Buss
1905 Gay Washerwoman
1908 The Washerwoman's Revenge

Washing machine
1899 Scrubbem's Washing Machine

Washington, George
1908 Washington at Valley Forge
1910 [Washington's Home and Ground at Mount Vernon]

Washington, D.C.
1897 Corcoran Cadets, Washington
A Part of Inaugural Parade, Washington
Pennsylvania Avenue, Washington
Pennsylvania Avenue, Washington, D.C.
Pile Driving, Washington Navy Yard [Washington, D.C.]
Washington Continental Guards
1901 A Composite Picture of the Principal Buildings in Washington, D.C.
Panoramic View of the Capitol, Washington, D.C.
Panoramic View of the White House, Washington, D.C.
President McKinley's Funeral Cortege at Washington, D.C.
1902 Funeral Procession of Admiral Sampson at Washington
President and Prince at Washington
Prince Henry [of Prussia] Arriving in Washington and Visiting the German Embassy
Unveiling the Rochambeau Statue in Washington, D.C.
Unveiling the Rochambeau Statue, Washington, D.C.
1903 Prince Henry at Washington
1906 Scenes Washington, D.C.
1909 A Day in Washington, the Capital of the United States, Showing Many Points of Interest
Washington Under the American Flag
Washington Under the British Flag

Washington (Lake), Seattle (Washington)
1907 Along the Shore Line of Lake Washington

Washington (Mountain), New Hampshire
1899 Sliding Down Mount Washington
Summit of Mt. Washington

Washington (State)
1897 First Avenue, Seattle, Washington, No. 8
1903 James Street, Seattle, Wash.
Pacific Avenue, Tacoma, Wash.
Riverside Avenue, Spokane, Wash.

Washington and New York Flyer
1897 Washington Flyer
1903 Rear View of the Washington and New York Flyer
Washington and New York Flyer

Washington Bridge (New York City)
1901 Washington Bridge and Speedway

Washington Committee of Arrangements
1899 Admiral Dewey Receiving the Washington and New York Committees
Admiral Dewey Taking Leave of Washington Committee on the U.S. Cruiser 'Olympia'

1904 The Providence of the Waves; or, The Dream of a Poor Fisherman
1907 Crime Wave
1909 On the Crest of the Waves
1910 Fury of the Waves
Gigantic Waves
Sea Waves
Wild Waves at St. Jean-de-Lux

Waving
1904 Girl Waving American Flag, National Cash Register Co.
Waving American Flag—National Cash Register Co.

Wawona Big Tree, Mariposa Grove (California)
1901 Wawona, Big Tree
1905 Arrival of the Stage at Wawona Hotel, Enroute to Yosemite
Stages Passing Through Wawona Big Tree, Mariposa Grove, California

Way
1898 Three Ways of Climbing over a Chair
'Way Down South
1899 Police Boats and Pleasure Craft on Way to Olympia
The Way French Bathing Girls Bathe
Where There's a Will, There's a Way
1900 Irish Way of Discussing Politics
1901 Train of Sugar Cane on Way to Crusher
1902 King Edward and Queen Alexandra on Their Way to Westminster
An Old Fashioned Way of Pulling a Tooth
1904 The Liberty Bell on Its Way to the Exposition
Love Will Find a Way
A Novel Way of Catching a Burglar
One Way of Taking a Girl's Picture
The Way to Sell Corsets
1905 Bringing Up a Girl in the Way She Should Go [No. 1]
Bringing Up a Girl in the Way She Should Go [No. 2]
1907 Asking His Way
The Red Man's Way
1908 The Determined Lovers; or, Where There's a Will, There's a Way
Different Ways of Smuggling
The Girl Across the Way
Love Will Find a Way
A New Way of Traveling
A New Way to Pay Debts
'Way Down East
The Way They Fooled Dad
A Woman's Way
1909 The Better Way
Her Generous Way
Love Finds a Way
The Way of Man
The Way of the Cross, the Story of Ancient Rome
The Way to Happiness
Where There's a Will There's a Way
A Woman's Way
1910 Her Winning Way
A Man's Way
Matilda's Winning Ways
A Mohawk's Way
The Other Way
So Runs the Way
The Way of Life
The Way of the Red Man
The Way of the Transgressor Is Hard
The Way of the West
The Way of the World
The Way to Win
A Western Woman's Way
A Westerner's Way

Wayback
1899 Farmer Wayback Entertains

Wayside
1910 The Wayside Shrine

Wayward
1908 A Wayward Daughter

Weak
1910 The Man with the Weak Heart

Wealth
1906 Ephemeral Wealth
Wealthy but Homeless Citizens of San Francisco Cooking Their Meals in the Open Air at Jefferson Sq.
1907 A Tramp's Dream of Wealth
1908 A Dream of Wealth, a Tale of the Gold Seekers of '49
1909 The Wealthy Rival; or A Summer Story That Needs No Explanation
1910 Floating to Wealth
Hobo's Dream of Wealth

Weapons
1909 Choice of Weapons
1910 Insidious Weapons

Wearing
1910 Wearing of the Green

Weary
1898 "Weary Raggles"
1902 The Weary Hunters and the Magician
The Weary Traveller and His Wonderful Dream
1908 House Cleaning Days; or, No Rest for the Weary
Weary Waggles' Busy Day
Weary's Christmas Dinner
1910 No Rest for the Weary

Weary Willie
1901 "Weary Willie" and the Gardener
1903 Weary Willie and the Policeman
1904 "Weary Willie" Kidnaps a Child
"Weary Willie" Kisses the Bride
1906 Weary Willie and His Pal
1908 Weary Willie's Revenge
1909 Weary Willie Wheeling

Wearybones
1909 Wearybones Seeks Rest, and Gets It

Weather
1901 The Automatic Weather Prophet
1908 Weather Changes at the Smiths
1910 A Rough Weather Courtship

Weaving
1903 Navajo Squaw Weaving Blanket
1907 Indian Basket Weavers

Web
1903 Noon Hour at Hope Webbing Company
Silveon and Emerie "On the Web"
1908 Caught in the Web
1909 The Web of Fate: An Incident of the French Revolution
1910 In the Web

Weber Canyon (Utah)
1899 East of Uintah in Weber Canyon
One Thousand Mile Tree, Weber Canyon
West of Peterson; Entrance to Weber Canyon

Wedding
1900 Those Wedding Bells Shall Not Ring Out
1901 Wedding Procession in Cairo
1903 Wedding Procession in a Church at Rome
1904 The Coster's Wedding
A Wedding of Correspondence
The Passion Play (Les noces de Cana)
1905 The Wedding
1906 Fun After the Wedding
No Wedding Bells for Him
The Silver Wedding
A Strenuous Wedding
1907 Late for His Wedding
The Tin Wedding
Tragic Wedding
Trouble at a Wedding
Wedding on Bicycles
Wooing and Wedding of a Coon
1908 Bachelor's Wedding Bells
The Countess' Wedding Day
Leap Year; or, She Would Be Wed
The Rag Pickers' Wedding
The Soldier's Wedding
A Strenuous Wedding
The Watchmaker's Wedding
Wedding in Brittany
A Wedding Under Terror
Why the Wedding Was Put Off
1909 The Belated Wedding
A Chinese Wedding
Eve of the Wedding
Fatal Wedding
A Georgia Wedding
His Wedding Morn
Holding Up the Wedding
Joel's Wedding
Off to the Wedding
Wedding Party in Luna Park
Why the Wedding Didn't Come Off
1910 Circle "C" Ranch Wedding Present
Her Mother's Wedding Gown
Miss Moneybags Wishes to Wed
Nancy's Wedding Trip
Tin Wedding Presents
A Wedding During the French Revolution
A Wedding Trip from Montreal Through Canada to Hong Kong

Wedge
1902 A Flying Wedge

Week
1908 His Week's Wages; or, Where's That Quarter?
Military Parade, Founders Week Celebration, Philadelphia
Rivals for a Week
Three Weeks
1909 The Martins Leave Home for a Week

Weep
1907 Onions Make People Weep
1909 The Fisherman; or, Men Must Work and Women Must Weep

Weighing
1901 Weighing Mutton
1902 Rube and the Weighing Machine
1903 Weighing the Baby
1906 Weighing the Anchor

Weird
1907 Weird Fancies
1908 Weird Symphony

Welch
1910 [Welch-Daniels Fight]

Welcome
1899 A Marblehead Welcome
A Welcome Home
Welcoming the Soldier Boys
1902 Welcome Prince Henry!
1908 H. R. H. The Prince of Wales Decorating the Monument of Champlain and Receiving Addresses of Welcome from the Mayor of Quebec, the Governor General of Canada and Vice-President Fairbanks, Representative of the United States
1909 The Welcome Burglar
1910 A Western Welcome

Welding
1904 Welding Big Ring

Well
1907 All's Well That Ends Well
1909 All's Well That Ends Well
A Case of Spirits; or, All's Well That Ends Well
Trick Well Played
A Well Earned Medal
1910 All's Well That Ends Well
A Thief Well Received

Well-bred
1907 Well-Bred

Wellington Arch, London (England)
1902 The New Crowned King and Queen Passing Through Wellington Arch and Down Constitution Hill

Wells
1899 "Ding, Dong, Dell, Johnny's in the Well"
Shooting an Artesian Well
1900 A Tramp in the Well
1901 California Oil Wells in Operation
1903 The Enchanted Well
1904 The Chappie at the Well
1908 Well-Thy Water
1909 The Cry from the Well
1910 The Lovers' Well
Shooting an Oil Well

Wells, Pauline
1908 The Two Traveling Bags; or, The Adventures of Percy White and Pauline Wells

Welsh rabbit
1903 Making a Welch Rabbit
A Welsh Rabbit
1908 A Sculptor's Welsh Rabbit Dream

Wenonah
1910 Wenonah

Wep-Ton-No-Mah
1909 Wep-Ton-No-Mah, the Indian Mail Carrier

Werther
1910 Werther

Werts, Charles
1897 Chas. Werts, Acrobat

Weser
1909 At the Weser (Song)

The West
1898 Parade of Buffalo Bill's Wild West Show, No. 1
Parade of Buffalo Bill's Wild West Show, No. 2
1900 Buffalo Bill's Wild West Parade
Buffalo Bill's Wild West Show

1904 Children and White Rats
1905 Black and White; or, The Mystery of a Brooklyn Baby Carriage
White Rat and Young
The White Rats
1906 White Fox Motor Boat
1907 Black-White
Light-Fight-White
Mother-in-Law at the White City
The White Shoes; or, Looking Out for His Banknote
1908 A Comedy in Black and White
The Mystery of the Bride, in Black and White
The Mystery of the Bride in White
1909 Lines of White on a Sullen Sea
A Pair of White Gloves
A White Lie
1910 A White Lie
White Roses

White Caps
1900 Indiana Whitecaps
1905 The White Caps

White-Doe
1910 White-Doe's Lover

White Fawn
1910 White Fawn's Devotion

White House (Washington, D.C.)
1901 Panoramic View of the White House, Washington, D.C.
President McKinley Leaving the White House for the Capitol
1902 Egg Rolling at the White House

White Mountains (New Hampshire)
1904 Coaching in the White Mountains

White Pass Railroad (Alaska)
1901 Panoramic View of the White Pass Railroad
1903 Through Tunnel on the White Pass Route
Tunnel Scene of the White Pass Route
Two Miles of the White Pass & Yukon Railroad
1905 Panorama from a Moving Train on White Pass & Yukon Railway, Alaska
Train on the White Pass & Yukon Railway, Alaska

White Star
1904 White Star S.S. Baltic Leaving Pier on First Eastern Voyage

White Wings
1903 White Wings on Review

Whiteface
1905 Everybody Works But Father (Whiteface)

Whitehead
1905 Railway Panorama Between Kilroot and Whitehead

Whitehead torpedo
1900 Discharging a Whitehead Torpedo
Exploding a Whitehead Torpedo

Whitehorse Rapids, Yukon (Canada)
1900 White Horse Rapids
1903 Captain Allard Shooting White Horse Rapids
Panorama of White Horse Rapids
Through White Horse Rapids
United States Mail Leaving Dawson City for White Horse

Whites
1900 Rescue of a White Girl from the Boxers
1907 White Man's First Smoke; or, Puritan Days in America
The White Slave
1908 The White Chief
The White Squaw
1909 Iona, the White Squaw
The Trial of the White Man
1910 Red Wing and the White Girl
The White Captive of the Sioux
White Man's Money, the Indian Curse
The White Princess of the Tribe
The White Squaw

Whitewash
1900 The Tramp Gets Whitewashed
1903 Whitewashing a Colored Baby
1904 The Bobby Whitewashed
The Postman Whitewashed

Whitler
1909 Whitler's Witless Wanderings

Whitney (Boat)
1898 Transport "Whitney" Leaving Dock

Whittier School, Kansas City (Missouri)
1904 Whittier School, Calisthenics, Missouri Commission

Whole
1905 I. B. Dam and the Whole Dam Family
The Whole Dam Family and the Dam Dog
1909 The Whole World Kin

Wicked
1899 The Wicked Sister and the Lobster
1910 The Wicked Baron and the Page

Wicker
1908 Madeira Wicker Chair Industry

Wide
1905 Wide Awake

Widow
1902 Target Practice, and What Happened to Widow Flaherty
1903 The Widow
1904 The Widow and the Only Man
1907 The Merry Widow
Seaman's Widow
1908 Consoling the Widow
The Merry Widow at a Supper Party
The Merry Widow Hat
The "Merry Widow" Hats
Merry Widow Waltz
The Merry Widow Waltz Craze
1909 The Widow
A Widow to Console
Winning a Widow
1910 The Courting of the Merry Widow
The Merry Widow Takes Another Partner
The Sage, the Cherub and the Widow
Who Wins the Widow?
The Widow
A Widow and Her Child
The Widow of Mill Creek Flat
Zeb, Zeke and the Widow

Widower
1908 The Merry Widower; or, The Rejuvenation of a Fossil
Troubles of a Grass Widower
1909 The Happy Widower

Wife
1899 How the Medium Materialized Elder Simpkin's Wife
President McKinley and Wife, Members of His Cabinet and Their Wives and Capt. Coghlan Leaving the Cruiser Raleigh
1900 Jones Interviews His Wife
Pierrot's Problem, or How To Make a Fat Wife Out of Two Lean Ones
Wifie Invades the Studio
1902 Pugilist McKeever and Wife Bag Punching
She Meets with Wife's Approval
1903 His Wife Has Neuralgia
How a Wife Gets Her Pocket Money
How to Get a Wife and Baby
How to Shut Up a Quarrelsome Wife
Murphy Has Trouble with His Wife
Neptune's Wife
Smith's Wife Inspects the New Typewriter
The Unfaithful Wife: Murder and Suicide [Part 3]
The Unfaithful Wife: The Fight [Part 2]
The Unfaithful Wife: The Lover [Part 1]
The Wrath of a Jealous Wife
1904 How a French Nobleman Got a Wife Through the New York Herald "Personal" Columns
Wifey's Christmas Gift
Wifey's Mistake
1905 Capt. John Hance Telling About His 14th Wife, Grand Cañon, Arizona
1906 The Murder of His Seventeen Wives
A Race for a Wife
Ten Wives for One Husband
1907 I Never Forget the Wife
If You Had a Wife Like This
Innkeeper and Wife
The Innkeeper's Wife
Making Love to the Coalman's Wife
My Wife's Birthday
To Tame His Wife
A Too Devoted Wife
Wife Wanted
Wrestler's Wife
Your Wife Is Unfaithful to Us
1908 The Cabby's Wife
The Captain's Wives
The Doctor's Wife
Don't Fool Your Wife
A Faithful Wife
For a Wife's Honor
The Gambler's Wife
Have You Seen My Wife?
The Jealous Wife
My Cabby Wife
My Wife's Dog
Outwitted by His Wife
The Planter's Wife
The Poacher's Wife
The Ringmaster's Wife
The Valet's Wife
A Wife's Devotion
Wifey's Strategy
1909 The Bachelor's Wife
The Blacksmith's Wife
The Cavalier's Wife
The Convict's Wife
Faithful Wife
He Can't Lose Wifie's Ma
He Fell in Love with His Wife
His Wife's Mother
His Wife's Troublesome Twitching
His Wife's Visitor
The Hypnotic Wife
I Love My Wife, but Oh, You Kid
An Indian Wife's Devotion
A Man with Three Wives
The Miner's Wife
My Wife's Gone to the Country
My Wife's Gone to the Country (Hooray! Hooray!)
A Poor Wife's Devotion
The Ranchman's Wife
Royalist's Wife
A Soldier's Wife
Two Chums Looking for Wives
Wife or Child
A Wife's Ordeal
Wifey Away, Hubby at Play
1910 Advertising for a Wife
The Bandit's Wife
The Captain's Wife
The Cigars His Wife Bought
A Cowboy's Race for a Wife
The Gambler's Wife
His Second Wife
His Spanish Wife
His Wife's Sweethearts
His Wife's Testimony
A Husband's Jealous Wife
A Jealous Wife
The Jealous Wife's New Year Day
Love Your Neighbor as Yourself, but Leave His Wife Alone!
The Merry Wives of Windsor
A Mountain Wife
"Oh! You Wives"
A Pair of Schemers; or, My Wife and My Uncle
The Preacher's Wife
The Romany Wife
The Sepoy's Wife
They Have Vanished My Wife
The Wife of Marcius
The Wife's Sacrifice
Wifie's Mamma
Wilson's Wife's Countenance

Wig
1904 The Fatal Wig
1906 The Wig
The Wig Chase
1907 A Wig Made To Order
1909 Sleuth and the Wig

Wig-wagging
1903 Signal Boys Wig-Wagging

Wikoff (Camp), Montauk Point, Long Island (New York)
1898 General Wheeler and Secretary of War Alger at Camp Wikoff
Panoramic View of Camp Wikoff
President McKinley's Inspection of Camp Wikoff

Wild
1901 Wild Bear in Yellowstone Park
1903 A Drove of Wild Welsh Mountain Ponies
"What Are the Wild Waves Saying Sister?"
Wild Mountain Ponies on Dartmoor
1905 Roping and Branding Wild Horses
1908 The Call of the Wild
1909 The Wild Ass's Skin
1910 A Child of the Wild
Mazeppa; or, The Wild Horse of Tartary
Taming Wild Horses at Buenos Aires
Wild Birds in Their Haunts
The Wild Coast of Belle Island

Windfall
1908 A Calamitous Elopement: How It Proved a Windfall for Burglar Bill

Winding
1898 Winding the Maypole
1904 Coil Winding Machines, Westinghouse Works
Coil Winding Section E, Westinghouse Works
Girls Winding Armatures, Westinghouse Works

Window
1903 The Girl at the Window
Window Cleaner's Mishap
Window Display Clown, National Cash Register Co.
Window Display Revolving Balls, National Cash Register Co.
1904 On the Window Shade
What the Window Cleaner Saw
1905 London Ladies Looking at Lingerie in Oxford Street Windows, London
1907 Window Cleaner
The Window Demonstration
1908 The Face in the Window
The Light in the Window
1909 In the Window Recess
1910 The Face at the Window
The Light in the Window

Windsor (England)
1899 Panoramic View of Windsor Castle
1901 The Complete Funeral Cortege Passing Through Windsor
1910 The Merry Wives of Windsor

Windsor Hotel (New York City)
1899 Ruins of the Windsor Hotel Fire

Wine
1896 Wine Garden Scene
1898 The Soubrettes' Wine Dinner
1902 The Burglars in the Wine Cellar
1903 The Monk in the Monastery Wine Cellar
1905 The Wine Opener
Wine, Women & Song [No. 2]
1906 Wine, Women & Song
1907 The Good Wine
Susan Tastes Our Wine
1908 What a Good Wine
1909 A Cask of Good Old Wine
Reformation of a Wine-Loving Artist
Wine a Gent
1910 Making Sherry Wine at Xeres

Wing
1910 The Wings of Love

Wing dance
1903 Buck and Wing Dance
Wing Dance

Winks
1907 Forty Winks; or, A Strenuous Dream

Winnisquam Lake (New Hampshire)
1899 Winnisquam Lake

Winona
1910 Winona

Winslow (Boat)
1898 Torpedo Boat Winslow
1903 Panoramic View of Torpedo Boat "Winslow" and Yacht "Constitution"

Winter
1899 Niagara Falls in Winter
1901 Winter Life in Sweden
1902 Winter in Germany
1903 Winter Sport on Snake River, Nome
Winter Sports on the Lake
1904 Circular Panorama of the Horse Shoe Falls in Winter
International Winter Sports
1905 Winter Sports
1906 A Winter Straw Ride
1907 Tyrolean Alps in the Winter
Universal Winter Sports
Winter Amusements
A Winter Day in the Country
Winter in Switzerland
1908 Niagara Falls in Winter
Winter Manoeuvres of the Norwegian Army
Winter Time in Northern Europe
1909 A Canadian Winter Carnival
Niagara in Winter Dress
Stripping a Forest in Winter
The Thames in Winter
Trollhattan in Winter
Winter Horseplay
Winter Landscapes Round Stockholm
Winter Sports
Winter Sports and Games at Stockholm, Sweden, 1909
Winter Sports in Hungary
A Winter's Tale
1910 In Winter's Grip
Winter Bathing in the West Indies
Winter Days in Sweden
A Winter Romance at Niagara Falls
The Winter's Tale

Winthrop (Boat)
1897 Ferryboat "Winthrop"

Wipe
1907 Wipe Off Your Feet, Please

Wire
1902 The Bibulous Wire Walker
1903 The Wire Walker
1904 DeVoy the Wire Walker
1910 Over the Wire

Wireless
use **Telegraph**

Wiring
1903 Wiring Pike in a Mill Stream

Wisconsin
1903 The Dells of Wisconsin

Wise
1903 The Wise Elephant
1909 Prof. Wise's Brain Serum Injector
1910 Hank and Lank: They Get Wise to a New Scheme
A Wise Guy

Wise men
1909 Four Wise Men

Wish
1908 His Girl's Last Wish
1909 Foolshead Wishes to Commit Suicide
The Wishing Charm
1910 Foolshead Wishes to Marry the Governor's Daughter
Miss Moneybags Wishes to Wed
The Three Wishes

Wishbone
1905 The Lucky Wishbone
1906 The Wishbone
1908 The Wish Bone

Wit
1908 By a Woman's Wit
Tit for Tat; or, Outwitted by Wit
The Witty Ghost
1909 A Woman's Wit
1910 Brave Hearts; or, Saved from the Indians by a Woman's Wit
A Woman's Wit

Witch
1903 The Witch's Revenge
1905 Bedelia and the Witch
1906 The Last Witch
Village Witch
The Witch
1907 The Black Witch
The Witch Kiss
1908 The Witch
Witch's Secret
1909 Cycle Rider and the Witch
In the Days of Witchcraft
Soldier and Witch
The Witch
The Witches' Cavern
The Witch's Donkey
1910 The Witch of Carabosse
The Witch of the Ruins
The Witch's Ballad
The Witch's Spectacles

Witch Rocks
1899 The "Overland Limited" Passing Witch Rocks

Witching hour
1909 'Tis Now the Very Witching Hour of Night

Witless
1909 Whitler's Witless Wanderings

Witness
1908 The Dumb Witness
1910 The Silent Witness

Wizard
1899 The Wizard and the Spirit of the Tree
1900 Allabad, the Arabian Wizard
1904 The Up-to-Date Wizard
1907 Wizard's World
1909 The Hand of a Wizard
The Wizard's Walking Stick
1910 The Wonderful Wizard of Oz

Woes
1908 The Woes of Roller Skates
1909 Woes of a Cinematographer

Woffington, Peg
1910 Peg Woffington

Wolf
1903 North American Grey Wolves
1906 The Wolf's Trap
1907 The Sea Wolf
1908 The Wolf Hunt
A Wolf in Sheep's Clothing
1909 The Wolf Hunt
1910 Lorenzo, the Wolf
Russian Wolf Hunt
The Sea Wolves
A Wolf in Sheep's Clothing

Wolfson Spice Mills, Toledo (Ohio)
1900 Employees of Wolfson's Spice Mills, Toledo

Wolgast, Ad
1910 Nelson-Wolgast Fight

Wolseley, Garnet Joseph, 1st Viscount Wolseley
1899 Lord Wolseley

Woman
1897 Ladies' Saddle Horses
Vanishing Lady
1898 Hungarian Women Plucking Geese
Vanishing Lady
1899 The Female Drummer
Female Prisoners: Detroit House of Correction
Judging Ladies' Saddle Horses
Lady Contortionist
An Up-to-Date Female Drummer
1900 The Perfect Woman
A Raid on a Woman's Poolroom
The Thief and the Pie Woman
Where the Female Smuggler Hid the Lace
1901 Firemen Rescuing Men and Women
Ladies Day at the Public Baths
Women of the Ghetto Bathing
1902 The Cook, Her Lover and the Lady of the House
Native Women of Fort de France at Work
Native Women Washing Clothes at Fort de France
Native Women Washing Clothes at the Gueydon Fountain, Fort de France, Martinique
The University College of Oxford Winning the Ladies' Challenge Plate
1903 Chiquita, the Smallest Woman in the World
Colored Woman Smoking a Pipe
The Cowboy and the Lady
Female Contortionist and Acrobatic Dog
How the Old Woman Caught the Omnibus
In My Lady's Boudoir
Miss Jessie Dogherty, Champion Female Highland Fling Dancer
Native Woman Washing a Negro Baby in Nassau, B. I.
Native Women Coaling a Ship and Scrambling for Money [West Indies]
Native Women Coaling a Ship at St. Thomas, D.W.I.
Native Women Washing Clothes at St. Vincent, B. W. I.
The New Dude and a Market Woman
Old Woman Who Lived in a Shoe
Passion Play: Jesus and the Woman of Samaria
An Unprotected Female
Wonderful Suspension and Evolution (La femme volante)
1904 The Apple Woman
Dance of the College Women's Club
Dunloe Women
Ladies of the Court Bathing
The Lady Juggler
The Market Woman's Mishap
Minuet and Dance—College Women's Club
Photographing a Female Crook
The Shadowy Lady
Woman's Bath
The Passion Play (L'ange et les saintes femmes)
1905 Female Crook and Her Easy Victim
Flap-Jack Lady of the Esquimaux, Cape Nome, Alaska
Lady Barber
London Ladies Looking at Lingerie in Oxford Street Windows, London

Worcester High School
1902 Worcester High School Eight-Oared Boat Crews in Action

Word
1904 And Pat Took Him at His Word
1910 Keeping His Word

Work
1896 Fire Engine at Work
1897 Mr. Edison at Work in His Chemical Laboratory
Threshing Machine at Work
The Workers
1898 Divers at Work on the Maine
1899 Coolies at Work
Crew of the "Shamrock," at Work
1900 The Iron Workers
Panoramic View, Rescue Work, Galveston
1901 The War in China—Coolies at Work
Working the Breeches Buoy
1902 Building Made Easy; or, How Mechanics Work in the Twentieth Century
Hydraulic Giants at Work
Let the Gold Dust Twins Do Your Work
Miners at Work Under Guard of Troops
Native Women of Fort de France at Work
Working Rotary Snow Ploughs on Lehigh Valley Railroad
1903 At Work in a Peat Bog
Carpenter Work, Albuquerque School
Carriers at Work, U.S.P.O.
Fire Engines at Work
The Kidnapper: At Work [Part 1]
Rock Drill at Work in Subway
Threshing Outfit at Work
Working a Long Tom Rocker on Bonanza Creek
Working the Rocker, Called a Jigger, on Poverty Bar, Fourteen Below Discovery Bonanza Creek
The Workman's Paradise
1904 Burglars at Work
Elephants at Work
Elephants at Work in India
Gymnasium Work, Kirksville, Mo.
Late for Work
Quick Work Behind the Scenes
Quick Work for the Soubrettes
Working in the Charcoal Mines in France
Jumping Horses (Travail d'ensemble des chevaux sauteurs)
1905 Gen'l Elec. No. 1 Employees Leaving Work
Potters at Work
Working a Scraper on Tailings Klondike
1906 The Tunnel Workers
1907 Modern Hercules at Work
The Parson of Hungry Gulch; or, The Right Man in the Right Place May Work Wonders
Union Workers Spoil the Food
Work for Your Grub
Work Made Easy
1908 Home Work in China
A Sacrifice for Work
A Workingman's Dream
A Workman's Honor
Workman's Revenge
1909 Calino Objects to Work
The Fisherman; or, Men Must Work and Women Must Weep
Jane Is Unwilling to Work
Out of Work
The Settlement Workers
1910 Magdalene; or, The Workman's Daughter
The Man Suffragette for the Abolition of Work for Women
A Sculptor Who Has Easy Work

Workhouse
1909 Workhouse to Mansion

Works
1898 Union Iron Works
1903 Employees Leaving Fall River Iron Works
Panoramic View of Herreshoff Works from Bristol Harbor
1904 Assembling a Generator, Westinghouse Works
Assembling and Testing Turbines, Westinghouse Works
Casting a Guide Box, Westinghouse Works
Coil Winding Machines, Westinghouse Works
Coil Winding Section E, Westinghouse Works
Girls Taking Time Checks, Westinghouse Works
Girls Winding Armatures, Westinghouse Works
Panorama Exterior Westinghouse Works
Panorama Motor Room, Westinghouse Works
Panorama of Machine Co. Aisle, Westinghouse Co. Works
Panoramic View Aisle B., Westinghouse Works
Railroad Panorama, Pittsburg to Stewart, Westinghouse Works
Steam Hammer, Westinghouse Works
Steam Whistle, Westinghouse Works
Taping Coils, Westinghouse Works
Tapping a Furnace, Westinghouse Works
Testing a Rotary, Westinghouse Works
Testing Gas Engine, Westinghouse Works
Testing Large Turbines, Westinghouse Co. Works
Testing Steam Engine, Westinghouse Works
Turning Panorama from Hill, Westinghouse Works
Westinghouse Air Brake Co. Westinghouse Works
Westinghouse Employees, Westinghouse Works
1905 Everybody Works but Father
Everybody Works But Father (Blackface)
Everybody Works But Father (Whiteface)
Steel Works
1906 Everybody Works but Mother
Everybody Works But Mother
Nobody Works Like Father

World
1897 The Crookedest Railroad Yard in the World
Fastest Wrecking Crew in the World
1899 Getting Up in the World
Liberty Enlightening the World
Smallest Train in the World
1902 Dr. Lehwis Automobile Leaving London for a Trip Around the World
Rulers of Half the World
1903 Chiquita, the Smallest Woman in the World
Giant Wilkins, the Largest Man in the World
Introduction of the Rough Riders of the World
Trial Run of the Fastest Boat in the World, "The Arrow"
Trick Elephant Bolivar, the Largest Elephant in the World, No. 1
Trick Elephant Bolivar, the Largest Elephant in the World, No. 2
1904 A Girl Who Wanted to Rise in the World
1905 Largest Fat Boy in the World
1906 A Detective's Trip Around the World
Naval Subjects, Merchant Marine, and From All over the World
Railway Panoramas from Every Port of the World
1907 How the World Lives
Marceline, the World-Renowned Clown of the N.Y. Hippodrome
Wizard's World
1908 Motoring Around the World
Nations of the World
Sport from All the World
Starting of Around the World Automobile Race
The World of Magic
1909 The Blind Foundling; or, Alone in the World
Different Rulers of the World
The Pigmy World
Rulers of the World
Scenes from the World's Largest Pigeon Farm
"Ursula," World's Fastest Motor Boat
The Whole World Kin
The World Upset
1910 All the World's a Stage
Bird's Eye View from World's Highest Buildings
The Way of the World
When the World Sleeps

World Series
1906 The World Series Baseball Games-White Sox and Cubs
1908 The World's Championship Baseball Series of 1910

World's championship
1899 The Battle of Jeffries and Sharkey for Championship of the World
1900 Kansas City Fire Department, Winners of the World's Championship at the Paris Exposition
1902 Broncho Busting Scene, Championship of the World
1909 World's Heavyweight Championship Pictures Between Tommy Burns and Jack Johnson
Police Dogs (Championnat du monde des chiens de police)
1910 Gotch-Zbyszko World's Championship Wrestling Match
Jeffries-Johnson World's Championship Boxing Contest, Held at Reno, Nevada, July 4, 1910
World's Championship Motor Races
World's Championship Series
World's Wrestling Champions

World's Fair
1904 Panorama from German Building, World's Fair
Speech by President Francis, World's Fair

Worldly
1904 The Illusionist (Illusionniste mondain)
Woman's Bath (Mondaine au bain)

Worm
1905 The Red Slug Worm
1907 The Book Worm
Even a Worm Will Turn
1909 The Silk Worm Series
The Worm Will Turn
1910 Turning of the Worm

Worn
1908 Head-Dresses Worn in Brittany

Worried
1910 Worried to Death

Worse
1909 It Might Have Been Worse

Worth
1907 Two Cents Worth of Cheese
1910 A Prince of Worth

Worth (Lake), Florida
1905 Speed Trial of Auto Boat Challenger, Lake Worth, Fla.

Worthing (England)
1898 Worthing Life-Saving Station

Worthless
1908 Two Broken Hearts, the Story of a Worthless Husband and a Faithful Dog

Would-be
1909 The Would-Be Acrobats
The Would-Be Champion

Wounded
1897 13th Infantry, U.S. Army—Scaling Walls with Wounded and Dying, Governors Island
1898 Wounded Soldiers Embarking in Row Boats
1900 Bringing in the Wounded During the Battle of Grobler's Kloof
1902 Taking Out the Dead and Wounded
1903 Taking Out the Dead and Wounded

Wrath
1903 The Wrath of a Jealous Wife

Wreath
1899 Chinese Sailors Placing a Wreath on the Monument
1902 The Mystic Wreath
1903 The Marvelous Wreath
1909 A Wreath in Time
1910 The Wreath

Wreck
1897 Fastest Wrecking Crew in the World
Wreck of the Schooner "Richmond"
1898 Wreck of the Battleship "Maine"
The Wreck of the "Maine"
Wreck of the "Vizcaya"
1899 Wreck of the "Mohican"
Wreck of the "Norseman"
Wreck of the S.S. "Paris"
1900 Birdseye View of Galveston, Showing Wreckage
Panorama of Wreckage of Water Front
Panoramic View, Wreckage Along Shore, Galveston
1901 The Mischievous Clerks; or, How the Office was Wrecked
1902 A Railroad Wreck (Imitation)
1903 Scenes of the Wreckage from the Water Front

Yellowstone National Park
1899 Coaches Going to Cinnabar from Yellowstone Park
Lower Falls, Grand Canyon, Yellowstone Park
Tourists Going Round Yellowstone Park
1901 In the Yellowstone
Riverside Geyser, Yellowstone Park
Upper Falls of the Yellowstone
Wild Bear in Yellowstone Park
1903 Arrival of Tourists at the Hotel in Yellowstone Park
Great Falls of the Yellowstone
On Yellowstone Lake
Panorama of Yellowstone Lake
Panoramic View of Hot Springs, Yellowstone Park
United States Troops in Yellowstone Park
1905 Bears Feeding at the Lake Hotel, Yellowstone Park
The "Black Growler" Steam Vent, Yellowstone Park
Brink of the Upper Falls of the Yellowstone River, Wyoming
The Castle Geyser, Yellowstone Park
The "Crazy" Steamer Yellowstone Park
The Great Falls of the Yellowstone
Great Fountain Geyser, Yellowstone Park
Herd of Bison, Yellowstone Park
Minuteman Geyser, Yellowstone Park
Old Faithful Geyser, Yellowstone Park
Rapids of the Silver Apron, Yellowstone Park
Riverside Geyser, Yellowstone Park
Stage Coaches, Yellowstone Park
Stages Leaving Fountain House, Yellowstone Park
Upper Fall of the Yellowstone River
1907 Through Yellowstone Park
A Trip Through the Yellowstone Park, U.S.A.
A Trip Through Yellowstone Park
1908 The Great Yellowstone Park Hold-Up
1909 Glimpses of Yellowstone Park

Yensen, Yens
1908 Yens Yensen, The Swedish Butcher Boy; or, Mistaken for a Burglar

Yiddish
use **Jews**

Yokel
1907 The Yokel's Love Affair

Yokohama (Japan)
1898 Going to the Yokohama Races
Railway Station at Yokohama
Street Scene in Yokohama, No. 1
Street Scene in Yokohama, No. 2
Theatre Road, Yokohama
1905 A Matsuri Procession, Yokohama, Japan
Matsuri Procession, Yokohama, Japan
1910 Fiftieth Anniversary of Yokohama

York (England)
1901 Duke and Duchess of Cornwall and York Landing at Queenstown, Ontario
The Duke and Duchess of York Arriving at Quebec
Duke and Duchess of York Leaving the Railroad Station at Montreal, Canada
Duke and Duchess of York Marching Through the Streets of Montreal
The Duke and Duchess of York Presenting Medals to Boer War Veterans at the Unveiling of the Queen's Statue
Duke of York at Montreal and Quebec
Garden Party in Honor of the Duke and Duchess of York
Royal Train with Duke and Duchess of York, Climbing Mt. Hector

Yorkshire (England)
1910 A Yorkshire School

Yorktown (Boat)
1904 Recruits on "Yorktown"

Yosemite National Park (California)
1901 Coaching Party, Yosemite Valley
Picturesque Yosemite
1903 Mammouth Paint Pot, Yosemite Valley
"Old Faithful," Yosemite Valley
U.S. Interior Dept.: Mail Coach Yosemite Valley
1905 Arrival of the Stage at Wawona Hotel, Enroute to Yosemite
Brink of the Vernal Fall, Yosemite Valley
Cavalcade Descending Eagle Peak Trail, Yosemite Valley
Cavalcade Descending the Nevada Trail, Yosemite Valley
Coaching Down the Merced Grade into Yosemite Valley
The "Crazy" Tourists on the Nevada Trail, Yosemite Valley
The "Crazy" Tourists Starting for the Trail, Yosemite Valley
"Dinner Time" at Camp Curry Yosemite Valley
Fourth of July Celebration, Yosemite California
Fourth of July Parade Yosemite California
Indian Pony Races, Yosemite Valley, California
Nevada Falls, Yosemite Valley
Vernal Falls, Yosemite Valley, California
1909 A Trip to Yosemite

Young Deer
1909 Young Deer's Bravery
1910 Young Deer's Gratitude
Young Deer's Return

Younger Brothers
1908 Younger Brothers

Youth
1897 Love's Young Dream
Young America
Young Men's Blaine Club of Cincinnati
1898 The Gallant Young Man
1900 Another Demonstration of the Cliff-Guibert Fire Hose Reel, Showing a Young Girl Coming from an Office, Detaching the Hose, Running with It 60 Feet, and Playing a Stream, All Inside of 30 Seconds
How the Young Man Got Stuck at Ocean Beach
1903 Young America Celebrating Dewey's Return
1904 The Young Farmer Girl
1905 White Rat and Young
The Young Tramps
1906 Young Apple Thief
1907 The Fountain of Youth
A Modern Youth
Young Americans
Youthful Hackenschmidts
The Waters of Life (La fontaine de jouvence)
1908 A Bashful Young Man
A Dream of Youth
Elixir of Youth
The Fair Young Lady's Telephone Communication
Flower of Youth
The Little Marchioness and the Young Shepherdess
A Plucky Young Woman
Susceptible Youth
The Young Artist
Young Heroes of the West
The Young Poacher
The Young Protector
The Young Tramp
Youthful Artist
The Youthful Benefactor
Youthful Samaritan
Youthful Treasure Seekers
1909 Fountain of Youth
The Frolic of Youth
The Gift of Youth, a Fairy Story
A Modest Young Man
Romance of the Crafty Usurper and the Young King
Two Frolicking Youths
Useful Young Man
The Young Bachelor's Dream
1910 Go West, Young Woman, Go West
Old Heads and Young Hearts
When Love Is Young
When Old New York Was Young
A Young Aviator's Dream
A Young Girl's Sacrifice
Young Lord Stanley

Yukon
1903 Dog Teams Hauling Wood to Dawson City, Up the Yukon
Team of Horses Hauling Wood to Dawson, Up the Yukon
Two Miles of the White Pass & Yukon Railroad

Yukon River (Alaska)
1903 Birds-eye View of Dawson City on the Yukon River, Alaska
1905 Wooding Up a River Steamer, Yukon River, Alaska

Yukoner (Boat)
1903 Steamer "Yukoner" Leaving Dawson

Yum-Yum-Yum
1904 Yum-Yum-Yum

Yuma dance
1902 Japanese Yuma Dance

Yusuf the Pirate
1908 Yusuf the Pirate

Yvonne
1909 Marriage of Yvonne
1910 Neighbors; or, Yvonne's Daughter

Zaccheus
1903 Passion Play: Christ Calling Zaccheus from the Tree

Zambesi River
1909 On the Zambesi

Zbyszko, Stanislaus
1910 Gotch-Zbyszko World's Championship Wrestling Match

Zeb
1910 Zeb, Zeke and the Widow

Zeke
1910 Zeb, Zeke and the Widow

Zeppelin
1909 Airship Zeppelin

Zeppelin, Ferdinand Adolf August Heinrich von
1908 Count Zeppelin's Aerostat

Zermatt (Switzerland)
1905 Panorama from Train on Visp-Zermatt Railway
1907 Torrents of Zermath
1908 The Viege Zermatt Railway

Zinc
1909 Lead and Zinc Mines

Zingari Gypsies
1897 A Camp of Zingari Gypsies

Zion (Mountain), Israel
1903 Jerusalem's Busiest Street, Showing Mt. Zion

Zip
1902 "Zip"

Zola, Émile
1897 The Zola-Rochefort Duel

Zoo
1897 Elephants at the Zoo
Pelicans at the Zoo
1903 Buffaloes Born in the Zoo Gardens
London Zoo
Scenes at the Zoo
A Visit to the London Zoo
A Visit to the Zoo
1904 Trip to the Zoo
Zoological Garden
1905 Scenes at the Zoo
Zoological Garden
1907 The Zoo at London, Part I
The Zoo at London, Part II
1909 A Bride and Groom's Visit to the New York Zoological Gardens
Copenhagen Zoo
A Visit to the London Zoological Gardens
A Walk Through the Zoo
Zoological Gardens
1910 [London Zoological Gardens]
Zoological Gardens in Antwerp

Zou-Zou
1909 Zou-Zou, the Lucky Dog

Zouaves
1898 Anderson Zouaves
Veteran Zouaves
1901 Street's Zouaves and Wall Scaling

Zuider Zee (Netherlands)
1909 On the Zuider Zee
1910 On the Banks of the Zuyder Zee, Holland

Zulu
1899 A Zulu War Dance
1908 The Zulu's Heart

Zululand
1910 Rastus in Zululand

Zuni
1910 The Sacred Turquoise of the Zuni

GEOGRAPHIC INDEX

★ Entries in the Geographic Index are arranged alphabetically according to location. Film titles listed herein are arranged first according to country, with films shot in the United States listed first, subdivided by state, then city or region. Films shot outside the United States are arranged alphabetically by country, then province, followed by city or region. An **asterisk** (*) indicates that the location listed is possible, but not definite.

The reader should note that, as in the Keyword Index, modern place names are used. Cross-references are also provided for place names that may have extended beyond the borders of one state or country, for example, Niagara Falls, which is situated in both the U.S. and Canada.

GEOGRAPHIC INDEX

Los Angeles
1898
Feb [day undetermined]
South Spring Street, Los Angeles, Cal.
1901
Dec [day undetermined]
Pigeon Farm at Los Angeles, Cal
1903 [month undetermined]
The California Limited of the Santa Fe Route
Parade of Roses
1906
Jun [day undetermined]
Floral Fiesta, Los Angeles, Cal.
Aug 25 Ostrich Farm
Pigeon Farm
Sep 20 A Daring Hold-Up in Southern California
Oct [day undetermined]
Railroad Collision at Los Angeles, Calif.
Dec [day undetermined]
O'Brien-Burns Contest, Los Angeles, Cal., Nov. 26th, 1906
1910
Mar 3 The Newlyweds
Mar 5 The Ostrich and the Lady
Mar 14 The Converts
Mar 17 The Man
Mar 21 Faithful
Mar 28 Gold Is Not All
Mar 31 The Smoker
Apr 14 The Kid
Apr 18 Thou Shalt Not
May 2 The Gold-Seekers
May 5 The Unchanging Sea
May 23 Ramona

Los Angeles—Griffith Park
1910
Dec 12 A Tale of the Sea

Marin County
1898
Mar [day undetermined]
Mount Tamalpais R.R., No. 1
Mount Tamalpais R.R., No. 2
1906
Apr [day undetermined]
A Trip Down Mount Tamalpais

Monterey
1897
Oct [day undetermined]
Hotel Del Monte
Surf at Monterey

Mt. Hamilton
1897
Oct [day undetermined]
Lick Observatory, Mt. Hamilton, Cal.

Mt. Lowe
1901
Dec [day undetermined]
Ascending Mt. Low, California
Panoramic View of Rubio Canyon, Mt. Low R.R.
1906
Aug 25 Ascent of Mount Lowe

Mount Tamalpais
1898
Mar [day undetermined]
Mount Taw R.R., No. 3

Oakland
1901
Dec [day undetermined]
Jeffries Exercising in His Gymnasium
1906
May 7 Arrival of Refugees at Oakland

Palo Alto
1897
Oct [day undetermined]
Stanford University, California

Pasadena
1898
Feb [day undetermined]
Ostriches Running, No. 1
Ostriches Running, No. 2
Parade of Coaches
Mar [day undetermined]
Procession of Floats
1901
Dec [day undetermined]
Ostrich Farms at Pasadena
1907
Apr [day undetermined]
Floral Parade at Pasadena, Calif.
1910
Mar 28 Gold Is Not All
Apr 11 A Romance of the Western Hills
Apr 18 Thou Shalt Not

Peru
1910
May 23 Ramona

Port Blakeley
1903
Mar [day undetermined]
Disposition of Slabs and Waste at Pt. Blakeley

Ranch Coles Grove
1906
Jun [day undetermined]
Spanish Barbecue

Sacramento Valley
1903
Mar [day undetermined]
Sacramento Valley, Cal. from Pilot of Engine

San Diego
1898
Feb [day undetermined]
Dogs Playing in the Surf
Off for the Rabbit Chase
Street Scene, San Diego

San Fernando
1910
May 16 Over Silent Paths

San Francisco
1897
Sep [day undetermined]
Sutro Baths, No. 2
Oct [day undetermined]
Arrest in Chinatown, San Francisco, Cal.
Capsize of Lifeboat
Cupid and Psyche
Launch of Life Boat
Launch of Surf Boat
Leander Sisters
Lurline Baths
Rescue—Resuscitation
Return of Lifeboat
The Sea Lions' Home
Sutro Baths, No. 1
1898
Mar [day undetermined]
Launch of Japanese Man-of-War "Chitosa"
Jun [day undetermined]
14th U.S. Infantry Drilling at the Presidio
Troop Ships for the Philippines*
Troops Embarking at San Francisco
1899
Oct [day undetermined]
Back from Manila
In Busy 'Frisco
Market Street
Orpheum Theatre, San Francisco
1900
Sep [day undetermined]
Orpheum Theatre
Scene in Chinatown
1901
Jun 8 Launching of the New Battleship "Ohio" at San Francisco, Cal. When President McKinley Was There
Nov [day undetermined]
Panorama, Golden Gate
Water Front of San Francisco
Dec 14 Ruhlin in His Training Quarters*
Dec 21 Jeffries and Ruhlin Sparring Contest at San Francisco, Cal., Nov. 15, 1901—Five Rounds
1902
Jan [day undetermined]
Bird's Eye View of San Francisco, Cal., from a Balloon
A Cable Road in San Francisco, Cal.
Panoramic View of Mt. Tamalpais
Panoramic View of Mt. Tamalpais Between Bow Knot and McKinley Cut
Panoramic View of the Golden Gate
Sea Gulls Following Fishing Boats
Sep [day undetermined]
California Naval Reserves
Mr. Grauman. For Private Use
1903
Mar [day undetermined]
Fourth and Market Sts., San Francisco
Unfair House, Butchers Boycotting, San Francisco
Jun [day undetermined]
Market Street Before Parade
Over Route of Roosevelt Parade in an Automobile
Panorama, Union Square, San Francisco
President Reviewing School Children
The President's Carriage
Sep [day undetermined]
Panorama of Beach and Cliff House
1904
Jan [day undetermined]
San Francisco Chinese Funeral
1906 [month undetermined]
Army Pack Train Bringing Supplies
Exploded Gas Tanks, U.S. Mint, Emporium and Spreckels' Bld'g.
May [day undetermined]
Scenes in San Francisco
Views in San Francisco
May 7 City Hall from Market St. and City Hall Ave.
The Doomed City
Effect of Earthquake
Feeding Chinese
The First Trolley Car After the Earthquake
Fun Among the Refugees
Going to the Fire, Showing Chief Sullivan during the Earthquake
The Mission
Panorama from Telegraph Hill
Panorama of Chinatown
Panorama of Market Street before the Fire
Panorama of Nob Hill
Panorama of San Francisco in Smoke and Fire
Panoramas of Market Street, the City Hall, Taken from the Roof of the U.S. Mint
Refugees at the Golden Gate Park
Refugees in Jefferson Square
Refugees on Market St.
St. Francis Hotel
The San Francisco Disaster
Shot for Looting
Thieves in Camp, Golden Gate Park
Waterfront, Refugees Leaving San Francisco
Jun [day undetermined]
Bird's Eye View from Hopkins Art Institute
Dynamiting Ruins and Rescuing Soldier Caught in Falling Walls
Earthquake Ruins, New Majestic Theatre and City Hall
Free Show on the Beach*
Panorama, City Hall, Van Ness Avenue and College of St. Ignatius
Panorama, Nob Hill and Ruins of Millionaire Residences
Panorama, Notorious "Barbary Coast"
Panorama, Ruins Aristocratic Apartments
Panorama, Russian and Nob Hill from an Automobile
Physical Culture Lesson*
Play Ball on the Beach*
Ruins Bulletin Building, California Theatre and Evening Post
Ruins of Chinatown
Vertical Panorama City Hall and Surroundings
1907 [month undetermined]
Panorama of Market Street, San Francisco
1910
Dec 24 Owen Moran vs. Battling Nelson

San Francisco Bay
1898
Mar [day undetermined]
Feeding Sea Gulls

San Gabriel—Mission
1910
Mar 7 The Thread of Destiny
Mar 14 The Converts
Apr 25 The Way of the World

San Jose
1897
Oct [day undetermined]
Hotel Vendome, San Jose, Cal.

San Juan Capistrano
1910
May 12 The Two Brothers

San Pedro
1901
Dec [day undetermined]
Building a Harbor at San Pedro

Santa Anita
1898
Feb [day undetermined]
California Limited, A.T. & S.F.R.R.

Santa Monica
1910
May 5 The Unchanging Sea

Shasta
1903
Mar [day undetermined]
Passengers Alighting and Drinking Shasta Water

Shasta Spring
1903
Mar [day undetermined]
Past Shasta Spring, California

Sierra Madre
1910
Mar 17 The Man
Mar 24 The Twisted Trail
Apr 11 A Romance of the Western Hills
May 2 The Gold-Seekers

Sierra Nevada Mountains
1910
Jun 27 The Long Trail

Venice
1910
Jun 20 Never Again

Verdugo
1910
Apr 21 The Tenderfoot's Triumph
May 19 An Affair of Hearts
May 26 A Knot in the Plot
Jun 20 May and December

Vernon
1910
Apr 15 Sam Langford and John Flynn Fight

Wawona
1901
Oct [day undetermined]
Wawona, Big Tree
Nov [day undetermined]
A Cavalry Manoeuvre
In the Yellowstone
A Wonderful Waterfall
1903
Oct [day undetermined]
U.S. Interior Dept.: Changing Coaches, Raymond Coach

Yosemite National Park
1901
Nov [day undetermined]
A Cavalry Manoeuvre
1903
Oct [day undetermined]
U.S. Interior Dept.: Bridal Veil Falls
U.S. Interior Dept.: Vernal Falls

Yosemite Valley
1901
Oct [day undetermined]
Bridal Veil Falls
Nevada Falls
Wawona, Big Tree
Nov [day undetermined]
Artist's Point
Coaching Party, Yosemite Valley
In the Yellowstone
Picturesque Yosemite
A Wonderful Waterfall
1903
Oct [day undetermined]
U.S. Interior Dept.: Mail Coach Yosemite Valley
U.S. Interior Dept.: Panorama from Artist's Point
U.S. Interior Dept.: Santa Fe Coach
1910
Sep 22 The Sergeant

Colorado

1898
Feb [day undetermined]
Royal Gorge
Serving Rations to the Indians, No. 1*
Serving Rations to the Indians, No. 2*
1902
Nov [day undetermined]
Arrival on Summit of Pike's Peak
Balloon Ascension
Burlington Flyer
Clear Creek Canyon
Climbing Hagerman Pass
Horse Toboggan Slide
Hydraulic Giants at Work
Lava Slides in Red Rock Canyon
Leaving the Summit of Pike's Peak
Panorama of Cog Railway
Panorama of the Famous Georgetown Loop
Panorama of the Royal Gorge
Panorama of Ute Pass
Panoramic View of Granite Canon
Panoramic View of Hell Gate
Panoramic View of Seven Castles
Pike's Peak Toboggan Slide
Train in Royal Gorge
Trains Leaving Manitou
Ute Pass Express
Where Golden Bars Are Cast
1903
Feb [day undetermined]
Ute Indian Snake Dance
1904
Apr [day undetermined]
Tracked by Bloodhounds; or, A Lynching at Cripple Creek
1905
Apr 29 The Hold-Up of the Leadville Stage
1907
Jul [day undetermined]
Over the Midland Terminal Railroad: Through Cripple Creek District
1908
Oct 8 The Ranchman's Love
1909
Mar 4 The Mad Miner

Denver
1898
Feb [day undetermined]
Cripple Creek Float
Decorated Carriages
Denver Fire Brigade
Masked Procession
Procession of Mounted Indians and Cowboys
1902
Nov [day undetermined]
Broncho Busting Scene, Championship of the World
Denver Firemen's Race for Life
1903
Feb [day undetermined]
Bucking Broncho Contest
Christian Endeavor Greeting
1907
Mar 9 The Girl from Montana

Georgetown
1901
Jul [day undetermined]
The Georgetown Loop

Glenwood Springs
1902
Nov [day undetermined]
Fun in the Glenwood Springs Pool
Runaway Stage Coach

Grand Junction
1910
Mar 15 Fruit Growing, Grand Valley, Colorado (The Results of Irrigation)

Gunnison
1904
Oct 22 The Girls in the Overalls

La Junta
1903 [month undetermined]
Overland Flyer
Feb [day undetermined]
California Limited

Marble
1910
Jan 11 Bear Hunt in the Rockies

Royal Gorge
1903 [month undetermined]
Freight Train in the Royal Gorge, Colo.
Royal Gorge

Connecticut

1908
Jun 10 The Blue and the Gray; or, The Days of '61
1910
Aug 3 A Colonial Belle

Claytons
1906
Jun 14 The Village Cut-Up

Connecticut River
1897
Mar [day undetermined]
S.S. "Middletown"

Cos Cob
1908
Oct 13 The Barbarian Ingomar
Nov 20 The Ingrate
1909
Jun 18 A Priest of the Wilderness: Father Jogue's Mission to the Iroquois

Danbury
1904
Nov [day undetermined]
Miss Lillian Shaffer and Her Dancing Horse
A Rube Couple at a County Fair

Greenwich
1907
Jan 5 The Lighthouse
1909
Jul 5 The Message
Jul 8 The Country Doctor
Jul 12 The Cardinal's Conspiracy
Jul 15 Tender Hearts
Jul 22 Sweet and Twenty
Oct 11 The Little Teacher
Oct 14 A Change of Heart
1910
Sep 19 A Summer Tragedy
Oct 31 Two Little Waifs
Dec 12 The Golden Supper

Hartford
1896
Nov [day undetermined]
Winchester Arms Factory at Noon Time
1897
Mar [day undetermined]
Columbia Bicycle Factory
Jumbo
Jumbo, Horseless Fire-Engine
Jul [day undetermined]
Free-for-All Race at Charter Oak Park

Mianus
1906
Jun 28 The Paymaster

New Haven
1896
Nov [day undetermined]
An Arrest at New Haven, Conn.
Fire Department, New Haven, Conn.
Yale Football Team at Practice, New Haven, Conn.
Dec [day undetermined]
Sack Race
1897
Feb [day undetermined]
Champion Rolla O. Heikes, Breaking the Record at Flying Targets with Winchester Shotgun
1899
May [day undetermined]
A Cock Fight
Hazing a Freshman
Running the Hurdles
Yale Athletes
Yale Athletes Broad Jumping
The Yale Crew
1901
Nov [day undetermined]
Yale Football, Practice Scrimmage
Yale Football Squad of 1901

1902
May [day undetermined]
Panoramic View of New Haven, Conn.
1903
Nov [day undetermined]
Princeton and Yale Football Game

New London
1905
Jun [day undetermined]
Drills and Exercises, Schoolship "St. Mary's"
1906 [month undetermined]
Yale Harvard Boat Race, New London, Conn., 1906

Ridgefield
1908
Mar 21 Animated Snowballs

Sound Beach
1905
Oct [day undetermined]
The Great Jewel Mystery
Nov [day undetermined]
A Kentucky Feud
1906
Jul 19 The Masqueraders
Aug 1 No Wedding Bells for Him
Oct 8 The Country Schoolmaster
Nov 1 Dr. Dippy's Sanitarium
1907
Jan [day undetermined]
The Moving Picture Man
1908
Jul 14 The Adventures of Dollie
1909
Oct 26 He Fell in Love with His Wife
1910
Jan 1 Cupid and the Motor Boat

Stamford
1906
Jun [day undetermined]
Maneuvering a Small Motor Boat
White Fox Motor Boat
1910
May 30 The Impalement
Jun 2 In the Season of Buds

Delaware

New Castle
1899
Jun [day undetermined]
The Lock-Step
Suckling Pigs
A Whipping Post

Wilmington
1903
Jul [day undetermined]
Policemen's Prank on Their Comrade
A Scrap in Black and White
Sep [day undetermined]
The Baby Review
Maypole Dance
Rube and the Fender
Tub Race
Turning the Tables

Wilmington Springs
1903
Jul [day undetermined]
Miniature Railway at Wilmington Springs, Delaware
Razzle Dazzle

District of Columbia

1897
Feb [day undetermined]
Pennsylvania Avenue, Washington, D.C.
Pile Driving, Washington Navy Yard [Washington, D.C.]
Mar [day undetermined]
Bicyclers in Inaugural Parade
Governor Bushnell of Ohio, and Staff
McKinley and Cleveland Going to the Capitol
McKinley and Others in Carriage
McKinley Train, Penn. R.R.
Marines from U.S. Cruiser "New York"
A Part of Inaugural Parade, Washington
President Cleveland and President McKinley
Return of McKinley from the Capitol
Review of Artillery
71st Regiment, N.G.S.N.Y.
71st Regiment, New York
Troop "A" in Inaugural Parade
Troop "A" of Cleveland, O.
Vice-President Hobart's Escort
Washington Continental Guards
Apr [day undetermined]
Pennsylvania Avenue, Washington
May [day undetermined]
Corcoran Cadets, Washington
1898
Apr [day undetermined]
Captain Sigsbee
Theodore Roosevelt
May 20 Secretary Long and Captain Sigsbee
1899
Oct [day undetermined]
Presentation of Nation's Sword to Admiral Dewey
1901
Mar [day undetermined]
President McKinley Leaving the White House for the Capitol
The Second Inauguration
Mar 16 President McKinley and Escort Going to the Capitol
President McKinley Taking the Oath
Apr [day undetermined]
Calisthenic Drill
Deaf Mute Recitation
Dressmaking
Energizing Drill
Forging
The High School Cadets
Kindergarten Methods
Laboratory Study
A Language Lesson
Manual Training
A Muffin Lesson
Nature Study, the Rabbit
Physical Training
Star Spangled Banner by a Deaf Mute
Jul [day undetermined]
A Composite Picture of the Principal Buildings in Washington, D.C.
Panoramic View of the Capitol, Washington, D.C.
Panoramic View of the White House, Washington, D.C.
Sep [day undetermined]
President McKinley's Funeral
Oct 5 President McKinley's Funeral Cortege at Washington, D.C.
1902 [month undetermined]
President and Prince at Washington
Feb [day undetermined]
Prince Henry [of Prussia] Arriving in Washington and Visiting the German Embassy
Apr [day undetermined]
Babies Rolling Eggs
Egg Rolling at the White House
Scrambling for Eggs
Tossing Eggs
May [day undetermined]
Funeral Procession of Admiral Sampson at Washington
Sep [day undetermined]
Unveiling the Rochambeau Statue in Washington, D.C.
Unveiling the Rochambeau Statue, Washington, D.C.
1903
Jan [day undetermined]
Prince Henry at Washington
Aug [day undetermined]
Cancelling Machine, U.S.P.O.
Carriers at Work, U.S.P.O.
Carriers Leaving Building, U.S.P.O.
Clerks Casing Mail for Bags, U.S.P.O.
Clerks Tying Bags, U.S.P.O.
Clerks Tying Up for Bags, U.S.P.O.
Coach at Rural Post Office, U.S.P.O.
Collecting Mail, U.S.P.O.
Loading Mail Car, U.S.P.O.
Mailing Platform, U.S.P.O.
Old Mail Coach at Ford, U.S.P.O.
Post Man Delivering Mail, U.S.P.O.
Routing Mail, U.S.P.O.
Special Delivery Messenger, U.S.P.O.
Street Mail Car, U.S.P.O.
Throwing Mail into Bags, U.S.P.O.
Transporting Internal Rev. Stamps, U.S.P.O.
Tying Up Bags for Train, U.S.P.O.
Wagons Loading Mail, U.S.P.O.
1904 [month undetermined]
The Late Senator Mark Hanna
Apr [day undetermined]
Review of U.S. Marine Band by Sec'y Moody, U.S. Navy
1905
Mar [day undetermined]
The Inauguration of President Roosevelt
Inauguration of President Roosevelt. Leaving the Capitol
Inauguration of President Roosevelt. President-Elect Roosevelt, Vice-President-Elect Fairbanks and Escort Going to the Capitol
Inauguration of President Roosevelt. Taking the Oath of Office
Inauguration of President Roosevelt. the Grand Inaugural Parade
President Roosevelt's Inauguration
1906
Mar [day undetermined]
Scenes Washington, D.C.
1909
Mar 6 A Day in Washington, the Capital of the United States, Showing Many Points of Interest
Inauguration of President William H. Taft

Florida

1909
Jan 29 The Octoroon: The Story of the Turpentine Forest
Feb 26 The New Minister; or, The Drunkard's Daughter
Mar 12 The Seminole's Vengeance; or The Slave Catchers of Florida
May 7 Love's Triumphs
May 14 Good for Evil
May 21 The Girl Spy: An Incident of the Civil War
Dec 31 A Slave to Drink
1910
Jan 7 The Deacon's Daughter
Jan 14 The Romance of a Trained Nurse
Jan 28 The Man who Lost
Mar 23 The Girl and the Bandit
May 20 The Seminole Halfbreeds
Jun 10 The Exiled Chief

Dry Tortugas
1898
May 20 Cruiser "Cincinnati"
Cruiser "Detroit"
U.S. Battleship "Indiana"
U.S. Battleship "Iowa"
U.S. Cruiser "Nashville"
U.S.S. "Castine"

Everglades
1910
Mar 16 The Seminole's Trust

Jacksonville
1898
Jul [day undetermined]
An Execution by Hanging
Gen. Fitzhugh Lee and Staff
Lasso Throwing
Rocky Mountain Riders Rough Riding
Rough Riding
Salt Lake City Company of Rocky Mt. Riders
1909
Feb 12 The High Diver
1910
Feb 17 A Honeymoon Through Snow to Sunshine

Key West
1898
Apr [day undetermined]
Tossing a Nigger in a Blanket
May 20 Burial of the "Maine" Victims
Cruiser "Marblehead"
Monitor "Terror"
War Correspondents
1903
Jan [day undetermined]
U.S. Monitor Miantonomah Steaming into Key West

Lake Worth
1905
Feb [day undetermined]
Speed Trial of Auto Boat Challenger, Lake Worth, Fla.

Miami
1910
Feb 17 A Honeymoon Through Snow to Sunshine

Ormond Beach
1905
Feb [day undetermined]
Automobile Races at Ormond, Fla.

Palm Beach
1905
Feb [day undetermined]
Boating Carnival, Palm Beach, Fla.
In the Swimming Pool, Palm Beach, Fla.
1910
Feb 17 A Honeymoon Through Snow to Sunshine

Roseland
1909
Jan 8 A Florida Feud; or, Love in the Everglades
1910
Feb 16 The Fisherman's Granddaughter

St. Augustine
1909
May 15 The Ponce de Leon Fete
1910
Feb 17 A Honeymoon Through Snow to Sunshine

St. John's River
1909
Apr 6 The Orange Grower's Daughter
1910
Feb 2 The Step-Mother
Feb 16 The Fisherman's Granddaughter
Feb 23 The Miser's Child

Tampa
1898
Mar [day undetermined]
Feeding the Ducks at Tampa Bay
Fighting Roosters; in Florida
Lawn Tennis in Florida
Tampa Bay Hotel, Tampa, Fla.
Apr [day undetermined]
In Camp, Tampa, Fla.
Pile Drivers; Tampa, Fla.
Practice Warfare
With the Army at Tampa
May [day undetermined]
Cuban Patriots
May 20 Battery B Arriving at Camp
Colored Troops Disembarking
Cuban Refugees Waiting for Rations
Cuban Volunteers Marching for Rations
Military Camp at Tampa, Taken from Train
9th Infantry Boys' Morning Wash
9th U.S. Cavalry Watering Horses
Steamer "Mascotte" Arriving at Tampa
10th U.S. Infantry Disembarking from Cars
U.S. Cavalry Supplies Unloading at Tampa, Florida
Jun [day undetermined]
Transport Ships at Port Tampa
Jul [day undetermined]
A Charge by Cavalry
Col. Torrey's "Rough Riders"
Col. Torrey's Rough Riders and Army Mules
Cuban Volunteers
Cubans Sharpening their Machetes
Gen. Fitzhugh Lee and Staff
Lasso Throwing
Roosevelt's Rough Riders
69th Regiment Passing in Review
Troop "H," Denver, Col.

Georgia

Savannah
1909
May 4 A Road to Love

Hawaii

Honolulu
1898
Jun [day undetermined]
Honolulu Street Scene
Kanakas Diving for Money [Honolulu], No. 1
Kanakas Diving for Money [Honolulu], No. 2
Wharf Scene, Honolulu
1899
Dec [day undetermined]
33rd Infantry, U.S.A.
1901
Aug [day undetermined]
Boys Diving
Cutting Sugar Cane
Loading Sugar Cane
Panorama of Water Front
Steamboat Leaving for Hilo
Train of Sugar Cane on Way to Crusher
Oct [day undetermined]
Panorama of Water Front

Illinois

Chicago
1897
Jul [day undetermined]
Armour's Electric Trolley
Cattle Driven to Slaughter
Corner Madison and State Streets, Chicago
Sheep Run, Chicago Stockyards
1898
Oct [day undetermined]
A Chicago Street
County Democracy
Peace Parade—Chicago
Stealing a Ham
Street Fight and Arrest
A Texas Steer
Nov [day undetermined]
Illinois Central Terminal
1900
Jan [day undetermined]
Another Picture Showing Demonstration of a Pneumatic Shell Riveter
Demonstrating the Action of the Chicago Pneumatic Tool Co.'s Deck Machine
Sep [day undetermined]
Lincoln Park
Oct [day undetermined]
President McKinley Laying Corner Stone
1901 [month undetermined]
Arrival of Train of Cattle
Beef Extract Room
Beef, Sheep and Hog Killing
Branding Hams
Bridge of Sighs
Bull on the Stampede
A Busy Corner at Armour's
Canned Meat Department. No. 1: Filling and Capping
Canned Meat Department. No. 2: Inspecting
Canned Meat Department. No. 5: Vacuum Process
Canned Meat Department. No. 6: Painting and Labeling
Chicago Fat Stock Parade
Chicago Police Parade
Cleaning Pig's Feet
Columbia Post
Coming Out of Scraping Machines and Cutting Off Heads
Cutting Beef
Cutting Meat for Sausage (Side View)
Cutting Pork
Dewey Parade
Dressing Beef
Driving Hogs to Slaughter
Drove of Western Cattle
Dumping and Lifting Cattle
Elevated Railroad
Entrance to Union Stock Yards
Export Packing
Feeding Time
Hog Slaughtering. No. 6: Opening and Splitting
Hogs on the Rail
Interior of Armour's Power House
Killing Sheep
Koshering Cattle, (Hebrew Method of Killing)
Labeling Cans
Lafayette Post of New York
Lambs Post of Phila.
Lard Refinery
Laundry and Sewing Room
Legging Sheep
Loading Cars
Machine and Can Tester
Mince Meat Room
Miscellaneous. No. 6: Panoramic View
Noon Time in Packing Town, (Panoramic)
Noon Time in Packing Town, (Whiskey Point)
Oleo Oil Melting
Oleo Oil Pressing
Parade of Horses
Pulling Wool
A Ride on the Elevated R.R. (Panoramic)
Sausage Department. No. 2: Chopping
Scalding and Scraping Hogs
Scenes and Incidents in the G.A.R. Encampment
Sheep Led to Slaughter by Goat
Shipping Department. No. 2: Loading
Singing Pigs Feet
Skinning Sheep
Slicing Hams and Bacon
Soldering Cans
Square Can Machine
Stamping Tin
Sticking Cattle
Sticking Hogs, (Front View)
Street Sweeping Brigade
Stuffing Cans by Machinery
Stuffing Sausage
Stunning Cattle
Sweating Cans
Testing Cans by Machinery
Testing Hams
Testing Horses
3 Can Testers (Side View)
Trimming Room
Weighing Mutton
Apr 13 Gans-McGovern Fight
1902
Mar [day undetermined]
Prince Henry [of Prussia] at Lincoln's Monument, Chicago, Ill.
1903 [month undetermined]
Business Rivalry
Chicago Fire Boats in Action
Chicago Fire Run
Deadwood Coach
The Girl in Blue
A Hot Time on the Bathing Beach
Launching a Steamer*
Parade through Chicago Streets
The Prince Leaving Chicago
State and Madison Sts., Chicago
Trip Around the Union Loop
View of State Street
1910
Jan 8 His Only Child
Jun 1 Levi's Dilemma
Jul 2 Gotch-Zbyszko World's Championship Wrestling Match
Aug 18 Knights Templars Conclave
Aug 30 The Templars Conclave

Elgin
1910
Sep 10 Elgin National Trophy Races

Forest Park
1910
Jul 8 Reproduction of Jeffries-Johnson Championship Contest

Fort Sheridan
1903 [month undetermined]
Military Fire Drill

Galena
1910
Dec 15 County Fair

Morton Grove
1903 [month undetermined]
Pioneer Limited

Indiana

Dune Park
1910
Aug 11 Lost in the Soudan

Kentucky

1903 [month undetermined]
Train on High Bridge

Cumberland Mountains
1910
Feb 5 Sensational Logging

Louisville
1901
Aug [day undetermined]
Knight Templars Parade at Louisville, Ky.
Knight Templars Parade Drill
1903 [month undetermined]
Louisville Fire Run
1906
Jun [day undetermined]
Attack on Fort Boonesboro

Louisiana

1909
Apr 29 Mephisto and the Maiden

New Orleans
1898
Feb [day undetermined]
City Hall
Down in Dixie
Loading a Mississippi Steamboat
Mardi Gras Carnival
Torpedo Boat, "Dupont"
'Way Down South
Mar [day undetermined]
Scene on the Steamship "Olivette"
Tampa Bay Hotel, Tampa, Fla.
1902 [month undetermined]
Arrival of Rex
The Continental Guards
Mardi Gras Parade
Panoramic View of the French Market
Turning Keys over to Rex

Maine

1906
Jun [day undetermined]
Canoeing in Maine
Logging in Maine
1909
Nov 16 Indian Basket Making

Kittery
1901
Mar [day undetermined]
Fertilizing Codfish Eggs
Unloading Cod

Kittery Point
1901
Mar [day undetermined]
Codfishing with Trawl
Drawing a Lobster Pot

Portland
1906
Jan [day undetermined]
Moose Hunt in New Brunswick
1907
Jun 8 A Caribou Hunt

Rangeley Lakes
1906
Jan [day undetermined]
Trout Fishing in Rangeley Lakes

St. Croix River
1910
Mar 5 The History of a Sardine Sandwich

Maryland

Annapolis
1898
Jul [day undetermined]
Admiral Cervera and Officers of the Spanish Fleet Leaving the "St. Louis"
Admiral McNair, U.S. N.
Spanish Sailors on the "St. Louis"
1901
Apr [day undetermined]
Artillery Drill at Annapolis
General Quarters for Action
U.S. Naval Cadets Marching in Review
May [day undetermined]
Boats Under Oars
Middies Shortening Sails
Steam Tactics
1906
May [day undetermined]
John Paul Jones Ceremonies

Baltimore
1904
Feb [day undetermined]
The Great Baltimore Fire
Panorama of Ruins from Baltimore and Charles Street
Panorama of Ruins from Lombard and Charles Street
Panorama of Ruins from Water Front
Feb 20 The Great Baltimore Fire
Mar [day undetermined]
Panorama of Ruins from Lombard and Hanover Streets, Baltimore, Md.
1906
Sep [day undetermined]
Hoe Printing Press in Action

Baltimore—Camden Station
1905
Apr [day undetermined]
General Electric Engine Hauling Freight

Baltimore—Fort McHenry
1910
Jun 15 A Child of the Regiment

Chesapeake Bay
1898
Jul [day undetermined]
Admiral Cervera and Officers of the Spanish Fleet Leaving the "St. Louis"

St. Georges
1903
Oct [day undetermined]
Inside Car, Showing Bag Catcher [U.S.P.O.]
Train Taking Up Mail Bag, U.S.P.O.

Westminster
1903
Aug [day undetermined]
Buying Stamps from Rural Wagon, U.S.P.O.
Exchange of Mail at Rural P.O., U.S.P.O.
Rural Wagon Delivering Mail, U.S.P.O.
Rural Wagon Giving Mail to Branch, U.S.P.O.

Massachusetts

Amherst
1906
Feb [day undetermined]
College Life at Amherst

Boston
1897
Jan [day undetermined]
New England Church Scene
May [day undetermined]
Ferryboat "Winthrop"
Shooting the Chutes
Throwing over a Wall
U.S.S. "Massachusetts"
Jun [day undetermined]
Fort Hill Fire Station
Oct [day undetermined]
Ancient and Honorable Artillery Co.
Boston's Subway
Fall River Boat Train
Fastest Wrecking Crew in the World
A Fishing Schooner
Jordan, Marsh & Co.'s Store
Keith's Theatre
Taking on the Pilot
1898
Jan [day undetermined]
Charge of the Light Brigade
Clearing a Drift
During the Blizzard
A Fine Day for Sleighing, Boston
Fishing Vessels After the Blizzard
Merry Sleigh Bells
Sleighing Scene
Trinity Church
Mar [day undetermined]
Boston Navy Yard
Harbor Defenses
Steamer "Boston"
1899
Mar [day undetermined]
McKinley Leaving State House, Boston
Apr [day undetermined]
Eighth Regiment, Mass. Volunteers
A High-school Horse
Tremont Street
May [day undetermined]
Ambulance Corps Drill
First Boston School Regiment
High Jumping
Hurdle Jumping
Schooling Hunters
Second Boston School Regiment
Steamship "Pavonia"
Third Boston School Regiment
Jun [day undetermined]
Feeding the Pigeons
"La Grande Duchesse"
Jul [day undetermined]
Aquatic Sports
Kilpatrick's Ride
Aug [day undetermined]
Miss Jewett and the Baker Family
Sep [day undetermined]
The Boston Horseless Fire Department
A Roll Lift Draw Bridge
Some Future Champions
1900
Oct [day undetermined]
"Courier"
1901
Jul [day undetermined]
The Boston Fire Boat in Action
Dec [day undetermined]
Panoramic View of Boston Subway from an Electric Car
1903
Oct [day undetermined]
Ancient and Honourable Artillery of London on Parade
The Ancient and Honourables Homeward Bound
1904
Jul [day undetermined]
Canoeing on the Charles River, Boston, Mass.
1905
Mar [day undetermined]
Bathing in the Ice at the L Street Bath, Boston
Gov. Wm. L. Douglas, of Mass.
1906
Feb [day undetermined]
Seeing Boston
Sep [day undetermined]
E. Forest Fish Gun Assn.

Boston—Charles River
1901
Aug [day undetermined]
Canoeing Scene

Boston—Charles River Park
1897
Oct [day undetermined]
A Multicycle Race
One-Third Mile Bicycle Race
Oriten
A Paced Bicycle Race

Brockton
1905
Mar [day undetermined]
Gov. Wm. L. Douglas, of Mass.

Brookline
1899
May [day undetermined]
A Flock of Sheep

Buzzards Bay
1896
Sep [day undetermined]
Awakening of Rip
Exit of Rip and the Dwarf
Rip Leaving Sleepy Hollow
Rip Meeting the Dwarf
Rip Passing over the Mountain
Rip's Toast
Rip's Toast to Hudson
Rip's Twenty Years' Sleep
Stable on Fire
1897
Jun [day undetermined]
The Biggest Fish He Ever Caught
The Picnic
A Rural Courtship
Still Waters Run Deep
The Tramp and the Bather
The Troubadour
Trout Poachers
Young America

Cambridge
1902
Mar [day undetermined]
Prince Henry [of Prussia] Visiting Cambridge, Mass. and Harvard University
1904

Marshall
1904
May [day undetermined]
Basket ball, Missouri Valley College
Fencing Class, Missouri Valley College

St. Joseph
1904
May [day undetermined]
Free Arm Movement, All Schools, Missouri Commission
High School Field Exercises, Missouri Commission
Panorama of Field St., St. Joseph, Mo., Missouri Commission
Panorama of 4th St., St. Joseph, Mo., Missouri Commission
Panorama of 3rd Street, St. Joseph, Mo., Missouri Commission

St. Louis
1901
Dec [day undetermined]
The Beginning of a Great Enterprise
1903
May [day undetermined]
Pres. Roosevelt at the Dedication Ceremonies, St. Louis Exposition
1904
May [day undetermined]
Igorotte Savages, St. Louis Exposition
Opening Ceremonies, St. Louis Exposition
Panorama from St. Louis Plaza, St. Louis Exposition
Panorama St. Louis Exposition from Launch
Parade of Characters (Asia in America) St. Louis Exposition
Parade of the Pikers, St. Louis Exposition
Sec'y Taft's Address & Panorama
Twenty Mule Team, St. Louis Exposition
Jun [day undetermined]
Dress Parade of the Filipino Scouts, St. Louis Exposition
Filipino Scouts, Musical Drill, St. Louis Exposition
Panorama of St. Louis Exposition from Wireless Tower
Princess Rajah Dance with Chair, St. Louis Exposition
Princess Rajah, Dance without Chair
West Point Cadets Escorting Liberty Bell, St. Louis Exposition
Jul [day undetermined]
Panorama of Race Track Crowd, St. Louis
Aug [day undetermined]
Parade of Floats, St. Louis Exposition
Parade of National Cash Register Co.'s Employees, St. Louis Exposition
Speech by President Francis, World's Fair
Sep [day undetermined]
Imitation Naval Battle—St. Louis Exposition
Panorama from German Building, World's Fair
Parade of Military, St. Louis Exposition

Montana

1903
Nov [day undetermined]
Crow Indian Festival Dance

Crow Agency
1903
Nov [day undetermined]
Crow Indian War Dance
Crow Indians Harvesting
Indian Horsemanship

Gardiner
1903
Nov [day undetermined]
Arrival of Train at Gardner

Helena
1900
Apr [day undetermined]
Overland Express Arriving at Helena, Mont.

Livingston
1897 [month undetermined]
Tourist Train Leaving Livingston, Mont.

Nebraska

Central City
1901
Jul [day undetermined]
Herd of Cattle

Grand Island
1901
Jul [day undetermined]
The Overland Limited
A Race with the Overland Limited

Lincoln
1900
Sep [day undetermined]
William J. Bryan in the Biograph
1903 [month undetermined]
Bryan at Home

Omaha
1899
Oct [day undetermined]
Overland Limited
1900
Dec [day undetermined]
From Council Bluffs to Omaha
Union Pacific Fast Mail

Nevada

Goldfield
1906 [month undetermined]
Gans-Nelson Contest, Goldfield, Nevada, September 3rd, 1906

Reno
1910
Jul 6 Jeffries-Johnson World's Championship Boxing Contest, Held at Reno, Nevada, July 4, 1910

Tonopah
1907
Jan 26 Gans-Herman Fight

New England Coast

1899
Apr [day undetermined]
Wreck of the "Norseman"

New Hampshire

Crawford
1899
Aug [day undetermined]
Crawford Notch

Frankenstein
1899
Aug [day undetermined]
The Frankenstein Trestle

Laconia
1899
Aug [day undetermined]
Winnisquam Lake

Mt. Washington
1899
Jul [day undetermined]
Glen House Stage
Aug [day undetermined]
Climbing Jacob's Ladder
Sliding Down Mount Washington
Summit of Mt. Washington
1904
Jul [day undetermined]
Coaching in the White Mountains
Aug [day undetermined]
Automobiling Among the Clouds

Portsmouth
1904
Jan [day undetermined]
Drill
Stretcher Race over Obstacles
1905
Aug [day undetermined]
Peace Envoys at Portsmouth, N.H.
Scenes and Incidents, Russo-Japanese Peace Conference, Portsmouth, N.H.
1907
Sep 16 An Acadian Elopement

Portsmouth—Navy Yard
1904
Jan [day undetermined]
Auction of Deserters' Effects
Awkward Squad
Bag Inspection
First Aid to the Injured
General Quarters
Obstacle Race
Recruits Embarking
Recruits on "Yorktown"
Sailors Dancing
Scrubbing Clothes
"Secure"
Serving Outfits to Recruits

New Jersey

1897
Oct [day undetermined]
Ambulance at the Accident*
Ambulance Call*
Nov [day undetermined]
Sad Sea Waves
Wreck of the Schooner "Richmond"
1903
Oct [day undetermined]
A Romance of the Rail
1905
May [day undetermined]
The Wedding
1907
Jun 17 Rube Brown in Town

Asbury Park
1899
Nov [day undetermined]
Jeffries and a Child at Play
Jeffries and Brother Boxing
Jeffries and Roeber Wrestling
Jeffries Being Rubbed Down
Jeffries Boxing with Tommy Ryan
Jeffries Running with His Trainers
Jeffries Training on Bicycle
1902
Aug [day undetermined]
Baby Parade
1904
Sep [day undetermined]
Annual Baby Parade, 1904, Asbury Park, N.J.
Nov [day undetermined]
The Suburbanite
Dec [day undetermined]
The Chicken Thief
1906
Oct [day undetermined]
Getting Evidence, Showing the Trials and Tribulations of a Private Detective
1907
Dec 4 The Elopement
1908
Apr [day undetermined]
The Hallroom Boys Received Queer Freight
Apr 29 The King's Messenger

Atlantic City
1896
Sep [day undetermined]
Atlantic City Bathers
Bathers and Lifeboat, Atlantic City
Boys Bathing, Leapfrog—Atlantic City
Busses Leaving R.R. Depot, Atlantic City
Fire Engine at Work
Getting Off Trolley at Atlantic City
Panoramic View from Trolley, Atlantic City
Sea Scene
"Shooting the Chutes"
Showing Group of Bathers, Atlantic City Beach
Taken from Trolley, Atlantic City
Dec [day undetermined]
Atlantic City Boardwalk
Wrestling Ponies
1897
Jul [day undetermined]
Beach Scene
Hauling a Scoop Net
In the Surf
A Jolly Crowd of Bathers Frolicking on the Beach at Atlantic City
On the Board Walk
Promenading on the Beach
Aug [day undetermined]
Atlantic City Fire Department
1900 [month undetermined]
Parade of the Order of Elks in Atlantic City
Jul [day undetermined]
Atlantic City Lodge, 276, B.P.O. Elks

Blue Ribbon Jumpers
Brooklyn Lodge, No. 22, B.P.O. Elks
Philadelphia Lodge, No. 2, B.P.O. Elks
Prize-Winning Coaches
The Promenaders
Rescue from the Surf
Washington Lodge, No. 15, B.P.O. Elks

1901
Aug [day undetermined]
Bathing at Atlantic City

1902 [month undetermined]
Life Rescue, Atlantic City
The Beach at Atlantic City
Caught in the Undertow
Floral Chair Parade
A Heavy Surf at Atlantic City

1903
Jan [day undetermined]
Atlantic City Bathers
Atlantic City Board Walk, Easter Morn
Atlantic City Floral Parade
Baby Show Atlantic City
Bathing at Atlantic City
Beach at Atlantic City
Colored Folks Bathing
Panoramic View of Atlantic City Beach
Yachting at Atlantic City
Aug [day undetermined]
Down Where the Wurzburger Flows
Seashore Frolics

1904
Jan 30 Alligator Farm
Jun [day undetermined]
Atlantic City Floral Parade
Parade, Fiftieth Anniversary Atlantic City, N.J.
Jul [day undetermined]
Outing, Mystic Shriners, Atlantic City, New Jersey
Parade, Mystic Shriners, Atlantic City, New Jersey

1910
Apr 18 When the Cat's Away
Aug 18 Shorty at the Shore

Bayonne
1900
Jul [day undetermined]
Burning of the Standard Oil Co. 's Tanks, Bayonne, N.J.
Burning of the Standard Oil Tanks

1905
Sep [day undetermined]
The Course of True Love

Branchport
1898
Oct [day undetermined]
An Innocent Victim
Nov [day undetermined]
Making an Impression

Cliffside
1908
Oct 6 The Zulu's Heart

Coytesville
1908
May 26 A Night of Terror
Jun 23 The Outlaw
Jul 7 The Kentuckian
Oct 27 The Call of the Wild
Nov 10 Taming of the Shrew
Nov 13 The Guerrilla
Nov 24 A Woman's Way

1909
Jan 14 A Rural Elopement
May 10 The French Duel
Jun 14 The Son's Return
Aug 9 Jones' Burglar
Aug 12 The Better Way
Nov 22 The Open Gate
Dec 2 The Death Disc: A Story of the Cromwellian Period
Dec 16 The Test

1910
Jan 24 The Honor of His Family
Feb 21 His Last Burglary
Feb 28 The Final Settlement
Jul 7 A Midnight Cupid
Aug 4 Her Father's Pride
Aug 8 The House with Closed Shutters
Aug 18 An Old Story with a New Ending
When We Were in Our Teens
Sep 1 Muggsy Becomes a Hero
Oct 13 The Masher
Oct 17 The Broken Doll

Deal Beach
1905
Apr [day undetermined]
Wanted: A Dog

Delaware Water Gap
see also
Delaware Water Gap (Pennsylvania)
1910
Jun 13 In the Border States
Jul 11 What the Daisy Said
Jul 21 Serious Sixteen
Sep 12 A Mohawk's Way
Sep 26 Rose O' Salem-Town

Demarest
1905
Sep [day undetermined]
The White Caps

Dover
1903
Dec [day undetermined]
The Great Train Robbery

East Orange
1904
Nov [day undetermined]
"Weary Willie" Kisses the Bride

1909
May 7 The Doctored Dinner Pail

Edgewater
1904
Jun [day undetermined]
"Personal"

1909
Feb 25 At the Altar
Jun 3 His Duty
Jun 10 A New Trick
Jun 28 The Way of Man
Sep 13 The Children's Friend
Getting Even
Sep 16 The Broken Locket
Sep 30 The Awakening
Oct 4 Pippa Passes; or, The Song of Conscience
Oct 25 In the Watches of the Night
Dec 6 Through the Breakers
Dec 16 In a Hempen Bag

1910
Jan 3 The Rocky Road
Jan 6 The Dancing Girl of Butte
Oct 27 The Passing of a Grouch

Englewood
1904
Sep [day undetermined]
How a French Nobleman Got a Wife Through the New York Herald "Personal" Columns

1905
Oct 5 Poor Algy

1909
Jun 21 Was Justice Served?
Nov 4 Nursing a Viper

Fair Haven
1902
Jun [day undetermined]
The Accomodating Cow
Alphonse and Gaston
Belles of the Beach
Biograph's Improved Incubator
The Lovers' Knot
Milking Time on the Farm
The Polite Frenchman
A Seashore Gymkana
A Spill
"A Sweet Little Home in the Country"
A Tub Race
Will He Marry the Girl?

1910
Sep 5 The Healing Faith

Forest River Hill
1904
Apr 20 Skirmish Between Russian and Japanese Advance Guards

Fort Lee
1898
Jul [day undetermined]
An Overloaded Donkey
A Ride on a Switchback
"Rushing the Growler"
"Teeter Tauter"
The Wheelbarrow Race
When the Girls Got Frisky
Aug [day undetermined]
The Last Round Ended in a Free Fight

1903
Nov [day undetermined]
What Happened in the Tunnel

1905
Jan [day undetermined]
The Gentlemen Highwaymen
Aug [day undetermined]
The Fire-Bug
Sep [day undetermined]
The White Caps

1908
Apr 15 The King of the Cannibal Islands
Aug 14 The Man and the Woman
Aug 18 The Fatal Hour
Aug 25 Balked at the Altar
Sep 8 The Girl and the Outlaw

1909
Jan 25 The Welcome Burglar
Jan 28 The Cord of Life
Feb 1 The Girls and Daddy
Feb 11 Tragic Love
Feb 15 The Curtain Pole
Feb 18 The Hindoo Dagger
Mar 11 The Salvation Army Lass
Mar 15 The Lure of the Gown
Apr 12 A Sound Sleeper
Apr 19 A Troublesome Satchel
Apr 22 The Drive for a Life
Apr 29 'Tis an Ill Wind that Blows No Good
May 6 One Busy Hour
May 27 The Cricket on the Hearth
May 31 What Drink Did
Jun 3 Eradicating Aunty
Jun 4 "Davy" Crockett in Hearts United
Jun 10 The Lonely Villa
Jun 24 The Peachbasket Hat
Jul 15 Tender Hearts
Jul 22 Jealousy and the Man
Jul 26 A Convict's Sacrifice
Nov 1 What's Your Hurry?
Nov 15 Two Women and a Man
Nov 29 In the Window Recess
Dec 20 A Trap for Santa Claus
Dec 23 In Little Italy
Dec 27 To Save Her Soul

1910
Jan 10 Her Terrible Ordeal
Jan 13 All on Account of the Milk
Jan 20 The Call
Feb 7 The Course of True Love
Feb 28 The Final Settlement
Sep 1 The Affair of an Egg
Sep 15 In Life's Cycle
Oct 27 The Proposal
Nov 10 Simple Charity
Nov 17 Love in Quarantine
Nov 24 Not So Bad as It Seemed
Dec 8 Happy Jack, a Hero
Turning the Tables
Dec 19 The Lesson
Dec 22 White Roses

Glen
1903
May [day undetermined]
Changing Horses at Glen

Gloucester
1901
Jun 29 Shad Fishing at Gloucester, N.J.

Grantwood
1905
Mar [day undetermined]
The Nihilists

1908
Jun 16 The Invisible Fluid

Guttenberg
1900
Sep [day undetermined]
Little Sister
Love in the Suburbs
A Water Duel

Hackensack
1910
Jan 3 The Rocky Road

Haddonfield
1896
Sep [day undetermined]
Pa. R.R., Hattonsfield

High Bridge
1905
Sep [day undetermined]
The Course of True Love

Highlands
1908
Nov 3 After Many Years
1909
Oct 28 Lines of White on a Sullen Sea
Nov 1 The Gibson Goddess
1910
Aug 11 A Salutary Lesson
Aug 22 The Sorrows of the Unfaithful
Nov 17 The Troublesome Baby

Highwood Park
1902
Nov [day undetermined]
A Romp on the Lawn

Hoboken
1900
Jul [day undetermined]
Hoboken Fire
The Hoboken Holocaust
Panoramic View of Burning Wharves and Warehouses [Hoboken]
1901
Aug [day undetermined]
Steamship "Deutschland"
1902
Mar [day undetermined]
Sailing of the "Deutschland" with Prince Henry [of Prussia] on Board
May [day undetermined]
The S.S. "Deutschland" Leaving Her Dock in Hoboken
Jun [day undetermined]
Over the Rail
The Summer Exodus
Dec [day undetermined]
After the Service
1906
May 1 The Subpoena Server
1907
Sep [day undetermined]
Blowing Hard
A Swell Time
Vanishing Friends
1908
Mar 11 The Boy Detective; or, The Abductors Foiled
Jul 15 The Boston Tea Party
Dec 11 The Reckoning
Dec 15 The Test of Friendship

Jersey City
1896
Sep [day undetermined]
Pa. R.R. Cliffs, Jersey City
1898
Jul [day undetermined]
Company "C," 1st Regiment, N.J.V.
1st Regiment, N.Y.V.
1900
Aug [day undetermined]
Demonstrating the Action of the Brown Hoisting and Conveying Machine in Unloading a Schooner of Iron Ore, and Loading the Material on the Cars
1901
Nov [day undetermined]
A Mighty Tumble

Keyport
1910
Aug 11 A Salutary Lesson

Leonia
1905
Aug [day undetermined]
The Summer Boarders
1908
Mar 18 Her First Adventure [Kidnapped with the Aid of a Street Piano]
1909
Jun 14 The Son's Return
Oct 11 The Little Teacher
1910
Dec 29 His Wife's Sweethearts

Linden
1903
May [day undetermined]
Changing Horses at Linden
On the Road
Private Picture for Mr. Hyde

Little Falls
1908
May [day undetermined]
Farmer Greene's Summer Boarders
Fun in the Hay
Jun 5 The Romance of an Egg
Jul 28 The Redman and the Child
Sep 15 The Red Girl
Oct 20 The Planter's Wife
Nov 24 A Woman's Way
1909
Aug 9 They Would Elope
Aug 30 The Heart of an Outlaw Pranks
Nov 8 The Restoration

Long Branch
1897
Oct [day undetermined]
Exhibition of Prize Winners
Single Harness Horses
Teams of Horses*
1898
Mar [day undetermined]
Sea Waves
1901
Sep [day undetermined]
Life Rescue at Long Branch

New Brunswick
1896
Sep [day undetermined]
Pennsylvania R.R., New Brunswick

Newark
1896
Nov [day undetermined]
Fighting the Fire*
Starting for the Fire
1898
Feb [day undetermined]
Coasting
Snowballing the Coasters*
1900
Mar [day undetermined]
Morning Fire Alarm
1901
Jul [day undetermined]
Great Newark Fire
1903
Jan [day undetermined]
Life of an American Fireman
Oct [day undetermined]
The Heavenly Twins at Lunch
The Heavenly Twins at Odds
1909
Nov 26 Annual Celebration of School Children at Newark, NJ

North Asbury Park
1905
Oct 24 The Watermelon Patch
Nov 2 Down on the Farm

North Bergen
1905
Jul [day undetermined]
Seeing Squashville

Orange
1898
May 20 Snow Storm
1900
Mar [day undetermined]
Foot Ball Game
1903
Jan [day undetermined]
Life of an American Fireman
1904
Dec [day undetermined]
The Ex-Convict
1906
Jun [day undetermined]
The Terrible Kids
Oct 18 The Fox-Hunt

Orange Mountains
1903
Dec [day undetermined]
The Great Train Robbery

Palisades
1907
Apr 27 The Fencing Master
1908
Jan 18 Rescued from an Eagle's Nest
1909
Jun 4 "Davy" Crockett in Hearts United

Palisades Park
1905
Nov [day undetermined]
The Barnstormers
1906
Aug 30 The Lone Highwayman
1909
Apr 5 Trying to Get Arrested

Paterson
1900
Mar [day undetermined]
Paterson Falls
1902
Feb [day undetermined]
A Big Blaze*
The Burning of Durland's Riding Academy
A Devastated City
Panorama of the Paterson [N.J.] Fire
The Paterson Fire
Paterson [N.J.] Fire, Showing the Y.M.C.A. and Library
Ruins of City Hall, Paterson [N.J.]
1903
Oct [day undetermined]
Flood Scene in Paterson, N.J.
1904
Jun [day undetermined]
"Personal"
1910
Jul 25 The Call to Arms
Sep 22 The Oath and the Man

Pleasure Bay
1898
Oct [day undetermined]
How the Gobbler Missed the Axe
Love in a Cornfield
Who's Got the Red Ear?
Nov [day undetermined]
A Happy Family
1902
Jan [day undetermined]
Eeling Through the Ice
Great Sport! Ice Yachting
Ice Yacht Racing
A Mile a Minute on an Ice Yacht
A Spill from an Ice Yacht

Princeton
1899
Jun [day undetermined]
A Football Tackle
1901
Oct [day undetermined]
Coaching for a Record

Red Bank
1901
Feb 23 Ice-Boat Racing at Redbank, N.J.
1904
Feb [day undetermined]
Ice Boating on the North Shrewsbury, Red Bank, N.J.
1908
Oct 2 Ten Pickaninnies

Ridgefield Park
1899
Sep [day undetermined]
Chickens Coming Out of the Shell
Eggs Hatching
Two Hours After Hatching

Ridgewood Park
1899
May [day undetermined]
A Unique Race

Rockaway
1905
Nov 27 The Train Wreckers

Sandy Hook
1897
Feb [day undetermined]
Projectile from Ten Inch Disappearing Gun Striking Water, Sandy Hook
Ten Inch Disappearing Carriage Gun Loading and Firing, Sandy Hook
1898
Feb [day undetermined]
Spanish Battleship "Viscaya"
1899
Sep [day undetermined]
The "Erin"
"Shamrock I"
Shamrock Starting on Trial Trip
Sir Thomas Lipton and Party on "Erin's" Launch
Sir Thomas Lipton's Steam Yacht "Erin"
Oct [day undetermined]
After the Race—Yachts Returning to Anchorage

New Mexico

New York

Nov [day undetermined]
Diving at Bath Beach
1899
Sep [day undetermined]
Diving Through Paper Screens
Fancy Diving
The Golding Family

Bay Shore
1901
Dec [day undetermined]
Expert Driving
Tally Ho!

Berkeley Oval
1901
Sep [day undetermined]
International Field Sports
International Field Sports—Oxford-Cambridge vs. Harvard-Yale
International Track Athletic Meeting—Start and Finish of the One Mile Run

Berlin
1901
Aug [day undetermined]
Gathering Gladioli

Bowery Bay
1897
Nov [day undetermined]
Scrub Yacht Race

Brighton Beach
1905
Sep [day undetermined]
The Boer War
General Cronje & Mystic Shriners
Ludlow's Aerodrome
1906 [month undetermined]
Head-On Collision at Brighton Beach Race Track, July 4th, 1906
May's Mechanical Race Track
1907
Sep [day undetermined]
Attack on Emigrant Train
Buffalo Hunt
The Punishment of the Horse Thief
[Ranch 101]
Scenes from Miller Bros.
1910
Sep 17 World's Championship Motor Races

Brighton Beach—Boer War Park
1905
Sep [day undetermined]
The Boer War
General Cronje & Mystic Shriners
Ludlow's Aerodrome
Nov [day undetermined]
Ludlow's Aerodrome, No. 2

Bronx
1904
Jan [day undetermined]
The Escaped Lunatic

Bronx Park
1900
Aug [day undetermined]
Chasing the Cherry Pickers
A Farmer's Imitation of Ching Ling Foo
Over the Fence and Out
1902
Apr [day undetermined]
Pontoon Bridge Building

Brooklyn
1898
Jul [day undetermined]
New York Naval Reserves
Oct [day undetermined]
Officers and Crew of the U.S. Cruiser "Brooklyn"
Return of Troop C, Brooklyn
Troop "C"
Twenty-Third Regiment, N.G.S.N.Y.
U.S. Marines
1899
Mar [day undetermined]
Across Brooklyn Bridge
May [day undetermined]
Elephants in a Circus Parade
Frank Melville's Trick Elephant
Hippopotamus "Babe"
Tent Pegging
A Unique Race
1900
Apr [day undetermined]
Demonstrating the Operation of the Harrington Rail Bonding System on the Line of the Coney Island and Brooklyn Railroad Co.
May [day undetermined]
Buffalo Bill's Wild West Parade
Jul [day undetermined]
Polo Game: Myopia vs. Dedham
1901
Nov [day undetermined]
Automobile Parade on the Coney Island Boulevard
Twentieth Century Flyers
1902
Dec [day undetermined]
Sheep and Lambs*
1903
Dec [day undetermined]
Burning of the Academy of Music, Brooklyn
1904
Aug [day undetermined]
The Widow and the Only Man
Oct [day undetermined]
The Lost Child
Nov [day undetermined]
Parsifal
1905
May [day undetermined]
Funeral of Hiram Cronk
1907
Jun 17 Rube Brown in Town
1908
Apr [day undetermined]
Crowded Street-Congested Street Society

Brooklyn—Ambrose Park
1899
Apr [day undetermined]
A Bucking Broncho
1900
Apr [day undetermined]
Buffalo Bill's Wild West Show

Brooklyn—Brooklyn Navy Yard
1897
Dec [day undetermined]
Battleships "Maine" and "Iowa"
1904
Oct [day undetermined]
Launching of the U.S.S. Battleship "Connecticut"

Brooklyn—Flatbush
1910
Mar 22 Capital vs. Labor

Brooklyn—Manhattan Beach
1901
Sep [day undetermined]
Sousa and His Band
1902
Sep [day undetermined]
Pain's Fireworks

Brooklyn—Prospect Park
1899
Jun [day undetermined]
Sunday School Parade

Brooklyn—Sheepshead Bay
1897
Jul [day undetermined]
Racing at Sheepshead Bay
Suburban Handicap, 1897
1899
Jun [day undetermined]
Finish of the Brooklyn Handicap, 1899
1900
Jun [day undetermined]
The Suburban of 1900
1901
Sep [day undetermined]
Finish of Futurity
Finish of Futurity, 1901
Parade to the Post
1902
Jun [day undetermined]
The Suburban of 1902
Sep [day undetermined]
The Futurity Crowd
The Futurity of 1902
Savable Wins
1903
Jun [day undetermined]
"Africander" Winning the Suburban Handicap, 1903
1909
May 28 Romance of a Fishermaid

Brooklyn Bridge
1899
Sep [day undetermined]
New Brooklyn to New York via Brooklyn Bridge, No. 1
1903
Oct [day undetermined]
An East River Novelty
Dec [day undetermined]
Battleship "Illinois" Passing Under Brooklyn Bridge

Buffalo
1896
Dec [day undetermined]
Hurdle Race—High Jumpers
Tally Ho—Arrival
Tally Ho—Departure
1897
Jul [day undetermined]
Buffalo Fire Department in Action
Buffalo Police on Parade
Buffalo Stockyards
1899
Jul [day undetermined]
Buffalo Fire Department
A Flock of Export Sheep
1900
Jul [day undetermined]
Fire Boat "John M. Hutchinson"
Oct [day undetermined]
Pan-American Exposition
1901
May [day undetermined]
At the Setting of the Sun
The Horticultural Building
In the Gypsy Camp
"Laughing Ben"
On the Old Plantation
Jun [day undetermined]
Bally-Hoo Cake Walk
Beautiful Orient
The Bridge of Sighs—Pan-American Exposition
The Court of Fountains—Pan-American Exposition
Esquimaux Dance
An Esquimaux Game
The Esquimaux Village
Fair Japan—Pan-American Exposition
Fountain, Tower, and Basins—Pan-American Exposition
The Indian Congress
Main Entrance to Pan-American Exp.
On the Midway—Pan-American Exposition
The Ostrich Farm—On the Midway
Panorama of Midway—Pan-American Exposition
Panoramic View Gov't Building, Pan. Am. Exp.
Propylaea and North End of Plaza, Pan. Am. Exp.
Scene in Beautiful Orient—Pan-American Exposition
Sevillenas Dance—Pan-American Exposition
Triumphal Bridge, Pan-American Exposition
Venice in America
Jun 8 Circular Panorama of the Base of the Electric Tower, Ending Looking Down the Mall
Circular Panorama of the Electric Tower and Pond
Circular Panorama of the Esplanade with the Electric Tower in the Background
Opening of the Pan-American Exposition Showing Vice President Roosevelt Leading the Procession
Panoramic View of the Temple of Music and Esplanade
View of the Midway
Jun 22 A Trip Around the Pan-American Exposition
Jun 29 Acrobats in Cairo
Buffalo Street Parade
Couchee Dance on the Midway
A Good Joke
Grand Entry, Indian Congress
Indians No. 1
Midway Dance
Panorama of the Exposition, No. 1

Panorama of the Exposition, No. 2
Turkish Dance
Wedding Procession in Cairo
Jul [day undetermined]
The Assembly in the Indian Village
Circular Panorama of the Esplanade and Forecourt
Circular Panorama of the Midway
The Esquimaux Village
Japanese Village
On the Midway—Pan-American Exposition
Ostrich Farm
Jul 9 Esquimaux Village
Panorama of a Philippine Village
Aug [day undetermined]
Circular Panorama of Electric Tower
Esquimaux Game of Snap-the-Whip
Esquimaux Leap-Frog
Panoramic View of Electric Tower from a Balloon
Tally-Ho Departing for the Races
Sep [day undetermined]
Arrival of Funeral Cortege at the City Hall, Buffalo, N.Y.
McKinley Funeral—In Solemn State
The Multitude Passing into the City Hall
Panoramic View of the Crowd Rushing for the City Hall, Buffalo, to View the Body of President McKinley
President McKinley at the Buffalo Exposition
President McKinley's Funeral
Sep 21 The Mob Outside the Temple of Music at the Pan-American Exposition [Buffalo]
President McKinley Reviewing the Troops at the Pan-American Exposition
President McKinley's Speech at the Pan-American Exposition
Oct [day undetermined]
Horse Parade at the Pan-American Exposition
Spanish Dancers at the Pan-American Exposition
Working the Breeches Buoy
Oct 5 President McKinley's Funeral Cortege at Buffalo, N.Y.
Oct 19 Pan-American Exposition by Night
Nov [day undetermined]
Panorama of Esplanade by Night
Sham Battle at the Pan-American Exposition
1902 [month undetermined]
Boating in Lakes of Philippine Village
Bostock's Educated Chimpanzee
Electric Tower
Fire Run, Exposition
Gipsies Dancing
Indians No. 2
Japanese Acrobats
The Miniature Railway
Opening Day Parade No. 1
Opening Day Parade No. 2
Opening Day Parade No. 3
Panorama City of Venice
Panorama of Esplanade from Bridge of Triumph
Panorama of Esquimaux Village
Panorama of Midway
Panorama of Venice
Ye Olde Mill
1903
Jan [day undetermined]
Lafayette Square, Buffalo, N.Y.
Main Street, Buffalo, N.Y.

Camp Black
1898
May [day undetermined]
Three Views of the 69th Regiment, N.G.S.N.Y.

Canastota
1896
Aug [day undetermined]
Sparring Contest, Canastota, N.Y.
Sep [day undetermined]
Engine and Pump
Threshing Machine
Oct [day undetermined]
Chicago Fast Mail NYC. R.R.
Empire State Express
Empire State Express No. 2
Empire State Express, N.Y. Central R.R.
Train Taking Water, N.Y. Central R.R.
1897
May [day undetermined]
"Ring Around a Rosie"
See Saw
Sep [day undetermined]
Threshing Machine at Work
Oct [day undetermined]
Harvesting Corn
1900
Feb [day undetermined]
Marvin and Casler's Laboratory
1901
Oct [day undetermined]
Mr. H. Casler and Baby. Experimental
1902
Jan [day undetermined]
Love in a Hammock

Catskill Mountains
1906
Jun 30 In the Haunts of Rip Van Winkle
In the Heart of the Catskills
Through Austin Glen, Catskill Railway
The Valley of Esopus

Cedarhurst
1900
Jul [day undetermined]
Champion Polo Players

City Island
1906
Aug [day undetermined]
Weighing the Anchor
Aug 23 The Cruise of the Gladys

College Point
1903
Feb [day undetermined]
Sack Race

Coney Island
1897 [month undetermined]
Shooting the Chutes
Sep [day undetermined]
Riding on the Merry-Go-Round
Oct [day undetermined]
The Aerial Slide at Coney Island
A Baby Merry-Go-Round
Fatima
Fun on the Steeple-Chase
1898
Aug [day undetermined]
The Bathing Girls Hurdle Race
1899
Jun [day undetermined]
Going to the Post
The Suburban
Sep [day undetermined]
The Diving Horse
"King" and "Queen," the Great High Diving Horses
Prof. Paul Boynton Feeding His Sea Lions
Shoot the Chutes Series
Nov [day undetermined]
Jeffries-Sharkey Contest
Test. Coney Island Athletic Club
1900
Sep [day undetermined]
Around the Flip-Flap Railroad
Capt. Boynton Feeding His Pets
1901
Jul [day undetermined]
Flip-Flap Railway
A Wagon Load of Babies
Aug [day undetermined]
Swimming Pool at Coney Island
1903
Jan [day undetermined]
Beach Scene, Coney Island
Electrocution of an Elephant
Loop the Loop
May [day undetermined]
Shooting the Chutes
Jul [day undetermined]
Shooting the Chutes, Luna Park
Aug [day undetermined]
A Funny Story on the Beach
A Little Tease
Rube and Mandy at Coney Island
The Waders
"What Are the Wild Waves Saying Sister?"
Sep [day undetermined]
Baby Class at Lunch
Orphans in the Surf
The Sand Baby
The Sand Fort
Oct [day undetermined]
Arab Act, Luna Park
Double Ring Act, Luna Park
Rattan Slide and General View of Luna Park
Shooting the Rapids at Luna Park
Slide for Life, Luna Park
The Vaidis Sisters, Luna Park
Nov [day undetermined]
The Great Fire Ruins, Coney Island
1904
Jul [day undetermined]
Alone
Beyond the Danger Line
A Couple of Lightweights at Coney Island
Fighting the Flames [An Attraction at Coney Island]
The First Baby
The Racing Chutes at Dreamland
The Seashore Baby
The Swimming Class
Aug [day undetermined]
The Baby and the Puppies
The Children in the Surf
The Coney Island Beach Patrol
Fighting the Flames, Dreamland
Orphan Children on the Beach at Coney Island
A Seaside Cakewalk
A Swimming Race at Coney Island
The Two Bottle Babies
The Widow and the Only Man
1905 [month undetermined]
Dial's Girls' Band, Luna Park
Jul [day undetermined]
Coney Island at Night
Hippodrome Races, Dreamland, Coney Island
Aug [day undetermined]
June's Birthday Party
Leap Frog Railway, Coney Island
Mystic Shriners' Day, Dreamland, Coney Island
Sep [day undetermined]
The Boarding School Girls
Girls and "Barrel of Love"
Girls Riding Camels
Oct [day undetermined]
Meet Me Down at Luna, Lena
1907
Sep [day undetermined]
Scenes from Luna Park
1908
Aug 5 Tales the Searchlight Told

Coney Island—Luna Park
1903
Jun [day undetermined]
Down the Bamboo Slide
"Holy Moses" the Camel
1904
Jun [day undetermined]
Elephants Shooting the Chutes at Luna Park [Coney Island]
Jul [day undetermined]
Boxing Horses, Luna Park, Coney Island
Elephants Shooting the Chutes, Luna Park, Coney Island, No. 2
Aug [day undetermined]
Fire and Flames at Luna Park, Coney Island [An Attraction at Coney Island]
Parade of Mystic Shriners, Luna Park, Coney Island
1910
Jul 5 Gone to Coney Island

Cuddebackville
1909
Aug 5 The Mended Lute
Aug 23 The Indian Runner's Romance
Sep 2 The Little Darling
Sep 6 "1776" or, The Hessian Renegades
Sep 9 Comata, the Sioux
Sep 20 In Old Kentucky
Sep 23 A Fair Exchange
Sep 27 Leather Stocking
Oct 7 Fools of Fate
Nov 25 The Mountaineer's Honor
1910
Aug 25 Wilful Peggy
Aug 29 The Modern Prodigal
Sep 1 Muggsy Becomes a Hero
Sep 5 A Summer Idyll

Sep 15 In Life's Cycle
Oct 6 A Gold Necklace
Oct 10 That Chink at Golden Gulch
Oct 17 The Broken Doll

Ellis Island
1903
Aug [day undetermined]
Immigrants Landing at Ellis Island
1906
May [day undetermined]
Arrival of Immigrants, Ellis Island

Elmira
1902
Feb [day undetermined]
Demonstrating the Action of a Mergenthaler-Horton Basket Making Machine

Elmont—Belmont Park
1905
May [day undetermined]
Opening of Belmont Park Race Course
1910
Dec 15 The Renowned International Aviation Meet

Esopus
1904
Aug [day undetermined]
Democratic National Committee at Esopus
Judge Parker & Mayor McClellan at Esopus
Judge Parker Receiving the Notification of His Nomination for the Presidency
Sep [day undetermined]
Democratic Presidential Candidate, Judge Parker, and Mayor McClellan, Esopus, N.Y.

Far Rockaway
1898
Aug [day undetermined]
The Bathing Girls Hurdle Race
The Coney Island Bikers
The Dude's Experience with a Girl on a Tandem
"Leapfrog" on the Beach
Making Love on the Beach
Ready for the Bath
Snap the Whip
Stolen Sweets

Fishers Island
1902
Sep [day undetermined]
A Ball on a Battleship
Bombardment of Newport

Fishkill
1910
Nov 7 The Fugitive
Nov 21 The Song of the Wildwood Flute

Forest Hills
1905
Jul [day undetermined]
[On] a [Good Ole] 5¢ Trolley Ride

Fort Hamilton
1904
Oct [day undetermined]
The Lost Child

Fulton Chain
1900
Aug [day undetermined]
Eccentricities of an Adirondack Canoe
A Launch Party in the Adirondacks
The Narrows
Steamer "Stowell" Running the Narrows

Glen Island
1903
Nov [day undetermined]
Battleship "Indiana" in Action
Boat Race
Feeding the Russian Bear
An Impartial Lover
A Juvenile Elephant Trainer
The Llamas at Play
Man Overboard! "INDIANA"

Gloversville
1906
Apr [day undetermined]
A Winter Straw Ride
1907
May 18 Lost in the Alps
1908
Nov 17 Colonial Virginia

Governors Island
1897
Feb [day undetermined]
13th Infantry, U.S. Army—Bayonet Exercise, Governors Island
13th Infantry, U.S. Army—Blanket Court Martial, Governors Island
13th Infantry, U.S. Army—Full Dress Parade and Manoeuvering, Governors Island
13th Infantry, U.S. Army—Full Dress Parade, Governors Island
13th Infantry, U.S. Army, in Heavy Marching Order, Double-Time, Governors Island
13th Infantry, U.S. Army—Manual of Arms, Governors Island
13th Infantry, U.S. Army—Marching and Counter Marching (Band and Troops), Governors Island
13th Infantry, U.S. Army Marching Through Sallyport, Governors Island
13th Infantry, U.S. Army—Musical Drill, Governors Island
13th Infantry, U.S. Army—Scaling Walls in Retreat, Governors Island
13th Infantry, U.S. Army—Scaling Walls with Wounded and Dying, Governors Island
1900
Jul [day undetermined]
15th Infantry
1907
May [day undetermined]
Governor's Island Taken U.S.N.

Gravesend
1897
Apr [day undetermined]
Finish of the Brooklyn Handicap
Going to the Post
Hurdle Race
Six Furlong Handicap
1901
Oct [day undetermined]
Finish of Flatbush Stakes, Gravesend Track
Match Race, Endurance by Right vs. Heno
1902
Sep [day undetermined]
Steeplechasing at the Brooklyn Handicap
1904
Jun [day undetermined]
The Brooklyn Handicap, 1904

Haines Falls
1897
Jul [day undetermined]
Waterfall in the Catskills

Hammondsport
1910
Oct 15 Aeroplanes in Flight and Construction

Hartsdale
1905
Sep [day undetermined]
High Jumping Horses—Sidney Holloway's Farm
The Horse-Thief

Hastings
1905
Sep [day undetermined]
The River Pirates

Haverstraw
1897
Oct [day undetermined]
The Haverstraw Tunnel
1903
Jan [day undetermined]
Panoramic View of Haverstraw Tunnel, N.Y.

Hempstead
1899
Apr [day undetermined]
Going to the Hunt
High Hurdle Jumping, at Meadowbrook Hunt Club
The Meadowbrook Hunt

Highwood Park
1902
Nov [day undetermined]
"All Hot"

Hudson River
1898
Oct [day undetermined]
South Gate of the Highlands
1903
Oct [day undetermined]
From Haverstraw to Newburg
1904
Jul [day undetermined]
Speed Test W. K. Vanderbilt, Jr.'s "Tarantula"
1905
Nov [day undetermined]
Reception of British Fleet
1908
Apr 15 The King of the Cannibal Islands

Huntington Bay
1903
Jul [day undetermined]
Pres. Roosevelt's Fourth of July Oration
1910
Dec 16 The International Motor Boat Races

Irvington
1899
Apr [day undetermined]
Frank Gould's Dogs
Prize Winning St. Bernards
1903
Feb [day undetermined]
Trial Run of the Fastest Boat in the World, "The Arrow"

Jamaica
1909
Dec 13 A Corner in Wheat

Jerome Park
1897
Jul [day undetermined]
Expert Driving

King's County
1903
Jan [day undetermined]
Panorama of King's County, N.Y.

Lake Ronkonkoma
1910
Apr 13 Ice Scooters on Lake Ronkonkoma

Larchmont
1897
Nov [day undetermined]
Scrub Yacht Race
1900
Mar [day undetermined]
Trial Race Columbia and Defender
Trial Race Columbia and Defender No. 2
1910
Dec 16 The International Motor Boat Races

Liberty Island
1898
Sep [day undetermined]
Statue of Liberty

Long Island
1902
Jan [day undetermined]
Feeding Geese at Newman's Poultry Farm
1904
Oct [day undetermined]
Automobile Race for the Vanderbilt Cup

Long Island Sound
1897
Oct [day undetermined]
Fall River Boat "Priscilla"
1899
Jul [day undetermined]
"Columbia" and "Defender" Rounding Stake-Boat
"Columbia" vs. "Defender"
Running Up the Topsail on the "Columbia"
1900
Jun [day undetermined]
Larchmont Regatta
1902
Nov [day undetermined]
An Unsinkable Skimmer

Loon Lake
1898
Oct [day undetermined]
In the Adirondacks

Manlius
1904
Mar [day undetermined]
The Battle of the Yalu
Butt's Manual, St. John's School
Dress Parade, St. John's Academy
Gun Drill St. John's Academy
Sep [day undetermined]
The Hero of Liao Yang

Manlius—St. John's Military Academy
1904
Mar [day undetermined]
Company Drill, St. John's Military Academy
Manual of Arms, St. John's Military Academy

Montauk Point
1898
Sep [day undetermined]
Capron's Battery
Col. Theodore Roosevelt and Officers of His Staff
Crew of the "Yankee"
Eighth Ohio Volunteers (the President's Own)
First Battalion of the 2nd Massachusetts Volunteers
Fourth Infantry, U.S. Regulars
General Wheeler and Secretary of War Alger at Camp Wikoff
Ninth Regiment, U.S. Regulars
Panoramic View of Camp Wikoff
President McKinley's Inspection of Camp Wikoff
Second Battalion; 2nd Massachusetts Volunteers
71st Regiment, N.G.S.N.Y. AT CAMP WIKOFF
Thirteenth Infantry, U.S. Regulars
33rd Regiment, Michigan Volunteers
Twenty-Fourth Infantry

Morris Park
1901
Oct [day undetermined]
Horses Jumping Water Jump
The Matron Stakes
1903
May [day undetermined]
Juvenile Stakes
Meadowbrook Steeplechase
Metropolitan Handicap

Mt. Beacon
1902
Sep [day undetermined]
Down the Mountain Side
A Stern Chase
Turning Panorama of Mt. Beacon
1909
Dec 9 The Redman's View

New Empire City Park
1899
Sep [day undetermined]
The Great Free-for-All Pacing Race
One Mile Dash

New Rochelle
1910
Jun 21 Thelma

New Suffolk
1904
Jul [day undetermined]
Holland Submarine Boat Tests

New York Bay
1899
Oct [day undetermined]
Mr. and Mrs. C. Oliver Iselin

New York City
1896
Sep [day undetermined]
Li Hung Chang at Grant's Tomb
Li Hung Chang Driving Through 4th St. and Broadway [New York City]
Li Hung Chang, 5th Avenue & 55th Street, N.Y.
On the Boulevard
Union Square and Fourth Avenue
Union Square—New York
View on Boulevard, New York City
Oct [day undetermined]
Park Police Drill Left Wheel and Forward
Park Police Drill Mount and Dismounting
Wine Garden Scene
Nov [day undetermined]
Fire Department, N.Y. City, 1st and 2nd Alarms
Mounted Police Charge
New York Fire Department
The Sound Money Parade
Sound Money Parade
Dec [day undetermined]
Broadway & Park Row, Front of U.S. Post Office, N.Y.
1897 [month undetermined]
East River, New York
Herald Square
Jan [day undetermined]
"Boys Will Be Boys"
Feb [day undetermined]
Broadway, New York, at Madison Square
Ferryboat and Tug Passing Governors Island, New York Harbor
Outbound Vessel Passing Governors Island, N.Y. Harbor
Mar [day undetermined]
Columbia School Girls
Fifth Avenue, New York
First Corps Cadets; Mass. National Guard
Glimpses of the Grant Parade
Gov. John A. Tanner, of Virginia, and Staff
Major-General Dodge and Staff
Major-General O. Howard, U.S.A., and Staff
The Old Guard of New York
7th Regiment, N.G.S.N.Y.
Sleighing in Central Park
Steamship "St. Paul" Outward Bound*
U.S. Cavalry and Artillery
U.S. Sailors
West Point Cadets
May [day undetermined]
National Lancers of Boston
President McKinley's Address
7th and 71st Regiment, New York
Jun [day undetermined]
Loading Hay
Trial Scene
Jul [day undetermined]
The Junior Republic on Parade
Oct [day undetermined]
New York Elevated Trains
Dec [day undetermined]
The Battery
Battleship "Texas"
Mulberry Bend
Ocean Greyhounds
Scrambling for Pennies
Side-Walks of New York
Tipping the Cart in Mulberry Bend
The Workers
1898 [month undetermined]
Battleship Indiana
Battleship Iowa
Battleship Massachusetts
Battleship Oregon
Battleship Texas
Cruiser Brooklyn
Cruiser New York
The Spanish Cruiser Vizcaya
Feb [day undetermined]
The Skyscrapers of New York
Apr [day undetermined]
The Tenth Battalion
Troop "A"; N.G.S.N.Y.
Twelfth Regiment, N.G.S.N.Y.
May [day undetermined]
In Front of "Journal" Building
May 20 N.Y. Journal Despatch Yacht "Buccaneer"
A Street Arab
Jun [day undetermined]
Anderson Zouaves
Chief Devery at Head of N.Y. Police Parade
Church Temperance League
Dalgren Post, G.A.R.
Hebrew Orphan Asylum Band
Irish Volunteers
John A. Dix Post, G.A.R.
Koltes' Camp, G.A.R.
N. L. Farnum Post, G.A.R.
Naval Post, G.A.R.
New York Mounted on Parade
New York Police on Parade
New York Police Parade
Veteran Zouaves
Jul [day undetermined]
A Chinese Opium Joint
Aug [day undetermined]
Naval Constructor Richmond P. Hobson
Victorious Squadron Firing Salute
Sep [day undetermined]
Close View of the "Brooklyn," Naval Parade
The Fleet Steaming up North River
The "Massachusetts," Naval Parade
Observation Train Following Parade*
Peace Jubilee Naval Parade, New York City
Police Boats Escorting Naval Parade
U.S. Battleship "Oregon"
U.S. Cruiser "Brooklyn," Naval Parade
Dec [day undetermined]
The Astor Battery
Sleighing Scene
1899
Jan [day undetermined]
Astor Battery on Parade
Fifth Avenue Entrance to Central Park
Feb [day undetermined]
Panoramic View of Brooklyn Bridge
Mar [day undetermined]
Across Brooklyn Bridge
Around the Big Curves
Around the Big Curves on the Manhattan Elevated R.R.
Getting Rid of the Surplus
In the Grip of the Blizzard
Ruins of the Windsor Hotel Fire
Apr [day undetermined]
Cruiser "Raleigh"
An Easter Parade
Elevated Railroad and Drawbridge
"Etruria"
Ferryboat "St. Louis"
"Graf Waldersee"
Greater New York
Liberty Enlightening the World
Off for China
104th Street Curve, New York, Elevated Railway
Pilot Boats in New York Harbor
Pole Vaulting at Columbia University
Third Avenue Elevated Railroad
A Trip over the Manhattan Elevated Railroad
Under Full Sail
View of Brooklyn Bridge from a Ferryboat
May [day undetermined]
Champion High Jumpers, "Chappie" and "Ben Bolt"
Distributing a War Extra
High Steppers in Harness
Judging Ladies' Saddle Horses
"Langton Performer 2nd"
New York Mounted Police
"Sampson" Champion High Stepper
Jun [day undetermined]
Chief Devery and Staff
Eighth Regiment, N.G.S.N.Y.
Lieutenant-General Nelson A. Miles
New York Naval Militia
New York Police
New York Police Parade, June 1st, 1899
Ninth Regiment, N.G.S.N.Y.
Twenty-Second Regiment, N.G.S.N.Y.
Aug [day undetermined]
Fancy Diving
The Fire Boat "New Yorker"
Professor Billy Opperman's Swimming School
Sep [day undetermined]
New Brooklyn to New York via Brooklyn Bridge, No. 2
Oct [day undetermined]
Admiral Dewey and Mayor Van Wyck Going Down Riverside Drive
Admiral Dewey Leading Land Parade
Admiral Dewey Leading Land Parade, (Eighth Ave.)
Admiral Dewey Passing Catholic Club Stand
Admiral Dewey's First Step on American Shore
Battery K Siege Guns

Col. John Jacob Astor, Staff and Veterans of the Spanish-American War
Connecticut Naval Reserves
The "Corsair"
"Corsair" in Wake of Tugboat
The Dandy Fifth
The Dewey Arch
Dewey Naval Parade
Dewey Parade, 10th Pennsylvania Volunteers
5th Ohio Volunteers of Cleveland
1st Penn' Volunteers of Philadelphia
Flagship Olympia and Cruiser New York in Naval Parade
Fourth Connecticut Volunteers, Dewey Parade
Gen. McCrosky Butt and Staff
Governor Roosevelt and Staff
The "Havana"
Marines of the Atlantic Fleet
The "Niagara"
Panorama at Grant's Tomb, Dewey Naval Procession
Panoramic View of Floral Float "Olympia"
Panoramic View of Olympia in New York Harbor
The "Pennsylvania"
Police Boats and Pleasure Craft on Way to Olympia
Presentation of Loving Cup at City Hall, New York
The "Richard Peck"
The "Sagamore"
Sailors of the Atlantic Fleet
2nd Battalion, 3rd New York Provisional Regiment, Rochester and Syracuse, Separate Companies
2nd Company Governor's Footguards, Conn.
7th Regiment, New York City
Steamer "Grandrepublic"
10th Penn'a Volunteers
Training Ship "Lancaster"
West Point Cadets
The West Point Cadets and Band

Nov [day undetermined]
U.S. Cruiser "Olympia" Leading Naval Parade

1900

Feb [day undetermined]
Automobile Parade
Dick Croker Leaving Tammany Hall

Mar [day undetermined]
Above the Speedway
Answering the Alarm
Bowling Green
Broadway at Post Office
A Brush on the Speedway
Dancing on the Bowery
14th Street and Broadway
Mr. and Mrs. Califf at Dinner
Opening of the Rapid Transit Tunnel
Panoramic View of the Dewey Arch, New York City
Panoramic View of the Ghetto, New York City
Rosedale
Sidewalks of New York
U.S. Marines in Dewey Land Parade

Apr [day undetermined]
The Croton Dam Strike
In Central Park

May [day undetermined]
A Speedway Parade

Sep [day undetermined]
H. N. Marvin's Family
Little Sister
Republican National Committee of 1900
The "St. Paul" Outward Bound

Nov [day undetermined]
The Fire at Tarrant & Co.'s Drug Store

1901

Feb [day undetermined]
Anawanda Club
Locked in the Ice
Sea Gulls

Apr [day undetermined]
Demolishing and Building Up the Star Theatre

May [day undetermined]
Fulton Market
The Slippery Slide
Unloading a Mackerel Schooner

Jun [day undetermined]
The Heart of New York
Washington Bridge and Speedway

Jul [day undetermined]
Boys Entering Free Bath
Boys Free Public Baths
The Falling Walls at the Tarrant Explosion
Firemen Fighting the Tarrant Fire
Ladies Day at the Public Baths
New York Sky-Line from East River and Battery
New York Sky-Line from the North River
Panorama of Brooklyn Bridge, River Front, and Tall Buildings from the East River
Parade on the Speedway
Saturday at the Free Baths
Searching the Ruins of the Tarrant Fire
Women of the Ghetto Bathing

Aug [day undetermined]
Broadway and Fourteenth St.
Experimental
Soubrette's Troubles on a Fifth Avenue Stage Coach
What Happened on Twenty-Third Street, New York City

Oct [day undetermined]
A Perilous Proceeding
Steam Yacht "American"

1902 [month undetermined]
Herald Square, New York
Panorama of Ninth Ave. Elevated R.R.

Jan [day undetermined]
Deer in Park
Starting a Skyscraper

Feb [day undetermined]
Battleship "Illinois"
A Big Blaze
Docking a Liner
Fire at Durland's Academy, N.Y. City
"Kronprinz Wilhelm" with Prince Henry [of Prussia] on Board Arriving in New York
New York City in a Blizzard
Panoramic View of the Hohenzollern
Park Avenue Explosion
The Royal Salute
Welcome Prince Henry!

Mar [day undetermined]
Ferryboat Entering Slip
Madison Square, New York City
Prince Henry
Prince Henry and President's Party

Apr [day undetermined]
Century Wheelman, N.Y. City
48th Highlanders Regiment
Installation Ceremonies, Columbia University
Installation Ceremonies of President Butler
St. Patrick's Cathedral and Fifth Avenue on Easter Sunday Morning [New York City]

May [day undetermined]
Appointment by Telephone
On the Speedway
Scene on Lower Broadway
The Speedway Parade
Street Scene

Jun [day undetermined]
Lower New York
Panorama of Lower New York

Aug [day undetermined]
Around the Mulberry Bush
At the Fountain
A Lawn Party
Old Volunteer Fire Dept.
Rex's Bath
Sweethearts
Wash Day
Water Nymphs

Sep [day undetermined]
St. John's Guild. Dock to Plank, 35th St.
St. John's Guild. Examination of Patients
St. John's Guild. Going to Salt-water Bath Room
St. John's Guild. Julliard and Tug in Narrows
St. John's Guild. Julliard Passing; Fire-Hose Playing
St. John's Guild. Plank to Deck, Floating Hospital

Oct [day undetermined]
The Eighth Wonder
General Booth
"Seeing New York"

Nov [day undetermined]
A Remarkable Fire

Dec [day undetermined]
Broadway & Union Square, New York
The Horse Market

1903 [month undetermined]
Automobile Parade

Jan [day undetermined]
Death Curve, New York City
Herald Square, New York
A Midwinter Blaze
Panorama from Elevated Train, New York
6th Ave. New York Elevated Railroad

Feb [day undetermined]
Children Coasting
A Sweep Across New York
25 Stories Up!

Mar [day undetermined]
In the Rapid-Transit Tunnel

May [day undetermined]
New York City Dumping Wharf
New York City "Ghetto" Fish Market
New York Harbor Police Boat Patrol Capturing Pirates
Run of N.Y. Fire Department
Skyscrapers of New York City, from the North River
Sorting Refuse at Incinerating Plant, New York City
The Still Alarm
White Wings on Review

Jun [day undetermined]
Rock Drill at Work in Subway
69th Regiment, N.G.N.Y.

Jul [day undetermined]
Battle Flags of the 9th U.S. Infantry
Bayonet Exercises
Musical Calisthenics
Musical Drill with Arms
Shelter Tent Drill

Sep [day undetermined]
New York Caledonian Club's Parade
Parade of Eagles, New York
Seeing New York by Yacht

Oct [day undetermined]
East Side Urchins Bathing in a Fountain
Move On
Seeing New York by Yacht
Two Chappies in a Box

Nov [day undetermined]
Lifting a Wagon from a New York Foundation
A Windy Day at the Flatiron Building

1904

Mar [day undetermined]
Buster and Tige Put a Balloon Vendor Out of Business

Jun [day undetermined]
Exhibition Fire Drill, Union Square, N.Y.
The Slocum Disaster
"Weary Willie" Kidnaps a Child

Jul [day undetermined]
Scenes in an Infant Orphan Asylum

Jul 16 White Star S.S. Baltic Leaving Pier on First Eastern Voyage

Sep [day undetermined]
European Rest Cure
How a French Nobleman Got a Wife Through the New York Herald "Personal" Columns

Oct [day undetermined]
Maniac Chase

Nov [day undetermined]
Opening Ceremonies, New York Subway, October 27, 1904
"Weary Willie" Kisses the Bride

Dec [day undetermined]
Bad Boy's Joke on the Nurse
The Ex-Convict
The "Strenuous" Life; or, Anti-Race Suicide

1905

Jan [day undetermined]
Around New York in 15 Minutes

Feb [day undetermined]
Across the New Viaduct of New York
The Kleptomaniac

Apr [day undetermined]
Bargain Day on 14th Street, New York
Employees Leaving Office

N.Y. Life Insurance Co. Pres. McCall & Officers
Panorama from the Roof of the Times Building, New York
Women Employee's Dining Room
May [day undetermined]
Funeral of Hiram Cronk
"Play Ball"—Opening Game, National League, N.Y. City, 1905—New York vs. Boston
Jun [day undetermined]
Interior N.Y. Subway, 14th St. to 42nd St.
Reuben in the Subway
Jul [day undetermined]
Departure of Peary for the North Pole
Lifting the Lid
Raffles, the Dog
Stolen by Gypsies
Aug [day undetermined]
Pennsylvania Tunnel Excavation
Scenes and Incidents, Russo-Japanese Peace Conference, Portsmouth, N.H.
Sep [day undetermined]
Stop Thief!
Oct [day undetermined]
Fire in New York's Bowery
Nov 6 The Miller's Daughter
Dec [day undetermined]
Spectacular Scenes during a New York City Fire
Dec 5 Desperate Encounter Between Burglar and Police
Life of an American Policeman
A River Tragedy

1906
Feb 19 A Friend in Need Is a Friend Indeed
Mar 29 The Black Hand
Jun [day undetermined]
The Terrible Kids
Jun 30 Grand Hotel to Big Indian
Jul [day undetermined]
Waiting at the Church
Aug [day undetermined]
How the Office Boy Saw the Ball Game
Kathleen Mavoureen
Water Tricycle
Sep [day undetermined]
Bryan
William Jennings Bryan
Oct [day undetermined]
Getting Evidence, Showing the Trials and Tribulations of a Private Detective
7th Regiment at 69th Army Dedication
Nov 15 The Tunnel Workers
Dec 8 Skyscrapers

1907 [month undetermined]
A Trip Up Broadway
Mar 2 The Teddy Bears
Apr [day undetermined]
Unloading Mail at Pier 13, N. R., N.Y.
Apr 6 Daniel Boone; or, Pioneer Days in America
Apr 27 The Fencing Master
Jun 17 Rube Brown in Town
Jun 29 Cohen's Fire Sale
Jul 20 The Hypnotist's Revenge
Aug 3 The Nine Lives of a Cat
Aug 17 The Deaf-Mutes' Ball
Aug 31 Stage Struck
Sep [day undetermined]
Congested Street Society
The Finish of Scrappy Patsey
A Tenement House Battle
Sep 12 Neighbors
Sep 14 Rivals
Sep 28 A Race for Millions
Oct 19 Jack the Kisser
Nov 2 Midnight Ride of Paul Revere
Nov 23 Three American Beauties [No. 2]
The Trainer's Daughter; or, A Race for Love
Dec 7 College Chums
Dec 14 Laughing Gas
Dec 21 The Little Girl who Did Not Believe in Santa Claus

1908
Jan 11 "Energizer"
Jan 18 The Suburbanite's Ingenious Alarm
Feb 1 Fireside Reminiscences
A Yankee Man-o-Warsman's Fight for Love
Feb 15 A Sculptor's Welsh Rabbit Dream
Mar 7 Playmates
Mar 14 Nellie, the Pretty Typewriter
Mar 21 Animated Snowballs
Stage Memories of an Old Theatrical Trunk
Mar 28 A Country Girl's Seminary Life and Experiences
Apr 11 Tale the Autumn Leaves Told
Apr 12 The Cowboy and the Schoolmarm
Apr 22 Nero and the Burning of Rome
Apr 29 The Merry Widow Waltz Craze
May 13 The Gentleman Burglar
May 20 Curious Mr. Curio
May 27 The Painter's Revenge
Jun 3 Skinny's Finish
Jun 10 The Blue and the Gray; or, The Days of '61
Jun 17 Honesty Is the Best Policy
Jun 24 Love Will Find a Way
Jul 1 Pioneers Crossing the Plains in '49
Jul 15 The Boston Tea Party
The Little Coxswain of the Varsity Eight
Jul 22 The Face on the Barroom Floor
Fly Paper
Jul 31 Deceived Slumming Party
Aug 5 Tales the Searchlight Told
Aug 7 A Calamitous Elopement: How It Proved a Windfall for Burglar Bill
Aug 19 When Ruben Comes to Town
Sep 2 A Comedy in Black and White
Heard over the Phone
Sep 9 The Devil
Sep 15 Wifey's Strategy
Sep 22 Buying a Title
Sep 25 A Smoked Husband
Sep 29 Pocahantas — A Child of the Forest
The Stolen Jewels
Oct 2 Sandy McPherson's Quiet Fishing Trip
Oct 9 A Voice from the Dead
Oct 16 Ex-Convict No. 900
Oct 20 Minstrel Mishaps; or, Late for Rehearsal
Oct 27 The Army of Two (An Incident during the American Revolution)
Nov 3 Saved by Love
Nov 10 The Lovers' Telegraphic Code
Nov 17 Colonial Virginia
The New Stenographer
Nov 27 The Clubman and the Tramp
The King's Pardon
Dec 4 Miss Sherlock Holmes
The Old Maids' Temperance Club
Dec 11 The Angel Child
Dec 15 Cocoa Industry, Trinidad, British West Indies
Dec 22 The Christmas Burglars
An Unexpected Santa Claus

1909
Jan 1 A Persistent Suitor
Jan 11 The Honor of Thieves
Jan 22 A Burglar Cupid
Jan 29 A Modest Young Man
Feb 8 A Wreath in Time
Feb 22 The Golden Louis
Mar 1 His Wife's Mother
Mar 18 The Voice of the Violin
Mar 29 Jones and His New Neighbors
May 14 The Pony Express
May 17 The Jilt
Sep 27 Grand Naval Parade
Sep 30 Historic Parade
Oct 4 Military Parade

1910
Apr 5 The Heart of a Rose
Jul 19 The Girls of the Ghetto
Nov 18 The City of Her Dreams

New York City—Battery Park

1900
May [day undetermined]
May Day Parade
Maypole Dance

1903
May [day undetermined]
Fireboat "New Yorker" Answering an Alarm

New York City—Broadway

1906
Dec [day undetermined]
Singer Building Foundation Co.

New York City—Caledonian Gardens

1903
Sep [day undetermined]
Throwing the Sixteen Pound Hammer

New York City—Central Park

1897
Jan [day undetermined]
Ye Merry Sleigh Bells

1900
Feb [day undetermined]
Skating in Central Park

1904
Jan [day undetermined]
Ice Skating in Central Park, N.Y.
Mar [day undetermined]
Sleighing in Central Park, New York

1907
Jan [day undetermined]
Man Being Run Over by Automobile
Feb 8 At the Monkey House
Mr. Hurry-Up

1908
Oct 9 Father Gets in the Game
Dec 29 The Helping Hand

1909
Feb 22 The Politician's Love Story
May 13 A Baby's Shoe
Nov 18 Sweet Revenge

New York City—City Hall

1903
May [day undetermined]
N.Y. Fire Department Returning

New York City—East River

1903
May [day undetermined]
Panorama of Blackwell's Island
Panorama Water Front and Brooklyn Bridge from East River
Dec [day undetermined]
Opening of New East River Bridge, New York

1904
Feb [day undetermined]
The Opening of the Williamsburg Bridge

1905
Oct [day undetermined]
Dream of the Race Track Fiend
How Millionaires Sometimes Entertain aboard Their Yachts

New York City—Fifth Avenue

1901
Apr [day undetermined]
Buffalo Bill's Wild West Parade

New York City—Grand Central Station

1909
Jan 21 Mr. Jones Has a Card Party

New York City—Grant's Tomb

1904
Jun [day undetermined]
"Personal"

New York City—Harbor

1897
Dec [day undetermined]
The "Amphitrite"
Battleships "Maine" and "Iowa"
Battleships "Marblehead" and "Miantonomah"

1898
Feb [day undetermined]
The Monitor "Terror"
Pilot Boat "New York"
A Three Masted Schooner
"Vizcaya" Under Full Headway
Sep [day undetermined]
Admiral Sampson on Board the Flagship
Excursion Boats, Naval Parade

1899
Sep [day undetermined]
The "Erin"
"Shamrock I"
Shamrock Starting on Trial Trip
Sir Thomas Lipton and Party on "Erin's" Launch
Sir Thomas Lipton's Steam Yacht "Erin"
Oct [day undetermined]
Admiral Dewey Receiving the Washington and New York Committees
Admiral Dewey Taking Leave of Washington Committee on the U.S. Cruiser 'Olympia'

1902
Mar [day undetermined]
"Deutschland" Leaving New York at Full Speed [with Prince Henry of Prussia]

1903
May [day undetermined]
Fireboat "New Yorker" in Action
1905
Nov [day undetermined]
Reception of British Fleet

New York City—Hudson River
1898
Sep [day undetermined]
The "Glen Island," Accompanying Parade
The "Texas," Naval Parade
1904
Jun [day undetermined]
Auto Boat Race on the Hudson River

New York City—Lower Broadway
1904
Apr [day undetermined]
Fire, Adams Express Co.

New York City—Lower East Side
1903
Oct [day undetermined]
New York City Public Bath

New York City—Madison Avenue
1905
Oct [day undetermined]
The Great Jewel Mystery

New York City—Madison Square Garden
1899
Oct [day undetermined]
Dewey Arch—Troops Passing Under Arch
1903
May [day undetermined]
New York City Police Parade
1904
May [day undetermined]
Annual Parade, New York Fire Department

New York City—Morris Heights
1906
Sep 29 Wanted—A Nurse

New York City—North River
1898
Sep [day undetermined]
The Battleship "Oregon"
The Men behind the Guns
U.S. Battleship "Oregon"
1899
Apr [day undetermined]
U.S. Cruiser "Raleigh"
1902
Feb [day undetermined]
The "Hohenzollern"
1903
May [day undetermined]
Steamscow "Cinderella" and Ferryboat "Cincinnati"
1907
Sep [day undetermined]
Casey on a Souse—Gives the Bunch a Douse
A Mash a Smash a Splash
What the Fisherman Caught

New York City—Union Square
1902
Nov [day undetermined]
New York's New Subway
1905
May [day undetermined]
N.Y. Police Parade, 1905
1906
Feb [day undetermined]
Volunteer Fire Department Parade
1907
Sep 25 Terrible Ted

New York City—Wall Street
1910
Sep 8 Little Angels of Luck

New York City—Washington Arch
1903
Oct [day undetermined]
Parade of "Exempt" Firemen

New York City—Williamsburg Bridge
1907
Sep [day undetermined]
The Crush at the Bridge Congested S.S.

Niagara Falls
see also
Niagara Falls (Canada—Ontario)
1896
Sep [day undetermined]
American Falls, Goat Island
American Falls, Luna Island
Canadian Falls, from American Side
Canadian Falls—Panoramic [View] from Michigan Central R.R.
Canadian Falls—Table Rock
Lower Rapids, Niagara Falls
Niagara Gorge from Erie R.R.
Panorama of American & Canadian Falls—Taken Opposite American Falls
Pointing Down Gorge, Niagara Falls
Taken from Trolley in Gorge, Niagara Falls
Upper Rapids, from Bridge
Dec [day undetermined]
American Falls—from Incline R.R.
Horseshoe Falls—From Luna Isle
Rapids at Cave of the Winds
1899
Mar [day undetermined]
Niagara Falls in Winter
Jul [day undetermined]
Lower Rapids of Niagara Falls
Niagara Falls Station
Panoramic View of Niagara Falls
Whirlpool Rapids
1900
May [day undetermined]
Panorama of Gorge Railway
1901
Aug [day undetermined]
Circular Panorama of Suspension Bridge and American Falls
Sep [day undetermined]
Arrival at Falls View Station
Oct [day undetermined]
Panorama, Great Gorge Route over Lewiston Bridge
1902
Mar [day undetermined]
Prince Henry [of Prussia] at Niagara Falls
May [day undetermined]
Carlysle D. Graham Swimming the Whirlpool Rapids
1903
Jan [day undetermined]
American Falls from Luna Island
Great Gorge R.R., Niagara
Horseshoe Falls from American Side
Panorama Looking Down Niagara from New Suspension Bridge
Rapids Above American Falls from American Side
Rapids Above American Falls from Bridge to Goat Island
Whirlpool Rapids
Feb [day undetermined]
C. D. Graham Swimming the Lower Rapids
Apr [day undetermined]
American Falls, Goat Island
American Falls, Luna Island
1904
Jan [day undetermined]
Circular Panorama of the Horse Shoe Falls in Winter
Crossing Ice Bridge at Niagara Falls
Sliding Down Ice Mound at Niagara Falls
1906
Nov [day undetermined]
The Honeymoon at Niagara Falls
Dec [day undetermined]
American Falls from Canadian Side, Niagara Falls, N.Y.
American Falls from Goat Island, Niagara Falls, N.Y.
Cave of the Winds
Horseshoe Falls from American Side, Niagara Falls, N.Y.
Horseshoe Falls from Canadian Side Niagara Falls, N.Y.
A Trip on the "Maid in the Mist," Niagara Falls, N.Y.
A Trip on the "Chippewa," Niagara Falls, N.Y.
Whirlpool Rapids

Niagara Falls Gorge
1901
Aug [day undetermined]
Circular Panoramic View of Whirlpool Rapids

Niagara River
1899
Feb [day undetermined]
Rapids below Suspension Bridge
1901
Aug [day undetermined]
Panoramic View of the Gorge Railroad

North Beach
1905
Oct [day undetermined]
A Country Courtship
1906
Aug 1 The Old Swimming Hole
Aug 6 Looking for John Smith

North Brother Island
1904
Jun [day undetermined]
The Slocum Disaster

Oyster Bay
1903
Sep [day undetermined]
Jack Tar Sewing a Patch on the Seat of His Trousers
Jack's Four Footed Friend. Mike the Ship's Mascot
One of Jack's Games aboard a Man o' War
Piping Down. Wash Clothes. Scrambling for Clothes
President Roosevelt Addressing Crew of "Kearsarge"
Pres. Roosevelt Leaving the Flagship
President Roosevelt's Arrival at "Kearsarge"
President Roosevelt's Departure from "Kearsarge"
Pres. Roosevelt's Sunday Visit to Kearsage
President Roosevelt's Visit to Admiral Barker
Signal Boys Wig-Wagging
Sparring Match on the "Kearsarge"
1904
Jul [day undetermined]
President Roosevelt's Home-coming
1905
Aug [day undetermined]
Scenes and Incidents, Russo-Japanese Peace Conference, Portsmouth, N.H.

Peekskill
1904
Jul [day undetermined]
"Pollywogs" 71st Regiment, N.G.S.N.Y., Initiating Raw Recruits
1905
Dec [day undetermined]
Climbing the American Alps

Phoenica
1906
Jun 30 Hold-Up of the Rocky Mt. Express

Pine Camp
1910
Sep 21 The Japanese Spy

Poughkeepsie
1897
Jun [day undetermined]
Albany Day Boats
Cornell-Yale-Harvard Boat-Race
Harvard Crew
Observation Train at the Inter-Collegiate Boat-Races
1904
Jul [day undetermined]
Inter-Collegiate Regatta, Poughkeepsie, N.Y., 1904
1908
Jul 15 The Little Coxswain of the Varsity Eight

Poughkeepsie—Hudson River
1906
Jun 26 Poughkeepsie Regatta

Riker's Island
1903
May [day undetermined]
Panorama of Riker's Island

Rochester
1899
Sep [day undetermined]
Arabis Patrol
Employes of Bausch, Lomb & Co.
Four Corners of Rochester
Guardians of the Peace
The Makers of the Kodak
Rochester Fire Department
Soldiers of the Future
A Thrilling Ride

Rye Beach
1907
Sep 16 An Acadian Elopement

Sackets Harbor
1898
Dec [day undetermined]
Ice Yachting

Scarsdale
1904
Aug [day undetermined]
The Moonshiner
1907
Jun [day undetermined]
Wyoming Girl

Schenectady
1897
Jul [day undetermined]
Sprague Electric Train
1904
Nov [day undetermined]
Electric Locomotive Tests and Races, Schenectady, N.Y.
1905
Apr [day undetermined]
Gen'l Elec. No. 1 Employees Leaving Work
Gen'l Elec. No. 2 Trolley Changing from Di. to Alter. Cur.
Gen'l Elec. No. 3 Handling Cars at the Barn
Aug [day undetermined]
The Electric Mule
Empire State Express, the Second, Taking Water on the Fly

Shadyside
1908
Aug 4 The Bandit's Waterloo: The Outwitting of an Andalusian Brigand by a Pretty Senora

Shooters Island
1902
Feb [day undetermined]
Christening and Launching Kaiser Wilhelm's Yacht "Meteor"
Launch of Meteor III
Mar [day undetermined]
Kaiser Wilhelm's Yacht, "Meteor," Entering the Water
"Meteor III" Afloat
Mar 15 Arrival of Prince Henry [of Prussia] and President Roosevelt at Shooter's Island

Sonyea
1905
Dec [day undetermined]
Threshing Scene
1906 [month undetermined]
Epileptic Seizure No. 8
Epileptic Seizure, No. 9

Spuyten Duyvil
1898
Nov [day undetermined]
The Rivals

Staten Island
1906
Jun [day undetermined]
Life of a Cowboy

Staten Island—Port Richmond
1905 [month undetermined]
[Launching the Ferryboat Richmond—Staten Island]

Syracuse
1898
Aug [day undetermined]
A Blast at the Solvay Quarries
Jumping Net Practice
Race Between a Multicycle and a Horse
1900
Jul [day undetermined]
The Farmer and the Trolley Car
Lawn Tennis

Thousand Islands
1898
Aug [day undetermined]
Steamer "Island Wanderer"
1906
Oct [day undetermined]
Motor Race
Thousand Islands

Travers Island
1905
Jun [day undetermined]
A Saturday Afternoon at Travers' Island with the New York Athletic Club
Dec [day undetermined]
Intercollegiate Cross Country Run

Watertown
1898
Nov [day undetermined]
A Narrow Escape
1899
Mar [day undetermined]
Bucking the Blizzard
Rotary Snowplow in Action*
Storming the Fort

Welfare Island
1902
Jul [day undetermined]
Thro' Hell Gate
1905
Sep [day undetermined]
Steamboat Travel on Long Island Sound

West Point
1896
Sep [day undetermined]
West Point Cadet Cavalry
West Point Cadet Drill
1902
Mar [day undetermined]
Prince Henry
Prince Henry at West Point
Prince Henry of Germany
Prince Henry [of Prussia] Arriving at West Point
Prince Henry [of Prussia] Reviewing the Cadets at West Point
Jun [day undetermined]
Daly, of West Point
Review of Cadets at West Point
Review of Cadets, West Point
1908
Jun 10 The Blue and the Gray; or, The Days of '61

Westbury
1899
Apr [day undetermined]
Going to the Hunt
High Hurdle Jumping, at Meadowbrook Hunt Club
The Meadowbrook Hunt

Westchester County
1898
Nov [day undetermined]
Around the Big Swing

White Plains
1908
Jul 15 The Boston Tea Party
Aug 19 When Ruben Comes to Town

Yonkers
1899
Aug [day undetermined]
A Volunteer Fire Company
Water Throwing Contest
1907
Nov 23 The Trainer's Daughter; or, A Race for Love

North Carolina

Asheville
1901
Oct 25 Convention of Railroad Passengers Agents
Panoramic View, Asheville, N. C.

Edenton—Greenfield Fishery
1901
May [day undetermined]
Hauling a Shad Net
A Large Haul of Fish

Pinehurst
1906
Jan [day undetermined]
Deer Stalking with a Camera
Quail Shooting at Pinehurst
Turkey Hunt at Pinehurst

Raleigh
1903
Jan [day undetermined]
Lieut. Bagley's Funeral. Escort of Lieut. Bagley's at Raleigh, N. C.

Ohio

Canton
1896
Sep [day undetermined]
McKinley at Home, Canton, Ohio
Parade, Americus Club, Canton Ohio
Parade at Canton O., Showing Major McKinley in Carriage
Parade, Elkins Cadets, Canton, O.
Parade, Sound Money Club, Canton, O.
1901
Sep [day undetermined]
Complete Funeral Cortege at Canton, Ohio
Funeral of President McKinley
Panoramic View of the McKinley Homestead
President McKinley's Funeral
Oct 5 Arrival of McKinley's Funeral Train at Canton, Ohio
Funeral Leaving the President's House and Church at Canton, Ohio
McKinley's Funeral Entering Westlawn Cemetery, Canton [Ohio]
Panoramic View of the President's House at Canton, Ohio
President Roosevelt at the Canton Station
Taking President McKinley's Body from Train at Canton, Ohio

Cincinnati
1900
Mar [day undetermined]
Dress Parade of the Woodward High School Cadets
Walnut Hill Cadets
May [day undetermined]
The Clown and the Mule
A Four-Horse Circus Act
Gatling Gun Drill
A Somersault on Horseback
Water Babies
1901
Sep [day undetermined]
Industrial Parade of the Cincinnati Fall Festival
Traveling Men's Association

Cleveland
1897
Jul [day undetermined]
Giant Coal Dumper
1900
Jun [day undetermined]
Public Square, Cleveland
Oct [day undetermined]
The Last Alarm
On the Cleveland and Eastern Railway
Nov [day undetermined]
Showing a Giant Crane Dumping a 40-Ton Car
1901
Sep [day undetermined]
Capt. Schuyler Post of Philadelphia
Chapin Post of Buffalo
Cuyahoga Gorge
The Empire Theatre
Farragut Naval Post, Ohio State
Headquarters, Staff and Band, Ohio State
Lambs Club, G.A.R.
The Living Flag
Lyttle Post of Cincinnati
Panorama, Public Square, Cleveland, O.

Columbus
1900
Jan [day undetermined]
Blaine Club of Cincinnati
Governor Nash of Ohio

Dayton
1903
Feb [day undetermined]
Envelope Folder and Sealer, National Cash Register Co.
German Flag Afloat, National Cash Register Co.
Girls Getting on Trolley, National Cash Register Co.
Girls Going to Lunch. National Cash Register Co.
Girls in Physical Culture, National Cash Register Co.
Jubilee, National Cash Register Co.
Little Wonder Printing Press, National Cash Register Co.
Men Getting on Trolley, National Cash Register Co.
Men in Physical Exercise, National Cash Register Co.
Men Leaving Factory, National Cash Register Co.
Mr. Bickford on Trolley, National Cash Register Co.
Mr. Carney and Friend, National Cash Register Co.
Mr. Carroll and Assistant, National Cash Register Co.
Mr. Chalmers and Mr. Gibbs Arrive at Club, National Cash Register Co.
Mr. Chalmers Going to Officers' Club, National Cash Register Co.
Mr. J. H. Crane, National Cash Register Co.
Mr. Lawer, National Cash Register Co.
Mr. Patterson and Mr. Mark Arriving, National Cash Register Co.
Officers Leaving Club, National Cash Register Co.
Panorama of Factory from Automobile, National Cash Register Co.
Patterson Children in Pony Wagon, National Cash Register Co.
Patterson Children Leaving Home, National Cash Register Co.
Patterson Children on Horseback, National Cash Register Co.
Porters in Parade, National Cash Register Co.
Steam Whistle, National Cash Register Co.
Testing Jacks, National Cash Register Co.
Visitors in Wheeling Chairs, National Cash Register Co.
Window Display Clown, National Cash Register Co.
Window Display Revolving Balls, National Cash Register Co.

Lorraine
1901
Jan [day undetermined]
Launch of the "Saturn"

Toledo
1900
Nov [day undetermined]
Employees of Wolfson's Spice Mills, Toledo
1909
Oct 8 United States Military Tournament

Youngstown
1903
Dec [day undetermined]
Dumping Iron Ore

Oklahoma

1908
Dec [day undetermined]
A Round-Up in Oklahoma
1909
Sep 6 The Stampede
1910
Dec 24 The Cattlemen's Feud

Bliss
1904
May [day undetermined]
Brush Between Cowboys and Indians
Bucking Broncos
Cowboys and Indians Fording River in a Wagon
Driving Cattle to Pasture
Herding Horses Across a River
Rounding Up and Branding Cattle
Western Stage Coach Hold Up
1905
Sep [day undetermined]
Great Buffalo Chase

Cache and Wichita Forest and Game Reserve
1908
Dec [day undetermined]
The Bank Robbery

Oregon

1903
Mar [day undetermined]
Hydraulic Mining in Oregon

Multnomah Falls
1904 [month undetermined]
Panoramic View of Multnomah Falls

Portland
1905
Nov [day undetermined]
President Roosevelt at Portland
1907
Jan [day undetermined]
Scene at "The Oaks," Portland, Oregon

Willamette Falls
1903
Mar [day undetermined]
Willamette Falls

Pennsylvania

1899
Jul [day undetermined]
A Ride Through Pack Saddle Mountains, Penna. R.R.
1903
Oct [day undetermined]
A Romance of the Rail

Allentown
1902
Apr [day undetermined]
The Swimming Ducks at Allentown [Pa.] Duck Farm
1910
Aug 15 The Duck Farm

Altoona
1899
Jun [day undetermined]
Panoramic View, Horseshoe Curve, From Penna. Ltd.
Jul [day undetermined]
Panoramic View, Horseshoe Curve, Penna. R.R., No. 2
1904
Jun [day undetermined]
Horse-Shoe Curve

Camp Meade
1898
Sep [day undetermined]
Behind the Firing Line
Charge by Rushes
Company "H," 3rd N.Y.V.
The Defence of the Flag
18th Pennsylvania Volunteers
Fifteenth Minnesota Volunteers
Fifth Massachusetts Volunteers
First Maryland Volunteers
First Rhode Island Volunteers
Free Tobacco
A Gallant Charge
In the Trenches
The Last Stand
Rapid Fire, Charge
The Red Cross
Tenth Regiment, Ohio Volunteers
22nd Regiment, Kansas Volunteers

Carlisle
1901
Apr [day undetermined]
Band and Battalion of the U.S. Indian School
Basket Ball
Club Swinging, Carlisle Indian School
Girls Dumbbell Drill
Heavy Gymnastics
The High Jump
Pole Vaulting

Delaware Water Gap
see also
Delaware Water Gap (New Jersey)
1906
Mar [day undetermined]
Phoebe Snow

Drifton
1904
Dec [day undetermined]
Mining Operations, Pennsylvania Coal Fields

East Pittsburgh
1904
May [day undetermined]
Panorama Motor Room, Westinghouse Works
Railroad Panorama, Pittsburg to Stewart, Westinghouse Works
Steam Hammer, Westinghouse Works
Steam Whistle, Westinghouse Works
Testing Gas Engine, Westinghouse Works
Testing Steam Engine, Westinghouse Works
Turning Panorama from Hill, Westinghouse Works
Westinghouse Employees Boarding Train
Westinghouse Employees, Westinghouse Works

Gallitzen
1899
Jul [day undetermined]
Running through Gallitzen Tunnel, Penna. R.R.

Garversville
1909
May 14 The Pony Express

Gettysburg
1901
Jun [day undetermined]
U.S. National Cemetery

Harrisburg
1901
Sep [day undetermined]
President McKinley's Funeral

Lancaster
1904 [month undetermined]
Convention of Red Men, Lancaster, Pa.

Lehigh Valley
1902
Feb [day undetermined]
Working Rotary Snow Ploughs on Lehigh Valley Railroad

Mauch Chunk
1901
Jul [day undetermined]
Circular Panorama of Mauch Chunk, Penna.
1902
May [day undetermined]
Panoramic View of Switchback, Mauch Chunk
1903
Jan [day undetermined]
Loading a Train with Stone

Perkasie
1903
Jan [day undetermined]
Perkasie Tunnel

Philadelphia
1896
Sep [day undetermined]
Pa. R.R. Train near Phila.
Train Coming out of Station, Philadelphia, Pa.
1897 [month undetermined]
Delaware River, Philadelphia
Mar [day undetermined]
Keystone Express
May [day undetermined]
Unveiling of the Washington Monument
Aug [day undetermined]
A Busy Corner
Catching a Runaway Team
Fire Boat "Edwin S. Stewart"
Fire Run
A Giant Steam-Shovel
High Diving
Making an Arrest
Mounted Police Drill
Returning from Drill
Rough Riding
Nov [day undetermined]
Philadelphia Police on Parade

Towanda
1903
May [day undetermined]
Lehigh Valley Black Diamond Express

Trafford
1904
May [day undetermined]
Casting a Guide Box, Westinghouse Works
Tapping a Furnace, Westinghouse Works

Versailles
1905
Sep [day undetermined]
The Little Train Robbery

Wilkes-Barre
1903
Jan [day undetermined]
Mitchell Day at Wilkes-Barre, Pa.
President Mitchell's Speech

Wilmerding
1904
May [day undetermined]
Operation of Westinghouse Block System
Westinghouse Air Brake Co., Casting Machine

Wysock
1900
May [day undetermined]
New Black Diamond Express

Potomac River

1903
May [day undetermined]
Stripping Shad U.S.F.C.

Bryans Point
1903
May [day undetermined]
Stripping Shad U.S.F.C.

Rhode Island

Newport
1900
Mar [day undetermined]
Drill of Naval Cadets at Newport
Military Scenes at Newport, R.I.
May [day undetermined]
Discharging a Whitehead Torpedo
Exploding a Whitehead Torpedo
Panoramic View of Newport [R.I.]
Torpedo Boat "Morris" Running
Nov [day undetermined]
Gun Drill by Naval Cadets at Newport [R.I., Naval] Training School
Gymnasium Exercises and Drill at Newport [R.I., Naval] Training School
Naval Apprentices at Sail Drill on Historic Ship "Constellation"
Sham Battle on Land by Cadets at Newport Naval Training School
1902
Sep [day undetermined]
Torpedo Boats Racing off Newport

Newport—Naval Training School
1900
Nov [day undetermined]
Naval Sham Battle at Newport

Newport—Newport Harbor
1903
Feb [day undetermined]
North Atlantic Fleet Bombarding Fort Adams, Newport Harbor

Pawtucket
1903
Dec [day undetermined]
Noon Hour at Hope Webbing Company
Run of Pawtucket Fire Dept.

Providence
1899
Apr [day undetermined]
Arrival of Boat, Providence, R.I.
Market Square, Providence, R.I.
Parade in Providence, R.I.
Providence Fire Department
Review of First Rhode Island Volunteers
1900
Oct [day undetermined]
School Fire Drill
"Three Ones"
A Visit to Baby Roger
Westminster Street
1901
Jul [day undetermined]
Shooting the Chutes at Providence, Rhode Island
1903
Oct [day undetermined]
The Honourable Artillery Company of London
The Providence Light Artillery
Dec [day undetermined]
Drill by Providence Police
1904
Jul [day undetermined]
Battery "A," Rhode Island Light Artillery

South Carolina

Charleston
1902
Apr [day undetermined]
Charleston Chain Gang
The Golden Chariots
Loading a Vessel at Charleston, S. C.
Midway of Charleston Exposition [South Carolina]
Miniature Railway
Panoramic View of Charleston Exposition [South Carolina]
President Roosevelt Reviewing the Troops at Charleston Exposition [South Carolina]

Tennessee

Memphis
1903 [month undetermined]
Memphis & Ft. Scott Railway Bridge
Memphis Fire Run
Memphis Water Front

Texas

1910
May 26 The Paleface Princess
Jun 9 Love's "C.Q.D."

Beaumont
1902
Apr [day undetermined]
New Sunset Limited

Galveston
1900
Sep [day undetermined]
Bird's-Eye View of Dock Front, Galveston
Galveston Disaster
The Galveston Disaster
Panorama of East Galveston
Panorama of Galveston Power House
Panorama of Orphans' Home, Galveston
Panorama of Wreckage of Water Front
Panoramic View of Tremont Hotel, Galveston
Panoramic View, Rescue Work, Galveston
Panoramic View, Wreckage Along Shore, Galveston
Searching Ruins on Broadway, Galveston, for Dead Bodies
1903
Jan [day undetermined]
Burning the Rubbish
Scenes of the Wreckage from the Water Front
Sunken Vessel in the Harbor
Taking Out the Dead and Wounded
View of the Residence Section

San Antonio
1910
Apr 7 Cyclone Pete's Matrimony

Sour Lake
1904 [month undetermined]
Sour Lake Oil Fields

Utah

1899
Dec [day undetermined]
Devil's Gate*
The "Overland Limited" Passing Witch Rocks*

Devil's Slide
1899
Dec [day undetermined]
Devil's Slide

Echo
1899
Dec [day undetermined]
By Pulpit Rock and Through the Town of Echo*

Green River
1899
Dec [day undetermined]
Toll Gate and Castle Rock near Green River

Peterson
1899
Dec [day undetermined]
West of Peterson; Entrance to Weber Canyon

Uintah
1899
Dec [day undetermined]
East of Uintah in Weber Canyon

Weber Canyon
1899
Dec [day undetermined]
One Thousand Mile Tree, Weber Canyon

Vermont

Fort Ethan Allen
1897
Mar [day undetermined]
Cavalry Charge
Cavalry Horses at Play
Cavalry Musical Drill
Charge, Through Intervals of Skirmishes
Fencing on Horseback
Jumping Hurdles
Musical Drill; Troop A., Third Cavalry
Standing in Stirrups
Troopers Hurdling
Wrestling, Bareback; 3rd Cavalry

Virginia

1901
May [day undetermined]
Bass Fishing

Camp Alger
1898 [month undetermined]
15,000 Soldiers Reviewed by the President at Camp Alger May 28
President McKinley and Cabinet at Camp Alger, May 28, 1898
1903
Jan [day undetermined]
Ohio Colored Troops at Camp Alger
Panorama of American Soldiers in Camp

Cumberland Mountains
1910
Feb 5 Sensational Logging

Fort Myer
1897
Apr [day undetermined]
Bareback Hurdle Jumping
1898
Apr [day undetermined]
Bareback Riding, 6th Cavalry, U.S.A.
1903
Jan [day undetermined]
Vaulting in Saddle and Jumping Hurdle

Hampton Roads
1909 [month undetermined]
The American Fleet in Hampton Roads, 1909, After Girdling the Globe

Jamestown
1907
May 11 Jamestown Exposition
Sep [day undetermined]
Pres. Roosevelt Reviewing U.S. Regulars
Pres. Roosevelt Reviewing West Point Cadets

Manassas
1904
Sep [day undetermined]
Military Maneuvers, Manassas, Va.

Mount Vernon
1910
Dec [day undetermined]
[Washington's Home and Ground at Mount Vernon]

Newport News
1898
Mar [day undetermined]
Launch, U.S. Battleship "Kentucky"
Apr [day undetermined]
Battleship "Massachusetts"
Launching of the "Kearsage"
S.S. "Columbia" Sailing
Oct [day undetermined]
Launch of the "Illinois"

Norfolk
1898
Apr [day undetermined]
Cruiser "Brooklyn"
Cruiser "Minneapolis"
Newport News Ship-Building Co.'s Shipyard
Ram "Katahdin"

Washington

1903
Feb [day undetermined]
Gravity Fountain
Harvesting Scene
Snoqualmie Falls
Mar [day undetermined]
A Rotary Snow Plow in the Great Northwest
Snow-Plow Bucking a 15-foot Snow Slide
Through Cascade Tunnel

Altoona
1903
Aug [day undetermined]
Horses Drawing in Seine
Horses Drawing Salmon Seine
Men Taking Fish from Salmon Seine
Sep [day undetermined]
Butchering and Cleaning Tables U.S.F.C.
Lifting Salmon Trap
Raising Salmon Trap U.S.F.C.
Salmon Seining on Columbia River U.S.F.C.

Columbia River
1904 [month undetermined]
Chicago Portland Special
Fish Traps Columbia River
Hauling in a Big Catch
Hauling in Seines and Pulling Seines into Boat
Mending Seines on the Columbia River
Panoramic View of the Columbia River
Unloading Fish at Cannery
1909
Jun 21 The Red Man

Lake Washington
1903
Feb [day undetermined]
Log-Rolling Contest

Seattle
1897
Oct [day undetermined]
First Avenue, Seattle, Washington, No. 8
Horses Loading for Klondike
Loading Baggage for Klondike
1903
Jan [day undetermined]
James Street, Seattle, Wash.
Feb [day undetermined]
Seattle Fire Department in Action
1905
Nov [day undetermined]
President Roosevelt at Seattle
1907 [month undetermined]
Along the Shore Line of Lake Washington

Spokane
1903
Jan [day undetermined]
Riverside Avenue, Spokane, Wash.
Spokane Falls, Spokane

Spokane River
1904 [month undetermined]
Panoramic View of Spokane Falls

Tacoma
1903
Jan [day undetermined]
Pacific Avenue, Tacoma, Wash.
1905
Nov [day undetermined]
President Roosevelt at Tacoma

Vancouver
1902
Jul [day undetermined]
Cavalry Swimming Columbia River

Walla Walla
1905
Nov [day undetermined]
President Roosevelt at Walla Walla

West Virginia

Harper's Ferry
1903 [month undetermined]
Harper's Ferry

Wisconsin

1903 [month undetermined]
The Dells of Wisconsin

Milwaukee
1903 [month undetermined]
Floral Parade
Fool's Parade

Wyoming

Cheyenne
1901
Jul [day undetermined]
Arrival of Train at Station
1903
Feb [day undetermined]
Shoshone Indians in Scalp Dance
1910
Sep 17 Cowboy and Indian Frontier Celebration

Dale Creek Valley
1901
Jul [day undetermined]
Through Gibraltar
Train Crossing Dale Creek Fill

Grand Island
1901
Jul [day undetermined]
Flock of Sheep

Green River
1901
Jul [day undetermined]
Fish Cut

Laramie
1901
Jul [day undetermined]
Pine Ridge Bluffs

Sheridan
1903
Feb [day undetermined]
Bucking Broncho Contest [Sheridan Contest]
Cavalry Parade
Indian Fire Dance
Indian Hideous Dance
Indian Parade
Indians Charging on the Photographer
Stage Hold-Up
Steer Roping Contest at Cheyenne, Wyo.

Sherman
1901
Jul [day undetermined]
Indian Fort, Sherman Hill Tunnel
Through Gibraltar

Yellowstone National Park
1899
Jan [day undetermined]
Coaches Going to Cinnabar from Yellowstone Park
Lower Falls, Grand Canyon, Yellowstone Park
Tourists Going Round Yellowstone Park
1901
May [day undetermined]
Old Faithful Geyser
Riverside Geyser, Yellowstone Park
May 4 Upper Falls of the Yellowstone
Jul [day undetermined]
Wild Bear in Yellowstone Park
1903
Nov [day undetermined]
Arrival of Tourists at the Hotel in Yellowstone Park
Fountain Geyser
Great Falls of the Yellowstone
Mammouth Paint Pot, Yosemite Valley
"Old Faithful," Yosemite Valley
On Yellowstone Lake
Panorama of Yellowstone Lake
Panoramic View of Hot Springs, Yellowstone Park
United States Troops in Yellowstone Park
1907
Jul [day undetermined]
Through Yellowstone Park
1909
Sep 9 Glimpses of Yellowstone Park

Yellowstone National Park—Mammoth Hot Springs
1899
Jan [day undetermined]
Coaches Arriving at Mammoth Hot Springs

Locations in Other Countries

Atlantic Ocean
1902
May [day undetermined]
The S.S. "Deutschland" in a Storm
The S.S. "Deutschland" in a Storm, No. 2
The S.S. "Deutschland" in Heavy Sea
1904
Jan [day undetermined]
Torpedo Attack

Australia

Sydney
1909
Apr 19 World's Heavyweight Championship Pictures Between Tommy Burns and Jack Johnson

Bahama Islands

Nassau
1903
Apr [day undetermined]
Native Woman Washing a Negro Baby in Nassau, B. I.

Nassau—Hog Island
1910
May 23 Winter Bathing in the West Indies

Belgium

Bruges
1904
Aug [day undetermined]
Procession of the "Holy Blood"

Oostende
1903
Feb [day undetermined]
Panorama and Bathing Scene of Ostend, Belgium

British West Indies
1910
May 9 Rastus in Zululand

Canada
1897
Dec [day undetermined]
Fast Mail, Northern Pacific Railroad
1899
Nov [day undetermined]
Bridge No. 804, and Daly's Grade
Caribou Bridge
1900
Feb [day undetermined]
Canadian Mounted Rifles on the March
1901
Oct [day undetermined]
The Duke and Duchess of York Presenting Medals to Boer War Veterans at the Unveiling of the Queen's Statue
Garden Party in Honor of the Duke and Duchess of York

1903
Mar 14 On the Bow River Horse Ranch at Cochrane, North West Territory
Spearing Salmon in the Rivers of the North West Territory
Apr [day undetermined]
Breaking a Bronco
1905
Nov [day undetermined]
By Rail Through Canadian Rockies
1909
Oct 29 The Girl Scout; or the Canadian Contingent in the Boer War
1910
Sep 16 A Leap for Life
Sep 20 An Unselfish Love

Alberta

1901
Nov [day undetermined]
Royal Train with Duke and Duchess of York, Climbing Mt. Hector

Banff
1899
Oct [day undetermined]
In the Canadian Rockies, near Banff

British Columbia

1899
Oct [day undetermined]
Beyond the Great Divide
The Eastern Slope of the Rockies, Passing Anthracite Station
Under the Shadow of Mt. Stephen, Passing Field's Station in the Rocky Mountains
Up the Big Grade in the Valley of the Kicking Horse
Nov [day undetermined]
Frazer Canyon, East of Yale
1901
May [day undetermined]
Panoramic View of the White Pass Railroad
1902
Jan [day undetermined]
Panoramic View Between Palliser and Field, B. C.
Panoramic View of the Canadian Pacific R.R. near Leauchoil, B. C.

Albert Cañon
1901
Dec [day undetermined]
Panoramic View, Albert Canyon

Bear Creek
1903
Mar 14 Logging in Canada

Golden
1901
Dec [day undetermined]
Panoramic View, Upper Kicking Horse Canyon
1902
Jan [day undetermined]
Panoramic View near Mt. Golden on the Canadian Pacific R.R.

Kicking Horse Canyon
1899
Oct [day undetermined]
Down the Western Slope of the Canadian Rockies Through Kicking Horse Pass
1901
Dec [day undetermined]
Panoramic View, Kicking Horse Canyon
Panoramic View, Lower Kicking Horse Canyon
Panoramic View, Lower Kicking Horse Valley
Panoramic View, Upper Kicking Horse Canyon
1902
Jan [day undetermined]
Panoramic View near Mt. Golden on the Canadian Pacific R.R.

Port Victoria
1903
Feb [day undetermined]
Arrival of H.I.M. The German Emperor, at Port Victoria

Vancouver
1899
Aug [day undetermined]
The Imperial Limited
"Imperial Limited." Canadian Pacific R.R.
Oct [day undetermined]
Chinamen Returning to China
Steamship "Empress of India"

Lake Superior

1899
Nov [day undetermined]
Around Gravel Bay

New Brunswick

1906
Jan [day undetermined]
Moose Hunt in New Brunswick
Salmon Fishing in Quebec

Bathurst
1906
Sep [day undetermined]
E. Forest Fish Gun Assn.

Newfoundland

Millertown
1907
Jun 8 A Caribou Hunt

Nova Scotia

Halifax
1900
Feb [day undetermined]
Departure of the Second Canadian Contingent
Mounted Rifles at Drill
Northwestern Mounted Rifles
The Royal Leinster Regiment
Royal Leinster Regiment on Parade
Royal Leinsters on Review
Mar [day undetermined]
Off for the Boer War
Nov [day undetermined]
Return of the Canadian Contingent
1901
Jul [day undetermined]
Snowballing Scene in Halifax

Ontario

Desbarats
1905
Nov [day undetermined]
Hiawatha

Hamilton
1909
Nov 5 The Cattle Thieves

Muskoka Lakes
1897
Jun [day undetermined]
Trout Poachers
1900
Jun [day undetermined]
Brook Trout Fishing
Aug [day undetermined]
Arrival of Train at Muskoka Wharf
Departure of Boats from Muskoka Wharf

Niagara Falls
see also
Niagara Falls (United States—New York)
1896
Dec [day undetermined]
American Falls from Bottom of Canadian Shore
Horseshoe Falls from Table Rock, Canadian Side
Whirlpool Rapids—from Bottom of Canadian Shore
1899
Feb [day undetermined]
Rapids below Suspension Bridge
Jul [day undetermined]
Steamship "Chippewa"
1902
Mar [day undetermined]
Prince Henry [of Prussia] at Niagara Falls
1903
Jan [day undetermined]
American Falls from Canadian Side
Great Gorge R.R., Niagara
Horseshoe Falls, from Canadian Side
Panorama Looking Down Niagara from New Suspension Bridge

Ottawa
1899
Aug [day undetermined]
43rd Rifles; Royal Canadian Infantry
In Fighting Trim
Lord and Lady Minto
1900
May [day undetermined]
The Great Ottawa Fire
Sep [day undetermined]
A Hand Car and the Imperial Limited
Imperial Limited

Pembroke
1900
Aug [day undetermined]
The Imperial Limited

Queenstown
1901
Oct [day undetermined]
Duke and Duchess of Cornwall and York Landing at Queenstown, Ontario
1903
Apr [day undetermined]
Panorama of Queenstown

Queenstown Heights
1899
Jul [day undetermined]
The Approach to Niagara

Sarnia
1900
Jun [day undetermined]
St. Clair Tunnel

Toronto
1900
Feb [day undetermined]
Toronto Mounted Rifles
Jun [day undetermined]
A Close Finish
Soldiers of Greater Britain
Steeple Chase, Toronto
1904 [month undetermined]
The Great Toronto Fire, Toronto, Canada, April 19, 1904
May [day undetermined]
Capsized Boat
War Canoe Race

Quebec

1898
Mar [day undetermined]
Canadian Artillery Marching on Snow Shoes
Canadian Outdoor Sports
Children Coasting
Coasting in Canada
Coasting Scene in Canada
Hockey Match; Quebec
Life Saving; Quebec Fire Department
Quebec Fire Department Drill
Apr [day undetermined]
Quebec Fire Department
Quebec Fire Department Drill
1899
Nov [day undetermined]
2nd Special Service Battalion, Canadian Infantry, Embarking for So. Africa
1901
Oct [day undetermined]
The Duke and Duchess of York Arriving at Quebec
1902
Feb [day undetermined]
Amateur Ski Jumpers
Arrival of the Governor General, Lord Minto, at Quebec
"Bouncing"
Dog Sleighing
A Husky Dog Team
Kent House Slide
Over the Crust
Quebec Fire Department on Sleds
Run of a Snow Shoe Club
Skiing Scene in Quebec
Toboggan Slide
"What Ho, She Bumps!"

Lachine Falls
1903
Feb [day undetermined]
Canoe Fight

Montmorency Falls
1898
Mar [day undetermined]
Coasting in Canada
The Snow Shoe Club
1902
Feb [day undetermined]
Coasting Scene at Montmorency Falls, Canada

Montreal
1900
Jun [day undetermined]
Victoria Jubilee Bridge
1901
Mar 23 Montreal Fire Department on Runners
Jul [day undetermined]
Hockey Match on the Ice at Montreal, Canada
Oct [day undetermined]
Duke and Duchess of York Leaving the Railroad Station at Montreal, Canada
Duke and Duchess of York Marching Through the Streets of Montreal
1902
Feb [day undetermined]
Skiing in Montreal
Tobogganing in Canada

St. Lawrence River
1898
Aug [day undetermined]
Shooting the Long Sault Rapids
Steamer "New York"

Yukon Territory
1901
May 4 Miles Canyon Tramway
Rocking Gold in the Klondike

Chilkoot Pass
1901
May 4 Burro Pack Train on the Chilcoot Pass

Dawson City
1901
Jul [day undetermined]
Burro Pack Train on Main Street, Dawson City
1903
Jan [day undetermined]
Birds-eye View of Dawson City on the Yukon River, Alaska
Feb [day undetermined]
Arrival of Lord and Lady Minto at the Barracks, Dawson
Dawson City Fire Department Going to a Fire
Firing the Royal Salute at Dawson City by the Northwest Mounted Police
1,000 Mile Ride over the Ice on a Bicycle
Race Between Dog Team, Bicycle and Cutter
A Sleigh Load of Squaws
United States Mail Leaving Dawson City for White Horse
Mar [day undetermined]
Steamer Susie Excursion to Moosehide
Steamer "Yukoner" Leaving Dawson

Klondike
1900
Apr [day undetermined]
White Horse Rapids
1901
May [day undetermined]
Packers on the Trail
May 4 Washing Gold on 20 Above Hunker, Klondike

China

Canton
1898
Jun [day undetermined]
Canton River Scene
Canton Steamboat Landing Chinese Passengers
Landing Wharf at Canton
Tourists Starting for Canton

Harbin
1904
Aug [day undetermined]
The Arrival of the 1st Siberian Sharpshooters at Harbin

Mukden
1904
Aug [day undetermined]
The Execution (Beheading) of One of the Hunchuses (Chinese Bandits) Outside the Walls of Mukden
Extraordinary Feats of Horsemanship

Peking
1901 [month undetermined]
Li Hung Chang
Jan [day undetermined]
The Bengal Lancers
Capt. Reilly's Battery, Bombardment of Pekin
Capt. Reilly's Battery Limbering
A Chinese Market
Cossack Cavalry
First Bengal Lancers, Distant View
Li Hung Chang
Reilly's Light Battery F
The War in China—An Army Transport Train
The War in China—Japanese Infantry
The War in China—Von Waldersee and Staff
The War in China—Von Waldersee's Review
Feb [day undetermined]
Charge by 1st Bengal Lancers
The Forbidden City
The Forbidden City, Pekin
The 9th Infantry, U.S.A.
6th Cavalry Assaulting South Gate of Pekin
Squad of Men Clearing the Road
The War in China
The War in China—First Bengal Lancers
The War in China—The Evacuation of Pekin
Oct 24 The Ch-ien-men Gate, Pekin
1903
May [day undetermined]
Procession of Chinamen in Pekin
1904
Apr 20 Camel Caravan, Pekin, China

Shanghai
1898
Jun [day undetermined]
Shanghai Street Scene No. 1
Shanghai Street Scene No. 2
1901
Jan [day undetermined]
The War in China—British Rajputs
Feb [day undetermined]
The 14th Sikhs
The Fourth Ghorkhas
In Old China
Second Queen's Rajputs
Shanghai from a Launch
Street in Shanghai
Street Scene in Shanghai
Street Scene, Shanghai
The War in China—First Bengal Lancers
The War in China—The Fourth Goorkhas
Oct 24 The Bund, Shanghai
Harbor of Shanghai
1910
Sep 21 Scenes in the Celestial Empire

Tientsin
1901
Jan [day undetermined]
Charge of Cossack Cavalry
Cossack Cavalry
The French Bridge
French Bridge, Tien-Tsin
Japanese Artillery
Japanese Infantry on the March
Japanese Soldiers on the Taku Road
An Oriental Highway
Review of Russian Artillery
Russian Sharp Shooters
Street Scene, Tientsin [China]
The Taku Road
Von Waldersee Reviewing Cossacks
The War in China—A British Donkey Train
The War in China—Bombay Cavalry
The War in China—British Light Artillery
The War in China—Coolies at Work
The War in China—Japanese Infantry
The War in China—Review of German Troops
The War in China—Ruins of Tien-Tsin
The War in China—Von Waldersee and Staff
The War in China—Von Waldersee's Review
Feb [day undetermined]
Charge by 1st Bengal Lancers
First Bengal Lancers
On the Pei-Ho
Tien-Tsin
The War in China—First Bengal Lancers
The War in China
The War in China—The German Contingent
Oct 24 Arrival of Tongkin Train

Yangtsin
1901
Jan [day undetermined]
Second Squad, Sixth U.S. Cavalry
Sixth U.S. Cavalry Charging
Sixth U.S. Cavalry, Skirmish Line

Cornwall
see **Great Britain**

Costa Rica
1908
Nov 7 Our Banana Supply

Cuba
1898 [month undetermined]
Battle of San Juan Hill
Red Cross at the Front
Sailors Landing Under Fire
Surrender of General Toral
May [day undetermined]
Battleship "Indiana"
Battleship "Iowa"
Jul [day undetermined]
A Landing Fight
"New York Journal's War Issue"
Aug [day undetermined]
Major General Shafter
Pack Mules with Ammunition on the Santiago Trail, Cuba
Shooting Captured Insurgents
1899
Jun [day undetermined]
Skirmish of Rough Riders
1910
May 17 The Princess and the Peasant
May 20 Sisters
Jun 24 The Judgment of the Mighty Deep
Jul 8 A Wireless Romance

Daiquiri
1898
Aug [day undetermined]
Mules Swimming Ashore at Daiquiri, Cuba
U.S. Troops Landing at Daiquiri, Cuba

Havana
1898
Mar [day undetermined]
Brigadier-General Fitz Hugh Lee
The Christian Herald's Relief Station, Havana
Cruiser "Montgomery"
Cuban Reconcentrados
Divers at Work on the Maine
A Run of the Havana Fire Department
Spanish Volunteers in Havana
Steamship "Olivette"
The Wreck of the "Maine"
May 20 Morro Castle, Havana Harbor
Wreck of the Battleship "Maine"
1899
Jan [day undetermined]
General Lee's Procession, Havana
Spaniards Evacuating
Troops at Evacuation of Havana
1903
Jan [day undetermined]
Burial of Maine Sailors
Apr [day undetermined]
Panorama of Morro Castle, Havana, Cuba

1910
Jul 15 A Vacation in Havana

Santiago
1898
Jul [day undetermined]
Wreck of the "Vizcaya"
Sep [day undetermined]
Troops Making Military Road in Front of Santiago

Siboney
1898
Jul [day undetermined]
U.S. Troop-Ships
Wounded Soldiers Embarking in Row Boats

Curacao

Willemstadt
1903
Apr [day undetermined]
Panorama of Willemstadt, Curacao, Taken from the River

Denmark

Helsingør
1902
Nov [day undetermined]
The Children of the Czar
King Edward VII at the Birthday Celebration of the King of Denmark

Helsingør—Fredensburg Castle
1902
Nov [day undetermined]
Promenade of the Kings
Rulers of Half the World

Dutch East Indies

Suarakarta
1909
Jun 9 The Race Course

Dutch West Indies

St. Thomas
1903
Apr [day undetermined]
West Indian Girls in Native Dance

St. Thomas—Charlotte Amalie
1903
Apr [day undetermined]
Wharf Scene and Natives Swimming at St. Thomas, D.W.I.

East China Sea

1901
Jan [day undetermined]
Chinese Junks

Egypt

Cairo
1903 [month undetermined]
Streets in Cairo, Egypt
Feb [day undetermined]
Market Scene in Cairo, Egypt
Jun [day undetermined]
Egyptian Fakir with Dancing Monkey
Egyptian Market Scene
Shearing a Donkey in Egypt

Cairo—Upper
1903
Jun [day undetermined]
Fording the River Nile on Donkeys
Panoramic View of an Egyptian Cattle Market
Primitive Irrigation in Egypt

Luxor
1903
Jun [day undetermined]
Egyptian Boys in Swimming Race
Going to Market, Luxor Egypt

Sakkarah
1903
Jun [day undetermined]
Excavating Scene at the Pyramids of Sakkarah
Tourists Starting on Donkeys for the Pyramids of Sakkarah

England

see **Great Britain**

Finland

Imaha
1904
Jul [day undetermined]
Chutes of Imaha, Finland

France

1898 [month undetermined]
The Late President Faure of France
1902
Nov [day undetermined]
Beautifyl Beaulieu
The Train to Villefranche

Auteuil
1905
Jul 29 Great Steeplechase

Cannes
1904 [month undetermined]
View of "La Croisette," Cannes, France

Lake Daumesnil
1903
Jan [day undetermined]
Skating Scene

Marseilles
1902
Nov [day undetermined]
The Longchamps Palace
The Old Port of Marseilles
On the Marseilles Tramway

Montreuil
1902
Sep [day undetermined]
Reproduction, Coronation Ceremonies—King Edward VII
1903
Jun 13 The Marvelous Wreath
Jun 27 The Enchanted Well
Jul 25 The Drawing Lesson; or, The Living Statue
The Mystical Flame
The Witch's Revenge
Aug 15 The Melomaniac
The Monster
The Oracle of Delphi
A Spiritualistic Photographer
Sep 5 The Fairyland; or, The Kingdom of the Fairies
Oct 17 The Apparition
The Infernal Caldron
Nov [day undetermined]
Alcrofrisbas, the Master Magician
Nov 7 Jack Jaggs & Dum Dum
Jupiter's Thunderbolts
10 Ladies in an Umbrella
Nov 21 Bob Kick, the Mischievous Kid
Extraordinary Illusions
Dec 9 The Ballet Master's Dream
Dec 12 The Damnation of Faust
Jack and Jim
Dec 19 The Magic Lantern
1904
Jan 9 The Terrible Turkish Executioner
Jan 23 A Moonlight Serenade; or, The Miser Punished.
Feb 6 Tit for Tat; or, A Good Joke on My Head
Mar 5 The Fugitive Apparitions
The Untamable Whiskers
Mar 12 The Clock Maker's Dream
Apr 2 Faust and Marguerite
Jun 4 The Cook in Trouble
Jul 2 The Mermaid

Nice
1899
Sep [day undetermined]
Admiral Dewey
Admiral Dewey Receiving His Mail
"Sagasta" Admiral Dewey's Pet Pig
1903
Apr [day undetermined]
Battle of Confetti at the Nice Carnival
Battle of Flowers at the Nice Carnival
Procession of Floats and Masqueraders at Nice Carnival

Paris
1897 [month undetermined]
The Zola-Rochefort Duel
Dec [day undetermined]
Charge of the French Cuirassieurs
French Cuirassieurs Charging a Field Battery
Place de la Concorde
1898 [month undetermined]
President Faure Shooting Pheasants
Jan [day undetermined]
Place de l'Opera
Aug [day undetermined]
A Hotel Fire in Paris, and Rescue by Parisian Pompiers
101st Regiment, French Infantry
Sep [day undetermined]
Agoust Family of Jugglers
Oct [day undetermined]
French Soldiers in a Wall-Climbing Drill
1900 [month undetermined]
Paris Exposition
Vesper Boat Club
Mar [day undetermined]
Scene on the Bois de Boulogne
Aug [day undetermined]
Annual French Military Carousal
Arrival of Train at Paris Exposition
Breaking of the Crowd at Military Review at Longchamps
Champs de Mars
Champs Elysees
Eiffel Tower from Trocadero Palace
Esplanade des Invalides
Palace of Electricity
Panorama from the Moving Boardwalk
Panorama of Eiffel Tower
Panorama of Place De L'Opera
Panorama of the Moving Boardwalk
Panorama of the Paris Exposition, from the Seine
Panoramic View of the Champs Elysees
Panoramic View of the Place de la Concorde
Scene from the Elevator Ascending Eiffel Tower
Scene in the Swiss Village at Paris Exposition
Scene on the Boulevard DeCapucines
Street Scene at Place de la Concorde, Paris, France
Swiss Village, No. 2
1901
Jul [day undetermined]
Feeding the Pigeons
Great Cavalry Charge
1902
Nov [day undetermined]
The Abbe and the Colonel
Allegorical Procession
Arrival of Major Marchand from the Soudan
An Automobile Parade in the Tuilleries Gardens
The Bon Vivant
Bridge of Alexander III
The Champs Elysees
A Dance by Kanaka Indians
A Dog's Cemetery
French Boxers
George J. Marck and His Lions
The Giant Constantin
The India-Rubber Man
Jo Jo, the Dog Faced Boy
A Mis-Adventure
Mr. Oldsport's Umbrella
M. Le Comte De Dion
Oom Paul
Paris Exposition
A Parisian Ballet
Prize-Winning Trip of the Santos-Dumont Airship No. 6
The Valiant Pig
A Water Carnival
"Zip"
1903
Jan [day undetermined]
The Aquarium
Boulevard St. Denis, Paris, France
Feb [day undetermined]
Panoramic View of the Streets of Paris, France
Jun [day undetermined]
King Edward's Visit to Paris
1904
Jul [day undetermined]
Easter Flower Parade in Bois de Boulogne, Paris

Oct [day undetermined]
Paris from the Seine
1910
May 26 Roosevelt in Paris

Pau
1909
May 12 Wilbur Wright and His Majesty King Edward VII

Rennes
1902
Nov [day undetermined]
Captain Dreyfus

Seine River
1909
Nov 13 The Rhymester's Ruse

Versailles
1905
Jan 14 Big Fountain at Versailles

Villefranche
1899
Sep [day undetermined]
Jack Tars Ashore
Officers of the "Olympia"
Oct [day undetermined]
A Dip in the Mediterranean
Harbor of Villefranche

Vincennes
1903
Jun [day undetermined]
King Edward and President Loubet Reviewing French Troops

Germany

1901
Jul [day undetermined]
Ammunition Wagons Arriving on the Battlefield
A German Cuirassier Regiment
Red Cross of the German Army on the Battlefield
1904
Aug [day undetermined]
The Great International Automobile Race for the Gordon-Bennett Trophy
Sep 3 Falls of the Rhine
1909
Jan 20 Balloon Races

Berlin
1897
Dec [day undetermined]
A Children's Carnival in Germany
1902
Nov [day undetermined]
The Attack
The Baby's Meal
"Be Good Again"
Berlin Fire Department
Bi-Centennial Jubilee Parade
A Blast in a Gravel Bed
The Bogie Man
Calling the Pigeons
The Children and the Frog
Children Playing with Lion Cubs
Dedication of the Alexander Grenadiers' Barracks
The Elephant's Bath
Elevated and Underground
Emperor and Empress of Germany
Emperor William II
Emperor William II on Horseback
Emperor William of Germany on Horseback
Field-Marshal Count Von Waldersee
Fun in a Clothes Basket
Fun on a Sand Hill
Ganswindt's Flying Machine
German Artillery in Action
German Cavalry Leaping Hurdles
German Garde Kurassiers
German Lancers
German Military Exercises
German Railway Service
The Gourmand
In the Friedrichstrasse
A Mermaid Dance
Panoramic View from the Stadtbahn
Panoramic View of the Siegesallee
Rare Fish in an Aquarium
The Rivals
A Run by the Berlin Fire Department, Berlin, Germany
A Tug of War
Unveiling of the Bismarck Monument
An Unwelcome Visitor
Visit of Emperor Francis Josef of Austria to Berlin
When the Bugle Sounds "Charge!"
Winter in Germany
With Emperor William's Army
1903
May [day undetermined]
Berlin Fire Department at Drill
1906
Sep [day undetermined]
Trip on Berlin Elevated R.R.

Bremen
1902
Nov [day undetermined]
The Flying Train

Breslau
1901
Jul [day undetermined]
Breslau Fire Department in Action
Fire Drills at Breslau, Germany
The Great Corpus Christi Procession in Breslau
Market Day in Breslau, Germany

Danzig
1902
Nov [day undetermined]
Emperor William as a Hussar
Emperor William Returning from Manoeuvres
Empress of Germany at Danzig
Prince Tsung of China

Dresden
1902
Nov [day undetermined]
Clever Horsemanship
A Hurdle Race
On the Elbe

Friedrichsruh
1901
Jul [day undetermined]
Opening of Bismarck's Museum

Greenwald
1902
Nov [day undetermined]
In the Heart of the Forest

Halensee
1902
Nov [day undetermined]
In a German Bath

Hamburg
1902
Nov [day undetermined]
Banks of the Elbe
Panoramic View of the Harbor of Hamburg, Germany
1904
Aug [day undetermined]
The Great International Automobile Race for the Gordon-Bennett Trophy
1907
Sep 23 Carl Hagenbeck's Wild Animal Park at Hamburg, Germany

Kiel
1902
Nov [day undetermined]
Aboard the Aegir
Battleship "Odin"
Between the Decks
The Emperor and Empress and Crown Prince of Germany
A Flying Wedge
German Navy Target Practice
A German Torpedo Boat Flotilla in Action
King Albert of Saxony
Launch of the "Koenig Albert"
Launching of the "Kaiser Wilhelm der Grosse"
On Board His Majesty's Battleship "Fuerst Bismark"
On Board His Majesty's Gunboat "Luchs"
A Rescue at Sea
Torpedo Boat "G-89"

Langfuhr
1902
Nov [day undetermined]
Emperor William at the Danzig Manoeuvres
Empress of Germany Driving to the Manoeuvres

Marienburg
1902
Nov [day undetermined]
The Emperor and Empress of Germany
When Knighthood Was in Flower

Potsdam
1902
Nov [day undetermined]
Funeral Procession of the Late Empress Frederick

River Spree
1902
Nov [day undetermined]
German Cavalry Fording a River

Schloss Altfranken
1902
Nov [day undetermined]
Marvelous Markmanship

Stettin
1902
Nov [day undetermined]
The Crown Prince of Germany

Vohwinkel
1902
Nov [day undetermined]
The Flying Train

Wilhelmshaven
1902
Nov [day undetermined]
Panorama of Wilhelmshaven
Return of the German China Fleet
Sailing of Battleship "Wurtemberg"

Gibraltar

1899
Sep [day undetermined]
Admiral Dewey
Admiral Dewey Receiving His Mail
Admiral Dewey's Dog, "Bob"

Great Britain

1909
Sep 29 Love, the Conqueror

Cornwall

1899
Jun [day undetermined]
Wreck of the S.S. "Paris"

England

1896 [month undetermined]
The Henley Regatta
1897 [month undetermined]
The Rocket Coach
Nov [day undetermined]
Finish of the English Derby of 1897
German Warship at Spithead
Maxim Firing Field Gun
1898
Jan [day undetermined]
Surf Dashing Against England's Rocky Coast
1899
Apr [day undetermined]
South Wales Express
Jun [day undetermined]
Launch of the Porthonstock Life-boat
Wreck of the "Mohican"
Sep [day undetermined]
Launch of the Battleship "Vengeance"
1903
Apr [day undetermined]
An English Prize-Fight
A Paper Chase
Stag Hunting in England
A Water Carnival

Aldershot
1897
Sep [day undetermined]
Aldershot Review
The Coldstream Guards
Gordon Highlanders
Oct [day undetermined]
His Majesty, King Edward VII
A Maxim Gun in Action
Dec [day undetermined]
The Alarm (Gordon Highlanders)
Bayonet Versus Bayonet
Gordon Highlanders Marching into Camp

Gymnastic Exercises in the British Army
The Highland Fling, by the Gordon Highlanders
A Regimental Calisthenic Drill in the British Army
1898
Apr [day undetermined]
A Terrible Spill
1899 [month undetermined]
The Prince of Wales (King Edward VII) at the Aldershot Review

Ambergate
1904 [month undetermined]
Arrival and Release of 40,000 Carrying Pigeons at Ambergate, England

Ascot
1897 [month undetermined]
A Race for the Gold Cup
Nov [day undetermined]
Arrival of His Majesty, King Edward VII (then Prince of Wales) at the Ascot Races, 1897

Blenheim
1901 [month undetermined]
Chamberlain and Balfour

Bolton
1900 [month undetermined]
Razing a Chimney

Bushey
1898
Apr [day undetermined]
The "Jennie Deans"

Chatham
1900 [month undetermined]
Mining Operations

Clapham Park
1902
Nov [day undetermined]
Dessert at Dan Leno's House
An Obstinate Cork

Depford
1903
Feb [day undetermined]
Cattle Bathing

Devonshire
1903
Apr [day undetermined]
A Devonshire Fair

East Cowes
1901
Feb [day undetermined]
Queen Victoria's Funeral [Number 1]

Epsom—Epsom Downs
1899
Jun [day undetermined]
The Derby
The Paddock
1901
Jun [day undetermined]
English Derby, 1901

Exmoor
1903
Apr [day undetermined]
A Majestic Stag

Henley
1901
Aug [day undetermined]
The Henley Regatta, 1901
1902
Sep [day undetermined]
Clearing the Course for the Henley Boat Races, July 10th, 1902
Third Trinity, Cambridge, Winning the Race for the Grand Challenge Cup. Taken at Henley on July 10th, 1902
The University College of Oxford Winning the Ladies' Challenge Plate

Hurlingham
1899
Sep [day undetermined]
Polo—A Dash for Goal
Polo—Hurlingham vs. Ranelagh

Liverpool
1899 [month undetermined]
Departure of the Gordon Highlanders
Apr [day undetermined]
Grand National Steeple-Chase

London
1897 [month undetermined]
Burglars in the Pantry
Elephants at the Zoo
"Has He Hit Me?"
The Horse Guards
Mr. C. N. Morton
Pelicans at the Zoo
Sir Wilfred Laurier and the New South Wales Lancers
"To the Death"
Jul [day undetermined]
Queen's Jubilee
Nov [day undetermined]
His Majesty, King Edward VII
Dec [day undetermined]
Trafalgar Square
1898
Jan [day undetermined]
Relieving the Guard at St. James Palace
1899 [month undetermined]
Amann
Amann, the Great Impersonator
Beerbohm Tree, the Great English Actor
Rt. Honorable Cecil Rhodes
Ritchie, the Tramp Bicyclist
Mar [day undetermined]
Lockhart's Performing Elephants
Apr [day undetermined]
English Fire Department Run
Fire Department Rescue Drill
The Humane Side of Modern Warfare
Oxford and Cambridge University Boat Crews
Oxford-Cambridge Boat-Race
Aug [day undetermined]
Stage Coaches Leaving the Hotel Victoria
1900 [month undetermined]
John Philip Sousa
Kansas City Fire Department, Winners of the World's Championship at the Paris Exposition
Jul [day undetermined]
Amateur Athletic Championships
Children of the Royal Family of England
Playing Soldier
Spirit of the Empire
Nov [day undetermined]
Keith's Theater, London
1901 [month undetermined]
Emar De Flon, the Champion Skater
Nabbed by the Nipper
Panoramic View of London Streets, Showing Coronation Decorations
Signor Marconi—Wireless Telegraphy
Their Majesties the King and Queen
Feb [day undetermined]
The First Procession in State of H. M. King Edward VII
First Procession in State of H. M. King Edward VII
Queen Victoria's Funeral [Number 2]
Jul [day undetermined]
Arrival of Funeral Cortege at St. George's Chapel
The Complete Funeral Cortege Passing Through Windsor
The Funeral Arriving at Hyde Park
The Funeral Cortege Arriving at Trinity Pier
London Fire Department
Piccadilly Circus, London, England
Royal Artillery and English Sailors Marching Through Hyde Park
Royal Exchange, London, England
1902
Sep [day undetermined]
Coronation Parade
Nov [day undetermined]
Mr. Dan Leno, Assisted by Mr. Herbert Campbell, Editing the "Sun"
The Murderer's Vision
Rare Fish in the Aquarium
Umbrella Dance, San Toy
1903
Jan [day undetermined]
The King's Guardsmen
Panorama of Thames River
Feb [day undetermined]
King Edward and Queen Alexandra Passing Through London, England
Apr [day undetermined]
England's Colonial Troops
A Kennel Club Parade
Looping the Loop
Man's Best Friend
Over London Bridge
Push Ball
A Visit to the London Zoo
May [day undetermined]
Game of Push Ball
Oct [day undetermined]
London Zoo
1904
Jul [day undetermined]
Push Ball on Horseback
Aug [day undetermined]
The International Congress of the Salvation Army
1908
Feb 29 Hackenschmidt-Rodgers Wrestling Match
1909
Mar 14 The Summers-Britt Fight Pictures
1910
Jun 18 [Welch-Daniels Fight]

London—Kensington
1901
Jul [day undetermined]
Edward VII, King of England

London—National Sporting Club
1907
Dec 27 Burns-Moir

London—Queens Club Grounds
1899
Sep [day undetermined]
International Collegiate Games
The International Collegiate Games
International Collegiate Games
International Collegiate Games—Half Mile Run
International Collegiate Games—110 Yards Hurdle Race
International Collegiate Games—100 Yards Dash

London—Worthing Baths
1898
Apr [day undetermined]
Water Polo

Maidenhead
1901
Jun [day undetermined]
Panoramic View of the Thames

Newcastle
1899 [month undetermined]
Tapping a Blast Furnace
1900
May [day undetermined]
Trial Speed of H. M. Torpedo Boat Destroyer "Viper"

Newlyn
1904
Oct [day undetermined]
Sea Gulls at Newlyn, Cornwall, England

Newmarket
1901
Jun [day undetermined]
"Volodyovski"

Portsmouth
1898
Apr [day undetermined]
"Away Aloft"

Putney
1900 [month undetermined]
Oxford-Cambridge Race

Sandown Park
1899
Mar [day undetermined]
Grand Military Steeple-Chase

Sheerness
1900 [month undetermined]
Speed Trial of the "Albatross"

Southampton
1899 [month undetermined]
Lord Roberts Embarking for South Africa
Lord Wolseley

Southead
1899
Apr [day undetermined]
A Zulu War Dance

Southsea
1901
Feb [day undetermined]
Departure of Duke and Duchess of Cornwall for Australia

Spithead
1897
Nov [day undetermined]
H. M. S. Powerful at Spithead
1898
Jun [day undetermined]
Naval Review Spithead

Stamford Bridge
1901 [month undetermined]
Amateur Athletic Association Sports

Thames River
1899
Aug [day undetermined]
"Between the Races"
The Henley Regatta

Tunbridge Wells
1903
Apr [day undetermined]
Acquatic Sports

Walton-on-Thames
1903
Nov 21 Saturday's Shopping
1904
Nov [day undetermined]
The Lover's Ruse
Over the Hedge
A Race for a Kiss
Dec [day undetermined]
The Honeymoon
1905
Jul [day undetermined]
Rescued by Rover

Windsor
1899 [month undetermined]
Church Parade of the Life Guards
"God Save the Queen"
Her Majesty, Queen Victoria
Her Majesty, Queen Victoria, Reviewing the Honorable Artillery
Her Majesty, Queen Victoria, Reviewing the Household Cavalry at Spital Barracks
Apr [day undetermined]
Panoramic View of Windsor Castle
1900
May [day undetermined]
The Queen's Reception to the Heroes of Ladysmith
1901
Feb [day undetermined]
Queen Victoria's Funeral [Number 3]

Worthing—Worthing Station
1898
Apr [day undetermined]
Idle Hours of the English Coast Guards
"Me and My Two Friends"
Worthing Life-Saving Station

English Channel

1898
Apr [day undetermined]
Three Men in a Boat
A Tug in a Heavy Sea
1899
Sep [day undetermined]
"Man Overboard!"

Scotland

Dumbarton
1901 [month undetermined]
The Builders of Shamrock II
Launch of Shamrock II

Edinburgh
1899
Apr [day undetermined]
The Gordon Highlanders
Scots Grey

Gourock
1903
Sep [day undetermined]
Sir Thomas Lipton's Yacht Fleet Leaving England

River Clyde
1901
Jun [day undetermined]
Emperor William's Yacht "Meteor"
International Yacht Races on the Clyde

Wales

Conway
1898
Apr [day undetermined]
Conway Castle

Greece

Athens
1906
Jun 23 The Olympic Games at Athens, Greece

Holland

see **The Netherlands**

Hong Kong

1898
Jun [day undetermined]
Government House at Hong Kong
Hong Kong Regiment, No. 1
Hong Kong Regiment, No. 2
Hong Kong, Wharf Scene
Street Scene in Hong Kong
1901
Sep [day undetermined]
In Old Hong Kong
The Queen's Road

Hungary

1897 [month undetermined]
Home Life of a Hungarian Family
Dec [day undetermined]
A Camp of Zingari Gypsies
1898
Oct [day undetermined]
Hungarian Women Plucking Geese

Budapest
1897
Oct [day undetermined]
Emperor Francis Joseph of Austria
Dec [day undetermined]
Austrian Mounted Police
Charge of Hungarian Hussars
Emperor William of Germany, and Emperor Franz Josef of Austria
Hungarian Cavalry Charge
1898
Jan [day undetermined]
Meeting of Emperor William of Germany and Emperor Franz Josef of Austria

India

1903
Apr [day undetermined]
A Gorgeous Pageant of Princes
May [day undetermined]
Fighting Rams
Sep [day undetermined]
The Galloping Tongas

Delhi
1903
Mar 14 The Delhi Camp Railway

Hyderabad
1903
Oct [day undetermined]
Street Scene in Hyderabad

Indonesia

Java
1909
Jun 11 Snake Skin Industry
Dec 4 The Crocodile Hunt

Ireland

1903
Apr [day undetermined]
Coaching in Ireland
Coaching Through the Tunnel on the Kenmere Road
1910
Nov 23 The Lad from Old Ireland

Cork
1904
Dec 17 Patrick Street, Cork

Dublin
1900 [month undetermined]
Queen Victoria's Last Visit to Ireland

Dunloe
1903
Apr [day undetermined]
On Horseback, Killarney

Queenstown
1903
Oct [day undetermined]
King Edward's Visit to Ireland

Tillaloe
1903
Apr [day undetermined]
The River Shannon

Israel

Jaffa
1903
Jun [day undetermined]
Street Scene at Jaffa
Tourists Embarking at Jaffa

Jericho
1903
Jun [day undetermined]
Tourists Taking Water from the River Jordan

Jerusalem
1903
Jan [day undetermined]
Leaving Jerusalem
Jun [day undetermined]
Jerusalem's Busiest Street, Showing Mt. Zion
A Jewish Dance at Jerusalem

Italy

Capri
1903
Jun [day undetermined]
Tourists Landing at Island of Capri, Italy

Genoa
1904
Jan [day undetermined]
Nautical Tournament

Lago Maggiore
1902
Apr [day undetermined]
Moonlight on Lake Maggiore, Italy

Naples
1903
Jun [day undetermined]
Eating Macaroni in the Streets of Naples

Orvieto
1898 [month undetermined]
Corpus Christi Procession, Orvieto

Rome
1898 [month undetermined]
The Armenian Archbishop, Rome
The Vatican Guards, Rome
1900 [month undetermined]
Panoramic View of Rome
1903
Jan [day undetermined]
Wedding Procession in a Church at Rome
Oct [day undetermined]
Rome and the Vatican

Tivoli
1903
Jun [day undetermined]
Panorama of Tivoli, Italy, Showing Seven Falls

Venice
1897 [month undetermined]
A Panoramic View in the Grand Canal
Panoramic View of Grand Canal
Panoramic View of Venice
1903
Jan [day undetermined]
Panorama of City of Venice
Apr [day undetermined]
The Grand Canal, Venice
On the Grand Canal, Venice
Jun [day undetermined]
Feeding Pigeons in Front of St. Mark's Cathedral, Venice, Italy

Oct [day undetermined]
Glimpses of Venice

Sicily

Syracuse
1903
Jun [day undetermined]
Washing Clothes at Sicily

Jamaica

Kingston
1903
Jan [day undetermined]
West Indian Boys Diving for Money
1910
Jul 8 Between Love and Honor

Spanishtown
1903
Apr [day undetermined]
Railroad Panorama near Spanishtown, Jamaica

Japan
1902 [month undetermined]
Black and White Hair Dance
Eight Japanese Dancing Girls
Four Hong Kong Sisters
Fu Tschi Dancers
Geisha Girls
Hu-Ki-Si, Japanese Dancer
Is Ka Trio
Japanese Bowery
Japanese Dancing Hall
Japanese Yuma Dance
1903
Jan [day undetermined]
Japanese Geisha Girls No. 1
Japanese Geisha Girls No. 2

Kanagarva
1904
Apr 20 Japanese Railroad Scene, Kanagarva, Japan

Kobe
1901
Sep [day undetermined]
Panorama of Kobe Harbor, Japan
Sampans Racing Toward Liner

Kyoto
1901
Sep [day undetermined]
Ox Carts
Oct [day undetermined]
Japanese Fencing
A Japanese Railway Train
Rickshaw Parade, Japan

Nagasaki
1898
Jun [day undetermined]
S.S. "Gaelic" at Nagasaki
1901
Oct 24 Coaling a Steamer, Nagasaki Bay, Japan

Nikko
1904
Sep [day undetermined]
Great Temple Procession, Nikko, Japan

Tokyo
1898
Jun [day undetermined]
Arrival of Tokyo Train
1901
Sep [day undetermined]
Street Scene, Tokio, Japan
Oct [day undetermined]
Asakusa Temple
Shimbashi R.R. Station
1902 [month undetermined]
Street Scene, Tokio
May [day undetermined]
The National Geisha Dance of Japan
1904
Aug [day undetermined]
A Fierce Sword Combat at Tokio
The Military Funeral of the "Standard Bearer of the Yalu"
Sep [day undetermined]
Japanese Fan Dance
Japanese Flag Dance

Yokohama
1898
Jun [day undetermined]
Going to the Yokohama Races
Returning from the Races
S.S. "Doric"
Street Scene in Yokohama, No. 1
Street Scene in Yokohama, No. 2
Theatre Road, Yokohama

Jordan
1903
Jun [day undetermined]
Herd of Sheep on the Road to Jerusalem

Mizpah
1903
Jun [day undetermined]
Tourists Returning on Donkeys from Mizpah

Korea

Seoul
1904
Apr 20 Panorama of Railroad Station at Seoul, Korea, from Departing Train

Lebanon

Beirut
1903
Jun [day undetermined]
Arabian Jewish Dance
Panoramic View of Beyrouth, Syria, Showing Holiday Festivities
Passengers Embarking from S.S. "Augusta Victoria" at Beyrouth

Macao
1898
Jun [day undetermined]
River Scene at Macao, China

Martinique

Carbet
1902
Sep [day undetermined]
Natives Unloading a Boat of Fire-Wood at Carbet (A Suburb of St. Pierre)

Fort de France
1902
Sep [day undetermined]
Circular Panoramic View of the Market Place at Fort de France, Showing S.S. Korona in the Background
Native Women of Fort de France at Work
Native Women Washing Clothes at Fort de France
Native Women Washing Clothes at the Gueydon Fountain, Fort de France, Martinique
Natives Unloading a Coaling Vessel at Fort de France, Martinique
Street Scene in Fort de France, Martinique

Morne Rouge
1902
Sep [day undetermined]
Native Bull Cart at Morne Rouge (A Suburb of St. Pierre)

St. Pierre
1902
Sep [day undetermined]
Circular Panoramic View of St. Pierre from the Lighthouse, Showing Mt. Pelee Smoking in the Distance
Circular Panoramic View of St. Pierre, Showing the Ruins of the Catholic Cathedral and Mt. Pelee Smoking in the Background
Storm at Sea near St. Pierre, Martinique
1903
Apr [day undetermined]
Panoramic View of St. Pierre, Martinique

Mexico
1898
Feb [day undetermined]
Mexican Fishing Scene
Mexican Rurales Charge
Sunday Morning in Mexico
Surface Transit, Mexico
Mar [day undetermined]
Mexico Street Scene

Durango
1898
Feb [day undetermined]
Train Hour in Durango, Mexico
Wash Day in Mexico*
Mar [day undetermined]
Bull Fight, No. 1
Bull Fight, No. 2
Bull Fight, No. 3

Juarez
1910
Sep 24 The Tout's Remembrance

Mexico City
1898
Feb [day undetermined]
Market Scene, City of Mexico
Repairing Streets in Mexico
1902
Apr [day undetermined]
Great Bull Fight
Las Viga Canal, Mexico

Santa Anita
1898
Feb [day undetermined]
Las Viga Canal, Mexico City

Monaco
1902
Nov [day undetermined]
Ten Minutes at Monte Carlo
1903
Feb [day undetermined]
Santos Dumont's Airship

Monte Carlo
1902
Nov [day undetermined]
From Monte Carlo to Monaco
1903
Apr [day undetermined]
Panoramic View of Monte Carlo

The Netherlands
1897 [month undetermined]
Dutch Fishing Boats

Hague
1898
Oct [day undetermined]
Coronation of Queen Wilhelmina of Holland

Scheveningen Baths
1897 [month undetermined]
Bath Scene

Northern Ireland

Belfast
1898 [month undetermined]
Launch of the "Oceanic"

Portrush
1898 [month undetermined]
Feeding the Pigs

Norway
1903
Apr [day undetermined]
Mountain Torrents
Sep [day undetermined]
Rising Panorama of a Norwegian Waterfall
1904
Dec 3 From Christiania to the North Cape

Holmenkollen
1901 [month undetermined]
Norway Ski Jumping Contests

Lake Brienz
1910
Jun 8 The Mountain Lake

Lucerne
1903
Jun [day undetermined]
Lake Lucerne, Switzerland

Montreux
1904 [month undetermined]
Panoramic View of Montreux, Switzerland

Mt. Blanc
1910
Jan 15 Railway on the Ice Sea

Mount Pilatus
1904
Oct 15 Ascending Mount Pilate

Schaffhausen
1901
Jul [day undetermined]
Great Waterfall of the Rhein at Schaffhausen, Switzerland

Zermatt
1907 [month undetermined]
Torrents of Zermath

Zurich
1903
Apr [day undetermined]
A Swiss Carnival

Trinidad

1908
Dec 15 Cocoa Industry, Trinidad, British West Indies

Vatican City

1903
Sep [day undetermined]
Pope [Leo XIII] in His Carriage
Pope [Leo XIII] Passing Through Upper Loggia

Vietnam

Hanoi
1903
May [day undetermined]
Market Scene in Hanoi, China

Virgin Islands

St. Thomas
1898
May [day undetermined]
Harbor of St. Thomas
1903
Apr [day undetermined]
Native Women Coaling a Ship at St. Thomas, D.W.I.

St. Vincent
1903
Apr [day undetermined]
Native Women Washing Clothes at St. Vincent, B. W. I.

Wales

see **Great Britain**

FOREIGN COUNTRY INDEX

★ Entries in the Foreign Country Index are arranged according to the country of origin of specific films, then chronologically according to year, month and date. An **asterisk** (*) indicates that the participation of the country is doubtful; a **dagger** (†) indicates that the film may have been a production of either France or Great Britain.

FOREIGN COUNTRY INDEX

Denmark

1907

Apr 20 Anarchist's Mother-in-Law
Auntie's Birthday
Polar Bear Hunt
True Until Death

1908

Feb 29 Iceboat Racing on Lake St. Clair
Mar 21 The Hot Temper
The Magic Bag
Apr 4 The Robber's Sweetheart
When the House Rent Was Due
Apr 11 Angelo, Tyrant of Padua
Lion Hunting
Stone Industry in Sweden
Willie's Magic Wand
Apr 25 Ihles & Antonio, Boxers
A Modern Naval-Hero
May 2 The Champagne Bottle
A Misalliance
May 9 Dog Training
When Honor Is Lost Everything Is Lost
May 16 Emperor Nero on the Warpath
Sport from All the World
May 23 The Flight from Seraglio
Winter Manoeuvres of the Norwegian Army
May 30 Mr. Drawee
The Will
Jun 7 Texas Tex
Jun 13 A Chance Shot
The Pupa Changes into a Butterfly
Two Gentlemen
Winter Time in Northern Europe
Aug 29 From Bagdad
Summer in North Europe
Sep 5 The Laplanders
The School of Life
Sep 12 The Hand
The Isle of Bornholm
Sep 19 The Lady with the Camellias
Sep 26 The Codfish Industry
The Magic Rubbers
Oct 3 From the Rococo Times
A Sport at the Music Hall
Oct 10 The Countess' Wedding Day
Oct 28 The Arab Band
Nov [day undetermined]
The Acrobats
Automatic Statue
The Bank Director
The Child and the Gigantic Animal
Cupboard Courtship
The Dance of Death
The Dancing Girl
Little Hannie's Last Dream
The Magic Ring
The Mill
On Roller Skates
The Photographer
Pierrot's Death
The Prima Donna of the Ballet Parody
Rheumatism
Rose That Makes Everybody Dance
Scandanavian North
Supper
The Tinder Box
Nov 1 Bear Hunting in Russia
Nov 4 Clearing the Mountain Track
The Watchmaker's Wedding
Nov 7 The Pillory
The Pilot's Daughter
Nov 14 Blind
Nov 18 Othello
Nov 25 Alexandrian Quadrille
Children of the East
Dec 2 Dummies on the Spree
A Sinner
Dec 9 Sherlock Holmes
Dec 16 The Changing of Souls
The Spring Lock
Dec 23 Count Zeppelin's Aerostat
Hercules the Athlete; or, Love Behind the Scenes
Dec 30 The Quack
The Queen's Love (La Tosca)

1909

Jan 6 "Mafia," the Secret Society; or, Sicilian Family Honor
On Guard at the Powder Magazine
Jan 20 Balloon Races
Jim Smith, the Champion Boxer
Life in Russia
The Stepmother: the Spirit of Unkindness and Jealousy Thwarted
Jan 27 Desert Life
The Gnomes
Feb 3 Moving Furniture
Sultan Abdul Hamid, and the Ladies of His Harem
Summer Sport
Feb 6 Badger Hunt
The Wild Man of Borneo
Feb 17 The Caliph's Adventures
Feb 19 The Barber's Christening
James and Catherine; or, Love on a Farm
Feb 26 Sherlock Holmes II: Raffles Escapes from Prison
Mar 3 The Blind Foundling; or, Alone in the World
The False Superintendent
Four Sweethearts
Sherlock Holmes III: The Detectives Adventure in the Gas Cellar
Mar 6 Two Violins
Mar 8 The Capricious Moment
The Chimney Sweep's Birthday
Round the Lake of Constanz and the Rhine Falls
Mar 9 The Student's Predicament
Mar 14 The Artist's Model's Sweetheart
For Love of a Fisher Girl
From the North Cape
Mar 20 The Grand Procession at the King of Siam Jubilee
Sold to Thieves; or, A Deathbed Confession
A Stage Romance; or, An Actor's Love
Mar 31 The Chauffeur's Adventure
In Ancient Egypt
The Non-Stop Motor Bicycle
William Tell: The Liberator of Switzerland
Apr 5 Nat Pinkerton: The Anarchists Plot
Apr 14 Canals of Copenhagen
A Sailor's Life
Apr 16 Bangkok
Apr 17 The Magic Purse
Apr 21 The Artist's Dream
A Walk Through the Zoo
Apr 24 Modern Egypt
The Viking's Love; or, True to His Chief
Apr 28 Nat Pinkerton [Series II]
May 1 Siamese Actors and Actresses Play a Siamese Drama
Winter Sports and Games at Stockholm, Sweden, 1909
May 5 Boxing Match [by Hallberg of Denmark and Young Joe Gaines "Baltimore Black"]
Hard Working Elephants
May 8 Danish Capitol Under Snow
Neptune's Daughter; or, The Shoemaker's Dream
May 12 The Beggarmaid
Moscow
May 17 Summering in the Austrian Alps
Winter Landscapes Round Stockholm
May 19 The Farmer's Grandson
May 22 The Master Detective; or, The Attack on the Strong Room
May 26 The Human Ape; or, Darwin's Triumph
May 29 The Hasty Tempered Father; or, The Blacksmith's Love
Motherly Love of Animals
Jun 2 Cab Number 519
Jun 9 The Brothers Laurento
The Convict
The General and the Sentry
Street Life in North Siam
Jun 12 The Brave Page Boy
Jun 16 The Wages of Sin
Jun 19 The Art of Fencing
Lesson in Cycling
Jun 23 A Woman of the People
Jul 3 A Mother's Grief
The Mouse
Policeman's Rest
The Prince and the Actor
Jul 10 Herring Fishing
The Persistent Lover
Jul 17 Carnival Merriment in the North
A Shadow of the Past
Jul 24 A Clever Nurse
Off the Coast of Norway
Aug 14 A Soldier's Wife
The Spy
Water Sports
Aug 21 False Alarm
Surroundings of Copenhagen
Aug 28 Cowboys in Argentina
The Shell; or, "A Madman's Revenge"
Sep 4 Cycle Rider and the Witch
The Henpecked Husband
Norrkobing
Sep 11 The Gray Dame
Sep 18 How Dr. Nicola Procured the Chinese Cane
Sep 22 Dr. Cook at Copenhagen
Sep 25 The Great Prize
Life on Board a Training Ship
Oct 2 The Cremation
Heroism Reconciles
Oct 9 Adventures of an Emigrant
Vagabond Life
Oct 16 The Red Domino
Oct 23 The Bracelet
Gotacanal—over Norway's Rockies
A Lunatic's Day Off
Nov 3 Dynamite
Hanson & Co.
Life in Dalerne (Sweden)
Nov 6 The Destiny of Paul Wang
Nov 10 The Short-Sighted Governess
The Suicide Woods
Yachting on the Baltic
Nov 13 A Message to Napoleon; or, An Episode in the Life of the Great Prisoner at Elba
Nov 20 A Girl's Cross Roads
Dec 1 A Boy Hero; or, The Fisherman's Son
Trollhattan
Dec 4 Little Willie's Trip to the North Pole
Wrestling
Dec 8 Gerhardi Mohr
Temptations of the Gold Fields; or, The Two Gold Diggers
Dec 18 The Butcher's Bill
In Southern Sweden
Mother-in-Law Crazy with Music
Dec 25 Father's Busy Papering
An Outcast's Christmas

1910

Jan 1 Refreshing Bath
Vengeance; or, The Forester's Sacrifice

Jan 8 Child as Benefactor
Jan 15 Death of the Brigand Chief
Naughty Boys
Jan 22 Anarchists on Board; or, The Thrilling Episode on the S.S. "Slavonia"
Jan 29 The Mystery of the Lama Convent; or, Dr. Nicola in Thibet
Feb 5 The Foxy Soldiers; or, How Schmidt Got to the Masquerade
A Woman's Destiny
Feb 12 Never Despair; or, From Misery to Happiness
Worried to Death
Feb 19 Ruined by His Son
Feb 26 Doctor's Sacrifice
Mar 5 The Mad Drainpipe
A Pleasant Walk
Mar 12 A Wedding During the French Revolution
Mar 19 A Quiet Honeymoon
The Theft of the Diamonds
Mar 26 Tsing Fu, the Yellow Devil
Apr 2 Madame Sans Gene; or, The Duchess of Danzig
Apr 9 Hustling Mr. Brown
A New Burglar Alarm
Apr 16 The Hidden Treasure
Apr 23 The Conjuror
A Day Off
The Four Seasons
Apr 30 Saved from the Sultan's Sentence
May 7 The Somnambulist
May 14 The Club of the Corpulent
The Marvelous Cure; or, The Wonderful Hair-Growing Fluid
May 21 A Father's Grief
May 28 The Eagle's Egg; or The Rival Lovers
Roosevelt in Denmark
Jun 4 The Carman's Dream
The Jump to Death
Jun 11 The Duel
Jun 18 How Brother Cook Was Taught a Lesson
Lake of Lucerne
Jun 25 The Captain's Wife
The Clown and His Dogs
Jul 2 The Sons of the Minister
Jul 9 The Laughing Machine
The Wonderful Cigar
Jul 16 The Prodigal Son
Jul 23 The Elopement
Fabian Cleaning Chimney
Jul 30 Fabian Arranging Curtain Rods
For the Sake of a Child
Aug 6 Magdalene; or, The Workman's Daughter
Aug 13 The Life Boat
The Stolen Policeman
Aug 27 Fabian's Hollow Tooth
A Society Sinner
Sep 3 Fabian Hunting Rats
The Little Drummer Boy
Sep 10 Robinson Crusoe
Sep 17 Danish Dragoons
Fabian Out for a Picnic
Sep 24 Dr. Jekyll and Mr. Hyde; or, A Strange Case
Oct 1 Bird's Eye View from World's Highest Buildings
The Flight Across the Atlantic
Oct 8 The Storms of Life
Oct 15 Saved by Bosco
Willie Visits a Moving Picture Show
Oct 22 The Artist's Luck
Oct 29 Who Is She?
Nov 5 A Fatal Picnic
The Jewel Case
Nov 12 Mother-in-Law Arrives
World's Wrestling Champions
Nov 19 The Diamond Swindler
Nov 26 Kean; or, The Prince and the Actor
Dec 3 The Birthday Present
The Ohami Troupe of Acrobats
Dec 10 The Poacher
Dec 17 A Christmas Letter
Dickey's Courtship
Dec 24 The Necklace of the Dead
Dec 31 Bearhunting
The Scarecrow

France

1897 [month undetermined]
Babies Quarrel

1898 [month undetermined]
The Late President Faure of France
President Faure Shooting Pheasants

1899
Feb 11 The Devil's Laboratory
The Infernal Palace
Apr 10 A Trip to the Moon
May 13 The Enchanted Inn
May 20 The Cavern of the Demons
Dec 25 Cinderella

1900
Feb [day undetermined]
Faust and Marguerite
Apr [day undetermined]
Birth of Venus
Apr 7 Four Heads Better Than One
Apr 21 X Rays
Jun 30 A Mysterious Portrait
Neptune and Amphitrite
The Power of the Cross
Spanish Inquisition
Wrestling Extraordinary
Nov 11 Joan of Arc

1901
Apr 6 The One Man Orchestra
Jul [day undetermined]
The Mysterious Blackboard
Oh! What a Night; or, The Sultan's Dream
The Statue of William Tell
Oct 26 Little Red Riding Hood
Nov 23 A Christmas Dream
Dec [day undetermined]
The Fat and the Lean Wrestling Match

1902 [month undetermined]
The Man with the Rubber Head
May [day undetermined]
The Burglars in the Wine Cellar
The Clown and the Automobile
The Clown with the Portable Body
The Darktown Comedians Trip to Paris
The Double Magician and the Magical Head
Gibson, the Eccentric American Actor
Going to Bed Under Difficulties
Herrmann, the Great Conjuror
The History of a Crime
The Magical Hen
The Magician and the Human Pump
Troubles in a Tenement House
What Happened to the Inquisitive Janitor
Wonderful Feats of Vivisection
The Wonderful Hair Restorer
May 3 Blue Beard
Oct 4 A Trip to the Moon
Nov [day undetermined]
The Abbe and the Colonel
Allegorical Procession
Arrival of Major Marchand from the Soudan
An Automobile Parade in the Tuilleries Gardens
Beautifyl Beaulieu
The Bon Vivant
Bridge of Alexander III
Captain Dreyfus
The Champs Elysees
The Children of the Czar
A Dance by Kanaka Indians
A Dog's Cemetery
A French Bicycle Corps
French Boxers
From Monte Carlo to Monaco
George J. Marck and His Lions
The Giant Constantin
The India-Rubber Man
Jo Jo, the Dog Faced Boy
King Edward VII at the Birthday Celebration of the King of Denmark
The Longchamps Palace
A Mis-Adventure
Mr. Oldsport's Umbrella
M. Le Comte De Dion
The Old Port of Marseilles
On the Marseilles Tramway
Oom Paul
Paris Exposition
A Parisian Ballet
Prize-Winning Trip of the Santos-Dumont Airship No. 6
Promenade of the Kings
Rulers of Half the World
Ten Minutes at Monte Carlo
The Train to Villefranche
The Valiant Pig
A Water Carnival
"Zip"
Nov 1 Ali Baba and the Forty Thieves

1903 [month undetermined]
Beggar's Dream
Black Magic
The Bridegroom's Dilemma
The Cabinet Trick of the Davenport Brothers
Christ Walking on the Water
The Famous Box Trick
Going to Bed Under Difficulties
The Infernal Meal
The Last Cartridges
The Lightning Change Artist
A Lively Cock Fight
A Maiden's Paradise
A Midnight Episode
The Seven Capital Sins
Summoning the Spirits
The Up-to-Date Spiritualism
Jan [day undetermined]
Andre at the North Pole
The Artist's Model
Bathing Horses
Boulevard St. Denis, Paris, France
Bullet vs. Whiskey
Cagliostro's Mirror
Climbing the Greasy Pole
Fantastic Dining Room
Hunting White Bear
Jewelry Robbery
Jolly Monks
Massage Treatment
The Philosopher's Stone
Pygmalion and Galatea
Quadrille in Drawers
Skating Scene
Snowballing
Spanish Dance
The Three Bacchantes
What Was Found in a High Hat
Jan 17 Picture Hanging Extraordinary
Jan 31 The Magical Egg
Wonderful Suspension and Evolution
Feb [day undetermined]
Cadet's First Smoke
The Human Fly
The Impossible Feat of Balancing
The Magician and the Imp
Mephistopheles' School of Magic
Santos Dumont's Airship
Twentieth Century Conjuring
Up-to-Date Surgery
Feb 14 Disagreeable Railroad Passengers
Mar 7 Robinson Crusoe
Mar 14 Buying a Baby
Apr [day undetermined]
Artist and the Dummy
Bachelor's Paradise
Bewitched Dungeon
The Brahmin and the Butterfly
Conjurer and 100 Tricks
Gigantic Devil
The House of Mystery
How He Missed His Train
The Long and Short of It
Miracles of Brahmin
The Miser
The Sorcerer, Prince and the Good Fairy
What Befell the Inventor's Visitor
Apr 11 Acrobatic Sisters Daines
Apr 13 Gulliver's Travels
May [day undetermined]
The Angler
Modern House Furnishing Methods
New Bull Fight
Resourceful Waiter
Window Cleaner's Mishap
May 16 The Gambler's Crime
Smiles and Tears
Jun 6 Little Tom Thumb
Jun 13 Beelzebub's Daughters
The Cake Walk Infernal
The Enchanted Basket
The Marvelous Wreath
Misfortune Never Comes Alone
The Mysterious Box
The Queen's Musketeers
Jun 27 The Enchanted Well
The Inn Where No Man Rests
Jul 11 Sleeping Beauty
Jul 25 The Drawing Lesson; or, The Living Statue
The Mystical Flame
The Witch's Revenge
Aug 15 The Melomaniac
The Monster
The Oracle of Delphi

A Spiritualistic Photographer
Sep 5 The Fairyland; or, The Kingdom of the Fairies
Sep 19 Pope Pius X [His Election and the Procession]
Sep 26 The Apothicareric Grotto
The Pigeons, Place St. Marc, Venice
Oct [day undetermined]
Ballet of the Nations
Oct 17 The Apparition
The Infernal Caldron
Nov [day undetermined]
Alcrofrisbas, the Master Magician
Nov 7 Jack Jaggs & Dum Dum
Jupiter's Thunderbolts
Life of Napoleon
10 Ladies in an Umbrella
Nov 21 Bob Kick, the Mischievous Kid
Extraordinary Illusions
Dec 9 The Ballet Master's Dream
Dec 12 The Damnation of Faust
Jack and Jim
Dec 19 The Magic Lantern
1904 [month undetermined]
Algerian Goums in the Desert
Bull Fight with Matadors Senor Don Luis Mazzantini and Bombita
Clowns
Cook's Joke
Engineers, French Army
Frivolity
Gavotte
Herring Fishing on French Coast
Highwaymen
The Interrupted Couple
Japanese Coaling a Man-of-War
Japanese Infantry Morning Drill
The Mischievous Kid, the Duck and the Gendarme
Mysterious Clock
Panoramic View of Chamonix, Alps
Panoramic View of La Mure, France
Panoramic View of Montreux, Switzerland
The Policeman's Mistake
Preparing the Codfish After the Catch
Secret Procession of the Algerian Tribes
Toys Competition
Trained Dogs
The Up-to-Date Wizard
View of "La Croisette," Cannes, France
Working in the Charcoal Mines in France
Jan 2 William Tell
Jan 9 The Terrible Turkish Executioner
Jan 16 A Burlesque Highway Robbery in "Gay Paree"
Puss in Boots
Jan 23 Amusing Changes
Charming Enchantment
A Moonlight Serenade; or, The Miser Punished.
Jan 30 Dogs and Rats
Feb 6 Devil's Pot
The Little Greedy Beggar
Marie Antoinette
Metamorphosis of the King of Spades
The Midgets
Tit for Tat; or, A Good Joke on My Head
Feb 13 Every Man His Own Cigar Lighter
The Invisible Sylvia
A Wager Between Two Magicians; or, Jealous of Myself
Mar 5 The Bewitched Trunk
The Fugitive Apparitions
The Untamable Whiskers
Mar 12 Babe and Dog
The Clock Maker's Dream
Scenes on Every Floor
Mar 26 Benvenuto Cellini; or, A Curious Evasion
The Imperceptible Transmutations
A Miracle Under the Inquisition
The Passion Play
Wonderful Hair Restorer
Apr [day undetermined]
How to Disperse the Crowd
Pierrot, Murderer
Apr 2 Faust and Marguerite
Apr 9 Living Dummy
The Revolving Table
Apr 25 The Prodigal Son
Samson and Delilah
Apr 30 The Jolly Russian Prophets
Tchin-Chao, the Chinese Conjuror
May 7 The Wonderful Living Fan
May 21 Barnum's Trunk
May 28 Fishing in Newfoundland—French Shore
Our Jolly French Students
The Restive Chicken
Typical Algerian 'Ouled Nails' Muslin Dance
Jun [day undetermined]
The Magic Hat
Jun 4 The Cook in Trouble
The Devilish Plank
Jun 18 A Disagreeable Remedy
European Idea of Christopher Columbus Discovering America
The Impossible Dinner
The Lyons Mail
Metamorphosis of a Butterfly
A Scandal on the Staircase
Jul [day undetermined]
Barber's Revenge
Giovanni and His Trained Parrots
Japanese Varieties
Jul 2 Don Quixote
The Mermaid
Jul 16 Mischances of a Drunkard
The Providence of the Waves; or, The Dream of a Poor Fisherman
Jul 23 Annie's Love Story
The Barber of Seville
Dance Plastiques
Japanese Ambush
The Nest Robbers
Tour in Italy
Jul 30 Uncle Rube's Birthday
Aug 20 Lookout at Port Arthur
Aug 27 A Boar Hunt
Orla and His Trained Dogs
Sep 3 Falls of the Rhine
Indians and Cowboys
The Strike
The Wrestling Donkey
Sep 10 Ghezzi and His Circus
Joseph Sold by His Brothers
Sep 24 The Devil's Seven Castles
Drama in the Air
The Fairy of the Spring
Fox and Rabbits
A Gambler's Quarrel
A Good Story
Ice Cream Eater
Quo Vadis
Ruffian's Dance
Oct [day undetermined]
Advance Guard Fight
Alarm
Alcohol and Its Victims
Amphitrite
Arabian Phantasia
Around Port Arthur (No. 2)
Arrival and Departure of a Train
Arrival of a Train
Attack on a Fortress
Attack on a Train
A Bad Rich Man
Battleship Leaving Harbor
The Bear and the Sentinel
The Bird Charmer
Boy's First Smoke
Bride Retiring
The Brothers Laure
Bullocks Swimming
Cakewalk
Capture of a Gun
Cavalry Crossing a River
Cavalry Fording a Stream
Charging Cuirassiers
Charley's Aunt
Cloth Dealer
Convoy of Oxen
Dance of the Sylphs
Death of Robert McCaire and Bertrand
Dranem Salutes the Audience
Drunkard and Statue
Eccentric Tight-rope Walker
Eccentric Waltz
Elephants at Work in India
The Enchanted Wardrobe
Extraordinary Fishing
Fairy of the Black Rocks
Fairy of the Lake
The False Cripple
Fire! Fire!
Flea
Gate Jumping by Unsaddled Horse
Grandma's Glass
Grinning Guillot
A Heavy Sea
Hedge Jumping
Honeymoon Trip
Horse Tied to a Post Jumping
The Illusionist
Impossible to Get a Plunge
Iroquois Theatre Fire in Chicago
Japanese Dance
Japanese Girls at Tea
Jumping Horses
Kickapoo
Kissing in a Tunnel
Ladies of the Court Bathing
Lahury, the Soldier
Living Statues; or, Marble Comes to Life
Looping the Loop
Masks and Faces
Mind! Madame Is Coming
Modern High School Riding
Mysterious Screen
Naval Fight
No Posters Allowed
Outpost Skirmishing
Painter's Misfortune
Passing Trains
Pedestrian Jugglers
Pole Jumping
The Porter's Horrible End
Rolling Bridge in Tunis
Russian Cavalry
Russian Dance
Russian Infantry
Scenes from My Balcony
The Shadowy Lady
The Shower Bath
Sisters Barrison
Soap Bubbles
A Sorcerer's Night
Spy's Arrest
Spy's Execution
Startling Pursuit
The Statue Dealer
Street in Canton, China
Street in Tokio
Swimming Horses
Too Hot
Too Late
Up-to-Date Burglars; or, The Mystified Cops
Vision of Art
Water Shoots
A Wedding of Correspondence
Woman's Bath
The Young Farmer Girl
Oct 1 Across the Alps
Dogs and Cats
The Opera Hat
Park in Barcelona by Moonlight
Smoker Too Small
Oct 8 Around Port Arthur
Fantastic Fishing
A Fight on the Yalu
Oct 15 Ascending Mount Pilate
Bathers at Joinville
Greedy Cat
Oct 22 The Animated Costumes
Behind the Lens
The Clever Baker
Disagreeable Five O'Clock
In a Hurry to Catch the Train
Mistake in the Door
Simple Simon's Surprise Party
Oct 29 An Impossible Voyage
Trained Hogs
Nov 12 August, the Monkey
A Princess in Disguise
Nov 19 A Cheeky Traveler
Dec [day undetermined]
The Firefall
The Grotto of Surprises
The Wandering Jew
Dec 3 From Christiania to the North Cape
Saluting the Flag
Dec 10 The Astonishing Frame
The Wonderful Rose Tree
Dec 24 Babies Bathing
Burglars at Work
Christmas Angel
His First Hunting Day
Louis XIV
Pilgrimage to Lourdes
Solomon's Judgment
The Swing
Vintage
Dec 31 Russian Antisemitic Atrocities

1905 [month undetermined]
The Angler's Nightmare
Different Hair Dresses
A Little Jules Verne
Love at Each Floor
Out Boating
Jan 14 Big Fountain at Versailles
Christmas, 1904
Wonderful Beehive
Wrestler and Bull
Feb 4 Fireworks
Innocent Flirtation
Prompting Phonograph
Feb 25 Bewitched Lover
From Cairo to the Pyramids
Last Attack on the Hill
Riots in St. Petersburg
Surrender at Port Arthur
Mar 4 Modern Style House Maids
Mar 11 Gluttonous Negro
Mar 25 Assassination of the Grand Duke Serge
The Nihilists in Russia
Apr 1 Winter Sports
Apr 8 Cards and Crime
The Incendiary
The King of Sharpshooters
The Living Playing Cards
The Sign of the Cross
Apr 22 The Black Imp
May 13 The Crystal Casket
The Lilliputian Minuet
The Moon-Lover
May 27 A Father's Honor
Jun 10 In the Mining District
Jun 17 A Mesmerian Experiment
Jun 24 Christian Martyrs
The Palace of the Arabian Nights
Jul 1 King of Dollars
A Pleasure Trip
Jul 15 The Gun License
Jul 22 Mr. Dauber and the Whimsical Picture
The Young Tramps
Jul 29 Great Steeplechase
Aug 5 The Chloroform Fiends
Mutiny on Man-of-War in Odessa
The Venetian Looking-Glass
Aug 19 An Adventurous Automobile Trip
Modern Brigandage
Aug 26 The Vendetta
Sep 16 Life of Moses
Sep 23 A Crazy Composer
Creusot's Metallurgy
The Enchanted Sedan-Chair
Sep 30 Countryman in Paris
Flower Fairy
Gay Washerwoman
Impatient Customer
Language of Flowers
Loie Fuller
Stunning Creations
Wonderful Album
Oct [day undetermined]
The Cheated Policeman
Chimney Sweep and Pastry Cook
Life Saving Up-to-Date
The Scheming Gambler's Paradise
Oct 14 Behind the Stage
A Henpecked Husband
Ill Rewarded Conjuror
The Vicar's Garden Party
Oct 28 The Tower of London
Nov [day undetermined]
"Clown Sidney on Stilts"
Defense of a Pagoda
Defense of Port Arthur
"A Frightful Night"
Horses Jumping over a Wall
The King and Queen of Italy in Paris
Pillow Fight
Russian Artillery
A Street in Lourdes
Through the Keyhole
Tight-Rope Walker Undressing
Turkish Atrocities in Macedonia
Yantai Episode
Nov 4 An Impracticable Journey
The Mysterious Island
The Pastry Cook's Practical Jokes
Unexpected Fireworks
Zoological Garden
Nov 25 Rip's Dream
Dec 9 The Hen with the Golden Eggs
Love Is Ingenious
The Postman's Christmas Box
Dec 16 Alcoholism Engenders Tuberculosis
Ceylon
Christmas Miracle
A Tragedy at Sea
Dec 23 The Christmas Goose
Disagreeable Mistake
A Great Discovery
The Photographing Bear
The Three Phases of the Moon
Dec 30 Custom House Search
Misadventures of a Hat

1906 [month undetermined]
Punch and Judy
Jan 6 The Tramp
Jan 13 The Bicycle Robber
Robbers of Children
Jan 20 Fire Cascades
The Wolf's Trap
Jan 27 The Deserter
The Opium Smoker's Dream
Feb 3 Socialism and Nihilism
Feb 10 Beware of My Husband
Tragedy in a Train
Feb 17 Tit-for-Tat
Victims of the Storm
Feb 24 The Heart Governs the Head
The Inventor Crazybrains and His Wonderful Airship
The Last Witch
Mar 3 Chimney Sweep
Mar 17 Another's Crime
Ascending Mt. Serrat in Spain
Descending Mt. Serrat in Spain
Engadin in Switzerland
I've Lost My Eyeglasses
Passing Trains
Street in Agra, India
Thibidado
A Trip from Naples to Vesuvius, Showing the Volcano in Action
A Trip Through the Island of Ceylon
Mar 31 A Boarding School Conspiracy
Apr [day undetermined]
The Absent-Minded Shoe Black
Acrobatic Elephant
Aerial Billiard Playing
Apaches in Paris
At Mukden
Baby's Bath
Bad Coffee
Bad Joke
Bad Lodgers
Bath of Sacred Elephants
Bird's Eye View of Paris
Boats on the Nile
Bull Fight
Captain's Inspection
Childish Tricks Baffled
Children's Quarrel
Clown's Revenge
Coal Man's Bath
Compromising Spots
Confession
A Courageous Husband
Dancing Sentry Box
Doorkeeper's Curiosity
Dranem's Dream
Drunkard
The Enchanted Melon
False Alarm
Fantastic Diver
First Night Out
Flying Machine
Frog Fishing
Funny Shave
Gaieties of Divorce
Good Pipe
Great Ballet
Hairdresser's Victim
Haunted House
A Heavy Sea
High Sea Fishing
Improvised Suit
In the Polar Regions
The Indiscreet Bathroom Maid
Indiscreet Mystified
Infernal Cave
Ingenious Dauber
Insolvable Guests
Irascible Fisherman
Jack the Bootblack
Japanese Soldier's Return
Joys of Marriage
Kids' Practical Jokes
Lady Undressing
Life on Board Ship
Liliputian Dance
Love Letter
Man with 36 Heads
Matrimonial Agency
Miniature Theatre
Motor-car and Cripple
Nautical Fancy
Nautical Game
Negro and Policeman
Neighbor's Lamp
Obstacle Jumping by Attached Horses
Obstinate Drunkard
Old Seducer
Pasha's Nightmare
Penny Milk
Phantom's Guard
Phenomenal Hen
Pierrot's Revenge
Practical Conjuror
Prince of Wales in India
Pussy's Breakfast
Remorse
Retaking a Fort
Revolution in Russia
Robbers Robbed
Room, Please
St. Bartholomew's Day
Sardine Fishing
Scenes of Convict Life
Scholar's Breakfast
Schoolboys' Practical Jokes
Ski Running
Sock
Stupendous Jugglers
Surgical Operation
Temptation of St. Anthony
Ten Wives for One Husband
Terrible Anguish
Topsy-Turvy Dance
Touching Pleading
Trained Bears
Troublesome Fishbone
Tunisian Dance
Two Drunkards
Unforeseen Meeting
Virtue Rewarded
Voice of Conscience
War of Children
When the Masters Are Out
Whence Does He Come?
Where Is My Horse?
The Wig
Young Apple Thief
Apr 7 The Maestro Do-Mi-Sol-Do
A Mix-Up in the Gallery
The Starvelings
Apr 14 Carnival Night
History of a Pair of Trousers
The Invisible Man
Jewel Robbers Mystified
Living Flowers
Old and New Style Conjurors
Apr 21 Hello! Hello! Grinder
Life in India
Spontaneous Generation
Apr 28 Monte Carlo to Monaco
Playing Truant
May [day undetermined]
Dance of Geishas
May 5 A Desperate Crime
Law of Pardon
May 12 A Shooting Expedition Accident
The Wig Chase
May 19 A Childish Match
May 26 My Hat
The Olympian Games†
Jun 2 Ephemeral Wealth
Escaped from the Cage
Mrs. Brown's Bad Luck
Jun 16 A Detective's Trip Around the World
The Holiday
Three Cent Leeks
The Troubles of a Fireman
Jun 23 The Angler's Dream
I Fetch the Bread
Marriage of Princess Ena and Alphonse XIII, King of Spain
The Rajah's Casket
The Riderless Bicycle
Jun 30 Who Looks, Pays
Jul 7 The Elections
Follower of Women
A Strange Engagement Bouquet
The Target
Jul 14 Butterfly Catching
Corsican Chastisement
Dogs Used as Smugglers
Extraordinary Dislocation
Honor Is Satisfied
The Tramp and the Mattress Maker
The Troublesome Flea

Jul 21 The Hilarious Posters
Rival Brothers
Jul 28 Letters Which Speak
Aug [day undetermined]
Pals; or, My Friend, the Dummy
Aug 11 Voyage Around a Star
Aug 18 Fayet-Chamonix: Trip on the New Trolley Line from Le Fayet-St. Gervais to Chamonix
From Menton to Nice
Les Gorges du Fier
Perefitte to Luz
Aug 25 The Paris-Bordeaux Auto Race
Playmates†
Sep 8 The Paris Students
Sep 22 The Accordion
Sep 29 A Spiritualistic Meeting
The Tenacious Cat
Oct 6 A Road Side Inn
Soap Bubbles
Oct 13 Custom Officials Bewitched
Fun After the Wedding
Ill Rewarded Honesty
Indian's Revenge
Mephisto's Son
The Merry Frolics of Satan
New Brother
Nov 3 The Bell Ringer's Daughter
Nov 24 An Artist's Dream
Caught in a Trap
Colonel's Bicycle
The Inexperienced Chauffeur
The Poor Tutor
A Seaside Flirtation
Travels of a Barrel
Dec 1 The Cab
Cross Country
Day in the Country
Honesty's Strange Reward
The Magic Flute
Man Without Scruple
Old Man's Darling
Poor Mother
The Rebellious Walking Stick
Stealing Tomatoes
The Telescope
The Troubadour
Village Witch
Dec 8 At the Seaside
Child's Revenge
Difficult Problem
Japanese Sports
Love's Thermometer
Magic Roses
Dec 15 Alladin and His Wonder Lamp
Bobby and His Family
Desperate Girl
The Female Spy
In Search of Adventure
The Mysterious Retort
The Poacher
Dec 20 The Witch
1907 [month undetermined]
Bakers in Trouble
Botanist's Misadventures
Delirium in a Studio
Jan [day undetermined]
Beaver Hunt†
Cheating Justice†
Deer Hunt†
The Little Globe Trotter†
Making Champagne†
Reformation†
The Stepmother
Trial Trip of the Airship "La Patrie"†
Whale Fishing†
Jan 5 Life of Christ
Jan 12 Between Two Fires
Cousin's Visit
Exciting Honeymoon Trip
Fine Birthday Cake
Forbidden Fruit
Friendship Better Than Riches
Gibelot's Hotel
Hot Chestnuts
Hypnotized Police Inspector
Life in Congo
My Wife's Birthday
Niagara Falls
Paris Slums
Pay Day
Saved by a Melon
Scales of Justice
Six Amorous Dragoons
Skating Lessons
Sportsmen and Lion
Strange Mount
Susan Tastes Our Wine
Tragic Wedding
Unexpected Meal
Venetian Tragedy
Wedding on Bicycles
Jan 19 Attempted Suicide
Cabby by the Hour
A Colored Man's Revenge
Crime on the Railroad
Little Blind Girl
Jan 26 Bad Mother
Fan in Japan
The Gypsies
Infants at Breakfast
Joined Lips
Misadventures of a Negro King in Paris
An Officer's Honor
Professor in Difficulties†
Servant's Strike
Stormy Winds Do Blow†
Wrestler's Wife
Wrestling Matches of 1906
Feb [day undetermined]
Animated Stamp Pad†
Baby Cries†
The Bad Son†
Burglar and Policeman†
Going Away for Holiday†
His First Cigarette†
Indian Customs†
Man Who Hangs Himself†
The Miner's Daughter†
Moonlight on the Ocean†
My Master's Coffee Service†
My Servant Is a Jewel†
My Wife's Birthday†
A New Toboggan†
Policeman Has an Idea†
Skiing in Norway†
Snowballing†
Soldier to Colonel†
Stolen Child†
Two Rival Peasants†
When Friends Meet†
Winter in Switzerland†
Wrestling Match, Hackenschmidt†
Feb 2 Carnival at Venice†
College Boy's First Love
Faces and Grimaces
The Little Rascal's Tricks
Playing a Trick on the Gardener†
Playing Truant†
Two Cabbies for One Passenger
The Underworld of Paris†
Wanted, a Governess
The Zoo at London, Part I†
The Zoo at London, Part II†
Feb 9 Bobby and His Balloon
The Charmer
Constructed Fishing Boat
Determined Creditor
False Coiners
For Mother's Birthday
Forbidden Sport
In the Cause of Faith
India Rubberman
Julia at the Barracks
Old Mashers
Policeman's Little Run
Spot at the 'Phone
Feb 16 Cavalry School
Difficult Arrest
Phial of Poison
Rat Catching
Robert Macaire and Bertrand; or, The Troubles of a Hobo and His Pal, in Paris
Sea by Moonlight
Two Little Scamps
Feb 23 The Pork Butcher's Nightmare
Mar [day undetermined]
Cassimir's Night Out†
The Electric Belt
His First Dinner at Father-in-Law's†
Little Lord Mayor†
Looking for Lodgings†
Mrs. Smithson's Portrait†
Moonlight on Lake†
Woman Up-to-Date†
Mar 2 The Birthday Celebration†
The Clever Thief
Little Tich
A Set of Dishes†
Mar 9 The Murderer†
Mar 16 Ascending Mt. Blanc
Cinderella
Hooligans of the Far West
The Life and Passion of Christ
Suicide Impossible
Tommy at Play
The Yawner
Mar 30 The Carving Doctor†
Flirting on the Sands†
The Jota
The Mischievous Sketch
Napoleon and Sentry†
An Old Coat Story†
Parody on Toreador†
Take Good Care of Baby†
Apr [day undetermined]
Curious Carriage of Klobenstein†
How the World Lives†
In a Picture Frame†
Picnic Hampers†
Tirolean Dance†
Apr 13 Street in Frankfort
Apr 20 Chasing a Sausage†
Rogues' Tricks
The Terrorist's Remorse†
Apr 27 Amateur Photographer
The Baby's First Outing
Boxing Matches in England
Clowns and Statue†
From Jealousy to Madness
Golden Beetle
Herring Fishing
Japanese Women
A Military Prison
Picturesque Canada
Pompeii
The Smugglers†
Tragic Rivalry
Wonderful Flames
May 4 The Skipping Cheeses
May 11 The Hundred Dollar Bill; or, The Tramp Couldn't Get It Changed†
May 18 Barometer of Love
Clever Detective
Cream Eating Contest
Interesting Reading
Kind-Hearted Girl
Robbing a Bird's Nest
Stealing Candies
Trouble at a Wedding
May 25 Beating the Landlord†
Buying a Ladder†
Catastrophe in the Alps†
A Child's Cunning†
The Cup and Ball†
Dog and the Tramp†
Janitor's Tea Party
Nurse Takes a Walk†
Rogie Falls and Salmon Fishing†
Salome†
Sign of the Times†
Two Cents Worth of Cheese†
The Village Celebration†
Jun 1 Anything to Oblige
Artful Husband
Betrothed's Nightmare
Blind Man's Dog
Brigand Story
Cowboys and Red-skins
Distress
Haunted Kitchen
Horrible Adventure
The Human Clock†
An Icy Day†
Julius, the Sandwich Man
Lawyer Enjoys Himself
Looking for Lodgings
Mines and Forge at Decazeville
Modern Burglars
A Perfect Nuisance†
To Tame His Wife
A Trip Through the Holy Land†
Winter Amusements†
Jun 10 Dressing in a Hurry†
The Faithful Dog; or, True to the End†
Saved from the Wreck†
The Substitute Drug Clerk†
Jun 15 Biker Does the Impossible
Costumes of Different Centuries
Dog Police
How Bridget's Lover Escaped
Poor Coat
Servant's Vengeance
Straw Hat Factory in Florence
Washings Badly Marked
Weird Fancies
Whose Hat Is It?†
Jun 22 Moving Under Difficulties†
She Won't Pay Her Rent†

Jun 24 Shoeing the Mail Carrier†
Jun 25 The Amateur Rider†
Mother-in-Law at the White City
Jun 26 The Legless Runner†
The Toilet of an Ocean Greyhound†
Jun 27 The Near-Sighted Cyclist
Jun 29 Alps of Chamonix
A Carmen in Danger
Charley Paints
Crime in the Mountains
Frolics of Ding Dong Imps
A Hooligan Idea
Mother-in-Law's Race
Nervous Kitchenmaid
No More Children
Palmistry
A Slave's Love
Struggle for Life
Tragic Moment
Under the Seas
Jul 6 Diabolo, the Japanese Top Spinner†
Jul 8 The Soldier's Helmet
Union Workers Spoil the Food
Jul 13 Drama on the Riviera
Life's Reality
A New Death Penalty
Quick, I'm on Fire
Seaman's Widow
Woodchopper's Daughter
Jul 20 The Dog Acrobats†
Don't Pay Rent—Move†
Drama in a Spanish Inn†
Harlequin's Story
Magic Drawing Room
Prisoner's Escape†
Sambo as Footman
Servant's Generosity†
Too Stout†
Unlucky Interference†
Victim of Science
Jul 27 Chasing a Motorist
Diabolo
Drawing Teacher†
Dunhard After All
Genevieve of Brabant
Lighthouse Keepers
Looking for the Medal†
The Poacher's Daughter†
Sham Beggars
Troubles of a Cook
Tunneling the English Channel
Vengeance of the Algerine
Window Cleaner
Aug 3 Buying a Donkey†
The Express Sculptor
A Kind Grandfather
Ostrich Farm
Poor Little Mites
Aug 10 Angling in Norway
The Dancing Swine
Discipline and Humanity
The Dummy†
First Success
From Barrel to Barrel
From Cairo to Khartoum†
A Glorious Start
The Gypsies; or, The Abduction†
The Helmet†
Life Boat Manoeuvres†
Life in a South African Gold Mine†
Looking at a Balloon†
A Lucky Heiress
The Magnetized Man
Spring Gardening†
Torpedo Attack on H. M. S. Dreadnought†
Aug 17 A Case of Arson
Cock Fight in Seville
The New Stag Hunt†
Poor but Proud†
The Red Spectre
The Servant Hypnotist
The Smoking Chimney
Aug 24 A Big Take of Tunny Fish†
The Blacksmith's Strike
Chrysanthemums
The Dervish's Revenge†
In an Armchair†
Nurses' Strike
Robber Robbed
Spanish Views, on Postals
Too Many Children
The Tooth Ache†
Wandering Willie's Luck†
Aug 31 Children's Reformatory
Half Caste's Revenge
I'll Dance the Cakewalk
Lost Umbrella
Modern Painters
Rival Sisters
Three Chatterboxes
Sep 7 The Bewildering Cabinet
A Drink!
Englishman in Harem
Irish Scenes and Types†
Knowing Dogs
Life in a Burmah Teak Forest†
The Life of Bee†
The Living Silhouette
A Modern Mother†
Mount Pilatus Railway†
Private Atkins Minds the Baby
Rail Lying at Crewe†
The Romance of a Singer
The Strength of Cheese†
Sep 14 At the Colonial Exhibition
Cambodian Customs
A Daring Maid
The Good Wine†
In Sevilla
The Two Fowls
Unlucky Substitution
Who Owns the Pear?
Sep 16 Absent Mindedness†
The Amateur Hunter†
Art Student's Frivolities†
The Fly†
Roumania, Its Citizens and Soldiers†
Woodcutter's Daughter†
Sep 21 The Blacksmith's Revenge
Charley's Dream
Dieppe Circuit
The Eclipse; or, The Courtship of the Sun and the Moon
The Fortune
Interrupted Card Party
A Pair of Boots, Please
Policeman's Boots
Wood Industry in Canada
Sep 23 Amongst the Reptiles†
Carl Hagenbeck's Wild Animal Park at Hamburg, Germany†
Dogs Tracking Burglars†
A First Class Restaurant†
Uncle's Heritage†
Winan's Horses†
Wipe Off Your Feet, Please†
Sep 26 The Persevering Lover†
Sep 28 The Adventuress
Enchanted Glasses
Indian Idyll
Maniac Juggler
Our Band's Going to the Competition
Poor Pig
Stilt Race
Sep 30 Coffee Plantation†
Tamer Hopkins†
Oct 1 A Doctor's Conscience†
Fisherman's Luck†
The Great Victoria Falls†
Oct 5 Highwaymen
Late for His Wedding†
Returning Good for Evil†
Riding School
Oct 7 The Foster Cabby†
Madame Goes Shopping†
Slavery by Circumstance†
Tyrolean Alps in the Winter†
A Would Be Champion†
Oct 12 Asking His Way†
Chopin's Funeral March, Burlesqued
Easter Eggs
The Heart's Bidding
The Japanese Girl
Making Pottery in Japan
The Prodigal Son
William, the Poacher
Oct 14 Crazed by a Fad†
Farmer Giles' Geese†
Rubberneck Reuben†
Oct 19 The Cigar Box
Clever Tailor
A Drama in Seville
Jane Is Furious
Jealousy Punished†
Naples to Vesuvius
Save the Pieces
A Story of Eggs
There Is a Rat in the Room†
West Africa
Oct 26 Andalusian Dances
Brain Storm
Burglary by Motor
A Crime in the Snow
Dog Avenges His Master
Hamlet, Prince of Denmark
Her First Bike Ride
Ice Cutting in Sweden
Magic Lantern
Making Love to the Coalman's Wife
My Mother-in-Law Is an Angel
Pleasant Thoughts
A Quiet Hotel
Red Riding Hood
Satan at Play
Tommy in Society
The Two Orphans
An Unpleasant Legacy
Wonderful Lion Killer
Oct 28 The Athletic Dude†
De Beers Diamond Mines, Kimberly, S.A.†
An Episode of the Paris Commune
Floor Polisher
A Four Year Old Heroine†
The Glue†
The Irresistible Piano
Naval Manoeuvres†
Onions Make People Weep†
Picturesque Brittany†
Smoke Without Fire†
The Thieving Umbrella†
Through Hong Kong†
Towed by an Automobile†
Volunteer's Betrothal†
Who Has Stolen My Bicycle†
Nov 2 Shakespeare Writing "Julius Caesar"
Nov 4 An Anonymous Letter†
A Good Husband†
The Lost Bass Drum; or, Where Is That Louie?†
Raising the Wind†
The White Shoes; or, Looking Out for His Banknote†
A Wig Made To Order†
Nov 9 The Elixir of Life
Good Glue Sticks
The Mysterious Armor
The Night Watchman
A Pressing Letter
Seek and You Shall Find...Trouble
Swedish Sports
Tunny Fisheries in Sicily
Nov 11 A Rolling Bed
The Stolen Shoes†
Nov 14 The Bomb
Grandfather and the Kitten†
Turning the Tables†
Nov 16 Sightseeing Through Whiskey
Nov 23 Airship Thieves
Ali Baba and the Forty Thieves
Artistic Woodcarver
The Baboon
Chemist's Mistake
Cripple's Duel
The Cupboard
Enchanted Pond
Inexhaustible Barrel
Innkeeper and Wife
The Innkeeper's Wife
Little Conjuror
Mysterious Boudoir
The Pirates
The Plank
Satan in Prison
Tippler's Race
Nov 30 Bad Boy's Joke†
The Clock-Maker's Secret
The Colonial Soldier
Comrade Rations†
Daughter's Lover in Difficulties†
Economical Trip
A Forester Made King
French Recruit
Master in General
Misadventures of a Street Singer†
Modern Hercules at Work
Simple-Minded Peasant†
Stolen Child's Career†
The Tattler†
Unlucky Trousers†
Ups and Downs of a Hat
Wood Industry in Norway
Your Wife Is Unfaithful to Us
Dec [day undetermined]
Against the Law†
An Angelic Servant
Bulgarian Army†
Cabman Mystified†
The Cashier†
Deaf and Dumb†

Hatred†
Highly Scented Bouquet†
Love Levels All Ranks†
Willing to Oblige
Dec 2 Darkest Hour†
Harvest Celebration†
Wrong Righted†
Dec 7 Bobby's Practical Jokes
Doings of a Maniac
An Exciting Ride
The Pearl Fisher
The Poor Old Couple
Dec 9 Notice to Quit†
Saving His Country's Flag†
Sunday with the Boss†
Dec 14 A Champion After All
Elephants in India
A Mother's Secret
Music, Forward!
Sailor's Practical Joke
A Super's Debut
Up to Date Burglars
Dec 21 The Daily Life of a French Sailor
Madam's Fancies
Manners and Customs of Australia
On the Grass
An Uncle by Marriage
Dec 23 Nurse's Travels†
A Red Hot Day†
The Romance of a Fisherman's Daughter†
The Waters of Life
Dec 28 The Bargeman's Child
The Black Witch
Blue Beard
Doings of a Poodle
Elegant Paris
The First Row
The Strong Man
The Talisman or Sheep's Foot
Thieves Caught in Their Own Trap
Thirteen at Table
Unknown Talent
The Witch Kiss
Wonderful Mirrors
Dec 30 Cook's Fiancé†
False Start†
A Tight Fix†

1908

Jan 4 Dog and His Various Merits
The Shrimper
The Tulips
Jan 6 The Affianced†
Buying a Cow
The Hypnotist's Pranks†
The Marvelous Powder†
Jan 11 Afraid of Microbes
Fatherhood and Drunkenness
Go, Little Cabin Boy
Lovers' Ill Luck
Military Tournament at Saumur
Jan 18 Adventures of an Overcoat
Bewitched Son-in-Law
The Diabolical Itching
First Cigar
Funny Faces Competition
Girl's Dream†
Going to Switzerland
Heavyweight's Race
In the Bogie Man's Cave
Ingenuity Conquers†
Kiri-Kis
The Knight of Black Art
Lady Doctor's Husband
Man Who Walks on the Water
Medal Winner†
Mr. Sleepy Head†
A Prince's Idea
Red Tapism
A Restful Ride†
Shipowner's Daughter
Tenor with Leather Lungs†
That Squally Beach
Valiant Son†
Witch's Secret
Jan 25 Animated Portraits
Charmed Sword
For a Flower
Good Luck for the Coming Year
The Hostage
A Kindhearted Gentleman
The King and the Jester
Picturesque Smyrna
The Pretty Typist
Skillful Policemen
Slave's Hate
Will He Overtake Them?
Feb 1 Dog's Music Hall
Excursion to Moon
A Gypsy's Revenge
London Streets
A Phlegmatic Gentleman
The Playful Tenant
Soldier's Antics
Feb 3 Ancient Headgear†
Gainsborough Hat†
Music Hath Charms†
The Scout†
Feb 8 Artistic Rag-Pickers
Flower of Youth
A Gamble for a Woman
The Good Luck of a "Souse"
The Runaway Horse
Sandwich Woman
Feb 10 The Strenuous War Veteran's Story†
Uncle's Clock†
Feb 15 Avenged by the Sea
Cabman's Delusion
Discharging the Maid
Electrocuted
Farman Aeroplane
Fire Maneuvers in Madrid
Forsaken
Incendiary Foreman
Making Charcoal
Man with Calf's Head
Mr. Shortsighted Goes Shrimping
Neapolitan's Revenge
Touaregs in Their Country
Feb 17 An Episode of the French Revolution†
Satan's Little Jaunt
Feb 22 Any Barrels to Sell?
I'm Mourning the Loss of Chloe
The Little Cripple
Scullion's Dream
Feb 29 Cruel Joke
Custom Officers Mystified
Hold-Up in Calabria
It Is Not the Cowl That Makes the Friar
Jerusalem
The One-Legged Man
Pierrot's Jealousy
Playing at Chess
Regattas in London
Troubles of a Grass Widower
Unlucky Old Flirt
Up-to-Date Removal
Mar 1 Launching the Roma
What a Razor Can Do
Mar 7 Betrayed by One's Feet
The Explosive Calf
The Mattress
Northern Venice
Only Thoughtlessness
A Statue on a Spree
A Workman's Honor
Mar 8 A Bewitching Woman
The Mummy
A New Way of Traveling
That Mother-in-Law Is a Bore
Mar 14 The Baby Show
Billy Is on Fire
A Briton's Promise
The Genii of Fire
In a Difficult Position
Lost, a Pretty Dog
Mr. and Mrs. Jollygood Go Tandeming
My Watch Is Slow
A Rape Under Louis XVI
Student's Joke on the Porter†
Suspicious Husband
Toula's Dream
Mar 15 Angel of the Village
The Frog
Mar 21 Beauty Parlors
The Devil's Three Sins
The Dream of an Opium Fiend
Engulfed in Quicksands
Gendarme Has a Keen Eye
A Good Joke
I Have Won a Pig
Orderly Jameson
The Vestal
Wedding in Brittany
Whimsical People
Mar 28 Avaricious Father
Different Ways of Smuggling
The Idler
Jim Gets a New Job
A Narrow Escape
Swedish Dances
Transformation of a Horse
Mar 29 A Modern Samson
The Waif
Apr 4 Amateur Acrobat
A Night with the Masqueraders in Paris
The Old Maid's Inheritance
What a Good Wine
Apr 5 Black Princess
Military Airship "Ville de Paris"
The Sacrifice
Sleeping Beauty
The Two Brothers
Apr 11 Antics of Two Spirited Citizens†
The Astrologer†
Boy and the Coalman
Champion Wrestling Bear
A Contagious Nervousness†
The Deserter
A Dislocated Veteran†
Doctor's Lunch†
The Dog's Scent
The Door-Keeper's Substitute
Dynamiters
The Enchanted Boots†
Free Admission
The Half-Moon Tavern†
A Lady Who Likes a Moustache†
Lion's Tilting Contest
Ma-in-Law Mesmerized†
The Novice Tight-Rope Walker†
The Professor's Secret†
Shanghai, China
Travels of a Flea
Trip to Norway†
The Videos
Wanted, a Maid
Apr 12 Champagne Industry
The Cossacks
Lottery Ticket
Modern Sculptors
Why That Actor Was Late
Will Grandfather Forgive?
Apr 18 The Accordion†
A Bear in the Flat†
Cider Industry
The Coal Man's Savings†
The Consequences of a Night Out
The Crusaders' Return†
The Drama on a Roof
The Enchanted Guitar†
Engaged Against His Will
False Money†
Hunchback Brings Luck
Improvised Servant
International Illusionist
Just Retribution
Love's Victim
The Miracle†
The Misadventures of an Equilibrist†
The Nomads
Peggy's Portrait
The Prophetess of Thebes
Railway Tragedy†
The Shepherd†
The Ski-ing Maniac†
The Spirit†
Thirsty Moving Men
Tony Has Eaten Garlic
Useful Present for a Child
A Visit to the Public Nursery
Woman's Forbearance
Youthful Treasure Seekers†
Apr 19 Christmas Eve
A Peaceful Inn
Apr 25 A Disastrous Oversight
A French Guard's Bride
Give Me Back My Dummy
Harry, the Country Postman
Long Distance Wireless Photography
A Miser's Punishment
A Mistaken Identity
The Poacher's Wife
A Poor Man's Romance
Under the Livery
Unwilling Chiropodist
Workman's Revenge
May 2 Alone at Last†
Biarritz†
Cat and Dog Show†
Clogmaking in Brittany
A Day in the Life of a Suffragette
Diabolical Pickpocket
Fiji Islanders†
For Kate's Health
Fox Hunting
Funeral of the Late King of Portugal†
The Hanging Lamp

Humanity Through Ages
In the Land of the Gold Mines
John Is No More a Child
Kidnapped by Gypsies†
Love's Sacrifice
Mandrel's Feats
Marvelous Pacifier†
Men and Women†
Mistaken Identity
Mr. Smith's Difficulties in the Shoe Store†
Mrs. Stebbins' Suspicions Unfounded†
Music Teacher
The Near-Sighted Hunter
The Outcast Heroine†
Oyster Farming†
The Pastry Cook
Poor Schoolmistress
A Ride in a Subway†
The Rival Lovers†
Ski Contest†
The Stolen Dagger†
The Sugar Industry†
Sweden
Tommy the Fireman†
A Useful Beard

May 9 The Bargee's Daughter
The Bargeman's Son
Bloodless Duel
Bogus Magic Powder†
The Boxing Englishman
Country About Rome†
Dreams and Realities
Each in His Turn
Environs of Naples†
The False Coin
Female Police Force
Gendarme's Honor
The Guileless Country Lassie†
Haunted Castle
In China (Hong Chu Fou)
In the Barber Shop
Indiscreetness of the Kinematograph
A Lover's Hazing
The Lover's Tribulation†
The Maid's Last Day
My Cabby Wife†
Spiritualistic Seance
Students' Jokes
Tommy Has the Spleen
The Two Guides†
The Two Rivals
The Wand Has Lost Its Magic

May 16 Always Too Late†
Artist's Inheritance
Australian Sports and Pastimes†
Awkward Orderly†
The Basket Maker's Daughter†
Bertie's Sweetheart†
A Bohemian Romance†
The Bond†
The Carnival at Nice
Chair, If You Please†
An Extraordinary Overcoat†
Fond of His Paper†
A Good Thief
Japanese Butterflies
Little Chimney Sweep
The Little Flower Girl†
Locked Up
Madam Is Capricious
The Magic Powder†
Meeting of Kings and Queens†
Motoring over the Alps†
Mountaineer's Son
Nobleman's Rights
Oscar's Elopement
The Perverse Statues
Pretty Dairymaid
Pretty Flower Girl
A Red Man's Justice†
Running for Office†
St. Patrick's Day in New York†
Schoolboy's Joke†
Stolen Boots†
Stolen Sausage
The Strong Man's Discretion†
These Gentlemen Are with Me†
Thirty Years After†
The Uncle from America
Why Smith Left Home†
The Winning Number†
The Young Protector†
Youthful Samaritan†

May 23 All for a Bird
Blind Woman's Story
Catholic Centennial Parade
End of a Dream
A Fake Diamond Swindler
Fashionable Hat
A Good Medicine
Imperial Canal
Justinian's Human Torches
Legend of a Ghost
Poverty and Probity
Unfortunate Pickpocket

May 30 Anti-Hair Powder
Around the Coast of Brittany
Artificial Preparation of the Diamond
Athletic Woman
Battle of Flowers in Nice
Burglar's New Trick
Carnival at Nice
A Complicated Duel
Expensive Marriage†
Fire! Fire!
Hedge Hog Coat†
Hide and Seek
In a Submarine
Inventor's Son's Downfall†
Lucky Accident
Magical Suit of Armor†
The Marriage of a French Soldier
A Mean Man†
The Minstrel's Sacrifice
Mischievous Diabolo
Mr. Farman's Airship†
An Occasional Porter
Oxford and Cambridge Boat Race†
The Persistent Beggar†
Red Man's Revenge†
River in Norway†
Steel Industry†
Story of a Foundling
Student's Predicament†
Unlucky Luck
Warsmen at Play†

Jun [day undetermined]
No Trifling with Love

Jun 6 Arabian Dagger
Don Juan
Family of Cats
Fish Preserving at Astrakhan
Justice of the Redskin
Lady Barrister
Mrs. Pimpernell's Gown
Tormented by His Mother-in-Law
Weird Symphony

Jun 13 Brazil—The Cascades
Cast Off by His Father†
The Cat's Revenge
Clarinet Solo†
Curiosity Punished
Drama in the Tyrol
Dynamite Duel
The Effective Hair Grower
Faithful Governess Rewarded†
Held for Ransom
Hunting Teddy Bears
Joyous Surprise
Magic Dice†
Messenger's Mistake
Misadventures of a Sheriff
The Miser
Music and Poetry
The Old Actor†
The Paralytic's Vengeance
Penniless Poet's Luck†
A Poor Knight and the Duke's Daughter†
The Ragpicker's Daughter
The Saloon-Keeper's Nightmare†
Side Show Wrestlers
A Tiresome Play
Tracked by the Police Dog
Up-to-Date Clothes Cleaning
Usefulness at an End†

Jun 20 Astrakhan Fisheries
Beatrice Cenci
The Book Agent†
Boston Normal School Pageant
Double Suicide
Driven by Hunger†
Grandfather's Pills
The Handy Man at Play†
The Little Peace-Maker
Lively Pranks with a Fake Python
The Matterhorn†
Music Which Hath No Charms†
The New Maid
Peculiar People
The Pony Express†
Poor Pussy
Ruffians Thrashed
A Russian Bear Hunt†
Swiss Peasants' Festival†
Tribulations of a Mayor†
A Trip on the Venetian Canals†
Unlucky Artist
Victim of His Honesty
The Viege Zermatt Railway†

Jun 27 The Fat Baby
For the Sake of a Crown
Magnetic Removal
Mr. Boozer Gets a Fright
Mysterious Flames
Nocturnal Thieves
Our Dog Friends
Troublesome Theft
Walks in Soudan

Jul [day undetermined]
Love and Molasses

Jul 4 Ancient Rome†
A Bird of Freedom†
The Blackmailer
Blessing the Boats in Arcachon†
Bull Fight in Arcachon†
Busy Fiancé
The Closing Hour
Constantinople
The Country of the "Bogoudens"
The Dressmaker's Surprise†
The Dreyfus Affair
A Fine Easter Egg
Fox Hunting†
French Dairy Farm
A Gendarme's Tribulations
Heavy Seas†
Husband Wanted
Interrupted Romance
Love and Fortune
Mr. Smith, the New Recruit†
Native Life in Sudan
Niagara Falls in Winter†
The Nihilist†
On Bad Terms with the Janitor
Precipitated Removal
Riviera in Motor Car
Scenes in Sicily†
Silk Hats Ironed†
The Specter
Swiss Alps†
They Want a Divorce†
An Unfortunate Mistake†
Unrequited Love†
Who Owns the Basket?†

Jul 6 Artificial Brooding
A Bad Boy†
A Costly Coat
Fountains of Rome†
Frightened by Burglars
In the Riviera†
Keenest of the Two
The Leaking Glue Pot
Lessons in Jiu Jitsu
Love and Hatred†
The Mediterranean Fleet
Nothing to Declare; or, Bested by Custom Officials
The Pastry Cook's Misfortune
A Poacher's Trick
Posthumous Jealousy
St. Marc Place†
A Second-Hand Camera
The Two Pickpockets
Views of New York†

Jul 11 The Accuser
The Candidate
Cumbersome Baby
Jealous Fiancé
Latest Style Airship
Noisy Neighbors
The Organ-Grinder's Daughter
The Perjurer
Professor Bric-a-Brac's Inventions
The Shipwreckers†
Stockholm
The Stone Breaker†
A Trip Through Savoy†
Unsuccessful Flirts

Jul 13 The Best Remedy†
Disappointing Rehearsal
Father Is Late! Go Fetch Him†
The Grand Canal in Venice†
His Girl's Last Wish†
The Lady with the Beard; or, Misfortune to Fortune†
Sammy's Idea†
The Simpleton†
The Substitute Automatic Servant†
The Triumph of Love†

Trying to Get Rid of a Bad Dollar†
A Walking Tree†
Wandering Musician†
Jul 18 A Bashful Young Man
Bothersome Husband
Contagious Nervous Twitching
The Father Is to Blame
In the Government Service
Korea
Motoring Around the World
Mystery of the Mountains
The Poor Officer
Runaway Mother-in-Law
Russian Review of the Fiftieth Regiment
Jul 25 The Affair of the Select Hotel
Crocodile Turns Thief
Cumbersome First Fight
Hard to Get Arrested
Home Work in China
I Won One Hundred Thousand†
It Sticks Everything—Even Iron
King Scatterbrain's Troubles
Living Posters
Matrimonial Stages†
Mr. Softhead Has a Good Time
A New Fruit†
Obeying Her Mother†
Off to Morocco†
On the War Path†
Physical Phenomena†
A Pleasant Evening at the Theatre†
Promoted Corporal†
The Saw Mill†
Story of a Fishermaiden
The Story of the King of Fregola†
Sturdy Sailor's Honor†
Too Polite†
The Torrent†
The Tyrant Feudal Lord†
A Wolf in Sheep's Clothing†
Aug [day undetermined]
French Cops Learning English
Oriental Black Art
Aug 1 Baffled Lover†
A Boarding House Acquaintance
The Chronic Life-Saver†
A Comical Execution
An Embarrassing Gift†
Fishing Boats in the Ocean†
Head over Heels in Politics
His Mother's Melody
An Interesting Conversation†
It Smells of Smoke
The Killing Remorse
The Learned Dr. Cornelius
The Little Magician
The Miraculous Flowers†
Out of Patience†
Picturesque Naples
The Roses†
Secret of Hypnotism
The Secret of the Iron Mask
Sensational Duel†
The Smuggler Automobilist
Too Hungry to Eat†
The Tramp's Daughter
The Uncle's Fortune
The Vacuum Cleaner
Wanted—A Son-in-Law on Trial
Water Cure
Aug 8 The Boundary
The Brigand's Daughter†
The Child's Forgiveness†
A Country Drama†
The Curse of Drink
Flower Fete on the Bois de Boulogne†
The French Airship La Republique†
German Dragoons Crossing the Elbe†
Grand Prix Motor Race at Dieppe†
The Gypsy and the Painter†
The Gypsy Model†
The Improvised Statue
The Inconvenience of Taking Moving Pictures
Jewel of a Servant
The Knowing Birds
The Masque Ball
Miss Hold's Puppets
Moscow Under Water†
The Rag Pickers' Wedding†
Reedham Boys' Festival Drill†
Royal Voyage to Canada†
Susceptible Youth
The Tempter†
Trooping the Colour†
Tyrolean Alps Customs†

A Wonderful Fluid
Aug 15 Army Dogs
The Cheese Race†
Dieppe Circuit, 1908
The Dog and the Pipe
A Kind-Hearted Policeman
Lady-Killer Foiled
Mother's Darling†
Music Hall Agent's Dream†
New York
The Poor Man, Homeless, Wants to Go to Prison†
The Powerful Tenor
Prospective Heirs
The Sailor's Dog
Aug 22 The Blue Bird
The Broken Violin
Brothers in Arms
The Forester's Remedy
Freedom for All
His First Job
The Indian Sorcerer
Jim Is Fond of Garlic
A Kindness Never Goes Unrewarded
The Magic of Catchy Songs
Manual of a Perfect Gentleman
The Miller, His Son and the Ass
The Mischances of a Photographer
The Mishaps of the New York-Paris Auto Race
The Mystery of the Garrison
A Trip Through Russia
Two Crazy Bugs
The Woes of Roller Skates
A Woman's Jealousy
Aug 29 The Bewitched Tricycle
A Country Lad
A Daughter's Honesty
The Duck's Finish†
The Enchanted Mantle
A False Alarm
A Good Dinner Badly Digested
The Hapless Hubby
The Happy Man's Shirt†
Head-Dresses Worn in Brittany
Mr. Fuzz
Mrs. Toney's Suitors
Troublesome Carbuncle
The Two Models
Yusuf the Pirate
Sep 1 Samson and Delilah
Sep 5 A Dozen of Fresh Eggs
The Gambler's Fate
The Hotel Mix-Up
The Marathon Race
Olympic Games
Two Talented Vagabonds
Sep 12 Amateur Brigands†
The Asphalters' Dilemma†
The Blind Woman's Daughter†
The Cabby's Wife
The Daughter of the Gypsy
The Dover Pageant†
The Ever-Laughing Gentleman†
Fighting the Flames
Goodwood Races†
Grotesques
The Hand-Cart Race†
King Edward and the German Emperor at Friedrichshof†
The Marathon Race†
The Mesmerist
Music Hath Its Charms
Olympic Regatta at Henley†
Quebec†
Quebec to Niagara†
The Signalman's Sweetheart†
The Son's Crime†
The Spiteful Groom
A Stern Father†
The Swimming Master†
Traveling Through Russia†
Tricksy, the Clever Princess
Two Clever Detectives
The Wrong Lottery Number†
Sep 19 Beginning of the Game of Diablo
How Glue Is Made
The Luckless Spike†
Paris Fire Brigade at Drill
Policeman's Vision
Salome
The Shepherdess
Unusual Cooking
Sep 20 Custom Officer's Revenge
Sep 22 Not Guilty
A Tricky Painter's Fate

Sep 26 The Brahmin's Miracle
Culture of Rice
Fatty's Follies
The Happiest Day of Her Life
Magic Dice
The Magistrate's Conscience
Motor Boat Races, 1908
Sep 29 Buncoed Stage Johnnie
Fun with the Bridal Party
Oct [day undetermined]
A Rude Awakening
Oct 3 The Blusterer†
Caught Red Handed
The Locket
Romeo and Juliet†
The Sailor's Sweetheart
Sammy's Saw†
Spooks Do the Moving
Oct 4 A Basket Party
Palermo and Its Surroundings
The Pardon
Parisian Life in Miniature
A Strong Gale
Oct 6 A Grandmother's Story
Oct 9 Fantastic Magic
Spending a Holiday
What a Funny Horse
Oct 10 Andalousie
Any Rags†
Deep Down within the Cellar†
Down in Jungle Town†
Harrigan†
The Helping Hand
I Want What I Want When I Want It†
I'm Sorry†
I've Taken Quite a Fancy to You†
Just Some One†
L-A-Z-Y†
A Lemon in the Garden of Love†
Lincoln's Speech at Gettysburg†
The Magic Mirror
Make Believe†
Making Arabian Pottery
Military Swimming Championship†
A Mother's Fault
The Old Footlight Favorite
Paris Fire Brigade
A Stiff Neck†
Stupid Mr. Cupid†
A Talk on Trousers†
Tricked into Giving His Consent
Whistle It†
Wouldn't You Like to Have Me for a Sweetheart†
You Got to Love Me a Lot†
Oct 11 Doll Making
The Fake Doctor
The Innkeeper's Remorse
Two Great Griefs
Oct 12 Federal Fete of Wrestling, and Alpino Sports
Oct 13 Jerusalem
Political Speeches†
Oct 14 Miscalculated Revenge
Oct 16 The Court in Session†
The Puppet's Nightmare
Victim of Heroism†
Oct 17 Crocodile Hunt
Elixir of Youth
For the Sake of the Uniform
Heart of a Gypsy Maid
His First Frock Coat
Honeymoon in a Balloon
Incident from Don Quixote
A Love Affair
The Mind Reader
Result of Eating Horseflesh
An Unselfish Guest (?)
Water Bailiff's Daughter†
Oct 19 A Treasure of a Pig†
The Witty Ghost†
Oct 20 Wheelwright's Daughter
Oct 21 Somnambulic (sic) Bell Ringer†
Oct 24 Caught with the Goods
The Fakir's Dream
How Mabel Found a Husband
Hunting for Her Better Half
Mysterious Knight
Pierrette's Talisman
The Power of Habit†
Preparing for Combat
A Sicilian Hermit
Oct 26 When Pa Went Fishing†
Oct 27 Bald Headed Actor and Fair Lady†
The Duke's Good Joke
He Did Not Know He Was a Monk

Oct 28 First Love Triumphs†
The Fortune Hunters
Oct 29 The Flower Thief†
Pa and the Girls†
Oct 30 Bear Hunt in Canada
Mabel's Beau in Trouble
The Sofa Bed†
Oct 31 Ambulance Dogs
Cuddle Up a Little Closer†
Cyrano de Bergerac
Don't You Think It's Time to Marry†
Hamlet, Duel Scene with Laertes
Hep Yo' Self, Peck-a-Boo†
The Honeybees' Honeymoon†
Ideal Policemen
I'm Afraid to Come Home in the Dark†
I'm Going on the War Path†
In the Barber Shop†
The Moon's Gift†
Precieuses Ridicules
Thunderbolt on the Mill
Tipperary†
Under Any Old Flag at All†
What It Might Have Been†
Who? Me?†
With Care†
Wouldn't You Like to Flirt with me†
Nov 1 I've Lost My Ball
Troubles of a Coat
Unyielding Parent
Nov 2 The Automatic Hotel†
The Fair Young Lady's Telephone Communication†
A House of Cards†
How the Pair Butted In
The Legend of Prometheus†
Magic Album
The Necklace†
The Penalty of His Crime
Sold by His Parents
Thou Shalt Not Love†
Nov 3 A Love Tragedy in Spain
Nov 4 Benvenuto Cellini
Don't Fool Your Wife
Maple Sugar
Nov 6 Gust of Wind
Pirate's Honor
Nov 7 The Four-Legged Thief†
The Peer's Fancy
Push Cart Race
Nov 8 Roman Colonel's Bravado
Nov 9 Beauty and the Beast
Feeding a Serpent†
The First Servant†
The Gorges of the Tarn†
The Grandfather's Tobacco†
Hurry Up, Please
The Lake of Garda, Italy†
Looking for the Bald Heads†
No Race Suicide†
Out to Nurse†
The Scare Crow†
A Tyrolean Paradise†
A Woman's Aid†
Nov 10 The Wonderful Charm
Nov 11 Blood Will Tell
Weather Changes at the Smiths
Nov 13 Reception of the American Fleet in Australia
Nov 14 We Close at Noon
Will They Ever Get to Town?
Nov 16 Bicycle Polo
Puss in Boots
Nov 17 Caesar Up-to-Date
The Doctor's Wife†
Having the Time of Their Lives†
The Prize Camel
A Serious Joke
A Visit to Compiegne and Pierrefond
Nov 18 Donkey's Skin
Nov 20 Race Prejudice
Wood Floating and Pulp Industry
Nov 21 Cave of the Spooks
A Love Affair in Toyland
Old College Chums
The Pirates
The Swimming Lesson
Nov 23 Marie Stewart
Nov 25 L'Arlesienne
Nov 27 Crack Riders of the Russian Cavalry
The Substitute
Nov 28 Merry Widow Waltz
The Vagabond
Nov 30 Her Flowers
The Magic Handkerchief
Dec 1 A Child's Devotion
Jack of All Trades
Looking for the Sea Serpent
Making Home Attractive
Dec 2 A Dear Old Grandma
Devils in the Farm
Every Age Has Its Trouble
The Nature Fakir Comes to Grief
Dec 4 The Jealous Fisherman
Paris as Seen from a Height of 2600 Feet
Dec 5 The Bewildered Professor†
Modern Magic
Surprise Package
Thompson's Night with the Police†
Dec 7 The Clown's Daughter
Rubber Heels
Dec 9 The Acrobatic Maid
The Deadly Plant
Dec 11 The Miniature Circus
Mother-in-Law Breaks All Records
Dec 12 Animated Matches
A Good Watch Dog†
The Madman of the Cliff
The Mohammedan at Home
The Quarry Man
Dec 14 No Petticoats for Him
Roman Idyl
Dec 16 The One Best Bet
A Plucky Young Woman
Dec 18 The Bee and the Rose
The Smuggler's Daughter
Dec 19 The Angel of Nativity
The Christmas of a Poacher†
Electric Hotel
The Good Playthings†
Grimsol, the Mischievous Goblin
Hobo on a Bike†
The Little Chimney Sweeps†
Misdeeds of a Tragical Part
The Police Band†
The Poor Singer Girl†
Some Dangerous Members of Bostock's Menagerie
Troubles of an Airship
Dec 21 Faithful Little Doggie
The Faun
George and Margaret
The Holy Hermit†
In Bondage†
The Little Marchioness and the Young Shepherdess†
My Laundress Inherits
Too Much Snuff
Dec 23 Antique Wardrobe
An Awkward Habit
Dec 25 The Gallant Guardsman
Silhouettes
Dec 26 Bill Wants to Marry a Toe Dancer
Water Sports
Dec 28 Acrobatic Toys
Bobby Has a Pipe Dream†
Current News Items†
The Devil's Sale
A Heavy Head Piece†
Mr. Soaker at the Seaside
Not Guilty†
St. Moritz
Dec 30 The Ragtag's Ball
The Sicilian's Revenge

1909

Jan 1 Anonymous Letter
Strasburg
Jan 2 Collection of Stamps
The Corsican's Revenge
Persistent Suitor
Jan 4 Mysterious Correspondent
Two Very Unlucky Thieves
Jan 6 A Lovely Lass
School Children's Strike
Jan 8 A Drunkard's Dream
The Wooden-Headed Veteran
Jan 9 Burning of Stamboul, Constantinople
For Baby's Sake
Ted and His Little Sister
Jan 11 The Bewitched Breton
Converted
Duel Under Richeleau
A Gypsy's Jealousy†
Spanish Blood
Visions of a Goldsmith
Jan 13 A Nervy Thief
The Prehistoric Lid
Stilt Walking
Jan 15 It's Only the Painter
Paper Cock-A-Doodles
Jan 16 The Captain's Love†
The Coiners, or Catching the Counterfeiters
The Hunchback
Mr. Pynhead Out for a Good Time
South African Gold Fields†
An Unprofitable Call
Jan 18 Champion Suffragist
A Hot Remedy
Married Twice
The Persevering Insurance Agent
A Pretty Little Milliner
The Sergeant's Stripes
Troubled Artists†
Jan 20 The Stepmother
Wonderful Eggs
Jan 22 Beginning of the Serpentine Dance
Buffin Wins First Prize
Jan 23 Bobby's Sketches
A Fish Story
For Mother's Sake
For Their Country's Cause
Lady Cabby's Romance
Messina After the Earthquake
The Pleasant Side of a Soldier's Life
Trip on Rhodesian Railway†
Jan 25 Sammy Celebrates
The Scar
Jan 27 Calling Day
Nick Carter's Double
Jan 29 Messina
A Put Up Job
Jan 30 The Frolic of Youth
On the Zambesi
Saved by His Dog
Feb 1 Gendarme's Horses
The Living Wreck†
A Mother's Heart
The Nurse's Romance
A Sure 'Nuff Tumbler
The Two Bandboxes
A Village Quarrel
Feb 3 Incriminating Evidence
Feb 5 Choosing a Life Partner
He Can Imitate Anything
Feb 6 The Banker
The Great Earthquake in Sicily
The Juggler
The Unwelcome Lover
Vulture Hunting in Africa
Why They Fell Out
Feb 8 Buster's Revenge
Les Ricochets
Women Chauffeurs
Feb 9 The Miner's Will
A Sportive Puppet
Feb 10 Adventures of a Bag of Coal
Charlotte Corday
The Double's Fate†
Feb 12 Bess and Her Goose
The Laplanders
Feb 13 The Ambassador's Dispatch Case
The Brazilian's Ring
An Evil Day
Jones Has Bought a Phonograph
Palmistry
They Lead the Cops on a Chase
Feb 15 The Hand
Feb 16 Outwitted†
Feb 17 The Assassination of the Duke of Guise
Grandfather
A Strong Draught
Feb 19 Choice of Weapons
His First Flight
How Mother-in-Law Got Even
Feb 20 Bernard Palissy
The Chinamen
Exacting Father-in-Law
Now I'm Here, I'll Stay
Feb 22 Grand Canal, Venice
The Miser
Feb 23 An Obstinate Umbrella
Some Milk for Baby
Feb 24 Joel's Wedding
A Little Coquette
What a Uniform Will Do
Feb 26 The Jolly Trio's Dream
Mr. Jonah Gets a Little Dust in His Eyes
Topsy-Turvy
Feb 27 A Day's Outing
Florrie's Birthday
The Foxy Husband
Her Daughter's Dowry
Hypnotic Subject
The Prince and the Dwarf
Mar 1 The Suffragette's Dream
The Test
Mar 2 The Piano Teacher

Mar 3 An Embarrassing Present†
The Guilty Guardian
The Man Monkey
The Sailor's Belt†
Mar 5 A Bad Shot
Behind in His Rent
Mar 6 Dr. Wright's Invention
Forced to Play Cop
In Sore Straits
Walking on His Toes
Mar 8 All's Well That Ends Well
When Love Will
Mar 9 The Blacksmith's Bride
The Postal Clerk
Mar 10 He Can't Lose Wifie's Ma
Little Cyril, the Runaway
Mother-in-Law's Day in the Country†
Rivalry†
South American Indians†
Mar 12 Convict's Revenge
Educating the Blind
He Is a Cousin Who Eats Truffle
Mar 13 Buttes Chaumont After a Snow Storm
The Irresolute Man
Sad Awakening
The Smoking Lamp
A Trip to Monte Carlo
Visit from the "Down Home Folks"
Mar 15 Unusual Elopement
Vampires of the Coast
Mar 16 Devotion and Its Reward
Innocent, but Found Guilty
Kid's Jest
The Musician's Dream
Mar 17 The Celebrated Mountain Climbers†
Cremation on the River Ganges†
Jealous Hubby
Master Goes Shopping†
The Ringleader
Mar 19 Child's Vision
Summer Home for the School Children of Paris
Tommy's Own Invention
Tramp's Defense
Mar 20 The Return of Ulysses
The Secretary's Revenge
The Survivor's Story
Mar 22 A Borrowed Suit
Brisquet
The Chambermaid and the Dwarf
Chasi Movement
Chasing the Helmet
Compassion
The Dragonad
Dream of Featart
The Duel
Duplicate Vases
The Elixir of Dreams
Five Minutes Interview
For Honor
The Ghost
House of Disagreement
In the Land of the Hindoo
Irritable Woman
Louis XVII
Magic French Horn
Main Clues
Marriage in Haste
Maternal Protection
Matrimonial Agency
The Mesmerist
Mother-in-law Too Kindhearted
Norseman
Lo Piferaro
Pity
Procession in Japan
The Prophecy
Recommended Servant
Removing
Rifle Bill No. 5
Runaway Dog
Service of a Friend
Shooting the Rapids in Japan
Soldier and Witch
State Secret
The Statue
The Stolen Inheritance
Taming a Husband
Tylda and Her Lions
United by Misfortune
Where Stormy Winds Do Blow
Zoological Gardens
Mar 23 Cross of Honor
Gift
Japanese Magic
Pocket Policeman
Mar 24 Chivalrous Beggar
I Have Lost Toby†
Mr. Pallet Goes Out Landscaping†
New Cut Roads Up Mt. Blanc
We Must Have a Butler
Mar 26 Jolly Sports
The Maid and the Millionaire
Mar 27 Across the Border
The Electric Belt
Life on a French Training Ship
On the Brink
The Warden's Nightmare
Mar 29 The Child of the Regiment
What Three Tots Saw in the Land of Nod
Mar 30 The Policewoman
The Politician
Mar 31 Arabian Horsemen†
Benevolent Employer†
His Last Illusion Gone
Whale Fishing in Southern Waters
Apr 2 Beware of Evil Companions
Larry, the Limit for Deviltry
Old Aunt Hanna's Cat
Apr 3 Benares
De Comtess de Valeria
Every Lass a Queen
King for an Hour
Lost in the Snow
The Martins Leave Home for a Week
Uncle's Palm Tree
Apr 5 The Schoolboy's Revenge
Vercingetorix—Gaul's Hero
Apr 6 The Prodigal Daughter
The Riviera
Apr 7 Inviting His Boss for Dinner†
The Kiss of Judas
On the Brink of the Precipice†
Apr 9 Contemptible Theft
Moscow Clad in Snow
Apr 10 Clarence and His Cigarette
Eagle's Prey
He Advertised for His Dog
Mishaps of Lover
Ponto Runs Away with the Milk Cart
Theodore Yearns to be a Tough
The Tramp at the Masquerade
Apr 12 Moonstruck
Pranks of a Mischievous Kid
Apr 13 Charlie Forced to Find a Job
In the Lime Light
Apr 14 Oliver Cromwell
Policeman in Action
Under Suspicion
Apr 16 The General's Fiancée
The Teamster's Daughter
We're Backing Up
Apr 17 A Bachelor's Persistence†
Jack's Successful Bluff
A Plot Foiled†
The State Secret
Story of a Calf's Head
A War Time Tale
Apr 19 The Legend of the Forget-Me-Not
Paul Has Decided to Marry
Apr 20 The Poet's Vision
Too Much Advice
Apr 21 Magic Eggs
A Pair of White Gloves
Sentenced to Death
Apr 23 There's No Fool Like an Old Fool
Apr 24 Burglary in the Year 2000
The Cabin Boy's Dog
Found on the Rocks†
Hungary
It Was a Beautiful Dream
The Magic of Music
The Magnetizer
Martyrdom of Louis XVII
The Squire and the Noble Lord†
Apr 26 The Clever Reporter
The Gold Prospectors
Apr 27 The Automatic Monkey
Before and After
How They Propose
Apr 28 The Fairy's Presents
The Love-sick Barber
The Suspicious Fencing Master
An Unwritten Letter
Apr 30 Playing Patience
Wilbur Wright's Aeroplane
May 1 The Bohemian Girl
The Donkey That Was Not an Ass
The Dragoons Under Louis XIV
Dream Spectres
Easter Bells
Hunting the Hippopotamus
Removal Under Difficulties
Two Ladies and a Beggar
May 3 Between Love and Honor
Your Turn, Marquis
May 5 Forgotten†
The Peddler's Reward†
Thanksgiving Turkey
Zou-Zou, the Lucky Dog
May 7 A Chinese Wedding
Haunted by the Cops
Instantaneous Nerve Powder
May 8 Earthly Paradise
Eddie Is a Real Live One
Ellen
Four Footed Hawkshaw
The Gambler's Vow
The Haunted Bridge
The Inheritance of Baptiste Durand
New Pain Killer
Sportsmen in Switzerland
Tribulations of a Lover
The Way to Happiness
May 10 Mirielle's Sincere Love
A Striking Resemblance
May 11 The Cyclone Sneezer
An Uneven Keel
May 12 Bamboo Pole Equilibrist†
The Hunter's Grief
A Timely Apparition†
Wilbur Wright and His Majesty King Edward VII†
May 14 A Faithful Old Horse
Manufacturing Steel Rails
May 15 The Actor's Mother
Disappointed Heirs
A Distracted Man
An Exciting Hunt
For Honor's Sake
Free Champagne
Magic Sack
On the French Littoral
The Two Donkeys
A Woman's Heart
May 17 The Beggar's Coin
Fountain of Youth
May 18 He Couldn't Lose Her
The Policeman Sleeps
The World Upset
May 19 Blessings Sometimes Come in Disguise
Caught on the Cliffs†
Objections Overcome†
Père Milon
May 21 Daunted by His First Love
Land of the Midnight Sun
May 22 Cartouche
A Guest's Predicament
Justice or Mercy
Longing for Gold
Neurasthenique
Perilous Expedition
May 24 The Bondsman's Fate
Cured by Gymnastics
Little Mother
May 25 A Blind Man of Jerusalem
The Glories of Sunset
May 26 How Jones Paid His Debts†
An Obliging Friend
Panther Hunting on the Isle of Java†
A Profitable Marriage
May 28 Alphonse Gets in Wrong
Miss Faust
May 29 The Accusing Double
Apostle of Gaul
Bottled Up
King's Jester
Nantilda
Reveler's Dream
The Suffragist Wants a Husband
Vaccination Against Injuries
A Visit to the London Zoological Gardens
May 31 Advantages of Aviation
An Uninvited Guest
Jun 1 The Cripple's Marriage
The Good Omen
Jun 2 Making Tambourines
Saved by a Waif
Tender Cords†
Jun 4 A Bruised Heart
Carnival at Nice, 1909
Jun 5 Debut of an Alpinist
Gambler's Honor
Legend of the Erring Jew
On the Zuider Zee
Protector of Animals
Saved from Conviction
A Soldier's Heart

Jun 7 The Blue Legend
The Pulverizer
Jun 8 A Mother's Choice
Jun 9 The Race Course†
La Tosca
Two Heroes†
Jun 11 Snake Skin Industry
A Woman's Intrigue
Jun 12 The Consequences of a Bad Action
Cyrano de Bergerac's Adventure
Drama at Messina
His Lucky Day
Historical Fan
Man with the Cut Throat
A Message from the Sea
Rapids and Falls of Tannfossen and Rista
Skylight Theater Seat
A Strong Diet
Too Clean a Servant
Jun 14 Cupid's Four Darts
The Dog Detective
Jun 15 Hunted to the End
A Paying Business
Jun 16 Don Juan; or, A War Drama of the Eighteenth Century
Life's Disappointment
Modern Algeria†
The New Footman†
The Reckoning
Strenuous Sneezer
Jun 18 Looking for His Umbrella
Mixed in His Dinner Dates
Jun 19 The Cry from the Well
A Good Birthday Present
Making Lace
Poor Little Kiddies
Jun 21 For His Daughter's Sake
Jun 22 A Good Hearted Policeman
The Troublesome Lamppost
Jun 23 The Grandfather
Mrs. Simpson's Attractiveness†
Winning a Princess†
Jun 25 An Affair of Honor
An Assortment of Aeroplanes
Jun 26 The Buffoon
Chimney Sweep's Debut
Dollar in Each Egg
Fratricide
Joan of Arc
Lover's Mistake
Maddened Players
Misadventures of a Bench
Police Dogs
Stung by a Bee
The Wrong Medicine
Jun 28 Broke Again
A Western Hero
Jun 29 No Appetite for Dinner
Saved from the Flames
Jun 30 The Phantom Sirens†
Psyche
Rulers of the World†
Jul 2 The Bogey Woman
Fun with a Manikin
Jul 3 American Squadron in France
Book Taught Hypnotism
Determined Wooer
The Hand Bell
An Inspiring Sunset
The Sentimental Burglar
The Snow Man
The Sunny South of France
Jul 5 A Child's Love
Spanish Army
Jul 6 The Coin Collector
Raised in the Country
Jul 7 Exciting Steeple-Chase†
The Pretty Fisher-Maiden†
A Tragic Ending of Shrove Tuesday
Tunisian Industries
Jul 9 The Fan
A Little Detective
Jul 10 A Bad Case
Gaffles, Vice King of Police
The Origin of Man
Pierrot as a Grocer
The Reason of the Strongest
Trained Falcon
A Tramp Show Heart
Visions of Mother
The Witch's Donkey
Jul 12 Different Rulers of the World
Wood Floating in Morvan
Jul 13 Only a Dream
A Sure Cure
Jul 14 Conchita, the Spanish Belle†
The Evil Spirit in a Girl's Boarding School
True to Her First Love
Jul 16 The Hand of Justice
Jul 17 Automatic Umbrella Seller
Ballad of the Pumpkin
In the Hands of the Enemy
The Invisible Thief
A Jealous Woman
A Kind Hearted Tough
The Lost Tie
Miraculous Fluid
The Poisoned Flower
The Punch Register
The Sacrifice
Jul 19 Behind the Mask
Catching Turtles
The Fiddlers
Jul 20 The Man in the Moon
True to His Master
Jul 21 Bewitched Manor House
The King's Conspiracy†
Little Busybody
Jul 23 A Case of Lumbago
Holding Up the Wedding
Sweet Toothed Dogs
Jul 24 Admirer of a Mustache
Brown's Moving Day
Columbine's Return
The Good Shepherd
John Maxwell's Medal
The Monk's Mother
Poor Kid
Professor of Dancing
Jul 26 Champion Heavyweight Lifter
Living Dolls
Sweet Dreams Intermingled with Nightmares
Jul 27 The Last Confession
Papa's Hat
Jul 28 Amazons of Different Periods
The Barber's Revenge
His Rival's Hand†
Parks in Berlin†
Jul 30 Charity Begins at Home
A Mother's Sorrow
Jul 31 An Easy Job
Game of Nine Pins
The Gamekeeper's Son
In Hot Water
Little Gypsy
Missionary
Wonderful Rose Designs
Aug 2 The Butler's Tricks
Fantastic Heads
Aug 3 The Morning After
The Sentinel on Duty
Aug 4 Stripping a Forest in Winter†
Thelly's Heart
The Turning Point†
Aug 6 The Tragedy of Meudon
Aug 7 Arabian Pilgrimage
Baby Is King†
Clever Horse Hans
The Hidden Treasure†
Japanese Prince
King of Spain
The Orphan of Messina
Sympathetic Tippler
Troubles of a Coachman
The Two Pigeons
Wonderful Compound
Aug 9 Charity Rewarded
The Sacrifice
Satan's Smithy
Aug 10 Cyclist's Horn
Dust in His Eye
Retaliation
Aug 11 Laurels
A Long Reach
Pompey's Dream
Aug 13 Cigar-Butt Pickers in Paris
A Trip to Jupiter
Aug 14 Black Hand
Bouquet Gallantly Offered
The Foxy Farmer
Her Beautiful Hair
The Mysterious Crime
A Near Tragedy
Nightmare of a Single Man
Peddling Shoes
A Smart Trick
A Trying Position
Why She Didn't Marry
The Wild Ass's Skin
Aug 16 A Cold Plunge in Moscow
A Heroic Father
Aug 17 The Cobbler and the Millionaire
The Little Drummer of 1792
Aug 18 Building Barrels†
Elastic Transformation
The Strikers†
Two Lovers and a Coquette
Aug 20 Doomed
Aug 21 Getting Even with Everybody
He Preferred to Smoke His Pipe
Honesty Rewarded
Hooligan Against His Will
The King's Protege†
The New General
Rival Sisters
Rover Turns Santa Claus
Up the Mountain from Hong Kong†
Aug 23 Dances of Various Countries
The Hat Juggler
Aug 24 The Frock Coat
Too Gentlemanly
Aug 25 Broken Ties
The Eternal Romance
Sevres Porcelain
Tennessee Guards
Aug 27 A Billposter's Trials
Manufacturing Bamboo Hats
Aug 28 Ancestral Treasures
A Generous Emperor
Grandmother's Birthday
Great Event at Podunk
The Horse and the Haystack
The Hypnotic Wife
The Professor's Dilemma
The Spy's Revenge
The Two Friends
Aug 30 The New Mail Carrier
Ralph Benefits by People's Curiosity
Aug 31 The French Battleship "Justice"†
Sep 1 An Awakened Conscience
The Little Street Singer
Magic Cartoons
Sam Not Wanted in the Family
Sep 3 Show Your License
A Visit to Biskra
Sep 4 An Apostle of Temperance
The Crusader's Return
Day After a Spree
A Grave Disappointment
In Hot Pursuit†
Launching the "Voltaire"
Mexican Drama
Romantic Italy†
A Strong Woman's Lover
Training Bulls for the Fight
Sep 6 They Robbed the Chief of Police
Versailles
Sep 7 First Airships Crossing the English Channel
The Mason's Paradise
Sep 8 Glimpses of Paris
The Little Soldier
The Stolen Gems
Sweden—Gotha Canal
Sep 10 Tom Thumb
Sep 11 Chasing a Sea Lion in the Arctics
How to Tame a Mother-in-Law
Mozart's Last Requiem
Sports in Java
Sep 13 The Amateur Detective
The Child's Prayer
Daughter of an Anarchist
From Millionaire to Porter
The Justifier
Love of Adventures
Sep 14 The Fiddle and the Fan
Her Busy Day
The Tricky Dummies
Sep 15 City of Naples
The Fatal Love†
Pontine Marshes, Italy†
The Pretty Girl of Nice
Sep 17 The Mountebank's Son
Sep 18 Aeroplane Contests at Rheims
The Arithmetic Lesson
Calino Objects to Work
Construction of Balloons
The Farmer's Treasure†
For My Children
The Fresh Kid
Making of a Sailor
Man with the Sack in Society
Oh, What a Beard!
Pietro, the Candy Kid
Pietro, the Mule Driver

Sep 20 Aviation Contests at Rheims
Blind Against His Will
The Bull Fight of Oran
Caught in His Own Trap
Tragical Love
Sep 21 Meskal, the Smuggler
Old Servants
Saved from the Quicksands
Strike Time in Paris
Taking in a Reef
Sep 22 Dropped from the Clouds
The Five Divorcees
The Legend of the Lighthouse
The Tower of Nesle
Sep 23 A Lucky Man
Sep 24 Careless Tramp
Caucasian Customs
Marriage of Yvonne
Sep 25 The Adopted Child
All for a Nickel
A Mother's Love
Not Wanted on Voyage
On the Crest of the Waves
Servant's Good Joke
Towards Immortalidated [sic]
Trained Birds
Sep 27 He Learns the Trick of Mesmerism
Suitor's Competition
Sep 28 Breach of Promise
Wife or Child†
Sep 29 The Blind Detective
Chasing the Ball†
Jane Is Unwilling to Work
Love, the Conqueror†
Pierrot, the Fuddler
Sep 30 Rats
Oct 1 An Eventful Trip
A Game of Chess
Oct 2 The Garbage of Paris
Good Cigars
The Masterpiece
The Poacher
Vendetta
Oct 4 The Story of a Banknote
Oct 5 Breaking the Bank
The Pill Box
Oct 6 Female Sleuth
Gambling Passion†
The Music Lesson
Yachting off Cowes†
Oct 8 How Jack Helped His Little Sister
Sister Angelica
Oct 9 Anti-Fat Sanitarium
The Dog Pickpocket
Napoleon
Sleuth and the Wig
Wedding Party in Luna Park
Oct 11 Maneuvers of Ambulance Corps.
The Trappers
Oct 12 Convicting Evidence
How He Earned His Medal
Oct 13 The Cook's Mistake
Liquid Air
The Love Trip
A Lucky Husband
Princess of the Sea
A Wonderful Remedy
Oct 15 Blessington's Bonny Babies
The Romance of a Poor Girl
Oct 16 Alphonse, the Dead Shot
The Broken Violin
Chums
One-Legged Pete and Pat
Physical Culture Fiend
Oct 18 The Belated Wedding
Bob's Electric Theater
Oct 19 His Helpmate
Husband's Strategy
Oct 20 Casting Bread upon the Water†
Crown Prince of Germany Drilling Battery†
A Good Trick
A Home Without Children
Hunting Jack Rabbits in Hungary
The Ogress
Oct 22 Drink
Oct 23 Country Life in a Flat
Tickled to Death
Oct 25 The Boating Party
The Bogus Heir
The Brigand's Repentance
The Indian Phantasy
Love and Vendetta
A Prince's Love
Romance in the Andes
The Strength of Love
The Would-Be Champion
Oct 26 Ambulance Ventilators
The Old Lord of Ventnor
Oct 27 Awakened Memories†
The Gambler
Grotesque Make-Up
The Plundered Museum
Sunday at Douarenez
Volcanoes of Java†
Oct 29 Buffalo Racing in Madoera
Life Behind the Scenes
Oct 30 A Barrow Race
Burglar in the Trunk
Mountebank's Watchcase
The Song of the Cradle
Nov 1 Across the Island of Ceylon
The Lonely Bachelor
Nov 2 Don Quixote
Honest John, the Coachman
Mystic Melodies
Nov 3 Eat Your Soup
The General's Birthday Present
Tale of the Fiddle†
"Ursula," World's Fastest Motor Boat†
Nov 5 The Prodigal Son
The Witch
Nov 6 Cops on a Strike
Elephant Hunting in Cambodge
Malicious Rival
The Sack Race
Two Brothers
The Warrior's Sacrifice
Nov 8 Bandits of the Atlas Gorges
The Bearskin
Boatman of the Riviera
Culture of Tea in Java
Lines of the Hand
Miracle of a Necklace
Misadventures of a Pair of Trousers
Woes of a Cinematographer
Nov 9 A Peace Agitator
The Pigmy World
Telltale Reflections
Nov 10 The Flight of Monsieur Valette
The Haunted Castle
A Heavy Gale at Biarritz
The Necklace of the Holy Virgin
The Robber Duke†
A Serious Error
Nov 11 Bertha's Birthday
Nov 12 Man with the Dolls
Running in Hard Luck
Nov 13 Good Lesson in Charity
Harlequin's Nightmare
Mischief of a Big Drum
Nana's Mother
Now Keep Smiling
The Rhymester's Ruse
Sam's Artistic Beard
Substitute Pig
Nov 14 Rigoletto
Nov 15 Electrified Hunchback
In India, Marriage of the Nephew of the Maharajah of Tagore
Two Chums Looking for Wives
Nov 16 A Convict's Heroism
Mysterious Luggage
A Set of Teeth
Nov 17 Fighting Suffragettes†
Goddess of the Sea
Her Dramatic Career
Nov 19 How French Perfumes Are Made
The Nobleman's Dog
Nov 20 Adonis Is Robbed of His Clothes
Moon for Your Love
The Patient from Punkville
Visions of a Nag
Nov 22 Honest Little Rag Picker
John Farley's Redemption
Late for the Recital
Legend of the Good Knight
Napoleon's Game of Chess
Nov 23 Belle of the Harvest
Marriage of Love†
Nov 24 A Convenient Lamp-Post
A Heart's Devotion
The Sleeper
Tulips
Nov 26 The Bigamist
Nov 27 Chinese Amusements
Mix-Up at Court
The Mixed Letters
The Village Scare
Nov 29 A Bunch of Lilacs
The Double Six
The Motor Cyclist
The Painter's Idol
Professor Short Sight's Surprise
Spanish Marriage
Nov 30 The Broken Vase
In the Consomme
Dec 1 Legend of Orpheus
The Wolf Hunt
Dec 3 Forced into Marriage
The Three Neighbors
Dec 4 A Cask of Good Old Wine
The Crocodile Hunt
From the Egg to the Spit
How to Get a City Job
Indiscreet Father and Son
Punishment of an Athlete
An Unlucky Acquisition
X-Ray Glasses
Dec 6 Captain Fracassee
The Disguised Bridegroom
The Heir of Clavencourt Castle
The Lady's Companion
Mr. Sadman's Cure
The Song That Reached Her Heart
Dec 7 In a Pickle
Listen
Top-Heavy Mary
Dec 8 The Evil Philter
Impossible to Get Sleep
The Secret Chamber†
Dec 10 Bear Hunt in Russia
Masquerader's Charity
Dec 11 Daughters of Poverty
Exploits of a Cowboy
Willyboy Gets His
Dec 12 La Grande Breteche
Dec 13 Beethoven
Dr. Lyvenemup's Elixir
Repairing the House
The Tramp's Romance
A Trip to the Arctic
Dec 14 The Life Buoy
Nothing Is Ever Lost
Dec 15 Punch and Judy
The Red Signal†
Switzerland, Conquering the Alps†
The Ugly Girl
Dec 17 The Lucky Number
The Strong Tonic
Dec 18 Cambyses, King of Persia
The Forced Loan
Hector, the Angel Child
The Honey Industry
Off to the Wedding
Reformed Thief
The Shepherd's Flute
Dec 20 The Chemist's Bell
The Death of the Duke D'Enghien
Explorer's Dream
Granny's Darling
Mac Nabb Wants to Get Arrested
A Persistent Lover
The Prisoner's Strategy
Dec 21 The Stranger
Dec 22 Contest for a Handkerchief
Fiorella, the Bandit's Daughter†
From the Fighting Top of a Battleship in Action†
The Love Token
Dec 24 Agriculture in Hungary
The Birth of Jesus
Dec 25 Absorbing Tale
Drama in the Far West
Drama of Villasgne
The Good Doctor
The Greek Slave's Passion
Gypsy Child
The Happy Widower
Mule Driver's Bride
Original Sausage Tale
Pork Butcher
Pretty Fisher-Woman
Real Brittany
Reincarnated Mummy
Repentance
The Sailor's Son
Spring Heeled Jack
Suicide Club
Turning Out of Time
Dec 27 A Bad Bargain
Marvellous Garlands
Dec 28 A Clever Sleuth
Hush Money
Mug Chump's Early Morning Excursion
Dec 29 The Gold Digger's Son
Oh, You Doggie!
The Park of Caserta†
A Well Earned Medal

Dec 30 The Rheumatic Bridegroom
Dec 31 Corsican Hospitality
The Emperor's Staff Officer
A Live Corpse

1910

Jan 1 The Legion of Honor
Tabby's Finish
Trials of a Schoolmaster
Jan 3 A Happy New Year
Madam's Favorite
The Marriage of the Cook
Seal and Walrus Hunting
The Strolling Players
A Victim of Circumstances
Jan 4 The Avenging Dentist
The Wreck at Sea
Jan 5 Drama at Sea
Football Craze
The King's Command
The Overzealous Domestic
Shanghai of To-day†
Tragedy at the Mill†
Jan 7 An English Boxing Bout
Modern Highwayman
Jan 8 His Opponent's Card
How the Dog Saved the Flag
The Last Look
On the Bank of the River
The Rivals
A Seat in the Balcony
Jan 10 Hotstuff Takes on the Champions
Miss Moneybags Wishes to Wed
Monarchs of All Nations
The Terrors of the Family
Toes and Teeth
Women in India
Jan 11 Shooting in the Haunted Woods
Towser's New Job
Jan 12 Broken Happiness
Home of the Gypsies†
My Aunt's Birthday
True to His Oath†
Jan 14 The Beggar's Repentance
Story of a Leg
Jan 15 At the Carnival
Bogus General
Church Robber
Consequence of a Lie
Decorated by the Emperor
The Double
Drama Under Richelieu
Follow Me
Foster Brothers
Good Tramp
Human Squib
On a Racket
Railway on the Ice Sea
Roast Chicken
A Stag Hunt in Java
Jan 17 Jealousy, a Bad Counsellor
Testing Their Love
A Visit to Bombay
Jan 18 Fatal Fascination
Getting Square with the Inventor
Jan 19 Adventures of a Sandwich Man
An Aerial Acrobat
The Bareback Rider
The Coast Guard†
The Refugee
Riva, Austria, and the Lake of Garda†
Jan 21 Fickle Fortune
The Painter's Sweetheart
Jan 22 Count Tolstoi
A Russian Heroine
Swallowed by the Deep
Jan 24 Acrobatic Exercises by the Colibris
Dwarfs
The Unlucky Fisherman
Jan 25 The Price of Patriotism
Seaside Adventures at Home
Jan 26 He Would Be an Acrobat
Motherless
Tommy in Dreamland†
Uncle Learns to Hypnotize
Jan 27 Bear Hunting
Jan 28 The Leather Industry
The Scarecrow
Jan 29 Cousin Lou for Mine
The Great Divide
The Strong Man
Wild Waves at St. Jean-de-Lux
Jan 31 Coffee Culture
Dick's a Winner
Feb 1 Ascending the Jura Mountains
The Golden Lily
Feb 2 Hamlet, Prince of Denmark
The Might of the Waters†
The Postmistress
Sheltered in the Woods†
Feb 4 The Model Drama
Roller Skating in Australia
Feb 5 Adam II — Miscellaneous
Civil War
A Critical Situation
Feb 7 The Bandit
The Child and the Dancing-Jack
Mr. Giddy's Revenge
The Two Raffles
Feb 8 Servant from the Country
Settled Out of Court
Feb 9 Coals of Fire†
The Consequence of a Nod
Cora, the Contraband's Daughter
In Ancient Greece
Pirate's Fiancée
Venetian Isles†
Feb 11 Before and After
The Troubadour
Feb 12 A Bag Race
The Foot Juggler
The Gambler's Doom
The Jockey
The Paris Disaster
Feb 14 Druid Remains in Brittany
The Enterprising Clerk
Feb 15 The Ghost
Pastoral Scenes
Feb 16 The Acrobatic Fly†
The Blue Swan Inn†
Her Dolly's Revenge
The Man Who Could Not Sit Down
Feb 17 Easy Job
Feb 18 The Little Beggar
A Panicky Picnic
Feb 19 Better Than Gold
The Comedy-Graph
Fate Against Her
Three Queens and a Jack
Feb 21 A Corsican's Revenge
The Gunby's Sojourn in the Country
Feb 22 Duped
His Fears Confirmed
Feb 23 The Buried Secret†
A Family Outing†
The Fisherman's Honour
The Lamp-Post Inspector
The Runaway Stove
Feb 25 The Harry Brothers
Ouchard, the Merchant
Feb 26 Blue Fishing Nets
Granny's Birthday
In the Gulf of Salerno
The Legend of King Midas
Feb 28 Joseph Sold by His Brethren
A Mica Mine, the Ullugura Mountains
Mar 1 The Plucky Suitor
The Vale of Aude
Mar 2 From Beyond the Seas†
The Golf Mania
The Sailor's Dog
The Violin Maker of Cremona
The Wrestling Match
Mar 4 Brittany Lassies
The Door
Mar 5 A Happy Turn
Pierrot
The Poet of the Revolution
Mar 7 The Cage (An Episode in the
Adventures of Morgan the Pirate)
Strenuous Massage
Tragic Idyl
Mar 8 The Great Scoop
The Legend of Daphne
Mar 9 The Arrest of Duchess de Berry
At the Bar of Justice†
A Father's Patriotism
He Knew Best
A Tragic Adventure
The Water-Flyer†
Mar 11 A Cure for Timidity
A Seaside Flirtation
Mar 12 The Pirate Airship
Rabelais' Joke
Sporty Dad
A Tale of a Tenement
Mar 14 The Revenge of Dupont L'Anguille
Tobacco Culture
Uncle's Money
Mar 15 In the Shadow of the Cliffs
The Saraband Dance
Mar 16 A Bullfight in Mexico
The Captive
The Country Schoolmaster†
Life in the Next Century
A Trip Along the Rhine†
The Two Brothers
Mar 18 The Exile
Mar 19 In the Foothills of Savoy
Little Jack's Letter
Wild Birds in Their Haunts
A Willful Dame
Mar 21 A Woman's Repentance
Mar 22 The Queen and the Mirror
The Wild Coast of Belle Island
Mar 23 For the King
The Horseshoe
A Maid of the Mountains†
Over the Appennines of Italy†
Mar 24 A Family Feud
How a Bad Tempered Man Was Cured
Mar 25 The Banks of the Ganges
Dwarf Detective
No Trifling with Love
Mar 26 A Conquest
The Fall of Babylon
Foxy Ernest
Mar 28 The Little Vixen
The Polar Bear Hunt in the Arctic Seas
Mar 29 The Diary of a Nurse
Mar 30 Cured by a Tip
Drama on the Reef
Driven to Steal
Making Sherry Wine at Xeres†
The Midnight Escape†
Out of Sight, Out of Mind
Apr 1 The Rhine Falls at Schaffhausen
A Woman's Caprice
Apr 2 Amateur Billiards
Athletic Sports in India
The Dreamer
Lorenzo, the Wolf
O'er Crag and Torrent
Apr 4 After the Fall of the "Eagle"
Agra
The Good Boss
Apr 5 A Drama of the Mountain Pass
Poetry of the Waters
Apr 6 The Duchess of Langeais
The Fly Pest†
Her Father's Choice†
Rico, the Jester
The Snake Man
The Vintage
Apr 8 The Hunchbacked Fiddler
Paula Peters and Her Trained Animals
Apr 9 A Hasty Operation
Honest Peggy
The Kiss Was Mightier Than the Sword
O'er Hill and Vale
Apr 11 Her Sister's Sin
One-Legged Acrobats
Apr 12 The Stubborn Lover
Vintage in Lanquedoc
The Volcano of Chinyero
Apr 13 The Attack upon the Train
Ice Scooters on Lake Ronkonkoma
The Lookout; or, Saved from the Sea†
The Miniature
A Ramble Through the Isle of
Sumatra†
Washed Ashore
Apr 15 Johnny's Pictures of the Polar Regions
The Mask Maker
Apr 16 The Bully
Mephisto at a Masquerade
The Pillagers
Touring the Canary Islands
Apr 18 The Greenhorns
Simone
Apr 19 A Penitent of Florence
Apr 20 Grandpa's Darling
The Lover's Oracle†
Trawler Fishing in a Hurricane†
A Young Aviator's Dream
Apr 22 Delhi
The Wreath
Apr 23 The Chivalrous Stranger
Judith and Holofernes
The Storm
Apr 25 The Parisian
Venice
Apr 26 Paying Attention
The Potter's Wheel
Solving the Puzzle
Apr 27 The Bagpipe Player
Jim Wants to Get Punched
The Rival Miners†
Volcanic Eruptions of Mt. Aetna†
Apr 28 Artist's Child
Tommy and the Powder

Apr 29 The Merry Medrano Circus Clowns
The Subterfuge
Apr 30 Bud's Escapade
The Captain of the Guard
The Cheese Box
Deep Sea Fishing
Hope of the Village
May 2 Only a Faded Flower
The Picturesque Pyrenees
May 3 The Banks of the Danube
The Money Bag
May 4 Called to the Sea†
Diamond Cut Diamond
Immigrants' Progress in Canada†
The Witch of the Ruins
May 5 The Little Beggar Maid
They Would Roller Skate
May 6 Customs of the Buddhists in India
A Romantic Girl
May 7 The Call of the Forest
The Cherries
Gigantic Waves
Medium Wanted as Son-in-Law
May 9 Pete Wants a Job
Villainy Defeated
May 10 A Little Vagrant
A Sea of Clouds
May 11 Cleopatra
Purged by Fire†
Roosevelt in Cairo†
May 12 Her Two Suitors
A Mother's Grief
May 13 Berlin
The Surgeon's Visit
May 14 Christopher Columbus
The Little Truant
The Wrong Road
May 17 Marvellous Waters
Racing for a Bride
May 18 The Girl Conscript†
The Gold Spider
Modern Railway Construction†
Who Will Win My Heart?
May 19 He Did Not Die
The Lace Maker's Dream
Werther
May 20 A Brave Little Girl
Gee I Am Late
May 21 The Centenarian
The Masher's Delirium
The Milk Industry in the Alps
A Tempestuous Adventure
May 23 Little Mary and Her Dolly
Romeo Turns Bandit
May 24 Floral Studies
Over the Cliffs
May 25 Capturing Cub Bears
His Wife's Testimony†
Max Leads Them a Novel Chase
A Sagacious Animal
May 26 Don Carlos
Midsummer Night's Dream
May 27 A Mirror of the Future
A Prince of Worth
May 28 The Messenger's Dog
Pete Has Nine Lives
A Sailor's Friendship
May 30 Down with the Women
Russia, the Caucasian Mountains
May 31 Jarnac's Treacherous Blow
The Little German Band
Won and Lost
Jun 1 Her Life for Her Love†
Ines de Castro
Making Salt†
One Can't Believe One's Eyes
Jun 2 A Stray Dog
Vitellius and Heliogabalus
Jun 3 Lillian and Anetta
The Slave's Love
The Two Portraits
What Happened to a Cinematograph Party
Jun 4 Beneath the Walls of Notre Dame
Burglar's Dog
[King Edward's Funeral]
Macbeth
The Office Seeker
Quarrelsome Man
A Trip on the Seine
Jun 7 The Monastery in the Forest
A Night on the Coast
Jun 8 The Empty Cradle
Lucy Consults the Oracle
The Mountain Lake†
The Nightmare†
Jun 9 The Children of Edward IV
Jun 10 Dmitri Donskoj
24-Hour Automobile Race
Jun 11 Floating to Wealth
Lerin's Abbey on St. Honorat's Island
The Marriage of Esther
An Unexpected Friend
Jun 13 Childish Escapade
Micro-Cinematography: Sleeping Sickness
Jun 14 At the Dawning; or, The Fear of the Comet
A Bitter Enemy
Jun 15 The Barry Sisters
The Bone-Setter's Daughter
The Gum-Shoe Kid†
A Trip to Brazil†
Jun 16 The Legend of the Holy Chapel
Jun 17 MacNab Visits the Comet
Max Makes a Touch
Poor, but Proud
Jun 18 Esther and Mordecai
The Spanish Frontier
Jun 20 Reconciliation of Foes
Jun 21 The Devil's Wand
Hercules and the Big Stick
Princess and Pigeon
Jun 22 A Child of the Squadron†
An Excursion into Wales†
Perseverance Rewarded
Riding School in Belgium
Jun 23 Oliver Twist
Jun 24 Catching Fish with Dynamite
A Curious Invention
An Exciting Yarn
We Want Your Vote
Jun 25 Does Nephew Get the Cash?
Lakes at Eventide
Jun 27 Caesar in Egypt
Save Us from Our Friends
Jun 28 The Elder Sister
The Unlimited Train
The Witch's Spectacles
Jun 29 Napoleon
St. Paul and the Centurion†
Jun 30 Fort Du Bitche
Jul 1 Charles the Fifth
Inside the Earth
A Quiet Pipe
Rebellious Betty
Jul 2 Max Foils the Police
Motoring Among the Cliffs and Gorges of France
On the Threshold
Riding Feats by Cossacks
Jul 4 The Rhine from Cologne to Bingen
The Runaway Dog
Jul 5 The Clink of Gold
Life in Senegal, Africa
Jul 6 Jinks Has the Shooting Mania
Love Ye One Another
A Russian Spy†
Tropical Java of the South Sea Islands†
Jul 7 Jemmy
Jul 8 Big-Hearted Mary
Colonel Roosevelt Reviewing French Troops
The Money Lender's Son
Must Be Without Encumbrance
Jul 9 The Invincible Sword
Ruins of Mediaeval Fortifications in France
Jul 11 The Faithless Lover
Just for Good Luck
Jul 12 A Hidden Serpent
In the Realm of the Czar
Jul 13 The Moonlight Flitting†
The Overland Coach Robbery
Verona
The Wicked Baron and the Page†
Jul 14 The End of a Dynasty
Jul 15 Bill's Serenade
The Greatest of These Is Charity
Please Take One
A Political Discussion
Jul 16 Algerian Stud
A Good Loser
The Jolly Whirl
Jupiter Smitten
Jul 18 An Awful Symphony
Mistaken Identity
Jul 19 The Failure of Success
Jul 20 Catching Lobsters
Manon
Pekin, the Walled City†
Through the Enemy's Line†
Jul 21 Andromache
Mateo Falcone
Jul 22 A Devoted Little Brother
Ma's New Dog
Jul 23 The Foxy Lawyer
More of Betty's Pranks
Pete Has a Good Time
The Princess and the Fishbone
Jul 25 Breaking Up Ice in Finland
Getting Even with the Lawyer
Jul 26 An Angler's Dream
The Beautiful Margaret
Making Wooden Shoes
Jul 27 The Art Lover's Strategy†
The Detective's Dream
Mexican Domain†
On the Ethiopian Frontier
Jul 28 The Hiding Place
Jul 29 The Bailiff
Jul 30 Cagliostro
The Forbidden Novel; or, Don't Do as I Do, Do as I Say
The Sculptor's Ideal
Aug 1 Betty as an Errand Girl
Hunting Bats in Sumatra
Aug 2 The Ace of Hearts
An Ancient Mariner
Aug 3 The Barrel Jumper
Camel and Horse Racing in Egypt†
The Witch of Carabosse†
Aug 4 The Eagle and the Eaglet
Aug 5 No Man's Land
No Rest for the Weary
Aug 6 Fiftieth Anniversary of Yokohama
The Lord's Prayer
Teneriffe, the Gem of the Canaries
Aug 8 Jewish Types in Russia
The Troubles of a Flirt
Aug 9 Picturesque Waters of Italy
The Water Cure
Aug 10 The "Ibis"
On the Banks of the Zuyder Zee, Holland†
The Silent Witness†
Aug 11 Charles Le Tremeraire
The Oedipus King
Aug 13 Drifts of Snow in Chamonix Valley
Entombed Alive
Oliver Twist
Aug 15 Back to Life After 2,000 Years
Max Has to Change
Aug 16 Across Russian Poland
The Estrangement
Aug 17 Paris Viewed from the Eiffel Tower†
The Rival Serenaders†
Aug 18 Carmen
Aug 19 The Eriks
A Short-Lived Triumph
Aug 20 Buying a Mother-in-Law
Refusing a Mansion
A School in New Guinea
The Shepherd's Dog
Aug 22 Butter Making in Normandy
A Miscalculation
Aug 23 Four Little Tailors
Neighbors; or, Yvonne's Daughter
Aug 24 Escape of the Royalists†
Scenes in Norway
Shipbuilders of Toulon
Aug 25 The Acrobat's Son
The Chemist's Mistake
In the Time of the First Christians
Aug 27 The Castaway's Return
How Jack Won His Bride
In the Pyrenees
The Vow, or, Jephthah's Daughter
Aug 29 Kids Will Be Kids
Memento of the Past
Aug 30 Ancient Castles of Austria
The Shepherd and the Maid
Aug 31 Advertising for a Wife
Buying a Bear†
A Cruise in the Mediterranean†
Sep 1 King of a Day
Sep 2 Deer Hunting in Celebes Islands
Saved from Ruin
Sep 3 Calino Takes New Lodgings
Maggie Hollihan Gets a Job
Unrequited Love
Sep 5 Who Is Boss?
Zoological Gardens in Antwerp
Sep 6 The Way of the Transgressor Is Hard
Sep 7 Ingratitude; or, The Justice of Providence†
Military Kite Flying at Rheims
Sep 8 Conscience of a Child
The Minister's Speech

Sep 9 The Belgian Army
Lucy at Boarding School
Sep 10 Robert the Devil
Sep 12 A Good Glue
Hunting the Panther
Sep 13 An Easy Winner
A Powerful Voice
Sep 14 The Artisan†
The Tramps†
The Two Sisters
Sep 15 Aunt Tabitha's Monkey
The Selfish Man's Lesson
The Temptation of Sam Bottler
Sep 16 Unconscious Heroism
Sep 17 A Dummy in Disguise
Poems in Pictures
The Vagaries of Love
Sep 19 The False Friend
Trip to the Isle of Jersey
Sep 20 Sunset
Tactics of Cupid
Sep 21 A Corsican Vendetta†
Scenes in the Celestial Empire†
Sep 22 The Bobby's Dream
Ma-in-Law as a Statue
Only a Bunch of Flowers
That Typist Again
Sep 23 Max in a Dilemma
The Mexican Tumblers
Sep 24 The Reserved Shot
The Times Are Out of Joint
Sep 26 Colombo and Its Environs
Max Is Absent-Minded
The Street Arab of Paris
Sep 27 The Sunken Submarine
Too Much Water
Sep 28 The Hoodoo
The Quarrel†
Sep 29 How Jones Won the Championship
Kindness Abused and Its Results
Sep 30 The Sick Baby
Oct 1 The Diver's Honor
A High-Speed Biker
Southern Tunis
Who Owns the Rug?
Oct 3 Betty Is Still at Her Old Tricks
Molucca Islands
Oct 4 Her Fiancé and the Dog
The Little Acrobat
Oct 5 City of the Hundred Mosques, Broussa, Asia Minor†
Different Trades in Bombay
The Dishonest Steward†
Mirth and Sorrow
Oct 6 Auntie in the Fashion
Mother's Portrait
Oct 7 A Life for Love
Slippery Jim
Oct 8 The Dunce Cap
A Skier Training
Oct 10 Betty Is Punished
The Stigma
Oct 11 The Lovers' Mill
The Three Friends
Oct 12 Foiled by a Cigarette; or, The Stolen Plans of the Fortress†
Oct 13 Bill and the Missing Key
Runaway Star
Oct 14 Werther
Oct 15 Aeroplanes in Flight and Construction
The Aviation Craze
The Romance of a Necklace
Oct 17 Jinks Wants to Be an Acrobat
One on Max
Oct 18 Grandmother's Plot
Phantom Ride from Aix-les-Bains
Oct 19 Around Pekin
In the Shadow of the Night
Tunny Fishing off Palermo, Italy†
Oct 20 Gilson and Those Boys
The Tyrant
Oct 21 His Life for His Queen
Oct 22 The Cheat
Oct 24 Another's Ghost
Hagenbeck's Menagerie
Oct 25 The Amazon
The First Gray Hair
Oct 26 Bruges, Belgium
In the Spreewald†
The Signet Ring†
Oct 27 Bewitched
She Required Strength and Got It
Where You Go I Go
Oct 28 Buffalo Fight
Max in the Alps
Oct 29 The Life of Molière
Oct 31 Darjiling
Max Has Trouble with His Eyes
New Style Inkwell
Nov 1 Both Were Stung
Picturesque Majorca
Nov 2 Crossing the Andes
The Facori Family
Tragical Concealment
Nov 3 Fatty Taking a Bath
Her Diary
Nov 4 The Woman of Samaria
Nov 5 The Fishing Smack
Nov 7 Micro-Cinematography: Recurrent Fever
Nov 8 Pharoah; or, Israel in Egypt
Nov 9 A Mexican Legend
Secret of the Cellar†
A Trip Through Scotland†
Nov 11 Bill as a Boxer
A Black Heart
Dutch Types
The Truth Revealed
Nov 12 Faithful Until Death
A Trip to the Blue Grotto, Capri, Italy
Nov 14 A Shadow of the Past
Nov 15 Nebuchadnezzar's Pride†
Nov 16 An Alpine Retreat†
Love Laughs at Locksmiths
The Rival Barons†
Russian Wolf Hunt
Nov 18 Bill as a Lover
Blopps in Search of the Black Hand
Military Cyclists of Belgium
Phaedra
Nov 19 Lisbon, Before and During the Revolution
Spanish Loyalty
Nov 21 New South Wales Gold Mine
The Old Longshoreman
Nov 22 Cast into the Flames
A Woman's Wit
Nov 23 Behind a Mask†
Nantes and Its Surroundings†
Wonderful Plates
Nov 25 A Dog's Instinct
In Friendship's Name
Isis
Nov 26 Calino Travels as a Prince
An Eleventh Hour Redemption
Samson's Betrayal
Nov 28 A Border Tale
A Freak
Nov 29 The Flat Next Door
Tarascon on the Rhone
Nov 30 Finland—Falls of Imatra
Ramble Through Ceylon†
The Return at Midnight
Who Is Nellie?
Dec 2 Bill as an Operator
Necessity Is the Mother of Invention
The Tale the Mirror Told
What a Dinner!
Dec 3 Lured by a Phantom; or, The King of Thule
Nancy's Wedding Trip
Dec 5 The Clever Domestic
Dec 6 A Man of Honor
Professor's Hat
Dec 7 An Animated Armchair
Cocoanut Plantation
The Death of Admiral Coligny†
Dec 9 And She Came Back
Saved in the Nick of Time
Soap in His Eyes
What Will It Be
Dec 10 Her First Husband's Return
The Revolt
Dec 12 In Her Father's Absence
The Julians
Dec 13 Closed Gate
The Phantom Rider
Dec 14 Charlie and Kitty in Brussels
Hoboes' Xmas
The Little Matchseller's Christmas†
Dec 16 Her Favorite Tune
How We Won Her
Little Snowdrop
Dec 17 Herod and the New Born King
Saved by Divine Providence
Dec 19 Get Rich Quick
Hunting Sea Lions in Tasmania
Dec 20 His Cinderella Girl
The Kingdom of Flowers
Dec 21 A Chamois Hunt†
Max Goes Skiing
The Tyrant of Florence†
Dec 23 Betty's Fireworks
Bill Plays Bowls
The Lucky Charm
Rosalie's Dowry
Dec 24 Cain and Abel
The Old Home
Dec 26 The Atonement
The Bowling Fiend
Dec 27 The Adventuress
Dec 28 The American Fleet in French Waters
In Full Cry
A Mexican Romance†
Dec 30 Aunt Julia's Portrait
Carnival of Japanese Firemen in Tokio
Catalan, the Minstrel
Tim Writes a Poem
Dec 31 The Doctor's Secretary
The Yaqui Girl

Germany

1902

Nov [day undetermined]
Aboard the Aegir
The Attack
The Baby's Meal
Banks of the Elbe
Battleship "Odin"
"Be Good Again"
Berlin Fire Department
Between the Decks
Bi-Centennial Jubilee Parade
A Blast in a Gravel Bed
The Bogie Man
Calling the Pigeons
The Children and the Frog
Children Playing with Lion Cubs
Clever Horsemanship
The Crown Prince of Germany
Dedication of the Alexander Grenadiers' Barracks
The Elephant's Bath
Elevated and Underground
The Emperor and Empress and Crown Prince of Germany
Emperor and Empress of Germany
The Emperor and Empress of Germany
Emperor William II
Emperor William II on Horseback
Emperor William as a Hussar
Emperor William at the Danzig Manoeuvres
Emperor William of Germany on Horseback
Emperor William Returning from Manoeuvres
Empress of Germany at Danzig
Empress of Germany Driving to the Manoeuvres
Field-Marshal Count Von Waldersee
The Flying Train
A Flying Wedge
Fun in a Clothes Basket
Fun on a Sand Hill
Funeral Procession of the Late Empress Frederick
Ganswindt's Flying Machine
German Artillery in Action
German Cavalry Fording a River
German Cavalry Leaping Hurdles
German Garde Kurassiers
German Lancers
German Military Exercises
German Navy Target Practice
German Railway Service
A German Torpedo Boat Flotilla in Action
The Gourmand
A Hurdle Race
In a German Bath
In the Friedrichstrasse
In the Heart of the Forest
King Albert of Saxony
Launch of the "Koenig Albert"
Launching of the "Kaiser Wilhelm der Grosse"
Marvelous Markmanship
A Mermaid Dance
On Board His Majesty's Battleship "Fuerst Bismark"
On Board His Majesty's Gunboat "Luchs"
On the Elbe
Panorama of Wilhelmshaven
Panoramic View from the Stadtbahn
Panoramic View of the Harbor of Hamburg, Germany
Panoramic View of the Siegesallee
Prince Tsung of China

Lord Dundonald's Cavalry Seizing a Kopje in Spion Kop
On to Ladysmith
Mar [day undetermined]
Photographing the Ghost
May [day undetermined]
Bringing in the Wounded During the Battle of Grobler's Kloof
The Queen's Reception to the Heroes of Ladysmith
The Relief of Ladysmith
Trial Speed of H. M. Torpedo Boat Destroyer "Viper"
Jul [day undetermined]
Amateur Athletic Championships
Children of the Royal Family of England
Playing Soldier
Spirit of the Empire
1901 [month undetermined]
Amateur Athletic Association Sports
"Bend Or"
The Builders of Shamrock II
Chamberlain and Balfour
Emar De Flon, the Champion Skater
Launch of Shamrock II
Nabbed by the Nipper
Norway Ski Jumping Contests
Panoramic View of London Streets, Showing Coronation Decorations
Signor Marconi—Wireless Telegraphy
Soot Versus Suds
Spanish Coronation Royal Bull-Fight
Their Majesties the King and Queen
Winter Life in Sweden
Feb [day undetermined]
Departure of Duke and Duchess of Cornwall for Australia
The First Procession in State of H. M. King Edward VII
First Procession in State of H. M. King Edward VII
Queen Victoria's Funeral [Number 1]
Queen Victoria's Funeral [Number 2]
Queen Victoria's Funeral [Number 3]
Jun [day undetermined]
Emperor William's Yacht "Meteor"
English Derby, 1901
International Yacht Races on the Clyde
Panoramic View of the Thames
"Volodyovski"
Jun 29 The Inexhaustible Cab
Aug [day undetermined]
The Henley Regatta, 1901
1902 [month undetermined]
Bathing Made Easy
A Frustrated Elopement
May [day undetermined]
The Absent Minded Clerk, Fly Paper and Silk Hat
The Cheese Mites; or, The Lilliputians in a London Restaurant
The Children's Tea Party
The Children's Toys That Came to Life
The Haunted Pawnshop
Magical Sword
Ora Pro Nobis Illustrated
The Pals and the Clothier's Dummy
A Railroad Wreck (Imitation)
The Tight Collar
Undressing Under Difficulties
The Wonderful Baby Incubator
Jul [day undetermined]
Explosion of an Automobile
Aug 30 Crowning of King Edward and Queen Alexandra
The King and Queen Arriving at Westminster Abbey
The King and Queen Leaving Westminster Abbey After the Crowning
King Edward Reviewing Coronation Naval Force at Spithead August 16, 1902
The King's Procession
The New Crowned King and Queen Passing Through Wellington Arch and Down Constitution Hill
Panoramic View of Westminster Abbey and Surroundings
Sep [day undetermined]
Coronation Parade
The Deonzo Brothers in Their Wonderful Barrel Jumping Act
The Dutchman's Interrupted Dinner
Grandma Threading Her Needle
The Hodcarriers' Ping Pong
A Photographic Contortion
Reproduction, Coronation Ceremonies—King Edward VII
A Telephone Romance
Nov [day undetermined]
Dessert at Dan Leno's House
His Morning Bath
Mr. Dan Leno, Assisted by Mr. Herbert Campbell, Editing the "Sun"
The Murderer's Vision
An Obstinate Cork
Rare Fish in the Aquarium
Umbrella Dance, San Toy
1903 [month undetermined]
Brothers of the Misericordia, Rome
Two Old Sports
Jan [day undetermined]
The Miller and Chimney Sweep
The Soldier's Return
Jan 17 The Ascent of Mount Blanc
Feb [day undetermined]
Mother Goose Nursery Rhymes
Policeman and Automobile
Reversible Donkey Cart
Mar 14 The Delhi Camp Railway
Logging in Canada
On the Bow River Horse Ranch at Cochrane, North West Territory
Spearing Salmon in the Rivers of the North West Territory
Mar 21 Life of a London Fireman
The Little Match Seller
The Workman's Paradise
Apr [day undetermined]
Acquatic Sports
Ascending a Rock-Chimney on the Grand Charmoz, 11,293 feet
Ascent and Descent of the Aiguilles Des Grandes Charmoz, 11,293 feet
Breaking a Bronco
The Broncho Horse Race
Coaching in Ireland
Coaching Through the Tunnel on the Kenmere Road
Coster Sports
"The Devil of the Deep" and the Sea Urchins
A Devonshire Fair
A Duel with Knives
England's Colonial Troops
An English Prize-Fight
A Gorgeous Pageant of Princes
The Grand Canal, Venice
The Grand Panorama from the Great Schreckhorn, 13,500 feet
The House That Jack Built
A Kennel Club Parade
A Kiss in the Tunnel
Landing Guns
Life and Passion of Christ
Looping the Loop
A Majestic Stag
Man's Best Friend
Mary Jane's Mishap; or, Don't Fool with the Parafin
The Monk in the Monastery Wine Cellar
Mountain Torrents
On Horseback, Killarney
On the Grand Canal, Venice
Over London Bridge
Panorama of Alpine Peaks
Panorama of Grindelwald
Panorama of Lucerne Lake
Panorama of Queenstown
Panorama on the St. Gothard Railway
A Paper Chase
Pa's Comment on the Morning News
The Pines of the Rockies
Push Ball
Review of Native Chiefs at the Durbar
Review of the Chiefs at the Durbar
The River Shannon
Ski Jumping Competition
Spanish Bull Fight
Stag Hunting in England
A Swiss Carnival
Through the Telescope
A Triple Balloon Ascent
A Two Handed Sword Contest
A Visit to the London Zoo
A Water Carnival
Weary Willie and the Policeman
With the Stag Hounds
May [day undetermined]
Life of an English Fireman
Miniature Prize Fighters
A Scarecrow Tramp
May 16 Spring Cleaning
May 23 Railway Ride in the Alps
Jul [day undetermined]
Laplanders at Home
Jul 18 The Life of a London Bobby
Aug [day undetermined]
Little Lillian, Toe Danseuse
Aug 1 The Elixir of Life
Fun on Board a Fishing Smack
Sep [day undetermined]
At Brighton Beach
At Terrific Speed
At the Ford, India. Across the Ravi River
The Busy Bee
Coasting in the Alps
A Daring Daylight Burglary
The Devonshire Fair
The Devonshire Hunt
The Diamond Robbery
From London to Brighton
The Galloping Tongas
How to Get a Wife and Baby
King Edward VII in France
The Llamas of Thibet
A Norwegian Waterfall
A Remarkable Group of Trained Animals
Rip Van Winkle
Rising Panorama of a Norwegian Waterfall
Start of the Gordon-Bennet Cup Race
A Terrific Race
Trained Baby Elephants
Trained Dogs and Elephants
An Unusual Spectacle
The Wise Elephant
Sep 18 Trailed by Bloodhounds
Oct [day undetermined]
Dextrous Hand
Photographer's Victim
Soap vs. Blacking
Washerwomen and Chimney-Sweep
Oct 17 Alice in Wonderland
Oct 31 Hop Picking
Moses in the Bullrushes
The Poachers
Nov [day undetermined]
The Professor
Nov 21 Animated Picture Studio
Automobile Explosion
Cruelty on the High Seas
The Deserter
Down Below
Fire and Rescue
The Ghost in the Graveyard
Hotel and Bath
Letter Came Too Late
Murphy's Wake
The New Cook
Nicholas Nickleby
Over the Garden Wall
A Pugilistic Parson
Quarrelsome Neighbors
Saturday's Shopping
A Trip to Southend
Nov 28 Attack on Chinese Mission
The Bather
Bicycle Dive
Jack's Return
Stop Thief
Dec [day undetermined]
How the Old Woman Caught the Omnibus
The Pickpocket
Dec 12 At Work in a Peat Bog
Cliff Scenery at the Fabbins
A Coach Drive from Glengariffe to Kenmore
A Drove of Wild Welsh Mountain Ponies
Elopement a la Mode
Irish Peasants Bringing Their Milk to a Cooperative Creamery
The Mono-Railway Between Listowel and Ballybunion, Ireland
Panorama of the Lakes of Killarney from Hotel
Polo Match for the Championship at Hurlingham
Scenes in an Irish Bacon Factory
Scenes in an Irish Market Place
Scenes of a New Forest Pony Fair
Scenes of Irish Cottage Life
Scenes on a Welsh Pony Farm
Shooting the Rapids of Killarney

A Trip Through the Gap of Dunloe
A Trip to the Giant's Causeway
Trout Fishing, Landing Three Pounder
Wild Mountain Ponies on Dartmoor
Wiring Pike in a Mill Stream

1904 [month undetermined]
Arrival and Release of 40,000 Carrying Pigeons at Ambergate, England
The Baby, the Monkey and the Milk Bottle
International Winter Sports
Manoeuvres by British Bluejackets, Afloat and Ashore
The Monkey and the Ice Cream
The Oxford and Cambridge Boat Race
The Russian Army in Manchuria

Jan [day undetermined]
Chameleon Climbing
The Cheese Mites
Pugilistic Toads
The Toad's Luncheon
Trick Bicycle Riding

Jan 2 The Somnambulist
Jan 23 The Kiddies and the Poultry

Feb [day undetermined]
Those Troublesome Boys

Feb 23 Diving Lucy
Jack Sheppard—The Robbery of the Mail Coach
The Salmon Fisheries of Vancouver

Mar 12 Behind a Big Gun
How the Japs Fought at Port Arthur
The Jap Behind the Guns
Japanese Jackies

Apr 20 Russian Outposts Attacked by Japanese
Apr 25 The Dear Boys Home for the Holidays
An Evil Doer's Sad End
Falls of the Clyde
Inspector's Birthday
Life Guards Responding to Distress Signals
No Room for Dad
Pleasant Breakfast
The Sailor's Rival
The Smugglers
That Busy Bee
What the Window Cleaner Saw
The Wrong Poison

Jun [day undetermined]
Deer Hunting in England*
The Devonshire Fair*
The Eviction
Military Tactics
Pushball Game*
Willful Murder

Jun 4 The Apple Woman
The Bobby Whitewashed
The Cook's Lovers
The Coster's Wedding

Jun 25 Chased by a Dog
The Child Stealers
Naval Attack on Port Arthur
The Office Boy's Revenge
The Postman Whitewashed
Raid on a Coiner's Den

Jul [day undetermined]
All for the Love of a Geisha
Boys Will Be Boys
Capture and Execution of Spies by Russians
The Chappie at the Well
A Circus Romance
College Sports in England
The Coster's Wedding
Courting and Caught
Dorothy's Dream
Driven from Home
Duck Hunt
Haunted Scene Painter
The Music Hall Manager's Dilemma
Old Maids and the Unfaithful Lovers
The Parson's Cooking Lesson
Push Ball on Horseback
Rum vs. Cherries
Smoked Out
The Snapshot Fiend
Stolen Puppy
Study, Smoke and Soot
Such Is Life
That Terrible Sneeze
Toy Maker and Good Fairy
Tragic Elopement
Two's Company, Three's None
Voyage of the "Arctic"

Jul 9 A Disaster in a Colliery

Aug [day undetermined]
Arrival and Departure of the Ice-Crushing Steamer "Baikal" at Baikal, Siberia
The Arrival of the 1st Siberian Sharpshooters at Harbin
Attempted Murder in a Train
Barber's Tricks
The Bewitched Traveler
Cairo and the Nile
Children Romping on the Lawn
Constantinople and the Bosporus
Curious Sights in Burmah and Cashmere (Section 1)
Curious Sights in Burmah and Cashmere (Section 2)
The Execution (Beheading) of One of the Hunchuses (Chinese Bandits) Outside the Walls of Mukden
Extraordinary Feats of Horsemanship
A Fierce Sword Combat at Tokio
The Great International Automobile Race for the Gordon-Bennett Trophy
"He Won't Be Happy till He Gets It"
The International Congress of the Salvation Army
The Japanese Ogre
The Japanese Standard Bearer
Late for Work
The Military Funeral of the "Standard Bearer of the Yalu"
Nobles Leaving the Kremlin, Moscow, After a Reception by Czar
Off for the Holidays
Piraeus and Athens (Greece). A Visit to Piraeus
Piraeus and Athens (Greece). Athens and the Acropolis
Piraeus and Athens (Greece). Hoisting Cattle on Steamer
A Regiment of the Japanese Imperial Guards and Engineer Corps off to the Front
A Trip to Palestine. Jaffa and Its Harbor
A Trip to Palestine. Jerusalem, the Holy City
The War Correspondent and the Two Bear Cubs

Sep [day undetermined]
Boys' Trick on Grandpa
The Miser's Daughter
The Pig That Came to Life
The Quarrelsome Washerwoman

Sep 7 Linen Shop
Sep 17 Burglar and Girls
The Convict's Escape
A Kiss and a Tumble

Oct [day undetermined]
Bobbie's Downfall
Cruelty to Horses
Decoyed
An Englishman's Trip to Paris from London
Fly Paper Vendors
Kissing the Blarney Stone
Lover's Crime
The Market Woman's Mishap
The Masher's Dilemma
Mixed Bathing
Night Duty
Paris from the Seine
Putting Up the Swing
Revenge!
Sculptor and Model
Shooting the Rapids of Killarney

Oct 15 A Railway Tragedy
Oct 17 A Little Boy Called "Taps"
Oct 29 The Fatal Wig
Three Little Maids

Nov [day undetermined]
Coal Heavers
Electric Doorbell
Illustrated Songs
The Lover's Ruse
Over the Hedge
Petticoat Lane on Sunday
A Race for a Kiss
Shanghaied by Pirates

Dec [day undetermined]
The Amorous Militiaman
At Brighton
Disturbed Picnic
Dunloe Women
Great Sea Serpent
Guy Fawkes' Day
The Honeymoon
Intresting Story
Lady Plumpton's Motor Car
Mary in the Dock
Oh! What a Surprise
Stowaway

Dec 3 Life of a Race Horse
Sandy McGregor

Dec 17 The Baltic Fleet and the North Sea Trawlers
Patrick Street, Cork

1905 [month undetermined]
Fine Feathers Make Fine Birds

Jan [day undetermined]
Soldier's Romance
Tramps in Clover

Feb 25 Love Letter

Mar [day undetermined]
Awful Donkey

May [day undetermined]
Behind the Scenes

Jul [day undetermined]
Bishop and Burglar
Cook and Chimney Sweep
An Eccentric Burglary
Fatal Necklace
Fixing the Derby Favorite
Only Her Brother
The Race for Bed
Rescued by Rover

Aug [day undetermined]
An Affair of Honor
Aylesbury Ducks*
Blind Man's Bluff
Dangerous Golfers
Falsely Accused
His Washing Day
How Jones Saw the Derby
Lady Barber
Masher and Nursemaid
Rehearsing a Play at Home
Robbing His Majesty's Mail
Terrible Flirt
Wide Awake*
Won't You Come Home?

Sep [day undetermined]
The Blacksmith's Daughter

Oct [day undetermined]
Devil's Dice
He Learned Ju Jitsu, So Did the Missus
Pilfered Porker

Nov [day undetermined]
Among the Snakes
Arrival of the Mail Steamer at Larne
The Baby Show
Brick Making Rotifier
The British Bull Dog
By Rail Through Canadian Rockies
Cake-Walk in Our Alley
Cir. of Blood, Frog's Foot
Cir. of Protoplasm in Waterweed
Coaches Starting from Larne and Passing Through Tunnel on the Antrim Coast Road
Convicts' Escape
The Curate's Adventures
Elopement
An English Gymkana
Father Neptune and Bear
Feeding the Otters
Fiscal Problem
Fresh Water Infusorian
Getting the Hay
Giant Tortoise Feeding
Head Hunters of Borneo
Hiawatha
Imp No. 2
In an English Hayfield
Indian Babies' Bath
The Intruders
Japanese Funeral
The King Planting a Tree at the Royal Agricultural Society's Show Yard
The Life Boat
The London Press
Magic Cone
Magic Hair Restorer
Market Day at Kenmore
The Midnight Sun at Scalo
Military Display at Hurlingham
Milking Time: A Kerry Herd
Mr. Martin Duncan
A Moorish Street Minstrel Performing at Morocco City
Motor Highwayman
The Naughty Boys and Curate
The Newt
An Old Maid's Darling
On a Borneo Railway
Over in Jersey
Overturning a Mammoth Chimney
Panorama of the Sultan of Morocco's Troop Forming a Square Awaiting the Arrival of H. M. S.

Panoramic Bird's Eye View of Montreal, Canada
Police Raid on a Club
Pond Life
Potters at Work
The Puppies
Railway Panorama Between Green Island and Kilroot
Railway Panorama Between Kilroot and Whitehead
The Red Slug Worm
The Red Snow Germs
Ride on Sprinkler Car
Rock Scene at Ballybunion
Roping and Branding Wild Horses
A Rough Sea on the Derry Coast
Russian Field Artillery
Russian Kirgis Troops
Russian Mounted Artillery
Sambo
Scenes at the Zoo
The Servant Girl's Dream
The Servant Question
Shooting the Chutes, Cork Exhibition
A Smart Captive
Snail, Tortoise, Toad
A Snake in the Grass
The Squire and the Maid
The Stolen Cake
Stork's Tug of War
A Study in Feet
The Three Honeymoons
Through Tunnel on the Antrim Coast
Tourists Leaving the Lake Hotel, Killarney
Two Imps
Typhoid Fever Germs
The Waterfalls of Glengariffe
White Rat and Young
The White Rats
Winning a Pair of Gloves
Wonderful Hat

Dec [day undetermined]
Freak Barber
Goaded to Anarchy
Hubby Tries to Keep House

1906

Jan [day undetermined]
Horse Stealing
A Misguided Bobby at a Fancy Garden Party
Moose Hunt in Canada*
Opium Smoker's Dream
The Peashooter
Shaving by Installments
Two Little Waifs

Jan 27 A False Alarm

May 26 The Lost Leg of Mutton
The Olympian Games†

Jul [day undetermined]
Fakir and Footpad
House Furnishing Made Easy

Jul 14 Anything for Peace and Quietness

Aug 25 The Henly Regatta
Playmates†

Sep 20 The Dog Detective
Rescued in Mid-Air

Nov 24 Algy's New Suit

Dec [day undetermined]
The Drunken Mattress
A Modern Diogenes

1907

Jan [day undetermined]
Beaver Hunt†
Cheating Justice†
Deer Hunt†
Following in Father's Footsteps
The Gardener's Nap
The Little Globe Trotter†
Making Champagne†
Reformation†
Trial Trip of the Airship "La Patrie"†
Whale Fishing†
Willie Goodchild Visits His Auntie

Jan 26 Professor in Difficulties†
The Stolen Bride
Stormy Winds Do Blow†

Feb [day undetermined]
Animated Stamp Pad†
Baby Cries†
The Bad Son†
Brown Goes to Mother
Burglar and Policeman†
Going Away for Holiday†
Her First Cake
His First Cigarette†
Indian Customs†
The Man Monkey
Man Who Hangs Himself†
Message from the Sea
The Miner's Daughter†
Moonlight on the Ocean†
My Master's Coffee Service†
My Servant Is a Jewel†
My Wife's Birthday†
A New Toboggan†
Policeman Has an Idea†
Skiing in Norway†
Snowballing†
Soldier to Colonel†
Stolen Child†
Two Rival Peasants†
When Friends Meet†
Winter in Switzerland†
Wrestling Match, Hackenschmidt†

Feb 2 The Artful Dodger
Carnival at Venice†
The Double Life
Playing a Trick on the Gardener†
Playing Truant†
The Underworld of Paris†
The Zoo at London, Part I†
The Zoo at London, Part II†

Mar [day undetermined]
Cassimir's Night Out†
The Conjuror's Pupil
Conquering the Dolomites
Disturbing His Rest
First Snowball
Flashes from Fun City
The Hand of the Artist
His First Camera
His First Dinner at Father-in-Law's†
Is Marriage a Failure?
Little Lord Mayor†
Looking for Lodgings†
Mrs. Smithson's Portrait†
Moonlight on Lake†
Oh! That Molar
Paying Off Scores
Puck's Pranks on Suburbanite
Quaint Holland
The Runaway Van
Traveling Menagerie
Trip to Borneo
Turkey Raffle
Woman Up-to-Date†
Wonders of Canada

Mar 2 The Birthday Celebration†
A Set of Dishes†

Mar 9 The Murderer†

Mar 30 After the Matinee
The Arlberg Railway
The Atlantic Voyage
Berlin to Rome
Black Beauty
Captain Kidd and His Pirates
The Carving Doctor†
A Championship Won on a Foul
Curfew Shall Not Ring Tonight
Dolomite Towers
Flirting on the Sands†
The Magic Bottle
Napoleon and Sentry†
An Old Coat Story†
Parody on Toreador†
Take Good Care of Baby†
Universal Winter Sports
The Yokel's Love Affair

Apr [day undetermined]
Curious Carriage of Klobenstein†
How the World Lives†
In a Picture Frame†
Miss Kellerman's Diving Feats
Picnic Hampers†
Tirolean Dance†

Apr 6 The Busy Man
Drink and Repentance
Father's Picnic
The Fishing Industry
Foiled by a Woman; or, Falsely Accused
Quarter Day Conjuring
She Would Sing
Signal Man's Son
Slippery Jim, the Burglar

Apr 13 The Animated Pill Box
Artist's Model
Baby's Peril
The Borrowed Ladder
An Early Round with the Milkman
The Tell-Tale Telephone
Traced by a Laundry Mark
The Vision of a Crime
A Woman's Sacrifice

Apr 20 The Bad Shilling
Cambridge-Oxford Race
Catch the Kid
Chasing a Sausage†
Chef's Revenge
Eggs
Father! Mother Wants You
Knight-Errant
Lady Cabby
Land of Bobby Burns
Life and Customs in India
A Mother's Sin
Murphy's Wake
The Naval Nursery
The Poet's Bid for Fame
Sailor's Return
The Terrorist's Remorse†
The Vacuum Cleaner
Village Fire Brigade
Wizard's World

Apr 27 Clowns and Statue†
The Doll's Revenge
Great Boxing Contest
A Pig in Society
Servant's Revenge
A Smart Capture
The Smugglers†

May [day undetermined]
A Little Bit of String

May 4 The Fatal Hand
Johnny's Run
The Park Keeper
The Romany's Revenge

May 11 The Hundred Dollar Bill; or, The Tramp Couldn't Get It Changed†

May 18 Father's Washing Day
Papa's Letter
Spring Cleaning
The Stolen Bicycle

May 25 Beating the Landlord†
Buying a Ladder†
Catastrophe in the Alps†
A Child's Cunning†
The Cup and Ball†
Dog and the Tramp†
Nurse Takes a Walk†
Rogie Falls and Salmon Fishing†
Salome†
Sign of the Times†
Two Cents Worth of Cheese†
The Village Celebration†

Jun 1 Fatal Leap
The Human Clock†
An Icy Day†
Mischievous Sammy
The New Policeman
A Perfect Nuisance†
The Tramp's Dream
A Trip Through the Holy Land†
Winter Amusements†
Won by Strategy
The Wrong Chimney; or, Every Man His Own Sweep

Jun 10 The Child Accuser
Dressing in a Hurry†
The Faithful Dog; or, True to the End†
Saved from the Wreck†
The Substitute Drug Clerk†

Jun 15 I Never Forget the Wife
Whose Hat Is It?†

Jun 22 The Blackmailer
His Cheap Watch
Moving Under Difficulties†
She Won't Pay Her Rent†
Willie's Dream

Jun 24 Comedy Cartoons
Shoeing the Mail Carrier†

Jun 25 The Amateur Rider†

Jun 26 The Legless Runner†
The Toilet of an Ocean Greyhound†

Jun 29 Bertie's Love Letter
The Comic Duel
Humors of Amateur Golf
The Orange Peel

Jul 6 Diabolo, the Japanese Top Spinner†

Jul 8 Fatality
Scratch My Back

Jul 18 Croker's Horse Winning the Derby

Jul 20 Dick Turpin
The Dog Acrobats†
Don't Pay Rent—Move†
Drama in a Spanish Inn†
Getting His Change
The Matinee Idol
A Poet and His Babies
Prisoner's Escape†

Servant's Generosity†
Too Stout†
Unlucky Interference†
Jul 27 Drawing Teacher†
Looking for the Medal†
The Poacher's Daughter†
Aug 3 Buying a Donkey†
Aug 10 The Dummy†
From Cairo to Khartoum†
The Gypsies; or, The Abduction†
The Helmet†
Life Boat Manoeuvres†
Life in a South Afrhcan Gold Mine†
Looking at a Balloon†
Spring Gardening†
Torpedo Attack on H. M. S. Dreadnought†
Aug 17 The New Stag Hunt†
Poor but Proud†
Aug 24 A Big Take of Tunny Fish†
The Dervish's Revenge†
The Doll Maker's Daughter
Hair Restorer
Her Friend, the Enemy
In an Armchair†
The Tooth Ache†
Wandering Willie's Luck†
Sep 7 After the Fancy Dress Ball
Hanky Panky Cards
Irish Scenes and Types†
Life in a Burmah Teak Forest†
The Life of Bee†
A Modern Mother†
The Motorcyclist
Mount Pilatus Railway†
Rail Lying at Crewe†
The Strength of Cheese†
The Warwick Pageant
Sep 14 The Cheater's Cheated
The Good Wine†
Sep 16 Absent Mindedness†
The Amateur Hunter†
Art Student's Frivolities†
A Baffled Burglar
The Fly†
Roumania, Its Citizens and Soldiers†
Woodcutter's Daughter†
Sep 21 The Ghost Holiday
His Second Childhood
The Pastry Cook and Musician
Slavery of Children
Sep 23 Amongst the Reptiles†
Carl Hagenbeck's Wild Animal Park at Hamburg, Germany†
A Chinaman Visits London
Conway to Dublin
Dogs Tracking Burglars†
A First Class Restaurant†
Glimpses of Erin
Those Boys Again
Uncle's Heritage†
Winan's Horses†
Wipe Off Your Feet, Please†
Sep 26 The Persevering Lover†
Sep 28 The Benediction of the Sea
Invalid's Adventure
Sep 30 Coffee Plantation†
The Horse That Ate the Baby
How Isaac Won the Cop
Tamer Hopkins†
The Undergraduate
Oct 1 A Doctor's Conscience†
Fisherman's Luck†
The Great Victoria Falls†
Oct 5 His First Topper
Late for His Wedding†
Returning Good for Evil†
Oct 7 The Foster Cabby†
The Haunted Bedroom
Madame Goes Shopping†
Slavery by Circumstance†
Tyrolean Alps in the Winter†
A Would Be Champion†
Oct 12 Asking His Way†
A Day of His Own
Drink
Little Meg and the Wonderful Lamp
Serving a Summons
The Sham Sword Swallower
A Soldier's Jealousy
A Too Devoted Wife
Oct 14 Crazed by a Fad†
Farmer Giles' Geese†
Rubberneck Reuben†
Oct 19 Cricket Terms Illustrated
Don't Go to the Law
Jealousy Punished†
Just in Time
Mischievous Girls
A Modern Don Juan
Picturesque Wales
A Sailor's Lass
A Seaside Girl
Slate Quarries in North Wales
There Is a Rat in the Room†
Wild Animals
Oct 26 The Lover's Charm
Oct 28 The Absent-Minded Professor
The Adventures of a Bath Chair
The Athletic Dude†
De Beers Diamond Mines, Kimberly, S.A.†
A Four Year Old Heroine†
The Glue†
Naval Manoeuvres†
Onions Make People Weep†
Picturesque Brittany†
Smoke Without Fire†
The Thieving Umbrella†
Through Hong Kong†
Towed by an Automobile†
Volunteer's Betrothal†
Who Has Stolen My Bicycle†
Nov 4 Accidents Will Happen
An Anonymous Letter†
A Good Husband†
King Edward on H.M.S. Dreadnought
Launch of the British Battleship Bellerophon
The Lost Bass Drum; or, Where Is That Louie?†
Raising the Wind†
The White Shoes; or, Looking Out for His Banknote†
A Wig Made To Order†
Nov 9 A Shilling Short in Wages
Nov 11 The Stolen Shoes†
Nov 14 Grandfather and the Kitten†
Turning the Tables†
Nov 16 A Drink Cure
Dumb Sagacity
Even a Worm Will Turn
Testing of a Lifeboat
A Tramp's Dream of Wealth
Nov 23 The Collar'd Herring
Nov 30 Bad Boy's Joke†
Comrade Rations†
Daughter's Lover in Difficulties†
Misadventures of a Street Singer†
Reedham Boys' Aquatic Sports
Simple-Minded Peasant†
Stolen Child's Career†
The Tattler†
Unlucky Trousers†
Dec [day undetermined]
Against the Law†
Bulgarian Army†
Cabman Mystified†
The Cashier†
Deaf and Dumb†
Diabolo Nightmare
Hatred†
Highly Scented Bouquet†
Love Levels All Ranks†
When the Devil Drives
Youthful Hackenschmidts
Dec 2 Darkest Hour†
Harvest Celebration†
The Lady Athlete; or, The Jiu Jitsu Downs the Footpads
Tommy's Box of Tools
Wrong Righted†
Dec 7 A Letter in the Sand
The Rebellious Schoolgirls
The Sticky Bicycle
Dec 9 Notice to Quit†
Saving His Country's Flag†
Sunday with the Boss†
Dec 21 Father Buys a Hand Roller
Dec 23 The Gamekeeper's Dog
Nurse's Travels†
A Red Hot Day†
The Romance of a Fisherman's Daughter†
Dec 27 Burns-Moir
Dec 30 Cook's Fiancé†
False Start†
A Tight Fix†

1908

Jan 6 The Affianced†
The Hypnotist's Pranks†
The Marvelous Powder†
Jan 18 Anxious Day for Mother
The Artful Lovers
Girl's Dream†
Ingenuity Conquers†
Medal Winner†
Mr. Sleepy Head†
Pied Piper of Hamlin
A Restful Ride†
Tenor with Leather Lungs†
Valiant Son†
The Viking's Bride
Jan 20 The Water Babies; or, The Little Chimney Sweep
Jan 25 Pa Takes Up Physical Culture
Why the Wedding Was Put Off
Feb 3 Ancient Headgear†
Gainsborough Hat†
Music Hath Charms†
Oh, That Cat
The Scout†
Feb 8 Gabriel Grub
Home for the Holidays
Feb 10 The Strenuous War Veteran's Story†
Uncle's Clock†
Feb 15 Bobby's Birthday
A Day at the Sea Shore
Rival Barbers
The Story of an Egg
Feb 17 An Episode of the French Revolution†
The Soldier's Wedding
Feb 22 Adventures of a Beggar
Feb 29 Hackenschmidt-Rodgers Wrestling Match
His Sweetheart When a Boy
Jealous Husband
Painless Extraction
Mar 7 The Boarder Got the Haddock
Duchess' Crime
Sad Awakening
The Tricky Twins
Mar 14 The Curate's Courtship
For the Baby's Sake
The Inquisitive Fly and the Bald Head
Our New Errand Boy
Remorse
Student's Joke on the Porter†
Mar 21 His Daughter's Voice
Poor Pa's Folly
The Robbers and the Jew
'Twixt Love and Duty; or, A Woman's Heroism
When Our Sailor Son Comes Home
Willie's Magic Wand
Apr 4 Big Bow Mystery
Boats
Brigand's Daughter
Getting Rid of His Dog
Moonbeams
The Orphans
The Soul Kiss
Starvelings
Struck
Terrors of the Deep
Apr 11 Antics of Two Spirited Citizens†
The Astrologer†
The Captain's Wives
A Contagious Nervousness†
A Dislocated Veteran†
Doctor's Lunch†
The Downfall of the Burglars' Trust
The Enchanted Boots†
The Half-Moon Tavern†
A Lady Who Likes a Moustache†
Ma-in-Law Mesmerized†
The Novice Tight-Rope Walker†
£100 Reward
The Professor's Secret†
The Scandalous Boys
Trip to Norway†
Apr 18 The Accordion†
A Bear in the Flat†
The Coal Man's Savings†
The Crusaders' Return†
The Enchanted Guitar†
False Money†
Ice Cream Jack
The Miracle†
The Misadventures of an Equilibrist†
Railway Tragedy†
The Shepherd†
The Ski-ing Maniac†
The Spirit†
Youthful Treasure Seekers†
May 2 Alone at Last†
Biarritz†
Cat and Dog Show†
Fiji Islanders†
Freddie's Little Love Affair
Funeral of the Late King of Portugal†

The Great Trunk Robbery
The Greedy Girl
Harvesting
Kidnapped by Gypsies†
Lazy Jim's Luck
Marvelous Pacifier†
Men and Women†
The Mission of a Flower
Mr. Smith's Difficulties in the Shoe Store†
Mrs. Stebbins' Suspicions Unfounded†
The Outcast Heroine†
Oyster Farming†
Poor Aunt Matilda
Portland Stone Industry
A Ride in a Subway†
The Rival Lovers†
A Sacrifice for Work
Ski Contest†
The Stolen Dagger†
The Sugar Industry†
Tell-Tale Cinematograph
Tommy the Fireman†
May 9 Bogus Magic Powder†
Country About Rome†
The Doctor's Dodge
Environs of Naples†
The Gambler's Wife
The Guileless Country Lassie†
The Interrupted Bath
Leap Year; or, She Would Be Wed
The Lover's Tribulation†
The Memory of His Mother
My Cabby Wife†
Professor Bounder's Pills
The Two Guides†
May 16 Always Too Late†
Australian Sports and Pastimes†
Awkward Orderly†
The Basket Maker's Daughter†
Bertie's Sweetheart†
A Bohemian Romance†
The Bond†
Canine Sagacity
Catching a Burglar
Chair, If You Please†
An Extraordinary Overcoat†
A Faithless Friend
Fond of His Paper†
The Little Flower Girl†
The Magic Powder†
Meeting of Kings and Queens†
Motoring over the Alps†
Nasty Sticky Stuff
The Ramming of H. M. S. Gladiator by the St. Paul
A Red Man's Justice†
Running for Office†
St. Patrick's Day in New York†
Schoolboy's Joke†
Scotland
Stolen Boots†
The Strong Man's Discretion†
These Gentlemen Are with Me†
Thirty Years After†
Why Smith Left Home†
The Winning Number†
The Young Protector†
Youthful Samaritan†
May 30 Expensive Marriage†
The Fireman's Daughter
Hedge Hog Coat†
Inventor's Son's Downfall†
Magical Suit of Armor†
A Mean Man†
Mr. Farman's Airship†
Oxford and Cambridge Boat Race†
The Persistent Beggar†
Red Man's Revenge†
River Avon
River in Norway†
Rugby Match
Sammy's Sucker
Steel Industry†
Student's Predicament†
Warsmen at Play†
Jun 6 Father's Lesson
Hunting Deer
The Prodigal Son
Jun 13 Cast Off by His Father†
Clarinet Solo†
Faithful Governess Rewarded†
Magic Dice†
The Man and His Bottle
Mr. Brown Has a Tile Loose
The Old Actor†
Penniless Poet's Luck†
A Poor Knight and the Duke's Daughter†
The Saloon-Keeper's Nightmare†
Three Sportsmen and a Hat
Usefulness at an End†
Jun 20 The Book Agent†
The Chauffeur's Dream
Driven by Hunger†
The Handy Man at Play†
The Matterhorn†
Music Which Hath No Charms†
The Pony Express†
A Russian Bear Hunt†
Swiss Peasants' Festival†
Tribulations of a Mayor†
A Trip on the Venetian Canals†
The Viege Zermatt Railway†
Jul 4 Ancient Rome†
A Bird of Freedom†
Blessing the Boats in Arcachon†
Bull Fight in Arcachon†
The Dressmaker's Surprise†
Fox Hunting†
Heavy Seas†
Mr. Smith, the New Recruit†
Niagara Falls in Winter†
The Nihilist†
Scenes in Sicily†
Silk Hats Ironed†
Swiss Alps†
They Want a Divorce†
An Unfortunate Mistake†
Unrequited Love†
Who Owns the Basket?†
Jul 6 A Bad Boy†
Fountains of Rome†
In the Riviera†
Love and Hatred†
St. Marc Place†
Views of New York†
Jul 11 The International Horse Show
Over the Sticks
The Shipwreckers†
The Stone Breaker†
A Trip Through Savoy†
Votes for Women
Jul 13 The Best Remedy†
Father Is Late! Go Fetch Him†
The Grand Canal in Venice†
His Girl's Last Wish†
The Lady with the Beard; or, Misfortune to Fortune†
Sammy's Idea†
The Simpleton†
The Substitute Automatic Servant†
The Triumph of Love†
Trying to Get Rid of a Bad Dollar†
Two Little Motorists
A Walking Tree†
Wandering Musician†
Jul 25 I Won One Hundred Thousand†
Matrimonial Stages†
A New Fruit†
Obeying Her Mother†
Off to Morocco†
On the War Path†
Physical Phenomena†
A Pleasant Evening at the Theatre†
Promoted Corporal†
The Saw Mill†
The Story of the King of Fregola†
Sturdy Sailor's Honor†
Three Maiden Ladies and a Bull
Too Polite†
The Torrent†
The Tyrant Feudal Lord†
A Wolf in Sheep's Clothing†
Aug 1 Baffled Lover†
Black Eyed Susan
The Chronic Life-Saver†
An Embarrassing Gift†
Fishing Boats in the Ocean†
Follow Your Leader and the Master Follows Last
An Interesting Conversation†
The Miraculous Flowers†
Out of Patience†
The Roses†
Sensational Duel†
Too Hungry to Eat†
Aug 8 The Brigand's Daughter†
The Child's Forgiveness†
A Country Drama†
Flower Fete on the Bois de Boulogne†
The French Airship La Republique†
German Dragoons Crossing the Elbe†
Grand Prix Motor Race at Dieppe†
The Gypsy and the Painter†
The Gypsy Model†
Moscow Under Water†
The Rag Pickers' Wedding†
Reedham Boys' Festival Drill†
Royal Voyage to Canada†
The Tempter†
Trooping the Colour†
Tyrolean Alps Customs†
Aug 15 The Cheese Race†
Mother's Darling†
Music Hall Agent's Dream†
The Poor Man, Homeless, Wants to Go to Prison†
Uncle's Rejected Present
Aug 29 The Duck's Finish†
The Happy Man's Shirt†
The Hayseed's Bargain
Napoleon and the English Sailor
Sep 5 The Hidden Hoard
The Tramp and the Purse
Sep 12 Amateur Brigands†
The Asphalters' Dilemma†
The Blind Woman's Daughter†
The Burglar and the Clock
The Diamond Thieves
The Dover Pageant†
The Ever-Laughing Gentleman†
Goodwood Races†
The Hand-Cart Race†
King Edward and the German Emperor at Friedrichshof†
The Lightning Postcard Artist
The Marathon Race†
Olympic Regatta at Henley†
Paper Tearing
Quebec†
Quebec to Niagara†
The Signalman's Sweetheart†
The Son's Crime†
A Stern Father†
The Swimming Master†
Traveling Through Russia†
The Wrong Lottery Number†
Sep 19 How the Poor Clown's Prayer Was Answered
The Luckless Spike†
Sep 26 The Artist's Nightmare
How the Coster Sold the Seeds
The Thief at the Casino
Oct 3 The Ayah's Revenge
The Blusterer†
My Wife's Dog
Romeo and Juliet†
Sammy's Saw†
Oct 10 Any Rags†
Deep Down within the Cellar†
A Den of Thieves
Down in Jungle Town†
Harrigan†
I Want What I Want When I Want It†
I Would Like to Marry You
I'm Sorry†
I've Taken Quite a Fancy to You†
Just Some One†
L-A-Z-Y†
A Lemon in the Garden of Love†
Lincoln's Speech at Gettysburg†
Make Believe†
Military Swimming Championship†
A Stiff Neck†
Stupid Mr. Cupid†
A Talk on Trousers†
Whistle It†
Wouldn't You Like to Have Me for a Sweetheart†
You Got to Love Me a Lot†
Oct 13 Political Speeches†
Oct 16 The Court in Session†
Victim of Heroism†
Oct 17 Chauncey Proves a Good Detective
Water Bailiff's Daughter†
When Other Lips
Oct 19 A Treasure of a Pig†
The Witty Ghost†
Oct 20 High Jumping at Hurlingham
Madeira Wicker Chair Industry
Oct 21 Picturesque Switzerland
Somnambulic (sic) Bell Ringer†
Oct 23 Over the Hubarthal Railroad
Oct 24 If I Catch You I Will
The Power of Habit†
The Red Barn Mystery: A Startling Portrayal of the Great Marie Martin Mystery
Sunny Madeira

Oct 26 The Convict and the Dove
Desperately in Love
When Pa Went Fishing†
The World of Magic
Oct 27 Bald Headed Actor and Fair Lady†
Jane Shore
Oct 28 First Love Triumphs†
Motor Boat Races
Oct 29 Closed on Sundays
The Flower Thief†
Pa and the Girls†
Oct 30 The Sofa Bed†
Oct 31 Cuddle Up a Little Closer†
Daisy, the Pretty Typewriter
Don't You Think It's Time to Marry†
Hep Yo' Self, Peck-a-Boo†
The Honeybees' Honeymoon†
I'm Afraid to Come Home in the Dark†
I'm Going on the War Path†
In the Barber Shop†
The Moon's Gift†
Tipperary†
Under Any Old Flag at All†
What It Might Have Been†
Who? Me?†
With Care†
Wouldn't You Like to Flirt with me†
Nov 2 The Automatic Hotel†
The Fair Young Lady's Telephone Communication†
A House of Cards†
The Legend of Prometheus†
The Mock Baronets
The Necklace†
Thou Shalt Not Love†
Nov 7 All That Trouble for a Drink
Archie Goes Shopping with the girls
The Four-Legged Thief†
His First Experiment in Chemistry
A Jilted Woman's Revenge
Mr. Simpson's Artful Ruse
A Night Alarm
Our Banana Supply
Our Village Club Holds a Marathon Race
'Round Brussels in Ten Minutes
Nov 9 Feeding a Serpent†
The First Servant†
The Gorges of the Tarn†
The Grandfather's Tobacco†
The Lake of Garda, Italy†
Looking for the Bald Heads†
Monty Buys a Motor
No Race Suicide†
Out to Nurse†
The Quick Change Mesmerist
The Scare Crow†
A Tyrolean Paradise†
A Woman's Aid†
Nov 12 Jack in Letter Box
When Women Rule
Nov 14 The Prehistoric Man
Nov 17 Champion Globe Trotter
Disappearing Watch
The Doctor's Wife†
Having the Time of Their Lives†
Waterproof Willie
Nov 21 The Devil's Bargain
Grandpa's Pension Day
Nov 25 Kind Old Lady
Soldier's Love Token
Dec 5 The Bewildered Professor†
Thompson's Night with the Police†
Dec 12 A Bike Chase
A Good Watch Dog†
It Serves Him Right
Dec 14 A Free Pardon
Harmless Lunatic's Escape
How the Dodger Secured a Meal
The Serpent's Tooth
Dec 19 The Christmas of a Poacher†
The Good Playthings†
Hobo on a Bike†
The Little Chimney Sweeps†
The Police Band†
The Poor Singer Girl†
Dec 21 The Baby and the Loafer
Baby's Playmate
Cabby's Sweetheart
The Holy Hermit†
In Bondage†
The Little Marchioness and the Young Shepherdess†
Spoof and His Monkey
Dec 28 Bobby Has a Pipe Dream†
Current News Items†
A Heavy Head Piece†
Not Guilty†

1909 [month undetermined]
Robin Hood and His Merry Men
Jan 9 Tit for Tat
Wright's Aeroplane
Jan 11 A Gypsy's Jealousy†
Jan 16 The Captain's Love†
South African Gold Fields†
Jan 18 Troubled Artists†
Jan 23 Trip on Rhodesian Railway†
Feb 1 The Guard's Alarm
The Living Wreck†
Feb 10 Baby's Exciting Ride
Dog Outwits Kidnapper
The Double's Fate†
Following Mother's Footsteps
Grandfather's Birthday
The Guardian of the Bank
Polly's Excursion
A Sign from Heaven
Feb 16 The American Fleet at Sydney, New South Wales
The Hand of a Wizard
Outwitted†
Feb 24 Polka on Brain
Feb 25 Holland Cheese
Mar 3 An Embarrassing Present†
The Sailor's Belt†
Mar 10 Mother-in-Law's Day in the Country†
Rivalry†
South American Indians†
Mar 17 The Celebrated Mountain Climbers†
Cremation on the River Ganges†
Master Goes Shopping†
Mar 22 Fairy Sword
Galileo
Goose Chase
High Game
Mail Carrier's Daughter
Master and Servant
Phantom Games
Royalist's Wife
Son and Mother-in-law
A Wild Goose Chase
Mar 24 I Have Lost Toby†
Mr. Pallet Goes Out Landscaping†
Mar 27 Hero of the Prussian War
Mar 31 Arabian Horsemen†
Benevolent Employer†
Apr [day undetermined]
Henpecked
Apr 7 Inviting His Boss for Dinner†
On the Brink of the Precipice†
Apr 17 A Bachelor's Persistence†
A Plot Foiled†
A Plucky Little Girl
Puritan Maid
A Traitor to the King
Apr 24 The Deserter
The Dog Came Back
Found on the Rocks†
A Heartless Mother
High Game
Last Year's Time Table
A Lover's Quarrel
Married Under Difficulties
Nancy; or, The Burglar's Daughter
Professor's Anti-Gravitation
The Rival Cyclists
Runaway Kids
The Squire and the Noble Lord†
A Thoughtless Beauty
The Unlucky Thief
The Villain's Wooing
May 1 The Anarchist's Sweetheart
Farmer Jones Goes to the Market
The Fickle Husband
An Unfortunate Bath
May 5 Forgotten†
The Peddler's Reward†
May 8 Baby's Chum
The Cavalier's Wife
I Will Have a Husband
The Immortal Goose
The Land of the Pharoah
The Milkman's Wooing
Romance of the Crafty Usurper and the Young King
Taking Home the Eggs
What William Did
May 12 Bamboo Pole Equilibrist†
A Timely Apparition†
Wilbur Wright and His Majesty King Edward VII†
May 15 The Detective's Ruse
In the Service of the King
The Spoilt Child
Tower of London
Unlucky Bridegroom
May 19 Caught on the Cliffs†
Objections Overcome†
May 22 Boys' Holiday
Copenhagen Zoo
Favorite Doll
In Quest of Health
Present for Her Husband
River Panorama
Scenes in Ceylon
Stratagem Rewarded
Why Father Learned to Ride
May 24 Soldier Manoeuvres in Morocco
May 26 How Jones Paid His Debts†
Panther Hunting on the Isle of Java†
May 29 Frost Bound Nature
His Only Quid
Lesson in Electricity
Morganatic Marriage
Jun 2 Magic Carpet
Tender Cords†
Jun 5 Cat Came Back
Dentist's Daughter
Gypsy's Child
Happy Man
Trollhattan in Winter
Jun 9 The Race Course†
Two Heroes†
Jun 12 Achill's Rocky Shores
The Birth of a Big Gun
Cingalese Village Life
A False Friend
How Jones Got a New Suit
Killarney's Lakes
The Man Housemaid
Only a Dart
Special License
Weary Willie Wheeling
Jun 16 Modern Algeria†
The New Footman†
Jun 19 The English Derby
Jun 23 Mrs. Simpson's Attractiveness†
Winning a Princess†
Jun 26 Bully and Recruit
His Wedding Morn
Moonlight on the Thames
Quiet Day at the Cafe
The Shepherd's Dog
Sunshine After Storm
To the Custody of the Father
Winter Horseplay
The Wrong Coat
Jun 30 The Phantom Sirens†
Rulers of the World†
Jul 3 Bee's Eviction
Dissolution of Parliament
The Dog and the Bone
The Egg Race
Fancy Dress Ball
A Joke on Teddy
Lighthouse
Modern Cinderella
A Pair of Truants
Ski Jumping
Jul 7 Exciting Steeple-Chase†
The Pretty Fisher-Maiden†
Jul 10 The Interrupted Jollification
Jul 14 Conchita, the Spanish Belle†
The Wizard's Walking Stick
Jul 17 Billy's Bugle
The Curate of the Races
Inexperienced Angler
Motor Skates
Mysterious Lodger
Never Gamble for Your Trousers
Too Much Lobster for Supper
Jul 21 The King's Conspiracy†
Jul 24 Territory on Brain
Treacherous Policeman
The Would-Be Acrobats
Jul 28 His Rival's Hand†
Parks in Berlin†
Aug 4 Stripping a Forest in Winter†
The Turning Point†
Aug 7 Baby Is King†
Butcher Boy
The Course of True Love
The Hidden Treasure†
Aug 14 The Burning Home
Mr. Isaacs and the Mice
Race for a Farmer's Cup
Aug 18 Building Barrels†
The Strikers†
Aug 21 The King's Protege†
The Spy
Story of a Picture

Up the Mountain from Hong Kong†
When Jack Gets His Pay
Aug 28 A Cheap Removal
The Farmer's Joke
Henpeck's Revolt
Rival Mesmerists
Squaring the Account
Aug 31 The French Battleship "Justice"†
Professor Puddenhead's Patents
Sep 4 Baby's Revenge
Bad Day for Lavinsky
Biskra, Garden of Allah
The Boy and His Kite
The Boy Scouts
How the Bulldog Paid the Rent
How the Page Boy Cured a Flirt
In Hot Pursuit†
A Jealous Husband
Little Jim
Love of a Hunchback
Only a Tramp
Romantic Italy†
A Troublesome Malady
Sep 13 The Boy and the Convict
The Rivals
Uncle Rube's Visit
Votes for Women
Sep 15 The Fatal Love†
Pontine Marshes, Italy†
Sep 18 Arab Life in South Algeria
A Dream of Paradise
The Farmer's Treasure†
If at First You Don't Succeed
Luck of the Cards
A Tricky Convict
A Villain's Downfall
Sep 21 Carlo and the Baby
Sep 23 An Aerial Elopement
Sep 24 Mrs. Minta's Husband
Sep 25 The Eccentric Barber
Father's Beautiful Beard
The Little Milliner and the Thief
Necessity Is the Mother of Invention
Sep 28 Wife or Child†
Sep 29 Chasing the Ball†
Love, the Conqueror†
Oct 4 Entertaining Grandfather
Oct 5 Hot Time in Cold Quarters
Oct 6 Gambling Passion†
The Mysterious Motor
Yachting off Cowes†
Oct 7 The Curse of Money
Was It a Snake Bite?
Oct 11 Invisibility
Mistaken Identity
Who Owned the Coat?
Oct 12 The New Servant
Oct 18 A Drunkard's Son
Escaped Lunatic
Lobster Fishing
Roosevelt's Route Through Africa
Oct 19 The Phantom Ship
Winter Sports in Hungary
Oct 20 Casting Bread upon the Water†
Crown Prince of Germany Drilling Battery†
Oct 21 Artful Dodger
Oct 27 Awakened Memories†
Volcanoes of Java†
Nov 3 Tale of the Fiddle†
"Ursula," World's Fastest Motor Boat†
Nov 6 Belgrade, Capital of Servia
Nov 8 Father's Holiday
Nov 10 The Robber Duke†
Nov 13 The Cabman's Good Fairy
The Invaders
The Street Arab
Two Little Runaways
Nov 17 Fighting Suffragettes†
Workhouse to Mansion
Nov 23 Marriage of Love†
Dec 1 Consul Crosses the Atlantic
Dec 8 Capturing the North Pole; or, How He Cook'ed Peary's Record
The Secret Chamber†
Dec 15 The Red Signal†
Switzerland, Conquering the Alps†
Dec 22 Fiorella, the Bandit's Daughter†
From the Fighting Top of a Battleship in Action†
Dec 25 The Kidnapped King
Silly Billy
The Thames in Winter
Dec 29 Battle in the Clouds
The Park of Caserta†
Dec 30 The Motherless Waif

1910
Jan 5 Shanghai of To-day†
Tragedy at the Mill†
Jan 12 Home of the Gypsies†
True to His Oath†
Jan 15 An Absorbing Tale
Boy Scouts
A Father's Love
Forced Treatment
Getting Rid of Uncle
Marvelous Indeed
Mind, I Catch You Smoking
Rivals
Simple Simon
Tyrolean Tragedy
Jan 17 Muggins
Jan 19 The Coast Guard†
Riva, Austria, and the Lake of Garda†
Jan 26 The Lass Who Loves a Sailor
Tommy in Dreamland†
Feb 2 The Might of the Waters†
Sheltered in the Woods†
Feb 4 Winter Days in Sweden
Feb 8 In Winter's Grip
Feb 9 Coals of Fire†
Venetian Isles†
Feb 16 The Acrobatic Fly†
The Blue Swan Inn†
Feb 23 The Buried Secret†
A Family Outing†
Mar 2 Baby Bet
From Beyond the Seas†
Lines of the Hand
Mar 9 At the Bar of Justice†
The Water-Flyer†
Mar 16 The Country Schoolmaster†
Peter's Patent Paint
A Trip Along the Rhine†
Mar 23 A Maid of the Mountains†
Over the Appennines of Italy†
Mar 30 Making Sherry Wine at Xeres†
The Midnight Escape†
Robber's Ruse
Apr 5 Boxing Fever
Apr 6 The Fly Pest†
Her Father's Choice†
Apr 13 The Lookout; or, Saved from the Sea†
A Ramble Through the Isle of Sumatra†
Apr 18 Roosevelt in Africa
Apr 20 The Lover's Oracle†
Trawler Fishing in a Hurricane†
Apr 26 The Penalty of Beauty
Apr 27 The Rival Miners†
Volcanic Eruptions of Mt. Aetna†
Apr 30 The Sculptor's Dream
May 2 Safety Suit for Skaters
May 4 Called to the Sea†
Immigrants' Progress in Canada†
May 7 Father's Crime
May 11 Purged by Fire†
Roosevelt in Cairo†
May 12 The Invisible Dog
Three Fingered Kate
May 14 Bobby, the Boy Scout
The Convict's Dream
May 18 The Electric Servant
The Girl Conscript†
Modern Railway Construction†
Wonderful Machine Oil
May 25 His Wife's Testimony†
Jun 1 Her Life for Her Love†
Making Salt†
Jun 4 Adopting a Child
Animated Cotton
Boy and Purse
A Drink of Goat's Milk
A Father's Mistake
Gipsy's Baby
The Last of the Dandies
A Race for a Bride
Scratch as Scratch Can
Teaching a Husband a Lesson
Jun 8 The Mountain Lake†
The Nightmare†
Jun 15 The Gum-Shoe Kid†
A Trip to Brazil†
Jun 18 [Welch-Daniels Fight]
Jun 21 Drowsy Dick's Dream
Tempered with Mercy
Jun 22 A Child of the Squadron†
An Excursion into Wales†
Jun 24 Lieutenant Rose, R. N.
Jun 29 Fishery in the North
St. Paul and the Centurion†
Jul 1 The Fresh Air Fiend
The Plumber
Jul 5 The Boy and His Teddy Bear
Jul 6 A Russian Spy†
Tropical Java of the South Sea Islands†
Jul 8 From Gypsy Hands
A New Hat for Nothing
Jul 12 A Deal in Broken China
Prince of Kyber
Jul 13 The Moonlight Flitting†
The Wicked Baron and the Page†
Jul 15 The Hindoo's Treachery
[Kinemacolor Films]
Jul 20 Pekin, the Walled City†
Through the Enemy's Line†
Jul 27 The Art Lover's Strategy†
Mexican Domain†
Aug 3 Camel and Horse Racing in Egypt†
The Witch of Carabosse†
Aug 10 On the Banks of the Zuyder Zee, Holland†
The Silent Witness†
Aug 17 Paris Viewed from the Eiffel Tower†
The Rival Serenaders†
Aug 24 Escape of the Royalists†
Aug 31 Buying a Bear†
A Cruise in the Mediterranean†
Sep 7 Ingratitude; or, The Justice of Providence†
Sep 14 The Artisan†
The Tramps†
Sep 21 A Corsican Vendetta†
Scenes in the Celestial Empire†
Sep 28 The Quarrel†
Reedham's Orphanage Festival, 1910
Oct 5 City of the Hundred Mosques, Broussa, Asia Minor†
The Dishonest Steward†
Oct 12 Foiled by a Cigarette; or, The Stolen Plans of the Fortress†
Oct 19 Tunny Fishing off Palermo, Italy†
Oct 26 In the Spreewald†
The Signet Ring†
Nov 9 Secret of the Cellar†
A Trip Through Scotland†
Nov 15 Nebuchadnezzar's Pride†
Nov 16 An Alpine Retreat†
The Rival Barons†
Nov 23 Behind a Mask†
Nantes and Its Surroundings†
Nov 30 Ramble Through Ceylon†
Dec [day undetermined]
[Liquors and Cigars]
[The London Fire Brigade]
[London Zoological Gardens]
[Picking Strawberries]
[The Richmond Horse Show]
A Visit to the Seaside at Brighton Beach, England
Dec 7 The Death of Admiral Coligny†
Dec 14 The Little Matchseller's Christmas†
Scenes in British India
Dec 21 A Chamois Hunt†
The Tyrant of Florence†
Dec 28 Coaching in Devonshire, England
A Mexican Romance†

Italy

1907
Aug 14 The Fireman
Fountains of Rome
Kidnapping a Bride
A Modern Youth
The Slavery of Children
Aug 19 The Barber's Daughter
Little Fregoli
Sep 14 Electric Pile
Hunting a Devil
A Modern Samson
Sep 28 Gitana; or, The Gypsy
Oct 12 Monk's Vengeance
Stolen Chickens
Oct 28 Adventures of a Lover
The Sylvan God
Nov 9 Beyond Criticism
Nov 22 In the Dreamland
Where Is My Head
Nov 23 Venetian Baker; or, Drama of Justice
Watchmaker's Secret
Dec 7 A Soldier Must Obey Orders
When Cherries Are Ripe
Dec 14 The Christmas
Dec 28 Hunting Above the Clouds
Japanese Vaudeville "The Flower Kingdom"

1908
Jan 4 A Brief Story
A Magistrate's Crime
Jan 11 The Farmer
The Rivals: A Love Drama of Pompeii

Jan 18 Adventures of a Countryman
The Gay Vagabonds
Jan 25 The Butterflies
Feb 15 A Country Drama
Lover and Bicycle
Woman's Army
Feb 29 Othello
Mar [day undetermined]
Comic Serenade
Duel After the Ball*
Winning the Gloves*
Mar 14 Custom Officer's Pull
Electric Sword
Mar 21 The Cook Wins
Gaston Visits Museum
Good-Hearted Sailor
The Skull and the Sentinel
Apr 4 A False Accusation
Pulcinella
Apr 6 Romeo and Juliet
Apr 11 The Bad Sister
Basket Mystery or the Traveler's Jest
The Doctor's Monkey
A Dream
The Edily
The Gambling Demon
Judith and Holopherne
A Magician's Love Test
The Mayor's Misfortune
Nephew's Luck
Pierrot and the Devil
Vengeance in Normandy
Apr 18 The Animated Dummy
Butler's Misdeed
Apr 22 The Grandmother's Fables
Apr 25 Rejoicing Dreams
Sausage
Tramp's Revenge
May 2 The Accusing Vision
The Baby Strike
Bad Bargain
Bad Boys
The Best Glue
Concealed Love
The First Kiss
The First Lottery Prize
Forgotten Ones
Frolicsome Powders
Generous Policeman
Greediness Punished
Life and Customs of Naples
A Mistake in the Dark
Modern Hotel
Mysterious Stranger
No Divorce Wanted
Panorama of Venice
The Price of a Favor
A Priest's Conscience
Rival Sherlock Holmes
Shooting Party
Soldiers in the Italian Alps
The Statue of Rocco
A Story of the 17th Century
Wrongly Charged
May 9 Gathering Indian Figs
Manoeuvres of Artillery
Peasant's Difficulties in Society
Sicily Illustrated
The Smokeless Stove
May 16 Lost Pocketbook
May 30 The Castle Ghosts
Remorseful Son
Jul 4 A Love Affair of the Olden Days
Jul 6 The Troublesome Fly
Wanted: A Colored Servant
Jul 13 Consoling the Widow
Good Night Clown
Through the Oural Mountains
A Tricky Uncle
The Two Brothers
Jul 25 Transformation with a Hat Rim
Venice and the Lagoon
Aug 1 The Dear Little Heart
Making of Tomato Sauce
Overflowing in Italy
Peasant and Prince
The Policeman and the Cook
War Episode
Aug 15 A Good Repentance
Aug 29 Pretty Flower Girl
Oct 3 Panic in a Village
Oct 6 The Chances of Life
A Wedding Under Terror
Oct 7 Manon Lescaut
Oct 10 Boxing Mania
Romance of a School Teacher
Oct 19 Shadows of Night
Oct 20 The Cashier's Romance
The Puppet Man's Dream
Trials of an Educator
Oct 21 A Father's Will
Prince Kin Kin's Malady
The Voice of the Heart
Oct 24 The Little Rope Dancer
The Revengeful Waiter
The Young Artist
Oct 26 The Queen's Lover
Oct 30 The Galley Slave's Return
Nov 9 At Night
Nov 17 The Jester's Daughter
Dec 5 She Could Be Happy with Either
Dec 12 Fighting for Gold
Timid Dwellers
Dec 14 A Fatal Present
An Interior Cyclone
Dec 19 Braving Death to Save a Life
Dec 21 The Black Sheep
In the Nick of Time
1909 [month undetermined]
Peasant and Princess
Jan 9 Soldier's Heroism
Jan 16 Holy Fires
Porcelain of Good Quality
Jan 23 Messina Disaster
Feb 6 Fatal Wedding
A Pirate of Turkey
Riding for Love
Feb 13 Circumstantial Evidence
The Showman's Drama
Feb 22 The Galley Slave
Feb 24 Drama Amongst Fishermen
Feb 27 Edgar and Lucy
The Shoemaker's Luck
Mar 7 Episode in Boer War
A Good Excuse
Mar 8 Hurricane of Lovers
A Widow to Console
Mar 9 A Providential Chance
Story of Every Day
Mar 10 Arrival at the Village
Chances of Life
For the Motherland
Giordono Bruno
Scenes of Morocco
Mar 11 Alcoholic Doctor
Love Letter
Prascovia
Salon in 1820
Mar 12 Love and the Motherland
Medieval Episode
Mar 13 Father and Son
Grand Maneuvers
Mar 22 Foolshead, King of Police
Foolshead Wishes to Commit Suicide
Hat Making
Italian Cavalry Maneuvers
Living Statue
Two Fathers
Apr 3 A Stormy Sea
Apr 17 Unforgiving Father
Apr 24 Artful Art
Foolshead Looks for a Duel
The Game of Pallone
A Marvelous Ointment
The Regimental Barber
Apr 27 The Bandits
Earthenware Industry
May 1 Countess Valleria of Issogne
May 8 Artillery Manoeuvers in the Mountains
An Awful Toothache
First Comes the Fatherland
House Full of Agreeables
Love with Love Is Paid
Snowball
May 15 Fishing Industry
Foolshead on the Alps
For a Woman's Sake
Galileo, Inventor of the Pendulum
Humble Heroes
Rosin Industry
Who Has Seen My Head?
May 22 A Clever Detective
In Sardinia
Sapho
You Shall Pay for It
May 29 The Bear in the Staircase
Count of Monte Cristo
The Emperor
Mimosa and the Good Prince
A Piano Lesson
Jun 5 Face to Face
Italian Artillery
Resuscitated
A True Friend
Jun 12 Ski Runners of the Italian Army
Jun 17 The Conjuror
Cyrano de Bergerac
The Girl Heroine
Officer's Revenge
Recompense
Jun 26 Foolshead Wrestling
Good for Nothing Nephew
Heroine of the Balkans
Louis the XI
The Mother-in-Law Phantasm
Officer's Lodgment
A Painful Joke
Jul 3 Bink's Toreador
Infernal Salamandre
Lord of Montmorency
Pity and Love
Jul 10 The Gambler's Son
Horse to the Rescue
The Life of a Pierrot
Phonographic Message of Love
Prince of Chalant
Jul 17 Brave Little Organ Boy
Count Ugolini
Expiation
His First Drink
Mr. Stubborn
Tragic Night
Jul 24 The Harp Player
Little Imp
Aug 14 An Amazing Story
Foolshead Sportsman of Love
A Hero of the Italian Independence
The Iron Mask
Satan's Retreat
Aug 21 False Lunatic
Madam Lydia's Little Trick
Niccolo' De' Lapi
Aug 28 Foolshead Matrimony
Little Seller of Cyclamens
Sep 4 Florian De Lys
Foolshead, King of Robbers
Louisa of Lucerne
Mr. A. Nutt
Mosimilla
Who Laughs Last
Sep 13 Don Carlos
Importune Neighbor
The Story of a Bad Cigar
Sep 18 The End of the Terror
How Money Circulates
Sep 20 His Wife's Troublesome Twitching
Sep 21 Eleanora
Sep 23 Jackson's Last Steeple Chase
Sep 25 From Portofino to Nervi
Phaedra
Sep 27 Mother-in-Law's Parrot
The Priest's Niece
Sep 29 An Embarrassing Portfolio
Oct 2 Arab Life
Mady Millicent's Visitor
Mr. Muddlehead's Mistake
Romance of a Pierrot
Oct 4 Careless Life
Eve of the Wedding
Love and Sacrifice
Oct 5 Forgiven at Last
Oct 6 Deputy
The Devil and the Painter
Oct 11 The Convict's Wife
Love Stronger Than Revenge
Oct 12 Noble and Commoner
Oct 13 The Two Sergeants
Oct 18 Berlin Jack the Ripper
Foolshead's Trousers
Reformation of a Wine-Loving Artist
Oct 19 Man in Pieces
Sardinian Brigand
Oct 25 The False Oath
Nov 1 Nero; or, The Burning of Rome
Nov 2 A Race for the Monkey
Nov 4 Napoleon and Princess Hatzfeld
Nov 5 A Very Attractive Gentleman
Nov 6 Princess and Slave
The Silk Worm Series
Spartacus
Nov 8 Enthusiastic Hand Ball Player
Force of Love
Henry the Third
Musical Waiter
Orange Growing in Palestine
Pirates of the Sea
Nov 9 Good for Evil
Nov 12 The Farmer's Son
Logging in the Italian Alps

Nov 13 Balloon Trip over Turin
A Broken Life
How Foolshead Paid His Debts
Life for a Life
Nov 15 The Cursed Cage
High Treason
Nov 18 Julius Caesar
Nov 19 The Love of Little Flora
Nov 20 A Mother's Heart
Nov 22 The Hostage
Nov 29 Leopard Hunting in Abyssinia
The Servant of the Actress
Dec 6 An Athlete of a New Kind
The Electric Safe
The Little Vendean
Dec 11 Macbeth
Dec 13 The Beggarman's Gratitude
The Smuggler's Sweetheart
Dec 18 Mr. Nosey Parker
Dec 20 A Little Disagreement
Lorenzi De Medica
Dec 25 Alberno & Rosamunda
Bath Chair
The Deserter
Electra
Interrupted Rendezvous
Magda
A Surprising Powder
Theodora
Who Seeks Finds
The Wonderful Pearl
Dec 27 Admiral Nelson's Son
Dec 28 Foolshead Pays a Visit
Dec 29 The Story of My Life
Dec 31 A Christmas Legend

1910

Jan 3 Foolshead's Holiday
Patrician and Slave
The Poem of Life
Jan 10 The Garibaldi Boy
The Law of Destiny
The Rebel's Fate
Rudolph of Hapsburg
Jan 12 Camille
An Episode of Napoleon's War with Spain
Jan 15 Amorous Minstrel
The Son of the Wilderness
The Twine
Jan 17 Arthur's Little Love Affair
Mammy's Boy Joins the Army
The Miners
A Young Girl's Sacrifice
Jan 19 Italian Artillery
Pauli
Jan 20 Martyrs of Pompeii
Jan 22 Football Player
The Tempting Collar
There Are Some Ghosts
Jan 26 Angler and the Cyclist
A Choice Policeman
The Last Keepsake
Walkaway's New Boots
Jan 29 A Good Winning
The Timid One
Feb 2 Hero and Leander
Feb 4 Strike Instigator
Feb 5 Love and Treason
Feb 9 The Longing for Gaol
The Strongest
Feb 12 Foolshead Preaches Temperance
Foolshead Receives
Feb 16 Carmen
I Have Lost My Latch Key
The Silent Piano
Feb 19 Louise Strozzi
Feb 23 The Dog of the Cheese Monger
Foolshead at the Ball
Feb 26 Why Fricot Was Sent to College
The Witch's Ballad
Mar 2 The Mysterious Track
The Two Mothers
Mar 5 Supreme Recognition
Mar 9 Foolshead Chief of the Reporters
The Town Traveler's Revenge
Mar 12 Fatal Imprudence
They Have Vanished My Wife
Mar 16 Insidious Weapons
The Shepherdess
Mar 19 The Betraying Mirror
Mar 23 Military Dirigible
The Sea's Vengeance
Mar 25 Double Six
Mar 26 Foolshead Wishes to Marry the Governor's Daughter
The Rivalry of the Two Guides
Mar 30 A Sudden Telephone Call
An Unworthy Fiancé
Apr 1 Andrea Chenier
Apr 2 The Servant and the Tutor
Apr 5 Love and Art
Apr 6 My Life Remembrances of a Dog
An Unpleasant Dream
Apr 7 Roosevelt at Messina
Apr 8 Come to Supper with Me
Motherless Waif
Apr 9 At the Farm
The Valuable Hat
Apr 11 Musical Masterpiece
Spanish Fandalgo
Apr 13 Fricot in College
The Legend of the Cross
Apr 16 A Mistake
The Three Brothers
Apr 18 The Queen's Attendant
Apr 20 The Heart of a Vagabond
Othello
Petit Jean Louis d'Or & Co.
Apr 23 Isabella of Arragon
Apr 26 Among the Snowy Mountains
Grandfather's Story
Apr 27 Bethlehem
A Doctor's Revenge
Fricot Is Learning a Handicraft
Apr 28 Twenty Francs
Apr 30 The False Friar
The Fashionable Sport
May 4 Blue Jackets' Manoeuvres on a Sailing Vessel
Who Killed Her?
May 5 Fury of the Waves
Village Beauty
May 7 Artist's Good Joke
How the Great Field Marshall Villars Had an Adopted Daughter
The Sentinel's Romance
May 9 Beatrice Cenci
May 11 Fricot Gets in a Libertine Mood
The Secret of the Lake
May 12 Two Betrothed
May 14 Foolshead Learns to Somersault
Honor of the Alpine Guide
That Gentleman Has Won a Million
May 17 Child's Doctor
May 18 The Devil on Two Sticks
May 19 In the Name of Allah
May 21 Conquered Again
May 25 Estrellita; or, The Invasion of the French Troops in Portugal
May 28 Foolshead Marries Against His Will
The Knot in the Handkerchief
Jun 1 A Just Revenge
Prascovia
Jun 4 Am I Mad?
Battles of Soul
A Fool's Paradise
Foolshead as a Porter
Jane of Montressor
Negro's Gratitude
A Pennyworth of Potatoes
Servant and Guardian
The Slave's Sacrifice
Two Friends
Jun 8 A Jealous Wife
The Shipwrecked Man
The Vivandiera
Jun 11 Linda of Chamouny
Jun 13 Artist's Dream
Jun 15 The Battle of Legnano; or, Barbarossa
The Emperor's Message
Jun 18 Distractions of Foolshead
The New Sign of the Globe Hotel
Jun 21 Love Is Stronger Than Life
Jun 22 The Story of Lulu Told by Her Feet
The Tricky Umbrella of Fricot
Jun 23 From Love to Martyrdom
Jun 24 Isis
Jun 25 The Man Suffragette for the Abolition of Work for Women
A White Lie
Jun 28 Under the Reign of Terror
Jun 29 The Taking of Saragossa
Jun 30 False Accusation
Faust
Jul 2 Catherine, Duchess of Guisa
Jul 4 The Derby
Jul 6 The Tamer; Alfred Schneider and His Lions
Jul 7 Giorgione
Jul 9 The Abyss
Jul 13 The Struggle of Two Souls
Tweedle Dum's Aeronautical Adventure
Jul 16 Mother-in-law, Son-in-law and Tanglefoot
The Voice of the Blood
Jul 20 The Romance of a Jockey
Some Riding Exercises of the Italian Cavalry
Jul 23 A Cannon Duel
Let Us Die Together
Jul 27 The Room of the Secret
Jul 30 The Two Bears
Where Can We Hang This Picture?
Aug 3 Fricot Drinks a Bottle of Horse Embrocation
The Glove
Aug 6 Louisa Miller
Aug 10 A Favour Admission to a Play
Truth Beyond Reach of Justice
Aug 13 A Cloud
Papa's Cane
Aug 17 The Hump's Secret
Tweedle Dum Has Missed the Train
Aug 20 Agnes Visconti
Aug 24 A Fatal Vengeance
Fricot's Itching Powder
Aug 27 The Cantiniere
An Enemy of the Dust
Foolshead in the Lion's Cage
Aug 31 The Fisherman's Crime
Tweedle Dum's Forged Bank Note
Sep 3 The Vestal
Sep 7 The Caprice of a Dame
Fricot Has Lost His Collar Button
Sep 10 Mr. Coward
A Thief Well Received
Sep 14 The Iron Foundry
Sep 16 The Sacking of Rome
Sep 17 The Falconer
Sep 21 The Last Friend
Molly at the Regiment—Her Adventures
Sep 23 Julie Colonna
Tontolini as a Ballet Dancer
Sep 24 The Bad Luck of an Old Rake
Foolshead as a Policeman
Sep 28 The Virgin of Babylon
Sep 30 Giovanni of Medici
Oct 1 Foolshead Employed in a Bank
Foolshead Has Been Presented with a Foot Ball
Oct 5 The Pit That Speaks
Tweedledum's Duel
Oct 8 Foolshead Fisherman
Mrs. Cannon Is Warm
Oct 12 The Betrothed's Secret
Tweedledum on His First Bicycle
Oct 13 Mysteries of Bridge of Sighs at Venice
Oct 14 The Mad Lady of Chester
Oct 15 Paid Boots and Stolen Boots
A Pearl of Boy
Oct 19 Excursion on the Chain of Mont Blanc
Tweedledum's Sleeping Sickness
Oct 20 The Calumny
Oct 21 The Last of the Savelli
Oct 22 The False Coin
Foolshead Between Two Fires
Oct 26 Launching the First Italian Dreadnought
Tweedledum Wants to be a Jockey
Oct 27 Ruin
Oct 28 The Pretty Dairy Maid
Tontolini Is in Love
Oct 29 An Excursion on the Lake of Garda
Foolshead Volunteer on the Red Cross
Nov 2 The Slave of Carthage
Nov 3 The Fault of Grandmother
Nov 4 A Wooden Sword
Nov 5 A Sufferer of Insomnia
Where Have I Put My Fountain Pen?
Nov 9 A Floating Message
Nov 10 The Black Gondola
A Stormy Seas
Nov 12 The Coalman's Soap
Foolshead Knows All and Does All
Nov 16 The Mermaid
Tweedledum Gets Employed in the Corporation Body
Nov 17 Judge and Father
Nov 19 Foolshead Victim of His Honesty
An Original Palette
Nov 23 Gounod's 'Ave Maria'
The Story of a Pair of Boots
Nov 24 Sacrificed
Nov 26 A Chosen Marksman
A Windy Day
Nov 30 The Judas Money; or, An Episode of the War in Vendee

Dec 1 A Painful Debt
Dec 3 The Big Drum
The Dog Keeper
Dec 7 The Tell-Tale Portrait
Tweedledum Learns a Tragical Part
Dec 8 The Soldier of the Cross
Dec 10 Foolshead Knows How to Take His Precautions
The Good Samaritan
Dec 14 Dido Forsaken by Aeneas
Dec 15 The False Accusation
Dec 17 The Mother's Shadow
Thieves as Quick Change Artists
Dec 21 Little Peter's Xmas Day
Tweedledum and Frothy Want to Get Married
Dec 22 Neapolitan Volcanic Islands
Who Was the Culprit?
Dec 24 Greediness Spoiled Foolshead's Christmas
In Norway
Dec 28 Drama of the Engine Driver
Grandfather's Pipe
Dec 29 The Rustic
Dec 31 The Jealous Wife's New Year Day
Norwegian Water Falls

Spain

1909

May 15 Carnival at Nice

Sweden

1907

Dec 27 "King Oscar II's Funeral Films"

Country of origin undetermined

1902

May [day undetermined]
The Aerial Railway at the Crystal Palace, London, England
Burlesque on Romeo and Juliet
The Burlesque Thieves
The Chinese Conjurer and the Devil's Head
A Chinese Mystery
The Clown and His Burlesque Horse
Devil's Prison
The Devil's Theatre
English Cavalry on the Battlefield
The Fat and Lean Comedians
The Giant and Pygmy
The Horrible Nightmare
The Magician and the Seven Hats
The Mermaid's Ballet
The Mystical Burglars
The Nurse Maid in the Tunnel
The Other Fellow's Laundry
Peasant Children and Their Rocking Horse
Tommy Atkins Bathing
Troubled Dream
Waves at Dover, England
The Weary Traveller and His Wonderful Dream

Sep [day undetermined]
Bathing at Kiel, Germany
Bologna Eating Contest
Ching Ling Foo's Greatest Feats
The Crazy Artist and the Pictures That Came to Life
Departure of the Bride and Groom
A Dutchman Shaving
German Soldiers Starting for War
The Haunted Dining Room
His First Dose of Medicine
Horse Racing in Germany
Kaiser Wilhelm and Emperor Franz Josef, and Prince Henry Riding Horseback
Kaiser Wilhelm and the Empress of Germany Reviewing Their Troops
Kaiser Wilhelm and the German Cuirrassiers Galloping
Kaiser Wilhelm at Stettin
Kaiser Wilhelm at the Launching of a German Battleship
Kaiser Wilhelm in the Tier Garten, Berlin, Germany
Kaiser Wilhelm Inspecting His Soldiers
Kaiser Wilhelm, of Germany, and Emperor Franz Josef, of Austria
Kaiser Wilhelm's Yacht "Meteor" Under Sail
Lightning Facial Changes
Loading Cattle in India
The Magical Dish Mender
An Old Fashioned Way of Pulling a Tooth
The Old Maid's Tea Party
Queen Wilhelmina and Kaiser Wilhelm Riding in the Tier Garten
Queen Wilhelmina Arriving at the Kaiser's Palace
Queen Wilhelmina, of Holland, in Berlin
Street Scene in Cairo
Tourists Climbing the Alps

1905

Nov [day undetermined]
Bedelia and the Witch

1907

Mar 30 Indian Basket Weavers
Apr [day undetermined]
Winning a Princess
May 4 Boss Away, Choppers Play
Roof to Cellar
Well-Bred
Jun 15 A Disturbed Dinner
The White Slave
A Woman's Duel
Jun 22 Revenge
That Awful Tooth
Jun 29 Because My Father's Dead
Rummy Robbers
Aug 31 Don Juan
Female Wrestlers
Great Lion Hunt
Happy Bob as a Boxer
Sep 14 For a Woman's Sake
Once Upon a Time There Was...
Sep 21 Arrival of Lusitania
Babes in the Woods
Sep 28 Cheekiest Man on Earth
Oct 5 The Petticoat Regiment

1908

Jul 4 Porcelain Industry
Aug 15 Human Vultures
Moscow Under Water
The Picture
Undesirable Tenants
Aug 29 Riches, Poverty and Honesty
Sep 12 Antiquary
The Beggar
Fencing Fiend
Hamlet
Little Walk in Rome
Lottery Ticket
The Model
Root in Mexico
Rose, the Flower Girl
Strange Inheritance
Who Is It?
Youthful Artist
Sep 19 His Sweetheart's Birthday
In the Time of Rebellion
Sep 26 Duchess of Bracciano
Oct 10 Rocanbole
Nov 2 A Child's Debt
My Daughter Will Only Marry a Strong Man
The Young Tramp
Nov 17 Tarn Mountains
The Young Poacher
Dec 5 Buying an Automobile
The Country Idyll
The Fast Train
Dec 14 Christmas: From the Birth of Christ to the Twentieth Century
Father and the Kids
Dec 26 Hermit

1909

Feb 6 The Delirious Patient
Mar 6 The Ashes of Hercules
The Miner's Wife
The Musician
The Story of a Life
Mar 20 Western Bill
Mar 27 The Magician
The Reprobate
May 8 Funeral of Joe Petrosino: The American Detective in Merino, Italy
Sep 4 Bad Brother
By Path of Love
Fancy Soldier
Gaffy's King of Detectives
Love and Revenge
Madwoman's Child
Sep 18 A Broken Heart
Dec 8 The End of the Tragedy

1910

Jan 15 Episode of French Revolution
Feb 11 Hard Heart
Souvenirs of Paris
Feb 12 False Oath
Nema Lescout
Feb 17 Camargo
Mar 1 Scenes of the Australian Gold Fields
Apr 7 Roosevelt's Reception
May 3 The Flood
May 16 Lucretia
Jun 4 Picturesque Sentari
Jun 13 Views of England
Jun 23 No Smoking

LITERARY AND DRAMATIC CREDIT INDEX

★ Entries listed herein are arranged according to the name of the author or playwright of the work used as a source for a specific film, then listed chronologically by year, month and day of release. All entries within the Literary and Dramatic Credit Index can also be located in the Personal Name Index. The reader should note that literary and dramatic credits were included only for those films which available sources indicated were based on literary or dramatic sources.

LITERARY AND DRAMATIC CREDIT INDEX

Falero, Louis
1900
Aug [day undetermined]
Living Pictures
Fechter, Charles
1908
Feb 15 Monte Cristo
Garros, Paul de
1909
Dec 25 Drama of Villasgne
Gautier, Théophile
1909
Dec 6 Captain Fracassee
Dec 25 Alberno & Rosamunda
Gérôme, Jean Léon
1900
Aug [day undetermined]
The Slave Market
Ginnett, Fred
1907
Jul 20 Dick Turpin
Goethe, Johann Wolfgang von
1909
Apr 29 Mephisto and the Maiden
1910
May 19 Werther
Jun 30 Faust
Jul 30 Cagliostro
Oct 14 Werther
Goldsmith, Oliver
1910
Aug 19 She Stoops to Conquer
Dec 27 The Vicar of Wakefield
Goodman, H. B.
1910
Dec 22 The Recreation of an Heiress
Gounod, Charles
1904
Apr 2 Faust and Marguerite
1909
Dec 24 Faust
Grimm, Jakob Ludwig Karl
1909
Oct 15 Hansel and Gretel
1910
Feb 4 The Little Old Men of the Woods
Grimm, Wilhelm
1909
Oct 15 Hansel and Gretel
1910
Feb 4 The Little Old Men of the Woods
Guéroult, Edmund
1909
Jun 23 The Grandfather
Haggard, H. Rider
1908
Nov 13 "She"
Hale, Edward Everett
1909
Jun 29 A Man Without a Country
Halévy, Ludovic
1910
Feb 16 Carmen
Halm, Friedrich
1908
Oct 13 The Barbarian Ingomar
Harte, Bret
1910
Jan 21 The Luck of Roaring Camp
Hawthorne, Nathaniel
1908
Mar 28 Scarlet Letter
1910
Oct 18 The House of the Seven Gables
Henderson, Dell
1910
Dec 8 Happy Jack, a Hero
Henry, O.
1909
Jan 14 The Sacrifice
Mar 22 The Deception
Apr 5 Trying to Get Arrested
1910
Sep 19 A Summer Tragedy
Holmes, Mary Jane
1910
Jun 28 Tempest and Sunshine
Aug 12 Lena Rivers
Hood, Thomas
1908
Oct 13 The Bridge of Sighs
Nov 17 The Song of the Shirt
Hubbard, Elbert
1910
Dec 29 Justinian and Theodora
Hugo, Victor
1908
Apr 11 Angelo, Tyrant of Padua
1909
Jan 19 Ruy Blas
Mar 4 A Fool's Revenge
Aug 13 The Price of a Soul
Sep 4 The Galley Slave
Sep 21 The Ordeal
Sep 25 Fantine; or, A Mother's Love
Oct 12 A New Life
Oct 23 Cosette
Nov 14 Rigoletto
Nov 27 Jean Valjean
Hunt, Clarence
1902
May [day undetermined]
Ora Pro Nobis Illustrated
Irving, Washington
1903
Sep [day undetermined]
Rip Van Winkle
1908
Apr 25 The Legend of Sleepy Hollow
May 2 Rip Van Winkle
1910
Dec 6 Rip Van Winkle
Jackson, Helen Hunt
1910
May 23 Ramona
Jerrold, Douglas
1908
Aug 1 Black Eyed Susan
Kingsley, Charles
1908
Jan 20 The Water Babies; or, The Little Chimney Sweep
1910
May 5 The Unchanging Sea
Kipling, Rudyard
1910
Nov 10 The Vampire
Knowles, James Sheridan
1909
Feb 6 Virginius
Landelle, Charles
1900
Aug [day undetermined]
Living Pictures
Lemaître, Jules
1909
Mar 20 The Return of Ulysses
London, Jack
1907
Aug 17 The Sea Wolf
1908
Aug 21 For Love of Gold
Dec 4 Money Mad
Long, John Luther
1910
Dec 9 The Captain's Bride
Longfellow, Henry Wadsworth
1908
Feb 8 Evangeline
1909
Oct 25 Hiawatha
1910
Jan 20 The Courtship of Miles Standish
Lorde, A. de
1909
Jun 10 The Lonely Villa
Lucas, Wilfred
1910
Nov 14 Sunshine Sue
McCay, Winsor
1906
Feb [day undetermined]
Dream of a Rarebit Fiend
Mary, Jules
1909
Aug 6 The Tragedy of Meudon
Matrowsky
1900
Aug [day undetermined]
Living Pictures
Maupassant, Guy de
1909
May 19 Père Milon
Jul 1 The Necklace
Aug 10 A Coward
1910
Feb 2 A Voice from the Fireplace
Meilhac, Henri
1910
Feb 16 Carmen
Mérimée, Prosper
1910
Feb 16 Carmen
May 3 The Cigarette Maker of Seville
Metenier, Oscar
1910
Mar 14 The Revenge of Dupont L'Anguille
Michealis, Sophus
1910
Mar 12 A Wedding During the French Revolution
Millet, Jean François
1910
Apr 28 The Angelus
Molnar, Ferenc
1908
Sep 9 The Devil
Oct 2 The Devil
Morton, Edward
1902
Nov [day undetermined]
Umbrella Dance, San Toy
Mulock, Dinah
1910
Dec 2 John Halifax, Gentleman
Munroe, James Montague
1909
Nov 26 The Governor's Daughter
Musset, Alfred de
1910
Mar 25 No Trifling with Love
Apr 16 The Bully
Apr 18 Simone
May 16 Barberine
Norris, Frank
1909
Dec 13 A Corner in Wheat
Norton, Roy
1910
Apr 8 Sandy the Substitute
Aug 16 His New Family
Nuitter, Charles Louis Etienne
1910
Jan 18 The Toymaker's Secret
Parkman, Francis
1910
Sep 23 The Conspiracy of Pontiac; or, At Fort Detroit in 1763
Perrault, Charles
1901
Oct 26 Little Red Riding Hood
1902
May 3 Blue Beard
1904
Jan 16 Puss in Boots
1907
Mar 16 Cinderella
1909
Aug 14 The Wild Ass's Skin
Sep 10 Tom Thumb
Perrot, Phillipe
1900
Aug [day undetermined]
Living Pictures
Philippe, D.
1908
Mar 14 Remorse
Pratt, William W.
1901
Jun [day undetermined]
Ten Nights in a Bar-Room: Death of Little Mary
Ten Nights in a Bar-Room: Death of Slade
Ten Nights in a Bar-Room: Murder of Willie
Ten Nights in a Bar-Room: The Fatal Blow
Ten Nights in a Bar-Room: Vision of Mary
1909
Jun 9 Ten Nights in a Bar-room
Prescott, William H.
1910
May 18 The Aztec Sacrifice

SELECTED BIBLIOGRAPHY

American Film-Index, 1908-1915. Einar Lauritzen and Gunnar Lundquist. Stockholm, Sweden, 1974.

Artificially Arranged Scenes: The Films of Georges Méliès. John Frazer. Boston: G. K. Hall, 1979

Beginnings of the Biograph. Gordon Hendricks. New York: Beginnings of American Film, 1964.

The Big V: A History of the Vitagraph Company. Anthony Slide with Alan Gevinson. Revised Edition. Metuchen, N.J.: The Scarecrow Press, Inc., 1987.

The British Film Catalogue, 1895-1970. Denis Gifford. Newton Abbot, England: David & Charles, 1973.

Buckwalter: The Colorado Scenes of a Pioneer Photojournalist, 1890-1920. William C. Jones and Elizabeth B. Jones. Boulder, CO: Pruett Publishing Company, 1989.

Cinema muto italiano 1905-1909. Aldo Bernardini. Roma, 1980.

D. W. Griffith and the Biograph Co. Cooper C. Graham, Steven Higgins, Elaine Mancini and Joao Luiz Vieira. Metuchen, N.J.: The Scarecrow Press, 1985.

Den Dansk Stumfilm 1903-1910. Marguerite Engberg. Copenhagen: Danske Filmmuseum, 1968.

Early Motion Pictures: The Paper Print Collection in the Library of Congress. Kemp Niver, Edited by Bebe Bergsten. Library of Congress: Washington, D.C., 1985.

Embattled Shadows: A History of Canadian Cinema, 1895-1966. Peter Morris. Montreal: McGill-Queen's University Press, 1978

Émile Cohl. Donald Crafton. Cambridge, MA: MIT Press, 1982.

Enciclopedia dello spettacolo. Roma: Casa Editrice Le Maschere, 1954-.

Essai de reconstitution du catalogue français de la star-film. Centre National de la cinématographie. Bois d'Arcy: Service des Archives du Film du Centre National de la Cinématographie, 1981.

The Film Catalog, Museum of Modern Art. Jon Gartenberg, General Editor. Boston, MA: G. K. Hall & Co., 1985.

Film History: Theory and Practice. Robert C. Allen and Douglas Gomery. New York: Alfred A. Knopf, 1985.

The George Kleine Collection. Prepared by Rita Horwitz and Harriet Harrison, with Wendy White. Washington, D.C.: Library of Congress, 1980.

The History of the British Film. Volume 1 (1896-1902) & Volume 2 (1906-1914). Rachel Low. London: Unwin, 1943-.

An Index to the Creative Work of Georges Méliès (1896-1912). Compiled with an introduction by Georges Sadoul. London: British Film Institute, 1947.

Marvelous Méliès. Paul Hammond. New York: St. Martin's Press, 1975.

Motion Pictures 1894-1912 Identified from the Records of the Copyright Office. Howard Lamarr Walls. Washington, D.C.: Copyright Office, Library of Congress, 1953.

Motion Pictures from the Library of Congress Paper Print Collection, 1894-1912. Kemp Niver, Edited by Bebe Bergsten. Berkeley, CA: University of California Press, 1967.

The Movies Begin: Making Movies in New Jersey 1887-1920. Paul C. Spehr. The Newark Museum, in cooperation with Morgan and Morgan, Inc., 1977.

Moving Pictures—How They Are Made and Worked. Frederick A. Talbot. Philadelphia: J. B. Lippincott, 1914.

Mutoscope. Gordon Hendricks. New York: The Beginnings of American Film, 1964.

National Film Archive Catalog. London: The British Film Institute.

Nickelodeon Theatres and Their Music. David Q. Bowers. Vestal, NY: The Vestal Press, Ltd., 1986.

One Reel a Week. Fred J. Balshofer and Arthur C. Miller. Berkeley, CA: University of California Press, 1967.

Los 500 films de Segundo de Chomón. Juan Gabriel Tharrats. Zaragoza: Universidad de Zaragoza, 1988.

Storia del cinema muto italiano. Maria Adriana Prolo. Milano: Poligono, 1951.

Treasures from the Film Archives. Ronald S. Magliozzi. Metuchen, N.J.: The Scarecrow Press, 1988.

Vitagraph Co. of America: Il cinema primi di Hollywood. Edited by Paolo Cherchi Usai. Pordenone: Studio Tessi, 1987.

Wonderful Inventions. Library of Congress. Washington, D. C.: Library of Congress, 1985.